D1609463

# Labor Law

# Labor Law

## *Cases, Materials, and Problems*

**Eighth Edition**

**Michael C. Harper**
*Professor of Law and Barreca Labor Relations Scholar*
*Boston University*

**Samuel Estreicher**
*Dwight D. Opperman Professor of Law*
*New York University*

**Kati Griffith**
*Associate Professor of Labor and Employment Law*
*Cornell University*

Wolters Kluwer

Published by Wolters Kluwer in New York.

Wolters Kluwer serves customers worldwide with CCH, Aspen Publishers, and Kluwer Law International products. (www.wolterskluwerlb.com)



To contact Customer Service, e-mail customer.service@wolterskluwer.com,
call 1-800-234-1660, fax 1-800-901-9075, or mail correspondence to:

Wolters Kluwer
Attn: Order Department
PO Box 990
Frederick, MD 21705

Printed in the United States of America.

2 3 4 5 6 7 8 9 0

ISBN 978-1-4548-4943-8

**Library of Congress Cataloging-in-Publication Data**

Harper, Michael C., 1948- author.
Labor law : cases, materials, and problems/Michael C. Harper, Professor of Law and Barreca Labor Relations Scholar, Boston University; Samuel Estreicher, Dwight D. Opperman Professor of Law New York University; Kati Griffith, Associate Professor of Labor and Employment Law, Cornell University. — 8th ed.
pages cm
Includes bibliographical references and index.
ISBN 978-1-4548-4943-8 (alk. paper)
I. Estreicher, Samuel, author. II. Griffith, Kati, author. III. Title.
KF3369.H348 2014
344.7301 — dc23

2014043928

# About Wolters Kluwer Law & Business

Wolters Kluwer Law & Business is a leading global provider of intelligent information and digital solutions for legal and business professionals in key specialty areas, and respected educational resources for professors and law students. Wolters Kluwer Law & Business connects legal and business professionals as well as those in the education market with timely, specialized authoritative content and information-enabled solutions to support success through productivity, accuracy and mobility.

Serving customers worldwide, Wolters Kluwer Law & Business products include those under the Aspen Publishers, CCH, Kluwer Law International, Loislaw, ftwilliam.com and MediRegs family of products.

**CCH** products have been a trusted resource since 1913, and are highly regarded resources for legal, securities, antitrust and trade regulation, government contracting, banking, pension, payroll, employment and labor, and healthcare reimbursement and compliance professionals.

**Aspen Publishers** products provide essential information to attorneys, business professionals and law students. Written by preeminent authorities, the product line offers analytical and practical information in a range of specialty practice areas from securities law and intellectual property to mergers and acquisitions and pension/benefits. Aspen's trusted legal education resources provide professors and students with high-quality, up-to-date and effective resources for successful instruction and study in all areas of the law.

**Kluwer Law International** products provide the global business community with reliable international legal information in English. Legal practitioners, corporate counsel and business executives around the world rely on Kluwer Law journals, looseleafs, books, and electronic products for comprehensive information in many areas of international legal practice.

**Loislaw** is a comprehensive online legal research product providing legal content to law firm practitioners of various specializations. Loislaw provides attorneys with the ability to quickly and efficiently find the necessary legal information they need, when and where they need it, by facilitating access to primary law as well as state-specific law, records, forms and treatises.

**ftwilliam.com** offers employee benefits professionals the highest quality plan documents (retirement, welfare and non-qualified) and government forms (5500/PBGC, 1099 and IRS) software at highly competitive prices.

**MediRegs** products provide integrated health care compliance content and software solutions for professionals in healthcare, higher education and life sciences, including professionals in accounting, law and consulting.

Wolters Kluwer Law & Business, a division of Wolters Kluwer, is headquartered in New York. Wolters Kluwer is a market-leading global information services company focused on professionals.

For Robert and Dorothea Harper, in loving appreciation

M.C.H.

For Chuna David Estreicher (December 4, 1917-January 19, 2003)

וְתַלְמוּד תּוֹרָה כְּנֶגֶד כֻּלָּם.

("And the study of Torah is the foundation of all.")

S.E.

For Jack and Joyce Griffith

K.L.G.

# Summary of Contents

# Contents

# 3 | Protection of Concerted Activity 115

# Preface

We have revised and updated our basic text in labor law to take account of developments since the publication of the seventh edition. With the help of our new coauthor, Professor Kati Griffith of the Cornell University School of Industrial and Labor Relations, we have added two new chapters – one on immigration and labor law and the other on cross-border issues in labor law.

*Michael C. Harper*
*Samuel Estreicher*
*Kati L. Griffith*

September 2014

# Acknowledgments

We appreciate the permission of the following publishers, authors, and periodicals to reprint excerpts from their publications:

George W. Brooks, The Strengths and Weaknesses of Compulsory Unionism, 11 New York University Review of Law and Social Change 32 (1982-1983). Reprinted by permission of the New York University Review of Law and Social Change. New York, N.Y.

Archibald Cox, Labor Decisions of the Supreme Court at the October Term, 1957, 44 Virginia Law Review 1051 (1958). Reprinted by permission of The Virginia Law Review Association, Charlottesville, Va. and Fred B. Rothman & Company, Littleton, Colo.

Samuel Estreicher, Collective Bargaining or "Collective Begging"?: Reflections on Antistrikebreaker Legislation, 93 Michigan Law Review 577 (1994). Reprinted by permission of The Michigan Law Review Association, Ann Arbor, Mich.

Samuel Estreicher, Deregulating Union Democracy, 21 Journal of Labor Research 247 (2000), reprinted in The Internal Governance and Organizational Effectiveness of Labor Unions, ch. 17 (Estreicher et al. eds., 2001). Reprinted by permission of the Journal of Labor Research, George Mason University, Fairfax, Va.

Samuel Estreicher, Policy Oscillation at the Labor Board, 37 Administrative Law Review 176 (1985). Reprinted by permission of the American Bar Association, Chicago, Ill.

Samuel Estreicher, Win-Win Labor Law Reform, 10 The Labor Lawyer 674 (1994). Reprinted by permission of the American Bar Association, Chicago, Ill.

William Forbath, Law and the Shaping of the American Labor Movement. Cambridge, Mass.: Harvard University Press. Copyright © 1989 by the Harvard Law Review Association. Copyright © 1991 by the President and Fellows of Harvard College. Reprinted by permission of Harvard University Press.

Mayer G. Freed et al., Unions, Fairness, and the Conundrums of Collective Choice, 56 Southern California Law Review 461 (1983). Reprinted with the permission of the Southern California Law Review, Los Angeles, Cal.

Michael C. Harper, The Consumer's Emerging Right to Boycott: NAACP v. Claiborne Hardware and Its Implications for American Labor Law, 93 Yale Law Journal 409 (1984). Reprinted by permission of The Yale Law Journal

Company, New Haven, Conn. and Fred B. Rothman & Company, Littleton, Colo.

Michael C. Harper, Leveling the Road from Borg-Warner to First National Maintenance: The Scope of Mandatory Bargaining, 68 Virginia Law Review 1447 (1982). Reprinted by permission of The Virginia Law Review Association, Charlottesville, Va. and Fred B. Rothman & Company, Littleton, Colo.

Michael C. Harper, Limiting Section 301 Preemption: Three Cheers for the Trilogy, Only One for Lingle and Lueck, 66 Chicago-Kent Law Review 685 (1990). Copyright © 1992. Reprinted by special permission of the Chicago-Kent College of Law, Illinois Institute of Technology.

Michael C. Harper, Union Waiver of Employee Rights, 4 Industrial Relations Law Journal 335 (1981). Copyright © 1981 by Industrial Relations Law Journal. Reprinted by permission.

Michael C. Harper & Ira Lupu, Fair Representation as Equal Protection, 98 Harvard Law Review 1212 (1985). Copyright © 1985 by the Harvard Law Review Association, Cambridge, Mass. Reprinted by permission.

Bruce Kaufman & Jorge Martinez-Vasquez, Monopoly, Efficient Contract and Median Voter Models of Union Wage Determination: A Critical Comparison, 11 Journal of Labor Research 401 (1990). Reprinted by permission of the Journal of Labor Research, George Mason University, Fairfax, Va.

Douglas L. Leslie, Right to Control: A Study in Secondary Boycotts and Labor Antitrust, 89 Harvard Law Review 904 (1976). Copyright © 1976 by the Harvard Law Review Association, Cambridge, Mass. Reprinted by permission.

Howard Lesnick, The Gravamen of the Secondary Boycott. Article originally appeared at 62 Columbia Law Review 1363 (1962). Reprinted by permission of the author, Professor Howard Lesnick at the University of Pennsylvania Law School, Philadelphia, Pa.

Mancur Olson, The Logic of Collective Action: Public Goods and the Theory of Groups. Cambridge, Mass.: Harvard University Press. Copyright © 1965 and 1971 by the President and Fellows of Harvard College. Reprinted by permission of Harvard University Press.

Paul C. Weiler, Governing the Workplace: The Future of Labor and Employment Law. Cambridge, Mass.: Harvard University Press. Copyright © 1990 by the President and Fellows of Harvard College. Reprinted by permission of Harvard University Press.

Paul C. Weiler, Promises to Keep: Securing Workers' Rights to Self-Organization Under the NLRA, 96 Harvard Law Review 1769 (1983). Copyright © 1983 by the Harvard Law Review Association. Reprinted by permission of the Harvard Law Review Association, Cambridge, Ma. and Professor Paul Weiler at the Harvard Law School, Cambridge, Mass.

# Labor Law

# 1 The Historical and Institutional Framework

This book is about the legal framework governing the organization of workers and the process of collective bargaining in private industries in the United States. Representing an important regulatory intervention into the operation of private markets, labor law has been (and continues to be) contested terrain. Its early history was marked by pitched battles between organizations of workers seeking to improve their compensation and other conditions of employment and employers seeking to maintain control over the costs and processes of production. The legal system evolved from an initial hostile legal reception of labor organizations to growing recognition of the legitimacy of worker organization and the law's role in facilitating the development of labor unions and collective bargaining.

Because our labor relations system, as well as its underlying legal framework, is a product of this history, the first chapter explores the historical underpinnings of the basic labor law governing private companies, the National Labor Relations Act of 1935 and the Railway Labor Act of 1926. It reflects the ways in which labor organizations evolved, the methods they used to attempt to further their goals, and the response they received in dealings with employers and in the courts and legislatures of this country. Particular features of the system—for example, a federal law restricting federal courts from issuing injunctions in labor disputes, and the relative unimportance of compulsory interest arbitration of the content of labor agreements and of legislated minimum terms—are understandable only through an appreciation of American labor history.

## A. THE COMMON LAW

### 1. The Evolution of Labor Organizations

Although guilds of craftsmen can be traced back to a much earlier period, trade unions in the United States did not begin to develop until the end of the eighteenth century. Unions first emerged in larger cities where relatively large numbers of employees were engaged in the same occupations, and distinct classes of employees and employers evolved. Organization initially embraced skilled workers. Such workers had the education necessary for organizing and running a union, and they desired to safeguard their investment in their apprenticeship. The relative scarcity of skilled workers impeded their replacement during strikes and increased the power of their organization.

The early unions were highly unstable. They often were formed to press a particular demand, such as increased wages during a period of rising prices. Organization frequently disappeared along with the occasion that generated it because of a lack of continuing interest on the part of the members or because of employer or judicial hostility. In addition, during depressions members drifted away because workers, fearing unemployment, sought to protect individual interests rather than those of the group.

The first permanent national unions were formed in the 1850s, beginning with the National Typographical Union in 1852. A national union was originally a federation of local unions representing one craft or occupation in various localities. (The term "international" was used to indicate affiliation with Canadian unions. Today, the terms "national" and "international" are interchangeable.) An important stimulus to the development of national unions came from improvements in transportation and communication, principally the growth of interstate railroads. Formation of such unions was, in part, an effort to deal with problems caused by the flow of goods produced at low wages into markets offering goods produced at higher wages. Such unions were also formed in response to problems raised by the movement of workers to new locations where they sought admission to the local of their trade. Rules for the admission of migratory workers were an important concern of many early national unions. Today, the national union in the mass-production industries is generally the most important unit of organization; in such industries it is usually more realistic to view the local as a subordinate division of the national union rather than to consider the national as a federation of locals. By contrast, in the construction trades, locals play a critically important role in bargaining and in other activities.

The strong demand for labor and the inflation accompanying the Civil War promoted the growth of established unions and the formation of new ones, both nationally and locally. In 1866, another central federation of American labor unions, the National Labor Union, was formed. It was a loose association of national social reform groups.

The Civil War also accelerated developments that were to influence significantly the workplace and union development. War profits laid the basis for increased capital formation and industrialization. New technology further stimulated two great capital-goods industries—iron-steel and machinery. Industrial establishments increased in size, and larger enterprises were employing a larger proportion of the workers. As cities became more important, a growing number of urban workers became completely dependent on wages. Those forces, and particularly the increased scale of enterprises, ended the personal relationship between employer and employed that was typical of smaller enterprises.

In the 1870s, financial panic and depression took its toll on unions. During that period, labor-management relations were turbulent. Substantial paralysis of traffic and extensive disruption resulted from large-scale railroad strikes in protest against wage cuts. After riots in several cities, federal troops and state militia were called out to restore order. Few railroad workers had been organized, and the strikes appeared to be largely spontaneous. They were unsuccessful, partly because violence alienated the public.

Between the formation and collapse of the National Labor Union, another effort to unite workers for economic and political action led to the formation of the Noble Order of the Knights of Labor, founded in 1869 as a secret society. The depression of 1870 contributed to its growth. The Knights began to abandon their secrecy in 1879, and the organization grew rapidly in the next few years. The Knights differed from most early organizations in several respects. They admitted not only skilled craftsmen but also the unskilled, women, farmers, and in some cases self-employed businessmen. Lawyers, doctors, liquor dealers, and other "non-workingmen" were ineligible. The Knights also emphasized political action and producer cooperatives rather than collective bargaining. In principle, they opposed strikes and advocated legislation and education to achieve their aims. In practice, the Knights achieved their greatest successes when some of their district assemblies, representing railroad workers of a particular craft or occupation, won major strikes against wage cuts and discriminatory discharges.

The Knights of Labor achieved their most dramatic victory in 1885 when various railroads controlled by Jay Gould, a symbol of unrestrained economic power, agreed to end discrimination against striking members of the Order. Thereafter, the organization's prestige and membership soared, and in 1886 reached a peak of 700,000—almost seven times the 1885 membership.

The decline of the Knights was even swifter than their rise. The organization embraced groups and interests that were difficult to reconcile. It suffered from weak and inexperienced leadership. In the second half of 1886, the Knights were also involved in important strikes that ended disastrously for labor and resulted in the loss of many members. The virtual disappearance of the Knights by the 1890s marked a major turning point in the history of American unions. Never again was a major union to advocate primary reliance on social reform and producer cooperation rather than on collective bargaining backed by economic weapons.

The Knights had become involved in jurisdictional controversies with craft unions and had recruited their members. As a defensive measure, those unions called a convention in 1881 and formed the Federation of Organized Trades and Labor Unions, which was reorganized in 1886 as the American Federation of Labor (AFL). At first the group largely appealed to craft unions. Its leaders, including Samuel Gompers, its first president, rejected the more utopian and radical features of earlier movements. The new federation adopted a philosophy of pure "job and wage consciousness" and "business unionism," which accepted capitalism and sought to enlarge "the bargaining power of the wage earner in the sale of his labor." See Selig Perlman, A Theory of the Labor Movement 197-207 (1928). The principles announced by Gompers included (1) autonomy in the internal affairs of each affiliated international union; (2) exclusive jurisdiction for each affiliate; (3) avoidance of a permanent commitment to any political party, and the use of labor's political influence to support its friends and punish its enemies regardless of their party affiliations; and (4) the principle of voluntarism, that is, the improvement of wages and hours through trade unions, as distinguished from legislative action. Those principles were so attractive that all national unions of any importance, except those representing railroad-operating employees, soon joined the AFL.

The Federation failed to secure the affiliation of at least one of the railroad brotherhoods because of Gompers's insistence on the elimination from national union constitutions of provisions discriminating against African-Americans — discrimination that was to persist on the railroads and lead to landmark litigation in the 1940s. See Henry Pelling, American Labor 84, 90 (1960). The AFL at first denied admission to unions whose constitutions explicitly provided for discrimination. But opposition to Gompers's policy caused him to modify it in order to increase the strength of the Federation.

Despite the victory for craft unionism reflected in the success of the Federation, the United Mine Workers in 1890 succeeded in organizing the first permanent industrial union, embracing all coal miners in the bituminous and anthracite fields irrespective of craft or skill. Later, the AFL was to recognize the UMW's right to organize certain skilled workers in and around the mining industry despite rival jurisdictional claims of craft unions.

The AFL, and its philosophy of business unionism, was also challenged by radical movements, including the Industrial Workers of the World (IWW), formed in 1905. The IWW developed a militant syndicalism encompassing strikes and other forms of direct action designed to eliminate the wage system and to replace existing institutions by organization of workers along industrial lines. Early in its history, most of its strength was in the West, especially among lumberjacks and migratory workers. It did, however, support several large, spontaneous, and successful strikes in the East. Nevertheless, its radical program appeared to divert it from building a permanent organization. It opposed American participation in World War I and military conscription. Those positions, along with mob violence against the IWW, federal prosecution of its leaders for hampering the government's war efforts, and state "criminal syndicalism" statutes, contributed to its virtual disappearance in the postwar period. Socialists, although a minority group, from 1890 to 1918 also challenged the AFL's established leadership and played a significant role in keeping the issue of industrial unionism alive.

## 2. Judicial Response to Labor Disputes

Labor's difficulties in the nineteenth century may have been principally the result of larger economic and social factors, such as the abundant supply of land, the continuing waves of immigration to this country, and the relative absence of a unifying working-class consciousness in a workforce that was ethnically and racially heterogeneous. However, the manner in which the law responded to the concerted efforts of working people to improve their wages also played an important role.

### *a. Criminal Conspiracy*

The law's initial response was to treat combinations of craftsmen (for virtually all were men at the time) as a criminal conspiracy. The early cases involved journeymen's associations.

**Philadelphia Cordwainers (Commonwealth v. Pullis)**
*Philadelphia Mayor's Court (1806), in 3 John R. Commons & Eugene A. Gilmore, A Documentary History of American Industrial Society 59-248 (1910)*

[The indictment in this celebrated case charged in substance that the defendants, journeymen and cordwainers of the city of Philadelphia, had conspired as follows: (1) They would work only at specified rates, higher than those that had customarily been paid. (2) They would, "by threats, menaces, and other unlawful means," try to prevent other workmen from working at different rates. (3) They would not work for any person who employed a workman who had broken any of the rules or bylaws of their association and, pursuant to that agreement, had refused to work for the usual rates and prices.

Recorder Levy charged the jury, in part, as follows:]

"It is proper to consider, is such a combination consistent with the principles of our law, and injurious to the public welfare? The usual means by which the prices of work are regulated, are the demand for the article and the excellence of its fabric. Where the work is well done, and the demand is considerable, the prices will necessarily be high. Where the work is ill done, and the demand is inconsiderable, they will unquestionably be low. If there are many to consume, and few to work, the price of the article will be high: but if there are few to consume, and many to work, the article must be low. . . . These are the means by which prices are regulated in the natural course of things. To make an artificial regulation, is not to regard the excellence of the work or quality of the material, but to fix a positive and arbitrary price, governed by no standard, controlled by no impartial person, but dependent on the will of the few who are interested; this is the unnatural way of raising the price of goods or work. This is independent of the number of customers, or of the quality of the material, or of the number who are to do the work. It is an unnatural, artificial means of raising the price of work beyond its standard, and taking an undue advantage of the public. Is the rule of law bottomed upon such principles, as to permit or protect such conduct? Consider it on the footing of the general commerce of the city. Is there any man who can calculate (if this is tolerated) at what price he may safely contract to deliver articles, for which he may receive orders, if he is to be regulated by the journeymen in an arbitrary jump from one price to another? It renders it impossible for a man, making a contract for a large quantity of such goods, to know whether he shall lose or gain by it. If he makes a large contract for goods today, for delivery at three, six, or nine months hence, can he calculate what the prices will be then, if the journeymen in the intermediate time, are permitted to meet and raise their prices, according to their caprice or pleasure? Can he fix the price of his commodity for a future day? It is impossible that any man can carry on commerce in this way. . . . What then is the operation of this kind of conduct upon the commerce of the city? It exposes it to inconveniences, if not to ruin; therefore, it is against the public welfare. . . ."

". . . One man determines not to work under a certain price and it may be individually the opinion of all: in such a case it would be lawful in each to refuse to do so, for if each stands, alone, either may extract from his determination when he pleases. In the turnout of last fall, if each member of the body had stood alone, fettered by no promises to the rest, many of them might have changed their opinion as to the price of wages and gone to work; but it has been given to you in evidence, that they were bound down by their agreement, and pledged by mutual engagements, to persist in it, however contrary to their own judgment. The continuance in improper conduct may therefore well be attributed to the combination. The good sense of those individuals was prevented by this agreement, from having its free exercise. . . . Is this like the formation of a society for the promotion of the general welfare of the community, such as to advance the interests of religion, or to accomplish acts of charity and benevolence? . . . [O]r the meeting of the city wards to nominate candidates for the legislature or the executive? These are for the benefit of third persons: [the object of] the society in question [is] to promote the selfish purposes of the members. . . . The journeymen shoemakers have not asked an increased price of work for an individual of their body, but they say that no one shall work unless he receives the wages they have fixed. They could not go farther than saying, no one should work unless they all got the wages demanded by the majority; is this freedom? Is it not restraining instead of promoting the spirit of '76 when men expected to have no law but the constitution, and laws adopted by it or enacted by the legislature in conformity to it? Was it the spirit of '76, that either masters or journeymen, in regulating the prices of their commodities should set up a rule contrary to the law of their country? General and individual liberty was the spirit of '76. . . . It is not a question, whether we shall have . . . besides our state legislature a new legislature consisting of journeymen shoemakers. It is of no consequence, whether the prosecutors are two or three, or whether the defendants are ten thousand, their numbers are not to prevent the execution of our laws . . . though we acknowledge it is the hard hand of labour that promises the wealth of a nation, though we acknowledge the usefulness of such a large body of tradesmen and agree they should have everything to which they are legally entitled; yet we conceive they ought to ask nothing more. They should neither be the slaves nor the governors of the community."

The jury found the defendants guilty, and the court fined them $8.00 each plus costs.

[Counsel for the prosecuting masters had told the jury that the masters wanted only to establish a principle and not to punish the defendants. The modest fine was presumably designed to keep that implied promise and to avoid exacerbation of popular feelings. See Walter Nelles, The First American Labor Case, 41 Yale L.J. 165, 193 (1931).]

### Commonwealth v. Hunt
*45 Mass. (4 Met.) 111 (1842)*

[The opinion in *Commonwealth v. Hunt* marked an important departure in the law's response to labor organization. The case arose from the conviction, after a jury trial, of seven members of the Boston Journeymen Bootmakers Society for criminal conspiracy. The prosecution had been instigated by a journeyman named Jeremiah Horne, who had accepted pay below the Society's rate schedule. After objection by the Society, Horne's master paid him what was due under that schedule. When Horne again broke its rules, the Society expelled him and required that he pay a fine of $7 and sign its rules as a condition of reinstatement. His employer, having failed to persuade Horne to capitulate, fired him at the union's insistence in order to avoid a strike. Horne then filed a complaint with the district attorney.

The essence of the five-count indictment was that the defendants had agreed to maintain what later was to be called a closed shop—that all must be members of the Society to continue to work—had brought about the discharge of Horne, and had formed a combination to exclude him from his trade as a bootmaker.

After the verdict of guilty, exceptions raised the issue of whether the indictment had stated a criminal offense. Those exceptions were sustained by Chief Justice Shaw on the basis of a highly technical construction of the indictment:]

SHAW, C.J.

The manifest intent of the association is, to induce all those engaged in the same occupation to become members of it. Such a purpose is not invalid. It would give them a power which might be exerted for useful and honorable purposes, or for dangerous and pernicious ones. If the latter were the real and actual object, and susceptible of proof, it should have been specially charged. . . .

Nor can we perceive that the objects of this association, whatever they may have been, were to be attained by criminal means. The means which they proposed to employ, as averred in this count, and which, as we are now to presume, were established by the proof, were, that they would not work for a person, who, after due notice, should employ a journeyman not a member of their society. Supposing the object of the association to be laudable and lawful or at least not unlawful, are these means criminal? The case presupposes that these persons are not bound by contract, but free to work for whom they please, or not to work, if they so prefer. In this state of things, we cannot perceive, that it is criminal for men to agree together to exercise their own acknowledged rights, in such a manner as best to subserve their own interests.

## *NOTES AND QUESTIONS*

**1. Means-Ends Distinction**. *Commonwealth v. Hunt* was a milestone in the decline of the criminal conspiracy doctrine. Although Shaw did not squarely repudiate the doctrine, his opinion has been hailed as a major advance for American trade unionism in that it arrested the tendency to identify a labor organization as ipso facto a criminal conspiracy and instead directed attention to the justifications for union objectives and the propriety of the means used. See Walter Nelles, *Commonwealth v. Hunt*, 32 Colum. L. Rev. 1128 (1932); Leonard W. Levy, The Law of the Commonwealth and Chief Justice Shaw, ch. 11 (1957).

In the 25 years after the decision in *Commonwealth v. Hunt*, no indictment against labor unions for criminal conspiracy appears to have been returned in Massachusetts. In other states, however, application of the criminal conspiracy doctrine continued—e.g., State v. Donaldson, 32 N.J.L. 151 (Sup. Ct. 1867) (indictment charging defendants with criminal conspiracy to quit working for their employer unless he fired two named employees)—until the labor injunction emerged as an effective weapon against harms attributed to labor unions.

**2. Strikes to Enforce a Closed Shop vs. Freedom of Contract?** Despite the sweeping charges used by the prosecutors, these were not cases involving simply the rights of a private association to govern its own affairs. In *Cordwainers,* the group had gone on strike to enforce what is called a "closed shop": the requirement that the employer engage only members of the association as journeymen. In *Hunt,* the union also sought to enforce a closed shop against a dissident worker by means of a strike threat. Historians have highlighted an emerging entrepreneurial spirit in the nineteenth century that "sanctified the liberty of individuals to use their property productively free of the restraints of collective regulation." See Christopher L. Tomlins, The State and the Unions: Labor Relations, Law and the Organized Labor Movement 1880-1960, at 35 (1985). Was it inconsistent with such liberty for a private organization to declare that it would withhold the labor of its members from an employer unless the employer ensured that all others in its employ belonged to the association and observed its rules? Rather than state intervention through its criminal law, why was an employer not simply allowed to decide whether the services of the union members were sufficiently valuable that it would prefer to live with the association's restrictions than be without those services? Shaw's opinion in *Hunt* arguably reflects this theme by drawing a line at the use of physical force or fraud to require the employer, Wait, to fire Horne, which "would have been a different case. . . ." Here, by contrast, "[i]t was the agreement not to work for him, by which they compelled Wait to decline employing Horne longer." 45 Mass. (4 Met.) at 133.

**3. Who Were the Complainants?** In both *Cordwainers* and *Hunt* "the complainants were not employers seeking to discipline unions but rather fellow employees whom union members had attempted to exclude from the labor market because of their willingness to work at too low a wage." Herbert Hovenkamp, Enterprise and American Law 1836-1937, at 227 (1991). To what extent did the conspiracy doctrine try to protect the nonunion worker? To what extent should the law protect this interest? The competing rights of strikers and replacements continue to be a source of controversy. See infra pages 522-560.

**4. Is There a Public Interest in Preventing Private Wage Setting?** Recorder Levy asserted that the Philadelphia association was setting up its own private law in derogation of state authority. By 1842, Chief Justice Shaw took a different view:

> [The indictment] does not aver a conspiracy or even an intention to raise wages; and it appears by the bill of the exceptions, that the case was not put on the footing of a conspiracy to raise wages. Such an agreement, as set forth in this count, would be perfectly justifiable under the recent English statute, by which this subject is regulated, 6 Geo. IV, c.129.

45 Mass. (4 Met.) at 131-132. The English statute cited was a revision of an 1824 law that eliminated price-setting regulations for a wide range of crafts and occupations. See Act to Repeal Laws Relative to the Combination of Workmen, 5 Geo. IV, c.95, §2. In 1825, Parliament enacted a new law that continued to treat labor combinations as lawful but prohibited workers from compelling or threatening to compel others to strike by "Violence to the Person or Property, or by Threats or Intimidation, or by molesting or in any way obstructing another." Act to Repeal the Law Relating to the Combination of Workmen, 6 Geo. IV, c.129, §1.

Where the state does not regulate wages and prices, does it still have an interest in ensuring that wages and prices will be determined by the marketplace rather than by concentrations of private power, whether they be groups of employers or workers? This issue will be explored infra pages 38-46 and further in Chapter 10.

### b. *The Labor Injunction*

The use of collective action to achieve union objectives typically inflicts harm — at least in the short run — on employers, nonunion employees, rival unions, or the general public. After the early doctrine of criminal conspiracy lapsed, civil actions were brought against unions for damages and, more typically, for injunctive relief restraining the strike or boycott.

#### Vegelahn v. Guntner
*167 Mass. 92, 44 N.E. 1077 (1896)*

[After a preliminary hearing, an injunction was issued pendente lite, restraining the respondents and their agents and servants] from "interfering with the plaintiff's business by patrolling the sidewalk in front or in the vicinity of the premises occupied by him, for the purpose of preventing any person in his employment, or desirous of entering the same, from entering it, or continuing in it . . . or by any scheme or conspiracy for the purpose of annoying, hindering, interfering with, or preventing any person in the employment of the plaintiff, or desirous of entering the same, from entering it, or from continuing therein." . . .

[After a hearing on the merits, Justice Holmes reported the case for the full court as follows:] "The facts admitted or proved are that, following upon a strike of the plaintiff's workmen, the defendants have conspired to prevent the plaintiff from getting workmen, and thereby to prevent him from carrying on his business unless and until he will adopt a schedule of prices which has been exhibited to him, and for the purpose of compelling him to accede to that schedule but for no other purpose. If he adopts that schedule, he will not be interfered with further. The means for preventing the plaintiff from getting workmen are, (1) in the first place, persuasion and social pressure. And these means are sufficient to affect the plaintiff disadvantageously, although it does not appear, if that be material, that they are sufficient to crush him. I ruled that the employment of these means for the said purpose was lawful, and for that reason refused an injunction against the employment of them. If the ruling was wrong, I find that an injunction ought to be granted.

(2) I find also, that as a further means for accomplishing the desired end, threats of personal injury or unlawful harm were conveyed to persons seeking employment or employed, although no actual violence was used beyond a technical battery, and although the threats were a good deal disguised, and express words were avoided. It appeared to me that there was danger of similar acts in the future. I ruled that conduct of this kind should be enjoined.

The defendants established a patrol of two men in front of the plaintiff's factory, as one of the instrumentalities of their plan. The patrol was changed every hour, and continued from half-past six in the morning until half-past five in the afternoon, on one of the busy streets of Boston. The number of men was greater at times, and at times showed some little inclination to stop the plaintiff's door, which was not serious, but seemed to me proper to be enjoined. The patrol proper at times went further than simple advice, not obtruded beyond the point where the other person was willing to listen, and conduct of that sort is covered by (2) above, but its main purpose was in aid of the plan held lawful in (1) above. I was satisfied that there was probability of the patrol being continued if not enjoined. I ruled that the patrol, so far as it confined itself to persuasion and giving notice of the strike, was not unlawful, and limited the injunction accordingly.

There was some evidence of persuasion to break existing contracts. I ruled that this was unlawful, and should be enjoined.

I made the final decree appended hereto. If, on the foregoing facts, it ought to be reversed or modified, such decree is to be entered as the full court may think proper; otherwise, the decree is to stand.

[The final decree was as follows:] . . . [I]t is ordered, adjudged, and decreed that the defendants, and each and every of them, their agents and servants, be restrained and enjoined from interfering with the plaintiff's business by obstructing or physically interfering with any persons in entering or leaving the plaintiff's premises numbered 141, 143, 145, 147 North Street in said Boston, or by intimidating, by threats, express or implied, of violence or physical harm to body or property, any person or persons who now are or hereafter may be in the employment of the plaintiff, or desirous of entering the same, from entering or continuing in it, or by in any way hindering, interfering with, or preventing any person or persons who now are in the employment of the plaintiff from continuing therein, so long as they may be found so to do by lawful contract. . . ."

ALLEN, J.

. . . The patrol was maintained as one of the means of carrying out the defendants' plan, and it was used in combination with social pressure, threats of personal injury or unlawful harm, and persuasion to break existing contracts. It was thus one means of intimidation, indirectly to the plaintiff, and directly to persons actually employed, or seeking to be employed, by the plaintiff, and of rendering such employment unpleasant or intolerable to such persons. Such an act is an unlawful interference with the rights both of employer and of employed. An employer has a right to engage all persons who are willing to work for him, at such prices as may be mutually agreed upon; and persons employed or seeking employment have a corresponding right to enter into or remain in the employment of any person or corporation willing to employ them. These rights are secured by the Constitution itself. . . . Patrolling or picketing, under the circumstances stated in the report, has elements of intimidation like those which were found to exist in Sherry v. Perkins, 147 Mass. 212. . . . The patrol was an unlawful interference both with the plaintiff and with the workmen, within the principle of many cases, and, when instituted for the purpose of interfering with his business, it became a private nuisance. . . .

[In the opinion of a majority of the court] the injunction should be in the form originally issued. So ordered.

[The dissenting opinion of Chief Justice Field is omitted.]

HOLMES, J. (dissenting).

. . . I agree, whatever may be the law in the case of a single defendant . . . that when a plaintiff proves that several persons have combined and conspired to injure his business, and have done acts producing that effect, he shows temporal damage and a cause of action, unless the facts disclose, or the defendants prove, some ground of excuse or justification. And I take it to be settled, and rightly settled, that doing that damage by combined persuasion is actionable, as well as doing it by falsehood or by force. . . .

Nevertheless, in numberless instances the law warrants the intentional infliction of temporal damage because it regards it as justified. It is on the question of what shall amount to a justification, and more especially on the nature of the considerations which really determine or ought to determine the answer to that question, that judicial reasoning seems to me often to be inadequate. The true grounds of decision are considerations of policy and of social advantage, and it is vain to suppose that solutions can be attained merely by logic and the general propositions of law which nobody disputes. Propositions as to public policy rarely are unanimously accepted, and still more rarely, if ever, are capable of unanswerable proof. They require a special training to enable any one even to form an intelligent opinion about them. In the early stages of law, at least, they generally are acted on rather as inarticulate instincts than as definite ideas, for which a rational defense is ready.

To illustrate what I have said in the last paragraph, it has been the law for centuries that a man may set up a business in a country town too small to support more than one, although he expects and intends thereby to ruin some one already there, and succeeds in his intent. In such a case he is not held to act "unlawfully and without justifiable cause." . . . The reason, of course, is that the doctrine generally has been accepted that free competition is worth more to society than it costs, and that on this ground the infliction of the damage is privileged. Commonwealth v. Hunt, 4 Met. 111, 134. . . .

I have chosen this illustration partly with reference to what I have to say next. It shows without the need of further authority that the policy of allowing free competition justifies the intentional inflicting of temporal damage, including the damage of interference with a man's business, by some means, when the damage is done not for its own sake, but as an instrumentality in reaching the end of victory in the battle of trade. In such a case it cannot matter whether the plaintiff is the only rival of the defendant, and so is aimed at specifically, or is one of a class all of whom are hit. The only debatable ground is the nature of the means by which such damage may be inflicted. We all agree that it cannot be done by force or threats of force. We all agree, I presume, that it may be done by persuasion to leave a rival's shop, and come to the defendant's. It may be done by the refusal or withdrawal of various pecuniary advantages, which, apart from this consequence, are within the defendant's lawful control. It may be done by the withdrawal of, or threat to withdraw, such advantages from third persons who have a right to deal or not to deal with the plaintiff, as a means of inducing them not to deal with him either as customers or servants. Commonwealth v. Hunt, 4 Met. 111, 132, 133. Bowen v. Matheson, 14 Allen, 499. Heywood v. Tillson, 75 Me. 225. [Mogul] Steamship Co. v. McGregor, [1892] App. Cas. 25. I have seen the suggestion made that the conflict between employers and employed is not competition. But I venture to assume that none of my brethren would rely on that suggestion. If the policy on which our law is founded is too narrowly expressed in the term free competition, we may substitute free struggle for life. Certainly the policy is not limited to struggles between persons of the same class competing for the same end. It applies to all conflicts of temporal interests. . . .

So far, I suppose, we are agreed. But there is a notion, which latterly has been insisted on a good deal, that a combination of persons to do what any one of them lawfully might do by himself will make the otherwise lawful conduct unlawful. It would be rash to say that some as yet unformulated truth may not be hidden under this proposition. But in the general form in which it has been presented and accepted by many courts, I think it plainly untrue, both on authority and on principle. Commonwealth v. Hunt, 4 Met. 111. Randall v. Hazelton, 12 Allen, 412, 414. There was combination of the most flagrant and dominant kind in *Bowen v. Matheson* and in the Mogul Steamship Company's case, and combination was essential to the success achieved. But it is not necessary to cite cases; it is plain from the slightest consideration of practical affairs, or the most superficial reading of industrial history, that free competition means combination, and that the organization of the world, now going on so fast, means an ever-increasing might and scope of combination. It seems to me futile to set our faces against this tendency. Whether beneficial on the whole, as I think it, or detrimental, it is inevitable, unless the fundamental axioms of society, and even the fundamental conditions of life, are to be changed.

One of the eternal conflicts out of which life is made up is that between the effort of every man to get the most he can for his services, and that of society, disguised under the name of capital, to get his services for the least possible return. Combination on the one side is patent and powerful. Combination on the other is the necessary and desirable counterpart, if the battle is to be carried on in a fair and equal way. . . .

## *NOTES AND QUESTIONS*

**1. Special Characteristics of the "Labor Injunction."** Employers typically preferred the injunction proceeding to the action in damages for a number of reasons. First, relief could be obtained quite quickly; indeed, temporary injunctions could issue on an ex parte showing. Second, the decree imposed personal obligations on strikers and picketers, avoiding the legal difficulties of the time in joining unions as legal entities or enforcing judgments against individuals of limited means. Third, the decree operated prospectively as an ongoing restraint during the pendency of the dispute. Fourth, jury trials were (and are) not available in equity, and judges were often more willing than the community at large to restrict labor protest. Finally, the decrees often were framed in broad, inclusive terms, casting a wide restraining net that could reach all supporters of the labor protest, whether or not they had previously engaged in tortious activity.

Between 1880 and 1930, the labor injunction became the characteristic form of legal intervention in labor strife. Abuses associated with the labor injunction, as cataloged in Felix Frankfurter and Nathan Greene's *The Labor Injunction* (1930), not only undermined the economic strength of unions but also placed in question the neutrality and prestige of the courts. Reflecting the labor movement's disquiet, Frankfurter and Greene criticized the courts for issuing ex parte temporary restraining orders (TROs) on the basis of allegations of union misconduct entered by employers, without giving the unions an opportunity to respond. They found that TROs were issued in 70 of 118 important cases in the first quarter of the twentieth century; a TRO was denied in only one. Id. at 60. Supporting affidavits were not even filed in 58 of the 70 cases in which TROs were granted, and the employers' allegations often were identical from case to case as if a legal form book were used. Id. at 64, 71. TROs could not become permanent until a full hearing was held but that often occurred only after a month of delay, and any delay could be critical for strikes that were part of the momentum of an organizing drive. Even if the injunction was lifted by the trial judge without the further delay of an appeal, the momentum of an organizing drive or strike would often have been dissipated.

Frankfurter and Greene's book identified other abuses, including the issuance of restraints and contempt citations against union leaders and supporters for actions not clearly authorized or ratified by the labor organization; the manipulation by courts of prolix, vague decrees to trap unwary union leaders and workers; the deputization of company guards and other agents to ensure compliance with injunctions; and the ability of employers to bypass juries and select judges with strong class identifications and a pro-business ideology predisposed against unions. The evolution of the labor injunction during the "Gilded Age" is recounted in William E. Forbath, Law and the Shaping of the American Labor Movement, ch. 3 (1991).

**2. Is Labor Picketing Inherently Coercive?** The opinions in *Vegelahn* take differing views of labor picketing. Is such picketing simply a means of communicating the labor group's protest to, and inviting expression of solidarity from, the community, or does it coerce the employer and nonstriking workers in some way other than the pressure that would ensue from any loss of patronage by community members supporting the protest? Can we assume that labor groups which honor such picket lines do so not out of agreement with picketing union's demands but because of background alliances between labor organizations requiring the honoring of each other's picket lines?

Although the *Vegelahn* majority's interdiction of peaceful picketing has few modern defenders, Professor Epstein has argued that it may have been justified as a prophylactic against disguised threats or use of force:

> [T]he broader injunction can be defended by pointing to the weaknesses of the finely tuned injunction that Holmes had adopted. Leaving the pickets in place by the plaintiff's business invites, or at least increases the likelihood of, the threat or use of force, which will go unredressed because the summary remedies available in principle are imperfect in practice. Case-by-case determinations are expensive to make, and are subject to very high error rates, especially where disguised threats are a substantial possibility.

Richard A. Epstein, A Common Law for Labor Relations: A Critique of New Deal Labor Legislation, 92 Yale L.J. 1357, 1377 (1983). Does Epstein's position adequately take into account the communicative aspects of picketing and the inhibiting effects of overbroad decrees on noncoercive protests? For further discussion of the line between "persuasion" and "intimidation," see Eileen Silverstein, Collective Action, Property Rights and Law Reform, 11 Hofstra Lab. L.J. 97, 104-106 (1993). For consideration of the constitutional status of labor picketing, see infra pages 576-583 and pages 608-623.

**3. Organizational vs. Immediate Economic Objectives.** Does the test formulated by Holmes provide an effective standard for common-law regulation of labor conflict, or is it subject to manipulation by judges bent on implementing their own policy preferences? Applying essentially the analytic framework espoused by Holmes in *Vegelahn*, the Massachusetts court in *Plant* upheld an injunction against strikes and threatened strikes to force employees belonging to a rival union to join the striking union or be discharged from their employment. We excerpt below from the majority opinion (by Justice Hammond) and the dissent (by Chief Justice Holmes):

> HAMMOND, J. . . . It is to be observed that this is not a case between the employer and employed, or, to use a hackneyed expression, between capital and labor, but between laborers all of the same craft, and each having the same right as any one of the others to pursue his calling. In this as in every other case of equal rights the right of each individual is to be exercised with due regard to the similar right of all others, and the right of one be said to end where that of another begins.
>
> The right involved is the right to dispose of one's labor with full freedom. This is a legal right, and it is entitled to legal protection. . . .
>
> . . . Without now indicating to what extent workmen may combine and in pursuance of an agreement may act by means of strikes and boycotts to get the hours of labor reduced, or their wages increased, or to procure from their employers any other concession directly and immediately affecting their own interests, or to help themselves in competition with their fellow workmen, we think this case must be governed by the [following] principles. . . . The purpose of these defendants was to force the plaintiffs to join the defendant association, and to that end they injured the plaintiffs in their business, and molested and disturbed them in their efforts to work at their trade. It is true they committed no acts of personal violence, or of physical injury to property,

although they threatened to do something which might reasonably be expected to lead to such results. In their threat, however, there was plainly that which was coercive in its effect upon the will. It is not necessary that the liberty of the body should be restrained. Restraint of the mind, provided it would be such as would be likely to force a man against his will to grant the thing demanded, and actually has that effect, is sufficient in cases like this. . . .

The defendants might make such lawful rules as they please for the regulation of their own conduct, but they had no right to force other persons to join them. . . .

HOLMES, C.J. (dissenting). . . . To come directly to the point, the issue is narrowed to the question whether, assuming that some purposes would be a justification, the purpose in this case of the threatened boycotts and strikes was such as to justify the threats. That purpose was not directly concerned with wages. It was one degree more remote. The immediate object and motive was to strengthen the defendants' society as a preliminary . . . means to enable it to make a better fight on questions of wages or other matters of clashing interests. I differ from my Brethren in thinking that the threats were as lawful for this preliminary purpose as for the final one to which strengthening the union was a means. I think that unity of organization is necessary to make the contest of labor effectual, and that societies of laborers lawfully may employ in their preparation the means which they might use in the final contest.

**4. Double Standard?** In a portion of the *Plant* opinion not excerpted above, the Massachusetts court distinguished two decisions involving combinations of shipowners. See Bowen v. Matheson, 14 Allen 499 (1867); Mogul Steamship Co. v. McGregor, 23 Q.B. Div. 598 (1889). In *Bowen,* for example, it was held to be within allowable competition for an association of shipowners to refuse to provide seamen for vessels belonging to the nonmembers of the association and to notify shippers and others of its boycott of nonmember ships. The court in that case dismissed the resulting injury to the nonmember shipowners: "If [the] effect is to destroy the business of shipping masters who are not members of the association, it is such a result as in the competition of business often follows from a course of proceeding that the law permits." 14 Allen at 503-504. The *Plant* court stated that "the primary object" of the defendants in *Bowen* was "to build up their own business, and this they might lawfully do to the extent disclosed in that case, even to the injury of their rivals"; whereas in the case before it, "the purpose was, in substance, to force the plaintiff to give his work to the defendants, and to extort from him a fine because he had given some of his work to other persons." 57 N.E. at 1015-16. Is this a persuasive ground for allowing firms to attempt to prop up their prices by boycotts of competing businesses, but preventing labor from attempting to prop up the price obtainable for its services by the picketing at issue in *Vegelahn* and *Plant*?

## 3. Judicial Response to Protective Labor Legislation

**Lochner v. New York**
*198 U.S. 45 (1905)*

[The Court held unconstitutional a New York statute providing that no employee shall "work in a biscuit, bread or cake bakery or confectionary establishment more than sixty hours in any one week, or more than ten hours in any one day."]

Mr. Justice PECKHAM . . . delivered the opinion of the court:

. . . The statute necessarily interferes with the right of contract between the employer and employees, concerning the number of hours in which the latter may labor in the bakery of the employer. The general right to make a contract in relation to his business is part of the liberty of the individual protected by the Fourteenth Amendment of the Federal Constitution. . . . Under that provision no State can deprive any person of life, liberty or property without due process of law. The right to purchase or to sell labor is part of the liberty protected by this amendment, unless there are circumstances which exclude the right. There are, however, certain powers, existing in the sovereignty of each State in the Union, somewhat vaguely termed police powers, the exact description and limitation of which have not been attempted by the courts. Those powers . . . relate to the safety, health, morals and general welfare of the public. Both property and liberty are held on such reasonable conditions as may be imposed by the governing power of the State in the exercise of those powers, and with such conditions the Fourteenth Amendment was not designed to interfere. . . .

The question whether [the New York law] is valid as a labor law, pure and simple, may be dismissed in a few words. There is no reasonable ground for interfering with the liberty of person or the right of free contract, by determining the hours of labor, in the occupation of a baker. There is no contention that bakers as a class are not equal in intelligence and capacity to men in other trades or manual occupations, or that they are not able to assert their rights and care for themselves without the protecting arm of the State, interfering with their independence of judgment and of action. They are in no sense wards of the State. Viewed in the light of a purely labor law, with no reference whatever to the question of health, we think that a law like the one before us involves neither the safety, the morals nor the welfare of the public, and that the interest of the public is not in the slightest degree affected by such an act. The law must be upheld, if at all, as a law pertaining to the health of the individual engaged in the occupation of a baker. It does not affect any other portion of the public than those who are engaged in that occupation. Clean and wholesome bread does not depend upon whether the baker works but ten hours per day or only sixty hours a week. . . .

We think that there can be no fair doubt that the trade of a baker, in and of itself, is not an unhealthy one to that degree which would authorize the legislature to interfere with the right to labor, and with the right of free contract on the part of the individual, either as employer or employee. . . . It might be safely affirmed that almost all occupations more or less affect the health. There must be more than the mere fact of the possible existence of some small amount of unhealthiness to warrant legislative interference with liberty. It is unfortunately true that labor, even in any department, may possibly carry with it the seeds of unhealthiness. But are we all, on that account, at the mercy of legislative majorities? . . .

[The dissenting opinion of Justice Harlan, with whom Justices White and Day concurred, is omitted.]

Mr. Justice HOLMES dissenting. . . .

. . . It is settled by various decisions of this court that state constitutions and state laws may regulate life in many ways which we as legislators might think as injudicious, or if you like as tyrannical, as this, and which, equally with this, interfere with the liberty to contract. Sunday laws and usury laws are ancient examples. A more modern one is the prohibition of lotteries. The liberty of the citizen to do as he likes so long as he does not interfere with the liberty of others to do the same, which has been a shibboleth for some well-known writers, is interfered with by school laws, by the Post Office, by every state or municipal institution which takes his money for purposes thought desirable, whether he likes it or not. The Fourteenth Amendment does not enact Mr. Herbert Spencer's Social Statics. . . . [A] constitution is not intended to embody a particular economic theory, whether of paternalism and the organic relation of the citizen to the State or of *laissez faire.* It is made for people of fundamentally differing views, and the accident of our finding certain opinions natural and familiar or novel and even shocking ought not to conclude our judgment upon the question whether statutes embodying them conflict with the Constitution of the United States.

. . . I think that the word liberty in the Fourteenth Amendment is perverted when it is held to prevent the natural outcome of a dominant opinion, unless it can be said that a rational and fair man necessarily would admit that the statute proposed would infringe fundamental principles as they have been understood by the traditions of our people and our law. It does not need research to show that no such sweeping condemnation can be passed upon the statute before us. A reasonable man might think it a proper measure on the score of health. Men whom I certainly could not pronounce unreasonable would uphold it as a first instalment of a general regulation of the hours of work. . . .

## *NOTES AND QUESTIONS*

**1. Origins of Labor's "Voluntarism" Strategy.** Decisions like *Lochner* in the federal and state courts had a profound impact on the evolution of the labor movement's attitude toward securing its objectives through protective labor legislation rather than economic action. Consider the following excerpt from Forbath, Law and the Shaping of the American Labor Movement, supra, at 37-42:

> Judicial review was the most visible and dramatic fashion in which courts curtailed labor's ability to use laws to redress asymmetries of power in the employment relationship. By the turn of the century state and federal courts had invalidated roughly sixty labor laws. During the 1880s and 1890s courts were far more likely than not to strike down the very laws that labor sought most avidly. For workers, judicial review—the invalidation of labor laws under the language of "liberty of contract" and "property rights"—became both evidence and symbol of the intractability of the American state from the perspective of labor reform.
>
> The decision of the New York Court of Appeals in In re Jacobs [98 N.Y. 98 (1885)], the first high court decision to strike down a piece of labor legislation for infringing a workingman's constitutional liberty, is a landmark in the history of "laissez-faire constitutionalism." Invalidating an 1884 statute prohibiting the manufacture of cigars in tenement dwellings, *Jacobs* is an eloquent, if ironic, statement of the Gilded Age courts' vision of "free labor" and workers' dignity and independence. . . .
>
> *Jacobs* also figured as a landmark in Samuel Gompers's political evolution. . . . Gompers and the Cigarmakers considered whether to return to the political-legislative fray [after *Jacobs*] but decided instead that they would henceforth pursue their ends solely through "strikes and agitation." In that fashion, . . . they forced the manufacturers "to abandon the tenement manufacturing system and carry on the industry in factories under decent conditions. Thus we accomplished through economic power what we had failed to achieve through legislation." In retrospect the experience became a nice text on the wisdom of voluntarism.
>
> By the end of the century, Gompers's and the Cigarmakers' experience with reform by legislation in the era of rising judicial supremacy had been repeated roughly sixty times and shared by trade unionists in almost every industrial state.

**2. The *Lochner* Era.** From the 1905 decision in *Lochner* until the New Deal period of the mid-1930s, the Supreme Court invalidated over 200 laws regulating the economy, typically under the implied "substantive" dimension of the Due Process Clause of the Fourteenth Amendment. Some of the notable "highlights" of this period include Adair v. United States, 208 U.S. 161 (1908), and Coppage v. Kansas, 236 U.S. 1 (1915), which invalidated, respectively, federal and state laws forbidding employers from requiring their workers to enter into "yellow-dog" contracts—i.e., agreements not to join a union — as a condition of employment. See also Adkins v. Children's Hospital, 261 U.S. 525 (1923), striking down a law establishing minimum wages for women. Some laws did overcome the constitutional hurdles imposed by the Court; a state law requiring an eight-hour day for miners was sustained in Holden v. Hardy, 169 U.S. 366 (1898), and a state law prohibiting the employment of women in laundries for more than ten hours a day was upheld in Muller v. Oregon, 208 U.S. 412 (1908). See generally Frank R. Strong, Substantive Due Process of Law: A Dichotomy of Sense and Nonsense (1986).

**3. The Theoretical Underpinnings of *Lochner*.** The *Lochner* Court took a limited view of legitimate state power. Government could properly act to (1) facilitate private undertakings by, for example, enforcing contracts; (2) require private actors to absorb costs imposed on third parties through the law of torts; (3) regulate health and safety in industries considered hazardous, as in *Holden v. Hardy*, 106 U.S. 366 (1898) (sustaining state statute limiting underground mining work to 8 hours per day) or (4) protect dependent groups like women, who were considered incapable of protecting themselves, as in *Muller v. Oregon*, supra. It was not permitted, however, to attempt to redistribute wealth from one class in society to another through law. As the Court stated in Coppage v. Kansas, supra, 236 U.S. at 17-18:

> [I]t is said . . . [that] "employees, as a rule, are not financially able to be as independent in making contracts for the sale of their labor as are employers in making contracts of purchase thereof." No doubt, wherever the right of private property exists, there must and will be inequalities of fortune. . . . [Thus, it is] impossible to uphold freedom of contract and the right of private property without at the same time recognizing as legitimate those inequalities of fortune that are the necessary result of the exercise of those rights.
>
> . . . And since a State may not strike [those rights] down directly it is clear that it may not do so indirectly, as by declaring in effect that the public good requires the removal of those inequalities that are but the normal and inevitable result of their exercise. . . . The police power is broad, . . . but it cannot be given the wide scope that is here asserted for it, without in effect nullifying the constitutional guaranty.

*Lochner*'s position on redistributive legislation is defended in Bernard Siegan, Economic Liberties and the Constitution (1980), and criticized in Cass R. Sunstein, *Lochner*'s Legacy, 87 Colum. L. Rev. 873 (1987). The exchange of views continued in David E. Bernstein, *Lochner's* Legacy, 82 Tex. L. Rev. 1 (2003) (critiquing Sunstein's article); and Cass R. Sunstein, Reply: *Lochnering*, supra, id. at 65.

**4. What's Wrong with *Lochner*?** *Lochner* is one of the most heavily criticized decisions in American constitutional law. Does the flaw lie in the Court's transformation of the proceduralist thrust of the Due Process Clause into a doctrine of "substantive due process" — that is, of substantive limitations on the power of the state? See John Hart Ely, Democracy and Distrust: A Theory of Judicial Review (1980). But see Samuel Estreicher, Platonic Guardians of Democracy: John Hart Ely's Role for the Supreme Court in the Constitution's Open Texture, 56 N.Y.U. L. Rev. 547 (1981). Or does it lie, rather, in the Court's treatment of liberty of contract as a fundamental right whose infringement requires a compelling justification? Even if liberty of contract is a fundamental right, should not the Court have taken more seriously New York's health and safety concerns? Professor Sunstein also questions *Lochner*'s political theory, arguing that the Court simply assumed that departures from the preexisting wealth distributions required extraordinary justification, whereas status quo entitlements were conclusively presumed to be legitimate. See Sunstein, *Lochner*'s Legacy, supra; Cass R. Sunstein, The Partial Constitution (1993).

Reconsider also Justice Holmes's dissent. Do the courts have the institutional competence to determine whether the benefits of economic legislation are outweighed by their probable costs, or to engage in an evaluation of the political process to determine whether the "winners" have an unfair advantage over the probable "losers"? For instance, assuming that minimum-wage and maximum-hour laws result in depressed employment levels, how can courts balance these costs against the benefits to employed workers? Furthermore, the effects of legislation are difficult to gauge. See, e.g., David E. Card & Alan B. Krueger, Myth and Measurement: The New Economics of the Minimum Wage (1995) (presenting evidence that while substantial boosts in minimum wages can create significant disincentives to hiring additional workers, modest increases have no effect on employment levels).

## B. THE ANTITRUST LAWS

### *Note: Union Growth and Industrial Strife in the 1890s and the Early Twentieth Century*

The physical output of American industry increased 14 times between 1870 and 1929, creating a demand for workers that attracted waves of immigration from Europe. At the outset of World War I, close to 60 percent of the industrial workforce was foreign-born. See David Brody, Workers in Industrial America: Essays on the Twentieth Century Struggle 14-15 (2d ed. 1993). In the prosperous years following the depressed 1890s, the labor movement experienced a major period of growth, climbing from 447,000 members in 1897 to 2 million in 1904. Construction unions grew from 67,000 in 1897 to 391,000 in 1904; transportation unions expanded from 116,000 to 446,000. The bituminous miners struck in 1897 and won the Central Competitive Field Agreement covering virtually the entire industry in Pennsylvania, Ohio, Indiana, and Illinois; the 1902 anthracite strike led to complete organization of the hard-coal fields. See Brody, Workers in Industrial America, supra, at 24.

Many of the famous strikes of this period, such as the Carnegie Steel and Pullman disputes, were accompanied by considerable violence on both sides. Moreover, where unions took hold in an industry, it often was the result of an agreement with an association of employers that sought to control competition. Control was often imperfect, and union efforts to regulate output and shop practices often spurred lower-cost, nonunion competitors, leading to a destabilization of many of these agreements.

In the late 1890s and early twentieth century, union success provoked a counteroffensive by employers, and one by one the trade associations broke with the unions. Some of these associations, like the National Founders' Association, provided strikebreaking and industrial espionage services for its members. Others, like the National Metal Trades Association, helped maintain for its members "an ample supply of skilled workers, while rigging the market, cheapening their price and increasing their flexibility by destroying workers' collective attempts to share in determining the rules under which they worked." Howell Harris, Employers' Collective Action in the Open Shop Era: The Metal Manufacturers' Association of Philadelphia, c. 1903-1933, at 117, 128, in The Power to Manage? Employers and Industrial Relations in a Comparative-Historical Perspective (Steven Tolliday & Jonathan Zeitlin eds., 1991). The courts also were enlisted in this struggle. In March 1893, in the first case to rely on the recently enacted Sherman Antitrust Act, a federal court in Louisiana issued an injunction against the Workingmen's Amalgamated Council of New Orleans arising out of the general strike of 1892. The court stated: "The evil, as well as the unlawfulness of the act of the defendants, consists in [the fact] that, until certain demands of theirs were complied with, they endeavored to prevent, and did prevent, everybody from moving the commerce of the country." United States v. Workingmen's Amalgamated Council, 54 F. 994, 1000 (C.C.E.D. La. 1893). The Supreme Court in In re Debs, 158 U.S. 564 (1895), held that federal courts had authority under the Commerce Clause to enjoin labor unions that threatened to disrupt interstate commercial transactions. The Court discussed but did not rest its decision on the Sherman Act.

## 1. The Sherman Act

### *Note:* Loewe v. Lawlor *(The* "Danbury Hatters" *Case)*

The passage of the Sherman Act in 1890 provided employers with an important weapon for curbing labor unions. Although Congress was principally concerned with restraints of trade and other acts of monopolization by large business enterprises, the statute's language was sufficiently broad to potentially cover agreements between laborers to exert control over a labor market. In particular, §1 of the Act states: "Every contract, combination in the form of trust or otherwise, or conspiracy, in restraint of trade or commerce among the several States, or with foreign nations, is declared to be illegal." Within the Act's first two decades the Supreme Court had an opportunity to consider whether this language reached at least some combinations of laborers.

During the 1890s and early 1900s, vigorous national boycott campaigns, organized by the Hatters, Ironmolders, and other national craft unions, were successful in wresting concessions from previously resistant large manufacturers. These successes prompted the creation of the American Anti-Boycott Association (AABA), founded by two nonunion hat manufacturers in Danbury, Connecticut, Dietrich Loewe and Charles Merritt. In 1902, Loewe refused to recognize the Hatters' union, and all but ten of his men struck in support of the union. Loewe then hired a new workforce and resumed production, leading the AFL to place his firm on its "We Don't Patronize" list. Wherever Loewe's hats were sold, union agents or rank-and-file activists were on the scene, pressuring the local labor groups to put the retailer on their unfair list. In the first *Danbury Hatters* decision, Loewe v. Lawlor, 208 U.S. 274 (1908), the Supreme Court held that the Sherman Act applied to combinations of workers, at least where the union boycotted goods that crossed state lines. Seven years later, the Court sustained a ruling that enabled Loewe to collect treble damages from 248 Connecticut members of the union. Lawlor v. Loewe, 235 U.S. 522 (1915). Walter Merritt, son of the AABA cofounder who was counsel for the plaintiffs, searched state real estate and bank records to determine which of the union's 2,000 Connecticut members had seizable assets. See David Bensman, The Practice of Solidarity: American Hat Finishers in the Nineteenth Century 202-203 (1985).

*Danbury Hatters* involved a "primary" dispute, between Loewe and his striking workers, and a "secondary boycott," in which the union sought a boycott of third parties not directly involved in the dispute but who were wholesalers and retailers of Loewe's hats. Is there a justification for attempting to limit the scope of industrial conflict by condemning secondary boycotts? Were the retailers truly neutrals in a dispute not of their own making? Did they benefit in some sense from the low-cost hats Loewe could produce with nonunion labor? Was the impact of the boycott on the retailers the same as if the Hatters' strike against Loewe had been wholly successful, or was the union seeking a broader boycott of the retailers' entire operations as a means of placing pressure on Loewe?

Note also that the *Danbury Hatters* case involved a secondary *consumer* boycott, where the union sought to encourage the public not to patronize hats produced by Loewe, rather than a secondary *producer* boycott, where the union would be calling on employees of Loewe's distributors or retailers to refuse to handle Loewe's hats. Should this distinction make a difference in defining the proper limits of a labor dispute? Could such a distinction readily be drawn under the Sherman Act?

Labor's supporters expressed outrage at the Supreme Court's application of the Sherman Act to labor disputes, and some commentators charged the Court with a usurpation of the legislative role. See, e.g., Edward Berman, Labor and the Sherman Act 11-51 (1930). Others, however, have defended *Danbury Hatters* based on legislative history indicating that Congress had declined to incorporate amendments expressly exempting agreements between or combinations of laborers. See Hovenkamp, Enterprise and American Law, supra, at 229; 21 Cong. Rec. 2611-2612, 2728-2731 (1890); Alpheus T. Mason, Organized Labor and the Law, ch. VII (1925).

## 2. The Clayton Act

### *Note: The Origins of the Labor Exemption*

*Danbury Hatters* alarmed the labor movement not so much because of its impact on the consumer boycott tactic as for its implications for a very important source of the economic leverage of AFL-affiliated unions — the industry-wide closed shop agreement. Through such agreements, the unions sought to control use of skilled labor and thereby attempt to prevent erosion of labor standards by new entrants into the industry. See Lloyd Ulman, The Rise of the National Labor Union 526-531 (2d ed. 1966). The efficacy of these agreements depended on an ongoing union campaign to ensure that all firms in the industry agreed to abide by union pay and work rules. In 1907, a state court had ordered a national trade union, the Amalgamated Window Glass Workers of America, dissolved on common-law antitrust grounds because the union's by-laws established a closed shop, limited the number of workers who could be employed by a firm, and regulated methods of production. See Kealey v. Faulkner, 18 Ohio Dec. 498 (1907). In the same year, the Hitchman Coal & Coke Co. v. Mitchell litigation was commenced to enjoin an alleged conspiracy between the United Mine Workers (UMW) and coal operators in western Pennsylvania, Ohio, Indiana, and Illinois, the so-called Competitive Coal Fields, to impose a closed shop on a nonunion West Virginia company. The litigation resulted in a 1913 final decree granting "a perpetual injunction," which was reversed pending review by the U.S. Supreme Court. In 1917, the Supreme Court sustained the injunction. 245 U.S. 229, 234-35 (1917). As AFL President Gompers explained in Congress, closed-shop agreements and pressure tactics to obtain such pacts were "a matter of self-defense"; the union's task was to compel the Loewes in an industry to conform to union pay and work rules or risk undercutting the competitive position of employers who had already agreed to those terms. See Daniel R. Ernst, The Labor Exemption, 1908-1914, 74 Iowa L. Rev. 1151, 1155-1156 (1989) and citations therein.

Despite some reverses in the courts, labor was enjoying considerable support among Progressive politicians and improved access to the political process. In order to determine the underlying causes of industrial strife, Congress in 1912 established a United States Commission on Industrial Relations, a tripartite body with broad investigatory power. 37 Stat. 415 (1912). A staff report signed in 1915 by the Commission's chair and labor representatives found that labor was not receiving a fair share of the nation's wealth; the growth of national corporations had made bargaining by individuals impossible; the inequality of income had reduced mass purchasing power; and labor's right to organize had been denied. The report recommended new laws to protect the rights of organization and collective bargaining. Near the end of his term, President William Howard Taft, who as a lower federal judge had been a strong voice in favor of the use of injunctions to restrain labor boycotts, signed the law creating the present Department of Labor. 37 Stat. 736 (1913).

In 1914, President Woodrow Wilson issued a call for changes in the antitrust laws and for creation of a federal trade commission. Labor saw this as an opportunity to revive its campaign for a labor exemption from the antitrust laws. Although Wilson rejected the demand for a wholesale exclusion and the Clayton bill that passed the House did not incorporate the AFL's broad exclusionary language, labor's supporters in the Senate were convinced that the bill legalized the secondary boycott and, in Gompers's terms, would be "Labor's Magna Carta."

### Duplex Printing Press Co. v. Deering
*254 U.S. 443 (1921)*

Mr. Justice Pitney delivered the opinion of the Court.

This was a suit in equity brought by appellant in the District Court for the Southern District of New York for an injunction to restrain a course of conduct carried on by defendants in that District and vicinity in maintaining a boycott against the products of complainant's factory, in furtherance of a conspiracy to injure and destroy its good will, trade, and business—especially to obstruct and destroy its interstate trade. . . .

. . . Complainant conducts its business [at a factory in Battle Creek, Michigan,] on the "open shop" policy, without discrimination against either union or non-union men. The individual defendants and the local organizations of which they are the representatives are affiliated with the International Association of Machinists, an unincorporated association having a membership of more than 60,000; and are united in a combination, to which the International Association also is a party, having the object of compelling complainant to unionize its factory and enforce the "closed shop," the eight-hour day, and the union scale of wages, by means of interfering with and restraining its interstate trade in the products of the factory. Complainant's principal manufacture is newspaper presses of large size and complicated mechanism, varying in weight from 10,000 to 100,000 pounds, and requiring a considerable force of labor and a considerable expenditure of time — a week or more — to handle, haul, and erect them at the point of delivery. These presses are sold throughout the United States and in foreign countries; and, as they are especially designed for the production of daily papers, there is a large market for them in and about the city of New York. They are delivered there in the ordinary course of interstate commerce, the handling, hauling, and installation work at destination being done by employees of the purchaser under the supervision of a specially skilled machinist supplied by complainant. The acts complained of and sought to be restrained have nothing to do with the conduct or management of the factory in Michigan, but solely with the installation and operation of the presses by complainant's customers. None of the defendants is or ever was an employee of complainant, and complainant at no time has had relations with either of the organizations that they represent. In August, 1913 (eight months before the filing of the bill), the International Association called a strike at complainant's factory in Battle Creek, as a result of which union machinists to the number of about eleven in the factory and three who supervised the erection of presses in the field left complainant's employ. But the defection of so small a number did not materially interfere with the operation of the factory, and sales and shipments in interstate commerce continued.

The acts complained of made up the details of an elaborate programme adopted and carried out by defendants and their organizations in and about the city of New York as part of a country-wide programme adopted by the International Association, for the purpose of enforcing a boycott of complainant's product. The acts embraced the following, with others: warning customers that it would be better for them not to purchase, or, having purchased not to install, presses made by complainant, and threatening them with loss should they do so; threatening customers with sympathetic strikes in other trades; notifying a trucking company usually employed by customers to haul the presses not to do so, and threatening it with trouble if it should; inciting employees of the trucking company, and other men employed by customers of complainant, to strike against their respective employers in order to interfere with the hauling and installation of presses, and thus bring pressure to bear upon the customers; notifying repair shops not to do repair work on Duplex presses; coercing union men, by threatening them with loss of union cards and with being blacklisted as "scabs" if they assisted in installing the presses; threatening an exposition company with a strike if it permitted complainant's presses to be exhibited; and resorting to a variety of other modes of preventing the sale of presses of complainant's manufacture in or about New York City, and delivery of them in interstate commerce, such as injuring and threatening to injure complainant's customers and prospective customers, and persons concerned in hauling, handling, or installing the presses. In some cases the threats were undisguised; in other cases polite in form but none the less sinister in purpose and effect. . . .

The substance of the matters here complained of is an interference with complainant's interstate trade, intended to have coercive effect upon complainant, and produced by what is commonly known as a "secondary boycott"; that is, a combination not merely to refrain from dealing with complainant, or to advise or by peaceful means persuade complainant's customers to refrain ("primary boycott"), but to exercise coercive pressure upon such customers, actual or prospective, in order to cause them to withhold or withdraw patronage from complainant through fear of loss or damage to themselves should they deal with it. . . .

Upon the question whether the provisions of the Clayton Act forbade the grant of an injunction under the circumstances of the present case, the Circuit Court of Appeals was divided; the majority holding that under section 20, "perhaps in conjunction with section 6," there could be no injunction. . . . Defendants seek to derive from them some authority for their conduct. As to section 6, it seems to us its principal importance in this discussion is for what it does *not* authorize, and for the limit it sets to the immunity conferred. The section assumes the normal objects of a labor organization to be legitimate, and declares that nothing in the anti-trust laws shall be construed to forbid the existence and operation of such organizations or to forbid their members from *lawfully* carrying out their *legitimate* objects; and that such an organization shall not be held in itself — merely because of its existence and operation — to be an illegal combination or conspiracy in restraint of trade. But there is nothing in the section to exempt such an organization or its members from accountability where it or they depart from its normal and legitimate objects and engage in an actual combination or conspiracy in restraint of trade. And by no fair or permissible construction can it be taken as authorizing any activity otherwise unlawful, or enabling a normally lawful organization to become a cloak for an illegal combination or conspiracy in restraint of trade as defined by the anti-trust laws.

The principal reliance is upon section 20. . . .

The first paragraph merely puts into statutory form familiar restrictions upon the granting of injunctions already established and of general application in the equity practice of the courts of the United States. It is but declaratory of the law as it stood before. The second paragraph declares that "no *such* restraining order or injunction" shall prohibit certain conduct specified — manifestly still referring to a "case between an employer and employees, . . . involving, or growing out of, a dispute concerning terms or condition of employment," as designated in the first paragraph. It is very clear that the restriction upon the use of the injunction is in favor only of those concerned as parties to such a dispute as is described. The words defining the permitted conduct include particular qualifications consistent with the general one respecting the nature of the case and dispute intended. . . . If the qualifying words are to have any effect, they must operate to confine the restriction upon the granting of injunctions, and also the relaxation of the provisions of the anti-trust and other laws of the United States, to parties standing in proximate relation to a controversy such as is particularly described.

The majority of the Circuit Court of Appeals appear to have entertained the view that the words "employers and employees," as used in section 20, should be treated as referring to "the business class or clan to which the parties litigant respectively belong," and that, as there had been a dispute at complainant's factory in Michigan concerning the conditions of employment there—a dispute created, it is said, if it did not exist before, by the act of the Machinist's Union in calling a strike at the factory—section 20 operated to permit members of the Machinists' Union elsewhere—some 60,000 in number—although standing in no relation of employment under complainant, past, present, or prospective, to make that dispute their own and proceed to instigate sympathetic strikes, picketing, and boycotting against employers wholly unconnected with complainant's factory and having relations with complainant only in the way of purchasing its product in the ordinary course of interstate commerce—and this where there was no dispute between such employers and their employees respecting terms or conditions of employment.

We deem this construction altogether inadmissible. Section 20 must be given full effect according to its terms as an expression of the purpose of Congress; but it must be borne in mind that the section imposes an exceptional and extraordinary restriction upon the equity powers of the courts of the United States and upon the general operation of the anti-trust laws, a restriction in the nature of a special privilege or immunity to a particular class, with corresponding detriment to the general public; and it would violate rules of statutory construction having general application and far-reaching importance to enlarge that special privilege by resorting to a loose construction of the section, not to speak of ignoring or slighting the qualifying words that are found in it. . . . Congress had in mind particular industrial controversies, not a general class war. "Terms or conditions of employment" are the only grounds of dispute recognized as adequate to bring into play the exemptions; and it would do violence to the guarded language employed were the exemption extended beyond the parties affected in a proximate and substantial, not merely a sentimental or sympathetic, sense by the cause of dispute. . . .

Decree reversed, and the cause remanded to the District Court for further proceedings in conformity with this opinion.

Mr. Justice BRANDEIS, dissenting, with whom Mr. Justice HOLMES and Mr. Justice CLARKE, concur.

. . . The defendants admit interference with plaintiff's business but justify [it] on the following ground: There are in the United States only four manufacturers of such presses; and they are in active competition. Between 1909 and 1913 the machinists' union induced three of them to recognize and deal with the union, to grant the eight-hour day, to establish a minimum wage scale, and to comply with other union requirements. The fourth, the Duplex Company, refused to recognize the union; insisted upon conducting its factory on the open shop principle; refused to introduce the eight-hour day and operated, for the most part, ten hours a day; refused to establish a minimum wage scale; and disregarded other union standards. Thereupon two of the three manufacturers, who had assented to union conditions, notified the union that they should be obliged to terminate their agreements with it unless their competitor, the Duplex Company, also entered into the agreement with the union, which, in giving more favorable terms to labor, imposed correspondingly greater burdens upon the employer. Because the Duplex Company refused to enter into such an agreement, and in order to induce it to do so, the machinists' union declared a strike at its factory, and in aid of that strike instructed its members and the members of affiliated unions not to work on the installation of presses which plaintiff had delivered in New York. . . .

First. As to the rights at common law: Defendants' justification is that of self-interest. They have supported the strike at the employer's factory by a strike elsewhere against its product. They have injured the plaintiff, not maliciously, but in self-defense. They contend that the Duplex Company's refusal to deal with the machinists' union and to observe its standards threatened the interest, not only of such union members as were its factory employees, but even more of all members of the several affiliated unions employed by plaintiff's competitors and by others whose more advanced standards the plaintiff was, in reality, attacking; and that none of the defendants and no person whom they are endeavoring to induce to refrain from working in connection with the setting up of presses made by plaintiff is an outsider, an interloper. In other words, that the contest between the company and the machinists' union involves vitally the interest of every person whose co-operation is sought. May not all with a common interest join in refusing to expend their labor upon articles whose very production constitutes an attack upon their standard of living and the institution which they are convinced supports it? Applying common law principles the answer should, in my opinion, be: Yes, if as a matter of fact those who so co-operate have a common interest. . . .

Second. As to the anti-trust laws of the United States . . . [t]his statute was the fruit of unceasing agitation, which extended over more than 20 years and was designed to equalize before the law the position of workingmen and employer as industrial combatants. . . .

. . . Congress did not restrict the provision to employers and workingmen *in their employ*. By including "employers and employees" and "persons employed and persons seeking employment" it showed that it was not aiming merely at a legal relationship between a specific employer and his employees. . . . The . . . contention that this case is not one arising out of a dispute concerning the conditions of work of one of the parties is, in my opinion, founded upon a misconception of the facts.

Because I have come to the conclusion that both the common law of a state and a statute of the United States declare the right of industrial combatants to push their struggle to the limits of the justification of self-interest, I do not wish to be understood as attaching any constitutional or moral sanction to that right. All rights are derived from the purposes of the society in which they exist; above all rights rises duty to the community. The conditions developed in industry may be such that those engaged in it cannot continue their struggle without danger to the community. But it is not for judges to determine whether such conditions exist, nor is it their function to set the limits of permissible contest and to declare the duties which the new situation demands. This is the function of the legislature which, while limiting individual and group rights of aggression and defense, may substitute processes of justice for the more primitive method of trial by combat.

## *NOTES AND QUESTIONS*

**1. Labor's "Magna Carta"?** Who had the better of the argument with respect to the reach of §20: Justice Pitney's opinion for the majority or Justice Brandeis's for the dissent? Is it likely, given the outcry over *Danbury Hatters*, that Congress intended a narrow definition of "labor dispute" that would also permit injunctions against consumer boycotts of the type involved in that case? What meaning does the majority give to the clause, "or between an employer and employees," in §20? Even with the qualifying language, permitting acts "which might lawfully be done in the absence of such disputes by any party thereto," do we have anything more here than a case of statutory ambiguity? What reasons does the majority give for the manner in which it resolves that ambiguity? For the view that, despite the "Magna Carta" rhetoric, labor's supporters opted for ambiguous language because they were unable to secure in Congress a clear-cut exclusion from the antitrust laws, see Ernst, The Labor Exemption, supra, at 1167.

**2. Section 6 and Labor Market vs. Product Market Restraints?** What effect does the majority give to the opening sentence of §6: "That the labor of a human being is not a commodity or article of commerce"? Does this language support an argument that restraints in the labor market—in the competition between union workers and nonunion workers—are not within the reach of the antitrust laws? Does §20 simply define the permissible reach of injunctions against union tactics that involve combinations with employer groups or violence or other disruptions that can be said to be unlawful, independent of their use in furtherance of a labor dispute? On the facts in *Duplex Printing*, was the union acting at the behest of organized employer groups? If so, is this enough to take the case out of the protection of §6? Is there a distinction between restraints on competition in product markets not based on the costs of labor inputs and restraints on competition based on labor costs? Reconsider this question after reading the *Hutcheson* and *Apex Hosiery* opinions below.

**3. "Hot Cargo" vs. Secondary Producer Boycotts?** What if the New York machinists had gone beyond refusing to work on the struck product—in labor terminology, a refusal to handle "hot cargo"—and had suspended all work for their employers until the latter broke off relations with the Michigan manufacturer? Would Justice Brandeis have held such a secondary producer boycott protected by the Clayton Act?

**4. The Primary Strike and the Antitrust Laws.** Unions employ secondary consumer and producer boycotts because a primary strike is unable to prevent a cessation of production at the struck employer. An apparent assumption of both *Danbury Hatters* and *Duplex Printing* was that the primary strike itself was beyond the reach of the antitrust laws. However, the Supreme Court in a 1925 decision, Coronado Coal Co. v. United Mine Workers, 268 U.S. 295, placed even that premise in question. In that case, an Arkansas mine that had been unionized reopened on a nonunion basis, provoking a violent strike. A jury returned a verdict of $200,000, which was trebled. On appeal, the Supreme Court remanded the case because it found evidence only of a "local" motive on the part of the UMW to reestablish a closed shop at the mine rather than an intent to restrain interstate commerce. 259 U.S. 344 (1922). On remand, evidence was presented that the union's objective in organizing the Arkansas mine was to eliminate competition from nonunion mines that was undermining closed shop agreements in adjacent states. This showing was held sufficient by the Supreme Court in its second *Coronado Coal* decision to violate the Sherman Act:

> We think there was substantial evidence at the second trial in this case tending to show that the purpose of the destruction of the mines was to stop the production of nonunion coal and prevent its shipment to markets of other states than Arkansas, where it would by competition tend to reduce the price of the commodity and affect injuriously the maintenance of wages for union labor in competing mines.

268 U.S. at 310. Under this rationale, would even a nonviolent strike be free from damages liability under the Sherman Act?

***Note: Labor Organization and the Management of Work from World War I Through the 1920s***

World War I and its immediate aftermath brought significant successes for the union movement. Membership increased rapidly, from about 2.5 million in 1914 to about 5 million in 1920. That growth was aided by a strong demand for workers and by rising prices, which produced both discontent and opportunities for unions to secure increases in wages and benefits. Moreover, the National War Labor Board legitimated organization by recognizing the "right of workers to organize in trade unions and to bargain collectively through chosen representatives." Although the Board lacked enforcement authority, President Wilson exercised his war powers to secure obedience to its decisions, threatening recalcitrant workers with conscription and in several cases seizing the plants of defiant employers. The policy of affirmative protection of labor organization was abandoned soon after the war, but it survived in the railroad industry, and during the Great Depression it was to become the cornerstone of national labor policy.

The wartime increase in union membership had been concentrated in relatively few trades, and the trade union movement had not organized the unskilled workers in heavy industries. The AFL's effort in 1917-1918 to organize the basic steel industry failed. Elbert Gary of the United States Steel Company (U.S. Steel), which dominated that industry, first stated that the corporation "does not confer . . . with or combat labor unions as such" and later insisted that the unions lacked authority to speak for its employees. See Philip Taft, The AFL in the Time of Gompers 387 (1957). Some employers resisted unionization with familiar weapons: espionage, discharge of union sympathizers, and other acts of intimidation and suppression. A strike called in 1919, despite Gompers' urging of caution and President Wilson's request for postponement, was honored by a majority of the steel workers in every region, and in seven weeks there were 367,000 strikers, according to union estimates. Violence erupted in many areas; 20 people, including 18 strikers, were killed, and martial law was imposed in some places. Replacements made the strike increasingly ineffective, and early in 1920 it was called off.

The 1919 U.S. Steel strike was part of a larger strike wave that swept the country, involving over 4 million workers or 20 percent of the labor force. The consequences of the strike wave for the labor movement were fairly devastating:

> When the smoke cleared, the labor movement had lost 1.5 million members. The entrenched unions had come through well enough, and some had scored notable gains, but labor's outbreak into open-shop territory had almost everywhere been smashed. The union movement fell back to the confined position it had occupied before the war.

Brody, Workers in Industrial America, supra, at 45.

The 1920s were a period of general decline for unions. In contrast to their gains in prior periods of prosperity, unions did not benefit from the vigorous economic activity and stable prices that prevailed from 1923 to 1929. Union membership declined from 5 million in 1920 to 3.4 million in 1929—a 23 percent decrease. Unions covered only fragments of the workforce, primarily in the traditional crafts with some penetration in basic industries such as coal, construction, and the railroads. In manufacturing and mechanical industries, unions were present only in printing, clothing, and shoe manufacturing, with almost no organization in steel, automobiles, electrical equipment, rubber, oil, or cement. Union membership in manufacturing fell from 1.9 million in 1920 to less than 800,000 by 1929, a decline of nearly 60 percent. Strike activity also declined, from 3,411 work stoppages in 1920 to 921 in 1929. See Sanford M. Jacoby, Employing Bureaucracy: Managers, Unions, and the Transformation of Work in American Industry, 1900-1945, at 172 (1985); Irving Bernstein, The New Deal Collective Bargaining Policy 2 (1950).

The union decline was due only in part to the inability of the AFL's craft orientation to adjust to the rise of mass production industries, and employer opposition of the type exemplified by Elbert Gary's response to the attempt to organize the steel industry in the postwar period. Employers used a carrot in addition to the stick. The general prosperity of the period led to improved wages and working conditions, despite some wage stagnation in manufacturing. See Jacoby, Employing Bureaucracy, supra, at 168-169. The leading firms in the mass production industries continued policies developed in the pre–World War I period to establish special personnel staffs as a means of curtailing the discretion of plant foremen and to promote "welfare capitalism," including profit-sharing, plant councils or shop committees, insurance plans, company housing, and recreation. These policies were limited to large companies, and there is some question whether diffusion occurred beyond a "progressive minority" of firms. See id. at 190-192; Brody, Workers in Industrial America, supra, at 59-60.

## C. THE NORRIS-LAGUARDIA ACT AND REEXAMINATION OF THE ANTITRUST LAWS: MANDATING GOVERNMENT NEUTRALITY IN LABOR DISPUTES

### 1. The Norris-LaGuardia Act of 1932

#### a. *The "Labor Injunction"*

The "labor injunction" reached new heights (or lows) during the 1920s, with employers able to secure the judiciary's assistance in labor disputes by the simple expedient of requiring their employees to agree not to join a union or be involved in union activities during the term of their employment—the so-called "yellow dog contract." The Supreme Court facilitated this process by striking down legislation that outlawed such agreements in Adair v. United States, 208 U.S. 161 (1908), and Coppage v. Kansas, 236 U.S. 1 (1915). In Hitchman Coal & Coke Co. v. Mitchell, 245 U.S. 229 (1917), with Justice Brandeis dissenting, the Court upheld an injunction against union organizers who sought to persuade employees of a once-unionized mine to again become union members despite their having signed such clauses. Justice Pitney wrote for the Court:

> Plaintiff, having in the exercise of its undoubted rights established a working agreement between it and its employees, with the free assent of the latter, is entitled to be protected in the enjoyment of the resulting status, as in any other legal right. That the employment was "at will," and terminable by either party at any time, is of no consequence. . . .
>
> The case involves no question of the rights of employees. Defendants have no agency for plaintiff's employees, nor do they assert any disagreement or grievance in their behalf. In fact, there is none; but, if there were, defendants could not, without agency, set up any rights that employees might have. The right of the latter to strike would not give to defendants the right to instigate a strike. The difference is fundamental. . . .
>
> But the facts render it plain that what the defendants were endeavoring to do at the Hitchman mine and neighboring mines cannot be treated as a bona fide effort to enlarge the membership of the union. There is no evidence to show, nor can it be inferred, that defendants intended or desired to have the men at these mines join the union, *unless they could organize the mines.* . . .
>
> The present is not a case of merely withholding from an employer an economic need—as a supply of labor—until he assents to be governed by union regulations. Defendants have no supply of labor of which plaintiff stands in need. . . . There is no reason to doubt that if defendants had been actuated by a genuine desire to increase the membership of the union without unnecessary injury to the known rights of plaintiff, they would have permitted their proselytes to withdraw from plaintiff's employ when and as they became affiliated with the union—as their contract of employment required them to

> do — and that in this event plaintiff would have been able to secure an adequate supply of non-union men to take their places. It was with knowledge of this, and because of it, that defendants . . . caused the new members to remain at work in plaintiff's mine until a sufficient number of men should be persuaded to join so as to bring about a strike and render it difficult if not practically impossible for plaintiff to continue to exercise its undoubted legal and constitutional right to run its mine "non-union."

245 U.S. at 251-253, 256-258 (emphasis in the original).

The labor injunction was used throughout the 1920s, with the courts in a sense assisting companies in their campaign to impose a nonunion shop throughout industry. See, e.g., United Mine Workers v. Red Jacket Consol. Coal & Coke Co., 18 F.2d 839 (4th Cir. 1927). According to the late Professor Bernstein, 1.25 million workers were required to sign these contracts during the decade, and some court orders "covered large segments of an industry, like the notorious Red Jacket injunction granted by Judge John J. Parker in 1927, which effectively barred the UMW from organizing in virtually the entire West Virginia coal industry." Irving Bernstein, The Lean Years: A History of the American Worker, 1920-1933, at 200 (1960).

The reputation of the federal judiciary was badly tarnished by its role during the 1920s, and indeed Judge Parker's nomination to the Supreme Court was rejected by the Senate in 1930 principally because of his *Red Jacket* decision. For the classic text on the federal labor injunction, see Frankfurter & Greene, The Labor Injunction, discussed supra. Increasingly, the federal courts' exercise of their equity power clashed with an emerging sentiment in Congress in favor of labor organization and collective bargaining. The Railway Labor Act had been enacted in 1926 to carry forward the unionization of the railroads that had occurred during World War I. Largely at the behest of the labor movement, Congress passed the Davis-Bacon Act of 1931, 40 U.S.C. §§3041 et seq., to require payment of "prevailing wages" — typically, union-set wages and work rules — on public projects funded by the federal government. The Great Depression of 1929 also increased public concern with the erosion of earnings and working conditions.

This was the setting for the enactment of the Norris-LaGuardia Act on March 23, 1932, 47 Stat. 70 (codified at 29 U.S.C. §§101-115). This statute outlawed the yellow-dog contract as a matter of public policy and gave recognition for the first time to labor's claim that individual employees bargaining on their own could not exercise "actual liberty of contract," thus undermining the theoretical underpinnings of *Hitchman Coal.*

Moreover, the statute also addressed many of the objections to labor injunctions raised by union leaders and other supporters of the labor movement. Section 4 barred federal courts from issuing any temporary or permanent injunctions or restraining orders against becoming or remaining a union member, engaging in strikes, nonviolent and nonfraudulent patrolling or other forms of publicizing labor disputes, peaceful assemblies for organizing in a labor dispute, or rendering advice or entering into an agreement to do any of the above.

Furthermore, §7 imposed procedural conditions on the issuance of injunctions in labor disputes (defined broadly in §13) in cases not covered by §4. First, ex parte orders could be issued only when "a substantial and irreparable injury to complainant's property will be unavoidable," after the posting of adequate security, and only for a maximum of five days. Second, the issuance of any injunction required findings of facts supporting the normal conditions of the exercise of equity power, including the lack of an adequate remedy at law, a likelihood of substantial and irreparable injury to the complainant's property, and the lesser impact on defendants from the grant of relief. Third, §7 required a specific finding that public officers charged with protecting the complainant's property were unwilling or unable to do so without the issuance of the injunction. Fourth, the injunction could only be issued against the particular persons or organizations actually committing, threatening, or authorizing the unlawful acts being enjoined.

The Norris-LaGuardia Act afforded other procedural protections as well. Section 6 provided that no officer or member of a union or a union itself could be made liable for the unlawful acts of individual members or agents, except upon proof of actual participation in, authorization of, or ratification of the acts. Section 9 required injunctions to cover only the specific act or acts complained of and to be supported by findings of fact. Section 8 imposed a clean-hands doctrine, barring injunctive relief when the complainant failed to comply with some legal obligation involved in the labor dispute or failed to make every reasonable effort to settle the dispute through private negotiation, government mediation, or voluntary arbitration. Section 10 required the certification of the appeal of temporary labor injunctions to the courts of appeals. Finally, §11 required jury trials in all contempt proceedings under the Act other than those for contempt committed in the presence of the court.

The Norris-LaGuardia Act can be characterized as an attempt to perfect the common-law model for regulating labor disputes rather than as an effort to promote labor organization directly. It has been described as a "monument to the spirit of complete free enterprise for unions." Charles O. Gregory & Harold A. Katz, Labor and the Law 197 (3d ed. 1979). It was designed to afford unions an opportunity to organize free of the restraints of government authority, but without attempting directly to restrain the power of private employers.

### *b. Modern Applications of the Norris-LaGuardia Act*

The modern application of the Norris-LaGuardia Act is discussed in detail in Chapter 8, infra pages 703-720. As that material indicates, the

Act has conferred upon labor unions a broad immunity from the issuance of federal injunctions in labor disputes. See, e.g., Jacksonville Bulk Terminals, Inc. v. Int'l Longshoremen's Ass'n, 457 U.S. 702 (1982), infra page 719 (term "labor dispute" defined to include even disputes that have their origin in political protests rather than economic self-interest). As explained in Chapter 8, moreover, in many cases it effectively immunizes unions from state injunctions as well. The Supreme Court, however, has significantly qualified the protection of the Norris-LaGuardia Act in decisions "accommodating" the Act to §301 of the Labor Management Relations Act, enacted in 1947. See especially Boys Markets, Inc. v. Retail Clerks Union, Local 770, 398 U.S. 235 (1970), infra pages 704-710 (injunction against strike over issue encompassed within contractual grievance-arbitration clause does not violate Norris-LaGuardia Act).

## 2. Reexamination of the Antitrust Laws

Despite the fact that the express terms of the Norris-LaGuardia Act only limit the injunctive power of federal courts, the Act also had implications for the applicability of the antitrust laws in labor disputes. Included below are excerpts from two leading decisions of the Supreme Court, which reflect both the influence of the new appointments of President Franklin D. Roosevelt, who was first elected in 1932, and the change in reigning conceptions of the proper role of the law and federal judges in labor disputes.

### Apex Hosiery Co. v. Leader
*310 U.S. 469 (1940)*

Mr. Justice Stone delivered the opinion of the Court.

Petitioner, a Pennsylvania corporation, is engaged in the manufacture, at its factory in Philadelphia, of hosiery, a substantial part of which is shipped in interstate commerce. It brought the present suit in the federal district court for Eastern Pennsylvania against respondent Federation, a labor organization, and its officers, to recover treble the amount of damage inflicted on it by respondents in conducting a strike at petitioner's factory alleged to be a conspiracy in violation of the Sherman Anti-Trust Act. [The trial resulted in a jury verdict of $237,310, which was trebled to the amount of $711,932.55. The judgment was reversed on appeal by the United States Court of Appeals for the Third Circuit] on the ground that the interstate commerce restrained or affected by respondents' acts was unsubstantial. . . .

The facts are undisputed. There was evidence from which the jury could have found as follows. Petitioner employs at its Philadelphia factory about twenty-five hundred persons in the manufacture of hosiery, and manufactures annually merchandise of the value of about $5,000,000. Its principal raw materials are silk and cotton, which are shipped to it from points outside the state. It ships interstate more than 80 per cent of its finished product, and in the last eight months of 1937 it shipped in all 274,791 dozen pairs of stockings. In April, 1937, petitioner was operating a nonunion shop. A demand of the respondent Federation at that time for a closed shop agreement came to nothing. On May 4, 1937, when only eight of petitioner's employees were members of the Federation, it ordered a strike. Shortly after midday on May 6, 1937, when petitioner's factory was shut down members of the union, employed by other factories in Philadelphia who had stopped work, gathered at petitioner's plant. Respondent Leader, president of the Federation, then made a further demand for a closed shop agreement. When this was refused Leader declared a "sit down strike." Immediately, acts of violence against petitioner's plant and the employees in charge of it were committed by the assembled mob. It forcibly seized the plant, whereupon, under union leadership, its members were organized to maintain themselves as sit-down strikers in possession of the plant, and it remained in possession until June 23, 1937, when the strikers were forcibly ejected pursuant to [a court injunction]. . . .

It is not denied, and we assume for present purposes, that respondents by substituting the primitive method of trial by combat, for the ordinary processes of justice and more civilized means of deciding an industrial dispute, violated the civil and penal laws of Pennsylvania which authorize the recovery of full compensation and impose criminal penalties for the wrongs done. But in this suit, in which no diversity of citizenship of the parties is alleged or shown, the federal courts are without authority to enforce state laws. Their only jurisdiction is to vindicate such federal right as Congress has conferred on petitioner by the Sherman Act and violence, as will appear hereafter, however reprehensible, does not give the federal courts jurisdiction. . . .

The critical words which circumscribe the judicial [role] so far as the present case is concerned are "Every . . . combination . . . or conspiracy, in restraint of trade or commerce." Since in the present case, as we have seen, the natural and predictable consequence of the strike was the restraint of interstate transportation the precise question which we are called upon to decide is whether that restraint resulting from the strike maintained to enforce union demands by compelling a shutdown of petitioner's factory is the kind of "restraint of trade or commerce" which the Act condemns.

In considering whether union activities like the present may fairly be deemed to be embraced within this phrase, three circumstances relating to the history and application of the Act which are of striking significance must first be taken into account. The legislative history of the Sherman Act as well as the decisions of this Court interpreting it, show that it was not aimed at policing interstate transportation or movement of goods and property. . . . It was enacted in the era of "trusts" and of "combinations" of businesses and of capital organized and directed to control of the market by suppression of competition in the marketing of goods and services, the monopolistic tendency of which had become a matter of public concern. The end sought was the prevention of restraints to free competition in business and commercial transactions which tended to restrict production, raise prices or otherwise control the market to the detriment of purchasers or consumers of goods and services, all of which had come to be regarded as a special form of public injury.

A second significant circumstance is that this Court has never applied the Sherman Act in any case, whether or not involving labor organizations or activities, unless the Court was of opinion that there was some form of restraint upon commercial competition in the marketing of goods or services and finally this Court has refused to apply the Sherman Act in cases like the present in which local strikes conducted by illegal means in a production industry prevented interstate shipment of substantial amounts of the product but in which it was not shown that the restrictions on shipments had operated to restrain commercial competition in some substantial way. . . .

The question remains whether the effect of the combination or conspiracy among respondents was a restraint of trade within the meaning of the Sherman Act. This is not a case of a labor organization being used by combinations of those engaged in an industry as the means or instrument for suppressing competition or fixing prices. See United States v. Brims, 272 U.S. 549; Local 167 v. United States, 291 U.S. 293. Here it is plain that the combination or conspiracy did not have as its purpose restraint upon competition in the market for petitioner's product. Its object was to compel petitioner to accede to the union demands and an effect of it, in consequence of the strikers' tortious acts, was the prevention of the removal of petitioner's product for interstate shipment. So far as appears the delay of these shipments was not intended to have and had no effect on prices of hosiery in the market, . . . because notwithstanding its effect upon the marketing of the [hosiery] it nevertheless was not intended to and did not affect market price.

A combination of employees necessarily restrains competition among themselves in the sale of their services to the employer; yet such a combination was not considered an illegal restraint of trade at common law when the Sherman Act was adopted, either because it was not thought to be unreasonable or because it was not deemed a "restraint of trade." Since the enactment of the declaration in §6 of the Clayton Act that "the labor of a human being is not a commodity or article of commerce . . . nor shall such (labor) organizations, or the members thereof, be held or construed to be illegal combinations or conspiracies in restraint of trade, under the anti-trust laws," it would seem plain that restraints on the sale of the employee's services to the employer, however much they curtail the competition among employees, are not in themselves combinations or conspiracies in restraint of trade or commerce under the Sherman Act. . . .

. . . Furthermore, successful union activity, as for example consummation of a wage agreement with employers, may have some influence on price competition by eliminating that part of such competition which is based on differences in labor standards. Since, in order to render a labor combination effective it must eliminate the competition from non-union made goods . . . an elimination of price competition based on differences in labor standards is the objective of any national labor organization. But this effect on competition has not been considered to be the kind of curtailment of price competition prohibited by the Sherman Act.[24]

This Court first applied the Sherman Act to a labor organization in Loewe v. Lawlor, 208 U.S. 274, in 1908, holding that the trial court had erroneously sustained a demurrer to the declaration in a suit for damages for violation of the Sherman Act on the ground that the combination alleged was not within the Act. The combination or conspiracy charged was that of a nation-wide labor organization to force all manufacturers of fur hats in the United States to organize their workers by maintaining a boycott against the purchase of the product of non-union manufacturers shipped in interstate commerce. The restraint alleged was not a strike or refusal to work in the complainants' plant, but a secondary boycott by which, through threats to the manufacturer's wholesale customers and their customers, the Union sought to compel or induce them not to deal in the product of the complainants, and to purchase the competing products of other unionized manufacturers. . . . The Court in the *Loewe* case held that the boycott operated as a restraint of trade or commerce within the meaning of the Sherman Act, and that the language of the Act, "every combination, etc." was broad enough to include a labor union imposing such a restraint. Like problems found a like solution in Duplex Printing Press Co. v. Deering, 254 U.S. 443, and in Bedford Cut Stone Company v. Journeyman Stone Cutters' Assn., 274 U.S. 37; where, in the one case, a secondary boycott, and in the other, the refusal of the union to work on a product in the hands of the purchaser, were carried on on a country-wide scale by a national labor organization, in order to induce the purchasers of a manufactured product shipped in interstate commerce to withdraw their patronage from the producer. . . .

---

24. Federal legislation [citing, inter alia, the Norris-LaGuardia Act, 29 U.S.C. §§101-115; Public Contracts Act, 41 U.S.C. §§35-48; and Fair Labor Standards Act of 1938, 29 U.S.C. §§201-219] aimed at protecting and favoring labor organizations and eliminating the competition of employers and employees based on labor conditions regarded as substandard, through the establishment of industry-wide standards both by collective bargaining and by legislation setting up minimum wage and hour standards, supports the conclusion that Congress does not regard the effects upon competition from such combinations and standards as against public policy or condemned by the Sherman Act. . . .

It will be observed that in each of these cases where the Act was held applicable to labor unions, the activities affecting interstate commerce were directed at control of the market and were so widespread as substantially to affect it. There was thus a suppression of competition in the market by methods which were deemed analogous to those found to be violations in the non-labor cases. . . . That the objective of the restraint in the boycott cases was the strengthening of the bargaining position of the union and not the elimination of business competition—which was the end in the non-labor cases—was thought to be immaterial because the Court viewed the restraint itself, in contrast to the interference with shipments caused by a local factory strike, to be of a kind regarded as offensive at common law because of its effect in curtailing a free market and it was held to offend against the Sherman Act because it effected and was aimed at suppression of competition with union made goods in the interstate market. . . .

If, without such effects on the market, we were to hold that a local factory strike, stopping production and shipment of its product interstate, violates the Sherman law, practically every strike in modern industry would be brought within the jurisdiction of the federal courts, under the Sherman Act, to remedy local law violations. The Act was plainly not intended to reach such a result. . . . The Sherman Act is concerned with the character of the prohibited restraints and with their effect on interstate commerce. It draws no distinction between the restraints effected by violence and those achieved by peaceful but oftentimes quite as effective means. Restraints not within the Act, when achieved by peaceful means, are not brought within its sweep merely because, without other differences, they are attended by violence.

### United States v. Hutcheson
*312 U.S. 219 (1941)*

Mr. Justice FRANKFURTER delivered the opinion of the Court.

. . . Summarizing the long indictment, these are the facts. Anheuser-Busch, Inc., operating a large plant in St. Louis, contracted with Borsari Tank Corporation for the erection of an additional facility. The Gaylord Container Corporation, a lessee of adjacent property from Anheuser-Busch, made a similar contract for a new building with the Stocker Company. Anheuser-Busch obtained the materials for its brewing and other operations and sold its finished products largely through interstate shipments. The Gaylord Corporation was equally dependent on interstate commerce for marketing its goods, as were the construction companies for their building materials. Among the employees of Anheuser-Busch were members of the United Brotherhood of Carpenters and Joiners of America and of the International Association of Machinists. The conflicting claims of these two organizations, affiliated with the American Federation of Labor, in regard to the erection and dismantling of machinery had long been a source of controversy between them. Anheuser-Busch had had agreements with both organizations whereby the Machinists were given the disputed jobs and the Carpenters agreed to submit all disputes to arbitration. But in 1939 the president of the Carpenters, their general representative, and two officials of the Carpenters' local organization, the four men under indictment, stood on the claims of the Carpenters for the jobs. Rejection by the employer of the Carpenters' demand and the refusal of the latter to submit to arbitration were followed by a strike of the Carpenters, called by the defendants against Anheuser-Busch and the construction companies, a picketing of Anheuser-Busch and its tenant, and a request through circular letters and the official publication of the Carpenters that union members and their friends refrain from buying Anheuser-Busch beer. . . .

The Norris-LaGuardia Act removed the fetters upon trade union activities, which according to judicial construction §20 of the Clayton Act had left untouched, by still further narrowing the circumstances under which the federal courts could grant injunctions in labor disputes. More especially, the Act explicitly formulated the "public policy of the United States" in regard to the industrial conflict, and by its light established that the allowable area of union activity was not to be restricted, as it had been in [*Duplex Printing*] to an immediate employer-employee relation. Therefore, whether trade union conduct constitutes a violation of the Sherman Law is to be determined only by reading the Sherman Law and §20 of the Clayton Act and the Norris-LaGuardia Act as a harmonizing text of outlawry of labor conduct.

Were then the acts charged against the defendants prohibited or permitted by these three interlacing statutes? If the facts laid in the indictment come within the conduct enumerated in §20 of the Clayton Act they do not constitute a crime within the general terms of the Sherman Law because of the explicit command of that section that such conduct shall not be "considered or held to be violations of any law of the United States." So long as a union acts in its self-interest and does not combine with non-labor groups, the licit and the illicit under §20 are not to be distinguished by any judgment regarding the wisdom or unwisdom, the rightness or wrongness, the selfishness or unselfishness of the end of which the particular union activities are the means. There is nothing remotely within the terms of §20 that differentiates between trade union conduct directed against an employer because of a controversy arising in the relation between employer and employee, as such, and conduct similarly directed but ultimately due to an internecine struggle between two unions seeking the favor of the same employer. . . .

In so far as the Clayton Act is concerned, we must therefore dispose of this case as though we had before us precisely the same conduct on the part of the defendants in pressing claims against Anheuser-Busch for increased wages, or shorter hours, or other elements of what are called working conditions. The fact that what was done was done in a competition for jobs against the Machinists rather than against, let us say, a company union is a differentiation which Congress has not put into the federal legislation and which therefore we cannot write into it.

It is at once apparent that the acts with which the defendants are charged are the kind of acts protected by §20 of the Clayton Act. The refusal of the Carpenters to work for Anheuser-Busch or on construction work being done for it and its adjoining tenant, and the peaceful attempt to get members of other unions similarly to refuse to work, are plainly within the free scope accorded to workers by §20 for "terminating any relation of employment," or "ceasing to perform any work or labor," or "recommending, advising or persuading others by peaceful means so to do." The picketing of Anheuser-Busch premises with signs to indicate that Anheuser-Busch was unfair to organized labor, a familiar practice in these situations, comes within the language "attending at any place where any such person or persons may lawfully be, for the purpose of peacefully obtaining or communicating information, or from peacefully persuading any person to work or to abstain from working." Finally, the recommendation to union members and their friends not to buy or use the product of Anheuser-Busch is explicitly covered by "ceasing to patronize . . . any party to such dispute, or from recommending, advising, or persuading others by peaceful and lawful means so to do."

Clearly, then, the facts here charged constitute lawful conduct under the Clayton Act unless the defendants cannot invoke that Act because outsiders to the immediate dispute also shared in the conduct. But we need not determine whether the conduct is legal within the restrictions which *Duplex Printing Press Co. v. Deering* gave to the immunities of §20 of the Clayton Act. Congress in the Norris-LaGuardia Act has expressed the public policy of the United States and defined its conception of a "labor dispute" in terms that no longer leave room for doubt. . . . Such a dispute, §13(c), 29 U.S.C. §113(c), provides, "includes any controversy concerning terms or conditions of employment, or concerning the association or representation of persons in negotiating, fixing, maintaining, changing, or seeking to arrange terms or conditions of employment, regardless of whether or not the disputants stand in the proximate relation of employer and employee." And under §13(b) a person is "participating or interested in a labor dispute" if he "is engaged in the same industry, trade, craft, or occupation in which such dispute occurs, or has a direct or indirect interest therein, or is a member, officer, or agent of any association composed in whole or in part of employers or employees engaged in such industry, trade, craft, or occupation."

To be sure, Congress expressed this national policy and determined the bounds of a labor dispute in an act explicitly dealing with the further withdrawal of injunctions in labor controversies. But to argue, as it was urged before us, that the *Duplex* case still governs for purposes of a criminal prosecution is to say that that which on the equity side of the court is allowable conduct may in a criminal proceeding become the road to prison. It would be strange indeed that although neither the Government nor Anheuser-Busch could have sought an injunction against the acts here challenged, the elaborate efforts to permit such conduct failed to prevent criminal liability punishable with imprisonment and heavy fines. That is not the way to read the will of Congress, particularly when expressed by a statute which, as we have already indicated, is practically and historically one of a series of enactments touching one of the most sensitive national problems. Such legislation must not be read in a spirit of mutilating narrowness. . . .

The relation of the Norris-LaGuardia Act to the Clayton Act is not that of a tightly drawn amendment to a technically phrased tax provision. The underlying aim of the Norris-LaGuardia Act was to restore the broad purpose which Congress thought it had formulated in the Clayton Act but which was frustrated, so Congress believed, by unduly restrictive judicial construction. . . . The Norris-LaGuardia Act reasserted the original purpose of the Clayton Act by infusing into it the immunized trade union activities as redefined by the later Act. In this light §20 removes all such allowable conduct from the taint of being "violations of any law of the United States," including the Sherman Law. . . .

## *NOTES AND QUESTIONS*

**1. Influence of New Deal Legislation.** Both *Apex Hosiery* (especially footnote 24) and *Hutcheson* reflect the influence not only of the Norris-LaGuardia Act but also of the spate of protective labor laws enacted during Franklin Roosevelt's first two administrations. These include the recognition of labor's right to organize and engage in collective bargaining in §7(a) of the National Industrial Recovery Act of 1933, 48 Stat. 195 (June 16, 1933), and the National Labor Relations Act of 1935 (NLRA); federal guarantees of minimum wages and overtime pay in the Fair Labor Standards Act of 1938; the federal program of retirement and survivors' benefits in the Social Security Act of 1935; and the "prevailing wage" laws for federally funded public projects in the Davis-Bacon Act of 1931 and the Walsh-Healy Act of 1936.

**2. Professor Frankfurter vs. Justice Frankfurter.** As a Harvard Law School professor, Felix Frankfurter was one of a group of academics advising the Senate Judiciary Committee on the drafting of the bill that became the Norris-LaGuardia Act. At the time, Professor Frankfurter favored a measure limited to "[curbing] the procedural abuses of the injunction," with ". . . modifications of the substantive law" to be "dealt with [in a separate bill], so far as necessary." Letter from Felix Frankfurter to Edwin Witte (May 20, 1928), quoted in Robert A. Gorman & Matthew W. Finkin, The Individual and the Requirement of "Concert" Under the National Labor Relations Act, 130 U. Pa. L. Rev. 286, 334 n.176 (1981). See also Frankfurter & Greene, The Labor Injunction, supra, at 215 (". . . it is not immunity from legal as distinguished from equitable remedies—hitherto unlawful conduct remains unlawful"). No such separate legislation was proposed by the group or considered by Congress at this time.

**3. Assistant Attorney General Arnold's Program.** The *Hutcheson* case grew out of a program developed by Assistant Attorney General Thurman Arnold to use the antitrust laws to curb certain labor abuses, including (a) union attempts to prevent the use of lower-cost materials and more efficient methods; (b) union attempts to require the hiring of redundant labor, a practice known as "featherbedding"; (c) union extortion of businesses; (d) union-management price-fixing schemes; and (e) strikes and other tactics used by one union to obtain work assigned to members of another union, or what are called jurisdictional disputes. See Thurman Arnold, The Bottlenecks of Business 251-252 (1940). To what extent are any of these practices reached by the antitrust laws as interpreted in *Apex Hosiery* and *Hutcheson*? To what extent should they be? Even if not regulated by the antitrust laws, should these practices go unregulated altogether? The original NLRA did not contain a set of prohibited union unfair labor practices. Congress, in 1947, amended the NLRA to reach some, though not all, of the labor abuses covered by Arnold's program. See infra pages 58-59.

**4. Comparing *Apex Hosiery* vs. *Hutcheson*.** Justice Stone in *Apex Hosiery* purported not to disturb *Danbury Hatters*, *Duplex Printing*, or the second *Coronado Coal* decision. Are there aspects of Justice Stone's rationale that undermine these rulings, however? Do these rulings survive *Hutcheson*? How would you articulate the difference between the tests in *Apex Hosiery* and *Hutcheson*? Which does a better job of reconciling the objectives and impact of unions with the pro-competition policy of the antitrust laws?

**5. "Taking Wages Out of Competition"?** Should the labor movement be free of any restraint under the antitrust laws in furthering its goals of taking wages out of competition, as long as it is not acting at the behest of business groups? Do restraints in labor market competition ultimately affect competitive forces in product markets? Even if so, in light of the difficulty unions will have maintaining a labor cartel (absent collusion with employers or affirmative government assistance), was the *Apex Hosiery-Hutcheson* Court essentially right to remove antitrust scrutiny? These matters are taken up in Chapter 10.

## D. MODERN LABOR LEGISLATION: AFFIRMATIVE PROTECTION OF COLLECTIVE REPRESENTATION

### 1. The Railway Labor Act (RLA)

Federal regulation of the national railroad system dates back to the Interstate Commerce Act of 1887. Recall the role of federal judges in enjoining railroad strikes and boycotts. The potential for a railroad labor dispute to tie up the nation's economy early on called for federal oversight of labor organization and collective bargaining. In 1888, Congress passed a law providing for voluntary arbitration and the appointment of investigating commissions by the President. 25 Stat. 101. Ten years later, Congress enacted the Erdman Act, adding mediation to voluntary arbitration and outlawing the yellow-dog contract. 30 Stat. 424. Continued labor strife on the railways led to passage of the Newlands Act in 1913, which added a permanent Board of Mediation and Conciliation. 38 Stat. 103.

Rail unionism enjoyed tremendous growth during World War I. Following federal seizure of the roads in 1917, the Railroad Administration recognized the right of workers to organize and bargain collectively, and the unions obtained national agreements and bipartite national boards of adjustment for the first time.

The Transportation Act of 1920 returned the roads to private operation and created a tripartite Railroad Labor Board to hear and decide disputes but with no means of enforcement. The rail carriers, however, began an open shop campaign, including the formation of company unions accompanied by yellow-dog contracts and discrimination against union activists. Company unionism made considerable inroads among shop and roundhouse employees but not the operating brotherhoods. The Board was powerless to deal with these developments. See Harry D. Wolf, The Railroad Labor Board (1927).

A process of negotiation between the operating brotherhoods and the rail carriers led to enactment of the Railway Labor Act of 1926 (RLA), 44 Stat. 577 (codified as amended at 45 U.S.C. §§151-188). The RLA made it the duty of the parties to exert every reasonable effort to "make and maintain agreements concerning rates of pay [and] working conditions" and to attempt to resolve differences by peaceful means. A five-person Board of Mediation was created to attempt mediation if the parties could not come to agreement by themselves. The board was instructed to urge voluntary arbitration if mediation proved unsuccessful, and if arbitration were declined, to notify the President, who could empanel an ad hoc emergency board to investigate and publish findings. During the pendency of these various proceedings, and for 30 days until after the report of the emergency board, the parties were under an obligation to maintain the status quo. The parties, however, were not obligated to accept the recommendations of the emergency board. The 1926 statute also provided for the creation of boards of adjustment to resolve grievances involving the interpretation or application of labor agreements, but these bipartite boards lacked a mechanism for breaking deadlocks.

Section 2, Third of the 1926 law provided that employees had a right to select their own representative "without interference, influence or coercion" from carriers, although it lacked a procedure for determining representatives or requiring carriers to deal solely with the representatives of the majority. In Texas & N.O. R. Co. v. Brotherhood of Railway and Steamship Clerks, 281 U.S. 548 (1930), the Supreme Court seemed to signal some greater receptivity toward federal regulation of private employment arrangements by upholding the constitutionality of this provision.

In 1934, Congress amended the RLA at the behest of the railway unions and over the bitter opposition of the carriers, many of whom were in bankruptcy. See Bernstein, New Deal Collective Bargaining Policy, supra, at 44. These amendments established the National Railroad Adjustment Board (NRAB), an agency comprised of carrier and union representatives to adjust grievances and disputes arising out of the interpretation of agreements (denominated by the RLA as "minor" disputes, to be contrasted with "major" disputes involving negotiations for basic contract changes). In the event of a deadlock, the NRAB members are to select a neutral referee or have one assigned by the National Mediation Board (NMB), also created at this time. The expenses of the NRAB, other than the salaries of its members, are paid for by the federal government. The 1934 measure also authorized the new NMB to resolve representation disputes and created a set of employer unfair labor practices to be enforced largely by the courts. (There is no corresponding set of union unfair labor practices, as there is under the NLRA by virtue of the 1947 Taft-Hartley amendments.)

In 1936, the airline industry was brought under the RLA. Pub. L. 74-487, 49 Stat. 1189. In lieu of the NRAB, the airlines and unions have established system-wide boards of adjustment that handle grievances and other minor disputes. (Although the 1936 amendments authorize the NMB to establish a National Air Transport Board, neither airline carriers nor unions have expressed an interest in industry-wide settlement of "minor" disputes.) The other provisions of the RLA also apply to airline labor disputes. See 45 U.S.C. §§181-188.

In 1934, the national railway unions successfully sought a prohibition of any requirement of union membership as a condition of employment as a means of undercutting the position of so-called nonstandard unions, typically company-dominated organizations that had been installed by carriers in nonoperating departments following the failed 1922 shopmen's strike. By 1951, the nonstandard unions had been eliminated, and at the urging of the rail and airline unions, the RLA was amended to authorize union shop and checkoff provisions (45 U.S.C. §152).

In 1966, the RLA was amended again to provide for the establishment of special adjustment boards (now called Public Law Boards) at the request of either unions or carriers to hear minor disputes otherwise referable to the NRAB, and to limit sharply the scope of judicial review of awards (45 U.S.C. §153). Additional amendments occurred in 1970, 1981, and 2012.

Although the railroad and airline industries remain areas of considerable union strength, each has undergone a major transformation. Employment levels have substantially declined in the railroads because of the growing use of trucks to move freight and the demise of for-profit passenger rail. Also, competitive forces within both industries have been unleashed by legislation passed during the 1970s removing federal regulatory authority over the rates charged and route entry by air and trucking carriers. See, e.g., Herbert R. Northrup, The Railway Labor Act—Time for Repeal?, 13 Harv. J.L. & Pub. Pol'y 441 (1990); Cleared for Takeoff: Airline Labor Relations Since Deregulation (Jean T. McKelvey ed., 1988).

## 2. The National Labor Relations Act (NLRA)

### *a. The Original NLRA: The Wagner Act of 1935*

#### i. The Origins of the Wagner Act

The Great Depression of 1929 fundamentally altered the American landscape. National income plummeted from $81 billion in 1929 to $49 billion in 1932, with wages sustaining the greatest losses. There were over 15 million unemployed in 1933. See Bernstein, New Deal Collective Bargaining Policy, supra, at 14-15. Although many firms tried to forestall wage reductions for a time, in the fall of 1931, U.S. Steel cut its wages, and the automobile, textile, and rubber tire industries quickly followed suit. The economic toll of the Depression also caused leading companies to abandon the "welfare capitalism" policies of the 1920s, typified by the announcement of layoffs of senior workers in addition to wage cuts. See Jacoby, Employing Bureaucracy, supra, at 217-223.

The Democrats gained the White House in 1932 on the promise they would bring the economic hemorrhaging to a halt. Franklin Delano Roosevelt's first New Deal administration embarked on an ambitious experimental program in the National Industrial Recovery Act of 1933 (NIRA). Industries were to organize themselves to eliminate cut-throat competition and stabilize prices. Private trade associations were to submit codes of fair competition to the National Recovery Administration. To boost purchasing power and reduce unemployment, the NIRA also called for the establishment of minimum-wage and maximum-hours standards in every industry. Section 7(a) of the NIRA declared that "employees shall have the right to organize and bargain collectively through representatives of their own choosing, and shall be free from the interference, restraint or coercion of employers . . . in the designation of such representatives or in self-organization or in other concerted activities for the purpose of collective bargaining."

A burst of organizing and surge of strikes occurred soon after passage of the NIRA. Strikes in the last half of 1933 reached levels not seen since 1921. Workers formed unions, often without assistance from AFL organizers. Unions in mining and clothing revived. New federal labor unions, directly chartered by the AFL, began to appear in the rubber tire, electrical manufacturing, automobile, and petroleum refining industries. Dramatic and violent strikes occurred in 1934 among auto parts workers in Toledo, longshoremen in San Francisco, and truckers in Minneapolis. By the end of 1934, union membership rose to 3.5 million — a gain approximating the loss between 1923 and 1933. See Jacoby, Employing Bureaucracy, supra, at 224; James A. Gross, The Making of the National Labor Relations Board: A Study in Economics, Politics and the Law, 1933-1937, at 62 (1974); Irving Bernstein, Turbulent Years: A History of the American Worker 1933-1941, chs. 2-3 (1969).

The NIRA provided no machinery for handling labor disputes. In August 1933, President Roosevelt created by executive order a National Labor Board (NLB) to conduct representation elections and hold hearings to determine whether firms had discriminated against employee organizers. The NLB, however, lacked any enforcement authority. In 1934, the NLB was replaced by the first National Labor Relations Board, and President Roosevelt appointed special boards in the automobile, steel, and petroleum industries.

The NIRA period would have a major influence on the shape and content of subsequent federal labor legislation. First, the NIRA experience pointed out the need for a strong administrative agency with enforcement authority rather than a body whose principal mission was to help adjust disputes. Second, despite President Roosevelt's acceptance of plural representation in crafting a 1934 settlement in the automobile industry, the first Labor Board established the principle in Houde Engineering Co., 1 N.L.R.B. (old) no. 12, at 39-44 (1934), that the representative of the majority of workers in an appropriate unit would be the *exclusive* representative of the workers in that unit. See Bernstein, New Deal Collective Bargaining Policy, supra, at 86; Gross, The Making of the National Labor Relations Board, supra, at 89-103. Third, the NIRA boards had a difficult time reconciling the guarantees of §7(a) with the growth of company unionism. Companies across the country formed in-house employee representation plans as a means of fending off organizing drives. A National Industrial Conference Board survey in November 1933 found that 45 percent of the employees in the manufacturing and mining firms studied were covered by such plans — a 169 percent increase over the previous year. Over 60 percent of these plans were established after the NIRA was enacted in June 1933. See National Industrial Conference Board, Individual and Collective Bargaining Under the N.I.R.A. 16-17 (1933); see also U.S. Dept. of Labor, Bureau of Labor Statistics, Characteristics of Company Unions, 1935, Bull. No. 634 (1937). Some firms insisted they would deal only with their in-house plans, even where the independent union enjoyed the overwhelming support of the workers. See, e.g., the *Edward G. Budd Mfg.* and *Weirton Steel Co.* cases, described in Gross, The Making of the National Labor Relations Board, at 37-39; Bernstein, Turbulent Years, at 177-179. (The *Budd* case is also discussed infra pages 116-119.)

On May 27, 1935, the Supreme Court invalidated the NIRA as both an unconstitutional delegation of legislative power and an invalid exercise of Congress's power under the Commerce Clause in Schechter Poultry Corp. v. United States, 295 U.S. 495. The collapse of the NIRA edifice made more urgent the case for the labor relations legislation that Senator Robert F. Wagner of New York, an ally of organized labor, had been shepherding through Congress. At the same time, as discussed in further detail below, the *Schechter* case raised serious concerns about whether Senator Wagner's legislation could survive a constitutional challenge.

President Roosevelt signed the National Labor Relations Act (NLRA or Wagner Act) on July 5, 1935. 49 Stat. 449 (codified at 29 U.S.C. §§151 et seq.). The centerpiece of the new law was §7, which originally provided:

> Employees shall have the right to self-organization, to form, join or assist labor organizations, to bargain collectively through representatives of their own choosing, and to engage in other concerted activities for the purpose of collective bargaining or other mutual aid or protection. . . .

As a means of giving content to §7 rights, the NLRA specified certain employer unfair labor practices:

- §8(1): interference, coercion, or restraint of employees in the exercise of §7 rights;
- §8(2): support or domination of a labor organization (as defined in §2(5));
- §8(3): discrimination for the purpose of encouraging or discouraging membership in a labor organization;
- §8(4): discharge or other discrimination against an employee for filing a charge or giving testimony; and
- §8(5): refusal to bargain collectively with the majority representative of the employees (as defined in §9 of the NLRA).

A new independent federal agency, the National Labor Relations Board (NLRB), was established to enforce the unfair labor practice provisions of §8 and to hold elections pursuant to §9 to determine whether the majority of workers in an appropriate unit wished to be represented for purposes of collective bargaining by a labor organization. Voluntary recognition of majority unions without elections was also permitted. A labor organization selected by employee vote (and certified by the NLRB) or recognized as the majority representative served as the exclusive bargaining agency with whom the employer was under a duty to bargain in good faith. Employers could play no role in the formation of labor organizations, and any support or domination would violate §8(2).

During the first two years of its existence, the Board's operations were hampered by serious doubts that the NLRA's constitutionality would be upheld. See Frank W. McCulloch & Tim Bornstein, The National Labor Relations Board 25-29 (1974). Between 1935 and 1937, the lower federal courts issued almost 100 injunctions against the NLRB based on the Supreme Court's 1935 decision in *Schechter Poultry*, supra page 52, and its 1936 decision in Carter v. Carter Coal Co., 298 U.S. 238. McCulloch & Bornstein, supra, at 26. In *Schechter*, the Court had held that Congress lacked authority under the Commerce Clause to regulate the wages and hours of slaughterhouse employees, reasoning that by the time the chickens purchased out of state arrived at Schechter's slaughterhouse for slaughter and subsequent sale to local retailers, the "flow in interstate commerce had ceased." 295 U.S. at 543. In *Carter Coal*, conversely, the Court held that the Commerce Clause did not authorize Congress to regulate the wages and working conditions of miners producing coal that had yet to be shipped across state lines, because the product was not yet moving in interstate commerce. "In the *Schechter* Case the flow [of interstate commerce] had ceased. Here it had not begun." 298 U.S. at 306. In the following decision, the NLRA's constitutionality was finally put to the test.

### NLRB v. Jones & Laughlin Steel Corp.
*301 U.S. 1 (1937)*

Mr. Chief Justice Hughes delivered the opinion of the Court.

. . . We think it clear that the National Labor Relations Act may be construed so as to operate within the sphere of constitutional authority. . . .

. . . [I]n its present application, the statute goes no further than to safeguard the right of employees to self-organization and to select representatives of their own choosing for collective bargaining or other mutual protection without restraint or coercion by their employer.

That is a fundamental right. Employees have as clear a right to organize and select their representatives for lawful purposes as the respondent has to organize its business and select its own officers and agents. Discrimination and coercion to prevent the free exercise of the right of employees to self-organization and representation is a proper subject for condemnation by competent legislative authority. Long ago we stated the reason for labor organizations. We said that they were organized out of the necessities of the situation; that a single employee was helpless in dealing with an employer; that he was dependent ordinarily on his daily wage for the maintenance of himself and family; that, if the employer refused to pay him the wages that he thought fair, he was nevertheless unable to leave the employ and resist arbitrary and unfair treatment; that union was essential to give laborers opportunity to deal on an equality with their employer. . . .

. . . The congressional authority to protect interstate commerce from burdens and obstructions is not limited to transactions which can be deemed to be an essential part of a "flow" of interstate or foreign commerce. . . . That power is plenary and may be exerted to protect interstate commerce "no matter what the source of the dangers which threaten it." Although activities may be intrastate in character when separately considered, if they have such a close and substantial relation to interstate commerce that their control is essential or appropriate to protect that commerce from burdens and obstructions, Congress cannot be denied the power to exercise that control. . . .

Experience has abundantly demonstrated that the recognition of the right of employees to self-organization and to have representatives of their own choosing for the purpose of collective bargaining is often an essential condition of industrial peace. Refusal to confer and negotiate has been one of the most prolific causes of strife. This is such an outstanding fact in the history of labor disturbances that it is a proper subject of judicial notice and requires no citation of instances. . . .

. . . It would seem that when employers freely recognize the right of their employees to their own organizations and their unrestricted right of representation there will be much less occasion for controversy in respect to the free and appropriate exercise of the right of selection and discharge.

[The dissenting opinion of Justice McReynolds, joined by Justices Van Devanter, Sutherland, and Butler, is omitted.]

### ii. Labor Organization During the New Deal Period

In 1933, 3 million workers were members of labor unions. By the early 1940s, over 12 million workers were organized. Union membership doubled between 1933 and 1937, but not all of this was due to the NLRA. Key organizational successes in rubber, auto, and steel were achieved well before the *Jones & Laughlin* decision. The change in public policy set a climate in favor of labor organization, but the process was driven by the workers themselves.

Labor organization was in the first instance a response to the severity of the Great Depression and in particular the corrosive effect of economic conditions on the "welfare capitalism" policies of the large manufacturing firms. As Professor Ulman has observed:

> The union organization was in part a response to the breaking of many implicit contracts, after early attempts by employers to hold the line on wages, to stabilize employment and to ration work by seniority or work-sharing had failed, and after pension plans and other benefit programmes had suffered a similar fate. The breaking of implicit contracts (albeit under duress) generated worker demands for the explicit variety—and for organizations that could negotiate and enforce them.

Lloyd Ulman, Why Should Human Resource Managers Pay High Wages?, 30 Brit. J. Indus. Rel. 177, 205 (1992).

The breakthrough of the 1936-1937 period was also due to the formation of the Congress of Industrial Organizations and the rise of the great industrial unions—i.e., unions organized by industry rather than craft. The AFL, contrary to its traditional focus on craft unions, had sought to take advantage of the upsurge in the mass production industries such as auto and rubber by chartering local industrial unions, which would otherwise likely have affiliated with existing national unions. The aim of these new locals, to represent all the workers in the plants, conflicted with the traditional jurisdictional claims of the established craft unions.

By the time of the 1935 AFL convention, the craft unions were in irreconcilable conflict both with the newly chartered local industrial unions and the older national industrial unions such as the United Mine Workers (UMW), led by John L. Lewis. At the convention, the jurisdictional claims of the craft unions were upheld, and the industrial unionists, led by Lewis, thereupon formed the Committee for Industrial Organization. Although that committee was formed within the framework of the AFL, the executive council of the AFL branded it a "dual organization" and ordered it to disband. Upon the Committee's refusal, its constituent unions were expelled from the AFL. In 1938, the insurgent group changed its name to the Congress of Industrial Organizations (CIO) and operated as a rival federation until the AFL-CIO merger in 1955.

The new industrial unions, upon being denied recognition in the auto and rubber industries, resorted to a dramatic form of the strike—the "sit down." Strikers occupied struck plants and were supplied by sympathizers outside the plants. Although the sit-down strike was uniformly held to be illegal, it contributed to the recognition of unions in these industries, including the celebrated recognition of the United Auto Workers by General Motors after a sit-down strike at the Flint Works in Michigan.

The CIO had also launched an organizing campaign in the basic steel industry through a new organization, the Steel Workers Organizing Committee (SWOC), to which John L. Lewis and the UMW supplied staff and funds. In 1937, U.S. Steel voluntarily recognized SWOC and signed an agreement providing wage increases and other concessions. Other steel producers, however, were more stubborn. Their resistance led to strikes marked by violent incidents, including the "Memorial Day Massacre" on May 30, 1937, at the South Chicago plant of the Republic Steel Company, where ten strikers were killed by police gunfire. SWOC lost the "Little Steel" strike. However, organizational activity at these steel companies continued, and in 1941 they recognized SWOC.

The CIO emerged as a political as well as an economic rival of the AFL and generally was bolder and more vigorous in its political action. Its leaders were prominent in the formation in 1936 of Labor's Non-Partisan League. The UMW contributed close to half a million dollars to the League's efforts in connection with the national elections in 1936. Labor's vigorous support of the Democratic ticket contributed to Roosevelt's sweeping victory.

### iii. The Purposes of the Wagner Act

#### *(a) Promoting Industrial Peace*

Prominent among the purposes listed in §1 of the NLRA (often referred to as the "preamble" to the Act) is the prevention of industrial strife. Indeed, some academics have criticized the Act for routinizing conflict and hence robbing the labor movement of the 1930s of what they believed was its radical potential to transform society. See, e.g., Karl E. Klare, Judicial Deradicalization of the Wagner Act and the Origins of Modern Legal Consciousness, 1937-1941, 62 Minn. L. Rev. 265 (1978).

By providing an administrative procedure for resolving recognitional disputes, the Act helped reduce industrial conflict. At the same time, however, it recognized the central role of the strike as a means of resolving economic disagreements. See §13 of the 1935 Act ("Nothing in this Act shall be construed so as either to interfere with or impede or diminish in any way the right to strike. . . ."). Unlike the RLA, the NLRA created no obligation to maintain agreements as such — no long drawn-out process of mandatory mediation awaiting a governmental declaration of impasse before the parties can resort to self-help and contractual terms may be changed. Moreover, unlike some of the current laws governing labor relations in the public sector (such as many state laws pertaining to police and firefighters), the Act does not provide for compulsory interest arbitration of economic disputes.

*(b) Redressing Inequality of Bargaining Power*

Section 1 speaks of "[t]he inequality of bargaining power between employees who do not possess full freedom of association or actual liberty of contract, and employers who are organized in the corporate or other forms of business association," and the depressing effect such inequality has had on "wage rates and the purchasing power of wage earners in industry." Senator Wagner and some of his advisers were certainly of the view that labor organization and collective bargaining could help increase the purchasing power of workers and thereby lift the nation out of the Depression. See Kenneth M. Casebeer, Holder of the Pen: An Interview with Leon Keyserling on Drafting the Wagner Act, 42 U. Miami L. Rev. 285 (1987). For a critical view of Senator Wagner's economic theory, see Daniel J.B. Mitchell, Inflation, Unemployment and the Wagner Act: A Critical Reappraisal, 38 Stan. L. Rev. 1065, redundant 1073-1076 (1986).

In important respects, however, the statute Wagner helped enact is largely a procedural measure. The NLRA assumes that inequality of bargaining power can be corrected by protecting workers' ability to obtain collective representation. There is, notably, no provision for government to set the terms of the labor contract, and no provision on the Continental European model to extend labor agreements to unorganized sectors of an industry. Senator Wagner initially omitted a good faith bargaining requirement from his bill, fearing it would be vulnerable to the charge that he was seeking a form of compulsory arbitration of labor disputes. See Gross, The Making of the National Labor Relations Board, supra, at 137. The bill as it emerged out of the Senate labor committee (and was enacted into law) contained such a requirement, but the committee took pains to

> dispel any possible false impression that this bill is designed to compel the making of agreements or to permit governmental supervision of their terms. It must be stressed that the duty to bargain collectively does not carry with it the duty to reach an agreement, because the essence of collective bargaining is that either party shall be free to decide whether proposals made to it are satisfactory.

S. Rep. No. 573, 74th Cong., 1st Sess. (1935), reprinted in 2 Legislative History of the National Labor Relations Act of 1935, at 2312 (1985).

### iv. The Orientation of the Wagner Act

The 1935 Wagner Act was framed to encourage collective bargaining. Section 1 states that it is "the policy of the United States to . . . *encourag[e] the practice and procedure of collective bargaining*" (emphasis added). Moreover, §8, the unfair labor practice provision, regulated only employer conduct; it set out five employer unfair labor practices, but did not outlaw any conduct on the part of unions.

### *b. The Taft-Hartley Act of 1947*

#### i. Labor Organization and the Administration of the NLRA from 1935 to 1947

The labor movement grew and collective bargaining spread between 1935 and 1947. The number of workers belonging to unions swelled from 3 million in 1935 to 15 million by 1947—including two-thirds of NLRA-covered employees in manufacturing industries and over four-fifths of those in coal mining, construction, and trucking, as well as railroading (covered by the RLA).

The challenge of the CIO and the protection to organization afforded by the Wagner Act stimulated new vigorous organizational campaigns by the AFL. The older federation soon made up for its loss of members to the CIO. Some AFL successes resulted from voluntary recognition by employers who wished to forestall bargaining with CIO unions, which were generally considered more militant than their AFL rivals. The rivalry between the two federations also blurred the distinction between craft and industrial unions, since the AFL, as a competitive measure, allowed craft unions to charter industrial locals. See supra page 53-54.

That rivalry also complicated the administration of the Wagner Act by the NLRB. In determining appropriate units for elections and collective bargaining, the Board was continually faced with competing claims by AFL-affiliated and CIO-affiliated unions. The AFL charged that the Board's resolution of these claims indicated a pro-CIO bias, while employers alleged that the Board was biased in favor of organized labor, period. These complaints ultimately contributed to the amendment of the Wagner Act by the Taft-Hartley Act of 1947. As discussed further below, Taft-Hartley changed both the statutory mechanisms for resolving representational issues and the internal structure of the NLRB.

World War II, like World War I, was a period of growth for the union movement. President Roosevelt promised to maintain the protections provided by the Wagner Act and the Fair Labor Standards Act of 1938, including minimum wages and premium pay for overtime. Unions, in turn, gave no-strike pledges designed to avoid interference with war production. Moreover, the prestige of the union movement was enhanced by the appointment of union leaders to important posts in mobilization agencies.

In 1942, the National War Labor Board (NWLB), a tripartite agency, was established "for adjusting and settling labor disputes which might interrupt work which contributes to the effective prosecution of the war." Later, its responsibility was extended to include wage stabilization as well as dispute settlement. The NWLB sought to "stabilize" wages without freezing them. Its basic guidelines were embodied in "the Little Steel formula," which in general sought to limit wage increases to those warranted by the 15 percent increase in the cost of living between January 1941 and May 1942. The NWLB's rulings also promoted adoption of union security and grievance arbitration clauses.

Following the war, the reconversion of the economy to a peace-time footing was accompanied by a wave of long and stubborn strikes. These strikes involved over 3 million workers in 1945 alone, and affected many important industries, including coal, electrical manufacturing, oil refining, longshoring, railroads, and steel. In 1946, the government took vigorous action to end the most significant strikes—those in coal and railroads. The coal strike led to government seizure of the mines and to the imposition of fines on both Mine Workers President John L. Lewis and the UMW for violating an injunction against the strike. These strikes created widespread support for curbing the power of and claimed abuses by organized labor, and contributed to the passage of the Taft-Hartley Act in 1947.

### ii. The Taft-Hartley Amendments

The Taft-Hartley amendments to the NLRA and the Labor Management Relations Act of 1947 (LMRA), 61 Stat. 136 (codified at 29 U.S.C. §§141-197), were in part a response to the strike wave of late 1945 and 1946 and the widespread public perception of abuse of union power. Note that following the 1941 *Hutcheson* decision, supra page 42-45, there was no federal law in effect regulating union conduct.

The 1947 amendments marked a clear shift in tone from the original Wagner Act, from a measure reflecting affirmative support of unionization and collective bargaining to one that appeared to take a more neutral position as to whether unions and collective bargaining were truly in the interests of all workers. Compare, e.g., NLRA §1, para. 3 (enacted 1935) ("Experience has proved that protection by law of the right of employees to organize and bargain collectively safeguards commerce from injury") with NLRA §1, para. 4 (added 1947) ("Experience has *further demonstrated* that certain practices by some *labor organizations* . . . have the intent or the necessary effect of burdening or obstructing commerce . . . [and] impair the interest of the public in the free flow of such commerce") (emphases added). Taft-Hartley retained, however, the Wagner Act's original findings and declaration of policy emphasizing the need to redress the inequality of bargaining power between labor and management and declaring it to be official U.S. policy to "encourag[e] the practice and procedure of collective bargaining."

The 1947 amendments significantly changed the substance of the Act as well. First, §7, the Act's core provision, was amended to make clear that employees "shall also have the right to refrain" from the activities listed. Second, Taft-Hartley added §8(b), establishing for the first time a number of union unfair labor practices under the NLRA. In addition to provisions paralleling certain of the employer ULPs set forth in §8(a), Taft-Hartley also outlawed the secondary boycott and required the Board's Regional offices to seek preliminary injunctions against such boycotts in federal court. See NLRA §10(l). In contrast, §10(j), also added in 1947, authorized but did not require the pursuit of injunctive relief in other unfair labor practice cases.

Taft-Hartley added a new §8(c) to clarify that employers have the right to express their views about unionization in response to a union organizing drive, and a new §8(d) to make clear that the Board lacks authority to infer that a party has not bargained in good faith from its failure to reach an agreement or to make particular concessions. It further amended the Act to exclude supervisors from the definition of covered employees, to admonish the Board not to equate its inquiry into an appropriate bargaining unit with the petitioning union's extent of organization, and to bar permanently replaced economic strikers from voting in NLRB elections.

In addition, Taft-Hartley outlawed the "closed shop" (where union membership is a prerequisite for employment), and permitted states to enact so-called "right to work" laws outlawing even the "union shop" (where union membership or its financial equivalent is required only after an initial period of employment). See NLRA §14(b). Moreover, in states that did not enact such laws, the union shop remained lawful only if authorized by the affected employees in an NLRB election. (In 1951, this last provision was deleted, and employers and unions were permitted to require, without a prior election, the payment of union dues or its financial equivalent as a condition of employment after 30 days on the job, while employees were given the right to petition the Board for a "deauthorization" election to remove this "union security" provision. See NLRA §§8(a)(3) and 9(e)(1) (as amended 1951).)

The 1947 amendments were framed not only to curb perceived abuses of union power. Congress also added a number of provisions aimed at furthering the statutory goal of promoting industrial peace. New §8(d), for instance, discussed above, required notification of the Federal Mediation and Conciliation Service of any proposed contract modification or termination and mandated a 60-day "cooling-off" period. LMRA §§206-210 (codified at 29 U.S.C., §§176-180) authorized the President to invoke special procedures where strikes or lockouts were deemed to create a national emergency. Finally, LMRA §301 granted the federal courts jurisdiction to resolve disputes arising out of the interpretation of collective bargaining agreements.

### c. *The Landrum-Griffin Act of 1959*

#### i. Labor Organization from 1947 to 1959

As discussed further at the conclusion of this chapter, the high-water mark for unionization occurred in the early 1950s; by 1953, 36 percent of American private sector workers were union members. The most significant development in labor organization during this period was the merger of the AFL and the CIO in 1955, and the attendant "no-raid" agreement in the constitution of the new organization. This agreement provided that no AFL-CIO affiliate would attempt to organize employees already represented or "claimed" by another affiliate, and further required the affiliates involved in any such dispute to submit to final and binding arbitration under AFL-CIO auspices. See AFL-CIO Const. articles XX, §§2, 3 and XXI, §2, discussed in greater detail in Samuel Estreicher, Disunity Within the House of Labor: Change to Win or Stay the Course?, 27 J. Lab. Res. 505 (2006). Following the AFL-CIO merger and the no-raid pact, the percentage of "rival union" elections decreased dramatically. See Kye D. Pawlenko, Reevaluating Inter-Union Competition: A Proposal to Resurrect Rival Unionism, 8 U. Pa. J. Lab. & Emp. L. 65, 65 & nn.8-9 (2006) (only 6 percent of NLRB elections in 2004 had more than one union on the ballot, compared to 21 percent of elections in 1955); compare 69 N.L.R.B. Ann. Rep. Table 13 (2004) with 20 N.L.R.B. Ann. Rep. Table 13A (1955).

#### ii. The Landrum-Griffin Act

Public concern over labor corruption, fueled by an inquiry of a Senate select committee chaired by Senator McClellan, escalated in the 1950s. The hearings ultimately resulted in the enactment of the Labor-Management Reporting and Disclosure Act of 1959 (LMRDA or Landrum-Griffin Act), 73 Stat. 519 (codified at 29 U.S.C. §§401-531), a measure that broadly regulates the internal affairs of labor organizations. Title I established a "bill of rights of members of labor organizations." Title II imposed reporting requirements on labor organizations and their officers and employers. Title III provided for regulation of union trusteeships (the practice whereby a parent union can assume control over a subordinate labor organization). Title IV created safeguards for the conduct of internal union elections, and Title V recognized fiduciary obligations for union officers.

The Landrum-Griffin amendments also affected the NLRA. Certain perceived loopholes in the secondary boycott prohibition enacted in 1947 were closed by outlawing "hot cargo" clauses. See NLRA §8(e). Congress added another union unfair labor practice (§8(b)(7)) to outlaw extended picketing for a recognitional or organizational objective. A new provision,

§8(f), was inserted to authorize building and construction industry employers to enter into "prehire" agreements with unions before the majority status of the union has been established.

In addition, the 1959 amendments partially reinstated the voting rights of permanently replaced economic strikers, which had been entirely eliminated by Taft-Hartley. Congress amended §9(c)(3) to authorize the NLRB to allow such strikers to vote in NLRB elections for a period of up to 12 months from the commencement of a strike.

#### d. *The 1974 Health Care Industry Amendments*

In 1974, Congress amended the NLRA to extend its jurisdiction to nonprofit health care institutions, including hospitals, health maintenance organizations (HMOs), and nursing homes. (Jurisdiction over for-profit institutions was already clearly established.) The amendments provided special rules for resolution of disputes in the health care industry, such as a requirement that a union give ten days' notice to the Federal Mediation and Conciliation Service before going on strike. See new §8(g).

#### e. *The Proposed Labor Reform Act of 1977, the Proposed Employee Free Choice Act, and Other Failed Legislative Bids*

Due to the sharp division between labor and management and the power of the interest groups on each side, as well as the fact that only rarely does the same party (a) control the presidency, (b) control both Houses of Congress, *and* (c) possess a filibuster-proof margin in the Senate (i.e., the 60 votes necessary to invoke cloture and cut off debate), it is extremely difficult to enact labor legislation of any significance. See Terry M. Moe, Interests, Institutions and Positive Theory: The Politics of the NLRB, in 2 Studies in American Political Development 236, 240-241, 262-263 (1987); see also Cynthia Estlund, The Ossification of American Labor Law, 102 Colum. L. Rev. 1527 (2002). Thus, although there have been a number of attempts to amend the Act since 1974, the health care amendments remain the last significant revision of the statute.

An attempt was made in the proposed Labor Reform Act of 1977 to strengthen NLRB remedies and speed up its election processes. After passing the heavily Democratic House by nearly 100 votes, it died in the Senate following a 19-day filibuster. Other significant efforts to amend the NLRA included bills in 1991 and 1993 that would have banned the hiring of permanent replacements for economic strikers, and the proposed Teamwork for Employees and Managers Act of 1995 (TEAM Act), which would have amended §8(a)(2) to allow employers greater latitude in creating employee participation or involvement committees. The bills banning permanent replacements, like the Labor Reform Act, passed the House but died via filibuster in the Senate. The TEAM Act actually passed both Houses of Congress, but was vetoed by President Clinton in July 1996.

With the election of Democrat Barack Obama as President in 2008, the labor movement made a strong, concerted effort to enact the Employee Free Choice Act (EFCA), S. 560, H.R. 1409, 111th Cong. (2009). EFCA passed the House in 2007 but was unable to marshal enough support in the Senate to ward off a threatened filibuster. EFCA had three titles: Title I provided for NLRB certification of unions without elections on the basis of a majority card-check; under present law, by contrast, the employer can insist on an election provided it has not committed serious unfair labor practices; Title II provided for mandatory interest arbitration in first-time bargaining situations; and Title III provided for enhanced remedies and penalties for employer unfair labor practices. For a defense of EFCA, see Benjamin I. Sachs, Enabling Employee Choice: A Structural Approach to the Rules of Union Organizing, 123 Harv. L. Rev. 655 (2010); and his Card Check 2.0, ch. 4, in Labor and Employment Law Initiatives and Proposals Under the Obama Administration: Proc. of the N.Y.U. 62d Ann. Conf. on Labor (Zev J. Eigen & Samuel Estreicher eds., 2011). For a critique from the employer's perspective, see Andrew M. Kramer, Jacqueline M. Holmes & R. Scott Medsker, Two Sentences, 104 Words: Congress's Folly in First Contract Arbitration and the Future of Free Collective Bargaining, ch 3, in id.

***Note: The Sharp Decline in Private Sector Unionism***

As previously discussed, the enactment of the NLRA in 1935 and the Supreme Court's upholding of the Act's constitutionality in the 1937 *Jones & Laughlin* decision were followed by sharp increases in union membership; the percentage of union members in the private sector work force jumped from 14 percent in 1935 to 23 percent in 1939, and to a peak of 36 percent in 1953. See Leo Troy & Neil Sheflin, Union Sourcebook: Membership, Structure, Finance, Directory A-1 (1st ed. 1985). The percentage then began a steady decline, and by 1979 had reached 22 percent, identical to that in the year following *Jones & Laughlin.* See id.

This decline accelerated even further in the 1980s; union density (i.e., the percentage of workers who are union members) in the private sector fell from 20 percent in 1980 to 12 percent in 1990, and as of 2013 stood at but 6.7 percent—a lower union density than existed prior to the enactment of the NLRA. See BLS, Union Members in 2013, USDL 14–0095 (Jan. 24, 2014); Macpherson, Union Membership and Earnings Data Book: Compilations from the Current Population Survey (2014) (Table 1c) (1973-2013); Barry T. Hirsch & Edward J. Schumacher, Private Sector Union Density and the Wage Premium: Past, Present, and Future, 22 J. Lab. Res. 487 (2001) (noting comparison to pre-NLRA days). Moreover, these percentages rise only a point or two if one includes employees who are covered by a collective bargaining agreement but are not themselves members of a union. The decline in union density cuts across all areas of private sector employment, including traditional areas of union strength such as manufacturing and construction. Hirsch & Macpherson, supra, Tables 1c & 1d (1973-2013) (manufacturing declines from 39% in 1973 to 28% in 1983 to 10.1% in 2013); (construction declines from 31% in 1980 to 20% in 1993 to 14.1% in 2013). Unions have had modest success organizing workers in service industries, the fastest growing sector of the economy, in recent years. The percentage of private sector service industry workers (including those in health care as well as in the leisure and hospitality industries — i.e., hotels and restaurants) belonging to unions was 5 percent in the year 2005 and 10.6 percent in the year 2013. See BLS, Union Members in 2005, USDL 6–99 (Jan. 20, 2006), Table 3; BLS, Union Members in 2013, supra, Table 3.

In 2013, unions represented 3.2 percent of workers in the leisure and hospitality industries and 8.1 percent of workers in healthcare and social assistance industries. In the last two decades, the total number of private sector union members has dropped even as tens of millions of jobs have been added to the American economy. Although over 30 million jobs were added to the private sector economy between 1983 and 2013, the number of union members in the private sector nonetheless declined by almost 3.5 million during that period. See BLS, Union Members in 2013, Table 3 (2013); U.S. Dep't of Labor, Employment and Earnings (1983).

In contrast, unions have fared considerably better in recent decades in the public sector (which is governed by state law rather than the NLRA and hence is largely beyond the purview of this book). In 2013, 35.3 percent of public sector workers were unionized, as compared to less than 7 percent of their private sector counterparts. BLS, Union Members in 2013, supra, Table 3. Moreover, the percentage of public sector employees belonging to unions, rather than undergoing a steep decline, has held steady during the past two decades. See id. (2013); Employment and Earnings, supra (1983). With the number of public sector jobs increasing by almost 5 million since 1983 and the percentage of union members staying constant, public sector unions have added over a million and a half members to their rolls during this period. Id.

In 2013, U.S. public sector workers had a union membership rate (35.3 percent) that was over five times that of private sector employees (6.7 percent) and accounted for half of total union membership, even though government work is only one-fifth the size of the private workforce. See BLS, Union Members in 2013, supra. In 2013, total U.S. union membership held steady at 11.3 percent from 2012. See id. In government jobs, unions represented 38.7 percent of all workers in 2013, a slight dip from 2012. Id. at Table 3.

The contrast with the public sector has highlighted the decline in American private sector unionism. Competing theories attempting to explain this decline abound, with the most prominent focusing on: (1) structural changes in the American economy; (2) changes in workers' preferences ("demand-side" changes); (3) employer opposition; and (4) the effects of global product and labor market competition. See generally Samuel Estreicher & Stewart J. Schwab, Foundations of Labor and Employment Law 85-120 (2000); Hirsch & Schumacher, supra, at 490-498 (summarizing various arguments and key research in this area).

The "structural change" proponents, most notably Rutgers University Professor Leo Troy, argue that changes in the American economy such as the shift of jobs out of the traditionally union-heavy manufacturing sector and into the service sector and from the more heavily unionized Northeast and Midwest to the less union-friendly South and Southwest, as well as demographic changes in the workforce, best account for the decline in private sector union density. See, e.g., Leo Troy, U.S. and Canadian Industrial Relations: Convergent or Divergent?, 39 Indus. Rel. 695 (2000); Leo Troy, Market Forces and Union Decline: A Response to Paul Weiler, 29 U. Chi. L. Rev. 681 (1992); see also Henry S. Farber & Bruce Western, Accounting for the Decline of Unions in the Private Sector, 1973-1998, 22 J. Lab. Res. 459 (2001) (pointing to slow net growth in union relative to nonunion employment as key factor in decline in union density).

Other work attempts to explain the decline of private sector union density by focusing on the changing preferences of American workers. Some studies have pointed to increased job satisfaction among nonunion workers. See Henry S. Farber & Alan B. Krueger, Union Membership in the United States: The Decline Continues, in Employee Representation: Alternatives and Future Directions 105 et seq. (Bruce E. Kaufman & Morris M. Kleiner eds., 1993). One reason for this increased satisfaction may be the broad array of workplace regulations governing issues such as discrimination, safety, family and medical leave, plant closings, overtime, and pension benefits that now provide job-related protection for all workers without need of unionization. See Samuel Estreicher, Models of Workplace Representation for an Era of Global Labor and Product Market Competition, in Labour Law: Human Rights and Social Justice 51 (Roger Blanpain ed., 2001); Hirsch & Schumacher, supra, at 497-498. Other work on employee preferences has focused on the American culture of individualism and its influence on U.S. workers. See Seymour Martin Lipset & Ivan Katchanovski, The Future of Private Sector Unions in the U.S., 22 J. Lab. Res. 229 (2001); Sharon Rabin-Margalioth, The Significance of Worker Attitudes: Individualism as a Cause for Labor's Decline, 16 Hofstra Lab. & Emp. L.J. 133 (1998). Still other research suggests that American workers may want a different "product" than that currently offered by unions—that workers want a greater voice in workplace decisions, but "want that voice to be exercised as a part of a *cooperative* rather than a confrontational relationship with management." Hirsch & Schumacher, supra, at 497 (summarizing findings of Richard B. Freeman & Joel Rogers, What Workers Want (1999)); see also Freeman & Rogers, What Workers Want (updated ed. 2006).

An opposing view identifies employer opposition to unions (both lawful and unlawful), in conjunction with the weak remedies available under the NLRA, as the principal cause of declining union density in private firms. The classic statement of this position is found in Paul C. Weiler, Promises to Keep: Securing Workers' Rights to Self-Organization Under the NLRA, 96 Harv. L. Rev. 1769 (1983); see also Paul C. Weiler, Governing the Workplace: The Future of Labor and Employment Law (1990); Richard B. Freeman & James L. Medoff, What Do Unions Do?, ch. 15 (1984); Richard B. Freeman, What Do Unions Do?: The 2004 M-Brane Stringtwister Edition (Nat. Bur. Econ. Res., Working Paper No. 11410, June 2005), available at http://www.nber.org/papers/w11410 (examining critiques of What Do Unions Do?, and reaffirming original claim regarding key role of employer opposition).

A fourth explanation of the decline in private sector union density emphasizes that many traditional union goals, including union wage premiums, shorter work weeks, staffing rules, and seniority systems are increasingly difficult to maintain in an era of global product and labor market competition. See Estreicher, Models of Workplace Representation, supra.

The decline in private sector union density is likely attributable to some combination of the above factors. For example, more competitive and often more global product markets may have stiffened employer resistance to unionization as well as affected workers' assessments of the potential costs and benefits of traditional union representation. See Samuel Estreicher, Labor Law Reform in a World of Competitive Product Markets, 69 Chi.-Kent L. Rev. 3 (1993); see also Thomas A. Kochan et al., The Transformation of American Industrial Relations, esp. ch. 3 (2d ed. 1994).

The decline in private sector union density is a worldwide phenomenon. In some European countries, the decline in union membership is masked by the effect of extension laws in extending contract coverage to a larger percentage of employees. See Samuel Estreicher, Global Issues in Labor Law 174-83 (2007). Even in Canada, with pro-unionization labor law in the federal sector and many of the provinces, union representation in private companies is declining, although the unionization rate is still considerably higher than in the United States. See Samuel Estreicher, Trade Unionization Under Globalization: The Demise of Voluntarism?, 54 St. Louis U. L.J. 415, 425 n.26 (Winter 2010); "Think Global, Act Local": Employee Representation in a World of Global Labor and Product Market Competition, 4 Va. L. & Bus. Rev. 81 (Spring 2009).

# 2 The Jurisdiction, Structure, and Procedure of the NLRB

## A. A BRIEF OVERVIEW OF NLRB STRUCTURE AND PROCEDURE

### 1. The Board

The National Labor Relations Board (NLRB or Board) is the federal agency that administers the National Labor Relations Act. The term "Board" formally refers to the five-member body that sits in Washington, D.C. However, the term is also used to refer to the entire agency, which includes approximately 34 Regional offices, the Office of the General Counsel, and the Division of Judges (formerly referred to as "Trial Examiners" but now known as "Administrative Law Judges" or "ALJs").

Board members are appointed by the President and must be confirmed by the Senate. The full term of an NLRB member is five years, but an individual chosen to fill a premature vacancy is appointed only for the remainder of the predecessor's unexpired term. See NLRA §3(a). As a matter of custom, but not statutory mandate, the Board has typically been made up of three members of the President's party and two members of the opposing party.

Up through the late 1970s, with rare exceptions, the Senate routinely confirmed the President's nominees to the Board. Since that time, however, the Senate has quite frequently refused to act on particular nominations, and in recent years it has often refused to vote on any Board nominations until the President and Senate leaders from both parties reach agreement on a "package" of appointments. See generally Joan Flynn, A Quiet Revolution at the Labor Board: The Transformation of the NLRB, 1935-2000, 61 Ohio St. L.J. 1361 (2000). The Senate's insistence on packaged appointments has led to continuing vacancies on the Board. Vacancies both slow the processing of routine cases, which (as a matter of agency practice) are heard by three-member Board panels, and prevent the Board from reaching the more controversial cases on its docket, which are typically decided by the full

Board, and very rarely by fewer than four Board members. The Supreme Court has held that the Board must have at least three members as a necessary quorum to conduct business. See New Process Steel v. NLRB, 560 U.S. 674 (2010).

In 2011, President Obama presented the Senate with three new nominees for the Board. After the Senate failed to act on the nominations, during a three-day recess on January 4, 2012, the President appointed all three, invoking the Recess Appointments Clause of the Constitution, Art. II, 3, cl. 3. The recess appointments were subjected to challenge in the courts. In NLRB v. Noel Canning Co., 134 S. Ct. 2550 (2014), the Supreme Court (per Justice Breyer) unanimously ruled that the January 4, 2012 appointments were invalid. The Court held that three days is too short a period to bring a recess within the scope of the Clause, and that the Senate was in "pro forma" session because it was capable of conducting business by unanimous consent. The Court's ruling rendered ineffective any decisions of the Board during the period in which any of the three recess-appointed members were necessary for a quorum. That period came to an end in August, 2013, when four new nominees joined the Board with the consent of the Senate. Delay in Senatorial confirmation of the President's appointees may be less common after a Senate resolution of November 21, 2013, changed the institution's rules to require only 51 votes for most executive and judicial appointments.

## 2. The General Counsel

The General Counsel (GC), who is appointed by the President with Senate consent to a four-year term, is in charge of the Regional offices and is the chief prosecutor of unfair labor practice (ULP) complaints. While the Regional Directors of the various Regional offices decide whether to issue a legal complaint in routine cases, novel or complex issues are referred to the General Counsel for that determination. The General Counsel's refusal to issue a complaint is completely unreviewable by either the Board or the courts. See NLRB v. United Food & Commercial Workers Union, 484 U.S. 112 (1987).

The General Counsel's authority over the issuance of complaints gives the GC a key role in the development of the law under the NLRA. An activist GC will present new legal theories to the Board and may well argue for the overruling of Board precedent in a substantial number of areas. While the Board may sometimes "reach out" to reverse precedent or otherwise establish new law in a case in which the General Counsel has not argued for such a change, many controversial issues that reach the Board do so as the result of a conscious effort by the General Counsel to bring the issue to the Board's attention.

The General Counsel also plays a key role in the Board's use of its power to seek preliminary injunctive relief under NLRA §10(j). Although the statute empowers "the Board" to seek 10(j) relief, under long-standing practice the Board considers authorizing the pursuit of such relief only upon a request by the General Counsel. During certain periods, the Board has delegated its 10(j) authority to the GC.

### 3. Unfair Labor Practice and Representation Proceedings

The Board has two principal functions: to prosecute and remedy unfair labor practices committed by either employers or unions (ULP or "complaint" proceedings), and to conduct elections to determine whether a majority of employees wish to be represented by a union ("representation" proceedings).

#### *a. Unfair Labor Practice Proceedings*

Unfair labor practice cases start with the filing of a charge by an individual, a union, or an employer with one of the Board's Regional offices. Regional employees investigate the charge, and the Regional Director then determines whether to dismiss the charge or issue a complaint. Complaint cases are litigated on behalf of the General Counsel by lawyers from the Regional office, and are heard by Board ALJs. ALJs issue written decisions in all but a small percentage of cases, and both sides have the opportunity to file "exceptions" to an ALJ's decision with the Board. The Board then issues its decision, which often takes the form of a one- or two-page opinion adopting the ALJ's decision except to the extent noted. A party "aggrieved by" a Board order may then file an appeal in the circuit in which the alleged ULP occurred, the D.C. Circuit, or any circuit in which that party "resides or is doing business." NLRA §10(f). Hence, nationwide employers have wide latitude to "circuit-shop." As discussed further infra pages 261-262, Board orders are not self-enforcing, so if a party refuses to comply with the Board's order (but does not file its own appeal), the Board must petition a court of appeals for enforcement. Under NLRA §10(e), the Board may petition in the circuit in which the alleged ULP occurred or in any circuit in which the respondent "resides or transacts business." The Board's general practice, however, is not to forum-shop, and to simply file in the circuit in which the alleged ULP occurred. See Samuel Estreicher & Richard L. Revesz, Nonacquiescence by Federal Administrative Agencies, 98 Yale L.J. 679, 706 & n.144 (1989). If a court of appeals does not enforce a Board's order, the Board's longstanding policy is to consider the ruling but decide for itself whether to acquiesce to the court of appeals or continue to adhere to its position until the Supreme Court rules to the contrary. See id. at 707.

Only three percent of ULP cases are resolved through a Board order. The other 97 percent are resolved at the Regional level through dismissals for lack of merit (28 percent), withdrawals (35 percent) or settlements between the parties (34 percent). NLRB, Disposition of Unfair Labor Practice Charges in FY13, available at http://www.nlrb.gov/news-outreach/graphs-data/charges-and-complaints/disposition-unfair-labor-practice-charges. Cases are handled fairly expeditiously at the Regional level but bottlenecks develop as cases move up the line. See Samuel Estreicher & Matthew T. Bodie, Review Essay—Administrative Delay at the NLRB: Some Modest Proposals, 23 J. Lab. Res. 87, 88-92 (2002); Edward B. Miller, An Administrative Appraisal of the NLRB (4th ed. 1999). In fiscal years 2007-2010, the median time from filing of a charge to issuance of a complaint ranged from 96-101 days (up from roughly 45 days in 1993). Compare 72-74 N.L.R.B. Ann. Rep. Table 23 (2007-2009) and N.L.R.B. Statistical Tables FY-2010 Table 23, with 58 N.L.R.B. Ann. Rep. Table 23 (1993). The median time from filing of a charge to issuance of an ALJ decision ranged from 295 to 340 days. See 72-74 N.L.R.B. Ann. Rep. Table 23 (2007-2009). In fiscal years 2011-2013, the median time from filing of charge to issuance of a Board decision ranged from 508 to 653 days, down from an average median of about two years for fiscal years 2007-2009. Compare 2011-2013 Data Received from NLRB (available upon request from authors) with 72-74 N.L.R.B. Ann. Rep. Table 23.

#### b. *Representation Proceedings*

Representation proceedings also commence at the Regional level. Given the volume of representation cases, the Board grants review only in those cases that raise a substantial question of law or policy. The courts' role in representation cases is also more circumscribed than in "ULP" cases. As discussed infra pages 258-262, representational issues such as bargaining unit determinations are not directly reviewable by the courts, although the employer, at least, may obtain review of such issues in the course of subsequent unfair labor practice proceedings. Procedure in representation cases is discussed more fully in Chapter 4.

### 4. Rulemaking Versus Adjudication

#### a. *The Procedures Contrasted*

There are two distinct procedures by which administrative agencies make legal policy pursuant to their enabling statute: adjudication and rule-making. Adjudication is the type of case-by-case decision making in which courts engage. In the case of agencies, the decision is generally based on the record developed before an ALJ, the ALJ's recommended decision, and the parties' briefs. Policies developed in adjudication typically apply not only to the parties before the agency, but also to all pending cases and other future cases presenting the same issue. But see infra page 72 regarding "retroactivity" problems when the agency has engaged in a policy reversal via adjudication.

Rulemaking works quite differently. A "rule" is a "statement of general or particular applicability and future effect." 5 U.S.C. §551(4). Under the Administrative Procedure Act (APA), before promulgating a rule, an agency must issue a notice of the proposed rulemaking proceeding setting forth either the substance of the proposed rule or a description of the issues involved, and then provide an opportunity for public comment. Any rule issued must contain a "concise general statement of [its] basis and purpose," and can take effect only after a minimum of 30 days following its publication in the *Federal Register.* 5 U.S.C. §553(b)-(d). In order to reverse or rescind a rule, an agency must follow the same procedures that govern the promulgation of an initial rule. 5 U.S.C. §551(5).

### *b. NLRB Preference for Adjudication over Rulemaking*

The NLRB has broad rulemaking powers; NLRA §6 authorizes the Board to "make, amend, and rescind, in the manner prescribed by the Administrative Procedure Act, such rules and regulations as may be necessary to carry out the provisions of the Act." Alone among the major federal agencies, however, the Board has instead chosen to make policy almost exclusively through adjudication. See Allentown Mack Sales & Service, Inc. v. NLRB, 522 U.S. 359, 374 (1998). Indeed, over its history the Board has promulgated only one significant substantive rule, which was upheld by a unanimous Supreme Court. See American Hosp. Ass'n v. NLRB, 499 U.S. 606 (1991), excerpted infra pages 234-238.

The Board's near-complete refusal to use its substantive rulemaking powers has long drawn criticism from some judges, the bar, and many academics. See, e.g., NLRB v. Federal Security, Inc., 154 F.3d 751, 754-755 (7th Cir. 1998); NLRB v. Majestic Weaving Co., 355 F.2d 854, 860 (2d Cir. 1966) (Friendly, J.); 16 Admin. L. Rev. 77 (1964) (resolution by Administrative Law Section of ABA); 42 Lab. Rel. Rep. 513 (BNA) (1958) (resolution by Labor Law Section of ABA); Samuel Estreicher, Improving the Administration of the National Labor Relations Act Without Statutory Change, 25 A.B.A. J. Lab. & Emp. L. 1, 12-14 (Fall 2009) and his Policy Oscillation at the Labor Board: A Plea for Rulemaking, 37 Admin. L. Rev. 163, 181 (1985); Merton C. Bernstein, The NLRB's Adjudication-Rule Making Dilemma Under the Administrative Procedure Act, 79 Yale L.J. 571 (1970); David Shapiro, The Choice of Rule Making or Adjudication in the Development of Administrative Law Policy, 78 Harv. L. Rev. 921, 942 (1965); Cornelius J.

Peck, The Atrophied Rule Making Powers of the National Labor Relations Board, 70 Yale L.J. 729 (1961).

Despite this criticism, the Supreme Court has made clear that the Board has broad discretion in choosing between rulemaking and adjudication as a policymaking vehicle. In NLRB v. Bell Aerospace Co., 416 U.S. 267, 294 (1974), the Court unanimously rejected the Second Circuit's position (per Judge Friendly) that the Board was required to use rulemaking where it was reversing long-standing precedent, stating that "the Board is not precluded from announcing new principles in an adjudication" and that "the choice between rulemaking and adjudication lies in the first instance within the Board's discretion." Nonetheless, the Board has sometimes encountered resistance from the circuit courts when it attempts to apply a new policy retroactively. See, e.g., Epilepsy Foundation of Northeast Ohio v. NLRB, 268 F. 3d 1095, 1102-1103 (D.C. Cir. 2001) (Edwards, J.) (enforcing Board's policy, but refusing to allow its retroactive application, noting that such application would render conduct that was entirely lawful when committed unlawful and subject employer to substantial sanctions).

When making policy through adjudication, the Board sometimes identifies particular cases as likely vehicles for reconsideration of existing policy or development of policy in a novel area. In those instances, it frequently schedules oral argument and provides an opportunity for interested employee and employer groups that are not parties to the case to file amicus briefs, and sometimes to participate in oral argument as well.

In Excelsior Underwear, Inc., 156 N.L.R.B. 1236 (1966), excerpted infra pages 271-274, the Board not only invited the participation of amici, but announced a general rule (requiring employers to disclose the names and addresses of unit employees within seven days of the approval or direction of an election) that was not to take effect until 30 days from the decision and hence was not applied to the parties to the case. In NLRB v. Wyman-Gordon Co., 394 U.S. 759 (1969), involving the Board's attempt to enforce a subpoena against an employer who had refused to produce the requisite "*Excelsior* list," six members of the Court found that the Board had acted improperly in *Excelsior* by promulgating a rule—"an agency statement of general or particular applicability and future effect"—without following the notice-and-comment procedures required by the APA. Nonetheless, four of those Justices joined with three other members of the Court to form a majority favoring enforcement of the subpoena; the four reasoned that whatever the improprieties in *Excelsior,* the disputed subpoena had been issued as part of a valid adjudicatory proceeding and should therefore be enforced.

### c. *The NLRB's Recent Experience with Rulemaking*

The Board's recent experience with rulemaking may offer a cautionary note. The agency issued two new rules in 2011, both of which were challenged in federal court. In August 2011, after receiving more than 7000 comments, the NLRB issued a final rule that required employers to post a notice advising employees of their rights under the NLRA. 76 Fed. Reg. 54,006. The D.C. Circuit held that the rule was invalid in Nat'l Ass'n of Mfrs. v. NLRB, 717 F.3d 947 (D.C. Cir. 2013). It concluded that that the rule, in effect, compelled employer speech and thus violated NLRA §8(c)'s requirement that noncoercive expression or the refusal to engage in expression cannot constitute an unfair labor practice. Id. at 955; 29 U.S.C. §158(c).

On December 22, 2011, the Board also issued a final rule intended to streamline representation election procedures. 76 Fed. Reg. 80138-89. In Chamber of Commerce of the U.S. v. NLRB, 879 F. Supp. 2d 18, 21, 24 (D.D.C. 2012), the court struck down the rule on the ground that there was no three-member quorum when the final rule was issued because Member Hayes was "absent"—rather than merely "abstaining"—from the vote, as the Board had asserted. On February 6, 2014, by a 3-2 vote the Board issued a Notice of Proposed Rulemaking that is essentially a reissuance of the 2011 proposal.

For further discussion of rulemaking and adjudication, see infra pages 234-240.

### 5. Delay at the NLRB

The amount of time that it takes the NLRB to dispose of contested unfair labor practice cases has long been a matter of considerable concern. See Estreicher & Bodie, Review Essay—Administrative Delay at the NLRB: Some Modest Proposals, 23 J. Lab. Res. 87 (2002); Edward B. Miller, An Administrative Appraisal of the NLRB (4th ed. 1999). The delay factor should be carefully weighed in appraising the following:

1. the Board's failure to index its jurisdictional standards to inflation;
2. the Board's penchant for highly fact-specific standards that encourage litigation without necessarily effectively serving the agency's regulatory objectives;
3. the Board's tendency to revisit some doctrines again and again, often for no other reason than a change in its own composition due to a new administration in the White House;
4. the Board's failure to make greater use of its rulemaking powers;
5. the degree to which the General Counsel and the Board have made use of §10(j) to seek preliminary injunctive relief against alleged unfair labor practices, and arguments that §10(j) has generally been underutilized;

6. the wisdom of Board policies that tend to channel disputes over a union's continued majority status into the unfair labor practice procedure rather than the representation process; and
7. the degree of respect (or lack thereof) shown the Board by the federal appellate courts.

## B. SCOPE OF REVIEW OF NLRB DETERMINATIONS

As discussed below, the standard of review applied by courts in NLRB cases depends on the nature of the issue in dispute.

### 1. "Substantial Evidence" Review

Section 10(e) of the Act provides that "findings of the Board with respect to questions of fact if supported by substantial evidence on the record considered as a whole shall be conclusive." NLRA §10(e), as amended 1947. In Universal Camera Corp. v. NLRB, 340 U.S. 474 (1951), the Supreme Court made clear that §10(e) requires courts to consider not only evidence in support of a finding, viewed in isolation, but also anything in the record that fairly detracts from the weight of such evidence. Nonetheless, the "substantial evidence" test requires deference to reasonable agency findings of fact. See, e.g., Allentown Mack Sales & Service, Inc. v. NLRB, 522 U.S. 359, 370 (1998) (application of substantial evidence test requires a court to decide "whether on this record it would have been possible for a reasonable trier of fact to reach the Board's conclusion").

Although both §10(e) and *Universal Camera* speak in terms of "factual findings," the substantial evidence test as a practical matter applies to two different kinds of Board determinations. The first category involves "pure" factual questions or questions of "adjudicative fact"—that is, questions regarding the conduct of the specific parties involved in the case, or "who did what, where, when, how, why, [and] with what motive or intent?" The second involves the Board's application of law to fact, or "mixed" questions of law and fact. Although there appears to be a certain amount of confusion regarding the proper standard of review in this context, see Samuel Estreicher, The Second Circuit and the NLRB 1980-81: A Case Study in Judicial Review of Agency Action, 48 Brook. L. Rev. 1063, 1069 (1982), the Supreme Court has indicated that the substantial evidence standard should apply. See Fall River Dyeing & Finishing Corp. v. NLRB, 482 U.S. 27, 42 (1987) (if Board's application of a properly adopted rule or policy is supported by substantial evidence, courts should enforce its order); Beth Israel Hosp. v. NLRB, 437 U.S. 483, 501 (1978) (same); *Allentown Mack,* 522 U.S. at 366, discussed further infra pages 340-348.

## 2. Review of Questions of "Law" or "Policy"

*Universal Camera* dealt with the reviewing function only with respect to "questions of fact" as distinguished from "questions of law" or "policy." The Supreme Court decision that is now most often cited by courts in reviewing an agency's legal and policy judgments is Chevron U.S.A. Inc. v. Natural Resources Defense Council, Inc., 467 U.S. 837 (1984). In *Chevron,* which involved a regulation promulgated by the Environmental Protection Agency, the Court formulated the appropriate standard of review as follows:

> When a court reviews an agency's construction of the statute which it administers, it is confronted with two questions. First, always, is the question whether Congress has directly spoken to the precise question at issue. If the intent of Congress is clear, that is the end of the matter, for the court, as well as the agency, must give effect to the unambiguously expressed intent of Congress. If, however, the court determines Congress has not directly addressed the precise question at issue, the court does not simply impose its own construction on the statute. . . . Rather, if the statute is silent or ambiguous with respect to the specific issue, the question for the court is whether the agency's answer is based on a permissible construction of the statute.

Id. at 842-843.

*Chevron* holds that courts are to show deference to agencies like the Board when they exercise policymaking authority that has been either explicitly or implicitly delegated to the agency by Congress. See also United States v. Mead Corp., 533 U.S. 218 (2001). The *Chevron* Court indicated that in order to uphold an agency when the court has determined that Congress did not directly address the precise question at issue, the court "need not conclude that the agency construction was the only one it permissibly could have adopted . . . , or even the reading the court would have reached if the question initially had arisen in a judicial proceeding"; it need only be "reasonable." 467 U.S. at 843 n.11. In addition, the Court rejected the argument that the agency's rule was not entitled to deference because the agency had changed its policy over time: "On the contrary, the agency, to engage in informed [policymaking], must consider varying interpretations and the wisdom of its policy on a continuing basis." Id. at 863-864.

The *Chevron* Court gave three reasons why courts should defer to reasonable agency interpretations where Congress has not spoken to the issue: (1) because "[t]he power of an administrative agency to administer a congressionally created . . . program necessarily requires the formulation of policy and the making of rules [or policies] to fill any gap left, implicitly or explicitly, by Congress"; (2) because a specialized agency generally has superior knowledge, compared to a court, regarding the practical impact of competing policies; and (3) because policy choices are more appropriately made by agencies, which are indirectly accountable to the people through the President, than by unelected federal judges. For an analysis of the extent to which courts can restrain Board policymaking and policy changes under *Chevron*, see Michael C. Harper, Judicial Control of the National Labor Relations Board's Lawmaking in the Age of *Chevron* and *Brand X*, 89 B.U. L. Rev. 189 (2009).

In studying the materials in this book, you should evaluate both whether the Board's efforts at policymaking are consistent with the statutory scheme, and also whether reviewing courts are respecting the proper limits of their role as opposed to imposing their own policy judgments on the statute.

## C. JURISDICTION

### 1. The Commerce Requirement and Other Limitations on NLRB Jurisdiction

#### *a. The Commerce Clause and the Board's Jurisdictional Self-Limitations*

Under §§10(a) and 9(c)(1) of the NLRA, as amended, the NLRB's jurisdiction extends to cases "affecting commerce," as that term is defined in §2(7) of the Act. In upholding the constitutionality of the Wagner Act, the Supreme Court announced that the Board's statutory jurisdiction was coextensive with the power of Congress under the Commerce Clause. See NLRB v. Jones & Laughlin Steel Corp., 301 U.S. 1 (1937). However, the Board, through its policy of jurisdictional self-limitation, has in general avoided serious tests of the limits that might be imposed on its reach under the commerce power.

The Board's two primary self-limiting standards, promulgated in 1958, are as follows:

1. *Retail concerns*: $500,000 annual gross volume of business.
2. *Nonretail companies* (e.g., manufacturers): $50,000 annual outflow or inflow, direct or indirect.

> Direct outflow refers to goods shipped or services furnished directly by the employer to entities outside the state, and direct inflow to goods or services furnished directly to the employer from entities outside the state. Indirect outflow includes sales within the state to entities who subsequently sell the goods or services outside the state. Indirect inflow refers to the purchase of goods or services which originated outside the employer's state but which it purchased from a seller within the state.

In 1996, the House attempted to index the Board's jurisdictional standards to account for inflation, which would have raised the $500,000 gross revenue standard for retail businesses to over $2.5 million, and the $50,000 inflow/outflow standard for nonretail enterprises to over $250,000. However, this effort, which would have effectively removed the Board's jurisdiction over many small businesses, was not successful, and the $500,000 and $50,000 standards remain in place.

As the above material suggests, the Board has the discretion to decline jurisdiction over entities that fall within §2(2)'s definition of "employer." That discretion, however, is not unlimited. In Office Employees, Local 11 v. NLRB, 353 U.S. 313 (1957), the Supreme Court rejected the Board's declination of jurisdiction over local labor unions, which the Board based on their nonprofit character. The Court noted §2(2)'s specific inclusion of a labor organization when "acting as an employer," and held that the Board's "arbitrary blanket exclusion of union employers as a class" ran contrary to Congress's clear intent. Id. at 318. The Court distinguished the categorical exclusion of labor unions from the Board's practices of excluding employers who do not meet its dollar volume jurisdictional standards and of declining jurisdiction in particular cases where it determines that the policies of the Act would not be effectuated by an assertion of jurisdiction. Note that NLRA §14(c), added in 1959, permits states to assert jurisdiction where the Board has declined as a discretionary matter to do so.

The NLRB's jurisdiction encompasses the American operations of foreign companies doing business in the United States. See Il Progresso Italo Americano Publishing Co., 299 N.L.R.B. 270 (1990). The statute, however, has been interpreted as excluding from coverage American citizens who are permanently employed by American companies outside the United States. See Computer Sciences Raytheon, 318 N.L.R.B. 966, 968 (1995) (citing McCulloch v. Sociedad Nacional, 372 U.S. 10 (1963)). Questions about the territorial limits of the NLRB's jurisdiction will be discussed further in Chapter 15 infra.

### *b. The Implied Religious Exemption: Avoiding First Amendment Issues*

The First Amendment imposes some limits on the Board's jurisdiction. In NLRB v. Catholic Bishop of Chicago, 440 U.S. 490 (1979), the Supreme Court rejected the Board's policy of declining jurisdiction over religiously sponsored organizations only if the organizations were "completely religious," not merely "religiously associated," and held that the Board lacked jurisdiction over teachers in church-operated schools in either case. The Court reasoned that both the inquiry required under the Board's test and the actual assertion of jurisdiction over teachers in church-operated schools could create serious First Amendment Free Exercise Clause problems. Finding no clear expression in the NLRA that Congress intended to bring teachers in church-operated schools within the Board's jurisdiction, and applying its policy of construing statutes so as to avoid constitutional issues wherever possible, the Court construed the Act to preclude such jurisdiction. For more recent significant cases in this area, see University of Great Falls v. NLRB, 278 F.3d 1335 (D.C. Cir. 2002) (rejecting Board's case-by-case inquiry in *Catholic Bishop* cases as overly intrusive and substituting bright-line test, including whether school holds itself out as providing a religious educational environment); St. Edmund's High School and St. Edmund's Roman Catholic Church, 337 N.L.R.B. 1260 (2002) (discussing application of *Catholic Bishop* to non-teaching employees at religious institutions, Board rejects inquiry into role of particular employees involved in furthering employer's religious purpose and endorses previous decisions "declin[ing] to assert jurisdiction over a church employer" even where employees at issue performed purely secular functions). In Pacific Lutheran University, Case 19-RC-102521, the Board is considering whether *Catholic Bishop* excludes NLRB jurisdiction only over teachers performing religious functions or whether the exclusion extends to entire institutions that have a "substantial religious character."

## 2. Statutory Exclusions

The NLRA expressly excludes several significant classes of employees from its coverage, including agricultural laborers; domestic service workers; employees of federal, state, and local governments, including wholly owned government corporations; and railroad and airline employees subject to the Railway Labor Act. Of the above exclusions, the one that has given the Board the most difficulty is that for governmental employees. Particularly troublesome have been issues concerning private companies performing under contract with governmental entities; the Board has struggled with the question of whether it should, as a discretionary matter, decline to assert jurisdiction over employers who have such close ties to an exempt governmental entity that their hands may be bound to some degree in collective bargaining negotiations. Under its prior *Res-Care* doctrine, 280 N.L.R.B. 670 (1986), the Board had examined the extent of control over essential terms and conditions maintained by the private employer and the exempt entity, respectively, to determine whether the private employer was capable of engaging in meaningful collective bargaining; if the Board thought not, it would exercise its discretion to decline jurisdiction.

In Management Training Corp., 317 N.L.R.B. 1355 (1995), however, the Board overruled *Res-Care*, reasoning that "whether there are sufficient employment matters over which unions and employers can bargain is a question better left to the parties at the bargaining table and ultimately, to the employee voters in each case." The Board concluded that its prior attempts to judge whether the number and nature of the issues controlled by the non-governmental employer would allow for meaningful bargaining had inappropriately injected it into the substantive aspects of the bargaining process, and had also resulted in much undesirable litigation. Hence, in *Management Training*, the Board decided that it would assert jurisdiction over the private employer as long as it met the statutory definition of "employer" under §2(2) and the applicable monetary thresholds. The Board's *Management Training* policy has been approved by every circuit to consider the matter. See NLRB v. Young Women's Christian Assn., 192 F.3d 1111 (8th Cir. 1999); Aramark Corp. v. NLRB, 179 F.3d 872 (10th Cir. 1999) (en banc); Pikeville United Methodist Hospital of Kentucky, Inc. v. NLRB, 109 F.3d 1146 (6th Cir. 1997); Teledyne Econ. Dev. v. NLRB, 108 F.3d 56 (4th Cir. 1997). In 2012, the Board asserted jurisdiction over nonprofit corporations that operate charter schools, concluding that they are not political subdivisions of the state under §2(2). See Chi. Mathematics & Sci. Acad. Charter Sch., Inc., 359 N.L.R.B. No. 41 (2012), invalidated due to lack of quorum by NLRB v. Noel Canning Co., 134 S. Ct. 2550 (2014); Pilsen Wellness Ctr., 359 N.L.R.B. No. 72 (2013), invalidated due to lack of quorum by NLRB v. Noel Canning Co., 134 S. Ct. 2550 (2014) (finding jurisdiction over private company that contracted with charter school to provide staff and educational services).

In addition, the 1947 Taft-Hartley amendments excluded "independent contractors" and "supervisors" from the Act's coverage. Determining whether borderline personnel fall within those excluded categories — or within categories covered by implied exclusions — has raised difficult interpretive issues, which are explored in the materials below.

### *a. Independent Contractors*

#### *Note:* NLRB v. Hearst *and Congress' Reaction*

The 1935 Wagner Act did not exclude independent contractors from the definition of "employee." In a 1944 case, NLRB v. Hearst Publications, Inc., 322 U.S. 111, 126-28, the Supreme Court upheld the Board's finding that the "newsboys" or news vendors in that case were statutory employees, stating as follows:

> The mischief at which the Act is aimed and the remedies it offers are not confined exclusively to "employees" within the traditional legal distinctions separating them from "independent contractors." . . . Unless the common-law tests are to be imported and made exclusively controlling, without regard to the statute's purposes, it cannot be irrelevant that the particular workers in these cases are subject, as a matter of economic fact, to the evils the statute was designed to eradicate and that the remedies it affords are appropriate for preventing them or curing their harmful effects in the special situation. . . .
>
> . . . Inequality of bargaining power in controversies over wages, hours and working conditions may as well characterize the status of the one group as of the

other. . . . In short, when . . . the economic facts of the relation make it more nearly one of employment than of independent business enterprise with respect to the ends sought to be accomplished by the legislation, those characteristics may outweigh technical legal classification for purposes unrelated to the statute's objectives and bring the relation within its protections. . . .

Congress voiced strong disapproval of the *Hearst* decision and amended the NLRA §2(3) in 1947 to expressly exclude "individuals having the status of an independent contractor" from the protections of the Act. The amendment did not, however, define "independent contractor." The House Committee Report on the Taft-Hartley amendments stated:

> . . . [I]n *Hearst Publications, Inc.*, the Board expanded the definition of the term "employee" beyond anything that it ever had included before, and the Supreme Court, relying upon the theoretic "expertness" of the Board, upheld the Board. In this case the Board held independent merchants who bought newspapers from the publisher and hired people to sell them to be "employees." The people the merchants hired to sell the papers were "employees" of the merchants, but holding the merchants to be "employees" of the publisher of the papers was most far reaching. . . . [W]hen Congress passed the Labor Act, it intended words it used to have the meanings that they had when Congress passed the act, not new meanings that, nine years later, the Labor Board might think up. In the law, there always had been a difference, and a big difference, between "employees" and "independent contractors." "Employees" work for wages or salaries under direct supervision. "Independent contractors" undertake to do a job for a price, decide how the work will be done, usually hire others to do the work, and depend for their income not upon wages, but upon the difference between what they pay for goods, materials, and labor and what they receive for the end result, that is, upon profits. . . . To correct what the Board has done, and what the Supreme Court, putting misplaced reliance upon the Board's expertness, has approved, the bill excludes "independent contractors" from the definition of "employee."

H.R. Rep. No. 245, 80th Cong., 1st Sess., on H.R. 3020, at 18 (1947).

In the following case, the Court considered the proper interpretation of the 1947 exclusion.

### NLRB v. United Insurance Co.
*390 U.S. 254 (1968)*

[The company contended that approximately 3,300 debit agents, who primarily collected premiums, prevented lapsing of policies, and sold new insurance, were independent contractors, and therefore refused to recognize a union certified by the Board as the agents' representative. The court of appeals, agreeing with the company, declined to enforce the Board's bargaining order. The Supreme Court reversed.]

Black, J. [After mentioning Congress's adverse reaction to the *Hearst* decision, stated in part:]

... On the one hand these debit agents perform their work primarily away from the company's offices and fix their own hours of work and work days; and clearly they are not as obviously employees as are production workers in a factory. On the other hand, however, they do not have the independence, nor are they allowed the initiative and decision-making authority, normally associated with an independent contractor. In such a situation as this there is no shorthand formula or magic phrase that can be applied to find the answer, but all of the incidents of the relationship must be assessed and weighed with no one factor being decisive. What is important is that the total factual context is assessed in light of the pertinent common-law agency principles. When this is done, the decisive factors in these cases become the following: the agents do not operate their own independent businesses, but perform functions that are an essential part of the company's normal operations; they need not have any prior training or experience, but are trained by company supervisory personnel; they do business in the company's name with considerable assistance and guidance from the company and its managerial personnel and ordinarily sell only the company's policies; the "Agent's Commission Plan" that contains the terms and conditions under which they operate is promulgated and changed unilaterally by the company; the agents account to the company for the funds they collect under an elaborate and regular reporting procedure; the agents receive the benefits of the company's vacation plan and group insurance and pension fund; and the agents have a permanent working arrangement with the company under which they may continue as long as their performance is satisfactory. Probably the best summation of what these factors mean in the reality of the actual working relationship was given by the chairman of the board of respondent company in a letter to debit agents about the time this unfair labor practice proceeding arose:

> if any agent believes he has the power to make his own rules and plan of handling the company's business, then that agent should hand in his resignation at once, and if we learn that said agent is not going to operate in accordance with the company's plan, then the company will be forced to make the agents final [sic]. . . .

The Board examined all of these facts and found that they showed the debit agents to be employees. This was not a purely factual finding by the Board, but involved the application of law to facts — what do the facts establish under the common law of agency: employee or independent contractor? . . . [S]uch a determination of pure agency law involved no special administrative expertise that a court does not possess. On the other hand, the Board's determination was a judgment made after a hearing with witnesses and oral argument . . . and on the basis of written briefs. Such a determination should not be set aside just because a court would, as an original matter, decide the case the other way. As we said in Universal Camera Corp. v. NLRB, 340 U.S. 474, "Nor does it [the requirement for canvassing the whole record] mean that even as to matters not requiring expertise a court may displace the Board's choice between two fairly conflicting views, even though the court would justifiably have made a different choice had the matter been before it de novo." 340 U.S., at 488. Here the least that can be said for the Board's decision is that it made a choice between two fairly conflicting views, and under these circumstances the Court of Appeals should have enforced the Board's order.

**Roadway Package System, Inc.**
*326 NLRB 842 (1998)*

Roadway . . . operates a nationwide pickup and delivery system for small packages. . . . The sole issue to be decided here is whether the drivers at Roadway's Ontario and Pomona terminals are employees under Section 2(3) of the Act or independent contractors not subject to the Board's jurisdiction. . . .

The parties and amici in the instant case rely on the Restatement [of Agency §220],[32] but they debate whether any of the factors listed in Section

32. This section provides, in pertinent part:

1) A servant is a person employed to perform services in the affairs of another and who with respect to the physical conduct in the performance of the services is subject to the other's control or right of control.
2) In determining whether one acting for another is a servant or an independent contractor, the following matters of fact, among others, are considered:

The extent of control which, by the agreement, the master may exercise over the details of the work.

Whether or not the one employed is engaged in a distinct occupation or business.

The kind of occupation, with reference to whether, in the locality, the work is usually done under the direction of the employer or by a specialist without supervision.

The skill required in the particular occupation.

Whether the employer or the workman supplies the instrumentalities, tools, and the place of work for the person doing the work.

The length of time for which the person is employed.

The method of payment, whether by the time or by the job.

Whether or not the work is part of the regular business of the employer.

Whether or not the parties believe they are creating the relation of master and servant.

Whether the principal is or is not in the business.

220 are more or less indicative of employee status. Citing the language contained in Subsections (1) and 2(a), Roadway and several amici argue that the "most important" or "predominant" factor to be considered is whether an employer has a "right to control" the manner and means of the work. In contrast, the Petitioner and the AFL-CIO assert that all the factors should be weighed in the equation, as evidenced by the opening paragraph of Subsection 2 of Section 220.

The Supreme Court has clearly stated that "all of the incidents of the relationship must be assessed and weighed with no one factor being decisive." See *United Insurance*, 390 U.S. at 258. . . . While we recognize that the common-law agency test described by the Restatement ultimately assesses the amount or degree of control exercised by an employing entity over an individual, we find insufficient basis for the proposition that those factors which do not include the concept of "control" are insignificant when compared to those that do. Section 220(2) of the Restatement refers to 10 pertinent factors as "among others," thereby specifically permitting the consideration of other relevant factors as well, depending on the factual circumstances presented. . . .

. . . [W]e now apply the common-law agency test to the present situation involving the Ontario and Pomona drivers. We find that the dealings and arrangements between these drivers and Roadway, including those reflective of the changes made by [the 1994 "Pickup and Delivery Contractor Operating Agreement"] have many of the same characteristics of the employee-employer relationship presented in *United Insurance*. . . .

As in *United Insurance*, the drivers here do not operate independent businesses, but perform functions that are an essential part of the company's normal operations; they need not have any prior training or experience, but receive training from the company; they do business in the company's name with assistance and guidance from it; they do not ordinarily engage in outside business; they constitute an integral part of the company's business under its substantial control; they have no substantial proprietary interest beyond their investment in their trucks; and they have no significant entrepreneurial opportunity for gain or loss. All these factors weigh heavily in favor of employee status, and are fully supported by the following facts.

The Ontario and Pomona drivers devote a substantial amount of their time, labor, and equipment to performing essential functions that allow Roadway to compete in the small package delivery market. . . . None of the drivers are required to have prior delivery training or experience. Those unfamiliar with Roadway's system can gain assistance and guidance from the new driver orientation meetings that are conducted by Roadway's personnel. While a few operate as incorporated businesses, all the Ontario and Pomona drivers do business in the name of Roadway. Wearing an "RPS-approved uniform," the drivers operate uniformly marked vehicles. In fact, the vehicles are custom designed by Roadway and produced to its specifications by Navistar. . . . All the vehicles clearly display Roadway's name, logo, and colors. Thus, the drivers' connection to and integration in Roadway's operations is highly visible and well publicized.

The drivers have a contractual right to use this customized truck in business activity outside their relationship with Roadway, though none of the Ontario and Pomona drivers (and only 3 out of Roadway's 5,000 drivers nationwide) have used their vehicles for other commercial purposes. This lack of pursuit of outside business activity appears to be less a reflection of entrepreneurial choice by the Ontario and Pomona drivers and more a matter of the obstacles created by their relationship with Roadway.[36]

Roadway's drivers are prohibited under the 1994 Agreement from conducting outside business for other companies throughout the day. The drivers' commitment to Roadway continues through the evening hours when they must return their vehicles to the terminal to interface with Roadway's evening line-haul operations. Typically, most drivers then . . . leave their vehicles overnight at the terminal to take advantage of loading of the next day's assignments by Roadway's package handlers. As a consequence, their vehicles remain out of service during these off-work hours. Even if the drivers want to use their vehicles for other purposes during their off-work hours, there are several obvious built-in hindrances. First, the vehicles are not readily available. Second, before the driver can use his vehicle for other purposes, he must mask any marking reflecting Roadway's name or business. . . . The vehicles are also not easily flexible or susceptible to modifications or adaptations to other types of use. Thus, these constraints on the drivers' use of their vehicles during their off-work hours "provide minimal play for entrepreneurial initiative and minimize the extent to which ownership of a truck gives its driver entrepreneurial independence." . . . Roadway has simply shifted certain capital costs to the drivers without providing them with the independence to engage in entrepreneurial opportunities.

Truck ownership can suggest independent contractor status where, for example, an entrepreneur with a truck puts it to use in serving his or another business' customers. But, the form of truck ownership, here, does not eliminate the Ontario and Pomona drivers' dependence on Roadway in acquiring their vehicles. Roadway . . . requires the drivers to acquire and maintain their own specialty vans, and Roadway eases the drivers' burden through its arrangement and promotion of Navistar vans sold or leased through Bush Leasing. Although it does not directly participate in these van transfers, Roadway's involvement in these deals undoubtedly facilitates and ensures

---

36. In [C.C. Eastern, Inc. v. NLRB, 60 F.3d 855, 860 (D.C. Cir. (1995),] the court agreed with the principle that "if a company offers its workers entrepreneurial opportunities that they cannot realistically take, then that does not add any weight to the Company's claim that the workers are independent contractors." We view the Ontario and Pomona drivers' contractual right to engage in outside business as falling within th[is] category. . . .

that a fleet of vehicles, built and maintained according to its specifications, is always readily available and recyclable among the drivers.

Roadway also encourages the sale of used vehicles from former to new drivers. In this way, Roadway eases the new driver's responsibility for obtaining a qualified vehicle . . . and increases the likelihood that there will be a qualified buyer for a costly specialty van no longer needed by the former driver. There is simply no ready market for these vehicles. Every feature, detail, and internal configuration has been dictated by Roadway's specifications. In short, Roadway has created a system which makes the necessary, custom vehicles readily available to prospective drivers, and enables drivers who want to end their relationship with it to easily transfer their vehicles to incoming drivers. . . .

Other support for employee status can be found in Roadway's compensation package for the drivers. Here, Roadway establishes, regulates, and controls the rate of compensation and financial assistance to the drivers as well as the rates charged to customers. Generally speaking, there is little room for the drivers to influence their income through their own efforts or ingenuity. Whatever potential for entrepreneurial profit does exist, Roadway suppresses through a system of minimum and maximum number of packages and customer stops assigned to the drivers. . . .

Weighing all the incidents of their relationship with Roadway, we conclude that the Ontario and Pomona drivers are employees and not independent contractors. . . .

## *NOTES AND QUESTIONS*

**1. Dial-A-Mattress.** In the companion case to *Roadway*, Dial-A-Mattress Operating Corp., 326 N.L.R.B. 884 (1998), the Board found the owner-operators at issue to be independent contractors rather than employees. In *Dial*, the company provided no training to the owner-operators, and imposed no requirements regarding the trucks used by them, which varied widely. Many of the owner-operators owned more than one truck, and a few owned several. The owner-operators hired their own helpers to assist with loading, and some hired other drivers. They had sole control over the hiring and terms and conditions of the helpers and any drivers hired. The owner-operators formed their own trucking companies, and the trucks displayed the company name of the owner-operator, not Dial-A-Mattress. They were not required to return to Dial's warehouse at the end of the day, and were allowed to use their vehicles to make deliveries for other companies — except for Dial's competitors — and to perform additional work for the customers to whom deliveries were made in exchange for separate payment. The owner-operators were paid a flat fee per delivery, there was no guaranteed minimum compensation, and there was a wide range in their annual compensation. In finding them to be independent contractors under the common-law agency test, the Board noted that they had significant entrepreneurial opportunity for gain or loss, and a separate identity and significant independence from Dial.

**2. "Right to Control" vs. Multi-Factored Test.** Consider the competing tests for independent contractor status discussed in *Roadway*: the multi-factored common law of agency test versus a test that focuses on whether the employer has a right to control the manner and means by which the job is to be done. The "manner and means" or "right to control" test derives from tort law, where it is used to determine whether a company is vicariously liable for torts committed by those who are acting in its interests. See Michael C. Harper, Defining the Economic Relationship Appropriate for Collective Bargaining, 39 B.C. L. Rev. 329, 334 (1998). Does such a test make sense for purposes of determining whether particular workers should be able to engage in collective bargaining with that company? On the other hand, are there disadvantages to the multi-factored test applied by the Board in *Roadway*? How predictable is it for employers and unions? Is it subject to manipulation by the employer? What is the policy goal underlying this test? See Harper, supra, at 335, 337-338.

**3. Significant Entrepreneurial Opportunity for Gain or Loss.** Does the Board in *Roadway* focus its common-law analysis on whether the drivers actually retained both significant entrepreneurial opportunity to achieve some independent economic gains and also exposure to potential independent losses? If so, is this focus consistent with the congressional command after the *Hearst* case to apply general common-law principles? In FedEx Home Delivery v. NLRB, 563 F.3d 492 (D.C. Cir. 2009), the court stressed that "it is the worker's retention of the right to engage in entrepreneurial activity rather than his regular exercise of that right that is most relevant for the purpose of determining whether he is an independent contractor." The court noted the FedEx drivers' ability to operate multiple routes, hire substitute drivers and helpers, and to sell routes without permission. Judge Garland, in dissent, stressed the Board's finding that there was in fact "little room for the contractors to influence their income through their own efforts or ingenuity" and that any abstract "rights" to make entrepreneurial decisions, like the use of trucks for shippers other than FedEx or the sale of a route for profit, were in practice foreclosed and not utilized. In FedEx Home Delivery, 361 N.L.R.B. No. 55 (2014), a case based on substantially similar facts, the Board disagreed with the D.C. Circuit. It clarified that the consideration of whether the putative independent contractor is providing services through an independent business should be made "in the context of weighing all relevant common-law factors." Similar to the dissent in the D.C. Circuit case, it stressed that it would only give weight to actual entrepreneurial opportunities, rather than theoretical opportunities, and would consider any constraints that the company places on the putative independent contractor's ability to pursue entrepreneurial opportunities.

**4. Restatement of Employment Law Test.** On May 21, 2014, the membership of the American Law Institute approved the following definition of employment status in §1.01 of the Restatement Third of Employment Law:

**§1.01. General Conditions for Existence of Employment Relationship**

(1) [A]n individual renders services as an employee of an employer if
  (a) the individual acts, at least in part, to serve the interests of the employer,
  (b) the employer consents to receive the individual's services, and
  (c) the employer controls the manner and means by which the individual renders his or her services or otherwise effectively prevents the individual from rendering the services as an independent businessperson.

(2) An individual renders services as an independent businessperson when the individual in his or her own interest exercises entrepreneurial control over important business decisions, including whether to hire and where to assign assistants, whether to purchase and where to deploy equipment, and whether and when to provide service to other customers.

How, if at all, does this test differ from the common-law "right to control" test? From the Board's approach in *Roadway*?

### *b. Supervisory, Managerial, and Confidential Personnel*

Repealing Packard Motor Car Co. v. NLRB, 330 U.S. 485 (1947), Congress in the Taft-Hartley amendments enacted an express exclusion in §2(11) for a company's supervisors. The decision that follows deals with the issue of whether managerial employees, even when not supervising employees within the express exclusion, are nevertheless implicitly excluded from the Act.

**NLRB v. Bell Aerospace Co.**
*416 U.S. 267 (1974)*

[In this case the Board had certified a union as the bargaining representative of 25 buyers in the purchasing and procurement department at the company's plant, which was engaged in the research and development of aerospace products. The Board rejected the company's argument that the buyers should be excluded from the coverage of the Act because they were managerial employees. The Board asserted the view that Congress intended to exclude from the Act only those "managerial employees" associated with the "formulation and implementation of labor relations policies." The Board held that the "fundamental touchstone" was "whether the duties and responsibilities of any managerial employee or group of managerial employees . . . include determinations which should be made free of any conflict of interest which could arise if the person involved was a participating member of a labor organization." The Supreme Court rejected the Board's position in favor of a broader exclusion of managerial employees.]

Powell, J. . . .

The relevant facts adduced at the representation hearing are as follows. The purchasing and procurement department receives requisition orders from other departments at the plant and is responsible for purchasing all of the company's needs from outside suppliers. Some items are standardized and may be purchased "off the shelf" from various distributors and suppliers. Other items must be made to the company's specifications, and the requisition orders may be accompanied by detailed blueprints and other technical plans. Requisitions often designate a particular vendor, and in some instances the buyer must obtain approval before selecting a different one. Where no vendor is specified, the buyer is free to choose one.

Absent specific instructions to the contrary, buyers have full discretion, without any dollar limit, to select prospective vendors, draft invitations to bid, evaluate submitted bids, negotiate price and terms, and prepare purchase orders. Buyers execute all purchase orders up to $50,000. They may place or cancel orders of less than $5,000 on their own signature. On commitments in excess of $5,000, buyers must obtain the approval of a superior, with higher levels of approval required as the purchase cost increases. For the Minute Man missile project, which represents 70% of the company's sales, purchase decisions are made by a team of personnel from the engineering, quality assurance, finance, and manufacturing departments. The buyer serves as team chairman and signs the purchase order, but a representative from the pricing and negotiation department participates in working out the terms.

After the representation hearing, the Regional Director transferred the case to the Board. On May 20, 1971, the Board issued its decision holding that the company's buyers constituted an appropriate unit for purposes of collective bargaining and directing an election. 190 N.L.R.B. 431. Relying on its recent decision in North Arkansas Electric Cooperative, Inc., 185 N.L.R.B. 550 (1970), the Board first stated that even though the company's buyers might be "managerial employees," they were nevertheless covered by the Act and entitled to its protections. . . .

On June 16, 1971, a representation election was conducted in which 15 of the buyers voted for the union and nine against. On August 12, the Board certified the union as the exclusive bargaining representative for the company's buyers. . . .

We begin with the question whether all "managerial employees," rather than just those in positions susceptible to conflicts of interest in labor relations, are excluded from the protections of the Act. . . .

The Wagner Act, 49 Stat. 449, did not expressly mention the term "managerial employee." After the Act's passage, however, the Board developed the concept of "managerial employee" in a series of cases involving the appropriateness of bargaining units. The first cases established that "managerial employees" were not to be included in a unit with rank-and-file employees. . . .

Whether the Board regarded all "managerial employees" as entirely outside the protection of the Act, as well as inappropriate for inclusion in a rank-and-file bargaining unit, is less certain. To be sure, at no time did the Board certify even a separate unit of "managerial employees" or state that such was possible. The Board was cautious, however, in determining which employees were "managerial." . . .

During this period the Board's policy with respect to the related but narrower category of "supervisory employees" manifested a progressive uncertainty. The Board first excluded supervisors from units of rank-and-file employees. . . . This trend was soon halted, however, by Maryland Drydock Co., 49 N.L.R.B. 733 (1943), where the Board held that supervisors, although literally "employees" under the Act, could not be organized in any unit. . . .

*Maryland Drydock*, supra, was subsequently overruled in Packard Motor Car Co., 61 N.L.R.B. 4, 64 N.L.R.B. 1212 (1945), where the Board held that foremen could constitute an appropriate unit for collective bargaining. The Board's position was upheld 5-4 by this Court in Packard Motor Car Co. v. NLRB, 330 U.S. 485 (1947).) In view of the subsequent legislative reversal of the *Packard* decision, the dissenting opinion of Mr. Justice Douglas is especially pertinent. Id., at 493. He stated:

> The present decision . . . tends to obliterate the line between management and labor. It lends the sanctions of federal law to unionization at all levels of the industrial hierarchy. It tends to emphasize that the basic opposing forces in industry are not management and labor but the operating group on the one hand and the stockholder and bondholder group on the other. The industrial problem as so defined comes down to a contest over a fair division of the gross receipts of industry between these two groups. The struggle for control or power between management and labor becomes secondary to a growing unity in their common demands on ownership. . . .

> [I]f Congress, when it enacted the National Labor Relations Act, had in mind such a basic change in industrial philosophy, it would have left some clear and unmistakable trace of that purpose. But I find none. Id., at 494-495. . . .

The *Packard* decision was a major factor in bringing about the Taft-Hartley Act of 1947. . . .

The legislative history of the Taft-Hartley Act . . . may be summarized as follows. The House wanted to include certain persons within the definition of "supervisors," such as straw bosses, whom the Senate believed should be protected by the Act. As to these persons, the Senate's view prevailed. There were other persons, however, who both the House and the Senate believed were plainly outside the Act. The House wanted to make the exclusion of certain of these persons explicit. In the conference agreement, representatives from both the House and the Senate agreed that a specific provision was unnecessary since the Board had long regarded such persons as outside the Act. Among those mentioned as impliedly excluded were persons working in "labor relations, personnel and employment departments," and "confidential employees." But assuredly this did not exhaust the universe of such excluded persons. The legislative history strongly suggests that there also were other employees, much higher in the managerial structure, who were likewise regarded as so clearly outside the Act that no specific exclusionary provision was thought necessary. For example, in its discussion of confidential employees, the House Report noted that "[m]ost of the people who would qualify as 'confidential' employees are *executives and are excluded from the act in any event.*" H.R. Rep. No. 245, p. 23 (emphasis added). We think the inference is plain that "managerial employees" were paramount among this impliedly excluded group. . . .

Following the passage of the Taft-Hartley Act, the Board itself adhered to the view that "managerial employees" were outside the Act. . . . Until its decision in *North Arkansas* in 1970, the Board consistently followed this reading of the Act. It never certified any unit of "managerial employees," separate or otherwise, and repeatedly stated that it was Congress' intent that such employees not be accorded bargaining rights under the Act. And it was this reading which was permitted to stand when Congress again amended the Act in 1959. 73 Stat. 519.

The Board's exclusion of "managerial employees" defined as those who "formulate and effectuate management policies by expressing and making operative the decisions of their employer," has also been approved by courts without exception. . . .

In sum, the Board's early decisions, the purpose and legislative history of the Taft-Hartley Act of 1947, the Board's subsequent and consistent construction of the Act for more than two decades, and the decisions of the courts of appeals all point unmistakably to the conclusion that "managerial employees" are not covered by the Act. We agree with the Court of Appeals below that the Board "is not now free" to read a new and more restrictive meaning into the Act. 475 F.2d, at 494.

In view of our conclusion, the case must be remanded to permit the Board to apply the proper legal standard.

[The dissent of Justice White, with whom Justices Brennan, Stewart, and Marshall joined, is omitted.]

## *NOTES AND QUESTIONS*

**1. Consequences of Treating Employees as Managers or Supervisors.** Determining whether particular employees are managers or supervisors is important under the NLRA for a number of reasons. First, supervisors and managers have no right to organize and are wholly unprotected by the Act. Second, they cannot be included in bargaining units with employees who are covered by the Act and cannot vote in certification elections. Third, the active involvement of supervisory or managerial employees in a union of protected employees can constitute employer interference with the administration of that union, a violation of §8(a)(2).

**2. The Managerial Exclusion After *Bell Aerospace*.** On remand, the Board concluded that the Bell Aerospace buyers did not exercise "sufficient independent discretion in their jobs to truly align them with management" and that they were therefore employees within the meaning of the Act. The Board noted "comprehensive manuals and instructions" restricting the buyers' discretion in making purchases, the ratio of one supervisor for every three buyers, and the buyers' lack of authority over their own hours and over secretaries. The Board also reaffirmed its definition of managerial employees as "those who formulate and effectuate management policies by expressing and making operative the decisions of their employer, and those who have discretion in the performance of their jobs independent of their employer's established policy. . . . [M]anagerial status is not conferred upon rank-and-file workers, or upon those who perform routinely, but rather it is reserved for those in executive-type positions, those who are closely aligned with management as true representatives of management." Bell Aerospace Corp., 219 N.L.R.B. 384, 385 (1975) (quoting General Dynamics Corp., 213 N.L.R.B. 851(1974)).

While determinations of the managerial exemption are "fact-based analyses," NLRB v. Cooper Union for Advancement of Science and Art, 783 F.2d 29, 31 (2d Cir. 1986), the Board's rejection of managerial status for employees whose discretion is bounded by the employer's established policy has been sustained by the courts of appeals in other cases. See, e.g., NLRB v. Solartec, Inc., 310 Fed. Appx. 829, 831 (6th Cir. 2009) (unpublished) (employee did not have managerial status under the NLRA, in part because the employee's "discretion was circumscribed"); Evergreen America Corp. v. N.L.R.B., 362 F.3d 827, 839-40 (2004) ("The . . . employees in question do not have "absolute authority" over anything—not even a ship's schedule. These employees exercise professional discretion in a few matters affecting the ships, but their decisions are closely monitored by and subject to the direction of the Section Manager"); Northeast Utils. Serv. Corp. v. NLRB, 35 F.3d 621, 626 (1st Cir. 1994) (employees with day-to-day discretion to buy and sell power between New England utilities not managerial because this discretion was bounded by formal policies that employees did not have authority to modify); NLRB v. Case Corp., 995 F.2d 700, 704 (7th Cir. 1993) (engineers with discretion to make technical recommendations not managerial because they lacked discretion to deviate from pre-established policies); Maccabees Mut. Life Ins. Co. v. NLRB, 757 F.2d 767 (6th Cir. 1985) (insurance representatives with authority to approve or deny claims not managerial because their decisions had to conform to employer's established policy). Reconsider these decisions after reading *Kentucky River*, infra page 97. See especially note 2, infra page 103.

**3. Uses of Legislative History.** Given Congress's failure to add managerial employees to the list of express exclusions in §2 of the Act, what were the Court's grounds for finding a broad implied exclusion for all managerial employees?

**4. Conflict of Interest vs. "Alignment."** Is there a plausible account of the congressional purpose that would exclude even first-level shop foremen from statutory coverage yet include individuals higher up in the firm's hierarchy who happen not to supervise anyone? Did Congress intend only to protect employees from being coerced by supervisors into opposing or supporting particular unions rather than to advance the broader notion of "alignment" suggested in Justice Douglas's *Packard* dissent, that capital has a right to "loyal" representatives of its interest aligned against labor's interest? See generally David M. Rabban, Distinguishing Excluded Managers from Covered Professionals Under the NLRA, 89 Colum. L. Rev. 1775 (1989). On the other hand, outside of the professional context, how often will employees who are considered "managerial" by their employers lack supervisory authority over other employees?

**5. *Bell Aerospace* and New Workplace Arrangements.** One important consequence of *Bell Aerospace* is that the NLRA establishes a sharp divide between employees covered by the Act and those falling outside of its protections based on whether they play a role in policymaking for the firm. The realm of unionization and collective bargaining is largely confined to "touch" employees, those engaged as operators, technicians, maintenance or service personnel, and clericals—implementers of the directives of supervisors, managers, and engineers. Middle managers and others engaged in knowledge-based, pro-active roles are outside of the statutory scheme, even if they have similar concerns over job security and fair treatment with no greater ability to influence the personnel decisions of department heads and other executives. Should the Act be amended to allow such employees to choose collective bargaining? See, e.g., Marion Crain, Building Solidarity Through Expansion of NLRA Coverage: A Blueprint for Worker Empowerment, 74 Minn. L. Rev. 953 (1990). Would allowing managers to bargain collectively radically change industrial relations or shift the economic balance between the providers of capital and labor? Would it make it more difficult for management to manage?

At some work sites "touch" workers have been given responsibilities on matters such as quality and inventory control and production process development that were previously the exclusive province of supervisors and managers. See Samuel Estreicher, Employee Involvement and the "Company Union" Prohibition: The Case for Partial Repeal of Section 8(a)(2) of the NLRA, 69 N.Y.U. L. Rev. 125 (1994). Given *Bell Aerospace* and the Board and judicial response set forth in note 2, does the exercise by "touch" workers of significant discretionary responsibilities require their exclusion from the coverage of the NLRA? Should it matter whether the workers exercise any discretionary authority collectively as a team? See NLRB v. Yeshiva Univ., 444 U.S. 672 (1980), discussed infra. See also Harold J. Krent, Note, Collective Authority and Technical Expertise: Reexamining the Managerial Employee Exclusion, 56 N.Y.U. L. Rev. 694 (1981). Is the contemporary delegation of traditional managerial responsibilities to rank-and-file workers a good reason to overrule *Bell Aerospace*? If so, should the definition of supervisor also be modified?

**6. "Confidential" Employees.** "Confidential" employees, like managerial employees and supervisors, are excluded from bargaining units. Under the Board's "labor nexus" test, confidential employees are those who "assist and act in a confidential capacity to persons who exercise 'managerial' functions in the field of labor relations." Ford Motor Co., 66 N.L.R.B. 1317, 1322 (1946). Those who have access only to confidential *business* information — as opposed to confidential information that is *labor-related* — are not excludable from a bargaining unit on that basis. Id. The Supreme Court upheld this "labor nexus" test in NLRB v. Hendricks County Rural Electric Membership Corp., 454 U.S. 170 (1981).

**7. Discharge of Supervisors to Intimidate Statutory Employees.** Although supervisors themselves are unprotected by the Act, the Board has held that the discharge of a supervisor may constitute an unfair labor practice in certain circumstances because of the effect on the rights of employees who *are* protected by the NLRA:

> Thus, an employer may not discharge a supervisor for giving testimony adverse to an employer's interest either at an NLRB proceeding or during the processing of an employee's grievance under the collective-bargaining agreement. Similarly, an employer may not discharge a supervisor for refusing to commit unfair labor practices, or because the supervisor fails to prevent unionization.

Parker-Robb Chevrolet, Inc., 262 N.L.R.B. 402, 402-403 (1982), enforced sub nom. Automobile Salesmen's Union, Local 1095 v. NLRB, 711 F.2d 383 (D.C. Cir. 1983).

However, in *Parker-Robb* the Board held that it would no longer extend protection to supervisors who had been discharged along with statutory employees for engaging in concerted activity with those employees, even when it could be shown that the employer's purpose in discharging the supervisor was to intimidate the NLRA-covered employees. Does *Parker-Robb* undermine the §7 protection of covered employees? Is the limitation necessary to ensure the loyalty of supervisors to management, or because of proof problems in disentangling proper employer motive (to ensure loyalty of supervisors) from improper motive (to intimidate rank-and-file employees)? See Richard B. Freeman, What Can We Learn from NLRA to Create Labor Law for the 21st Century, The Labor and Worklife Program at Harvard Law School, at 9 (Oct. 28, 2010), available at http://www.law.harvard.edu/programs/lwp/people/staffPapers/freeman/2010%20Freeman%20NLRB.pdf (urging "legal protection for supervisors to act neutrally in the NLRB election" as one of four reforms that "would go a long way to modernizing the labor law").

**8. Protection of Employee Seeking Promotion to Supervisor?** An employer rejects a statutory employee's bid for promotion to supervisor solely because of the employee's vigorous participation in concerted activity. Has the employer violated the Act? If so, is the employee entitled to a Board-ordered promotion as well as an award of the salary differential? See NLRB v. Ford Motor Co., 683 F.2d 156 (6th Cir. 1982), enforcing as modified 251 N.L.R.B. 413 (1981) (affirming Board's conclusion that employer violated Act because employees were statutory employees at time of adverse action, but refusing to uphold "compelled promotion" to supervisory position; requiring management to promote a specific employee to a supervisory position is not within Act's intent); see also United Exposition Service Co., 300 N.L.R.B. 211, 221 (1990) (discussing and adhering to line drawn by Sixth Circuit in *Ford*), enforced, 945 F.2d 1057 (8th Cir. 1991).

*Note: The Tension Between Coverage of Professional Employees and Exclusion of Supervisors and Managers*

**1. The Basic Tension Explained.** The Taft-Hartley Act, which expressly excluded supervisors from the protection of the NLRA, simultaneously clearly contemplated the inclusion of at least some professional employees. Taft-Hartley added a proviso to §9(b) requiring the Board not to include professional workers within bargaining units that encompass nonprofessional employees "unless a majority of such professional employees vote for inclusion in such a unit." It also added, at §2(12) of the NLRA, a definition of "professional employees."

Compare the statutory definitions of supervisors in §2(11) and professional employees in §2(12), and recall the definition of managerial employees under *Bell Aerospace.* Note that Taft-Hartley's coverage of professional employees is somewhat in tension with the express exclusion of supervisory employees and the implied exclusion of managerial employees. As for supervisory functions, employees who meet the definition of professional almost always have at least some authority over less experienced professional coworkers, such as the authority to "assign [them work]" or "responsibly to direct" them. Moreover, because of the tradition of "peer review," many professionals have hiring and performance evaluation responsibilities. Many professionals also have authority to direct at least some nonprofessional employees, such as secretaries in an office or orderlies or nurses' aides in a hospital.

In addition, many professionals can be said to have at least some authority to "formulate and effectuate management policies" by the exercise of some degree of independent discretion. Consider, for instance, the role that engineers and chemists may have in product design and development or the discretion that doctors and nurses must exercise in the treatment of patients. At what point, then, does a professional worker's performance of his or her responsibilities constitute the exercise of "managerial" functions under *Bell Aerospace* or "supervisory" functions under §2(11)?

In dealing with the tensions discussed above, the Supreme Court has three times rejected attempts by the Board to broadly define professionals as nonmanagerial or nonsupervisory. Each of these cases was decided by a 5-4 margin. The first two cases, NLRB v. Yeshiva Univ., 444 U.S. 672 (1980), and NLRB v. Health Care & Retirement Corp. of Am., 511 U.S. 576 (1994), are discussed just below. The Court's most recent foray into this area, NLRB v. Kentucky River Community Care, Inc., 532 U.S. 706 (2001), is set out at greater length infra page 97 et seq.

**2. Professionals as Managers: *NLRB v. Yeshiva.*** In *Yeshiva,* the Court held that full-time faculty members at a large private university were all "managerial" employees because of the faculty's role in such matters as faculty appointments and the setting of curriculum, admission standards, and degree requirements. Justice Powell's opinion for the majority rejected the Board's argument that the faculty's discharge of its duties on these matters did not align it with management because the faculty was expected to exercise "independent professional judgment" and to pursue professional values rather than "conform to management policies" and serve institutional interests. Justice Powell explained:

> In arguing that a faculty member exercising independent judgment acts primarily in his own interest and therefore does not represent the interest of his employer, the Board assumes that the professional interests of the faculty and the interests of the institution are distinct, separable entities with which a faculty could not simultaneously be aligned. The Court of Appeals found no justification for this distinction, and we perceive none. In fact, the faculty's professional interests—as applied to governance at a university like Yeshiva—cannot be separated from those of the institution. . . . The "business" of a university is education.

444 U.S. at 688. Justice Powell also dismissed as inconsistent with other precedent a rationale used by the Board in prior cases for treating members of university faculties as employees: the fact that faculty authority is generally exercised collectively. Id. at 685 n.22.

The *Yeshiva* Court, however, indicated that the "routine discharge of professional duties" by professional employees would not be sufficient to establish managerial (or supervisory) status, "even if union membership arguably may involve some divided loyalty." As an example, the Court noted in a footnote that "architects and engineers functioning as project captains for work performed by teams of professionals are deemed employees despite substantial planning responsibility and authority to direct and evaluate team members." The Court concluded that "only if an employee's activities fall outside of the scope of the duties routinely performed by similarly situated professionals will he be found aligned with management." Id. at 690 & n.30.

Adjunct teachers in colleges and universities are generally held to be NLRA employees. However, in *Point Park University*, No. 6-RC-12276, the Board invited briefing addressing whether adjunct faculty members, because of their ability to vote in certain faculty meetings, are excluded managerial employees, and what weight the NLRB should assign to various factors identified by the Supreme Court in its *Yeshiva* ruling.

**3. Professionals as Supervisors?: "In the Interest of the Employer."** In the second decision, NLRB v. Health Care & Retirement Corp. of Am., 511 U.S. 576 (1994), the Court rejected the Board's view that licensed practical nurses' direction of less skilled employees "in the exercise of professional judgment incident to the treatment of patients" does not establish supervisory status because it is not authority exercised "in the interest of the employer," one of the three requirements for supervisory status within the meaning of §2(11). Justice Kennedy, writing for the majority, found this view to be inconsistent with the rejection in *Yeshiva* of any distinction between professional and institutional interests. Thus, the nurses' professional interests in patient care were not distinct from the interests of the nursing home that employed them, and their direction of subordinate nurses' aides had to be considered "in the interest of the employer" for purposes of determining supervisory status.

Justice Ginsburg's dissent took the Court to task for failing to recognize the statutory overlap between the coverage of professional employees and the criteria for supervisory status under §2(11): "The categories 'supervisor' and 'professional' necessarily overlap. . . . If the term 'supervisor' is construed broadly, to reach everyone with any authority to use 'independent judgment' to assign and 'responsibly . . . direct' the work of other employees, then most professionals would be supervisors, for most have *some* authority to assign and direct others' work. If the term 'supervisor' is understood that broadly, however, Congress' inclusion of professionals within the Act's protections would effectively be nullified."

**4. Professionals as Supervisors: Exercise of "Independent Judgment."** Following the rejection of its "patient care" approach in *Health Care & Retirement Corp.*, the Board developed a new approach to cases involving the potential supervisory status of professional and technical employees that emphasized their lack of "independent judgment" for §2(2) purposes. See, e.g., Providence Hospital, 320 N.L.R.B. 717 (1996), enforced, 121 F.3d 548 (9th Cir. 1997); see also Mississippi Power & Light Co., 328 N.L.R.B. 965 (1999). In the following case, the Supreme Court considered the Board's new approach.

### NLRB v. Kentucky River Community Care, Inc.
*532 U.S. 706 (2001)*

SCALIA, J. . . .

#### I

[R]espondent Kentucky River Community Care, Inc., operates a care facility for residents who suffer from mental retardation and mental illness. The facility, named . . . Caney Creek . . . , employs approximately 110 professional and nonprofessional employees [, including six registered nurses (RNs)]. When a union sought to represent all of Caney Creek's employees, Kentucky River argued that the RNs were supervisors under NLRA §2(11) and must therefore be excluded from the unit. The Board's

Regional Director made the following findings of fact, which were adopted by the Board:

> The Caney Creek facility is staffed 24 hours per day, 7 days per week, but apparently is only fully staffed on the first shift. . . . There are two RNs on each of the three shifts. The RNs are responsible for dispensing medication to the residents and for providing any other medical services ordered by a resident's physician or psychiatrist.
>
> The two RNs on duty during each shift are responsible for servicing the entire facility[, which has four 20-bed units]. The RNs assigned to the second and third shift also serve as "building supervisors" and the first shift RNs occupy this position on weekends. The RNs do not receive any extra compensation for serving as "building supervisors" and do not have keys to the facility. . . .
>
> [T]he only extra responsibility assumed by the RNs when serving as "building supervisors" is to obtain needed help if for some reason a shift is not fully staffed. In the event a shift is understaffed, the RNs on duty will first attempt to find a volunteer to stay over from among the employees on the preceding shift. If a volunteer cannot be obtained from the employees on the preceding shift, the "building supervisor," using a list containing the names, telephone numbers and addresses of the employees, will attempt to reach an off-duty employee who lives nearby to come in and cover the shift. The "building supervisors" do not have any authority, however, to compel an employee to stay over or come in to fill a vacancy under threat of discipline.
>
> It appears that the RNs may occasionally request other employees to perform routine tasks, but they apparently have no authority to take any action if the employee refuses their directives. The RNs may also complete incident reports, but so can any other employee. All incident reports are independently investigated by the nursing or unit coordinators to determine if any disciplinary action is warranted and it does not appear that these management officials seek any input from the RNs involved. Although the Employer asserts in its brief that RNs can "write-up" employees, there is no evidence in the record that they have ever done so. Indeed, [in the case of] the only record evidence where an RN made a complaint about another employee it was apparently ignored. . . .
>
> The RNs in their normal capacity or as "building supervisors" do not have the authority to hire, fire, reward, promote or independently discipline employees or to effectively recommend such action. They do not evaluate employees or take any action which would affect their employment status. Indeed, the RNs, including when they are serving as "building supervisors," for the most part, work independently and by themselves without any subordinates.

[The Board found that the nurses were not supervisors, but the Sixth Circuit reversed.]

## III

... The text of §2(11) of the Act ... sets forth a three-part test for determining supervisory status. Employees are statutory supervisors if (1) they hold the authority to engage in any 1 of the 12 listed supervisory functions, (2) their "exercise of such authority is not of a merely routine or clerical nature, but requires the use of independent judgment," and (3) their authority is held "in the interest of the employer." NLRB v. Health Care & Retirement Corp. of America, 511 U.S. 571, 573-574 (1994). The only basis asserted by the Board, before the Court of Appeals and here, for rejecting respondent's proof of supervisory status ... was the Board's interpretation of the second part of the test—to wit, that employees do not use "independent judgment" when they exercise "ordinary professional or technical judgment in directing less-skilled employees to deliver services in accordance with employer-specified standards." The Court of Appeals rejected that interpretation, and so do we.

Two aspects of the Board's interpretation are reasonable, and hence controlling on this Court, see ... Chevron U.S.A. Inc. v. Natural Resources Defense Council, Inc., 467 U.S. 837, 842-844 (1984). First, it is certainly true that the statutory term "independent judgment" is ambiguous with respect to the degree of discretion required for supervisory status. See NLRB v. Health Care & Retirement Corp. of America, supra, at 579. Many nominally supervisory functions may be performed without the "exercis[e of] such a degree of ... judgment or discretion ... as would warrant a finding" of supervisory status under the Act. Weyerhaeuser Timber Co., 85 N.L.R.B. 1170, 1173 (1949). It falls clearly within the Board's discretion to determine, within reason, what scope of discretion qualifies. Second, as reflected in the Board's phrase "in accordance with employer-specified standards," it is also undoubtedly true that the degree of judgment that might ordinarily be required to conduct a particular task may be reduced below the statutory threshold by detailed orders and regulations issued by the employer. So, for example, in Chevron Shipping Co., 317 N.L.R.B. 379, 381 (1995), the Board concluded that "although the contested licensed officers are imbued with a great deal of responsibility, their use of independent judgment and discretion is circumscribed by the master's standing orders, and the Operating Regulations, which require the watch officer to contact a superior officer when anything unusual occurs or when problems occur."

The Board, however, argues further that the judgment even of employees who are permitted by their employer to exercise a sufficient degree of discretion is not "independent judgment" if it is a particular kind of judgment, namely, "ordinary professional or technical judgment in directing less-skilled employees to deliver services." ... The text [of §2(11)], by focusing on the "clerical" or "routine" (as opposed to "independent") nature of the judgment, introduces the question of degree of judgment that we have agreed falls within the reasonable discretion of the Board to resolve. But the Board's categorical exclusion turns on factors that have nothing to do with the degree of discretion an employee exercises. . . . Let the judgment be significant and only loosely constrained by the employer; if it is "professional or technical" it will nonetheless not be independent. The breadth of this exclusion is made all the more startling by virtue of the Board's extension of it to judgment based on greater "experience" as well as formal training. What supervisory judgment worth exercising, one must wonder, does not rest on "professional or technical skill or experience"? If the Board applied this aspect of its test to every exercise of a supervisory function, it would virtually eliminate "supervisors" from the Act. Cf. NLRB v. Yeshiva Univ., 444 U.S. 672, 687 (1980) (Excluding "decisions . . . based on . . . professional expertise" would risk "the indiscriminate recharacterization as covered employees of professionals working in supervisory and managerial capacities").

As it happens, though, only one class of supervisors would be eliminated in practice, because the Board . . . would apply its restriction upon "independent judgment" to just 1 of the 12 listed [supervisory] functions: "responsibly to direct." There is no apparent textual justification for this asymmetrical limitation, and the Board has offered none. Surely no conceptual justification can be found in the proposition that supervisors exercise professional, technical, or experienced judgment only when they direct other employees. Decisions "to hire, . . . suspend, lay off, recall, promote, discharge, . . . or discipline" other employees, [§2(11)], must often depend upon that same judgment, which enables assessment of the employee's proficiency in performing his job. See *NLRB v. Yeshiva Univ.*, supra, at 686 ("[M]ost professionals in managerial positions continue to draw on their special skills and training"). Yet in no opinion that we were able to discover has the Board held that a supervisor's judgment in hiring, disciplining, or promoting another employee ceased to be "independent judgment" because it depended upon the supervisor's professional or technical training or experience. When an employee exercises one of these functions with judgment that possesses a sufficient degree of independence, the Board invariably finds supervisory status. See, e.g., Trustees of Noble Hospital, 218 N.L.R.B. 1441, 1442 (1975).

The Board's refusal to apply its limiting interpretation of "independent judgment" to any supervisory function other than responsibly directing other employees is particularly troubling because just seven years ago we rejected the Board's interpretation of part three of the supervisory test that similarly was applied only to the same supervisory function. See NLRB v. Health Care & Retirement Corp. of America, 511 U.S. 571 (1994). In *Health Care*, the Board argued that nurses did not exercise their authority "in the interest of the employer," as §152(11) requires, when their "independent judgment [was] exercised incidental to professional or technical judgment" instead of for "disciplinary or other matters, i.e., in addition to treatment of patients."

Northcrest Nursing Home, 313 N.L.R.B. 491, 505 (1993). It did not escape our notice that the target of this analysis was the supervisory function of responsible direction. . . . We . . . rejected the Board's analysis as "inconsistent with . . . the statutory language," because it "read the responsible direction portion of §2(11) out of the statute in nurse cases." Id. at 579-580. It is impossible to avoid the conclusion that the Board's interpretation of "independent judgment," applied to nurses for the first time after our decision in *Health Care,* has precisely the same object. This interpretation of "independent judgment" is no less strained than the interpretation of "in the interest of the employer" that it has succeeded. . . .

When the Taft-Hartley Act added the term "supervisor" to the Act in 1947, it largely borrowed the Board's [prior] definition of the term, with one notable exception: Whereas the Board [had] required a supervisor to direct the work of other employees and perform another listed function, the Act permitted direction alone to suffice. "The term 'supervisor' means any individual having authority . . . to hire, transfer, suspend, lay off, recall, promote, discharge, assign, reward, or discipline other employees, or responsibly to direct them, or to adjust their grievances." Taft-Hartley Act §2(11), as amended. . . . It is the Act's alteration of precisely that aspect of the Board's jurisprudence that has pushed the Board into a running struggle to limit the impact of "responsibly to direct" on the number of employees qualifying for supervisory status — presumably driven by the policy concern that otherwise the proper balance of labor-management power will be disrupted.

It is upon that policy concern that the Board ultimately rests its defense of its interpretation of "independent judgment." In arguments that parallel those expressed by the dissent in *Health Care,* see 511 U.S. at 588-590 (Ginsburg, J., dissenting), and which are adopted by Justice Stevens in this case, the Board contends that its interpretation is necessary to preserve the inclusion of "professional employees" within the coverage of the Act. See §2(12), 29 U.S.C. §152(12). Professional employees by definition engage in work "involving the consistent exercise of discretion and judgment." §152(12)(a)(ii). Therefore, the Board argues . . . , if judgment of that sort makes one a supervisor under §152(11), then Congress's intent to include professionals in the Act will be frustrated, because "many professional employees (such as lawyers, doctors, and nurses) customarily give judgment-based direction to the less-skilled employees with whom they work." The problem with the argument is not the soundness of its labor policy (the Board is entitled to judge that without our constant second-guessing, see, e.g., NLRB v. Curtin Matheson Scientific, Inc., 494 U.S. 775, 786 (1990)). It is that the policy cannot be given effect through this statutory text. See *Health Care,* supra, at 581 ("There may be 'some tension between the Act's exclusion of [supervisory and] managerial employees and its inclusion of professionals,' but we find no authority for 'suggesting that that tension can be resolved' by distorting the statutory language in the manner proposed by the Board") (quoting *NLRB v. Yeshiva Univ.*, supra, at 686). Perhaps the Board could offer a limiting interpretation of the supervisory function of responsible direction by distinguishing employees who direct the manner of others' performance of discrete tasks from employees who direct other employees, as §152(11) requires. Certain of the Board's decisions appear to have drawn that distinction in the past, see., e.g., Providence Hospital, 320 N.L.R.B. 717, 729 (1996). We have no occasion to consider it here, however, because the Board has carefully insisted that the proper interpretation of "responsibly to direct" is not at issue in this case. . . .

[The Board's] contentions [here] contradict both the text and structure of the statute, and they contradict as well the rule of *Health Care* that the test for supervisory status applies no differently to professionals than to other employees. 511 U.S. at 581. We therefore find the Board's interpretation unlawful.

STEVENS, J., with whom SOUTER, GINSBURG, and BREYER, JJ., join, concurring in part and dissenting in part.

[The dissenting Justices agreed with the majority that the Sixth Circuit had erred in rejecting the Board's allocation of the burden of proof on the supervisory issue; the Court unanimously upheld as a reasonable interpretation of the Act the Board's position that the burden always lies with the party attempting to prove supervisory status. The dissent, however, would also have upheld as reasonable the Board's interpretation of the term "independent judgment" and its conclusion that the RNs were not supervisors.]

Even if I shared the majority's view that the term "independent judgment" should be given the same meaning when applied to each of the 12 supervisory functions and when applied to professional and nonprofessional employees, I would not simply affirm the judgment of the Court of Appeals. Cf. NLRB v. Bell Aerospace Co., 416 U.S. 267, 289-290 (1974); SEC v. Chenery Corp., 318 U.S. 80, 87-88 (1943). The Court's rejection of the Board's interpretation of the term "independent judgment" does not justify a categorical affirmance of the Sixth Circuit's decision, which rests in part on an erroneous allocation of the burden of proof. In any case, I do not agree with the majority's view. Given the Regional Director's findings that the RNs' duties as building supervisors do not qualify them as "supervisors" within the meaning of 29 U.S.C. §152(11), and that they, "for the most part, work independently and by themselves without any subordinates," it is absolutely clear that the nurses in question are covered by the NLRA. . . .

## NOTES AND QUESTIONS

1. ***Chevron* and *Kentucky River*.** Recall the *Chevron* two-step analysis set out supra page 75. How did the *Kentucky River* majority apply the *Chevron* framework? The dissent? Which side was correct?

**2. Pathways Open to the Board?**

a. *Exercise of "Independent Judgment."* In *Kentucky River*, the Court noted two bases on which the Board might still find in a particular case that individuals do not exercise the "independent judgment" necessary for supervisory status. What are they? Had the case been remanded, could the RNs have been found nonsupervisory on either of these grounds?

b. *"Responsible Direction."* Near the end of *Kentucky River*, the Court mentions, without deciding the issue, a third possible route open to the Board: "Perhaps the Board could offer a limiting interpretation of the supervisory function of responsible direction by distinguishing employees who direct the manner of others' performance of discrete *tasks* from employees who direct other *employees*, as [§2(11)] requires." 532 U.S. at 720 (emphasis in original). Here Justice Scalia cites to Providence Hospital, 320 N.L.R.B. 717, 729 (1996), enforced sub nom. Providence Alaska Medical Center v. NLRB, 121 F.3d 548 (9th Cir. 1997). In *Providence*, the Board stated that:

> Section 2(11) supervisory authority does not include the authority of an employee to direct another to perform discrete tasks stemming from the directing employee's experience, skills, training, or position, such as the direction which is given by a lead or journey level employee to another or apprentice employee, the direction which is given by an employee with specialized skills and training which is incidental to the directing employee's ability to carry out that skill and training, and the direction which is given by an employee with specialized skills and training to coordinate the activities of other employees with similar specialized skills and training.

What is the significance of the Court's citation to *Providence* on this point? Is the possible route laid out consistent with *Kentucky River* as a whole? With the Court's earlier decisions in this area? How might an approach suggested in *Providence* apply to the following situations?

(a) A senior associate who gives more junior lawyers directions regarding which potential arguments to include in briefs in cases on which they are both working;
(b) A senior associate who decides which of several junior lawyers is to write the initial draft of the brief;

(c) A television producer who assigns writers, reporters, photographers, and graphic artists to particular stories, and determines which co-anchors will read which stories;

(d) A producer who lacks the above authority but does instruct other employees as to how a story should be covered, including the desired length, whether it should be shot live or use taped footage, and what graphics should accompany the story.

Consider also how these cases would be decided under the doctrine fashioned and applied under the following Board decisions. Do these decisions take the *Providence* approach?

***Note: The Board's 2006 Rulings on Supervisory Status***

The Board articulated its most significant post–*Kentucky River* interpretation of supervisory status in Oakwood Healthcare, Inc., 348 N.L.R.B. 686 (2006), a 3-2 decision involving charge nurses. The Board majority in *Oakwood*, "consistent with the Supreme Court's instructions in *Kentucky River*," sought to "adopt definitions for the terms 'assign,' 'responsibly to direct,' and 'independent judgment' as those terms are used in Section 2(11) of the Act."

> [W]e construe the term "assign" to refer to the act of designating an employee to a place (such as a location, department, or wing), appointing an employee to a time (such as a shift or overtime period), or giving significant overall duties, i.e., tasks, to an employee. That is, the place, time, and work of an employee are part of his/her terms and conditions of employment. In the health care setting, the term "assign" encompasses the charge nurses' responsibility to assign nurses and aides to particular patients. It follows that the decision or effective recommendation to affect one of these—place, time, or overall tasks—can be a supervisory function.
>
> The assignment of an employee to a certain department (e.g., housewares) or to a certain shift (e.g., night) or to certain significant overall tasks (e.g., restocking shelves) would generally qualify as "assign" within our construction. However, choosing the order in which the employee will perform discrete tasks within those assignments (e.g., restocking toasters before coffeemakers) would not be indicative of exercising the authority to "assign." To illustrate our point in the health care setting, if a charge nurse designates a [nurse] to be the person who will regularly administer medications to a patient or a group of patients, the giving of that overall duty to the [nurse] is an assignment. On the other hand, the charge nurse's ordering a [nurse] to immediately give a sedative to a particular patient does not constitute an assignment. In sum, to "assign" for purposes of Section 2(11) refers to the charge nurse's designation of significant overall duties to an employee, not to the charge nurse's ad hoc instructions that the employee perform a discrete task. . . .
>
> We . . . find that for direction to be "responsible," the person directing and performing the oversight of the employee must be accountable for the

> performance of the task by the other, such that some adverse consequences may befall the one providing the oversight if the tasks performed by the employee are not performed properly. . . .
>
> Thus, to establish accountability for purposes of responsible direction, it must be shown that the employer delegated to the putative supervisor the authority to direct the work and the authority to take corrective action, if necessary. It also must be shown that there is a prospect of adverse consequences for the putative supervisor if he/she does not take these steps. . . .
>
> [W]e find that a judgment is not independent if it is dictated or controlled by detailed instructions, whether set forth in company policies or rules, the verbal instructions of a higher authority, or in the provisions of a collective bargaining agreement. Thus, for example, a decision to staff a shift with a certain number of nurses would not involve independent judgment if it is determined by a fixed nurse-to-patient ratio. Similarly, if a collective bargaining agreement required that only seniority be followed in making an assignment, that act of assignment would not be supervisory.
>
> On the other hand, the mere existence of company policies does not eliminate independent judgment from decision-making if the policies allow for discretionary choices. Thus, a registered nurse, when exercising his/her authority to recommend a person for hire, may be called upon to assess the applicants' experience, ability, attitude, and character references, among other factors. If so, the nurse's hiring recommendations likely involve the exercise of independent judgment. Similarly, if the registered nurse weighs the individualized condition and needs of a patient against the skills or special training of available nursing personnel, the nurse's assignment involves the exercise of independent judgment. . . .
>
> Where an individual is engaged a part of the time as a supervisor and the rest of the time as a unit employee, the legal standard for a supervisory determination is whether the individual spends a regular and substantial portion of his/her work time performing supervisory functions. Under the Board's standard, "regular" means according to a pattern or schedule, as opposed to sporadic substitution. The Board has not adopted a strict numerical definition of substantiality and has found supervisory status where the individuals have served in a supervisory role for at least 10-15 percent of their total work time. We find no reason to depart from this established precedent.

The Board in *Oakwood* determined that the employer failed to establish that it actually held the charge nurses in that case accountable for the work of the staff members that they directed; "[t]here is no indication that the charge nurses are subject to discipline or lower evaluations if other staff members fail to adequately perform. . . ." The agency found, however, that the permanent charge nurses were supervisors because Oakwood did establish that these nurses exercised independent judgment to assign nursing personnel to patients and to specific geographic locations in the emergency room. The Board also concluded that "rotating" charge nurses were not supervisors because the employer offered inadequate evidence that these nurses served in a charge role according to a "pattern or structured schedule." Absent this showing of "regularity," the question whether their duties as a charge nurse were "substantial" did not have to be decided.

In Croft Metals, Inc., 348 N.L.R.B. 717 (2006), the Board applied *Oakwood* in a non-healthcare context—to "lead persons" at a manufacturing facility. It ruled that Croft Metals's "lead persons" did not have any authority to assign other employees to "production lines or departments or to shifts or overtime periods" and that "the occasional switching of tasks . . . does not implicate the authority to 'assign' as that term is described in *Oakwood Healthcare.*" The Board found that the record showed that "lead persons" did "responsibly direct" other employees because some had been "disciplined" with "written warnings . . . because of the failure of their crews to meet production goals or because of other shortcomings of their crews." The employer, however, did not demonstrate that this responsible direction was exercised with "independent judgment" involving "a degree of discretion that rises above the "'merely routine or clerical.'" "For example, the testimony reflects that, in loading trucks, the lead persons follow a pre-established delivery schedule and generally employ a standard loading pattern that dictates the placement of different products in the trucks." For a discussion of these cases, see Harper, Judicial Control, supra, at 239-248.

## *NOTES AND QUESTIONS*

**1. Post-*Oakwood* nurse cases?** Recently, the courts have resisted the Board's approach in its charge nurse cases. See GGNSC Springfield LLC v. NLRB, 721 F.3d 403 (6th Cir. 2013) (refusing to enforce the Board's order to bargain because charge nurses, when faced with a certified nurse assistant's misconduct, use independent judgment to decide whether to initiate the first step of the hospital's progressive disciplinary procedures); Lakeland Health Care Assocs. v. NLRB, 696 F.3d 1332 (11th Cir. 2012) (refusing to enforce Board's order because Licensed Practical Nurses used independent judgment in responsibly directing and assigning Certified Nursing Assistants as well as deciding whether to initiate formal discipline against them through the employer's "coaching program"). But see Frenchtown Acquisition Co. v. NLRB, 683 F.3d 298 (6th Cir. 2012) (enforcing the Board's order to bargain because charge nurses' participation in "one-on-one in services" to improve the performance of nursing aides was not part of the formal disciplinary procedure and occasionally sending home aides for "egregious conduct" was not sufficient to establish that they had the power to formally discipline).

**2. Board Response to *Kentucky River*?** Is the Board doctrine articulated in *Oakwood Healthcare* consistent with the Court's opinion in *Kentucky River*? Is it required by the Court's holding or reasoning in *Kentucky River*? Could the Board, after *Kentucky River*, have provided narrower definitions of "assign" and "responsibly direct"? The dissenters in *Oakwood* argued that the term "assign" was intended by Congress to cover only the allocation of workers "to shifts, departments, and job classifications" and not to particular daily job duties. Relying on an accompanying statement of the Senator who offered the "responsibly to direct" phrase as a floor amendment, the *Oakwood* dissenters also argued that this phrase was intended only to insure the coverage of those with "substantial authority" over an entire "work unit" rather than "straw bosses, lead men, set-up men, and other minor supervisory employees" with authority over only a few other employees. Would such alternative definitions also have been consistent with the *Kentucky River* decision?

**3. Impact of *Oakwood Healthcare* on Employer Personnel Policies?** Might the Board's *Oakwood Healthcare* doctrine lead employers to modify their personnel policies in order to have many more of their employees excluded as supervisors from the protection of the NLRA? Is such a goal likely to cause employers to delegate to more workers discretion to assign other workers to general job duties? Is it likely to cause employers to evaluate more workers by the performance of other workers whom the former workers may have some discretion to direct and control with some form of corrective action? Do the answers to these questions turn on whether the workers with authority to assign or direct are professional or skilled employees? In accord with *Croft Metals*, the Board has found manufacturing and construction workers not to be supervisors notwithstanding their authority over other workers, because the authority did not require the use of "independent judgment." See, e.g., Pacific Coast M.S. Industries Co., 355 N.L.R.B. 1422 (2010); Shaw, Inc., 350 N.L.R.B. 354 (2007); Austal USA, L.L.C., 349 N.L.R.B. 561 (2007). Cf. Loparex LLC v. NLRB, 591 F.3d 540, 550-551 (7th Cir. 2009) (Board may treat as employees shift leaders who lack authority to direct other employees through some form of even informal corrective action such as staying late to finish a task).

**4. Impact of *Kentucky River* and *Oakwood Healthcare* on Board Precedent?** Do the following precedents survive *Kentucky River* and *Oakwood Healthcare*?

a. *Power Plant Dispatchers.* Mississippi Power & Light Co., 328 N.L.R.B. 965 (1999), involved "distribution dispatchers" and "systems dispatchers" at a power plant. Distribution dispatchers "direct[] field employees in repairing faults and performing switching procedures," "set priorities for work requests and orders, coordinate the response of trouble-shooting personnel, monitor building security after hours, and decide whether to call out meter readers or servicemen for any after-hour reconnection of customers." Systems dispatchers coordinate outages on power transmission lines. In the course of this work:

> They call a day ahead to the service supervisor, local manager, or clerk of the affected district to have field employees in place the next day. In overseeing the work as it is performed, the system dispatchers are in continuous communication with the field employees to direct the switching activity, to make certain that the switching sequences are completed step-by-step, and to handle unforeseen problems.

Is the Board's determination that the dispatchers are nonsupervisory still good law? See Entergy Gulf States, Inc. v. NLRB, 253 F.3d 203, 211 (5th Cir. 2001) (finding operations coordinators at electrical utility with responsibilities similar to *Mississippi Power* dispatchers to be supervisors; Board's attempt to find individuals nonsupervisory on ground that they "use their technical expertise and judgment . . . but do not necessarily exercise supervisory judgment in assigning and directing others . . . is no longer viable [under] *Kentucky River*"); see also Public Serv. Co. of Colorado v. NLRB, 271 F.3d 1213, 1218-1221 (10th Cir. 2001) (similar).

b. *Television News Directors and Producers.* In McGraw-Hill Broadcasting Co. d/b/a KGTV, 329 N.L.R.B. 454 (1999), the Board found "producer/directors" who made determinations regarding camera shots and editing and "communicat[ed] necessary directions" to reporters, photographers, and technicians to be nonsupervisory, stating:

> The Employer's producer/directors . . . work as part of an integrated production team, each member of which is independently capable of executing his own assignment. Thus, their relationship to the other employees necessary to the successful production of the newscasts or special projects is not supervisory, but rather one of coworkers involved in separate but sequential functions in the development of a single product. [O]nly where the facts of a particular case have shown that similar producers or directors additionally played a role in, for example, hiring or disciplining employees, have such producers been found to be supervisors.

Following *Kentucky River* and *Oakwood Healthcare,* do you think that producer/directors with duties like those in *McGraw-Hill* would be found nonsupervisory? What other information would you like to have to make this determination?

### c. *Students/Trainees as Employees?*

#### i. Medical Interns and Residents

In Cedars-Sinai Medical Center, 223 N.L.R.B. 251 (1976), and St. Clare's Hospital & Health Center, 229 N.L.R.B. 1000 (1977), the Board held that medical interns, residents, and fellows (collectively referred to as "house staff") were "primarily students" and therefore not employees within §2(3) of the Act. In Boston Medical Center Corp., 330 N.L.R.B. 152 (1999), the Clinton Board reconsidered that position. As explained in *Boston Medical,* interns and residents have their medical degrees. A one-year internship, however, is necessary to practice medicine outside a residency program, and completion of a residency program is necessary to become eligible to take the Board exam in any medical specialty. Failure to become "Board-certified" (by passing the exam) may limit a doctor's professional opportunities. Interns and residents are the "work horses" of teaching hospitals; they work notoriously long hours, and those at Boston Medical spent 80 percent of their time in direct patient care. Although they consulted with full-fledged "attending physicians" regarding their patients, 80-90 percent of their patient care work was performed outside an attending physician's presence. The house staff were paid $34,000-$44,000 per year, from which taxes were withheld, and they also received paid vacation, sick leave, health insurance, and other benefits.

In *Boston Medical,* the Board voted 3-2 to overrule its prior decisions, holding that while house staff may be students, they are also statutory employees. The majority noted the broad definition of "employee" in §2(3) and the absence of any exclusion for "students," and that house staff were compensated for their services and spent a very large percentage of their time providing patient care. The Board pointed out that the Act's definition of professional employees expressly includes those who have completed their coursework and are performing related work under a professional's supervision "in an institution of higher learning *or a hospital*" in order to become fully qualified for their profession. See NLRA §2(12) (emphasis added). Finally, it noted that house staff are unlike many students in that they do not pay tuition, take examinations in a classroom setting, or receive grades, and that interns and residents working in public hospitals are routinely treated as "employees" under state public sector labor laws.

#### ii. Graduate Teaching Assistants

A year after *Boston Medical,* the Board held in New York University, 332 N.L.R.B. 1205 (2000) (*NYU*), that the university's graduate teaching assistants (TAs) were statutory employees. *NYU,* like *Boston Medical,* overturned long-standing precedent that had held professionals-in-training whom the Board characterized as "primarily students" to be non-employees. See Leland Stanford Junior University, 214 N.L.R.B. 621 (1974) (overruled by *NYU*) (physics research assistants are not statutory employees).

A reconstituted Board returned to its pre-*NYU* stance that graduate assistants are not employees in Brown University, 342 N.L.R.B. 483 (2004). In *Brown* the Board stated flatly that "graduate student assistants, including those at Brown, . . . have a primarily educational, not economic, relationship with their university," and "declare[d] the Federal law to be that graduate student assistants are not employees within the meaning of Section 2(3) of the Act." Id. at 487, 493. The *Brown* ruling made no distinction between the roughly two-thirds (69 percent) of Brown TAs or research assistants who were required to serve in those roles in order to obtain their degree, and the remaining one-third, who were subject to no such requirement.

Dissenting Members Liebman and Walsh argued that the majority had ignored not only the "plain language" of §2(3), but also "contemporary academic reality" and pertinent empirical evidence, citing statistics indicating that 23 percent of college instructors were graduate assistants. See id. at 493, 497. In response to concerns expressed by the majority that bargaining by TAs would threaten academic freedom, they noted that the Board was free to "take account of the academic enterprise" in deciding which subjects the university and the union were legally required to bargain over. Id. at 499 n.28; see also Chapter 6 infra (discussing in greater detail the distinction between "mandatory" and "permissive" subjects of bargaining). They pointed out that the New York University TAs permitted to bargain by the Board's previous decision had entered into a contract with the university addressing stipends, health insurance, discipline and discharge, and a grievance/arbitration procedure. In a "management and academic rights" clause, however, the union waived any right to bargain over decisions regarding "'who is taught, what is taught, how it is taught and who does the teaching. . . . '" Id. at 499.

The Board limited the reach of the *Brown* decision in two cases granting employee status to research assistants who worked for and were paid by private research foundations independent from but affiliated with the universities in which they were enrolled as students. See Research Foundation of the City University of New York, 350 N.L.R.B. 201 (2007); Research Foundation of State University of New York, 350 N.L.R.B. 197 (2007). The foundations, the Board stressed, were not themselves academic institutions. In the latter case the Regional Director had found the assistants were not employees because they were required to be enrolled at the university, their work was related to their dissertations, and their work was to end upon the conferral of degrees. The Board, however, found the researchers to have only an economic relationship with the foundation, not an academic one.

The Board has also indicated a willingness to revisit the *Brown* decision's classification of TAs by reversing a decision of a Regional Director denying a union's request to represent a unit of graduate students in New York University, 356 N.L.R.B. No. 7 (2010). The Board in this case directed the Regional Director to hold a hearing on the question of employee status. In December 2013, TAs from New York University withdrew their NLRB petition after the university agreed, among other things, to recognize the union if it won majority support.

### *NOTES AND QUESTIONS*

1. **Co-Existence of *Boston Medical* and *Brown*?** *Brown* did not purport to overrule *Boston Medical.* Can the two decisions be harmonized? In St. Barnabas Hospital, 355 N.L.R.B. 233 (2010), the Board rejected the argument that *Brown* required reversal of *Boston Medical.*

2. **Are Student Athletes Receiving Scholarships Statutory "Employees"?** In March 2014, a NLRB Regional Director (RD) concluded that a union representing Northwestern University football players who receive scholarships could move forward with an NLRB-supervised representation election. The RD reasoned that the scholarship players were NLRA "employees," in part, because the players provide non-educational services to the university, the university controls their day-to-day activities and they receive compensation in the form of tuition, fees, room, board and books in exchange for their services. The Board subsequently granted Northwestern University's request to review the decision. The players cast ballots on the question of union representation in April 2014, but the Board subsequently impounded the votes until the resolution of its review. Is *Brown* relevant or can it be distinguished because football duties, unlike teaching assistant duties, are unrelated to academic studies? In August 2015, the Board declined to rule on the question of whether Northwestern's scholarship football players were NLRA "employees." See Northwestern Univ. & College Athletes Players Ass'n, 362 N.L.R.B. No. 167 (2015). Instead, the Board declined to assert jurisdiction in the case. It stated that "because of the nature of sports leagues (namely the control exercised by the leagues over the individual teams) and the composition and structure of FBS football (in which the overwhelming majority of competitors are public colleges and universities over which the Board cannot assert jurisdiction), it would not promote stability in labor relations to assert jurisdiction in this case."

3. **Status of "Primarily Rehabilitative" Workers?** Brevard Achievement Center, Inc., 342 N.L.R.B. 982 (2004), involved mentally disabled workers

who, pursuant to a federal statute intended to assist adults with severe disabilities and a contract entered into in accordance with that law, provided compensated janitorial services at Cape Canaveral Air Station. The disabled workers performed the same work under the same supervision as their non-disabled coworkers. Is *Brown* relevant to the question whether the disabled workers are statutory employees? See *Brevard*, 342 N.L.R.B. at 985 (3-2) (citing *Brown* in support of holding that the disabled workers are not "employees" because their relationship with their employer is "primarily rehabilitative" rather than "primarily economic"). Should it matter that the disabled workers were not, unlike their non-disabled coworkers, subject to progressive discipline, and were not held to the same work pace as their coworkers? If so, are these factors relevant to "employee" status or only to whether these workers could properly be included in the same bargaining unit as the non-disabled janitors? See also note 5 infra. For a discussion of unit determination principles, see Chapter 4 infra.

**4. Does the Board Have Discretion to Exclude Common-Law Employees from Coverage?** At least for purposes of employer vicarious liability, the common law seems not to have recognized an exclusion of compensated students from employee status based on their having a primarily educational rather than economic relationship with the entity for which they perform work. Should this common law determine the status of TAs under the NLRA, or does the Board have discretion to exclude from coverage any common-law employees not expressly excluded by Congress? Does the *Bell Aerospace* decision, supra page 87, settle this question? If the Board does have discretion to exclude certain classes of common-law employees from coverage, on what ground can it base that exclusion? Would it be sufficient if it determined, as a policy matter, that collective bargaining is not appropriate for these employees? Or would it have to base its argument on NLRA §14(c)(1), referenced supra, which explicitly states that the Board "in its discretion" can "decline to assert jurisdiction over any labor dispute involving any class or category of employers, where . . . the effect of such labor dispute on commerce is not sufficiently substantial to warrant the exercise of its jurisdiction." For discussion of these issues, see Harper, Judicial Control, supra, at 214-222.

**5. Can a Group of Employees Be Denied Collective Bargaining Rights Yet Otherwise Be Protected by the NLRA?** Under *Brown*'s ruling that all TAs are "non-employees," a university may, for instance, retaliate against TAs who act together in any manner to better their working conditions—such as asking about the possibility of increased wages or improved health insurance—without any repercussions under the NLRA. In his *Boston Medical* dissent, however, Member Hurtgen seemed to suggest that house staff denied collective bargaining rights under the Act as a discretionary matter might be treated as "employees" for other purposes. See 330 N.L.R.B. at 152, 170 ("I am not necessarily suggesting that house staff cannot fall within the statutory definition. Rather, I conclude that, as a policy matter, the Board should continue to exercise its discretion to exclude them for purposes of collective bargaining."); see also *Brown*, 342 N.L.R.B. at 492; *St. Clare's Hospital*, supra page 109, 229 N.L.R.B. at 1003 (acknowledging possibility that Board could treat TAs and house staff, respectively, as "employees" while denying them right to engage in bargaining on policy grounds).

Does the Board have the authority to decline as a discretionary matter to assert jurisdiction over certain individuals for purposes of collective bargaining, but to extend the Act's protection to those individuals when they engage in concerted activity for "mutual aid or protection" that is unrelated to collective bargaining? If so, what is the statutory basis for this authority?

# 3 | Protection of Concerted Activity

As explained above, the NLRA is structured to serve several separable, albeit interrelated, principal purposes: (1) the protection of employees' choice of whether to join together to attempt to improve the terms of their employment; (2) the facilitation of employees' choice of whether to be represented by an exclusive bargaining agent; and (3) the encouragement of bona fide collective bargaining for employees who choose such exclusive representation. The next several chapters are divided along these lines.

## A. THE CONCEPTS OF DISCRIMINATION AND OF INTERFERENCE, RESTRAINT, OR COERCION

The material that follows involves two different kinds of violations of the Act: violations based on an unlawful motive and violations based on the impact of employer (or union) conduct on employees' ability to exercise their §7 rights.

### 1. Violations Based on Employer (or Union) Motivation

The following cases focus on §8(a)(3) of the Act. (The *Budd* case also involves a violation of §8(a)(2), a provision that is taken up in more detail in Section E of this chapter.) It is in §8(a)(3) that the NLRA most resembles federal employment discrimination statutes such as Title VII of the Civil Rights Act of 1964 and the Age Discrimination in Employment Act (ADEA). In all three statutes, the employer commits a violation if it is improperly motivated. The essential difference is that under the NLRA, the forbidden basis of discrimination is union activity rather than a status such as race, color, religion, sex, or national origin (Title VII), or age (the ADEA). For a comparison of the concepts of "discrimination" applied under the NLRA and Title VII, see

Rebecca Hanner White, Modern Discrimination Theory and the National Labor Relations Act, 39 Wm. & Mary L. Rev. 99 (1997).

## Edward G. Budd Manufacturing Co. v. NLRB

*138 F.2d 86 (3d Cir. 1943)*

Biggs, J.

[On September 5, 1933,] the management caused to be placed in the time card rack of each employee the following: a pamphlet entitled "Proposed Plan of Employee Representation," a folder entitled "Preliminary Announcement of the Establishment of a Budd Employee Representation Association" signed by President Edward G. Budd, and a ballot to be used for nominating employee representatives. On September 7th the election was held and nineteen employee representatives were elected. The expenses of this election were paid by the petitioner and it was held on company time and on company property.

The plan provided a method according to which the representatives should represent their constituents, the workmen, and divided the plant geographically into eleven election districts. . . . Five management representatives were appointed by the petitioner and these sat with the employee representatives at meetings, but were not entitled to vote except on amendments to the plan [, which] could be amended at any time by a vote of a majority of the employee representatives with the concurrence of a majority of the management representatives. Numerous committees were set up and these negotiated with the management in respect to wages, grievances and conditions of employment. The company paid $2 to each representative per month for attending meetings of the representatives. . . .

Meetings of the representatives were held from time to time; the committees which had been appointed functioned actively. The management adopted a most cooperative attitude toward the Association. This was to be expected. What had happened was that the management had found a group of its own employees who desired to create a labor organization and the company had sponsored and created the Association at their request. The petitioner's attitude toward its employees seems to have been one of friendly interest. Nevertheless, we entertain no doubt that the plan and the Association were in fact sponsored, largely created and supported by the petitioner. The Association could not have continued to exist had the Budd Company withdrawn its support. . . .

. . . The petitioner treated the employee representatives with extraordinary leniency. The testimony shows to what very great lengths the employer went in its parental treatment of the Association and its officers. The petitioner permitted the employee representatives to conduct themselves about as they wished. They left the plant at will whether on personal business or on the business of the Association. Some of them did very little or no work but they received full pay. It is clear that some of them, Walter Weigand for example, were not disciplined because they were representatives. We can scarcely believe that the petitioner would have displayed such an attitude toward officers of an undominated "adversary" labor organization.

In our opinion the decision of the Board to the effect that the Association was and is subject to the petitioner's domination and control [in violation of §8(a)(2)] is amply supported by the evidence. . . .

The case of Walter Weigand is extraordinary. If ever a workman deserved summary discharge it was he. He was under the influence of liquor while on duty. He came to work when he chose and he left the plant and his shift as he pleased. In fact, a foreman on one occasion was agreeably surprised to find Weigand at work and commented upon it. Weigand amiably stated that he was enjoying it. He brought a woman (apparently generally known as the "Duchess") to the rear of the plant yard and introduced some of the employees to her. He took another employee to visit her and when this man got too drunk to be able to go home, punched his time-card for him and put him on the table in the representatives' meeting room in the plant in order to sleep off his intoxication. Weigand's immediate superiors demanded again and again that he be discharged, but each time higher officials intervened on Weigand's behalf because as was naively stated he was "a representative." In return for not working at the job for which he was hired, the petitioner gave him full pay and on five separate occasions raised his wages. One of these raises was general; that is to say, Weigand profited by a general wage increase throughout the plant, but the other four raises were given Weigand at times when other employees in the plant did not receive wage increases.

The petitioner contends that Weigand was discharged because of cumulative grievances against him. But about the time of the discharge it was suspected by some of the representatives that Weigand had joined the complaining CIO union. One of the representatives taxed him with this fact and Weigand offered to bet a hundred dollars that it could not be proved. On July 22, 1941 Weigand did disclose his union membership to the vice-chairman (Rattigan) of the Association and to another representative (Mullen) and apparently tried to persuade them to support the union. Weigand asserts that the next day he with Rattigan and Mullen, were seen talking to CIO organizer Reichwein on a street corner. The following day, according to Weigand's testimony, Mullen came to Weigand at the plant and stated that Weigand, Rattigan and himself had been seen talking to Reichwein and that he, Mullen, had just had an interview with Personnel Director McIlvain and Plant Manager Mahan. According to Weigand, Mullen said to him, "Maybe you didn't get me in a jam." And, "We were seen down there." The following day Weigand was discharged.

As this court stated in National Labor Relations Board v. Condenser Corp. [128 F.2d 67 (1942)], an employer may discharge an employee for a good reason, a poor reason or no reason at all so long as the provisions of the National Labor Relations Act are not violated. It is, of course, a violation to discharge an employee because he has engaged in activities on behalf of a union. Conversely an employer may retain an employee for a good reason, a bad reason or no reason at all and the reason is not a concern of the Board. But it is certainly too great a strain on our credulity to assert, as does the petitioner, that Weigand was discharged for an accumulation of offenses. We think that he was discharged because his work on behalf of the CIO had become known to the plant manager. That ended his sinecure at the Budd plant. The Board found that he was discharged because of his activities on behalf of the union. The record shows that the Board's finding was based on sufficient evidence.

## *NOTES AND QUESTIONS*

**1. "Derivative" §8(a)(1) Violations.** The Budd Co. was charged with violating §8(a)(1) of the Act as well as §§8(a)(3) and 8(a)(2). All violations of §§8(a)(2)-(5) also violate §8(a)(1), because all such violations necessarily "interfere with, restrain, or coerce employees" in the exercise of their §7 rights. Such §8(a)(1) violations are known as "derivative" (as distinct from "independent") §8(a)(1) violations.

**2. "Discrimination" under §8(a)(3).** Consider the language of §8(a)(3). Was Walter Weigand the victim of Budd's "discrimination in regard to . . . tenure of employment . . . to encourage or discourage membership in any labor organization"? Would he have been discharged had he not begun to support the CIO union? Would the company have retained Weigand had he not been a representative of the Employee Association?

**3. Encouragement vs. Discouragement of Union Activity.** Should the Act prohibit employer encouragement of employee involvement in labor organizations in the same way that it prohibits employer discouragement of such involvement? How might the §7 rights of employees be affected by the company's lenient treatment of representatives of the Association?

**4. Dual Motive.** What if Budd argued that it took action against Weigand because it no longer wished to tolerate his conduct, and would have taken this action even if Weigand remained loyal to the Association?

How should the Board handle a discharge that is motivated in part by lawful considerations (Weigand's misconduct) and in part by unlawful considerations (Weigand's joining an independent union)? The problem of dual motives is discussed further in the case just below.

**5. Investigating a §8(a)(3) Discharge Case.** If you were investigating a §8(a)(3) discharge case for an NLRB field office, what types of evidence would you look to or attempt to gather that might shed light on the motivation for the discharge?

**6. Is Reinstatement an Appropriate Remedy?** The Board ordered Weigand's reinstatement as well as backpay. Was the Board's purpose to compensate him for some unjust treatment or to serve some broader public purpose? If the latter, is the remedy adequate? How long do you think Weigand probably remained in Budd's employ after this decision? Is the remedy appropriate? How long must Budd keep Weigand on the job if Weigand continues to engage in misconduct?

**7. Section 8(a)(2) Violation.** Note the prohibition expressed in §8(a)(2), which the Board and the court found was also violated in this case. Other than its lenient treatment of Association representatives like Weigand, how did the company transgress this provision? How might these actions have interfered with the §7 rights of employees? For further discussion of §8(a)(2) issues, see infra pages 219-230.

## NLRB v. Transportation Management Corp.

*462 U.S. 393 (1983)*

WHITE, J. . . .

[In response to] a complaint alleging that an employee was discharged because of his union activities, the employer may assert legitimate motives for his decision. In Wright Line, 251 N.L.R.B. 1083 (1980), enforced, 662 F.2d 899 (CA1 1981), cert. denied, 455 U.S. 989 (1982), the [NLRB] reformulated the allocation of the burden of proof in such cases. It determined that the General Counsel carried the burden of persuading the Board that an anti-union animus contributed to the employer's decision to discharge an employee, a burden that does not shift, but that the employer, even if it failed to meet or neutralize the General Counsel's showing, could avoid the finding that it violated the statute by demonstrating by a preponderance of the evidence that the worker would have been fired even if he had not been involved with the Union. The question presented . . . is whether the burden placed on the employer in *Wright Line* is consistent with §§8(a)(1) and 8(a)(3), as well as with §10(c) of the NLRA, which provides that the Board must prove an unlawful labor practice by a "preponderance of the evidence."

... [The ALJ] determined by a preponderance of the evidence that Patterson [who supervised Santillo and other drivers] clearly had an anti-union animus and that Santillo's discharge was motivated by a desire to discourage union activities. ... While acknowledging that Santillo had engaged in some unsatisfactory conduct, the ALJ was not persuaded that Santillo would have been fired had it not been for his union activities.

The Board affirmed, ... applying its *Wright Line* decision. It stated that respondent had failed to carry its burden of persuading the Board that the discharge would have taken place had Santillo not engaged in activity protected by the Act. The First Circuit ... refused to enforce the Board's order and remanded for consideration of whether the General Counsel had proved by a preponderance of the evidence that Santillo would not have been fired had it not been for his union activities. ... We now reverse. ...

The ... First Circuit refused enforcement of the *Wright Line* decision because in its view it was error to place the burden on the employer to prove that the discharge would have occurred had the forbidden motive not been present. The General Counsel, the Court of Appeals held, had the burden of showing not only that a forbidden motivation contributed to the discharge but also that the discharge would not have taken place independently of the protected conduct of the employee. The Court of Appeals was quite correct, and the Board does not disagree, that throughout the proceedings, the General Counsel carries the burden of proving the elements of an unfair labor practice. Section 10(c) expressly directs that violations may be adjudicated only "upon the preponderance of the testimony" taken by the Board. ... We are quite sure, however, that the Court of Appeals erred in holding that §10(c) forbids placing the burden on the employer to prove that absent the improper motivation he would have acted in the same manner for wholly legitimate reasons.

As we understand the Board's decisions, they have consistently held that the unfair labor practice consists of a discharge or other adverse action that is based in whole or in part on anti-union animus—or as the Board now puts it, that the employee's protected conduct was a substantial or motivating factor in the adverse action. The General Counsel has the burden of proving these elements under §10(c). But the Board's construction of the statute permits an employer to avoid being adjudicated a violator by showing what his actions would have been regardless of his forbidden motivation. It extends to the employer what the Board considers to be an affirmative defense but does not change or add to the elements of the unfair labor practice that the General Counsel has the burden of proving under §10(c).[6] We assume that

---

6. The language of the [NLRA] requiring that the Board act on a preponderance of the testimony taken was added by the [Labor Management Relations Act (LMRA)] in 1947. A closely related provision directed that no order of the Board reinstate or compensate

the Board could reasonably have construed the Act in the manner insisted on by the Court of Appeals. We also assume that the Board might have considered a showing by the employer that the adverse action would have occurred in any event as not obviating a violation adjudication but as going only to the permissible remedy, in which event the burden of proof could surely have been put on the employer. The Board has instead chosen to recognize, as it insists it has done for many years, what it designates as an affirmative defense that the employer has the burden of sustaining. We are unprepared to hold that this is an impermissible construction of the Act. "[T]he Board's construction here, while it may not be required by the Act, is at least permissible under it . . . ," and in these circumstances its position is entitled to deference. NLRB v. Weingarten, Inc., 420 U.S. 251, 266-267 (1975); NLRB v. Erie Resistor Corp., 373 U.S. 221, 236 (1963).

The Board's allocation of the burden of proof is clearly reasonable in this context. . . . The employer is a wrong-doer; he has acted out of a motive that is declared illegitimate by the statute. It is fair that he bear the risk that the influence of legal and illegal motives cannot be separated, because he knowingly created the risk and because the risk was created not by innocent activity but by his own wrongdoing.

In Mount Healthy City Board of Education v. Doyle, 429 U.S. 274 (1977), we found it prudent, albeit in a case implicating the Constitution, to set up an allocation of the burden of proof which the Board heavily relied

---

any employee who was fired for cause. Section 10(c) places the burden on the General Counsel only to prove the unfair labor practice, not to disprove an affirmative defense. Furthermore, it is clear from the legislative history of the [LMRA] that the drafters of §10(c) were not thinking of the mixed motive case. Their discussions reflected the assumption that discharges were either "for cause" or punishment for protected activity. Read fairly, the legislative history does not indicate whether, in mixed motive cases, the employer or the General Counsel has the burden of proof on the issue of what would have happened if the employer had not been influenced by his unlawful motives; on that point the legislative history is silent.

The "for cause" proviso was not meant to apply to cases in which both legitimate and illegitimate causes contributed to the discharge. The amendment was sparked by a concern over the Board's perceived practice of inferring from the fact that someone was active in a union that he was fired because of anti-union animus even though the worker had been guilty of gross misconduct. The House Report explained the change in the following terms:

> A third change forbids the Board to reinstate an individual unless the weight of the evidence shows that the individual was not suspended or discharged for cause. In the past, the Board, admitting that an employee was guilty of gross misconduct, nevertheless frequently reinstated him, "inferring" that, because he was a member or an official of a union, this, not his misconduct, was the reason for his discharge.

H.R. Rep. No. 245, 80th Cong., 1st Sess., at 42 (April 11, 1947) (emphasis added).

The proviso was thus a reaction to the Board's readiness to infer anti-union animus from the fact that the discharged person was active in the union, and thus has little to do with the situation in which the Board has soundly concluded that the employer had an anti-union animus and that such feelings played a role in a worker's discharge.

on and borrowed from in its *Wright Line* decision. . . . The analogy to *Mount Healthy* drawn by the Board was a fair one.

For these reasons, we conclude that the Court of Appeals erred in refusing to enforce the Board's orders, which rested on the Board's *Wright Line* decision.

. . . At least two of the transgressions that purportedly would have in any event prompted Santillo's discharge were commonplace, and yet no transgressor had ever before received any kind of discipline. Moreover, the employer departed from its usual practice in dealing with rules infractions; indeed, not only did the employer not warn Santillo that his actions would result in being subjected to discipline, it never even expressed its disapproval of his conduct. In addition, Patterson, the person who made the initial decision to discharge Santillo, was obviously upset with Santillo for engaging in such protected activity. It is thus clear that the Board's finding that Santillo would not have been fired even if the employer had not had an anti-union animus was "supported by substantial evidence on the record considered as a whole."

## *NOTES AND QUESTIONS*

**1. Deference to NLRB Interpretation?** To what extent does the Court's decision turn on deference to the Board's delegated authority in interpreting the Act? What are the limits on the Board's authority? Would the Court also have upheld a Board policy or rule that required the General Counsel to prove that a discharge would not have taken place but for the employer's consideration of the discharged employee's union affiliation? Would the Court have upheld a Board policy or rule that predicated a statutory violation solely on proof that an employee's union affiliation played a role in a discharge decision, regardless of whether the employer would have discharged the employee in any event?

**2. Is "But For" Causation a Necessary Element of a §8(a)(3) Violation?** The Board construes the elements of a §8(a)(3) violation to include proof that the employee's §7 activity played a "substantial" or "motivating" role in the employer's decision. The General Counsel is not required to show that "but for" the employee's §7 activity, the employee would not have been discharged. An employer, however, may avert liability by proving the absence of such "but for" causation. Yet, once the Board has interpreted §8 to *not* include a "but for" causation element—and the Supreme Court approves this as a permissible reading—what is the statutory basis for allowing employers a "same decision" affirmative defense?

**3. Constitutional vs. Statutory Violations.** As indicated in *Transportation Management*, the Board "borrowed" its *Wright Line* approach from

Mount Healthy City Sch. Dist. Bd. of Educ. v. Doyle, 429 U.S. 274 (1977), a First Amendment case involving the discharge of a public employee. Was it appropriate for the Board in *Wright Line* to rely on a judicial interpretation of a constitutional provision when interpreting the meaning of specific statutory provisions? Should liability for a constitutional violation be easier or harder to establish than liability for a statutory violation?

**4. Complete Defense vs. Limitation on Recovery?** Under the *Wright Line* approach, an employer who establishes a "same decision" defense defeats liability entirely. In 1989, the Supreme Court adopted a similar approach for discrimination claims under Title VII of the 1964 Civil Rights Act in Price Waterhouse v. Hopkins, 490 U.S. 228. In 1991, however, Congress amended Title VII to provide that "an unlawful employment practice is established when the complaining party demonstrates that race, color, religion, sex, or national origin was a motivating factor for any employment practice, even though other factors also motivated the practice." Title VII, §703(m), 42 U.S.C. §2000e-2(m). The 1991 amendment also provides, however, that an employer who proves that it "would have taken the same action in the absence of the impermissible motivating factor" shall not be required to reinstate the employee or be liable for backpay or damages. Title VII, §706(g)(2)(B), 42 U.S.C. §2000e-5(g)(2)(B).

In view of these changes in Title VII law, could the Board now change its approach to the same-decision defense, making it relevant only to the appropriate remedy for unfair labor practices? Under such an approach, even where an employer established a same-decision defense, there could still be a statutory violation and basis for a prospective remedial order. How much practical impact would legal condemnation and a prospective cease-and-desist order be likely to have?

The Supreme Court has also ruled with respect to the Age Discrimination in Employment Act and the anti-retaliation provision of Title VII that plaintiffs are required to prove that their age or protected activity was the "but for" cause of the adverse action they suffered. See Gross v. FBL Financial Services, Inc., 557 U.S. 167 (2009); Univ. of Texas Southwestern Medical Ctr. v. Nassar, 133 S.Ct. 2517 (2013). Could the NLRB now reverse its *Wright Line* approach and require that an employee's §7 activity be the "but for" cause for the employee's discharge or other adverse action? Is this foreclosed by *Transportation Management*?

**5. Shield Against Anticipated Discipline?** Does §8(a)(3) in effect enable employees who anticipate discharge or other discipline for cause to avert such consequences by getting involved in union activity? Can employers address any such strategic behavior by having clear workplace rules and consistently enforcing them? Should the Board take into account that this is not always practical for small employers lacking personnel departments and formal procedures for handling discipline?

**6. Application to Hiring Cases.** For discussion of the Board's use of burden shifting in cases where hiring discrimination is alleged, see note 4, infra page 156.

**7. "After-Acquired" Evidence.** Should an employer have a complete defense to liability for an unlawfully motivated employment decision if it learns *after* the decision of misrepresentations on an employee's employment application or other misconduct that would have justified the decision? In 1995, in a case arising under federal age discrimination law, the Supreme Court ruled that "after-acquired" evidence of employee misconduct does not provide a complete defense to liability; generally, plaintiffs may still obtain back pay for the period *before* the employer discovered the grounds that would have justified termination, although they are barred from reinstatement and from recovering back pay for the period following the discovery. See McKennon v. Nashville Banner Publishing Co., 513 U.S. 352 (1995). The Board, with judicial approval, applies *McKennon* to its cases. See, e.g., Hartman Bros. v. NLRB, 280 F.3d 1110 (7th Cir. 2002) (Posner, J.). See generally Samuel Estreicher, The Doctrine of After-Acquired Evidence, N.Y.L.J., Apr. 29, 1993, at 1, 4, 41.

In a related case, ABF Freight System, Inc. v. NLRB, 510 U.S. 317 (1994), the Court held that a former employee's false testimony under oath in an NLRB hearing did not preclude the Board from granting him reinstatement with back pay upon a finding that he was discharged for union activities. Justice Stevens, writing for the majority, reasoned that the question whether relief for statutory violations should be afforded notwithstanding such misconduct was a matter committed by Congress to the agency's discretion. In Hoffman Plastic Compounds v. NLRB, 535 U.S. 137 (2002), infra pp. 1056-1062, the Court held that an unauthorized immigrant employee's use of false identity documentation to gain employment, a fact that the employer became aware of during NLRB proceedings, did preclude the Board from awarding the employee reinstatement with backpay. Unlike ABF, the Court reasoned, the immigration violation at issue in *Hoffman* was "serious misconduct unrelated to Board proceedings." Id. at 146.

### *Note: NLRA Remedies in Discharge and Failure to Hire Cases*

**1. *Phelps Dodge* and Make-Whole Relief.** In Phelps Dodge Corp. v. NLRB, 313 U.S. 177 (1941), the Court upheld a §8(a)(3) order calling for the hiring of applicants for employment who had been rejected because of their union affiliations, even though the applicants in the interim had obtained substantially equivalent employment elsewhere. Note that §2(3) of the Act defines an "employee" as a person "who has not obtained . . . other regular and substantially equivalent employment"; and §10(c) speaks of "reinstatement of employees." The Court reasoned that the hiring order, although not necessary to protect the rejected applicants against monetary loss in that particular case, was warranted because the Act was designed to effectuate the public policy in favor of self-organization and was not confined to remedying private losses. The Court also held, however, that the computation of lost pay should reflect a deduction not only of the actual earnings of the discriminatees but also of the amounts they could have earned by making reasonable efforts to secure alternative employment. While acknowledging that the Board possesses broad remedial discretion under §10(c) of the Act, the Court nonetheless rejected the Board's contention that such a requirement of mitigation of damages would be administratively burdensome.

*Phelps Dodge* defined the remedial goal in §8(a)(3) cases as "a restoration of the situation, as nearly as possible, to that which would have obtained but for the illegal discrimination." If an employee is discriminatorily discharged, the usual remedy is an order of reinstatement and an award of back pay, with interest, from the date of the discharge to the date of an offer of reinstatement less monies earned or that could have been earned through alternative employment. In 2010, the Board adopted a new policy requiring interest on back pay awards to be compounded on a daily basis. Jackson Hospital Corp., 356 N.L.R.B. No. 8 (2010). Several months later, the Acting General Counsel advised the Regional Directors how to comply with this policy, and directed them to include in the overall back pay award search-for-work and work-related expenses, also with daily compounded interest. This conforms NLRB practice with that of the Equal Employment Opportunity Commission and the Department of Labor. NLRB General Counsel, GC Mem. 11-08: Changes to the Methods Used to Calculate Backpay in Light of *Kentucky River Medical Center* and to Better Effectuate the Remedial Purposes of the Act (Mar. 11, 2011).

**2. Problems with the NLRA's Remedial Scheme?**

a. *Reinstatement.* Consider the practical problems inherent in the reinstatement remedy. How likely is it that a government agency can reconstruct a solid and enduring employment relationship between an employer who has illegally fired an employee and the victim of the illegal firing? Will an employer who was willing to break the law in the first place be able to find another reason to get rid of the victim after her return? Is an employee likely to be anxious to return to the employ of someone who has illegally fired her, especially if she has obtained another job in the meantime? See Weiler, Promises to Keep, at 1791 (discussing these issues).

Should the Board use front pay as an alternative remedy in lieu of reinstatement? Front pay is commonly awarded in Title VII cases compensating discriminatees for the income they would have received in the absence of the violation until they obtain or could reasonably have obtained a new position. Front pay is regarded for Title VII purposes as an equitable remedy, See Pollard v. E.I. du Pont de Nemours & Co., 532 U.S. 843 (2001), and would be treated similarly under §10(c) of the NLRA. In 2013, the Board's Acting General Counsel issued a memorandum modifying the agency's opposition to front pay as a remedy by allowing it to be included in Board settlements in lieu of reinstatement. Inclusion of Front Pay in Board Settlements, GC Mem. 13-02 (Jan. 9, 2013).

b. *Back Pay Awards.* As noted above, an employee's failure to exercise reasonable diligence in mitigating her loss by seeking alternate employment will result in a reduction in the back pay award. The mitigation requirement detracts from the deterrence value of the NLRA's back pay remedy by deducting from an employer's financial responsibility income the discriminatee earns or would have earned—a factor unrelated to the employer's culpability. The *Phelps Dodge* Court held that mitigation was a necessary part of the NLRA's back pay remedy because of the remedy's compensatory goal. Should compensatory principles control in this statutory context? The mitigation requirement also has affected the NLRB's coverage authority. In Hoffman Plastic Compounds v. NLRB, 535 U.S. 137 (2002), infra pages 1056-1062, the Supreme Court reasoned that employees without authorization to work in the U.S. who have been discharged in violation of the NLRA cannot recover back pay, in part because they cannot mitigate backpay awards without encouraging a violation of immigration law. The relationship between immigration and labor law is covered in Chapter 14.

**3. NLRA Remedies vs. Title VII Remedies.** Prior to 1991, the remedy for a discharge in violation of Title VII mirrored that under the NLRA. See Title VII, §706(g), 42 U.S.C. §2000e-5(g). In 1991, however, Congress amended Title VII to allow for compensatory and punitive damages (with a "cap" of $50,000-$300,000 depending on the employer's size) in addition to make-whole relief for cases of intentional discrimination. See 42 U.S.C. §§1981a(a)(1) & (b)(3).

Section 4 of the proposed, but not enacted, Employee Free Choice Act (EFCA) of 2009, S.560, H.R. 1409, 111th Cong. would have provided that employees receive backpay and "2 times that amount as liquidated damages" for §8(a)(3) violations. It also would have provided for additional "civil penalties," not to exceed $20,000, for willful or repeated violations. The adequacy of NLRB remedies for §8(a)(3) violations is discussed further in Chapter 4, infra pages 324-328.

## 2. Violations Based on Impact of Employer (or Union) Actions

**Radio Officers' Union v. NLRB**
*347 U.S. 17 (1954)*

[This case involved a consolidation of three appeals raising the issue whether an employer violates §8(a)(3), and a union correspondingly violates §§8(b)(1)(A) and 8(b)(2), by making employment decisions that treat union members in "good standing" differently from nonmembers or members not in "good standing" without additional proof that the employer's specific purpose in agreeing to such differential treatment was "to encourage or discourage membership in any labor organization." Although the case raises issues concerning the relationship between the individual and his or her union and the scope of union security obligations that are covered in Chapter 12, it is included here because of the light it sheds on the scope of the NLRA's antidiscrimination principle. In all three of these cases the employer was not motivated by hostility to the union and yet it was found in violation of §8(a)(3):

1. In *Teamsters*, the union maintained a hiring hall under which it referred drivers to the employer on the basis of a seniority list that included members and nonmembers. Boston, a union member, was placed at the bottom of the list and denied driving assignments because he was in arrears in his dues.

2. In *Radio Officers*, the employer agreed to fill vacancies for radio officer positions from union members in "good standing." Fowler, a union member, was denied a job with the employer because he had not previously obtained clearance from the union and thus was deemed not in good standing with the union.

3. In *Gaynor*, Loner, a nonunion employee covered by a collective bargaining agreement between the Newspaper and Mail Deliverers' Union and his employer, was denied a retroactive wage increase and vacation payments that had been granted to all employees covered by the agreement who were union members.]

Reed, J. . . .

The language of §8(a)(3) is not ambiguous. The unfair labor practice is for an employer to encourage or discourage membership by means of discrimination. Thus this section does not outlaw all encouragement or discouragement of membership in labor organizations; only such as is accomplished by discrimination is prohibited. Nor does this section outlaw discrimination in employment as such; only such discrimination as encourages or discourages membership in a labor organization is proscribed. . . .

But it is also clear that specific evidence of intent to encourage or discourage is not an indispensable element of proof of violation of §8(a)(3). . . . Th[e] recognition that specific proof of intent is unnecessary where employer conduct inherently encourages or discourages union membership is but an application of the common-law rule that a man is held to intend the foreseeable consequences of his conduct. . . . Thus an employer's protestation that he did not intend to encourage or discourage must be unavailing where a natural consequence of his action was such encouragement or discouragement. Concluding that encouragement or discouragement will result, it is presumed that he intended such consequence. In such circumstances intent to encourage is sufficiently established. . . .

In *Gaynor*, the Second Circuit . . . properly applied this principle. The court there held that disparate wage treatment . . . based solely on union membership status is "inherently conducive to increased union membership." In holding that a natural consequence of discrimination, based solely on union membership or lack thereof, is discouragement or encouragement of membership in such union, the court merely recognized a fact of common experience—that the desire of employees to unionize is directly proportional to the advantages thought to be obtained from such action. No more striking example of discrimination so foreseeably causing employee response as to obviate the need for any other proof of intent is apparent than the payment of different wages to union employees doing a job than to nonunion employees doing the same job. . . .

We express no opinion as to the legality of disparate payments where the union is not exclusive bargaining agent, since that case is not before us. We do hold that in the circumstances of this case, the union being exclusive bargaining agent for both member and nonmember employees, the employer could not, without violating §8(a)(3), discriminate in wages solely on the basis of such membership even though it had executed a contract with the union prescribing such action. . . . Such discriminatory contracts are illegal and provide no defense to an action under §8(a)(3). . . .

Petitioners in *Gaynor* and *Radio Officers* contend that the Board's orders in these cases should not have been enforced by the Second Circuit because the records do not include "independent proof that encouragement of Union membership actually occurred." . . .

. . . We have held that a natural result of the disparate wage treatment in *Gaynor* was encouragement of union membership; thus it would be unreasonable to draw any inference other than that encouragement would result from such action. The company complains that it could have disproved this natural result if allowed to prove that Loner, the employee who filed the charges against it, had previously applied for and been denied membership in the union. But it is clear that such evidence would not have rebutted the inference: not only would it have failed to disprove an increase in desire on the part of other employees, union members or nonmembers, to join or retain good standing in the union, but it would not have shown lack of encouragement of Loner. In rejecting this argument the Second Circuit noted that union admission policies are not necessarily static and that employees may be encouraged to join when conditions change. . . .

The circumstances in *Radio Officers* and *Teamsters* are nearly identical. In each case the employer discriminated upon the instigation of the union. The purposes of the unions in causing such discrimination clearly were to encourage members to perform obligations or supposed obligations of membership. Obviously, the unions would not have invoked such a sanction had they not considered it an effective method of coercing compliance with union obligations or practices. Both Boston and Fowler were denied jobs by employers solely because of the union's actions. Since encouragement of union membership is obviously a natural and foreseeable consequence of any employer discrimination at the request of a union, those employers must be presumed to have intended such encouragement. It follows that it was eminently reasonable for the Board to infer encouragement of union membership, and the [court of appeals] erred in holding encouragement not proved. . . .

FRANKFURTER, J., concurring. . . .

The lower courts have given conflicting interpretations to the phrase, "by discrimination . . . to encourage or discourage membership in any labor organization," contained in §8(a)(3). We should settle this conflict without giving rise to avoidable new controversies.

The phrase in its relevant setting is susceptible of alternative constructions of decisively different scope:

> (a) On the basis of the employer's disparate treatment of his employees standing alone, or as supplemented by evidence of the particular circumstances under which the employer acted, it is open for the Board to conclude that the conduct of the employer tends to encourage or discourage union membership, thereby establishing a violation of the statute.
>
> (b) Even though the evidence of disparate treatment is sufficient to warrant the Board's conclusion set forth in (a), there must be a specific finding by the Board in all cases that the actual aim of the employer was to encourage or discourage union membership.

I think (a) is the correct interpretation. In many cases a conclusion by the Board that the employer's acts are likely to help or hurt a union will be so compelling that a further and separate finding characterizing the employer's state of mind would be an unnecessary and fictive formality. In such a case the employer may fairly be judged by his acts and the inferences to be drawn from them. . . .

What I have written and the Court's opinion, as I read it, are not in disagreement. In any event, I concur in its judgment.

BURTON and MINTON, JJ., having joined in the opinion of the Court, also join this opinion.

[Justice Black, with whom Justice Douglas joined, dissented, urging that §8(a)(3) "forbids an employer to discriminate" only when he does so *in order to* "encourage or discourage" union membership and that the evidence did not establish and, indeed, may have controverted the existence of the proscribed purpose.]

## *NOTES AND QUESTIONS*

**1. "Membership in Any Labor Organization."** Section 8(a)(3) speaks in terms of union "membership." However, in a portion of the opinion not excerpted above, the *Radio Officers* Court broadly interpreted the phrase "membership in any labor organization" to include some concerted activities beyond formal union membership. Does this mean that any disparate treatment of an employee because of that employee's exercise of his or her §7 rights is reached by §8(a)(3), or are there some concerted activities within the scope of §7's language that cannot be connected to "membership in any labor organization"?

**2. Is Proof of a Motive to Encourage or Discourage Union Activity Always Required?** NLRA §8(a)(3) indicates that there are two elements to a violation: (1) discrimination in regard to hiring or tenure or some term or condition of employment; and (2) a resulting encouragement or discouragement of union membership. Which of these two elements was at issue in *Radio Officers*? Was there any question in the three cases there under review that the employer discriminated against particular employees in the sense of treating them differently because of their membership status with a union? Did any of the employers, like the employers in *Budd* and *Transportation Management*, attempt to argue that its challenged disparate treatment was based on some legitimate consideration, such as work performance or ability, rather than a response to a union's determination of membership status?

a. *Inferring Unlawful Discrimination from Impact?* Does the *Radio Officers* Court hold that the General Counsel need not prove that an employer's *motive* was to encourage or discourage union membership, as long as it can reasonably be inferred that the employer's discrimination on the basis of union status would likely have the *effect* of such encouragement or discouragement?

b. *Inferring Unlawful Impact from Discrimination?* Does *Radio Officers* hold that discriminatory treatment alone will always suffice to establish a §8(a)(3) violation—i.e., that where an employer is found to be discriminating on the basis of union or other §7 activity, an illegal resulting encouragement or discouragement of such activity can always be inferred? If not, what else must be proven to establish illegality?

c. *Further Exploration of the Relationship Between Motive and Impact.* The Court returned to the relationship between motive and impact in establishing a §8(a)(3) violation in *NLRB v. Erie Resistor Corp.*, infra page 536, and *NLRB v. Great Dane Trailers*, infra page 543. See also the *Darlington* case, infra page 161. For commentary on the motive-impact relationship and the elements of a §8(a)(3) violation, see White, Modern Discrimination Theory, supra; Samuel Estreicher, Strikers and Replacements, 3 Lab. Law. 897 (1987); Paul V. Barron, A Theory of Protected Employer Rights: A Revisionist Analysis of the Supreme Court's Interpretation of the National Labor Relations Act, 59 Tex. L. Rev. 421 (1981); Thomas G.S. Christensen & Andrea H. Svanoe, Motive and Intent in the Commission of Unfair Labor Practices: The Supreme Court and the Fictive Formality, 77 Yale L.J. 1269 (1968).

**3. Derivative §8(b)(2) Theory?** Note that while the employers in *Radio Officers* may not have intended to encourage union membership, surely the unions requesting that the employers act in discriminatory ways were so motivated. Could the Court more simply have held that an employer violates §8(a)(3) when it implements a union request to discriminate among employees with respect to their union membership or other §7-protected activity? How well does this approach square with the language of §8(b)(2)?

## Republic Aviation Corp. v. NLRB
*324 U.S. 793 (1945)*

REED, J.

In the Republic Aviation Corporation case, the employer, a large and rapidly growing military aircraft manufacturer, adopted, well before any union activity at the plant, a general rule against soliciting which read as follows: "Soliciting of any type cannot be permitted in the factory or offices." . . . The Republic plant was located in a built-up section of Suffolk County, New York. An employee persisted after being warned of the rule in soliciting union membership in the plant by passing out application cards to employees on his own time during lunch periods. The employee was discharged for infraction of the rule and, as the [NLRB] found, without discrimination on the part of the employer toward union activity.

Three other employees were discharged for wearing UAW-CIO union steward buttons in the plant after being requested to remove the insignia. The union was at that time active in seeking to organize the plant. The reason which the employer gave for the request was that, as the union was not then the duly designated representative of the employees, the wearing of the steward buttons in the plant indicated an acknowledgment by the management of the authority of the stewards to represent the employees in dealing with the management and might impinge upon the employer's policy of strict neutrality in union matters and might interfere with the existing grievance system of the corporation.

The Board was of the view that wearing union steward buttons by employees did not carry any implication of recognition of that union by the employer where, as here, there was no competing labor organization in the plant. The discharges of the stewards, however, were found not to be motivated by opposition to the particular union or, we deduce, to unionism.

The Board determined that the promulgation and enforcement of the "no solicitation" rule violated §8(1) of the [NLRA] as it interfered with, restrained and coerced employees in their rights under §7 and discriminated against the discharged employee under §8(3). It determined also that the discharge of the stewards violated §§8(1) and 8(3). As a consequence of its conclusions as to the solicitation and the wearing of the insignia, the Board entered the usual cease and desist order and directed the reinstatement of the discharged employees with back pay and also the rescission of "the rule against solicitation in so far as it prohibits union activity and solicitation on company property during the employees' own time." 51 N.L.R.B. 1186, 1189. The . . . Court of Appeals for the Second Circuit affirmed. . . .

In the case of *Le Tourneau Company of Georgia*, two employees were suspended two days each for distributing union literature or circulars on the employees' own time on company owned and policed parking lots, adjacent to the company's fenced-in plant, in violation of a long-standing and strictly enforced rule, adopted prior to union organization activity about the premises, which read as follows: "In the future no Merchants, Concern, Company, or Individual or Individuals will be permitted to distribute, post, or otherwise circulate handbills or posters, or any literature of any description, on Company property without first securing permission from the Personnel Department." . . . The rule was adopted to control littering and petty pilfering from parked autos by distributors. The Board determined that there was no union bias or discrimination by the company in enforcing the rule.

The company's plant for the manufacture of earth-moving machinery and other products for the war is in the country on a six thousand acre tract. The plant is bisected by one public road and built along another. There is one hundred feet of company-owned land for parking or other use between the highways and the employee entrances to the fenced enclosures where the work is done, so that contact on public ways or on noncompany property with employees at or about the establishment is limited to those employees, less than 800 out of 2100, who are likely to walk across the public highway near the plant on their way to work, or to those employees who will stop their private automobiles, buses or other conveyances on the public roads for communications. The employees' dwellings are widely scattered.

The Board found that the application of the rule to the distribution of union literature by the employees on company property which resulted in the layoffs was an unfair labor practice under §§8(1) and 8(3). Cease and desist, and rule rescission orders, with directions to pay the employees for their lost time, followed. 54 N.L.R.B. 1253. The Court of Appeals for the Fifth Circuit reversed the Board. . . .

These cases bring here for review the action of the . . . Board in working out an adjustment between the undisputed right of self-organization assured to employees under the Wagner Act and the equally undisputed right of employers to maintain discipline in their establishments. Like so many others, these rights are not unlimited in the sense that they can be exercised without regard to any duty which the existence of rights in others may place upon employer or employee. Opportunity to organize and proper discipline are both essential elements in a balanced society.

The Wagner Act did not undertake the impossible task of specifying in precise and unmistakable language each incident which would constitute an unfair labor practice. On the contrary, that Act left to the Board the work of applying the Act's general prohibitory language in the light of the infinite combinations of events which might be charged as violative of its terms. Thus a "rigid scheme of remedies" is avoided and administrative flexibility within appropriate statutory limitations obtained to accomplish the dominant purpose of the legislation. Phelps Dodge Corp. v. Labor Board, 313 U.S. 177, 194. So far as we are here concerned, that purpose is the right of employees to organize for mutual aid without employer interference. This is the principle of labor relations which the Board is to foster.

The gravamen of the objection of both *Republic* and *Le Tourneau* to the Board's orders is that they rest on a policy formulated without due administrative procedure. To be more specific it is that the Board cannot substitute its knowledge of industrial relations for substantive evidence. The contention is that there must be evidence before the Board to show that the rules and orders of the employers interfered with and discouraged union organization in the circumstances and situation of each company. Neither in the *Republic* nor the *Le Tourneau* cases can it properly be said that there was evidence or a finding that the plant's physical location made solicitation away from company property ineffective to reach prospective union members. Neither of these is like a mining or lumber camp where the employees pass their rest as well as their work time on the employer's premises, so that union organization must proceed upon the employer's premises or be seriously handicapped.

... [The] statutory plan for an adversary proceeding requires that the Board's orders on complaints of unfair labor practices be based upon evidence which is placed before the Board by witnesses who are subject to cross-examination by opposing parties. Such procedure strengthens assurance of fairness by requiring findings on known evidence. Such a requirement does not go beyond the necessity for the production of evidential facts, however, and compel evidence as to the result which may flow from such facts. An administrative agency with power after hearings to determine on the evidence in adversary proceedings whether violations of statutory commands have occurred may infer within the limits of the inquiry from the proven facts such conclusions as reasonably may be based upon the facts proven. One of the purposes which lead to the creation of such boards is to have decisions based upon evidential facts under the particular statute made by experienced officials with an adequate appreciation of the complexities of the subject which is entrusted to their administration. . . .

In the *Republic* . . . case the evidence showed that the petitioner was in early 1943 a nonurban manufacturing establishment for military production which employed thousands. It was growing rapidly. Trains and automobiles gathered daily many employees for the plant from an area on Long Island, certainly larger than walking distance. The rule against solicitation was introduced in evidence and the circumstances of its violation by the dismissed employee after warning [were] detailed.

As to the employees who were discharged for wearing the buttons of a union steward, the evidence showed in addition the discussion in regard to their right to wear the insignia when the union had not been recognized by the petitioner as the representative of the employees. Petitioner looked upon a steward as a union representative for the adjustment of grievances with the management after employer recognition of the stewards' union. Until such recognition petitioner felt it would violate its neutrality in labor organization if it permitted the display of a steward button by an employee. From its point of view, such display represented to other employees that the union already was recognized.

No evidence was offered that any unusual conditions existed in labor relations, the plant location or otherwise to support any contention that conditions at this plant differed from those occurring normally at any other large establishment.

The *Le Tourneau* . . . case also is barren of special circumstances. The evidence which was introduced tends to prove the simple facts heretofore set out as to the circumstances surrounding the discharge of the two employees for distributing union circulars.

These were the facts upon which the Board reached its conclusions as to unfair labor practices. . . . The Board's reasons for concluding that the petitioner's insistence that its employees refrain from wearing steward buttons [was unlawful] appear at page 1187 of the report.[7] In the *Le Tourneau Company* case the discussion of the reasons underlying the findings was much more extended. 54 N.L.R.B. 1253, 1258, et seq. We insert in the note below a quotation which shows the character of the Board's opinion.[8] Furthermore, in both opinions of the Board full citation of authorities was given, including the Matter of Peyton Packing Co., 49 N.L.R.B. 828, 50 N.L.R.B. 355. . . .

The Board has fairly, we think, explicated . . . the theory which moved it to its conclusions in these cases. The excerpts from its opinions just quoted show this.

Not only has the Board in these cases sufficiently expressed the theory upon which it concludes that rules against solicitation or prohibitions against the wearing of insignia must fall as interferences with union organization, but, in so far as rules against solicitation are concerned, it had theretofore succinctly expressed the requirements of proof which it considered appropriate to outweigh or overcome the presumption as to rules against solicitation. In the Peyton Packing Company case, 49 N.L.R.B. 828, at 843, hereinbefore referred to, the presumption adopted by the Board is set forth.[10] . . .

---

7. We quote an illustrative portion. 51 N.L.R.B. 1187-1188: "We do not believe that the wearing of a steward button is a representation that the employer either approves or recognizes the union in question as the representative of the employees, especially when, as here, there is no competing labor organization in the plant. Furthermore, there is no evidence in the record herein that the respondent's employees so understood the steward buttons or that the appearance of union stewards in the plant affected the normal operation of the respondent's grievance procedure. . . ."

8. 54 N.L.R.B. at 1259-1260: ". . . The Board . . . has held that the employer's right to control his property does not permit him to deny access to his property to persons whose presence is necessary there to enable the employees effectively to exercise their right to self-organization and collective bargaining, and in those decisions which have reached the courts, the Board's position has been sustained. Similarly, the Board has held that, while it was 'within the province of an employer to promulgate and enforce a rule prohibiting union solicitation during working hours,' it was 'not within the province of an employer to promulgate and enforce a rule prohibiting union solicitation by an employee outside of working hours, although on company property,' the latter restriction being deemed an unreasonable impediment to the exercise of the right to self-organization."

10. 49 N.L.R.B. at 843-844: "The Act, of course, does not prevent an employer from making and enforcing reasonable rules covering the conduct of employees on company time. Working time is for work. It is therefore within the province of an employer to promulgate and enforce a rule prohibiting union solicitation during working hours. Such a rule must be presumed to be valid in the absence of evidence that it was adopted for a discriminatory purpose. It is no less true that time outside working hours, whether before or after work, or during luncheon or rest periods, is an employee's time to use as he wishes without unreasonable restraint, although the employee is on company property. It is therefore not within the province of an employer to promulgate and enforce a rule prohibiting union solicitation by an employee outside of working hours, although on company property. Such a rule must be presumed to be an unreasonable

In the Republic Aviation case, petitioner urges that irrespective of the validity of the rule against solicitation, its application in this instance did not violate §8(3) . . . because the rule was not discriminatorily applied against union solicitation but was impartially enforced against all solicitors. It seems clear, however, that if a rule against solicitation is invalid as to union solicitation on the employer's premises during the employee's own time, a discharge because of violation of that rule discriminates within the meaning of §8(3) in that it discourages membership in a labor organization. . . .

ROBERTS, J., dissents. . . .

## NOTES AND QUESTIONS

**1. Section 8(a)(3) Violation Without Proof of "Discrimination"?** Given the Board's findings that neither Republic Aviation nor Le Tourneau was motivated by anti-union animus in either its adoption or application of the facially neutral no-solicitation and no-distribution rules at issue, why did the Board find that the disciplining of employees who had disobeyed these rules violated §8(a)(3) of the Act, and why did the Court uphold these findings? In what sense did these employers engage in "discrimination" within the meaning of §8(a)(3)?

**2. Distinction Between §8(a)(3) and §8(a)(1).** The employers' telling their employees they could not solicit on company property on nonwork time would have constituted §8(a)(1) violations even without any ensuing discriminatory discharges or suspensions. There were also §8(a)(3) violations in these cases because the employers discharged or suspended employees for continuing to engage in the onsite solicitation held to be protected in *Republic Aviation.*

**3. Section 8(a)(1)'s Role in Discharge Cases?** In NLRB v. Burnup & Sims, Inc., 379 U.S. 21 (1964), the employer discharged two employees after it had been told that, while recruiting during an organizing campaign, they had threatened to use dynamite, if necessary, to achieve recognition. The Board found that the reported threat had not been made, ruled that the employer's honest belief to the contrary was not a defense, concluded that the discharges had violated both §8(a)(1) and §8(a)(3), and ordered reinstatement and back pay. The Court affirmed the Board's order solely on the basis of §8(a)(1), stating (at 22-24):

---

impediment to self-organization and therefore discriminatory in the absence of evidence that special circumstances make the rule necessary in order to maintain production or discipline."

> We find it unnecessary to reach . . . §8(a)(3) for . . . §8(a)(1) was plainly violated, whatever the employer's motive. . . . A protected activity acquires a precarious status if innocent employees can be discharged while engaging in it, even though the employer acts in good faith. It is the tendency of [such] discharges to weaken or destroy the §8(a)(1) right that is controlling. We are not in the realm of managerial prerogatives. . . . Had the alleged dynamiting threats been wholly disassociated from §7 activities quite different considerations might apply.

Does *Burnup & Sims* stand for the proposition that §8(a)(1) protects employee organizers from discharge for reasons that are later determined to be erroneous despite the absence of discriminatory motivation by the employer? Is it preferable to read *Burnup & Sims* as imposing liability not for the discharge decision but rather for the employer's unwillingness to reinstate the employees in question once it learned that its grounds for the discharge were erroneous?

**4. The NLRB's "Gap-Filling" Function.** Note the Court's discussion in *Republic Aviation* of the NLRB's role in applying the Act's extremely broad language to "the infinite combinations of events which might be charged as violative of its terms," and of the appropriateness of having "experienced officials with an adequate appreciation of the complexities of the subject" make the determination in the first instance of precisely what conduct shall be found to contravene the Act. On what basis did the Board determine that prohibitions against solicitation or distribution on nonworking time generally violate the Act? Is the *Peyton Packing* presumption upheld by the Court in *Republic Aviation* because of the Court's deference to the Board's expert determination that employee solicitation during nonwork time poses no interference with legitimate employer interests in the typical industrial establishment, or in deference to the Board's policy judgment that whatever interference does occur must be tolerated because of the strength of the employees' §7 interest in being able to discuss union representation while on the job? Would either reason for deference be appropriate under *Chevron*, see pp. 75 supra?

### *Note: Restrictions on Workplace Solicitation and Distribution*

**The *Peyton Packing* Presumption.** The Board's approach in *Republic Aviation* does not hold that every employer restraint on §7 activity violates §8(a)(1). Rather, the Board purports to balance employer interests in the maintenance of "production or discipline" against the Act's protection of the free exercise of §7 rights. The Board's "*Peyton Packing* presumption," set forth at footnote 10 of *Republic Aviation*, in fact incorporates two rebuttable presumptions. First, a neutral rule prohibiting solicitation *during working hours* can be applied against employee union solicitation in the absence of proof that it was adopted for the purpose of discouraging §7 protected activity. Second, enforcement against union solicitation of even a neutral rule prohibiting all solicitation *outside of working hours* on company property is illegal, unless the company demonstrates "special circumstances [that] make the rule necessary in order to maintain production or discipline." This doctrine has been further elaborated and developed by the Board and courts along several significant lines.

**"Working Time" vs. "Working Hours."** To be presumptively valid, a rule restricting organizational activity must state with reasonable clarity that it does not apply during periods when employees are not scheduled for work—for example, lunch and break periods. As *Republic Aviation* illustrates, rules can be unlawful on their face because they are overly broad. Furthermore, the Board has taken the view that since unclear, overbroad restrictions can deter protected activity, ambiguities should be resolved against the employer. See, e.g., St. George Warehouse, Inc., 331 N.L.R.B. 454 (2000). Although *Peyton Packing* and *Republic Aviation* used the term "working hours," the Board will find restrictions on solicitation or distribution during "working hours," as opposed to "working time," invalid. See Our Way, Inc., 268 N.L.R.B. 394 (1983). It believes that "working hours" may be construed by employees as covering lunch and break periods, whereas "working time" will be clearly understood to cover only periods of actual work. Similarly, the Board has ruled that restrictions on the use of social media during "Company time" are presumptively invalid because they fail to convey that solicitation could happen through social media outlets "during breaks and other nonworking hours at the enterprise." Dish Network Corp., 359 N.L.R.B. No. 108 (2013), invalidated due to lack of quorum under NLRB v. Noel Canning Co., 134 S. Ct. 2550 (2014).

**Solicitation vs. Distribution.** The Board has distinguished between oral solicitation and distribution of literature by employees and has recognized the presumptive validity of plant rules restricting such "distribution" to *nonworking areas* of the plant regardless of whether such distribution occurs during nonworking time. Distribution raises issues of littering and possible cluttering of company equipment not present with most instances of on-site solicitation. The Board treats the handing out of union solicitation cards as a form of solicitation because these cards are likely to be collected by the solicitor. See Stoddard-Quirk Mfg. Co., 138 N.L.R.B. 615 (1962) (two members dissenting). See also National Semiconductor Corp., 272 N.L.R.B. 973 (1984) (distribution of a petition to garner employee signatures in protest of a personnel action treated as solicitation).

**Union Buttons or Insignia.** As *Republic Aviation* itself illustrates, the wearing of union buttons or insignia is an exception to the rule that an employer may generally restrict solicitation during working time. The line between active solicitation, which may be lawfully confined to nonworking time, and the wearing of insignia, which may not be so confined, is not always clear, however. See, e.g., Wal-Mart Stores, Inc., 340 N.L.R.B. 637 (2003), enforced in relevant part, 400 F.3d 1093 (8th Cir. 2005) (employee may not be disciplined for wearing T-shirt stating "Sign a Card . . . Ask Me How," as wearing shirt did not constitute solicitation calling for "immediate response from other employees").

Restrictions on the wearing of union buttons or insignia at any time are presumptively unlawful in the absence of "special circumstances" showing that the rule is necessary to maintain production, discipline, or customer relations. See, e.g., In re Eckert Fire Protection, Inc., 332 N.L.R.B. 198 (2000); Pepsi Cola Bottling Co., Inc., of Norton, 301 N.L.R.B. 1008 (1991). See also Meijer, Inc. v. NLRB, 130 F.3d 1209, 1216 (6th Cir. 1997) (referring to employees' "near-absolute" right to wear insignia). The Board's view is that an employee's contact with customers is not per se a "special circumstance" justifying a total ban on wearing union buttons. See, e.g., Flamingo Hilton-Laughlin, 330 N.L.R.B. 287 (1999); Albertson's, Inc., 300 N.L.R.B. 1013 (1990); but see NLRB v. Starbucks Corp., 679 F.3d 70, 78 (2d Cir. 2012) (Starbucks's one-button dress code was permissible because multiple "union buttons would risk serious dilution of the information contained on Starbucks's buttons"), and Starwood Hotel & Resorts Worldwide, Inc., 348 N.L.R.B. 372 (2006) (employer may prohibit employee from wearing a button on a completely black uniform designed to create special atmosphere during in-room delivery service). The Board has suggested that the wearing of certain union buttons by employees who regularly interact with customers may be prohibited because the particular message on the button would threaten to "produce a divisive customer atmosphere." *Albertson's*, supra, 300 N.L.R.B. at 1016. Should it matter whether a union button says "Help us organize this sweat shop" or simply "Win with the Union"? Should the size of the button or insignia matter? See Fabri-Tek, Inc. v. NLRB, 352 F.2d 577, 583-584 (8th Cir. 1965) (employer may prohibit extremely large buttons and "out-size letters" stenciled on back of employees' shirts); Virginia Elec. & Power Co. v. NLRB, 703 F.2d 79 (4th Cir. 1983) (employer may require receptionist to wear smaller and "less gaudy" union pin while on duty).

**Privileged Broad No-Solicitation or Distribution Rules**. Broader restrictions on solicitation and distribution are presumptively valid in certain types of establishments such as retail department stores and hospitals. Thus, rules banning employee solicitation even during nonworking time in selling areas of department stores are generally valid. See, e.g., Gayfers Dep't Store, 324 N.L.R.B. 1246, 1250 (1997); J.C. Penney Co., 266 N.L.R.B. 1223, 1224 (1983). The Board also applies this "selling areas" exception to working areas of other establishments such as hotels and casinos. See Flamingo Hilton-Laughlin, 330 N.L.R.B. at 294.

As for hospitals and other health care facilities, the Board generally permits bans on all buttons, solicitation, and distribution (even during non-working time) in "immediate patient care" areas such as patients' rooms, operating rooms, and other treatment areas. See Cooper Health Systems, 327 N.L.R.B. 1159 (1999); Doctors Hospital of Staten Island, 325 N.L.R.B. 730 (1998). In contrast, bans on buttons or on solicitation or distribution on nonworking time in "patient access" or "visitor access" areas such as cafeterias, gift shops, and hospital entrances are presumed invalid absent a showing by the hospital that such a ban is necessary to avoid disrupting patient care or disturbing patients. Cooper Health Systems, supra; Eastern Maine Medical Center, 253 N.L.R.B. 224 (1980). In Sacred Heart Medical Center, 347 N.L.R.B. 531 (2006), the Board ruled that the wearing of buttons stating "RNs Demand Safe Staffing" could be banned even outside immediate patient care areas because of the buttons' "disruptive" message. Was the message on the buttons disruptive because it suggested that the care patients were receiving was unsafe?

The Supreme Court has approved the Board's distinction between "immediate patient care" versus "patient access" or "visitor access" areas. See NLRB v. Baptist Hospital, 442 U.S. 773 (1979); Beth Israel Hospital v. NLRB, 437 U.S. 483 (1978). It has also indicated that, unlike the approach for normal industrial establishments approved in *Republic Aviation*, the availability of other areas for on-site organizational activity in a healthcare facility is relevant in evaluating the permissibility of restrictions in "immediate patient care" areas of that facility. See Beth Israel, 437 U.S. at 505.

In *Beth Israel*, the Court upheld a Board order barring enforcement of a rule that prohibited union solicitation and distribution by employees in the hospital cafeteria and restricted such activities to locations next to employees' lockers and rest rooms. Only about 600 of the 2,200 regular employees were accessible to solicitation in the scattered locker areas, and a union survey had shown that of the cafeteria's patrons, 77 percent were employees while only 9 percent were visitors and 1.5 percent were patients. In *Baptist Hospital*, however, the Court disagreed with the Board's characterization of certain areas, finding that corridors and sitting rooms on floors of the hospital that contain patient rooms or operating or other treatment areas should be treated as immediate patient care areas in which solicitation may be banned.

**Facial Challenges to Use of Employer Equipment, Including E-mail Systems.** Do employees who use their employers' e-mail systems for work purposes have a statutory right to use such systems for Section 7 purposes? The Board and the courts have upheld employer restrictions, even during nonworking time, on the use of other company-owned equipment or property to facilitate communication. See, e.g., Union Carbide Corp. v.

NLRB, 714 F.2d 657 (6th Cir. 1983) (telephones); Eaton Technologies, 322 N.L.R.B. 848, 853 (1997) (bulletin boards); Champion Int'l Corp., 303 N.L.R.B. 102 (1991) (copy machines). In Register Guard, 351 N.L.R.B. 192 (2007), reversed in part on other grounds, 571 F.3d 53 (D.C. Cir. 2009), the Board upheld an employer's restrictions on the use of its e-mail system. The Board majority viewed the e-mail system as another example of company-owned instrumentalities that do not trigger employee access under Republic Aviation. In 2014, however, a new Board (3-2) majority reversed *Register Guard* in Purple Communications, Inc. 361 N.L.R.B. No. 126 (2014). It held that employers who give employees access to their e-mail systems must permit employees to use that system during nonworking time "for statutorily protected communications." The Board majority essentially equated the e-mail system with a brake room or cafeteria where employees during nonworking time can engage in solicitation. According to *Purple Communications,* "an employer may justify a total ban on nonwork use of email, including Section 7 use on nonworking time, by demonstrating that special circumstances make the ban necessary to maintain production or discipline. Absent justification for a total ban, the employer may apply uniform and consistently enforced controls over its email system to the extent such controls are necessary to maintain production and discipline." Under this ruling, does an employer that bars all employee use of e-mails for non-business purposes violate the NLRA by not permitting employee use for organizing purposes? Does *Purple Communications* require a similar approach to company telephone systems, Xerox and scanning facilities?

**Facial Challenges to Rules Governing the Content or Civility of Employee Communications.** The Board has held that an employer can illegally interfere with the exercise of §7 rights not only by directly prohibiting organizational activity, but also by chilling such activity through regulation of the content or tone of employee communications. Thus, the Board has proscribed restrictions on the discussion of wages or other terms and conditions of employment. See, e.g., Double Eagle Hotel & Casino, 341 N.L.R.B. 112 (2004); Waco, Inc., 273 N.L.R.B. 746 (1984). The Board also has invalidated facially neutral decorum rules that could chill vigorous protected activity. See, e.g., Adtranz, ABB Daimler-Benz Transportation, N.A., Inc., 331 N.L.R.B. 291 (2000) (rule against the use of "abusive . . . language"), enforcement denied, 253 F.3d 19 (D.C. Cir. 2001); Lafayette Park Hotel, 326 N.L.R.B. 824 (1998) (rule prohibiting "false, vicious, profane or malicious statements"), enforced, 203 F.3d 52 (D.C. Cir. 1999). In Martin Luther Memorial Home, Inc., 343 N.L.R.B. 1044 (2004), however, the Board, accepting the D.C. Circuit's analysis in *Adtranz,* held that rules prohibiting "abusive and profane language," "harassment," and "verbal, mental, and physical abuse" are lawful so long as employees would not reasonably construe them to prohibit §7 conduct and the rules are not adopted or applied to do so. See generally Michael C. Harper, Judicial Control of the National Labor Relations Board's Lawmaking in the Age of *Chevron* and *Brand X*, 89 B.U. L. Rev. 189, 229-233 (2009). Since *Martin Luther Memorial,* the Board has found illegal employer rules requiring all complaints to be made through the employer's "chain of command," see Guardsmark, LLC v. NLRB, enforced, 475 F.3d 369 (D.C. Cir. 2007); prohibiting "negative comments" about co-workers, Hills & Dales Gen. Hosp., 360 N.L.R.B. No. 70 (2014) or "negative conversations" about other employees or managers, see KSL Claremont Resort, Inc., 344 N.L.R.B. 832 (2005); prohibiting commentary via social media and other electronic communications that contains "inappropriate discussions about the company, management, and/or coworkers," Triple Play Sports Bar and Grille, 361 N.L.R.B. No. 31 (2014), is "disparaging or defamatory" to the employer, Costco Wholesale Corp., 358 N.L.R.B No. 106 (2012), invalidated due to lack of quorum under NLRB v. Noel Canning Co., 134 S. Ct. 2550 (2014), or that "disrespectful" language "which injuries the image or reputation" of the employer, Karl Knauz Motors, 358 N.L.R.B. No. 164 (2012), invalidated due to lack of quorum under NLRB v. Noel Canning Co., 134 S. Ct. 2550 (2014).

Rules requiring confidentiality with respect to business information might also run afoul of §7 on the ground that employees might construe them to restrict discussion of wages and other conditions of employment. See Cintas Corp., 344 N.L.R.B. 943 (2005), enforced, 482 F.3d 463 (D.C. Cir. 2007); Flex Frac Logistics 358 N.L.R.B. No. 127 (2012), enforced, 746 F.3d 205 (5th Cir. 2014); Verso Paper, Case 30-CA-089350, NLRB Office of the General Counsel Advice Memorandum (Jan. 29, 2013).

**Discriminatory Enforcement of Valid No-Solicitation/No-Distribution Rules.** The Board holds that an otherwise valid no-solicitation or no-distribution rule is unlawful if it is enforced in a discriminatory manner. See, e.g., Cooper Health Systems, 327 N.L.R.B. at 1164 (1999); Reno Hilton Resorts, 320 N.L.R.B. 197, 208 (1995).

The Board's view had been that an exception even for charitable organizations or for employees' personal solicitations is a form of discriminatory application that undermines the business justification for an otherwise valid no-solicitation rule and precludes enforcement of the rule against employee §7 solicitations. The Board's position here has encountered some judicial resistance, particularly in the Seventh Circuit. See Fleming Co. v. NLRB, 349 F.3d 968 (7th Cir. 2003) (employer that allows posting on company bulletin board of personal announcements and for-sale notices may ban posting of union literature as employer consistently banned posting by any organizations or groups), and Guardian Indus. v. NLRB, 49 F.3d 317, 319-321 (7th Cir. 1995) (company may permit "swap-and-shop" notices on company bulletin boards without being required to post notices of union meetings, as company did not permit notices of other groups' meetings). In *Register Guard*, supra, the Board adopted the position of the Seventh Circuit; it held that it would find solicitation rules to be discriminatory only if the rules were applied differently to solicitations on different sides of Section 7 related matters, such as allowing solicitations by pro-union employees but not anti-union employees. The Board's 2014 *Purple Communications* decision, supra, did not address this aspect of *Register Guard.*

## B. THE ACCOMMODATION OF §7 RIGHTS AND EMPLOYER INTERESTS

### 1. Interest in Maintaining Production and Discipline

As *Republic Aviation* and the accompanying material on no-solicitation/no-distribution rules indicates, although there is no express mention in §§7 or 8 of employer interests or rights, the Board and the courts have assumed that Congress did not intend by these provisions to interfere with legitimate employer interests in the running of business enterprises. Thus, determining whether an employer interfered with a §7 right in violation of §8(a)(1), or illegally discouraged union activity through discrimination in violation of §8(a)(3), requires some consideration and accommodation of legitimate employer interests.

### 2. Interest in Excluding Non-Invitees: Employer Property Rights

Because employees are already rightfully on the employer's premises, solicitation and distribution by employees are thought not to implicate the employer's property rights. State-law property rights clearly do come into play, however, whenever those who have not been invited on the company premises, including non-employee union organizers, seek access to the employer's premises.

#### *Note:* NLRB v. Babcock & Wilcox Co.

The Court first confronted the issue of the extent to which an employer's property rights could be asserted to bar access to its property by non-employee union organizers in NLRB v. Babcock & Wilcox Co., 351 U.S. 105 (1956), decided 11 years after *Republic Aviation.* In *Babcock*, the Court (per Justice Reed, who had also authored *Republic* Aviation), held the Board must "make a distinction between rules of law applicable to employees and those applicable to nonemployees."

The distinction is one of substance. No restriction may be placed on the employees' right to discuss self-organization among themselves, unless the employer can demonstrate that a restriction is necessary to maintain production or discipline. Republic Aviation Corp. v. Labor Board, 324 U.S. 793, 803. But no such obligation is owed nonemployee organizers. Their access to company property is governed by a different consideration. The right of self-organization depends in some measure on the ability of employees to learn the advantages of self-organization from others. Consequently, if the location of a plant and the living quarters of the employees place the employees beyond the reach of reasonable union efforts to communicate with them, the employer must allow the union to approach his employees on his property. No such conditions are shown [here].

The plants are close to small well-settled communities where a large percentage of the employees live. The usual methods of imparting information are available. . . . The various instruments of publicity are at hand. Though the quarters of the employees are scattered they are in reasonable reach. The Act requires only that the employer refrain from interference, discrimination, restraint or coercion in the employees' exercise of their own rights. It does not require that the employer permit the use of its facilities for organization when other means are readily available. Id. at 112-114.

The following decision is the Supreme Court's most recent pronouncement on the issue of union access to an employer's property.

## Lechmere, Inc. v. NLRB
*502 U.S. 527 (1992)*

Justice Thomas delivered the opinion of the Court.

This case stems from the efforts of Local 919 of the United Food and Commercial Workers Union, AFL-CIO, to organize employees at a retail store in Newington, Connecticut, owned and operated by petitioner Lechmere, Inc. The store is located in the Lechmere Shopping Plaza, which occupies a roughly rectangular tract measuring approximately 880 feet from north to south and 740 feet from east to west. Lechmere's store is situated at the Plaza's south end, with the main parking lot to its north. A strip of 13 smaller "satellite stores" not owned by Lechmere runs along the west side of the Plaza, facing the parking lot. To the Plaza's east (where the main entrance is located) runs the Berlin Turnpike, a four-lane divided highway. The parking lot, however, does not abut the Turnpike; they are separated by a 46-foot-wide grassy strip, broken only by the Plaza's entrance. The parking lot is owned jointly by Lechmere and the developer of the satellite stores. The grassy strip is public property. . . .

The union began its campaign to organize the store's 200 employees, none of whom was represented by a union, in June 1987. After a full-page advertisement in a local newspaper drew little response, nonemployee union organizers entered Lechmere's parking lot and began placing handbills on the windshields of cars parked in a corner of the lot used mostly by employees. Lechmere's manager immediately confronted the organizers, informed them that Lechmere prohibited solicitation or handbill distribution of any kind on its property,[1] and asked them to leave. They did so, and Lechmere personnel removed the handbills. The union organizers renewed this handbilling effort in the parking lot on several subsequent occasions; each time they were asked to leave and the handbills were removed. The organizers then relocated to the public grassy strip, from where they attempted to pass out handbills to cars entering the lot during hours (before opening and after closing) when the drivers were assumed to be primarily store employees. For one month, the union organizers returned daily to the grassy strip to picket Lechmere; after that, they picketed intermittently for another six months. They also recorded the license plate numbers of cars parked in the employee parking area; with the cooperation of the Connecticut Department of Motor Vehicles, they thus secured the names and addresses of some 41 nonsupervisory employees (roughly 20% of the store's total). The union sent four mailings to these employees; it also made some attempts to contact them by phone or home visits. These mailings and visits resulted in one signed union authorization card.

Alleging that Lechmere had violated the NLRA by barring the nonemployee organizers from its property, the union filed an unfair labor practice charge with respondent National Labor Relations Board (Board). . . . The Board affirmed the ALJ's judgment and adopted the recommended order in the union's favor, applying the analysis set forth in its opinion in Jean Country, 291 N.L.R.B. 11 (1988). . . . A divided panel of the United States Court of Appeals for the First Circuit denied Lechmere's petition for review and enforced the Board's order.

. . . By its plain terms, . . . the NLRA confers rights only on *employees*, not on unions or their nonemployee organizers. In NLRB v. Babcock & Wilcox Co., 351 U.S. 105 (1956), however, we recognized that insofar as the

---

1. Lechmere had established this policy several years prior to the union's organizing efforts. The store's official policy statement provided, in relevant part:

> Non-associates [i.e., nonemployees] are prohibited from soliciting and distributing literature at all times anywhere on Company properly, including parking lots. Non-associates have no right of access to the non-working areas and only to the public and selling areas of the store in connection with its public use.

On each door to the store Lechmere had posted a 6- by 8-inch sign reading: "TO THE PUBLIC. No Soliciting, Canvassing, Distribution of Literature or Trespassing by Non-Employees in or on Premises." Lechmere consistently enforced this policy inside the store as well as on the parking lot (against, among others, the Salvation Army and the Girl Scouts).

employees' "right of self-organization depends in some measure on [their] ability . . . to learn the advantages of self-organization from others," id., at 113, §7 of the NLRA may, in certain limited circumstances, restrict an employer's right to exclude nonemployee union organizers from his property. It is the nature of those circumstances that we explore today. . . .

*Jean Country* . . . represents the Board's latest attempt to implement the rights guaranteed by §7. It sets forth a three-factor balancing test:

> [I]n all access cases our essential concern will be [1] the degree of impairment of the Section 7 right if access should be denied, as it balances against [2] the degree of impairment of the private property right if access should be granted. We view the consideration of [3] the availability of reasonably effective alternative means as especially significant in this balancing process. 291 N.L.R.B., at 14.

. . . The Board maintains in this case that *Jean Country* is a reasonable interpretation of the NLRA entitled to judicial deference. . . . Chevron U.S.A. Inc. v. Natural Resources Defense Council, Inc., 467 U.S. 837, 842-843 (1984).

Before we reach any issue of deference to the Board, however, we must first determine whether *Jean Country*—at least as applied to nonemployee organizational trespassing—is consistent with our past interpretation of §7. . . . In *Babcock*, . . . we held that the Act drew a distinction "of substance," 351 U.S., at 113, between the union activities of employees and nonemployees. In cases involving *employee* activities, we noted with approval, the Board "balanced the conflicting interests of employees to receive information on self-organization on the company's property from fellow employees during nonworking time, with the employer's right to control the use of his property." Id., at 109-110. In cases involving *nonemployee* activities (like those at issue in *Babcock* itself), however, the Board was not permitted to engage in that same balancing (and we reversed the Board for having done so). By reversing the Board's interpretation of the statute for failing to distinguish between the organizing activities of employees and nonemployees, we were saying, in *Chevron* terms, that §7 speaks to the issue of nonemployee access to an employer's property. *Babcock*'s teaching is straightforward: §7 simply does not protect nonemployee union organizers *except* in the rare case where "the inaccessibility of employees makes ineffective the reasonable attempts by nonemployees to communicate with them through the usual channels," 351 U.S., at 112. Our reference to "reasonable" attempts was nothing more than a commonsense recognition that unions need not engage in extraordinary feats to communicate with inaccessible employees—*not* an endorsement of the view (which we expressly rejected) that the Act protects "reasonable" trespasses. Where reasonable alternative means of access exist, §7's guarantees do not authorize trespasses by nonemployee organizers, *even* (as we noted in *Babcock*, ibid.) "under . . . reasonable regulations" established by the Board.

. . . To say that our cases require accommodation between employees' and employers' rights is a true but incomplete statement, for the cases also go far in establishing the locus of that accommodation where nonemployee organizing is at issue. So long as nonemployee union organizers have reasonable access to employees outside an employer's property, the requisite accommodation has taken place. It is *only* where such access is infeasible that it becomes necessary and proper to take the accommodation inquiry to a second level, balancing the employees' and employers' rights. . . . At least as applied to nonemployees, *Jean Country* impermissibly conflates these two stages of the inquiry—thereby significantly eroding *Babcock*'s general rule that "an employer may validly post his property against nonemployee distribution of union literature," 351 U.S., at 112. We reaffirm that general rule today, and reject the Board's attempt to recast it as a multifactor balancing test.

The threshold inquiry in this case, then, is whether the facts here justify application of *Babcock*'s inaccessibility exception. . . . As we have explained, the exception to *Babcock*'s rule is a narrow one. It does not apply wherever nontrespassory access to employees may be cumbersome or less-than-ideally effective, but only where "the *location of a plant and the living quarters of the employees* place the employees *beyond the reach* of reasonable union efforts to communicate with them," 351 U.S., at 113 (emphasis added). Classic examples include logging camps, mining camps, and mountain resort hotels. [Citations omitted.] *Babcock*'s exception was crafted precisely to protect the §7 rights of those employees who, by virtue of their employment, are isolated from the ordinary flow of information that characterizes our society. The union's burden of establishing such isolation is, as we have explained, "a heavy one," [Sears, Roebuck & Co. v. Carpenters, 436 U.S. 180, 205 (1978),] and one not satisfied by mere conjecture or the expression of doubts concerning the effectiveness of nontrespassory means of communication.

The Board's conclusion in this case that the union had no reasonable means short of trespass to make Lechmere's employees aware of its organizational efforts is based on a misunderstanding of the limited scope of this exception. Because the employees do not reside on Lechmere's property, they are presumptively not "beyond the reach," *Babcock*, supra, at 113, of the union's message. Although the employees live in a large metropolitan area (Greater Hartford), that fact does not in itself render them "inaccessible" in the sense contemplated by *Babcock*. See Monogram Models, Inc., 192 N.L.R.B. 705, 706 (1971). Their accessibility is suggested by the union's success in contacting a substantial percentage of them directly, via mailings, phone calls, and home visits. Such direct contact, of course, is not a necessary element of "reasonably effective" communication; signs or advertising also may suffice. In this case, the union tried advertising in local newspapers; the

Board said that this was not reasonably effective because it was expensive and might not reach the employees. 295 N.L.R.B., at 93. Whatever the merits of that conclusion, other alternative means of communication were readily available. Thus, signs (displayed, for example, from the public grassy strip adjoining Lechmere's parking lot) would have informed the employees about the union's organizational efforts. (Indeed, union organizers picketed the shopping center's main entrance for months as employees came and went every day.) *Access* to employees, not *success* in winning them over, is the critical issue — although success, or lack thereof, may be relevant in determining whether reasonable access exists. Because the union in this case failed to establish the existence of any "unique obstacles," *Sears*, 436 U.S., at 205-206, n.41, that frustrated access to Lechmere's employees, the Board erred in concluding that Lechmere committed an unfair labor practice by barring the nonemployee organizers from its property.

The judgment of the First Circuit is therefore reversed, and enforcement of the Board's order is denied.

Justice WHITE, with whom Justice BLACKMUN joins, dissenting.

"We will uphold a Board rule so long as it is rational and consistent with the Act, . . . even if we would have formulated a different rule had we sat on the Board." NLRB v. Curtin Matheson Scientific, Inc., 494 U.S. 775, 787 (1990). The judicial role is narrow: The Board's application of the rule, if supported by substantial evidence on the record as a whole, must be enforced. Beth Israel Hospital v. NLRB, 437 U.S. 483, 501 (1978). . . .

For several reasons, the Court errs in this case. First, that *Babcock* stated that inaccessibility would be a reason to grant access does not indicate that there would be no other circumstance that would warrant entry to the employer's parking lot and would satisfy the Court's admonition that accommodation must be made with as little destruction of property rights as is consistent with the right of employees to learn the advantages of self-organization from others. . . . If the Court in *Babcock* indicated that nonemployee access to a logging camp would be required, it did not say that only in such situations could nonemployee access be permitted. Nor did *Babcock* require the Board to ignore the substantial difference between the entirely private parking lot of a secluded manufacturing plant and a shopping center lot which is open to the public without substantial limitation. Nor indeed did *Babcock* indicate that the Board could not consider the fact that employees' residences are scattered throughout a major metropolitan area; *Babcock* itself relied on the fact that the employees in that case lived in a compact area which made them easily accessible.

Moreover, the Court in *Babcock* recognized that actual communication with nonemployee organizers, not mere notice that an organizing campaign exists, is necessary to vindicate §7 rights. 351 U.S., at 113. If employees are entitled to learn from others the advantages of self-organization, ibid., it is singularly unpersuasive to suggest that the union has sufficient access for this purpose by being able to hold up signs from a public grassy strip adjacent to the highway leading to the parking lot. . . .

. . . [M]ore fundamentally, *Babcock* is at odds with modern concepts of deference to an administrative agency charged with administering a statute. See Chevron U.S.A. Inc. v. Natural Resources Defense Council, Inc., 467 U.S. 837 (1984). When reviewing an agency's construction of a statute, we ask first whether Congress has spoken to the precise question at issue. Id., at 842. If it has not, we do not simply impose our own construction on the statute; rather, we determine if the agency's view is based on a permissible construction of the statute. Id., at 843. *Babcock* did not ask if Congress had specifically spoken to the issue of access by third parties and did not purport to explain how the NLRA specifically dealt with what the access rule should be where third parties are concerned. If it had made such an inquiry, the only basis for finding statutory language that settled the issue would have been the language of §7, which speaks only of the rights of employees; i.e., the Court might have found that §7 extends no access rights at all to union representatives. But *Babcock* itself recognized that employees have a right to learn from others about self-organization, 351 U.S., at 113, and itself recognized that in some circumstances, §§7 and 8 required the employer to grant the union access to parking lots. . . .

That being the case, the *Babcock* Court should have recognized that the Board's construction of the statute was a permissible one and deferred to its judgment. . . .

Under the law that governs today, it is *Babcock* that rests on questionable legal foundations. The Board's decision in *Jean Country*, by contrast, is both rational and consistent with the governing statute. The Court should therefore defer to the Board, rather than resurrecting and extending the reach of a decision which embodies principles which the law has long since passed by.

[The opinion of Justice Stevens, dissenting, is omitted.]

## *NOTES AND QUESTIONS*

**1. Who Does the Balancing?** The view that unions have only derivative §7 rights that depend on the ability of employees "to learn the advantages of self-organization" from other sources may support a narrower access right for unions than for employees. But does it support the Court's assumption of the authority to strike the balance between §7 rights and employer interests on its own? Does the Board have less authority here than in *Republic Aviation* to strike the balance because non-employee access may impinge on the employer's state-law property right to exclude "outsiders"?

Does *Republic Aviation* itself not have an impact on the common law right of employers to control solicitation by those invited onto their property for other reasons?

**2. Role of State Law.** Would the *Lechmere* Court have ruled differently if Connecticut trespass law had not granted property owners a right to exclude outsiders from shopping center parking lots? Does state law define the property interest that overweighs §7 rights or does the NLRA set a nationally uniform balance? The decisions hold that if state law does not recognize the employer's right to exclude non-invitees, *Lechmere* is not implicated. See Roundy's Inc. v. NLRB, 674 F.3d 638, 655 (7th Cir. 2012) (employer's burden to prove that state property interest is sufficient to oust nonemployees and affirming Board's conclusion "that a store owner who has only a nonexclusive easement in the common areas violates Section 8(a)(1) when excluding peaceful, nondisruptive handbillers engaged in protected Section 7 activities"); Thunder Basin Coal Co. v. Reich, 510 U.S. 200, 217 n.21 (1994) (dicta: the "right of employers to exclude union organizers from their private property emanates from state common law, and while this right is not superseded by the NLRA, nothing in the NLRA expressly protects it"); United Brotherhood of Carpenters v. NLRB, 540 F.3d 957 (9th Cir. 2008) (California law); United Food & Commercial Workers v. NLRB (Farm Fresh, Inc.), 222 F.3d 1030 (D.C. Cir. 2000) (Virginia law); O'Neil Mkts., Inc. v. United Food & Commercial Workers Union Meatcutters Local 88, 95 F.3d 733 (8th Cir. 1996) (Missouri law). See Jeffrey M. Hirsch, Taking State Property Rights Out of Federal Labor Law, 47 B.C. L. Rev. 891(2006).

**3. Stare Decisis?** Was the result in *Lechmere* required as a matter of respect for the 36-year old precedent in *Babcock & Wilcox*? Did *Lechmere* present a materially different factual situation?

**4. Strength of Employer's Interest.** Would placing handbills on cars parked in the corner of a shopping center parking lot be likely to impair in any way the operation of the retail stores at the shopping center whether by disrupting business, by discouraging customers from entering the shopping center, or by subverting employee discipline? Would it have been reasonable for the Board to have weighed Lechmere's interest in controlling access to the parking lot at its shopping mall less heavily than Babcock & Wilcox's interest in controlling access to the parking lot at its isolated industrial plant? Under the *Jean Country* analysis rejected in *Lechmere,* the Board had considered the extent to which the employer's property was generally open to the public in weighing the degree of impairment of the employer's property interest.

**5. "Reasonable Access" to Employees?** The *Lechmere* Court held that the Board may not force an employer to allow nonemployee union organizers onto its property (or even engage in any balancing of §7 rights and property rights) unless the organizers do not "have reasonable access to employees" outside the property. Does "reasonable access" mean alternatives that are equally effective in reaching employees and not difficult or expensive for a union to employ? Or does it mean any feasible access, even if considerably less likely to reach employees or more expensive or burdensome for the union? The Court cites logging and mining camps and resort hotels as examples of work sites that would provide no alternative "reasonable access"; it also rejects a per se exception to the *Babcock & Wilcox* rule for large metropolitan areas. Would it have made a difference in *Lechmere* if the organizers had had no means of obtaining the names, addresses, and phone numbers of any employees and had been relegated to the use of the grassy strip and advertisements in the local media? What if there were no grassy strip or other area from which to picket or post signs and the only option was expensive advertisements in local media that might not even be seen or heard by the affected employees? For a post-*Lechmere* case finding no reasonably effective alternative means of reaching the employees, see Nabors Alaska Drilling, Inc., 325 N.L.R.B. 574 (1998) (where employees live variously on oil drilling rig, offshore oil platform, or in employer-owned camp, Board engages in balancing of rights and concludes that access is required), enforced, 190 F.3d 1008 (9th Cir. 1999).

**6. Employees Communicating with Non-Employee Organizers?** Can the NLRA §2(3) provision that statutory employees "shall not be limited to the employees of a particular employer" be reconciled with the Court's reasoning in *Lechmere*? Does *Lechmere* mean that an employer not only can remove non-employee organizers from its property, but also can discipline employees for speaking with any such organizers on company property to which the organizers are not authorized to have access? In North Hills Office Services, Inc., 345 N.L.R.B. 1262 (2005), the Board held that an employer did not commit an unfair labor practice by instructing an employee to discontinue talking to a union organizer while he was trespassing on company property. If the employee had defied these instructions, could the employer have lawfully fired her?

**7. Impact on §7 Rights?** How much impact do the *Lechmere* and *Babcock & Wilcox* decisions have on the effectiveness of union organization campaigns, given employees' rights to engage in oral solicitation and to distribute literature on employer premises? If the union does not have at least some pre-campaign, in-plant supporters who are willing to initiate solicitation, is the organizational campaign doomed to fail in any event?

Does the answer to these questions turn on the degree to which employees are likely to feel protected from employer retaliation for engaging in on-premises solicitation? On whether employees are likely to be as effective as trained organizers in conveying the union's message? See generally Jay Gresham, Still as Strangers: Nonemployee Union Organizers on Private Commercial Property, 62 Tex. L. Rev. 111 (1983); Leonard Bierman, Justice Thomas and *Lechmere Inc. v. NLRB:* A Reply to Professor Robert A. Gorman, 10 Hofstra Lab. L.J. 299 (1992).

**8. Labor Organizations Seeking Access to Employer Property to Reach Customers vs. Employees?** Does *Lechmere* apply where a labor organization seeks access not to employees for organizing purposes, but to consumers for purposes such as publicizing and protesting an employer's failure to meet the so-called "area standards" for wages and other benefits? In Leslie Homes, Inc., 316 N.L.R.B. 123, enforced sub nom. Metropolitan District Council v. NLRB, 68 F.3d 71 (3d Cir. 1995), the Board held 3-2 that *Lechmere* applies to nonemployee appeals to customers. The dissent argued that *Lechmere* should not apply to appeals by non-employees to customers because the non-employee §7 rights in *Lechmere* were only derivative of those of the employees to be organized, while non-employees attempting to protect area standards may be engaging in concerted activity for their own mutual aid or protection. The dissenters also stressed the greater difficulties non-employees may have reaching a diffuse group of consumers, rather than a limited number of identifiable employees, without going onto the employer's property.

**9. Solicitation by Off-Duty Employees and Employees of Business Invitees.** It will sometimes be unclear whether a case involves a question of employee access under *Republic Aviation* or one of non-employee access under *Lechmere.*

a. Which presumptive rule should apply to off-duty employees who return to their work site to organize for a union in the middle of another shift? See Tri-County Medical Center, Inc., 222 N.L.R.B. 1089 (1976) (off-duty employees are protected as long as their organizational activity is conducted outside "the interior of the plant and other working areas"); Automotive Plastic Technologies, Inc., 313 N.L.R.B. 462 (1993) (affirming *Tri-County* after *Lechmere*); NLRB v. Pizza Crust Co. of Pa., Inc., 862 F.2d 49 (3rd Cir. 1988) (accord). Should it make a difference if these off-duty employees are also *off-site* employees—that is, if they work at another of the employer's facilities? See ITT Indus. v. NLRB, 413 F.3d 64 (D.C. Cir. 2005); First Healthcare Corp. v. NLRB, 344 F.3d 523 (6th Cir. 2003) (both upholding Board's treatment of the rights of off-site employees as "non-derivative," like those of on-site employees, as long as consideration is given to any special legitimate employer concerns such as security or traffic control problems that cannot be otherwise addressed).

b. Which rule applies if an employer restricts solicitations on its property by the employees of another employer who have been invited onto its property to assist in the property owner's conduct of its business or as employees of a tenant? What if Lechmere, for instance, had prohibited solicitations in its parking lot by employees of another store that rented space in its shopping center? In New York, New York, LLC v. NLRB, 313 F.3d 585 (D.C. Cir. 2002), the court asked the Board to reconsider in light of *Lechmere* its position treating the access rights of employees of contractors under the approach of *Republic Aviation.* On remand the Board held that contractor employees who work regularly on another employer's property may be lawfully excluded from engaging in organizational handbilling in nonwork areas directed at customers of the property owner or contractor "only where the owner is able to demonstrate that the activity significantly interferes with his use of the property or where exclusion is justified by another legal business reason. . . ." New York New York Hotel & Casino, 356 N.L.R.B. No. 119 (2011), enforced, 676 F.3d 193 (D.C. Cir. 2012).

**10. Effect of Discriminatory Application of No-Access Rules.** Note that the employer in *Lechmere* had kept *all* non-employee solicitors off its property. May an employer bar union personnel from its property if it has allowed access to non-employees soliciting for other purposes? Does it matter whether the employer or property owner has previously allowed access only to charitable organizations, or to non-charitable entities as well?

There has been a significant split between the Board and the courts on this issue. For instance, in Cleveland Real Estate Partners, 316 N.L.R.B. 158, 166 (1995), the Board held that a mall owner who had permitted solicitation by the Girl Scouts, the Knights of Columbus, and political candidates could not lawfully eject union handbillers from its property. The Board's ruling rested on the Court's statement in *Babcock* that its holding applied only where "the employer . . . does not discriminate against the union by allowing other [solicitation or] distribution." See *Babcock,* 351 U.S. at 112. The Sixth Circuit denied enforcement, asserting that "the Court could not have meant to give the word 'discrimination' the import the Board has chosen to give it. . . . The term 'discrimination' as used in *Babcock* means favoring one union over another, or allowing employer-related information while barring similar union-related information." 95 F.3d 457, 465 (6th Cir. 1996). See also Sandusky Mall Co., 329 N.L.R.B. 618 (1999) (mall owner who had permitted substantial civic, charitable, and promotional activities unlawfully discriminated in ejecting union representatives engaged in area standards handbilling), enforcement denied, 242 F.3d 682 (6th Cir. 2001).

**11. First Amendment Interests.** In Amalgamated Food Employees Union, Local 1590 v. Logan Valley Plaza, 391 U.S. 308 (1968), the Court held that the First Amendment provides protection to expressive activity in private shopping centers deemed to be the modern "functional equivalent" of the downtown business areas whose public sidewalks historically provided a "public forum" for the free exchange of views. The Court, however, overruled *Logan Valley* in Hudgens v. NLRB, 424 U.S. 507 (1976), on the ground that exclusions from privately owned shopping centers did not involve governmental action and hence did not implicate First Amendment rights. Whether or not *Logan Valley* made good constitutional law, was its social analysis correct? Has the demise of downtown urban centers in favor of privately owned shopping malls reduced the opportunities to engage in public communication? Does this change support a different balancing of employer and employee interests than that struck in *Lechmere*?

A few state courts have interpreted the free-speech guarantee in their state constitutions as a limitation on the rights of certain private property owners to exclude nondisruptive picketing or leafletting. See Jones v. Memorial Hosp. System, 677 S.W.2d 221 (Tex. App. 1984). Cf. PruneYard Shopping Center v. Robbins, 447 U.S. 74 (1980) (upholding against federal constitutional challenge California state constitution's protection of speech at privately owned shopping center). See generally Note, Private Abridgement of Speech and the State Constitution, 90 Yale L.J. 165 (1980).

### *Note:* NLRB v. Town & Country Electric, Inc. *and Paid Union Organizers as Protected Employees*

Can unions attempt to overcome the impediments to organizing presented by *Babcock & Wilcox* and *Lechmere* by having paid union organizers become employees of nonunion employers in order to conduct organizational campaigns? In NLRB v. Town & Country Electric, Inc., 516 U.S. 85 (1995), a unanimous Supreme Court upheld the Board's interpretation of the definition of "employee" in §2(3) of the NLRA to include "salts"—workers who are also paid union organizers. It thus affirmed the Board's finding that Town & Country had violated §§8(a)(1) and (3) by refusing to hire union members who were going to be paid by the union while they attempted to organize the employer. The Court rejected Town & Country's argument that under the common law of agency a worker could not be the servant of both an employer and a union at the same time. The Court asserted that "union organizing, when done for pay but during nonwork hours, would seem equivalent to simple moonlighting, a practice wholly consistent with a company's control over its workers as to their assigned duties." 516 U.S. at 91. The Court was also unsympathetic to Town & Country's argument that "salts" might quit at a particularly inopportune time, or even try to harm the company through acts of sabotage or other unlawful activity. Justice Breyer pointed out (id. at 96):

> If a paid union organizer might quit, leaving a company . . . in the lurch, so too might an unpaid organizer, or a worker who has found a better job, or one whose family wants to move elsewhere. And if an overly zealous union organizer might hurt the company through unlawful acts, so might another unpaid zealot (who might know less about the law), or a dissatisfied worker. . . . This does not mean they are not "employees."

## *NOTES AND QUESTIONS*

1. ***Town & Country* and *Lechmere*.** To what extent does *Town & Country* soften the impact of *Lechmere* for union organizers? Will unions always be able to take advantage of the strategy apparently afforded by the Court's acceptance of a broad definition of "employee"? Consider the notes below.

2. **Use of Facially Neutral Policies to Avert "Salts."** Following *Town & Country*, can employers use facially neutral hiring policies to effectively counter union attempts to "salt" their workforce with paid organizers? A facially neutral hiring policy violates the Act only if it is adopted for an anti-union purpose or applied in a discriminatory manner. See Tualatin Electric, 319 N.L.R.B. 1237 (1995) (facially neutral anti-moonlighting policy against hiring applicants holding another job held unlawful). How might one prove that a facially neutral policy was adopted or is being used for a discriminatory purpose? Is it sufficient, for example, that the policy was implemented after the union began its salting campaign? What if the policy was adopted initially before any union organizing was attempted but the employer had been advised of the *Town & Country* decision and was trying to avoid its impact?

Although the Board has found at least some facially neutral hiring policies to be unlawful because of their effect on union activity, see *Tualatin Electric*, supra, and note 3 infra, the courts have required proof of anti-union purpose. See, e.g., Indep. Elec. Contrs. of Houston, Inc. v. NLRB, 720 F.3d 543 (5th Cir. 2013) (not unlawful for member contractors to utilize referral service and "shared man program" which allows them to "borrow workers" from other contractors); Int'l Union of Operating Engineers, Local 150 v. NLRB, 325 F.3d 818 (7th Cir. 2003) (not unlawful to give preference in hiring to referred applicants over walk-in or unknown applicants, regardless of comparative skill level); Contractor's Labor Pool, Inc. v. NLRB, 323 F.3d 1051 (D.C. Cir. 2003) (policy of refusing to consider applicants whose recent wages exceeded company's by 30 percent or more, which effectively barred those who had recently worked for unionized employers, not unlawful); BE & K Construction Co. v. NLRB, 133 F.3d 1372 (11th Cir. 1997) (rejection of applications submitted in "batch" rather than individually not unlawful).

**3. "Covert" and "Overt" Salting.** Salting can be either "covert" or "overt." Covert salts attempt to keep their union position secret until they are hired. Overt salts, in contrast, intentionally put the employer on notice that they work for the union. What is their purpose in doing so?

In Hartman Brothers Heating & Air Conditioning, Inc. v. NLRB, 280 F.3d 1110 (7th Cir. 2002), the Seventh Circuit ruled that "covert" salts may lie on their employment application about their status as paid union organizers, as long as they do not misrepresent facts relevant to their job qualifications. Chief Judge Posner reasoned that such a lie was irrelevant to legitimate employer concerns since an employer cannot lawfully refuse to hire an applicant on the basis that he or she is a salt. Do you agree?

One technique that employers have used to defend against overt salting is the adoption of "no extraneous information" policies that disqualify from consideration applications that contain information not requested by the employer. The Clinton Board found such policies, when applied to applicants who wrote "union organizer" or similar words on their application, unlawful even without proof of anti-union motivation. See H.B. Zachary Co., 319 N.L.R.B. 967 (1995); see also Mainline Contracting Corp., 334 N.L.R.B. 922 (2001) (applying same analysis to policy barring consideration of applications that indicate "race, color, religion, creed, sex, national origin, age . . . or protected concerted activity under the [NLRA]"). The courts, however, have sustained such employer policies in the absence of a showing of anti-union discrimination in the adoption or enforcement of the policies. See Int'l Brotherhood of Boilermakers v. NLRB (H.B. Zachary Co.), 127 F.3d 1300 (11th Cir. 1997); TIC—The Industrial Co. Southeast, Inc. v. NLRB, 126 F.3d 334 (D.C. Cir. 1997).

**4. General Counsel's Burden of Proof in Salting Cases.** In Toering Electric Co., 351 N.L.R.B. 225 (2007), the Board (3-2) held that an applicant entitled to statutory protection is "someone genuinely interested in seeking to establish an employment relationship with the employer." Those who submit applications "solely to create a basis for unfair labor practice charges and thereby to inflict substantial litigation costs on the targeted employer" are not protected by the Act. The *Toering Electric* Board thus enlarged the General Counsel's burden of proof in salting cases to include demonstrating that an applicant had a "genuine interest" in "establishing an employment relationship." In FES (A Division of Thermo Power), 331 N.L.R.B. 9 (2000), enforced, 301 F.3d 83 (3d Cir. 2003), the Board had earlier ruled that to establish a discriminatory refusal to hire the General Counsel must show that the employer was hiring or had concrete plans to hire at the time of the application, that the applicant had relevant experience or training, and that anti-union animus contributed to the employer's failure to hire. If the General Counsel carries this burden, the employer may still avoid liability if it proves by a preponderance of the evidence that it would not have hired the applicant even in the absence of his or her union activities or affiliations.

**5. Remedial Issues.**

a. Cases in which the number of applicants exceeds the number of job openings, which are particularly common in but not confined to the "salting" area, present difficult issues under §8(a)(3). As stated by the Board in *FES*, a showing that one applicant was discriminated against establishes a violation warranting a cease-and-desist order, but back pay and hiring orders for specific applicants require showing that sufficient openings existed for those applicants. See Starcon, Inc. v. NLRB, 176 F.3d 948 (7th Cir. 1999).

b. In Oil Capitol Sheet Metal, Inc., 349 N.L.R.B. 1348 (2007), the Board (3-2) refused to accept for salting cases the Board's usual rebuttable presumption that the back pay period continues indefinitely from the date of the discriminatory act until a valid offer of employment is made. The Board in *Oil Capitol* instead shifted to the General Counsel the burden of proving that a salt/discriminatee, if hired, would have worked for the employer for a particular period. The Board reasoned that "[u]nlike other applicants for employment . . . , salts often do not seek employment for an indefinite duration; rather, . . . many salts remain or intend to remain with the targeted employer only until the union's defined objectives are achieved or abandoned."

**6. Other Access Rules.** Additional issues involving access to employees are dealt with in Chapter 4 in the section on "Access to the Employee Electorate." See infra pages 265-275 (discussing *Nutone* and *Avondale* decision, captive audience speeches, and union access to the "*Excelsior*" list).

## 3. Interest in Entrepreneurial Discretion

### NLRB v. J.M. Lassing

*284 F.2d 781 (6th Cir. 1960)*

Per Curiam.

. . . The respondent is a partnership operating an independent chain of retail gas and service stations in Tennessee and Kentucky. During the latter part of 1958 it had considered and studied the problem of whether it should continue to truck gas with its own equipment and employees, particularly in the light of mounting costs and what it deemed to be inadequate equipment, and had decided to adopt a common carrier system of gas delivery as soon as anything occurred which would increase costs and, in any event, when the truck licenses expired on April 1, 1959.

On January 1, 1959, three of respondent's drivers joined the Union. The Union requested recognition and a meeting for the purpose of negotiating a collective bargaining agreement. A meeting was arranged for January 20, 1959. On January 19, 1959, the drivers were instructed to report at the respondent's office at 8:30 A.M. When they arrived respondent told them that it was going to contract with a common carrier to transport the gasoline and gave the three drivers herein involved their separation notices and final checks. The three drivers thereupon left and have not since been in respondent's employ.

When the Union and respondent met later that morning, the Union renewed its request for recognition. Respondent refused, announcing that it had for a time contemplated abandoning its method of shipping gas and that the coming of the Union, with the added payroll expense thereby entailed, was, in effect, the straw that broke the camel's back.

This case presents basically the same question considered by this Court and decided adversely to the Board's contention in NLRB v. Adkins Transfer Co., 6 Cir., 226 F.2d 324, and NLRB v. R.C. Mahon Co., 6 Cir., 269 F.2d 44. We there held that a company may suspend its operations or change its method of doing business, with the resulting loss of employment on the part of certain employees, so long as its change in operations is not motivated by the illegal intention to avoid its obligations under the National Labor Relations Act. A change in operations motivated by financial or economic reasons is not an unfair labor practice under the Act.

The Board contends that this case is not controlled by the ruling in the *Adkins* and *Mahon* cases because the respondent accelerated its proposed change in operations upon its learning that the three employees had joined the Union and before any demands for increased pay for said employees had been made upon it by the Union, and that such action constituted the discrimination found by the Board to exist.

We do not agree. Although the Union had made no demand for increased pay, the evidence fully justified respondent's belief that such demands would be made and could not be met. Under the circumstances we do not believe it was incumbent upon the respondent to delay the effective date of its new method of operation previously decided upon before the advent of the Union. It will be noticed that the respondent's decision to change its method of operation did not include a commitment to continue under its existing method of operations until April 1, 1959. That date fixed the maximum period of time which would elapse before the change would become effective. The respondent had decided to make the change effective before that date if anything occurred which would increase its costs. The advent of the Union was a new economic factor which necessarily had to be evaluated by the respondent as a part of the overall picture pertaining to costs of operation. It is completely unrealistic in the field of business to say that management is acting arbitrarily or unreasonably in changing its method of operations based on reasonably anticipated increased costs, instead of waiting until such increased costs actually materialize.

There is no evidence in the present case, and there is no contention made, that there was any anti-union background on the part of the respondent. Fundamentally, the change was made because of reasonably anticipated increased costs, regardless of whether this increased costs was caused by the advent of the Union or by some other factor entering into the picture. This did not constitute discrimination against the three employees with respect to their tenure of employment because of membership in the Union, within the provisions of Section 8(a)(1) and (3) of the Act. NLRB v. Houston Chronicle Pub. Co., 5 Cir., 211 F.2d 848, 854.

Since that division of the respondent's business was discontinued and the employment of the three drivers legally terminated, there was no basis for a meeting with the Union later for the purpose of collective bargaining.

## *NOTES AND QUESTIONS*

**1. Why Was Proof of Anti-Union Animus Required?** Consider again the two basic elements of a §8(a)(3) violation discussed in note 2, page 130, after the *Radio Officers* case. Is there any doubt in the *Lassing* case that the employer treated its driver employees differently because of their decision to join a union, and that the effect of the decision to subcontract was to discourage further union activity by the discharged employees and probably other employees of the company as well? Why, then, does the *Lassing* court require the Board to have substantial evidence that the employer was motivated by a desire to discourage union affiliation? Is the *Lassing* court insisting on proof of anti-union animus because of the strength of the employer's interest in being able to shut down part of its operations for legitimate cost-based business reasons, as contrasted with the lack of any comparably strong employer interest in cases like *Radio Officers* and *Republic Aviation*? Does this "entrepreneurial" interest of the employer also provide the best justification for the *Lassing* court's refusal to uphold the Board's finding of a §8(a)(1) violation, even though this section does not require proof of anti-union motivation?

**2. Anti-Union Motivation vs. Economic Motivation?** The *Lassing* court, in accord with rulings of the Board and other courts, assumes that the shutdown or transfer of facilities because of higher labor costs resulting from unionization does not, without more, violate §8(a)(3). What reasons other than a concern with higher labor costs might employers have for opposing unions? An unwillingness to share power? Purely ideological opposition? Is it likely that these other reasons exist in the absence of a concern with higher labor costs?

Should *Lassing* be read not as allowing employers to escape §8(a)(3) liability whenever they equate unionization with higher labor costs, but rather as allowing a particular type of decision — a partial plant closing or other significant withdrawal of capital — to be made in the absence of proof of anti-union animosity? Can such a reading be justified on the ground that it can be assumed that a decision to incur the significant costs of shutting down a business must be a response to felt business necessity rather than a reflection of mere hostility to unionism or to the sharing of authority or even a vague concern with higher costs? On the facts of *Lassing*, however, did the employer incur any losses in deciding to subcontract the delivery operation?

**3. Labor Costs vs. Costs of Protected Activity?** Would the case have been treated differently if Lassing had announced that its decision to subcontract was based on its concern with the disruption and other costs of strikes rather than its determination that it could not pay the high wages and benefits the union would demand? What if an employer states publicly the following reason for locating production for a major contract at a nonunion facility: "The overriding factor (in transferring the line) was not the business climate. And it was not the wages we're paying today. It was that we cannot afford to have a work stoppage, you know, every three years." Does the employer without additional actions violate the Act? See Boeing Co., 19-CA32421 (Complaint and Notice of Hearing, April 20, 2011).

**4. The Significance of the Failure to Bargain?**

a. Note that the Board found in *Lassing* that the company had failed to bargain in good faith as well as violated §8(a)(3). Why did the company have to terminate the three drivers before at least meeting with the union to find out the union's negotiating position? Did management know that it could not have worked out some sort of plan with the union to avoid increasing labor costs? Note that the employer's duty to bargain under the Act does not require that an agreement be reached with the union or that any particular concessions be made. See NLRA §8(d), discussed further in Chapter 6. Does the opinion suggest that the company was under any particular time pressure that did not allow testing of the union's intentions and resolve during negotiations? How critical was it to the court that the company had decided in the latter part of 1958 — before being presented with a request for recognition — to subcontract its gas shipping by April 1959? Would it be relevant whether management knew of the union's organizational efforts when it announced this decision?

b. In the *NLRB v. Adkins Transfer Co.* case on which the *Lassing* court relied, the company met with Teamsters Union representatives twice before announcing its decision to subcontract the work of the truck maintenance and service employees that the Teamsters had just organized. Furthermore, the Teamsters were already the bargaining agent for all of Adkins's truck drivers, and the union had presented and was likely to insist on a uniform contract for the maintenance and service workers to which other companies in the area had agreed. Did the *Adkins Transfer* decision necessarily require the holding in *Lassing*? See generally Cynthia L. Estlund, Economic Rationality and Union Avoidance: Misunderstanding the National Labor Relations Act, 71 Tex. L. Rev. 921 (1993).

## Textile Workers Union v. Darlington Manufacturing Co.
*380 U.S. 263 (1965)*

HARLAN, J. . . .

Darlington Manufacturing Company was a South Carolina corporation operating one textile mill. A majority of Darlington's stock was held by Deering Milliken, a New York "selling house" marketing textiles produced by others. Deering Milliken in turn was controlled by Roger Milliken, president of Darlington, and by other members of the Milliken family. The National Labor Relations Board found that the Milliken family, through Deering Milliken, operated 17 textile manufacturers, including Darlington, whose products, manufactured in 27 different mills, were marketed through Deering Milliken.

In March 1956 petitioner Textile Workers Union initiated an organizational campaign at Darlington which the company resisted vigorously in various ways, including threats to close the mill if the union won a representation election. On September 6, 1956, the union won an election by a narrow margin. When Roger Milliken was advised of the union victory, he decided to call a meeting of the Darlington board of directors to consider closing the mill. Mr. Milliken testified before the Labor Board:

> I felt that as a result of the campaign that had been conducted and the promises and statements made in these letters that had been distributed [favoring unionization], that if before we had had some hope, possible hope of achieving competitive [costs] . . . by taking advantage of new machinery that was being put in, that this hope had diminished as a result of the election because a majority of the employees had voted in favor of the union. . . .

The board of directors met on September 12 and voted to liquidate the corporation, an action which was approved by the stockholders on October 17. The plant ceased operations entirely in November, and all plant machinery and equipment were sold piecemeal at auction in December.

The union filed charges with the Labor Board claiming that Darlington had violated §§8(a)(1) and (3) . . . by closing its plant; and §8(a)(5) by refusing to bargain with the union after the election.[5] The Board, by a divided vote, found that Darlington had been closed because of the anti-union animus of Roger Milliken, and held that to be a violation of §8(a)(3). The Board also found Darlington to be part of a single integrated employer group controlled by the Milliken family through Deering Milliken; therefore Deering Milliken could be held liable for the unfair labor practices of Darlington. Alternatively, since Darlington was a part of the Deering Milliken enterprise, Deering Milliken had violated the Act by closing part of its business for a discriminatory purpose. The Board ordered back pay for all Darlington employees until they obtained substantially equivalent work or were put on preferential hiring lists at the other Deering Milliken mills. Respondent Deering Milliken was ordered to bargain with the union in regard to details of compliance with the Board order. 139 N.L.R.B. 241.

On review, the Court of Appeals, sitting en banc, set aside the order and denied enforcement by a divided vote. The Court of Appeals held that even accepting arguendo the Board's determination that Deering Milliken had the status of a single employer, a company has the absolute right to close out a part or all of its business regardless of anti-union motives. The court therefore did not review the Board's finding that Deering Milliken was a single integrated employer. We granted certiorari to consider the important questions involved. We hold that so far as the Labor Relations Act is concerned, an employer has the absolute right to terminate his entire business for any reason he pleases, but disagree with the Court of Appeals that such right includes the ability to close part of a business no matter what the reason. We conclude that the cause must be remanded to the Board for further proceedings.

Preliminarily it should be observed that both petitioners argue that the Darlington closing violated §8(a)(1) as well as §8(a)(3). . . . We think, however, that the Board was correct in treating the closing only under §8(a)(3).[8] Section 8(a)(1) provides that it is an unfair labor practice for an employer "to interfere with, restrain, or coerce employees in the exercise of"

5. The union asked for a bargaining conference on September 12, 1956 (the day that the board of directors voted to liquidate), but was told to await certification by the Board. The union was certified on October 24, and did meet with Darlington officials in November, but no actual bargaining took place. The Board found this to be a violation of §8(a)(5). Such a finding was in part based on the determination that the plant closing was an unfair labor practice, and no argument is made that §8(a)(5) requires an employer to bargain concerning a purely business decision to terminate his enterprise. Cf. Fibreboard Paper Products Corp. v. Labor Board, 379 U.S. 203.

8. The Board did find that Darlington's discharges of employees following the decision to close violated §8(a)(1). . . .

§7 rights. Naturally, certain business decisions will, to some degree, interfere with concerted activities by employees. But it is only when the interference with §7 rights outweighs the business justification for the employer's action that §8(a)(1) is violated. See, e.g., Labor Board v. Steelworkers, 357 U.S. 357; Republic Aviation Corp. v. Labor Board, 324 U.S. 793. A violation of §8(a)(1) alone therefore presupposes an act which is unlawful even absent a discriminatory motive. Whatever may be the limits of §8(a)(1), some employer decisions are so peculiarly matters of management prerogative that they would never constitute violations of §8(a)(1), whether or not they involved sound business judgment, unless they also violated §8(a)(3). Thus it is not questioned in this case that an employer has the right to terminate his business, whatever the impact of such action on concerted activities, if the decision to close is motivated by other than discriminatory reasons.[10] But such action, if discriminatorily motivated, is encompassed within the literal language of §8(a)(3). We therefore deal with the Darlington closing under that section.

We consider first the argument, advanced by the petitioner union but not by the Board, and rejected by the Court of Appeals, that an employer may not go completely out of business without running afoul of the Labor Relations Act if such action is prompted by a desire to avoid unionization. Given the Board's findings on the issue of motive, acceptance of this contention would carry the day for the Board's conclusion that the closing of this plant was an unfair labor practice, even on the assumption that Darlington is to be regarded as an independent unrelated employer. A proposition that a single businessman cannot choose to go out of business if he wants to would represent such a startling innovation that it should not be entertained without the clearest manifestation of legislative intent or unequivocal judicial precedent so construing the Labor Relations Act. We find neither. . . .

The AFL-CIO suggests in its amicus brief that Darlington's action was similar to a discriminatory lockout, which is prohibited "because designed to frustrate organizational efforts, to destroy or undermine bargaining representation, or to evade the duty to bargain." One of the purposes of the Labor Relations Act is to prohibit the discriminatory use of economic weapons in an effort to obtain future benefits. The discriminatory lockout designed to destroy a union, like a "runaway shop," is a lever which has been used to discourage collective employee activities in the future. But a complete liquidation of a business yields no such future benefit for the employer, if the

---

10. It is also clear that the ambiguous act of closing a plant following the election of a union is not, absent an inquiry into the employer's motive, inherently discriminatory. We are thus not confronted with a situation where the employer "must be held to intend the very consequences which foreseeably and inescapably flow from his actions . . ." (Labor Board v. Erie Resistor Corp., 373 U.S. 221, 228), in which the Board could find a violation of §8(a)(3) without an examination into motive. See Radio Officers v. Labor Board, 347 U.S. 17, 42-43; Teamsters Local 357 v. Labor Board, 365 U.S. 667, 674-676.

termination is bona fide.[14] It may be motivated more by spite against the union than by business reasons, but it is not the type of discrimination which is prohibited by the Act. The personal satisfaction that such an employer may derive from standing on his beliefs and the mere possibility that other employers will follow his example are surely too remote to be considered dangers at which the labor statutes were aimed.[15] Although employees may be prohibited from engaging in a strike under certain conditions, no one would consider it a violation of the Act for the same employees to quit their employment en masse, even if motivated by a desire to ruin the employer. The very permanence of such action would negate any future economic benefit to the employees. The employer's right to go out of business is no different.

We are not presented here with the case of a "runaway shop," whereby Darlington would transfer its work to another plant or open a new plant in another locality to replace its closed plant. Nor are we concerned with a shutdown where the employees, by renouncing the union, could cause the plant to reopen. Such cases would involve discriminatory employer action for the purpose of obtaining some benefit from the employees in the future. We hold here only that when an employer closes his entire business, even if the liquidation is motivated by vindictiveness toward the union, such action is not an unfair labor practice.[20]

While we thus agree with the Court of Appeals that viewing Darlington as an independent employer the liquidation of its business was not an unfair

---

14. The Darlington property and equipment could not be sold as a unit, and were eventually auctioned off piecemeal. We therefore are not confronted with a sale of a going concern, which might present different considerations under §§8(a)(3) and (5). Cf. John Wiley & Sons, Inc. v. Livingston, 376 U.S. 543; Labor Board v. Deena Artware, Inc., 361 U.S. 398.

15. Cf. NLRA §8(c). Different considerations would arise were it made to appear that the closing employer was acting pursuant to some arrangement or understanding with other employers to discourage employee organizational activities in their businesses.

20. Nothing we have said in this opinion would justify an employer's interfering with employee organizational activities by threatening to close his plant, as distinguished from announcing a decision to close already reached by the board of directors or other management authority empowered to make such a decision. We recognize that this safeguard does not wholly remove the possibility that our holding may result in some deterrent effect on organizational activities independent of that arising from the closing itself. An employer may be encouraged to make a definitive decision to close on the theory that its mere announcement before a representation election will discourage the employees from voting for the union, and thus his decision may not have to be implemented. Such a possibility is not likely to occur, however, except in a marginal business; a solidly successful employer is not apt to hazard the possibility that the employees will call his bluff by voting to organize. We see no practical way of eliminating this possible consequence of our holding short of allowing the Board to order an employer who chooses so to gamble with his employees not to carry out his announced intention to close. We do not consider the matter of sufficient significance in the overall labor-management relations picture to require or justify a decision different from the one we have made.

labor practice, we cannot accept the lower court's view that the same conclusion necessarily follows if Darlington is regarded as an integral part of the Deering Milliken enterprise.

The closing of an entire business, even though discriminatory, ends the employer-employee relationship; the force of such a closing is entirely spent as to that business when termination of the enterprise takes place. On the other hand, a discriminatory partial closing may have repercussions on what remains of the business, affording employer leverage for discouraging the free exercise of §7 rights among remaining employees of much the same kind as that found to exist in the "runaway shop" and "temporary closing" cases. . . . Moreover, a possible remedy open to the Board in such a case, like remedies available in the "runaway shop" and "temporary closing" cases, is to order reinstatement of the discharged employees in the other parts of the business. No such remedy is available when an entire business has been terminated. By analogy to those cases involving a continuing enterprise we are constrained to hold, in disagreement with the Court of Appeals, that a partial closing is an unfair labor practice under §8(a)(3) if motivated by a purpose to chill unionism in any of the remaining plants of the single employer and if the employer may reasonably have foreseen that such closing would likely have that effect.

While we have spoken in terms of a "partial closing" in the context of the Board's finding that Darlington was part of a larger single enterprise controlled by the Milliken family, we do not mean to suggest that an organizational integration of plants or corporations is a necessary prerequisite to the establishment of such a violation of §8(a)(3). If the persons exercising control over a plant that is being closed for antiunion reasons (1) have an interest in another business, whether or not affiliated with or engaged in the same line of commercial activity as the closed plant, of sufficient substantiality to give promise of their reaping a benefit from the discouragement of unionization in that business; (2) act to close their plant with the purpose of producing such a result; and (3) occupy a relationship to the other business which makes it realistically foreseeable that its employees will fear that such business will also be closed down if they persist in organizational activities, we think that an unfair labor practice has been made out.

Although the Board's single employer finding necessarily embraced findings as to Roger Milliken and the Milliken family which, if sustained by the Court of Appeals, would satisfy the elements of "interest" and "relationship" with respect to other parts of the Deering Milliken enterprise, that and the other Board findings fall short of establishing the factors of "purpose" and "effect" which are vital requisites of the general principles that govern a case of this kind.

Thus, the Board's findings as to the purpose and foreseeable effect of the Darlington closing pertained *only* to its impact on the Darlington employees. No findings were made as to the purpose and effect of the closing with respect to the employees in the other plants comprising the Deering Milliken group. It does not suffice to establish the unfair labor practice charged here to argue that the Darlington closing necessarily had an adverse impact upon unionization in such other plants. We have heretofore observed that employer action which has a foreseeable consequence of discouraging concerted activities generally does not amount to a violation of §8(a)(3) in the absence of a showing of motivation which is aimed at achieving the prohibited effect. In an area which trenches so closely upon otherwise legitimate employer prerogatives, we consider the absence of Board findings on this score a fatal defect in its decision. The Court of Appeals for its part did not deal with the question of purpose and effect at all, since it concluded that an employer's right to close down his entire business because of distaste for unionism, also embraced a partial closing so motivated.

Apart from this, the Board's holding should not be accepted or rejected without court review of its single employer finding, judged, however, in accordance with the general principles set forth above. . . .

[On remand, the ALJ concluded that the evidence did not establish a violation under the Court's tests. In rejecting that conclusion, the Board relied on Roger Milliken's anti-union speeches to Kiwanis clubs and other non-employee groups and stated that the legislative background of §8(c) indicated that it "left unrestricted the Board's right to consider employer statements for purposes for which they ordinarily would be admissible in courts of law." The Board's order was enforced (5-2) by the Court of Appeals for the Fourth Circuit sitting en banc; in January 1969, the Supreme Court denied the company's request to review the decision. Darlington Mfg. Co. v. NLRB, 397 F.2d 760 (4th Cir. 1968), cert. denied, 393 U.S. 1023 (1969). The back pay phase of *Darlington* began in the early 1970s, involved 400 hearing days spread over a period of years, and produced a record that reached 37,000 pages. In December 1980, the NLRB's General Counsel announced the company's agreement to his proposed back pay settlement of $5,000,000, which the affected employees also approved. See generally NLRB Office of the General Counsel, Release No. 1625, Dec. 3, 1980; Patricia E. Eames, The History of the Litigation of *Darlington* as an Exercise in Administrative Procedure, 5 U. Tol. L. Rev. 595 (1974).]

## *NOTES AND QUESTIONS*

**1. Does §8(a)(3) Always Require Anti-Union Motivation?** Note Justice Harlan's assertion that "employer action which has a foreseeable consequence of discouraging concerted activities generally does not amount to a violation of §8(a)(3) in the absence of a showing of motivation which is aimed at achieving the prohibited effect." In an omitted footnote, Justice Harlan cited *Radio Officers*, supra p. 127, as support. Is this a correct reading of *Radio Officers*?

**2. Why Was §8(a)(1) Inapplicable?** Do you understand Justice Harlan's reason for treating the *Darlington* case only under §8(a)(3)? Is this because for certain major employer decisions the balancing of interests contemplated by §8(a)(1) must always favor the employer's interests, unless the typically strong legitimate reasons for such decisions are impeached by proof of illegitimate anti-union motivation? Does this at least in part also explain the approach of the *Lassing* court? Does the Court offer guidance to help the Board determine which employer decisions are "so peculiarly matters of management prerogative that they would never constitute violations of §8(a)(1) . . . unless they also violated §8(a)(3)"?

**3. Why Are Discriminatory Total Shutdowns Beyond the Reach of §8(a)(3)?** What is the justification for Justice Harlan's conclusion that an employer does not commit an unfair labor practice by closing its entire business, "even if the liquidation is motivated by vindictiveness toward the union"? Are not all the elements of §8(a)(3) satisfied? Consider the following:

a. *No "Future Benefit?"* Why does the Court require some showing of possible "future benefit" to the employer? Does the encouragement/discouragement element of §8(a)(3) require some future benefit to the employer? Can the possibility of "future benefit" ever be ruled out even in the case of total shutdown given the ability of the owners of the shutdown enterprise to invest in other companies and perhaps derive some reputational benefit from being known as "tough on unions"?

b. *No Effective Remedy?* Do remedial considerations drive this portion of the *Darlington* decision? Even if, as the Court suggests, the Board would find it difficult to require companies to stay in business against their will, is there any reason why the back pay claims of employees who lose their jobs as a result of a discriminatory shutdown cannot be assessed against the assets of the business in any liquidation proceeding?

c. *Fear of Error Costs?* What do you make of the suggestion in footnote 15 as well as the sentence to which it is attached? Are employers being accorded virtually unlimited discretion to shut down totally to avoid the risk that the Board will make faulty findings of anti-union motives concerning decisions that the Court believes are unlikely to be animated by such considerations?

**4. Threatened Total Shutdowns.** How does the Court in footnote 20 qualify an employer's ability to threaten to shut down its business? Why does it do so? Given the relative costs of threats and actual closures, is it more likely that an employer will threaten to close for a vindictive anti-union reason than that it will actually close?

Is the line drawn in footnote 20 between threats and decisions already arrived at the right one? In many situations, businesses will not lightly announce decisions to close. However, given the prospect that an announced contingent decision to close might dissuade employees from voting for the union, will there be situations where a contingent shutdown decision is made for entirely strategic purposes, with an expectation of retraction if the employees actually do choose the union? Yet would the prohibition of all announcements of an intent to close deprive employees of critical information given the fact that actual closures are not illegal?

**5. Partial Shutdowns: Why Require Proof of a Motive to Chill Rights Elsewhere?** Why does the *Darlington* Court hold that partial closures should be treated differently than total closures? Why does it require proof that the employer was motivated by "a purpose to chill unionism" in any of the remaining parts of its business, as well as proof of the reasonable foreseeability of such a chilling effect? In view of the purposes of the statutory scheme, why isn't it sufficient that the discriminatory shutdown is likely to discourage future interest in unionization bids by employees of the facility that is shut down?

**6. Is the Motive to Chill Rights Elsewhere Always Present?** Is it likely that an employer would shut down a plant in order to rid itself of a union unless it was reasonably foreseeable that the shutdown would chill further union organization at other plants in which the employer had a substantial interest? Might an employer who does not anticipate organizing drives at its other facilities simply be seeking to avoid the costs of dealing with the union at the particular facility undergoing an organizing effort? Or be seeking a reputation as a union-free employer, thereby avoiding the spread of unionization at other facilities even if an organizing drive at those facilities is not imminent or reasonably foreseeable?

**7. Applicability of *Darlington* to Decisions Other Than Plant Shutdowns?** Is the Court's "chill rights elsewhere" test limited to plant shutdowns? Does *Darlington* suggest that the Board should have to present some special proof that the discharge of an employee for union organizing chilled organizational efforts by other employees? In *Lassing*, would it have been sufficient for the General Counsel to prove that the company decided to subcontract its gas shipping because it did not want to deal with the union, irrespective of any concerns about the costs of the shipping operation, or would the Board have had to prove that the company wanted to chill union efforts by its remaining employees? See George Lithograph Co., 204 N.L.R.B. 431 (1973) (motivation to have chilling effect on remaining employees may be reasonably inferred without direct proof where general anti-union motive is shown and discharged employees worked in same plant and under same management as other employees). Should *Darlington*'s holding govern an employer's decision to transfer work from a recently unionized plant to a nonunion plant, such that the General Counsel would have to prove an intent to chill unions at the nonunion transferee plant rather than just at the unionized transferor plant? See Local 57, International Ladies Garment Workers Union v. NLRB (Garwin Corp.), 374 F.2d 295 (D.C. Cir. 1967); Lear Siegler, Inc., 295 N.L.R.B. 857 (1989) (Board's view is that *Darlington* is not applicable to discriminatory relocation of work or subcontracting).

**8. "Runaway Shops": Remedial Considerations.** In "runaway shop" cases, if the Board does find sufficient anti-union motivation to support an unfair labor practice, should it routinely order the employer to reopen a closed plant? What if the plant and its machinery have already been sold? Can the Board order the employer to recognize the union as the bargaining representative at the new plant? Should the remedy depend on proof that the employer was trying to chill unionization at the transferee plant? That it did chill unionization there? Is a bargaining order at the new plant proper without proof that a majority of the employees there want to be represented by that particular union? See also infra page 325. Does the difficulty in fashioning an ex post remedy suggest that the Board should readily seek (and the district courts should readily grant) preliminary injunctive relief under §10(j) of the Act? See infra page 328.

**9. The Duty to Bargain and "Entrepreneurial Decisions."** Does the *Darlington* Court hold in footnote 5 that the company had no duty to bargain over the decision to close the plant? See page 162 supra. The duty to bargain over "entrepreneurial" decisions such as plant closings is taken up in Chapter 6, infra pages 475-496.

## C. THE SCOPE OF PROTECTED EMPLOYEE ACTIVITY

In the cases treated earlier in this chapter there was no question of §7's coverage of the activity that the employer allegedly subjected to discrimination or restraint. Union affiliation or organizational activity and striking to achieve bargaining goals are at the core of §7. Section 7, however, grants employees not only the right to "self-organization, to form, join or assist labor organizations, [and] to bargain through representatives of their own choosing," but also the right to "engage in *other concerted activities* for the purpose of collective bargaining or *other mutual aid or protection.*" NLRA §7 (emphases added). This section explores this latter part of §7 and the three elements thereof: concert, object or purpose, and means. The first two of these elements stem directly from the language of §7 itself. The means test, however, was read into the statute by the Board and the courts.

## 1. "Protected" Concerted Activity: Means Test

**NLRB v. Washington Aluminum Co.**
*370 U.S. 9 (1962)*

Mr. Justice Black delivered the opinion of the Court.

The Court of Appeals for the Fourth Circuit, with Chief Judge Sobeloff dissenting, refused to enforce an order of the National Labor Relations Board directing the respondent Washington Aluminum Company to reinstate and make whole seven employees whom the company had discharged for leaving their work in the machine shop without permission on claims that the shop was too cold to work in.[1] . . . The machine shop in which the seven discharged employees worked was not insulated and had a number of doors to the outside that had to be opened frequently. An oil furnace located in an adjoining building was the chief source of heat for the shop, although there were two gas-fired space heaters that contributed heat to a lesser extent. The heat produced by these units was not always satisfactory and, even prior to the day of the walkout involved here, several of the eight machinists who made up the day shift at the shop had complained from time to time to the company's foreman "over the cold working conditions."

January 5, 1959, was an extraordinarily cold day for Baltimore, with unusually high winds and a low temperature of 11 degrees followed by a high of 22. When the employees on the day shift came to work that morning, they found the shop bitterly cold, due not only to the unusually harsh weather, but also to the fact that the large oil furnace had broken down

1. The Court of Appeals also refused to enforce another Board order requiring the respondent company to bargain collectively with the Industrial Union of Marine & Shipbuilding Workers of America, AFL-CIO, as the certified bargaining representative of its employees. Since the Union's status as majority bargaining representative turns on the ballots cast in the Board election by four of the seven discharged employees, the enforceability of that order depends upon the validity of the discharges being challenged in the principal part of the case. Our decision on the discharge question will therefore also govern the refusal-to-bargain issue.

the night before and had not as yet been put back into operation. As the workers gathered in the shop just before the starting hour of 7:30, one of them, a Mr. Caron, went into the office of Mr. Jarvis, the foreman, hoping to warm himself but, instead, found the foreman's quarters as uncomfortable as the rest of the shop. As Caron and Jarvis sat in Jarvis' office discussing how bitingly cold the building was, some of the other machinists walked by the office window "huddled" together in a fashion that caused Jarvis to exclaim that "[i]f those fellows had any guts at all, they would go home." When the starting buzzer sounded a few moments later, Caron walked back to his working place in the shop and found all the other machinists "huddled there, shaking a little, cold." Caron then said to these workers, ". . . Dave [Jarvis] told me if we had any guts, we would go home. . . . I am going home, it is too damned cold to work." Caron asked the other workers what they were going to do and, after some discussion among themselves, they decided to leave with him. One of these workers, testifying before the Board, summarized their entire discussion this way: "And we had all got together and thought it would be a good idea to go home; maybe we could get some heat brought into the plant that way." As they started to leave, Jarvis approached and persuaded one of the workers to remain at the job. But Caron and the other six workers on the day shift left practically in a body in a matter of minutes after the 7:30 buzzer.

On these facts the Board found that the conduct of the workers was a concerted activity to protest the company's failure to supply adequate heat in its machine shop, that such conduct is protected under the provision of §7 of the National Labor Relations Act . . . and that the discharge of these workers by the company amounted to an unfair labor practice under §8(a)(1) of the Act. . . .

In denying enforcement of this order, the majority of the Court of Appeals took the position that because the workers simply "summarily left their place of employment" without affording the company an "opportunity to avoid the work stoppage by granting a concession to a demand," their walkout did not amount to a concerted activity protected by §7 of the Act. . . .

We cannot agree that employees necessarily lose their right to engage in concerted activities under §7 merely because they do not present a specific demand upon their employer to remedy a condition they find objectionable. The language of §7 is broad enough to protect concerted activities whether they take place before, after, or at the same time such a demand is made. To compel the Board to interpret and apply that language in the restricted fashion suggested by the respondent here would only tend to frustrate the policy of the Act to protect the right of workers to act together to better their working conditions. Indeed, as indicated by this very case, such an interpretation of §7 might place burdens upon employees so great that it would effectively nullify the right to engage in concerted activities which that section protects. The seven employees here were part of a small group of employees who were wholly unorganized. They had no bargaining representative and, in fact, no representative of any kind to present their grievances to their employer. Under these circumstances, they had to speak for themselves as best they could. As pointed out above, prior to the day they left the shop, several of them had repeatedly complained to company officials about the cold working conditions in the shop. . . .

. . . Having no bargaining representative and no established procedure by which they could take full advantage of their unanimity of opinion in negotiations with the company, the men took the most direct course to let the company know that they wanted a warmer place in which to work. So, after talking among themselves, they walked out together in the hope that this action might spotlight their complaint and bring about some improvement in what they considered to be the "miserable" conditions of their employment. This we think was enough to justify the Board's holding that they were not required to make any more specific demand than they did to be entitled to the protection of §7.

Although the company contends to the contrary, we think that the walkout involved here did grow out of a "labor dispute" within the plain meaning of the definition of that term in §2(9) of the Act, which declares that it includes "any controversy concerning terms, tenure or *conditions of employment*. . . ." The fact that the company was already making every effort to repair the furnace and bring heat into the shop that morning does not change the nature of the controversy that caused the walkout. At the very most, that fact might tend to indicate that the conduct of the men in leaving was unnecessary and unwise, and it has long been settled that the reasonableness of workers' decisions to engage in concerted activity is irrelevant to the determination of whether a labor dispute exists or not. Moreover, the evidence here shows that the conduct of these workers was far from unjustified under the circumstances. The company's own foreman expressed the opinion that the shop was so cold that the men should go home. This statement by the foreman but emphasizes the obvious — that is, that the conditions of coldness about which complaint had been made before had been so aggravated on the day of the walkout that the concerted action of the men in leaving their jobs seemed like a perfectly natural and reasonable thing to do.

It is of course true that §7 does not protect all concerted activities, but that aspect of the section is not involved in this case. The activities engaged in here do not fall within the normal categories of unprotected concerted activities such as those that are unlawful,[14] violent[15] or in breach of contract.[16] Nor can they be brought under this Court's more recent pronouncement which denied the protection of §7 to activities characterized as "indefensible" because they were there found to show a disloyalty to the workers' employer which this Court deemed unnecessary to carry on the

14. Southern Steamship Co. v. Labor Board, 316 U.S. 31.
15. Labor Board v. Fansteel Metallurgical Corp., 306 U.S. 240.
16. Labor Board v. Sands Manufacturing Co., 306 U.S. 332.

workers' legitimate concerted activities.[17] The activities of these seven employees cannot be classified as "indefensible" by any recognized standard of conduct. Indeed, concerted activities by employees for the purpose of trying to protect themselves from working conditions as uncomfortable as the testimony and Board findings showed them to be in this case are unquestionably activities to correct conditions which modern labor-management legislation treats as too bad to have to be tolerated in a humane and civilized society like ours.

### *Note: Categorical Limitations on the Means Employed*

*Washington Aluminum* lists certain means that are generally considered impermissible, and thus will remove concerted activity from §7 protection.

**Unlawful Activity**. The NLRA does not protect conduct that is illegal under the Act itself, such as union conduct barred by §8(b), or under other federal laws, such as the federal criminal anti-mutiny provisions violated in the *Southern Steamship* case cited in *Washington Aluminum.* Nor does it protect concerted efforts to compel an employer to violate the Act or another federal law. See, e.g., American News Co., Inc., 55 N.L.R.B. 1302 (1944) (strike aimed at forcing employer to grant wage increase in violation of federal wage and price control law unprotected).

In contrast, activity that is unlawful under state law is not automatically removed from §7 protection because, as discussed in Chapter 11, state laws that restrict activity protected by the NLRA or the Railway Labor Act are preempted by those federal laws. Nonetheless, because Congress is considered to have drafted the NLRA against a backdrop of general state criminal and tort laws, some concerted activity that violates state laws protecting property and reputation, for instance, will be deemed unprotected under the Act.

**Violent Activity**. Actual or threatened violence against persons is also a ground for excluding concerted activity from §7 protection. However, the Board has recognized that "the right to strike . . . would be unduly jeopardized if any misconduct, without regard for [its] seriousness . . . , would deprive the employee of [statutory protections]." Coronet Casuals, 207 N.L.R.B. 304, 305 (1973). Under Clear Pine Mouldings, Inc., 268 N.L.R.B. 1044 (1984), enforced, 765 F.2d 148 (9th Cir. 1985), strike-related misconduct will result in loss of the Act's protections where the conduct "may reasonably tend to coerce or intimidate [other] employees in the exercise of [their] rights . . . under the Act"—an objective test that does

17. Labor Board v. Local Union No. 1229, International Brotherhood of Electrical Workers (Jefferson Standard), 346 U.S. 464, 477.

not require inquiry into whether any particular employee was in fact coerced or intimidated. See Mohawk Liqueur Co., 300 N.L.R.B. 1075 (1990). *Clear Pine* holds that even verbal threats unaccompanied by any physical gestures may be unprotected. For further discussion of the consequences of strike misconduct, see infra page 533.

The Court in *Washington Aluminum* cited the *Fansteel* case as an example of unprotected violent activity. The case involved a "sit down" strike that became violent after the employees discharged the strikers and called in the state police to remove them from the property. The *Fansteel* decision makes clear that the "sit down" was illegal under state law and because it involved a seizure of the employer's property and presumably would have been unprotected even if further violence had not pursed. The Board's principal argument in that case, rejected by the Court, was that the employer's unfair labor practices had precipitated the sit-down strike. See Henry M. Hart & E.F. Pritchard, The *Fansteel* Case: Employee Misconduct and the Remedial Powers of the National Labor Relations Board (1939). In a related vein, walkouts that threaten physical damages to the employer's property have been held unprotected. See, e.g., Marshall Car Wheel & Foundry Co., 218 F.2d 409 (5th Cir. 1955) (walkout unprotected where employees left molten iron in the cupola, which could have resulted in significant damage).

**Breach of Contract.** The third basis noted in *Washington Aluminum* for excluding concerted employee activity from §7 protection is a contractual breach. Here the Court cited NLRB v. Sands Mfg. Co., 306 U.S. 332 (1938), which involved the discharge of employees for refusing to do assigned work as required by the terms of their collective bargaining agreement. The Board and the courts generally have considered contractual commitments by unions not to engage in certain protected activity, including strikes, during the term of a collective agreement to constitute what amounts to an effective waiver of represented employees' §7 right. See, e.g., NLRB v. Rockaway News Supply Co., 345 U.S. 71 (1953) (no-strike clause renders concerted strike unprotected). However, there are limits on the union's ability to waive all of the §7 rights of the employees whom they represent. See pp. 210-219 infra.

**"Indefensible" or "Disloyal" Conduct?** The *Washington Aluminum* opinion also noted that §7 does not protect activities "characterized as 'indefensible' because they were found to show a disloyalty to the workers' employer which this Court deemed unnecessary to carry on the workers' legitimate concerted activities." 370 U.S. at 17. Here, the Court was referring to the *Jefferson Standard* case, excerpted infra at page 177.

## *NOTES AND QUESTIONS*

**1. Relevance of "Reasonableness" of Employees' Walkout?** Note that the employees' conduct in *Washington Aluminum* did not fall within any of the prohibited categories discussed in the Note above. Thus, the Court had to decide whether it should be deemed unprotected for some other reason. The court of appeals had ruled that the employees' conduct was unprotected because they did not present any demand to their employer before walking out, and hence gave the employer no chance to remedy the situation. The Supreme Court, however, reversed. Why did the Court deem such a demand unnecessary in this context? The Court also found it irrelevant that the employer was making "every effort" to repair the furnace and get heat into the shop at the time of the walkout. Did the Court hold that the reasonableness of the employees' act was irrelevant in determining whether that conduct was protected? What is the import of the Court's statement that the employees' act was "far from unjustified" after it had established that reasonableness was not relevant?

The Board generally extends protection to isolated spontaneous employee walkouts without assessing whether the employees' response was reasonable or proportional to the employer conduct being protested. See, e.g., QSI, Inc., 346 N.L.R.B. 1117 (2006); Accel, Inc., 338 N.L.R.B. 1052 (2003); Triad Management Corp., 287 N.L.R.B. 1239 (1988). Several courts of appeals, however, have held in cases involving nonunion employee protests over the termination of supervisors that the reasonableness of the protests must be considered. See, e.g., Smithfield Packing Co. v. NLRB, 510 F.3d 507 (4th Cir. 2007) (concluding that *Washington Aluminum's* rejection of reasonableness was *dicta* and otherwise inapplicable to the special circumstance of personnel decisions regarding supervisors); Bob Evans Farms, Inc. v. NLRB, 163 F.3d 1012, 1022-1023 (7th Cir. 1998) (also a protest regarding the identity of the supervisor; concluding, without directly distinguishing *Washington Aluminum's* apparent rejection of a reasonableness test, that a failure to consider reasonableness in supervisor termination cases would contradict "the objectives of industrial harmony" and would give employees "liberty to resort to the most disruptive form of industrial action to protest even a trivial grievance over working conditions."). See page 190 note 7 infra for further treatment of whether protests related to personnel decisions involving supervisors or managers fall within the scope of §7.

**2. Relevance of Spontaneous Protesters' Refusal to Leave Premises?** Even if the *Washington Aluminum* holding does not contemplate a general "reasonableness" or "proportionality" limitation on the protection of spontaneous employee walkouts, does it allow other limitations on the scope of protection of spontaneous protests? For instance, can an employer discharge employees for refusing to leave its premises after spontaneously walking off the job? Should it matter whether the employees refuse to leave a work area or instead congregate in a nonwork area? Whether the employer has offered to meet with them to discuss their grievances? The Board has treated the refusal to leave an employer's premises differently than walking off the job and off the employer's property. For instance, in Quietflex Manufacturing Co., 344 N.L.R.B. 1055 (2005), the Board found unprotected the refusal of 83 nonunion Hispanic-surnamed employees to leave the employer's parking lot for 12 hours after walking off work in protest of their pay being lower than that of Vietnamese coworkers. The employer had warned them twice that they had to leave or return to work and had offered to discuss their complaints with them. The Board held that an employer may insist that employee protesters leave its property, including nonwork areas, after a reasonable period of time that varies, inter alia, with the purpose and disruptive impact of the protest.

**3. Concerted Activity by Non-Union Workers**. *Washington Aluminum* would seem to stand for the proposition that activity may be protected by §7, regardless of whether it is intended to lead to unionization or collective bargaining. Could §7 have been interpreted to protect only union-led protests? Would such a limit be consistent with the Section's protection of the right to "self-organization" as something independent of the right to "form, join, or assist labor organizations"? Can an outside tribunal, in any event, ever be certain that protest activity will not lead ultimately to organization and collective bargaining? Consider, for instance, footnote 1 in the *Washington Aluminum* opinion. Chapter 14 will discuss the NLRA's protection of employee participation in "worker centers" and other non-traditional worker groups, which sometimes focus on workplace issues but often do not attempt to acquire bargaining authority under the NLRA.

**4. Partial or Intermittent Strike vs. Full Work Stoppages.** The Board, without judicial dissent, has declined to find partial or intermittent strikes or work slowdowns protected under the Act. See, e.g., Yale University, 330 N.L.R.B. 246 (1999); Elk Lumber Co., 91 N.L.R.B. 333 (1950). Such partial work stoppages are considered an interference with the employer's ability to control its property. In *Elk Lumber* the Board stated: "the objective of the carloaders' concerted activity—to induce the Respondent to increase their hourly rate of pay or to return to the piecework rate—was a lawful one. To achieve this objective, however, they adopted the plan of decreasing their production to the amount they considered adequate for the pay they were then receiving. In effect, this constituted a refusal on their part to accept the terms of employment set by their employer without engaging in a stoppage, but to continue rather to work on their own terms. . . ." *Elk Lumber Co.*, 91 N.L.R.B. at 337. In the *Yale* case, 200 graduate teaching fellows went on a "grade strike" in mid-December, refusing to submit students' final grades to the university while at the same time continuing to perform other duties such as meeting with students, writing letters of recommendation, and preparing for the next term's classes. The Board found that since the teaching fellows were both working and striking at the same time, their conduct was a "partial strike" unprotected by §7.

Even if it is assumed that partial work stoppages or slowdowns interfere more significantly with employer property interests than do full work stoppages or strikes, should the former be categorically excluded from §7 protection, or should the Board still have authority to determine whether an employer's response to partial strike activity exceeded what was needed to meet its legitimate concerns in maintaining operations? See generally Craig Becker, "Better Than a Strike": Protecting New Forms of Collective Work Stoppages Under the National Labor Relations Act, 61 U. Chi. L. Rev. 351 (1994); Samuel Estreicher, Strikers and Replacements, 3 Lab. Law. 897 (1987); Julius G. Getman, The Protected Status of Partial Strikes After *Lodge 76*: A Comment, 29 Stan. L. Rev. 205 (1977).

**5. "Condonation."** Despite an employee's unprotected activity, the NLRB may order reinstatement on the basis of the doctrine of "condonation" whereby an employer is held to have waived its rights to discipline if it expressly or impliedly condoned employee misconduct. Claims of condonation have usually arisen in strike situations, typically when an employer invites strikers to return to work without reserving its rights to discipline them for strike misconduct. See, e.g., *Marshall Car Wheel*, supra page 174; White Oak Coal Co., Inc., 295 N.L.R.B. 567 (1989). The Board holds that there must be clear, convincing, and positive evidence that the employer agreed to forgive the unprotected conduct—to "wipe the slate clean"—and that an offer of reinstatement alone, at least before the company completes its investigations, does not constitute such evidence. See, e.g., International Paper Co., 309 N.L.R.B. 31 (1992), enforced sub nom. Local 14, United Paperworkers Intl. Union v. NLRB, 4 F.3d 982 (1st Cir. 1993) (table decision); Fibreboard Corp., 283 N.L.R.B. 1093 (1987).

## NLRB v. Local 1229, IBEW (*Jefferson Standard*)

*346 U.S. 464 (1953)*

[After an impasse in negotiations for a renewal agreement with the Jefferson Standard Broadcasting Co., members of Local 1229, which represented 22 television technicians, engaged in the activities described below.]

Burton, J.

July 9, 1949, the union began daily peaceful picketing of the company's station. Placards and handbills on the picket line charged the company with unfairness to its technicians and emphasized the company's refusal to renew the provision for arbitration of discharges. The placards and handbills named the union as the representative of the WBT technicians. The employees did not strike. They confined their respective tours of picketing to their off-duty hours and continued to draw full pay. There was no violence or threat of violence and no one has taken exception to any of the above conduct.

But on August 24, 1949, a new procedure made its appearance. Without warning, several of its technicians launched a vitriolic attack on the quality of the company's television broadcasts. Five thousand handbills were printed over the designation "WBT Technicians." These were distributed on the picket line, on the public square two or three blocks from the company's premises, in barber shops, restaurants and busses. Some were mailed to local businessmen. The handbills made no reference to the union, to a labor controversy or to collective bargaining. They read:

**Is Charlotte a Second-Class City?**

> You might think so from the kind of Television programs being presented by the Jefferson Standard Broadcasting Co. over WBTV. Have you seen one of their television programs lately? Did you know that all the programs presented over WBTV are on film and may be from one day to five years old. There are no local programs presented by WBTV. You cannot receive the local baseball games, football games or other local events because WBTV does not have the proper equipment to make these pickups. Cities like New York, Boston, Philadelphia, Washington receive such programs nightly. Why doesn't the Jefferson Standard Broadcasting Company purchase the needed equipment to bring you the same type of programs enjoyed by other leading American cities? Could it be that they consider Charlotte a second-class community and only entitled to the pictures now being presented to them?
>
> WBT Technicians

This attack continued until September 3, 1949, when the company discharged ten of its technicians, whom it charged with sponsoring or distributing these handbills.

In its essence, the issue is simple. It is whether these employees, whose contracts of employment had expired, were discharged "for cause." They were discharged solely because at a critical time in the initiation of the company's television service, they sponsored or distributed 5,000 handbills making a sharp, public, disparaging attack upon the quality of the company's product and its business policies, in a manner reasonably calculated to harm the company's reputation and reduce its income. . . .

The company . . . interpreted the handbill as a demonstration of such detrimental disloyalty as to provide "cause" for its refusal to continue in its employ the perpetrators of the attack. We agree.

Section 10(c) of the Taft-Hartley Act expressly provides that: "No order of the Board shall require the reinstatement of any individual as an employee who has been suspended or discharged, or the payment to him of any back pay, if such individual was suspended or discharged for cause." There is no more elemental cause for discharge of an employee than disloyalty to his employer. . . .

Assuming that there had been no pending labor controversy, the conduct of the "WBT TECHNICIANS" from August 24 through September 3 unquestionably would have provided adequate cause for their disciplinary discharge within the meaning of §10(c). Their attack related itself to no labor practice of the company. It made no reference to wages, hours or working conditions. The policies attacked were those of finance and public relations for which management, not technicians, must be responsible. The attack asked for no public sympathy or support. It was a continuing attack, initiated while off duty, upon the very interests which the attackers were being paid to conserve and develop. Nothing could be further from the purpose of the Act than to require an employer to finance such activities. Nothing would contribute less to the Act's declared purpose of promoting industrial peace and stability.

The fortuity of the coexistence of a labor dispute affords these technicians no substantial defense. While they were also union men and leaders in the labor controversy, they took pains to separate those categories. In contrast to their claims on the picket line as to the labor controversy, their handbill of August 24 omitted all reference to it. The handbill diverted attention from the labor controversy. It attacked public policies of the company which had no discernible relation to that controversy. The only connection between the handbill and the labor controversy was an ultimate and undisclosed purpose or motive on the part of some of the sponsors that, by the hoped-for financial pressure, the attack might extract from the company some future concession. A disclosure of that motive might have lost more public support for the employees than it would have gained, for it would have given the handbill more the character of coercion than of collective bargaining. Referring to the attack, the Board said "In our judgment, these tactics, in the circumstances of this case, were hardly less "indefensible' than acts of physical sabotage." 94 N.L.R.B., at 1511. In any event, the findings of the Board effectively separate the attack from the labor controversy and treat it solely as one made by the company's technical experts upon the quality of the company's product. As such, it was as adequate a cause for the discharge of its sponsors as if the labor controversy had not been pending. The technicians, themselves, so handled their attack as thus to bring their discharge under §10(c).

The Board stated "We . . . do not decide whether the disparagement of product involved here would have justified the employer in discharging the employees responsible for it, had it been uttered in the context of a conventional appeal for support of the union in the labor dispute." Id., at 1512, n.18. This underscored the Board's factual conclusion that the attack of August 24 was not part of an appeal for support in the pending dispute. . . .

Frankfurter, J., whom Black and Douglas, JJ., join, dissenting. . . .

[T]he Court, relying on §10(c) which permits discharges "for cause," points to the "disloyalty" of the employees and finds sufficient "cause" regardless of whether the handbill was a "concerted activity" within §7. Section 10(c) does not speak of discharge "for disloyalty." If Congress had so written that section, it would have overturned much of the law that had been developed by the Board and the courts in the twelve years preceding the Taft-Hartley Act. . . . Many of the legally recognized tactics and weapons of labor would readily be condemned for "disloyalty" were they employed between man and man in friendly personal relations. . . .

## *NOTES AND QUESTIONS*

**1. The Nexus Requirement: Connection Between Labor Dispute and Product Disparagement?** During a strike prompted by a bargaining impasse, the company, a paint manufacturer, continued to operate with supervisors. Thereupon, various strikers distributed circulars entitled "Beware Paint Substitute." Those circulars, after referring to the strike, advised customers that the company was not manufacturing paint with "the well-trained, experienced employees who have made the paint you have always bought" and warned that the other paint might peel and crack. The circular concluded with the statement that customers would be told when they could again buy paint made by the company's regular employees. Was the distribution of the circular protected activity? See Patterson Sargent Co., 115 N.L.R.B. 1627 (1956) (holding that is was not).

Later decisions of the Board and courts suggest that *Patterson Sargent* would now be distinguished from *Jefferson Standard* as a case in which a sufficient connection between the labor dispute and the product disparagement was made. See, e.g., Sierra Publishing Co. v. NLRB, 889 F.2d 210, 216 (9th Cir. 1989); NLRB v. Mount Desert Island Hosp., 695 F.2d 634 (1st Cir. 1982); Misericordia Hosp. Medical Ctr. v. NLRB, 623 F.2d 808 (2d Cir. 1980); Mountain Shadows Golf Resort, 330 N.L.R.B. 1238 (2000); SAS Ambulance Serv., Inc., 255 N.L.R.B. 286 (1981); Allied Aviation Serv. Co. of N.J., 248 N.L.R.B. 229, enforced, 636 F.2d 1210 (3d Cir. 1980). Do you think the *Jefferson Standard* case would have, or should have, come out differently had the handbills simply stated that the technicians responsible for their distribution were in a labor dispute with the station?

**2. "Disloyalty"?** Why is disloyalty a sufficient ground for excluding the technicians' product disparagement from the compass of §7? Was the product disparagement unlawful or tortious under state law? Does the employer have some state-law-based right to employee loyalty, analogous to a property right, that must be balanced in the interpretation of §7? If the product disparagement is viewed as an act of insubordination, is this not also true of strikes and union organization drives against the wishes of an employer?

**3. "Bounded Conflict"?** Is the product disparagement in *Jefferson Standard* distinguishable from those in a case like *Patterson Sargent* where the employees' criticisms are tied to the labor dispute and hence will no longer be apt when the dispute is settled? The former disparagement can be said to threaten the long-term success of the enterprise in which the employer and employees are both engaged, while the latter, like a strike, may harm the company in the short run but is consistent with a continuation of the relationship at the strike's end. See Estreicher, Strikers and Replacements, supra. See also Jimmy John's & Indus. Workers of the World, 361 N.L.R.B. No. 27 (2014) (public statements that sandwich shop workers did not receive sick days and that this policy had implications for food safety were tied to the labor dispute over sick days and not disloyal enough to lose protection); Endicott Interconnect Technologies, Inc. v. NLRB, 453 F.3d 532 (D.C. Cir. 2006) (vacating Board's order because it protected "disloyal" employee who charged management with causing business to be "tanked" and allowing "gaping holes" and "voids in the critical knowledge base" after layoffs); Diamond Walnut Growers, Inc. v. NLRB, 113 F.3d 1259, 1267 (D.C. Cir. 1997) (en banc) (suggesting that damage to company's business due to "visceral fear" created in public mind by strikers' campaign claiming that "scab"-packaged walnuts were contaminated with "mold, dirt, oil, worms and debris" would not be eliminated by settlement of strike). Reconsider this notion of reciprocal loyalty and "bounded conflict" after the treatment below of employer countermeasures to strikes, including the legality of hiring permanent replacements for strikers. See 522-536 infra.

**4. "Scurrilous" Disparagement?** Should product disparagement that is related to a labor controversy ever be unprotected because of the sharp or vituperative tone of its criticism? See, e.g., Coca Cola Bottling Works, Inc., 186 N.L.R.B 1050, 1054 (1970), modified on other grounds sub nom. Retail, Wholesale & Dep't Store Union v. NLRB, 466 F.2d 380 (D.C. Cir. 1972) (distribution of leaflets warning public of roaches and dead mice in soda bottles while an inadequate number of stop-gap employees did inspections during strike); American Arbitration Ass'n, 233 N.L.R.B. 71, 75 (1977) (sending questionnaire to lawyer-clients "mention[ing] dogs and other animals in the same breath as lawyers and insurance adjusters"). See also *Diamond Walnut,* cited supra note 3, 113 F.3d at 1267 & n.8.

**5. False Disparagement?** Should product disparagement that is related to a labor dispute lose its protection because it includes false claims? What if the false claims are made maliciously, that is with knowledge of their falsity or with reckless disregard of their accuracy? The Board applies an intentionally or recklessly false standard. See, e.g., Simplex Wire & Cable Co., 313 N.L.R.B. 1311 (1994); see also, e.g., Joliff v. NLRB, 513 F.3d 600 (6th Cir. 2008); NLRB v. Cement Transp., Inc., 490 F.2d 1024 (6th Cir. 1974) (both finding maliciously false standard not met; comments protected). Cf. Old Dominion Branch No. 496, Nat'l Ass'n of Letter Carriers v. Austin, 418 U.S. 264 (1974) (protecting from state libel law action rhetoric in union organizing campaign that is not deliberately or recklessly false).

**6. Application to Social Media?** Does the *Jefferson Standard* doctrine apply in the same way to social media postings to, say, Facebook "friends," as it does to employee communications directed to customers and the general public? Is the reputational harm to companies less direct and more attenuated? See Triple Play Sports Bar and Grille, 361 N.L.R.B. No. 31, at 4 (2014) (applying *Jefferson Standard* doctrine to "employees' off-duty, offsite use of social media").

**7. Reach of "Disloyalty" Rationale Beyond Product Disparagement?** Does *Jefferson Standard*'s "disloyalty" rationale have any application to cases not involving product disparagement? Employees generally have a common law duty of loyalty to their employer, the breach of which can be a basis for employer discharge or other discipline. See generally Restatement of Employment Law §8.01. Can the duty of loyalty provide a basis for excluding certain kinds of strikes from §7 protection? What about a sudden strike by restaurant workers responsible for placing perishable products under refrigeration, or a sudden strike by employees assembling the sections of a Sunday newspaper? Or a strike against a department store during the Christmas shopping season? Would excluding protection in such cases be consistent with §7's affirmative protection of the right to engage in concerted activity even where it leads to economic losses to the employer?

**8. Union "Corporate Campaigns."** The *Jefferson Standard* doctrine has become increasingly important as unions have attempted to gain leverage with particular employers by directing economic pressure or other appeals to the employer's suppliers, creditors, or customers. These appeals sometimes involve disparagement of the target employer's products, services, or financial condition. See generally Melinda J. Branscomb, Labor, Loyalty, and the Corporate Campaign, 73 B.U. L. Rev. 291 (1993); Jarol B. Manheim, The Death of a Thousand Cuts: Corporate Campaigns and the Attack on the Corporation (2000). The relevance of §8(b)(4) to such appeals is treated infra pages 608-623.

## 2. "Protected" Concerted Activity: Purpose or Object Test

**Eastex, Inc. v. NLRB**
*437 U.S. 556 (1978)*

Powell, J. . . .

[Petitioner] manufacturers paper products in Silsbee, Tex. Since 1954, petitioner's production employees have been represented by Local 801 of the United Paperworkers International Union. . . . Since Texas is a "right-to-work" state by statute, Local 801 is barred from obtaining an agreement with petitioner requiring all production employees to become union members.

In March 1974, officers of Local 801, seeking to strengthen employee support for the union and perhaps recruit new members in anticipation of upcoming contract negotiations with petitioner, decided to distribute a union newsletter to petitioner's production employees. . . . The first and fourth sections urged employees to support and participate in the union and, more generally, extolled the benefits of union solidarity. The second section encouraged employees to write their legislators to oppose incorporation of the state "right-to-work" statute into a revised state constitution then under consideration, warning that incorporation would "weaken[] Unions and improv[e] the edge business has at the bargaining table." The third section noted that the President recently had vetoed a bill to increase the federal minimum wage from $1.60 to $2.00 per hour, compared this action to the increase of prices and profits in the oil industry under administration policies, and admonished, "As working men and women we must defeat our enemies and elect our friends. If you haven't registered to vote, please do so today.". . .

[In March and April 1974, certain employees as well as union officers were denied permission by the company to distribute the newsletter in the plant's nonworking areas. The union filed unfair labor practice charges.]

At a hearing on the charge, [the company's personnel director] testified that he had no objection to the first and fourth sections of the newsletter. He had denied permission to distribute the newsletter because he "didn't see any way in which [the second and third sections were] related to our association with the Union." The [ALJ] held that although not all of the newsletter had immediate bearing on the relationship between petitioner and Local 801, distribution of all its contents was protected under §7 as concerted activity for the "mutual aid or protection" of employees. Because petitioner had presented no evidence of "special circumstances" to justify a ban on the distribution of protected matter by employees in nonworking areas during nonworking time, the [ALJ] held that petitioner had violated §8(a)(1). . . . The Board affirmed . . . , 215 N.L.R.B. 271 (1974).

The Court of Appeals enforced the order.

Two distinct questions are presented. The first is whether, apart from the location of the activity, distribution of the newsletter is the kind of concerted activity that is protected from employer interference by §§7 and 8(a)(1) of the National Labor Relations Act. If it is, then the second question is whether the fact that the activity takes place on petitioner's property gives rise to a countervailing interest that outweighs the exercise of §7 rights in that location. . . . We address these questions in turn. . . . Petitioner contends that the activity here is not within the "mutual aid or protection" language [of §7] because it does not relate to a "specific dispute" between employees and their own employer "over an issue which the employer has the right or power to affect." . . .

We believe that petitioner misconceives the reach of the "mutual aid or protection" clause. The "employees" who may engage in concerted activities for "mutual aid or protection" are defined by §2(3) of the Act to "include any employee, and shall not be limited to the employees of a particular employer, unless the Act explicitly states otherwise. . . ." This definition was intended to protect employees when they engage in otherwise proper concerted activities in support of employees of employers other than their own. In recognition of this intent, the Board and the courts long have held that the "mutual aid or protection" clause encompasses such activity. Petitioner's argument on this point ignores the language of the Act and its settled construction.

We also find no warrant for petitioner's view that employees lose their protection under the "mutual aid or protection" clause when they seek to improve terms and conditions of employment or otherwise improve their lot as employees through channels outside the immediate employee-employer relationship. The 74th Congress knew well enough that labor's cause often is advanced on fronts other than collective bargaining and grievance settlement within the immediate employment context. It recognized this fact by choosing, as the language of §7 makes clear, to protect concerted activities for the somewhat broader purpose of "mutual aid or protection" as well as for the narrower purposes of "self-organization" and "collective bargaining." Thus, it has been held that the "mutual aid or protection" clause protects employees from retaliation by their employers when they seek to improve working conditions through resort to administrative and judicial forums, and that employees' appeals to legislators to protect their interests as employees are within the scope of this clause. To hold that activity of this nature is entirely unprotected—irrespective of location or the means employed—would leave employees open to retaliation for much legitimate activity that could improve their lot as employees. As this could "frustrate the policy of the Act to protect the right of workers to act together to better their working conditions," NLRB v. Washington Aluminum Co., 370 U.S. 9, 14 (1962), we do not think that Congress could have intended the protection of §7 to be as narrow as petitioner insists.

It is true . . . that some concerted activity bears a less immediate relationship to employees' interests as employees than other such activity. We may assume that at some point the relationship becomes so attenuated that an activity cannot fairly be deemed to come within the "mutual aid or protection" clause. It is neither necessary nor appropriate, however, for us to attempt to delineate precisely the boundaries of the "mutual aid or protection" clause. That task is for the Board to perform in the first instance as it considers the wide variety of cases that come before it.[18] . . . To decide this case, it is enough to determine whether the Board erred in holding that distribution of the second and third sections of the newsletter is for the purpose of "mutual aid or protection."

The Board determined that distribution of the second section, urging employees to write their legislators to oppose incorporation of the state "right-to-work" statute into a revised state constitution, was protected because union security is "central to the union concept of strength through solidarity" and "a mandatory subject of bargaining in other than right-to-work states." 215 N.L.R.B., at 274. The newsletter warned that incorporation could affect employees adversely "by weakening Unions and improving the edge business has at the bargaining table." The fact that Texas already has a "right-to-work" statute does not render employees' interest in this matter any less strong, for, as the Court of Appeals noted, it is "one thing to face a legislative scheme which is

18. See Ford Motor Co., 221 N.L.R.B. 663, 666 (1975), enforced, 546 F.2d 418 (3rd Cir. 1976) (holding distribution on employer's premises of a "purely political tract" unprotected even though "the election of any political candidate may have an ultimate effect on employment conditions"); cf. Ford Motor Co. (Rouge Complex), 233 N.L.R.B. No. 102 (1977), decision of [ALJ], at 8 (concession of General Counsel that distributions on employer's premises of literature urging participation in Revolutionary Communist Party celebration, and of Party's newspaper, were unprotected). The Board has not yet made clear whether it considers distributions like those in the above-cited cases to be unprotected altogether, or only on the employer's premises. In addition, even when concerted activity comes within the scope of the "mutual aid or protection" clause, the forms such activity permissibly may take may well depend on the object of the activity. "The argument that the employer's lack of interest or control affords a legitimate basis for holding that a subject does not come within 'mutual aid or protection' is unconvincing. The argument that economic pressure should be unprotected in such cases is more convincing." Getman, The Protection of Economic Pressure by Section 7 of the National Labor Relations Act, 115 U. Pa. L. Rev. 1195, 1221 (1967).

open to legislative modification or repeal" and "quite another thing to face the prospect that such a scheme will be frozen in a concrete constitutional mandate." 550 F.2d, at 205. We cannot say that the Board erred in holding that this section of the newsletter bears such a relation to employees' interests as to come within the guarantee of the "mutual aid or protection" clause. . . .

The Board held that distribution of the third section, criticizing a presidential veto of an increase in the federal minimum wage and urging employees to register to vote to "defeat our enemies and elect our friends," was protected despite the fact that petitioner's employees were paid more than the vetoed minimum wage. It reasoned that the "minimum wage inevitably influences wage levels derived from collective bargaining, even those far above the minimum," and that "concern by [petitioner's] employees for the plight of other employees might gain support for them at some future time when they might have a dispute with their employer." 215 N.L.R.B., at 274. We think that the Board acted within the range of its discretion in so holding. Few topics are of such immediate concern to employees as the level of their wages. The Board was entitled to note the widely recognized impact that a rise in the minimum wage may have on the level of negotiated wages generally, a phenomenon that would not have been lost on petitioner's employees. The union's call [regarding] the minimum wage . . . fairly is characterized as concerted activity for the "mutual aid or protection" of petitioner's employees and of employees generally. . . .

The question that remains is whether the Board erred in holding that petitioner's employees may distribute the newsletter in nonworking areas of petitioner's property during nonworking time. Consideration of this issue must begin with the Court's decisions in Republic Aviation Corp. v. NLRB, 324 U.S. 793 (1945), and NLRB v. Babcock & Wilcox Co., 351 U.S. 105 (1956). . . . It is apparent that the instant case resembles *Republic Aviation* rather closely. . . .

The only possible ground of distinction is that part of the newsletter in this case does not address purely organizational matters, but rather concerns other activity protected by §7. The question, then, is whether this difference required the Board to apply a different rule here than it applied in *Republic Aviation.*

Petitioner contends that the Board must distinguish among distributions of protected matter by employees on an employer's property on the basis of the content of each distribution. Echoing its earlier argument, petitioner urges that the *Republic Aviation* rule should not be applied if a distribution "does not involve a request for any action on the part of the employer, or does not concern a matter over which the employer has any degree of control." . . . In petitioner's view, distribution of any other matter protected by §7 would be an "unnecessary intrusion on the employer's property rights," . . . in the absence of a showing by employees that no alternative channels of communication with fellow employees are available.

We hold that the Board was not required to adopt this view in the case at hand. In the first place, petitioner's reliance on its property right is largely misplaced. Here, as in *Republic Aviation*, petitioner's employees are "already rightfully on the employer's property," so that in the context of this case it is the "employer's management interests rather than [its] property interests" that primarily are implicated. As already noted, petitioner made no attempt to show that its management interests would be prejudiced in any way by the exercise of §7 rights proposed by its employees here. Even if the mere distribution by employees of material protected by §7 can be said to intrude on petitioner's property rights in any meaningful sense, the degree of intrusion does not vary with the content of the material. Petitioner's only cognizable property right in this respect is in preventing employees from bringing literature onto its property and distributing it there — not in choosing which distributions protected by §7 it wishes to suppress.

On the other side of the balance, it may be argued that the employees' interest in distributing literature that deals with matters affecting them as employees, but not with self-organization or collective bargaining, is so removed from the central concerns of the Act as to justify application of a different rule than in *Republic Aviation*. Although such an argument may have force in some circumstances, . . . the Board to date generally has chosen not to engage in such refinement of its rules regarding the distribution of literature by employees during nonworking time in nonworking areas of their employer's property. We are not prepared to say in this case that the Board erred in the view it took.

It is apparent that the complexity of the Board's rules and the difficulty of the Board's task might be compounded greatly if it were required to distinguish not only between literature that is within and without the protection of §7, but also among subcategories of literature within that protection. In addition, whatever the strength of the employees' §7 interest in distributing particular literature, the Board is entitled to view the intrusion by employees on the property rights of their employer as quite limited in this context as long as the employer's management interests are adequately protected. . . .

We need not go so far in this case, however, as to hold that the *Republic Aviation* rule properly is applied to every in-plant distribution of literature that falls within the protective ambit of §7. This is a new area for the Board and the courts which has not yet received mature consideration. . . . For this reason, we confine our holding to the facts of this case.

Petitioner concedes that its employees were entitled to distribute a substantial portion of this newsletter on its property. In addition, as we have held above, the sections to which petitioner objected concern activity which petitioner, in the absence of a countervailing interest of its own, is not entitled to suppress. Yet petitioner made no attempt to show that its management interests would be prejudiced in any manner by distribution of these sections, and in our view any incremental intrusion on petitioner's property rights from their distribution together with the other sections would be minimal. Moreover, it is undisputed that the Union undertook the distribution in order to boost its support and improve its bargaining position in upcoming contract negotiations with petitioner. Thus, viewed in context, the distribution was closely tied to vital concerns of the Act. In these circumstances, we hold that the Board did not err in applying the *Republic Aviation* rule to the facts of this case. The judgment of the Court of Appeals therefore is affirmed.

[The concurring opinion of Justice White and the dissenting opinion of Justice Rehnquist, joined by Chief Justice Burger, are omitted.]

## *NOTES AND QUESTIONS*

**1. In-Plant Distribution of "Partisan" Political Appeals?** Consider the cases cited in footnote 18 of *Eastex,* as well as Local 174, UAW v. NLRB, 645 F.2d 1151 (D.C. Cir. 1981), where the court held that the distribution of leaflets promoting particular political candidates was unprotected, even though the leaflets noted government decisions that could affect working conditions. Are such rulings viable after *Eastex*? Can the Board or a court ever be certain that speech on any political issue would not assist employees in organizing for their own ultimate benefit? Could organizing around a political issue help organization for collective bargaining as well? Can it always be argued plausibly that political results might ultimately affect the well-being of employees? Should the willingness of employees and unions to spend resources on certain public issues be viewed as the best evidence that organizing around these issues could benefit employees? See Alan Hyde, Economic Labor Law v. Political Labor Relations: Dilemmas for Liberal Legalism, 60 Tex. L. Rev. 1 (1981). Furthermore, does the Board's authority to deny protection to certain political literature because of its content raise First Amendment concerns?

Even after *Eastex,* however, do employers have sufficiently strong countervailing property and business interests to impose some limitations on the content of employee distributions in the workplace? For instance, does an employer have a legitimate interest in barring certain distributions because they address the employees in their role as citizens of the polity rather than in their role as workers? Or because there is a fair chance that a subgroup of the workforce might object to the message? How would you advise an employer who has been asked by a group of workers for permission to distribute in the plant the literature of the "Right to Work" Committee? The literature of an anti-affirmative action group? The literature of a pro- or anti-immigrant rights group? For more extensive treatment of this latter question, see Chapter 14. See also Kati L. Griffith & Tamara L. Lee, Immigration Advocacy as Labor Advocacy, 33 Berk. J. Emp. & Lab. L. 73 (2012) (surveying NLRA political advocacy cases and identifying three categories of issues that typically fall within "mutual aid or protection": issues framed as affecting (1) workers' legal rights, (2) wages and working conditions above minumum legal standards or (3) job opportunities and job security).

**2. Balancing Employer Interests Under §8(a)(1) or §7?** Might the Board better balance the employer concerns raised by the preceding note under §8(a)(1) rather than through the definition of "mutual aid or protection" under §7? Exclusion from §7 protection altogether, for example, would seem to allow employers to permit solicitations or distributions for some political candidates but not for others. See footnote 18 in *Eastex.*

**3. Distribution Rights in Nonunion Settings?** What if a group of workers in a *nonunion* plant seeks to distribute a newsletter urging an increase in the statutory minimum wage or defeat of an effort to insert the state's "right-to-work" law into the state constitution? Given *Washington Aluminum,* must a nonunion employer permit such in-plant distributions? The NLRA's application to nonunion worker groups is discussed further in Chapter 14, infra.

**4. "Whistleblowing" and Other Protests of Nonlabor Management Policies.** The Board and the courts have denied protection to employee protests of the managerial practices of their employer when the employees are motivated not by their own interests but by the interests of the public or of their customers, clients, or patients. See, e.g., Vincent v. Trend Western Technical Corp., 828 F.2d 563 (9th Cir. 1987) (whistleblowing on employer's breach of government contract); Orchard Park Health Care Center, Inc., 341 N.L.R.B. 642 (2004) (employees' call to report excessive heat at nursing home to state health department expressed concern only for patients not for themselves); Lutheran Social Serv. of Minn., Inc., 250 N.L.R.B. 35 (1980) (employee complaints about management concerned the welfare of troubled youth clients, not of employees themselves). But see Squier Distributing Co. v. Local 7, 801 F.2d 238 (6th Cir. 1986) (citing *Eastex* to protect employees who, because of fear that they would lose their jobs if the company failed, provided law enforcement officials with information about vice president's involvement in embezzlement). For the case for extending §7 protection to whistleblowing, see Cynthia L. Estlund, What Do Workers Want? Employee Interests, Public Interests, and Freedom of Expression Under the National Labor Relations Act, 140 U. Pa. L. Rev. 921, 938-960 (1992).

**5. Off-Premises Political Activity.** Is there a basis for reading §7 to protect employees against discipline for engaging in off-premises political or other speech not directly tied to their interests as employees, even when in-plant activity of this type need not be tolerated by the employer under *Eastex?* Consider the last sentence in *Eastex* footnote 18, paragraph one. Is the Court suggesting that the Board might protect distributions for political candidates off the employer's premises but not on its property? Would such a distinction mean that purely political expression is within "mutual aid or protection," but not sufficiently connected to workplace concerns to render unlawful an employer's refusal to allow such activity to disrupt the workplace? Can such an interpretation be reconciled with the Act's language, structure, and focus?

**6. Strikes for "Political" Objectives.** Consider the last paragraph in footnote 18 in the *Eastex* opinion. Assume that the Eastex employees joined in a state-wide, week-long strike to protest anti-union legislation being considered by the Texas legislature. Should the strike receive §7 protection? What if the Eastex employees refused to complete orders for Chinese customers until China modified its trade policies to open its markets more fully to American goods? See NLRB General Counsel, GC Mem. 08-10: Guideline Memorandum Concerning Unfair Labor Practice Charges Involving Political Advocacy, p. 10 (July 22, 2008):

> [W]hen employees leave work in support of a political cause, either to mobilize public sentiment or to urge governmental action (in either case a matter outside their employer's control), they are not withholding their services as an economic weapon in the employment relationship. It is primarily because the employees' underlying grievance is not usually one which their employer can address that the employees' conduct, while resembling a strike, is distinctly different from the typical strike specifically protected under Section 13. Indeed, in *Eastex* the Court in dicta suggested that economic pressure in support of a political dispute may not be protected when it is exerted on an employer with no control over the outcome of that dispute. We agree with that principle.

See also infra pages 581-582.

**7. Protests over Identity of Supervisor.** To what extent does §7 protect employee protests regarding the selection or termination of supervisors or managers? The general rule is that employee action to influence the identity of management is unprotected because it "lies outside the sphere of legitimate employee interest." NLRB v. Oakes Machine Corp., 897 F.2d 84, 89 (2d Cir. 1990); see also Smithfield Packing Co. v. NLRB, 510 F.3d 507 (4th Cir. 2007) (protests over supervisors only protected when a "protest over the actual conditions of the employees' employment"); *Bob Evans Farms,* supra note 1, page 175, 163 F.3d at 1021. Thus, protests may be protected only where the supervisor or manager has a "direct impact on the employees' own job interests and [work] performance." Dobbs Houses, 135 N.L.R.B. 885 (1962) (assistant restaurant manager who acted as buffer between employees and verbally abusive manager), enforcement denied on other grounds, 325 F.2d 53 (5th Cir. 1963); see *Bob Evans,* 163 F.3d at 1021-1022 (restaurant supervisor who repeatedly advocated employees' causes with other supervisors—a "self-appointed [and successful] mediator" of employee grievances). Is this more likely to be the case where a low-level or a high-level supervisor is the focus of the protest? See Plastilite Corp., 153 N.L.R.B. 180 (1965), enforced in relevant part, 375 F.2d 343 (8th Cir. 1967). Could an attenuated §7 interest in supervisory personnel decisions explain why some courts of appeals have embraced a consideration of reasonableness in this context despite *Washington Aluminum*? See p. 175 note 1 supra. See also Trompler, Inc. v. NLRB, 338 F.3d 747 (7th Cir. 2003) (stating that "'combat' model of labor relations [on which Act is modeled] does not sort well with a requirement that the combatants act 'reasonably,'" but choosing to limit reasonableness considerations to cases involving supervisory personnel decisions, partially in deference to *Washington Aluminum*).

**8. "Entrepreneurial" Objectives.** In Harrah's Lake Tahoe Resort Casino, 307 N.L.R.B. 182 (1992), an employee sought his coworkers' support for a proposal that the employee stock option plan (ESOP) buy 50 percent of the employer's parent corporation. The Board held his conduct unprotected, reasoning that although the proposal envisioned enhanced benefits for current employees, "[its thrust] was to cast employees in the role of owners with ultimate corporate control, and thus fundamentally to change how and by whom the corporation would be managed. The current employees would not enjoy any of the envisioned benefits unless and until they, through the ESOP, effectively controlled the corporation." Is this too cramped a view of §7 after *Eastex*?

**9. Refusal to Cross "Stranger" Picket Lines.** Two truck drivers, not themselves members of or represented by a union, refuse to follow their employer's order to deliver inventory to a customer whose plant driveway is blocked by a picket line set up by the customer's employees, who themselves are on strike for a better contract. Should the refusal to cross the line be protected by §7? How might the truck drivers view their refusal to be for their own "mutual aid or protection"? See, e.g., NLRB v. Browning-Ferris Industries Chemical Servs., Inc., 700 F.2d 385 (7th Cir. 1983) (finding protection but noting that employer can respond by hiring replacements for the drivers); Overnite Transp. Co., 154 N.L.R.B. 1271 (1965), enforced sub nom. Teamsters Local 728 v. NLRB, 364 F.2d 682 (4th Cir. 1966) (replacement of employee for refusing to cross picket line was not justified because employer's business was not significantly disrupted). For further discussion, see infra pages 534-536.

**10. Employee Litigation.** Employees may engage in protected activity by filing or otherwise participating in litigation with other employees on workplace issues. See, e.g., Le Madri Restaurant, 331 N.L.R.B. 269 (2000) (two employees filing suit for 17 other employees alleging violation of federal and state labor laws); Novotel New York, 321 N.L.R.B. 624 (1996) (class action suits alleging FLSA violations are protected activity). Section 7 protects the employees' right to bring a collective or class action, but it is less clear whether the NLRA protects the employees from otherwise legally recognized waivers of the right to a judicial forum or to maintain a class or collective action. See NLRB General Counsel, GC Mem. 10-06: Guideline Memorandum Concerning Unfair Labor Practice Charges Involving Employee Waivers in the Context of Employers' Mandatory Arbitration Policies (June 16, 2010); D.R. Horton, Inc. 357 N.L.R.B. No. 184 (2012) (concluding that such waivers interfere with §7 protected activity), enforcement denied 737 F.3d 344 (5th Cir. 2014) (concluding that disallowing such waivers conflicts with the Federal Arbitration Act, 9 U.S.C. §§1 et seq.); Murphy Oil USA, 361 N.C.R.B. No. 72 (2014) (reaffirming its 2010 *D.R. Horton, Inc.* decision). See infra pages 210-219 and 747.

**11. Petitioning the Government and Use of Other Channels Outside the Employer/Employee Relationship.** The newsletter in *Eastex* encouraged employees to petition the government by writing their legislators. What other sorts of "petitions to government" are protected? See Riverboat Services of Indiana, 345 N.L.R.B. 1286 (2005) (solicitation of letters to the U.S. Coast Guard protected). Employment law-related lawsuits or complaints to administrative agencies? What about the filing of an injunctive petition by employees seeking protection against abuse by a subcontractor's agents? See Mojave Electric Cooperative, Inc. v. NLRB, 206 F.3d 1183, 1189 (D.C. Cir. 2000) (protected unless done with malice or bad faith). Are concerted work-related appeals to *non*-governmental entities protected under *Eastex*? What about a letter-writing campaign to newspapers about working conditions at the company? About a need to raise the minimum wage?

## 3. Individual Employee Action as "Concerted" Activity

The cases covered thus far have involved joint action by two or more employees. Thus, the "concert" requirement of §7 has not been at issue. The following section turns to the question of when conduct engaged in by an individual employee is nonetheless deemed "concerted" activity under §7.

**NLRB v. City Disposal Systems, Inc.**
*465 U.S. 822 (1984)*

BRENNAN, J.

James Brown . . . was discharged when he refused to drive a truck that he . . . believed to be unsafe because of faulty brakes. Article XXI of the collective-bargaining agreement between respondent and [Teamsters] Local 247, which covered Brown, provides:

> [t]he Employer shall not require employees to take out on the streets or highways any vehicle that is not in safe operating condition or equipped with safety appliances prescribed by law. It shall not be a violation of the Agreement where employees refuse to operate such equipment unless such refusal is unjustified.[1]

The question . . . is whether Brown's honest and reasonable assertion of his right to be free of the obligation to drive unsafe trucks constituted "concerted activit[y]" within the meaning of §7 of the [NLRA]. . . .

. . . Respondent, City Disposal System, Inc. . . . hauls garbage for the City of Detroit . . . to a land fill. . . . On Saturday, May 12, 1979, Brown observed that a fellow driver had difficulty with the brakes of . . . truck No. 244. As a result of the brake problem, truck No. 244 nearly collided with Brown's truck. After unloading their garbage at the land fill, Brown and the driver of truck No. 244 brought No. 244 to respondent's truck-repair facility, where they were told that the brakes would be repaired [by] the morning of Monday, May 14.

Early in the morning of [that] Monday, . . . while transporting a load of garbage to the land fill, Brown experienced difficulty with one of the wheels of his own truck — No. 245 — and brought that truck in for repair. . . . Brown was told that, because of a backlog at the facility, No. 245 could not be repaired that day. Brown reported the situation to his supervisor, Otto Jasmund, who ordered Brown to punch out and go home. Before Brown could leave, however, Jasmund changed his mind and asked Brown to drive truck No. 244 instead. Brown refused, explaining that "there's something wrong with that truck . . . with the brakes . . . there was a grease seal or something leaking causing it to be affecting the brakes." Brown did not, however, explicitly refer to Article XXI of the collective-bargaining agreement or to the agreement in general. In response to Brown's refusal to drive truck No. 244, Jasmund angrily told Brown to go home. At that point, an argument ensued and Robert Madary, another supervisor, intervened, repeating

---

1. Article XXI also provides that "[t]he Employer shall not ask or require any employee to take out equipment that has been reported by any other employee as being in an unsafe operating condition until same has been approved as being safe by the mechanical department."

Jasmund's request that Brown drive truck No. 244. Again, Brown refused, explaining that No. 244 "has got problems and I don't want to drive it." Madary replied that half the trucks had problems and that if respondent tried to fix all of them it would be unable to do business. He went on to tell Brown that "[w]e've got all this garbage out here to haul and you tell me about you don't want to drive." Brown responded, "Bob, what you going to do, put the garbage ahead of the safety of the men?" Finally, Madary went to his office and Brown went home. Later that day, Brown received word that he had been discharged. . . .

. . . [The next day] Brown filed a written grievance, pursuant to the collective-bargaining agreement, asserting that truck No. 244 was defective, that it had been improper for him to have been ordered to drive the truck, and that his discharge was therefore also improper. The union, however, found no objective merit in the grievance and declined to process it.

On September 7, 1979, Brown filed [a] charge with the NLRB. . . . The [ALJ] found that Brown had been discharged for refusing to operate truck No. 244, that Brown's refusal was covered by §7 . . . , and that respondent had therefore [violated] §8(a)(1). The ALJ held that an employee who acts alone in asserting a contractual right can nevertheless be engaged in concerted activity within the meaning of §7. . . . The NLRB adopted the findings and conclusions of the ALJ and ordered that Brown be reinstated with backpay.

. . . [T]he Court of Appeals disagreed with the ALJ and the Board. Finding that Brown's refusal to drive truck No. 244 was an action taken solely on his own behalf, the [court] concluded that the refusal was not a concerted activity within the meaning of §7. . . .

. . . The NLRB's decision in this case applied the Board's long-standing "*Interboro* doctrine," under which an individual's assertion of a right grounded in a collective-bargaining agreement is recognized as "concerted activit[y]" and therefore accorded the protection of §7.[6] See Interboro Contractors, Inc., 157 N.L.R.B. 1295, 1298 (1966), enforced, 388 F.2d 495 (CA2 1967). . . . The Board has relied on two justifications for the doctrine: First, the assertion of a right contained in a collective-bargaining agreement is an extension of the concerted action that produced the agreement . . . ; and second, the assertion of such a right affects the rights of all employees covered by the collective-bargaining agreement.

We have often reaffirmed that the task of defining the scope of §7 "is for the Board to perform in the first instance . . . ," Eastex, Inc. v. NLRB, 437

---

6. The NLRB has recently held that, where a group of employees are not unionized and there is no collective-bargaining agreement, an employee's assertion of a right that can only be presumed to be of interest to other employees is not concerted activity. Meyers Industries, 268 N.L.R.B. No. 73 (1984) ["*Meyers I*"]. The Board, however, distinguished that case from the cases involving the Interboro doctrine, which is based on the existence of a collective-bargaining agreement. The *Meyers* case is thus of no relevance here.

U.S. 556, 568 (1978), and, on an issue that implicates its expertise in labor relations, a reasonable construction by the Board is entitled to considerable deference. . . . The question . . . is thus narrowed to whether the Board's application of §7 to Brown's refusal to drive truck No. 244 is reasonable. . . .

. . . The term "concerted activit[y]" is not defined in the Act but it clearly enough embraces the activities of employees who have joined together in order to achieve common goals. See, e.g., Meyers Industries, 268 N.L.R.B. No. 73, at 3 (1984). What is not self-evident from the language of the Act, however, . . . is the precise manner in which particular actions of an individual employee must be linked to the actions of fellow employees in order to permit it to be said that the individual is engaged in concerted activity. . . .

Although one could interpret the phrase, "to engage in concerted activities," to refer to a situation in which two or more employees are working together at the same time and the same place toward a common goal, the language of §7 does not confine itself to such a narrow meaning. In fact, §7 itself defines both joining and assisting labor organizations—activities in which a single employee can engage—as concerted activities.[8] Indeed, even the courts that have rejected the *Interboro* doctrine recognize the possibility that an individual employee may be engaged in concerted activity when he acts alone. They have limited their recognition of this type of concerted activity, however, to two situations: (1) that in which the lone employee intends to induce group activity, and (2) that in which the employee acts as a representative of at least one other employee. See, e.g., Aro, Inc. v. NLRB, 596 F.2d, at 713, 717 (CA6 1979); NLRB v. Northern Metal Co., 440 F.2d 881, 884 (CA3 1971). The disagreement over the *Interboro* doctrine, therefore, merely reflects differing views regarding the nature of the relationship that must exist between the action of the individual employee and the actions of the group in order for §7 to apply. We cannot say that the Board's view of that relationship, as applied in the *Interboro* doctrine, is unreasonable.

The invocation of a right rooted in a collective-bargaining agreement is unquestionably an integral part of the process that gave rise to the agreement. That process—beginning with the organization of a union, continuing into the negotiation of a collective-bargaining agreement, and extending through the enforcement of the agreement—is a single, collective activity. Obviously, an employee could not invoke a right grounded in a collective-bargaining agreement were it not for the prior negotiating activities of his fellow employees. Nor would it make sense for a union to negotiate a collective-bargaining agreement if individual employees could

---

8. Section 7 lists these and other activities initially and concludes the list with the phrase "other concerted activities," thereby indicating that the enumerated activities are deemed to be "concerted."

not invoke the rights thereby created against their employer. Moreover, when an employee invokes a right grounded in the collective-bargaining agreement, he does not stand alone. Instead, he brings to bear on his employer the power and resolve of all his fellow employees. . . .

Furthermore, the acts of joining and assisting a labor organization, which §7 explicitly recognizes as concerted, are related to collective action in essentially the same way that the invocation of a collectively bargained right is related to collective action. When an employee joins or assists a labor organization, his actions may be divorced in time, and in location as well, from the actions of fellow employees. Because of the integral relationship among the employees' actions, however, Congress viewed each employee as engaged in concerted activity.

. . . [I]t is evident that, in enacting §7 of the NLRA, Congress sought generally to equalize the bargaining power of the employee with that of his employer by allowing employees to band together in confronting an employer regarding the terms and conditions of their employment. . . .

The Board's *Interboro* doctrine, based on a recognition that the potential inequality in the relationship between the employee and the employer continues beyond the point at which a collective-bargaining agreement is signed, mitigates that inequality throughout the duration of the employment relationship, and is, therefore, fully consistent with congressional intent. Moreover, by applying §7 to the actions of individual employees invoking their rights under a collective-bargaining agreement, the *Interboro* doctrine preserves the integrity of the entire collective-bargaining process; for by invoking a right grounded in a collective-bargaining agreement, the employee makes that right a reality, and breathes life, not only into the promises contained in the collective-bargaining agreement, but also into the entire process envisioned by Congress as the means by which to achieve industrial peace.

To be sure, the principal tool by which an employee invokes the rights granted him in a collective-bargaining agreement is the processing of a grievance according to whatever procedures his collective-bargaining agreement establishes. No one doubts that the processing of a grievance in such a manner is concerted activity within the meaning of §7. . . .

In practice, however, there is unlikely to be a bright-line distinction between an incipient grievance, a complaint to an employer, and perhaps even an employee's initial refusal to perform a certain job that he believes he has no duty to perform. It is reasonable to expect that an employee's first response to a situation that he believes violates his collective-bargaining agreement will be a protest to his employer. Whether he files a grievance will depend in part on his employer's reaction and in part upon the nature of the right at issue. In addition, certain rights might not be susceptible of enforcement by the filing of a grievance. In such a case, the collective-bargaining agreement might provide for an alternative method of enforcement, as did the agreement involved in this case, or the agreement might be silent on the matter. Thus, for a variety of reasons, an employee's initial statement to an employer to the effect that he believes a collectively bargained right is being violated, or the employee's initial refusal to do that which he believes he is not obligated to do, might serve as both a natural prelude to, and an efficient substitute for, the filing of a formal grievance. As long as the employee's statement or action is based on a reasonable and honest belief that he is being, or has been, asked to perform a task that he is not required to perform under his collective-bargaining agreement, and the statement or action is reasonably directed toward the enforcement of a collectively bargained right, there is no justification for overturning the Board's judgment that the employee is engaged in concerted activity, just as he would have been had he filed a formal grievance.

The fact that an activity is concerted, however, does not necessarily mean that an employee can engage in the activity with impunity. An employee may engage in concerted activity in such an abusive manner that he loses the protection of §7. See, e.g., Crown Central Petroleum Corp. v. NLRB, 430 F.2d 724, 729 (CA5 1970).... Furthermore, if an employer does not wish to tolerate certain methods by which employees invoke their collectively bargained rights, he is free to negotiate a provision in his collective-bargaining agreement that limits the availability of such methods. No-strike provisions, for instance, are a common mechanism by which employers and employees agree that the latter will not invoke their rights by refusing to work.... Whether Brown's action in this case was unprotected, however, is not before us.

Respondent argues that the *Interboro* doctrine undermines the arbitration process by providing employees with the possibility of provoking a discharge and then filing an unfair labor practice claim. This argument, however, misses the mark for several reasons. [A]n employee who purposefully follows this route would run the risk that the Board would find his actions concerted but nonetheless unprotected, as discussed above....

[Moreover,] to the extent that the factual issues raised in an unfair labor practice action have been, or can be, addressed through the grievance process, the Board may defer to that process. See Collyer Insulated Wire, 192 N.L.R.B. 837 (1971); Spielberg Manufacturing Co., 112 N.L.R.B. 1080 (1955). There is no reason, therefore, for the Board's interpretation of "concerted activit[y]" in §7 to be constrained by a concern for maintaining the integrity of the grievance and arbitration process.

... Respondent argues that Brown's action was not concerted because he did not explicitly refer to the collective-bargaining agreement as a basis for his refusal to drive the truck. The Board, however, has never held that an employee must make such an explicit reference for his actions to be covered by the *Interboro* doctrine, and we find that position reasonable....

Respondent further argues that the Board erred in finding Brown's action concerted based only on Brown's reasonable and honest belief that truck No. 244 was unsafe. Respondent bases its argument on the language of the collective-bargaining agreement, which provides that an employee may refuse to drive an unsafe truck "unless such refusal is unjustified." In the view of respondent, this language allows a driver to refuse to drive a truck only if the truck is objectively unsafe. Regardless of whether respondent's interpretation of the agreement is correct, a question as to which we express no view, this argument confuses the threshold question whether Brown's conduct was concerted with the ultimate question whether that conduct was protected. The rationale of the *Interboro* doctrine compels the conclusion that an honest and reasonable invocation of a collectively bargained right constitutes concerted activity, regardless of whether the employee turns out to have been correct in his belief that his right was violated. No one would suggest, for instance, that the filing of a grievance is concerted only if the grievance turns out to be meritorious. As long as the grievance is based on an honest and reasonable belief that a right had been violated, its filing is a concerted activity because it is an integral part of the process by which the collective-bargaining agreement is enforced. The same is true of other methods by which an employee enforces the agreement. On the other hand, if the collective-bargaining agreement imposes a limitation on the means by which a right may be invoked, the concerted activity would be unprotected if it went beyond that limitation.

. . . [B]ecause Brown reasonably and honestly invoked his right to avoid driving unsafe trucks, his action was concerted. It may be that the collective-bargaining agreement prohibits an employee from refusing to drive a truck that he reasonably believes to be unsafe, but that is, in fact, perfectly safe. If so, Brown's action was concerted but unprotected. . . . [H]owever, the only issue before this Court and the only issue passed upon by the Board or the Court of Appeals is whether Brown's action was concerted, not whether it was protected.

[The dissenting opinion of Justice O'Connor, joined by Chief Justice Burger and Justices Powell and Rehnquist, is omitted.]

## *NOTES AND QUESTIONS*

**1. Individual vs. Concerted Protests.** The courts and the Board have consistently read the "concerted activities" phrase in §7 as words of limitation and have generally excluded from §7 protection complaints of a sole employee that he or she is being treated unfairly as an individual. See, e.g., Tabernacle Community Hosp. & Health Ctr., 233 N.L.R.B. 1425 (1977); Ontario Knife Co. v. NLRB, 637 F.2d 840 (2d Cir. 1980) (Friendly, J.) (discussing distinction between individual and concerted activity and finding one-person walkout unprotected). *City Disposal* is one of the recognized exceptions to the nonprotection of individual protests. Other exceptions are discussed in note 6 infra.

**2. Why Are Individual Protests Generally Unprotected?** Why might Congress have included the word "concerted" in §7? Are protests by two or more employees, as in *Washington Aluminum*, any less disruptive than lone employee protests? Are group protests more likely to have some reasonable basis? More likely to put the employer on notice that it is dealing with NLRA-protected activity? For an argument that Congress used "concerted" not as a word of limitation but rather to emphasize the Act's rejection of common law actions against labor conspiracies, see Robert A. Gorman & Matthew W. Finkin, The Individual and the Requirement of "Concert" Under the National Labor Relations Act, 130 U. Pa. L. Rev. 286 (1981).

**3. Statutory Right vs. Contractual Right?** Note that Brown's union in *City Disposal* found his grievance to be without merit and declined to process it further. The *City Disposal* decision thus may seem to suggest that Brown has a statutory right based on the existence of a collective agreement negotiated by a collective representative when that representative does not find the collective agreement to have been violated in his case. The *City Disposal* Court, however, holds only that the invocation of the collective agreement made Brown's refusal to work concerted, not that it necessarily made it protected. Does the union's failure to process mean that the company ultimately could have fired Brown for refusing to work, just not for filing the grievance or otherwise invoking the contract? Is *City Disposal* best understood as recognizing a statutory right to begin the contractual grievance process, even if the grievance ultimately is found to lack merit?

**4. "Obey Now, Grieve Later."** In *City Disposal*, the Court notes that if employers do not wish "to tolerate certain methods by which employees invoke their collectively bargained rights," they may seek contractual language limiting the availability of such methods. One such means of limitation, as further noted, is a no-strike clause. See infra page 703-721.

Even absent express contractual language, labor agreements are conventionally read to permit employers to insist that workers not ignore job assignments, even if such assignments violate the contract. See infra note 9, page 656. This principle is referred to as "obey now, grieve later." An exception is commonly inferred when the assignment poses an imminent safety threat. Footnote 1 of *City Disposal* indicates that the contract in that case contained an express clause embodying this exception.

**5. Individual Protests Asserting Noncontractual Workplace Rights: From *Alleluia Cushion* to *Meyers Industries*.** In Alleluia Cushion Co., 221

N.L.R.B. 999 (1975), the Board went beyond its *Interboro* doctrine to offer protection to an employee in an unorganized plant who, acting solely from his own concerns about plant safety and without seeking or obtaining any express support from any other employee, sought to enforce state safety regulations applicable to his plant by writing a letter of complaint to an appropriate regulatory agency. The Board concluded that "where an employee speaks up and seeks to enforce statutory provisions relating to occupational safety designed for the benefit of all employees, in the absence of any evidence that fellow employees disavow such representation, we will find an implied consent thereto and deem such activity to be concerted." Id. at 1000.

However, a decade later a new Board appointed by President Reagan repudiated *Alleluia Cushion.* It instead required proof that an activity was "engaged in with or on the authority of other employees," without the benefit of any presumption of such authority, and maintained that this construction of the statute was *mandated* by the Act. See Meyers Indus., Inc. ("*Meyers I*"), 268 N.L.R.B. 493 (1984). The D.C. Circuit rejected the notion that the Board's *Meyers I* interpretation was required by the Act, and remanded "to afford the Board a full opportunity to consider" the issue, and with instructions to articulate its rationale more fully. See Prill v. NLRB ("*Prill I*"), 755 F.2d 941 (D.C. Cir. 1985). On remand, the Board decided to adhere to the *Meyers I* definition of concerted activity as a discretionary matter. See Meyers Indus., Inc. ("*Meyers II*"), 281 N.L.R.B. 882 (1986). The D.C. Circuit then deferred to the *Meyers II* decision as a reasonable interpretation of the statute entitled to deference under the Supreme Court's *Chevron* doctrine, supra page 75. See Prill v. NLRB ("*Prill II*"), 835 F.2d 1481 (D.C. Cir. 1987); see also Ewing v. NLRB, 861 F.2d 353 (2d Cir. 1988) (accepting Board's interpretation as within its discretion).

**6. Individual Action as a Prelude to or Logical Outgrowth of Group Action: *Mushroom Transportation* and Related Doctrines.** In *Meyers II,* the Board noted its continued endorsement of the *Mushroom Transportation* doctrine, making clear that concerted activity "encompasses those circumstances where individual employees seek to initiate or to induce or to prepare for group action, as well as individual employees bringing truly group complaints to the attention of management." 281 N.L.R.B. at 887 (citing Mushroom Transp. Co. v. NLRB, 330 F.2d 683 (3d Cir. 1964)). Should an employee's criticism of management and of a newly implemented policy in a group meeting be deemed concerted under this doctrine? See NLRB v. Caval Tool Division, Chromalloy Gas Turbine Corp., 262 F.3d 184, 190 (2d Cir. 2000) (holding yes; intent to initiate or induce group action inferred in context of group meeting concerning conditions of employment). An e-mail message to fellow employees complaining of a proposed vacation policy change? See Timekeeping Systems, Inc., 323

N.L.R.B. 244 (1997) (conduct deemed "concerted" as implicit attempt to induce group action; object of inducing group action need not be express). What if an individual employee discusses working conditions or the treatment of a coworker with fellow employees without addressing the possibility of group action? See Adelphi Inst., Inc., 287 N.L.R.B. 1073 (1988); Parke Care of Finneytown, Inc., 287 N.L.R.B. 710 (1987) (both requiring evidence of contemplation of group action and finding activity not concerted). Can *Adelphi* and *Parke Care* be reconciled with *Timekeeping Systems*? With *Caval Tool*?

Another line of cases has recognized that conduct by an individual that is a "logical outgrowth" of group activity is also "concerted" activity. See, e.g., Salisbury Hotel, Inc., 283 N.L.R.B. 685 (1987) (individual employee contacts U.S. Department of Labor after employees had tacitly agreed to complain to management); Every Woman's Place, Inc., 282 N.L.R.B. 413 (1986) (single employee contacts Labor Department after several employees had complained to management about issue). For a discussion of both these lines of cases and of the doctrine of "protected concerted activity" generally, see Charles J. Morris, NLRB Protection in the Nonunion Workplace: A Glimpse at a General Theory of Section 7 Conduct, 137 U. Pa. L. Rev. 1673 (1989).

**7. "Posts" on Facebook or Other Social Media Outlets as "Concerted" Activity?** Should an employee's post on Facebook that solicits support from other employees be treated as concerted? The Board has treated social media like Facebook as similar to other means of communication. For example, in Triple Play Sports Bar and Grille, 361 N.L.R.B. No. 31 (2014), the Board found that it was unlawful for an employer to fire both an employee who posted about perceived errors in the employer's calculations of tax withholdings and also an employee who responded to the post.

**8. Must an Employer Have Knowledge of the Concerted Nature of the Individual Protest?** In *Meyers I* the Board also stated that the employer must know of the concerted nature of an individual employee's protest for that protest to be protected. See 268 N.L.R.B. at 497; see also Tradesmen Int'l, Inc., 332 N.L.R.B. 1158 (2000), enforcement denied on other grounds, 275 F.3d 1137 (D.C. Cir. 2002). Does recognition of a scienter requirement expose an employee engaged in concerted activity to a risk of job loss simply because the General Counsel cannot prove the employer's awareness that others are also involved? If scienter were not required, would such employers have to assume that individual protests were concerted in order to avoid liability? Would that necessarily be undesirable?

**9. Can an Employee's Self-Interested Actions Be Concerted and for Mutual Aid or Protection?** Are an employee's efforts to enlist the assistance of her fellow workers in the assertion of her interests at work necessarily for "mutual aid or protection" as well as "concerted"? Should the law assume that an employee's assistance to another employee could ultimately benefit other workers as well as the employee directly assisted? Is this assumption necessary? Appropriate in all situations? In at least recurring ones? See Fresh & Easy Neighborhood Mkt., Inc., 361 N.L.R.B. No. 12 (2014) (finding an employee's solicitation of other employees to support a sexual harassment complaint concerted and for mutual aid or protection even though no other employees experienced harassment).

### NLRB v. J. Weingarten, Inc.
*420 U.S. 251 (1975)*

BRENNAN, J. . . .

Respondent operates a chain of . . . retail stores with lunch counters at some, and so-called lobby food operations at others. . . . Respondent's sales personnel are represented . . . by Retail Clerks Union, Local 455. Leura Collins . . . worked at the lunch counter at Store No. 2 from 1961 to 1970 when she was transferred to the lobby operation at Store No. 98. Respondent maintains a companywide security department staffed by "Loss Prevention Specialists" who work undercover . . . to guard against . . . shoplifting and employee dishonesty. In June 1972, "Specialist" Hardy, without the knowledge of the store manager, spent two days observing the lobby operation at Store No. 98 investigating a report that Collins was taking money from a cash register. When Hardy's surveillance of Collins . . . turned up no evidence to support the report, Hardy disclosed his presence to the store manager and reported that he could find nothing wrong. The store manager then told him that a fellow lobby employee . . . had just reported that Collins had purchased a box of chicken that sold for $2.98, but had placed only $1 in the cash register. Collins was summoned to an interview with Specialist Hardy and the store manager, and Hardy questioned her. The Board found that several times during the questioning she asked the store manager to call the union shop steward or some other union representative to the interview, and that her requests were denied. Collins admitted that she had purchased some chicken, a loaf of bread, and some cake which she said she paid for and donated to her church for a church dinner. She explained that she purchased four pieces of chicken for which the price was $1, but that because the lobby department was out of the small-size boxes in which such purchases were usually packaged she put the chicken into the larger box normally used for packaging larger quantities. Specialist Hardy left the interview to check Collins' explanation with the fellow employee who had reported Collins. This employee confirmed that the lobby department had run out of small boxes and also said that she did not know how many pieces of chicken Collins had put in the larger box. Specialist Hardy returned to the interview, told Collins that her explanation had checked out, that he was sorry if he had inconvenienced her, and that the matter was closed.

Collins thereupon burst into tears and blurted out that the only thing she had ever gotten from the store without paying for it was her free lunch. . . . [T]he store manager and Specialist Hardy closely interrogated Collins about violations of the policy [against free lunches] in the lobby department at Store No. 98. Collins again asked that a shop steward be called to the interview, but the store manager denied her request. Based on her answers to his questions, Specialist Hardy prepared a written statement which included a computation that Collins owed the store approximately $160 for lunches. Collins refused to sign the statement. The Board found that Collins, as well as most, if not all, employees in the lobby department of Store No. 98, including the manager of that department, took lunch from the lobby without paying for it, apparently because no contrary policy was ever made known to them. Indeed, when company headquarters advised Specialist Hardy by telephone during the interview that headquarters itself was uncertain whether the policy against providing free lunches at lobby departments was in effect at Store No. 98, he terminated his interrogation of Collins. . . . [After Collins informed the union of this interview, this unfair labor practice proceeding was initiated. The NLRB held that the employer had violated §8(a)(1) by denying Collins's request for the presence of her union representative at an investigatory interview that the employee had reasonably believed might result in discipline. The Fifth Circuit denied enforcement.]

The Board's construction that §7 creates a statutory right in an employee to refuse to submit without union representation to an interview which he reasonably fears may result in his discipline was announced in its decision and order of January 28, 1972, in Quality Mfg. Co., 195 N.L.R.B. 197. . . . In its opinion in that case and in Mobil Oil Corp., 196 N.L.R.B. 1052, . . . three months later, the Board shaped the contours and limits of the statutory right.

First, the right inheres in §7's guarantee of the right of employees to act in concert for mutual aid and protection.

Second, the right arises only in situations where the employee requests representation. . . .

Third, the employee's right to request representation as a condition of participation in an interview is limited to situations where the employee reasonably believes the investigation will result in disciplinary action. . . .

Fourth, exercise of the right may not interfere with legitimate employer prerogatives. The employer has no obligation to justify his refusal to allow union representation, and despite refusal, the employer is free to carry on his inquiry without interviewing the employee, and thus leave to the employee the choice between having an interview unaccompanied by his representative, or having no interview and forgoing any benefits that might be derived from one. . . .

Fifth, the employer has no duty to bargain with any union representative who may be permitted to attend the investigatory interview. The Board said in *Mobil,* "we are not giving the Union any particular rights with respect to predisciplinary discussions which it otherwise was not able to secure during collective bargaining negotiations." 196 N.L.R.B., at 1052 n.3. . . . "The representative is present to assist the employee, and may attempt to clarify the facts or suggest other employees who may have knowledge of them. The employer, however, is free to insist that he is only interested, at that time, in hearing the employee's own account of the matter under investigation."

The Board's holding is a permissible construction of "concerted activities for . . . mutual aid or protection" . . . , and should have been sustained.

The action of an employee in seeking to have the assistance of his union representative at a confrontation with his employer clearly falls within the literal wording of §7 that "[e]mployees shall have the right . . . to engage in . . . concerted activities for the purpose of . . . mutual aid or protection." This is true even though the employee alone may have an immediate stake in the outcome; he seeks "aid or protection" against a perceived threat to his employment security. The union representative whose participation he seeks is, however, safeguarding not only the particular employee's interest, but also the interests of the entire bargaining unit by exercising vigilance to make certain that the employer does not initiate or continue a practice of imposing punishment unjustly. The representative's presence is an assurance to other employees in the bargaining unit that they, too, can obtain his aid and protection if called upon to attend a like interview. . . .

The Board's construction plainly effectuates the most fundamental purposes of the Act [paraphrasing §1]. . . . Requiring a lone employee to attend an investigatory interview which he reasonably believes may result in the imposition of discipline perpetuates the inequality the Act was designed to eliminate, and bars recourse to the safeguards the Act provided "to redress the perceived imbalance of economic power between labor and management.". . . .

The Board's construction also gives recognition to the right when it is most useful to both employee and employer. A single employee confronted by an employer investigating whether certain conduct deserves discipline may be too fearful or inarticulate to relate accurately the incident being investigated, or too ignorant to raise extenuating factors. A knowledgeable union representative could assist the employer by eliciting favorable facts, and save the employer production time by getting to the bottom of the incident occasioning the interview. Certainly his presence need not transform the interview into an adversary contest. Respondent suggests nonetheless that union representation at this stage is unnecessary because a decision as to employee culpability or disciplinary action can be corrected after the decision to impose discipline has become final. In other words, respondent would defer representation until the filing of a formal grievance challenging the employer's determination of guilt after the employee has been discharged or otherwise disciplined. At that point, however, it becomes increasingly difficult for the employee to vindicate himself, and the value of representation is correspondingly diminished. The employer may then be more concerned with justifying his actions than reexamining them. . . .

The responsibility to adapt the Act to changing patterns of industrial life is entrusted to the Board. The Court of Appeals impermissibly encroached upon the Board's function in determining for itself that an employee has no "need" for union assistance at an investigatory interview. . . . [T]he Board's construction here, while it may not be required by the Act, is at least permissible under it, and insofar as the Board's application of that meaning engages in the "difficult and delicate responsibility" of reconciling conflicting interests of labor and management, the balance struck by the Board is "subject to limited judicial review." NLRB v. Truck Drivers, 353 U.S. 87, 96 (1957).

The statutory right confirmed today is in full harmony with actual industrial practice. Many important collective bargaining agreements . . . accord employees rights of union representation at investigatory interviews. Even where such a right is not explicitly provided in the agreement a "well-established current of arbitral authority" sustains the right of union representation at investigatory interviews which the employee reasonably believes may result in disciplinary action against him. Chevron Chemical Co., 60 Lab. Arb. 1066, 1071 (1973).

The judgment is reversed and the case is remanded with direction to enter a judgment enforcing the Board's order. . . .

[The dissenting opinions of Justice Powell, joined by Justice Stewart, and of Chief Justice Burger are omitted.]

## *NOTES AND QUESTIONS*

**1. Section 7 Right to a Particular Term of Employment?** The §7 protected activity in the other cases in this chapter involved employee protests or complaints or organizational efforts or solicitations. Does *Weingarten* affirm the Board's taking an additional step by also protecting a particular procedure that is more in the nature of an actual condition of employment rather than an effort to obtain better conditions? Note that the Board protects employees from being disciplined not only for asking for a union representative at an investigatory interview that the employee reasonably fears will lead to discipline, but also for refusing to submit to such an interview without the representative. Note also, however, that the Board does not require the employer to provide an opportunity for the employee to be interviewed.

**2. Rationale for *Weingarten*?** In *Weingarten,* the Court acknowledged that "the employee alone may have an immediate stake in the outcome [of the interview]." Why then was Collins's request for "mutual aid or protection"? What precisely is the rationale underlying the recognition of *Weingarten* rights?

**3. *Weingarten* Terminology: "Investigatory" vs. "Disciplinary" Interviews?** When discussing *Weingarten* rights, the Board, courts and commentators often use the term "investigatory" interview—and occasionally "disciplinary" interview—as a shorthand reference. The decision itself, however, states that the right to request representation attaches "where the employee reasonably believes the investigation will lead to disciplinary action." *Weingarten,* then, applies only where both elements are present: (1) an investigatory interview (2) that may lead to disciplinary action. The limitations on this concept are explored in the notes below.

**4. Why Only One Procedural Right?** If §7 creates the procedural right recognized in *Weingarten,* why not other procedural rights to the assistance of union representatives? For instance, should employees be able to insist on an opportunity to respond with the aid of a union representative to charges against them even where the employer does not want to conduct an investigatory interview? To insist on an adjudicatory hearing with union representation as a precondition to any discipline? To insist on the presence of union representatives during training or corrections of work technique to ensure that instructions have been adequately conveyed? Do you understand why these claims are conceptually distinguishable from the *Weingarten* right as formulated at the end of note 1? Would expanding *Weingarten* to include procedural rights such as these restrict the personnel policies of employers without allowing them the give and take of collective bargaining?

**5. Meetings to Inform Employees of a Disciplinary Decision.** The Board does not protect the right to union representation at meetings the sole purpose of which is to inform an employee of a previously determined disciplinary decision. See Baton Rouge Water Works Co., 246 N.L.R.B. 995 (1979). Accord Alfred M. Lewis, Inc. v. NLRB, 587 F.2d 403 (9th Cir. 1978). Why not? On what basis are such meetings distinguishable from the types of interviews to which *Weingarten* applies?

**6. Individualized Drug Testing.** Should *Weingarten* rights apply to the administration of a drug test to an individual employee? See Safeway Stores, Inc., 303 N.L.R.B. 989 (1991) (Board does not pass on ALJ's "apparent conclusion that a drug test, standing alone, would constitute an investigatory interview under *Weingarten,*" but finds *Weingarten* applicable where test is part of broader investigation of employee's absenteeism record). What role would the union representative play during the administration of a drug or other medical test?

**7. Covert Investigations.** Are *Weingarten* rights infringed by a covert investigatory interview conducted, at management's request, by a fellow employee? See National Treasury Employees' Union v. FLRA, 835 F.2d 1446 (D.C. Cir. 1987) (holding *Weingarten* does not apply because employee could have no fear of discipline from covert interview).

**8. Limitation on Remedies for *Weingarten* Violations; §10(c).** An employee cannot be discharged or otherwise disciplined for invoking *Weingarten* rights, but does the employer's *Weingarten* violation shield the employee from discipline for the investigated conduct? In Taracorp Indus., 273 N.L.R.B. 221 (1984), overruling Kraft Food, Inc., 251 N.L.R.B. 598 (1980), the Board held that §10(c) of the Act bars reinstatement and back pay whenever an employee has been discharged for cause, and that the Board will order these remedies only when the employee would not have been discharged but for requesting representation. What if the decision to discipline is based primarily on a written confession obtained during an interview in which *Weingarten* rights were denied; should the employee at least be able to get the confession "expunged"? See N.J. Bell Telephone Co., 300 N.L.R.B. 42 (1990) (rejecting expungement remedy as inconsistent with *Taracorp* and §10(c)). From what disciplinary actions are employees protected by *Weingarten* after the *Taracorp* decision? Cf. Preferred Transportation, Inc., 339 N.L.R.B. 1 (2003) (unlike in *Taracorp* "the discharge here was not based on misconduct *uncovered* by the investigation, but rather on misconduct that was triggered by and elicited during the investigation").

Does *Taracorp* express a general principle pursuant to §10(c) that the Board cannot order make-whole relief as a remedy for a discharge based on an employer's discovery of discharge-justified misconduct through an unlawful means? In Anheuser-Busch Inc., 351 N.L.R.B. 644 (2007), review denied sub nom. Brewers & Malters, Local Union No. 6 v. NLRB, 303 Fed. Appx. 899 (D.C. Cir. 2008), the Board, relying on *Taracorp,* held that an employer who unlawfully installed hidden cameras without bargaining with the union could not be compelled to rescind the discharge of employees whose misconduct warranting discharge had been revealed by the cameras.

**9. Role of the Union Representative?** What is the union representative's role in the investigatory interview? The Board has required employers to allow union representatives to be more than passive observers, to give advice to employees, and even to advise against answering particular questions "as abusive, misleading, badgering, confusing, or harassing." New Jersey Bell Telephone Co., 308 N.L.R.B. 277, 279 (1992). But a union representative may lose his or her §7 protection through disruptive tactics that prevent the interview from being conducted. See, e.g., Yellow Freight Systems, Inc., 317 N.L.R.B. 115 (1995). See generally Jodie Meade Michalski, Knowing When to Keep Quiet: *Weingarten* and the Limitation on Representative Participation, 26 Hofstra Lab. & Emp. L.J. 163 (2008).

### *Note:* **Weingarten** *Rights in the Nonunion Setting?*

Should nonunion employees have the right to refuse to submit to an investigatory interview without the presence of a fellow employee? The Board has gone back and forth on this issue. See Materials Research Corp., 262 N.L.R.B. 1010 (1982) (3-2) (extending *Weingarten* to nonunion setting); Sears, Roebuck & Co., 274 N.L.R.B. 230 (1985) (Act mandates opposite result of confining *Weingarten* to union context); E.I. DuPont de Nemours, 289 N.L.R.B. 627 (1988), on remand from 794 F.2d 120 (3d Cir. 1986) (adhering to *Sears* rule as discretionary matter following circuit's rejection of conclusion that *Sears* interpretation was required by Act); Epilepsy Foundation of Northeast Ohio, 331 N.L.R.B. 676 (2000) (3-2) (returning to rule that *Weingarten* extends to nonunion employees), enforced in relevant part, 268 F.3d 1095 (D.C. Cir. 2001); IBM Corp., 341 N.L.R.B. 1288 (2004) (returning to earlier Board precedent holding *Weingarten* inapplicable in nonunion workplace).

In *IBM* the Board allowed that *Epilepsy Foundation* was based on a permissible construction of the Act, but concluded that the national labor relations policy would be "best served" by the permissible alternative construction that *Weingarten* rights do not apply in a nonunionized workplace. The Board's conclusion was based on several factors that weighed against extending *Weingarten* rights to nonunion shops. First, the Board noted that coworkers in a nonunion setting, unlike union representatives, have no obligation to represent the entire work force. Second, nonunion coworkers have no leverage to redress the balance of power between employers and employees. Third, coworkers do not have the same skills as a union representative. Fourth, a nonunion coworker may compromise the confidentiality of information, while union representatives, by virtue of their legal duty of fair representation, may not, in bad faith, reveal or misuse the information obtained in an employee interview. The Board confirmed that employees have the right to *seek* coworker representation, and cannot be disciplined for doing so. The nonunion employer, however, has no obligation to accede to the request, and can therefore discipline an employee for refusing to submit to the interview without representation.

In dissent, Members Liebman and Walsh argued that the presumed reduced efficacy of the *Weingarten* right in the absence of a union should not affect its availability. They also faulted the majority for failing to produce any evidence "that unions have interfered with employers' investigatory obligations since 1975, when *Weingarten* was decided, or that coworker representatives have caused harm since *Epilepsy Foundation* issued in 2000. Nothing in the record shows that investigations have come to a halt because of the presence of a coworker at an investigatory interview, or that information obtained during such an interview has been compromised."

## *NOTES AND QUESTIONS*

**1. Policy Oscillation at the Labor Board.** Could or should the type of "policy oscillation" exhibited by the Board on this issue be reined in by the Board committing to use rulemaking rather than adjudication when it wishes to reverse existing policy? See Estreicher, Policy Oscillation at the Labor Board, supra. Are these policy changes by the Board, with Democratic-appointed Boards favoring the extension of *Weingarten* rights to the nonunion setting (*Materials Research* and *Epilepsy Foundation*) and Republican Boards (*Sears, DuPont,* and *IBM*) opposing it, an example of acceptable rebalancing of employee and employer interests? See *Chevron,* supra page 75, 467 U.S. at 865; see also Harper, Judicial Control of the National Labor Relations Board's Lawmaking in the Age of *Chevron* and *Brand X,* supra, at 233-239; Ralph K. Winter, Jr., Judicial Review of Agency Decisions: The Labor Board and the Court, 1968 S. Ct. Rev. 53, 64-67. Even if the Board's policy changes are appropriate, would the Board and the constituencies it serves be better served by announcing in advance an agenda of issues for prospective change, to be effected either through rulemaking or adjudication, and remitting all other cases to be decided under existing Board law? See Estreicher, Improving the Administration of the NLRA, supra, at 13-1. For the view that political or ideological voting on the Board has become more pronounced, see Ronald Turner, Ideological Voting on the National Labor Relations Board, 8 U. Pa. J. Lab. & Emp. L. 707 (2006); James J. Brudney, Isolated and Politicized: The NLRB's Uncertain Future, 26 Comp. Lab. L. & Pol'y J. 221 (2005).

**2. An Ideological or Practical Dispute?** Of how much practical significance is the Board's continuing debate over the existence of *Weingarten* rights in the nonunion sector? How likely are nonunion employees to be aware of such rights if and when they do exist? How likely are they to invoke them? How many nonunion employees, if they do attempt to invoke such a right and the employer refuses, will insist on the presence of a coworker at the risk of being fired? Finally, if the employee does insist and refuses to be interviewed alone, is the employer more likely to fire her for insubordination or to finish the investigation without the interview and then discipline or discharge her for the underlying conduct? In this regard, recall both *Weingarten* itself and the remedial rule of *Taracorp Indus.*, supra note 8, page 207.

## D. UNION WAIVERS OF EMPLOYEE RIGHTS TO ENGAGE IN PROTECTED ACTIVITY

**NLRB v. Magnavox Co. of Tennessee**
*415 U.S. 322 (1974)*

Mr. Justice DOUGLAS delivered the opinion of the Court.

In 1954, the International Union of Electrical, Radio, and Machine Workers (IUE) became the collective-bargaining representative of respondent's employees. At that time respondent had a rule prohibiting employees from distributing literature on any of its property, including parking lots and other nonwork areas. The collective agreement authorized the company to issue rules for the "maintenance of orderly conditions on plant property," provided the rules were not "unfair" or "discriminatory." It also provided that bulletin boards would be available for the posting of union notices, subject to the company's right to reject "controversial" notices. All subsequent contracts contained similar provisions. Throughout the period since 1954 respondent has prohibited employees from distributing literature even in nonworking areas during nonworking time.

In due course, the IUE challenged the validity of the company's rule and requested that the rule be changed. The request was denied and the IUE filed charges against respondent for unfair labor practices in violation of §8(a)(1) of the National Labor Relations Act. The Board held for the IUE, following its earlier decision in Gale Products, 142 N.L.R.B. 1246, where it had said:

> Their place of work is the one location where employees are brought together on a daily basis. It is the one place where they clearly share common interests and where they traditionally seek to persuade fellow workers in matters affecting their union organizational life and other matters related to their status as employees. [Id., at 1249.]

The remedy in *Gale Products* ran in favor of employees whose distribution project was *to reject* a union representative. The Board in the present case, however, broadened the relief to embrace those who wanted *to support* a union representative, 195 N.L.R.B. 265. The Court of Appeals denied enforcement of the Board's order, because in its view the union had waived objection to the ban on on-premises distribution of literature and had the authority to do so. . . .

Employees have the right recognized in §7 of the Act "to form, join, or assist labor organizations" or "to refrain" from such activities. 29 U.S.C. §157. We agree that a ban on the distribution of union literature or the solicitation of union support by employees at the plant during nonworking time may constitute an interference with §7 rights. . . . No contention is made here that considerations of production or discipline make respondent's rule necessary. The sole issue concerns the power of the collective-bargaining representative to waive those rights.

The union may, of course, reach an agreement as to wages and other employment benefits and waive the right to strike during the time of the agreement as the quid pro quo for the employer's acceptance of the grievance and arbitration procedure. Textile Workers v. Lincoln Mills, 353 U.S. 448, 455. Such agreements, however, rest on "the premise of fair representation" and presuppose that the selection of the bargaining representative "remains free." Mastro Plastics Corp. v. NLRB, 350 U.S. 270, 280. In that case we held that the waiver of the "right to strike" did not embrace a waiver of the right to strike "against unlawful practices destructive of the foundation on which collective bargaining must rest." Id., at 281. We dealt there with rights in the economic area. Yet, . . . a different rule should obtain where the rights of the employees to exercise their choice of a bargaining representative is involved—whether to have no bargaining representative, or to retain the present one, or to obtain a new one. When the right to such a choice is at issue, it is difficult to assume that the incumbent union has no self-interest of its own to serve by perpetuating itself as the bargaining representative. The place of work is a place uniquely appropriate for dissemination of views concerning the bargaining representative and the various options open to the employees. So long as the distribution is by employees to employees and so long as the in-plant solicitation is on nonworking time, banning of that solicitation might seriously dilute §7 rights. For Congress declared in §1 of the Act that it was the policy of the United States to protect "the exercise by workers of full freedom of association, self-organization, and designation of representatives of their own choosing." 29 U.S.C. §151. . . .

Moreover, a limitation of the right of in-plant distribution of literature to employees opposing the union does not give a fair balance to §7 rights, as the Board ruled in the present case. For employees supporting the union have as secure §7 rights as those in opposition. . . .

Mr. Justice STEWART, with whom Mr. Justice POWELL and Mr. Justice REHNQUIST join, concurring in part and dissenting in part.

To the extent the Court holds that a union cannot contractually waive the right of disaffected employees to distribute in non-work areas and during nonwork time literature advocating the displacement of the incumbent collective-bargaining representative, I am in complete agreement. This is the essence of the Board's decision in Gale Products, 142 N.L.R.B. 1246. But it seems to me wholly inconsistent with the letter and spirit of the National Labor Relations Act to relieve the union of its promise that its own self-serving literature will not be so distributed in the plant. . . .

. . . Contractual waivers against a union's own interests are seldom if ever gratuitously granted in the give and take of the collective-bargaining process. In return, the union typically exacts some form of quid pro quo from the management negotiators. Since it is usually impossible to identify the consideration given in return for a particular union concession, the result of nullifying a union's agreement to waive the §7 rights of its supporters will necessarily be to deprive management of the benefit of its bargain and to leave the union with a windfall. This sort of invalidation of bargained-for concessions does not promote stability in the collective-bargaining process and must certainly have a negative effect on labor-management relations. For this reason, the Board and the courts should not relieve the parties of the promises they have made unless a contractual provision violates a specific section of the Act or a clear underlying policy of federal labor law.* . . .

## *NOTES AND QUESTIONS*

**1. An Agency-Cost Explanation?** Why should a union not be able to determine whether it can best maintain employees' support by sacrificing its rights to distribute promotional literature in exchange for some economic benefit? The Court relies on an equality of access explanation: If union critics have a right to distribute oppositional literature, union supporters must have a countervailing right. Does the opinion also imply that an identity of interest cannot be assumed between union supporters and the union leadership? Is this absence of identity likely?

**2. A Rights-Based Explanation?** Can *Magnavox* be better explained by analysis of why the NLRA protects certain types of rights? Consider the following:

> [T]he statutory policies supportive of the assignment of authority to exclusive majority bargaining representatives do not support the suppression of the otherwise protected expression of employees' views, even views supported by the exclusive representative, and even in exchange for collective benefits for the

---

* The Board held, and I presume the Court agrees, that the union could waive any right that the employees might have to distribute union institutional literature. The only question in this case relates to the waivability of rights to distribute literature regarding the proposed selection, retention, or displacement of the collective-bargaining agent. [Footnote relocated in text. — EDS.]

> bargaining unit. True, the authority of exclusive bargaining representatives rests on the Act's policy of "encouraging the practice and procedure of collective bargaining." But, as the Supreme Court stressed in *Mastro Plastics v. NLRB*, the Act has a "complementary" policy of "protecting the exercise by workers of full freedom of association, self-organization and designation of representatives of their own choosing." . . . Moreover, assurance of "full freedom of association" is the "foundation" of both policies of the Act; without it the effectiveness and the democratic legitimacy of exclusive representatives are undermined. Restricting the authority of exclusive representatives to waive the free-association and free-expression §7 rights of employees supports free and effective collective bargaining by insuring that economically strong employers cannot force unions to sacrifice at the bargaining table any of the rights upon which the unions' continued existence as effective bargaining agents may depend.

Michael C. Harper, Union Waiver of Employee Rights Under the NLRA: Part I, 4 Indus. Rel. L.J. 335, 345 (1981).

**3. Applications.**

a. How should the Board and the courts treat the waivability of rights to distribute literature regarding internal union affairs, such as the election of union officers? See, e.g., General Motors Corp. v. NLRB, 512 F.2d 447 (6th Cir. 1975) (nonwaivable). How about §7 rights to lead, support, associate, or refuse to associate with a labor organization? The right to wear or refrain from wearing a union logo on a company uniform? See Lee v. NLRB, 393 F.3d 491 (4th Cir. 2005) (nonwaivable). The right to distribute political literature relevant to the employees' conditions of employment as protected by *Eastex*, supra page 183?

b. Should unions be able to waive the §7-protected right recognized in *Weingarten* to insist on the presence of a union representative at any employer interview that an employee reasonably fears could result in disciplinary action?

c. A two-year collective bargaining agreement between an employer and an NLRB-certified union contains the following clause: "During the term of this Agreement, no union other than the employees' certified representative shall be granted access to the Employer's premises or bulletin boards; provided, however, that the certified representative's exclusive right of access shall not affect the statutory rights of employees to make distributions or solicitations on the Employer's premises." Does *Magnavox* answer the question whether this provision violates the NLRA? Cf. Perry Educ. Ass'n v. Perry Local Educators' Ass'n, 460 U.S. 37 (1983), where the Court, holding that the First Amendment was not violated by a bargaining agreement's grant to a recognized public sector union of an exclusive right of access to teachers' mailboxes and interschool mail systems, noted that exclusive-access provisions for private sector bargaining representatives "have yet to be expressly approved." Id. at 51 n.11.

**Metropolitan Edison Co. v. NLRB**
*460 U.S. 693 (1983)*

[The company was building a nuclear generating station at Three Mile Island. A series of bargaining agreements with the IBEW provided that "the Brotherhood and its members agree that during the term of this agreement there shall be no strikes or walkouts." Between 1970 and 1974, union members participated in four work stoppages violating that provision. On each occasion the company disciplined participating union officers more severely than the other participants. Two resultant arbitration awards had upheld the company's disparate treatment. In both cases the arbitrator determined that union officials have an "affirmative duty" to uphold the bargaining agreement, breach of which justifies greater discipline.

In August 1977, IBEW members refused to cross another union's informational picket line at the construction site. The company "repeatedly" ordered the local IBEW president to cross the picket line in order to demonstrate to other employees the IBEW's compliance with the no-strike clause. He refused to do so, choosing instead to attempt to persuade the other union to remove the picket line. Within four hours the IBEW president and vice-president had negotiated a settlement of the other union's dispute with the company, and the line was removed. The company imposed 5- to 10-day suspensions on all employees who had refused to cross the picket line. The local union president and vice-president, however, each received 25-day suspensions and warnings that future participation in any unlawful work stoppage would result in immediate discharge.

The NLRB ruled that selective discipline of union officials violates §§8(a)(1) and 8(a)(3). 252 N.L.R.B. 1030 (1980). The Third Circuit enforced the Board's order, holding that an employer may impose greater discipline on union officials only when the collective agreement expressly states that the officials have an "affirmative duty" to prevent work stoppages. The Supreme Court affirmed.]

POWELL, J. . . .

This case does not present the question whether an employer may impose stricter penalties on union officials who take a leadership role in an unlawful strike. The [ALJ] found that neither Light nor Lang [the local's president and vice-president] acted as a strike leader.[6] Nor does this case

---

6. The Board has held that employees who instigate or provide leadership for unprotected strikes may be subject to more severe discipline than other employees. See Midwest Precision Castings Co., 244 N.L.R.B. 597, 598 (1979); Chrysler Corp., 232 N.L.R.B. 466, 474 (1977). In making this factual determination the Board has recognized that a remark made by

question the employer's right to discipline union officials who engage in unprotected activity. Neither the union nor the Board has argued that union officials who fail to honor a no-strike clause are immunized from being disciplined in the same manner as other strike participants. The narrow question presented is whether an employer unilaterally may define the actions a union official is required to take to enforce a no-strike clause and penalize him for his failure to comply. . . .

The Board has found that disciplining union officials more severely than other employees for participating in an unlawful work stoppage "is contrary to the plain meaning of §8(a)(3) and would frustrate the policies of the Act if allowed to stand." Precision Castings Co., 233 N.L.R.B. [183] at 184 [(1979)]. This conduct, in the Board's view, is "inherently destructive" of protected individual rights because it discriminates solely on the basis of union status. See Consolidation Coal Co., 263 N.L.R.B. 1306 (1982); Indiana & Michigan Electric Co., 237 N.L.R.B. 226 (1978), enf. denied, 599 F.2d 227 (CA7 1979). The Board has concluded that an employer's contractual right to be free of unauthorized strikes does not counterbalance the "discriminatory effects of singling out union officers for especially harsh treatment." Consolidation Coal Co., 263 N.L.R.B., at 1309. Disciplining union officials discriminatorily may have only an indirect effect on the rank and file's decision to strike, but it may well deter qualified employees from seeking union office. See ibid.

We defer to the Board's conclusion that conduct such as Metropolitan Edison's adversely affects protected employee interests. Section 8(a)(3) not only proscribes discrimination that affects union membership, it also makes unlawful discrimination against employees who participate in concerted activities protected by §7. . . . See Radio Officers' Union v. NLRB, 347 U.S. 17, 39-40 (1954). Holding union office clearly falls within the activities protected by §7, . . . and there can be little doubt that an employer's unilateral imposition of discipline on union officials inhibits qualified employees from holding office. . . .

Determining that such conduct adversely affects protected employee interests does not conclude the inquiry. If the employer comes forward with a legitimate explanation for its conduct, the Board must "strike the proper balance between the asserted business justifications and the invasion of employee rights." NLRB v. Great Dane Trailers, Inc., 388 U.S. [26, 33-34 (1967)]. . . . [T]he company has argued that its actions were justified because there is an implied duty on the part of the union officials to uphold

---

a union official may have greater significance than one made by a rank-and-file member. See Midwest Precision Castings, supra, at 599.

In this case the Board accepted the [ALJ's] finding that Light and Lang were not strike leaders, and the Court of Appeals affirmed that finding. . . .

the terms of the collective-bargaining agreement. Unquestionably there is support for the proposition that union officials, as leaders of the rank and file, have a legal obligation to support the terms of the contract and to set a responsible example for their members. See Indiana & Michigan Electric Co. v. NLRB, 599 F.2d, at 230-232. And in view of the disruptive effects of wildcat strikes, the importance of ensuring compliance with no-strike clauses is self-evident. . . . But it does not follow that an employer may assume that a union official is required to attempt to enforce a no-strike clause by complying with the employer's directions and impose a penalty on the official for declining to comply. . . .

The company argues that even if §8(a)(3) would prohibit it from imposing a more severe penalty on union officials than on other employees, the union in effect has waived the [statutory] protection. . . . The substance of this contention is that, in this case, the prior arbitration awards and the union's acquiescence in the harsher sanctions imposed on its officials are sufficient to establish a corresponding contractual duty. . . . [T]he union's response [is] that the statutory right to be free from discrimination may never be waived. . . .

. . . [A] union may waive a member's statutorily protected rights, including "his right to strike during the contract term, and his right to refuse to cross a lawful picket line." NLRB v. Allis-Chalmers Manufacturing Co., 388 U.S. 175, 180 (1967). Such waivers are valid because they "rest on 'the premise of fair representation' and presuppose that the selection of the bargaining representative 'remains free.'" NLRB v. Magnavox Co., 415 U.S. 322, 325 (1974) (quoting Mastro Plastics Corp. v. NLRB, 350 U.S. 270, 280 (1956)). . . . Waiver should not undermine these premises. Thus a union may bargain away its members' economic rights, but it may not surrender rights that impair the employees' choice of their bargaining representative. See NLRB v. Magnavox Co., 415 U.S., at 325.

We think a union's decision to bind its officials to take affirmative steps to end an unlawful work stoppage is consistent with "the premise of fair representation." Such a waiver imposes no constraints on the employees' ability to choose which union will represent them. Imposition of this duty is more closely related to the economic decision a union makes when it waives its members' right to strike. It merely requires union officials to take steps that are ancillary to the union's promise not to strike and provides the employer with an additional means of enforcing this promise. . . .

We will not infer from a general contractual provision that the parties intended to waive a statutorily protected right unless the undertaking is "explicitly stated." More succinctly, the waiver must be clear and unmistakable.

. . . Metropolitan Edison does not contend that the general no-strike clause included in the bargaining agreement imposed any explicit duty on the union officials. Rather it argues that the union's failure to change the relevant contractual language in the face of two prior arbitration decisions constitutes an implicit contractual waiver. . . .

. . . [W]e do not doubt that prior arbitration decisions may be relevant—both to other arbitrators and to the Board—in interpreting bargaining agreements. But to waive a statutory right the duty must be established clearly and unmistakably. Where prior arbitration decisions have been inconsistent, sporadic, or ambiguous, there would be little basis for determining that the parties intended to incorporate them in subsequent agreements. Assessing the clarity with which a party's duties have been defined of course will require consideration of the specific circumstances of each case. Cf. Carbon Fuel Co. v. Mine Workers, 444 U.S. 212, 221-222 (1979).

. . . [T]he company argues that when the prior bargaining agreement was renegotiated, the union's silence manifested a clear acceptance of the earlier arbitration decisions. During the history of collective bargaining between these two parties, however, . . . only two arbitration decisions . . . imposed a higher duty on union officials. We do not think that two arbitration awards establish a pattern of decisions clear enough to convert the union's silence into binding waiver. This is especially so in light of the provision in the bargaining agreement that "[a] decision [by an arbitrator] shall be binding . . . for the term of *this* agreement" (emphasis added). We conclude that there is no showing that the parties intended to incorporate the two prior arbitration decisions into the subsequent agreement.

## *NOTES AND QUESTIONS*

**1. Should the Right to Be Free of Special Penalties as a Union Officer Be Waivable?** The *Metropolitan Edison* Court seems to accept the Board's conclusion that imposing greater penalties on union officers than on other employees discriminates against those who choose to be more active in the union and thus infringes on the §7 right to be a union leader. The Court also cites its prior decision in *Magnavox* for the proposition that unions "may not surrender rights that impair the employees' choice of their bargaining representative." Why, then, does the Court endorse a union's authority to accept greater penalties on union officers? Presumably, employees' free choice of bargaining representative entails the free choice of that representative's leadership, and special penalties on officers for illegal strikes are likely to discourage some people more than others from becoming union officers. Is it a sufficient response to assert that unions can be counted on to vigorously protect the institutional position of their leaders and organizers?

**2. Rule of "Clear and Unmistakable" Waiver.** Given the Court's premise that the right involved in *Metropolitan Edison* is akin to an economic right that is subject to contractual waiver or modification by the union, what is the justification for requiring that any waiver be expressed "clearly and unmistakably"? Does this requirement express a factual presumption that waivers of statutory rights are exceptional occurrences? Is such a presumption reasonable in light of the widespread negotiation of clauses waiving the fundamental §7 right to strike? Does the requirement of clear and unmistakable waiver instead express a legal presumption based on a statutory policy that union waivers of statutory rights should not be implied but rather should be the product of an express bargain struck by the union in exchange for some valuable concession?

**3. Are Rights to Engage in Some Strikes Waivable?**

a. *Unfair Labor Practice Strikes.* To what extent should unions be able to waive the rights of represented employees to engage in strikes in protest of unfair labor practices? In Mastro Plastics Corp. v. NLRB, 350 U.S. 270, 281 (1956), a case involving an employer's discharge of a supporter of the signatory union and unlawful assistance to an insurgent union, the Supreme Court held that general no-strike clauses should not be presumed to have the effect of waiving employee rights to engage in strikes "against unlawful practices destructive of the foundation on which collective bargaining must rest."

*Mastro Plastics* leaves open several questions. First, because the case involved an employer's attempt to oust the bargaining representative, it may be argued that strikes over less serious unfair labor practices capable of being redressed as contract breaches might be covered by a general no-strike clause. Indeed, in Arlan's Department Store, 133 N.L.R.B. 802 (1961), the Board held that only strikes protesting "serious" unfair labor practices are beyond the reach of a general no-strike clause. See also Dow Chemical Co., 244 N.L.R.B. 1060 (1979) (reaffirming *Arlan's*), enf. denied, 636 F.2d 1352 (3d Cir. 1980). What, then, is a "serious" unfair labor practice? Compare *Arlan's* (general no-strike clause covers strike protesting discharge of steward for circulating a decertification petition), with *Dow Chemical* (general no-strike clause does not cover strike protesting employer's unilateral change in work schedules). Second, even where a no-strike clause explicitly covers strikes against unfair practices, the rationale of the *Magnavox* decision suggests that where the employer's violation involves the abridgement of a nonwaivable right, such as the right to press for the selection or rejection of a bargaining representative, a purported contractual waiver should be held ineffective. For instance, a strike to protest an unlawful recognition or withdrawal of recognition of a bargaining representative would be deemed beyond the reach of any no-strike clause.

b. *Sympathy Strikes.* Consider also the waivability by unions of represented employees' rights to refuse to cross picket lines established on behalf of other employees in different bargaining units. For discussion of this issue, see infra Note, *Honoring Picket Lines,* page 534.

## E. EMPLOYER "SUPPORT" OR "DOMINATION" OF A "LABOR ORGANIZATION"

The framers of the NLRA viewed §8(a)(2)'s prohibition of "company unions" as a key element in the protection of the organizing process. This provision, which was invoked in the *Budd* case, supra page 116, was enacted in part as a response to the experience with employer-initiated representation plans that mushroomed in growth after the enactment of the National Industrial Recovery Act of 1933 (NIRA), which announced in §7(a) that employees had a right to organize and engage in collective bargaining. Because the NIRA did not provide an effective enforcement mechanism, many companies openly flouted §7(a), using in-house representation plans as part of an arsenal of tactics that also included spies, professional strikebreakers, and mass discharges of union supporters.

For instance, in an earlier phase of the Budd Employee Representation Association's history, the company insisted that it would deal only with its employee association in the face of overwhelming evidence that a majority of the employees supported an independent union: "When management told the United Automobile Federal Labor Union, which claimed 1,000 Budd employees as members, that the company 'could not recognize the American Federation of Labor inasmuch as Budd had employee representation that was operating satisfactorily,' approximately 1,500 Budd employees went on strike." Edward G. Budd Mfg. Co., 1 N.L.R.B. 58, 59 (1933). See also James A. Gross, The Making of the National: A Study in Economics, Politics, and the Law (1933-1937), at 37 (1974); Irving Bernstein, The Turbulent Years: A History of the American Worker 1933-1941, 179 (1969); Hearings on S. 2926 Before the Comm. on Education and Labor, U.S. Sen., 73d Cong., 2d Sess. 104-106 (1934) (testimony of William Green), reprinted in 1 NLRB Legislative History of the National Labor Relations Act, 1935, at 134-136 (1985).

By enacting §8(a)(2) as an independent prohibition, Congress sought to bar any employer involvement in the process of selecting or maintaining a bargaining representative of the employees, even where employers did not use their in-plant systems as a justification for refusing to deal with an independent union. For a consideration of the justifications in 1935 for the breadth of the §8(a)(2) prohibition and the question of its continued relevance to contemporary conditions, compare Samuel Estreicher, Employee Involvement and the "Company Union" Prohibition: The Case for Partial Repeal of Section 8(a)(2) of the NLRA, 69 N.Y.U. L. Rev. 101 (1994), with Michael C. Harper, The Continuing Relevance of Section 8(a)(2) to the Contemporary Workplace, 96 Mich. L. Rev. 2322 (1998);

Mark Barenberg's essays, Democracy and Domination in the Law of Workplace Cooperation: From Bureaucratic to Flexible Production, 94 Colum. L. Rev. 753 (1994); The Political Economy of the Wagner Act: Power, Symbol and Workplace Cooperation, 106 Harv. L. Rev. 1379 (1993); and Laurence Gold, The Legal Status of "Employee Participation" Programs After the Labor Board's *Electromation* and *du Pont* Decisions, in Proc., 46th N.Y.U. Ann. Conf. on Lab. 21, 24 (Bruno Stein ed., 1993).

Although employer recognition of minority unions may remain a resistant problem in some industries, §8(a)(2) has effectively eliminated actual collective bargaining with company unions. The broader reach of §8(a)(2) has continued to generate controversy, however. With the decline of private sector union density and the expression by American employers of a growing desire to enlist the participation of more employees at some level of firm management, appeals have been made to revisit the judgments underlying §8(a)(2). The specifics of such appeals or proposals are discussed infra page 230.

**Crown Cork & Seal Co.**
*334 N.L.R.B. 699 (2001)*

. . . The Respondent employs approximately 150 employees at its aluminum can manufacturing plant in Sugar Land, Texas. Ever since the plant opened in 1984, a system of employee management has been utilized known as the "Socio-Tech System." The central purpose of the Socio-Tech System is to delegate to employees substantial authority to operate the plant through their participation on numerous standing and temporary teams, committees, and boards (collectively committees). There was no union organizational activity occurring at the time the Socio-Tech System was adopted or at the time of the events in issue here.

The seven committees discussed below are alleged to be employer-dominated labor organizations. All seven committees make decisions by a process of discussion and consensus. If a member of a committee cannot join in a consensus, he abstains on the issue. The management members of a committee have no greater authority than other committee members.

[The] four production teams "decide and do" on a wide variety of workplace issues, "including production, quality, training, attendance, safety, maintenance, and discipline short of suspension or discharge." For example, the teams have the authority to stop the production lines without management approval. With respect to quality issues, [Plant Manager] De Young testified that if team members working in the shipping area were concerned that scratched cans may have been shipped to a customer, "they're empowered to call up the customer and stop that delivery and turn it around." Regarding training, the teams have the authority to decide which members are given formal and informal training. The production teams administer the plant's absentee program, deciding whether to grant a team member's request for time off and whether an absence is excused or unexcused.

With respect to safety, the production teams have the authority to investigate accidents and correct safety-related problems. For example, Plant Manager De Young testified that production teams would correct the problem of a piece of machinery "eating people's fingers" by building and installing a guard without further review by anyone else in the plant. . . .

The production teams decide what disciplinary action to take against a team member failing to meet team norms with respect to performance or behavior. The team can counsel the member and, if necessary, require the member to enter into a "social contract." A "social contract" can be verbal or written and is designed to modify the member's behavior. If the social contract does not have the desired effect and the team believes that suspension or discharge is warranted, the decision is in the form of a recommendation to the Organizational Review Board discussed below.

. . . [T]hree [other] committees exist at one administrative level above the production teams. Each one has about a dozen members, including two members from each of the four teams and some members of management. Many of the decisions made by these three committees are reviewed by the Management Team composed of 15 members of management. The plant manager is above the Management Team. He has the ultimate authority to review all decisions made by the three committees.

Under the Socio-Tech System, the *Organizational Review Board* (ORB) is charged with monitoring plant policies to insure that they are administered consistently among the four teams. The ORB also suggests modifications to plant norms, including hours, layoff procedures, smoking policies, vacations, and all terms and conditions of employment. Decisions of the ORB are in the form of recommendations forwarded to the Management Team or the plant manager. Plant Manager De Young testified that he could not recall a single instance when he over-ruled the ORB. "I just haven't done it." Further, De Young testified that decisions of the ORB often have been implemented by the time they reach him. . . .

In addition, the ORB reviews production team recommendations to suspend or discipline a team member. Again, the record shows that the plant manager gives great weight to the recommendation of the ORB. . . .

Like the other committees, the ORB must operate within established parameters. The record indicates that one of the roles of management is to ensure that the committees do not exceed their delegated authority. For example, when the ORB recommended a layoff procedure that contained a provision for seniority, the Management Team returned the matter to the ORB with the following comment: "We do not have seniority in this plant." The final version of the layoff policy did not include seniority as an independent factor.

The Socio-Tech System delegates to the *Advancement Certification Board* (ACB) the authority to administer the Respondent's "Pay for Acquired Skills

Program." The ACB certifies that employees have advanced to higher skill levels and recommends pay increases to the plant manager. De Young has never overruled a recommendation of the ACB.

The Socio-Tech System delegates to the *Safety Committee* the authority to review production team accident reports and consider the best methods to ensure a safe workplace. The plant manager has never overruled a recommendation of the Safety Committee. In fact, De Young indicated that he would defer to the Safety Committee on an issue even if he did not agree with it. . . .

By its terms, Section 8(a)(2) provides that it is an unfair labor practice for an employer to dominate or support "any labor organization." Consequently, before a violation of Section 8(a)(2) can be found, the entity involved must be a statutory "labor organization."

One of the required elements for "labor organization" status under Section 2(5) is that the entity "exists for the purpose, in whole or in part, of dealing with employers concerning grievances, labor disputes, wages, rates of pay, hours of employment, or conditions of work." (Emphasis added.) The Board has explained that "dealing with" contemplates "a bilateral mechanism involving proposals from the employee committee concerning the subjects listed in Section 2(5), coupled with real or apparent consideration of those proposals by management." Electromation, Inc., 309 N.L.R.B. 990, 995 n. 21 (1992), enfd. 35 F.3d 1148 (7th Cir. 1994). "That 'bilateral mechanism' ordinarily entails a pattern or practice in which a group of employees, over time, makes proposals to management, [and] management responds to these proposals by acceptance or rejection by word or deed. . . ." E. I. du Pont & Co., 311 N.L.R.B. 893, 894 (1993).

Keeler Brass Co., 317 NLRB 1110 (1995), illustrates the concept of "dealing." In that case, an employee grievance committee decided that the company's decision to discharge an employee under its "no-call, no-show" policy was too harsh. The committee recommended that the employee be rehired and that the policy be reexamined. The company considered the committee's proposal, changed the no-call, no-show policy, but decided that the discharge was justified by past practice. The grievance committee then heard additional testimony on the past-practice issue, reversed itself, and denied the grievance. On these facts, the Board found that statutory "dealing" was present with respect to the discharge grievance and the no-call, no-show policy because the committee and the company "went back and forth explaining themselves until an acceptable result was achieved." *Id.* at 1114.

By contrast, the element of "dealing" was absent in General Foods Corp., 231 N.L.R.B. 1232 (1977). That case involved a "job enrichment program" designed "to enlarge the powers and responsibilities of all its rank-and-file employees and to give them certain powers or controls over their job situations which are normally not assigned to manual laborers." Id. at 1232-1233. Employees were divided into four teams. Acting by consensus, the teams made job assignments to individual team members, assigned job rotations, and scheduled overtime. Individual team members also served on ad hoc committees that interviewed job applicants, made safety inspections of the plant, and, within certain limits, set starting and quitting times.

The *General Foods* Board found that "these are managerial functions being flatly delegated to employees and do not involve any dealing with the employer on a group basis within the meaning of Section 2(5), however expansively that term is applied." Id. at 1235. The decision continued as follows: While the employer could withdraw the powers delegated to employees to perform these functions on its behalf, the withdrawal of authority would be wholly unilateral on its part just as was Respondent's original delegation. There was no dealing between employer and employee (or employee group) involved in these matters. These functions were just other assignments of job duties, albeit duties not normally granted to rank-and-file personnel.

In its subsequent *Electromation* decision, the Board cited *General Foods* for the proposition that there is no "dealing" if the organization's "purpose is limited to performing essentially a managerial" function. 309 N.L.R.B. at 995. . . .

[T]he facts of the instant case resemble those of *General Foods*. . . . As in *General Foods*, management has delegated to the committees in issue the authority to operate the plant within certain parameters. This is the essence of the Socio-Tech System. As the judge recognized, the Socio-Tech System represents a significant variation on the traditional plant organizational structure where authority is delegated to descending levels of managers who make decisions on an individual basis. Under the Socio-Tech System, authority is delegated to descending levels of committees which make decisions by consensus.

Nevertheless, the two systems have an important element in common and that is that at each level the authority being exercised is unquestionably managerial. With respect to the four production teams, Plant Manager De Young testified, the [ALJ] found, and we agree, that the authority they exercise is comparable to that of the front-line supervisor in the traditional plant setting. Similarly, given De Young's credited testimony that he has rarely, if ever, overruled one of the recommendations of the ORB, the ACB, or the Safety Committee, it cannot be doubted that each committee exercises as a group authority that in the traditional plant setting would be considered to be supervisory. Therefore, we conclude that the rationale of *General Foods* applies here and that the seven committees are not labor organizations because their purpose is to perform essentially managerial functions, and thus they do not "deal with" the Respondent within the meaning of Section 2(5) of the Act.

In contending otherwise, the General Counsel maintains that because one of the seven committees possess authority that is final and absolute, "dealing" must necessarily be occurring when their recommendations are passed on to the Management Team and the plant manager. Like the judge, we reject this contention. Few, if any, supervisors in a conventional plant possess authority that is final and absolute. At the Respondent's facility, just as in a more traditional plant, one level of management (e.g., the ORB), acting within its sphere of delegated authority, forwards for review its recommendations to a higher level of authority (e.g., the plant manager). But it would not be accurate to characterize that exchange as "dealing" within the meaning of Section 2(5) of the Act. Rather, what is occurring in the Respondent's facility is the familiar process of a managerial recommendation making its way up the chain of command. Higher-management review of a recommendation made by lower management cannot be equated to the "dealing" between an employer and a representative of its employees contemplated by the statute. Indeed, it is the fact that the interaction is occurring between two management bodies that distinguishes this case from cases such as *Keeler Brass* and persuades us that the statutory element of dealing is absent. . . .

## *NOTES AND QUESTIONS*

**1. Delegation of Managerial Authority?** In *General Foods Corp.*, 231 N.L.R.B. 1232 (1977), relied on in *Crown Cork*, the Board suggested that employee committees do not "deal with" management where firms are willing to delegate fully managerial tasks to the employees. In what sense were Crown Cork's employee committees acting as "management bodies"? Were managerial tasks fully delegated to Crown Cork employees through the committees? Is it critical that supervisors "rarely, if ever, overruled one of the recommendations" of the Organizational Review Board, the Advancement Certification Board, and the Safety Committee? Contrast Crown Cork's committees with the Action Committees in *Electromation*, 309 N.L.R.B. 990 (1992), enforced 35 F.3d 1148 (7th Cir. 1994). The *Electromation* Board, concluding that the Action Committees were nonmanagerial "labor organizations," described them as:

> . . . consist[ing] of six employees and one or two members of management, as well as the Respondent's Employees Benefits Manager . . . who would coordinate all the Action Committees. The sign-up sheets explained the responsibilities and goals of each Committee. No employees were involved in the drafting of the policy goals expressed in the sign-up sheets. The Respondent determined the number of employees permitted to sign-up for the Action Committees. The Respondent informed two employees who had signed up for more than one Committee that each would be limited to participation on one Committee. After the Action Committees were organized, the Respondent posted a notice to all employees announcing the members of each Committee and the dates of the initial Committee meetings. The Action Committees were designated as (1) Absenteeism/Infractions, (2) No Smoking Policy, (3) Communication Network, (4) Pay Progression for Premium Positions, and (5) Attendance Bonus Program.

> The Action Committees began meeting in late January and early February. The Respondent's coordinator of the Action Committees, Dickey, testified that management expected that employee members on the Committees would "kind of talk back and forth" with the other employees in the plant, get their ideas, and that, indeed, the purpose of the Respondent's postings was to ensure that "anyone [who] wanted to know what was going on, they could go to these people" on the Action Committees. Other management representatives, as well as Dickey, participated in the Action Committees' meetings, which were scheduled to meet on a weekly basis in a conference room on the Respondent's premises. The Respondent paid employees for their time spent participating and supplied necessary materials. Dickey's role in the meetings was to facilitate the discussions. . . .
>
> . . . The Attendance Bonus Committee's proposal was one of two proposals that the employees had developed concerning attendance bonuses. The first one, developed at the committee's second or third meeting, was pronounced unacceptable by the Respondent's controller, a member of that committee, because it was too costly. Thereafter the employees devised a second proposal, which the controller deemed fiscally sound. The proposal was not presented to [the company] President because the Union's campaign to secure recognition had intervened.

Why did the Board determine that Crown Cork's committees were integrated into the management structure but that Electromation's Action Committees were not?

**2. Peer Review Grievance Systems.** The Board has upheld peer review grievance committees when the review body can make a final decision in the employee's favor without management override. See Sparks Nugget, Inc., 230 N.L.R.B. 275 (1977) (employees participated in joint grievance committee that presided over grievance hearings and rendered binding decisions), enforced sub nom. NLRB v. Silver Spur Casino, 623 F.2d 571 (9th Cir. 1980); Mercy Memorial, 231 N.L.R.B. 1108 (1977) (employee grievance committee lawful because binding unless grievant successfully appealed decision to highest level of management); Syracuse Univ., 350 N.L.R.B. 755 (2007) (employee grievance committee lawful because even though it had to submit its proposed decisions to management for input it was not required to abide by that input).

**3. "Dealing With" vs. Communication Devices?** Citing *Electromation* and E. I. du Pont & Co., 311 N.L.R.B. 893 (1993), the *Crown Cork* Board stated that "dealing with" contemplates "a bilateral mechanism involving proposals from the employee committee concerning subjects listed in 2(5), coupled with real or apparent consideration of those proposals by management," to which "management responds . . . by acceptance or rejection by word or deed." What is the difference between "dealing with" and mere "communication"? What if an employer solicits suggestions from individual employees, perhaps through suggestion boxes or brainstorming sessions? Should a plant committee's presentation to management of employee views on working conditions, without specific recommendations for accommodating those views, be permissible? In other words, as a practical matter, can communication vehicles avoid give-and-take between managers and employees? Are Crown Cork's committees such an example? Chapter 14 considers whether new actors on the labor relations scene, such a "worker centers," fall within the definition of "labor organization."

For other applications of the "dealing with" concept, compare Polaroid Corp., 329 N.L.R.B. 424 (1999); EFCO Corp., 327 N.L.R.B. 372 (1998), enforced, 215 F.3d 1318 (4th Cir. 2000); and V & S ProGalv v. NLRB, 168 F.3d 270 (6th Cir. 1999) (all finding "dealing with" requirement met where employer-created committees made proposals to management, which management would subsequently accept or reject), with E.I. DuPont de Nemours & Co., 311 N.L.R.B. 893 (1993) (soliciting individual employee views in safety conferences not "dealing with" where no specific joint proposals were developed for management response; such conferences were permissible "brainstorming groups"); and *EFCO*, supra ("employee suggestion screening committee" that reviewed suggestions made by individual employees and forwarded them to management without recommendation was not "dealing with" employer; committee "functioned essentially as a screening portion of an employee 'suggestion box' program"). See generally *Polaroid*, supra (describing certain "safe havens" for employee involvement programs).

**4. Relevance of Employer Motive?** The Board generally does not view anti-union motive as a necessary element of a §8(a)(2) violation. Is this position required by the statutory language and intent? The Sixth Circuit once considered the lack of "anti-union animus to be a factor" in the assessment of the legality of employer-initiated employee representational programs. See NLRB v. Streamway Division, Scott & Fetzer Co., 691 F.2d 288 (6th Cir. 1982). In NLRB v. Webcor Packaging, Inc., 118 F.3d 1115, 1122 (6th Cir. 1997), however, the Sixth Circuit rejected *Scott & Fetzer*'s treatment of motive as contrary to both statutory text and Supreme Court precedent.

**5. Relevance of Employee "Free Choice" and Satisfaction?** The Sixth Circuit in *Scott & Fetzer* also deemed an infringement on "employee free choice" essential to a finding of an unlawful interference or domination of a "labor organization." It asserted that no interference with employee free choice occurs "unless employees are encouraged in the mistaken belief" that an employee committee is "truly representative and afford[s] an agency for collective bargaining." Is this a proper reading of §8(a)(2) and §2(5)? Other courts have held that employee satisfaction is relevant to the question of whether the "labor organization" is in fact unlawfully "dominate[d]" or "support[ed]" by the employer. See, e.g., Hertzka & Knowles v. NLRB, 503

F.2d 625, 630 (9th Cir. 1974); Chicago Rawhide Mfg. Co. v. NLRB, 221 F.2d 165, 168 (7th Cir. 1955). Do such rulings take proper account of NLRB v. Newport News Shipbuilding Co., 308 U.S. 241 (1939), where the Supreme Court held that an employer-controlled representation plan violated §8(a)(2) even though the employees in question overwhelmingly approved of the committees? For criticism of the appeals court decisions, see Thomas C. Kohler, Models of Worker Participation: The Uncertain Significance of Section 8(a)(2), 27 B.C. L. Rev. 499, 543-545 (1986).

The Board rejected *Scott & Fetzer*'s "infringement on employee free choice" standard in its *Electromation* decision. If employees are aware that the organization is not a "real union" and that they remain free to choose such a representative under §9(a), why should the Labor Board intervene? Is the Board being overly paternalistic or is there reason to think that employers use representative organizations to undermine the employees' ability to opt for independent unions? For an inside account of such use of an employee representational scheme, see Guillermo J. Greiner, Inhuman Relations: Quality Circles and Anti-Unionism in American Industry (1988).

**6. Representational Capacity?** Is it an element of the §2(5) definition of "labor organization" that the employer-initiated committees function in a representational capacity? Does the language of §2(5) support such a requirement? Do the policies underlying §8(a)(2)? The Board has declined on several occasions to decide this question. See *Polaroid,* 329 N.L.R.B. at 424 (citing cases). What if Crown Cork had held an election among the workforce to determine who would sit on the teams? Would that have changed the outcome? See Webcor Packaging, Inc., 319 N.L.R.B. 1203, 1204 n.6 (1995) (holding that Plant Council acted in representational capacity "because its employee-members were elected by the [company's] workforce," and further noting that Council members canvassed other employees for their opinion of policy changes being considered by the Council, e.g., by circulating copy of proposed attendance program with attached comment form and request for employee response), enforced, 118 F.3d 1115 (6th Cir. 1997).

As reflected in *Crown Cork,* some companies have sought to delegate traditional supervisor and engineering roles by training front-line workers to function as "self-directed work teams" responsible for task assignments, scheduling of work, maintaining and improving performance levels, cost and quality controls, and safety—usually with a minimum of supervision by traditional lower-level managers. See Estreicher, Employee Involvement, supra, at 138-139, and authorities cited therein; Paul Osterman, How Common Is Workplace Transformation and Who Adopts It?, 47 Indus. & Lab. Rel. Rev. 173 (1994); Edward E. Lawler III, High-Involvement Management: Participation Strategies for Improving Organizational Performance 175-176 (1986). Does the fact that these teams often have management-appointed or employee-selected team leaders who serve representative or liaison functions with the rest of the company satisfy any "representational capacity" requirement under §2(5)?

**7. "Quality" and "Efficiency" vs. §2(5) Subjects?** Can employers interested in obtaining the benefits of employee involvement avoid §8(a)(2) strictures simply by limiting the subjects considered by employee committees to matters implicating only "quality" and "efficiency" concerns rather than working conditions? Can a meaningful line be drawn in this manner? How would you characterize safety issues? Work-shift changes?

**8. Employer's Financial or Other Assistance to a Union?** The Board typically adopts a more permissive attitude toward employer financial and other assistance to a legitimately recognized, independent union—including the allowance of payment for time spent on grievance adjustment and the provision of company facilities for union meetings. Is such a permissive attitude justified under the language of §8(a)(2)? By the policies of the NLRA? Even in union-represented firms, payment to union officials for time spent on union business may raise issues under NLRA §8(a)(2), Labor Management Relations Act §302 (LMRA), and Labor-Management Reporting and Disclosure Act §§202 and 203. In Caterpillar v. Int'l Union, United Auto., Aerospace & Agric. Implement Workers of Am., et al., 107 F.3d 1052 (3d Cir. 1997) (en banc), an appeals court held that an employer's provision of paid leaves of absence for employees who became the union's full-time grievance chairpersons did not violate LMRA §302 because the payments arose from "the collective bargaining agreement itself," not from a "back-door deal." The Supreme Court granted review, Caterpillar, Inc., v. Int'l Union, United Auto., Aerospace & Agric. Implement Workers of Am., et al., 521 U.S. 1152 (1997), but later dismissed the case because the parties settled, 523 U.S. 1015 (1998).

**9. Employer-Initiated Participation Programs in the Union Setting.** Where a union is present, should employers have more, less, or the same latitude to establish employee participation programs? Is the consent of the union always required? Can employers implement such programs after satisfying their bargaining obligations under the Act? (For discussion of bargaining obligations, see infra page 468.) Would it matter if the employer-initiated vehicle did not include a representational feature and addressed only "quality" and "efficiency" concerns? Cf. *DuPont,* supra note 3, 311 N.L.R.B. 893.

**10. Involvement of Union Leaders in Firm Management.** Does §8(a)(2) permit the same individuals to serve simultaneously in both union leadership and management positions? See, e.g., Jeffrey Mfg. Co.,

208 N.L.R.B. 75, 83 (1974) (permitting supervisor to serve as union president and handle disputes arising under the collective bargaining agreement violates §8(a)(2)). Is a union president barred from taking a traditional seat on the board of directors of a corporation whose employees his union represents? Should it matter whether the firm involved is employee-owned? These questions are explored in Michael C. Harper, Reconciling Collective Bargaining with Employee Supervision of Management, 137 U. Pa. L. Rev. 1, 21, 52 (1988): even "lifelong union officials could be influenced by the experience of making decisions from the perspectives of the interests of an entire corporation and its shareholders," and even in an employee-owned firm, those serving union roles should not also serve managerial functions because "collective bargaining provides the most realistic check on any emerging employee-managerial elite."

**11. Involvement of Workers and Employers in "German-style" Work Councils?** A German auto-maker, Volkswagen (VW), has expressed interest in establishing work councils in its U.S.-based plants. Work councils take many forms but they always involve both management and employee representatives and typically make decisions about shop-floor issues such as safety, working conditions and how to respond to production changes. In the German model wages and benefit negotiations typically occur at the industry level and are within the purview of unions, not work councils. Employers typically pay the work council representatives' salaries. If VW sets up this type of work council in its Chattanooga, Tennessee plant, would it violate 8(a)(2)? What if the company initially set up the councils with the assistance of a U.S. union that did not have majority support? Would involvement of a union that did have majority support ameliorate all of the §8(a)(2) issues? In November 2014, VW promulgated a "Community Organization Engagement" policy which allows organizations which primarily represent employees and their interests "to engage in constructive dialogue with Volkswagon and its employees." See VW, Community Organization Engagement policy, available at http://op.bna.com/dlrcases.nsf/id/bpen9qsnql/$File/Community%20Organization%20Engagement.pdf; Ben Pen, VW Issues Policy Offering Groups Varying Levels of Management-Worker Engagement, 2014 Daily Lab. Rep. (BNA) No. 218, at A9 (November 12, 2014). Depending on the level of membership support that the organization has (>15, >30 or >45), these groups can achieve a graduated scale of access to the facility and opportunity for meetings with the Company's Executive Committee to "discuss topics of general interest to their membership." If VW considers proposals that are raised at these meetings and responds with counter-proposals, would such conduct be considered "dealing with" under the NLRA's definition of "labor organization"? Given the §8(a)(2) material discussed above, how would you advise VW with respect to its implementation of this policy?

**12. A Right to Refuse to Participate?** In a nonunion setting, do employees have a right to refuse to participate in employee involvement programs initiated by an employer? Would it matter whether the scheme was a labor organization within the meaning of §2(5)? Whether the scheme was an integral part of the production or service delivery process? See Estreicher, Employee Involvement, supra, at 156-157 & nn.93-95.

**13. Section 8(a)(2) Remedies: "Domination" vs. "Interference and Support."** Since 1948, the Board has taken the following approach to remedies for §8(a)(2) violations:

> Where we find that an employer's unfair labor practices have been so extensive as to constitute *domination* of the organization, we shall order its disestablishment, whether or not it be affiliated. . . . But when the Board finds that an employer's unfair labor practices were limited to interference and support and never reached the point of domination, we shall only order that recognition be withheld until certification, again without regard to whether the organization happens to be affiliated.

Carpenter Steel Co., 76 N.L.R.B. 670, 673 (1948) (emphasis in original).

### *Note: Amending §8(a)(2)?*

In the mid-1990s, Congress passed the Teamwork for Employees and Managers Act (TEAM Act), H.R. 743, 104th Cong., 2d Sess. (1996), but President Clinton vetoed the legislation. The TEAM Act would have added the following proviso to §8(a)(2):

> [T]hat it shall not constitute or be evidence of an unfair labor practice . . . for an employer to establish, assist, maintain, or participate in any organization or entity of any kind, in which employees . . . participate, to address matters of mutual interest, including, but not limited to, issues of quality, productivity, efficiency, and safety and health, and which does not have, claim, or seek authority to be the exclusive bargaining representative of the employees or to negotiate or enter into collective bargaining agreements with the employer or to amend existing collective bargaining agreements between the employer and any labor organization, except that in a case in which a labor organization is the representative of such employees as provided in §9(a), this proviso shall not apply.

In view of *Crown Cork*, what sort of organizations would be permitted by the TEAM Act proposal that are not already permitted under the NLRA? Would the amendment effectively have codified the *Scott & Fetzer* approach? Would it have validated the committees struck down in *Electromation*?

# 4 | NLRB Determination of Bargaining Authority

The protection of concerted employee activity from employer interference, restraint, coercion, and discrimination is clearly a core function of the National Labor Relations Act. However, Congress also designed the Act to have a second central thrust: protecting employees' choice and requiring employers to recognize labor organizations as exclusive bargaining agents when a majority of employees in common groupings express a preference for such representation. The decision to protect concerted activity did not necessarily require the regulation of employer recognition of unions' bargaining agency or the process of collective bargaining; employer recognition of unions as collective bargaining agents could have been made completely dependent on the impact of any economic power that labor organizations could muster under the protection of §§7 and 8.

While most other industrialized countries prohibit discrimination against employees for affiliating with unions, few regulate the process by which unions obtain representational authority. This is due to the fact that most systems outside of the United States and Canada view labor unions as private associations representing the interests of their members only. The laws in these countries do not impose a legal duty on employers to recognize and bargain with unions. Whether bargaining occurs is a function of the union's economic leverage, enhanced in some countries by laws providing for administrative extension of standards achieved in collective bargaining to unorganized segments of an industry. See Samuel Estreicher, Global Issues in Labor Law (2007). In the United States and Canada, by contrast, while members-only unionism is lawful, labor organizations can, and typically do, seek to become exclusive bargaining agents for all workers in particular bargaining units; employers have a legal duty to recognize and bargain only with exclusive bargaining agents. This exclusivity principle does not necessarily require elections but Congress believed that government provision of elections would minimize conflict among rival organizations, make it more difficult for employers to impose a company-supported union or play one group of employees against another, and in general reduce conflict over recognitional issues. The meaning of exclusive representation under the NLRA and the Act's regulation of collective bargaining will be treated in Chapter 6.

Although this chapter deals with the process by which labor organizations obtain recognition via NLRB elections, it is important to keep in mind that elections are not the sole means by which labor organizations obtain bargaining authority. Section 9(c) of the Act authorizes the Board to conduct secret-ballot elections to determine majority status and to certify the results. However, §9(a) provides that "[r]epresentatives designated or selected for the purposes of collective bargaining by the majority of the employees in a unit appropriate for such purposes, shall be the exclusive representatives of all the employees in such unit. . . ." The Act does not specify that majority status be "designated" in any particular manner. Thus, labor organizations may also gain representative status by means of voluntary recognition by the employer—a topic taken up in Chapter 5.

## A. OBTAINING REPRESENTATIVE STATUS THROUGH THE NLRB'S ELECTION PROCEDURE

### 1. Question Concerning Representation

The NLRB will conduct a representation election only in circumstances where it believes a question concerning representation (QCR) exists. A petitioner, typically a labor organization, has to present evidence (usually through authorization cards) that "a substantial number of employees . . . wish to be represented for collective bargaining and that their employer declines to recognize their representative" as their exclusive bargaining agent under §9(a) of the NLRA. The Board, as an administrative matter, requires that at least 30 percent of the employees in an appropriate unit support the petitioning organization. Although the Board will not disclose the name of or permit cross-examination of employees who signed the petition, the employer can present payroll information or handwriting samples if it thinks forgery may be involved.

There are other elements to the QCR determination relevant to whether the Board will hold a representation election. The first is the statutory one-year election bar of §9(c)(3), which the Board extends to a year after certification in the event of union success in the election. See pages 332-336 infra. Where a collective agreement has been reached, the Board recognizes up to a three year "contract bar" to holding another election. See page 337 infra. Where a union has been voluntarily recognized by the employer but there is yet no collective agreement, the Board will recognize a virtually irrebuttable presumption of continued majority support for the recognized union for a "reasonable period". In the case of a new facility, the Board requires that a "representative complement" of the ultimate workforce has been hired. General Extrusion Co., 121 N.L.R.B. 1165, 1167 (1958). Under the Board's "blocking charge" policy, the agency also generally declines to proceed with an election when unfair labor practice charges involving the unit are pending. See NLRB Casehandling Manual, Pt. 2, Representation Proceedings, §11730 (2007). For exceptions to the Board's blocking charge policy, see id. at §11731. Unfair labor practice charges are considered "pending" and thus continue to block an election until they have been withdrawn or dismissed, or, in the case of meritorious charges, until the litigation (up to and including a circuit court ruling if sought) is complete.

The block may also be lifted if the Regional Director finds that a fair election can still be held under the circumstances presented, or, in some instances, if the charging party files a "Request to Proceed." A Request to Proceed does not waive the charging party's right to assert the alleged unlawful conduct as a basis for objections to the election, as long as the conduct occurred after the filing of the election petition. See Ed Chandler Ford, Inc., 241 N.L.R.B. 1201 (1979); Form NLRB-4551 (1994) (Request to Proceed form). In its February 6, 2014 Notice of Proposed Rulemaking related to streamlining election procedures, the Board invited comment about whether amendments to the proposed rule should change the Board's current blocking charge policy. See 79 Fed. Reg. 7334-35.

The courts have on occasion criticized the Board's application of the blocking charge policy as overly "mechanical" or "dogmatic," or simply as irrational. See Templeton v. Dixie Color Printing Co., 444 F.2d 1064, 1068, 1069 (5th Cir. 1971); Surratt v. NLRB, 463 F.2d 378, 381 (5th Cir. 1972); Johns-Manville Sales Corp. v. NLRB, 906 F.2d 1428, 1431 n.7 (10th Cir. 1990) (questioning rationality). The policy, however, is nearly immune to judicial review. See *Leedom v. Kyne*, infra page 258; see also Bishop v. NLRB, 502 F.2d 1024, 1027-1028 (5th Cir. 1974). For criticism, see Samuel Estreicher, Improving the Administration of the National Labor Relations Act Without Statutory Change, 25 A.B.A. J. Lab. & Emp. L. 1, 9 (2009); Berton B. Subrin, The NLRB's Blocking Charge Policy: Wisdom or Folly?, 39 Lab. L.J. 651 (1988).

If a QCR is present, the next significant issue will be whether the petitioner has filed for an election in an appropriate unit under §9(a).

## 2. Appropriate Bargaining Units

### *a. NLRB Unit Determinations*

Before an NLRB-sponsored election can be held, there must be a determination regarding an appropriate electoral unit. Such a unit is defined by job classifications rather than by the particular holders of jobs. Section 9(a) requires "a unit appropriate" "for the purposes of collective bargaining"—in common parlance, "an appropriate bargaining unit."

Unit questions arise in two basic contexts: (1) within a single facility, and (2) single-facility versus multi-facility units. In the first situation, the question may be whether all nonsupervisory employees in a particular facility (such as a warehouse or factory) should be grouped together in a single unit (a "wall-to-wall" unit), or whether the unit should include only a limited number of job classifications within that facility. In the second situation, the question is whether the employees at one facility (such as a restaurant) should constitute a separate unit, or whether all of the employees in that job classification at other of the employer's facilities within a particular geographic area (such as a metropolitan area) should be grouped together.

NLRB unit determinations are of considerable strategic importance. In formulating their respective positions as to the bargaining unit, unions and employers are focused on two distinct phases: the organizational phase and the representational phase. That is, each side wants the unit that will both: (1) maximize its chances of winning the election; and (2) should the union win the election and bargaining ensue, give it the strongest possible hand in contract negotiations and administration.

The union "takes the first shot" in defining the unit; it must list the unit sought in the petition form that it files with the NLRB's Regional office, a copy of which is included in your Supplement. The statute does not require that the unit ultimately approved be the "*most* appropriate" unit; §9(a) requires only "a unit appropriate for [collective bargaining] purposes." The employer, however, will often seek to alter the petitioned-for unit (usually by expanding the number of job categories or the number of facilities in the unit), and negotiations on the issue then ensue. If the parties reach agreement on the unit and enter into a "stipulated election agreement," the Regional Director will approve the agreed-upon unit unless it is manifestly inappropriate. However, if the parties cannot reach agreement, a hearing is held at the Regional office, and the Regional Director makes the unit determination subject to discretionary review by the Board, which is granted only rarely. Unit determination questions arise, then, when the employer does not agree to the unit sought by the union and the parties cannot agree on a compromise unit.

#### i. Rulemaking vs. Adjudication

**American Hospital Ass'n v. NLRB**
*499 U.S. 606 (1991)*

STEVENS, J., delivered the opinion for a unanimous Court.

For the first time since the National Labor Relations Board (Board or NLRB) was established in 1935, the Board has promulgated a substantive rule defining the employee units appropriate for collective bargaining in a particular line of commerce. The rule is applicable to acute care hospitals and provides, with three exceptions, that eight, and only eight, units shall be appropriate in any such hospital. The three exceptions are for cases that present extraordinary circumstances, cases in which nonconforming units already exist, and cases in which labor organizations seek to combine two or more of the eight specified units. The extraordinary circumstances exception applies automatically to hospitals in which the eight-unit rule will produce a unit of five or fewer employees. See 29 CFR §103.30 (1990).

Petitioner, American Hospital Association, brought this action challenging the facial validity of the rule on three grounds: First, petitioner argues that §9(b) of the National Labor Relations Act (NLRA or Act) requires the Board to make a separate bargaining unit determination "in each case" and therefore prohibits the Board from using general rules to define bargaining units; second, petitioner contends that the rule that the Board has formulated violates a congressional admonition to the Board to avoid the undue proliferation of bargaining units in the health care industry; and, finally, petitioner maintains that the rule is arbitrary and capricious. . . .

## I

Petitioner's first argument is a general challenge to the Board's rule-making authority in connection with bargaining unit determinations based on the terms of the National Labor Relations Act . . . The central purpose of the Act was to protect and facilitate employees' opportunity to organize unions to represent them in collective-bargaining negotiations.

Sections 3, 4, and 5 of the Act created the Board and generally described its powers. §§153-155. Section 6 granted the Board the "authority from time to time to make, amend, and rescind . . . such rules and regulations as may be necessary to carry out the provisions" of the Act. §156. This grant was unquestionably sufficient to authorize the rule at issue in this case unless limited by some other provision in the Act.

Petitioner argues that §9(b) provides such a limitation because this section requires the Board to determine the appropriate bargaining unit "in each case." §159(b). We are not persuaded. Petitioner would have us put more weight on these three words than they can reasonably carry.

* * *

The more natural reading of these three words is simply to indicate that whenever there is a disagreement about the appropriateness of a unit, the Board shall resolve the dispute. Under this reading, the words "in each case" are synonymous with "whenever necessary" or "in any case in which there is a dispute." Congress chose not to enact a general rule that would require plant unions, craft unions, or industry-wide unions for every employer in every line of commerce, but also chose not to leave the decision up to employees or employers alone. Instead, the decision "in each case" in which a dispute arises is to be made by the Board.

In resolving such a dispute, the Board's decision is presumably to be guided not simply by the basic policy of the Act but also by the rules that the Board develops to circumscribe and to guide its discretion either in the process of case-by-case adjudication or by the exercise of its rulemaking authority. The requirement that the Board exercise its discretion in every disputed case cannot fairly or logically be read to command the Board to exercise standardless discretion in each case. . . .

Even petitioner acknowledges that "the Board could adopt rules establishing general principles to guide the required case-by-case bargaining unit determinations." Petitioner further acknowledges that the Board has created many such rules in the half-century during which it has adjudicated bargaining unit disputes. Petitioner contends, however, that a rule delineating the appropriate bargaining unit for an entire industry is qualitatively different from these prior rules, which at most established rebuttable presumptions that certain units would be considered appropriate in certain circumstances.

We simply cannot find in the three words "in each case" any basis for the fine distinction that petitioner would have us draw. Contrary to petitioner's contention, the Board's rule is not an irrebuttable presumption; instead, it contains an exception for "extraordinary circumstances." Even if the rule did establish an irrebuttable presumption, it would not differ significantly from the prior rules adopted by the Board. As with its prior rules, the Board must still apply the rule "in each case." For example, the Board must decide in each case, among a host of other issues, whether a given facility is properly classified as an acute care hospital and whether particular employees are properly placed in particular units. . . .

## II

Consideration of petitioner's second argument requires a brief historical review of the application of federal labor law to acute care hospitals. Hospitals were "employers" under the terms of the NLRA as enacted in 1935, but in 1947 Congress excepted not-for-profit hospitals from the coverage of the Act. [This provision was repealed in 1974, 88 Stat. 395, as discussed below.] In 1960, the Board decided that proprietary hospitals should also be excepted. . . .

Congress addressed [in 1973] the issue and considered bills that would have extended the Act's coverage to all private health care institutions, including not-for-profit hospitals. The proposed legislation was highly controversial, largely because of the concern that labor unrest in the health care industry might be especially harmful to the public. Moreover, the fact that so many specialists are employed in the industry created the potential for a large number of bargaining units, in each of which separate union representation might multiply management's burden in negotiation and might also increase the risk of strikes. Motivated by these concerns, Senator Taft introduced a bill that would have repealed the exemption for hospitals, but also would have placed a limit of five on the number of bargaining units in nonprofit health care institutions. S. 2292, 93d Cong., 1st Sess. (1973). Senator Taft's bill did not pass.

In the second session of the same Congress, however, the National Labor Relations Act Amendments of 1974 were enacted. See 88 Stat. 395. These amendments subjected all acute care hospitals to the coverage of the Act but made no change in the Board's authority to determine the appropriate bargaining unit in each case. See *ibid.* Both the House and the Senate Committee Reports on the legislation contained this statement:

> **EFFECT ON EXISTING LAW**
>
> Bargaining Units
>
> Due consideration should be given by the Board to preventing proliferation of bargaining units in the health care industry. In this connection, the Committee notes with approval the recent Board decisions in *Four Seasons Nursing Center,* 208 NLRB No. 50, 85 LRRM 1093 (1974), and *Woodland Park Hospital,* 205 NLRB No.144, 84 LRRM 1075 (1973), as well as the trend toward broader units enunciated in *Extendicare of West Virginia,* 203 NLRB No. 170, 83 LRRM 1242 (1973).

Petitioner does not—and obviously could not—contend that this statement in the Committee Reports has the force of law, for the Constitution is quite explicit about the procedure that Congress must follow in legislating. Nor, in view of the fact that Congress refused to enact the Taft bill that would have placed a limit of five on the number of hospital bargaining units, does petitioner argue that eight units necessarily constitute proliferation. Rather, petitioner's primary argument is that the admonition, when coupled with the rejection of a general rule imposing a five-unit limit, evinces Congress' intent to emphasize the importance of the "in each case" requirement in §9(b). . . .

Petitioner also suggests that the admonition "is an authoritative statement of what Congress intended when it extended the Act's coverage to include nonproprietary hospitals." Even if we accepted this suggestion, we read the admonition as an expression by the Committees of their desire that the Board give "due consideration" to the special problems that "proliferation" might create in acute care hospitals. Examining the record of the Board's rulemaking proceeding, we find that it gave extensive consideration to this very issue. . . .

In any event, we think that the admonition in the Committee Reports is best understood as a form of notice to the Board that if it did not give appropriate consideration to the problem of proliferation in this industry, Congress might respond with a legislative remedy. So read, the remedy for noncompliance with the admonition is in the hands of the body that issued it. . . .

### III

Petitioner's final argument is that the rule is arbitrary and capricious because "it ignores critical differences among the more than 4,000 acute-care hospitals in the United States, including differences in size, location, operations, and workforce organization." . . .

The Board responds to this argument by relying on the extensive record developed during the rulemaking proceedings, as well as its experience in the adjudication of health care cases during the 13-year period between the enactment of the health care amendments and its notice of proposed rulemaking. Based on that experience, the Board formed the "considered judgment" that "acute care hospitals do not differ in substantial, significant ways relating to the appropriateness of units." Moreover, the Board argues, the exception for "extraordinary circumstances" is adequate to take care of the unusual case in which a particular application of the rule might be arbitrary. . . .

The fact that petitioner can point to a hypothetical case in which the rule might lead to an arbitrary result does not render the rule "arbitrary or capricious." This case is a challenge to the validity of the entire rule in all its applications. We consider it likely that presented with the case of an acute care hospital to which its application would be arbitrary, the Board would conclude that "extraordinary circumstances" justified a departure from the rule. See 29 C.F.R. §§103.30(a), (b)(1990).

In this opinion, we have deliberately avoided any extended comment on the wisdom of the rule, the propriety of the specific unit determinations, or the importance of avoiding work stoppages in acute care hospitals. We have pretermitted such discussion not because these matters are unimportant but because they primarily concern the Board's exercise of its authority rather than the limited scope of our review of the legal arguments presented by petitioner. Because we find no merit in any of these legal arguments, the judgment of the Court of Appeals is affirmed. . . .

### *NOTES AND QUESTIONS*

1. **Agency's Decision to Use Rulemaking.** The rule at issue in *American Hospital Ass'n* represented the Board's first exercise of its powers under §6 of the Act to promulgate substantive rules. For an account of the Board's

decision to use rulemaking in the healthcare area and the rulemaking proceedings themselves, see Mark H. Grunewald, The NLRB's First Rulemaking: An Exercise in Pragmatism, 41 Duke L.J. 274 (1991).

**2. The Effect of the Healthcare Unit Rule.** It has been suggested that the primary effect of the healthcare rule approved in *American Hospital Ass'n* has not been an increase in unionization of hospitals, but a decrease in time spent processing representation cases in the industry. See Michelle Amber et al., Health Care Organizing—A Two Year Perspective, BNA Special Supplement to Labor Relations Week, vol. 7, no. 19, May 12, 1993. Elections can be more quickly processed because the Board will refuse to take evidence in pre-election hearings where the employer's arguments for departing from the rule are similar to arguments already considered and rejected by the agency in promulgating the rule. See, e.g., St. Margaret Memorial Hospital, 303 N.L.R.B. 923 (1991), approved, 991 F.2d 1146 (3d Cir. 1993); see also 54 Fed. Reg. 16336, 16338 (1989) (final rule) (explaining that while other issues such as whether certain employees are supervisory or managerial will be resolved based on testimony taken at hearing, scope of appropriate unit will generally be resolved based upon the rule rather than adjudication).

**3. Nonacute Care Facilities.** The healthcare unit rule, sustained in *American Hospital Ass'n,* expressly excludes from the definition of an acute care hospital "facilities that are primarily nursing homes." 29 C.F.R. §103.30(f)(2). For those facilities as well as all other nonacute care facilities, as defined in §2(14) of the NLRA, the Board stated it would determine appropriate units "by adjudication." 29 C.F.R. §103.30(g). In Specialty Healthcare and Rehab. Ctr., 357 N.L.R.B. No. 83 (2011), enfd. sub nom. Kindred Nursing Centers East, LLC v. NLRB, 727 F.3d 552 (6th Cir. 2013), a case involving a union's request for a unit of certified nursing associates (CNAs) in a nursing home, the Board considered whether the CNAs were "clearly identifiable as a group and share a community of interest" and approved the petitioned for unit. For more discussion of *Specialty Healthcare,* see infra page 244. The Board's *Specialty Healthcare* standard considers whether the employees are "clearly identifiable as a group and share a community of interest."

**4. Strategic Considerations.** As the acute care rulemaking suggests, the parties have their own strategic considerations in proposing or opposing certain bargaining units. Unions often prefer smaller, more cohesive units because they are easier to organize for election purposes and are more likely to maintain solidarity during bargaining. In the healthcare area, unions that specialize among certain professional groups will prefer a bargaining unit comprised only of, say, registered nurses (RNs) to an all professional unit, or will prefer a unit comprised only of LPNs, who are not grouped together with other technical employees or with a service-and-maintenance grouping. Review the eight-unit structure sustained in *American Hospital Ass'n* with these considerations in mind.

### ii. Standards for an Appropriate Unit

**Friendly Ice Cream Corp. v. NLRB**
*705 F.2d 570 (1st Cir. 1983)*

BOWNES, J. . . .

Friendly, a Massachusetts corporation, owns and operates a chain of 605 restaurants in sixteen states. The eastern region of the chain is headquartered in Wilbraham, Massachusetts. Executive personnel at Wilbraham formulate standard policies applicable to all restaurants in the chain, covering such matters as: menus, pricing, food preparation, formulas, interior and exterior decor, employee uniforms, maintenance, marketing, advertising, purchasing, inventory, cash accounting, security, hours of operation and personnel. The eastern region is divided into twelve divisions, each supervised by a Division Manager. Division I, covering portions of eastern and southern Massachusetts, is further subdivided into nine districts. Each district comprises from four to nine restaurants, for a total of sixty-five restaurants within Division I. A District Manager supervises the operations of the restaurants within each district, and reports to the Division Manager.

The store involved in this proceeding, the Weymouth restaurant, is part of a district comprised of eight restaurants. The restaurant employs approximately twenty-four part-time and three full-time employees. The supervisory hierarchy of the Weymouth restaurant begins with the Shift Supervisor, who acts as the Store Manager's delegate when she or he is not present. The Store Manager, who works between fifty and fifty-five hours per week, bears overall responsibility for the day-to-day operation of the restaurant. The Store Manager is supervised by the District Manager, who regularly visits the eight restaurants within the district. While at a restaurant, the District Manager checks the supplies, sales, service, cleanliness and employees. Estimates of the frequency of the District Manager's visits range from one to three times per week, and estimates of the length of the visits range from fifteen minutes to several hours. The District Manager reports to the Division Manager, located in Braintree, Massachusetts, who visits the Weymouth restaurant about once a month.

On April 5, 1979, the Union filed a representation petition seeking certification as the collective bargaining representative of specified employees at the Weymouth restaurant.[2] Friendly did not dispute the composition

---

2. The unit consisted of:

All full time and regular part time waiters, waitresses, cooks, busboys, busgirls, cashiers and shift supervisors employed by the Employer at its 435 Washington Street, Weymouth,

of this unit, but argued that the scope of the unit was inappropriate because it covered only a single restaurant within the chain. Friendly argued that the most appropriate unit would be one encompassing all of its restaurants in the United States. Four alternative units were also proposed: a unit composed of all restaurants within the Boston Standard Metropolitan Statistical Area; all restaurants within Division I; all restaurants within a county; or a cluster of restaurants within a defined geographical area.

[The Regional Director, after extensive hearings, determined that the single-store unit was an appropriate unit for bargaining. The Board declined to review the decision. An election ensued. The union prevailed 11-10, but Friendly refused to bargain with the certified union. The Board then issued a bargaining order and Friendly appealed, again claiming that the Weymouth restaurant was an inappropriate unit for bargaining. Such refusals to bargain as the means for employer appeals of unit determinations are discussed infra pages 258-262.]

The Board is not required to select the most appropriate unit in a particular factual setting; it need only select *an* appropriate unit from the range of units appropriate under the circumstances. . . . An employer seeking to challenge the Board's unit determination cannot merely point to a more appropriate unit. Rather, the burden of proof is on the employer to show that the Board's unit is clearly inappropriate. . . .

In making a unit determination, the Board's primary duty is to effect the Act's overriding policy of assuring employees the fullest freedom in exercising their right to bargain collectively. [See NLRA §9(b).] At the same time, the Board must "respect the interest of an integrated multi-unit employer in maintaining enterprise-wide labor relations." NLRB v. Solis Theatre Corp., 403 F.2d 381, 382 (2d Cir. 1968). Accordingly, the Board must grant some minimum consideration to the employer's interest in avoiding the disruptive effects of piecemeal unionization. NLRB v. Purity Food Stores, Inc., 354 F.2d 926, 931 (1st Cir. 1965). An employer with a central labor policy can be expected to prefer a bargaining unit which corresponds to the company's internal organization. While an employer's interest in bargaining with the most convenient possible unit should be accommodated when feasible, the Board is free to grant greater weight to the employees' interest in being represented by a representative of their own choosing. The Act expressly dictates that employee freedom of choice must be paramount in any unit determination. Thus, this factor of employee freedom can legitimately tip the balance in determining which of two equally appropriate units should be preferred.

The critical consideration in determining the appropriateness of a proposed unit is whether the employees comprising the unit share a

---

Massachusetts location but excluding all bookkeepers, managers, manager trainees, assistant managers, guards and all supervisors as defined in the Act.

"community of interest." In determining whether the requisite community of interest exists, the Board considers several criteria, no single factor alone being determinative. The factors include:

(a) geographic proximity of the stores in relation to each other;
(b) level of employee interchange between various stores;
(c) degree of autonomy exercised by the local store manager, especially with respect to labor relations;
(d) extent of union organization;
(e) history of collective bargaining;
(f) desires of the affected employees;
(g) employer's organizational framework;
(h) similarity in skills, employee benefits, wages and hours of work.

In weighing these factors and determining what group of employees constitutes an appropriate unit, the Board is not bound to follow any rigid rule laid down by the law or prior decisions. Since each unit determination is dependent upon factual variations, the Board is free to decide each case on an ad hoc basis. The Board has, however, developed certain administrative policies which guide it in making unit determinations. When considering the appropriateness of a single store bargaining unit in a multistore retail operation, the Board is aided by its policy that a single store is "presumptively an appropriate unit for bargaining." Haag Drug Co., Inc., 169 N.L.R.B. 877, 878 (1968). This rebuttable presumption is consistent with the Act, has a rational foundation, and reflects the Board's expertise. Thus, in an appropriate case, the Board is entitled to invoke this presumption. NLRB v. Baptist Hospital, Inc., 442 U.S. 773, 787 (1979). . . .

The administration of the Friendly chain is a casebook study in centralized control. Like most retail chains, Friendly relies upon uniform policies which regulate practically every aspect of the individual stores' operations. But the company's determination of the most efficient form of organization cannot be ascribed controlling significance in matters of unit determination. Otherwise, "an employer, by centralizing all matters of labor policy, [could] prevent the NLRB from selecting as appropriate a unit of smaller dimensions than the employer's whole enterprise even though that smaller unit was the one which in light of all the relevant factors the NLRB determined would be appropriate under [the Act]." NLRB v. Living and Learning Centers, Inc., 652 F.2d [209, 215 (1st Cir. 1981)].

In the context of a retail chain operation, one of the most weighty factors in determining the appropriateness of a single store unit is the degree of control vested in the local store manager. Such control does not specifically refer to the local manager's freedom to establish prices, decor or menus—though control of these decisions might be indicative of the level of integration of the employer's business. Rather, the Board considers as significant the local manager's effective control of those areas "which most directly affect the restaurant's employees." Magic Pan, Inc. v. NLRB, 627 F.2d 105, 108 (7th Cir. 1980) (per curiam). Here, the Board reasonably found that the Weymouth Store Manager exercised significant, albeit limited, authority in those matters which most directly affect the Weymouth employees.

Our independent review of the record convinces us that the Board had ample grounds for concluding that the Store Manager was, in fact, autonomous. The evidence can be summarized as follows. Employees at the Weymouth restaurant perform their day-to-day work under the immediate supervision of the Store Manager. The Store Manager is usually the only company official who interviews prospective applicants for employment. On his own, the Store Manager can decide not to grant a second interview. Job applicants receive a conditional offer of employment from the Store Manager and, in some cases, an immediate offer following the first interview.

Once hired, employees receive most of their training from the Store Manager or his designee. He regularly reviews their work and fills out quarterly written evaluations which are used as the basis for recommending wage increases. According to company policy, the District Manager must approve all wage increases, but, in practice, the Store Manager, at times, grants wage increases on the spot. . . .

In sum, the Board's determination that the employees at the Weymouth restaurant constituted an appropriate bargaining unit was within its discretion and supported by substantial evidence in the record.

## *NOTES AND QUESTIONS*

1. **"An Appropriate Unit."** The Board requires that the petitioning labor organization seek an election in an appropriate unit even if it is not the only appropriate unit, or even the most appropriate unit:

> The Board . . . examine[s] first the petitioned-for unit. If that unit is appropriate, then the inquiry into the appropriate unit ends. If the petitioned-for unit is not appropriate, the Board may examine the alternative units suggested by the parties, but it also has the discretion to select an appropriate unit that is different from the alternative proposals of the parties. The Board generally attempts to select a unit that is the smallest appropriate unit encompassing the petitioned-for employee classifications.

Boeing Co., 337 N.L.R.B. 152, 153 (2001); Bartlett Collins Co., 334 N.L.R.B. 484 (2001) (internal citations omitted). What is the Board's basis for choosing the smallest unit covering the petitioned-for employees? Is the Board's policy consistent with the Congressional judgment in §9(c)(5) that in determining whether a unit is appropriate, "the extent to which the employees have organized shall not be controlling"? Does the provision apply if the Board has independently determined that the petitioned-for unit is appropriate? Is it likely, however, that the Board will be influenced by the extent of organization in making its decision?

**2. Is a Petitioned-for Unit That Shares a Community of Interest Inappropriate Because it Does Not Include Additional Employees Who Also Share a Community of Interest?** The Board addressed this question in *Specialty Healthcare,* Note 3, supra page 239. This case involved an employer's challenge to a Regional Director's finding that a petitioned-for bargaining unit of certified nursing assistants (CNAs) was appropriate. The employer argued that the only appropriate unit for the CNAs also would include all of the maintenance and nonprofessional service workers at the facility. The *Specialty Healthcare* Board denied the employer's request for a larger unit and set out a heightened burden for challenges to petitioned-for units that propose inclusion of additional employees. In such situations, the challenger must demonstrate that "the excluded employees share an overwhelming community of interest with the included employees." The dissent argued, among other things, that *Specialty Healthcare*'s heightened burden makes it nearly impossible to challenge the petitioned-for unit and is thus "in contravention of Section 9(c)(5)," which states that "the extent to which the employees have organized" shall not control whether a unit is appropriate. Is the *Specialty Healthcare* rule, as the dissent suggests, likely to lead "to an extraordinary fragmentation of the work force for collective-bargaining purposes, a situation that cannot lend itself to . . . labor relations stability"?

**3. Should the Board Consider Employer Interests in Unit Determinations?** Why does the *Friendly* court state that the "Board must grant some minimum consideration to the employer's interest in avoiding the disruptive effects of piecemeal unionization"? Does the language of §9(b) support the Board weighing employer interests? Does the addition of §9(c)(5) in 1947 suggest that employee interests in securing collective bargaining cannot always be controlling? Does the provision speak to employer interests? If employer interests may be considered, how is the employer's interest in maintaining centralized operations compromised by allowing union organization on a single-store basis? Does the court's emphasis on the extent of the individual store manager's autonomy effectively address such employer concerns?

**4. Employee Interests in Broader Units?** Are employee interests also involved in the congressional judgment in §9(c)(5) that the extent of organization cannot be a controlling factor in unit determination? Are there ways in which a smaller unit might compromise employee exercise of rights guaranteed by the NLRA even in cases where a larger unit is not a realistic alternative for the organizing union? What weight should be given to the effect on employees excluded from the unit who may not be able to form a viable unit of their own and thus to *their* freedom to exercise the rights guaranteed by the Act? To the degree of interchange of employees in and out of a proposed small unit? Will bargaining on the basis of a smaller unit be effective where an employer maintains a highly centralized operation? Will it be stable?

**5. Geographical Proximity as Countervailing Factor?** If we assume in a given case decentralized control of personnel decisions and a low degree of interchange of employees, should the geographical proximity of stores count as a general matter against single-store units and in favor of multi-store units, or only when the broader unit is sought by unions? Would it be consistent with the Board's §9 authority, as limited by §9(c)(5), to treat geographical proximity as favoring multi-store units, while not treating it as disfavoring single-store units?

**6. "Merged" Units?** Assume that after gaining certification as the representative of the employees of one store in a multi-store chain, a union also achieves certification as the representative of the employees at a second store in the chain. Should the union now be able to insist that the employer bargain with it as a representative of a two-store unit? The Board holds that one party cannot lawfully pressure the other party to merge existing units. See, e.g., Chicago Truck Drivers (Signal Delivery), 279 N.L.R.B. 904 (1986); Note on Coalition and Coordinated Bargaining, infra pages 504-505. Although the union cannot force the employer to agree to bargain on a two-store basis, absent an NLRB certification of a two-store unit, the parties can agree to bargain on the broader basis. What effect should be given to a history of successful bargaining on a multi-store basis if employees in one of the stores timely petition for an election for that store to decertify the union or bring in a new labor organization? Should the unit determination standard for initial organization and severance bids be the same? See generally George Brooks, Stability Versus Employee Free Choice, 61 Cornell L. Rev. 344 (1976). Do the considerations differ when the parties negotiate a "new location" clause which automatically applies the collective agreement to a newly-established or acquired, but unorganized facility upon proof of majority support at the new location? See Kroger Co., infra page 473.

**7. The "Community of Interest" Standard vs. a Strong Presumption.** Note the general "community of interest" standard discussed in *Friendly*.

One commentator suggests that "there are a few applicable presumptions" but "no hard-and-fast rules regarding unit appropriateness." See Douglas L. Leslie, Labor Bargaining Units, 70 Va. L. Rev. 353, 381 (1984). A former longtime director of the Board's Office of Representation Appeals argues to the contrary that the Board's flexible, "totality of the circumstances" approach is illusory—that in most areas, the Board's decisions are guided by strong presumptions or other relatively fixed principles. See Berton B. Subrin, Conserving Energy at the Labor Board: The Case for Making Rules on Collective Bargaining Units, 32 Lab. L.J. 105, 110 (1981). Subrin argued that unit determinations are thus particularly good candidates for rulemaking.

**8. Proposed Single Location Bargaining Unit Rule.** In 1995, the Board proposed a rule to govern single-location units in all industries except public utilities, construction, and ocean-going maritime firms. Under the proposed rule, absent "extraordinary circumstances," a single-location unit, if petitioned for by the union, would have been deemed appropriate if (a) 15 or more employees were employed at that location; (b) no other location of the employer was located within one mile; and (c) at least one §2(11) supervisor was present at the location. See 60 Fed. Reg. 50146 (1995), withdrawn, 63 Fed. Reg. 8890 (1998).

The proposed single-location rule never became law. For three straight years following its proposal, the Republican majority in Congress attached "riders" to the Board's budget preventing the Board from spending any money on the single-facility proceeding, in effect killing it. The Board ultimately withdrew the proposed rule, with Chairman Gould dissenting. See Joan Flynn, "Expertness for What?": The Gould Years at the NLRB and the Irrepressible Myth of the "Independent" Agency, 52 Admin. L. Rev. 465, 501-502 & nn.151-152 (2000). Is it likely that Congressional opponents of the Board would have injected themselves into this debate had the Clinton Board simply continued its predecessors' practice of adjudicating single-facility cases and approving single-facility units in the vast majority of such cases? See Joan Flynn, The Costs and Benefits of 'Hiding the Ball': NLRB Policymaking and the Failure of Judicial Review, 75 B.U. L. Rev. 387, 425, 433 (1995).

**9. Petitioned-for Multi-location Units**. When a union petitions for a multi-location unit, the single-facility presumption has no applicability. The Board uses its traditional community of interest criteria. See NLRB v. Carson Cable TV, 795 F.2d 879, 887 (9th Cir. 1986); Capital Coors Co., 309 N.L.R.B. 322, 322 n. 1 (1992).

**10. The Relevant Majority.** Section 9(c)(3), in stipulating the rules for a run-off election, assumes that the Board may certify the majority winner of all the votes cast in a representation election, presumably even if the winner receives only a plurality of the members in the unit. The Board has on occasion refused to hold an election or certify results because those actually voting on a given day did not represent a reasonable complement of the unit. It has never, however, required that the certified winner receive votes of a majority of the unit. In a 2010 rulemaking, the National Mediation Board (NMB), the agency responsible for holding representation elections under the Railway Labor Act (RLA), revoked its longstanding requirement that a union must garner votes from a majority of eligible voters to win an election. Under the NMB's new rule unions need only garner a majority of the votes cast. See 75 Fed. Reg. 26062 (May 11, 2010). See Air Transport Ass'n v. National Mediation Board, 188 L.R.R.M. 3053 (D.D.C. June 28, 2010).

**11. Can Unauthorized Immigrant Employees Share a Community of Interest with Authorized Employees?** The D.C. Circuit, agreeing with the Board, concluded that the employees' immigration status should not preclude them from being in the bargaining unit. Despite the possibility that their immigration status may affect expectations with respect to continued future employment, their wages and working conditions were similar to their authorized counterparts. Agri Processor Co., Inc. v. NLRB, 514 F.3d 1, 5 (D.C. Cir. 2008).

### iii. Craft vs. Industrial Units

In the Board's early years, the major unit issue involved competing claims by AFL unions seeking units of skilled craft workers and CIO unions seeking "wall-to-wall" or industrial units. In Globe Machine & Stamping Co., 3 N.L.R.B. 294 (1937), the Board ruled that when rival union petitions seeking equally appropriate units were filed, an election would be held to determine the employees' desires. A "*Globe*" election gave craft employees a chance to vote in favor of "be[ing] established as a separate bargaining unit, apart from a broader industrial unit in which they would otherwise be included, by voting for the craft union that seeks to represent them separately, as against the industrial union that desires to represent them as part of the larger unit." 15 NLRB Ann. Rep. 33 n.26 (1950). The craft employees, like other employees, could also vote for "no union."

In American Can Co., 13 N.L.R.B. 1252 (1939), the Board held that once craft employees were represented as part of a broader industrial unit, it would not permit them to sever themselves from the broader unit. A proviso to §9(b)(2) passed in 1947, curbs this policy, stating that "the Board shall . . . not decide that any craft unit is inappropriate . . . on the ground that a different unit has been established by a prior Board determination, unless a majority of the employees in the proposed craft unit votes against separate representation." The Board continued for a time to deny craft severance and even initial establishment of craft units in four basic industries (aluminum, steel, lumber, and wet milling) on the rationale that these industries were so highly integrated that craft severance would interfere with stable labor relations. See National Tube Co., 76 N.L.R.B. 1199 (1948). The Board adopted a pro-craft severance position in American Potash & Chemical, 107 N.L.R.B. 1418 (1954). Departing from this pro-severance preference in Mallinckrodt Chemical Works, 162 N.L.R.B. 387, 397 (1966), however, the Board held that craft severance determinations would henceforth be based on a multi-factor analysis:

1. Whether or not the proposed unit consists of a distinct and homogeneous group of skilled journeymen craftsmen performing the functions of their craft on a nonrepetitive basis, or of employees constituting a functionally distinct department, working in trades or occupations for which a tradition of separate representation exists.
2. The history of collective bargaining of the employees sought and at the plant involved, and at other plants of the employer, with emphasis on whether the existing patterns of bargaining are productive of stability in labor relations, and whether such stability will be unduly disrupted by the destruction of the existing patterns of representation.
3. The extent to which the employees in the proposed unit have established and maintained their separate identity during the period of inclusion in a broader unit, and the extent of their participation or lack of participation in the establishment and maintenance of the existing pattern of representation and the prior opportunities, if any, afforded them to obtain separate representation.
4. The history and pattern of collective bargaining in the industry involved.
5. The degree of integration of the employer's production processes, including the extent to which the continued normal operation of the production processes is dependent upon the performance of the assigned functions of the employees in the proposed unit.
6. The qualifications of the union seeking to "carve out" a separate unit, including that union's experience in representing employees like those involved in the severance action.

The 1955 merger of the AFL and CIO, interunion no-raiding agreements, and the decline in union organizational activity have reduced craft-industrial rivalries. Nonetheless, the Board continues to use the *Mallinckrodt* test to assess—and generally deny—craft-severance petitions. See John E. Abodeely, NLRB Craft Severance Policies: Preeminence of the Bargaining History Factor After *Mallinckrodt*, 11 B.C. Indus. & Comp. L. Rev.

411 (1970). For a decision rebuffing the Board's receptivity to a severance bid, see Williamette Industries, Inc. v. NLRB, 144 F.3d 877 (D.C. Cir. 1998) (Board failed adequately to explain why it was departing from its practice of certifying wall-to-wall units in the lumber industry when it certified a unit of skilled maintenance employees in this case). When unions seek to organize craft units where there is no preexisting bargaining relationship, the Board typically finds such units appropriate under its general unit determination criteria.

The Board also has relied on *Mallinckrodt* to deny severance petitions in other industries. See, e.g., Metropolitan Opera Ass'n, 327 N.L.R.B. 740 (1999) (choristers' attempt to sever from unit of opera's choristers, soloists, dancers, stage managers, stage directors, and choreographers); Kaiser Foundation Hospitals, 312 N.L.R.B. 933 (1993) (skilled maintenance employees' attempt to sever from preexisting broader unit).

### iv. Accretion

When a unionized employer adds employees with new skills in an existing plant or establishes or acquires a new plant or facility, the Board must decide whether the new group of employees should be incorporated into an existing bargaining unit through "accretion" or whether, instead, they constitute a separate unit that must be independently organized. An accretion question may be raised in various ways: by a charge under §8(a)(5); a petition to the Board for an election covering potentially accretable employees; or a petition for "unit clarification." Such issues may also be presented to an arbitrator depending on the language of the parties' labor agreement. However, a ruling from an arbitrator that the existing collective bargaining agreement covers the new group of employees, does not prevent the NLRB from reviewing the award for conformity with the NLRA. See Marion Power Shovel Co., 230 N.L.R.B. 576, 577-578 (1977) (stating that questions of accretion "are matters for decision of the Board rather than an arbitrator.").

Because a finding of accretion precludes the employees at issue from expressing their preferences in a secret-ballot election, the NLRB's accretion standards are more restrictive than its general unit determination criteria. The Board states that it will find a valid accretion "only when the additional employees have little or no separate group identity . . . and when the additional employees share an *overwhelming* community of interest with the preexisting unit to which they are accreted." Super Valu Stores, Inc., 283 N.L.R.B. 134, 136 (1987) (quoting Safeway Stores, 256 N.L.R.B. 918 (1981) (emphasis supplied)).

Furthermore, accretion may be barred if "the group sought to be accreted ha[d] been in existence at the time of recognition or certification, yet [was] not covered in an ensuing contract, or, having [subsequently] come into existence, ha[d] not been part of the larger unit to which their accretion is sought." Laconia Shoe Co., 215 N.L.R.B. 573 (1974); see also United Parcel Serv., 303 N.L.R.B. 326 (1991), enforced sub nom. Teamsters National United Parcel Serv. Negotiating Committee v. NLRB, 17 F.3d 1518 (D.C. Cir. 1994). The Board's accretion policy reflects a reluctance "to deprive employees of their basic right to select their own bargaining representative." Gitano Group, Inc., 308 N.L.R.B. 1172 (1992).

### v. Joint Employers, and Multiemployer Units

*Joint Employers*

In recent years, a more salient issue for the Board has been how to treat workers whose terms of employment are set by multiple entities. Such workers include many "contingent" workers, such as employees of temporary agencies who work for long periods of time at a single user company. Some employees in more permanent employment relationships also may have the terms of their employment determined by more than one entity. The Board therefore in some cases has found appropriate bargaining units that impose bargaining obligations on multiple companies as joint employers. The Board finds joint-employer status when two separate entities "share or co-determine those matters governing the essential terms and conditions of employment." See NLRB v. Browning-Ferris Indus., 691 F.2d 1117 (3d Cir. 1982). In Boire v. Greyhound Corp., 376 U.S. 473 (1964), for instance, the Board found that janitorial employees at four Greyhound bus terminals, who previously had been employed directly by Greyhound until the work was subcontracted to a cleaning company, Floors, were co-employees of Floors and Greyhound. As a result, it directed an election to determine their support for the petitioning union.

> [W]hile Floors hired, paid, disciplined, transferred, promoted and discharged maintenance employees at a bus terminal operated by Greyhound, Greyhound took part in setting up work schedules, in determining the number of employees required to meet those schedules, and in directing the work of the employees in question. The Board also found that Floors' supervisors visited the terminals only irregularly—on occasion not appearing for as much as two days at a time—and that in at least one instance Greyhound had prompted the discharge of an employee whom it regarded as unsatisfactory. On this basis, the Board . . . concluded that Greyhound and Floors were joint employers, because they exercised common control over the employees, and that the unit consisting of all employees under the joint employer relationship was an appropriate unit in which to hold an election. Id. at 475.

Although the agency's order directing an election was overturned by the court of appeals, the Supreme Court vacated that ruling for lack of jurisdiction on the basis of Leedom v. Kyne, 358 U.S. 184 (1958), infra page 258.

On remand, the court of appeals upheld the Board's joint-employer determination. 368 F.2d 778 (5th Cir. 1966).

The Reagan administration Board tightened the standard for joint employment, announcing that the two entities "must meaningfully affect[] matters relating to the employment relationship such as hiring, firing, discipline, supervision and direction," Laerco Transportation, 269 N.L.R.B. 324, 325 (1984), and the control must be direct and immediate, TLI, Inc. 271 N.L.R.B. 798, 798-799 (1984), enfd. 772 F.2d 894 (3d Cir. 1985). In *TLI*, for instance, the Board declined to treat a company leasing drivers from an employment agency as a joint employer of the agency's employees even though the leasing agreement granted the leasing company the authority to direct and supervise the drivers, including the scheduling of all their work and the initiation of discipline, and the leasing company had made clear that the leasing contract was dependent upon a reduction in expenses. See 271 N.L.R.B. at 798-799. The *TLI* Board found the leasing company's exercise of its authority to be "limited and routine" and that it had not dictated how expenses were to be reduced.

In August 2015, the Board altered its joint employment standard. It stated that two or more employers can be joint employers of the same employees if they "share or codetermine those matters governing the essential terms and conditions of employment." Browning-Ferris, 362 NLRB No. 186 (2015) (3-2). If a common-law employment relationship exists between the parties, the Board will then inquire "whether the putative joint employer possesses sufficient control over employees' essential terms and conditions of employment to permit meaningful collective bargaining." It will also "no longer require that a joint employer not only possess the authority to control employees' terms and conditions of employment, but also exercise that authority." Should the Board find a company to be a joint employer based on its legal authority to affect employment terms, regardless of the degree to which that authority has been exercised? Should a company that has outsourced its business to a subcontractor or sold a part of its business to franchisee be treated as a joint employer for purposes of bargaining merely because the bargaining unit realistically cannot attain higher wages, increased benefits, or better working conditions without the participation of that company? See generally Michael C. Harper, Defining the Economic Relationship Appropriate for Collective Bargaining, 39 B.C. L. Rev. 329, 345-46 (1998).

Joint-employment status may have relevance under the Act beyond defining bargaining responsibilities. First, if a company is a joint employer, it may not be considered a "neutral" protected from secondary pressure in the other employer's labor disputes with joint employees. See page 585 infra. Second, joint employment status also may be relevant to determining responsibility for unfair labor practices. For instance, in July, 2014, the General Counsel filed complaints against McDonald's USA as a joint employer of some of its franchisees' employees who allegedly suffered §8(a)(1) or §8(a)(3) violations. Is it clear, however, that employers with the responsibility to bargain jointly should be subject to ULP charges and liable for all unfair labor practice engaged in by a joint employer? Is the NLRA's definition of "employer," which refers to persons acting directly or indirectly as an agent of an employer, and its definition of "employee," which is not "limited to the employees of a particular employer," instructive here? Should a leasing company that sets and pays wages and benefits for a leased group of employees, for instance, necessarily be liable for a user company's suspension of two of the leased employees for protesting an overly harsh supervisor? See, e.g., Capitol EMI Music, Inc., 311 N.L.R.B. 997 (1993), enforced 23 F.3d 399 (4th Cir. 1994) (joint employer that can prove that it did not know of and should not have known of other employer's action is not liable for that action). Conversely, might the Board find that a company's anti-union pressure on another company interfered with the §7 rights of the second company's employees even without finding the first company to be a joint employer? Cf. Bowling Transportation, Inc., 336 N.L.R.B. 393 (2001), enforced, 352 F.3d 274 (6th Cir. 2003) (regardless of joint employer status, "supplier" company liable for unfair labor practice even if "user" company required the "supplier" to take the action).

*Multiemployer Units*

Many employees covered by collective agreements are in multiemployer units, in which a single master agreement is worked out for the employer group (perhaps supplemented by individual agreements dealing with issues pertaining to particular employers). Such units are most common in industries with large numbers of relatively small firms operating in local or regional labor and product markets, such as construction, retail stores, and the service industries. In industries dominated by relatively few firms, such as the auto industry, such bargaining has rarely developed. Far more significant in such industries is "pattern" bargaining, that is, the spread throughout the industry of a bargain worked out with one employer. See generally John W. Budd, The Determinants and Extent of UAW Pattern Bargaining, 45 Indus. & Lab. Rel. Rev. 523 (1992).

The NLRA does not explicitly authorize the formation of multiemployer units; §9(b) refers to units defined by employer, craft, or plant (or subdivision thereof). Nonetheless, early in its history the Board, with judicial assent, asserted the authority to recognize multiemployer units. See Shipowners' Ass'n of the Pacific Coast, 7 N.L.R.B. 1002 (1938), enforced sub nom. AFL v. NLRB, 103 F.2d 933 (D.C. Cir. 1939), affirmed, 308 U.S. 401 (1940); NLRB v. Truck Drivers Local 449 (Buffalo Linen Supply Co.), 353 U.S. 87 (1957). However, unlike other bargaining units, the multiemployer unit requires the consent both of each employer and of the union representative. This means that the Board does not conduct initial certification elections in multiemployer units. The union must have established its majority status for the employees of each employer member of the unit.

The formation of multiemployer units has been explained in part as an effort by employers to blunt the power of unions by preventing them from singling out one employer, extracting concessions from it by actual or threatened strikes, and thereafter relying on the coercive impact of the initial bargain to secure the same concessions from competitors. See Clark Kerr & Lloyd H. Fisher, Multi-Employer Bargaining: The San Francisco Experience, in Insights into Labor Issues 25 (Richard Lester & Joseph Shister eds., 1948). The multiemployer unit is designed to avoid such whipsawing and to expand the scope of an actual or threatened stoppage and thereby increase its costs to the union and the employees involved. Such expansion may also reduce the pressure that otherwise would operate on a single struck employer to settle in order to avoid giving its competitors an opportunity to divert its customers.

However, it also has been argued that multiemployer bargaining permits employer concessions that would otherwise be withheld out of fear that competitors might make a better bargain. On this view, a multiemployer unit strengthens rather than weakens the union's hand. See Gottfried Haberler, Wage Policy, Employment and Economic Stability, in The Impact of the Union 34, 41 (David McCord Wright ed., 1951). For good general treatments, see Douglas L. Leslie, Multiemployer Bargaining Rules, 75 Va. L. Rev. 241 (1989); Jan Vetter, Commentary on "Multiemployer Bargaining Rules": Searching for the Right Questions, 75 Va. L. Rev. 285 (1989); Bernard D. Meltzer, Single-Employer and Multi-Employer Lockouts Under the Taft-Hartley Act, 24 U. Chi. L. Rev. 70, 85-86 (1956).

### *Note:* M.B. Sturgis, Inc. *and* Oakwood Care Center

In M.B. Sturgis, Inc., 331 N.L.R.B. 1298 (2000), the Board addressed the question of whether, and under what circumstances, employees provided by a "supplier" employer (such as a temporary agency) to perform services for a "user" employer can be included in the same bargaining unit with employees who are solely employed by the user employer. In the typical situation, the supplier employer hires and fires the temporary employees and determines their pay and benefits, while the user employer is responsible for their day-to-day supervision and direction. Unlike the joint employer situation described above, however, the issue in *Sturgis* was whether the presence of jointly employed employees in the same bargaining unit as the user employer's solely employed employees constituted a multiemployer unit requiring the consent of both employers.

In *Sturgis,* the Board reexamined its earlier decisions in Greenhoot, Inc., 205 N.L.R.B. 250 (1973), and Lee Hospital, 300 N.L.R.B. 947 (1990). In *Greenhoot,* a union sought to represent engineering and maintenance employees at 14 area office buildings managed by Greenhoot. The Board held that the employees were jointly employed by Greenhoot and the 14 separate building owners, and that the requested unit was necessarily a multi-employer unit requiring the consent of both Greenhoot and each of the building owners. In *Lee Hospital*, a union sought to represent nurse anesthetists who were jointly employed by the hospital and a supplier employer, Anesthesiology Associates, Inc., in a unit with other employees who were solely employed by the hospital. Extending *Greenhoot*, the *Lee Hospital* Board deemed this a multiemployer unit requiring the consent of both employers.

*Sturgis* involved two consolidated cases. In the first, the union sought to represent 35 permanent, solely employed employees of the M.B. Sturgis Co., a producer of flexible gas hoses. The company, however, asserted that the unit was inappropriate unless it also included 10-15 temporary employees supplied and paid by the temporary agency Interim. These employees worked side by side with the permanent employees and performed the same work under the same supervisors. The union, in contrast, argued that a unit including the temporaries would be inappropriate. The Regional Director dismissed the petition because it sought a multiemployer unit without obtaining the consent of both Sturgis and Interim. In *Jeffboat Division*, the companion case, the union sought to accrete 30 welders and steamfitters supplied to Jeffboat, a shipbuilder, by the temporary agency TT&O, into a unit of 600 production and maintenance employees covered by a collective bargaining agreement between Jeffboat and the union. The acting Regional Director concluded that Jeffboat controlled nearly every aspect of the temporary employees' daily working environment, and that they were jointly employed by Jeffboat and TT&O. He further found that they shared a strong community of interest with Jeffboat's permanent employees. Because neither Jeffboat nor TT&O consented to joint bargaining, however, the petition was dismissed under *Greenhoot* and *Lee Hospital*.

The Clinton administration Board overruled *Lee Hospital*, holding that multiemployer principles do not apply where a union seeks to represent a unit combining employees who are jointly employed by a supplier and a user employer and employees who are solely employed by the user employer. In that situation, the Board ruled, it would not require either employer's consent to the unit, but rather would apply its traditional community of interest principles to determine whether the requested unit was appropriate. The agency reasoned that the scope of a bargaining unit is delineated by the work being performed for a particular employer, and that in the *Lee Hospital/Sturgis* situation, all of the work is being performed for the user employer and all the employees are employed by it, either wholly or in part. A unit of employees performing work for one user employer, it concluded, is an "employer unit" for purposes of NLRA §9(b).

As to the mechanics of bargaining in this situation, the Board stated that each employer is obligated to bargain with the union over the terms and conditions that it controls. Thus, the user employer must bargain over all terms and conditions of its solely employed employees, and over those conditions (generally workplace conditions such as supervision, direction, and safety rather than pay and benefits) of the jointly employed temporary employees that are under its control. The supplier employer, in turn, must bargain over the terms and conditions of the temporary employees that it controls (typically pay and benefits). The Board remanded both *Sturgis* and *Jeffboat* for application of its traditional bargaining unit principles.

In H.S. Care, Inc. d/b/a Oakwood Care Center, 343 N.L.R.B. No. 76 (2004), the Bush administration Board overruled *Sturgis* and reinstated the consent rule. The majority reasoned as follows:

> The *Sturgis* Board's reinterpretation of the concept of an "employer unit" severed that term from its statutory moorings. . . .
>
> Section 9(b) of the Act establishes the Board's authority to determine appropriate units . . .
>
> Of these permissible categories of units, the broadest is the "employer unit," with each of the other delineated types of appropriate units representing subgroups of the work force of an employer. Thus, the text of the Act reflects that Congress has not authorized the Board to direct elections in units encompassing the employees of more than one employer. The legislative history supports this interpretation of the plain language of the Act. Specifically, Congress included the phrase "or subdivision thereof" to authorize other units "not as broad as 'employer unit,' yet not necessarily coincident with the phrases 'craft unit' or 'plant unit.'"
>
> Where the parties voluntarily agree to multiemployer bargaining, however, the Board has long recognized the legitimacy of such units. . . .
>
> *Sturgis* left in place the fundamental principle that Section 9(b) permits the Board to find multiemployer units appropriate only with the consent of the parties but restricted the situations in which that principle would be applied through a strained interpretation of the phrase "employer unit." The *Sturgis* majority held that a unit composed of the employees of a user employer and employees jointly employed by the user and a supplier employer consists of employees of one employer. We disagree with this redefinition of terms, as it is inconsistent with the plain meaning of "employer unit" in the Act. Returning to prior precedent under both *Greenhoot* and *Lee Hospital*, we conclude that solely employed employees and jointly employed employees are employees of different employers and that their inclusion in the same bargaining unit creates a multiemployer unit.
>
> A joint employer, under the Board's traditional definition, is comprised of two or more employers (e.g., A and B) that "share or codetermine those matters governing essential terms and conditions of employment" for bargaining unit employees. All of the unit employees work for a single employer, i.e., the joint employer entity A/B. Therefore, a joint employer unit of A/B is not a multiemployer unit. In a *Sturgis* unit, in contrast, some of the employees are employed by A, and others are employed by A/B. It may be that, as to the latter

group, A and B jointly set all terms and conditions of employment. Or, it may be that, as to that group, A sets some terms and B sets others. The critical point is that the one group has its terms set by A/B. The other group has its terms set only by A. Thus, the entity that the two groups of employees look to as their employer is not the same. No amount of legal legerdemain can alter this fact. . . .

Although *Sturgis* anticipates that each employer will bargain with respect to employees whom it employs and as to the terms and conditions of employment that it controls, the reality of collective bargaining defies such neat classifications. Two examples illustrate this point. First, the wages paid to the jointly employed employees, which are frequently controlled by the supplier, could certainly have an effect on the negotiation of the wages of the solely employed employees, a matter controlled by the user. Second, the user employer would likely determine the holiday schedule for its facility, but the supplier might control whether the jointly employed employees are paid for those holidays. These are merely examples of how the bifurcation of bargaining regarding employees in the same unit hampers the give-and-take process of negotiation between a union and an employer, and places the employers in the position of negotiating with one another as well as with the union. The user employer's status as the customer of the supplier may effectively restrict the supplier's options in bargaining as to those subjects that appear to be within its purview. This fragmentation thus undermines effective bargaining.

The bargaining regime posited in *Sturgis* also fails to adequately protect employee rights. It combines jointly employed and solely employed employees in a single unit, with a single union negotiating with two different employers, each of which controls only a portion of the terms and conditions of employment for the unit. Such a structure subjects employees to fragmented bargaining and inherently conflicting interests, a result that is inconsistent with the Act's animating principles.

## *NOTES AND QUESTIONS*

**1. Multiemployer Bargaining and Employer Consent.** Why is the consent of each employer a condition of multiemployer bargaining under the Act? Is consent required because of Congress' failure to mention a unit of more than one employer in §9(b) of the Act? If the reference to "employer unit" excludes units of more than one employer, is there a statutory basis for multiemployer units formed with consent or for joint employer units? Is there a policy basis for requiring consent in a case like *Sturgis* where the employees at issue work jointly for two employers who are not competitors? Is the situation different in principle from that in *Greenhoot* where the employees work for competing employers? See Harper, Defining the Economic Relationship, supra, at 352-56.

**2. Units of Some Jointly-Employed and Some Solely-Employed Employees?** The *Oakwood* Board appears to draw a hard-and-fast distinction between units of jointly-employed employees, which do not require employer consent, and units of some jointly-employed and some solely-employed, which do require such consent: "All of the unit employees work for a single employer, i.e., the joint employer entity A/B." Therefore, a joint employer unit of A/B is not a multiemployer unit. In footnote 15 of its opinion (not reprinted above), the Board cites to Boire v. Greyhound Corp., 376 U.S. 473 (1964), described supra page 250. While the Board emphasized the fact that the union in *Greyhound* was not seeking to represent Floors employees who were not working at the Greyhound terminals, there seems no indication in any of the opinions that the joint employers functioned as an "entity" or that the unit sought by the union contained only employees common to the joint employers. Nor is this latter factor—the presence of only commonly employed employees—identified in other widely cited joint-employer rulings such as NLRB v. Browning-Ferris Indus., 691 F.2d 1117 (3d Cir. 1982). In any event, is the *Oakwood* Board's stress on this factor—which turns on the additional presence of solely employed employees rather than an additional employer—consistent with its rationale that units comprising employees of more than one employer should be viewed as multiemployer units triggering the consent rule? For further treatment, see Michael C. Harper, Judicial Control of the National Labor Relations Board's Lawmaking in the Age of *Chevron* and *Brand X*, 89 B.U. L. Rev. 189, 223-233 (2009).

**3. Community of Interest Between Temporary and Permanent Employees or Between Solely-Employed and Jointly-Employed Employees?** Even if the *Oakwood* Board's underlying concern is the presence of solely-employed employees among a unit of those jointly-employed, the Board would have authority, with or without the consent rule, to evaluate whether the proposed unit comprised an appropriate unit. Is it possible that in some instances that either a unit of the permanent employees only (those solely employed by the user employer) or a unit combining the permanent and temporary employees (who are jointly employed by the user and supplier employers) would be appropriate under the community of interest analysis? If so, on what will the unit determination turn? See Engineered Storage Prods. Co., 334 N.L.R.B. 1063 (2001) (petitioned-for unit of permanents-only approved; while unit including temporaries might also be appropriate, temporaries do not share such a strong community of interest with permanents as to require their inclusion in unit). Is this decision still good law after *Oakwood*? Are user and supplier employers likely in any event to consent to the inclusion of jointly-employed temporary employees in units including employees solely employed by the user?

**4. Who Would *Sturgis* Have Helped?** *Sturgis* clearly would aid unions that wish to organize temporary employees but have found it difficult to do so because of their high rate of turnover; including the temporaries in units with permanent employees may be the only means of organizing them at all. But as the facts of *Sturgis* itself indicate, there will be situations where user employers will find it tactically useful to argue that employees of a supplier employer should be included in an election involving its employees. In any event, after *Oakwood*, won't employees provided by a supplier employer to a user employer have to be organized separately from both the user's other employees and from the employees supplied to other users?

### *b. Judicial Review of Unit Determinations and Other Representational Issues*

**Leedom v. Kyne**
*358 U.S. 184 (1958)*

WHITTAKER, J. . . .

Buffalo Section, Westinghouse Engineers Association, Engineers and Scientists of America, a voluntary unincorporated labor organization, hereafter called the Association, was created for the purpose of promoting the economic and professional status of the nonsupervisory professional employees of Westinghouse Electric Corporation at its plant in Cheektowaga, New York, through collective bargaining with their employer. In October 1955, the Association petitioned the [NLRB] for certification as the exclusive collective bargaining agent of all nonsupervisory professional employees, being then 233 in number, . . . [at the Cheektowaga plant]. . . . A hearing was held by the Board upon that petition. A competing labor organization was permitted by the Board to intervene. It asked the Board to expand the unit to include employees in five other categories who performed technical work and were thought by it to be "professional employees" within the meaning of §2(12) of the Act.

The Board found that they were not professional employees within the meaning of the Act. However, it found that nine employees in three of those categories should nevertheless be included in the unit because they "share a close community of employment interests with [the professional employees, and their inclusion would not] destroy the predominantly professional character of such a unit." The Board, after denying the Association's request to take a vote among the professional employees to determine whether a majority of them favored "inclusion in such unit," included the 233 professional employees and the nine nonprofessional employees in the unit and directed an election to determine whether they desired to be represented by the Association, by the other labor organization, or by neither. The Association moved the Board to stay the election and to amend its decision by excluding the nonprofessional employees from the unit. The Board denied that motion and went ahead with the election at which the Association received a majority of the valid votes cast and was thereafter certified. . . .

Thereafter respondent, individually, and as president of the Association, brought this suit in the District Court against the members of the Board, alleging the foregoing facts and asserting that the Board had exceeded its statutory power in including the professional employees, without their consent, in a unit with nonprofessional employees in violation of §9(b)(1) which commands that the Board "shall not" do so, and praying, among other things, that the Board's action be set aside. . . .

On the Board's appeal it did not contest the trial court's conclusion that the Board, in commingling professional with nonprofessional employees in the unit, had acted in excess of its powers and had thereby worked injury to the statutory rights of the professional employees. Instead, it contended only that the District Court lacked jurisdiction to entertain the suit. The Court of Appeals held that the District Court did have jurisdiction and affirmed its judgment.

Petitioners, members of the Board, concede here that the District Court had jurisdiction of the suit under §24(8) of the Judicial Code, 28 U.S.C. §1337, unless the review provisions of the [NLRA] destroyed it. In American Federation of Labor v. Labor Board, 308 U.S. 401, this Court held that a Board order in certification proceedings under §9 is not "a final order" and therefore is not subject to judicial review except as it may be drawn in question by a petition for enforcement or review of an order, made under §10(c) of the Act, restraining an unfair labor practice. But the Court was at pains to point out in that case that "[t]he question [there presented was] distinct from . . . whether petitioners are precluded by the provisions of the Wagner Act from maintaining an independent suit in a district court to set aside the Board's action because contrary to the statute. . . ." Id., at 404. . . .

The record in this case squarely presents the question found not to have been presented by the record in *American Federation of Labor v. Labor Board*, supra. This case, in its posture before us, involves "unlawful action of the Board [which] has inflicted an injury on the [respondent]." Does the law, "apart from the review provisions of the . . . Act," afford a remedy? We think the answer surely must be yes. This suit is not one to "review," in the sense of that term as used in the Act, a decision of the Board made within its jurisdiction. Rather it is one to strike down an order of the Board made in excess of its delegated powers and contrary to a specific prohibition in the Act. Section 9(b)(1) is clear and mandatory. It says that, in determining the unit appropriate for the purposes of collective bargaining, "the Board *shall not* (1) decide that any unit is appropriate for such purposes if such unit includes both professional employees and employees who are not professional employees unless a majority of such professional employees vote for inclusion in such unit." (Emphasis added.) Yet the Board included in the unit employees whom it found were not professional employees, after refusing to determine whether a majority of the professional employees would "vote for inclusion in such unit." Plainly, this was an attempted exercise of power that had been specifically withheld. It deprived the professional employees of a "right" assured to them by Congress. Surely, in these circumstances, a Federal District Court has jurisdiction of an original suit to prevent deprivation of a right so given. . . .

Here, . . . "absence of jurisdiction of the federal courts" would mean "a sacrifice or obliteration of a right which Congress" has given professional employees, for there is no other means, within their control, to protect and enforce that right. And "the inference (is) strong that Congress intended the statutory provisions governing the general jurisdiction of those courts to control." 320 U.S. at page 300. This Court cannot lightly infer that Congress does not intend judicial protection of rights it confers against agency action taken in excess of delegated powers. . . .

Where, as here, Congress has given a "right" to the professional employees it must be held that it intended that right to be enforced. . . .

[The dissenting opinion of Justice Brennan, joined in by Justice Frankfurter, is omitted.]

## *NOTES AND QUESTIONS*

**1. The Limits of *Leedom v. Kyne*.** Note that the injunction in *Kyne* was sought by the union. Approving the assertion of jurisdiction by the district court, the Court noted that the Board's order was "in excess of its delegated powers and contrary to a specific prohibition in the Act." It also pointed out that under the *American Federation of Labor v. Labor Board* case, holding that orders in representation cases are not "final orders" reviewable under NLRA §10, both the professional employees and the union otherwise would have lacked any avenue for enforcing their rights under §9. (Unions' ability, or lack thereof, to obtain judicial review of representation issues is discussed in note 3 below.)

In Board of Governors of the Federal Reserve System v. MCorp Financial, Inc., 502 U.S. 32, 43-44 (1991), the Court stated that "central to our decision in *Kyne* was the fact that the Board's interpretation of the Act would wholly deprive the union of a meaningful and adequate means of vindicating its statutory rights." In holding that "nonstatutory" review under *Kyne* was unavailable, the Court in *MCorp* relied heavily on the fact that the plaintiff corporation was statutorily entitled (albeit at a later point) to review of the Board of Governors' decision in the court of appeals. For an NLRB case applying *MCorp*, see Detroit Newspaper Agency v. NLRB, 286 F.3d 391, 399 (6th Cir. 2002) (reversing district court's assertion of jurisdiction under *Kyne* on ground that plaintiff-employer ultimately would have an opportunity to appeal Board's decision to court of appeals under NLRA §10(f), "thereby making jurisdiction under *Leedom* improper on this basis alone").

**2. Indirect Review of Unit-Determination and Other Representational Issues: "Technical 8(a)(5)" Cases.** Employers can gain judicial review of representational issues by refusing to bargain and converting the case into an unfair labor practice proceeding. NLRA §9(d) provides that if the final order in a ULP proceeding "is based in whole or in part upon facts certified" in a representation proceeding, the certification and the record in the underlying representation case is included in the record transmitted to the court of appeals for a proceeding under NLRA §10(e) or §10(f). Hence, an employer that loses an election and wishes to raise a representational issue such as a unit determination may refuse to bargain with the union, thus forcing the union to file a charge under §8(a)(5) with the Board. In processing the ULP charge, the Board will not revisit the underlying representational issue; it will affirm its earlier determination via a summary judgment proceeding, find the employer guilty of a refusal to bargain, and order it to bargain with the union. (Such cases are known as "technical 8(a)(5)" cases.) Also, because Board orders are not self-enforcing, the employer may wait for the Board to petition for enforcement of its order under NLRA §10(e), or it may file its own petition in a court of appeals under §10(f). The court will then review the underlying representational issue in the course of deciding whether to uphold the Board's finding of a §8(a)(5) violation. (The same procedure is followed if the employer files objections to the conduct of the election.) Note that judicial review, including the technical 8(a)(5) procedure, delays bargaining for well over a year.

The Wagner Act Congress declined to provide for direct review of Board certification decisions because it concluded that employers had used the mechanism for pre-election review of certifications available under a precursor of the NLRA to delay elections, often for a year or more. Did its failure to provide for direct post-election review of certification decisions, however, exacerbate the delay at that end of the process? See Michael C. Harper, The Case for Limiting Judicial Review of Labor Board Certification Decisions, 55 Geo. Wash. L. Rev. 262, 281-282 & n.99 (1987) (concluding that despite Board's use of summary judgment procedure in technical 8(a)(5) cases, requiring filing and processing of unfair labor practice charge rather than allowing direct post-election review of certification decisions likely adds six months of delay to review process).

**3. Union-Initiated Review of Representational Issues?** Unions, in contrast, have no comparable means of converting a representational issue into an unfair labor practice case and thereby obtaining judicial review under §10(e) or §10(f); the narrow doctrine of *Leedom v. Kyne* is more or less all that is available to them. Would direct review, which would require statutory change, be of much value to unions that have lost elections given that they can seek a new election in the bargaining unit once the one-year election bar of §9(c)(3) has passed? Direct review would obviate the delay entailed in a technical ULP proceeding, but a court of appeals determination in the union's favor almost certainly would take over a year to obtain, and would achieve the same result obtainable by filing a new petition: a new election. There may be cases, however, where the court disagrees with the Board's grounds for overturning a union election victory.

**4. Eliminating §10 Review?** Should indirect review of representation decisions under §10 be eliminated completely, leaving *Kyne* as the sole avenue of judicial review of representational issues for employers and unions alike? If not, should review of certification decisions at least be much more narrowly circumscribed on the ground that Board decisions in representation cases largely involve fact-intensive inquiries? See Harper, Limiting Judicial Review, supra, at 305-320 (setting forth proposal for very narrow review).

## 3. Two Tracks for Regulating NLRA Elections

Before moving on to the law governing union access to the electorate and various campaign tactics, it is important to understand that the NLRB has essentially two routes by which representation election issues can be addressed: (1) the exercise of the agency's §9 authority in regulating the conduct of elections; and (2) the exercise of the agency's §§8 and 10 authority in prohibiting and providing remedies for unfair labor practices. The independence of these routes was established in the principal reading.

### General Shoe Corp.

*77 N.L.R.B. 124 (1948)*

. . . Conduct that creates an atmosphere which renders improbable a free choice will sometimes warrant invalidating an election, even though that conduct may not constitute an unfair labor practice. An election can serve its true purpose only if the surrounding conditions enable employees to register a free and untrammeled choice for or against a bargaining representative. For this reason the Board has sometimes set elections aside . . . in the absence of any charges or proof of unfair labor practice. When a record reveals conduct so glaring that it is almost certain to have impaired employees' freedom of choice, we have set an election aside and directed a new one. . . .

On this record, therefore, although the respondent's activities immediately before the election . . . are not held to constitute unfair labor practices . . . , certain of them created an atmosphere calculated to prevent a free and untrammeled choice by the employees. . . . The significant element is the method selected by this Company's president to express his antiunion views to the employees on the day before the election. He had them brought to his own office in some 25 groups of 20 to 25 individuals, and there, in the very room which each employee must have regarded as the locus of final authority in the plant, read every small group the same intemperate antiunion address. In our opinion, this conduct, and the Employer's instructions to its foremen to propagandize employees in their homes, went so far beyond the presently accepted custom of campaigns directed at employees' reasoning faculties that we are not justified in assuming that the election results represented the employees' own true wishes.

. . . [T]he criteria applied by the Board in a representation proceeding to determine whether certain alleged misconduct interfered with an election need [not] necessarily be identical to those employed in testing whether an unfair labor practice was committed, although the result will ordinarily be the same.[10] In election proceedings, it is the Board's function to provide a laboratory in which an experiment may be conducted, under conditions as nearly ideal as possible, to determine the uninhibited desires of the employees. It is our duty to establish those conditions; it is also our duty to determine whether they have been fulfilled. When, in the rare extreme case, the standard drops too low, because of our fault or that of others, the requisite laboratory conditions are not present and the experiment must be conducted over again. That is the situation here. We find the circumstances surrounding the election . . . raise substantial doubts as to whether [its results reflect] the employees' free choice. . . . Accordingly, we shall set it aside. . . .

## *NOTES AND QUESTIONS*

**1. Regulatory Authority Free of §8(c) Strictures?** Note 10 suggests that the Board has authority to set aside the election in *General Shoe* for conduct that may be protected by §8(c). Does it make sense to protect employer

10. . . . It should be noted that Congress only applied the new §8(c) to unfair labor practice cases. Matters which are not available to prove a violation of law, and therefore to impose a penalty upon a respondent, may still be pertinent, if extreme enough, in determining whether an election satisfies the Board's own administrative standards. . . .

speech under §8(c) and at the same time permit such speech to be a basis for invalidating "no union" votes? On the other hand, is there an argument that because the Board's authority under §9 does not involve branding a party a violator of the law or imposing any sanctions on it and requires the Board to affirmatively certify the results of an election, this authority should be treated differently than the Board's authority under §8? Moreover, does the precise wording of §8(c) lend support to the Board's position? For developments under the Railway Labor Act, see US Airways, Inc. v. NMB, 177 F.3d 985 (D.C. Cir. 1999) (holding NMB's order for rerun election on grounds of employer interference violated employer's free speech rights); Shawn J. Larsen-Bright, First Amendment and NLRB's Laboratory Conditions Doctrine, 77 N.Y.U. L. Rev. 204 (2002). Reconsider these issues after reading *NLRB v. Gissel Packing Co.*, infra, page 283.

**2. Unfair Labor Practices as Per Se Violations of "Laboratory Conditions"?** In Dal-Tex Optical Co., 137 N.L.R.B. 1782, 1786-1787 (1962), the Board declared that conduct constituting an unfair labor practice is a per se violation of fair election conditions under *General Shoe.* Should a pre-election unfair labor practice automatically constitute grounds for voiding an election? Suppose, for example, that an employer made a single §8(a)(1) threat, or subjected one employee to coercive interrogation, see infra pages 310-315, in a bargaining unit of 300 employees? In Caron Int'l, 246 N.L.R.B. 1120 (1979), the agency rejected a per se approach, ruling that whether misconduct warrants setting the election aside requires an assessment of "the number of violations, their severity, the extent of dissemination, the size of the unit, and other relevant factors."); see also Waste Automation and Waste Management of Pennsylvania, 314 N.L.R.B. 376 (1994) (closeness of election results is a relevant factor).

**3. Two Procedural Routes, Two Remedies.** When a new election is sought, objections must be filed within seven days of the challenged election. Ordinarily such objections must be based on conduct occurring during the "critical period," that is, the period between the filing of the petition and the election. See Ideal Electric & Mfg. Co., 134 N.L.R.B. 1275 (1961); Goodyear Tire & Rubber Co., 138 N.L.R.B. 453 (1962). Pre-petition conduct may be considered if it adds "meaning and dimension" to related post-petition conduct. Vestal Nursing Center, 328 N.L.R.B. 87, 103 n.34 (1999); see also National League of Professional Baseball Clubs, 330 N.L.R.B. 670 (2000) (extensive discussion of case law).

Conversely, §8(a)(1) cases, which can reach pre-petition conduct, proceed according to the Board's unfair labor practice procedure. Unfair labor practice charges must be filed within six months of the alleged unfair labor practice. See NLRA §10(b). The standard remedy in a §8(a)(1) case is a cease-and-desist order and the posting of an NLRB notice stating that the employer has been found guilty of violating the Act, and giving assurances to employees that it will respect their rights under the Act in the future.

### 4. Access to the Employee Electorate

Recall the discussion in Chapter 3 of no-solicitation/no-distribution rules, *Lechmere*, and salting. All of these present "access" issues; they concern employees' ability to communicate with each other or the union at the worksite. Access to employees is a critical issue in organizing campaigns. This section focuses on the *employer's* access to employees to communicate *its* message during a campaign, and on the relative degree of access to employees enjoyed by employers and unions. Such access issues tend to arise in the exercise of the Board's authority under the *General Shoe* doctrine.

#### NLRB v. United Steelworkers of America (*Nutone* and *Avondale*)
*357 U.S. 357 (1958)*

Frankfurter, J. . . .

No. 81.—In April of 1953 the respondent Steelworkers instituted a campaign to organize the employees of respondent NuTone, Inc., a manufacturer of electrical devices. In the early stages of the campaign, supervisory personnel of the company interrogated employees and solicited reports concerning the organizational activities of other employees. Several employees were discharged; the Board later found that the discharges had been the result of their organizational activities. In June the company began to distribute, through its supervisory personnel, literature that, although not coercive, was clearly antiunion in tenor. In August, while continuing to distribute such material, the company announced its intention of enforcing its rule against employees' posting signs or distributing literature on company property or soliciting or campaigning on company time. The rule, according to these posted announcements, applied to "all employees—whether they are for or against the union." Later the same month a representation election was held, which the Steelworkers lost.

In a proceeding before the Board commenced at the instance of the Steelworkers, the company was charged with a number of violations of the [NLRA] alleged to have taken place both before and after the election, including the discriminatory application of the no-solicitation rule. The Board found that the preelection interrogation and solicitation by supervisory personnel and the discharge of employees were unfair labor practices; it also found that the company had, in violation of the Act, assisted and supported an employee organization formed after the election. However, the

Board dismissed the allegation that the company had discriminatorily enforced its no-solicitation rule. 112 N.L.R.B. 1153. . . . The Court of Appeals concluded that it was an unfair labor practice for the company to prohibit the distribution of organizational literature on company property during nonworking hours while the company was itself distributing antiunion literature; and it directed that the Board's order be modified accordingly and enforced as modified.

No. 289.—In the fall of 1954 the Textile Workers conducted an organizational campaign at several of the plants of respondent Avondale Mills. A number of individual employees were called before supervisory personnel of the company, on the ground that they had been soliciting union membership, and informed that such solicitation was in violation of plant rules and would not be tolerated in the future. The rule [against solicitation] had not been promulgated in written form, but there was evidence that it had been previously invoked in a nonorganizational context. During this same period, both in these interviews concerning the rule and at the employees' places of work, supervisory personnel interrogated employees concerning their organizational views and activities and solicited employees to withdraw their membership cards from the union. This conduct was in many cases accompanied by threats that the mill would close down or that various employee benefits would be lost if the mill should become organized. Subsequently three employees, each of whom had been informed of the no-solicitation rule, were laid off and eventually discharged for violating the rule.

. . . The Board found that the interrogation, solicitation and threatening of employees by the company's supervisory personnel were unfair labor practices. Moreover, it found that resort to the no-solicitation rule and discharge of the three employees for its violation were discriminatory and therefore in violation of the Act; it further held that, even if the rule had not been invoked discriminatorily, the discharge of one of the employees had resulted solely from his organizational activities apart from any violation of the rule and was therefore an unfair labor practice. The Board ordered the cessation of these practices and the reinstatement of the discharged employees. 115 N.L.R.B. 840. Upon the Board's petitioning for enforcement in the Court of Appeals for the Fifth Circuit, the company contested only the portions of the Board's findings and order relating to the rule and the discharges. The [c]ourt . . . finding insufficient evidence of discrimination in the application of the no-solicitation rule, denied enforcement to the portion of the order relating to the rule and to . . . the discharges [resulting from violations of the rule]. . . .

. . . In neither of the cases before us did the party attacking the enforcement of the no-solicitation rule contest its validity. Nor is the claim made that an employer may not, under proper circumstances, engage in noncoercive antiunion solicitation; indeed, his right to do so is protected by the so-called "employer free speech" provision of §8(c) of the Act. Contrariwise, as both cases before us show, coercive antiunion solicitation and other similar conduct run afoul of the Act and constitute unfair labor practices irrespective of the bearing of such practices on enforcement of a no-solicitation rule. The very narrow and almost abstract question here derives from the claim that, when the employer himself engages in antiunion solicitation that if engaged in by employees would constitute a violation of the rule — particularly when his solicitation is coercive or accompanied by other unfair labor practices — his enforcement of an otherwise valid no-solicitation rule against the employees is itself an unfair labor practice. We are asked to rule that the coincidence of these circumstances necessarily violates the Act, regardless of the way in which the particular controversy arose or whether the employer's conduct to any considerable degree created an imbalance in the opportunities for organizational communication. . . .

There is no indication in the record in either of these cases that the employees, or the union on their behalf, requested the employer, himself engaging in antiunion solicitation, to make an exception to the rule for prounion solicitation. There is evidence in both cases that the employers had in the past made exceptions to their rules for charitable solicitation. Notwithstanding the clear antiunion bias of both employers, it is not for us to conclude as a matter of law — although it might well have been open to the Board to conclude as a matter of industrial experience — that a request for a similar qualification upon the rule for organizational solicitation would have been rejected. Certainly the employer is not obliged voluntarily and without any request to offer the use of his facilities and the time of his employees for prounion solicitation. He may very well be wary of a charge that he is interfering with, or contributing support to, a labor organization in violation of §8(a)(2) of the Act.

No attempt was made in either of these cases to make a showing that the no-solicitation rules truly diminished the ability of the labor organizations involved to carry their messages to the employees. Just as that is a vital consideration in determining the validity of a no-solicitation rule, it is highly relevant in determining whether a valid rule has been fairly applied. Of course the rules had the effect of closing off one channel of communication; but the Taft-Hartley Act does not command that labor organizations as a matter of abstract law, under all circumstances, be protected in the use of every possible means of reaching the minds of individual workers, nor that they are entitled to use a medium of communication simply because the employer is using it. Cf. Bonwit Teller, Inc. v. Labor Board, 197 F.2d 640, 646; Labor Board v. F.W. Woolworth Co., 214 F.2d 78, 84 (concurring opinion). No such mechanical answers will avail for the solution of this nonmechanical, complex problem in labor-management relations. If, by virtue of the location of the plant and of the facilities and resources available to the union, the opportunities for effectively reaching the employees with a prounion message, in spite of a no-solicitation rule, are at least as great as the employer's ability to promote the legally authorized expression of his anti-union views, there is no basis for invalidating these "otherwise valid" rules. The Board, in determining whether or not the enforcement of such a rule in the circumstances of an individual case is an unfair labor practice, may find relevant alternative channels available for communications on the right to organize. When this important issue is not even raised before the Board and no evidence bearing on it adduced, the concrete basis for appraising the significance of the employer's conduct is wanting.

We do not at all imply that the enforcement of a valid no-solicitation rule by an employer who is at the same time engaging in antiunion solicitation may not constitute an unfair labor practice. All we hold is that there must be some basis, in the actualities of industrial relations, for such a finding. The records in both cases — the issues raised in the proceedings — are barren of the ingredients for such a finding. Accordingly the judgment in No. 81 is reversed, insofar as it sets aside and requires the Board to modify its order, and the cause is remanded to the Court of Appeals for proceedings not inconsistent with this opinion; in all other respects, it is affirmed. The judgment in No. 289 is affirmed.

[The opinion of Chief Justice Warren (joined by Justices Black and Douglas) dissenting in *Avondale Mills* and concurring in the result in *Nutone* is omitted.]

## *NOTES AND QUESTIONS*

**1. What Can the Board Do to Promote Greater Union Access After *Nutone*?** To what extent does *Steelworkers* (generally referred to as *Nutone* and *Avondale*) turn on deference to the Board's judgment? Note the Court's statement that "no attempt was made . . . to . . . show[] that the no-solicitation rules truly diminished the ability of the labor organizations involved to carry their messages to the employees." Assume that the Board subsequently determined, in an exercise of its industrial expertise, that restricting employee solicitation to nonworking time while allowing company agents to engage in unlimited noncoercive anti-union solicitation at work significantly diminishes the ability of unions to communicate with employees. Would it then be free to decide that such discriminatory application of no-solicitation rules interferes with employees' §7 rights to learn of the potential benefits of unionization and thereby violates §8(a)(1), or at least sufficiently marred fair election conditions to warrant a rerun election under its *General Shoe* doctrine? Would such a rule be consistent with the employer's free speech rights under §8(c) of the Act, which is discussed infra pages 276-283? With the Court's ruling in *Lechmere*, supra page 144?

**2. "Captive Audience" Speeches and Broad, Privileged No-Solicitation Rules.** In Bonwit-Teller, Inc., 96 N.L.R.B. 608 (1951), the Board held that although an employer may assemble and address a captive audience of employees, it violates the Act by denying a union's request to reply to a similar assembly. However, in Livingston Shirt Corp., 107 N.L.R.B. 400, 409 (1953), a reconstituted Board reversed course, and finding "nothing improper in an employer's refusing to grant to the union a right equal to his own in his plant," required an employer to grant such requests to reply only in "special circumstances"; namely, when an employer maintains "either an unlawful broad no-solicitation rule . . . or a privileged no-solicitation rule (broad, but not unlawful because of the character of the business)." See generally Paul M. Secunda, The Contemporary "Fist Inside the Velvet Glove"—Employer Captive Audience Meetings Under the NLRA, 5 Fla. Int'l U. L. Rev. 385 (2010).

**3. Employer Control of Employee Audience.** The Board also has generally declined to regulate the number of required-attendance speeches regarding organizational issues an employer can hold on its property or an employer's control of its employee audience during these meetings. The Board has ruled that employees have "no statutorily protected right to leave a meeting which the employees were required by management to attend on company time and property to listen to management's noncoercive antiunion speech designed to influence the outcome of a union election." Litton Systems, Inc., 173 N.L.R.B. 1024, 1030 (1968). Employers also can prohibit questions during captive-audience meetings. See F.W. Woolworth Co., 251 N.L.R.B. 1111 (1980), enforced, 655 F.2d 151 (8th Cir. 1981); Luxuray of New York, 185 N.L.R.B. 100 (1970), enforced in part, 447 F.2d 112 (2d Cir. 1971). An employer can discipline an employee for asking a question if it involves "violent conduct, improper motive, or bad faith," if it is "an attempt to turn the meetings into a union forum," or the misconduct is of "such serious character as to render the employee unfit for further service." Woolworth Co., 251 N.L.R.B. at 1114. Do these holdings inhibit or encourage the free flow of ideas in representation elections? Are they necessary to enable employers to present their views? Are they required by §8(c) of the Act? Are they best understood as an application of the principle articulated in *Babcock & Wilcox* and confirmed in *Lechmere* that §7 rights must be accommodated to employer property rights? If the latter, do they strike an appropriate balance?

**4. Last-Minute "Mass Assembly" Speeches.** Invoking *General Shoe*, the agency ruled in Peerless Plywood Co., 107 N.L.R.B. 427 (1953), that it will set aside an election when an employer or a union has delivered a speech "on company time to massed assemblies of employees within 24 hours before the scheduled . . . election." Id. at 429. A last-minute speech on company time, the Board reasoned, tends to create a "mass psychology" incompatible with "sober and thoughtful choice" and to give an "unfair advantage" to the party who enjoys the last opportunity to talk to the voters. Id. Note, however, the relative narrowness of the *Peerless Plywood* rule. It does not, for instance, reach other forms of captive campaigning within a day of the election. Thus, management may address voters individually at their work stations or in a managerial office within this period. See, e.g., Flex Prods., Inc., 280 N.L.R.B. 1117 (1986); Land O'Frost of Arkansas, Inc., 252 N.L.R.B. 1 (1980). Moreover, *Peerless Plywood* does not prohibit either employers or unions from making campaign speeches on or off company premises during the 24-hour period if the employees are on their own time and their attendance is voluntary. In addition, leafletting and other forms of campaigning may take place without restriction during this period. Does the Board have authority under *General Shoe* to issue a broader ban on 24-hour electioneering or to bar all electioneering, say, within a week of the election? What if a union broadcasts union anthems such as "Proud to be a Teamster" from a sound truck across from the employer's facility on election day, at sufficiently high volume that the songs could be heard at many employees' work stations, although not in the polling area itself? Is this grounds for overturning a union victory under *Peerless Plywood*? See Bro-Tech Corp., 330 N.L.R.B. 37 (1999), on remand from 105 F.3d 890 (3d Cir. 1997).

**5. Union Access "at Least as Great" as the Employer's?** The Court states in *Nutone* and *Avondale* that if "the opportunities for effectively reaching the employees with a pro-union message . . . are at least as great as the employer's ability to promote the legally authorized expression of his antiunion views, there is no basis for invalidating" rules that allow employer, but not union, speech during work time. What is the basis for this seeming equal-access rule? Is it likely that union opportunities for reaching employees outside of work can ever be equal to an employer's ability to reach employees through work-time speeches to which the captive workers must listen—especially when one factors in the *Lechmere* decision, supra page 144? Is the Court's reference to access to the employee electorate "at least as great as the employer's" part of the holding in that case? Is there a basis for requiring greater union access to employees in the election context than is required at the organizational stage? Review after considering the Board's reasoning in *Excelsior Underwear, Inc.* below.

**6. Holding Elections at the Work Site vs. Mail Balloting?** In order to encourage a maximum voter turnout, the Board usually obtains company consent to hold representation elections at the unit's work site. Does this practice aggravate the effect of unequal access on unions' chances? Consider Craig Becker, Democracy in the Workplace: Union Representation Elections and Federal Labor Law, 77 Minn. L. Rev. 495, 566 (1993) ("[I]f the polling takes place at work, the employer may lawfully keep the union at a distance from the balloting. . . . The practical effect is that employers can campaign among employees on election day, and even during the polling, but unions cannot.").

To avoid this effect, should the Board implement mail or electronic balloting in all cases? Does it have the authority to do so? The Board's regulations provide that Regional Directors should consider mail ballots where eligible voters are "scattered" because of job duties over a wide geographic area, where eligible voters are "scattered" in the sense that their work schedules vary significantly, so that they are not present at a common location at common times; and if there is a strike, a lockout or picketing in progress. NLRB, Representation Casehandling Manual §11301.2. The National Mediation Board (NMB), the agency that regulates representation elections under the Railway Labor Act, has long used mail and now electronic balloting. See National Mediation Board Representation Manual 14.02 (2009); In re Continental Airlines, 35 N.M.B. 42 (2008) (introducing Internet voting). Would such a procedure in the NLRA context significantly reduce employee voter turnout?

**7. Access Remedies for Serious Unfair Labor Practices.** Where an employer's response to an organizing effort is a series of egregious unlawful acts, the Board has ordered certain forms of union access to the employer's premises as a remedial measure—for example, access to plant bulletin boards, to nonworking areas during nonworking periods, or to a work time forum to reply to any captive audience speeches. Such access is usually limited to the site at which the unfair labor practices were committed. The Board's view is that such orders are an exercise of its §10(c) remedial authority and do not require a showing that the union has no other reasonable means of reaching the employees. For a thorough discussion of access remedies, see United Steelworkers v. NLRB (Florida Steel Corp.), 646 F.2d 616 (D.C. Cir. 1981).

## Excelsior Underwear, Inc.
*156 N.L.R.B. 1236 (1966)*

[In *Excelsior*, after an election in which 246 of 247 eligible employees voted and 206 votes were against the union, the union filed objections based, inter alia, on the employer's failure to supply the union with the employees' names and addresses. The Regional Director recommended overruling the objections. The Chamber of Commerce, the National Association of Manufacturers, the AFL-CIO, and various international unions, pursuant to the

Board's invitation, filed amicus curiae briefs and participated in oral argument in *Excelsior* and a companion case raising the same issue.]

... [E]ach of these cases poses the question whether an employer's refusal to provide a union with the names and addresses of employees eligible to vote in a representation election should be grounds on which to set that election aside. The Board has not in the past set elections aside on this ground. ...

We are persuaded ... that higher standards of disclosure than we have heretofore imposed are necessary, and that prompt disclosure of the information here sought by the Petitioners should be required in all representation elections. Accordingly, we now establish a requirement that will be applied in all election cases. That is, within seven days after the Regional Director has approved a consent-election agreement entered into by the parties ..., or after the Regional Director or the Board has directed an election ..., the employer must file with the Regional Director an election eligibility list, containing the names and addresses of all the eligible voters. The Regional Director, in turn, shall make this information available to all parties in the case. Failure to comply with this requirement shall be grounds for setting aside the election whenever proper objections are filed.[5]

The considerations that impel us to adopt the foregoing rule are these: ... [W]e regard it as the Board's function to conduct elections in which employees have the opportunity to cast their ballots for or against representation under circumstances that are free not only from interference, restraint, or coercion violative of the Act, but also from other elements that prevent or impede a free and reasoned choice. Among the factors that undoubtedly tend to impede such a choice is a lack of information with respect to one of the choices available. In other words, an employee who has had an effective opportunity to hear the arguments concerning representation is in a better position to make a more fully informed and reasonable choice. Accordingly, we think that it is appropriate for us to remove the impediment to communication to which our new rule is directed.

... [A]n employer, through his possession of employee names and home addresses as well as his ability to communicate with employees on plant premises, is assured of the continuing opportunity to inform the entire electorate of his views. ... [A] labor organization, whose organizers normally have no right of access to plant premises, has no method by which it can be certain of reaching all the employees with its arguments in favor of representation. ... In other words, by providing all parties with employees' names and addresses, we maximize the likelihood that all the voters will be exposed to the arguments for, as well as against, union representation. ...

5. However, the rule we have here announced is to be applied prospectively only. It will not apply in the instant cases but only in those elections that are directed, or consented to, subsequent to 30 days from the date of this Decision. ...

The arguments against imposing a requirement of disclosure are of little force especially when weighed against the benefits resulting therefrom. Initially, we are able to perceive no substantial infringement of employer interests that would flow from such a requirement. A list of employee names and addresses is not like a customer list, and an employer would appear to have no significant interest in keeping the names and addresses of his employees secret (other than a desire to prevent the union from communicating with his employees — an interest we see no reason to protect). Such legitimate interest in secrecy as an employer may have is, in any event, plainly outweighed by the substantial public interest in favor of disclosure. . . .

The main arguments that have been presented to us by the Employers and the amici curiae supporting the Employers relate not to any infringement of *employer* rights flowing from a disclosure requirement but rather to an asserted infringement of *employee* rights. . . . We regard this argument as without merit. An employee's failure to provide a union with his name and address, whether due to inertia, fear of employer reprisal, or an initial predisposition to vote against union representation, is not, as we view it, an exercise of [his §7 right] to refrain from union activity. Rather, in the context with which we are here concerned — a Board-conducted representation election — an employee exercises this right by voting for or against union representation.

Similarly, we reject the argument that to provide the union with employee names and addresses subjects employees to the dangers of harassment and coercion in their homes. We cannot assume that a union, seeking to obtain employees' votes in a secret ballot election, will engage in conduct of this nature; if it does, we shall provide an appropriate remedy. We do not, in any event, regard the mere possibility that a union will abuse the opportunity to communicate with employees in their homes as sufficient basis for denying this opportunity altogether. . . .

The argument is also made (by the Employer in the *Excelsior* case) that under the decisions of the Supreme Court in *NLRB v. The Babcock & Wilcox Company*, and *NLRB v. United Steelworkers of America* (*Nutone Inc.*), the Board may not require employer disclosure of employee names and addresses unless, in the particular case involved the union would otherwise be unable to reach the employees with its message. . . .

Initially, as we read *Babcock* and *Nutone*, the existence of alternative channels of communication is relevant only when the opportunity to communicate made available by the Board would interfere with a significant employer interest — such as the employer's interest in controlling the use of property owned by him. Here, as we have shown, the employer has no significant interest in the secrecy of employee names and addresses. Hence, there is no necessity for the Board to consider the existence of alternative channels of communication before requiring disclosure of that information.

Moreover, even assuming that there is some legitimate employer interest in nondisclosure, we think it relevant that the subordination of that interest which we here require is limited to a situation in which employee interests in self-organization are shown to be substantial. For, whenever an election is directed (the precondition to disclosure) the Regional Director has found that a real question concerning representation exists; when the employer consents to an election, he has impliedly admitted this fact. The opportunity to communicate on company premises sought in *Babcock* and *Nutone* was not limited to the situation in which employee organizational interests were substantial; i.e., in which an election had been directed; we think that on this ground also the cases are distinguishable. . . .

[The Board certified that a majority of valid ballots had not been cast for the unions participating in each of the elections involved.]

## *NOTES AND QUESTIONS*

**1. An Exercise of the *General Shoe* Doctrine.** The *Excelsior* rule is not predicated on the commission of any unfair labor practices, but rather is an example of the Board's authority to prescribe fair election conditions under *General Shoe.* As the Board notes, failure to comply with the requirement is grounds for overturning an employer victory in the election.

**2. Pseudo-Rulemaking?** Note the procedure used by the Board as described at the outset of the decision and in footnote 5. In *Excelsior,* was the Board in effect substituting its own rulemaking procedure for the one set forth in §553 of the Administrative Procedure Act (APA)?

In NLRB v. Wyman-Gordon Co., 394 U.S. 759 (1969), an employer refused to submit an "*Excelsior* list," and the Board issued a subpoena requiring its submission. The issue before the Supreme Court was whether the subpoena, which was based on *Excelsior,* was unenforceable because the *Excelsior* Board had not followed APA rulemaking procedures. Six Justices agreed that the "one-size-fits-all," prospective-only decision in *Excelsior* was a "rule" subject to the APA's notice-and-comment requirements, which the Board had not followed. However, four of those Justices nonetheless voted to enforce the subpoena in the *Wyman-Gordon* proceeding, reasoning that it had been the product of a valid adjudication. In effect, a majority of the Justices, while not agreeing on the same rationale, were in favor of enforcement of the *Excelsior* requirement in the *Wyman-Gordon* litigation.

**3. Earlier Access to *Excelsior* Lists?** Note when the *Excelsior* decision requires an employer to provide a list of eligible voters. Should the Board require employers to provide union organizers with an *Excelsior* list earlier in the process? Would this be consistent with the Board's reasoning in

*Excelsior*? Is *Lechmere* relevant here? If the Board has the authority to require earlier access, at what point in the process should the employer be required to provide the *Excelsior* list? Should the Board consider requiring earlier disclosure of the list at least in circumstances where the employees are unusually difficult to reach? See Technology Serv. Solutions, 324 N.L.R.B. 298, 303-306 (1997) (Chairman Gould, concurring). See generally Estreicher, Improving the Administration of the NLRA, supra.

**4. Should the *Excelsior* List Include Employees' E-mail Addresses?** The Board's proposed rule on election procedures, discussed infra, would compel employers to provide e-mail addresses, where available. The Notice of Proposed Rulemaking states that "[t]he provision of only a physical address no longer serves the primary purpose of the *Excelsior* list." Does the rationale of *Excelsior* support this position? 79 Fed. Reg. 7326.

**5. Impact of *Excelsior* on the Board's "Captive Audience" Rulings?** In General Elec. Co., 156 N.L.R.B. 1247 (1966), decided the same day as *Excelsior*, the Board declined to reinstate the "equal opportunity" right to reply doctrine of *Bonwit-Teller*, supra page 269, note 2, preferring "to defer any reconsideration of current Board doctrine in the area of plant access until after the effects of *Excelsior* become known." Id. at 1251. In view of *Lechmere*, should the Board now revive the *Bonwit-Teller* doctrine? Can it do so after *Nutone* and *Avondale*? Can it do so consistent with §8(c)? Can it do so as a condition certifying election results under its *General Shoe* doctrine? Do the home visits facilitated by *Excelsior* effectively equalize the union's ability to communicate with employees with that enjoyed by employers at the workplace?

**6. Other Access Rights?** What do you think of the following proposal:

> Elections require an informed electorate. The NLRB has authority under current law to give a union limited access to employees once the required showing of interest for an election has been demonstrated. Presently, the agency requires only that the employer provide contact information for unit employees. This could be extended to requiring union access to nonwork areas like the parking lot, cafeteria, and break room, and could be conditioned on compliance with reasonable security procedures.

Samuel Estreicher: "Easy In, Easy Out": A Future for U.S. Workplace Representation, 98 Minn. L. Rev. 1615, 1632-33 (2014). Is this approach maintainable after *Lechmere*? As an exercise of authority under *General Shoe*?

## 5. Regulation of the Conduct of the Election

The previous section, as well as the material in Chapter 3 on no-solicitation/no-distribution rules, access to the employer's property, and salting, dealt with the ability of employees, non-employee union organizers, and the employer to communicate with employees about the campaign. It did not, however, focus on the legality of the *content* of the message communicated; for instance, *Nutone* and *Avondale* and the captive-audience doctrine addressed the employer's ability to engage in *noncoercive* anti-union solicitation. This section, in contrast, deals largely with the content of both oral and written communications with employees, and the line between what is permissible and what is not. It also addresses the legality of certain employer and union conduct such as grants of benefits and surveillance. As you read through this material, pay close attention to the Board's and the courts' views of how much impact employer and union campaign tactics actually have on employees, and ask yourself whether these views are consistent across cases and different substantive areas.

### a. *Threatening Speech*

**NLRB v. Golub Corp.**
*388 F.2d 921 (2d Cir. 1967)*

Friendly, J. . . .

On January 18, 1965, the Regional Director ordered an election for February 17. The company sent employees three letters, dated February 2, 8 and 12, arguing against the union. In another letter of February 11 it invited employees and their spouses to attend a dinner meeting on February 16, advising that they would be paid for their time. After dinner William Golub delivered a speech again arguing against the union.

The union lost the election 24-4 but the Regional Director set the vote aside because Golub's speech violated the 24 hour rule set forth in Peerless Plywood Co., 107 N.L.R.B. 427 (1953). Later he approved the union's request to withdraw its certification petition. Meanwhile unfair labor practice charges had been filed and a complaint issued. The Trial Examiner found that . . . certain passages in the letters of February 2 and 8 and the speech of February 16 to violate §8(a)(1). The Board agreed. . . .

In contrast to many §8(a)(1) proceedings, the violations here found consisted solely of writings and a speech addressed to the employees as a group—there was no finding of interrogation or surveillance, of discriminatory discharge, or of the grant of benefits. The case thus sharply raises the issue how far the Board may go in curbing speech consistently with §8(c) and the First Amendment.

The Board had no criticism of the company's letters of February 11 and 12, and only faulted portions of the letters of February 2 and 8 and a rather small part of Golub's speech of February 16. To quote simply the contested passages would create a false impression; it is necessary to place them in their setting by summarizing the entire communications.

The February 2 letter began by telling the employees of the forthcoming election. It accused the union of making false promises which "you can easily find out about . . . from others" and of picking on a single store to avoid a vote for all the chain's employees. It assured employees that the ballot would be absolutely secret, that they were "protected by law from anyone who attempts to interfere with your making a free choice," and that they were not bound by having signed a union card. It then went on to say "To get you to vote for them, the Union has been making many promises — promises to make demands which could be excessive. Companies that have been forced to meet excessive Union demands have been known to be forced out of business. The employees at the other local chain (Saveway) were not fooled by Union promises and flatly rejected them just a short time ago."[7] After arguing that union membership would mean dues, assessments, other financial burdens, and possibly sympathy strikes, the letter continued:

> The retail food business is the most competitive business in the world. Customers, not Unions, help pay your wages. We bring customers into our stores if we attract them with competitive prices. Even the large chains cannot meet these Union demands without making drastic adjustments because they also have to remain competitive. Large chains which have been forced to sign up with the Unions have been known to increase the workload of all their individual employees by reducing the number of employees in order to offset the higher costs. They find that they have to get the same amount of work done by fewer people to remain competitive.[8]

In conclusion the company promised to write again and asked the employees to keep an open mind.

The February 8 letter began by asking the employees to "look at the true facts of what outside interference would mean to you." The first set of facts consisted of the payment of dues and other union obligations, much as the earlier letter had depicted. Then came a paragraph found to have violated §8(a)(1) which we quote in the margin.[9] The letter went on to challenge "two false arguments" — that employees who did not sign up or vote for the

7. The last two sentences were found to have violated §8(a)(1).

8. The last two sentences were found to have violated §8(a)(1).

9. "2. What does the choice of a union do to personal relationships? It means the end of a close relationship between you and your manager — or other management personnel. You certainly must recall that from time to time you may have asked the manager for some special personal arrangement or privilege which he probably gladly granted, such as time off

union would be fired if the union won and that [Golub's] owners really wanted a union. It urged employees not to put their future in the hands of union representatives with little interest in their needs or problems, and warned that a union might cook up a dispute "just to keep 'the pot boiling' or perhaps to help one of their favorites in your store," and that choice of a union "possibly could mean long drawn out strikes." It told the employees who planned to make their careers with the company that they did not need a union "to get the greatest benefits which this company can give and which it gives without unions" and appealed to those employees who were working their way through school or college not to foist a burden on their fellows. The letter concluded by asking how a union can "truthfully promise job security," arguing that "their exorbitant, excessive and outlandish demands often result in layoffs and even force companies out of business," and that job security really rested in sales and service to customers. Golub promised to write again, and requested the employees to "keep an open mind until the election."

Only two excerpts [in Golub's long February 16 speech] were found to have violated §8(a)(1). The first we quote in the margin.[10] In the second Golub dealt with the small 1% profit margin characteristic of grocery chains and the correspondingly narrow leeway for "many additional unrealistic demands which add to your overhead and expenses." He then told of a large chain which had raised prices after negotiating a union contract and as a result had been required to discharge around 25% of its help and make the remaining staff "do a tougher job because they have got to do the work those who were let out have to do," and of another market, and also a discount store, that were being forced out of business due to a union contract.

. . . [T]he basic issue is whether an employer coerces his employees in the exercise of §7 rights, as forbidden by §8(a)(1), when he prophesies that

---

when your children were sick, weddings, for haircuts, a school prom, emergencies at home, and to catch up on studies. If there were a union contract, such personal privileges most likely could not be granted. Special privileges could be forbidden under a contract and be in violation of the contract. In such cases, we could not deal directly with you, but only through your union representative. You will not be able to solve problems directly as we have been doing. Do not be fooled by those who tell you otherwise — especially those fellow employees who might try to frighten you into thinking that they can control your job."

10. "We have never had tensions or misunderstanding. We have always been able to talk them out, and they are here. They bring in these tensions and these difficulties which you would be subject to under their regime. Now, don't forget also that if they were to come in that many of the human things that we are now doing as a matter of course would no longer be possible if they were here under contract. Many of the little human things like we do, like giving you privileges where you want to go out to dances or if you have to play in a basketball game, or a child is sick, or [any] of a dozen reasons. We will always give you reasonable consideration. Under a contract we would be subject to the rules of that contract. If we did these things, we could be charged with favoritism, we would be violating our contract. These things could well go by the board as a result. . . ."

unionization will decrease or wholly eliminate work opportunities, increase workloads, or create greater rigidity in personnel relationships, or whether such predictions come within the protection [of] §8(c). . . . While the answer would seem easy enough, the trend of Board decisions toward ever increasing restrictions on employer speech makes it desirable to attain perspective by a brief historical survey.

Under the Wagner Act, which contained §8(a)(1) but nothing like §8(c), the Board condemned almost any antiunion expression by an employer. It was sustained against First Amendment attack by some courts including this one, on the basis that employer arguments have "an ambivalent character." Since "what to an outsider will be no more than the vigorous presentation of a conviction, to an employee may be the manifestation of a determination which it is not safe to thwart," we held that "the Board must decide how far the second aspect obliterates the first," with the substantial evidence rule available to support its decision. NLRB v. Federbush Co., 121 F.2d 954, 957 (2d Cir. 1941). The Supreme Court evidently thought otherwise. NLRB v. Virginia Electric & Power Co., 314 U.S. 469 (1941), dealt with employer notices pointing out that in the fifteen years since an organization strike had failed, confidence and understanding had reigned without the existence of a labor organization in any department. It went on to state that the company would freely entertain employee grievances and that it believed the mutual interest of all could "best be promoted through confidence and cooperation." The Board found the communications a violation of §8(1). The Court interpreted the words of the Wagner Act to avoid constitutional doubts arising from the First Amendment. It held that speech, which by its own terms was not coercive, did not violate the Act unless part of a course of conduct that was coercive.[12] As the Board appeared to have found the employer's words had violated the Act in and of themselves, the Court remanded to the Board so that it could determine whether the totality of the employer's conduct, of which his communications were a part, coerced [the] employees in violation of the statute. The Board later held that it did. See Virginia Electric & Power Co. v. NLRB, 319 U.S. 533 (1943).

This decision and the Board's rather halting response to it . . . constituted the background for §8(c) of the Taft-Hartley Act. . . .

In the light of this history and the Supreme Court's more recent warning of the dangers of ever finding an unfair labor practice in employer argument alone, see NLRB v. Exchange Parts Co., 375 U.S. 405 (1964), we find the approach here taken unacceptable. In holding the passages we have cited to be violations, the Trial Examiner stated simply that "the letters and

---

12. The Court, in a dictum in Thomas v. Collins, 323 U.S. 516, 537 (1945), interpreted *Virginia Electric* as deciding that an employer's attempts to persuade employees to join or not to join a union are "within the First Amendment's guaranty" and can be restricted only when "other things are added which bring about coercion, or give it that character."

speech . . . were calculated to create and instill in the minds of employees a fear of loss of privileges and economic suffering as a result of their adherence to the Union, and constituted interferences, restraint, and coercion within the meaning of §8(a)(1) of the Act." This is reading the Act as if §8(c) did not exist; while there is a risk that an employer's prediction of adverse consequences from unionization may be taken as a threat to produce them, to hold that this danger alone suffices to convert a prediction into a threat of reprisal would go back to the very position of the early 1940s which §8(c) was adopted to change. . . . Only if respondent's words contained a "threat of reprisal" did they go beyond the bounds of §8(c). But, as the dictionaries tell us, a "threat of reprisal" means a "threat of retaliation" and this in turn means not a prediction that adverse consequences will develop but a threat that they will be deliberately inflicted in return for an injury— "to return evil for evil." Whatever vitality decisions . . . giving weight to an agency's construction of statutory language may have generally, . . . such considerations have little weight when the statute being enforced approaches the limits of constitutional power. In such a case we encounter the overriding principle of construction requiring that statutes be read so as to avoid serious constitutional doubt. . . .

The error of the Board in finding violations of the Act in the two passages from the letter of February 2 and the second set of remarks in the speech of February 16 predicting loss of work, harder work, or even a close-down as a result of unionization is apparent. Nothing in these communications could reasonably be interpreted as a threat to make the employees' lot harder in retaliation for their voting for the union. . . . The only fair reading is that the employer would take these steps solely from economic necessity and with regret. . . .

Although the case as to the prediction of the effect of unionization on the grant of special privileges is a shade closer, we reach the same conclusion. Golub's speech made it clear enough that he would not aim to withdraw special privileges if a union contract were signed, and certainly not to withdraw them in retaliation for the union contract, but that he feared that the rules of the contract or the union's administration of it might forbid giving such benefits to one employee unless they were uniformly given to all. The same is true of the letter of February 8 when this is read as a whole. While these fears may have been unwarranted, they were not shown to have so far transcended the bounds of reason as to justify the Board in finding them to be disguised threats of reprisal. . . .

HAYS, J., dissenting.

The majority opinion demonstrates once more the inescapable truth that United States Circuit Judges safely ensconced in their chambers do not feel threatened by what employers tell their employees. An employer can dress up his threats in the language of prediction ("You will lose your job" rather than "I will fire you") and fool judges. He doesn't fool his employees; they know perfectly clearly what he means. . . .

The error into which the majority falls is to believe that one can identify threatening language regardless of the circumstances in which the language is used and regardless of the ears to which it is directed. A dictionary definition will suffice because it makes no difference whether the words are addressed to a judge or to a machine hand, they must mean the same thing. . . .

The extent to which the majority will go in defending the employer's rights is indicated by their treatment of the employer's threats to discontinue making "special personal arrangement[s]" and granting privileges "such as time off when your children [are] sick, weddings, for haircuts, a school prom, emergencies at home, and to catch up on studies." These "fears" (of the employer) may have been "unwarranted" says the majority, but "they were not shown" to be unreasonable. If it is not obvious on its face that no employee would believe that the *union* would interfere with his taking time off for a haircut, and that the employees undoubtedly (and correctly) understood that it was the *employer* who was going to withdraw these privileges, then certainly such a matter ought to be left to the Board's expertise, without requiring a "showing" that the Board was right. . . .

## *NOTES AND QUESTIONS*

1. **Predictions vs. Threats?** Do you agree with Judge Friendly's majority opinion or with Judge Hays's dissent concerning an employee's likely understanding of the employer's predictions in this case? Is Judge Hays right that the line drawn by the *Golub* majority enables employers to communicate implied threats to employees simply by stating that circumstances occasioned by the union's certification will dictate particular untoward consequences? What precisely is the line drawn by the majority?

2. **Relevance of Union's Opportunity to Reply?** Is it relevant to the coercive-speech inquiry that the union had at least five days to respond to the employer's letters, while it had considerably less opportunity to respond to Golub's February 16 speech? Although the union presumably could have countered the employer's prediction of the loss of informal privileges by articulating the position it would take on such practices, what could it have said to address the employer's profit concerns and account of store closings elsewhere?

3. **Employer Neutrality?** As noted in *Golub,* before the Supreme Court's 1941 decision in *Virginia Elec. & Power,* the NLRB was sufficiently concerned about the effect of employer participation in representation

elections on employee free choice to veer close to a rule mandating employer neutrality. Presumably, the Taft-Hartley addition of §8(c) forecloses such a rule. Might a policy of employer neutrality nonetheless be undesirable, even apart from First Amendment and §8(c) concerns? If employers were not allowed to describe possible undesirable consequences that could result from union certification (including the employer's withdrawal of capital), would employees be likely to be fully informed about the disadvantages, as well as the advantages, of choosing a union representative?

**4. First Amendment Concerns?** To what extent does §8(c)'s protection of employer speech reflect what the First Amendment would require in any event? Are representation elections materially different from general political elections? Could Congress, if it wished, ban employer speech about union affiliation on the grounds that such speech inevitably has a coercive impact on employees? Note that employers are sovereigns in the workplace who cannot be voted out of office in union certification elections. Moreover, unlike politicians who must secure legislative majorities before they can implement regulatory change, employers often have the ability to unilaterally implement their adverse predictions. Review these questions after reading *NLRB v. Gissel Packing Co.*, infra page 283.

**5. Was Loss of Special Privileges Likely?** Should the *Golub* court have treated the company's predictions of loss of special privileges differently from the other predictions it found protected by §8(c)?

**6. How Should the Board Determine the Likely Impact of Employer Speech?** Ordinarily, the Board does not concern itself with the actual impact of speech or other conduct on the specific employees involved. See 33 NLRB Ann. Rep. 60 (1968). Instead, it determines, based on its understanding of "industrial reality," whether the conduct was reasonably likely to have interfered with, restrained, or coerced them in the exercise of their §7 rights. Why is the Board apparently reluctant to attempt to determine the subjective impact of the employer's conduct? What type of evidence would the Board need to make this determination? Would it, for instance, need to rely on employee testimony regarding the impact of the employer's statements? Are there disadvantages to seeking or relying on this type of evidence?

**7. Evidentiary Use of §8(c) Speech?** Note that §8(c) bars any evidentiary use of protected speech in unfair labor practice proceedings. Consider the following hypothetical: After an organizing campaign began, the employer fired a union-proponent Eager, ostensibly for violating a plant rule that had not been enforced for some time. The next day the employer posted the following notice on the employee bulletin board: "I've treated you fairly and will continue to do so. But a union in this plant would not be good for you or for the company. Its demands could lead to the loss of jobs. Don't sign up with dues-hungry union bosses." Could the Board's General Counsel use the notice as evidence that Eager's discharge was motivated by anti-union animus and thus violated §8(a)(3)? Could the General Counsel use other evidence that Eager was discharged to discourage unionization to prove that the employer's notice was coercive and thus not protected by §8(c)?

**NLRB v. Gissel Packing Co.**
*395 U.S. 575 (1969)*

[Each of the four cases before the Court raised the question of the validity of a bargaining order entered (under §8(a)(5)) against an employer who had both rejected a recognition demand by a union with an authorization card-based majority and engaged in an anti-union campaign involving unfair labor practices. The portion of the Court's opinion considering the bargaining order appears infra page 316. Here the Court deals with the reach of §8(c) and the First Amendment—a question raised by the Sinclair Company, a petitioner challenging the finding that its communications to employees violated §8(a)(1).]

WARREN, C.J. . . .

In July 1965, the International Brotherhood of Teamsters, Local Union No. 404, began an organizing campaign among petitioner's Holyoke employees. . . .

When petitioner's president first learned of the Union's drive in July, he talked with all of his employees in an effort to dissuade them from joining a union. He particularly emphasized the results of the long 1952 strike, which he claimed "almost put our company out of business," and expressed worry that the employees were forgetting the "lessons of the past." He emphasized, secondly, that the Company was still on "thin ice" financially, that the Union's "only weapon is to strike," and that a strike "could lead to the closing of the plant," since the parent company had ample manufacturing facilities elsewhere. He noted, thirdly, that because of their age and the limited usefulness of their skills outside their craft, the employees might not be able to find reemployment if they lost their jobs as a result of a strike. Finally, he warned those who did not believe that the plant could go out of business to "look around Holyoke and see a lot of them out of business." The president sent letters to the same effect to the employees in early November, emphasizing that the parent company had no reason to stay in Massachusetts if profits went down.

During the two or three weeks immediately prior to the election on December 9, the president sent the employees a pamphlet captioned: "Do you want another 13-week strike?" stating, inter alia, that: "We have no doubt that the Teamsters Union can again close the Wire Weaving Department and the entire plant by a strike. We have no hopes that the Teamsters Union Bosses will not call a strike. . . . The Teamsters Union is a strike-happy outfit." Similar communications followed in late November, including one stressing the Teamsters' "hoodlum control." Two days before the election, the Company sent out another pamphlet that was entitled: "Let's Look at the Record," and that purported to be an obituary of companies in the Holyoke-Springfield, Massachusetts, area that had allegedly gone out of business because of union demands, eliminating some 3,500 jobs; the first page carried a large cartoon showing the preparation of a grave for the Sinclair Company and other headstones containing the names of other plants allegedly victimized by the unions. Finally, on the day before the election, the president made another personal appeal to his employees to reject the Union. He repeated that the Company's financial condition was precarious; that a possible strike would jeopardize the continued operation of the plant; and that age and lack of education would make reemployment difficult. The Union lost the election 7 to 6, and then filed both objections to the election and unfair labor practice charges which were consolidated for hearing before the trial examiner.

The Board agreed with the trial examiner that the president's communications with his employees, when considered as a whole, "reasonably tended to convey to the employees the belief or impression that selection of the Union in the forthcoming election could lead [the Company] to close its plant, or to the transfer of the weaving production, with the resultant loss of jobs to the wire weavers." Thus, the Board found that under the "totality of the circumstances" petitioner's activities constituted a violation of §8(a)(1) of the Act. The Board further agreed with the trial examiner that petitioner's activities, because they "also interfered with the exercise of a free and untrammeled choice in the election," and "tended to foreclose the possibility" of holding a fair election, required that the election be set aside. . . . [T]he First Circuit sustained the Board's findings and conclusions and enforced its order in full. . . .

. . . [A]n employer's free speech right to communicate his views to his employees is firmly established and cannot be infringed by a union or the Board. Thus, §8(c) merely implements the First Amendment.

Any assessment of the precise scope of employer expression, of course, must be made in the context of its labor relations setting. Thus, an employer's rights cannot outweigh the equal rights of the employees to associate freely, as those rights are embodied in §7 and protected by §8(a)(1) and the proviso to §8(c). And any balancing of those rights must take into account the economic dependence of the employees on their employers, and the necessary tendency of the former, because of that relationship, to pick up intended implications of the latter that might be more readily dismissed by a more disinterested ear. Stating these obvious principles is but another way of recognizing that what is basically at stake is the establishment of a nonpermanent, limited relationship between the employer, his economically dependent employee and his union agent, not the election of legislators or the enactment of legislation whereby that relationship is ultimately defined and where the independent voter may be freer to listen more objectively and employers as a class freer to talk. Cf. New York Times Co. v. Sullivan, 376 U.S. 254 (1964).

Within this framework, we must reject the Company's challenge to the decision below and the findings of the Board on which it was based. The standards used below for evaluating the impact of an employer's statements are not seriously questioned by petitioner and we see no need to tamper with them here. Thus, an employer is free to communicate to his employees any of his general views about unionism or any of his specific views about a particular union, so long as the communications do not contain a "threat of reprisal or force or promise of benefit." He may even make a prediction as to the precise effects he believes unionization will have on his company. In such a case, however, the prediction must be carefully phrased on the basis of objective fact to convey an employer's belief as to demonstrably probable consequences beyond his control or to convey a management decision already arrived at to close the plant in case of unionization. See Textile Workers v. Darlington Mfg. Co., 380 U.S. 263, 274, n.20 (1965). If there is any implication that an employer may or may not take action solely on his own initiative for reasons unrelated to economic necessities and known only to him, the statement is no longer a reasonable prediction based on available facts but a threat of retaliation based on misrepresentation and coercion, and as such without the protection of the First Amendment. We therefore agree with the court below that "[c]onveyance of the employer's belief, even though sincere, that unionization will or may result in the closing of the plant is not a statement of fact unless, which is most improbable, the eventuality of closing is capable of proof." As stated elsewhere, an employer is free only to tell "what he reasonably believes will be the likely economic consequences of unionization that are outside his control," and not "threats of economic reprisal to be taken solely on his own volition." NLRB v. River Togs, Inc., 382 F.2d 198, 202 (2d Cir. 1967).

Equally valid was the finding by the court and the Board that petitioner's statements and communications were not cast as a prediction of demonstrable "economic consequences," but rather as a threat of retaliatory action. The Board found that petitioner's speeches, pamphlets, leaflets, and letters conveyed the following message: that the company was in a precarious financial condition; that the "strike-happy" union would in all likelihood have to obtain its potentially unreasonable demands by striking, the probable result of which would be a plant shutdown, as the past history of labor relations in the area indicated; and that the employees in such a case would have great difficulty finding employment elsewhere. In carrying out its duty to focus on the question: "[W]hat did the speaker intend and the listener understand?" (A. Cox, Law and the National Labor Policy 44 (1960)), the Board could reasonably conclude that the intended and understood import of that message was not to predict that unionization would inevitably cause the plant to close but to threaten to throw employees out of work regardless of the economic realities. In this connection, we need go no further than to point out (1) that petitioner had no support for its basic assumption that the union, which had not yet even presented any demands, would have to strike to be heard, and that it admitted at the hearing that it had no basis for attributing other plant closings in the area to unionism; and (2) that the Board has often found that employees, who are particularly sensitive to rumors of plant closings, take such hints as coercive threats rather than honest forecasts.

Petitioner argues that the line between so-called permitted predictions and proscribed threats is too vague to stand up under traditional First Amendment analysis and that the Board's discretion to curtail free speech rights is correspondingly too uncontrolled. It is true that a reviewing court must recognize the Board's competence in the first instance to judge the impact of utterances made in the context of the employer-employee relationship, see NLRB v. Virginia Electric & Power Co., 314 U.S. 469, 479 (1941). But an employer, who has control over that relationship and therefore knows it best, cannot be heard to complain that he is without an adequate guide for his behavior. He can easily make his views known without engaging in "'brinkmanship'" when it becomes all too easy to "overstep and tumble [over] the brink," Wausau Steel Corp. v. NLRB, 377 F.2d 369, 372 (7th Cir. 1967). At the least he can avoid coercive speech simply by avoiding conscious overstatements he has reason to believe will mislead his employees. . . .

## *NOTES AND QUESTIONS*

**1. Employee Perceptions of Employer Speech.** Is the *Gissel* Court's notion of how employees tend to perceive employer "predictions" closer to Judge Friendly's or Judge Hays's views in *Golub*? Is *Golub* still good law after *Gissel*?

**2. The *Gissel* Test.** Note the elements of the Court's standard for when an employer may make predictions concerning the effects of unionization on the company (apart from conveying a settled management decision to close the plant as permitted under footnote 20 of *Darlington*, supra page 161): (1) careful phrasing on the basis of objective fact (2) to convey an employer's belief (3) as to demonstrably probable consequences (4) that are beyond the employer's control. Does this test apply when an employer recounts the consequences of unionization at *other companies* (as in *Golub*), without making any specific predictions about the likely effects of unionization at its own company? If not, what is the dividing line between an impermissible threat and a lawful prediction in the latter category of cases? Review the *Gissel* opinion on this point as well as notes 3-4 below.

**3. Analysis of the *Gissel* Elements.** What is the purpose of each of the four *Gissel* elements? Do they strike an appropriate balance, allowing employers to provide potentially useful information to employees without intimidation? Do elements (1) and (3) require the employer's predictions to be sound or just phrased objectively? If the employer must have a good basis for a dire prediction, such as a loss of business if the union wins, should the Board require the employer to offer proof of this basis? See NLRB v. Pentre Electric, 998 F.2d 363 (6th Cir. 1993) (citing Board cases going both ways, and holding that such a requirement is improper), questioned as to standard of review applied, NLRB v. Webcor Packaging, Inc., 118 F.3d 1115, 1119 n.2 (6th Cir. 1997).

Does element (2) require a determination of an employer's intent in some cases? Does the quotation from Professor Cox suggest such a requirement? Should the employer's intent—or motive—be relevant in a §8(a)(1) case? Recall the discussion of §8(a)(1) cases in Chapter 3.

What does element (4) require? Recall the *Lassing* decision at page 157 above. Should an employer be able to announce that it has decided to shut down a marginally profitable department if a strong union is elected and then presents substantial cost-increasing demands? Are profitability considerations beyond the employer's control under *Gissel*? See Crown Cork & Seal Co. v. NLRB, 36 F.3d 1130 (D.C. Cir. 1994) (holding that employer did not commit unfair labor practice by predicting that the union would insist on terms similar to those found in its 12-plant master agreement with the employer and that such terms would imperil two extremely cost-sensitive projects that were necessary to maintain current employment levels).

**4. Applying *Gissel*.**

a. *The "Wall of Shame."* During a United Auto Workers (UAW) organizing campaign, the employer displayed a banner reading "PLANT CLOSURES: UAW WALL OF SHAME." The banner contained paper tombstones, each of which had "RIP" and the name of a UAW-represented plant that had closed written on it. Every day, the employer added to the banner another tombstone containing the name of another closed plant.

On the day before the election, the employer, Eldorado Tool, posted a tombstone reading, "ELDORADO?" Unlawful threat, or a permissible exercise of §8(c) speech rights? See Eldorado Tool, 325 N.L.R.B. 222 (1997) (2-1). Would this case come out differently without the explicit reference to Eldorado?

b. *The Mock Pink Slip.* During a United Food and Commercial Workers Union (UFCW) effort to organize a chain of 30 grocery stores, the employer distributed a "mock pink slip" to employees containing the following language: "Dear Unionized Employees: I regret to inform you that because we have lost our ability to compete in this extremely competitive market, we shall be forced to close this store and put you out of work." The pink slip contained the logos of three area grocery stores that had been closed after being organized by the UFCW (Colonial Stores, Big Star, and Safeway), and was signed "Sincerely, Colonial Stores/Big Star/Safeway." The pink slip was accompanied by a cover letter stating, "[Y]ou may want to take another look at what the UNITED FOOD AND COMMERCIAL WORKERS UNION got for their former dues payers in the area—A PINK SLIP." The letter (but not the pink slip) also stated, "We will do everything we can to prevent this from happening to you . . . , but you should consider what the union has DELIVERED in the past before you believe what they PROMISE in the future." See Be-Lo Stores, 318 N.L.R.B. 1 (1995), enforcement denied in relevant part, 126 F.3d 268 (4th Cir. 1997).

**5. Messages of Bargaining Futility and "Bargaining from Scratch."** An employer's assertion that it would not fulfill its statutory obligations to bargain in good faith with an elected representative is unlawful. Thus, an employer cannot, for instance, state that it would continue to impose uniform benefits on all its plants even if the union is voted in. See American Telecommunications Corp., Electromechanical Division, 249 N.L.R.B. 1135 (1980).

However, as will be discussed in Chapter 6, the NLRA does not require employers to make concessions in bargaining. Under what circumstances should an employer's statement that bargaining with a union would begin "from scratch," "from ground zero," or "with a blank sheet of paper" be held to violate the Act or warrant a new election? In evaluating such statements, the Board purports to distinguish between situations in which a reasonable employee would construe the statement, in context, as a threat to discontinue existing benefits without economic justification should the union prevail, from those in which the employer is merely lawfully informing employees that unionization alone is no guarantee of increased benefits. See Host Int'l, Inc., 195 N.L.R.B. 348 (1972); see also Shaw's Supermarkets, Inc. v. NLRB, 884 F.2d 34, 37, 40 (1st Cir. 1989) (Breyer, J.) (noting that the

Board is much more likely to find a violation where employer has committed other serious ULPs).

**6. A Drafting Exercise.** Should the following speech by a company official constitute an unfair labor practice and/or grounds for setting aside a union election loss?

> There is no magic in unions. If a company is competitive, if it manufactures a good product, there is going to be job security. If it does not, there will be no jobs. The union can only hurt your job prospects. We will bargain with the union if it wins the election, but the law gives us the right to bargain hard and we will do so, insisting on the reduction of benefits that we now grant in exchange for any new benefit the union seeks. We doubt that the union can achieve any increase in benefits without attempting a lengthy strike. After all, we provide better benefits now than most union plants in our industry. If there is a lengthy strike, we have the right to hire permanent replacements and you will not be able to collect unemployment compensation. Furthermore, a lengthy strike could cost the company business and force a retrenchment in our operations. If we allowed the union to increase your benefits, we would have to raise our prices and this would also cost us business and require cutbacks. We won't mess around. If we determine that we can't operate without incurring higher labor costs, we will completely shut the plant down. There is no way that the union can help you. There are lots of ways it can hurt you.

If you find problems with parts of this speech, how would you redraft it to avoid those problems with minimal sacrifice to the company's message?

### *b. Factual Misrepresentations*

Utilizing its §9 authority, the Board ruled in 1962 that misrepresentations "which involve a serious departure from the truth, at a time which prevents the other party or parties from making an effective reply," justify the holding of a new election. Hollywood Ceramics Co., Inc., 140 N.L.R.B. 221, 224 (1962). In 1977, after 15 years of experience under this rule, the Board announced that it would no longer probe into the truth or falsity of campaign propaganda, except where deceptive practices "improperly involve the Board and its processes, or the use of forged documents which render the voters unable to recognize the propaganda for what it is." Shopping Kart Food Market, Inc., 228 N.L.R.B. 1311, 1313 (1977). Twenty months later, the Board reversed itself and reinstated the *Hollywood Ceramics* standard, finding that the *Shopping Kart* approach involved a derogation of its responsibility to ensure fair elections. General Knit of California, 239 N.L.R.B. 619 (1978). In the decision that follows, the Board changed its mind again, reverting to the deregulatory approach of *Shopping Kart.*

**Midland National Life Insurance Co.**
*263 N.L.R.B. 127 (1982)*

[On the union's application, the Board, finding unfair labor practices and objectionable campaigning by the employer, set aside an election held on April 28, 1978, that had been won by the employer, 127 to 75. Following court enforcement of the Board's order against the employer, a second election was held on October 16, 1980. There were 107 votes for and 107 votes against the union. The union also filed objections to this election. The Board, rejecting the Hearing Officer's recommendations, overruled the union's objections and certified the results of the second election.]

... On the afternoon of October 15, 1980, the day before the election, the Employer distributed campaign literature to its employees with their paychecks. One of the distributions was a six-page document which included photographs and text depicting three local employers and their involvements with the Petitioner. The document also contained a reproduction of a portion of the Petitioner's 1979 financial report (hereinafter LMRDA report) submitted to the Department of Labor pursuant to the provisions of the Labor Management Reporting and Disclosure Act of 1959. The Petitioner learned of the document the next morning, 3½ hours before the polls were to open.

The first subject of the document, Meilman Food, Inc., was portrayed in "recent" pictures as a deserted facility, and was described in accompanying text as follows: "They too employed between 200 and 300 employees. This Local 304A struck this plant—violence ensued. *Now all of the workers are gone!* What did the Local 304A do for them? Where is the 304A union job security?" (Emphasis in original.) Jack Smith, the Petitioner's business representative, testified that Local 304A, the Petitioner, had been the representative of Meilman's employees, but that neither the Petitioner nor Meilman's employees had been on strike when the plant closed. He added that the employees had been working for at least 1½ years following the strike and prior to the closure of the facility.

... [The] document [also referred to] Luther Manor Nursing Home and Blue Cross/Blue Shield. The text accompanying the pictures of Luther Manor explained that:

> [a]lmost a year ago this same union that tells you they will "make job security" (we believe you are the only ones who can do that) and will get you more pay, told the employees of LUTHER MANOR (again, here in Sioux Falls) . . . the union would get them a contract with job security and more money. Unfortunately Local 304A did not tell the Luther Manor employees what year or century they were talking about. Today the employees have no contract. Most of the union leaders left to work elsewhere. Their job security is the same (depends upon the individual as it always has). There has been no change or increase in

> wages or hours. The union has sent in three different sets of negotiators. Again, promises and performance are two different things. All wages, fringes, working conditions are remaining the same while negotiations continue.

The text accompanying the pictures of Blue Cross stated that "this same Local union won an election at Blue Cross/Blue Shield after promising less restrictive policies, better pay and more job security. Since the election a good percentage of its former employees are no longer working there. Ask them! The employees have been offered a wage increase — *next year* of 5%. . . ." (Emphasis in original.)

Smith testified that the Petitioner took over negotiations at Luther Manor and at Blue Cross on or about July 1, 1980, after the Petitioner had merged with Retail Clerks, Local 1665, and that Retail Clerks, Local 1665, not the Petitioner, had conducted the prior negotiations and won the election at Blue Cross.

. . . [T]he Hearing Officer concluded that, in its description of Meilman Food, the Employer intended to instill in the minds of its employees the false impression that the Petitioner had conducted a strike at Meilman, that violence had ensued, and that, as a direct result of the strike, all of the employees at Meilman were terminated. . . . [T]he Hearing Officer [also] found that the Employer had misrepresented the labor organization involved [at Luther Manor and Blue Cross]. . . .

The Employer's distribution also [reproduced] a portion of the Petitioner's 1979 LMRDA report. . . . Three entries on the reproduced page were underlined: total receipts, reported at $508,946; disbursements "On Behalf of Individual Members," reported at zero; and total disbursements, reported at $492,701. Other entries on the reproduced page showed disbursements of $93,185 to officers, and $22,662 to employees. The accompanying text stated that $141,000 of the Petitioner's funds went to "union officers and officials and those who worked for them," and that "NOTHING— according to the report they filed with the U.S. Government—was spent 'on behalf of the individual members' [sic]."

The Hearing Officer found that the report actually showed that the Petitioner disbursed only $115,847 to its officers and employees, a difference of $25,000, and that the Employer's statement attributed 19 percent more in income to the officials and employees than was actually received. He further found that, while the report showed that no sums had been spent "on behalf of the individual members," the instructions for the LMRDA report require that entry to reflect disbursements for "other than normal operating purposes," and that the Employer failed to include this fact in its distribution.

. . . [T]he Hearing Officer concluded that the document distributed by the Employer contained numerous misrepresentations of fact of a substantial nature designed to portray the Petitioner as . . . staffed by highly paid officials and employees who were ineffectual as bargaining representatives, and that as a consequence employees would suffer with respect to job security and compensation. . . . The Hearing Officer also determined [that] the Petitioner did not have sufficient time to respond effectively. Applying the standard found in *General Knit of California, Inc.*, and *Hollywood Ceramics Co., Inc.*, the Hearing Officer . . . recommended that the objection be sustained and that a third election be directed.

We have decided to reject the Hearing Officer's recommendations and to certify the results of the election. We do so because, after painstaking evaluation . . . we have resolved to return to the sound rule announced in *Shopping Kart Food Market, Inc.*, and to overrule *General Knit* and *Hollywood Ceramics*. . . .

In sharp contrast to the *Hollywood Ceramics* standard, *Shopping Kart* "draws a clear line between what is and what is not objectionable." Thus, "elections will be set aside" not on the basis of the substance of the representation, but the deceptive *manner* in which it was made. . . . As long as the campaign material is what it purports to be, i.e., mere propaganda of a particular party, the Board would leave the task of evaluating its contents solely to the employees. Where, due to forgery, no voter could recognize the propaganda "for what it is," Board intervention is warranted. Further, unlike *Hollywood Ceramics*, the rule in *Shopping Kart* lends itself to definite results which are both predictable and speedy. The incentive for protracted litigation is greatly reduced, as is the possibility of disagreement between the Board and the courts. Because objections alleging false or inaccurate statements can be summarily rejected at the first stage of Board proceedings, the opportunity for delay is almost nonexistent. Finally, the rule in *Shopping Kart* "furthers the goal of consistent and equitable adjudications" by applying uniformly to the objections of both unions and employers. . . . [W]e also consider [the *Hollywood Ceramics* rule] to [reflect] an unrealistic view of the ability of voters to assess misleading campaign propaganda. . . . The "protectionism" propounded by the . . . rule is simply not warranted. On the contrary, as we found in *Shopping Kart*, "we believe that Board rules in this area must be based on a view of employees as mature individuals who are capable of recognizing campaign propaganda for what it is and discounting it." . . .

In sum, we rule today that we will no longer probe into the truth or falsity of the parties' campaign statements, and that we will not set elections aside on the basis of misleading campaign statements. We will, however, intervene in cases where a party has used forged documents which render the voters unable to recognize propaganda for what it is. . . . Accordingly, inasmuch as the Petitioner's objection alleges nothing more than misrepresentations, it is hereby overruled.[26]

---

26. With respect to the LMRDA report, our dissenting colleagues' attempted analogy to the rule set forth in Formco, Inc., 233 N.L.R.B. 61 (1977), misses the mark. . . . *Formco* clearly is inapposite, since here there is no Board document involved. In any event, there is no

Members Fanning and Jenkins, dissenting. . . .

. . . Albeit today's American employees may be better educated, in the formal sense, than those of previous generations, and may be in certain respects more sophisticated, we do not honor them by abandoning them utterly to the mercies of unscrupulous campaigners, including the expert cadre of professional opinion molders who devise campaigns for many of our representation elections. In political campaigns, which are conducted over a much longer period of time and are subject to extensive media scrutiny, the voters have ready access to independent sources of information concerning the issues. In representation campaigns, they do not. . . .

## *NOTES AND QUESTIONS*

**1. "Policy Oscillation" at the Labor Board.** The Board's flip-flopping on last-minute misrepresentations drew considerable criticism from the courts of appeals in the early eighties. See Estreicher, Policy Oscillation at the Labor Board, supra, at 171 & n.30; see, e.g., Mosey Mfg. Co. v. NLRB, 701 F.2d 610 (7th Cir. 1983). Is such "policy oscillation" among the consequences of the Board's failure to make policy through rulemaking rather than adjudication?

One of us has urged as a policy matter that rulemaking should be the predominant vehicle for reversing a prior Board policy. See Estreicher, Improving the Administration of the NLRA, supra, at 12-14. Because rulemaking operates prospectively only, the parties at least know the applicable rules of the game when they decide to use particular campaign tactics. In *Midland*, in contrast, the *Shopping Kart* deregulatory approach applied at the time the misrepresentations were made, but the more regulatory regime of *Hollywood Ceramics* was in force when the Hearing Officer ruled (and found the conduct objectionable). By the time the case reached the Board, however, the law had changed back (per *Midland*) to what it had been at the time of the primary conduct being regulated. See also *Mosey Mfg.*, supra (policy changed three times during course of litigation).

**2. Factual Misrepresentation or Implied Threat?** Could the Board have found that the six-page document at issue in *Midland* contained illegal implied threats, or did the employer merely exercise its §8(c) right to inform employees of the possible downside of unionization?

---

basis for describing—as the dissenters do—the Employer's presentation of the Form LM-2 excerpt as "an elaborately conceived fraud." The portion of the form distributed by the Employer appeared exactly as submitted by the Petitioner. We categorically reject the dissenters' suggestion that any misrepresentation of any document constitutes a fraud. . . .

**3. Preserving the "Integrity" of NLRB Elections?** Even if we assume that employee voters are usually able to discount last-minute campaign misrepresentations, is there nevertheless a case for regulation in order to promote the integrity of the Board's electoral process and hence the acceptability of NLRB election results? Is regulation on the basis of this "integrity" rationale consistent with the way we treat general political elections? See also Edward B. Miller, The Getman, Goldberg and Herman Questions, 28 Stan. L. Rev. 1163, 1172-1174 (1976) (former Board chair questions whether Board should "reduce its standards" to those followed in political elections).

**4. Whom Does Regulation Help?** Does regulation of misrepresentations help unions or management more? Recall that while employers can eventually obtain judicial review of a Board decision certifying a union victory, a union cannot obtain review of a decision setting aside a union victory. Consider also the following:

> [R]egulation of campaign tactics leads in many instances to the overturning of elections, and it must be understood that overturning a union victory is a more serious matter than is overturning an employer victory. In the latter case, the company continues to operate free of the union — the same result as the election would have provided — until a new election is held and the union is victorious. In the former, however, employees who voted for the union are denied representation. Thus, a rule which was purportedly created to insure even-handedness has in reality worked against unions.

Julius G. Getman, Ruminations on Union Organizing in the Private Sector, 53 U. Chi. L. Rev. 45, 70 (1986). Do you agree?

**5. The *Midland* Doctrine in the Courts.** With the notable exception of the Sixth Circuit, the *Midland* doctrine has won widespread acceptance in the courts. The Sixth Circuit will overturn elections even in the absence of forgery where the misrepresentation is "so pervasive and the deception so artful that employees will be unable to separate truth from untruth," and their right to free choice is thereby affected. See Van Dorn Plastic Machinery Co. v. NLRB, 736 F.2d 343 (6th Cir. 1984); see also NLRB v. Gormac Custom Manufacturing, Inc., 190 F.3d 742 (6th Cir. 1999); NLRB v. St. Francis Healthcare Centre, 212 F.3d 945 (6th Cir. 2000) (both applying five-factor test that implements *Van Dorn*). Given that regulation for misrepresentation is premised on the Board's *General Shoe* doctrine, what is the source of the court's authority for, in essence, forcing an application of *General Shoe*? Cf. also Savair Mfg. Co., infra page 306.

**6. The *Formco* Doctrine.** Under its *Formco* doctrine, which survives *Midland*, the Board holds that "any substantial mischaracterization or misuse of a Board document for partisan election purposes is a serious misrepresentation warranting setting an election aside." Formco, Inc., 233 N.L.R.B. 61 (1977). *Formco* is particularly concerned with any alterations or mischaracterizations that have the potential of placing the Board's neutrality in question. Id. at 62. The *Midland* dissenters analogized the company's use of the LMRDA financial report to misrepresentations of Board documents that would warrant a new election under *Formco*. See *Midland*, 263 N.L.R.B. at 135. Do you agree?

a. Consider whether in the course of the following union effort to organize dealers at Trump Plaza the union's appeal violated the *Formco* doctrine:

> [S]ix days before the election, the Union held a rally and 'mock card-check ceremony,' at which three public officials . . . signed a document entitled 'Certification of Majority Status.' According to the document, the officials had 'conducted a confidential examination of Union authorization cards . . . in accordance with NLRB rules' and had determined that a majority of Trump Plaza's dealers 'authorized the [Union] to represent them for the purposes of collective bargaining.' . . . After the rally [which received coverage in the local news], the Union displayed a copy of the 'Certification of Majority Status' poster in its office and printed leaflet-sized photocopies, which were 'made available to dealers who came into the union hall so they could read [them] and take [them].'

Trump Plaza Associates v. NLRB, 679 F.3d 822, 825 (D.C. Cir. 2012).The Board reviewing this case concluded that the card-check certification was not unlawful because few voters were aware of it and the union won the election by a wide margin. The Court of Appeals refused to enforce the Board's order and remanded the case for the Board to consider more fully whether the card-check certification breached Board neutrality and misled voters by conveying that the election was already decided. Id. at 831-832.

b. In Albertson's, Inc., 344 N.L.R.B. No. 158 (2005), the Board overturned a union election victory because the union had distributed to key employees an anonymous fax message purporting to be from the employer's corporate headquarters and listing non-union stores targeted for shutdown. The Board emphasized that the company had provided proof that the fax was a forgery but the union took no steps to inform employees of the forgery: "The nature and contents of the letter, the Union's role in its distribution, and the Union's decision to remain silent rather than inform employees of the forgery all prevented employees from reasonably recognizing the letter as a forgery, despite the Employer's efforts." Would the case come out differently if the union had not been responsible for disseminating the fax? Were the employees likely to have given special weight to the union's silence in view of the employer's repeated disavowal of the fax? Is this decision consistent with *Midland*?

### *Note: Are Employees Influenced by Campaign Conduct?: A Review of the Empirical Literature*

The best-known empirical study of the effect of the Board's campaign regulations on employee voting behavior is Julius G. Getman, Stephen B. Goldberg & Jeanne B. Herman, Union Representation Elections: Law and Reality (1976) ("Getman study"). The authors conducted pre- and post-campaign interviews with over 1,000 employees voting in 31 NLRB elections held in Midwestern states in 1972 and 1973. They concluded that election campaigns have a limited effect on voting behavior because most employees approach the issue of union representation with strong prior dispositions. The Getman study also found that workers "did not vote against union representation in significantly greater numbers in [elections resulting in NLRB bargaining orders because they were marred by serious unfair labor practices] than in clean elections or elections characterized by lesser unlawful campaigning. Nor did a greater proportion of employees report unlawful campaigning when the Board found it had occurred than when the Board did not find it had occurred." Id. at 129.

Some critics questioned whether the sample was representative of hotly contested elections and the design of the study. See James E. Martin, Employee Characteristics and Representation Election Outcomes, 38 Indus. & Lab. Rel. Rev. 365, 375 (1985); Thomas A. Kochan, Legal Nonsense, Empirical Examination and Policy Evaluation, 29 Stan. L. Rev. 1115 (1977); Patricia Eames, An Analysis of the Union Voting Study from a Trade-Unionist's Point of View, 28 Stan. L. Rev. 1181 (1976).

Others argued that the study drew conclusions that were not warranted by its own data; that while the study's data did not provide statistically significant proof that coercive campaigning affected the votes of individual employees; it did not neither was it sufficient to prove the opposite—that coercive campaigning did *not* affect votes. Conducting a computer simulation using the Getman study's data, one researcher found that "unions would have won 46 percent to 47 percent of the [31] elections if the employer had campaigned entirely cleanly (and 53 percent to 75 percent of the elections if there had been no campaign at all), but only 3 percent to 10 percent if every employer had campaigned with the highest intensity and greatest illegality identified in the sample." Weiler, Promises to Keep, supra, at 1786 (reporting on William Dickens, Union Representation Elections: Campaign and Vote (Oct. 1980) (unpublished Ph.D. dissertation, Department of Economics, Massachusetts Institute of Technology)).

The authors of the Getman study responded to their critics in Goldberg, Getman & Brett, Union Representation Elections: The Authors Respond to the Critics, 79 Mich. L. Rev. 564 (1981), and The Relationship Between Free

Choice and Labor Board Doctrine: Differing Empirical Approaches, 79 Nw. U. L. Rev. 721 (1984).

Two Board members relied on the Getman study in *Shopping Kart.* See 228 N.L.R.B. at 1313. In *General Knit,* however, the Board dismissed the study as "1 study of only 31 elections in 1 area of the country," and further noted that 19 percent of the voters in the study—a sizeable percentage—had decided which way to vote during the campaign. See 239 N.L.R.B. at 622. In *Midland,* the Getman study was not mentioned.

### c. *Racial and Religiously Based Speech*

**Honeyville Grain, Inc. v. NLRB**
*444 F.3d 1269 (10th Cir. 2006)*

Henry, Circuit Judge.

The Board conducted a secret-ballot election at Rancho Cucamonga on April 12, 2002. All thirty-two eligible voters cast ballots; twenty-three voted in favor of the Union, seven voted against the Union, and two ballots were challenged. . . . [Challenging the election,] Honeyville objected to comments made in a meeting held at the Union's office five days before the election; twenty to twenty-five of the drivers attended. Meeting attendees testified that two Union agents, Rene Torres and David Acosta, stated:

1. Honeyville is run by Mormons;
2. Honeyville is giving its money to the Mormon Church;
3. Companies have tax incentive to give profits to churches, which should be shared with the workers instead;
4. Honeyville's Mormon owners not only give their money to the Mormon Church, but they also give money to the Mormon missionaries; and
5. Mormons are missionaries, and missionaries speak good Spanish.

Mr. Torres is a driver with Honeyville Grain, and Mr. Acosta is a business agent and organizer for the Teamsters Local 396. Mr. Acosta claimed that he made no reference to missionaries or the Mormon Church at the meeting.

The most extensive testimony came from Enrique Erazo, a Honeyville driver who attended the meeting where the religious remarks were made. At a Board hearing, Mr. Erazo testified that Mr. Torres stated:

> [The drivers] have rights to benefits. So, the money the Company was making—was a rich Company and so, the money that the Company was making, they needed to share it with every worker and improve the benefits to workers. [sic]

> Since the Company was a Company run by Mormons, [the Union] said they would . . . see to it that they would make better contributions — they did to the church and they would also distribute or share that money with Missionaries going out of the country and because the money was tax deductible and that is why they would give part of that money to the Mormon Church, instead of giving it to — sharing it with the workers — the opportunity that they have in order to better their way of life. [sic]

Mr. Erazo further testified that the meeting attendees applauded after Mr. Torres discussed the distribution of the company's profits and referenced the religious beliefs of its owners. Neither party has put forward any evidence about the religious makeup of the unit employees. The religious remarks were made at one of about ten Union meetings held prior to the election.

. . . After the hearing, the Hearing Officer recommended that the Board overrule . . . the objection about the religious remarks, and certify the Union. . . .

The Board adopted the Recommendations and certified the Union. . . .

The . . . seminal case describing when an appeal to racial or religious prejudice warrants overturning an election is Sewell Manufacturing Co., 138 N.L.R.B. 66 (1982). The Board in *Sewell* set aside an election where a union had lost 985 to 331. . . . For four months, employers distributed anti-African-American propaganda materials focused on the union's support for the civil rights movement, including a photo (mailed two weeks before the election) of a white union official dancing with an African-American woman, together with a story about "race mixing." Id. at 66-68.

In *Sewell*, the Board described which types of racial references are allowed and which types warrant setting aside an election. It stated:

> So long . . . as a party limits itself to truthfully setting forth another party's position on matters of racial interest and does not deliberately seek to overstress and exacerbate racial feelings by irrelevant, inflammatory appeals, we shall not set aside an election on this ground. However, the burden will be on the party making use of a racial message to establish that it was truthful and germane, and where there is doubt as to whether the total conduct of such party is within the described bounds, the doubt will be resolved against him.

Id. at 71-72. Appeals to racial or religious prejudices constitute grounds for setting aside election results if "the challenged propaganda has lowered the standards of campaigning to the point where it may be said that *the uninhibited desires of the employees cannot be determined in an election.*" Id. at 70-71 (emphasis added). . . .

. . . *Sewell* and the appellate courts interpreting that decision require a party challenging a representative election first to demonstrate that the religious remarks were inflammatory or formed the core of the campaign. If this burden is satisfied, the burden then shifts to the party making the remarks to prove that such comments were "truthful and germane," as *Sewell* explains. 138 N.L.R.B. at 72. Remarks not found to be inflammatory or the core or theme of the campaign are reviewed under standards applied to other types of misrepresentations. . . .

[We now] examine whether the Board had substantial evidence to conclude that the religious remarks were not inflammatory or the theme of the Union's campaign. . . . In *Sewell*, the Board was concerned with a party's "deliberate" attempt to "overstress and exacerbate racial feelings by irrelevant, inflammatory appeals," 138 N.L.R.B. at 72, but it did not define what constituted "inflammatory appeals." The Board did make it clear, however, that it works to conduct elections free from "elements which prevent or impede a reasoned choice," id. at 70, and it will not "tolerate as 'electoral propaganda' appeals or arguments which can have no purpose except to inflame the racial feelings of voters in [an] election," id. at 71. Furthermore, the Seventh Circuit has explained that "[a] statement is racially inflammatory on its face if it is intended to produce or exploit strong racial prejudice, and is in fact likely to produce or exploit such racial prejudice." State Bank of India v. NLRB, 808 F.2d 526, 541 (7th Cir. 1986). These principles described by the Board and the Seventh Circuit apply similarly to inflammatory religious comments.

With this advice in mind, we look at the Board's findings about the Union's religious remarks:

> The Board in *Sewell* distinguished between sustained, deliberate, calculated appeals to racial prejudice (as in that case) and isolated, casual remarks appealing to prejudice. . . . Accordingly, since *Sewell*, the Board has consistently refused to overturn elections on the basis of comments with racial or religious overtones, even when they were inaccurate or gratuitous, when the comments were not inflammatory or part of a sustained, persistent attempt to appeal to the racial or religious prejudices of eligible voters. Relevant to the inquiry are the context in which the statements are made, and the "total conduct" of the person making the comments.

Applying these principles, we adopt the hearing officer's conclusion that the [Union's] conduct here did not so lower the standards of campaigning that the uninhibited desires of the employees could not be determined in an election. We find that, even if the evidence were fully credited, [Honeyville] has failed to demonstrate that the [Union's] conduct amounted to a "sustained inflammatory appeal" or a "systematic attempt to inject religious issues into the campaign."

Considering both the context and the [Union's] total conduct, we find that the [Union] did not overstress or exacerbate religious prejudice. The comments at issue were made at only one of about 10 union meetings. [Honeyville] offered no evidence that there was any other injection of religious comment into the campaign (through literature or other means); thus, religion was neither the core nor the theme of the campaign. Nor did [Honeyville] offer any evidence showing a history of preelection tension. Any appeal to religious prejudice — if, indeed, there was such an appeal — certainly does not appear to have been a deliberate and calculated attempt to so inflame religious prejudice that the employees would vote against [Honeyville] on religious grounds alone. In any event, we find that the [Union's] remarks would not have the "likely effect" of "preventing or impeding" employees from making a "reasoned choice" in the election. . . .

## *NOTES AND QUESTIONS*

**1. Racially or Religiously Inflammatory Statements as Destructive of "Laboratory Conditions"?** "Inflammatory" statements are statements tending "to excite to excessive or uncontrollable action or feeling." See Webster's Ninth New Collegiate Dictionary 619 (1985). Is the Board's regulation of inflammatory statements thus linked with the notion underlying *General Shoe* that the Board should ensure that elections are decided based on employees' assessments of the relative costs and benefits of unionization, and that conduct that renders this unlikely interferes with true freedom of choice?

Other than the text of the message, what factors should go into the determination of whether a given message is inflammatory under *Sewell*? Would the Board or the court have come out differently in *Honeyville* if the remarks in question had not been confined to one of ten union meetings but were repeatedly stressed at every meeting with employees? Would the analysis change if a minority of the employees were Mormon? If the employer was an Arab-American business and the union's remarks questioned the commitment of Arab-Americans to this country?

**2. Motive or Effect?** Look carefully at the language the *Honeyville* court uses: (a) in describing the *Sewell* case and (b) in resolving the case before it. Does the *Sewell* test rest on motive or effect, or both? Should the employer's or union's motive be relevant in determining whether laboratory conditions have been destroyed?

**3. Reconciling *Sewell* with *Midland*?** The Board has continued to apply its *Sewell* doctrine to irrelevant, inflammatory speech related to national origin, religion, or ethnic background as well as race, even after settling on the *Midland National* approach to factual misrepresentations. See, e.g., Durham School Services, 360 N.L.R.B. No. 86 (2014); Zartic, Inc., 315

N.L.R.B. 495 (1994); YKK (U.S.A.) Inc., 269 N.L.R.B. 82 (1984). Should racially or ethnically charged statements be treated differently than other misrepresentations? If so, why? Are racially or religiously based misrepresentations inherently more likely to distort the election process?

**4. Racial Solidarity vs. Racially Divisive Appeals.** Consider the facts in Archer Laundry Co., 150 N.L.R.B. 1427 (1965). In that case, a union seeking to organize predominantly African-American Baltimore laundry workers distributed a leaflet captioned "What Does Martin Luther King Have to Say About Labor Unions?" The leaflet concluded: "The labor hater is always a twin-headed creature spewing anti-Negro talk from one mouth and anti-union propaganda from the other." Another leaflet stated: "Be a free person, not a 'handkerchiefhead Uncle Tom.'" Other leaflets featured illustrations of police dogs and police brutality. The Board, in rejecting the employer's objections to the election, reasoned that the union campaign appealed to racial self-consciousness rather than to racial hatred. Was this a proper application of the *Sewell* doctrine?

**5. Can Inflammatory Third-party Statements Provide Grounds to Overturn an Election?** The Seventh Circuit answered this question in the affirmative, concluding that elections should be invalidated "if the inflammatory remarks could have impaired the employees' freedom of choice in the subsequent election." NLRB v. Katz, 701 F.2d 703, 707 (7th Cir. 1983). In contrast, the Fourth Circuit refused to extend *Sewell* to third-party statements and instituted a heightened standard. Ashland Facility Operations, LLC v. NLRB, 701 F.3d 983 (4th Cir. 2012). It held that these statements can only invalidate the election "if the appeal made a rational, uncoerced expression of free choice impossible." Id. at 993. The Fourth Circuit noted that an application of *Sewell* to third parties would be unworkable because the Board could not require the third party to show that the statements were "truthful and germane," leaving the employer or labor organization to defend statements it did not make. Id.

#### *d. Promises and Grants of Benefits*

**NLRB v. Exchange Parts Co.**
*375 U.S. 405 (1964)*

HARLAN, J.

. . . The respondent, Exchange Parts Company, is engaged in the business of rebuilding automobile parts in Fort Worth, Texas. Prior to November 1959 its employees were not represented by a union. On November 9, 1959, the International Brotherhood of Boilermakers, Iron Shipbuilders, Blacksmiths, Forgers and Helpers, AFL-CIO, advised Exchange Parts that the union was conducting an organizational campaign at the plant and that a majority of the employees had designated the union as their bargaining representative. On November 16 the union petitioned . . . for a representation election. The Board conducted a hearing on December 29, and on February 19, 1960, issued an order directing . . . an election. . . . The election was held on March 18, 1960.

At two meetings on November 4 and 5, 1959, C.V. McDonald, the Vice-President and General Manager of Exchange Parts, announced to the employees that their "floating holiday" in 1959 would fall on December 26 and that there would be an additional "floating holiday" in 1960. On February 25, six days after the Board issued its election order, Exchange Parts held a dinner for employees at which Vice-President McDonald told the employees that they could decide whether the extra day of vacation in 1960 would be a "floating holiday" or would be taken on their birthdays. The employees voted for the latter. McDonald also referred to the forthcoming representation election as one in which, in the words of the trial examiner, the employees would "determine whether . . . [they] wished to hand over their right to speak and act for themselves." He stated that the union had distorted some of the facts and pointed out the benefits obtained by the employees without a union. He urged all the employees to vote in the election.

On March 4, Exchange Parts sent its employees a letter which spoke of "the *Empty Promises* of the Union" and "the *fact* that *it is the Company that puts things in your envelope. . . .*" After mentioning a number of benefits, the letter said: "The Union can't put any of those things in your envelope — *only the Company can do that.*"[2] Further on, the letter stated: ". . . [I]t didn't take a Union to get any of those things and . . . it won't take a Union to get additional improvements in the future." Accompanying the letter was a detailed statement of the benefits granted by the company since 1949 and an estimate of the monetary value of such benefits to the employees. Included in the statement of benefits for 1960 were the birthday holiday, a new system for computing overtime during holiday weeks which had the effect of increasing wages for those weeks, and a new vacation schedule which enabled employees to extend their vacations by sandwiching them between two weekends. Although Exchange Parts asserts that the policy behind the latter two benefits was established earlier, it is clear that the letter of March 4 was the first general announcement of the changes to the employees. In the ensuing election the union lost.

The Board, affirming the findings of the trial examiner, found that the announcement of the birthday holiday and the grant and announcement of overtime and vacation benefits were arranged by Exchange Parts with the intention of inducing the employees to vote against the union. It found that

2. The italics appear in the original letter.

this conduct violated §8(a)(1) . . . and issued an appropriate order. On the Board's petition for enforcement of the order, the Court of Appeals rejected the finding that the announcement of the birthday holiday was timed to influence the outcome of the election. It accepted the Board's findings with respect to the overtime and vacation benefits, and the propriety of those findings is not in controversy here. However, noting that "the benefits were put into effect unconditionally on a permanent basis, and no one has suggested that there was any implication the benefits would be withdrawn if the workers voted for the union," 304 F.2d 368, 375, the court denied enforcement of the Board's order. . . .

. . . We have no doubt that [§8(a)(1)] prohibits not only intrusive threats and promises but also conduct immediately favorable to employees which is undertaken with the express purpose of impinging upon their freedom of choice for or against unionization and is reasonably calculated to have that effect. . . . The danger inherent in well-timed increases in benefits is the suggestion of a fist inside the velvet glove. Employees are not likely to miss the inference that the source of benefits now conferred is also the source from which future benefits must flow and which may dry up if it is not obliged. The danger may be diminished, if, as in this case, the benefits are conferred permanently and unconditionally. But the absence of conditions or threats pertaining to the particular benefits conferred would be of controlling significance only if it could be presumed that no question of additional benefits or renegotiation of existing benefits would arise in the future; and, of course, no such presumption is tenable.

. . . It is true . . . that in most cases of this kind the increase in benefits could be regarded as "one part of an overall program of interference and restraint by the employer," 304 F.2d, at 372, and that in this case the questioned conduct stood in isolation. Other unlawful conduct may often be an indication of the motive behind a grant of benefits while an election is pending, and to that extent it is relevant to the legality of the grant; but when as here the motive is otherwise established, an employer is not free to violate §8(a)(1) by conferring benefits simply because it refrains from other, more obvious violations. We cannot agree with the Court of Appeals that enforcement of the Board's order will have the "ironic" result of "discouraging benefits for labor." 304 F.2d, at 376. The beneficence of an employer is likely to be ephemeral if prompted by a threat of unionization which is subsequently removed. Insulating the right of collective organization from calculated good will of this sort deprives employees of little that has lasting value.

## *NOTES AND QUESTIONS*

**1. Unconditional Improvements as "Threats"?** The Board and the courts have consistently held that an employer's offer of a benefit to employees conditioned on their opposition to or rejection of a union should be treated the same as threats against their support of a union. See, e.g., Del Rey Tortilleria, 272 N.L.R.B. 1106 (1984), enforced, 787 F.2d 1118 (7th Cir. 1986) (promise of wage increase if union is rejected); Maid in New York, 289 N.L.R.B. 524 (1988) (employee promised management position if she ceased supporting union). Note that §8(c) excepts a "promise of a benefit" as well as threats from its insulation of employer speech. *Exchange Parts,* however, did not involve a conditional bribe. The company's new holiday and vacation benefits were not made dependent on the outcome of the pending union election. Why then was an unconditional grant of benefits held to be an unfair labor practice?

**2. Unconditional Improvements as "Strategic" Behavior or "Bribery"?** Is it a better explanation for *Exchange Parts* that employers should not be able to make purely "strategic" improvements that are spurred by union organizing drives and do not reflect enduring changes in employer policies, but have the effect of depriving unions of any gains from their investment in organizational expenditures and discouraging future attempts at organization? Put slightly differently, is *Exchange Parts* premised at least in part on the notion that it is unfair to allow employers to "bribe" employees during the campaign when the union, which does not control wages and working conditions, does not have the same tactic available to it?

**3. Discouraging Benefits for Labor?** Does *Exchange Parts,* in effect, prevent employees from reaping gains in wages and other terms of employment at the point when they have the maximum possible leverage with their employer? Should the law allow employers to raise pay or improve benefits during the period before an election, and then let the employees judge, via their vote in the union election, whether or not the benefits were only strategically granted and likely to be "ephemeral"? If the employer wins the election and then takes the benefits away, the employees have some recourse, do they not, at least after a year has passed? On the other hand, is a union that has invested in one unsuccessful campaign at a workplace likely to be eager to invest in another one, knowing that the employer may once again "buy off" the employees, and that the employees may be more interested in using the union as a pawn in their own strategic game than in long-term representation?

**4. Motive vs. Impact?** Why does the Court require that the employer be motivated by a desire to influence the election for any change in terms and conditions to be held violative of the Act? Is this consistent with the text of §8(a)(1) or with other §8(a)(1) decisions? Does the Court implicitly hold that any legitimate employer motives for granting benefits during representation election campaigns would outweigh any possible effects of such grants on §7 rights? Is the Court suggesting that terms and conditions of employment are always undergoing change and thus, like discipline, are facts of industrial life that trigger statutory concern only when motivated by opposition to §7 activity?

**5. "Dynamic Status Quo"?** The Board's practice is to infer that a grant of benefits that coincides with employee union activity was improperly motivated and interfered with the employees' §7 rights. See Walter Garcon, Jr. & Assocs., 276 N.L.R.B. 1226, 1240-1241 (1985). The burden rests with the employer to establish "that the timing of the action was governed by factors other than the pendency of the election." American Sunroof Corp., 248 N.L.R.B. 748 (1980), modified on other grounds, 667 F.2d 20 (6th Cir. 1981); see also Waste Management of Palm Beach, 329 N.L.R.B. 198 (1999). The employer can meet this burden by showing, for example, that the grant of benefits was the product of a previously established company policy, and that it did not deviate from that policy following the onset of the union campaign. First Student, Inc., 359 N.L.R.B. No. 120 (2013), invalidated due to lack of quorum under NLRB v. Noel Canning Co., 134 S. Ct. 2550 (2014), (employer failed to meet this burden because it withheld annual pay increase, erroneously arguing that it could not make "unilateral changes to the current pay scale when there is a union election pending"). The employer can, however, tell employees that implementation of expected benefits will be deferred until after the election regardless of the outcome "to avoid creating the appearance of interfering with the election." Noah's Bay Area Bagels, LLC, 331 N.L.R.B. 188, 189 (2000). Would it be sufficient for the company to prove that it was responding to a union-negotiated wage increase by its competitors in accord with a long-standing policy of maintaining a wage premium over its unionized competitors? Indeed, is continued adherence to such a policy during an election *required* by *Exchange Parts*? Would it matter if the policy were initially adopted to make unionization less attractive to employees?

*Application*: During 1994-2001, the employer, on the basis of an annual wage survey, granted wage increases to all employees during the first week of April. An election petition covering employees in the shipping department was filed on December 8, 2001, and an election was conducted on May 26, 2002. During the first week in April 2002, on the basis of the customary wage survey, the employer instituted annual wage increases for only those departments not involved in the pending election proceedings, including departments already represented by the petitioning union. At the same time, the employer distributed a notice that wage adjustments for employees involved in the election proceedings were being postponed, on advice of counsel, in order to avoid the appearance of vote-buying and possible unfair labor practices. The union lost the election and objected thereto on the basis of the foregoing notice. How should the Board rule? See *Noah's Bay*, supra. Should it depend on whether wage increases have always been based on a formula allowing no discretion to the employer? See Uarco, Inc., 169 N.L.R.B. 1153 (1968) (refusing to set aside election). See NLRB v. Otis Hosp., 545 F.2d 252, 254-255 (1st Cir. 1976) (withholding benefits during organizational campaign is unlawful "if the increase was promised by the employer prior to the union's appearance; if it normally would be granted as part of a schedule of increases established by the employer's past practice; or if the employer attempts to blame the union for the withholding.").

**6. Solicitation of Grievances.** Can management hold meetings with employees during organizing campaigns to solicit their complaints and grievances if it had not done so before the campaign? Should it matter whether management makes any promises about redressing the employees' complaints? See Torbitt & Castleman, Inc., 320 N.L.R.B. 907 (1996); see also DTR Industries, 311 N.L.R.B. 833, 834 (1993), enforced in relevant part, 39 F.3d 106 (6th Cir. 1994) (both finding violations). Should the Board be prohibiting employers from running "positive" campaigns such as these? Is the employer's conduct distinguishable from the unconditional grants of benefits?

## NLRB v. Savair Manufacturing Co.
*414 U.S. 270 (1973)*

DOUGLAS, J. . . .

. . . It appeared that prior to the election [which the union won resulting in its certification by the NLRB], "recognition slips" were circulated among employees. An employee who signed the slip before the election became a member of the Union and would not have to pay what at times was called an "initiation fee" and at times a "fine." If the Union was voted in, those who had not signed a recognition slip would have to pay.

The actual solicitation of signatures on the "recognition slips" was not done by Union officials. Union officials, however, explained to employees at meetings that those who signed the slips would not be required to pay an initiation fee, while those who did not would have to pay. Those officials also picked out some five employees to do the soliciting and authorized them to explain the Union's initiation-fee policy. Those solicited were told that there would be no initiation fee charged those who signed the slip before the election. Under the bylaws of the Union, an initiation fee apparently was not to be higher than $10; but the employees who testified at the hearing (1) did not know how large the fee would be and (2) said that their understanding was that the fee was a "fine" or an "assessment." . . .

The Board originally took the position that preelection solicitation of memberships by a union with a promise to waive the initiation fee of the union was not consistent with a fair and free choice of bargaining representatives. Lobue Bros., 109 N.L.R.B. 1182 [(1954)]. Later in DIT-MCO, Inc., 163 N.L.R.B. 1019 [(1967)], the Board explained its changed position as follows:

> We shall assume, arguendo, that employees who sign cards when offered a waiver of initiation fees do so solely because no cost is thus involved; that they in fact do not at that point really want the union to be their bargaining representative. . . . [However,] whatever kindly feeling toward the union may be generated by the cost-reduction offer, when consideration is given only to the question of initiation fees, it is completely illogical to characterize as improper inducement or coercion to vote "Yes" a waiver of something that can be avoided simply by voting "No."

. . . [T]he Board's analysis ignores the realities of the situation. Whatever his true intentions, an employee who signs a recognition slip prior to an election is indicating to other workers that he supports the union. His outward manifestation of support must often serve as a useful campaign tool in the union's hands to convince other employees to vote for the union, if only because many employees respect their coworkers' views on the unionization issue. By permitting the union to offer to waive an initiation fee for those employees signing a recognition slip prior to the election, the Board allows the union to buy endorsements and paint a false portrait of employee support during its election campaign. . . .

In addition, while it is correct that the employee who signs a recognition slip is not legally bound to vote for the union and has not promised to do so in any formal sense, certainly there may be some employees who would feel obliged to carry through on their stated intention to support the union. And on the facts of this case, the change of just one vote would have resulted in a 21 to 21 election rather than a 22 to 20 election. . . .

Whether it would be an "unfair" labor practice for a union to promise a special benefit to those who sign up for a union seems not to have been squarely resolved. The right of free choice is, however, inherent in the principles reflected in §9(c)(1)(A). . . .

. . . In the *Exchange Parts* case we said that, although the benefits granted by the employer were permanent and unconditional, employees were "not likely to miss the inference that the source of benefits not conferred is also the source from which future benefits must flow and which may dry up if not obliged." 375 U.S., at 409. If we respect, as we must, the statutory right of employees to resist efforts to unionize a plant, we cannot assume that unions exercising powers are wholly benign towards their antagonists whether they be nonunion protagonists or the employer. The failure to sign a recognition slip may well seem ominous to nonunionists who fear that if they do not sign, they will face a wrathful union regime, should the union win. That influence may have had a decisive impact in this case where the change of one vote would have changed the result.

White, Jr., with whom Brennan and Blackmun, JJ., join, dissenting. . . .

. . . The majority places heavy reliance on the supposed analogy between the waiver of fees in this case and an actual increase in benefits made by an employer during the course of an election campaign. NLRB v. Exchange Parts Co., 375 U.S. 405 (1964). . . . A number of important differences exist between that case and the instant one. First, the employer actually gave his employees substantial increased benefits, whereas here the benefit is only contingent and small; the union glove is not very velvet. Secondly, in the union context, the fist is missing. When the employer increased benefits, the threat was made "that the source of benefits now conferred is also the source from which future benefits must flow and which may dry up if it is not obliged." Ibid. The Union, on the other hand, since it was not the representative of the employees, and would not be if it were unsuccessful in the election, could not make the same threat by offering a benefit which it would take away if it *lost* the election. A union can only make its own victory more desirable in the minds of the employees.

## *NOTES AND QUESTIONS*

**1. Court-Imposed "Laboratory Conditions"?** *Savair* is a case where the Board declined to find that a particular union practice violated "laboratory conditions" under its *General Shoe* doctrine rather than a case where the Board finds that one of the parties to the election campaign committed an unfair labor practice. Is the Court's decision consistent with the discretionary character of the *General Shoe* doctrine and the deferential review that courts normally accord to the Board's §9 decisions, particularly when they rest on judgments about likely employee reactions?

**2. *Savair*'s Rationale.**

a. *Exchange Parts Analogy?* Justice Douglas states that "[t]he failure to sign a recognition slip may well seem ominous to non-unionists who fear that if they do not sign they will face a wrathful union regime, should the union win." Is this claimed effect tied to the union's offer to waive the initiation fee to card-signers or to the timing of that offer? Would the Court's argument here call into question any use of union-solicited authorization cards?

b. *A Moral Obligation?* Would some employees who have signed waiver-induced recognition cards feel morally obligated to vote for the union in a secret-ballot election? Can creating a sense of obligation impair fair election conditions? The Board itself relied in part on a similar "moral obligation" theory in Atlantic Limousine, Inc., 331 N.L.R.B. 1025, 1029 (2000) (3-2) (holding election day raffles sponsored by either side objectionable per se; "employees would reasonably perceive the offer to win a raffle prize as a 'reward' or 'favor' . . . which the[y] might feel obligated to repay" at the polls).

c. *Relevance of Authorization Cards? Savair* holds that the Board should have overturned an NLRB election because of the union's initiation fee waiver. In this case, however, the authorization cards were not used as a basis for obtaining bargaining authority without an election or despite a no-union vote in an election. Are the Court's concerns more relevant where the union seeks to obtain bargaining authority on the basis of such cards without an election?

**3. No Legitimate Union Interest?** Can *Savair* be justified on the ground that the impact on elections of pre-election waiver of fees, however slight, is an avoidable cost because any legitimate union interest would be equally well served by waivers that are not conditioned on signing a card before the election? Such unconditional waivers (that is, waiver offers that are left open for some time after the election) have traditionally been permitted. See, e.g., NLRB v. River City Elevator Co., 289 F.3d 1029 (7th Cir. 2002). Does the union have a legitimate interest in offering only pre-election waivers of its fees?

**4. Application.** A union has a policy of not filing election petitions until a majority of unit employees tender a reduced initiation fee and one month's dues. If the union loses the election, it will use the funds to pay its NLRB election campaign expenses. If it wins, it applies the dues payments to the first month's dues payable after the first contract is signed. It also keeps the reduction in initiation fees open until that time. If the union wins the election, should the employer be able to obtain a new election based on the union's conduct? See Aladdin Hotel Corp., 229 N.L.R.B. 499 (1977), enforcement denied, 584 F.2d 891 (9th Cir. 1978).

**5. Union Promises vs. Employer Promises.** A union's promise to negotiate better employee benefits if it is elected is not unlawful and will not be considered to taint a representation election. An employer, however, may not make even *unconditional* promises of benefits during the union campaign. See Greenwood Health Center v. NLRB, 139 F.3d 135, 140-141 (2d Cir. 1998); see also *Exchange Parts,* supra page 301. Are these rules reconcilable? See Fleet Boston Pavilion, 333 N.L.R.B. No. 655 (2001).

**6. Other Union Grants of Benefit.** The Board has been stringent in policing union grants of benefit. For decisions overturning an election on this basis, see Mailing Services, Inc., 293 N.L.R.B. 565 (1989) (free medical screening); Owens-Illinois, Inc., 271 N.L.R.B. 1235 (1984) (election-day gift of $16 union jackets). If a gift of a jacket is impermissible, what about a union T-shirt? Is there a point at which a grant of benefit is considered de minimis? See R.L. White Co., 262 N.L.R.B. 575 (1982) (distribution of union T-shirts, buttons, and stickers not objectionable).

**7. Union-Financed Litigation as a *Savair* Violation?** Assume that a union learns that the employer is or may be violating the minimum-wage and overtime provisions of the Fair Labor Standards Act. May union lawyers file a lawsuit on behalf of unit employees for the purpose in part of influencing the outcome of the NLRB election by demonstrating the benefits of union representation? Is the effect of filing such a suit no different than an employer's unconditional grant of benefits? Compare Novotel New York, 321 N.L.R.B. 624 (1996) (filing of lawsuit a week before election not objectionable; while union's action may influence employee votes, it goes to the heart of question facing employees in election), with Freund Baking Co. v. NLRB, 165 F.3d 928, 933 (D.C. Cir. 1999) (overturning election on similar facts; "although a union is free to advertise the benefits for which its members are eligible, it may not give voters 'free samples'" during pre-election period). In Stericycle, Inc., 357 N.L.R.B. No. 61 (2011), the Board overruled *Novotel* and followed *Freund Baking*. The Board found that wage-and-hour lawsuits during the critical pre-election period are objectionable and warrant a second election because they could be viewed as "a gratuitous grant of benefits" and infringe on employee's free choice to decide whether to vote in favor of unionization. According to the *Stericycle* Board, a union can educate workers about their employment rights and refer them to outside counsel during the critical pre-election period. The Board also clarified that these lawsuits are permissible if initiated before the filing of an election petition or after the election is held. See generally Catherine L. Fisk, Union Lawyers and Employment Law, 23 Berkeley J. of Emp. & Lab. L. 57 (2002).

### e. *Interrogation, Polling, and Surveillance*

**Timsco Inc. v. NLRB**
*819 F.2d 1173 (D.C. Cir. 1987)*

MIKVA, J.

The central issue in this case is the appropriateness of the Board's order in July 1985 setting aside the tie-vote secret ballot election held in December 1984 on the basis of coercive interrogation of employees by their employer. If the Board acted reasonably in ordering a new election, the Company has a duty to bargain with the duly certified union [which won the rerun election]. In order to evaluate the reasonableness of the Board's action, we must consider the findings upon which it was based, which are not in dispute among the parties. The Hearing Officer found and the Board adopted his findings that the following chronologically ordered conversations occurred:

1) On November 10, 1984, during the election campaign, Keith Pritchard, Timsco's general manager and the son of its president, approached John Marhefka, a maintenance employee, and asked, "What's going on?" Marhefka responded, "What?" K. Pritchard then said to him, "You know, who's ever behind this organizing is going to screw up a lot of jobs for a lot of people."

2) On November 20, 1984, Marhefka approached K. Pritchard outside of K. Pritchard's office to discuss an anticipated leave of absence. Marhefka followed K. Pritchard into his office, and following the discussion about the leave of absence, K. Pritchard said, "Since you asked me a question, I would like to ask you a question. I know the Union is well organized and they have told you not to say anything. I would like to know why the people want to start a union. We pay them a good wage." Pritchard prefaced this portion of the conversation by asking Marhefka to keep it "in confidence"; Marhefka agreed.

3) During the week of November 23-30, K. Pritchard approached Marhefka at his work area and asked, "What do these people want? Is it money?" Marhefka responded, "What I would like to have is hospitalization." K. Pritchard replied, "If you wanted this, why didn't you come to me when you had your evaluation and ask for it? Like Vince, because Vince came to me and—during review time and wasn't satisfied, and he was given an increase."

4) During the week of December 3, 1984 K. Pritchard and Marhefka had an exchange about whether the Union would challenge the vote of maintenance employee David Ehrenfried at the scheduled election. K. Pritchard said, "I heard that they are going to challenge Dave's vote." Marhefka responded, "I don't know." K. Pritchard then asked, "You know, what grounds do they have to challenge Dave's vote?" Marhefka responded, "I think Dave can vote." K. Pritchard then asked, "Would you hate Dave if he voted no [against representation]?" Marhefka responded, "No. . . ."

5) On December 6, 1984 Walter Pritchard, Keith's father and president of Timsco, approached Marhefka and asked, "Weren't you a union member?" W. Pritchard also asked where Marhefka had been employed and what union he had belonged to. Marhefka responded that while employed at U.S. Steel's Clairton Works he had been a member of the United Steelworkers of America. W. Pritchard told Marhefka that he didn't think that the Union was good for the Company and that he would like Marhefka's support.

6) On December 6, 1984 W. Pritchard approached Dorothea Green, a graphic artist for the company, and said, "I understand that you are active in organizing getting the Union in." Green responded, "You mean, you're discounting my vote." W. Pritchard told her that he was disappointed that she felt she had to contact the Union and that he would much rather have her come in to see him, that his door was always open.

7) After lunch on the same day, December 6, 1984, W. Pritchard again approached Green and said to her, "I'm surprised at you Dorothea. How did you come about contacting the Union?" Green responded that she had telephoned the Union after finding it listed in the telephone directory. W. Pritchard told Green that he was surprised that Green had done this and that he didn't think she had it in her. . . .

All recent significant precedent on coercive questioning begins with a discussion of Bourne v. NLRB, 332 F.2d 47 (2d Cir. 1964), which articulated criteria for assessing the legality of employer questioning under the National Labor Relations Act. The "*Bourne* standards" require that we consider:

(1) The background, i.e., is there a history of employer hostility and discrimination?
(2) The nature of the information sought. . . .
(3) The identity of the questioner, i.e. how high was he in the company hierarchy?
(4) Place and method of interrogation. . . .
(5) Truthfulness of the reply.

Id. at 48. In 1980 the Board briefly stepped away from the *Bourne* standards to create a per se rule that declared all questioning by an employer about an employee's union sympathies to be inherently coercive. See PPG Industries, 251 N.L.R.B. 1156 (1980). But the Board overturned *PPG* in its recent decision in Rossmore House, 269 N.L.R.B. 1176 (1984), embracing instead a flexible "totality of the circumstances" test and citing *Bourne* for relevant areas of inquiry. Id. at 1178 & n.20. . . .

The Board clearly acted reasonably in deeming coercive the first conversation between K. Pritchard and Marhefka, in which K. Pritchard said that the union organizers were "going to screw up a lot of jobs for a lot of people." The Hearing Officer found this statement to be a threat, all the more effective because directed at an employee who was not an open and active union supporter. . . .

Given the context here (small workplace, interrogator was general manager, employee was maintenance worker and not active union supporter), we accept the Board's conclusion that Marhefka was threatened in this first conversation.

This threat impacts the next three conversations between Marhefka and K. Pritchard. Repeated questioning about union sympathies in light of the early threat of jobs being "screwed up" can reasonably be deemed coercive even if any *single* exchange, taken out of context, could not itself support a finding of coercion. Moreover, the exchanges between Marhefka and K. Pritchard exhibited many of the characteristics earmarked as coercive by *Bourne.* For example, the November 20 conversation took place in K. Pritchard's office, where Pritchard extracted a promise of confidentiality from Marhefka. *Bourne* identified the importance of the place of interrogation, and clearly the employer's office is "the locus of authority." NLRB v. Knogo Corp., 727 F.2d 55, 58 (2d Cir. 1984). The promise of confidentiality extracted by Pritchard, the Board could reasonably conclude, added to the coerciveness of the closed-door chat by increasing Marhefka's isolation in the face of managerial pressure. In addition, K. Pritchard sought information from Marhefka about the Union's plans to challenge another employee's vote. In light of the circumstances, the Board could reasonably conclude that the questions were motivated by the purpose — improper under *Bourne* — to elicit specific information concerning union strategy so that the Company could better plan its own antiunion strategy.

The last three incidents of questioning involved W. Pritchard, the president of Timsco, and his involvement by itself has a coercive air under the *Bourne* standards because he is the highest ranking officer in the Company hierarchy. Although the smallness of the unit in this case might suggest that a conversation with the president is not a particularly unusual or intimidating event, the record reveals that the president's previous contacts with employees were limited to conversations about the weather. . . .

We grant that with the exception of the first threatening conversation between Marhefka and K. Pritchard, none of the exchanges, taken individually and out of context, sounds especially coercive on its face. But it is the Board's job, not ours, to assess the cumulative effect of the seven exchanges — the "totality of the circumstances." Our task is not to reassess independently the coerciveness of the questions, but rather to assess the reasonableness of the Board's conclusion. . . .

We find reasonable the Board's conclusion that the questioning was coercive enough to disrupt laboratory conditions so as to require a rerun election.

## *NOTES AND QUESTIONS*

**1. The Board's "Totality of the Circumstances" Test for Interrogation.** The Board has adopted a "totality of the circumstances" test that incorporates the *Bourne* factors. Both *Rossmore House* and Sunnyvale Medical Clinic, Inc., 277 N.L.R.B. 1217 (1985) suggest that employees' open support for the union or obvious lack of concern with hiding their pro-union stance cut against a finding that the interrogation was coercive. However, can it be argued in some cases that the interrogation of only the most open and active union supporters could be more coercive than random interrogation of employees? The Board conducts fact-intensive analyses in these cases and often stresses that the *Bourne* "factors are not to be mechanically applied." See e.g., Phillips 66 (Sweeny Refinery), 360 N.L.R.B. No. 26 (2014).

**2. Employer Motive Behind Interrogation?** Whether interrogation will be found coercive or not depends on impact rather than motive. Nonetheless, can an employer have legitimate motives for questioning employees about their attitude toward the union or related matters? What kinds of employer reactions might ensue after learning that an employee is a union supporter? Or that while he is not one, the union is actively organizing the workforce?

**3. Systematic Polling of Employees: The *Struksnes* Safeguards.** A systematic poll involves questioning a group of employees on their attitudes towards union representation. The leading Board decision is Struksnes Construction Co., 165 N.L.R.B. 1062 (1967):

> Absent unusual circumstances, the polling of employees by an employer will be violative of Section 8(a)(1) of the Act unless the following safeguards are observed: (1) the purpose of the poll is to determine the truth of a union's claim of majority, (2) this purpose is communicated to the employees, (3) assurances against reprisal are given, (4) the employees are polled by secret ballot, and (5) the employer has not engaged in unfair labor practices or otherwise created a coercive atmosphere.

Id. at 1063. Along with the five *Struksnes* factors, the Board considers whether the employer provided reasonable advanced notice to the union about the time and place of the poll. See, e.g., Grenada Stamping & Assembly, 351 N.L.R.B. 1152 (2007). Employer polling is discussed further infra page 349.

**4. Surveillance or Creating Impression of Surveillance.** The Board has consistently held, with the courts' approval, that an employer's surveillance of its employees' union activities is unlawful regardless of whether the employees are aware of the surveillance. See, e.g., NLRB v. J.P. Stevens & Co., 563 F.2d 8 (2d Cir. 1977); Bethlehem Steel Co. v. NLRB, 120 F.2d 641 (D.C. Cir. 1941). Why? How can employees be affected by activity of which they are unaware? It should be noted that creating the impression that employees' union activities are under surveillance also violates the Act. See, e.g., Newlonbro, LLC (Connecticut's Own) Milford, 332 N.L.R.B. 1559 (2000) (supervisor told employee that "I understand you went to the Union meeting"); Seton Co., 332 N.L.R.B. 979 (2000).

**5. Employer Photographing or Videotaping of Protected Activity.** Employer photographing or videotaping of employees engaged in peaceful picketing or other protected activities such as handbilling is generally considered to have coercive tendencies, and hence violates §8(a)(1) absent a showing of proper justification. See National Steel & Shipbuilding Co. v. NLRB, 156 F.3d 1268, 1271 (D.C. Cir. 1998); F.W. Woolworth, 310 N.L.R.B. 1194 (1993); see also Randell Warehouse of Arizona, Inc., 328 N.L.R.B. 1034, 1039-1041 (1999), enforcement denied, 252 F.3d 445 (D.C. Cir. 2001). Proper justification exists, for example, where an employer has a "reasonable basis for anticipating picket line misconduct," or where it is documenting unlawful secondary activity by the union. See *National Steel*, supra, at 1271; see also Colonial Haven Nursing Home, 542 F.2d 691, 701 (7th Cir. 1976).

**6. Union Photographing or Videotaping of Employees?** Should union photographing or videotaping of employees be judged by the same standard as employer photographing and videotaping? In Pepsi-Cola Bottling Co., 289 N.L.R.B. 736 (1988), the Board held that absent a legitimate explanation to the employees, union photographing or videotaping of employees' §7 activities is, without more, objectionable conduct. In *Randell Warehouse*, 328 N.L.R.B. at 1035-1036, the Board overruled *Pepsi-Cola Bottling*, reasoning that it was inconsistent with Board and court precedent permitting unions (unlike employers) to ask or to poll employees about their support for the union, to visit employees at home, or to ask pro-union employees to report back to them on anti-union activities by their coworkers. The D.C. Circuit denied enforcement, however, noting that the Board's Hearing Officer had found at least three instances of potentially threatening conduct. 252 F.3d 445 (2001).

## B. NLRB-COMPELLED RECOGNITION WITHOUT AN ELECTION

The principal way in which a union obtains recognition without an election is by the employer's voluntary recognition of the union when presented with evidence of the union's majority support among its employees in an appropriate bargaining unit. Issues concerning voluntary recognition are discussed in the next chapter. This section focuses on the extent to which the Board can *require* recognition and bargaining in the absence of voluntary recognition or union victory in an election.

## 1. The *Gissel* Bargaining Order

**NLRB v. Gissel Packing Co.**
*395 U.S. 575 (1969); see previous excerpt at page 283.*

Warren, C.J. . . .

The specific questions facing us here are whether the duty to bargain can arise without a Board election under the Act; whether union authorization cards, if obtained from a majority of employees without misrepresentation or coercion, are reliable enough generally to provide a valid, alternate route to majority status; whether a bargaining order is an appropriate and authorized remedy where an employer rejects a card majority while at the same time committing unfair labor practices that tend to undermine the union's majority and make a fair election an unlikely possibility; and whether certain specific statements made by an employer to his employees constituted such an election-voiding unfair labor practice and thus fell outside the protection of the First Amendment and §8(c) of the Act. . . . For reasons given below, we answer each of these questions in the affirmative. . . .

### Nos. 573 and 691

In each of the cases from the Fourth Circuit, the course of action followed by the Union and the employer and the Board's response were similar. In each case, the Union waged an organizational campaign, obtained authorization cards from a majority of employees in the appropriate bargaining unit, and then, on the basis of the cards, demanded recognition by the employer. All three employers refused to bargain on the ground that authorization cards were inherently unreliable indicators of employee desires; and they either embarked on, or continued, vigorous antiunion campaigns that gave rise to numerous unfair labor practice charges. In *Gissel*, where the employer's campaign began almost at the outset of the Union's organizational drive, the Union (petitioner in No. 691), did not seek an election, but instead filed three unfair labor practice charges against the employer, for refusing to bargain in violation of §8(a)(5), for coercion and intimidation of employees in violation of §8(a)(1), and for discharge of Union adherents in violation of §8(a)(3). In *Heck's* an election sought by the Union was never held because of nearly identical unfair labor practice charges later filed by the Union as a result of the employer's antiunion campaign, initiated after the Union's recognition demand. And in *General Steel*, an election petitioned for by the Union and won by the employer was set aside by the Board because of the unfair labor practices committed by the employer in the pre-election period.

In each case, the Board's primary response was an order to bargain directed at the employers, despite the absence of an election in *Gissel* and *Heck's* and the employer's victory in *General Steel.* More specifically, the Board found in each case (1) that the Union had obtained valid authorization cards from a majority of the employees in the bargaining unit and was thus entitled to represent the employees for collective bargaining purposes; and (2) that the employer's refusal to bargain with the Union in violation of §8(a)(5) was motivated, not by a "good faith" doubt of the Union's majority status, but by a desire to gain time to dissipate that status. The Board based its conclusion as to the lack of good faith doubt on the fact that the employers had committed substantial unfair labor practices during their antiunion campaign efforts to resist recognition. Thus, the Board found that all three employers had engaged in restraint and coercion of employees in violation of §8(a)(1)—in *Gissel*, for coercively interrogating employees about Union activities, threatening them with discharge, and promising them benefits; in *Heck's*, for coercively interrogating employees, threatening reprisals, creating the appearance of surveillance, and offering benefits for opposing the Union; and in *General Steel*, for coercive interrogation and threats of reprisals, including discharge. In addition, the Board found that the employers in *Gissel* and *Heck's* had wrongfully discharged employees for engaging in Union activities in violation of §8(a)(3). And, because the employers had rejected the card-based bargaining demand in bad faith, the Board found that all three had refused to recognize the Unions in violation of §8(a)(5). . . .

Consequently, the Board ordered the companies to cease and desist from their unfair labor practices, to offer reinstatement and back pay to the employees who had been discriminatorily discharged, to bargain with the Unions on request, and to post the appropriate notices.

On appeal, [the Fourth Circuit], in per curiam opinions in each of the three cases, sustained the Board's findings as to the §§8(a)(1) and (3) violations, but rejected the Board's findings that the employers' refusal to bargain violated §8(a)(5) and declined to enforce those portions of the Board's orders directing the respondent companies to bargain in good faith. . . . [The court's position was] that the 1947 Taft-Hartley amendments to the Act, which permitted the Board to resolve representation disputes by certification under §9(c) only by secret ballot election, withdrew from the Board the authority to order an employer to bargain under §8(a)(5) on the basis of cards, in the absence of NLRB certification, unless the employer knows independently of the cards that there is in fact no representation dispute. . . .

## No. 585

... In July 1965, [Teamsters, Local Union No. 404] began an organizing campaign among petitioner's Holyoke employees and by the end of the summer had obtained authorization cards from 11 of the Company's 14 journeymen wire weavers choosing the Union as their bargaining agent. On September 20, the Union notified petitioner that it represented a majority of its wire weavers, requested that the Company bargain with it, and offered to submit the signed cards to a neutral third party for authentication. After petitioner's president declined the Union's request a week later, claiming, *inter alia,* that he had a good faith doubt of majority status because of the cards' inherent unreliability, the Union petitioned, on November 8, for an election that was ultimately set for December 9.

... The Union lost the election 7 to 6, and then filed both objections to the election and unfair labor practice charges which were consolidated for hearing before the trial examiner.

The Board agreed with the trial examiner that the president's communications with his employees, when considered as a whole, "reasonably tended to convey to the employees the belief or impression that selection of the Union in the forthcoming election could lead [the Company] to close its plant, or to the transfer of the weaving production, with the resultant loss of jobs to the wire weavers." Thus, the Board found that under the "totality of the circumstances" petitioner's activities constituted a violation of §8(a)(1) of the Act. The Board further agreed with the trial examiner that petitioner's activities, because they "also interfered with the exercise of a free and untrammeled choice in the election," and "tended to foreclose the possibility" of holding a fair election, required that the election be set aside. The Board also found that the Union had a valid card majority ... when it demanded recognition initially and that the Company declined recognition, not because of a good faith doubt as to the majority status, but, as the §8(a)(1) violations indicated, in order to gain time to dissipate that status—in violation of §8(a)(5). Consequently, the Board set the election aside, entered a cease-and-desist order, and ordered the Company to bargain on request.

On appeal, the [First Circuit] sustained the Board's findings and conclusions and enforced its order in full. ...

## II

In urging us to reverse the Fourth Circuit and to affirm the First Circuit, the [NLRB] contends that we should approve its interpretation and administration of the duties and obligations imposed by the Act in authorization card cases. The Board argues (1) that unions have never been limited under

§9(c) of either the Wagner Act or the 1947 amendments to certified elections as the sole route to attaining representative status. Unions may, the Board contends, impose a duty to bargain on the employer under §8(a)(5) by reliance on other evidence of majority employee support, such as authorization cards. Contrary to the Fourth Circuit's holding, the Board asserts, the 1947 amendments did not eliminate the alternative routes to majority status. The Board contends (2) that the cards themselves, when solicited in accordance with Board standards which adequately insure against union misrepresentation, are sufficiently reliable indicators of employee desires to support a bargaining order against an employer who refuses to recognize a card majority in violation of §8(a)(5). The Board argues (3) that a bargaining order is the appropriate remedy for the §8(a)(5) violation, where the employer commits other unfair labor practices that tend to undermine union support and render a fair election improbable. . . .

The traditional approach utilized by the Board for many years has been known as the *Joy Silk* doctrine. Joy Silk Mills, Inc., 85 N.L.R.B. 1263 (1949), enforced, 185 F.2d 732 (1950). Under that rule, an employer could lawfully refuse to bargain with a union claiming representative status through possession of authorization cards [only] if he had a "good faith doubt" as to the union's majority status. . . . [Under *Joy Silk*,] an employer could not refuse a bargaining demand and seek an election instead "without a valid ground therefor."

The leading case codifying modifications to the *Joy Silk* doctrine was Aaron Brothers, 158 N.L.R.B. 1077 (1966). There the Board made it clear that . . . an employer "will not be held to have violated his bargaining obligation . . . simply because he refuses to rely upon cards, rather than an election, as the method for determining the union's majority." 158 N.L.R.B., at 1078. . . . The Board pointed out, however, that a bargaining order would issue if . . . an employer's "course of conduct" gave indications as to the employer's bad faith. As examples of such a "course of conduct," the Board cited [inter alia Snow & Sons, 134 N.L.R.B. 709 (1961), enforced, 308 F.2d 687 (9th Cir. 1962), where the employer reneged on its agreement to bargain if a third party verified the presence of a card majority and instead insisted on an election despite such verification]. . . .

. . . [T]he Board [indicated] at oral argument that [u]nder [its] current practice, an employer's good faith doubt is largely irrelevant, and the key to the issuance of a bargaining order is the commission of serious unfair labor practices that interfere with the election processes and tend to preclude the holding of a fair election. Thus, an employer can insist that a union go to an election, regardless of his subjective motivation, so long as he is not guilty of misconduct; he need give no affirmative reasons for rejecting a recognition request, and he can demand an election with a simple "no comment" to the union. The Board pointed out, however, (1) that an employer could not refuse to bargain if he *knew,* through a personal poll for instance, that a majority of his employees supported the union, and (2) that an employer could not refuse recognition initially because of questions as to the appropriateness of the unit and then later claim, as an afterthought, that he doubted the union's strength. . . .

### III

The first issue facing us is whether a union can establish a bargaining obligation by means other than a Board election and whether the validity of alternate routes to majority status, such as cards, was affected by the 1947 Taft-Hartley amendments. The most commonly traveled route for a union to obtain recognition as the exclusive bargaining representative of an unorganized group of employees is through the Board's election and certification procedures under §9(c) . . . ; it is also, from the Board's point of view, the preferred route. A union is not limited to a Board election, however, for, in addition to §9, the present Act provides in §8(a)(5), as did the Wagner Act in §8(5), that "[i]t shall be an unfair labor practice for an employer . . . to refuse to bargain collectively with the representatives of his employees, subject to the provisions of §9(a)." Since §9(a), in both the Wagner Act and the present Act, refers to the representative as the one "designated or selected" by a majority of the employees without specifying precisely how that representative is to be chosen, it was clearly recognized that an employer had a duty to bargain whenever the union representative presented "convincing evidence of majority support." Almost from the inception of the Act, then, it was recognized that a union did not have to be certified as the winner of a Board election to invoke a bargaining obligation; it could establish majority status by other means under the unfair labor practice provision of §8(a)(5)—by showing convincing support, for instance, by a union-called strike or strike vote, or, as here, by possession of cards signed by a majority of the employees authorizing the union to represent them for collective bargaining purposes.

. . . We have consistently accepted this interpretation of the Wagner Act and the present [A]ct, particularly as to the use of authorization cards. . . . [T]he 1947 amendments weaken rather than strengthen the position taken by the employers here and the Fourth Circuit below. An early version of the bill in the House would have amended §8(5) of the Wagner Act to permit the Board to find a refusal-to-bargain violation only where an employer had failed to bargain with a union "currently recognized by the employer or certified as such [through an election] under section 9." Section 8(a)(5) of H.R. 3020, 80th Cong., 1st Sess. (1947). The proposed change, which would have eliminated the use of cards, was rejected in Conference (H.R. Conf. Rep. No. 510, 80th Cong., 1st Sess., 41 (1947)), however, and we cannot make a similar change in the Act simply because, as the employers assert, Congress did not expressly approve the use of cards in rejecting the House amendment. Nor can we accept the Fourth Circuit's conclusion that the change was wrought when Congress amended §9(c) to make election the sole basis for *certification* by eliminating the phrase "any other suitable method to ascertain such representatives," under which the Board had occasionally used cards as a certification basis. A certified union has the benefit of numerous special privileges which are not accorded unions recognized voluntarily or under a bargaining order and which, Congress could determine, should not be dispensed unless a union has survived the crucible of a secret ballot election.

The employers rely finally on the addition to §9(c) of subparagraph (B), which allows an employer to petition for an election whenever "one or more individuals or labor organizations have presented to him a claim to be recognized as the representative defined in section 9(a)." That provision was not added, as the employers assert, to give them an absolute right to an election at any time; rather, it was intended, as the legislative history indicates, to allow them, after being asked to bargain, to test out their doubts as to a union's majority in a secret election which they would then presumably not cause to be set aside by illegal antiunion activity. We agree with the Board's assertion here that there is no suggestion that Congress intended §9(c)(1)(B) to relieve any employer of his §8(a)(5) bargaining obligation where, without good faith, he engaged in unfair labor practices disruptive of the Board's election machinery. And we agree that the policies reflected in §9(c)(1)(B) fully support the Board's present administration of the Act . . . ; for an employer can insist on a secret ballot election, unless, in the words of the Board, he engages "in contemporaneous unfair labor practices likely to destroy the union's majority and seriously impede the election." . . .

. . . Remaining before us is the propriety of a bargaining order as a remedy for a §8(a)(5) refusal to bargain where an employer has committed independent unfair labor practices which have made the holding of a fair election unlikely or which have in fact undermined a union's majority and caused an election to be set aside. We have long held that the Board is not limited to a cease-and-desist order in such cases, but has the authority to issue a bargaining order without first requiring the union to show that it has been able to maintain its majority status. And we have held that the Board has the same authority even where it is clear that the union, which once had possession of cards from a majority of the employees, represents only a minority when the bargaining order is entered. Franks Bros. Co. v. NLRB, 321 U.S. 702 (1944). We see no reason now to withdraw this authority from the Board. If the Board could enter only a cease-and-desist order and direct an election or a rerun, it would in effect be rewarding the employer and allowing him "to profit from [his] own wrongful refusal to bargain," *Franks Bros.*, supra, at 704, while at the same time severely curtailing the employees' right freely to determine whether they desire a representative. The employer could continue to delay or disrupt the election process and put off indefinitely his obligation to bargain, and any election held under these circumstances would not be likely to demonstrate the employees' true, undistorted desires.

The employers argue that . . . the bargaining order is an unnecessarily harsh remedy that needlessly prejudices employees' §7 rights solely for the purpose of punishing or restraining an employer. Such an argument ignores that a bargaining order is designed as much to remedy past election damage as it is to deter future misconduct. If an employer has succeeded in undermining a union's strength and destroying the laboratory conditions necessary for a fair election, he may see no need to violate a cease-and-desist order by further unlawful activity.

The damage will have been done, and perhaps the only fair way to effectuate employee rights is to reestablish the conditions as they existed before the employer's unlawful campaign. There is, after all, nothing permanent in a bargaining order, and if, after the effects of the employer's acts have worn off, the employees clearly desire to disavow the union, they can do so by filing a representation petition.

. . . Despite our reversal of the Fourth Circuit below in Nos. 573 and 691 on all major issues, the actual area of disagreement between our position here and that of the Fourth Circuit is not large as a practical matter. While refusing to validate the general use of a bargaining order in reliance on cards, the Fourth Circuit nevertheless left open the possibility of imposing a bargaining order, without need of inquiry into majority status on the basis of cards or otherwise, in "exceptional" cases marked by "outrageous" and "pervasive" unfair labor practices. . . . The Board itself, we should add, has long had a similar policy of issuing a bargaining order, in the absence of a §8(a)(5) violation or even a bargaining demand, when that was the only available, effective remedy for substantial unfair labor practices. . . .

The only effect of our holding here is to approve the Board's use of the bargaining order in less extraordinary cases marked by less pervasive practices which nonetheless still have the tendency to undermine majority strength and impede the election processes. The Board's authority to issue such an order on a lesser showing of employer misconduct is appropriate, we should reemphasize, where there is also a showing that at one point the union had a majority; in such a case, of course, effectuating ascertainable employee free choice becomes as important a goal as deterring employer misbehavior. In fashioning a remedy in the exercise of its discretion, then, the Board can properly take into consideration the extensiveness of an employer's unfair practices in terms of their past effect on election conditions and the likelihood of their recurrence in the future. If the Board finds that the possibility of erasing the effects of past practices and of ensuring a fair election (or a fair rerun) by the use of traditional remedies, though present, is slight and that employee sentiment once expressed through cards would, on balance, be better protected by a bargaining order, then such an order should issue.

We emphasize that under the Board's remedial power there is still a third category of minor or less extensive unfair labor practices, which, because of their minimal impact on the election machinery, will not sustain a bargaining order. There is, the Board says, no per se rule that the commission of any unfair practice will automatically result in a §8(a)(5) violation and the issuance of an order to bargain. . . .

With these considerations in mind, we turn to an examination of the orders in these cases. In *Sinclair*, No. 585, the Board made a finding, left undisturbed by the First Circuit, that the employer's threats of reprisal were so coercive that, even in the absence of a §8(a)(5) violation, a bargaining order would have been necessary to repair the unlawful effect of those threats. The Board therefore did not have to make the determination called for in the intermediate situation above that the risks that a fair rerun election might not be possible were too great to disregard the desires of the employees already expressed through the cards. . . .

In the three cases in Nos. 573 and 691 from the Fourth Circuit, on the other hand, the Board did not make a similar finding that a bargaining order would have been necessary in the absence of an unlawful refusal to bargain. Nor did it make a finding that, even though traditional remedies might be able to ensure a fair election, there was insufficient indication that an election (or a rerun in *General Steel*) would definitely be a more reliable test of the employees' desires than the card count taken before the unfair labor practices occurred. . . . Because the Board's current practice at the time required it to phrase its findings in terms of an employer's good or bad faith doubts (see Part II, supra), however, the precise analysis the Board now puts forth was not employed below, and we therefore remand these cases for proper findings. . . .

### *Note:* Linden Lumber

In Linden Lumber Div., Summer & Co. v. NLRB, 419 U.S. 301 (1974), decided five years after *Gissel*, the Court addressed the issue whether employers confronted with bargaining demands by unions presenting strong proof of majority support — in that case, a recognitional strike — must either bargain or themselves exercise their rights under §9(c)(1)(B) of the Act to file for an election. A sharply divided Court (5-4) upheld two Board rulings. First, an employer, otherwise guiltless of unfair labor practices, does not violate §8(a)(5) merely by refusing to recognize a union even though the employer at the time had "independent knowledge" of the union's valid card majority. Second, notwithstanding such independent knowledge, the union seeking recognition (rather than the employer) has the burden of filing an election petition. The Court reserved (419 U.S. at 310 n.10) "the question whether the same result obtains if the employer breaches his agreement to permit majority status to be determined by means other than a Board election. See Snow & Sons, 134 N.L.R.B. 709 (1961), enforced, 308 F.2d 687 (CA9, 1962)."

## *NOTES AND QUESTIONS*

**1. Is the Board's Election-Preference Policy Required or Permitted by the NLRA?** What are the justifications for the Board's election-preference policy, and do they outweigh conceivable associated costs? After *Gissel* and *Linden Lumber*, is the Board free to return to the approach it had taken in *Joy Silk*? Is this an appropriate area for judicial deference to the agency's statutory interpretation or policy judgments?

**2. Theory of the *Gissel* Bargaining Order: Remedy for Failure to Bargain or for Other Unfair Labor Practices?** Did the *Gissel* Court uphold the Board's authority to issue bargaining orders as remedies for refusals to bargain with unrecognized unions in violation of §8(a)(5) of the Act, as additional remedies for violations of §§8(a)(1)-(4), or as both? As indicated by the following note, the answer to these questions may have more than academic import.

**3. Commencement Date for Back Pay Remedies?** On February 1, a union requested recognition in an appropriate unit and (truthfully) advised the employer of its valid card majority. The employer promptly said "No." On February 2, a supervisor asked several employees their opinion of "the union business" and received noncommittal replies. On February 6, a management consultant, following a three-month study of the employer's wage costs and those of his competitors, (truthfully) advised the employer that his wages would have to be cut by 19 percent if he were to remain competitive. On February 8, the employer instituted such a cut. On February 10, the employer asked employees suspected of having attended a union meeting whether the union bosses were making "pie-in-the-sky" promises. Later he threatened many employees with plant closure if the union came in; he also discharged well-known union supporters.

Assume that the violations otherwise warrant a bargaining order under *Gissel*, does the Board also have the authority to order the employer to pay employees back pay to compensate for its February 8 unilateral pay cut? To what date should the Board make its *Gissel* bargaining orders retroactive: (1) when the employer declined to recognize the union; (2) when the employer's unlawful conduct began; (3) when the employer succeeded in undermining the union's preexisting majority; or (4) when the employer's conduct became serious enough to impede future election processes? See Trading Port, Inc., 219 N.L.R.B. 298 (1975); Power Inc. v. NLRB, 40

F.3d 409 (D.C. Cir. 1994) (obligation to bargain runs from date employer received union's request for recognition); Road Sprinkler Fitters Local Union No. 669 v. NLRB (John Cuneo, Inc.), 681 F.2d 11 (D.C. Cir. 1982), cert. denied, 459 U.S. 1178 (1983) (enforcing a Board bargaining order, retroactive to the date the union requested recognition; Justices Rehnquist and Powell dissenting from the denial of certiorari).

**4. Effectuation of Employee Free Choice or Deterrent to Employer Illegality?** Are *Gissel* bargaining orders a means of implementing the best measure available (given the employer's unlawful conduct) of ascertaining the preferences of a majority of the employees? Is their purpose also to deter serious unfair labor practices by employers during representational campaigns? Given the nature of the Board's traditional remedies, does the *Gissel* bargaining order provide needed additional deterrence? How likely is such deterrence if *Gissel* bargaining orders require on average two years of litigation during which employee support for the union has likely attenuated? Does the deterrence rationale provide an independent basis for a bargaining order even where a fair rerun could be held?

**5. The Question of Non-majority Bargaining Orders.** Note the Court's delineation near the end of *Gissel* of three categories of cases. What is the difference between the first category, commonly referred to as "*Gissel I*" cases, and the second, "*Gissel II*" cases? Does the Court suggest that a bargaining order might issue in a *Gissel I* case without proof that the union had achieved majority support before the illegal conduct? If a non-majority bargaining order can issue, should its issuance depend on evidence indicating that the union probably would have achieved majority status absent the illegal conduct, such as evidence of substantial minority support that was growing quickly before the employer's coercive response?

In Conair Corp., 261 N.L.R.B. 1189 (1982), a split Board ruled that it had the authority to issue non-majority bargaining orders in *Gissel I* cases, those marked by "outrageous" and "pervasive" unfair labor practices, and issued such an order. The D.C. Circuit disagreed, denying enforcement, 721 F.2d 1355 (D.C. Cir. 1983). In Gourmet Foods, Inc., 270 N.L.R.B. 578 (1984), the Board reversed course and held that it lacked authority under the Act to impose a bargaining order where the union had never demonstrated majority status. But see United Dairy Farmers Coop. Ass'n v. NLRB, 633 F.2d 1054 (3d Cir. 1980) (maintaining that the Board does possess such authority). Is *Gourmet Foods*, to which the Board continues to adhere, consistent with *Gissel*? See First Legal Support Services, 342 N.L.R.B. 350 (2004) (Member Liebman, dissenting, urged the overruling of *Gourmet Foods* as inconsistent with *Gissel*). Does *Gissel* give a clear answer to the question presented in *Conair* and *Gourmet Foods*?

**6. Which Unfair Labor Practices Warrant a *Gissel* Bargaining Order?** Where the union did possess a card majority at one time, which unfair labor practices are so "outrageous" and "pervasive" as to warrant a *Gissel I* bargaining order? Perhaps more importantly, given the relative infrequency of *Gissel I* orders, how is the Board to determine in which potential *Gissel II* cases fair election conditions for a rerun cannot be restored through traditional remedies such as reinstatement with back pay of unlawfully discharged employees? Some Board decisions refer to "hallmark violations," thought to be particularly coercive and likely to have a lasting effect, as especially likely to support issuance of a bargaining order. See NLRB v. Jamaica Towing, 632 F.2d 208, 212-213 (2d Cir. 1980). Among these are actual or threatened plant closure, other threats of job loss, and §8(a)(3) discharges. See, e.g., Michael's Painting, Inc., 337 N.L.R.B. 860 (2002); M.J. Metal Products, 328 N.L.R.B. 1184 (1999), enforced, 267 F.3d 1059 (10th Cir. 2001); General Fabrications Corp., 328 N.L.R.B. 1114 (1999), enforced, 222 F.3d 218 (6th Cir. 2000); Debbie Reynolds Hotel, Inc., 332 N.L.R.B. 466 (2000).

The presence of hallmark violations does not always lead to judicial enforcement. The circuits have repeatedly rebuked the Board for failing to adequately explain why, on the facts of the case before it, its traditional remedies are insufficient to ensure a fair election. See, e.g., Overnite Trans. Co. v. NLRB, 280 F.3d 417, 438 (4th Cir. 2002) (en banc); Douglas Foods Corp. v. NLRB, 251 F.3d 1056, 1065-1067 (D.C. Cir. 2001); see also James J. Brudney, A Famous Victory: Collective Bargaining Protections and the Statutory Aging Process, 74 N.C. L. Rev. 939, 1003-1005 (1996). The D.C. Circuit, to which any party "aggrieved by" a Board order may appeal, see NLRA §10(f), has been particularly adamant on this point, remanding numerous bargaining order cases for a more thorough explanation. See *Douglas Foods*, 280 F.3d at 1067 (noting court's "sense of deja vu" in remanding for adequate justification, but stating that "[s]o long as the Board [continues to ignore us] we have no choice but to remand each offending order"); see also Skyline Distributors, Inc. v. NLRB, 99 F.3d 403, 410 (D.C. Cir. 1996). The Board "begrudgingly adopted the approach" mandated by several circuit courts and now provides the following information to assist reviewing courts:

> (1) that it gave due consideration to the employee's section 7 rights, which are, after all, one of the fundamental purposes of the Act, (2) why it concluded that other purposes must override the rights of the employees to choose their bargaining representatives and (3) why other remedies, less destructive of employees' rights, are not adequate.

NLRB v. Goya Foods, 525 F.3d 1117, 1130 (11th Cir. 2008).

**7. Relevance of Subsequent Events and the Passage of Time?** Should the Board consider events occurring between the commission of the violations and the Board's decision—such as employee turnover, the removal of the company officials responsible for the illegal conduct, as well as the sheer passage of time—in determining whether a bargaining order is warranted? Emphasizing the deterrence objective of the *Gissel* bargaining order, the Board has traditionally viewed "changed circumstances" as irrelevant to the determination of whether a bargaining order should issue. See Overnite Transp. Co., 329 N.L.R.B. 990, 994-995 (1999), enforcement denied in relevant part, 280 F.3d 417 (4th Cir. 2002) (en banc); see also Intersweet, Inc., 321 N.L.R.B. 1 (1996), enforced, 125 F.3d 1064 (7th Cir. 1997). The circuits have tended, however, to decline enforcement of the agency's order, believing that changed circumstances permit a fair rerun election and thus obviate a bargaining order. See NLRB v. Cell Agricultural Mfg. Co., 41 F.3d 389, 398 (8th Cir. 1994) (noting that eight circuits have rejected Board's position); NLRB v. U.S.A. Polymer Corp., 272 F.3d 289, 293 (5th Cir. 2001) (discussing conflict). Are the courts in these cases overstating the significance of the Board's election preference policy and failing to respect the agency's need to balance that preference with the need to deter serious violations?

**8. Are *Gissel* Bargaining Orders "Worth the Candle"?** When the Board does secure judicial enforcement, how valuable is a bargaining order to the union? As we discuss in Chapter 6, the Act does not compel employers or unions to reach agreement on a contract or even to make concessions; it only requires them to "meet . . . and confer in good faith." See NLRA §8(d). How likely is it that a union will be able to build a lasting constructive relationship or even reach a first contract with an employer where serious unfair labor practices have occurred warranting a bargaining order? See Brudney, A Famous Victory, at 1008-1009 (discussing why bargaining orders are "hardly a panacea"); Weiler, Promises to Keep, at 1794 (similar).

**9. "Card-Check" Agreements.** As to the question reserved in *Linden*, the Board has consistently held, both pre- and post-*Linden*, that an employer that agrees to be bound by a means of determining majority status other than a Board election—such as a poll or a "card check"—cannot disavow the results because they are not to its liking. See Sullivan Elec. Co., 199 N.L.R.B. 809 (1972), enforced, 479 F.2d 1270 (6th Cir. 1973); Rockwell Int'l Corp., 220 N.L.R.B. 1262 (1975); Cam Indus., Inc., 251 N.L.R.B. 11 (1980), enforced, 666 F.2d 411 (9th Cir. 1982). Similarly, an employer that unilaterally attempts to determine majority status, for instance, through a poll, must extend recognition if the union receives majority support. See Montgomery Ward & Co., 210 N.L.R.B. 717, 724 n.18 (1974). A union, conversely, is not bound by a "loss" in a unilateral poll; it remains free to seek certification via a Board election. See Texas Petrochemicals Corp., 296 N.L.R.B. 1057 (1989), remanded as modified on other grounds, 923 F.2d 398 (5th Cir. 1991). Polling in the incumbent union context is discussed infra pages 340-349. Related issues arising in the context of "neutrality" and "card-check" agreements are considered in the next chapter at pages 380-384.

### *Note: Section 10(j): An Underutilized Tool in Organizing Cases?*

The proposed Labor Law Reform Act of 1977 would have required the General Counsel to seek §10(j) relief in all discriminatory discharge cases arising in organizing campaigns. Absent a settlement, only through the use of §10(j) will such discriminatees be reinstated prior to the Board election—arguably a key factor in the effectiveness of the reinstatement remedy. Even without new legislation, should the General Counsel be more aggressive in seeking §10(j) relief in organizing campaign cases, in part to send a strong deterrent signal to employers? Might a stepped-up use of §10(j) be more effective than *Gissel* bargaining orders in such cases? See Estreicher, Improving the Administration of the NLRA, supra, at 17-19; and his Labor Law Reform in a World of Competitive Product Markets, 69 Chi.-Kent L. Rev. 3, 36 & n.117 (1993). See Affirmation of 10(j) Program, GC Mem. 14-03 (April 30, 2014); Effective Section 10(j) Remedies for Unlawful Discharges in Organizing Campaigns, GC Mem. 10-07 (Sept. 20, 2010).

## 2. The Canadian Model: Mandating Recognition Without Elections

**Paul C. Weiler, Promises to Keep: Securing Workers' Rights to Self-Organization Under the NLRA**
*96 Harv. L. Rev. 1769 (1983)*

The most typical version of the Canadian model relies on union authorization cards. Once the provincial labor relations board confirms that a majority of the employees in a unit have signed cards authorizing a union to bargain on their behalf, it certifies the union as the bargaining agent. The aim of this approach is most clearly reflected in the British Columbia statute, which stipulates that the union's cards are to be counted as of the date of the application for certification. Thus, when the union surfaces with a majority of the bargaining unit signed up, the statutory condition for certification is satisfied. The employer is afforded no opportunity to campaign against the union. The antidote to employer intimidation, then, is not a heavy battery of regulations and sanctions, but rather a simple change in the legal environment—a change that, by making coercive tactics fruitless, eliminates the temptation to use them. . . .

. . . The system does, however, have one major drawback. . . . A secret ballot vote has a symbolic value that a card check can never have. It clears the air of any doubts about the unions' majority and also confers a measure of legitimacy on the union's bargaining authority, especially among minority pockets of employees who were never contacted in the initial organizational drive.

The Province of Nova Scotia has devised a procedure — the "instant vote" — that achieves these values while still avoiding the trauma of the bitter representation battle. The Nova Scotia Labour Board must conduct an election no more than five days after it receives a certification petition. In this highly compressed interval, it is nearly impossible for the employer to mount a sustained offensive aimed at turning employee sentiments around through intimidation and discrimination.

Comparison of the Nova Scotia experiment with the procedure used in the United States brings out the true contrast between the Canadian and American representation models. The difference consists not so much in the Canadian use of cards as in the elimination of the election campaign. . . .

My reading of the evidence about the current American experience leaves me unpersuaded of the supposed advantages of the extended campaign. In the first place, the employer has had ample opportunity and incentive to demonstrate the advantages of an individual bargaining regime before the union comes on the scene. Second, American workers are not typically unsophisticated about unionization. They are quite aware of the negative features that their employer may point out to them: dues, strikes, job losses, and so on. . . . By the time the employees make up their minds about what they wish to do in negotiations, the issues will be more focused, and the choice will be more informed than it could possibly be at the certification stage. The contribution made by the election campaign to the enlightenment of the employees is marginal at best.

## *NOTES AND QUESTIONS*

**1. Premises of the Canadian Model.** Is Professor Weiler's proposal based on the view that (a) employers have no legitimate interest in having a say on the question of who shall represent their workforces, and (b) contested elections provide no significant contribution to an informed employee choice. If so, do you agree?

**2. Rules Governing Exit.** Does the attractiveness of the Canadian model in part depend on how easy the law makes it for employers or employees to obtain a decertification election? For instance, what if card-check certification were coupled with a change in the law to permit employers to obtain an election after a year of bargaining, or at least at the end of a first contract, without any required demonstration of a reason to doubt the union's majority? See Joan Flynn, *Allentown Mack*: A Happy Exemplar of the Law of Unintended Consequences?, 49 Lab. L.J. 983, 995-996 (1998) (arguing for lower barriers to both entry and exit under NLRA); Samuel Estreicher, "Easy In, Easy Out": A Future for U.S. Workplace Regulation; and his Deregulating Union Democracy, 21 J. Lab. Res. 247 (2000) (discussing an "easy in, easy out" system whereby a union's bargaining authority would be subject to periodic reauthorization elections without requiring employees to file a decertification petition).

### *Note: The Proposed Employee Free Choice Act (EFCA)*

Borrowing from the Canadians, §2 of EFCA, H.R. 1409, 111th Cong., 1st Sess. (Mar. 10, 2009), would have amended §9(a) to provide:

> Notwithstanding any other provision of this section, whenever a petition shall have been filed by an employee or group of employees or any individual or labor organization acting in their behalf alleging that a majority of employees in a unit appropriate for the purposes of collective bargaining wish to be represented by an individual or labor organization for such purposes, the Board shall investigate the petition. If the Board finds that a majority of the employees in a unit appropriate for bargaining has signed valid authorizations designating the individual or labor organization specified in the petition as their bargaining representative and that no other individual or labor organization is currently certified or recognized as the exclusive representative of any of the employees in the unit, the Board shall not direct an election but shall certify the individual or labor organization as the representative described in subsection (a).

EFCA passed in the House of Representatives but was unable to elicit enough Senate support to close off debate.

### *Note: Reducing the Gap Between Petition and Election Without Statutory Change*

The Board's 2014 Notice of Proposed Rulemaking regarding election procedures aims to simplify the procedures in representation cases and eliminate unnecessary barriers to prompt resolutions or elections. The proposed rule changes include allowing for electronic filing, setting the pre-election hearing for seven days after a hearing notice is served (except when special circumstances exist) and setting the post-election hearing for fourteen days after the votes are tallied (or as soon as practicable). To streamline the process, the rule also requires parties to state their positions at the outset of the hearing and consolidates requests for Board review of Regional Directors' pre- and post-election determinations into a single, post-election request. Voter eligibility questions (such as supervisory status) that involve less than 20 percent of the bargaining unit would be addressed (if necessary) after the election, rather than before. 79 Fed. Reg. 7318 et seq.

Consider Professor Estreicher's proposal for reducing the period of time between the filing of an election petition and the holding of the election without statutory change. See Estreicher, Improving the Administration of the NLRA, supra, 5-9:

> How long is the gap between petition and election? The Dunlop Commission noted in 1994 that the "median time from petitioning for an election to a vote has been roughly fifty days for the last two decades (down considerably from the time taken in the 1940s and 1950s)." The Board has made considerable progress in this area. In fiscal year 2008, initial elections in representation cases were held in a median of thirty-eight days from the filing of the petition, and 95.1% of all initial elections were conducted within fifty-six days of the filing of the petition.
>
> The NLRA does not prescribe when an election must be held after a petition has been filed. The Dunlop Commission recommended that representation elections should be conducted "as promptly as administratively feasible, typically no later than two weeks after a petition is filed." The 1977 proposed labor reform legislation would have required an election between twenty-one days (under the House bill) or thirty days (under the Senate bill) from the filing of a petition if the petitioned-for unit was appropriate under a Board regulation. Presumably, the Board could implement even a fourteen-day proposal on its own. It is not clear, however, that decreasing the existing median from thirty-eight days to fourteen days would be administratively feasible or otherwise desirable.
>
> Where cases do not involve significant issues (or the parties stipulate to an accelerated schedule), the Regional Director should be able to hold a fairly prompt election, perhaps within a two-week period. It is doubtful, however, whether two weeks would be sufficient time, even with a strong administrative hand, to address difficult unit and supervisor-exclusion issues responsibly. To reduce the number of such cases, the Board might consider changing the sequence in which it considers unit and exclusion issues. Currently, supervisor-exclusion issues are addressed in a hearing before an election is conducted. Perhaps in many cases the election could happen first, based on an electorate that reflects well-established Board decisions as to the presumptively appropriate unit and likely disposition of eligibility issues. This could be possible in many cases, even in the absence of a consent-election agreement between the parties. The election results would not be certified, however, until the unit and eligibility issues were properly resolved in a hearing at the regional level with limited discretionary review by the Board. In some cases, the results of the post-balloting hearing might require a second election; in most cases, they would not. . . .
>
> Section 9(c)(1) plainly requires the Board to hold "an appropriate hearing" prior to the election to satisfy itself that a question concerning representation exists. The issue is whether more is required in this pre-election hearing other than to determine whether the labor organization has petitioned for an election in a unit whose appropriateness is well-established under agency case

law, whether the agency has statutory jurisdiction in the particular case, and to mandate the sealing of any challenged ballots, including challenges based on eligibility issues. If the respondent believes that the facts of its case require some variance from well-established Board law, that matter, if properly preserved, could be taken up after the election in a second-stage pre-certification inquiry. Functionally, this pre-certification inquiry would be similar to the situation where the Board grants a request for review from the regional director's decision directing an election. Neither the request nor the grant of the request operates as a stay of the election. . . .

The problem of delay in representation cases may have less to do with the median cases than with highly contested cases. . . . The Board should study the characteristics of the cases that take the longest time. For example, in 2008, 12.4 percent of the cases took longer than the median time to go to election and took longer than three weeks from the election for the results to be certified. [I]n 284 of the 2,024 petitions that proceeded to election in 2008, allegations of employer violations triggered the filing of a "blocking charge" by a labor organization, delaying the holding of the election. The median for this subset was 139 days compared to thirty-eight days overall. To the extent the Board's blocking-charge policy is exploited by charging parties unreasonably to delay elections, the Board should reexamine that policy and hold elections sooner even in the face of outstanding unfair labor practices.

## C. OUSTING AN INCUMBENT UNION

Thus far, this chapter has been concerned with the means by which a union may obtain representational status. This section turns to the means by which a union, once it has obtained bargaining authority, may have that authority revoked, and the question of when the union's authority is subject to challenge by the employer, disaffected employees, or a rival union. As you read the following materials, keep in mind the issues that were raised earlier in the chapter, such as the strength of the Board's election preference in various contexts, the relevance or lack thereof of good faith, and the relationship between the rules governing union "entry" and "exit."

### 1. Bars to an Election

#### *a. The Certification, Election, and Recognition Bars*

**Brooks v. NLRB**
*348 U.S. 96 (1954)*

Frankfurter, J.

The [NLRB] conducted a representation election in petitioner's Chrysler-Plymouth agency on April 12, 1951. [Machinists'] District Lodge

No. 727 won by a vote of eight to five, and the Labor Board certified it as the exclusive bargaining representative on April 20. A week after the election and the day before the certification, petitioner received a handwritten letter signed by nine of the 13 employees in the bargaining unit stating: "We, the undersigned majority of the employees . . . are not in favor of being represented by Union Local No. 727 as a bargaining agent."

Relying on this letter . . . , petitioner refused to bargain with the union. The Labor Board found that petitioner had thereby committed an unfair labor practice in violation of §§8(a)(1) and 8(a)(5) . . . and the Court of Appeals for the Ninth Circuit enforced the Board's order to bargain. . . .

The issue before us is the duty of an employer toward a duly certified bargaining agent if, shortly after the election which resulted in the certification, the union has lost, without the employer's fault, a majority of the employees from its membership.

Under the original Wagner Act, the Labor Board was given the power to certify a union as the exclusive representative of the employees in a bargaining unit when it had determined, by election or "any other suitable method," that the union commanded majority support. §9(c). . . . In exercising this authority the Board evolved a number of working rules, of which the following are relevant to our purpose:

(a) A certification, if based on a Board-conducted election, must be honored for a "reasonable" period, ordinarily "one year," in the absence of "unusual circumstances."

(b) "Unusual circumstances" were found in at least three situations: (1) the certified union dissolved or became defunct; (2) as a result of a schism, substantially all the members and officers of the certified union transferred their affiliation to a new local or international; (3) the size of the bargaining unit fluctuated radically within a short time.

(c) Loss of majority support after the "reasonable" period could be questioned in two ways: (1) employer's refusal to bargain, or (2) petition by a rival union for a new election.

(d) If the initial election resulted in a majority for "no union," the election — unlike a certification — did not bar a second election within a year. [Since abrogated by §9(c)(3) — Eds.]

The Board uniformly found an unfair labor practice where, during the so-called "certification year," an employer refused to bargain on the ground that the certified union no longer possessed a majority. While the courts in the main enforced the Board's decision, they did not commit themselves to one year as the determinate content of reasonableness. The Board and the courts proceeded along this line of reasoning:

(a) In the political and business spheres, the choice of the voters in an election binds them for a fixed time. This promotes a sense of responsibility in the electorate and needed coherence in administration. These considerations are equally relevant to healthy labor relations.

(b) Since an election is a solemn and costly occasion, conducted under safeguards to [protect] voluntary choice, revocation of authority should occur by a procedure no less solemn than that of the initial designation. A petition or a public meeting—in which those voting for and against unionism are disclosed to management, and in which the influences of mass psychology are present—is not comparable to the privacy and independence of the voting booth.

(c) A union should be given ample time for carrying out its mandate on behalf of its members, and should not be under exigent pressure to produce hothouse results or be turned out.

(d) It is scarcely conducive to bargaining in good faith for an employer to know that, if he dillydallies or subtly undermines, union strength may erode and thereby relieve him of his statutory duties at any time, while if he works conscientiously toward agreement, the rank and file may, at the last moment, repudiate their agent.

(e) In situations, not wholly rare, where unions are competing, raiding and strife will be minimized if elections are not at the hazard of informal and short-term recall.

Certain aspects of the Labor Board's representation procedures came under scrutiny in the Congress that enacted the Taft-Hartley Act in 1947. . . . Congress was mindful that, once employees had chosen a union, they could not vote to revoke its authority and refrain from union activities, while if they voted against having a union in the first place, the union could begin at once to agitate for a new election. The [NLRA] was amended to provide that (a) employees could petition the Board for a decertification election, at which they would have an opportunity to choose no longer to be represented by a union [§9(c)(1)(A)(ii)]; (b) an employer, if in doubt as to the majority claimed by a union without formal election or beset by the conflicting claims of rival unions, could likewise petition the Board for an election [§9(c)(1)(B)]; (c) after a valid certification or decertification election had been conducted, the Board could not hold a second election in the same bargaining unit until a year had elapsed [§9(c)(3)]; (d) Board certification could only be granted as the result of an election [§9(c)(1)], though an employer would presumably still be under a duty to bargain with an uncertified union that had a clear majority. . . .

The Board continued to apply its "one-year certification" rule after the Taft-Hartley Act came into force, except that even "unusual circumstances" no longer left the Board free to order an election where one had taken place within the preceding 12 months. . . .

Petitioner contends that whenever an employer is presented with evidence that his employees have deserted their certified union, he may forthwith refuse to bargain. In effect, he seeks to vindicate the rights of his employees to select their bargaining representative. If the employees are dissatisfied with their chosen union, they may submit their own grievance to the Board. If an employer has doubts about his duty to continue bargaining, it is his responsibility to petition the Board for relief, while continuing to bargain in good faith at least until the Board has given some indication that his claim has merit. Although the Board may, if the facts warrant, revoke a certification or agree not to pursue a charge of an unfair labor practice, these are matters for the Board; they do not justify employer self-help or judicial intervention. The underlying purpose of this statute is industrial peace. To allow employers to rely on employees' rights in refusing to bargain with the formally designated union is not conducive to that end, it is inimical to it. Congress has devised a formal mode for selection and rejection of bargaining agents and has fixed the spacing of elections, with a view of furthering industrial stability and with due regard to administrative prudence. . . .

To be sure, what we have said has special pertinence only to the period during which a second election is impossible. But the Board's view that the one-year period should run from the date of certification rather than the date of election seems within the allowable area of the Board's discretion in carrying out congressional policy. . . . Otherwise, encouragement would be given to management or a rival union to delay certification by spurious objections to the conduct of an election and thereby diminish the duration of the duty to bargain. Furthermore, the Board has ruled that one year after certification the employer can ask for an election or, if he has fair doubts about the union's continuing majority, he may refuse to bargain further with it. This, too, is a matter appropriately determined by the Board's administrative authority. . . .

## *NOTES AND QUESTIONS*

**1. "Certification Year" vs. "Election Year" Bar: A Policy Gloss on §9(c)(3)?** Is the holding of *Brooks* mandated by §9(c)(3)? If not, does the Board's doctrine in this case advance the general purposes of the statute? Is the Board free to reverse its "certification year" approach and hold that a union's virtually irrebuttable presumption of majority status continues only for the one-year election bar stipulated in §9(c)(3)?

**2. The "Recognition Bar."** Recall that under *Linden Lumber*, page 323, an employer is under no obligation to recognize a union that demonstrates majority support via a card showing or any means other than a Board election. Assume, however, that the employer in *Brooks* had chosen to recognize the union based on a card showing. Assume further that a week later the employer received the letter described in the first paragraph of *Brooks*. Should the employer be able to withdraw recognition? If not, for how long should it be required to recognize and bargain with the union? See Keller Plastics Eastern, 157 N.L.R.B. 583, 587 (1966) (voluntary recognition constitutes bar to election for a "reasonable time" for parties to reach agreement on first contract).

In *Dana Corp.* (often referred to as *Dana/Metaldyne*), 351 N.L.R.B. 434 (2007), the Board modified its recognition bar principles and held that the recognition bar does not begin until the employer provides notice that it has recognized a union and a 45-day period runs that gives employees or a rival union an opportunity to petition for a secret ballot election. In 2011, however, the Board reversed *Dana/Metaldyne* and returned to its *Keller Plastics* reasonable period of time standard, which it now defines as "no less than 6 months after the parties' first bargaining session and no more than 1 year." Lamons Gasket, 357 N.L.R.B. 72 (2011).

**3. Starting the Recognition Year Only After Good-Faith Bargaining Begins.** If the employer refuses to bargain after a certification, should the certification year begin to run on the date of certification or on the date the employer agrees to commence good-faith bargaining? See Mar-Jac Poultry, 136 N.L.R.B. 785 (1962) (granting "the union a period of at least one year of actual bargaining from the date of the settlement agreement").

What if an employer withdraws recognition after the certification year has expired, but in so doing relies on an anti-union petition circulated and presented to the employer during the certification year? Is such a withdrawal lawful? Should it be? See Chelsea Indus., Inc., 331 N.L.R.B. 1648 (2000) (withdrawal unlawful under *Brooks*), enforced, 285 F.3d 1073 (D.C. Cir. 2002).

**4. Employer's Interest in Withdrawing Recognition?** Whose interests did the employer purport to rely on in withdrawing recognition in *Brooks*? How does the Court respond to this argument? Does the Court's response in any way suggest that only employees should be able to take action to oust an incumbent union? Do employers have a legitimate interest in being able to ascertain whether the union retains majority support or not? For further discussion of the decertification procedure, see infra pages 339-353.

**5. Employer Challenges Following the Certification Year.** After the certification year, the union's presumption of continuing majority status becomes rebuttable. What does the Court in *Brooks* indicate about the employer's ability to challenge the union's bargaining authority at that point? Is this a matter of statutory mandate or the Board's discretion?

### b. *The Contract Bar*

The Board's "contract bar" doctrine, which is designed to promote stable labor relations, generally bars an election among employees covered by a valid and operative collective agreement of reasonable duration.

**Requirements and Duration.** To operate as a bar, an agreement must be in writing and properly executed. See Appalachian Shale Prods. Co., 121 N.L.R.B. 1160 (1958). It must also contain "substantial terms and conditions of employment" sufficient "to stabilize the bargaining relationship," including a termination date. See Cind-R-Lite Co., 239 N.L.R.B. 1255 (1979); see, e.g., Stur-Dee Health Prods., 248 N.L.R.B. 1100 (1980) (bar effect given to agreement arising from established relationship and providing for grievance arbitration along with no-strike pledge, union security, and various fringe items, but leaving wages for arbitral determination).

A contract for a fixed term will bar a petition filed by a rival union or by employees seeking decertification for only three years even if the contract term is longer and contracts for a longer term are customary in the industry or geographic area involved. General Cable Corp., 139 N.L.R.B. 1123 (1962). However, the contracting employer and union are barred from filing a petition for the entire contract term. Montgomery Ward & Co., 137 N.L.R.B. 346 (1962).

**The "Window" and "Insulated" Periods.** A petition filed by a rival union, by the employer, or by employees seeking decertification generally must be filed in a narrow "window" or "open" period — no more than 90 days, but no less than 60 days, prior to the expiration date of the contract (or so much of its term as does not exceed three years). The 60-day period following the expiration of this 30-day window is referred to as the "insulated period." The purpose of this period is to give the parties 60 days to negotiate "free from the 'threat of overhanging rivalry and uncertainty.'" Deluxe Metal Furn. Co., 121 N.L.R.B. 995, 1001 (1958). Health care institutions have their own, slightly different "window" and "insulated" periods. See Trinity Lutheran Hosp., 218 N.L.R.B. 199 (1975) (120-90 day rather than 90-60 day window period, and insulated period of 90 days). After an agreement expires, petitions can once again be filed until a new contract is executed. Neither of these periods is mandated by the terms of the NLRA. Should the Board revisit these periods to facilitate decertification and rival union petitions? See Kye D. Pawlenko, Reevaluating Inter-Union Competition: A Proposal to Resurrect Rival Unionism, 8 U. Pa. J. Lab. & Emp. L. 651, 692-697 (2006).

**Premature Extension and Premature Recognition.** "Premature extension" of a prior agreement consists of its extension, with or without modifications, prior to the beginning of the insulated period as measured by the original agreement. Premature extensions do not bar an election if the petition is timely filed during the 30-day period as measured from the expiration term of the original agreement. If, however, a petition is filed after that point, the extended agreement will constitute a new three-year contract bar (assuming the new agreement is for at least three years). See Republic Aviation, 122 N.L.R.B. 998 (1959). In premature recognition cases involving personnel increases, the existing contract bars an election "if at least 30 percent of the complement employed at the time of the hearing had been employed at the time the contract was executed, and 50 percent of the job classifications in existence at the time of the hearing were in existence at the time the contract was executed." General Extrusion Co., 121 N.L.R.B. 1165, 1167 (1958).

**Lifting the Contract Bar**. In certain limited circumstances, the contract bar may be lifted during the life of the contract due to some change in the union's status—namely, schism, defunctness, or disclaimer. "Schism" exists when a local union seeks changes to its affiliation "in the context of a basic intraunion conflict over fundamental policy considerations, involving an entire international union or a federation of unions." Hershey Chocolate Corp., 121 N.L.R.B. 901, 906-07 (1958). A "defunct" union is one that is no longer able or willing to represent the employees; a temporary inability to function will not suffice. *Hershey Chocolate*, supra at 911-912. Finally, the contract bar will sometimes be lifted if a union affirmatively disclaims interest in continuing to represent the employees, even though it is capable of doing so. See American Sunroof Corp., 243 N.L.R.B. 1128 (1979). If, however, the Board determines that the disclaimer is the result of collusion between two unions, with the incumbent disclaiming interest in order to disavow an unfavorable contract and give another union a chance to negotiate a more favorable one, the contract bar will remain in place. Id.

**Withdrawals of Recognition During the Contract Term**. The "contract bar," strictly speaking, applies only to election petitions, not to employer withdrawals of recognition. The Board, however, has long held, with Supreme Court approval, that a union's continuing majority status is irrebuttably presumed during the term of a contract, up to a three-year maximum. See NLRB v. Burns Int'l Security Servs., Inc., 406 U.S. 272, 290 n.12 (1972); Auciello Iron Works, Inc. v. NLRB, 517 U.S. 781 (1996). In *Auciello,* after the union had accepted the employer's contract offer, the employer withdrew recognition based on evidence casting doubt on the union's majority status that it had gathered just *before* the union accepted the contract. The Court agreed with the Board that the withdrawal was unlawful in light of the new contract:

> As Auciello would have it, any employer with genuine doubt about a union's hold on its employees would be invited to go right on bargaining, with the prospect of locking in a favorable contract that it could, if it wished, then challenge. Here, for example, if Auciello had acted before the Union's telegram by withdrawing its offer and declining further negotiation based on its doubt (or petitioning for decertification), flames would have been fanned,

> and if it ultimately had been obliged to bargain further, a favorable agreement would have been more difficult to obtain. But by saving its challenge until after a contract had apparently been formed, it could not end up with a worse agreement than the one it had. The Board could reasonably say that giving employers some flexibility in raising their scruples would not be worth skewing bargaining relationships by such one-sided leverage, and the fact that any collective-bargaining agreement might be vulnerable to such a postformation challenge would hardly serve the Act's goal of achieving industrial peace by promoting stable collective-bargaining relationships. . . .

Id. at 789-790.

**The Special Case of Construction Industry Prehire Agreements.** Prehire agreements in the construction industry, see infra note 3, page 365, are treated differently from other collective bargaining agreements. Under John Deklewa & Sons, 282 N.L.R.B. 1375 (1987), enforced sub nom. Int'l Ass'n of Bridge Workers, Local 3 v. NLRB, 843 F.2d 770 (3d Cir. 1988), although §8(f) agreements are enforceable through §§8(a)(5) and 8(b)(3) of the Act, they do not erect a contract bar to decertification or other representation petitions. In *Deklewa,* the Board further ruled that upon the expiration of a §8(f) agreement, the union enjoys no presumption of continuing majority status, and either party may repudiate the §8(f) bargaining relationship. Compare, e.g., *Fall River Dyeing & Finishing,* infra page 761 (discussing presumption of continuing majority status that applies outside §8(f) context). For further discussion of *Deklewa,* including its mixed reception in the circuits, see McKenzie Engineering Co. v. NLRB, 303 F.3d 902 (8th Cir. 2002).

## 2. The Means of Ousting an Incumbent Union

The previous section made clear that a union may not be challenged during certain periods such as the certification year or the term of a collective bargaining agreement of three years or less. It also introduced the various means that may be used to challenge the union's majority status outside the certification and contract-bar periods. This section examines those means in greater detail. After a brief discussion of employee-initiated decertification petitions, it focuses on the rules governing employer attempts to oust an incumbent union, which have been closely examined (or reexamined) by both the Supreme Court and the NLRB in recent years.

### *Note: Employee-Initiated Decertification Petitions*

As discussed in *Brooks* and the notes following, employees may seek to oust their union via a decertification petition under §9(c)(1)(A)(ii). The petition must be supported by a 30 percent "showing of interest" — that is, evidence that 30 percent or more of the unit employees do not wish to be represented by the union.

Between 2004 and 2011 unions won only 40 percent of decertification elections. See Decertification Petitions, NLRB, http://www.nlrb.gov/news-outreach/graphs-data/petitions-and-elections/decertification-petitions-rd (average union win rate of 42% from 2011-2013). Roughly 50 percent of decertification petitions, however, never culminate in an election. See id.; see also William A. Krupman & Gregory I. Rasin, Decertification: Removing the Shroud, 30 Lab. L.J. 231, 231 (1979) (over half of petitions filed in 1967 and 1977 did not result in election). One reason nearly half of decertification petitions do not lead to an election is the Board's "blocking charge" policy, discussed supra page 233. Unions have a strong incentive to file unfair labor practice charges that will stave off an election that may well result in their ouster. Among the charges that unions may file are §8(a)(1) charges alleging that the employer either instigated or gave employees "more than ministerial aid" in connection with the filing of the petition. See Catherine Meeker, Note, Defining "Ministerial Aid": Union Decertification Under the National Labor Relations Act, 66 U. Chi. L. Rev. 999 (1999) (discussing law in detail, and asserting that Board is inconsistent both in stating and applying test for what constitutes "more than ministerial aid").

Recall also the contract-bar rules, which allow election petitions (including decertification petitions) to be filed only within a "90-60" window period before the contract's expiration (no more than 90 days before expiration, but no less than 60 days before), or else following expiration but before a new agreement has been reached. Note that the NLRB does not notify employees of the window period (or even of the existence of the decertification procedure); it is up to them to acquire the necessary information and to conform to the Board's requirements. Should the Board, in order to effectuate employee free choice, inform employees of their decertification rights and the specifics of the procedure? See Douglas Ray, Industrial Stability and Decertification Elections: Need for Reform, 1984 Ariz. St. L.J. 257, 259. If so, when should this be done: during the organizing campaign, or after the union is certified?

### Allentown Mack Sales & Service, Inc. v. NLRB
*522 U.S. 359 (1998)*

SCALIA, J., delivered the opinion of the Court.

Under longstanding precedent of the National Labor Relations Board, an employer who believes that an incumbent union no longer enjoys the support of a majority of its employees has three options: to request a formal, Board-supervised election, to withdraw recognition from the union and refuse to bargain, or to conduct an internal poll of employee support for the union. The Board has held that the latter two are unfair labor practices unless the employer can show that it had a "good faith reasonable doubt" about the union's majority support. We must decide whether the Board's standard for employer polling is rational and consistent with the National Labor Relations Act, and whether the Board's factual determinations in this case are supported by substantial evidence in the record.

# I

Mack Trucks, Inc., had a factory branch in Allentown, Pennsylvania, whose service and parts employees were represented by Local Lodge 724 of the International Association of Machinists and Aerospace Workers, AFL-CIO. Mack notified its Allentown managers in May of 1990 that it intended to sell the branch, and several of those managers formed Allentown Mack Sales, Inc., the petitioner here, which purchased the assets of the business on December 20, 1990, and began to operate it as an independent dealership. From December 21, 1990, to January 1, 1991, Allentown hired 32 of the original 45 Mack employees.

During the period before and immediately after the sale, a number of Mack employees made statements to the prospective owners of Allentown Mack Sales suggesting that the incumbent union had lost support among employees in the bargaining unit. In job interviews, eight employees made statements indicating, or at least arguably indicating, that they personally no longer supported the union. In addition, Ron Mohr, a member of the union's bargaining committee and shop steward for the Mack Trucks service department, told an Allentown manager that it was his feeling that the employees did not want a union, and that "with a new company, if a vote was taken, the Union would lose." 316 N.L.R.B. 1199, 1207 (1995). And Kermit Bloch, who worked for Mack Trucks as a mechanic on the night shift, told a manager that the entire night shift (then 5 or 6 employees) did not want the union.

On January 2, 1991, Local Lodge 724 asked Allentown Mack Sales to recognize it as the employees' collective-bargaining representative, and to begin negotiations for a contract. The new employer rejected that request by letter dated January 25, claiming a "good faith doubt as to support of the Union among the employees." Id., at 1205. The letter also announced that Allentown had "arranged for an independent poll by secret ballot of its hourly employees to be conducted under guidelines prescribed by the National Labor Relations Board." Ibid. The poll, supervised by a Roman Catholic priest, was conducted on February 8, 1991; the union lost 19 to 13. Shortly thereafter, the union filed an unfair-labor-practice charge with the Board.

The Administrative Law Judge (ALJ) concluded that Allentown was a "successor" employer to Mack Trucks, Inc., and therefore inherited Mack's bargaining obligation and a presumption of continuing majority support for the union. Id., at 1203. The ALJ held that Allentown's poll was conducted in compliance with the procedural standards enunciated by the Board in *Struksnes Construction Co.* [discussed at note 3, page 314], but that it violated §§8(a)(1) and 8(a)(5) of the National Labor Relations Act (Act) because Allentown did not have an "objective reasonable doubt" about the majority status of the union. The Board adopted the ALJ's findings and agreed with his conclusion . . . [and] ordered Allentown to recognize and bargain with Local 724. . . . [The Court of Appeals] enforced the Board's bargaining order, over a vigorous dissent. . . .

## II

Allentown challenges the Board's decision in this case on several grounds. First, it contends that because the Board's "reasonable doubt" standard for employer polls is the same as its standard for unilateral withdrawal of recognition and for employer initiation of a Board-supervised election (a so-called "Representation Management," or "RM" election), the Board irrationally permits employers to poll only when it would be unnecessary and legally pointless to do so. Second, Allentown argues that the record evidence clearly demonstrates that it had a good-faith reasonable doubt about the union's claim to majority support. Finally, it asserts that the Board has, sub silentio (and presumably in violation of law), abandoned the "reasonable doubt" prong of its polling standard, and recognizes an employer's "reasonable doubt" only if a majority of the unit employees renounce the union.[a]

. . . Allentown argues that it is irrational to require the same factual showing to justify a poll as to justify an outright withdrawal of recognition, because that leaves the employer with no legal incentive to poll. Under the Board's framework, the results of a poll can never supply an otherwise lacking "good faith reasonable doubt" necessary to justify a withdrawal of recognition, since the employer must already have that same reasonable doubt before he is permitted to conduct a poll. . . . While the Board's adoption of a unitary standard for polling, RM elections, and withdrawals of recognition is in some respects a puzzling policy, we do not find it so irrational as to be "arbitrary [or] capricious" within the meaning of the Administrative Procedure Act, 5 U.S.C. §706. The Board believes that employer polling is potentially "disruptive" to established bargaining relationships and "unsettling"

a. [The other prong of the standard at issue is the "loss-of-majority-in-fact" prong. See *Levitz* note, infra page 349. — Eds.]

to employees, and so has chosen to limit severely the circumstances under which it may be conducted. Texas Petrochemicals Corp., 296 N.L.R.B. 1057, 1061 (1989), enf'd as modified, 923 F.2d 398 (CA5 1991). The unitary standard reflects the Board's apparent conclusion that polling should be tolerated only when the employer might otherwise simply withdraw recognition and refuse to bargain.

It is true enough that this makes polling useless as a means of insulating a contemplated withdrawal of recognition against an unfair-labor-practice charge — but there is more to life (and even to business) than escaping unfair-labor-practice findings. An employer concerned with good employee relations might recognize that abrupt withdrawal of recognition — even from a union that no longer has majority support — will certainly antagonize union supporters, and perhaps even alienate employees who are on the fence. Preceding that action with a careful, unbiased poll can prevent these consequences. The "polls are useless" argument falsely assumes, moreover, that every employer will want to withdraw recognition as soon as he has enough evidence of lack of union support to defend against an unfair-labor-practice charge. It seems to us that an employer whose evidence met the "good-faith reasonable doubt" standard might nonetheless want to withdraw recognition only if he had conclusive evidence that the union in fact lacked majority support, lest he go through the time and expense of an (ultimately victorious) unfair-labor-practice suit for a benefit that will only last until the next election. . . . And finally, it is probably the case that, though the standard for conviction of an unfair labor practice with regard to polling is identical to the standard with regard to withdrawal of recognition, the chance that a charge will be filed is significantly less with regard to the polling, particularly if the union wins.

It must be acknowledged that the Board's avowed preference for RM elections over polls fits uncomfortably with its unitary standard; as the Court of Appeals pointed out, that preference should logically produce a more rigorous standard for polling. But there are other reasons why the standard for polling ought to be less rigorous than the standard for Board elections. For one thing, the consequences of an election are more severe: if the union loses an employer poll it can still request a Board election, but if the union loses a formal election it is barred from seeking another for a year. See 29 U.S.C. §159(c)(3). If it would be rational for the Board to set the polling standard either higher or lower than the threshold for an RM election, then surely it is not irrational for the Board to split the difference.

### III.

The Board held Allentown guilty of an unfair labor practice in its conduct of the polling because it "had not demonstrated that it held a reasonable doubt, based on objective considerations, that the Union continued to enjoy the support of a majority of the bargaining unit employees." 316 N.L.R.B. at 1199. We must decide whether that conclusion is supported by substantial evidence on the record as a whole. . . . Universal Camera Corp. v. NLRB, 340 U.S. 474 (1951). Put differently, we must decide whether on this record it would have been possible for a reasonable jury to reach the Board's conclusion. . . .

. . . A doubt is an uncertain, tentative, or provisional disbelief. . . . The question . . . , therefore, is whether . . . a reasonable jury could have found that Allentown lacked a genuine, reasonable uncertainty about whether Local 724 enjoyed the continuing support of a majority of unit employees. In our view, the answer is no. The Board's finding to the contrary rests on a refusal to credit probative circumstantial evidence, and on evidentiary demands that go beyond the substantive standard the Board purports to apply.

The Board adopted the ALJ's finding that 6 of Allentown's 32 employees had made "statements which could be used as objective considerations supporting a good-faith reasonable doubt" [and] seemingly also accepted . . . the ALJ's willingness to assume that the statement of a seventh employee . . . supported [such a] doubt. . . . And it presumably accepted the ALJ's assessment that "7 of 32, or roughly 20 percent of the involved employees" was not alone sufficient to create "an objective reasonable doubt of union majority support," id., at 1207. The Board did not specify how many express disavowals would have been enough to establish reasonable doubt, but the number must presumably be less than 16 (half of the bargaining unit), since that would establish reasonable *certainty*. Still, we would not say that 20% first-hand-confirmed opposition (even with no countering evidence of union support) is alone enough to *require* a conclusion of reasonable doubt. But there was much more.

For one thing, the ALJ and the Board totally disregarded . . . the statement of an eighth employee, Dennis Marsh, who said that "he was not being represented for the $35 he was paying." Ibid. The ALJ, whose findings were adopted by the Board, said that this statement "seems more an expression of a desire for better representation than one for no representation at all." Ibid. It seems to us that it is, more accurately, simply an expression of dissatisfaction with the union's performance—which could reflect the speaker's desire that the union represent him more effectively, but could also reflect the speaker's desire to save his $35 and get rid of the union. The statement would assuredly engender an uncertainty whether the speaker supported the union, and so could not be entirely ignored.

But the most significant evidence excluded from consideration . . . consisted of statements of two employees regarding not merely their own support of the union, but support among the work force in general. Kermit Bloch, who worked on the night shift, told an Allentown manager "that the entire night shift did not want the Union." Ibid. The ALJ refused to credit this, because "Bloch did not testify and thus could not explain how he formed his opinion about the views of his fellow employees." Ibid. Unsubstantiated assertions that other employees do not support the union certainly do not establish the fact of that disfavor. . . . But under the Board's enunciated test for polling, it is not the fact of disfavor that is at issue (the poll itself is meant to establish that), but rather the existence of a reasonable uncertainty on the part of the employer regarding that fact. On that issue, absent some reason for the employer to know that Bloch had no basis for his information, or that Bloch was lying, reason demands that the statement be given considerable weight.

Another employee who gave information concerning overall support for the union was Ron Mohr, who told Allentown managers that "if a vote was taken, the Union would lose" and that "it was his feeling that the employees did not want a union." Ibid. The ALJ again objected irrelevantly that "there is no evidence with respect to how he gained this knowledge." Id., at 1208. . . .

. . . [T]he issue here is not whether Mohr's statement clearly establishes a majority in opposition to the union, but whether it contributes to a reasonable uncertainty whether a majority in favor of the union existed. We think it surely does. Allentown would reasonably have given great credence to Mohr's assertion of lack of union support, since he was not hostile to the union, and was in a good position to assess antiunion sentiment. Mohr was a union shop steward for the service department, and a member of the union's bargaining committee; according to the ALJ, he "did not indicate personal dissatisfaction with the Union." 316 N.L.R.B. 1208. It seems to us that Mohr's statement has undeniable and substantial probative value on the issue of "reasonable doubt."

Accepting the Board's apparent (and in our view inescapable) concession that Allentown received reliable information that 7 of the bargaining-unit employees did not support the union, the remaining 25 would have had to support the union by a margin of 17 to 8 — a ratio of more than 2 to 1 — if the union commanded majority support. The statements of Bloch and Mohr would cause anyone to doubt that degree of support, and neither the Board nor the ALJ discussed any evidence that Allentown should have weighed on the other side. . . . Giving fair weight to Allentown's circumstantial evidence, we think it quite impossible for a rational factfinder to avoid the conclusion that Allentown had reasonable, good-faith grounds to doubt — to be uncertain about — the union's retention of majority support.

## IV

That conclusion would make this a fairly straightforward administrative-law case, except for the contention that the Board's factfinding here was not an aberration. Allentown asserts that, although "the Board continues to cite the words of the good faith doubt branch of its withdrawal of recognition standard," a systematic review of the Board's decisions will reveal that "it has in practice eliminated the good faith doubt branch in favor of a strict head count." ... The Board denies (not too persuasively) that it has insisted upon a strict head count, but does defend its factfinding in this case by saying that it has regularly rejected similarly persuasive demonstrations of reasonable good-faith doubt in prior decisions.

The Court of Appeals in fact accepted that defense, relying on those earlier, similar decisions to conclude that the Board's findings were supported by substantial evidence here. ...

The question arises, then, whether ... we ought to measure the evidentiary support for the Board's decision against the standards consistently applied rather than the standards recited. ...

A ... practice [of] divorcing ... the rule announced from the rule applied ... frustrates judicial review. ... An agency should not be able to impede judicial review, and indeed even political oversight, by disguising its policymaking as factfinding.

[Thus,] the Board must be required to apply in fact the clearly understood legal standards that it enunciates in principle, such as good-faith reasonable doubt. ... Reviewing courts are entitled to take those standards to mean what they say, and to conduct substantial-evidence review on that basis. ...

The Board can, of course, forthrightly and explicitly adopt counterfactual evidentiary presumptions (which are in effect substantive rules of law) as a way of furthering particular legal or policy goals — for example, the Board's irrebutable presumption of majority support for the union during the year following certification. The Board might also be justified in forthrightly and explicitly adopting a rule of evidence that categorically excludes certain testimony on policy grounds, without reference to its inherent probative value. ... That is not the sort of Board action at issue here, however. ...

... When the Board purports to be engaged in simple factfinding, ... it is not free to prescribe what inferences from the evidence it will accept and reject, but must draw all those inferences that the evidence fairly demands.

... Of course the Board is entitled to be skeptical about the employer's claimed reliance on second-hand reports when the reporter has little basis for knowledge, or has some incentive to mislead. But that is a matter of logic and sound inference from all the circumstances, not an arbitrary rule of disregard to be extracted from prior Board decisions. ...

We conclude that the Board's "reasonable doubt" test for employer polls is facially rational and consistent with the Act. But the Board's factual finding that Allentown Mack Sales lacked such a doubt is not supported by substantial evidence on the record as a whole. ...

Chief Justice Rehnquist, with whom Justice O'Connor, Justice Kennedy, and Justice Thomas join, concurring in part and dissenting in part.

I concur in the judgment of the Court and in Parts I, III, and IV. However, I disagree that the Board's standard is rational and consistent with the [Act], and I therefore dissent as to Part II. . . .

. . . [E]ven conceding some remaining value to polling, the Board . . . fails to address the basic inconsistency of imposing the same standard on two actions [polling and unilateral withdrawals of recognition] having dramatically different effects. . . . [T]he standard for unilateral withdrawals should surely be higher.

. . . [H]aving the same standard for RM elections and polls is [also irrational, because an] RM election is binding on a losing union for one year, . . . while a union losing a poll may petition for a Board election at any time. [This] suggest[s] the standard for polling should be lower. The Board's "avowed preference for RM elections," without . . . further . . . support, would not appear to justify a higher standard for polling. . . . [I]n any event, that the Board could perhaps justify a higher standard for polling does not mean that it is rational to have the two standards equal. . . .

JUSTICE BREYER, with whom JUSTICE STEVENS, JUSTICE SOUTER, and JUSTICE GINSBURG join, concurring in part and dissenting in part.

I concur in Parts I and II and dissent from Parts III and IV of the Court's opinion. In Parts III and IV, the Court holds unlawful an agency conclusion on the ground that it is "not supported by substantial evidence." . . . That question was not presented to us in the petition for certiorari. In deciding it, the Court has departed from the half-century old legal standard governing this type of review. See Universal Camera Corp. v. NLRB, 340 U.S. 474, 490-491 (1951). . . . And it has failed to give the kind of leeway to the Board's factfinding authority that the Court's precedents mandate. . . .

. . . The majority . . . take[s] issue with the ALJ's decision not to count in Allentown's favor . . . statements . . . made by employees Marsh, Bloch, and Mohr. The majority says that these statements required the ALJ and the Board to find for Allentown. I cannot agree.

Consider Marsh's statement . . . that "he was not being represented for the $35 he was paying." . . . The majority says that the ALJ was wrong not to count this statement in the employer's favor. . . . But the majority fails to mention that Marsh made this statement to an Allentown manager while the manager was interviewing Marsh to determine whether he would, or would not, be one of the 32 employees whom Allentown would re-employ. The ALJ, when evaluating all the employee statements, wrote that statements made to the Allentown managers during the job interviews were "somewhat tainted as it is likely that a job applicant will say whatever he believes the prospective employer wants to hear." 316 N.L.R.B. at 1206. In so stating, the ALJ was reiterating the Board's own normative general finding that employers should not "rely in asserting a good-faith doubt" upon "statements made by employees during the course of an interview with a prospective employer." [Citation omitted.] The Board also has found that "employee statements of dissatisfaction with a union are not deemed the equivalent of withdrawal of support for the union." Torch Operating Co., 322 N.L.R.B. 939, 943 (1997).... Either of these general Board findings (presumably known to employers advised by the labor bar), applied by the ALJ in this particular case, provides more than adequate support for the ALJ's conclusion that the employer could not properly rely upon Marsh's statement....

I do not see how, on the record before us, one could plausibly argue that these relevant general findings of the Board fall outside the Board's lawfully delegated authority. The Board in effect has said that an employee statement made during a job interview with an employer who has expressed an interest in a nonunionized work force will often tell us precisely *nothing* about that employee's true feelings. That Board conclusion represents an exercise of the kind of discretionary authority that Congress placed squarely within the Board's administrative and fact-finding powers and responsibilities.... Nor is it procedurally improper for an agency, ... drawing upon its accumulated expertise and exercising its administrative responsibilities[,] to use adjudicatory proceedings to develop rules of thumb about the likely weight assigned to different kinds of evidence.... Consider next Bloch's statement, made during his job interview ... that those on the night shift (five or six employees) "did not want the Union." ...

... The majority says that "reason demands" that Bloch's statement "be given considerable weight." But why? The Board, drawing upon both reason and experience, has said it will "view with suspicion and caution" one employee's statements "purporting to represent the views of other employees." [Citations omitted.]

How is it unreasonable for the Board to provide this kind of guidance, about what kinds of evidence are more likely, and what kinds are less likely, to support an "objective reasonable doubt" ... ? Why is it unreasonable for an ALJ to disregard a highly general conclusory statement such as Bloch's, a statement that names no names, is unsupported by any other concrete testimony, and was made during a job interview by an interviewer who foresees a nonunionized workforce? To put the matter more directly, how can the majority substitute its own judgment for that of the Board and the ALJ in respect to such detailed workplace-related matters, particularly on the basis of this record, where the question of whether we should set aside this kind of Board rule has not even been argued? ...

## *NOTES AND QUESTIONS*

**1. Successorship.** Note that *Allentown Mack* arose in the context of a "successorship" relationship, discussed fully infra in Chapter 9. Challenges to the union's majority status are particularly common in this context.

**2. The "Unitary" Standard?** Is it irrational for the Board to require the same showing for polling as for withdrawals of recognition? Should the Board be more lenient in allowing polling?

**3. Polling as Suspect Activity?** What is the policy reason for treating polling as problematic employer activity, even when conducted consistent with the *Struksnes* safeguards? Does the problem lie in the fact that the employer should not be able to control the timing of raising a question concerning the union's majority unless it has sufficient antecedent reasonable doubt? Does the problem lie more in the employer's ability to undermine the union's position by engaging in repeated polling? If the latter, are there other ways of dealing with repeated polls?

**4. Unfair Labor Practice vs. Election Routes.** Consider the "unitary standard" upheld in *Allentown Mack,* and factor in the Board's blocking charge policy, discussed supra page 233. Does this overall regulatory scheme tend to channel disputes about the union's majority status away from the election procedure and into the unfair labor practice procedure? Is this a desirable result? See Joan Flynn, A Triple Standard at the NLRB: Employer Challenges to an Incumbent Union, 1991 Wis. L. Rev. 653. See also discussion of *General Shoe* doctrine, supra page 262.

**5. Standard for Review of NLRB Factfinding?** Note the Court's reformulation of the Board's "good faith doubt" test, and in particular, its treatment of the Board's "categorical approach." Is Justice Scalia correct that if an agency purports to be engaged in a purely fact-based "totality of the circumstances" inquiry, it must assess each relevant piece of evidence in the context of the specific case and cannot simply disregard entire categories of evidence? Or is Justice Breyer correct that determining the weight to be given particular kinds of evidence — such as employee statements made in job interviews — is precisely the kind of determination that specialized agencies are expected to make, and to which courts should defer?

### *Note:* Levitz Furniture Co.: *Curbing Unilateral Withdrawal of Recognition by Employers*

Since its 1951 decision in Celanese Corp., 95 N.L.R.B. 664 (1951), the Board had held that absent a contract bar, an employer could withdraw recognition following the certification year by showing either that the union had in fact lost majority support, or that the employer had a good-faith reasonable doubt regarding the union's majority status. In Levitz Furniture Co. of the Pacific, 333 N.L.R.B. 717 (2001), the Board overruled *Celanese* and eliminated the "good faith doubt" defense construed by the

Supreme Court in *Allentown Mack*; it ruled that henceforward (the decision was not made retroactive), loss of majority in fact would be the only valid defense to an unlawful withdrawal of recognition charge. As for employer polls and RM elections, the Board stated that it was "adopt[ing] a different, more lenient standard for obtaining RM elections," the "reasonable uncertainty" standard, and that it would leave any reconsideration of the polling standard for a future Board. The Board also stated that its blocking charge policy would remain unaltered.

Perhaps most significantly, the *Levitz* Board declined to adopt the General Counsel's position, also advocated by the charging party union and the AFL-CIO, that elections should be made the sole means of ousting an incumbent union:

> [The General Counsel and the unions] contend that, having abandoned the *Joy Silk* rule with regard to [the grant] of initial recognition, the Board should follow an analogous course with respect to withdrawals of recognition. Under *Linden Lumber*, when a union seeks to change the status quo ante by demanding recognition, the employer may insist that the union prove its majority status in a Board election, irrespective of the employer's good faith. By analogy, the General Counsel and the unions urge that, when an employer seeks to change the status quo ante by withdrawing recognition, the union should be entitled to insist that its majority support first be tested in a Board election, again regardless of the employer's good faith.
>
> While we acknowledge the logic of this argument, as well as the possibility that the suggested approach might minimize litigation, we decline to adopt such a rule at this time. We agree with the General Counsel and the unions that Board elections are the preferred means of testing employees' support. But we anticipate that as a result of our decision today, employers will be likely to withdraw recognition only if the evidence before them clearly indicates that unions have lost majority support. Similarly, by adopting a "good-faith uncertainty" standard for processing RM petitions, we are lowering the showing necessary for employers to obtain elections and reducing the temptation to act unilaterally. Accordingly, we believe that the interests of employees and incumbent unions will be adequately protected by our ruling today. If future experience proves us wrong, the Board can revisit this issue.

## *NOTES AND QUESTIONS*

**1. The "Rules of the Game" Following *Levitz*?** Consider *Levitz* in conjunction with *Allentown Mack*.

a. *Withdrawals of Recognition.* How does the standard for withdrawals of recognition adopted in *Levitz* compare with prior Board law as described in *Allentown Mack*?

b. *RM Elections.* When the Board states that it is adopting a "more lenient" standard for RM elections — "reasonable uncertainty," or as the Board sometimes refers to it, "good faith uncertainty" — does it mean "more lenient" than the pre-*Levitz* standard for RM elections, or only "more lenient" than the new standard for withdrawals of recognition?

c. *Employer Polls.* The Board states that it will leave for another day the question of the proper evidentiary standard for employer polls. What, then, is the law *now*? Following *Levitz,* how does the polling standard compare to that for withdrawals of recognition and RM elections? What should be the standard for polling?

**2. Employer Incentives Following *Levitz*?** Consider the relationship among the evidentiary standards discussed above, as well as the Board's blocking charge policy. What incentives does *Levitz* hold out to an employer wishing to challenge the status of an incumbent union? How much of an improvement is *Levitz,* if any, over the "unitary standard"? Is the Board correct that *Levitz* is likely to greatly increase the use of its RM election procedure? Why or why not? Which means of challenging the union do you think that employers are most likely to rely upon following *Levitz,* and why?

**3. Effect of Filing of Petition on Employer's Bargaining Obligation.** As Member Hurtgen indicates, the filing of an RM petition does not in itself relieve the employer of its bargaining obligation; the status quo continues in effect. Cf. Dresser Indus., 264 N.L.R.B. 1088 (1982) (holding that mere filing of decertification petition does not authorize employer to cease bargaining or to delay execution of an agreement). How is this rule likely to affect the option chosen by the employer?

**4. Rejection of the "Elections-Only" Rule.** As noted, the *Levitz* Board declined to accept the "elections-only" rule advocated by the General Counsel, which is based on an analogy to *Linden Lumber,* supra page 323. Why did the Board reject this rule? Was its reasoning persuasive? Is Member Hurtgen correct that the blocking charge policy presents an insuperable barrier to the implementation of an "elections-only" rule? See Flynn, A Triple Standard, supra, at 699-704 (asserting that modification of blocking charge policy is necessary element of "elections-only" regime).

### *Note: Remedy for Unlawful Withdrawal of Recognition*

**1. Bargaining Order as an "Extreme Remedy"?** The Board's standard remedy for an unlawful withdrawal of recognition (whether an outright withdrawal or a withdrawal following a poll that is later found to be unlawful) is a cease-and-desist order and an order that the employer resume bargaining with the union. See Caterair Int'l, 322 N.L.R.B. 64 (1996). Although the issuance of an affirmative bargaining order has been the Board's standard remedy for over 50 years, id. at 65, it has encountered substantial resistance in the courts of appeals, especially the D.C. Circuit. See, e.g., Vincent Industrial Plastics, Inc. v. NLRB, 209 F.3d 727 (D.C. Cir. 2000); Lee Lumber & Bldg. Material v. NLRB, 117 F.3d 1454 (D.C. Cir. 1997) ("*Lee Lumber I*"); Exxel/Atmos v. NLRB, 28 F.3d 1243 (D.C. Cir. 1994). That court views such orders, which implicitly include a bar for a "reasonable period of time" on any challenge to the union's majority status (including an employee-initiated decertification petition), as an "extreme remedy" that must be justified on a case-by-case basis. See *Vincent Industrial,* 209 F.3d at 738 (order must be justified by "a reasoned analysis that includes an explicit balancing of . . . 1) the employees' §7 rights; 2) whether other purposes of the Act override the rights of employees to choose their bargaining representatives; and 3) whether alternative remedies are adequate to remedy the violations of the Act"). In *Caterair,* the Board acknowledged the court's position but reaffirmed its stance that this remedy should be routine because:

> In such cases, the Board's paramount concerns are to restore to the union the bargaining opportunity which it should have had in the absence of unlawful conduct and to prevent the possibility that the wrongdoing employer would ultimately escape its bargaining obligations as the result of the predictably adverse effects of its unlawful conduct on employee support for the union.

Caterair, 322 N.L.R.B. at 65 (quoting Williams Enterprises, Inc., 312 N.L.R.B. 937, 940 (1993)). What statutory value does the D.C. Circuit appear most concerned with here? What policy concern appears most important to the Board? Should a bargaining order be considered an "extreme remedy" in this situation?

**2. A "Reasonable Time" to Bargain After an Unlawful Withdrawal of Recognition?** In Lee Lumber & Bldg. Material Corp., 334 N.L.R.B. 399 (2001), enforced on other grounds, 310 F.3d 209 (D.C. Cir. 2002) ("*Lee Lumber II*"), the Board for the first time quantified the "reasonable period" of time during which, after an unlawful withdrawal of recognition has been found, the union's majority status cannot be challenged. That period is to be "no less than 6 months, but no more than 1 year." Whether the six-month minimum or a longer period will apply in a given case is to be judged by a multi-factor analysis focusing on "the need to give unions a fair chance to succeed in contract negotiations before their representative status can be challenged." The Board based the six-month minimum period both on its own judgment and on data from the FMCS indicating that six months is the typical amount of time needed to negotiate a renewal agreement.

In *Lee Lumber,* the Board stated that the newly defined period would "provide a measure of certainty" and help to minimize litigation. In light of these goals, should the Board have chosen a bright-line period rather than a six-month range? Should it also establish either a bright-line period or a *Lee*-type range for the "recognition bar" that applies in the voluntary recognition situation?

**3. Other Remedies for Unlawful Withdrawal of Recognition?** As will be discussed further in Chapter 6, where an employer has unlawfully refused to bargain in making unilateral downward changes in the employees' wages or working conditions, the remedy will include an order to make the employees whole for those changes. In the absence of such changes, what relief are employees due for the loss of their bargaining agent during an unlawful cessation of bargaining? What relief, if any, is the union entitled to for its wrongful loss of representative status? See Flynn, A Triple Standard, supra, at 681-682 (noting lack of remedy for either of these losses).

# 5 Obtaining Bargaining Authority Outside of the NLRB Election Process

Under §9, as the Supreme Court reaffirmed in *NLRB v. Gissel Packing Co.*, supra page 316, labor organizations can obtain authority to act as exclusive bargaining agents without NLRB elections when they are "designated" as representatives by a majority of employees in an appropriate unit. As *Gissel* recounts, the Board in its early years certified unions on the basis of majority card showings. Because of employer objections, questions about the reliability of the cards as indicators of employee preferences, and the Taft-Hartley amendments (which provided that certification could only follow from a Board election), the agency developed a policy preference for resolving representational disputes by elections. It has been common, however, both before and after the 1947 legislation and into the present, for labor organizations to obtain voluntary recognition from employers by demonstrating majority support through cards or other means. Believing that voluntary recognition promoted statutory goals favoring voluntarism and collective bargaining, the Board has never applied its election-preference policy to bar voluntary recognition of majority unions.

The practice of voluntary recognition has taken on even greater salience in recent years as many labor organizations have sought to bypass the Board's election machinery entirely by obtaining so-called "card check" agreements from employers promising to abide by the results of a card showing. These agreements often also require the parties not to disparage each other or to maintain "neutrality" during the card solicitation process and may even stipulate other terms governing bargaining in the event majority status is demonstrated. The legal issues arising from the negotiation and enforcement of card-check/neutrality agreements are explored further in this chapter. We begin with a discussion of the law governing when employers may voluntarily recognize labor organizations as exclusive bargaining agents for their employees.

## A. VOLUNTARY RECOGNITION

### 1. Bars to Voluntary Recognition

As the Supreme Court made clear in *NLRB v. Gissel Packing Co.*, the final part of which is excerpted below, under §9(a) exclusive bargaining agents can be "designated or selected for the purposes of collective bargaining by the majority of employees in a unit appropriate for such purposes. . . ." The term "selected" usually refers to selection through a secret-ballot election; the term "designated" refers to selection by less formal means, such as signatures on authorization cards or in some cases participating in a collective action indicating the preferences of the affected employees. During consideration of the Taft-Hartley amendments, an attempt was made to limit the employer's duty to bargain to union representatives certified through the NLRB process, but that proposal did not become law.

For an employer's voluntary recognition of a labor organization as a §9(a) exclusive bargaining agency to be lawful, the union must be a representative of the majority of employees in an appropriate unit. The appropriate-unit inquiry was addressed in Chapter 4 and is equally applicable here; materials on how the union demonstrates majority support will follow below. In addition to these requirements, for the recognition to be lawful, the employer must have hired a representative complement of its ultimate workforce, see General Extrusion Co., 121 N.L.R.B. 116 (1955). The *General Extrusion* doctrine formally applies only as a condition of a valid contract bar to an election should an agreement be executed, but its requirements apply also to premature voluntary recognitions, which raise issues of employer recognition of a minority union (discussed below). Moreover, an employer's recognition of a second union at a time when a question concerning representation ("QCR") cannot be raised due to the operation of the certification year of insulated bargaining, a valid contract bar, or the presence of an incumbent union enjoying a presumption of majority support will raise difficulties for the employer under §§8(a)(2) and 8(a)(1) and for the recognized union under §8(b)(1)(A), and will likely taint the recognized union's later acquisition of majority support.

### 2. Validity of Authorization Cards

**NLRB v. Gissel Packing Co.**
*395 U.S. 575 (1969); prior excerpts supra pages 283-286, 316-321*

Warren, C.J. . . .

Only in *General Steel* [one of the companion cases decided here] was there any objection by an employer to the validity of the cards and the manner in which they had been solicited, and the doubt raised by the evidence was resolved in the following manner. The customary approach of the Board in dealing with allegations of misrepresentation by the Union and misunderstanding by the employees of the purpose for which the cards were being solicited has been set out in Cumberland Shoe Corp., 144 N.L.R.B. 1268 (1963) and reaffirmed in Levi Strauss & Co., 172 N.L.R.B. No. 57, 68 L.R.R.M. 1338 (1968). Under the *Cumberland Shoe* doctrine, if the card itself is unambiguous (i.e., states on its face that the signer authorizes the Union to represent the employee for collective bargaining purposes and not to seek an election), it will be counted unless it is proved that the employee was told that the card was to be used *solely* for the purpose of obtaining an election.[4] In *General Steel*, the trial examiner considered the allegations of misrepresentation at length and, applying the Board's customary analysis, rejected the claims with findings that were adopted by the Board and are reprinted in the margin.[5]

On September 20, the Union notified petitioner that it represented a majority of its wire weavers, requested that the Company bargain with it, and offered to submit the signed cards to a neutral third party for authentication. After petitioner's president declined the Union's request a week later, claiming, inter alia, that he had a good faith doubt of majority status because of the cards' inherent unreliability, the Union petitioned, on November 8, for an election that was ultimately set for December 9. . . .

[The Court first reaffirms in Part III of its opinion that unions can establish a bargaining relationship by means other than a Board election; this part of the opinion is excerpted at pages 316-321.]

---

4. The cards used . . . unambiguously authorized the Union to represent the signing employee for collective bargaining purposes; there was no reference to elections. Typical of the cards was the one used in the Charleston campaign in *Heck's* [another of the companion cases], and it stated in relevant part:

> "Desiring to become a member of the above Union of the International Brotherhood of Teamsters, Chauffeurs, Warehousemen and Helpers of America, I hereby make application for admission to membership. I hereby authorize you, your agents or representatives to act for me as collective bargaining agent on all matters pertaining to rates of pay, hours, or any other conditions of employment."

5. "Accordingly, I reject Respondent's contention 'that if a man is told that his card will be secret, or will be shown only to the Labor Board for the purpose of obtaining election, that this is the absolute equivalent of telling him that it will be used "only" for purposes of obtaining an election.' . . .

"With respect to 97 employees . . . Respondent in its brief contends, in substance, that their cards should be rejected because each of these employees was told *one or more* of the following: (1) that the card would be used to get an election (2) that he had the right to vote either way, even though he signed the card (3) that the card would be kept secret and not shown to anybody except to the Board in order to get an election. For reasons heretofore explicated, I conclude that these statements, singly or jointly, do not foreclose use of the cards for the purpose designated on their face."

We next consider the question whether authorization cards are such inherently unreliable indicators of employee desires that, whatever the validity of other alternate routes to representative status, the cards themselves may never be used to determine a union's majority and to support an order to bargain. In this context, the employers urge us to take the step the 1947 amendments and their legislative history indicate Congress did not take, namely, to rule out completely the use of cards in the bargaining arena. . . .

The objections to the use of cards voiced by the employers and the Fourth Circuit boil down to two contentions: (1) that, as contrasted with the election procedure, the cards cannot accurately reflect an employee's wishes, either because an employer has not had a chance to present his views and thus a chance to insure that the employee choice was an informed one, or because the choice was the result of group pressures and not individual decision made in the privacy of a voting booth; and (2) that quite apart from the election comparison, the cards are too often obtained through misrepresentation and coercion which compound the cards' inherent inferiority to the election process. Neither contention is persuasive, and each proves too much. The Board itself has recognized, and continues to do so here, that secret elections are generally the most satisfactory—indeed the preferred—method of ascertaining whether a union has majority support. The acknowledged superiority of the election process, however, does not mean that cards are thereby rendered totally invalid, for where an employer engages in conduct disruptive of the election process, cards may be the most effective—perhaps the only—way of assuring employee choice. . . .

That the cards, though admittedly inferior to the election process, can adequately reflect employee sentiment when that process has been impeded, needs no extended discussion, for the employers' contentions cannot withstand close examination. The employers argue that their employees cannot make an informed choice because the card drive will be over before the employer has had a chance to present his side of the unionization issues. Normally, however, the union will inform the employer of its organization drive early in order to subject the employer to the unfair labor practice provisions of the Act; the union must be able to show the employer's awareness of the drive in order to prove that his contemporaneous conduct constituted unfair labor practices on which a bargaining order can be based if the drive is ultimately successful. . . . Further, the employers argue that without a secret ballot an employee may, in a card drive, succumb to group pressures or sign simply to get the union "off his back" and then be unable to change his mind as he would be free to do once inside a voting booth. But the same pressures are likely to be equally present in an election, for election cases arise most often with small bargaining units where virtually every voter's sentiments can be carefully and individually canvassed. And no voter, of course, can change his mind after casting a ballot in an election even though he may think better of his choice shortly thereafter.

The employers' second complaint, that the cards are too often obtained through misrepresentation and coercion, must be rejected also in view of the Board's present rules for controlling card solicitation, which we view as adequate to the task where the cards involved state their purpose clearly and unambiguously on their face. We would be closing our eyes to obvious difficulties, of course, if we did not recognize that there have been abuses, primarily arising out of misrepresentation by union organizers as to whether the effect of signing a card was to designate the union to represent the employee for collective bargaining purposes or merely to authorize it to seek an election to determine that issue. And we would be equally blind if we did not recognize that various courts of appeals and commentators have differed significantly as to the effectiveness of the Board's *Cumberland Shoe* doctrine to cure such abuses. . . .

We need make no decision as to the conflicting approaches used with regard to dual-purpose cards, for in each of the five organization campaigns in the four cases before us the cards used were single-purpose cards, stating clearly and unambiguously on their face that the signer designated the union as his representative. . . .

In resolving the conflict among the circuits in favor of approving the Board's *Cumberland* rule, we think it sufficient to point out that employees should be bound by the clear language of what they sign unless that language is deliberately and clearly canceled by a union adherent with words calculated to direct the signer to disregard and forget the language above his signature. There is nothing inconsistent in handing an employee a card that says the signer authorizes the union to represent him and then telling him that the card will probably be used first to get an election. . . . We cannot agree with the employers here that employees as a rule are too unsophisticated to be bound by what they sign unless expressly told that their act of signing represents something else. . . .

We agree, however, with the Board's own warnings in Levi Strauss & Co., 172 N.L.R.B. 732 and n.7 (1968), that in hearing testimony concerning a card challenge, trial examiners should not neglect their obligation to ensure employee free choice by a too easy mechanical application of the *Cumberland* rule. We also accept the observation that employees are more likely than not, many months after a card drive and in response to questions by company counsel, to give testimony damaging to the union, particularly where company officials have previously threatened reprisals for union activity in violation of §8(a)(1). We therefore reject any rule that requires a probe of an employee's subjective motivations as involving an endless and unreliable inquiry. . . . We emphasize that the Board should be careful to guard against an approach any more rigid than that in *General Steel.* And we reiterate that nothing we say here indicates our approval of the *Cumberland Shoe* rule when applied to ambiguous, dual-purpose cards. . . .

## *NOTES AND QUESTIONS*

**1. Inherent Dual Purpose of Authorization Cards?** The Court recognizes the presumptive validity of single-purpose authorization cards—cards that make clear that the signer is authorizing the union to act as his or her collective bargaining agent. (Consider here the text of the card quoted in footnote 4 of the opinion.) Is this an accurate characterization of such cards when in most cases the cards will be used as a showing of interest to support a petition for an election? Can we assume in this context that the greater includes the lesser—that an employee willing to authorize a union for collective bargaining purposes necessarily also supports the filing of a petition that gives the employee an opportunity to change his or her mind in a secret-ballot election?

In the interest of clear notice to employees of the import of their card signature, could the NLRB require unions seeking only an election to use a form of authorization card that limits the employee's authorization to the seeking of an election and that therefore could not be used as a basis for recognition? Under §9(c)(1)(A), the petition filed by the employees or any individual or labor organization must "alleg[e] that a substantial number of employees wish to be represented for collective bargaining. . . ." Does this mean that the Board does not have authority to hold an election under this provision without a "substantial number" of employees authorizing representation for collective bargaining purposes? What statutory objective would be served by such a restriction?

**2. Cutting Off Inquiry into Organizer Representations?** Why does the Court purport to cut off extended inquiry into what organizers said to obtain card signatures and what employees understood when they signed the cards? The Court states that none of the following representations undermines the validity of a single-purpose card: "(1) that the card would be used to get an election (2) that he had the right to vote either way, even though he signed the card (3) that the card would be kept secret and not shown to anybody except to the Board in order to get an election." Are these statements facially consistent with the text of the authorization card? Will the average employee be likely to understand that there will be circumstances where he will have authorized the union's bargaining role even if no election is ever held? In the context of card-check agreements, where the parties do not envision resort to NLRB elections, should the Board require a clear statement in the text of the authorization card that an election will not be held if the union is able to obtain signatures from a majority of the employees? Are the concerns raised by the Court in *Savair*, supra page 306, applicable here?

**3. Signing Cards for More than One Union.** The Board does not count as evidence of majority support authorization cards signed by employees who also have signed in support of another union. See Human Dev. Ass'n v. NLRB, 937 F.2d 657 (D.C. Cir. 1991). The agency, however, will count cards that repudiate cards previously signed for a rival union. See Wavecrest Home for Adults, 217 N.L.R.B. 227 (1975).

**4. Revocation Period?** To mitigate concerns about whether employees understand what they are signing and to allow employees an opportunity to discuss with each other the merits of the particular organizing drive, would it be desirable for the Board to rule that employees should be given a limited time period during which they could freely revoke their authorizations?

### 3. Requirement of Majority Status at the Time of Recognition

Outside of the construction industry, an employer may recognize and bargain with a union as exclusive bargaining agent for its employees only if the union is the representative of a majority of employees in an appropriate unit. In Chapter 3 we considered the role of §8(a)(2) in the statutory scheme and its impact on the modes of interaction between employers and employees. As the following case indicates, §8(a)(2) places significant restraints on an employer's relationship even with a fully independent labor organization.

**International Ladies' Garment Workers Union (Bernhard-Altmann) v. NLRB**
*366 U.S. 731 (1961)*

Clark, J.

. . . In October 1956 the petitioner union initiated an organizational campaign at Bernhard-Altmann Texas Corporation's knitwear manufacturing plant in San Antonio, Texas. No other labor organization was similarly engaged at that time. During the course of that campaign, on July 29, 1957, certain of the company's Topping Department employees went on strike in protest against a wage reduction. That dispute was in no way related to the union campaign, however, and the organizational efforts were continued during the strike. Some of the striking employees had signed authorization cards solicited by the union during its drive, and, while the strike was in progress, the union entered upon a course of negotiations with the employer. As a result of those negotiations, held in New York City where the home offices of both were located, on August 30, 1957, the employer and union signed a "memorandum of understanding." In that memorandum the company recognized the union as exclusive bargaining representative of "all production and shipping employees." The union representative asserted that the union's comparison of the employee authorization cards in its possession with the number of eligible employees [that] representatives of the company furnished it indicated that the union had in fact secured such cards from a majority of employees in the unit. Neither employer nor union made any effort at that time to check the cards in the union's possession against the employee roll, or otherwise, to ascertain with any degree of certainty that the union's assertion, later found by the Board to be erroneous, was founded on fact rather than upon good-faith assumption. The agreement, containing no union security provision, called for the ending of the strike and for certain improved wages and conditions of employment. It also provided that a "formal agreement containing these terms" would "be promptly drafted . . . and signed by both parties within the next two weeks."

Thereafter, on October 10, 1957, a formal collective bargaining agreement, embodying the terms of the August 30 memorandum, was signed by the parties. . . . It is not disputed that as of execution of the formal contract the union in fact represented a clear majority of employees in the appropriate unit. In upholding the complaints filed against the employer and union by the General Counsel, the Board decided that the employer's good-faith belief that the union in fact represented a majority of employees in the unit on the critical date of the memorandum of understanding was not a defense, "particularly where, as here, the Company made no effort to check the authorization cards against its payroll records." 122 N.L.R.B. 1289, 1292. Noting that the union was "actively seeking recognition at the time such recognition was granted," and that "the Union was [not] the passive recipient of an unsolicited gift bestowed by the Company," the Board found that the union's execution of the August 30 agreement was a "direct deprivation" of the nonconsenting majority employees' organizational and bargaining rights. Accordingly, the Board ordered the employer to withhold all recognition from the union and to cease giving effect to agreements entered into with the union; the union was ordered to cease acting as bargaining representative of any of the employees until such time as a Board-conducted election demonstrated its majority status, and to refrain from seeking to enforce the agreements previously entered.

At the outset, we reject as without relevance to our decision the fact that, as of the execution date of the formal agreement on October 10, petitioner represented a majority of the employees. As the Court of Appeals indicated, the recognition of the minority union on August 30, 1957, was "a fait accompli depriving the majority of the employees of their guaranteed right to choose their own representative." 280 F.2d, at 621. It is, therefore, of no consequence that petitioner may have acquired by October 10 the necessary majority if, during the interim, it was acting unlawfully. Indeed, such acquisition of majority status itself might indicate that the recognition secured by the August 30 agreement afforded petitioner a deceptive cloak of authority with which to persuasively elicit additional employee support. . . .

In their selection of a bargaining representative, §9(a) of the Wagner Act guarantees employees freedom of choice and majority rule. . . . In short, as we said in Brooks v. Labor Board, 348 U.S. 96, 103, the Act placed "a nonconsenting minority under the bargaining responsibility of an agency selected by a majority of the workers." Here, however, the reverse has been shown to be the case. Bernhard-Altmann granted exclusive bargaining status to an agency selected by a minority of its employees, thereby impressing that agent upon the nonconsenting majority. There could be no clearer abridgment of §7 of the Act, assuring employees the right "to bargain collectively through representatives of their own choosing" or "to refrain from" such activity. It follows, without need of further demonstration, that the employer activity found present here violated §8(a)(1). . . . Section 8(a)(2) of the Act makes it an unfair labor practice for an employer to "contribute . . . support" to a labor organization. The law has long been settled that a grant of exclusive recognition to a minority union constitutes unlawful support in violation of that section, because the union so favored is given "a marked advantage over any other in securing the adherence of employees." Labor Board v. Pennsylvania Greyhound Lines, 303 U.S. 261, 267. In the Taft-Hartley Law, Congress added §8(b)(1)(A) to the Wagner Act, prohibiting, as the Court of Appeals held, "unions from invading the rights of employees under §7 in a fashion comparable to the activities of employers prohibited under §8(a)(1)." 280 F.2d, at 620. It was the intent of Congress to impose upon unions the same restrictions which the Wagner Act imposed on employers with respect to violations of employee rights.

The petitioner, while taking no issue with the fact of its minority status on the critical date, maintains that both Bernhard-Altmann's and its own good-faith beliefs in petitioner's majority status are a complete defense. To countenance such an excuse would place in permissibly careless employer and union hands the power to completely frustrate employee realization of the premise of the Act—that its prohibitions will go far to assure freedom of choice and majority rule in employee selection of representatives.[11] We find nothing in the statutory language prescribing scienter as an element of the unfair labor practices here involved. The act made unlawful by §8(a)(2) is employer support of a minority union. Here that support is an accomplished fact. More need not be shown, for, even if

11. Although it is of no significance to our holding, we note that there was made no reasonable effort to determine whether in fact petitioner represented a majority of the employees.

mistakenly, the employees' rights have been invaded. It follows that prohibited conduct cannot be excused by a showing of good faith.

This conclusion . . . places no particular hardship on the employer or the union. It merely requires that recognition be withheld until the Board-conducted election results in majority selection of a representative. . . . We do not share petitioner's apprehension that holding such conduct unlawful will somehow induce a breakdown, or seriously impede the progress of collective bargaining. If an employer takes reasonable steps to verify union claims, themselves advanced only after careful estimate — precisely what Bernhard-Altmann and petitioner failed to do here — he can readily ascertain their validity and obviate a Board election. We fail to see any onerous burden involved in requiring responsible negotiators to be careful, by cross-checking, for example, well-analyzed employer records with union listings on authorization cards. Individual and collective employee rights may not be trampled upon merely because it is inconvenient to avoid doing so. Moreover, no penalty is attached to the violation. Assuming that an employer in good faith accepts or rejects a union claim of majority status, the validity of his decision may be tested in an unfair labor practice proceeding. If he is found to have erred in extending or withholding recognition, he is subject only to a remedial order requiring him to conform his conduct to the norms set out in the Act, as was the case here. No further penalty results. We believe the Board's remedial order is the proper one in such cases. . . .

[The opinion of Justice DOUGLAS, with whom Justice BLACK concurred, dissenting in part, is omitted.]

## *NOTES AND QUESTIONS*

**1. Ex Ante vs. Ex Post Authorization?** Why wasn't the majority support that the Garment Workers enjoyed as of the execution date of the bargaining agreement with the company a better indication of the employees' true preferences than the level of support the union had at the time of its recognition? At which point did the employees have more information about what the union could do for them? If collective bargaining was working at the later date, how were the purposes of the Labor Act served by the Board's ordering the cessation of recognition? If we are concerned about employers favoring particular unions through voluntary recognition and cooperative bargaining, why should we not be concerned about such favoritism whether or not the union starts off with a showing of majority support? See generally Samuel Estreicher, Freedom of Contract and Labor Law Reform: Opening Up the Possibilities for Value-Added Unionism, 71 N.Y.U. L. Rev. 827 (1996).

**2. Exit vs. Entry Rules?** Is the concern over the recognition of minority unions based on a fear of company-favored unions preempting independent unions? Or is it principally a product of the difficulties employees face in removing or "decertifying" an incumbent union? See supra pages 332-351. If the latter, would it be better to lower the barriers to decertification than to preclude employer favoritism at the initial recognition stage? For a proposal to amend the labor laws to allow employers and unions to negotiate "prehire" contracts and accretion agreements permitting recognition prior to a showing of majority support provided that the Board holds a secret-ballot "authorization" vote within a year after such recognition, see Samuel Estreicher, Labor Law Reform, supra, at 42-43.

**3. "Prehire" Contracts in the Construction Industry.** Section 8(f) of the Act, added in 1959, allows an employer engaged primarily in the building and construction industry to enter into a collective bargaining agreement with an independent (that is, not otherwise employer-supported) union *before* the union has demonstrated majority support. Such an agreement may also require membership in the union within seven days of employment. Section 8(f) further provides, however, that such prehire agreements shall not act as a bar to representation petitions (or to decertification petitions). The construction industry is given special treatment because of the short tenure of most jobs in the industry and the common use of union hiring halls. On the union's ability to convert from §8(f) status to §9 status, see Brian A. Caufield, Reversion to Conversion? The Board's Interpretation of the Interplay Between Sections 8(f) and 9(a) in the Construction Industry, 8 U. Pa. Lab. & Emp. L. 413 (2006).

**4. Voluntary Recognition Bar.** Assume that an employer has chosen voluntarily to recognize a union based on a card showing. Assume further that a week later the employer receives a letter signed by most of its employees disavowing representation by the union. Should the employer be able to withdraw recognition? If not, for how long should it be required to recognize and bargain with the union? In order to give a validly recognized union an opportunity to negotiate a contract free of challenges to its representation authority, the Board has long held that voluntary recognition erects a bar to an election or withdrawal of recognition for a "reasonable time." See Keller Plastics Eastern, 157 N.L.R.B. 583, 587 (1966). For an interesting case applying *Keller Plastics* where the employees filed a petition opposing representation before recognition occurred but after the card-counting arbitrator (designated by the parties) had completed his card check, see Baseball Club of Seattle Mariners, 335 N.L.R.B. 563 (2001).

Is the "recognition bar" policy required by the NLRA? In order to promote a preference for elections, could the Board rule that voluntarily recognized unions: (a) enjoy only a rebuttable presumption of continuing majority status until they achieve a collective bargaining agreement, or (b) enjoy no presumption whatsoever until that time? Would either of these positions conflict with other policies that the NLRB seeks to promote?

Should the recognition bar apply in a case where a union obtains bargaining authority pursuant to a card-check agreement? In *Dana Corp.* (often referred to as *Dana/Metaldyne*), 351 N.L.R.B. 434 (2007), discussed supra page 336, the Board modified its recognition bar principles and held that the recognition bar does not begin until the employer provides notice that it has recognized a union (to be filed with the Board) and a 45-day period runs that gives employees or a rival union an opportunity to petition for a secret ballot election. The Board subsequently returned to its earlier rule of barring election petitions for a reasonable period of time after voluntary recognition. Lamons Gasket, 357 N.L.R.B. No. 72 (2011). The *Lamons Gasket* Board altered the *Keller Plastics* rule "in one respect" by defining a reasonable period of time as "no less than 6 months after the parties' first bargaining session and no more than 1 year." The Board will now rely on the multifactor test set out in Lee Lumber & Building Material Corp., 334 N.L.R.B. 399 (2001), supra pages 352-353, to determine a reasonable period in each case and the General Counsel will have the burden of proof to establish that further bargaining should be required.

**5. Recognition Conditioned on a Subsequent Majority?** Would the Court have come out differently in *Bernhard-Altmann* if the employer's recognition of the union had been expressly conditioned on its subsequent demonstration of majority support? Would this have eliminated or minimized the "deceptive cloak of authority" that troubled the Court? Consider Majestic Weaving, 147 N.L.R.B. 859, 859-860 (1964), enforcement denied on other grounds, 355 F.2d 854 (2d Cir. 1966):

> . . . The majority support which Local 815 had on April 26, 1963, when the contract was signed, was an assisted majority. All cards signed up to that time were secured through the effort of Felter, who during this critical period of initial hiring . . . admittedly acted in a lead capacity for the general laborers then being hired and had the cooperation of the [employer] in his organizing efforts. . . .
>
> In addition, the [employer] in the meantime negotiated with Local 815, despite its minority status, as the exclusive representative of its employees. . . . As stated by the Supreme Court in the *Bernhard-Altmann* case, Section 9(a) of the Act "guarantees employees freedom of choice and majority rule." The Court also observed that there "could be no clear abridgment" of the section 7 right of employees than impressing upon a

> non-consenting majority an agent granted exclusive bargaining status. That is precisely what the [employer] did here, and the fact that it conditioned the actual signing of a contract with Local 815 on the latter achieving a majority at the "conclusion" of negotiations is immaterial. In the *Bernhard-Altmann* case an interim agreement without union-security provisions was the vehicle for prematurely granting a union exclusive bargaining status which was found objectionable . . . in this case contract negotiation following an oral recognition agreement was the method. We see no difference between the two in the effect upon employee rights. Accordingly, we hold that the [employer's] contract negotiation with a nonmajority union constituted unlawful support within the meaning of Section 8(a)(2) of the Act.

The Second Circuit rejected for lack of substantial evidence the §8(a)(2) violation premised on Felter's organizing activity that, the court believed, was not conducted on the employer's behalf. It also denied enforcement because the Board had announced a new rule—that the mere fact of negotiation with a nonmajority union constituted unlawful assistance—requiring overturning prior Board precedent (Julius Resnick, Inc., 86 N.L.R.B. 38 (1949)) without having undertaken rulemaking or providing proper notice to the employer in the General Counsel's complaint that it would be doing so. 355 F.2d at 859-862. Recall that the Supreme Court in *Bell Aerospace*, supra page 87, rejected the Second Circuit's effort in a later case to compel the agency to engage in rulemaking when it altered prior Board law.

Is the Board right, as it later stated, that "the premature grant of exclusive bargaining status to a union, even if negotiated on attainment of a majority before execution of a contract, is similar to formal recognition with respect to the deleterious effect upon employee rights"? 29 N.L.R.B. Ann. Rep. 69 (1964) (discussing *Majestic Weaving* rule). Was the problem in *Majestic Weaving* that the parties had not made clear to the employees that they were negotiating terms expressly conditioned on the union's obtaining majority support and that the employees could express their disapproval of those terms by withholding support from the union?

### *Note: The* Kroger *"After-Acquired" Facility Doctrine*

The Board has held that the parties to a collective bargaining agreement (CBA) may lawfully agree to "new facility" or "after-acquired facility" clauses whereby the CBA automatically extends to the new facility upon proof of the union's majority support among the affected employees. See Kroger Co., 219 N.L.R.B. 388 (1978). Whether unions will insist on such extension is often an issue in organizing campaigns. See, e.g., Crown Cork & Seal Co. v. NLRB, 36 F.3d 1130 (D.C. Cir. 1994), discussed supra pages 220-230.)

Even where the parties have not expressly conditioned application of the CBA to the new facility on proof of majority support, the Board will read that condition into the agreement as a matter of law. See *Kroger,* supra (implying majority status condition on the assumption that parties intended agreement to be lawful); Harte & Co., 278 N.L.R.B. 947 (1986) (given likelihood of movement of employees from old plant to new, employer may recognize union at new facility when it decides to move production from unionized plant there, even before hiring of employees).

Does *Kroger* permit the parties to negotiate a variation from their master agreement to apply to the new facility? Consider the following: General Motors (GM) decides to open a new car manufacturing facility using new production processes in Tennessee. GM enters into an agreement with the United Auto Workers (UAW), which represents most of its production workers at its other plants, stating that to ensure a fully qualified workforce, the new facility will hire all its production workers from other GM-UAW bargaining units. The contract also states that GM will recognize the UAW as the representative of the new facility's production workers, and sets forth a wage scale and certain other working conditions, but contains very different terms from the national GM-UAW agreement, including a "co-management" structure providing for union input in supervisory and managerial decisions of the company, the absence of a seniority clause to govern work assignments and vacation picks, and the absence of a termination date.

Does the agreement violate §8(a)(2)? The NLRB General Counsel declined to issue a complaint in this case, relying substantially on the *Kroger* doctrine and the fact that the employees at the Saturn plant were all previously laid-off UAW-represented employees from other GM plants. See NLRB Office of General Counsel, 1986 GCM LEXIS 112 (Advice Mem., June 2, 1986).

**Post-Agreement Authorization Elections?** Would *Bernhard-Altmann* and *Majestic Weaving* have come out differently if the parties had given the affected employees a secret-ballot opportunity to decide whether to authorize the bargaining agency and the agreement? Would the acceptability of the *Kroger* doctrine and the Saturn determination also be furthered by provision of a post-recognition authorization election? See generally Samuel Estreicher, Deregulating Union Democracy, 2000 Colum. Bus. L. Rev. 501; and his "Easy In, Easy Out": A Future for U.S. Workplace Representation, 98 Minn. L. Rev. 1615 (2014). Would requiring an authorization election discourage either employers or unions from entering into such agreements? If so, should this matter?

### *Note:* Dana II *Litigation*

In Dana Corp., 356 N.L.R.B. No. 49 (2010), petition for review denied, Montague v. NLRB, 698 F.3d 307 (6th Cir. 2012), commonly referred to as "*Dana II,*" the parties to an established collective bargaining relationship at several plants throughout the country negotiated a framework "Letter of Agreement" (LOA) governing organizing at certain of the employer's non-union plants. The General Counsel did not challenge the card-check and neutrality provisions; rather, he issued a complaint challenging Article 4 of the LOA because it "sets forth terms and conditions of employment to be negotiated in a collective bargaining agreement [before] Respondent Union obtain[ed] majority status as the exclusive bargaining representative of certain of Respondent Employer's employees." Article 4, expressly applicable to the situation "Following Proof of Majority," states in general language the principles that would inform future bargaining on particular substantive topics:

> That in the labor agreements bargained pursuant to this Letter, the following conditions must be included for the facility to have a reasonable chance to succeed and grow.
>
> Healthcare costs that reflect the competitive reality of the supplier industry and the product(s) involved.
> Minimum classifications.
> Team-based approaches.
> The importance of attendance to productivity and quality.
> Dana's idea program (two ideas per month and 80% implementation).
> Continuous improvement.
> Flexible Compensation.
> Mandatory overtime when necessary (after qualified volunteers) to support the customer.

The parties also agreed to submit to interest arbitration should they be unable to reach a first contract on their own following presentation of a card majority from employees at a particular plant. The Board (2-1) agreed with the ALJ that the General Counsel's complaint should be dismissed:

### Dana Corp.
*356 N.L.R.B. 49 (2010)*

. . . Although it is clear that an employer may not render unlawful support, "it is also clear—and the Board has so held with court approval—that a certain amount of employer cooperation with the efforts of a union to organize is insufficient to constitute unlawful assistance." Steak and Brew of Huntington, 205 N.L.R.B. 1025, 1031 (1973). "The quantum of employer cooperation which surpasses the line and becomes unlawful support is not susceptible to precise measurement. Each case must stand or fall on its own particular facts." Id. at 1031.

The Board and courts have long recognized that various types of agreements and understandings between employers and unrecognized unions fall within the framework of permissible cooperation . . .

An employer is . . . permitted to express to employees a desire to enter into a bargaining relationship with a particular union and, essentially, to inform employees that it will enter into a bargaining agreement upon proof of majority support. Coamo Knitting Mills, 150 N.L.R.B. 579 (1964).

Outside the Section 8(a)(2) context, the Board and courts have also considered and enforced agreements between employers and unrecognized unions. For example, an employer may agree that it will voluntarily recognize a union in the future if the union demonstrates majority support by means other than an election, including signed authorization cards. See, e.g., Snow & Sons, 134 N.L.R.B. 709, 710 (1961) (employer bound by agreement to honor results of card check), enfd. 308 F.2d 687 (9th Cir. 1962); Hotel & Restaurant Employees Local 217 v. J.P. Morgan Hotel, 996 F.2d 561 (2d Cir. 1993) (enforcing card-check and neutrality agreement pursuant to Sec. 301 of Labor-Management Relations Act). . . . Finally, a multifacility employer and a union may lawfully provide in a collective-bargaining agreement that the employer will recognize the union as the representative of, and apply the collective-bargaining agreement to, employees in facilities the employer acquires in the future [relying on *Kroger*].

. . . The General Counsel and the Charging Parties argue that *Majestic Weaving* creates a per se rule that negotiation with a union "over substantive terms and conditions of employment" is unlawful if it occurs before the union has attained majority support. Such negotiations, they contend, grant the union "privileged" status in the eyes of employees and present the sort of "fait accompli" prohibited by *Majestic Weaving*, because "give and take negotiations" resulting in an agreement like the one involved here amount to "tacit recognition" of the union.

We reject this broad reading of *Majestic Weaving*. Neither *Majestic Weaving*, nor the decision on which it rests, *Bernhard-Altmann*, compels a finding that the conduct at issue here violated Section 8(a)(2). . . .

Here, the LOA did no more than create a framework for future collective bargaining, if (as specified in the agreement) the UAW were first able to provide proof of majority status by means of a card-check conducted by a neutral third party. The LOA did not contain an exclusive-representation provision (the "vice" of the agreement in *Bernhard-Altmann*). Indeed, the LOA expressly prohibited Dana from recognizing the UAW without a showing of majority support. Only the negotiation of the LOA, and no other conduct, is alleged to be an unfair labor practice interfering with employee free choice.

The crux of the General Counsel's position is that the negotiation of the LOA itself precluded a truly free choice. That position has no real support in *Majestic Weaving* or *Bernhard-Altmann*. In those cases, a premature grant of exclusive recognition by the employer gave the union, in the Supreme Court's words, a "deceptive cloak of authority" as it sought employee support. But neither the negotiation of the LOA nor the Agreement itself can be equated with a grant of exclusive recognition as that concept has been long understood in our law.

That the LOA set forth certain principles that would inform future bargaining on particular topics — bargaining contingent on a showing of majority support, as verified by a neutral third party — is not enough to constitute exclusive recognition. The UAW did not purport to speak for a majority of Dana's employees, nor was it treated as if it did. On the contrary, the LOA unmistakably disclaimed exclusive recognition by setting forth the process by which such status could be achieved. Nothing in the LOA affected employees' existing terms and conditions of employment or obligated Dana to alter them. Any potential effect on employees would have required substantial negotiations, following recognition pursuant to the terms of the Agreement.[18] Nothing in the Agreement, its context, or the parties' conduct would reasonably have led employees to believe that recognition of the UAW was a foregone conclusion or, by the same token, that rejection of UAW representation by employees was futile.

The General Counsel's position is rooted in the assumption that any employer conduct having the potential to enhance an unrecognized union's status in the employees' eyes is unlawful. But that is contrary to our law. For example . . . an employer may negotiate nonexclusive "members-only" agreements, may agree to remain neutral in an organizing campaign, may agree to voluntarily recognize the union upon proof of majority support, and may state its preference for unionization. In each of those scenarios, the employer's cooperation with the union could enhance the union's prestige, yet none of them is unlawful.

All of the decisions relied upon by the General Counsel for the proposition that negotiation of the LOA amounted to "tacit recognition" are easily distinguishable. None involves a situation where recognition is attacked as unlawful under Section 8(a)(2). Rather, they involve employers that reviewed a union's proffered evidence of majority support and either began bargaining or agreed to bargain, but later denied that a legally binding recognition had occurred. Plainly, those circumstances are not present here. The UAW has not claimed majority status, let alone presented proof to Dana, and neither the UAW nor Dana claims that recognition has taken place. . . .

In practice, an employer's willingness to voluntarily recognize a union may turn on the employer's ability to predict the consequences of doing

---

18. Notably, under existing law, the LOA — even if it had granted exclusive recognition to the UAW — would not be sufficient to bar a petition for a Board election, given its limited scope and general provisions. Appalachian Shale Products Co., 121 N.L.R.B. 1160, 1163-1164 (1958) ("[T]o serve as a bar, a contract must contain substantial terms and conditions of employment deemed sufficient to stabilize the bargaining relationship; it will not constitute a bar if it is limited to wages only, or to one or several provisions not deemed substantial."). In *Bernhard-Altmann*, in contrast, the Supreme Court pointed out that the agreement at issue would have barred an election petition under the Board's contract-bar doctrine. 366 U.S. at 737 fn. 8.

so. . . . Categorically prohibiting prerecognition negotiations over substantive issues would needlessly preclude unions and employers from confronting workplace challenges in a strategic manner that serves the employer's needs, creates a more hospitable environment for collective bargaining, and—because no recognition is granted unless and until the union has majority support—still preserves employee free choice. . . .

The essential premise of the dissent is that employees, made aware of an agreement like the one at issue here, "could reasonably believe they had no choice but to agree to [union] representation." Our colleague offers no evidence in support of this hypothesis—and the evidence here certainly tends to refute it: a majority of the employees subsequently rejected the UAW. Where, as in this case, an agreement expressly requires a showing of majority support, as determined by a neutral third party, before the union can be recognized, and where no unfair labor practices have been committed, it is hard to believe that a reasonable employee—a rational actor presumed by federal labor law to be capable of exercising free choice—would feel compelled to sign a union-authorization card simply because the agreement prospectively addresses some substantive terms and conditions of employment. If anything, such an agreement tends to promote an informed choice by employees. They presumably will reject the union if they conclude (or suspect) that it has agreed to a bad deal or that it is otherwise compromised by the agreement from representing them effectively.

## *NOTES AND QUESTIONS*

**1. Distinguishing *Kroger*?** What are the differences, if any, from the standpoint of NLRA policy between the framework agreement sustained in the principal case and the extension of preexisting agreements to new facilities in *Kroger*?

**2. Employee Expression of Disquiet vs. "Deceptive Cloak of Authority."** Footnote 25 in *Dana II* states:

> According to the General Counsel's own proffer, . . . employees reacted to the news of the [LOA framework agreement] and the lack of detail provided about it by circulating an antiunion petition. Thus, far from giving the UAW a "deceptive cloak of authority," the announcement of the agreement appears to have mobilized employees against the UAW. Therefore, we find that the excluded evidence would not affect our decision that the LOA was lawful. At most, the exclusion was harmless error. . . .

Does this level of disquiet preclude the union's later acquisition of a "deceptive cloak of authority," as the Board majority suggests? The framework agreement in *Dana II* received considerable publicity and triggered litigation by the National Right to Work League. Is this likely to occur in other cases?

**3. Open Questions?** Consider Andrew M. Kramer & Samuel Estreicher, NLRB Allows Pre-Recognition Framework Agreements Between Employer and Labor Union, N.Y.L.J., Feb. 23, 2011, p. 4:

> Although the Board "leave[s] for another day the adoption of a general standard for regulating prerecognition negotiation between unions and employer," the constraints placed on pre-recognition framework agreements by decisions like *Majestic Weaving*, likely to be overturned if the current Board membership is unchanged, appear to have been lifted at least for now. . . .
>
> At least two important legal issues remain open. First, the Board will need to decide in a future case whether the pre-recognition framework agreement should be made readily available to the affected employees before they are asked to vote on unionization or solicited by the union to sign authorization cards. We believe such a requirement would be salutary because transparency and an informed vote by the employees are especially important in this context. A second issue is whether the union can enter into such a framework agreement with an employer with whom it has no prior relationship. Because the *Dana* majority did not rely on the *Kroger* doctrine, the absence of a preexisting relationship should not make a legal difference. Of course, the parties need to be careful to act in an above-board manner to minimize charges of unlawful assistance.

## 4. The Doctrine of Employer Neutrality

**Bruckner Nursing Home**
*262 N.L.R.B. 955 (1982)*

. . . In the spring of 1974, Local 144, Hotel, Hospital, Nursing Home & Allied Health Services Union, S.E.I.U., AFL-CIO (hereinafter referred to as Local 144), and Local 1115, Joint Board, Nursing Home and Hospital Employees Division (hereinafter referred to as Local 1115), began organizational activities at Respondent Employer's nursing home facility in New York, New York. In early September 1974, Local 144 notified the Employer that it possessed a majority of signed authorization cards, and a date was set for a card count. Shortly thereafter, Local 1115 sent a mailgram to the Employer which stated that it was engaged in organizational activity among the Employer's employees and that the Employer should not extend recognition to any other labor organization. On September 23, 1974, Local 1115 filed charges against the Employer and Local 144 alleging violations of Sections 8(a)(1) and 8(b)(1)(A) through interference with the employees' right to select a union of their choice.

The card count was conducted on September 27, 1974, by an extension specialist of the New York State School of Industrial and Labor Relations.

Thereafter, the extension specialist informed the Employer that Local 144 represented a majority of its employees. Local 144 subsequently requested negotiations, but the Employer refused pending the outcome of the unfair labor practice charges filed by Local 1115.

On November 29, 1974, the unfair labor practice charges filed by Local 1115 were dismissed by the Regional Director. Negotiations between Local 144 and the Employer commenced shortly thereafter and culminated in the execution of a collective-bargaining agreement on December 18, 1974. Local 1115 then filed, on March 7, 1975, the charges at issue in this proceeding.

On September 27, 1974, the date of the card check, Respondent Employer had approximately 125 people in its employ. At that time, Local 1115 had two authorization cards, while Local 144 possessed signed authorization cards from approximately 80 to 90 percent of the Employer's employees. No representation petition was filed on behalf of either labor organization in this proceeding.

With respect to the foregoing facts, the Administrative Law Judge found that Local 1115 possessed a "colorable claim" to representation herein based on its continuous efforts to obtain employee support during the fall of 1974, and the fact that it had actually obtained a few authorization cards. The Administrative Law Judge concluded that the Employer "by executing a collective-bargaining agreement . . . in the face of a real question concerning representation which had not been settled [by] the special procedures of the Act" had rendered unlawful assistance to Local 144 in violation of Section 8(a)(2) of the Act. In what has become a standard remedy in this type of setting, the Administrative Law Judge ordered that the Employer cease giving effect to the collective-bargaining agreement with Local 144, and further ordered the Employer to withdraw and withhold recognition from Local 144 unless and until it has been certified in a Board-conducted election.

In this and a companion case, RCA del Caribe, Inc., 262 N.L.R.B. No. 116 (1982) (Chairman Van de Water and Member Jenkins dissenting), we undertake a reevaluation of what has come to be known as the *Midwest Piping* doctrine [Midwest Piping & Supply Co., Inc., 63 N.L.R.B. 1060 (1945)], a rule which, in one form or another, has been part of Board law for over 35 years. In *RCA del Caribe,* we set forth a new policy with respect to the requirements of employer neutrality when an incumbent union is challenged by an "outside" union. In this case, we will focus our attention on initial organizing situations involving two or more rival labor organizations.

As originally formulated, the "*Midwest Piping* doctrine" was an attempt by the Board to insure that, in a rival union situation, an employer would not render "aid" to one of two or more unions competing for exclusive bargaining representative status through a grant of recognition in advance of a Board-conducted election. In *Midwest Piping* itself, the Board found that an employer gave unlawful assistance to a labor organization when the employer recognized one of two competing labor organizations, both of which had filed representation petitions, and both of which had campaigned extensively for the mantle of exclusive bargaining representative. In the context of that case, we held that the employer had arrogated the resolution of the representation issue, and that a Board-conducted election was the "best" means of ascertaining the true desires of employees. We further stated that employers presented with rival claims from competing unions (in the form of representation petitions) should follow a course of strict neutrality with respect to the competing unions until such time as the "real question concerning representation" had been resolved through the mechanism of a Board-conducted election. . . .

In subsequent decisions, the Board removed the requirement that a representation petition actually be filed, stating that a petition was not a prerequisite to the finding of a "real" or "genuine" question concerning representation. The removal of the prerequisite of a petition stemmed in part from the need to recognize the existence of a rival union contest even before formal invocation of the Board's election procedures so as to insure that those procedures would be available. . . . We defined the "interest" that a union must have to trigger the operation of the *Midwest Piping* doctrine as a "colorable claim," a claim that was not "clearly unsupportable" or a claim that was not "naked." . . .

Extending the *Midwest Piping* doctrine frequently allowed a minority union possessing a few cards to forestall the recognition of a majority union in an effort either to buy time to gather more support for itself or simply to frustrate its rivals. For instance, here, where one union enjoys overwhelming support and the other has but a few cards, collective bargaining would be delayed until the 8(a)(2) charge has been resolved and the results of a later Board-conducted election have been certified. This delay would occur simply because an employer has done what in the absence of a rival claimant it may (but by no means has to) do in recognizing a majority union based on authorization cards. Ironically, in this factual setting, invoking "employee free choice" to justify Board intervention would clearly impede and frustrate the expression of employee preference, as well as the collective-bargaining process. For here, where employees have made a free choice and the employer has recognized that choice, the ultimate aim of that choice — the establishment of a collective-bargaining relationship and the benefits flowing therefrom — could not be achieved because another union has a "colorable claim" to representation.

Meanwhile, circuit courts refused to enforce many of our decisions based on "modified" *Midwest Piping* violations. . . .

We have reviewed the Board's experience with *Midwest Piping* with a desire to accommodate the view of the courts of appeals in light of our statutory mandate to protect employees' freedom to select their bargaining representatives and in harmony with our statutory mandate to encourage collective bargaining. Having identified the difficult problems in this area, it is the Board's task to reconcile the various interests of policy and law involved in fashioning a rule which will give, as far as possible, equal consideration to each of those interests in the light of industrial reality. We have concluded that this task has not been accomplished through the modified *Midwest Piping* doctrine. Accordingly, we will no longer find 8(a)(2) violations in rival union, initial organizing situations when an employer recognizes a labor organization which represents an uncoerced, unassisted majority, before a valid petition for an election has been filed with the Board.[13] However, once notified of a valid petition, an employer must refrain from recognizing any of the rival unions. Of course, we will continue to process timely filed petitions and to conduct elections in the most expeditious manner possible, following our normal procedures with respect to intervention and placement of parties on the ballot.

Making the filing of a valid petition the operative event for the imposition of strict employer neutrality in rival union, initial organizing situations will establish a clearly defined rule of conduct and encourage both employee free choice and industrial stability. Where one of several rival labor organizations cannot command the support of even 30 percent of the unit, it will no longer be permitted to forestall an employer's recognition of another labor organization which represents an uncoerced majority of employees and thereby frustrate the establishment of a collective-bargaining relationship. Likewise, an employer will no longer have to guess whether a real question concerning representation has been raised but will be able to recognize a labor organization unless it has received notice of a properly filed petition.

On the other hand, where a labor organization has filed a petition, both the Act and our administrative experience dictate the need for resolution of the representation issue through a Board election rather than through employer recognition. When a union has demonstrated substantial support by filing a valid petition, an active contest exists for the employees' allegiance. This contest takes on special significance where rival unions are involved since there an employer's grant of recognition may unduly influence or effectively end a contest between labor organizations. . . .

In addition to avoiding potential undue influence by an employer, our new approach provides a satisfactory answer to problems created by execution of dual authorization cards. It is our experience that employees

---

13. Although an employer will no longer automatically violate Sec. 8(a)(2) by recognizing one of several rival unions before an election petition has been filed, we emphasize that an employer will still be found liable under Sec. 8(a)(2) for recognizing a labor organization which does not actually have majority employee support. International Ladies' Garment Workers' Union [Bernhard-Altmann Texas Corporation] v. N.L.R.B., 366 U.S. 731 (1961). This longstanding principle applies in either a single or rival union organizational context and is unaffected by the revised *Midwest Piping* doctrine announced in this case. . . .

confronted by solicitations from rival unions will frequently sign authorization cards for more than one union. Dual cards reflect the competing organizational campaigns. They may indicate shifting employee sentiments or employee desire to be represented by either of two rival unions. In this situation, authorization cards are less reliable as indications of employee preference. When a petition supported by a 30-percent showing of interest has been filed by one union, the reliability of a rival's expression of a card majority is sufficiently doubtful to require resolution of the competing claims through the Board's election process. . . .

Applying the principles outlined above to the facts of the instant case, it is clear that no petition was filed by either of the rival unions and that the Employer recognized a clear majority claimant in extending recognition to Local 144. Accordingly, inasmuch as no petition was filed and recognition was granted to a labor organization with an uncoerced, unassisted majority, we shall dismiss the instant complaint in its entirety.

## *NOTES AND QUESTIONS*

**1. The Board's Election-Preference Policy in the Rival Union Context.** Is the *Midwest Piping* doctrine, even as softened in *Bruckner*, consistent with the Board's recognition that Congress did not insist on elections as the only means by which unions could obtain majority status? If employers normally can recognize unions as exclusive representatives on the basis of valid authorization cards from a majority of employees, why should they not be able to do so when a second union is competing for bargaining authority? Consider the following account of the reasoning underlying the *Midwest Piping* rule:

> [The Board's] regulatory assumption, presumably reflecting the institution's accumulated expertise, is that the decision to opt for unionization vel non represents a deliberate, profound, fairly fixed position (absent employer ULPs undermining the environment for free choice), whereas an employee's choice of one union over another represents a relatively unstable, mutable, preference. In many rival union campaign situations, even if the most sophisticated and politically active employees are generally in favor of unionization, they may have not yet made a firm commitment to support one union over another. . . .
>
> . . . Thus, where employee preference for one union is not clear, employer recognition prior to the election could easily cause employees to vote differently . . . than they would have if the election campaign had continued without employer interference. . . .
>
> A second related, although often unstated, purpose of the *Midwest Piping* rule is to prevent the employer from distorting employee decisionmaking through control of the timing of his recognition in a rival union context. If

> the employer enjoys untrammeled freedom in choosing when to recognize one union over another, it will be in a position to control the organizational process. It can thus "observe the ebb and flow of fluctuating sentiment" and make "timely recognition of the favored union."

Samuel Estreicher & Suzanne Telsey, A Recast *Midwest Piping* Doctrine: The Case for Judicial Acceptance, 36 Lab. L.J. 14, 18-19 (1985) (endorsing the Board's modification of the *Midwest Piping* doctrine in *Bruckner*); see also Julius Getman, *Midwest Piping* Doctrine: An Example of the Need for Reappraisal of Labor Board Dogma, 31 U. Chi. L. Rev. 292, 307-308 (1964) (arguing that recognition of one of two rival unions is not likely to be more coercive of employee choice "than a direct statement of preference by the employer").

**2. The Costs of the *Midwest Piping* Doctrine**? *Midwest Piping* itself involved a situation where rival unions had both filed petitions for an election; in this context, the employer is required to be neutral in order to permit the Board's election process to proceed unimpaired. As *Bruckner* discusses, the Board in subsequent cases extended *Midwest Piping* to require employer neutrality even in the absence of a filing of a petition by the non-recognized union. To understand why this extension was resisted by the courts of appeals, consider the following example: An employer has 100 production employees. On December 1, Union *A* asks the employer for a bargaining session and tenders verifiable evidence that 60 production employees have signed valid authorization cards. On December 3, Union *B*, which has a reputation for more aggressive bargaining than Union *A*, tells the employer that while Union *A* has been organizing for a month, it has just begun and already has collected authorizations from 20 employees. Neither union has filed an election petition. On December 4, the employer recognizes Union *A* and within a few days enters into a three-year contract covering the production employees. Has the employer been able to choose the union it prefers and prevent the organizational process from reaching its final conclusion? Can the approach taken in *Bruckner* be justified as a bright-line rule that reduces the ability of rival unions with no real basis of support to delay the commencement of collective bargaining by filing unfair labor practice charges? Note that the pre-*Bruckner* rule would have triggered the Board's blocking charge policy, supra pages 233, thus not only forestalling collective bargaining with a majority union (as evidenced by a valid card showing) but also preventing an election from being held to resolve the representational issue. The courts of appeals generally have accepted *Bruckner*. See, e.g., Haddon House Food Prods., Inc. v. NLRB, 764 F.2d 182 (3d Cir. 1985); see also NLRB v. Katz's Deli, 80 F.3d 755, 768 (2d Cir. 1996).

**3. *Midwest Piping* and Rival Union Challenges to an Incumbent Union.** Should the filing of a valid representation petition by a second union permit an employer to cease bargaining with an incumbent union? Does such a petition present adequate grounds for overcoming the presumption of continuing majority status that ordinarily attaches to incumbent unions? See supra pages 339-353. Does the principle of employer neutrality *require* the cessation of bargaining? Does it make sense to speak of employer neutrality in this situation? If the challenging union prevails in the representation election after a new agreement has just been negotiated with the old union, should that agreement be enforceable? See RCA del Caribe, Inc., 262 N.L.R.B. 963 (1982) (holding that mere filing of a representation petition by a rival union does not permit an employer to cease bargaining, and any contract executed after the petition has been filed will be null and void if the challenging union wins the election).

**4. *Midwest Piping* and Decertification Petitions.** For a time the Board held that *Midwest Piping*'s duty of neutrality was triggered by a timely filing of a decertification petition. See Telautograph Corp., 199 N.L.R.B. 892 (1972), overruling Shea Chemical Corp., 122 N.L.R.B. 1027 (1958). The theory was that the employer and the incumbent union should not be able to influence the results of an impending decertification election by negotiating an unusually favorable agreement. As part of the Board's retrenching of its *Midwest Piping* policy, and in keeping with the Board's approach to rival union petitions, the agency's rule of over three decades' standing is that a decertification petition does not require the suspension of bargaining with the incumbent. The employer remains under a duty to bargain in good faith, see Dresser Indus., Inc., 264 N.L.R.B. 1088 (1982), subject to the actual-loss-of-majority exception recognized in *Levitz*, supra page 349.

**5. "Members' Only" Agreements and the Issue of Employer Favoritism.** As a general matter, the employer does not violate §8(a)(2) by dealing with a union on a "members only" basis as long such dealing does not constitute exclusive bargaining with that union. See Consolidated Edison Co, v. NLRB, 305 U.S. 197, 236-237 (1938):

> The Act contemplates the making of contracts with labor organizations. That is the manifest objective in providing for collective bargaining. Under §7 the employees of the companies are entitled to self-organization, to join labor organizations and to bargain collectively through representatives of their own choosing. The 80 per cent of the employees who were members of the Brotherhood and its locals, had that right. They had the right to choose the Brotherhood as their representative for collective bargaining and to have contracts made as the result of that bargaining. Nothing that the employers

had done deprived them of that right. Nor did the contracts make the Brotherhood and its locals exclusive representatives for collective bargaining. On this point the contracts speak for themselves. They simply constitute the Brotherhood the collective bargaining agency for those employees who are its members. . . . Upon this record there is nothing to show that the employees' selection as indicated by the Brotherhood contracts has been superseded by any other selection by a majority of employees of the companies so as to create an exclusive agency for bargaining under the statute, and in the absence of such an exclusive agency the employees represented by the Brotherhood, even if they were a minority, clearly had the right to make their own choice. . . .

**6. Card-Check/Neutrality Agreements and the Issue of Employer Favoritism.** The vast majority of card-check and neutrality agreements cover organizing only by the signatory union. Does the fact that an employer provides favorable treatment to a particular union violate §8(a)(2)? Should an employer's agreement to recognize the union based on a card showing or to refrain from negative campaigning against it constitute illegal "assistance" or "support" of that union under §8(a)(2)? Should it matter whether there is a rival union on the scene, or at least a potential rival? Can the Board assume, without more, that the employer would not extend similar arrangements to other unions? Is the employer required to offer to do so? To agree to such access on request?

### *Note: Card-Check and Neutrality Agreements*

As noted above, some unions, dissatisfied with the NLRB's election procedure, have made substantial efforts to bypass the Board by negotiating agreements with target employers providing for recognition upon presentation of a majority card showing ("card-check" arrangements) and/or to some alteration of traditional campaign rules through so-called "neutrality agreements." See generally James J. Brudney, Neutrality Agreements and Card Check Recognition: Prospects for Changing Paradigms, 90 Iowa L. Rev. 819 (2005); Roger C. Hartley, Non-Legislative Labor Law Reform and Pre-Recognition Neutrality Agreements: The Newest Civil Rights Movement, 22 Berkeley J. Emp. & Lab. L. 369 (2001); for a critical review of these developments, see Charles I. Cohen, Joseph E. Santucci, Jr. & Jonathan C. Fritts, Resisting Its Own Obsolescence—How the National Labor Relations Board Is Questioning the Existing Law of Neutrality Agreements, 20 Notre Dame J.L. Ethics & Pub. Pol'y 521 (2006); Jarol B. Manheim, The Death of a Thousand Cuts: Corporate Campaigns and the Attack on the Corporation (2000). An early comprehensive empirical study of these agreements is Adrienne E. Eaton & Jill Kriesky, Union Organizing Under Neutrality Card Check Agreements, 55 Indus. & Lab. Rel. Rev. 42 (2001) (drawing on 118 such agreements).

**1. Contents of the Agreements.** Card-check agreements have been in use since the enactment of the NLRA; they provide for recognition of the union once the employer or a neutral third party has confirmed that the union has obtained authorization cards from a specified percentage of the bargaining unit, which ranged from a simple majority to 65 percent in the Eaton-Kriesky sample. Eaton & Kriesky, supra at 48 & n.6. There is much greater variation in "neutrality" provisions. Some provide that neither party will state anything derogatory about the other party; this might include any management communication of opposition to the union. Others define neutrality as "neither helping nor hindering" the union's organizing effort. Some may permit management to communicate factual information to its employees concerning the union and the organizing drive, although in some instances only in response to employee inquiries. Over three-quarters in the Eaton-Kriesky sample set limits on union campaign tactics as well, for instance, by requiring not only that the employer keep its statements "pro-company," but that the union restrict itself to "pro-union" assertions. Id. at 47-48.

Card-check/neutrality agreements also commonly provide for greater union access to employees than the NLRA requires. (Recall the *Lechmere* case, supra page 144, and the material on access to the employee electorate, supra pages 265-275.) Two-thirds of the agreements in the Eaton-Kriesky sample provide for union access to the employer's property, and slightly over one-third provide for early access to employee rosters. Ninety percent of the agreements stipulate to a particular dispute resolution mechanism—usually arbitration—to resolve any disagreements over issues such as the composition of the bargaining unit or whether the parties had complied with the neutrality provisions.

**2. Obtaining an Agreement.** Unions have obtained card-check or neutrality agreements both from employers with whom they have an existing relationship, and those with whom they lack such a relationship. In either case, why would an employer agree to a card-check or neutrality agreement? Unions that lack a preexisting relationship with the employer may be able to obtain agreements by using their political connections. For instance, if a union has allies on a city council, it may be able to get legislation passed requiring city contractors or other entities that receive public funds to agree to union recognition based on a card check. Or, the union may be able to put together a coalition of community leaders (politicians, religious leaders, etc.) to pressure a company to enter into a card check or neutrality agreement. Or in some cases the union uses what is often termed a "corporate campaign"—some combination of a consumer and community boycott of the company's product, shareholder pressure on the company's management, and leverage with government regulators from whom the company may need permission to build a facility or change the level or nature of its services to the public.

Card-check or neutrality agreements with companies with whom the union already has a relationship are products of the collective bargaining process. A union obtains these agreements, which by definition involve the coverage of currently unorganized employees at the company or employees of facilities opened or acquired in the future, by using its economic leverage at the bargaining table, as possibly supplemented by political influence or a corporate campaign. The employer may acquiesce in order to avoid a threatened strike or corporate campaign, or as a tradeoff for concessions that it is seeking. Whether such agreements are "mandatory" or "permissive" subjects of bargaining is discussed infra pages 473-474.

**3. Effectiveness of Agreements?** One of Eaton and Kriesky's major findings was that card-check agreements, especially when supplemented by neutrality provisions, are more effective than neutrality-only agreements in achieving recognition for the union. They found that unions' success rate in organizing under neutrality-only agreements was 46 percent, no higher than their overall success rate in NLRB elections during the same time period. Eaton & Kriesky, supra at 51-52. In contrast, card-check-only campaigns resulted in recognition 63 percent of the time, and card-check with neutrality agreements 78 percent of the time, both well above the union success rate in Board elections. Id. at 52. Unions were particularly successful in organizing under card-check agreements that also provided for broad access to employee rosters or limited the campaign's duration. Id. at 53.

As to a union's ultimate goal — the negotiation of a collective bargaining agreement with the employer — unions that successfully organized under a card-check and/or neutrality agreement obtained a first contract nearly 100 percent of the time. Id. In contrast, studies of unions' overall success in obtaining a first contract have generally found much lower rates. See infra page 433-434 (reporting rates of 55-57 percent). The situations may not be entirely comparable because unions presumably target particular companies for card-check/neutrality agreements where they have special economic or other leverage that induces employers to come to terms with them.

**4. Enforceability of Agreements?** Card-check/neutrality agreements raise a number of interesting and difficult issues, in addition to those already discussed. Recall that, even after *Linden Lumber*, supra page 323, the Board's election-preference policy does not extend to agreements to abide by a poll or card check: An employer that agrees to honor the results of a poll or card check and then refuses to bargain after the union has made the requisite showing violates §8(a)(5). See Sullivan Elec. Co., 199 N.L.R.B. 809

(1972), enforced, 479 F.2d 1270 (6th Cir. 1973); Rockwell Int'l Corp., 220 N.L.R.B. 1262 (1975); Cam Indus., Inc., 251 N.L.R.B. 11 (1980), enforced, 666 F.2d 411 (9th Cir. 1982); supra page 327. What if a *union* that has entered into a card-check agreement attempts to abort the process and instead files an election petition with the Board? See Verizon Information Systems, 335 N.L.R.B. 558 (2001) (petition dismissed). The Board also requires employers to honor agreements to recognize the union as the representative of employees in "after-acquired" stores and to apply the collective bargaining agreement to them upon proof of majority support for the union. See Kroger Co., 219 N.L.R.B. 388 (1975), supra pages 367-368. What if a union agrees, as part of a card-check or neutrality agreement covering certain facilities, that it will not attempt to organize the employees at some other facility, but subsequently files a petition seeking to represent those employees? Should the Board defer to the agreement? See Lexington House, 328 N.L.R.B. 894 (1999) (dismissing petition as barred by parties' express agreement).

Do neutrality agreements, which often preclude employers from engaging in "anti-union" as opposed to "pro-employer" campaigning, run afoul of §8(c) or general federal labor policy? See Int'l Union, UAW v. Dana Corp., 278 F.3d 548, 558 (6th Cir. 2002) (rejecting argument that arbitral decision enforcing such agreement is contrary to federal labor policy as expressed in §8(c) because employer voluntarily agreed to neutrality provision); Hotel Employees, Restaurant Employees Union, Local 2 v. Marriott Corp., 961 F.2d 1464, 1470 & n.9 (9th Cir. 1992) (nothing in Act "suggests employers may not agree to remain silent during a union's organizational campaign—something an employer is certainly free to do in the absence of such an agreement"; §8(c) in no way suggests that employer's agreement not to express its views is unenforceable).

**5. When Employers Agree to Neutrality Agreements, Are They Providing a "Thing of Value" to Unions, in Violation of Section 302 of the Taft-Hartley Act?** In Mulhall v. Unite Here Local 255, 667 F.3d 1211 (11th Cir. 2012), the court concluded that a neutrality agreement can be "a thing of value" in some circumstances. The employer-union agreement at issue provided union representatives with access to the workplace during non-work hours, provided a list of employees and an agreement to remain neutral. In return, the union agreed to financially support a ballot initiative favorable to the employer. The court concluded that "a jury could find that [employer] assistance had monetary value" because the money the union spent on the ballot initiative could be viewed as "consideration for the organizing assistance." Other Courts of Appeals have held that promises by an employer to assist or avoid opposing a union's organizing campaign fall outside the scope of §302. See Adcock v. Freightliner LLC, 550 F. 3d 369 (4th Cir. 2008); Hotel Employees & Restaurant Employees Union, Local

57 v. Sage Hospitality Resources, LLC, 390 F. 3d 206 (3rd Cir. 2004). The Supreme Court initially agreed to review the *Mulhall* decision, but then dismissed the writ of certiorari as improvidently granted. Unite Here Local 355 v. Mulhall, 134 S. Ct. 594 (2013). Justice Breyer, writing for himself and Justices Sotomayor and Kagan, would have asked for additional briefing instead of dismissing the writ. One of the questions on which the dissenting justices would have sought briefing was whether LMRA §302 authorized a private right of action rather than simply criminal penalties.

## B. REGULATION OF ORGANIZATIONAL AND RECOGNITIONAL PICKETING

Can the leaders of a particular union, frustrated in organizational campaigns at several work sites by legal and illegal employer opposition, set up peaceful pickets around a plant that they wish to organize and demand recognition as the bargaining representative of the plant's employees as the condition for removing the pickets? Alternatively, can they use such picketing to pressure the employer to accept card-check/neutrality agreements?

It might seem that allowing such picketing would be inconsistent with the Act. If the union does not in fact have the allegiance of a majority of employees at the plant, employer recognition of the union would constitute illegal support of a minority union. Allowing recognitional picketing thus could force employers to choose between economic loss from the picketing and violation of the Act. Moreover, even if the union does have compelling evidence of majority support, at least since *Gissel* and *Linden Lumber* the Board and the courts have interpreted the Act to favor elections as the means of testing union support in the absence of independent unfair labor practices undermining fair election conditions.

The Wagner Act, however, did not include any union unfair labor practices, and even the Taft-Hartley Act, which secured the right of employees to refrain from collective bargaining and also delineated a number of union unfair labor practices, expressly proscribed recognitional picketing only when another union had been certified by the Board. See §8(b)(4)(C) (added 1947). In 1957, the Board interpreted the broadly worded §8(b)(1)(A) to prohibit recognitional picketing by minority unions, see Teamsters Union (Curtis Bros.), 119 N.L.R.B. 232 (1957), but this interpretation was rejected by the Supreme Court in NLRB v. Drivers Local No. 639, 362 U.S. 274 (1960).

However, in 1959, Congress in the Landrum-Griffin Act comprehensively addressed organizational and recognitional picketing by amending the NLRA to include §8(b)(7) as a new union unfair labor practice. That section is reviewed and interpreted in the following case.

**International Hod Carriers, Local 840 (*Blinne Construction*)**
*135 N.L.R.B. 1153 (1962), supplementing 130 N.L.R.B. 587 (1961)*

[On February 20, 1961, the Board, in a divided opinion, concluded that the respondent union had violated §8(b)(7)(C). The Board later granted the union's motion for reconsideration.]

... [I]t is essential to note the interplay of the several subsections of §8(b)(7), of which subparagraph (C) is only a constituent part.

The section as a whole, as is apparent from its opening phrases, prescribes limitations only on picketing for an object of "recognition" or "bargaining" (both of which terms will hereinafter be subsumed under the single term "recognition") or for an object of organization. Picketing for other objects is not proscribed by this section. Moreover, not all picketing for recognition or organization is proscribed. A "currently certified" union may picket for recognition or organization of employees for whom it is certified. And even a union which is not certified is barred from recognition or organization picketing only in three general areas. The first area, defined in subparagraph (A) of §8(b)(7), relates to situations where another union has been lawfully recognized and a question concerning representation cannot appropriately be raised.[5] The second area, defined in subparagraph (B), relates to situations where, within the preceding 12 months, a "valid election" has been held.

The intent of subparagraphs (A) and (B) is fairly clear. Congress concluded that where a union has been lawfully recognized and a question concerning representation cannot appropriately be raised, or where the employees within the preceding 12 months have made known their views concerning representation, both the employer and employees are entitled to immunity from recognition or organization picketing for prescribed periods.

... Deeply concerned with other abuses, most particularly "blackmail" picketing, Congress concluded that it would be salutary to impose even further limitations on picketing for recognition or organization. Accordingly, subparagraph (C) provides that even where such picketing is not barred by the provisions of (A) or (B) so that picketing for recognition or organization would otherwise be permissible, such picketing is limited to a reasonable period not to exceed 30 days unless a representation petition is filed prior to the expiration of that period. Absent the filing of such a timely

5. ... Subparagraph (A) represents a substantial enlargement upon the prohibition already embodied in §8(b)(4)(C) of the Taft-Hartley Act which merely insulates certified unions from proscribed "raiding" by rival labor organizations. Subparagraph (A) affords protection to lawfully recognized unions which do not have certified status, and also incorporates, in effect, the Board's contract-bar rules [see supra pages 337-339 — Eds.] relating to the existence of a question concerning representation.

petition, continuation of the picketing beyond the reasonable period becomes an unfair labor practice. On the other hand, the filing of a timely petition stays the limitation and picketing may continue pending the processing of the petition. Even here, however, Congress by the addition of the first proviso to subparagraph (C) made it possible to foreshorten the period of permissible picketing by directing the holding of an expedited election pursuant to the representation petition.

The expedited election procedure is applicable, of course, only in a §8(b)(7)(C) proceeding, i.e., where an 8(b)(7)(C) unfair labor practice charge has been filed. Congress rejected efforts to amend the provisions of §9(c) . . . so as to dispense generally with preelection hearings. Thus, in the absence of an 8(b)(7)(C) unfair labor practice charge, a union will not be enabled to obtain an expedited election by the mere device of engaging in recognition or organization picketing and filing a representation petition. And on the other hand, a picketing union which files a representation petition pursuant to the mandate of §8(b)(7)(C) and to avoid its sanctions will not be propelled into an expedited election, which it may not desire, merely because it has filed such a petition. In both the above situations, the normal representation procedures are applicable; the showing of a substantial interest will be required, and the preelection hearing directed in §9(c)(1) will be held. . . .

Subparagraphs (B) and (C) serve different purposes. But it is especially significant to note their interrelationship. Congress was particularly concerned, even where picketing for recognition or organization was otherwise permissible, that the question concerning representation which gave rise to the picketing be resolved as quickly as possible. It was for this reason that it provided for the filing of a petition pursuant to which the Board could direct an expedited election in which the employees could freely indicate their desires as to representation. If, in the free exercise of their choice, they designate the picketing union as their bargaining representative, that union will be certified and it will by the express terms of Section 8(b)(7) be exonerated from the strictures of that section. If, conversely, the employees reject the picketing union, that union will be barred from picketing for 12 months thereafter under the provisions of subparagraph (B).

The scheme which Congress thus devised represents what that legislative body deemed a practical accommodation between the right of a union to engage in legitimate picketing for recognition or organization and abuse of that right. One caveat must be noted. . . . The congressional scheme is, perforce, based on the premise that the election to be conducted under the first proviso to subparagraph (C) represents the free and uncoerced choice of the employee electorate. Absent such a free and uncoerced choice, the underlying question concerning representation is not resolved and, more particularly, subparagraph (B) which turns on the holding of a "valid election" does not become operative.

There remains to be considered only the second proviso to subparagraph (C). In sum, that proviso removes the time limitation imposed upon, and preserves the legality of, recognition or organization picketing falling within the ambit of subparagraph (C), where that picketing merely advises the public that an employer does not employ members of, or have a contract with, a union unless an effect of such picketing is to halt pickups or deliveries, or the performance of services. Needless to add, picketing which meets the requirements of the proviso also renders the expedited election procedure inapplicable. . . .

. . . [I]t is important to note that structurally, as well as grammatically, subparagraphs (A), (B), and (C) are subordinate to and controlled by the opening phrases of §8(b)(7). In other words, the thrust of all the §8(b)(7) provisions is only upon picketing for an object of recognition or organization, and not upon picketing for other objects. Similarly, both structurally and grammatically, the two provisos in subparagraph (C) appertain only to the situation defined in the principal clause of that subparagraph. . . .

[W]e . . . turn to a consideration of the instant case. . . .

. . . On February 2, 1960, all three common laborers employed by Blinne at the Fort Leonard Wood jobsite signed cards designating the Union to represent them for purposes of collective bargaining. The next day the Union demanded that Blinne recognize the Union as the bargaining agent for the three laborers. Blinne not only refused recognition but told the Union it would transfer one of the laborers, Wann, in order to destroy the Union's majority. Blinne carried out this threat and transferred Wann 5 days later, on February 8. Following this refusal to recognize the Union and the transfer of Wann the Union started picketing at Fort Wood. The picketing, which began on February 8, immediately following the transfer of Wann, had three announced objectives: (1) recognition of the Union; (2) payment of the Davis-Bacon scale of wages; and (3) protest against Blinne's unfair labor practices in refusing to recognize the Union and in threatening to transfer and transferring Wann.

The picketing continued, with interruptions due to bad weather, until at least March 11, 1960, a period of more than 30 days from the date the picketing commenced. The picketing was peaceful, only one picket was on duty, and the picket sign he carried read "C.A. Blinne Construction Company, unfair." The three laborers on the job (one was the replacement for Wann) struck when the picketing started.

The Union, of course, was not the certified bargaining representative of the employees. Moreover, no representation petition was filed during the more than 30 days in which picketing was taking place. On March 1, however, about 3 weeks after the picketing commenced and well within the statutory 30-day period, the Union filed unfair labor practice charges against Blinne, alleging violations of §8(a)(1), (2), (3), and (5). On March 22, the Regional Director dismissed the 8(a)(2) and (5) charges, whereupon the Union forthwith filed a representation petition under §9(c). . . . Subsequently, on April 20, the Regional Director approved a unilateral settlement agreement with Blinne with respect to the §8(a)(1) and (3) charges which had not been dismissed. In the settlement agreement, Blinne neither admitted nor denied that it had committed unfair labor practices. . . .

Respondent, urging the self-evident proposition that a statute should be read as a whole, argues that §8(b)(7)(C) was not designed to prohibit picketing for recognition by a union enjoying majority status in an appropriate unit. Such picketing is for a lawful purpose inasmuch as §8(a)(5) and 9(a) of the Act specifically impose upon an employer the duty to recognize and bargain with a union which enjoys that status. Accordingly, Respondent contends, absent express language requiring such a result, §8(b)(7)(C) should not be read in derogation of the duty so imposed.

There is grave doubt that the argument here made is apposite in this case. But, assuming its relevance, we find it to be without merit. To be sure, the legislative history is replete with references that Congress in framing the 1959 amendments was primarily concerned with "blackmail" picketing where the picketing union represented none or few of the employees whose allegiance it sought. Legislative references susceptible to an interpretation that Congress was concerned with the evils of majority picketing are sparse. Yet it cannot be gainsaid that §8(b)(7) by its explicit language exempts only "currently certified" unions from its proscriptions. . . . [S]uch a construction is consonant with the underlying statutory scheme which is to resolve disputed issues of majority status, whenever possible, by the machinery of a Board election. . . .

We turn now to the second issue, namely, whether employer unfair labor practices are a defense to an 8(b)(7)(C) violation. . . . [T]he Union argues that Blinne was engaged in unfair labor practices within the meaning of §8(a)(1) and (3) . . . ; that it filed appropriate unfair labor practice charges against Blinne within a reasonable period of time after the commencement of the picketing; that it filed a representation petition as soon as the 8(a)(2) and (5) allegations of the charges were dismissed; that the 8(a)(1) and (3) allegations were in effect sustained and a settlement agreement was subsequently entered into with the approval of the Board; and that, therefore, this sequence of events should satisfy the requirements of §8(b)(7)(C). . . .

. . . It seems fair to say that Congress was unwilling to write an exemption into §8(b)(7)(C) dispensing with the necessity for filing a representation petition wherever employer unfair labor practices were alleged. . . .

. . . Upon careful reappraisal of the statutory scheme we are satisfied that Congress meant to require, and did require, in an 8(b)(7)(C) situation, that a representation petition be filed within a reasonable period, not to exceed 30 days. By this device machinery can quickly be set in motion to resolve by a free and fair election the underlying question concerning representation out of which the picketing arises. This is the normal situation, and the situation which it is basically designed to serve.

There is legitimate concern, however, with the abnormal situation, that is, the situation where because of unremedied unfair labor practices a free and fair election cannot be held. We believe Congress anticipated this contingency also. Thus, we find no mandate in the legislative scheme to compel the holding of an election pursuant to a representation petition where, because of unremedied unfair labor practices or for other valid reason, a free and uncoerced election cannot be held. On the contrary, the interrelated provisions of subparagraphs (B) and (C), by their respective references to a "valid election" and to a "certif[ication of] results" presuppose that Congress contemplated only a fair and free election. Only after such an election could the Board certify the results and only after such an election could the salutary provisions of subparagraph (B) become operative.

In our view, therefore, Congress intended that, except to the limited extent set forth in the first proviso, the Board in 8(b)(7)(C) cases follow the tried and familiar procedures it typically follows in representation cases where unfair labor practice charges are filed. That procedure, as already set forth, is to hold the representation case in abeyance and refrain from holding an election pending the resolution of the unfair labor practice charges. Thus, the fears that the statutory requirement for filing a timely petition will compel a union which has been the victim of unfair labor practices to undergo a coerced election are groundless. No action will be taken on that petition while unfair labor practice charges are pending, and until a valid election is held pursuant to that petition, the union's right to picket under the statutory scheme is unimpaired.

On the other side of the coin, it may safely be assumed that groundless unfair labor practice charges in this area, because of the statutory priority accorded §8(b)(7) violations, will be quickly dismissed. Following such dismissal an election can be directed forthwith upon the subsisting petition, thereby effectuating the congressional purpose. Moreover, . . . a timely petition . . . on file will protect the innocent union, which through a mistake of fact or law has filed a groundless unfair labor practice charge, from a finding of an 8(b)(7)(C) violation. Thus, the policy of the entire Act is effectuated and all rights guaranteed by its several provisions are appropriately safeguarded. . . .

The facts of the instant case may be utilized to demonstrate the practical operation of the legislative scheme. Here the union had filed unfair labor practice charges alleging violations by the employer of §§8(a)(1), (2), (3), and (5). . . . General Counsel found the allegations of 8(a)(2) and (5) violations groundless. Hence had these allegations stood alone and had a timely petition been on file, an election could have been directed forthwith and the underlying question concerning representation out of which the picketing arose could have been resolved pursuant to the statutory scheme. The failure to file a timely petition frustrated that scheme.

On the other hand, the §8(a)(1) and (3) charges were found meritorious. Under these circumstances, and again consistent with uniform practice, no election would have been directed notwithstanding the currency of a timely petition; the petition would be held in abeyance pending a satisfactory resolution of the unfair labor practice charges. The aggrieved union's right to picket would not be abated in the interim and the sole prejudice to the employer would be the delay engendered by its own unfair labor practices. The absence of a timely petition, however, precludes disposition of the underlying question concerning representation which thus remains unresolved even after the §8(a)(1) and (3) charges are satisfactorily disposed of. Accordingly, to condone the refusal to file a timely petition in such situations would be to condone the flouting of a legislative judgment. Moreover, and most important, to impose a lesser requirement would fly in the face of the public interest which prompted that judgment.

Because we read §8(b)(7)(C) as requiring in the instant case the filing of a timely petition and because such a petition was admittedly not filed until more than 30 days after the commencement of the picketing, we find that Respondent violated §8(b)(7)(C). . . . As previously noted it is undisputed that "an object" of the picketing was for recognition. It affords Respondent no comfort that its picketing was also in protest against the discriminatory transfer of an employee and against payment of wages at a rate lower than that prescribed by law. Had Respondent confined its picketing to these objectives rather than, as it did, include a demand for recognition, we believe none of the provisions of §8(b)(7) would be applicable.[29] Under the circumstances here, however, §8(b)(7)(C) is applicable.

## *NOTES AND QUESTIONS*

**1. Employer's Charge as Prerequisite to Expedited Election.** As confirmed in *Blinne,* a union cannot obtain an expedited election by engaging in recognitional picketing unless the employer files a

29. . . . Section 8(b)(7) is directed only at recognition and organization picketing and not at picketing for other objects including so-called protest picketing against unfair labor practices. . . . It follows that a cease-and-desist order issued against picketing in violation of Section 8(b)(7) will enjoin only picketing for recognition, bargaining, or organization and will not be a bar to protest picketing against unfair labor practices. . . .

§8(b)(7)(C) charge. Is it clear that when a petition has been filed by the union or the employer, an employer may secure an expedited election by also filing a charge even though it does so at the beginning of the "reasonable period" provided for in §8(b)(7)(C)? What considerations will be relevant to an employer's decision to seek an expedited election? If recognitional picketing continues for more than 30 days without the filing of a petition, can an expedited election be secured? If not, what action can be taken to stop the picketing? See §10(*l*) of the Act.

**2. "Reasonable Period" of Time?** When should the Board find that a "reasonable period" of time for the filing of an election petition by a union picketing for recognition is less than 30 days? When the employer's economic losses are particularly severe? When the picketing is accompanied by violence? When the picketing has been intermittent, totaling more than 30 days? When unions take turns doing "relay picketing" at a common work site? See Cuneo v. United Shoe Workers, Joint Council No. 13, 181 F. Supp. 324 (D.N.J. 1960); Elliot v. Typographical Union No. 619, 45 L.R.R.M. 2400 (N.D. Okla. 1959); Int'l Union of Operating Engrs., Local 4 (Seaward Construction Co.), 193 N.L.R.B. 632 (1971); Int'l Bhd. of Elec. Workers, Local 113 (I.C.G. Elec., Inc.), 142 N.L.R.B. 1418 (1963); see also NVE Constructors, Inc. v. NLRB, 934 F.2d 1084, 1090-1091 (9th Cir. 1991).

**3. Recognitional Picketing and the Board's Election-Preference Policy.** Did the *Blinne* Board properly read §8(b)(7)(C) to cover recognitional picketing by unions that have majority support? Note that such picketing does not place employers in the dilemma of choosing between sustaining the economic impact of picketing and violating the Act by recognizing a minority union. Can the provision be read to exclude majority but uncertified unions from its reach? Does the Board's reading of §8(b)(7)(C), however, accord with the rule of *Linden Lumber* (decided 12 years after *Blinne*) that employers may lawfully insist that even unions whom they know to possess majority support seek a Board election? Does *Linden Lumber* in fact require the *Blinne* Board's reading of §8(b)(7)? Does the Board remain free to reverse *Linden* and alter its interpretation of §8(b)(7) to permit majority unions to engage in recognitional picketing as a means of discouraging employers from insisting on unnecessary elections to delay bargaining? If it can, should it do so?

**4. Unfair Labor Practice Protest Picketing.** Do you agree with the Board's holding in *Blinne* that while unfair labor practice charges are pending, and until a valid election is held, a union's right to picket for recognition should not be impaired by §8(b)(7)(C)? Consider the economic loss that an employer may suffer while the Board delays an election for the purpose of resolving pending unfair labor practice charges, many of which may not be meritorious. Might such losses cause economically weak employers to recognize minority unions? Would it be preferable for the Board to condition suspension of the expedited election called for by §8(b)(7)(C) on the union's abandonment of recognitional picketing? See Bernard D. Meltzer, Organizational Picketing and the NLRB: Five on a Seesaw, 30 U. Chi. L. Rev. 78, 87 (1962). Would this allow employers to escape both picketing and expedited elections by committing unfair labor practices against unions who had not yet achieved majority status and thus could not qualify for a *Gissel* bargaining order?

**5. The Requirement of a Recognitional or Organizational Object.** Note that, as explained in footnote 29 in *Blinne*, §8(b)(7) does not cover picketing that does not have a recognitional or organizational objective.

a. *Picketing by Incumbent Unions for Economic Concessions.* A union that has been recognized by an employer clearly may picket over particular economic demands that have been topics of bargaining. However, if a union wants to protest an employer's withdrawal of recognition during bargaining, will the union be subject to §8(b)(7)(C) if it is unable to make a meritorious §8(a)(5) charge that the employer had no adequate grounds to doubt the union's continuing majority support? What is the effect of *Levitz*, supra page 349, here? Is §8(b)(7) limited to initial contests for recognition? Compare Warehouse Emp., Local 570 (Whitaker Paper Co.), 149 N.L.R.B. 731 (1964) (§8(b)(7) reaches only picketing to gain initial acceptance of union as bargaining agent), with Penello v. Warehouse Employees Union, Local No. 575, 230 F. Supp. 900 (D. Md. 1964) (after General Counsel's rejection of §8(a)(5) charge, picketing became recognitional and subject to §8(b)(7)(C)). See also Soft Drink Workers Union Local 812 v. NLRB, 937 F.2d 684 (D.C. Cir. 1991) (Board may prohibit picketing after union loses a decertification election).

b. *Picketing to Protest Unfair Labor Practices.* Footnote 29 states that §8(b)(7) does not bar picketing to protest unfair labor practices, such as discriminatory discharges or coercive interrogations. Thus, picketing that demands only particular remedies for illegal employer actions, rather than general recognition and bargaining, does not require the filing of an election petition. The Board has held that a union can even picket to publicize unfair labor practice charges after they are settled and election objections have been overruled. See Teamsters General Local 200 (Bachman Furniture Co.), 134 N.L.R.B. 670 (1961). Does this seem a sensible interpretation of §8(b)(7)? Does unfair labor practice picketing place employers in the same dilemma as that created by recognitional picketing? Does it compromise the regulatory system's preference for elections to determine majority status? Is its indulgence nonetheless necessary given other available remedies?

c. *Picketing in Support of a Particular Demand Not Requiring Recognition.* Footnote 29 also suggests that picketing by an unrecognized union in support of a particular demand, such as the reinstatement of a discharged employee, may not be regulated by §8(b)(7) even in the absence of an unfair labor practice charge. As long as a union makes only particular remedial demands on an employer that can be satisfied without recognition of the union, its picketing is not covered by §8(b)(7) whether or not the actions protested were illegal. See also Waiters Local 500 (Mission Valley Inn), 140 N.L.R.B. 433 (1963). Is this limitation on the reach of §8(b)(7) in accord with the congressional purpose underlying that section? Is it good policy?

d. *"Area Standards" Picketing.* The Board has held since 1961 that "area standards" picketing—"picketing aimed at causing the picketed employer to adopt employment terms at his enterprise commensurate with those prevailing in his locale," Bernard Dunau, Some Aspects of the Current Interpretation of Section 8(b)(7), 52 Geo. L.J. 220, 227 (1964)—is not for recognitional purposes. See Hod Carriers, Local 41 (Calumet Contractors Ass'n), 133 N.L.R.B. 512 (1961) (§8(b)(4)(C) case); Houston Bldg. & Constr. Trades Council, 136 N.L.R.B. 321 (1962) (§8(b)(7)(C) case); see also New Otani Hotel & Garden, 331 N.L.R.B. 1078, 1079 (2000). Why would a union engage in a protest of substandard wages or working conditions without also trying to compel the employer to recognize it as a bargaining agent? Consider the economic constraints on unions that bargain with employers whose competitors are free of unions. Is allowing unions to use economic pressure to advance the objectives of "area standards" picketing consonant with the purposes of §8(b)(7)? Note that "area standards" picketing, like other picketing deemed not to be for a recognitional or organizational object, may be engaged in indefinitely, may elicit work stoppages by delivery personnel, and cannot be regulated by state law because of federal preemption.

e. *Worker-Center Picketing.* Worker centers, which advocate on behalf of workplace and other concerns of immigrant workers and other low-income individuals, often picket employers to protest an employer's behavior toward one or more of their constituents. These centers typically do not seek to become the employees' bargaining agent. Does §8(b)(7) reach some worker center picketing? Do centers picket for a recognitional or organizational object when they seek resolution of a grievance of a constituent? Worker centers and alternative labor groups are discussed supra, Chapter 14.

**6. Picketing to Obtain a Card-Check/Neutrality Agreement.** Is it clear that a union acts with the requisite recognitional or organizational object if the objective of the picketing is to obtain a card-check/neutrality agreement? Does it matter that such picketing seeks a process for determining representational status but does not itself seek recognition? Should the union's ultimate objective be determinative here?

**7. "Publicity" Proviso.** The second proviso to §8(b)(7)(C) covers picketing that has the purpose of truthfully advising consumers and others in the general public that an employer does not employ union members or have a contract with a union, as long as the effect of such picketing is not to induce any worker to refrain from performing any services.

a. *Application Outside Subparagraph (C)?* Less than a month after losing a certification election at a large grocery store, the union stations a few peaceful pickets around the customer entrances to the store announcing that the store does not have union employees and asking those sympathetic to unions not to shop there. The union does not picket delivery entrances and asks the local Teamsters union to continue to make deliveries. All deliveries are made. Has the union violated §8(b)(7)?

b. *First Amendment Considerations.* If the publicity proviso does not protect the picketing described in the above paragraph, is it constitutional to ban such picketing under §8(b)(7)? Consider the following argument:

> The meaning of free speech—and picketing is at least in part free speech—is that the firm and the union may both seek customer support by appealing for it. Accordingly, if the union's propaganda wins enough adherents among consumers, the business pinch that the firm and its employees may then feel may cause them to reconsider the wisdom of their nonunion preference. The employees may choose and the firm is free to persuade them to choose, union representation. If the employees prefer retention of their nonunion status to alleviation of the pinch, that too is their right, but it is just as much the right of the union to continue to persuade the consumers to shun the nonunion product.

Bernard Dunau, Some Aspects of Section 8(b)(7), supra, at 234. For an elaborate development of this argument in light of a Supreme Court decision protecting an economically coercive civil rights consumer boycott implemented in part through picketing, see Michael C. Harper, The Consumer's Emerging Right to Boycott: *NAACP v. Claiborne Hardware* and Its Implications for American Labor Law, 93 Yale L.J. 409, 448-453 (1984).

c. *Test for Labor "Effect."* In determining whether informational picketing is protected by the second proviso of §8(b)(7)(C), the NLRB, at least in the case of retail firms, has considered the actual impact on the business and has rejected a quantitative test based solely on the number of deliveries aborted or services withheld. See NLRB General Counsel Mem., 1992 WL 340643 (N.L.R.B.G.C.) (Oct. 30, 1992). The memorandum relied on a case in which the union picketed 18 stores for about 12 weeks and took steps to ensure no interruption of services. The Board held that three delivery stoppages, two work delays, and several delivery delays did not constitute the "effect" contemplated by the proviso, absent specific evidence that the picketing disrupted, interfered with, or curtailed the employer's business. Retail Clerks (Barker Bros. Corp. and Gold's, Inc.), 138 N.L.R.B. 478 (1962), enforced, 328 F.2d 431 (9th Cir. 1964).

**8. Recognitional Picketing and Prehire Agreements.** Does a construction industry union violate §8(b)(7)(C) if, without filing an election petition, it engages in recognitional picketing for more than 30 days to enforce compliance with a §8(f) prehire agreement? In NLRB v. Iron Workers Local 103 (Higdon Contracting Co.), 434 U.S. 335 (1978), the Court sustained the Board's finding of a violation. In the Board's view, until a union actually acquires majority support, §8(f) agreements are voidable pacts, and signatory unions are minority unions subject to the strictures of §8(b)(7). The Court found that this was a permissible, even if not required, reading of the Act, to which it owed deference.

**9. Why Do We Not See More Recognitional Picketing?** Would unions be wise to engage more routinely than they presently do in recognitional picketing as a means of protesting election results they believe were marred by serious unfair labor practices? Are they likely to be able to attract employees to engage in such picketing? Would such picketing by employees of the target employer be protected concerted activity? In any event, do unions need to use a target's employees for this purpose? Does the efficacy of recognitional picketing depend on the ability of the union to obtain the agreement of other unions to honor the picket line? Is this a function of the union density rate in the region? Are there contractual or other legal restrictions on the ability of other unions to honor such picket lines?

# 6 Regulation of the Process of Collective Bargaining

For the framers of the National Labor Relations Act, the statutory duty to bargain was essential to give effect to the declared preference of employees to be represented in collective bargaining by an organization of their own choosing. The right of workers to insist on collective bargaining was thought to impose a corollary obligation on an employer to meet with the designated representative of its employees and proceed to negotiate a collective agreement. Indeed, Senator Wagner's original bill did not contain an express duty to bargain, in the belief that the NLRB would establish such a duty as necessarily implied by the statutory scheme. See Irving Bernstein, The New Deal Collective Bargaining Policy 95 (1950); James A. Gross, The Making of the National Labor Relations Board: A Study in Economics, Politics, and the Law (1933-1937), at 136 (1974).

Viewed as a corollary of the employer's duty to recognize the workers' collective bargaining agent, the duty to bargain suggests certain process-based obligations. First, without the designated representative's consent, the employer may not deal with any other agent and presumably may not negotiate terms with employees on an individual basis. Second, the employer has to act in a way that suggests a serious regard for its workers' preference for collective bargaining. It has to make itself available for meetings to discuss terms and conditions of employment, and have representatives at that meeting who possess the authority to bind the employer. Moreover, once an agreement is reached, the employer must not unreasonably delay its execution. Following the Taft-Hartley amendments, the Act also imposes good faith bargaining obligations on the union.

The first issue we examine is the principle of exclusive bargaining agency, i.e., that the labor organization with majority support among the employees in an appropriate unit is an exclusive representative of all the employees in that unit.

## A. EXCLUSIVE REPRESENTATION: AN OVERVIEW

**J.I. Case Co. v. NLRB**
*321 U.S. 332 (1944)*

Jackson, J. . . .

The petitioner, J.I. Case Company, . . . from 1937 offered each employee an individual contract of employment. The contracts were uniform and for a term of one year. The Company agreed to furnish employment as steadily as conditions permitted, to pay a specified rate, which the Company might redetermine if the job changed, and to maintain certain hospital facilities. The employee agreed to accept the provisions, to serve faithfully and honestly for the term, to comply with factory rules, and that defective work should not be paid for. About 75% of the employees accepted and worked under these agreements.

. . . [T]he execution of the contracts was not a condition of employment, nor was the status of individual employees affected by reason of signing or failing to sign the contracts. It is not found or contended that the agreements were coerced, obtained by any unfair labor practice, or that they were not valid under the circumstances in which they were made.

While the individual contracts executed August 1, 1941 were in effect, a CIO union petitioned the Board for certification as the exclusive bargaining representative of the production and maintenance employees. On December 17, 1941 a hearing was held, at which the Company urged the individual contracts as a bar to representation proceedings. The Board, however, directed an election, which was won by the union. The union was thereupon certified as the exclusive bargaining representative of the employees in question. . . .

The union then asked the Company to bargain. It refused, declaring that it could not deal with the union in any manner affecting rights and obligations under the individual contracts while they remained in effect. It offered to negotiate on matters which did not affect rights under the individual contracts, and said that upon the expiration of the contracts it would bargain as to all matters. Twice the Company sent circulars to its employees asserting the validity of the individual contracts and stating the position that it took before the Board in reference to them.

The Board held that the Company had refused to bargain collectively, in violation of [NLRA] §8(5) . . . ; and that the contracts had been utilized, by means of the circulars, to impede employees in the exercise of rights guaranteed by §7 . . . , with the result that the Company had engaged in unfair labor practices within the meaning of §8(1). . . .

Contract in labor law is a term the implications of which must be determined from the connection in which it appears. Collective bargaining between employer and the representatives of a unit, usually a union, results in an accord as to terms which will govern hiring and work and pay in that unit. The result is not, however, a contract of employment except in rare cases; no one has a job by reason of it and no obligation to any individual ordinarily comes into existence from it alone. . . .

After the collective trade agreement is made, the individuals who shall benefit by it are identified by individual hirings. The employer, except as restricted by the collective agreement itself and except that he must engage in no unfair labor practice or discrimination, is free to select those he will employ or discharge. But the terms of the employment already have been traded out. There is little left to individual agreement except the act of hiring. This hiring may be by writing or by word of mouth or may be implied from conduct. In the sense of contracts of hiring, individual contracts between the employer and employee are not forbidden, but indeed are necessitated by the collective bargaining procedure.

But, however engaged, an employee becomes entitled by virtue of the Labor Relations Act somewhat as a third party beneficiary to all benefits of the collective trade agreement, even if on his own he would yield to less favorable terms. The individual hiring contract is subsidiary to the terms of the trade agreement and may not waive any of its benefits. . . .

Care has been taken in the opinions of the Court to reserve a field for the individual contract, even in industries covered by the [NLRA], not merely as an act or evidence of hiring, but also in the sense of a completely individually bargained contract setting out terms of employment, because there are circumstances in which it may legally be used, in fact, in which there is no alternative. Without limiting the possibilities, instances such as the following will occur: Men may continue work after a collective agreement expires and, despite negotiations in good faith, the negotiation may be deadlocked or delayed; in the interim express or implied individual agreements may be held to govern. The conditions for collective bargaining may not exist; . . . a majority of the employees may refuse to join a union or to agree upon or designate bargaining representatives, or the majority may not be demonstrable by the means prescribed by the statute, or a previously existent majority may have been lost without unlawful interference by the employer and no new majority have been formed. As the employer in these circumstances may be under no legal obligation to bargain collectively, he may be free to enter into individual contracts.

Individual contracts, no matter what the circumstances that justify their execution or what their terms, may not be availed of to defeat or delay the procedures prescribed by the National Labor Relations Act looking to collective bargaining, nor to exclude the contracting employee from a duly ascertained bargaining unit; nor may they be used to forestall bargaining or to limit or condition the terms of the collective agreement. . . . Wherever private contracts conflict with [the Act's policies], they obviously must yield or the Act would be reduced to a futility.

It is equally clear [that] . . . the individual contract cannot be effective as a waiver of any benefit to which the employee otherwise would be entitled under the [collective] agreement. The very purpose of providing by statute for the collective agreement is to supersede the terms of separate agreements of employees with terms which reflect the strength and bargaining power and serve the welfare of the group. Its benefits and advantages are open to every employee of the represented unit, whatever the type or terms of his preexisting contract of employment.

But it is urged that some employees may lose by the collective agreement, that an individual workman may sometimes have, or be capable of getting, better terms than those obtainable by the group and that his freedom of contract must be respected on that account. We are not called upon to say that under no circumstances can an individual enforce an agreement more advantageous than a collective agreement, but we find the mere possibility that such agreements might be made no ground for holding generally that individual contracts may survive or surmount collective ones. The practice and philosophy of collective bargaining looks with suspicion on such individual advantages. Of course, where there is great variation in circumstances of employment or capacity of employees, it is possible for the collective bargain to prescribe only minimum rates or maximum hours or expressly to leave certain areas open to individual bargaining. But except as so provided, advantages to individuals may prove as disruptive of industrial peace as disadvantages. . . . They are a fruitful way of interfering with organization and choice of representatives; increased compensation, if individually deserved, is often earned at the cost of breaking down some other standard thought to be for the welfare of the group, and always creates the suspicion of being paid at the long-range expense of the group as a whole. Such discriminations not infrequently amount to unfair labor practices. The workman is free, if he values his own bargaining position more than that of the group, to vote against representation; but the majority rules, and if it collectivizes the employment bargain, individual advantages or favors will generally in practice go in as a contribution to the collective result. We cannot except individual contracts generally from the operation of collective ones because some may be more individually advantageous. Individual contracts cannot subtract from collective ones, and whether under some circumstances they may add to them in matters covered by the collective bargain, we leave to be determined by appropriate forums under the laws of contracts applicable, and to the Labor Board if they constitute unfair labor practices.

. . . Hence we find that the contentions of the Company that the individual contracts precluded a choice of representatives and warranted refusal to bargain during their duration were properly overruled. It follows that representation to the employees by circular letter that they had such legal effect was improper and could properly be prohibited by the Board.

[The dissenting opinion of Justice Roberts is omitted.]

## *NOTES AND QUESTIONS*

**1. Holding of J.I. Case?** Did the Court simply hold that employers could not invoke contracts negotiated with individual employees as a justification for refusing to bargain, or for limiting the scope of bargaining, with the majority representative? Does the decision also stand for the broader proposition that absent the union's consent, employers may not deal directly with their individual employees over wages, hours, and working conditions, even where the employees are attempting to extract better terms than those negotiated by their exclusive representative? If so, what is the justification for such a rule? See also Medo Photo Supply Corp. v. NLRB, 321 U.S. 678 (1944) (employer may not negotiate a wage increase with individual employees represented by a union, even if negotiation is initiated by the employees).

**2. Exceptions to the Direct-Dealing Prohibition?** In the entertainment and sports industries, it is customary for the labor agreement to set minimum terms while allowing the employer to bargain with individual "talent" for terms above the union scale. Under *J.I. Case,* does such individualized bargaining require explicit authorization in the labor agreement? What if the union acquiesced to a well-established custom by not seeking to change it? Is *J.I. Case* different from the "talent" union context because of the absence of a practice of individual employment contracts in the typical industrial setting? Are there situations where even in the absence of such a custom, agreements with individual workers should be permitted because those workers possess key skills and are threatening to leave for other employment?

**3. Impact of Direct-Dealing Prohibition on Bargaining Positions?** To what extent does the rationale of *J.I. Case* prevent employers from insisting on proposals that envision further second-tier bargaining with individual employees? For instance, can an employer insist in bargaining on the following clause?

> The Company shall have the right to offer some retirement and/or separation incentives in amounts under terms and conditions, and for periods of time, that the Company shall in its sole discretion deem appropriate, and the Union waives the right to raise a dispute or arbitrate with respect thereto.

See Toledo Blade Co., 295 N.L.R.B. 626 (1989) (holding clause lawful under *American National Insurance,* infra page 417), reversed sub nom. Toledo Typographical Union No. 63 v. NLRB, 907 F.2d 1220, 1223 (D.C. Cir. 1990) (direct-dealing clause is different in kind from management rights clause where decisions are made unilaterally; "[b]y allowing the Employer to bargain directly with its employees, Toledo Blade's proposal would deprive the Union *pro tanto* of its central statutory role as their representative in dealing with the Employer"); Retlaw Broadcasting Co. d/b/a KJEO-TV, 324 N.L.R.B. 138 (1997) (adopting D.C. Circuit view), enforced, 172 F.3d 660 (9th Cir. 1999). For further discussion, see infra note 5b, page 407.

**4. Direct Dealing and Employer Communications.** Section 8(c) of the Act protects an employer's right to communicate its views about labor issues, presumably including bargaining proposals, to employees in a noncoercive fashion. Does there come a point, however, where this right collides with the prohibition against direct dealing? For instance, may an employer lawfully communicate its proposal and arguments in support of its acceptance to employees before the union has had a chance to consider the proposal? See Americare Pine Lodging Nursing and Rehabilitation Center, 325 N.L.R.B. 98, 103-104 (1997) (simultaneous communication of offer to union and employees constitutes direct dealing, because union had no meaningful opportunity to consider proposal first), enforcement denied in relevant part, 164 F.3d 867, 876-877 (4th Cir. 1999) (finding "no support" in the Act for Board's interpretation). May an employer directly solicit employees' views about wages or working conditions before formulating its contract proposal or in the course of negotiations? See, e.g., Ryan Iron Works, Inc. v. NLRB, 257 F.3d 1, 7 (4th Cir. 2001) (company president's solicitation of employees' views on "laundry list of issues" that were subject of negotiations was unlawful attempt to "gain intelligence on employees' views and to gauge the level of support for a particular position, [thus] undermining the [union's] exclusive right to perform these functions"). The essence of direct dealing was described in NLRB v. General Elec., 418 F.2d 736, 759 (2d Cir. 1969), discussed further infra pages 428-429, as follows: "The fundamental inquiry . . . is whether the employer has chosen to deal with the Union through the employees, rather than with the employees through the Union."

### *Note: Nonmajority Collective Bargaining*

Where there is no majority representative, an employer does not violate the NLRA by agreeing to negotiate a "members only" agreement with a labor organization representing less than a majority of the workers in an appropriate unit. See Consolidated Edison Co. v. NLRB, 305 U.S. 197 (1938). Indeed, such agreements were common in the Act's very early days. See Charles J. Morris, The Blue Eagle at Work: Reclaiming Democratic Rights in the American Workplace 82 (2005). They were the basis, for instance, of a landmark agreement between U.S. Steel and the CIO's Steelworkers Organizing Committee, and of General Motors's recognition of the UAW, both in 1937. See Morris, supra, at 82-83; Irving Bernstein, Turbulent Years: A History of the American Worker, 1933-1941, at 471 (1970).

Does the legality of members-only agreements mean that employees who strike in support of a demand for such an agreement are protected by §7 from discipline or discharge for such activity? Some early Board decisions extended such protection. See Union-Buffalo Mills Co., 58 N.L.R.B. 384 (1944); Pennypower Shopping News, Inc., 244 N.L.R.B. 536 (1979); see also Alan Hyde et al., After *Smyrna*: Rights and Powers of Unions That Represent Less Than a Majority, 45 Rutgers L. Rev. 637 (1993). The Supreme Court's recognition of the rights of nonunion workers in *Washington Aluminum*, supra page 170, would seem to offer further support. Where a §9 representative is present, however, employees striking to obtain a members-only agreement may lose NLRA protection because they are striking to compel the employer's direct dealing with them in circumvention of the exclusive representative. See the *Emporium Capwell* decision below.

The more difficult question is whether the NLRA *requires* an employer to bargain with a minority union, at least in the absence of a majority representative, as opposed to merely refraining from disciplining the minority union's members for their union-related activities. Section 7's recognition of the employees' right to self-organization, standing alone, might arguably have supported such an obligation. Does the language of §8(a)(5), however, making it an unfair labor practice "to refuse to bargain collectively with the representatives of his employees, *subject to the provisions of section 9(a)*" (emphasis added), foreclose this avenue? It has been the consistent view of the NLRB that the employer has no duty to bargain with a members-only union. See, e.g., Mooresville Cotton Mills, 2 N.L.R.B. 952, 955 (1937), modified and enforced, 94 F.2d 61 (4th Cir.), modified, 97 F.2d 959 (1938), modified and enforced, 110 F.2d 179 (1940); *Pennypower*, supra, at 537 n.4. This view is questioned in Charles J. Morris, The Blue Eagle, supra; Clyde W. Summers, Unions Without Majority—A Black Hole?, 66 Chi.-Kent L. Rev. 531, 536, 538 (1990).

Proposals have been offered to amend the NLRA to mandate collective bargaining with nonmajority unions in the absence of a §9 representative. See, e.g., Matthew W. Finkin, The Road Not Taken: Some Thoughts on Nonmajority Employee Representation, 69 Chi.-Kent L. Rev. 195, 198 n.18 (1993); Richard R. Carlson, The Origin and Future of Exclusive Representation in American Labor Law, 30 Duq. L. Rev. 779 (1992). One difficulty with such proposals is the cost to the firm of dealing with a proliferation of bargaining obligations in a particular plant. The same costs are not present in foreign labor systems where collective bargaining occurs, if at all, at the multi-enterprise, regional level and typically sets only minimum terms of employment. See Samuel Estreicher, Labor Law Reform in a World of Competitive Product Markets, 69 Chi.-Kent L. Rev. 3, 33-34 (1993). Professor Finkin attempts to avoid some of these difficulties by permitting employers to insist on joint bargaining among labor groups "with respect to matters which have customarily been provided on a uniform basis"; absent consent to such joint bargaining, employers could bargain with the organization that represents the largest number of employees and impose the agreement on the other organizations. See Finkin, The Road Not Taken, supra, at 205-206. Do you see any problems with this proposal?

### Emporium Capwell Co. v. Western Addition Community Organization
*420 U.S. 50 (1975)*

MARSHALL, J. . . .

The Emporium Capwell Co. (Company) operates a department store in San Francisco. . . . [I]t was a party to the collective bargaining agreement negotiated by the San Francisco Retailer's Council, of which it was a member, and the Department Store Employees Union (Union) which represented all stock and marking area employees of the Company. The agreement, in which the Union was recognized as the sole collective bargaining agency for all covered employees, prohibited employment discrimination by reason of race, color, creed, national origin, age, or sex, as well as union activity. It had a no-strike or lockout clause, and it established grievance and arbitration machinery for processing any claimed violation of the contract, including a violation of the antidiscrimination clause.

On April 3, 1968, a group of Company employees covered by the agreement met with the secretary-treasurer of the Union, Walter Johnson, to present a list of grievances including a claim that the Company was discriminating on the basis of race in making assignments and promotions. The Union official agreed to take certain of the grievances and to investigate the charge of racial discrimination. He appointed an investigating committee and prepared a report on the employees' grievances, which he submitted to the Retailer's Council and which the Council in turn referred to the Company. The report described "the possibility of racial discrimination" as perhaps the most important issue raised by the employees and termed the situation at the Company as potentially explosive if corrective action were not taken. . . .

Shortly after receiving the report, the Company's labor relations director met with Union representatives and agreed to "look into the matter" of discrimination and see what needed to be done. Apparently unsatisfied with these representations, the Union held a meeting in September attended by Union officials, Company employees, and representatives of the California Fair Employment Practices Committee . . . and the local antipoverty agency. The secretary-treasurer of the Union announced that the Union had concluded that the Company was discriminating, and that it would process every such grievance through to arbitration if necessary. Testimony about the Company's practices was taken and transcribed by a court reporter, and the next day the Union notified the Company of its formal charge and demanded that the joint union-management Adjustment Board be convened "to hear the entire case."

At the September meeting some of the Company's employees had expressed their view that the contract procedures were inadequate to handle a systemic grievance of this sort; they suggested that the Union instead begin picketing the store in protest. Johnson explained that the collective agreement bound the Union to its processes and expressed his view that successful grievants would be helping not only themselves but all others who might be the victims of invidious discrimination as well. . . . Nonetheless, when the Adjustment Board meeting convened on October 16, James Joseph Hollins, Tom Hawkins, and two other employees whose testimony the Union had intended to elicit refused to participate in the grievance procedure. Instead, Hollins read a statement objecting to reliance on correction of individual inequities as an approach to the problem of discrimination at the store and demanding that the president of the Company meet with the four protestants to work out a broader agreement for dealing with the issue as they saw it. The four employees then walked out of the hearing.

Hollins attempted to discuss the question of racial discrimination with the Company president shortly after the incidents of October 16. The president refused to be drawn into such a discussion but suggested to Hollins that he see the personnel director about the matter. Hollins, who had spoken to the personnel director before, made no effort to do so again. Rather, he and Hawkins and several other dissident employees held a press conference on October 22 at which they denounced the store's employment policy as racist, reiterated their desire to deal directly with "the top management" of the Company over minority employment conditions, and announced their intention to picket and institute a boycott of the store. On Saturday, November 2, Hollins, Hawkins, and at least two other employees picketed the store throughout the day and distributed at the entrance handbills urging consumers not to patronize the store.[2] Johnson encountered the

---

2. The full text of the handbill read:

***BEWARE***BEWARE***BEWARE***
"EMPORIUM SHOPPERS
"'Boycott Is On' 'Boycott Is On' 'Boycott Is On'

"For years at The Emporium black, brown, yellow and red people have worked at the lowest jobs, at the lowest levels. Time and time again we have seen intelligent, hard working brothers and sisters denied promotions and respect.

"The Emporium is a 20th Century colonial plantation. The brothers and sisters are being treated the same way as our brothers are being treated in the slave mines of Africa.

"Whenever the racist pig at The Emporium injures or harms a black sister or brother, they injure and insult all black people. THE EMPORIUM MUST PAY FOR THESE INSULTS. Therefore, we encourage all of our people to take their money out of this racist store, until black people have full employment and are promoted justly through out The Emporium.

"We welcome the support of our brothers and sisters from the churches, unions, sororities, fraternities, social clubs, Afro-American Institute, Black Panther Party, W.A.C.O. and the Poor Peoples Institute."

picketing employees, again urged them to rely on the grievance process, and warned that they might be fired for their activities. The pickets, however, were not dissuaded, and they continued to press their demand to deal directly with the Company president.

On November 7, Hollins and Hawkins were given written warnings that a repetition of the picketing or public statements about the Company could lead to their discharge. When the conduct was repeated the following Saturday, the two employees were fired.

Western Addition Community Organization (hereinafter respondent), a local civil rights association of which Hollins and Hawkins were members, filed a charge against the Company with the National Labor Relations Board. . . . After a hearing, the NLRB Trial Examiner found that the [employees' protest] activity was not protected by §7 of the Act and that their discharges did not, therefore, violate §8(a)(l).

The Board, after oral argument, adopted the findings and conclusions of its Trial Examiner and dismissed the complaint. Among the findings adopted by the Board was that the discharged employees' course of conduct

> was no mere presentation of a grievance but nothing short of a demand that the [Company] bargain with the picketing employees for the entire group of minority employees.[5]

The Board concluded that protection of such an attempt to bargain would undermine the statutory system of bargaining through an exclusive, elected representative, . . . "and place on the Employer an unreasonable burden of attempting to placate self-designated representatives of minority groups while abiding by the terms of a valid bargaining agreement. . . ."[6]

5. 192 N.L.R.B., at 185. The evidence marshaled in support of this finding consisted of Hollins' meeting with the Company president in which he said that he wanted to discuss the problem perceived by minority employees; his statement that the pickets would not desist until the president treated with them; Hawkins' testimony that their purpose in picketing was to "talk to the top management to get better conditions"; and his statement that they wanted to achieve their purpose through "group talk and through the president if we could talk to him," as opposed to use of the grievance-arbitration machinery.

6. The Board considered but stopped short of resolving the question of whether the employees' invective and call for a boycott of the Company bespoke so malicious an attempt to harm their employer as to deprive them of the protection of the Act. The Board decision is therefore grounded squarely on the view that a minority group member may not bypass the Union and bargain directly over matters affecting minority employees, and not at all on the tactics used in this particular attempt to obtain such bargaining.

Member Jenkins dissented on the ground that the employees' activity was protected by §7 because it concerned the terms and conditions of their employment. Member Brown agreed but expressly relied upon his view that the facts revealed no attempt to bargain "but simply to urge [the Company] to take action to correct conditions of racial discrimination which the employees reasonably believed existed at the Emporium." 192 N.L.R.B., at 179. [Footnote relocated in text. — Eds.]

On respondent's petition for review the Court of Appeals reversed and remanded. The court was of the view that concerted activity directed against racial discrimination enjoys a "unique status" by virtue of the national labor policy against discrimination, as expressed in both the NLRA, see United Packinghouse Workers v. NLRB, 416 F.2d 1126, and in Title VII of the Civil Rights Act of 1964, and that the Board had not adequately taken account of the necessity to accommodate the exclusive bargaining principle of the NLRA to the national policy of protecting action taken in opposition to discrimination from employer retaliation. . . .

. . . [T]he Board found that the employees were discharged for attempting to bargain with the Company over the terms and conditions of employment as they affected racial minorities. Although the Court of Appeals expressly declined to set aside this finding, respondent has devoted considerable effort to attacking it in this Court, on the theory that the employees were attempting only to present a grievance to their employer within the meaning of the first proviso to §9(a).[12] We see no occasion to disturb the finding of the Board. The issue, then, is whether such attempts to engage in separate bargaining are protected by §7 of the Act or proscribed by §9(a).

. . . [The rights guaranteed by §7] are, for the most part, collective rights, rights to act in concert with one's fellow employees; they are protected not for their own sake but as an instrument of the national labor policy of minimizing industrial strife "by encouraging the practice and procedure of collective bargaining."

Central to the policy of fostering collective bargaining, where the employees elect that course, is the principle of majority rule. . . . [In] establishing a regime of majority rule, Congress sought to secure to all members of the unit the benefits of their collective strength and bargaining power, in full awareness that the superior strength of some individuals or groups might be subordinated to the interest of the majority. As a result, "[t]he complete satisfaction of all who are represented is hardly to be expected." Ford Motor Co. v. Huffman, 345 U.S. 330, 338 (1953). . . .

---

12. . . . Respondent clearly misapprehends the nature of the "right" conferred by this section. The intendment of the proviso is to permit employees to present grievances and to authorize the employer to entertain them without opening itself to liability for dealing directly with employees in derogation of the duty to bargain only with the exclusive bargaining representative, a violation of §8(a)(5). The Act nowhere protects this "right" by making it an unfair labor practice for an employer to refuse to entertain such a presentation, nor can it be read to authorize resort to economic coercion. This matter is fully explicated in Black-Clawson Co. v. Machinists, 313 F.2d 179 (2d Cir. 1962). If the employees' activity in the present litigation is to be deemed protected, therefore, it must be so by reason of the reading given to the main part of §9(a), in light of Title VII and the national policy against employment discrimination, and not by burdening the proviso to that section with a load it was not meant to carry.

In vesting the representatives of the majority with this broad power Congress did not, of course, authorize a tyranny of the majority over minority interests. First, it confined the exercise of these powers to the context of a "unit appropriate for the purposes of collective bargaining," i.e., a group of employees with a sufficient commonality of circumstances to ensure against the submergence of a minority with distinctively different interests in the terms and conditions of their employment. Second, it undertook in the 1959 Landrum-Griffin amendments . . . to assure that minority voices are heard as they are in the functioning of a democratic institution. Third, we have held, by the very nature of the exclusive bargaining representative's status as representative of *all* unit employees, Congress implicitly imposed upon it a duty fairly and in good faith to represent the interests of minorities within the unit. And the Board has taken the position that a union's refusal to process grievances against racial discrimination, in violation of that duty, is an unfair labor practice. Hughes Tool Co., 147 N.L.R.B. 1573 (1964); see Miranda Fuel Co., 140 N.L.R.B. 181 (1962), enforcement denied, 326 F.2d 172 (CA2 1963). . . .

Against this background of long and consistent adherence to the principle of exclusive representation tempered by safeguards for the protection of minority interests, respondent urges this Court to fashion a limited exception to that principle: employees who seek to bargain separately with their employer as to the elimination of racially discriminatory employment practices peculiarly affecting them, should be free from the constraints of the exclusivity principle of §9(a). Essentially because established procedures under Title VII or, as in this case, a grievance machinery, are too time consuming, the national labor policy against discrimination requires this exception, respondent argues, and its adoption would not unduly compromise the legitimate interests of either unions or employers. . . .

The decision by a handful of employees to bypass the grievance procedure in favor of attempting to bargain with their employer . . . may or may not be predicated upon the actual existence of discrimination. An employer confronted with bargaining demands from each of several minority groups would not necessarily, or even probably, be able to agree to remedial steps satisfactory to all at once. Competing claims on the employer's ability to accommodate each group's demands, e.g., for reassignments and promotions to a limited number of positions, could only set one group against the other even if it is not the employer's intention to divide and overcome them. Having divided themselves, the minority employees will not be in position to advance their cause unless it be by recourse seriatim to economic coercion, which can only have the effect of further dividing them along racial or other lines. Nor is the situation materially different where, as apparently happened here, self-designated representatives purport to speak for all groups that might consider themselves to be victims of discrimination. Even if in actual bargaining the various groups did not perceive their interests as divergent and further subdivide themselves, the employer would be bound to bargain with them in a field largely preempted by the current collective bargaining agreement with the elected bargaining representative. In this instance we do not know precisely what form the demands advanced by Hollins, Hawkins, et al. would take, but the nature of the grievance that motivated them indicates that the demands would have included the transfer of some minority employees to sales areas in which higher commissions were paid. Yet the collective bargaining agreement provided that no employee would be transferred from a higher-paying to a lower-paying classification except by consent or in the course of a layoff or reduction in force. The potential for conflict between the minority and other employees in this situation is manifest. With each group able to enforce its conflicting demands — the incumbent employees by resort to contractual processes and the minority employees by economic coercion — the probability of strife and deadlock is high; the likelihood of making headway against discriminatory practices would be minimal. . . .

[The dissenting opinion of Justice Douglas is omitted.]

## *NOTES AND QUESTIONS*

1. **Means vs. Object?** Did Hollins and Hawkins engage in unprotected activity because of the methods they used or simply because they sought a form of "direct dealing" with the employer? Would the convening of the October 22 press conference — standing alone, without any picketing or handbilling — have been sufficient to deprive Hollins and Hawkins of §7 protection? Or could Hollins and Hawkins have been discharged for any attempt to deal directly with management in circumvention of the union, even if no economic pressure or product disparagement was involved?

2. **Section 9(a) Proviso.** Would the result in *Emporium Capwell* have been different if the Court had accepted the argument of the discharged employees that they were only attempting to present a grievance under the collective agreement rather than attempting to bargain for a modification of the agreement? Consider the Court's treatment of the §9(a) proviso in footnote 12. Does the reference to "economic coercion" in that footnote suggest that the employees would not have been protected in pressing a contractual grievance, at least to the extent they engaged in picketing and handbilling? Why does the proviso allow the employer to entertain employee grievances, and yet render the forceful airing of those grievances unprotected?

**3. Impact of Exclusive Representation on §7 Rights?** In light of the cases discussed in Chapter 3, including *Washington Aluminum*, supra page 170, and *Jefferson Standard*, supra page 177, would Hollins's and Hawkins's activity have been protected by §7 if the store's employees had not been represented by an exclusive bargaining agent? To what extent does the presence of a §9 representative affect the §7 right of employees to engage in concerted activity? Presumably, workers cannot engage in "wildcat" strikes to protest the union's actions or otherwise to compel direct dealing with an agent other than the §9 representative. But are they protected in striking without the union's authorization if they are acting in support of the union's objectives at the bargaining table? See Judge Posner's discussion in East Chicago Rehabilitation Ctr. v. NLRB, 710 F.2d 397, 402 (7th Cir. 1983):

> Although §9(a) qualifies §7, it qualifies that part of §7 that gives workers the right to bargain collectively. It does not — not explicitly anyway — qualify their §7 right to engage in other concerted activities for mutual aid or protection. Unless, therefore, a wildcat strike is called for the purpose of asserting a right to bargain collectively in the union's place or is likely, regardless of its purpose, to impair the union's performance as exclusive bargaining representative, §9(a) does not put the strikers beyond the pale of §7.

Compare NLRB v. Shop Rite Foods, Inc., 430 F.2d 786 (5th Cir. 1970) (finding no protection where union had not approved walkout and had not articulated as an "established objective" any challenge to discharge that prompted walkout), with NLRB v. R.C. Can Co., 328 F.2d 974 (5th Cir. 1964) (walkout in support of union's objectives protected).

Do you see any practical difficulties with the *East Chicago Rehabilitation Center* position? How is the employer to determine whether the employees are acting in a manner congruent with the objectives of the union when the union disavows authorization of the walkout? Will rulings like *East Chicago Rehabilitation Ctr.* provide a vehicle for unions to evade obligations they have undertaken to maintain production pending the outcome of bargaining? Or is it sufficient that any walkout in violation of a no-strike pledge would be unprotected for that reason?

For the argument that the NLRA protects all dissident employees' strike activity aimed at supporting the union's objectives but makes such protection waivable by the union, see Michael C. Harper, Union Waiver of Employee Rights Under the NLRA: Part I, 4 Indus. Rel. L.J. 335, 368-371 (1981). For further discussion of group activities not sanctioned by the bargaining agent, see Norman L. Cantor, Dissident Worker Action After *The Emporium*, 29 Rutgers L. Rev. 35 (1975); James B. Atleson, Work Group Behavior and Wildcat Strikes: The Causes and Functions of Industrial Civil Disobedience, 34 Ohio St. L.J. 751 (1973).

## B. THE REQUIREMENT OF GOOD FAITH: BARGAINING POSITIONS AND PRACTICES

### 1. Models of the Bargaining Process

**NLRB v. Insurance Agents' International Union**
*361 U.S. 477 (1960)*

Brennan, J. . . .

Since 1949 the respondent Insurance Agents' International Union and the Prudential Insurance Company have negotiated collective bargaining agreements covering district agents employed by Prudential in thirty-five States and the District of Columbia. The principal duties of a Prudential district agent are to collect premiums and to solicit new business in an assigned locality known in the trade as his "debit." He has no fixed or regular working hours except that he must report at his district office two mornings a week and remain for two or three hours to deposit his collections, prepare and submit reports, and attend meetings to receive sales and other instructions. He is paid commissions on collections made and on new policies written; his only fixed compensation is a weekly payment of $4.50 intended primarily to cover his expenses.

In January 1956 Prudential and the union began the negotiation of a new contract to replace an agreement expiring in the following March. Bargaining was carried on continuously for six months before the terms of the new contract were agreed upon on July 17, 1956. It is not questioned that, if it stood alone, the record of negotiations would establish that the union conferred in good faith for the purpose and with the desire of reaching agreement with Prudential on a contract.

However, in April 1956, Prudential filed a §8(b)(3) charge of refusal to bargain collectively against the union. The charge was based upon actions of the union and its members outside the conference room, occurring after the old contract expired in March. The union had announced in February that if agreement on the terms of the new contract was not reached when the old contract expired, the union members would then participate in a "Work Without a Contract" program—which meant that they would engage in certain planned, concerted on-the-job activities designed to harass the company.

A complaint of violation of §8(b)(3) issued on the charge and hearings began before the bargaining was concluded. [The evidence showed] that the union's harassing tactics involved activities by the member agents such as these: refusal for a time to solicit new business, and refusal (after the writing of new business was resumed) to comply with the company's reporting procedures; refusal to participate in the company's "May Policyholders' Month

Campaign"; reporting late at district offices the days the agents were scheduled to attend them, and refusing to perform customary duties at the offices, instead engaging there in "sit-in-mornings," "doing what comes naturally" and leaving at noon as a group; absenting themselves from special business conferences arranged by the company; picketing and distributing leaflets outside the various offices of the company on specified days and hours as directed by the union; distributing leaflets each day to policyholders and others and soliciting policyholders' signatures on petitions directed to the company; and presenting the signed policyholders' petitions to the company at its home office while simultaneously engaging in mass demonstrations there.

[The Board found a refusal to bargain and entered a cease-and-desist order against the union. 119 N.L.R.B. 768. The Court of Appeals set aside that order.]

. . . [T]he Board's view is that irrespective of the union's good faith in conferring with the employer at the bargaining table for the purpose and with the desire of reaching agreement on contract terms, its tactics during the course of the negotiations constituted per se a violation of §8(b)(3). Accordingly, as is said in the Board's brief, "The issue here . . . comes down to whether the Board is authorized under the Act to hold that such tactics, which the Act does not specifically forbid but §7 does not protect, support a finding of a failure to bargain in good faith as required by §8(b)(3)."

*First*. . . . [T]he nature of the duty to bargain in good faith imposed upon employers by §8(5) of the original Act was not sweepingly conceived. The Chairman of the Senate Committee declared:

> When the employees have chosen their organization, when they have selected their representatives, all the bill proposes to do is to escort them to the door of their employer and say, "Here they are, the legal representatives of your employees." What happens behind those doors is not inquired into, and the bill does not seek to inquire into it.[9]

The limitation implied by the last sentence has not been in practice maintained—practically, it could hardly have been—but the underlying purpose of the remark has remained the most basic purpose of the statutory provision. That purpose is the making effective of the duty of management to extend recognition to the union; the duty of management to bargain in good faith is essentially a corollary of its duty to recognize the union. . . .

But at the same time, Congress was generally not concerned with the substantive terms on which the parties contracted. Cf. Terminal Railroad Ass'n v. Brotherhood of Railroad Trainmen, 318 U.S. 1, 6. Obviously

9. Senator Walsh, at 79 Cong. Rec. 7660.

there is tension between the principle that the parties need not contract on any specific terms and a practical enforcement of the principle that they are bound to deal with each other in a serious attempt to resolve differences and reach a common ground. And in fact criticism of the Board's application of the "good-faith" test arose from the belief that it was forcing employers to yield to union demands if they were to avoid a successful charge of unfair labor practice. Thus, in 1947 in Congress the fear was expressed that the Board had "gone very far, in the guise of determining whether or not employers had bargained in good faith, in setting itself up as the judge of what concessions an employer must make and of the proposals and counter-proposals that he may or may not make." H.R. Rep. No. 245, 80th Cong., 1st Sess., p.19. Since the Board was not viewed by Congress as an agency which should exercise its powers to arbitrate the parties' substantive solutions of the issues in their bargaining, a check on this apprehended trend was provided by writing the good-faith test of bargaining into §8(d) of the Act. . . .

*Second.* At the same time as it was statutorily defining the duty to bargain collectively, Congress, by adding §8(b)(3) . . . through the Taft-Hartley amendments, imposed that duty on labor organizations. . . .

*Third.* It is apparent from the legislative history of the whole Act that the policy of Congress is to impose a mutual duty upon the parties to confer in good faith with a desire to reach agreement, in the belief that such an approach from both sides of the table promotes the over-all design of achieving industrial peace. Discussion conducted under that standard of good faith may narrow the issues, making the real demands of the parties clearer to each other, and perhaps to themselves, and may encourage an attitude of settlement through give and take. The mainstream of cases before the Board and in the courts reviewing its orders, under the provisions fixing the duty to bargain collectively, is concerned with insuring that the parties approach the bargaining table with this attitude. But apart from this essential standard of conduct, Congress intended that the parties should have wide latitude in their negotiations, unrestricted by any governmental power to regulate the substantive solution of their differences.

We believe that the Board's approach in this case — unless it can be defended, in terms of §8(b)(3), as resting on some unique character of the union tactics involved here — must be taken as proceeding from an erroneous view of collective bargaining. It must be realized that collective bargaining, under a system where the Government does not attempt to control the results of negotiations, cannot be equated with an academic collective search for truth — or even with what might be thought to be the ideal of one. The parties — even granting the modification of views that may come from a realization of economic interdependence — still proceed from contrary and to an extent antagonistic viewpoints and concepts of self-interest. The system has not reached the ideal of the philosophic notion that perfect understanding among people would lead to perfect agreement among them on values. The presence of economic weapons in reserve, and their actual exercise on occasion by the parties, is part and parcel of the system that the Wagner and Taft-Hartley Acts have recognized. . . .

For similar reasons, we think the Board's approach involves an intrusion into the substantive aspects of the bargaining process — again, unless there is some specific warrant for its condemnation of the precise tactics involved here. The scope of §8(b)(3) and the limitations on Board power which were the design of §8(d) are exceeded, we hold, by inferring a lack of good faith not from any deficiencies of the union's performance at the bargaining table by reason of its attempted use of economic pressure, but solely and simply because tactics designed to exert economic pressure were employed during the course of the good-faith negotiations. Thus the Board in the guise of determining good or bad faith in negotiations could regulate what economic weapons a party might summon to its aid. And if the Board could regulate the choice of economic weapons that may be used as part of collective bargaining, it would be in a position to exercise considerable influence upon the substantive terms on which the parties contract. As the parties' own devices became more limited, the Government might have to enter even more directly into the negotiation of collective agreements. Our labor policy is not presently erected on a foundation of government control of the results of negotiations. . . . Nor does it contain a charter for the [NLRB] to act at large in equalizing disparities of bargaining power between employer and union.

*Fourth.* The use of economic pressure . . . is of itself not at all inconsistent with the duty of bargaining in good faith. But in . . . recent years, the Board has assumed the power to label particular union economic weapons inconsistent with that duty. . . . The Board freely (and we think correctly) conceded here that a "total" strike called by the union would not have subjected it to sanctions under §8(b)(3), at least if it were called after the old contract, with its no-strike clause, had expired. . . . But in the light of [that concession] and the principles we have enunciated, we must evaluate the claim of the Board to power, under §8(b)(3), to distinguish among various economic pressure tactics and brand the ones at bar inconsistent with good-faith collective bargaining. We conclude its claim is without foundation.

(a) The Board contends that the distinction between a total strike and the conduct at bar is that a total strike is a concerted activity protected against employer interference by §§7 and 8(a)(1) of the Act, while the activity at bar is not a protected concerted activity. We may agree arguendo with the Board that this Court's decision in the *Briggs-Stratton* case, Automobile Workers v. Wisconsin Board, 336 U.S. 245, establishes that the employee conduct here was not a protected concerted activity. On this assumption the employer could have discharged or taken other appropriate disciplinary action against the employees participating in these "slow-down," "sit-in," and arguably unprotected disloyal tactics. See Labor Board v. Fansteel Metallurgical Corp., 306 U.S. 240; Labor Board v. Electrical Workers, 346 U.S. 464. But surely that a union activity is not protected against disciplinary action does not mean that it constitutes a refusal to bargain in good faith. The reason why the ordinary economic strike is not evidence of a failure to bargain in good faith is not that it constitutes a protected activity but that, as we have developed, there is simply no inconsistency between the application of economic pressure and good-faith collective bargaining. The Board suggests that since (on the assumption we make) the union members' activities here were unprotected, and they could have been discharged, the activities should also be deemed unfair labor practices, since thus the remedy of a cease-and-desist order, milder than mass discharges of personnel and less disruptive of commerce, would be available. The argument is not persuasive. There is little logic in assuming that because Congress was willing to allow employers to use self-help against union tactics, if they were willing to face the economic consequences of its use, it also impliedly declared these tactics unlawful as a matter of federal law. Our problem remains that of construing §8(b)(3)'s terms, and we do not see how the availability of self-help to the employer has anything to do with the matter.

(b) The Board contends that because an orthodox "total" strike is "traditional" its use must be taken as being consistent with §8(b)(3); but since the tactics here are not "traditional" or "normal," they need not be so viewed. Further, the Board cites what it conceives to be the public's moral condemnation of the sort of employee tactics involved here. But again we cannot see how these distinctions can be made under a statute which simply enjoins a duty to bargain in good faith. . . . [W]e fail to see the relevance of whether the practice in question is time-honored or whether its exercise is generally supported by public opinion. It may be that the tactics used here deserve condemnation, but this would not justify attempting to pour that condemnation into a vessel not designed to hold it. The same may be said for the Board's contention that these activities, as opposed to a "normal" strike, are inconsistent with §8(b)(3) because they offer maximum pressure on the employer at minimum economic cost to the union. One may doubt whether this was so here, but the matter does not turn on that. Surely it cannot be said that the only economic weapons consistent with good-faith bargaining are those which minimize the pressure on the other party or maximize the disadvantage to the party using them. The catalog of union and employer weapons that might thus fall under ban would be most extensive.

*Fifth*. . . . [W]hen the Board moves in this area, with only §8(b)(3) for support, it is functioning as an arbiter of the sort of economic weapons the parties can use in seeking to gain acceptance of their bargaining demands. It has sought to introduce some standard of properly "balanced" bargaining power, or some new distinction of justifiable and unjustifiable, proper and "abusive" economic weapons into the collective bargaining duty imposed by the Act. The Board's assertion of power under §8(b)(3) allows it to sit in judgment upon every economic weapon the parties to a labor contract negotiation employ, judging it on the very general standard of that section, not drafted with reference to specific forms of economic pressure. We have expressed our belief that this amounts to the Board's entrance into the substantive aspects of the bargaining process to an extent Congress has not countenanced. . . .

[The opinion of Justice Frankfurter, with whom Justices Harlan and Whittaker concurred, is omitted.]

## *NOTES AND QUESTIONS*

**1. Free Play of Economic Forces vs. Good-Faith Bargaining?** What sense do you make of the Court's distinction between the good-faith bargaining required at the table and the unregulated state of affairs that apparently governs resort to economic conflict? Is there a greater danger of substantive control of the terms of employment when the state regulates economic conflict than when it regulates bargaining table conduct? Are there other reasons to hold that adversarial actions should occur only away from the bargaining table? One question to consider throughout this chapter is whether the emphasis on private determination of terms and conditions of employment—or "voluntarism"—emphasized in *Insurance Agents'* is also reflected in other areas of duty-to-bargain law.

**2. Motive vs. Impact?** Does *Insurance Agents'* support the position that the Board's regulatory authority under §§8(a)(5) and 8(b)(3) is limited to ascertaining whether the parties acted with an appropriate subjective state of mind, and that the Board cannot assess the impact of economic weapons used by the parties on employee willingness to engage in §7 activity or on the employer's ability to compete in the marketplace?

**3. Free Play of Economic Forces vs. Market Reconstruction?** Note the Court's clear statement that the NLRB lacks the authority to attempt to equalize disparities of bargaining power. If so, what is left of the promise in §1 of the Wagner Act that the statute will redress the inequality of power that characterizes bargaining between employers and individual employees? Is it enough to grant workers the right to insist on collective representation and a period of good-faith bargaining concerning a collective agreement, while in all other respects letting market valuations of bargaining power control?

## 2. The Problem of "Surface Bargaining"

### NLRB v. American National Insurance Co.
*343 U.S. 395 (1952)*

Vinson, C.J. . . .

The Office Employees International Union, A.F. of L., Local 27, certified . . . as the exclusive bargaining representative of respondent's office employees, requested a meeting with respondent for the purpose of negotiating an agreement. . . . At the first meetings, beginning on November 30, 1948, the Union submitted a proposed contract covering wages, hours, promotions, vacations and other provisions commonly found in collective bargaining agreements, including a clause establishing a procedure for settling grievances arising under the contract by successive appeals to management with ultimate resort to an arbitrator.

On January 10, 1949, following a recess for study of the Union's contract proposals, respondent objected to the provisions calling for unlimited arbitration. To meet this objection, respondent proposed a so-called management functions clause listing matters such as promotions, discipline and work scheduling as the responsibility of management and excluding such matters from arbitration. The Union's representative took the position "as soon as [he] heard [the proposed clause]" that the Union would not agree to such a clause so long as it covered matters subject to the duty to bargain collectively under the Labor Act.

Several further bargaining sessions were held without reaching agreement on the Union's proposal or respondent's counterproposal to unlimited arbitration. As a result, the management functions clause was "bypassed" for bargaining on other terms of the Union's contract proposal. On January 17, 1949, respondent stated in writing its agreement with some of the terms proposed by the Union and, where there was disagreement, respondent offered counterproposals, including a clause entitled "Functions and Prerogatives of Management" along the lines suggested at the meeting of January 10th. The Union objected to the portion of the clause providing:

> The right to select and hire, to promote to a better position, to discharge, demote or discipline for cause, and to maintain discipline and efficiency of employees and to determine the schedules of work is recognized by both union and company as the proper responsibility and prerogative of management . . . , and while it is agreed that an employee feeling himself to have been aggrieved by any decision of the company in respect to such matters, or the union in his behalf, shall have the right to have such decision reviewed by top management officials . . . under the grievance machinery hereinafter set forth, it is further agreed that the final decision of the

company made by such top management officials shall not be further reviewable by arbitration.

... [N]egotiations between the Union and respondent continued with the management functions clause remaining an obstacle to agreement. During the negotiations, respondent established new night shifts and introduced a new system of lunch hours without consulting the Union.

On May 19, 1949, a Union representative offered a second contract proposal which included a management functions clause containing much of the language found in respondent's second counterproposal, quoted above, with the vital difference that questions arising under the Union's proposed clause would be subject to arbitration as in the case of other grievances. Finally, on January 13, 1950 . . . an agreement between the Union and respondent was signed. The agreement contained a management functions clause that rendered nonarbitrable matters of discipline, work schedules and other matters covered by the clause. The subject of promotions and demotions was deleted from the clause and made the subject of a special clause establishing a union-management committee to pass upon promotion matters.

While these negotiations were in progress, the Board's Trial Examiner . . . held that respondent had a right to bargain for inclusion of a management functions clause in a contract. However, upon review of the entire negotiations, including respondent's unilateral action in changing working conditions during the bargaining, the Examiner found that from and after November 30, 1948, respondent had refused to bargain in a good faith effort to reach agreement. The Examiner recommended that respondent be ordered in general terms to bargain collectively with the Union. . . . [T]he Board rejected the Examiner's views on an employer's right to bargain for a management functions clause and held that respondent's action in bargaining for inclusion of any such clause "constituted, quite [apart from] Respondent's demonstrated bad faith, per se violations of §§8(a)(5) and (1)." Accordingly, the Board not only ordered respondent in general terms to bargain collectively with the Union . . . , but also included in its order a paragraph designed to prohibit bargaining for any management functions clause covering a condition of employment. . . . 89 N.L.R.B. 185. . . .

Enforcement of the obligation to bargain collectively is crucial to the statutory scheme. And, as has long been recognized, performance of the duty to bargain requires more than a willingness to enter upon a sterile discussion of union-management differences. Before the [NLRA], it was held that the duty of an employer to bargain collectively required the employer "to negotiate in good faith with his employees' representatives; to match their proposals, if unacceptable, with counter-proposals; and to make every reasonable effort to reach an agreement."[9] The duty to bargain collectively, implicit in the Wagner Act as introduced in Congress, was made express by the insertion of the fifth employer unfair labor practice accompanied by an explanation of the purpose and meaning of the phrase "bargain collectively in a good faith effort to reach an agreement."[10] This understanding of the duty to bargain collectively has been accepted and applied throughout the administration of the Wagner Act by the [NLRB] and the Courts of Appeal.

In 1947, the fear was expressed in Congress that the Board "has gone very far, in the guise of determining whether or not employers had bargained in good faith, in setting itself up as the judge of what concessions an employer must make and of the proposals and counterproposals that he may or may not make."[12] Accordingly, the Hartley Bill, passed by the House, eliminated the good faith test and expressly provided that the duty to bargain collectively did not require submission of counterproposals. As amended in the Senate and passed as the Taft-Hartley Act, the good faith test of bargaining was retained and written into Section 8(d). . . . That Section contains the express provision that the obligation to bargain collectively does not compel either party to agree to a proposal or require the making of a concession.

The Board offers . . . before this Court a theory quite apart from the test of good faith bargaining prescribed in §8(d) . . . , a theory that respondent's bargaining for a management functions clause as a counterproposal to the Union's demand for unlimited arbitration was, "per se," a violation of the Act.

. . . The Board's argument is a technical one for it is conceded that respondent would not be guilty of an unfair labor practice if, instead of proposing a clause that removed some matters from arbitration, it simply refused in good faith to agree to the Union proposal for unlimited arbitration. The argument starts with a finding, not challenged by the court below or by respondent, that at least some of the matters covered by the management functions clause proposed by respondent are "conditions of

9. Houde Engineering Corp., 1 N.L.R.B. (old) 35 (1934), decided by the National Labor Relations Board organized under 48 Stat. 1183 (1934).

. . . Section 8(5) was inserted at the suggestion of the Chairman of the Board that decided *Houde.* Id., at 79, 136-137. The insertion of §8(5) was described by the Senate Committee as follows:

> . . . [T]he committee has concluded that this fifth unfair labor practice should be inserted in the bill. . . . [A] guarantee of the right of employees to bargain collectively through representatives of their own choosing is a mere delusion if it is not accompanied by the correlative duty on the part of the other party to recognize such representatives as they have been designated . . . and to negotiate with them in a bona fide effort to arrive at a collective agreement. . . . S. Rep. No. 573, 74th Cong., 1st Sess. 12 (1935). . . .

12. H. R. Rep. No. 245, 80th Cong., 1st Sess. 19 (1947).

employment" which are appropriate subjects of collective bargaining under §§8(a)(5), 8(d) and 9(a). . . . The Board considers that employer bargaining for a clause under which management retains initial responsibility for work scheduling, a "condition of employment," for the duration of the contract is an unfair labor practice because it is "in derogation of" employees' statutory rights to bargain collectively as to conditions of employment.[22]

Conceding that there is nothing unlawful in including a management functions clause in a labor agreement, the Board would permit an employer to "propose" such a clause. But the Board would forbid bargaining for any such clause when the Union declines to accept the proposal, even where the clause is offered as a counterproposal to a Union demand for unlimited arbitration. Ignoring the nature of the Union's demand in this case, the Board takes the position that employers . . . must agree to include in any labor agreement provisions establishing fixed standards for work schedules or any other condition of employment. An employer would be permitted to bargain as to the content of the standard so long as he agrees to freeze a standard into a contract. Bargaining for more flexible treatment of such matters would be denied employers even though the result may be contrary to common collective bargaining practice in the industry. The Board was not empowered so to disrupt collective bargaining practices. . . .

Congress provided expressly that the Board should not pass upon the desirability of the substantive terms of labor agreements. Whether a contract should contain a clause fixing standards for such matters as work scheduling or should provide for more flexible treatment of such matters is an issue for determination across the bargaining table, not by the Board. If the latter approach is agreed upon, the extent of union and management participation in the administration of such matters is itself a condition of employment to be settled by bargaining.

Accordingly, we reject the Board's holding that bargaining for the management functions clause proposed by respondent was, per se, an unfair labor practice. Any fears the Board may entertain that use of management functions clauses will lead to evasion of an employer's duty to bargain collectively as to "rates of pay, wages, hours and conditions of employment" do not justify condemning all bargaining for management functions clauses covering any "condition of employment" as per se violations of the Act. The duty to bargain collectively is to be enforced by application of the good faith bargaining standards of §8(d) to the facts of each case rather

---

22. The Board's argument would seem to prevent an employer from bargaining for a "no-strike" clause, commonly found in labor agreements, requiring a union to forego for the duration of the contract the right to strike expressly granted by §7. . . . However, the Board has permitted an employer to bargain in good faith for such a clause. Shell Oil Co., 77 N.L.R.B. 1306 (1948). This result is explained by referring to the "salutary objective" of such a clause. Bethlehem Steel Co., 89 N.L.R.B. 341, 345 (1950).

than by prohibiting all employers in every industry from bargaining for management functions clauses altogether. . . .

MINTON, J. with whom BLACK and DOUGLAS, JJ., join, dissenting.

. . . No one suggests that an employer is guilty of an unfair labor practice when it proposes that it be given unilateral control over certain working conditions and the union accepts the proposal in return for various other benefits. But where, as here, the employer tells the union that the only way to obtain a contract as to wages is to agree not to bargain about certain other working conditions, the employer has refused to bargain about those other working conditions. . . .

I need not and do not take issue with the Court of Appeals' conclusion that there was no absence of good faith. Where there is a refusal to bargain, the Act does not require an inquiry as to whether that refusal was in good faith or bad faith. . . . The majority seems to suggest that an employer could be found guilty of bad faith if it used a "management functions" clause to close off bargaining about all topics of discussion. Whether the employer closes off all bargaining or, as in this case, only a certain area of bargaining, he has refused to bargain as to whatever he has closed off, and any discussion of his good faith is pointless. . . .

## NLRB v. A-1 King Size Sandwiches, Inc.

*732 F.2d 872 (11th Cir. 1984)*

DYER, J.

This case is before us upon the application of the National Labor Relations Board . . . for enforcement of its order issued against A-1 King Size Sandwiches, Inc. . . . The Board affirmed the administrative law judge's [conclusion that the company had failed to bargain in good faith with the Union.]

. . . The question to be decided is a narrow one: Whether the content of the Company's bargaining proposals together with the positions taken by the Company are sufficient to establish that it entered into bargaining with no real intention of concluding a collective bargaining agreement. We defer to the Board to make the initial determination, but we are required to review the proposals to determine whether the Board's findings are supported by substantial evidence on the record as a whole.

### WAGES

. . . The Company insisted that it remain in total control over wages. Its proposal to continue granting wage increases on the basis of semiannual wage reviews, in which the Company would make the final decision, coupled with the Company's Management Rights clause, infra, under which it had the exclusive right to evaluate, reward, promote and demote employees, left the Union's "participation" in the process meaningless. The Union was foreclosed from introducing factors other than merit into the equation. It had no contractual remedies since the granting or withholding of merit increases would not be arbitrable. The Union could not strike and, in fact, it had no leverage to require its views to be taken into account. Moreover, once an employee's wage rate increased above the level of the rate existing at the time of the contract, the Company could unilaterally reduce that which had been given in a previous merit increase and the Union could not grieve such action. It could not strike, and under the Zipper Clause, infra, it could not even discuss the matter with the Company. Thus, the Company's unalterable position was that it remain in total control of this mandatory subject of bargaining.

### MANAGEMENT RIGHTS

The Company submitted a management rights clause which initially provided that the Company retained exclusively all of its normal inherent rights and exempted the Company's decisions concerning these rights from the grievance procedure. Later the Company proposed a new management rights clause, which was much broader than the first proposal, and which reserved exclusively to the Company all authority customarily exercised by Management and "each and every right, power and privilege that it had ever enjoyed, whether exercised or not, except insofar as [the Company] has, by express and specific terms of the agreement, agreed to limitations." . . .

The new proposal further expanded the original by providing that the Company could exercise all of its reserved rights without advising the Union of any such proposed action, change or modification, and exempted the Company from any requirement to negotiate over the decision, or its effects on employees except as altered by the Agreement. The substituted proposal no longer contained a clause expressly excluding the Company's decisions from the grievance and arbitration procedure.

This proposal gave the Company the absolute right to subcontract work, assign it to supervisors, abolish jobs, and transfer, discontinue or assign any or all of its operations. It also required the Union to relinquish the employees' statutory right to notice and bargaining over such actions and their effects. Finally, the grievance and arbitration procedure was largely illusory because actions taken under this clause were subject to that procedure only if the right was limited by express contractual provision, and there was no such limitation. . . .

### Zipper Clause

The Company proposed a "zipper" clause under which "the parties [waived the] right to bargain during the life of the agreement regarding any subject or any matter referred to or covered in the agreement or any other subject matter which could be considered mandatory or permissive subject of bargaining under existing law." The Union offered to agree to the clause if the latter portion waiving the right to bargain over any other mandatory or permissive bargaining subject was deleted. The Company refused.

### No Strike Clause

The Company proposed a no strike clause that prohibited both the Union and employees from calling, encouraging, ratifying, participating in or engaging in any primary or sympathy strike, slow down, boycott, picketing or any other work interruption for any reason, including but not limited to alleged or actual unfair labor practices, alleged or actual unfair employment practices under any anti-discrimination law, alleged or actual breaches of contract, and showing support or sympathy for other employees or Union or their activities. The Union, although conceding that any contract would contain a no-strike clause, objected to waiving employees' right to strike over unfair labor practices or unfair employment practices. The Company declined to change the proposal. This extremely broad "no strike" clause clearly prohibited any strike for any reason.

### Discharge and Discipline

The Union proposed that the Company have the right to discipline an employee for any just or sufficient cause. The Company, citing meritless discrimination charges filed against it, refused the proposal because it would subject all of the discipline and discharge actions to grievance-arbitration. This is a common non-controversial clause. When considered with the rights expressly reserved in the management rights [c]lause, to suspend, reprimand, discharge, or otherwise discipline employees, the Company retained unfettered control over discharges and discipline.

### Layoff and Recall

With respect to layoff and recall, the Company proposed that the layoff of employees would be at the Company's sole discretion. Company-wide seniority would be considered but not controlling. Selection for layoff would not be the subject of grievance or arbitration. Recall from layoff was to be at the discretion of the Company and it was not required to consider seniority. The Company insisted on the clause as presented because it wanted to make the decisions on the basis of productivity and not seniority and not make the ability question subject to grievance and arbitration.

This clause gave the Company absolute control over the selection of employees for layoff and recall and freed it from its statutory obligation to bargain over these subjects.

### Dues Check-off

The Union proposed a dues check-off clause which the Company rejected as being nothing more than a Union security device and because it made employees' earnings appear lower . . .

The Union finally proposed a "swap off." The Union would agree to some type of management rights, no strike and zipper clauses if the Company would agree to a just cause for discipline and discharge provision, and seniority for layoff and recall provision. The Company refused.

Deciding when a party has reached the "point when hard bargaining ends and obstructionist intransigence begins," NLRB v. Big Three Industries, 497 F.2d 43, 47 (5th Cir. 1974), is "an inescapably elusive inquiry." Id. at 46. But it is clear from our extended recital of the proposals made over a ten-month period that the Company insisted on unilateral control over virtually all significant terms and conditions of employment, including discharge, discipline, layoff, recall, subcontracting and assignment of unit work to supervisors.

Its efforts were focused on requiring the employees to surrender statutory rights to bargain, or strike, without offering any real incentive for a surrender of such rights.

The Company refused to give the Union any voice whatsoever concerning employee work and safety rules, time studies, production quotas, overtime assignments, transfers, retirement, demotions and employee qualifications—all mandatory subjects of bargaining. Elimination of unit work, discipline or discharge of employees, layoff and recall were all exempted from the grievance and arbitration procedure. . . .

Finally, it is worthy of note that the Company responded to the Union's objections to the breadth of its original management rights . . . and zipper clauses by submitting new proposals that were even broader. Such bargaining is clearly an indicia that the Company had little desire to work towards agreement [on] a contract.

The Board correctly inferred bad faith from the Company's insistence on proposals that are so unusually harsh and unreasonable that they are predictably unworkable. See NLRB v. Wright Motors, 603 F.2d [604, 610 (7th Cir. 1979)]. They would have left the Union and the employees with substantially fewer rights and less protection than they would have had if they had relied solely upon the Union's certification. See NLRB v. Johnson Mfg. Co. of Lubbock, 458 F.2d 453 (5th Cir. 1972). . . .

## *NOTES AND QUESTIONS*

1. **Response to "Unlimited Arbitration" Demand?** Should *American National Insurance* be viewed as a case allowing an employer to insist on a broad management functions clause only as a counter to a union's prior insistence on an "unlimited" arbitration clause? Does the Court explain what was unusual about the union's proposed language? Are there other aspects of the opinion suggesting that the employer's proposed clause would have been consistent with good-faith bargaining, even in the absence of a prior union demand? What is the Court's explanation for why management could not refuse to bargain over certain working conditions, but it could refuse to sign any agreement that did not give it unlimited control over those conditions? From the Board's perspective, why could management insist on a fixed standard on promotions, work schedules, and discipline, but could not insist on preserving its discretion on these matters?

2. **Breadth of Management Functions Clause?** Given the language of §8(d) and the *American National Insurance* case, is there any basis for distinguishing the situation in *A-1 King Size Sandwiches*? Does it boil down to a matter of degree — that management can reserve a few, though important, subjects for unilateral decision making but cannot insist on preserving unilateral control over virtually all terms and conditions of employment? See Archibald Cox & John T. Dunlop, Regulation of Collective Bargaining by the National Labor Relations Board, 63 Harv. L. Rev. 389, 403-405, 421-422 (1950). Is this a satisfactory explanation given the fact that the subjects listed in the management functions clause in *American National Insurance* were promotions, work schedules, and discipline? Other than compensation, these are likely to be the most important matters over which a union might bargain. Would (or should) *A-1 King Size Sandwiches* have been decided differently if, for instance, the employer had been willing to negotiate fixed wage rates?

3. **No-Improvement Proposals?** Is the critical factor in *A-1 King Size Sandwiches* the contemporaneous insistence on a no-improvement contract along with a no-strike clause? In other words, can an employer insist on a contract that provides for no improvement over the status quo as long as

the union is free to call a strike during the term of the agreement? Note that "concessionary" bargaining, resulting in agreements providing for reductions in wages or benefits achieved in prior contracts while preserving no-strike clauses, is not uncommon. Should a distinction be drawn between first-time bargaining situations and contract renewal negotiations?

**4. "Some Reasonable Effort in Some Direction."** Are *A-1 King Size Sandwiches* and the similar decisions cited therein consistent with the Taft-Hartley Act's admonition in §8(d) that the duty to bargain in good faith "does not compel either party to agree to a proposal or require the making of a concession"? Consider the rationale offered by a former general counsel for the predecessor to the NLRB in NLRB v. Reed & Prince Mfg. Co., 205 F.2d 131, 134-135 (1st Cir. 1953) (Magruder, J.) (emphasis in original):

> Thus if an employer can find nothing whatever to agree to in an ordinary current-day contract submitted to him, or in some of the union's related minor requests, and if the employer makes not a single serious proposal meeting the union at least part way, then certainly the Board must be able to conclude that this is at least some evidence of bad faith, that is, of a desire not to reach an agreement with the union. In other words, while the Board cannot force an employer to make a "concession" on any specific issue or to adopt any particular position, the employer is obliged to make *some* reasonable effort in *some* direction to compose his differences with the union, if §8(a)(5) is to be read as imposing any substantial obligation at all.

Does this rationale support only a requirement of evidence of "some" willingness to compromise, or does it also suggest that the employees' act of designating a collective representative imposes on the employer a duty not to offer an agreement that no "self-respecting union"—a celebrated phrase from the *Reed & Prince* decision—could be expected to accept? 205 F.2d at 139. Employing similar reasoning, some decisions suggest that an employer's insistence on unilateral determination of grievances is inconsistent with good-faith bargaining. See, e.g., Continental Ins. Co. v. NLRB, 495 F.2d 44 (2d Cir. 1974); Vanderbilt Prods., Inc. v. NLRB, 297 F.2d 833 (2d Cir. 1961); White v. NLRB, 255 F.2d 564 (5th Cir. 1958). A per se rule along these lines may be difficult to reconcile with §8(d), but does the duty to bargain at least support a requirement that the employer "provide a[] justification for placing subjects of such importance to the employees beyond the influence of the bargaining representative"? Sparks Nugget, Inc., 298 N.L.R.B. 524, 527 (1990), enforced, 968 F.2d 991, 995 (9th Cir. 1992). Is it a sufficient "justification" that the employer strongly prefers to retain management control? See Public Serv. Co. v. NLRB, 318 F.3d 1173, 1176 (10th Cir. 2003) (company's statement that management control was necessary to stay competitive in a soon-to-be deregulated market not sufficient to overcome bad faith because positions "required the Union to cede substantially all of its representational function."); Latino Express, Inc., 360 N.L.R.B. No. 112 (2014) (regardless of the employer's justification, bad faith is inferred when the employer's proposals "would leave the union and the employees it represents with substantially fewer rights and less protection than provided by law without a contract.").

**5. Predictability of Bargaining Obligations and Unfair Labor Practice Strikes.** As the above questions indicate, the Board and the courts have as yet failed to develop predictable standards in this area. Thus, the criticisms set forth in James A. Gross et al., Good Faith in Labor Negotiations: Tests and Remedies, 53 Cornell L. Rev. 1009 (1968), are just as apt today.

Although the Board's remedies for §8(a)(5) violations are generally limited to bargaining orders and do not include imposition of substantive terms, see infra pages 429-440, if the employees strike and it is later determined that they struck to protest unlawful bad-faith bargaining—as opposed to simply in support of economic demands—at strike's end they can displace any replacements hired during the strike and will be owed back pay if reinstatement is denied. Conversely, if the strike is determined to have been motivated purely by economics, the strikers will not be entitled to displace the replacements, or to back pay. See infra pages 532-534 (discussing distinction between unfair labor practice strikes and economic strikes).

Should employees have to "bet" their jobs in support of what they believe to be an unfair labor practice strike? Should employers have to "bet" their business in maintaining their bargaining positions and responding to such walkouts? Given the potential costs to parties of acting without the benefit of clear and predictable rules, should there be a greater receptivity to per se rules rather than a "totality of the circumstances" approach in determining whether an employer engaged in bad-faith bargaining? Are per se rules consistent, however, with a statutory provision that speaks in terms of the parties' "good faith"?

**6. Procedural Rigidity.** Both of the principal cases deal with the difficult issue of substantive rigidity. The Board's authority to review the procedural aspects of the parties' negotiations, however, would seem to fit within §8(d)'s statement of the "mutual obligation" of the parties "to meet at reasonable times and confer in good faith." Thus, for example, where the union relies on employee negotiators, a company's refusal to release employees during working hours to perform this bargaining function would seem inconsistent with good-faith bargaining, at least in the absence of a basis for claiming that the employees in question are performing tasks for which no substitutes can be obtained on particular days. See, e.g., Borg-Warner Controls, 198 N.L.R.B. 726 (1972). Difficult questions can arise even on the procedural front. Consider the following examples:

a. *Recording Bargaining Sessions.* Does an employer or union violate the Act by insisting on using a stenographer or tape recorder to record the bargaining sessions? See Bartlett-Collins Co., 237 N.L.R.B. 770 (1978) (holding yes); see also Latrobe Steel Co. v. NLRB, 630 F.2d 171 (3d Cir. 1980) (upholding *Bartlett-Collins* rule). Does the NLRA necessarily envision a bargaining process where negotiators are free to make statements and "feel out" each other without creating a publicly accessible verbatim record? See Bartlett-Collins, 237 N.L.R.B. at 774 n.9.; cf. Pennsylvania Tel. Guild, 277 N.L.R.B. 501, 501 (1985) (finding union's insistence on recording of grievance meetings violated §8(b)(3) and noting the importance of protecting "informal dialogue," "spontaneity and flexibility," and "sensitive or confidential matters").

b. *Mixed-Union Bargaining Committees.* The unit certified by the NLRB in representation proceedings constitutes the unit of mandatory bargaining. It is not always, however, the unit for which actual bargaining takes place. The parties can agree to a broadening of the arena of bargaining to encompass other bargaining units, other divisions of the company, or other companies, although neither party can *insist* that bargaining take place on the broader level. Given these principles, may an employer refuse to bargain if a union includes as members of its negotiating team officials from other unions that represent other employees at the company? See General Elec. Co. v. NLRB, 412 F.2d 512 (2d Cir. 1969) (employer's outright refusal to bargain not excused by composition of union team; party objecting to other side's representatives must demonstrate "clear and present danger to the bargaining process"). For further discussion, see Note on Coalition and Coordinated Bargaining, infra page 504.

**7. "Boulwarism."** Lemuel R. Boulware, who for many years had been vice-president for labor relations for General Electric, adopted a bargaining strategy in the 1960 contract negotiations to dispense with the typical "horse-trading" scenario where the union would present a laundry list of demands that it had no expectation of securing and the company would respond with extreme "lowball" offers, and serious bargaining would commence only at the eleventh hour of the contract termination date. His strategy, known as "Boulwarism," was to have the company poll employees to ascertain their desires, to formulate a "firm, fair" offer from which it would not budge unless the union presented new information, and then to market the offer aggressively to the employees. See NLRB v. General Elec. Co., 418 F.2d 736, 740-741 (2d Cir. 1969):

> Through a veritable avalanche of publicity, reaching awesome proportions prior to and during negotiations, GE sought to tell its side of the issues to its employees. . . . In negotiations, GE announced that it would have nothing

> to do with the "blood-and-threat-and-thunder" approach, in which each side presented patently unreasonable demands, and finally choose a middle ground that both knew would be the probable outcome even before the beginning of the bargaining. The Company believed that such tactics diminished the company's credibility in the eyes of its employees, and at the same time appeared to give the union credit for wringing from the Company what it had been willing to offer all along. Henceforth GE would hold nothing back when it made its offer to the Union; it would take all the facts into consideration, and make that offer it thought right under all the circumstances. Though willing to accept Union suggestions based on facts the Company might have overlooked, once the basic outlines of the proposal had been set, the mere fact that the Union disagreed would be no ground for change. When GE said firm, it meant firm.

The Second Circuit, over a dissent by Judge Friendly, sustained the NLRB's finding of a §8(a)(5) violation in part because GE's communications to the employees caused it to be so locked into its initial position that alternative proposals made by the Union entailing no additional costs were rejected out of hand. Does the Boulwarism approach violate the NLRA even absent this unreasonable rigidity? Is there a requirement implicit in the Act that bargaining occur in a manner that does not denigrate the union's representative status? See supra note 4, page 402 (discussing "direct dealing").

**8. Union "Boulwarism"?** Say the Teamsters Union has organized a small manufacturing firm in New York City and on the first day presents its standard contract to the employer:

> This is the contract we use in the City for all light manufacturers. We are certainly willing to talk about terms, but it is Union policy that the standard we negotiate is the standard for everyone in the industry. We are not about to let you undercut our other employers. You are free to disagree. But we will not budge, and you should expect a strike.

Has the union violated §8(b)(3)? See, e.g., Kankakee-Iroquois County Employers' Ass'n v. NLRB, 825 F.2d 1091 (7th Cir. 1987).

### 3. Remedies for Bad-Faith Bargaining

**H.K. Porter Co. v. NLRB**
*397 U.S. 99 (1970)*

Black, J.

After an election respondent United Steelworkers Union was, on October 5, 1961, certified . . . as the bargaining agent for certain employees at the Danville, Virginia, plant of the petitioner, H.K. Porter Co. Thereafter negotiations commenced for a collective-bargaining agreement. Since that time the controversy has seesawed between the Board, the [D.C. Circuit] Court of Appeals, and this Court. This delay of over eight years is not because the case is exceedingly complex, but appears to have occurred chiefly because of the skill of the company's negotiators in taking advantage of every opportunity for delay in an Act more noticeable for its generality than for its precise prescriptions. The entire lengthy dispute mainly revolves around the union's desire to have the company agree to "check off" the dues owed to the union by its members, that is, to deduct those dues periodically from the company's wage payments to the employees. The record shows, as the Board found, that the company's objection to a checkoff was not due to any general principle or policy against making deductions from employees' wages. The company does deduct charges for things like insurance, taxes, and contributions to charities, and at some other plants it has a checkoff arrangement for union dues. The evidence shows, and the court below found, that the company's objection was not because of inconvenience, but solely on the ground that the company was "not going to aid and comfort the union." Efforts by the union to obtain some kind of compromise on the checkoff request were all met with the same staccato response to the effect that the collection of union dues was the "union's business" and the company was not going to provide any assistance. Based on this and other evidence the Board found, and the Court of Appeals approved the finding, that the refusal of the company to bargain about the checkoff was not made in good faith, but was done solely to frustrate the making of any collective bargaining agreement. In May 1966, the Court of Appeals upheld the Board's order requiring the company to cease and desist from refusing to bargain in good faith and directing it to engage in further collective bargaining, if requested by the union to do so, over the checkoff. . . .

The case was then remanded to the Board and on July 3, 1968, the Board issued a supplemental order requiring the petitioner to "[g]rant to the Union a contract clause providing for the checkoff of union dues." 172 N.L.R.B. No. 72. The Court of Appeals affirmed. . . . For reasons to be stated we hold that while the Board does have power under the [NLRA] . . . to require employers and employees to negotiate, it is without power to compel a company or a union to agree to any substantive contractual provision of a collective bargaining agreement. . . .

The object of [the Wagner] Act was not to allow governmental regulation of the terms and conditions of employment, but rather to ensure that employers and their employees could work together to establish mutually satisfactory conditions. . . . In 1947 Congress reviewed the experience under the Act and concluded that certain amendments were in order. In the House committee report accompanying what eventually became the [LMRA], the committee . . . said:

> Notwithstanding [certain] language of the [Supreme] Court, the present Board has gone very far, in the guise of determining whether or not employers had bargained in good faith, in setting itself up as the judge of what concessions an employer must make and of the proposals and counterproposals that he may or may not make. . . . [U]nless Congress writes into the law guides for the Board to follow, the Board may attempt to carry this process still further and seek to control more and more the terms of collective bargaining agreements.[3]

Accordingly Congress amended the provisions defining unfair labor practices and said in §8(d) that: ". . . *such obligation* [to bargain collectively] *does not compel either party to agree to a proposal or require the making of a concession.*" [emphasis added by the Court]. . . .

. . . We may agree with the Court of Appeals that as a matter of strict, literal interpretation that section refers only to deciding when a violation has occurred, but we do not agree that that observation justifies the conclusion that the remedial powers of the Board are not also limited by the same considerations that led Congress to enact §8(d). It is implicit in the entire structure of the Act that the Board acts to oversee and referee the process of collective bargaining, leaving the results of the contest to the bargaining strengths of the parties. It would be anomalous indeed to hold that while §8(d) prohibits the Board from relying on a refusal to agree as the sole evidence of bad-faith bargaining, the Act permits the Board to compel agreement in that same dispute. The Board's remedial powers under §10 of the Act are broad, but they are limited to carrying out the policies of the Act itself. One of these fundamental policies is freedom of contract. While the parties' freedom of contract is not absolute under the Act, allowing the Board to compel agreement when the parties themselves are unable to agree would violate the fundamental premise on which the Act is based—private bargaining under governmental supervision of the procedure alone, without any official compulsion over the actual terms of the contract. . . .

WHITE, J., took no part in the decision of this case.

MARSHALL, J., took no part in the consideration or decision of this case.

[The concurring opinion of Justice Harlan is omitted.]

DOUGLAS, J., with whom STEWART, J., concurs, dissenting. . . .

Here the employer did not refuse the checkoff for any business reason, whether cost, inconvenience, or what not. Nor did the employer refuse the checkoff as a factor in its bargaining strategy, hoping that delay and denial

---

3. H.R. Rep. No. 245, 80th Cong., 1st Sess., 19-20 (1947).

might bring it in exchange favorable terms and conditions. Its reason was a resolve to avoid reaching any agreement with the union.

In those narrow and specialized circumstances, I see no answer to the power of the Board in its discretion to impose the checkoff as "affirmative action" necessary to remedy the flagrant refusal of the employer to bargain in good faith. . . .

## *NOTES AND QUESTIONS*

**1. Refusal to Bargain?**

a. Do you agree with the Board's finding that the employer's refusal to accede to a checkoff was in bad faith? Is this consistent with §8(d) and the previous materials on "surface bargaining"? What justification does the employer have for rejecting such a clause if no additional cost is required in its payroll operations? Does the employer need an objection? Can it be a "principled," noneconomic objection?

b. An employer, otherwise in compliance with §8(a)(5), rejects the union's demand for a "union security" clause requiring represented employees to pay union dues or their monetary equivalent after their 30th day of employment) (a lawful, mandatory subject of bargaining) urging that (1) the recruitment of members or the securing of financial support should be the union's own business; (2) compulsory unionism is repugnant to the employer's principles; (3) compulsory unionism destroys employee morale; (4) compulsory unionism would give the union excessive power; or (5) that the employer, as the champion of the nonunion employees in the unit, had to resist that demand.

In each instance, has the employer satisfied the Act's bargaining requirements? Would it be material that the parties, for a considerable time, had entered into agreements not containing a union security clause? Or that the union had just been certified by the Board, after an extremely close election preceded by vigorous anti-union propaganda from the employer, and had failed to secure a collective agreement?

**2. Section 8(d) and the NLRB's Remedial Authority.** Why does the Court hold that §8(d) implicates the Board's remedial authority under §10(c)? Was the Board's position on remedial authority tainted by the fact that the remedy imposed was the very same disputed checkoff provision that led to the finding of a bargaining violation in the first case?

**3. Comparison: Restoration of Status Quo Remedies.** In some instances, the Board is permitted to require restoration of the status quo ante as a remedy. For instance, in Fibreboard Paper Products Corp. v. NLRB, 379 U.S. 203 (1964), excerpted infra page 475, the Board, with the Court's approval, ordered an employer who had unilaterally contracted out the unit work (a mandatory subject of bargaining) and laid off the unit employees to reinstitute the closed operation and reinstate the employees with back pay pending the outcome of good-faith bargaining over the subcontracting decision. If the rationale of *H.K. Porter* is that the Board should not write contracts for the parties even when exercising its remedial authority, does this raise questions about the remedy in *Fibreboard*? Is *Fibreboard* different because the Board there required a restoration of the status quo? Should this make a difference even though there was no assurance that had the employer bargained in good faith over the subcontracting decision, the maintenance work would have continued in the unit for the period of time reflected in the Board's back pay and reinstitution order? Is the only difference between the two cases that there is no status quo to restore in a first-time bargaining situation? Would the *H.K. Porter* Court have allowed the Board to impose the checkoff provisionally for the interim period between the date of the violation and the completion of good-faith bargaining? Why or why not?

### *Note: The Problem of First-Time Bargaining Relationships and Extraordinary Remedies*

**Rate at Which First Contracts Are Achieved.** In 1994, the Dunlop Commission reported that between 1986 and 1993, newly-certified units had achieved a first contract in only 56 percent of the cases in which the Federal Mediation and Conciliation Service (FMCS) had received a certification notice. See U.S. Dep't of Labor & U.S. Dep't of Commerce, Commission on the Future of Worker-Management Relations, Fact Finding Report 73 (1994). After 1995, the FMCS was immediately notified of all NLRB certifications and placed special emphasis on the mediation of first contracts. See 52 FMCS Ann. Rep. 14 (1999); 57 FMCS Ann. Rep. 18 (2004). For fiscal years 2000-2004, the rate at which new NLRB certifications resulted in a first contract hovered in the 55-57 percent range. See 57 FMCS Ann. Rep. 19. See generally John-Paul Ferguson, The Eyes of the Needles: A Sequential Model of Union Organizing Drives, 1999-2004, 62 Indus. & Lab. Rel. Rev. 3 (2008).

In 2006, the NLRB's General Counsel expressed concern about the high incidence of unfair labor practice charges in the first-contract setting. See First Contract Bargaining Cases, GC Mem. 06-05 (April 19, 2006). The General Counsel instructed the Regional Offices in first-contract cases to consider the possibility of seeking §10(j) relief and/or additional special remedies beyond the Board's standard order directing the employer to cease its unlawful refusal to bargain (such as bad-faith "surface bargaining") and to commence good-faith negotiations with the union (i.e., "prospective-only" relief). The additional special remedies have been referenced in a series of General Counsel memoranda since 2006, most recently on April

30, 2014. See Affirmation of 10(j) Program, GC Mem. 14-03, 2 n.4 (2014). The special remedies suggested in the memoranda include requiring bargaining on a prescribed or compressed schedule; periodic reports on bargaining status; a minimum six-month extension of the certification year; requiring a responsible management official to read to employees a notice of the Board's finding and remedies; requiring reimbursement of bargaining expenses; and requiring reimbursement of litigation expenses. See First Contract Bargaining Cases, GC Mem. 11-06 (2011).

**"Make-Whole" Relief? The *Ex-Cell-O* Rule**. In Ex-Cell-O Corp., 185 N.L.R.B. 107 (1970), the employer unlawfully refused to bargain with a union certified after an NLRB election in October 1965. The ALJ recommended that the Board order the employer to make the employees whole for any monetary losses sustained as a result of the company's unlawful refusal to bargain. After hearing oral argument to consider whether it had authority to award such a remedy, the Board ruled that it lacked authority "to permit the punishment of a particular respondent or class of respondents" and that the employer's refusal to bargain with the newly certified union was in the exercise of its right to seek judicial review of the Board's rejection of its objections to the election (regarding alleged union misrepresentations). On the propriety of the "make-whole" remedy, the Board majority stated:

> It is argued that the instant case is distinguishable from *H.K. Porter* in that the requested remedy merely would require the employer to compensate employees for losses they incurred as a consequence of their employer's *failure to agree* to a contract he *would* have agreed to *if* he had bargained in good faith. In our view, the distinction is more illusory than real. The remedy in *H.K. Porter* operates prospectively to bind an employer to a specific contractual term. The remedy in the instant case operates retroactively to impose financial liability upon an employer flowing from a *presumed* contractual agreement. . . . In either case the employer has not agreed to the contractual provision for which he must accept responsibility *as though he had agreed to it*. . . . It does not help to argue that the remedy could not be applied unless there was substantial evidence that the employer would have yielded to these demands during bargaining sessions. Who is to say in a specific case how much an employer is prepared to give and how much a union is willing to take? Who is to say that a favorable contract would, in any event, result from the negotiations? And it is only the employer of such good will as to whom the Board might conclude that he, at least, would have given his employees a fair increase, who can be made subject to a financial reparations order; should such an employer be singled out for the imposition of such an order? To answer these questions the Board would be required to engage in the most general, if not entirely speculative, inferences to reach the conclusion that employees were deprived of specific benefits as a consequence of their employer's refusal to bargain.

Id. at 110 (emphasis in original).

Members McCulloch and Brown dissented in part. On the speculative character of the "make-whole" remedy, the dissenters stated:

> It is well established that the rule which precludes recovery of "uncertain damages" refers to uncertainty as to the fact of injury, rather than to the amount. Where, as here, the employer has deprived its employees of a statutory right, there is by definition a legal injury suffered by them, and any uncertainty concerns only the amount of the accompanying reimbursable financial loss. . . .
>
> [S]ome reasonable method or basis of computation can be worked out as part of the compliance procedure. . . . [T]he following methods for measuring such loss do appear to be available, although these are neither exhaustive nor exclusive. Thus, if the particular employer and union involved have contracts covering other plants of the employer, possibly in the same or a relevant area, the terms of such agreements may serve to show what the employees could probably have obtained by bargaining. The parties could also make comparisons with compensation patterns achieved through collective bargaining for other employees in the same geographic area or industry. Or the parties might employ the national average percentage changes in straight time hourly wages computed by the Bureau of Labor Statistics.

Id. at 117, 118. Who has the better of the argument? Was the "speculative" character of the remedy the real problem in *Ex-Cell-O*?

As for the Board majority's reading of *H.K. Porter*, note that in Int'l Union of Electrical, Radio & Machine Workers (Tiidee Products, Inc.) v. NLRB, 426 F.2d 1243 (1970) ("*Tiidee I*"), decided before *Ex-Cell-O*, the D.C. Circuit held that *H.K. Porter* did not preclude the Board from awarding make-whole relief in first-contract refusal to bargain cases. In remanding for consideration of such relief, the court emphasized that "we have specifically limited the scope of our remand first, to consideration of past damages, not to compulsion of a future contract term, and second, to relate to damages based upon a determination of what the parties themselves would have agreed to if they had engaged in the kind of bargaining process required by the Act." Id. at 1253. Do you find the court's distinguishing of *H.K. Porter* convincing? The facts of *Tiidee* were particularly egregious, and on such facts, the court agreed with the union that the Board had not satisfactorily explained why its standard remedy was adequate:

> . . . Effective redress for a statutory wrong should both compensate the party wronged and withhold from the wrongdoer the "fruits of its violation." . . .
>
> Employee interest in a union can wane quickly as working conditions remain apparently unaffected by the union or collective bargaining. When the company is finally ordered to bargain with the union some years later, the union may find that it represents only a small fraction of the

> employees. . . . Thus the employer may reap a second benefit from his original refusal to comply with the law: he may continue to enjoy lower labor expenses after the order to bargain either because the union is gone or because it is too weak to bargain effectively.

Id. at 1249. The court instructed the Board to consider make-whole relief on remand, but did not mandate it. The Board ultimately declined to issue such relief on the ground that it was impossible to determine with even approximate accuracy what the parties "would have agreed to" had they bargained in good faith, but did order other "extraordinary" relief, discussed below. See 194 N.L.R.B. 1234, 1235 (1972).

Following *Tiidee I,* the same court remanded *Ex-Cell-O* on the union's petition for review for a determination regarding the propriety of make-whole relief or some other special remedy. Int'l Union, UAW v. NLRB, 449 F.2d 1046 (D.C. Cir. 1971). Before the Board could decide the case on remand, however, the court issued a separate ruling on the employer's petition for review, concluding that the employer's objections were, in fact, "fairly debatable" and that a compensatory award was therefore inappropriate. Ex-Cell-O Corp. v. NLRB, 449 F.2d 1058 (D.C. Cir. 1971).

Despite the D.C. Circuit's view that the Board may order make-whole relief in at least some cases, the Board has never reexamined its *Ex-Cell-O* rule. See Micah Berul, To Bargain or Not to Bargain Should Not Be the Question: Deterring Section 8(a)(5) Violations in First-Time Bargaining Situations Through a Liberalized Standard for the Award of Litigation and Negotiation Costs, 18 Lab. Law. 27, 35 (2002). Should it?

**Litigation Expenses, Negotiation Expenses, and Access Remedies.** Despite denying make-whole relief, on remand in *Tiidee* the Board ordered the employer to pay to the Board and the union the costs of litigation, to mail a copy of the Board-ordered notice to each employee, to give the union access to company bulletin boards, and to supply the union with an up-to-date list of employee names and addresses. In "*Tiidee II,*" the D.C. Circuit approved the notice and access aspects of the Board's order, but denied reimbursement of the Board's expenses on the ground that the employer had not been a habitual offender, and limited the union's recovery of litigation expenses to the period during which the employer had engaged in "frivolous" litigation. See Int'l Union of Elec., Radio & Mach. Workers v. NLRB, 502 F.2d 349 (D.C. Cir. 1974). In *Unbelievable, Inc. v. NLRB,* 118 F.3d 795 (D.C. Cir. 1997), denying enforcement in relevant part to Frontier Hotel & Casino, 318 N.L.R.B. 857 (1995), however, the same court held that the Board lacks any authority under NLRA §10(c) to award litigation expenses, the bulk of which are generally attorney's fees. In *Unbelievable,* the court relied on Summit Valley Industries, Inc. v. Carpenters, 456 U.S. 717 (1982), which held that the presumption against an award of attorneys' fees erected by the "American rule" that each side bears its own expenses can be overridden only by express Congressional authorization. The court found no such authorization in §10(c) or the Act's legislative history. The court did not, however, reach the question of the Board's authority to award litigation expenses under the "bad faith" exception to the American rule, finding that the Board had not relied on this potential alternative theory. 118 F.3d at 800 n.l.

Since *Unbelievable,* the Board has continued to award litigation expenses where it finds that a party has acted in bad faith in its actions leading up to the litigation (such as a refusal to bargain) or in the conduct of the litigation itself (such as raising "frivolous" defenses), relying both on §10(c) and on its "inherent authority to control its own proceedings through an application of the 'bad faith' exception to the American rule." See Alwin Mfg. Co., 326 N.L.R.B. 646, 647 (1998), enforced, 192 F.2d 133 (D.C. Cir. 1999) (court lacked jurisdiction to consider remedy because no objection was raised before Board); Lake Holiday Manor, 325 N.L.R.B. 469 (1998) (awarding litigation expenses to General Counsel on basis of bad-faith exception); cf. Teamsters Local Union No. 122 (August A. Busch & Co.), 334 N.L.R.B. 1190 (2001) (awarding litigation as well as negotiation costs to both General Counsel and employer in §8(b)(3) surface bargaining case, citing both §10(c) and bad faith exception).

Consider the fact that small employers and unions that prevail in litigation before the Board can recover *their* litigation expenses if the General Counsel cannot show that his position was "substantially justified." See Equal Access to Justice Act (EAJA), 28 U.S.C. §§2412(d)(1)(A), d(2)(D) (2000) (covering entities with fewer than 500 employees and less than $7 million in net worth); see also Samuel Estreicher & Richard L. Revesz, Nonacquiescence by Federal Administrative Agencies, 98 Yale L.J. 679, 758 & nn.347-48 (1989). The EAJA does not, however, provide for similar recovery by the agency or the charging party where the respondent's position was "substantially unjustified." Should it? See Berul, To Bargain or Not to Bargain, supra, at 44-46.

Finally, the Board on occasion has awarded negotiation expenses to the union where an employer has engaged in bad-faith bargaining. See *Frontier Hotel,* supra, 318 N.L.R.B. 857, 859 (1995) (reimbursement warranted "both to make the charging party whole for the resources that were wasted because of the unlawful conduct, and to restore the economic strength that is necessary to ensure a return to the status quo ante at the bargaining table"), enforced in relevant part, 118 F.3d 795. In *Frontier,* however, the Board made clear that such awards are confined to cases of "unusually aggravated misconduct." Id.

**Proposals for Reform**

a. *Make-Whole Relief.* The proposed Labor Reform Act of 1977 would have authorized the Board to award a make-whole remedy in the case of bad-faith bargaining in a first-contract situation. The award would have been calculated using Bureau of Labor Statistics data on average wage and benefit settlements reached during the period of bad-faith bargaining. See H.R. 8410, 95th Cong., 1st Sess. §8(3)(3) (1977) (as passed House) (amending NLRA §10(c)). Note that make-whole relief is authorized by the California Agricultural Labor Relations Act. See Cal. Lab. Code §1160.3 (2010); see also George Arakelian Farms, Inc. v. NLRB, 49 Cal. 3d 1279, 265 Cal. Rptr. 162, 783 P.2d 749 (1989).

b. *Interest Arbitration.* Since 2002, the California statute has also required interest arbitration when agricultural employers and the unions representing their employees have been unable to agree on the terms of a first contract. See Cal. Labor Code §§1164 et seq. (2010); see also Hess Collection Winery v. Cal. Agr. Labor Relations Bd., 140 Cal. App. 4th 1584, 45 Cal. Rptr. 3d 609, 179 L.R.R.M. (BNA) 3225 (Cal. App. 3d Dist. 2006) (2-1) (rejecting challenge under federal and state constitutions to provision), review denied, Sept. 13, 2006.

The proposed Employee Free Choice Act of 2009 (EFCA) would have provided for mandatory mediation, and if necessary, arbitration of initial agreements following certification or recognition. EFCA would have empowered either party after ninety days of bargaining to ask the FMCS to attempt to mediate an agreement and if it could not do so after an additional 30 days, to "refer the dispute to an arbitration board established in accordance with such regulations as may be prescribed by the Service." The arbitration panel's "decision settling the dispute" would have been "binding upon the parties for a period of 2 years, unless amended during such period by written consent of the parties." This provision is criticized in Andrew M. Kramer, et al., Two Sentences, 104 Words: Congress's Folly in First Contract Arbitration and the Future of Free Collective Bargaining, ch. 3 in Labor and Employment Law Initiatives and Proposals under the Obama Administration: Proceedings of the New York University 62nd Annual Conference on Labor 117 (Zev J. Eigen ed., 2011).

The interest-arbitration provision of EFCA was modeled in part on legislation in the Canadian federal sector and a number of Canadian provinces. See William B. Gould IV, Agenda for Reform: The Future of Employment Relationships and the Law 222-230 (1993); Paul C. Weiler, Striking a New Balance: Freedom of Contract and the Prospects for Union Representation, 98 Harv. L. Rev. 351, 405-412 (1984). While some provinces confined interest arbitration to a remedy for bad-faith bargaining, British Columbia for a time expanded its law to allow parties to apply for arbitration to resolve impasses in first-contract negotiations, and at least one other province provided almost automatic access to interest arbitration in first-contract situations. The Canadian experience with first-contract interest arbitration is assessed in Roy L. Heenan & Danny J. Kaufer, Card Majority Certification and First Contract Arbitration: Lessons from the Canadian Experience, ch. 9 in Eigen, Labor and Employment Law Initiatives, supra, at 431.

It is unclear whether agreements that are the product of first-contract arbitration awards result in enduring relationships. Compare Gary N. Chaison & Joseph B. Rose, The Canadian Perspective on Workers' Rights to Form a Union and Bargain Collectively, in Restoring the Promise of American Labor Law 241, 246 (Friedman et al. eds., 1994), with Errol Black & Craig Hosea, First Contract Legislation in Manitoba: A Model for the United States?, 45 Lab. L.J. 33, 36-38 (1994); see also Sabrina Sills, First Contract Arbitration in Ontario: Success or Failure? 1986-1990 (Master's Thesis, Queen's Univ., Kingston, Ont., Aug. 1991), 29-30. At a minimum, however, there is some suggestion that the prospect of first-contract arbitration may deter bad-faith bargaining and general foot-dragging and increase the overall first-contract success rate. See Chaison & Rose, supra, at 246; Joseph B. Rose & Gary N. Chaison, Canadian Labor Policy as a Model for Legislative Reform in the United States, 46 Lab. L.J. 259, 265-266 (1995). For additional assessments of the Canadian experience, see A.P. Macdonald, First Contract Arbitration in Canada, School of Indus. Rel. Research Essay Series No. 17 (Indus. Rel. Centre, Queen's Univ., Kingston, Ont., 1988); Jean Sexton, First Contract Arbitration in Canada, 38 Lab. L.J. 508 (1987).

Even if interest arbitration were strictly available only as a remedy for bad-faith bargaining, do you see any difficulties with the proposal? Where are arbitrators to find principles for deciding the content of first contracts? Can we be confident that arbitrators will craft agreements that provide a stable context for continuing relationships by reflecting the market pressures on firms or the preferences of the employees? Would it make more sense for Congress to authorize the Board to impose on employers and unions who cannot reach agreement on a first contract collective agreements that "include just-cause and grievance-arbitration clauses, based on due-process standards and industry practices, in addition to no-strike clauses," but that do not specify substantive work place rules or wages or fringe benefit plans? Would such authority enable the Board to protect a new collective bargaining relationship from being aborted short of a first contract, without the problems posed by make-whole relief or general first-contract arbitration? See Michael C. Harper, A Framework for the Rejuvenation of the American Labor Movement, 76 Ind. L.J. 103, 125-126 (2001).

Should interest arbitration also be available as a remedy for bad-faith bargaining during contract renewal talks? Former NLRB Chair Gould thinks so. See Gould, Agenda for Reform, supra, at 230. Would we still have collective bargaining rather than government stipulation of the terms and conditions of employment if renewal agreements were also subject to interest arbitration? See Samuel Estreicher, The Dunlop Report and the Future of Labor Law Reform, 18 Regulation 28, 34 (No. 1, Winter 1995), 28, 34; 12 Lab. Law. 117 (1996). Despite these formidable difficulties, is there any alternative approach that offers a comparable promise of remedying bargaining violations that frustrate the declared preferences of workers for collective representation?

## 4. Disclosure Obligations

**NLRB v. Truitt Manufacturing Co.**
*351 U.S. 149 (1956)*

Black, J. . . .

The question presented by this case is whether the [NLRB] may find that an employer has not bargained in good faith where the employer claims it cannot afford to pay higher wages but refuses requests to produce information substantiating its claim.

The dispute here arose when a union [representative] . . . asked for a wage increase of 10 cents per hour. The company answered that it could not afford to pay such an increase, it was undercapitalized, had never paid dividends, and that an increase of more than 2 cents per hour would put it out of business. The union asked the company to produce some evidence substantiating these statements, requesting permission to have a certified public accountant examine the company's books, financial data, etc. This request being denied, the union asked that the company submit "full and complete information with respect to its financial standing and profits," insisting that such information was pertinent and essential for the employees to determine whether or not they should continue to press their demand for a wage increase. A union official testified before the trial examiner that "[W]e were wanting anything relating to the Company's position, any records or what have you, books, accounting sheets, cost expenditures, what not, anything to back the Company's position that they were unable to give any more money." The company refused all the requests, relying solely on the statement that "the information . . . is not pertinent to this discussion and the company declines to give you such information; you have no legal right to such."

On the basis of these facts the [Board] found that the company had "failed to bargain in good faith with respect to wages in violation of §8(a)(5) of the Act." 110 N.L.R.B. 856. The Board ordered the company to supply the union with such information as would "substantiate the Respondent's position of its economic inability to pay the requested wage increase." The Court of Appeals refused to enforce the Board's order, agreeing with respondent that it could not be held guilty of an unfair labor practice because of its refusal to furnish the information requested by the union. . . .

The company raised no objection to the Board's order on the ground that the scope of information required was too broad or that disclosure would put an undue burden on the company. Its major argument throughout has been that the information requested was irrelevant to the bargaining process and related to matters exclusively within the province of management. Thus we lay to one side the suggestion by the company here that the Board's order might be unduly burdensome or injurious to its business. In any event, the Board has heretofore taken the position in cases such as this that "It is sufficient if the information is made available in a manner not so burdensome or time-consuming as to impede the process of bargaining." And in this case the Board has held substantiation of the company's position requires no more than "reasonable proof."

We think that in determining whether the obligation of good-faith bargaining has been met the Board has a right to consider an employer's refusal to give information about its financial status. While Congress did not compel agreement between employers and bargaining representatives, it did require collective bargaining in the hope that agreements would result. Section 204(a)(1) of the [1947 Labor Management Relations] Act admonishes both employers and employees to "exert every reasonable effort to make and maintain agreements concerning rates of pay, hours, and working conditions. . . ." In their effort to reach an agreement here both the union and the company treated the company's ability to pay increased wages as highly relevant. The ability of an employer to increase wages without injury to his business is a commonly considered factor in wage negotiations. Claims for increased wages have sometimes been abandoned because of an employer's unsatisfactory business condition; employees have even voted to accept wage decreases because of such conditions.

Good-faith bargaining necessarily requires that claims made by either bargainer should be honest claims. This is true about an asserted inability to pay an increase in wages. If such an argument is important enough to present in the give and take of bargaining, it is important enough to require some sort of proof of its accuracy. And it would certainly not be farfetched for a trier of fact to reach the conclusion that bargaining lacks good faith when an employer mechanically repeats a claim of inability to pay without making the slightest effort to substantiate the claim. . . . We agree with the Board that a refusal to attempt to substantiate a claim of inability to pay increased wages may support a finding of a failure to bargain in good faith.

The Board concluded that under the facts and circumstances of this case the respondent was guilty of an unfair labor practice in failing to bargain in good faith. We see no reason to disturb the findings of the Board. We do not hold, however, that in every case in which economic inability is raised as an argument against increased wages it automatically follows that the employees are entitled to substantiating evidence. Each case must turn upon its particular facts. . . .

FRANKFURTER, J., whom CLARK and HARLAN, JJ., join, concurring in part and dissenting in part. . . .

"Good faith" means more than merely going through the motions of negotiating; it is inconsistent with a predetermined resolve not to budge from an initial position. But it is not necessarily incompatible with stubbornness or even with what to an outsider may seem unreasonableness. A determination of good faith or of want of good faith normally can rest only on an inference based upon more or less persuasive manifestations of another's state of mind. The previous relations of the parties, antecedent events explaining behavior at the bargaining table, and the course of negotiations constitute the raw facts for reaching such a determination. The appropriate inferences to be drawn from what is often confused and tangled testimony about all this makes a finding of absence of good faith one for the judgment of the Labor Board, unless the record as a whole leaves such judgment without reasonable foundation.

An examination of the Board's opinion and the position taken by its counsel here disclose that the Board did not so conceive the issue of good-faith bargaining in this case. The totality of the conduct of the negotiation was apparently deemed irrelevant to the question; one fact alone disposed of the case. . . .

Since the Board applied the wrong standard here, by ruling that Truitt's failure to supply financial information to the union constituted per se a refusal to bargain in good faith, the case should be returned to the Board. There is substantial evidence in the record which indicates that Truitt tried to reach an agreement. It offered a 2[.5]-cent wage increase, it expressed willingness to discuss with the union "at any time the problem of how our wages compare with those of our competition," and it continued throughout to meet and discuss the controversy with the union. . . . I would return the case to the Board so that it may apply the relevant standard for determining "good faith."

## *NOTES AND QUESTIONS*

**1. Duty to Substantiate Bargaining Positions?** Why does the *Truitt* Court state that good-faith bargaining requires some measure of honest bargaining, that claims made at the bargaining table be "honest claims"? Bargaining in other contexts often involves elements of exaggeration, bluff, and even outright deceit. Is the Court attempting to use the duty to substantiate bargaining positions to encourage practices that it believes will promote a successful, long-term bargaining relationship? How broad is the duty to substantiate positions? Does it apply to any factual claim made by either side? Does it apply only to claims like the "inability to pay" position that employees and their bargaining agents will not be able to accurately assess on their own? For the view that *Truitt*'s honesty-in-bargaining policy should also be understood as an effort to prevent some employers from taking advantage of the trust generated by the honest bargaining engaged in by other employers with their unions, see Keith N. Hylton, An Economic Theory of the Duty to Bargain, 83 Geo. L.J. 19, 37-42 (1994).

**2. Areas of "Presumptive Relevancy" and "Presumptive Irrelevancy."** The Board's approach to disclosure obligations is to categorize certain items of information as "presumptively relevant" to the union's collective bargaining or grievance adjustment functions and other items as "presumptively irrelevant." Generally, data about unit employees' wages, benefits, and job classifications are presumptively relevant; in order to resist disclosure, the employer must prove lack of relevance. See Curtiss-Wright Corp., 145 N.L.R.B. 152 (1963), enforced, 347 F.2d 61 (3d Cir. 1965); Fairfield Daily Republic, 275 N.L.R.B. 7, 8-9 (1985), enforced, 782 F.2d 1052 (9th Cir. 1986). In contrast, there are other areas where the Board will not presume relevancy but will require the union (or employer) affirmatively to prove relevancy. For example, a union is generally presumed to have no legitimate interest in information about employees whom it does not represent. See, e.g., *Fairfield*, supra (such information is presumptively irrelevant). But consider a situation where the union wants information about wage rates and fringe benefits paid to employees at another plant of the employer because it fears the employer may be diverting bargaining-unit work to the other plant because of its lower labor costs. On the assumption that the employer has to bargain about an employer's diversion of bargaining-unit work elsewhere, see infra pages 491-493, is it obligated to disclose the requested information? Compare E.I. duPont de Nemours & Co., 268 N.L.R.B. 1031 (1984) (information on pay of non-unit personnel doing work similar to bargaining unit is relevant); NLRB v. Leonard B. Hebert Jr. & Co., 696 F.2d 1120 (5th Cir. 1983) (applying liberal discovery rule standard of probable relevance), with Bohemia, Inc., 272 N.L.R.B. 1128 (1984) (suspicion of work transfer without objective evidence not sufficient basis for obligation to disclose).

**3. Employer's Financial Records: "Competitive Disadvantage" vs. "Inability to Pay."** What sort of claims of an employer about its financial condition are necessary to render its financial records relevant under *Truitt*? Is the *Truitt* obligation triggered by a claim that the employer will be put at a "competitive disadvantage" if it accedes to the union's demands, or will only a claim of "inability to pay" suffice? The Board at one time found relatively broad pleas of competitive disadvantage sufficient. See Cincinnati Cordage & Paper Co., 141 N.L.R.B. 72 (1963); Harvstone Mfg. Corp., 272 N.L.R.B. 939 (1984). It found difficulty, however, securing judicial enforcement of its orders. See ConAgra, Inc. v. NLRB, 117 F.3d 1435

(D.C. Cir. 1997) (recounting cases in this area). For example, in NLRB v. Harvstone Mfg. Corp., 785 F.2d 570, 575 (7th Cir. 1986), the Seventh Circuit ruled that *Truitt* is not triggered when "the employer said it 'would not' as opposed to 'could not' pay the employees' proposed demands." After initially resisting the Seventh Circuit's *Harvstone* position, see Nielsen Lithographing Co., 279 N.L.R.B. 877 (1986), enforcement denied and case remanded, 854 F.2d 1063 (7th Cir. 1988) ("*Nielsen I*"), the Board adopted it as its own. In Nielsen Lithographing Co., 305 N.L.R.B. 697, 701 (1991), enforced sub nom. Graphic Communications Int'l Union Local 508 v. NLRB, 977 F.2d 1168 (7th Cir. 1992) ("*Nielsen II*"), the Board stated "that an employer's obligation under *Truitt* to provide a union with information by which it may fulfill its representative function in bargaining does not extend to information concerning the employer's projections of its future ability to compete."

In KLB Industries, 357 N.L.R.B. No. 8 (2011), enforced 700 F.3d 551 (D.C. Cir. 2012), the employer had proposed significant wage reductions during negotiations over a successor bargaining agreement, claiming that it was confronting competition from Asia, reduced production and increased production costs. The Board ruled that the union was entitled to information related to these claims, including lists of current and former customers, product prices, bids for new work and its cost saving report related to the projected wage concessions. Unlike in *Nielsen*, these requests did not involve balance sheets or information about the company's revenue and profits. The agency also found it crucial that the employer's competitiveness claims related to "a present and pressing lack of competitiveness in specific markets," rather than an "abstract proposition" or "routine negotiating verbiage" about competitiveness.

Is the "inability to pay" versus "competitive disadvantage" distinction sensible in determining when unions can obtain financial information from the employer? Consider Judge Posner's opinion for the panel in *Nielsen II*:

> All that we take *Truitt* to hold is that the union is entitled to obtain from the employer information that is relevant to substantiating the claims made by the employer in the bargaining process. If the employer claims that it cannot afford to pay a higher wage or, as here, the existing wage, the union is entitled to demand substantiation in the employer's financial records. Otherwise the employer would have an unfair advantage in bargaining, because it would be making an express or implied threat (of bankruptcy) that the union could not evaluate. That was *Truitt.* But there isn't a hint of it here. . . . All that [the company] was claiming was that if it didn't do anything about its labor costs it would continue to lose business and lay off workers. It didn't claim that it was in any financial trouble. . . . The union had all the information it needed to decide whether to knuckle under to the company's demands or call a strike.

977 F.2d at 1170-1171. If a union has a legitimate interest in knowing whether a strike could terminate operations, does it not also have an interest in knowing whether a strike might cause a substantial contraction of available work? Can the union obtain by other means information about demand conditions and the firm's costs and debt structure? The firm's ability to shift production elsewhere? The firm's plans for doing so? For a contrasting view to that of Judge Posner's, see Judge Wald's concurrence in *ConAgra,* 117 F.3d at 1447-1449 (urging Board to revisit *Nielsen II*).

**4. Applications of *Truitt.***

a. In the course of negotiations over wages and other benefits, an employer makes statements that it was "not going to be able to survive," "might have to close the business" and was a "bleeding, distressed asset—a losing proposition." It also made statements that it would "take [its] toy and . . . leave" unless the union made concessions, but that the preferred option was "to try to improve the company's financial condition" and "return it to profitable condition." Are these claims of the employer's inability to pay, prompting an employer duty to disclose its audited financial statement to the union? See Stella D'Oro Biscuit Co., 355 N.L.R.B. 769 (2010), enforcement denied sub nom. SDBC Holdings, Inc. v. NLRB, 711 F.3d 281 (2d Cir. 2013) (no duty because statements viewed in context show unwillingness, not inability, to pay). Assuming these are not inability-to-pay claims, are these claims "routine negotiating verbiage" or more specific claims of a present lack of competiveness which might prompt some information disclosure under *KLB,* supra page 444?

b. The employer, operator of a private bus line, submits a final offer providing for an extended wage freeze, a decrease in the amount of overtime available, and a $500 one-time payment in exchange for the overtime decrease. The company president writes a letter to employees noting that the company has lost 7,500 riders per week to a newly established public transit line. The letter states that "we are asking for help . . . so we may retain your jobs and get back in the black in the short term," and asks the employees to ratify the final offer, stating that "The future of Lakeland depends on it." Is this an inability-to-pay claim triggering the employer's duty to allow the union's accountant to inspect its books and records? See Lakeland Bus Lines, Inc., 335 N.L.R.B. 322 (2001), enforcement denied, 347 F.3d 955 (D.C. Cir. 2003).

c. In response to union proposals on benefits that the employer says will cost an extra $3 per hour per employee, the employer responds that the union is "asking for pie in the sky," that the employer had purchased the company "in distress a year and a half earlier, and that the company was still in distress," and that it was "fighting to stay alive." A subsequent union proposal to change the wholly discretionary wage increase policy to a guaranteed increase of $1/year in each year of a three-year contract elicited similar statements. Is this an inability-to-pay claim under *Truitt*? See AMF Trucking & Warehousing, Inc., 342 N.L.R.B. 1125 (2004) (no duty because company never said "survival was at stake").

d. Following an employer counterproposal that includes a one-year suspension of its matching pension contributions, the union representative asks the company's chief negotiator whether she is saying that the company could not afford the union's proposal. She replies, "No, I can't. I'd go broke." In a letter the next day responding to the union's written information request, the company's negotiator denies making any such statement and asserts that "at no time have I ever told you we cannot afford your proposals." If the union's account of the negotiation session is credited, was a *Truitt* obligation triggered? If so, did the letter effectively retract any asserted claim of an inability to pay and negate any potential duty to disclose? Compare American Polystyrene Corp., 341 N.L.R.B. 508 (2004) (finding a retraction), with Int'l Chemical Workers Union Council v. NLRB, 447 F.3d 1153 (9th Cir. 2006) (reversing Board's finding because company continued to claim it could not pay); see also Central Management Co., 314 N.L.R.B. 763, 768-769 (1994); Lakeland Bus Lines, Inc. v. NLRB, 347 F.3d 955, 961 (D.C. Cir. 2003) (both confirming that employer may retract claim of inability-to-pay by a clear statement to union).

**5. Evidence of Bad Faith vs. Per Se Violation?** Where an employer has asserted an "inability to pay" and then refused to disclose financial information following a union request, will a §8(a)(5) violation automatically be found? Note the *Truitt* Court's express limitation on the reach of its holding. Compare Ameron Pipe Prods., 305 N.L.R.B. 105, 109 n.7 (1991) ("Although the Supreme Court limited its holding, the case has become widely accepted as establishing for all practical purposes . . . an 'automatic' rule"), with *American Polystyrene,* supra note 4d, 341 N.L.R.B. at 509 (2004) ("*Truitt* . . . recognized that this general rule is not to be applied mechanically"); see also *Chemical Workers,* supra note 4d, 447 F.3d at 1159 n.3 & 1161-1163 (contrasting its totality of circumstances approach with that of other circuits).

**6. Disclosure Obligations and Trust.** Do the decisions on disclosure of financial data discussed in the preceding notes reflect a vision of the bargaining process in which labor and management are engaged exclusively in "distributional bargaining," in the sense that one side's gain must come at the other side's expense? Is there a role for the law to play in encouraging "integrative bargaining"—the search for outcomes that improve the positions of both sides or at least minimize loss to one side? Cf. Richard E. Walton & Robert B. McKersie, A Behavioral Theory of Labor Negotiations: An Analysis of Social Interaction Systems 129 (1991 ed.) (defining integrative bargaining). Walton and McKersie suggest that integrative bargaining is not possible without a "maximum exchange of information about the problems perceived by each party in order that these problems be identified and defined in their essentials." Id. at 137. They also stress that integrative bargaining is not possible without trust, and that trust requires the full sharing of information. Id. at 358.

Can it be assumed that employers will share information with unions where there are strong prospects of integrative bargaining and will avoid disclosures where such prospects are dim? Might employers avoid disclosures because of legitimate concerns that unions, as multiemployer organizations, might share nonpublic financial information with representatives of employees of competitor firms, or that unions might use disclosure obligations strategically as a means of triggering additional rounds of disclosure for the purpose of delaying resolution of the dispute? Could these concerns be dealt with directly "by preventing disputes over financial information from being used to protract bargaining and requiring safeguards to prevent unions from sharing proprietary information with competitor firms or the general public"? See Samuel Estreicher, Labor Law Reform in a World of Competitive Product Markets, 69 Chi.-Kent L. Rev. 3, 41-42 (1993).

**7. Can Interests in Confidentiality Overcome a Claim of Presumptive Access to Relevant Information?** The Supreme Court, in Detroit Edison Co. v. NLRB, 440 U.S. 301 (1979), answered in the affirmative. The *Detroit Edison* principle calls for a balancing between the employees' interests in gaining access to the information and the employer's confidentiality interests. The case involved a dispute about whether the employer was giving adequate weight to seniority in deciding promotions. In the course of this dispute, the union challenged the employer's use of a battery of aptitude tests in allotting promotions. During arbitration, the union requested test-related materials, including the test battery, the applicants' test papers and scores. The employer refused to turn over the materials directly to the union, although it did offer to turn the materials over to an industrial psychologist selected by the union. The company claimed that preserving the confidentiality of the materials was necessary to ensure the integrity of the tests for future use. The Supreme Court agreed. With respect to the test battery and answer sheets, the Court stated:

> The future validity of the tests is tied to secrecy, and disclosure to employees would not only threaten the Company's investment but would also leave the Company with no valid means of measuring employee aptitude.

440 U.S. at 313. With respect to the scores received by individual employees, the Court concluded that the Company satisfied its duty by offering to

release the scores only if it received consents from the examinees. The Court reasoned:

> The sensitivity of any human being to disclosure of information that may be taken to bear on his or her basic competence is sufficiently well known to be an appropriate subject of judicial notice. There is nothing in this record to suggest that the Company promised the examinees that their scores would remain confidential in order to further parochial concerns or to frustrate subsequent union attempts to process employee grievances. And it has not been suggested at any point in this proceeding that the Company's unilateral promise of confidentiality was in itself violative of the terms of the collective-bargaining agreement. Indeed, the Company presented evidence that disclosure of individual scores had in the past resulted in the harassment of some lower scoring examinees who had, as a result, left the Company.

Id. at 318-319. Along with the confidentiality and privacy concerns at issue in *Detroit Edison*, other factors can overcome the presumptive access to relevant information. See, e.g., NLRB v. Wachter Constr., Inc., 23 F.3d 1378 (8th Cir. 1994) (when the party's primary purpose is to harass the other party); Cincinnati Steel Castings Co., 86 N.L.R.B. 592 (1949) (when the request is unduly burdensome).

**8. Employer Confidentiality.**

a. *Use of Intermediaries.* Did *Detroit Edison*'s approval of providing relevant information to an industrial psychologist suggest an approach to addressing union demands for access to relevant information while still meeting legitimate employer concerns over preserving confidentiality? Did the union have any need for direct access to the test validation data beyond what information would be obtained from scrutiny of the data by an industrial psychologist of its choosing? See also Hercules, Inc. v. NLRB, 833 F.2d 426 (2d Cir. 1987) (requiring employer to provide access to union's nonemployee industrial hygienist to investigate fatal explosion, conditioned on union's executing standard trade secrets agreement required of all employees and contractors working in the plant).

b. *Redacted Documents.* Consider also the situation in NLRB v. New England Newspapers, Inc., 856 F.2d 409 (1st Cir. 1988). In that case the union sought access to a sales agreement to determine whether adequate reserves had been established to meet liabilities under the labor agreement; whether the sales agreement provided for preferential rehiring or seniority carry-over for existing employees; and whether the union would continue to have bargaining authority once the purchaser took over. Notably, the union agreed to allow the employer to redact the sales price and agreed not to reveal the information to third parties.

**9. Employee Confidentiality.** Does *Detroit Edison* give adequate weight to the union's responsibility as the collective bargaining agent of the employees? Will unions be able to secure consents from all unit employees when they are in competition with each other for the disputed promotions, and some have been promoted on the basis of the test scores and others have not? If under *J.I. Case* unions can compromise the individual contractual entitlements of employees, why can they not also be privy to private, work-related information about the employees, at least where the information is relevant to the union's bargaining or grievance functions and there is no history of prior harassment or other misuse? Is *Detroit Edison* a case where the union made no showing why it needed to be able to identify which individuals received particular test scores or that requiring employee consents would undermine its ability to process effectively the promotion grievance? Does *Detroit Edison* support recognition of a strong employee interest in the confidentiality of personnel records maintained by the employer? Would consents be required in a case where a union seeks access to the personnel records of coworkers in order to show discriminatory application of company rules? Compare New Jersey Bell Tel. Co. v. NLRB, 720 F.2d 789 (3d Cir. 1983) (employer need not release coworker attendance records, some of which contain sensitive medical information, without securing coworkers' consent), with New Jersey Bell Tel. Co., 289 N.L.R.B. 318 (1988) (compelling disclosure without consent where no showing was made that records contained sensitive personal information, union agreed to accept records with employee names redacted, and Board concluded that company was using its "employee privacy protection plan" as pretext for denying union information to which it was entitled). What about an employer's interview notes taken during an investigation of misconduct? See also Northern Indiana Public Service Co., 347 N.L.R.B. 210 (2006) (employer need not furnish union with interview notes made in investigation of threatening conduct in workplace).

## 5. The Concept of "Impasse"

### NLRB v. Katz
*369 U.S. 736 (1962)*

Brennan, J.

Is it a violation of the duty "to bargain collectively" . . . for an employer, without first consulting a union with which it is carrying on bona fide contract negotiations, to institute changes regarding matters which are subjects of mandatory bargaining under §8(d) and which are in fact under discussion? The [NLRB] answered the question affirmatively in this case, in a decision which expressly disclaimed any finding that the totality of the respondents' conduct manifested bad faith in the pending negotiations. 126 N.L.R.B. 288. . . . [T]he Second Circuit denied enforcement of the Board's [order], finding in our decision in Labor Board v. Insurance Agents' Union, 361 U.S. 477, a broad rule that the statutory duty to bargain cannot be held to be violated, when bargaining is in fact being carried on, without a finding of the respondent's subjective bad faith in negotiating. . . . We find nothing in the Board's decision inconsistent with *Insurance Agents* and hold that the Court of Appeals erred in refusing to enforce the Board's order. . . .

. . . As amended and amplified at the hearing and construed by the Board, the complaint's charge of unfair labor practices particularly referred to three acts by the company: unilaterally granting numerous merit increases in October 1956 and January 1957; unilaterally announcing a change in sick-leave policy in March 1957; and unilaterally instituting a new system of automatic wage increases during April 1957. . . . [T]he company has defended against the charges along two fronts: First, it asserts that the unilateral changes occurred after a bargaining impasse had developed through the union's fault in adopting obstructive tactics.[7] According to the Board, however, "the evidence is clear that the Respondent undertook its unilateral actions before negotiations were discontinued in May 1957, or before, as we find on the record, the existence of any possible impasse." 126 N.L.R.B., at 289-290. There is ample support in the record considered as a whole for this finding of fact, . . . which the Court of Appeals did not question.

The second line of defense was that the Board could not hinge a conclusion that §8(a)(5) had been violated on unilateral actions alone, without making a finding of the employer's subjective bad faith at the bargaining table; and that the unilateral actions were merely evidence relevant to the issue of subjective good faith. This argument prevailed in the Court of Appeals which remanded the cases to the Board. . . .

The duty "to bargain collectively" enjoined by §8(a)(5) is defined by §8(d) as the duty to "meet . . . and confer in good faith with respect to wages, hours, and other terms and conditions of employment." Clearly, the duty thus defined may be violated without a general failure of subjective good faith; for there is no occasion to consider the issue of good faith if a party has refused even to negotiate *in fact*—"to meet . . . and confer"—about any of the mandatory subjects. A refusal to negotiate *in fact* as to any subject which is within §8(d), and about which the union seeks to negotiate, violates §8(a)(5) though the employer has every desire to reach agreement with the union

7. The Examiner rejected the company's offer to prove union-instigated slowdowns. But such proof would not have justified the company's refusal to bargain. Since, as we held in Labor Board v. Insurance Agents' Union, 361 U.S. 477, the Board may not brand partial strike activity as illegitimate and forbid its use in support of bargaining, an *employer* cannot be free to refuse to negotiate when the union resorts to such tactics. Engaging in partial strikes is not inherently inconsistent with a continued willingness to negotiate; and as long as there is such willingness and no impasse has developed, the employer's obligation continues.

upon an over-all collective agreement and earnestly and in all good faith bargains to that end. We hold that an employer's unilateral change in conditions of employment under negotiation is similarly a violation of §8(a)(5), for it is a circumvention of the duty to negotiate which frustrates the objectives of §8(a)(5) much as does a flat refusal.

The unilateral actions of the respondent illustrate the policy and practical considerations which support our conclusion.

We consider first the matter of sick leave. A sick-leave plan had been in effect since May 1956, under which employees were allowed ten paid sick-leave days annually and could accumulate half the unused days, or up to five days each year. Changes in the plan were sought and proposals and counterproposals had come up at three bargaining conferences. In March 1957, the company, without first notifying or consulting the union, announced changes in the plan, which reduced from ten to five the number of paid sick-leave days per year, but allowed accumulation of twice the unused days, thus increasing to ten the number of days which might be carried over. This action plainly frustrated the statutory objective of establishing working conditions through bargaining. Some employees might view the change to be a diminution of benefits. Others, more interested in accumulating sick-leave days, might regard the change as an improvement. If one view or the other clearly prevailed among the employees, the unilateral action might well mean that the employer had either uselessly dissipated trading material or aggravated the sick-leave issue. On the other hand, if the employees were more evenly divided on the merits of the company's changes the union negotiators, beset by conflicting factions, might be led to adopt a protective vagueness on the issue of sick leave, which also would inhibit the useful discussion contemplated by Congress in imposing the specific obligation to bargain collectively.

Other considerations appear from consideration of the respondents' unilateral action in increasing wages. At the April 4, 1957, meeting the employers offered, and the union rejected, a three-year contract with an immediate across-the-board increase of $7.50 per week, to be followed at the end of the first year and again at the end of the second by further increases of $5 for employees earning less than $90 at those times. Shortly thereafter, without having advised or consulted with the union, the company announced a new system of automatic wage increases whereby there would be an increase of $5 every three months up to $74.99 per week; an increase of $5 every six months between $75 and $90 per week; and a merit review every six months for employees earning over $90 per week. It is clear at a glance that the automatic wage increase system which was instituted unilaterally was considerably more generous than that which had shortly theretofore been offered to and rejected by the union. Such action conclusively manifested bad faith in the negotiations, Labor Board v. Crompton-Highland Mills, 337 U.S. 217, and so would have violated §8(a)(5) even on the Court of Appeals' interpretation, though no additional evidence of bad faith appeared. An employer is not required to lead with his best offer; he is free to bargain. But even after an impasse is reached he has no license to grant wage increases greater than any he has ever offered the union at the bargaining table, for such action is necessarily inconsistent with a sincere desire to conclude an agreement with the union.[12]

The respondents' third unilateral action related to merit increases, which are also a subject of mandatory bargaining. Labor Board v. Allison & Co., 165 F.2d 766. The matter of merit increases had been raised at three of the conferences during 1956 but no final understanding had been reached. In January 1957, the company, without notice to the union, granted merit increases to 20 employees out of the approximately 50 in the unit, the increases ranging between $2 and $10. This action too must be viewed as tantamount to an outright refusal to negotiate on that subject, and therefore as a violation of §8(a)(5), unless the fact that the January raises were in line with the company's long-standing practice of granting quarterly or semiannual merit reviews — in effect, were a mere continuation of the status quo — differentiates them from the wage increases and the changes in the sick-leave plan. We do not think it does. Whatever might be the case as to so-called "merit raises" which are in fact simply automatic increases to which the employer has already committed himself, the raises here in question were in no sense automatic, but were informed by a large measure of discretion. There simply is no way in such case for a union to know whether or not there has been a substantial departure from practice, and therefore the union may properly insist that the company negotiate as to the procedures and criteria for determining such increases.

[I]n *Insurance Agents*, . . . [w]e held that Congress had not . . . empowered the Board to pass judgment on the legitimacy of any particular economic weapon used in support of genuine negotiations. But the Board *is* authorized to order the cessation of behavior which is in effect a refusal to negotiate, or which directly obstructs or inhibits the actual process of discussion, or which reflects a cast of mind against reaching agreement. Unilateral action by an employer without prior discussion with the union does amount to a refusal to negotiate about the affected conditions of employment under negotiation and must of necessity obstruct bargaining, contrary to the congressional policy. It will often disclose an unwillingness to agree with the union. It will rarely be justified by any reason of substance. It follows that the Board may hold such unilateral action to be an unfair labor practice in

---

12. Of course, there is no resemblance between this situation and the one wherein an employer, after notice and consultation, "unilaterally" institutes a wage increase identical with one which the union has rejected as too low. See National Labor Relations Board v. Bradley Washfountain Co., 192 F.2d 144, 150-152; National Labor Relations Board v. Landis Tool Co., 193 F.2d 279.

violation of §8(a)(5), without also finding the employer guilty of overall subjective bad faith.

[The case was reversed and remanded with direction to the Court of Appeals to enforce the Board's order.

Justices Frankfurter and White took no part in the decision of this case.]

## *NOTES AND QUESTIONS*

**1. "Flat Refusal" to Bargain "in Fact"?** Are you persuaded by the *Katz* Court's rationale that an inquiry into the employer's good faith was not required because the employer had refused to bargain at all with respect to the unilateral changes? Weren't these changes modifiable in subsequent bargaining with the union? Why are unilateral changes problematic? Is the underlying concern that unilateral changes might provoke a strike before the union is ready to call one? Is this likely in the case of unilateral improvements as opposed to unilateral reductions in existing wages and other terms? Is the Court's concern instead that the employer should not be able to denigrate the status of the collective bargaining representative by conveying the impression to the employees that such improvements are due to the employer's generosity rather than to pressure from the bargaining agent? If so, how can the Board know that employees are likely to be deceived? Is it also possible that unilateral improvements will encourage employees to believe there is more to be had? Do employers have strong legitimate reasons in most cases for unilaterally changing working conditions during collective bargaining?

**2. Is an "Impasse" Required?** Does *Katz* hold that a bargaining deadlock, known as an "impasse," must occur before an employer may institute changes in terms and conditions consistent with its final offer to the union? Consider footnote 12. Or is it sufficient that the employer give the union prior notice and an opportunity to meet and confer over proposed changes? In Litton Financial Printing Div. v. NLRB, 501 U.S. 190, 198 (1991), excerpted infra page 681, the Supreme Court stated in dicta, citing *Katz*: "The Board has determined, with our acceptance, that an employer commits an unfair labor practice if, without bargaining to impasse, it effects a unilateral change of an existing term or condition of employment." The Fifth Circuit holds (even after *Litton*) that:

> [T]here is no violation of [§8(a)(5)], even in the absence of an impasse, if the employer notifies the union that it intends to institute the change and gives the union the opportunity to respond to that notice.

Nabors Trailers, Inc. v. NLRB, 910 F.2d 268, 273 (5th Cir. 1990) (citation omitted); see also NLRB v. Pinkston-Hollar Construction Services, Inc., 954 F.2d 306, 311-312 & n.6 (5th Cir. 1992). The Board and all other circuits require bargaining to impasse, however. See Duffy Tool & Stamping, LLC v. NLRB, 233 F.3d 995, 996-998 (7th Cir. 2000) (citing cases).

**3. Why Allow Implementation upon Impasse?** The Board has not changed the rule on implementation. Why should an employer be able to unilaterally implement after impasse a change in a term or condition of employment? Does the Board have authority to rule that an employer must maintain the status quo until the employer and the union agree bilaterally to changes? Consider Judge Silberman's discussion in McClatchy Newspapers, Inc. v. NLRB, 131 F.3d 1026, 1032 (D.C. Cir. 1997):

> The Board has told us that its rationale for permitting an employer to unilaterally implement its final offer after impasse is that such an action breaks the impasse and therefore encourages future collective bargaining. The theory . . . does not explain why the Board decides to handle impasse with this rule instead of another. The Board could have adopted, for example, a rule requiring the status quo to remain in effect until either the union or the employer was willing to resume negotiations. Stagnancy might pressure both the employer and the union to bend. But the rule it did choose — allowing the employer to implement its final offer — moves the process forward by giving one party, the employer, economic leverage.

Is there a stronger rationale than that offered by the Board to the *McClatchy* court? If employers could not implement unilaterally after impasse, would unions have the ability to prevent employers from responding to labor or product market developments in time to retain valuable employees or otherwise maintain a competitive business position? Would it be consistent with the Act to grant unions such leverage?

Note that the Railway Labor Act (RLA), which became law before the NLRA was enacted, imposes an express "status quo" obligation; contracts must be maintained until the National Mediation Board declares impasse by proffering voluntary mediation. See RLA §§2, 5; but see LMRA §204. Contracts are very difficult to change in the RLA-governed rail and airline industries. See generally Herbert R. Northrup, The Railway Labor Act–Time for Repeal?, 13 Harv. J. L. & Soc. Pol'y 441 (1990). This feature is applauded in Katherine Van Wesel Stone, Labor Relations in the Airlines: The Railway Labor Act in an Era of Deregulation, 42 Stan. L. Rev. 1485 (1990). See also Note on Impasse Procedures, infra pages 459-460.

**4. Overall vs. Piecemeal Impasse.** What type of impasse is necessary before the employer can unilaterally implement its final offer? Once the parties are deadlocked on a particular issue (piecemeal impasse), may the employer implement its final offer on that issue—or is it precluded from unilateral implementation of any part of its final offer until the parties have reached an *overall* impasse in negotiations? See *Duffy Tool*, supra note 2, 233 F.3d 995 (7th Cir. 2000) (joining Board and other circuits in holding overall impasse is required; Fifth Circuit's piecemeal approach rejected).

**5. Implementation of Less Attractive Proposals than Were Proposed to the Union.** In Taft Broadcasting Co., 163 N.L.R.B. 475, 478 (1967), enforced sub nom. AFTRA v. NLRB, 395 F.2d 622 (D.C. Cir. 1968), the Board stated that following impasse, an employer may lawfully implement "proposals reasonably comprehended within those it offered before impasse." *Taft* plainly permits an employer to implement its final offer. Does it permit implementation of proposals that are less favorable to the union than those contained in the final offer? Would an employer have any reason for implementation of a less favorable proposal other than pressuring the union to compromise further at the bargaining table? Is such a motivation in any event necessarily inconsistent with good faith bargaining? Consider again the rationales for allowing unilateral implementation suggested in note 3 above.

In Telescope Casual Furniture Co., 326 N.L.R.B. 588 (1998), the Board indicated that an employer may use the implementation of less favorable proposals as a bargaining tactic. The employer in *Telescope* presented the union with both a final offer and a less favorable alternative. After several bargaining sessions, it stated that if the final offer was not accepted within two days, it would implement the alternative proposal. After the union membership rejected the final offer and the union refused to bargain over the alternative proposal, the employer implemented the alternative. The Board (2-1) concluded that the use of the alternative proposal as a means of pressuring the union to agree to the primary proposal did not render its unilateral implementation an unfair labor practice. The concurring opinion of then-Chairman Gould characterized the employer's conduct as "hard ball bargaining," but stated that "tough and sometimes distasteful tactics . . . are frequently not unlawful." Both the majority and concurring opinions stressed that the employer used the less favorable alternative proposal to attempt to achieve an agreement, rather than to frustrate bargaining. Indeed, the employer had used the threat of unilateral implementation of a less attractive proposal in the three previous negotiations, all of which had culminated in a contract without resort to a strike.

**6. Other Legal Consequences of Impasse.** In addition to enabling the employer to implement proposals "reasonably comprehended within [its] pre-impasse proposals," a valid impasse suspends the parties' duty to bargain. That suspension is only temporary, however. As the Court has explained: "As a recurring feature in the bargaining process, impasse is only a temporary deadlock or hiatus in the negotiations 'which in almost all cases is eventually broken, through either a change of mind or the application of economic force.'" Charles D. Bonanno Linen Service, Inc. v. NLRB, 454 U.S. 404, 412 (1982), excerpted infra page 497. Although the NLRB has held that unions may engage in strikes prior to impasse, there is some question whether pre-impasse lockouts by the employer are lawful. See infra note 1, page 567.

**7. Determining When an Impasse Has Occurred.** Sometimes both parties agree that an impasse has occurred. More typically, however, one of the parties (usually the employer) unilaterally declares impasse and implements changes in terms and conditions. Unlike the RLA, the NLRA provides no advance mechanism for determining whether an impasse has occurred. Rather, this determination occurs in a post hoc unfair labor practice proceeding, which turns on a highly fact-specific inquiry. See TruServ Corp. v. NLRB, 254 F.3d 1105, 1114 (D.C. Cir. 2001); *Taft Broadcasting*, 163 N.L.R.B. at 478 (among the factors considered are "the bargaining history, the good faith of the parties in negotiations, the length of the negotiations, the importance of the issue or issues as to which there is disagreement, [and] the contemporaneous understanding of the parties as to the state of negotiations"). The absence of any advance mechanism affects the behavior of the parties, for an employer eager to implement changes will attempt to structure its meetings with the union to develop a record to support its ultimate declaration of impasse. If the union wishes to forestall such changes, it may use information requests as a strategic tool for creating a basis for a §8(a)(5) charge.

**8. Impact of Unprotected Union Activity on the Employer's *Katz* Obligation.** Prior to *Katz*, the Board had held that slowdowns, or strikes in the face of a no-strike clause (whether or not sponsored by the union), suspended the employer's duty to bargain and justified unilateral action. See, e.g., Valley City Furniture Co., 110 N.L.R.B. 1589, 1592 (1954). Does footnote 7 of the *Katz* opinion reject those decisions? Does that footnote rest on the premise that only *unlawful* activity (such as a strike that does not comply with the notice requirements of §8(d) and hence violates §8(b)(3)), see infra page 459, as distinguished from *unprotected* activity, suspends the duty to bargain? Is that premise sound? In any event, the NLRB, without mentioning *Katz*, has held that an employer's duty to bargain is suspended during a strike that is unprotected because it violates an interim no-strike pledge. See Arundel Corp., 210 N.L.R.B. 525 (1974); see also Stamford Taxi, Inc., 332 N.L.R.B. 1372 (2000) (citing *Arundel* and similar cases with approval).

**9. Defining the Operational Status Quo for *Katz* Purposes After Contract Expiration.** An expired collective bargaining agreement continues, in general, to govern the employment relationship; its provisions covering mandatory subjects of bargaining under §8(d) define the status quo that *Katz* holds must not be changed unilaterally before bargaining to impasse.

a. *Union Security and Dues Checkoff Clauses.* Not all contractual obligations, however, survive contract expiration. For example, the Board has long held that following the contract's expiration an employer need not enforce union security and dues checkoff provisions (discussed further in Chapter 12). See Litton Financial Printing Div. v. NLRB, 501 U.S. 190 (1991), excerpted infra page 681; Bethlehem Steel Co., 136 N.L.R.B. 1500, 1502 (1962), enforced in relevant part sub nom. Shipbuilders v. NLRB, 320 F.2d 615 (3d Cir. 1963). The Board's rationale, as explained in *Litton,* is that union security and checkoff clauses are governed by specific statutory provisions that permit these obligations to be imposed only when authorized by the express terms of a collective bargaining agreement. See NLRA §8(a)(3) (union security conditioned upon agreement of parties); LMRA, 29 U.S.C. §186(c)(4) (checkoff valid only if employees given opportunity to revoke at termination of agreement); see also infra pages 683-684. In 2012, the Board overturned its *Bethlehem Steel* rule on dues checkoff. Unlike other exceptions to the status-quo rule (such as no-strike and management-rights clauses), dues checkoff, "does not involve the contractual surrender of any statutory or nonstatutory right." WKYC-TV, Inc., 359 N.L.R.B. No. 30 (2012), invalidated due to lack of quorum under NLRB v. Noel Canning, 134 S. Ct. 2550 (2014).

b. *No-Strike Clauses.* Because they waive a core statutory right, no-strike clauses do not survive the expiration of a contract. They are, however, a mandatory subject of bargaining, see footnote 22 of *American National Insurance,* supra page 420. Does *Katz* thus permit an employer to unilaterally implement a no-strike clause at impasse if its final offer contained such a clause? See McClatchy Newspapers, Inc. v. NLRB, 131 F.3d 1026 (D.C. Cir. 1997):

> The Board has held that because the right to strike is "fundamental," it cannot be relinquished by employees except by . . . a specific contractual waiver. Gary-Hobart Water Corp., 210 N.L.R.B. [742], 744 (1974). It follows, therefore — although the Board has never expressly so held — that an employer could not impose no-strike conditions post-impasse even if embodied in the final contract proposal.

Id. at 1031 (citation omitted). Recall that waivers of a statutory right must be "clear and unmistakable." See Metropolitan Edison Co. v. NLRB, 460 U.S. 693 (1983), supra page 214; see also infra page 718 (noting "the Board's general rule that no-strike promises do not persist after the expiration date of a contract").

c. *Management-Rights Clauses.* Do management-rights clauses survive the expiration of a contract? See Beverly Health & Rehabilitation Services v. NLRB, 297 F.3d 468, 480-482 (6th Cir. 2002) (upholding Board's position that because such clauses involve waiver of statutory right to bargain, under *Metropolitan Edison* they generally expire with the term of the contract). If the management rights clause expires with the contract, however, what defines the status quo following expiration? See id. at 481 (employer's past practice under management rights clause defines status quo; employer that has engaged in pattern of unilateral changes under management rights clause during contract term may continue to make such changes following expiration as part of maintenance of status quo, while employer that had no such pattern during contract term may not make such unilateral changes post-expiration). How is this rule different in practice from the rule that would have applied if the management rights clause were still in effect? See also note 5b infra page 467.

d. *Grievance and Arbitration Clauses.* Does the employer's agreement to arbitrate grievances survive contract expiration? In Hilton-Davis Chem. Co., 185 N.L.R.B. 241 (1970), the Board formulated the following guidelines for grievance adjustment during a bargaining hiatus: An employer is not required either to adhere to the arbitration procedure of an expired agreement or to bargain to an impasse over the suspension of that procedure. Such a requirement would run counter to the essentially consensual nature of arbitration. The parties, however, are under a statutory duty to confer about grievances arising after the expiration of their contract, and they may not abandon established grievance procedures (short of arbitration) even though such procedures had their genesis in the contract. See further discussion of the *Hilton-Davis* doctrine in the *Litton* decision, infra page 681.

**10. Remedy for *Katz* Violations.** The standard remedy for a pre-impasse unilateral change in a mandatory subject of bargaining that represents a "downward" departure from the status quo (such as a wage cut or increase in employee insurance premiums) is rescission of the change and make-whole relief for the unit employees, as well as an order to resume bargaining. Should even "positive" unilateral changes—i.e., those that are more favorable to the employees than the status quo—be rescinded? See Fresno Bee, 339 N.L.R.B. 1214, 1216 n.6 (2003) (Board will order rescission of changes deemed beneficial to employees only if union so requests); CJC Holdings, Inc., 320 N.L.R.B. 1041, 1047 (1996), enforced, 110 F.3d 794 (5th Cir. 1997) (same).

*Note: Impasse Procedures*

**Notice and "Cooling-Off" Periods.** In §8(d) of the NLRA, added in 1947, Congress sought to provide an opportunity for third-party mediation and conciliation services to help resolve labor disputes. Section 8(d)(1) requires a party desiring to terminate or modify an existing contract to serve written notice on the other side within at least 60 days of the termination (or reopener) date. Under §8(d)(3), within 30 days of submitting the written notice, the party must also notify the Federal Mediation and Conciliation Service (FMCS) together with any comparable state agency. Section 8(d)(4) provides for a 60-day "cooling-off" period in which neither strikes nor lockouts may occur. A failure to comply with these procedures constitutes an unlawful refusal to bargain. A strike within any notice period prescribed by §8(d)(4) renders the strike unprotected and causes the striker to lose his or her protection as a statutory "employee." Because of the special concerns raised by a disruption of medical services, somewhat expanded notice requirements — including a requirement of ten days' notice of any strike, following the expiration of a 90-day "cooling off" period — apply in the case of nonprofit hospitals, which were brought within the Act's jurisdiction in 1974. See NLRA §§8(d) (as amended 1974) & 8(g) (added 1974); see also §2(2) (as amended 1974) (repealing former exclusion for nonprofit hospitals). See also, e.g., SEIU, United Healthcare Workers-West v. NLRB, 574 F.3d 1213 (9th Cir. 2009) (holding that ten-day notice is required before a union may call for a concerted refusal to work voluntary overtime); CSEA Local 1000 v. NLRB, 569 F.3d 88 (2d Cir. 2009) (holding that those who picket but do not strike within notice period are protected from discharge). For an argument that the ten-day notice requirement for a strike in the health care industry should be legislatively extended to any institution that is part of the nation's "critical infrastructure," see Ross E. Davies, Strike Season: Protecting Labor-Management Conflict in the Age of Terror, 93 Geo. L.J. 1783 (2005).

**Conciliation, Mediation, and Fact-Finding Boards.** The NLRB is barred from providing mediation services under NLRA §4(a). The FMCS, authorized under LMRA §§202-203, and the RLA's National Mediation Board (NMB) supply neutral professionals who provide mediation and conciliation services — that is, help the parties identify areas of agreement and disagreement, mitigate failures of communication, and sometimes suggest a framework for possible resolution of the dispute. In addition, third parties may also be called on to act as fact-finding boards. Under the RLA, if the NMB reports that its mediation efforts have failed to resolve a dispute threatening essential services, the President may appoint an Emergency Board to investigate and report on the facts. See generally Chris A. Hollinger, The Railway Labor Act (2012). Often the legislation passed by Congress to resolve a railroad or airline strike is based on the recommendations of the Emergency Board. Similarly, under §213 of the Labor Management Relations Act (LMRA), the director of the FMCS is authorized to appoint an impartial board of inquiry if a dispute threatens to substantially disrupt the delivery of health care in a particular locality. Fact-finding boards are also quite common in the resolution of disputes in the public sector.

**National Emergencies**. Under §§206-210 of the LMRA, a product of the 1947 Taft-Hartley legislation, if the President feels a strike (or lockout) will imperil the national health or safety, he may impanel a board of inquiry to investigate the causes and circumstances of the controversy. If after receiving the report the President concludes that the strike will indeed imperil the national health or safety, he can direct the Attorney General to seek a federal court injunction (notwithstanding the Norris-LaGuardia Act) against the strike. The district court's role is limited to determining whether the strike will have the requisite effect on national health or safety. See United Steelworkers of America v. United States, 361 U.S. 39 (1959). Sixty days after issuance of an injunction, the board of inquiry must submit a further report setting forth the current status of the dispute and the employer's last offer of settlement. The employees then have an opportunity to vote on the employer's last offer in a secret ballot administered by the NLRB. Upon the certification of the results of such a ballot or a settlement being reached, whichever occurs sooner, the Attorney General must move the court to discharge the injunction, "which motion shall then be granted and the injunction discharged." Upon dissolution of the injunction, the President submits a report with recommendations to Congress. See generally Donald E. Cullen, National Emergency Strikes (1968).

After being invoked over 30 times between 1947 and 1978, resulting in injunctions in all but two cases, the emergency provisions lay dormant until 2002, when President Bush obtained an injunction against a lockout of West Coast dockworkers — the first time the emergency provisions had been invoked in a lockout rather than a strike. See Catherine Hollingsworth, Judge Extends Injunction at Ports During 80-Day "Cooling Off" Period, 2002 Daily Lab. Rep. (BNA) No. 202, at A-9 (Oct. 18, 2002). For commentary on the emergency provisions, see Michael H. LeRoy & John H. Johnson IV, Death by Lethal Injunction: National Emergency Strikes Under the Taft-Hartley Act and the Moribund Right to Strike, 43 Ariz. L. Rev. 63 (2001).

## C. SUBJECTS OF "MANDATORY BARGAINING"

### 1. The Mandatory/Permissive Framework

**NLRB v. Wooster Division of Borg-Warner Corp.**
*356 U.S. 342 (1958)*

Burton, J. . . .

[A]n employer insisted that its collective bargaining contract . . . include: (1) a "ballot" clause calling for a pre-strike secret vote of [the] employees (union and nonunion) as to the employer's last offer, and (2) a "recognition" clause which excluded, as a party to the contract, the International Union which has been certified by the [NLRB] as the employees' exclusive bargaining agent, and substituted for it the agent's uncertified local affiliate. The Board held that the employer's insistence upon either of such clauses amounted to a . . . violation of §8(a)(5). . . . The issue turns on whether either of these clauses comes within the scope of mandatory collective bargaining as defined in §8(d). . . . [W]e agree with the Board that neither clause comes within that definition. . . .

Late in 1952, the International Union, United Automobile, Aircraft and Agricultural Implement Workers of America, CIO (here called International) was certified by the Board to the Wooster (Ohio) Division of the Borg-Warner Corporation (here called the company) as the elected representative of an appropriate unit of the company's employees. Shortly thereafter, International chartered Local No. 1239, UAW-CIO (here called the Local). Together the unions presented the company with a comprehensive collective bargaining agreement. In the "recognition" clause, the unions described themselves as both the "International Union, United Automobile, Aircraft and Agricultural Implement Workers of America and its Local Union No. 1239, UAW-CIO. . . ."

The company submitted a counterproposal which recognized as the sole representative of the employees "Local Union 1239, affiliated with the International Union, United Automobile, Aircraft and Agricultural Implement Workers of America (UAW-CIO)." The unions' negotiators objected because such a clause disregarded the Board's certification of International as the employees' representative. The negotiators declared that the employees would accept no agreement which excluded International as a party.

The company's counterproposal also contained the "ballot" clause. . . . [T]his clause provided that, as to all nonarbitrable issues . . . there would be a 30-day negotiation period after which, before the union could strike, there would have to be a secret ballot taken among all employees in the unit (union and nonunion) on the company's last offer. In the event a majority of the employees rejected the company's last offer, the company would have an opportunity, within 72 hours, of making a new proposal and having a vote on it prior to any strike. The unions' negotiators announced they would not accept this clause "under any conditions."

. . . The company's representatives made it equally clear that no agreement would be entered into by it unless the agreement contained both clauses. In view of this impasse, there was little further discussion of the clauses, although the parties continued to bargain as to other matters. The company submitted a "package" proposal covering economic issues but made the offer contingent upon the satisfactory settlement of "all other issues. . . ." The "package" included both of the controversial clauses.

On March 15, 1953, the unions rejected that proposal and the membership voted to strike on March 20 unless a settlement were reached by then. None was reached and the unions struck. Negotiations, nevertheless, continued. . . . Finally, on May 5, the Local, upon the recommendation of International, gave in and entered into an agreement containing both controversial clauses. . . .

Read together, [§§8(a)(5) and 8(d)] . . . establish the obligation of the employer and the representative of its employees to bargain with each other in good faith with respect to "wages, hours, and other terms and conditions of employment. . . ." The duty is limited to those subjects, and within that area neither party is legally obligated to yield. Labor Board v. American Insurance Co., 343 U.S. 395. As to other matters, however, each party is free to bargain or not to bargain, and to agree or not to agree.

The company's good faith has met the requirements of the statute as to the subjects of mandatory bargaining. But that good faith does not license the employer to refuse to enter into agreements on the ground that they do not include some proposal which is not a mandatory subject of bargaining. We agree with the Board that such conduct is, in substance, a refusal to bargain about the subjects that are within the scope of mandatory bargaining. This does not mean that bargaining is to be confined to the statutory subjects. Each of the two controversial clauses is lawful in itself. Each would be enforceable if agreed to by the unions. But it does not follow that, because the company may propose these clauses, it can lawfully insist upon them as a condition to any agreement.

Since it is lawful to insist upon matters within the scope of mandatory bargaining and unlawful to insist upon matters without, the issue here is whether either the "ballot" or the "recognition" clause is a subject within the phrase "wages, hours, and other terms and conditions of employment" which defines mandatory bargaining. The "ballot" clause is not within that definition. It relates only to the procedure to be followed by the employees among themselves before their representative may call a strike or refuse a final offer. It settles no term or condition of employment—it merely calls for an advisory vote of the employees. It is not a partial "no-strike" clause. A "no-strike" clause prohibits the employees from striking during the life of the contract. It regulates the relations between the employer and the employees. The "ballot" clause, on the other hand, deals only with relations between the employees and their unions. It substantially modifies the collective bargaining system provided for in the statute by weakening the independence of the "representative" chosen by the employees. It enables the employer, in effect, to deal with its employees rather than with their statutory representative.

The "recognition" clause likewise does not come within the definition of mandatory bargaining. The statute requires the company to bargain with the certified representative of its employees. It is an evasion of that duty to insist that the certified agent not be a party to the collective bargaining contract. The Act does not prohibit the voluntary addition of a party, but that does not authorize the employer to exclude the certified representative from the contract. . . .

FRANKFURTER, J., joins this opinion insofar as it holds that insistence by the company on the "recognition" clause, in conflict with the provisions of the Act requiring an employer to bargain with the representative of his employees, constituted an unfair labor practice. He agrees with the views of Harlan, J., regarding the "ballot" clause. The subject matter of that clause is not so clearly outside the reasonable range of industrial bargaining as to establish a refusal to bargain in good faith, and is not prohibited simply because not deemed to be within the rather vague scope of the obligatory provisions of §8(d).

HARLAN, J., whom CLARK and WHITTAKER, JJ., join, concurring in part and dissenting in part. . . .

[I]n light of the finding below that the company bargained in "good faith," I dissent from the view that its insistence on the "ballot" clause can support the charge of an unfair labor practice.

Preliminarily, I must state that I am unable to grasp a concept of "bargaining" which enables one to "propose" a particular point, but not to "insist" on it as a condition to agreement. The right to bargain becomes illusory if one is not free to press a proposal in good faith to the point of insistence. Surely adoption of so inherently vague and fluid a standard is apt to inhibit the entire bargaining process because of a party's fear that strenuous argument might shade into forbidden insistence and thereby produce a charge of an unfair labor practice. This watered-down notion of "bargaining" which the Court imports into the Act with reference to matters not within the scope of §8(d) appears as foreign to the labor field as it would be to the commercial world. To me all of this adds up to saying that the Act limits *effective* "bargaining" to subjects within the three fields referred to in §8(d), that is "wages, hours, and other terms and conditions of employment," even though the Court expressly disclaims so holding. . . .

. . . I question the Court's conclusion that the "ballot" clause does not come within the "other terms and conditions of employment" provision of §8(d). The phrase is inherently vague and prior to this decision has been accorded by the Board and courts an expansive rather than a grudging interpretation. Many matters which might have been thought to be the sole concern of management are now dealt with as compulsory bargaining topics. E.g., Labor Board v. J.H. Allison & Co., 165 F.2d 766 (merit increases). And since a "no-strike" clause is something about which an employer can concededly bargain to the point of insistence, see Shell Oil Co., 77 N.L.R.B. 1306, I find it difficult to understand even under the Court's analysis of this problem why the "ballot" clause should not be considered within the area of bargaining described in §8(d). It affects the employer-employee relationship in much the same way, in that it may determine the timing of strikes or even whether a strike will occur by requiring a vote to ascertain the employees' sentiment prior to the union's decision.

Nonetheless I shall accept the Court's holding that this clause is not a condition of employment, for even though the union would accordingly not be *obliged* under §8(d) to bargain over it, in my view it does not follow that the company was *prohibited* from insisting on its inclusion in the collective bargaining agreement. In other words, I think the clause was a permissible, even if not an obligatory, subject of good faith bargaining. . . .

The most cursory view of decisions of the Board and the circuit courts under the [Act] reveals the unsettled and evolving character of collective bargaining agreements. Provisions which two decades ago might have been thought to be the exclusive concern of labor or management are today commonplace in such agreements. The bargaining process should be left fluid, free from intervention of the Board leading to premature crystallization of labor agreements into any one pattern of contract provisions, so that these agreements can be adapted through collective bargaining to the changing needs of our society and to the changing concepts of the responsibilities of labor and management. What the Court does today may impede this evolutionary process. Under the facts of this case, an employer is precluded from attempting to limit the likelihood of a strike. But by the same token it would seem to follow that unions which bargain in good faith would be precluded from insisting upon contract clauses which might not be deemed statutory subjects within §8(d). . . .

. . . A determination that a party bargained as to statutory or nonstatutory subjects in good or bad faith must depend upon an evaluation of the total circumstances surrounding any given situation. I do not deny that there may be instances where unyielding insistence on a particular item may be a relevant consideration in the over-all picture in determining "good faith," for the demands of a party might in the context of a particular industry be so extreme as to constitute some evidence of an unwillingness to bargain. But no such situation is presented in this instance by the "ballot" clause. "No-strike" clauses, and other provisions analogous to the "ballot" clause limiting the right to strike, are hardly novel to labor agreements. And in any event the uncontested finding of "good faith" by the Trial Examiner forecloses that issue here. . . .

The company's insistence on the "recognition" clause, which had the effect of excluding the International Union as a party signatory to agreement and making Local 1239 the sole contracting party on the union side, presents a different problem. In my opinion the company's action in this regard did constitute an unfair labor practice since it contravened specific requirements of the Act.

## *NOTES AND QUESTIONS*

**1. Consequences of Defining a Subject as "Mandatory" or "Permissive."** There are at least five consequences to defining a subject as "mandatory": (1) "the party who would control the topic unilaterally absent bargaining obligations [must] bargain about decisions concerning the topic with a sincere desire to reach an agreement"; (2) the noncontrolling party may "use economic leverage to attempt to compel the controlling party to compromise"; (3) if employees strike over the employer's failure to bargain over a mandatory subject, they will be treated as unfair labor practices strikers free to regain their jobs at strike's end; (4) midterm modifications of terms dealing with mandatory subjects contained in the collective agreement are unlawful without the consent of the other party; and (5) the controlling party must bargain in good faith to impasse before implementing changes concerning a mandatory subject. See Michael C. Harper, The Scope of the Duty to Bargain Concerning Business Transformations, in Labor Law and Business Change: Theoretical and Transactional Perspectives 25, 26-27 (Samuel Estreicher & Daniel G. Collins eds., 1988).

**2. Costs and Benefits of the Mandatory/Permissive Distinction.** One way to understand the Court's decision in *Borg-Warner* is as an attempt to promote collective bargaining by forcing the parties to deal with issues central to their relationship without allowing other issues to be used either to prolong discussions or as deal-breakers. Another explanation is that the distinction places limits on one party's use of its bargaining power to invade the sphere of control of the other party over its internal affairs. Thus, for example, the "ballot" clause is treated as a permissive subject in order to prevent strong employers from compelling changes in the way the union interacts with its represented employees. Other subjects thought to be at the core of employers' entrepreneurial discretion have been defined as permissive to prevent unions from using economic coercion to affect managerial control.

The *Borg-Warner* approach has not been without its critics. Consider the following objections as you study the materials in this section:

a. "*Borg-Warner* encourages deception because if a party feels strongly about a matter it will make clear to the other side that agreement on a mandatory subject is conditioned on the other side's yielding on the so-called 'permissive' subject."

b. "[I]nasmuch as there is no provision for declaratory judgments or advisory opinions under the Act permitting the parties to know in advance what the status of an item on the table is (i.e., whether mandatory or non-mandatory), the parties must guess as best they can and attempt to bargain intelligently in light of this." Gould, Agenda for Reform, supra, at 172.

c. "A line drawn by statutory interpretation is unduly rigid because of its permanence as well as its uniformity. Once made decisions can be altered only by revision of the statute. . . . Collective bargaining is too dynamic for us to decide today what should be required or permissible subjects of collective bargaining tomorrow." Archibald Cox, Labor Decisions of the Supreme Court at the October Term, 1957, 44 Va. L. Rev. 1057, 1083-1084 (1958).

d. "If collective bargaining is to succeed, the parties should be able to shape a deal that meets their needs without the government deciding which subjects can be deal-breakers. Such reform might unleash the creative potential of collective bargaining—for example, agreements over wages and job-bidding rights for a seat on the corporate board and enforceable guarantees of job security." Estreicher, Labor Law Reform, supra, at 39-40.

**3. Illegal Bargaining Topics.** Some topics of bargaining are neither mandatory nor permissive but rather illegal. Such subjects cannot be agreed to because the agreement would be in conflict with the NLRA or other laws. For example, consider NLRB v. Magnavox, 415 U.S. 322 (1974), supra page 210, where the Court agreed with the Board that unions could not waive certain on-site distribution rights of their opponents or their supporters. Was the recognition clause sought by the employer in *Borg-Warner* another example of an illegal subject?

**4. Waiver of Statutory Rights.** Some of the rights established by the NLRA are waivable by collective agreement, and some proposals that involve a waiver of those rights have been held to be mandatory subjects. See Michael C. Harper, Union Waiver of Employee Rights Under the NLRA (Pts. 1 & 2), 4 Indus. Rel. L.J. 335, 680 (1981). Prominent examples are management-rights clauses and clauses barring strikes during the term of the agreement. The status of a right as waivable and subject to mandatory bargaining does not necessarily render it subject to change through the employer's unilateral implementation, however. The no-strike clause is an example of a mandatory subject involving a union waiver of NLRA rights that cannot be unilaterally implemented by the employer; the proposal can be insisted on as a "deal breaker" under *Borg-Warner* but it requires the union's consent as the "controlling" party on the issue to be implemented. See notes 1 supra and 5b. infra.

**5. Applications: Effects on the Union-Employee Relationship.**

a. *"Ballot" Clause.* Was the "ballot" clause held to be a permissive subject in *Borg-Warner* really an attempt to achieve a form of direct dealing with the employees in derogation of the exclusive bargaining agent? The ballot clause would have limited what the union could do on its own in communicating final offers to the represented employees and setting its own ground rules with respect to matters such as strike votes and contract ratification votes. However, the balloting would not occur until after bargaining with the union and the employer's transmittal of a final offer to the union, and the union would still make the ultimate decision on whether to strike. How is the ballot clause different from no-strike clauses, which the Court acknowledges are mandatory items?

Note that §209 of the LMRA, discussed supra page 460, stipulates that the NLRB shall hold a secret ballot vote of employees on the employer's final offer as a condition for discharging a "national emergency" injunction. Moreover, both Ontario and the United Kingdom require strike ballot votes by law. See §§42, 79, Ontario Labour Rels. Law (2009); Vince Toman, Industrial Dispute, New L.J. 1474, 1475 (Oct. 2005).

b. *Discretionary Merit-Pay Systems.* Consider the following situation: The parties had a long-standing collective bargaining relationship. The most recent agreement contained a merit-pay system for employees who reached the top step of their classification. Although the union had the right to comment on the employer's individual merit-pay decisions during the review and appeals process, the employer retained the ultimate discretion over the timing and amount of individual merit-pay increases; merit-pay disputes were excluded from the grievance and arbitration process. In the renewal negotiations, the employer proposed moving to an entirely merit-based wage system, while the union wanted to eliminate the merit system aspect of the previous agreement. Following impasse, the employer stated that it was implementing its proposal and began granting merit increases to employees without consulting the union. Has the employer violated §8(a)(5) by insisting to impasse on its proposal? By unilaterally implementing that proposal following impasse? See McClatchy Newspapers, Publisher of the Sacramento Bee, 321 N.L.R.B. 1386 (1996) ("*McClatchy II*"), enforced, 131 F.3d 1026 (D.C. Cir. 1997); see also McClatchy Newspapers, Publisher of the Modesto Bee, 322 N.L.R.B. 812 (1996), enforced in relevant part, 131 F.3d 1026 (D.C. Cir. 1997).

In *McClatchy II*, the Board held that the employer could lawfully insist to impasse on the proposal, but could not unilaterally implement it following impasse. The Board formulated this "narrow exception" to the general "implementation following impasse" rule because of its concerns about a destructive impact on the collective bargaining process and disparagement of the union's role in that process. It emphasized the standardless discretion claimed by the employer in *McClatchy*, stating that "nothing in our decision precludes an employer from making merit wage determinations if definable objective procedures and criteria have been negotiated to . . . impasse." 321 N.L.R.B. at 1391.

Consider also the following. After impasse, the employer implements a proposal specifying that wage increases would average 4 percent in the contract's first year and 3 percent thereafter, that merit-pay determinations would be based on annual employee evaluations pursuant to an extensive evaluation form and be effective on fixed dates, and that employees would be permitted to contest the size of raises through a grievance procedure. Has the employer violated §8(a)(5) under *McClatchy II*? See Detroit Typographical Union No. 18 v. NLRB, 216 F.3d 109 (D.C. Cir. 2000) (holding that proposal contains sufficient criteria limiting employer's discretion). What about a proposal stating that employees "shall be paid a base rate of not less than $8.90 an hour, however, the Company may continue its current marketplace pay practices for the term of this contract"? See Quirk Tire, 340 N.L.R.B. 301 (2003), on remand from 241 F.3d 41 (1st Cir. 2001) (use of word "may" impermissibly permits employer to make recurring unilateral decisions over employees' wages in allowing employer to choose between $8.90 and "marketplace pay" and precludes meaningful review of whether wage change constitutes departure from unilaterally implemented proposal, thus violating principle that employer may institute one set of unilateral changes per impasse, but must again bargain with union before making further changes). For additional discussion, see Laurence M. Goodman, Merit Pay Proposals and Related Compensation Plans, *Detroit Typographical Union v. NLRB* and *McClatchy Newspapers* Revisited, 18 Lab. Law. 1 (2002).

c. *Productivity Committees.* Assume that employers are under no duty to bargain over decisions to introduce new technology or to redesign work systems in order to enhance productivity. If an employer wants to establish employee-manager committees to develop suggestions for work system changes, such as combinations of jobs that might improve productivity (but pledges to steer clear of mandatory items that the union designates as appropriate only for collective bargaining), does the employer have to bargain with the union prior to establishment of such committees? Does the employer violate §8(a)(5) by insisting to the point of impasse on the establishment of such committees? Can the committees be established by the employer after reaching a good-faith impasse? What if the employer's plan provides for employees in each department to select representatives to the productivity committees?

**6. Applications: Interference with Collective Bargaining Process.**

a. *Interest Arbitration.* Since the 1930s, following the custom in the newspaper industry, the parties have agreed that any issues unresolved by negotiations would be submitted for determination by an arbitrator, that is, by "interest" arbitration. Upon the expiration of the 1970-1973 agreement, the parties agree on all matters, except whether their renewal agreement should contain the provision for interest arbitration. The employer refuses to sign a contract embodying the parties' agreement on other matters unless the union agrees to deletion of the interest-arbitration clause. The union counters by seeking to initiate an arbitration proceeding under the expired prior agreement to resolve the parties' deadlock. The employer files a timely §8(b)(3) charge; the union files a §8(a)(5) charge. What result? Would the analysis change if the parties were also deadlocked on wages and the union sought interest arbitration under the expired prior agreement only on the issue of wages? See Columbus Printing Pressmen & Assistants' Union No. 252, 219 N.L.R.B. 268 (1975), enforced, 543 F.2d 1161 (5th Cir. 1976); Sheet Metal Workers Int'l Ass'n, Local 59, 227 N.L.R.B. 520 (1976); Mechanical Contractors Ass'n of Newburgh, 202 N.L.R.B. 1 (1973); see also Sheet Metal Workers Int'l Ass'n, Local 14 v. Aldrich Air Conditioning, 717 F.2d 456 (8th Cir. 1983) (all holding that interest arbitration is a permissive subject that may not be insisted on in bargaining or be the basis of a claim in arbitration after the expiration of the collective agreement). Former NLRB Chairs Murphy and Gould have expressed the view that interest arbitration should be a mandatory subject. See Columbus Printing Pressmen, 219 N.L.R.B. at 272-275 (Chair Murphy, dissenting); Sheet Metal Workers Int'l Ass'n, Local 162, 314 N.L.R.B. 923, 926 n.12 (1994) (Chairman Gould, dissenting).

b. *Salary Arbitration System.* Historically, major league baseball players have been employed under a "reserve" system that restricted their ability to play for other clubs. Through collective bargaining, the players' union has succeeded in negotiating limitations on this system. Players with six years or more of service have a right of "free agency" and can offer their services to, and seek competing bids from, all clubs. In addition, players with three or more years of service but less than six have the right to have their salaries determined through a salary arbitration process. In negotiations over a renewal agreement, the parties have deadlocked over the clubs' insistence that the players agree to a "salary cap" on the total compensation any club can pay its players; no change had been sought in the salary arbitration provision, as such, during the talks. After declaring good faith impasse, the clubs have announced they will not agree to submit individual player contracts to the salary arbitration process, at least until an overall agreement is reached on a renewal of the collective agreement. Have the clubs violated §8(a)(5) by implementing a change in the salary arbitration provision without bargaining to impasse on that issue? See Silverman v. Major League Player Relations Comm., Inc., 67 F.3d 1054, 1062 (2d Cir. 1995) (§10(j) case; finding "reasonable cause to believe" that provision was mandatory subject, distinguishing conventional interest arbitration clauses).

c. *Indemnity Bonds and Security Deposits.* The Board has held that demands for indemnity bonds or security deposits to ensure performance of contractual obligations are outside the area of mandatory bargaining.

See Radiator Specialty Co. v. NLRB, 336 F.2d 495 (4th Cir. 1964) (employer's demand for bond covering union liability under no-strike clause); Carpenters' Dist. Council, 145 N.L.R.B. 663 (1963) (union's demand for money deposit to secure wage obligations). Is "remoteness" from the employment relationship sufficient to explain these decisions? What if the union wants an indemnity or performance bond because it is concerned about the solvency of the signatory employer? Same result? Can the union insist to the point of impasse on the inclusion of the parent corporation as well as the actual employer as a signatory to the collective agreement?

**7. Applications: Remoteness from Employment Relationship and Effects on Third Parties.**

a. *Discretionary Bonuses.* In general, bonuses are a form of compensation subject to mandatory bargaining. The Board, however, has carved out an exception for bonuses that are not tied to an employment-related factor and are not "of such a fixed nature . . . to have become a reasonable expectation of the employees and, therefore, part of their anticipated remuneration." Phelps Dodge Mining Co. v. NLRB, 22 F3d 1493, 1496 (10th Cir. 1994). See also UNITE HERE v. NLRB, 546 F.3d 239 (2d Cir. 2008) (one-time stock award given in equal amounts to all employees after an initial public offering was a "gift" that did not require bargaining with the union).

b. *In-Plant Vending Machine Prices.* The employer provides in-plant eating facilities and vending machines owned and operated by a third-party vendor. Must the employer bargain over the vendor's food quality and prices? Even if the employer just rents space to the vendor without reserving any other control? Would the employer have to bargain over the institution of facilities that did not exist in the first place? See Ford Motor Co. v. NLRB, 441 U.S. 488, 497, 502 (1979) (sustaining "the Board's consistent view that in-plant food prices and services are mandatory bargaining subjects," at least where management in its own interest provides such in-plant facilities, but noting that management need not bargain over every change in price or service as long as it "honors a specific union request for bargaining about changes that have been made or are to be made").

c. *Retiree Benefits.* In Allied Chem. & Alkali Workers v. Pittsburgh Plate Glass Co., 404 U.S. 157 (1971), the collective agreement provided that the company would contribute $4 per month toward the cost of medical insurance for retired employees, but that it could reduce its monthly contribution by $2 if Congress enacted a national retiree medical insurance program. In 1965, Congress enacted such a program, Medicare, and the employer announced that it was canceling its program for retirees and would substitute a $3 monthly subscription fee for supplemental Medicare coverage. The union challenged the employer's unilateral decision to substitute supplemental Medicare coverage for the negotiated health plan. The Supreme Court, per Justice Brennan, held that retiree benefits were nonmandatory subjects and, as such, could be modified midterm without violating §8(a)(5), regardless of any contractual violation:

> *First.* . . . The inequality of bargaining power that Congress sought to remedy was that of the "working" man, and the labor disputes that it ordered to be subjected to collective bargaining were those of employers and their active employees. Nowhere in the history of the [Act] is there any evidence that retired workers are to be considered as within the ambit of the collective bargaining obligations of the statute. . . .
>
> *Second.* Section 9(a) . . . accords representative status only to the labor organization selected or designated by the majority of employees in a "unit appropriate" "for the purposes of collective bargaining." . . . [W]e hold that [pensioners] were not and could not be "employees" included in the bargaining unit. The unit determined by the Board to be appropriate was composed of "employees of the Employer's plant . . . working on hourly rates, including group leaders who work on hourly rates of pay. . . ."
>
> *Third.* The Board found that bargaining over pensioners' rights has become an established industrial practice. But industrial practice cannot alter the conclusions that retirees are neither "employees" nor bargaining unit members. . . .
>
> Even if pensioners are not bargaining unit "employees," are their benefits, nonetheless, a mandatory subject of collective bargaining as "terms and conditions of employment" of the active employees who remain in the unit? The Board held, alternatively, that they are, on the ground that they "vitally" affect the "terms and conditions of employment" of active employees principally by influencing the value of both their current and future benefits.
>
> The benefits that active workers may reap by including retired employees under the same health insurance contract are speculative and insubstantial at best. . . . [T]he relationship between the inclusion of retirees and the overall insurance rate is uncertain. Adding individuals increases the group experience and thereby generally tends to lower the rate, but including pensioners, who are likely to have higher medical expenses, may more than offset that effect. . . .
>
> . . . Under the Board's theory, active employees undertake to represent pensioners in order to protect their own retirement benefits, just as if they were bargaining for, say, a cost-of-living escalation clause. But there is a crucial difference. Having once found it advantageous to bargain for improvements in pensioners' benefits, active workers are not forever thereafter bound to that view or obliged to negotiate in behalf of retirees again. To the contrary, they are free to decide, for example, that current income is preferable to greater

> certainty in their own retirement benefits or, indeed, to their retirement benefits altogether. By advancing pensioners' interests now, active employees, therefore, have no assurance that they will be the beneficiaries of similar representation when they retire. . . .

404 U.S. at 165-176, 180-181.

In view of the Court's reasoning in *Pittsburgh Plate Glass*, why are unions representing active employees even permitted to bargain over the benefits of retirees? Would retirees as a group be better or worse off if the benefits of retirees could not be increased or adjusted through collective bargaining? What if the employer seeks to reduce or eliminate retiree benefits?

d. *The "Vitally Affects" Standard.* As the preceding note illustrates, third-party concerns are typically not mandatory subjects of bargaining. However, they can become mandatory when they "vitally affect" bargaining unit employees' terms and conditions of employment. In adopting this standard, the *Pittsburgh Plate Glass* Court relied on Teamsters Union v. Oliver, 358 U.S. 283 (1959), a case in which the Court concluded that an agreement between truck carriers and independent contractors was a mandatory subject of bargaining with the carriers' employees because the terms of the agreement were "integral to the establishment of a stable wage structure."

e. *Hiring Decisions.* The Board has ruled that employers have a duty to bargain before implementing a drug-testing program for existing employees, see Johnson-Bateman Co., 295 N.L.R.B. 180 (1989) and United Hoisting & Scaffolding, Inc., 360 N.L.R.B. No. 137 (2014), but need not bargain over the testing of job applicants who are not yet part of the bargaining unit, see Star Tribune, 295 N.L.R.B. 543 (1989). *Star Tribune* involved an application of the *Pittsburgh Plate Glass* "vitally affects" principle that bargaining is required only over the terms and conditions of "employees" in the unit that the union represents, or, where the individuals are not bargaining unit employees, where the subject of bargaining would nonetheless "vitally affect" the terms and conditions of the unit employees. The Board held that applicants are clearly not "employees" under *Pittsburgh Plate Glass,* and also rejected the ALJ's determination that testing of applicants would nonetheless "vitally affect" the unit employees' interests.

Are employers required to bargain over union proposals that all hires come from referrals from the union hiring hall? Does this depend on a showing of irregular periods of employment such that existing employees may in the near future return to the hiring hall for future referrals? Is bargaining required over a union proposal that the employer not discriminate on grounds of race, gender, national origin, age, or disability in any of its employment decisions, including hiring?

### *Note: Card-Check and Neutrality Provisions*

Recall the card-check and neutrality agreements discussed in Chapter 5, pages 380-384. By definition, such agreements pertain to non-unit employees — either currently unorganized employees of the company or employees of facilities that may be opened or acquired in the future. Given *Pittsburgh Plate Glass,* are card-check or "neutrality" provisions mandatory subjects of bargaining? In Pall Biomedical Products Corp., 331 N.L.R.B. 1674 (2000), the Board considered a union proposal that provided for recognition at another company facility if the employer "employs one or more employees performing unit work at that facility." Implying a condition that recognition at the other facility would be based on majority support, the Board found the proposal to be a mandatory subject under Kroger Co., 219 N.L.R.B. 388 (1975). In *Kroger,* after implying a similar condition, the Board had deemed a clause providing for inclusion in the unit and extending the contract to employees of after-acquired stores to be a mandatory subject of bargaining. The *Pall* Board also held the clause mandatory on the theory that it would "vitally affect" the unit employees' terms and conditions by removing economic incentives that might otherwise encourage the employer to transfer work out of the bargaining unit. The D.C. Circuit reversed, noting that the clause did not provide for extension of the contract to employees at the other facility (but instead required the union to negotiate any such contract de novo) and that the Supreme Court in *Pittsburgh Plate Glass* and earlier cases had held that the "vitally affects" doctrine applies only where the proposal is a "direct frontal attack" upon the perceived problem. See Pall Corp. v. NLRB, 275 F.3d 116, 120-122 (D.C. Cir. 2002). In the court's view, while clauses that provide for automatic extension of the contract to employees of additional facilities upon a showing of majority support constitute a "direct frontal attack" on the issue of the transfer of unit work, a clause that merely provides for recognition based on cards without extension of the contract does not. Id. at 121. Do you agree?

In 1995, the General Counsel issued an Advice Memorandum — later withdrawn when the case became moot — dealing with the following three clauses on which the union had insisted to impasse: (1) an "employer-speech clause" stating that the employer "will advise [employees at newly acquired facilities] that it welcomes their selection of a collective bargaining agent," and will not state or imply in any way that it opposes the employees' selection of a bargaining agent, or state or imply any preference for or opposition to any particular union as the bargaining agent; (2) an "access clause" permitting union access to new facilities "to the extent such access is permitted by the Employer's lawful solicitation rules"; and (3) a "roster clause" providing that the employer would furnish the union a list of the "target" employees' names, addresses, job classifications, and departments within 10-14 days of a union request. See Local Joint Exec. Bd. of Las Vegas, Culinary Workers

Union, Local 226 and Bartenders Union, Local 165 (Sahara Hotel and Casino), 28-CB-4349, available at 1995 WL 937191 (Nov. 30, 1995) (GC Adv. Mem.); 1996 WL 931978 (Feb. 13, 1996) (case now moot). These clauses were accompanied by an "after-acquired" clause providing for inclusion in the unit and extension of the contract to employees at newly acquired facilities.

In *Sahara Hotel*, the General Counsel deemed the "after-acquired" clause mandatory under *Kroger*, supra. In *Kroger*, the parties had defined the bargaining unit to include "all stores." Should the parties be able to redefine or expand the unit without Board approval? Should either party be able to insist to impasse on such redefinition or expansion? The General Counsel found the speech clause in *Sahara* to be permissive on the ground that a union should not be able to insist to impasse on a provision that involved the waiver of an employer's statutory rights under §8(c), stating that "The [B]oard has held in a wide variety of situations that a proposal which would waive another party's statutory rights constitutes a permissive subject of bargaining." Id. at 6. But is this always the case? Consider supra note 4, page 466. The General Counsel also ordered that a complaint issue on the union's insistence to impasse on the access and roster clauses. He did so, however, only in order to present the issue to the Board, stating that "the better view is that [these] clauses, when coupled with the after-acquired clause, are mandatory subjects" because they "are merely . . . methods of implementing the *Kroger* clause, which is a mandatory subject." Id. at 7. Could the speech clause also be deemed mandatory on such a theory? For further discussion of *Sahara*, see Charles I. Cohen, Neutrality Agreements: Will the NLRB Sanction Its Own Obsolescence?, 16 Lab. Law. 201, 204-211 (2000) (also discussing other types of "neutrality" provisions and whether they should be considered mandatory or permissive); Hartley, Non-Legislative Labor Law Reform, supra, at 397-399.

### *Note: Alternatives to* Borg-Warner

**Mandatory Bargaining over All Subjects?** Former NLRB Chair Gould, while a labor law professor, advocated that the law "compel bargaining over all subjects." Gould, Agenda for Reform, supra, at 172. For parties seeking to obstruct agreement—such as employers who wish to frustrate their employees' decision to opt for collective representation or unions who wish to assert control over entrepreneurial decisions—would this approach create incentives for protracted bargaining? Will both sides be under a duty to make global disclosures on demand? Are these problems adequately addressed by an overall inquiry into good-faith bargaining conduct?

**Justice Harlan's Approach: Separate the "Right to Insist" from the "Duty to Bargain"?** Under Justice Harlan's approach, the "right to insist" would be broader than the "duty to bargain"; either party could insist, and presumably use economic coercion, on subjects outside of the scope of mandatory bargaining, subject to an overall duty to bargain in good faith. Does this approach invite strategic insistence on matters of little underlying substantive interest in order to gain leverage or delay signing contracts? Can these difficulties be mitigated? See Estreicher, Labor Law Reform, supra, at 39-40 n.134 (favoring Harlan's approach, but suggesting that certain subjects should be placed "beyond the reach of either party's insistence, such as proposals to alter or dilute the representative status of the union"). See also Samuel Estreicher, Freedom of Contract and Labor Law Reform: Opening Up the Possibilities for Value-Added Unionism, 71 N.Y.U. L. Rev. 827 (1996).

**Duty to "Meet and Confer" over Nonmandatory Subjects?** Yet another approach is to retain much of the *Borg-Warner* framework while requiring some diluted form of bargaining—a duty to "meet and confer" but without the need to await impasse—over nonmandatory subjects. To what extent does this approach promote bargaining beyond what the parties would do on their own? Are there ways of defining the consultation obligation that will avoid strategic behavior and prolongation of disputes? Would a meet-and-confer obligation ultimately be worth the costs of regulation?

## 2. Status of Major Entrepreneurial Decisions

### Fibreboard Paper Products Corp. v. NLRB
*379 U.S. 203 (1964)*

Warren, C. J. . . .

The primary issue is whether the "contracting out" of work being performed by employees in the bargaining unit is a statutory subject of collective bargaining under [§§8(a)(5) and 8(d)].

. . . Since 1937 the [Union] has been the exclusive bargaining representative for a unit of the Company's maintenance employees. In September 1958, the Union and the Company entered the latest of a series of collective bargaining agreements which was to expire on July 31, 1959. . . . Efforts by the Union to schedule a bargaining session met with no success until July 27, four days before the expiration of the contract, when the Company notified the Union of its desire to meet.

The Company, concerned with the high cost of its maintenance operation, had undertaken a study of the possibility of effecting cost savings by engaging an independent contractor to do the maintenance work. At the July 27 meeting, the Company informed the Union that it had determined that substantial savings could be effected by contracting out the work. . . . The Company delivered to the [Union] a letter which stated in pertinent part: "For some time we had been seriously considering the question of letting out our Emeryville maintenance work . . . , and have now reached a definite decision to do so effective August 1, 1959. In these circumstances, we are sure you will realize that negotiation of a new contract would be pointless. However, if you have any questions, we will be glad to discuss them with you." After some discussion . . . , the meeting concluded with the understanding that the parties would meet again on July 30.

By July 30, the Company had selected Fluor Maintenance, Inc., to do the maintenance work. Fluor had assured the Company that maintenance costs could be curtailed by reducing the work force, decreasing fringe benefits and overtime payments, and by preplanning and scheduling the services to be performed. The contract provided that Fluor would:

> . . . furnish all labor, supervision and office help required for the performance of maintenance work . . . at the Emeryville plant of Owner as Owner shall from time to time assign to Contractor during the period of this contract; and shall also furnish such tools, supplies and equipment in connection therewith as Owner shall order from Contractor, it being understood however that Owner shall ordinarily do its own purchasing of tools, supplies and equipment.

The contract further provided that the Company would pay Fluor the costs of the operation plus a fixed fee of $2,250 per month.

At the July 30 meeting, the Company's representative, in explaining the decision to contract out the maintenance work, remarked that during bargaining negotiations in previous years the Company had endeavored to point out . . . "just how expensive and costly our maintenance work was and how it was creating quite a terrific burden upon the Emeryville plant." He further stated that unions representing other Company employees "had joined hands with management in an effort to bring about an economical and efficient operation," but "we had not been able to attain that in our discussions with this particular Local." The Company also distributed a letter stating that "since we will have no employees in the bargaining unit covered by our present Agreement, negotiation of a new or renewed Agreement would appear to us to be pointless." On July 31, the employment of the maintenance employees represented by the Union was terminated and Fluor employees took over. That evening the Union established a picket line at the Company's plant.

The Union filed . . . charges against the Company, alleging violations of §§8(a)(1), 8(a)(3) and 8(a)(5). . . . The Board . . . adhered to the Trial Examiner's finding that the Company's motive . . . was economic rather than antiunion but [ultimately] found nonetheless that the Company's "failure to negotiate with . . . [the Union] concerning its decision to subcontract its maintenance work constituted a violation of §8(a)(5). . . ."

. . . The Board ordered the Company to reinstitute the maintenance operation . . . , to reinstate the employees to their former or substantially equivalent positions with back pay computed from the date of the Board's supplemental decision, and to fulfill its statutory obligation to bargain. . . . [T]he District of Columbia Circuit granted the Board's petition for enforcement. . . .

. . . Because of the limited grant of certiorari, we are concerned here only with whether the subject upon which the employer allegedly refused to bargain — contracting out of plant maintenance work previously performed by employees in the bargaining unit, which the employees were capable of continuing to perform — is covered by the phrase "terms and conditions of employment" within the meaning of §8(d).

The subject matter of the present dispute is well within the literal meaning of the phrase "terms and conditions of employment." See Order of Railroad Telegraphers v. Chicago & N.W.R. Co., 362 U.S. 330. A stipulation with respect to the contracting out of work performed by members of the bargaining unit might appropriately be called a "condition of employment." The words even more plainly cover termination of employment which, as the facts of this case indicate, necessarily results from the contracting out of work performed by members of the established bargaining unit.

The inclusion of "contracting out" within the statutory scope of collective bargaining also seems well designed to effectuate the purposes of the [NLRA]. . . . The Act was framed with an awareness that refusals to confer and negotiate had been one of the most prolific causes of industrial strife. . . . To hold, as the Board has done, that contracting out is a mandatory subject of collective bargaining would promote the fundamental purpose of the Act by bringing a problem of vital concern to labor and management within the framework established by Congress as most conducive to industrial peace.

The conclusion that "contracting out" is a statutory subject of collective bargaining is further reinforced by industrial practices in this country. While not determinative, it is appropriate to look to industrial bargaining practices in appraising the propriety of including a particular subject within the scope of mandatory bargaining. Labor Board v. American Nat'l Ins. Co., 343 U.S. 395, 408. Industrial experience is not only reflective of the interests of labor and management in the subject matter but is also indicative of the amenability of such subjects to the collective bargaining process. Experience illustrates that contracting out in one form or another has been brought, widely and successfully, within the collective bargaining framework. . . .

The facts of the present case illustrate the propriety of submitting the dispute to collective negotiation. The Company's decision to contract out the maintenance work did not alter the Company's basic operation. The maintenance work still had to be performed in the plant. No capital investment was contemplated; the Company merely replaced existing employees with those of an independent contractor to do the same work under similar conditions of employment. Therefore, to require the employer to bargain about the matter would not significantly abridge his freedom to manage the business.

The Company was concerned with the high cost of its maintenance operation. It was induced to contract out the work by assurances from independent contractors that economies could be derived by reducing the work force, decreasing fringe benefits, and eliminating overtime payments. These have long been regarded as matters peculiarly suitable for resolution within the collective bargaining framework. . . . Yet, it is contended that when an employer can effect cost savings in these respects by contracting the work out, there is no need to attempt to achieve similar economies through negotiation with existing employees or to provide them with an opportunity to negotiate a mutually acceptable alternative. The short answer is that, although it is not possible to say whether a satisfactory solution could be reached, national labor policy is founded upon the congressional determination that the chances are good enough to warrant subjecting such issues to the process of collective negotiation. . . .

We are thus not expanding the scope of mandatory bargaining to hold, as we do now, that the type of "contracting out" involved in this case — the replacement of employees in the existing bargaining unit with those of an independent contractor to do the same work under similar conditions of employment — is a statutory subject of collective bargaining under §8(d). Our decision need not and does not encompass other forms of "contracting out" or "subcontracting" which arise daily in our complex economy.

The only question remaining is whether, upon a finding that the Company had refused to bargain about a . . . statutory subject of collective bargaining, the Board was empowered to order the resumption of maintenance operations and reinstatement with back pay. We believe that it was so empowered. . . .

GOLDBERG, J., took no part in the consideration or decision of this case.

STEWART, J., with whom DOUGLAS and HARLAN, JJ., join, concurring.

. . . The Court holds no more than that this employer's decision to subcontract this work, involving "the replacement of employees in the existing bargaining unit with those of an independent contractor to do the same work under similar conditions of employment," is subject to the duty to bargain collectively. Within the narrow limitations implicit in the specific facts of this case, I agree with the Court's decision. . . .

It is important to note that the words of the statute are words of limitation. The [Act] does not say that the employer and employees are bound to confer upon any subject which interests either of them; the specification of wages, hours, and other terms and conditions of employment defines a limited category of issues subject to compulsory bargaining. The limiting purpose of the statute's language is made clear by the legislative history of the present Act. As originally passed, the Wagner Act contained no definition of the duty to bargain collectively. In the 1947 revision of the Act, the House bill contained a detailed but limited list of subjects of the duty to bargain, excluding all others.[4] In conference the present language was substituted for the House's detailed specification. While the language thus incorporated in the 1947 legislation as enacted is not so stringent as that contained in the House bill, it nonetheless adopts the same basic approach in seeking to define a limited class of bargainable issues.

The phrase "conditions of employment" is no doubt susceptible of diverse interpretations. At the extreme, the phrase could be construed to apply to any subject which is insisted upon as a prerequisite for continued employment. Such an interpretation . . . would be contrary to the intent of Congress, as reflected in this legislative history. Yet there are passages in the Court's opinion today which suggest just such an expansive interpretation, for the Court's opinion seems to imply that any issue which may reasonably divide an employer and his employees must be the subject of compulsory collective bargaining.

Only a narrower concept of "conditions of employment" will serve the statutory purpose of delineating a limited category of issues which are subject to the duty to bargain collectively. In common parlance, the conditions of a person's employment are most obviously the various physical dimensions of his working environment. What one's hours are to be, what amount of work is expected during those hours, what periods of relief are available, what safety practices are observed, would all seem conditions of one's employment. There are other less tangible but no less important characteristics of a person's employment which might also be deemed "conditions" — most prominently the characteristic involved in this case, the security of one's employment. On one view of the matter, it can be argued that the question whether there is to be a job is not a condition of employment; the question is not one of imposing conditions on employment, but the more fundamental question whether there is to be employment at all. However, it is clear that the Board and the courts have on numerous occasions recognized that union demands for provisions limiting an employer's power to discharge employees are mandatorily bargainable. Thus, freedom from discriminatory discharge, seniority rights, the imposition of a compulsory retirement age, have been recognized as subjects upon which an employer must bargain, although all of these concern the very existence of the employment itself.

While employment security has thus properly been recognized in various circumstances as a condition of employment, it surely does not follow that every decision which may affect job security is a subject of compulsory

4. H.R. 3020, 80th Cong., 1st Sess., §2(11)(B)(vi) (1947), in I Legislative History of the Labor Management Relations Act, 1947, at 166-167 (1948). . . .

collective bargaining. Many decisions made by management affect the job security of employees. Decisions concerning the volume and kind of advertising expenditures, product design, the manner of financing, and sales, all may bear upon the security of the workers' jobs. Yet it is hardly conceivable that such decisions so involve "conditions of employment" that they must be negotiated with the employees' bargaining representative.

In many of these areas the impact of a particular management decision upon job security may be extremely indirect and uncertain, and this alone may be sufficient reason to conclude that such decisions are not "with respect to . . . conditions of employment." Yet there are other areas where decisions by management may quite clearly imperil job security, or indeed terminate employment entirely. An enterprise may decide to invest in labor-saving machinery. Another may resolve to liquidate its assets and go out of business. Nothing the Court holds today should be understood as imposing a duty to bargain collectively regarding such managerial decisions, which lie at the core of entrepreneurial control. Decisions concerning the commitment of investment capital and the basic scope of the enterprise are not in themselves primarily about conditions of employment though the effect of the decision may be necessarily to terminate employment. If, as I think clear, the purpose of §8(d) is to describe a limited area subject to the duty of collective bargaining, those management decisions which are fundamental to the basic direction of a corporate enterprise or which impinge only indirectly upon employment security should be excluded from that area.

Applying these concepts to the case at hand, I do not believe that an employer's subcontracting practices are, as a general matter, in themselves conditions of employment. . . . On the facts of this case, [however,] I join the Court's judgment, because all that is involved is the substitution of one group of workers for another to perform the same task in the same plant under the ultimate control of the same employer. . . .

Analytically, this case is not far from that which would be presented if the employer had merely discharged all its employees and replaced them with other workers willing to work on the same job in the same plant without the various fringe benefits so costly to the company. While such a situation might well be considered a §8(a)(3) violation upon a finding that the employer discriminated against the discharged employees because of their union affiliation, it would be equally possible to regard the employer's action as a unilateral act frustrating negotiation on the underlying questions of work scheduling and remuneration, and so an evasion of its duty to bargain on these questions, which are concededly subject to compulsory collective bargaining. Similarly, had the employer in this case chosen to bargain with the union about the proposed subcontract, negotiations would have inevitably turned to the underlying question of cost, which prompted the subcontracting. Insofar as the employer frustrated collective bargaining with respect to these concededly [compulsory] issues by its unilateral act of subcontracting this work, it can properly be found to have violated its statutory duty under §8(a)(5). . . .

## *NOTES AND QUESTIONS*

**1. Subcontracting of Bargaining-Unit Work.** Doesn't subcontracting always involve a removal of work previously performed by the bargaining unit? Why not require bargaining whenever the employer's decision threatens the job security of unit employees? Is this the majority's position? How do the majority and concurring opinions differ, if at all, on this score? Are you persuaded by Justice Stewart's reliance on the Taft-Hartley legislative history? Does the history actually support a broader conception of bargaining duties than that offered in his concurring opinion?

**2. Decisions at the "Core of Entrepreneurial Control."** Why does Justice Stewart suggest that decisions lying at the "core of entrepreneurial control" are beyond the scope of mandatory bargaining? Is this because such decisions lack a sufficiently direct impact on job security and working conditions? Because bargaining is not likely to make a contribution to the decision-making process? Because unions should not be able to influence such decisions through exertion of economic pressure? Because employer "rights" are left undisturbed by the NLRA?

**3. Sale and Franchise Arrangements.** Consider General Motors Corp., 191 N.L.R.B. 951 (1971), review denied, 470 F.2d 422 (D.C. Cir. 1972): GM, after taking over a franchised dealer, operated a retail outlet in Houston for the sale and servicing of GM trucks and parts. Subsequently GM reestablished a dealership by selling certain of the outlet's assets and subleasing its premises under an agreement permitting cancellation of the sublease by either party and the transfer of the assets to GM if the buyer ceased to be a GM-franchised truck dealer. GM rejected the incumbent union's request for bargaining over the proposed sale while sale negotiations were in progress.

Is this transaction akin to subcontracting or does it lie outside the scope of mandatory bargaining because it involves a decision to handle retailing differently through use of an independent business? Is it relevant how much control GM retains over the dealership? Or what role labor cost considerations played in GM's decision?

**4. Consistency with Past Practice.** In Westinghouse Electric Corp., 150 N.L.R.B. 1574 (1965), the company, without notice to the union, had for many years regularly engaged in extensive subcontracting. The union had sought contract restrictions on that practice, but the union always dropped this demand during bargaining, and ensuing agreements were silent on the issue. In the period covered by the instant §8(a)(5) proceeding, the company had awarded over 7,000 subcontracts involving work its own employees could have performed. The Board declared:

> . . . [B]earing in mind particularly that the recurrent contracting out of work here in question was motivated solely by economic considerations; that it comported with the [Respondent's] traditional methods . . . ; that it did not during the period here in question vary significantly in kind or degree from what had been customary under past established practice; that it had no demonstrable adverse impact on employees in the unit; and that the Union had the opportunity to bargain about changes in existing subcontracting practices at general negotiating meetings — for all these reasons cumulatively, we conclude that Respondent did not violate its statutory bargaining obligation by failing to invite union participation in individual subcontracting decisions.

### First National Maintenance Corp. v. NLRB
*452 U.S. 666 (1981)*

BLACKMUN, J.

Must an employer, under its duty to bargain in good faith "with respect to wages, hours, and other terms and conditions of employment" [§§8(d) and 8(a)(5)], negotiate with the certified representative of its employees over its decision to close a part of its business? In this case, the [NLRB] imposed such a duty on petitioner with respect to its decision to terminate a contract with a customer, and the . . . Court of Appeals, although differing over the appropriate rationale, enforced its order.

#### I

Petitioner, First National Maintenance Corporation (FNM) . . . [provides] housekeeping, cleaning, maintenance, and related services for commercial customers in the New York City area. It supplies each of its customers, at the customer's premises, [a] contracted-for labor force and supervision in return for reimbursement of its labor costs (gross salaries, [employment] taxes, and insurance) and payment of a set fee. It contracts for and hires personnel separately for each customer, and it does not transfer employees between locations.

During the Spring of 1977, petitioner was performing maintenance work for the Greenpark Care Center, a nursing home in Brooklyn. Its written agreement dated April 28, 1976, with Greenpark specified that Greenpark "shall furnish all tools, equipment [sic], materials, and supplies," and would pay petitioner weekly "the sum of five hundred dollars plus the gross weekly payroll and fringe benefits." Its weekly fee, however, had been reduced to $250 effective November 1, 1976. The contract prohibited Greenpark from hiring any of petitioner's employees during the term of the contract and for 90 days thereafter. Petitioner employed approximately 35 workers in its Greenpark operation.

Petitioner's business relationship with Greenpark, seemingly, was not very remunerative or smooth. In March 1977, Greenpark gave petitioner the 30 days' written notice of cancellation specified by the contract, because of "lack of efficiency." This cancellation did not become effective, for FNM's work continued after the expiration of that 30-day period. Petitioner, however, became aware that it was losing money at Greenpark. On June 30, by telephone, it asked that its weekly fee be restored at the $500 figure and, on July 6, it informed Greenpark in writing that it would discontinue its operations there on August 1 unless the increase were granted. By telegram on July 25, petitioner gave final notice of termination.

While FNM was experiencing these difficulties, District 1199, National Union of Hospital and Health Care Employees, Retail, Wholesale and Department Store Union, AFL-CIO (the union), was conducting an organization campaign among petitioner's Greenpark employees. On March 31, 1977, at a Board-conducted election, a majority of the employees selected the union as their bargaining agent. On July 12, the union's vice president, Edward Wecker, wrote petitioner, notifying it of the certification and of the union's right to bargain, and stating: "We look forward to meeting with you or your representative for that purpose. Please advise when it will be convenient." Petitioner neither responded nor sought to consult with the union.

On July 28, petitioner notified its Greenpark employees that they would be discharged 3 days later. Wecker immediately telephoned petitioner's secretary-treasurer, Leonard Marsh, to request a delay for the purpose of bargaining. Marsh refused the offer to bargain and told Wecker that the termination of the Greenpark operation was purely a matter of money, and final, and that the 30-days' notice provision of the Greenpark contract made staying on beyond August 1 prohibitively expensive. Wecker discussed the matter with Greenpark's management that same day, but was unable to obtain a waiver of the notice provision. Greenpark also was unwilling itself to hire the FNM employees because of the contract's 90-day limitation on hiring. With nothing but perfunctory further discussion, petitioner on July 31 discontinued its Greenpark operation and discharged the employees.

. . . Relying on Ozark Trailers, Inc., 161 N.L.R.B. 561 (1966), [the ALJ] ruled that petitioner had failed to satisfy its duty to bargain concerning both the decision to terminate the Greenpark contract and the effect of that change upon the unit employees. . . . [The] Board adopted the [ALJ's] findings without further analysis. . . .

The . . . Second Circuit, with one judge dissenting in part, enforced the Board's order, although it adopted an analysis different from that espoused by the Board. 627 F.2d 596 (1980). The Court of Appeals reasoned that no per se rule could be formulated to govern an employer's decision to close part of its business. Rather, the court said, §8(d) creates a *presumption* in favor of mandatory bargaining over such a decision, a presumption that is rebuttable "by showing that the purposes of the statute would not be furthered by imposition of a duty to bargain," for example, by demonstrating that "bargaining over the decision would be futile," or that the decision was due to "emergency financial circumstances," or that the "custom of the industry, shown by the absence of such an obligation from typical collective bargaining agreements, is not to bargain over such decisions." Id., at 601-602. . . .

## II

. . . [I]n establishing what issues must be submitted to the process of bargaining, Congress had no expectation that the elected union representative would become an equal partner in the running of the business enterprise. . . . [T]here is an undeniable limit to the subjects about which bargaining must take place. . . .

Some management decisions, such as choice of advertising and promotion, product type and design, and financing arrangements, have only an indirect and attenuated impact on the employment relationship. See [Fibreboard Paper Prods. Corp. v. NLRB, 379 U.S. 203, 223 (1964)] (Stewart, J., concurring). Other management decisions, such as the order of succession of layoffs and recalls, production quotas, and work rules, are almost exclusively "an aspect of the relationship" between employer and employee. [Allied Chem. & Alkali Workers v. Pittsburgh Plate Glass Co., 404 U.S. 157, 178 (1971).] The present case concerns a third type of management decision, one that had a direct impact on employment, since jobs were inexorably eliminated by the termination, but had as its focus only the economic profitability of the contract with Greenpark, a concern under these facts wholly apart from the employment relationship. This decision, involving a change in the scope and direction of the enterprise, is akin to the decision whether to be in business at all, "not in [itself] primarily about conditions of employment, though the effect of the decision may be necessarily to terminate employment." *Fibreboard,* 379 U.S., at 223 (Stewart, J., concurring). Cf. Textile Workers v. Darlington Co., 380 U.S. 263, 268 (1965) ("an employer has the absolute right to terminate his entire business for any reason he pleases"). At the same time, this decision touches on a matter of central and pressing concern to the union and its member employees: the possibility of continued employment and the retention of the employees' very jobs. . . .

Petitioner contends it had no duty to bargain about its decision to terminate its operations at Greenpark. This contention requires that we determine whether the decision itself should be considered part of petitioner's retained freedom to manage its affairs unrelated to employment. . . . The concept of mandatory bargaining is premised on the belief that collective discussions backed by the parties' economic weapons will result in decisions that are better for both management and labor and for society as a whole. . . . This will be true, however, only if the subject proposed for discussion is amenable to resolution through the bargaining process. Management must be free from the constraints of the bargaining process to the extent essential for the running of a profitable business. It also must have some degree of certainty beforehand as to when it may proceed to reach decisions without fear of later evaluations labeling its conduct an unfair labor practice. Congress did not explicitly state what issues of mutual concern to union and management it intended to exclude from mandatory bargaining. Nonetheless, in view of an employer's need for unencumbered decisionmaking, bargaining over management decisions that have a substantial impact on the continued availability of employment should be required only if the benefit, for labor-management relations and the collective bargaining process, outweighs the burden placed on the conduct of the business. . . .

With this approach in mind, we turn to the specific issue at hand: an economically-motivated decision to shut down part of a business.

### III

#### A

. . . A union's interest in participating in the decision to close a particular facility or part of an employer's operations springs from its legitimate concern over job security. The Court has observed: "The words of [§8(d)] . . . plainly cover termination of employment which . . . necessarily results" from closing an operation. *Fibreboard,* 379 U.S., at 210. The union's practical purpose in participating, however, will be largely uniform: it will seek to delay or halt the closing. No doubt it will be impelled, in seeking these ends, to offer concessions, information, and alternatives that might be helpful to management or forestall or prevent the termination of jobs. It is unlikely, however, that requiring bargaining over the decision itself, as well as its effects, will augment this flow of information and suggestions. There is no dispute that the union must be given a significant opportunity to bargain about these matters of job security as part of the "effects" bargaining mandated by §8(a)(5). . . . And, under §8(a)(5), bargaining over the effects of a decision must be conducted in a meaningful manner and at a meaningful time, and the Board may impose sanctions to insure its adequacy. A union, by pursuing such bargaining rights, may achieve valuable concessions from an employer engaged in a partial closing. It also may secure in contract negotiations provisions implementing rights to notice, information, and fair bargaining. . . .

Moreover, the union's legitimate interest in fair dealing is protected by §8(a)(3), which prohibits partial closings motivated by anti-union animus, when done to gain an unfair advantage. Textile Workers v. Darlington Co., 380 U.S. 263 (1965). . . . An employer may not simply shut down part of its business and mask its desire to weaken and circumvent the union by labeling its decision "purely economic." . . .

Management's interest in whether it should discuss a decision of this kind is much more complex and varies with the particular circumstances. If labor costs are an important factor in a failing operation and the decision to close, management will have an incentive to confer voluntarily with the union to seek concessions that may make continuing the business profitable. Cf. U.S. News & World Report, Feb. 9, 1981, p.74; BNA, Labor Relations Yearbook-1979, p.5 (UAW agreement with Chrysler Corp. to make concessions on wages and fringe benefits). At other times, management may have great need for speed, flexibility, and secrecy in meeting business opportunities and exigencies. It may face significant tax or securities consequences that hinge on confidentiality, the timing of a plant closing, or a reorganization of the corporate structure. The publicity incident to the normal process of bargaining may injure the possibility of a successful transition or increase the economic damage to the business. The employer also may have no feasible alternative to the closing, and even good-faith bargaining over it may be both futile and cause the employer additional loss.

There is an important difference, also, between permitted bargaining and mandated bargaining. Labeling this type of decision mandatory could afford a union a powerful tool for achieving delay, a power that might be used to thwart management's intentions in a manner unrelated to any feasible solution the union might propose. . . .

While evidence of current labor practice is only an indication of what is feasible through collective bargaining, and not a binding guide, see *Chemical Workers*, 404 U.S., at 176, that evidence supports the apparent imbalance weighing against mandatory bargaining. We note that provisions giving unions a right to participate in the decisionmaking process concerning alteration of the scope of an enterprise appear to be relatively rare. Provisions concerning notice or "effects" bargaining are more prevalent. . . .

Further, the presumption analysis adopted by the Court of Appeals seems ill suited to advance harmonious relations between employer and employee. An employer would have difficulty determining beforehand whether it was faced with a situation requiring bargaining or one that involved economic necessity sufficiently compelling to obviate the duty to bargain. If it should decide to risk not bargaining, it might be faced ultimately with harsh remedies forcing it to pay large amounts of backpay to employees who likely would have been discharged regardless of bargaining, or even to consider reopening a failing operation. . . . A union, too, would have difficulty determining the limits of its prerogatives, whether and when it could use its economic powers to try to alter an employer's decision, or whether, in doing so, it would trigger sanctions from the Board. . . .

We conclude that the harm likely to be done to an employer's need to operate freely in deciding whether to shut down part of its business purely for economic reasons outweighs the incremental benefit that might be gained through the union's participation in making the decision,[22] and we hold that the decision itself is *not* part of §8(d)'s "terms and conditions," over which Congress has mandated bargaining.

B

In order to illustrate the limits of our holding, we turn again to the specific facts of this case. First, we note that when petitioner decided to terminate its Greenpark contract, it had no intention to replace the discharged employees or to move that operation elsewhere. Petitioner's sole purpose was to reduce its economic loss, and the union made no claim of anti-union animus. In addition, petitioner's dispute with Greenpark was solely over the size of the management fee Greenpark was willing to pay. The union had no control or authority over that fee. The most that the union could have offered would have been advice and concessions that Greenpark, the third party upon whom rested the success or failure of the contract, had no duty even to consider. These facts in particular distinguish this case from the subcontracting issue presented in *Fibreboard.* Further, the union was not selected as the bargaining representative or certified until well after petitioner's economic difficulties at Greenpark had begun. We thus are not faced with an employer's abrogation of ongoing negotiations or an existing bargaining agreement. Finally, while petitioner's business enterprise did not involve the investment of large amounts of capital in single locations, we do not believe that the absence of "significant investment or withdrawal of capital," General Motors Corp., GMC Truck & Coach Div., 191 N.L.R.B., at 952, is crucial. The decision to halt work at this specific location represented a significant change in petitioner's operations, a change not unlike opening a new line of business or going out of business entirely.

The judgment of the Court of Appeals, accordingly, is reversed and the case is remanded to that court for further proceedings consistent with this opinion.

---

22. In this opinion we of course intimate no view as to other types of management decisions, such as plant relocations, sales, other kinds of subcontracting, automation, etc., which are to be considered on their particular facts. . . .

BRENNAN, J., with whom MARSHALL, J., joins, dissenting. . . .

The Court bases its decision on a balancing test. . . . I cannot agree with this test, because it takes into account only the interests of *management*; it fails to consider the legitimate employment interests of the workers and their Union. . . .

Even if the Court's statement of the test were accurate, I could not join in its application, which is based solely on speculation. Apparently, the Court concludes that the benefit to labor-management relations and the collective-bargaining process from negotiation over partial closings is minimal, but it provides no evidence to that effect. The Court acknowledges that the Union might be able to offer concessions, information, and alternatives that might obviate or forestall the closing, but it then asserts that "[i]t is unlikely, however, that requiring bargaining over the decision . . . will augment this flow of information and suggestions." . . .

The Court further presumes that management's need for "speed, flexibility, and secrecy" in making partial closing decisions would be frustrated by a requirement to bargain. In some cases the Court might be correct. In others, however, the decision will be made openly and deliberately, and considerations of "speed, flexibility, and secrecy" will be inapposite. . . .

## *NOTES AND QUESTIONS*

**1. Holding of *First National Maintenance*?** Justice Blackmun emphasizes some of the special facts in the case in Part III-B of his opinion for the Court. Does this suggest that on different facts partial plant closing decisions might indeed be mandatory subjects of bargaining? Or is the Court's holding better captured by Part III-A of the opinion?

**2. Pointlessness of Requiring Concessionary Bargaining in Plant Closure Cases?** Is the Court engaging in a form of categorical cost-benefit analysis that holds that where an employer is uninterested in negotiating with a union over a partial closing decision, collective bargaining is not likely to make a contribution to the decisionmaking process, and the costs of requiring bargaining are likely to outweigh any conceivable benefits? Is such a determination better made by the Board? Does this reading of *First National Maintenance* argue for the Second Circuit's use of a presumption rather than a per se rule? Did the lower court correctly apply its approach to the facts before it?

If we change the facts of the case slightly and assume there had been a prior bargaining relationship with the union respecting the Greenpark project, are you convinced that the dispute between First National Maintenance and Greenpark could not have been obviated if the union had been willing to agree to concessions amounting to the $250 difference in the weekly maintenance fee? Should the law require employers to pursue the possibility of union concessions before closing facilities, or is Justice Blackmun right that we can count on employers to do this on their own whenever there is reason to believe that an appeal to the union is likely to be fruitful?

**3. Requiring an Opportunity for the Union to Exert Pressure?** Is the *First National Maintenance* Court misdirected in its emphasis on concessionary bargaining, when its focus should be on whether partial closings are the kind of decision that the NLRA permits to be influenced by union economic pressure? Consider the analysis in Michael C. Harper, Leveling the Road from *Borg-Warner* to *First National Maintenance*: The Scope of Mandatory Bargaining, 68 Va. L. Rev. 1447, 1462-1464, 1471-1472 (1982) (emphasis in original):

> Any principled exclusion of a class of management decisions from the scope of mandatory bargaining must . . . accept the primary policy of the Labor Act—to facilitate employees engaging in certain legitimate concerted efforts, such as collective bargaining, in extracting from their employers more compensation for their work.
>
> The acceptance of this policy precludes suppressing full bargaining over certain forms of compensation simply because of the potential economic impact on employers. Two factors support this conclusion. First, topics that are clearly within the scope of mandatory bargaining, such as wage levels, often represent the most substantial production cost of employers. Second, the Act is not concerned with the economic impact of collective bargaining on employers; it requires employers to rely on their own economic power to protect their interests in collective bargaining. . . .
>
> It is possible nevertheless to carve out a set of management decisions that are inappropriate for compulsory bargaining, although potentially important to employees. This principle rests on a social policy allowing consumers, and only consumers, to influence management's product market decisions. This principle would exclude from compulsory bargaining *all decisions to determine what products are created and sold, in what quantities, for which markets, and at what prices.* These product market decisions are distinct from decisions concerning how employers are to compensate organized laborers from the wealth generated by their work. Employees can use economic pressure to direct to themselves as much of the economic resources of the employer as they can, as long as they do not attempt to coerce the employer's decisions concerning what goods will be produced and offered to which markets.
>
> The product market principle accords with a strong social policy that the Act does not subordinate. According to that social policy, consumers should decide which goods employers will produce by expressing their preferences in the marketplace, unless our general democratic institutions restrict these preferences by legislation. The Labor Act does encourage restrictions on the "free" play of employers' labor market and production decisions; indeed, Congress designed the Act to help employees escape disadvantageous labor

markets by allowing unions to extract greater compensation from employers. The Act therefore encourages employee efforts that might influence the product market indirectly by affecting the costs of producing goods. No language or policy of the Act, however, reveals an intention to facilitate employees' efforts to control product markets directly. It is consistent with the Act, therefore, to prohibit employees from coercing an employer with any demand that the employer could not satisfy, even with unlimited resources, without directly changing the product offered to the public. . . .

The product market principle does not exclude from mandatory bargaining all partial closing decisions based on decisions to reduce marketing. Some partial termination decisions, such as the one in [*First National Maintenance* [(FNM)], are inseparable from the product market decisions on which they are based. Many partial termination decisions, however, are distinct from underlying product market decisions. *Ozark Trailers* [161 N.L.R.B. 561 (1966)] is such a decision. Ozark and associated companies manufactured refrigerated truck bodies in at least two plants. Presumably for economic reasons, Ozark closed one of these plants without bargaining with certified union representatives of the employees of the closed plant. The Board's decision indicates that Ozark may have transferred the work of the closed plant either to another plant or to another company on contract. Yet even assuming that Ozark did decide to reduce the number of trucks that it marketed, its decision to close the plant represented by the union was not a product market decision. Ozark could have reduced production proportionately at all plants, or it could have curtailed operation of another plant. The decision to shut down the union plant was simply a production decision. The company could have satisfied a union demand to keep the plant open without changing any decision to reduce product sales. To be sure, keeping the plant open probably would have been more expensive for Ozark than closing it, but as noted previously, matters of production expense cannot be distinguished from mandatory topics such as wage or benefit levels. Therefore, the Board decided *Ozark* correctly, and its decision can be reconciled with the result in [FNM].

**4. "Effects" Bargaining.** Why isn't the opportunity for "effects" bargaining, which the *FNM* Court states "must be conducted in a meaningful manner and at a meaningful time," sufficient to protect employee interests? Is the problem that this opportunity is likely to come too late for the union to be able to offer adequate concessions or that it will come too late for the union effectively to exert any pressure to block the decision? See Thomas C. Kohler, Distinctions Without Differences: Effects Bargaining in Light of *First National Maintenance*, 5 Indus. Rel. L.J. 402 (1983). Consider also Professor Harper's criticism:

For effects bargaining to be truly meaningful, employers should notify unions of a contemplated unilateral action at least as soon as serious planning begins. This would give the union an opportunity to threaten or commence a strike before the employer unilaterally terminates the plant's operation. . . . Once

> the employer has implemented its decision to terminate operations, most of the union's economic leverage will dissipate, and an effects bargaining order from the Board will probably not help the union do much more than request special severance pay.

Harper, Leveling the Road, supra, at 1483. If employers are required to give early notice of plant closures, and unions are permitted to use economic pressure to press their position in "effects" bargaining, will this enable unions effectively to use coercion to influence the underlying decision?

**5. WARN Legislation.** The Worker Adjustment Retraining and Notification Act of 1988 (WARN), P.L. 100-379, 102 Stat. 890 (codified at 29 U.S.C. §§2101-2109), applies to firms with at least 100 employees, and requires 60 days' advance notice of any facility shutdown causing job loss for at least 50 employees within a 30-day period or any "mass layoff" (when, at a single site, either 500 employees or 50 employees representing at least 33 percent of the workforce are terminated or laid off during a 30-day period). If the employees are represented by a union, the employers must give 60 days' notice to the union. Advance notice is not required if the employer is "actively seeking capital or business which, if obtained, would have enabled the employer to avoid or postpone the shutdown, and the employer reasonably and in good faith believes that giving the notice would have precluded the employer from obtaining the needed capital or business," or if the shutdown or layoff is caused by "business circumstances that were not reasonably foreseeable as of the time that notice would have been required." The Act is enforced by suit in federal district court brought by the union or affected employees. For the Secretary of Labor's interpretative regulations, see 20 C.F.R. §§639.1-639.10. Unions have standing to bring WARN Act suits on behalf of affected employees. See United Food & Commercial Workers Union Local 751 v. Brown Group, Inc., 517 U.S. 544 (1996).

Does the WARN Act facilitate collective bargaining over the decision to shut down plants? Over the effects of such shutdowns?

**6. The Board's *Dubuque* Test.** In Dubuque Packing Co., 303 N.L.R.B. 386 (1991), enforced sub nom. United Food & Commercial Workers Int'l Union, Local 150-A v. NLRB, 1 F.3d 24 (D.C. Cir. 1993), the Board announced a new test for the bargainability of plant relocations and transfers of unit work. Dubuque Packing, after previously obtaining concessions from the union in an effort to stave off a closing of its hog kill and cut department at its Dubuque, Iowa, home plant, announced on March 30, 1981, that it intended to close the department. After the union made clear its rejection of a wage freeze proposal, the company stated on June 10, 1981, that it was considering relocating—rather than closing—the department, and that it was also considering relocating up to 900 plant pork processing jobs. The company also advised the employees that they could save their jobs by agreeing to a wage freeze. The union urged a vote against a wage freeze until the company opened its books. After the workers voted overwhelmingly in support of the union's position, the company informed the union that its decision to close the hog kill and cut department was "irrevocable." Over the next few months the parties continued to negotiate over the proposed relocation of the pork processing operations. On October 1, 1981, the company opened a hog kill and cut operation at its newly acquired Rochelle, Illinois, plant, and two days later eliminated approximately 530 hog kill and cut jobs at the Dubuque plant. On October 19, 1981, an agreement was signed providing for wage concessions, retention of 900 pork processing jobs in Dubuque, and an extension of the current labor agreement. However, because the company was unable to obtain new financing, it closed and sold the Dubuque and Rochelle plants on October 15, 1982.

The Board initially ruled that the employer had committed no unfair labor practice because it was under no duty to bargain over its decision to relocate. Although the Board had ruled that this result would obtain no matter which of three possible tests were used, the D.C. Circuit remanded, instructing the Board to articulate a single test to be applied in *Dubuque* and similar cases. See 880 F.2d 1422 (D.C. Cir. 1989), remanding 287 N.L.R.B. 499 (1987) ("*Dubuque I*"). In "*Dubuque II*," the Board approved a new test for bargaining over relocation decisions and held that the employer had breached its duty to bargain under that test. As a remedy it ordered the company to pay back wages to all employees terminated as a result of its relocation decision, from the date of their termination to the date operations ceased at Dubuque and Rochelle.

The Board's *Dubuque II* test states (303 N.L.R.B. at 391):

> Initially, the burden is on the General Counsel to establish that the employer's decision involved a relocation of unit work unaccompanied by a basic change in the nature of the employer's operation. If the General Counsel successfully carries his burden in this regard, he will have established prima facie that the employer's relocation decision is a mandatory subject of bargaining. At this juncture, the employer may produce evidence rebutting the prima facie case by establishing that the work performed at the new location varies significantly from the work performed at the former plant, establishing that the work performed at the former plant is to be discontinued entirely and not moved to the new location, or establishing that the employer's decision involves a change in the scope and direction of the enterprise. Alternatively, the employer may proffer a defense to show by a preponderance of evidence: (1) that labor costs (direct and/or indirect) were not a factor in the decision or (2) that even if labor costs were a factor in the decision, the union could not

have offered labor cost concessions that could have changed the employer's decision to relocate.

Is *Dubuque II* consistent with *First National Maintenance*? Does it impermissibly shift the burden of proof to the employer to prove the nonmandatory nature of the work relocation? On the other hand, why should the fact that the work at the former location has been discontinued provide a complete defense? Moreover, does the alternative defense implicitly adopt the view that the only purpose of bargaining is to extract concessions from the union rather than also allow the union to exert economic pressure to forestall a unit work removal? Does the test satisfy the legal system's need for legal certainty so that employers do not risk having business decisions undone in post hoc proceedings and employees do not bet their jobs on the hope that the Board will find they have engaged in a protected strike over a mandatory subject? In this regard, what is meant by a decision involving "a change in the scope and direction of the enterprise"?

As indicated above, the D.C. Circuit approved the Board's *Dubuque* test. Approval has not, however, been unanimous across the courts of appeals. In Dorsey Trailers, Inc. v. NLRB, 233 F.3d 831 (4th Cir. 2000), the Fourth Circuit rejected *Dubuque* and held that an employer had no duty to bargain over its decision to close one plant and transfer the unit work to a new plant. In its view, a plant closure resulting in relocation of unit work is not a "term or condition of employment" within §8(d), even though it may affect employees' "tenure" of employment. Id. at 843. Do you agree? Can *Dorsey* be reconciled with *Fibreboard*?

**7. Applications.**

a. *Subcontracting of Unit Work.* Is the *Dubuque* approach limited to relocation decisions, or is it also applicable to subcontracting decisions? In Torrington Indus., 307 N.L.R.B. 809 (1992), the Board held that *Fibreboard,* not *Dubuque,* applies to subcontracting decisions that involve little more than the substitution of one group of workers for another. See also Finch, Pruyn & Co., 349 N.L.R.B. 270 (2007) (subcontracting not akin to opening or closing new line of work, and hence not governed by *First National Maintenance*); Mi Pueblo Foods, 360 N.L.R.B. No. 116 (2014) (affirming that *Dubuque* applies only to relocation decisions). The Board in *Torrington* further stated, however, that some subcontracting decisions might be nonmandatory because motivated by a change in the scope and direction of the business. How should subcontracting decisions motivated to a significant degree by factors other than labor costs be treated? Compare *Torrington* (rejecting view that *Fibreboard* is inapplicable where decision turns on other than labor costs; key is whether decision is entrepreneurial one involving change in scope and direction of business), with Furniture Rentors of America, Inc. v. NLRB, 36 F.3d 1240, 1248-1250 (3d Cir. 1994) (reversing Board, stating that *Fibreboard* applies only where subcontracting is motivated by labor costs or other issues amenable to collective bargaining). The Board has also held that the subcontracting of unit work can be a mandatory subject of bargaining even if it does not result in the termination or layoff of unit employees. In *Mi Pueblo Foods,* supra, for instance, the Board concluded that the parties could have bargained over the modification of unit employees' schedules and the provision of overtime as alternatives to the subcontracting of additional work to non-unit employees. See also Spurlino Materials, LLC, 353 N.L.R.B. 1198 (2009), affirmed 355 N.L.R.B. 409 (2010), enforced 645 F.3d 870 (7th Cir. 2011).

b. *Consolidation of Plants in a New Facility.* Otis Elevator has decided to shut down its research facility in New Jersey and transfer research operations to its technologically up-to-date, expanded facility in Connecticut. There is no evidence that labor costs played a role in the decision. Should Otis have bargained with the union at the New Jersey facility before making the relocation decision? Before implementing the decision? If bargaining over the relocation decision has not occurred and the union requests financial and planning documents bearing on the decision, must the company provide this information? If the union calls a strike at the New Jersey facility in the hope of placing pressure on Otis to reconsider, is the strike protected activity? See Otis Elevator Co., 269 N.L.R.B. 891 (1984) ("*Otis II*"), reversing 255 N.L.R.B. 235 (1981).

c. *Corporate Code of Ethics.* Must an employer bargain over a code of ethics for employees prohibiting such things as receiving gifts from firms providing services to the employer? If bargaining over the promulgation of the code is not required, must the employer nevertheless bargain over the propriety of imposing the code and the level of sanctions in a particular case? See American Elec. Power Co., 302 N.L.R.B. 1021 (1991); Peerless Publications, Inc., 283 N.L.R.B. 334 (1987), on remand sub nom. Newspaper Guild Local 10 v. NLRB, 636 F.2d 550 (D.C. Cir. 1980).

d. *Hidden Surveillance Cameras.* Does the employer have a duty to bargain over the installation and use of hidden surveillance cameras intended to detect employee misconduct? See Colgate-Palmolive Co., 323 N.L.R.B. 515 (1997); Anheuser-Busch, Inc., 342 N.L.R.B. 560 (2004), enforced in relevant part sub nom. Brewers & Malters, Local Union No. 6 v. NLRB, 414 F.3d 36 (D.C. Cir. 2005) (holding mandatory); see also National Steel Corp., 335 N.L.R.B. 747 (2001), enforced, 324 F.3d 928 (7th Cir. 2003) (same).

e. *Employee Representatives on the Corporate Board.* Must an employer bargain over a union proposal to place employee representatives on the corporate board of directors? What if they are to be nonvoting directors?

What about union proposals that the company issue stock to employees? See Harper, The Scope of the Duty to Bargain, supra, at 35-39.

f. *Successorship Clauses.* Collective bargaining agreements often provide for successorship clauses that require the employer, in the event of a sale, to ensure that the purchaser agrees to assume the obligations of the labor agreement. Are such clauses subject to mandatory bargaining?

g. *Notice and Opportunity for Consultation Over Plant Shutdowns.* Must an employer bargain over a union proposal requiring advance notice and opportunity for consultation in the event of a plant shutdown? Would Article XXII, §5(a) of General Electric's agreement with the International Union of Electronic, Electrical, Salaried, Machine and Furniture Workers, set forth in your Supplement, be a matter for mandatory bargaining?

h. *Automation.* Does an employer have an obligation to bargain over a capital investment decision to automate work, if doing so will lead to layoffs of unit members? Is this management decision similar to the partial-closing decision at issue in *First National Maintenance,* which also led to the loss of unit jobs? Or is it more similar to the subcontracting decision, driven by labor costs, at issue in *Fibreboard*? Would the decision hinge on whether the automation changed the scope and direction of the business? Compare Noblit Brothers, Inc., 305 N.L.R.B. 329 (1992) (no bargaining obligation over employer decision to create a new telemarketing division and to introduce new computer advancements that would impact unit jobs), with The Winchell Co., 315 N.L.R.B. 526 (1994) (bargaining obligation over introduction of computers, which resulted in layoffs).

**8. Commentary.** For a detailed account of *First National*'s background as well as a critique of the Court's decision, see Alan Hyde, The Story of *First National Maintenance Corp. v. NLRB*: Eliminating Bargaining for Low-Wage Service Workers, in Labor Law Stories (Laura J. Cooper & Catherine L. Fisk eds., 2005). For literature on the "law and economics" perspective on bargaining duties, see, e.g., Michael L. Wachter & George M. Cohen, The Law and Economics of Collective Bargaining: An Introduction and Application to Problems of Subcontracting, Partial Closure, and Relocation, 136 U. Pa. L. Rev. 1349 (1988); Stewart J. Schwab, Collective Bargaining and the Coase Theorem, 72 Cornell L. Rev. 245 (1987); Armen A. Alchian, Decision Sharing and Expropriable Specific Quasi-Rents: A Theory of *First National Maintenance v. NLRB*, 1 Sup. Ct. Econ. Rev. 235 (1982).

### *Note: Remedies for Refusals to Bargain over Mandatory Entrepreneurial Decisions*

In *Fibreboard,* supra page 475, the Board required a restoration of the status quo ante; the employer was ordered to reinstitute the bargaining-unit work pending the outcome of good-faith bargaining over the subcontracting decision, and to reinstate the terminated employees with back pay going back to the date of their terminations. The Supreme Court approved the restoration order, noting that the employer had submitted no evidence casting doubt on the Board's conclusion that restoration would not pose an "undue or unfair burden" on the company. *Fibreboard*, 376 U.S. at 216 & n.10.

The Board will not always order restoration of the former operations for refusals to bargain over a mandatory subject. It will generally decline to do so where it finds that restoration would be "unduly burdensome." See, e.g., Owens-Brockway Plastic Products, Inc., 311 N.L.R.B. 519, 535 (1993); Atlantic Brands, Inc., 297 N.L.R.B. No. 22 (1989). For example, an employer who fails to bargain in good faith over a plant closure and relocation of the unit work to other plants will not necessarily be required to restart operations at the now closed former location. See, e.g., *Owens-Brockway*, supra (not requiring resumption of operations at former location, while ordering employer to offer employees terminated as result of plant closure same or substantially equivalent employment at plants to which work has been relocated, travel expenses and relocation costs, plus back pay from date of termination until offer of employment at other plants — or, for employees who choose not to relocate, until they secure regular and substantially equivalent employment with other employers).

For a failure to engage in "effects" bargaining, the Board will order the employer to bargain over the effects of the decision at the union's request and order a so-called "*Transmarine*" remedy: back pay from five days after the Board's order until the earliest of: (a) the parties' agreement on the "effects" issue; (b) a bona fide impasse; (c) the union's failure to make a timely request for bargaining; or (d) subsequent bad-faith bargaining by the union. See Transmarine Navigation Corp., 170 N.L.R.B. 389 (1968); see also, e.g., North Star Steel Co., 347 N.L.R.B. No. 119 (2006).

Are the Board's remedies in this area adequate? Does its limited remedial arsenal call for greater use of §10(j) interim injunctions or an advisory ruling procedure to halt plant shutdowns before they occur or to allow shutdowns to occur without pointless litigation? For criticisms of the Board's remedies, see, e.g., Charles J. Morris, The Role of the NLRB and the Courts in the Collective Bargaining Process: A Fresh Look at Conventional Wisdom and Unconventional Remedies, 30 Vand. L. Rev. 661 (1977); Frank W. McCulloch, Past, Present, and Future Remedies Under Section 8(a)(5) of the NLRA, 19 Lab. L.J. 131 (1968).

## D. MULTIEMPLOYER AND MULTIUNION BARGAINING

### Charles D. Bonanno Linen Service, Inc. v. NLRB
*454 U.S. 404 (1982)*

WHITE, J.

The issue here is whether a bargaining impasse justifies an employer's unilateral withdrawal from a multiemployer bargaining unit. The . . . Petitioner, Charles D. Bonanno Linen Service, Inc. (Bonanno), is a Massachusetts corporation engaged in laundering, renting, and distributing linens and uniforms. Teamsters Local No. 25 (Union) represents its drivers and helpers as well as those of other linen supply companies in the area. For several years, Bonanno has been a member of the New England Linen Supply Association (Association), a group of 10 employers formed to negotiate with the Union as a multiemployer unit and a signatory of the contracts negotiated between the Union and the Association. On February 19, 1975, Bonanno authorized the Association's negotiating committee to represent it in the anticipated negotiations for a new contract. Bonanno's president became a member of the committee.

The Union and the Association held 10 bargaining sessions during March and April. On April 30, the negotiators agreed upon a proposed contract, but four days later the Union members rejected it. By May 15, according to the stipulations of the parties, the Union and the Association had reached an impasse over the method of compensation: the Union demanded that the drivers be paid on commission, while the Association insisted on continuing payment at an hourly rate.

Several subsequent meetings failed to break the impasse. On June 23, the Union initiated a selective strike against Bonanno. In response, most of [the] Association members locked out their drivers. Despite sporadic meetings, the stalemate continued throughout the summer. During this period two of the employers met secretly with the Union, presumably in an effort to reach a separate settlement. These meetings, however, never reached the level of negotiations.

Bonanno hired permanent replacements for all of its striking drivers. On November 21, it notified the Association by letter that it was "withdrawing from the association with respect to negotiations at this time because of an ongoing impasse with Teamsters Local 25." Bonanno mailed a copy of its revocation letter to the Union and read the letter over the phone to a Union representative.

Soon after Bonanno's putative withdrawal, the Association ended the lockout. It told the Union that it wished to continue multiemployer negotiations. Several negotiating sessions took place between December and April, without Bonanno participating. In the middle of April, the Union abandoned its demand for payment on commission and accepted the

Association's offer of a revised hourly wage rate. With this development, the parties quickly agreed on a new contract, dated April 23, 1976, and given retroactive effect to April 18, 1975.

Meanwhile, on April 9, 1976, the Union had filed the present action, alleging that Bonanno's purported withdrawal from the bargaining unit constituted an unfair labor practice. In a letter dated April 29, the Union informed Bonanno that because the Union had never consented to the withdrawal, it considered Bonanno to be bound by the settlement just reached. In a reply letter, Bonanno denied that it was bound by the contract.

An [ALJ] concluded, after a hearing, that no unusual circumstances excused Bonanno's withdrawal from the multiemployer bargaining unit. The Board affirmed, ordering Bonanno to sign and implement the contract retroactively. In a supplemental decision, the Board explained the basis of its decision that Bonanno's attempt to withdraw from the multiemployer unit was untimely and ineffective. 243 N.L.R.B. 1093 (1979). The Court of Appeals enforced the Board's order.

. . . [M]ultiemployer bargaining ha[s] "long antedated the Wagner Act" and . . . become more common as employers, in the course of complying with their duty to bargain under the Act, "sought through group bargaining to match increased union strength." [Labor Board v. Truck Drivers Union,] 353 U.S. [87,] 94-95 [(1957)]. . . . Furthermore, at the time of the debates on the Taft-Hartley amendments, Congress had rejected a proposal to limit or outlaw multiemployer bargaining. The debates and their results offered "cogent evidence that in many industries multiemployer bargaining was a vital factor in the effectuation of the national policy of promoting labor peace through strengthened collective bargaining." 353 U.S., at 95. Congress' refusal to intervene indicated that it intended to leave to the Board's specialized judgment the resolution of conflicts between union and employer rights that were bound to arise in multiemployer bargaining. . . .

Multiemployer bargaining has continued to be the preferred bargaining mechanism in many industries, and . . . it has raised a variety of problems requiring resolution. One critical question concerns the rights of the union and the employers to terminate the multiemployer bargaining arrangement. Until 1958, the Board permitted both employers and the Union to abandon the unit even in the midst of bargaining. Bearing & Rim Supply Co., 107 N.L.R.B. 101, 102-103 (1953). . . . But in Retail Associates, Inc., 120 N.L.R.B. 388 (1958), the Board announced guidelines for withdrawal from multiemployer units. These rules, which reflect an increasing emphasis on the stability of multiemployer units, permit any party to withdraw prior to the date set for negotiation of a new contract or the date on which negotiations actually begin, provided that adequate notice is given. Once negotiations for a new contract have commenced, however, withdrawal is permitted only if there is "mutual consent" or "unusual circumstances" exist. Id., at 395.

. . . After equivocating for a time, the Board squarely held that an impasse is not such an unusual circumstance. Hi-Way Billboards, Inc., 206 N.L.R.B. 22 (1973). The [Fifth Circuit] refused enforcement of that decision, 500 F.2d 181 (CA5 1974), although it has since modified its views and now supports the Board. Similar decisions by the Board were also overturned by the Courts of Appeals in three other circuits. . . . [I]n this case, the Board [reaffirmed] its position that an impasse is not an unusual circumstance justifying withdrawal. Its decision was sustained and enforced by the [First Circuit].

We agree with the Board and with the Court of Appeals. The Board has recognized the voluntary nature of multiemployer bargaining. It neither forces employers into multiemployer units nor erects barriers to withdrawal prior to bargaining. At the same time, it has sought to further the utility of multiemployer bargaining as an instrument of labor peace by limiting the circumstances under which any party may unilaterally withdraw during negotiations. Thus, it has reiterated the view expressed in *Hi-Way Billboards* that an impasse is not sufficiently destructive of group bargaining to justify unilateral withdrawal. As a recurring feature in the bargaining process, impasse is only a temporary deadlock or hiatus in negotiations "which in almost all cases is eventually broken either through a change of mind or the application of economic force." Charles D. Bonanno Linen Service, 243 N.L.R.B. 1093, 1093-1094 (1979). Furthermore, an impasse may be "brought about intentionally by one or both parties as a device to further, rather than destroy, the bargaining process." Id., at 1094. Hence, "there is little warrant for regarding an impasse as a rupture of the bargaining relation which leaves the parties free to go their own ways." Ibid. As the Board sees it, permitting withdrawal at impasse would as a practical matter undermine the utility of multiemployer bargaining.[8]

Of course, the ground rules for multiemployer bargaining have not come into being overnight. They have evolved and are still evolving, as the Board, employing its expertise in the light of experience, has sought to balance the "conflicting legitimate interests" in pursuit of the "national policy of promoting labor peace through strengthened collective bargaining." *Buffalo Linen*, supra, 353 U.S., at 96, 97. The Board might have struck a different balance from the one it has, and it may be that some or all of us would prefer that it had done so. But assessing the significance of impasse and the dynamics of collective bargaining is precisely the kind of judgment

8. The Board explains that if withdrawal were permitted at impasse, the parties would bargain under the threat of withdrawal by any party who was not completely satisfied with the results of the negotiations. That is, parties could precipitate an impasse in order to escape any agreement less favorable than the one expected. In addition, it is precisely at and during impasse, when bargaining is temporarily replaced by economic warfare, that the need for a stable, predictable bargaining unit becomes acute in order that the parties can weigh the costs and possible benefits of their conduct.

that *Buffalo Linen* ruled should be left to the Board. We cannot say that the Board's current resolution of the issue is arbitrary or contrary to law.

If the Board's refusal to accept an impasse, standing alone, as an unusual circumstance warranting withdrawal were the only issue in this case, we would affirm without more. But several Courts of Appeals have rejected *Hi-Way Billboards* on the grounds that impasse may precipitate a strike against one or all members of the unit and that upon impasse the Board permits the union to execute interim agreements with individual employers. These Courts of Appeals consider the possibility of such events as sufficient grounds for any employer in the unit to withdraw. . . .

The Board's reasons for adhering to its *Hi-Way Billboards* position are telling. They are surely adequate to survive judicial review. First, it is said that strikes and interim agreements often occur in the course of negotiations prior to impasse and that neither tactic is necessarily associated with impasse. Second, it is "vital" to understand that the Board distinguishes "between interim agreements which contemplate adherence to a final unitwide contract and are thus not antithetical to group bargaining and individual agreements which are clearly inconsistent with, and destructive of, group bargaining." 243 N.L.R.B., at 1096. . . .

On the other hand, where the union, not content with interim agreements that expire with the execution of a unitwide contract, executes separate agreements that will survive unit negotiations, the union has so "effectively fragmented and destroyed the integrity of the bargaining unit," id., as to create an "unusual circumstance" under *Retail Associates* rules. Cf. Typographic Service Co., 238 N.L.R.B. 1565 (1978). Furthermore, the Board has held that the execution of separate agreements that would permit either the union or the employer to escape the binding effect of an agreement resulting from group bargaining is a refusal to bargain and an unfair labor practice on the part of both the union and any employer executing such an agreement. Teamsters Union Local No. 378 (Olympia Automobile Dealers Assn.), 243 N.L.R.B. 1086 (1979). The remaining members of the unit thus can insist that parties remain subject to unit negotiations in accordance with their original understanding.

The Board therefore emphatically rejects the proposition that the negotiation of truly interim, temporary agreements, as distinguished from separate, final contracts, are "inconsistent with the concept of multiemployer bargaining units." Charles D. Bonanno Linen Service, 243 N.L.R.B. 1093, 1096 (1979). Although interim agreements establish terms and conditions of employment for one or more employer members of the unit pending the outcome of renewed group bargaining, all employers, including those executing interim agreements, have an "equivalent stake" in the final outcome because "the resulting group agreement would then apply to all employers, including each signer of an interim agreement." Ibid. Such interim arrangements "preclude a finding that the early signers had withdrawn from the unit." Ibid. Although the Board concedes that interim agreements exert economic pressure on struck employers, this fact should no more warrant withdrawal than the refusal of one employer to join with others in a lockout. In any event, the Board's view is that interim agreements, on balance, tend to deter rather than promote unit fragmentation since they preserve a continuing mutual interest by all employer members in a final association-wide contract.

. . . The balance [the Board] has struck is not inconsistent with the terms or purposes of the Act, and its decision should therefore be enforced. . . .

STEVENS, J., concurring. . . .

The Court's holding does not preclude an employer from explicitly conditioning its participation in group bargaining on any special terms of its own design. Presumably, an employer could refuse to participate in multiemployer bargaining unless the union accepted the employer's right to withdraw from the bargaining unit should an impasse develop. The union or the other members of the bargaining unit of course may reject such a condition; in such a case, however, the employer simply would be forced to choose between agreeing to be bound by the terms of group negotiation without a right of withdrawal at impasse, or foregoing the advantages of multiemployer bargaining and bargaining on its own. . . .

[The opinion of Chief Justice Burger, with whom Justice Rehnquist joins, dissenting, is omitted.]

## *NOTES AND QUESTIONS*

1. **Bargaining Obligations and Economic Weapons.** Does *Bonanno Linen,* contrary to the Court's earlier *Insurance Agents'* decision, supra page 411, support the use of §§8(a)(5) and (b)(3) to regulate the weapons of economic conflict? Is the employer's ability to withdraw from multiemployer bargaining simply a question of permissible tactics for imposing the costs of disagreement on the union, and hence no different in principle from questions of the legality of the union's "whipsaw" strike? Or is the case best understood as being only concerned with the structure of bargaining and with rules on entry and withdrawal from bargaining units? If the Board has authority to protect the structure of bargaining, does it also have the authority to rule certain economic weapons out of bounds in the interest of preserving the process of collective bargaining as a means of resolving disputes rather than terminating relationships? Review these questions after studying the materials in the next chapter on weapons of economic conflict.

**2. "Unusual Circumstances."**

a. Bonanno was awarded approximately $124,000 as compensatory damages in an action against Local 125, among others, resulting from serious violence, actual and threatened, during the selective strike authorized or ratified by the union; the violence included physical damage to Bonanno's trucks and plant and threats of physical injury to employees that culminated in brutal attacks against substitute drivers and a security guard. Bonanno himself and his supervisory and professional employees were also the targets of threats. See Charles D. Bonanno Linen Serv., Inc. v. McCarthy, 550 F. Supp. 231 (D. Mass. 1982), affirmed in part and reversed in part, 708 F.2d 1 (1st Cir. 1983).

Should the "unusual circumstances" justification for withdrawal include serious and antecedent union violence? Should serious union violence, whether before or after withdrawal, constitute a defense against a bargaining order? Cf. NLRB v. Triumph Curing Ctr., 571 F.2d 462 (9th Cir. 1978).

b. In NLRB v. Siebler Heating & Air Conditioning, 563 F.2d 366 (8th Cir. 1977), the court, reversing the Board, upheld withdrawal by residential contractors from a multiemployer unit after negotiations for a renewal agreement began. The court recognized that dissatisfaction with the results of group bargaining does not justify withdrawal but found "unusual circumstances" in the association's failure fairly to represent the defectors, specifically in sacrificing their interests to the majority by feebly supporting the defectors' efforts to get a lower wage rate for certain residential construction in order to meet nonunion competition.

**3. Contracting Out of *Bonanno Linen*?** All members of a multiemployer unit have, for many years, bargained with a union through their association. Recently, these members agreed to by-laws barring any individual firm from abandoning a lawful lockout or from entering into "interim" or "separate" agreements without the permission of the multiemployer association's executive committee, which, under the applicable by-laws, is to be the exclusive bargaining agent for all the member firms. Prior to the time set for negotiations for a renewal agreement, the union was formally advised of the new by-laws. Following protracted negotiations and compliance with the notice and waiting periods of §8(d) of the Act, the union called a strike against Target, Inc., a member of the unit. The association's executive committee, pursuant to the by-laws, then activated a lockout by all members of the unit.

Would these by-laws affect the legality under the NLRA of another unit member's lifting the lockout and executing either an interim agreement or a separate agreement with the union, without prior permission from the association's executive committee? See NLRB v. Teamsters Local No. 378, 672 F.2d 741 (9th Cir. 1982) (remanding the Board's order in Olympia

Automobile Dealers Ass'n, 243 N.L.R.B. 1086 (1979), which was cited with approval in *Bonanno*). Would your answer change if the union had not been given early notice of the by-laws? If the employers conditioned their acceptance of the multiemployer unit on their operating under those by-laws and the union's acquiescence?

**4. 1980 Multiemployer Pension Legislation.** Under the Multiemployer Pension Plan Amendments Act of 1980, Pub. L. No. 96-364, 94 Stat. 1208 (1980), withdrawal from a multiemployer unit, even though proper under the NLRA, will in general require a withdrawing employer to fund a share of the unfunded vested benefits of the multiemployer defined-benefit pension plan. "Withdrawal" for this purpose may also arise from decertification of a union previously representing employees covered by the multiemployer plan, plant closure, or sale of assets. The 1980 Act has a substantial effect on the parties to multiemployer pension plans. See especially 26 U.S.C. §§412, 414, 418-418E, 4971, 4975, 6511 (2011). See generally Alicia H. Munnell & Jean-Pierre Aubry, Private Sector Multiemployer Pension Plans—a Primer (Center for Retirement Research of Boston College, August 2014, No. 14-13).

**5. Why Don't We Have More Multiemployer Bargaining?** In continental Europe multiemployer bargaining is quite pervasive, although the extent of centralization has diminished. See generally Samuel Estreicher & Stewart J. Schwab, Foundations of Labor and Employment Law 330-331 (2000).

Multiemployer collective bargaining in the United States would seem to offer considerable benefits to the parties—savings on administrative costs, assurances to employers that union-negotiated wages will be extended to competitors, and a general insulation of unions from threats to their institutional position. See Douglas L. Leslie, Multiemployer Bargaining Rules, 75 Va. L. Rev. 241 (1989); Jan Vetter, Commentary on "Multiemployer Bargaining Rules": Searching for the Right Questions, 75 Va. L. Rev. 285 (1989). Yet, despite these features, multiemployer bargaining here has never reached European levels and is on the wane in some industries such as trucking and construction because of competitive forces. In an effort to counter such forces (with mixed results), some European systems provide for government extension of collective agreements to unorganized firms. See Manfred Weiss et al., The Settlement of Labour Disputes in the Federal Republic of Germany, in Industrial Conflict Resolution in Market Economies (Hanami & Blanpain eds., 2d ed. 1989), at 94-95; Michael Despax & Jacques Rojot, France, in International Encyclopedia of Labour Law 265-272 (Roger Blanpain ed., 1987). Should similar laws be adopted here? Compare Joel Rogers, Reforming U.S. Labor Relations, 69 Chi.-Kent L. Rev. 97, 115-116 (1993), with Estreicher, Labor Law Reform, supra, at 34 n.112; Samuel Estreicher, Global Issues in Labor Law (2007).

**6. Remedy for Untimely Withdrawal.** An employer makes an untimely withdrawal from a multiemployer bargaining unit under the *Retail Associates* rule sustained in *Bonanno Linen,* and then refuses to honor the agreement later reached between the multiemployer association and the union. Can the Board require the employer to sign the agreement and comply with the benefits schedule therein? See NLRB v. Strong, 393 U.S. 357 (1969) (sustaining such an order without discussion of §8(d)).

***Note: Coalition and Coordinated Bargaining***

We have seen that employers, in connection with multiemployer bargaining, have drawn on considerations typically invoked by unions—the need for redressing power imbalances and for protection against divide-and-conquer tactics. Unions have stressed similar considerations in connection with "coordinated" or "coalition" bargaining. These terms are sometimes used interchangeably to describe various forms of cooperative communication or parallel action by unions that are bargaining for different bargaining units of the same employer (or, less frequently, by employers bargaining with a single union). "Coordinated" bargaining, however, would better describe communication among different bargaining representatives who nevertheless retain the power of independent decision making. "Coalition" bargaining, by contrast, would fairly describe an effort by unions to force the consolidation of separate bargaining units. Such efforts are more likely to run afoul of the rule that makes it unlawful for a union to insist on, or strike for, the expansion of the bargaining unit certified by the NLRB or agreed to by the union and the employer. See Douds v. International Longshoremen's Ass'n, 241 F.2d 278 (2d Cir. 1957).

General Elec. Co. v. NLRB, 412 F.2d 512 (2d Cir. 1969), involved the interplay of that rule and interunion cooperative arrangements. The IUE, which represented about 90,000 GE employees in 150 bargaining units, had formed a Committee for Collective Bargaining (CCB) with seven other international unions, whose locals had agreements with GE covering seven separate bargaining units. CCB's avowed purposes included the coordination of bargaining with GE and Westinghouse (GE's chief competitor), the formulation of national goals, and the creation of reciprocal support among the participating unions, which represented GE employees in 50 states. The court of appeals upheld the NLRB's position that it was proper for the IUE to include on its bargaining committee representatives of the seven other unions. Consequently, GE's refusal to bargain with the "mixed committee" violated §8(a)(5).

Although, as *General Electric* indicates, unions have been given considerable leeway in choosing their bargaining representatives, the Board and courts have rebuffed direct efforts by unions to consolidate separate bargaining units of a single employer. See Oil, Chem. & Atomic Workers v. NLRB, 486 F.2d 1266 (D.C. Cir. 1973) (affirming the Board's decision that upheld a company's refusal to bargain at a single time and place with an international union and its locals regarding pension benefits for 19 separate bargaining units represented by locals of the international).

## E. MIDTERM BARGAINING

### *Note: Permissive Subjects and Midterm Modification*

In Allied Chem. & Alkali Workers v. Pittsburgh Plate Glass Co., 404 U.S. 157 (1971), supra page 470-471, the Supreme Court made clear that mid-term modifications of clauses in a labor agreement dealing with permissive subjects do not violate the statutory duty to bargain:

> Paragraph (4) of §8(d) . . . requires that a party proposing a modification continue "in full force and effect . . . all the terms and conditions of the existing contract" until its expiration. Viewed in isolation from the rest of the provision, that language would preclude any distinction between contract obligations that are "terms and conditions of employment" and those that are not. But in construing §8(d), "'we must not be guided by a single sentence or member of a sentence, but look to the provisions of the whole law, and to its object and policy.'" Mastro Plastics Corp. v. NLRB, 350 U.S. 270, 285 (1956). . . . Seen in that light, §8(d) embraces only mandatory topics of bargaining. The provision begins by defining "to bargain collectively" as meeting and conferring "with respect to wages, hours, and other terms and conditions of employment." It then goes on to state that "the duty to bargain collectively shall also mean" that mid-term unilateral modifications and terminations are prohibited. Although this part of the section is introduced by a "proviso" clause, . . . it quite plainly is to be construed in pari materia with the preceding definition. Accordingly, just as §8(d) defines the obligation to bargain to be with respect to mandatory terms alone, so it prescribes the duty to maintain only mandatory terms without unilateral modification for the duration of the collective bargaining agreement. . . .
>
> The structure and language of §8(d) point to a more specialized purpose than merely promoting general contract compliance. The conditions . . . set out in paragraphs (1) through (4) plainly are designed to regulate modifications and terminations so as to facilitate agreement in place of economic warfare. . . .
>
> If that is correct, the distinction that we draw between mandatory and permissive terms of bargaining fits the statutory purpose. By once bargaining and agreeing on a permissive subject, the parties, naturally, do not make the subject a mandatory topic of future bargaining. When a proposed modification is to a permissive term, therefore, the purpose of facilitating accord on the proposal is not at all in point, since the parties are not required under the

statute to bargain with respect to it. The irrelevance of the purpose is demonstrated by the irrelevance of the procedures themselves of §8(d).... The remedy for a unilateral mid-term modification to a permissive term lies in an action for breach of contract, ... not in an unfair-labor-practice proceeding.

## Jacobs Manufacturing Co.

*94 N.L.R.B. 1214 (1951)*

... In July 1948, the Respondent and the Union executed a 2-year bargaining contract which, by its terms, could be reopened one year after its execution date for discussion of "wage rates." In July 1949 the Union invoked the reopening clause ... and thereafter gave the Respondent written notice of its "wage demands." In addition to a request for a wage increase, these demands included a request that the Respondent undertake the entire cost of an existing group insurance program, and another request for the establishment of a pension plan for the Respondent's employees. When the parties met thereafter to consider the Union's demands, the Respondent refused to discuss the Union's pension and insurance requests on the ground that they were not appropriate items of discussion under the reopening clause of the 1948 contract.

The group insurance program to which the Union alluded in its demands was established by the Respondent before 1948. It was underwritten by an insurance company, and provided life, accident, health, surgical, and hospital protection. All the Respondent's employees were eligible to participate in the program, and the employees shared its costs with the Respondent. When the 1948 contract was being negotiated, the Respondent and the Union had discussed changes in this *insurance program,* and had agreed to increase certain of the benefits as well as the costs. However, neither the changes thereby effected, nor the insurance program itself, was mentioned in the 1948 contract.

As indicated by the Union's request, there was no *pension* plan for the Respondent's employees in existence in 1949. The subject of pensions, moreover, had not been discussed during the 1948 negotiations; and, like insurance, that subject is not mentioned in the 1948 contract.

a. For the reasons stated below, Chairman Herzog and Members Houston and Styles agree with the Trial Examiner's conclusion that the Respondent violated §8(a)(5) ... by refusing to discuss the matter of *pensions* with the Union....

We are satisfied ... that the 1948 contract did not in itself impose on the Respondent any obligation to discuss pensions or insurance. The reopening clause of that contract refers to *wage rates,* and thus its intention appears to have been narrowly limited to matters directly related to the amount and manner of compensation for work....

On the other hand, a majority of the Board believes that, regardless of the character of the reopening clause, the Act itself imposed upon the Respondent the duty to discuss *pensions* with the Union during the period in question.

It is now established . . . [that] . . . pensions [fall] within the area where the statute requires bargaining. And, as noted above, the 1948 contract between the Respondent and the Union was silent with respect to the subject of pensions; indeed, the matter had never been raised or discussed by the parties. The issue raised, therefore, is whether the Respondent was absolved of the obligation to discuss pensions because of the [§8(d)] limitation . . . dealing with the duty to discuss or agree to the modification of an existing bargaining contract. . . . Section 8(d) does not itself license a party . . . to refuse, during the life of the contract, to discuss a bargainable subject unless it has been made a part of the agreement itself. . . . [T]herefore, the *Tide Water* [85 N.L.R.B. 1096 (1949)] construction of §8(d) means that the Respondent was obligated to discuss the Union's pension demand.

Members Houston and Styles have carefully reexamined the Board's construction of §8(d) in the *Tide Water* case, and are persuaded that the view the Board adopted [there] best effectuates the declared policy of the Act. Chairman Herzog, while joining in the result with respect to the obligation to bargain here concerning pensions — never previously discussed by the parties — joins in the rationale herein *only* to the extent that it is consistent with his views separately recited below, concerning the insurance program.

By making mandatory the discussion of bargainable subjects not already covered by a contract, the parties to the contract are encouraged to arrive at joint decisions with respect to bargainable matters, that, at least to the party requesting discussion, appear at the time to be of some importance. The Act's policy of "encouraging the practice and procedure of collective bargaining" is consequently furthered. A different construction of §8(d) in the circumstances — one that would permit a party to a bargaining contract to avoid discussion when it was sought on subject matters not contained in the contract — would serve, at its best, only to dissipate whatever . . . good will that had been engendered by the previous bargaining negotiations that led to the execution of a bargaining contract; at its worst, it could bring about the industrial strife and the production interruptions that . . . the Act also seeks to avert. . . .

The construction of §8(d) adopted . . . in the *Tide Water* case serves also to simplify, and thus to speed, the bargaining process. It eliminates the pressure upon the parties at the time when a contract is being negotiated to raise those subjects that may not then be of controlling importance, but which might in the future assume a more significant status. It also assures to both unions and employers that, if future conditions require some agreement as to matters about which the parties have not sought, or have not been able to obtain agreement, then some discussion of those matters will be forthcoming when necessary.

. . . What §8(d) does is to reject the pronouncements contained in some pre-1947 Board and court decisions . . . to the effect that the duty to bargain continues even as to those matters upon which the parties have reached agreement and which are set forth in the terms of a written contract. But we believe it does no more. Those bargainable issues which have never been discussed by the parties, and which are in no way treated in the contract, remain matters which both the union and the employer are obliged to discuss at any time.

. . . [I]f the parties originally desire to avoid later discussion with respect to matters not specifically covered in the terms of an executed contract, they need only so specify in the terms of the contract itself. Nothing in our construction of §8(d) precludes such an agreement, entered into in good faith, from foreclosing future discussion of matters not contained in the agreement.[13]

b. Chairman Herzog . . . believes that — unlike the pensions issue — the Respondent was under no obligation to bargain concerning the *group insurance program.*

However, Members Houston and Styles — a minority of the Board on this issue — are of the further opinion that the considerations discussed above leading to the conclusion that the Respondent was obligated to discuss the matter of pensions, also impel the conclusion that the Respondent was obligated to discuss the Union's group insurance demand. Like pensions, the matter of group insurance benefits is a subject which has been held to be within the area of compulsory bargaining; and like pensions, the Respondent's group insurance program was not mentioned in the terms of the 1948 contract. Members Houston and Styles therefore believe that so far as the controlling facts are concerned, the ultimate issues presented by the Union's pension and group insurance demands are identical. . . .

. . . Members Houston and Styles are constrained to reject the view of Chairman Herzog for the further reason that it would establish a rule which is administratively unworkable, and would inject dangerous uncertainty into the process of collective bargaining. Apart from the extremely difficult problems of proof — illustrated in this very case — which would constantly confront the Board in cases of this type, the parties to collective bargaining negotiations would always be faced with this question after a subject has been *discussed* — "Have we really *negotiated,* or are we under an obligation to discuss the subject further if asked to"? To this query the rule of the *Tide Water* case gives a clear and concise answer: "You are obligated to discuss any bargainable subject upon request unless you have reduced your agreement

---

13. [This footnote presented "an example of such a provision," a typical "zipper" clause, discussed in note 3 following this case. — Eds.]

on that subject to writing or unless you have agreed in writing not to bargain about it during the term of the contract."

[Chairman Herzog, concurring and dissenting in part, argued as follows: After the union had advanced the disputed insurance proposal during the prior negotiations, the respondent had rejected it but had improved the insurance benefits outside the written contract. Hence, rejection of the insurance proposal had been part of the bargain. Without regard to "the niceties of construing [§8(d)]," imposition of a bargaining duty in such situations would be inequitable and unwise.]

Member Reynolds, concurring separately and dissenting in part.

... [I]t is my opinion that §8(d) imposes no obligation on either party to a contract to bargain on any matter during the term of the contract except as the express provisions of the contract may demand. This is a result reasonably compatible with the particular §8(d) language involved, as well as with §8(d) as a whole. Moreover, not only does the result accord stability and dignity to collective bargaining agreements, but it also gives substance to the practice and procedure of collective bargaining. . . . Contractually stabilized industrial relations enable employers, because of fixed labor costs, to engage in sound long-range production planning, and employees, because of fixed wage, seniority, promotion, and grievance provisions, to anticipate secure employment tenure. . . .

[The opinion of Member Murdock, dissenting in part, is omitted.]

## *NOTES AND QUESTIONS*

**1. "Clear and Unmistakable" Waiver.** The Board's view that §8(d) does not relieve an employer of the duty to bargain over subjects neither discussed in negotiations nor incorporated as terms of the agreement was affirmed in NLRB v. Jacobs Mfg. Co., 196 F.2d 680 (2d Cir. 1952). Although that court found it unnecessary to determine whether "discussion" of an item during negotiations relieves the employer of a midterm duty to bargain about inclusion of a provision on the item, subsequent Board and court decisions make clear that only discussions constituting a "waiver" of the union's right to insist on midterm bargaining will have that effect. See, e.g., NL Indus., 220 N.L.R.B. 41, 43 (1975), enforced, 536 F.2d 786 (8th Cir. 1976). The Board's customary "clear and unmistakable" test of waiver is applicable; thus, the item in issue must have been "fully discussed" or "consciously explored," and the union must have "consciously yielded or relinquished" in the "give and take" of negotiations. See Rockwell Int'l Corp., 260 N.L.R.B. 1346, 1347 (1982); Angelus Block Co., 250 N.L.R.B. 868, 877 (1980). See also Pepsi-Cola Distrib. Co., 241 N.L.R.B. 869, 870 (1979) (what is said during negotiations must "put the union on notice that its failure to include a provision would preclude it from future bargaining on the subject"). Do you think that this approach may sometimes cause employers to raise and discuss matters that both sides would prefer to lie dormant?

Would it be desirable to shift the presumption and treat collective agreements as suspending any duty to bargain until their expiration date, unless there has been an express reservation of an issue for possible midterm bargaining? Would this promote industrial peace or would it make it more difficult for parties to finalize agreements? Yet does the Board's position, in any event, also impede completion of agreements because unions have the ability to raise issues, test management's reactions, and then withdraw the subject for possible use midterm? Does it matter which approach applies as long as the law is clear? See Schwab, Collective Bargaining and the Coase Theorem, supra. For the argument that "informational asymmetry" — the employer's generally greater knowledge of the likelihood that a particular issue will become salient during the term of an agreement—justifies imposing a midterm bargaining obligation on the employer over a mandatory issue not resolved in the agreement, see Hylton, An Economic Theory of the Duty to Bargain, supra, at 47-50. But cf. Wachter & Cohen, The Law and Economics of Collective Bargaining, supra, at 1409, 1417 (narrowing the scope of midterm bargaining is generally efficient).

**2. Effect of *Jacobs* on Midterm Modifications.** Assume that Jacobs Manufacturing wanted to change its group insurance system during the term of the collective bargaining agreement. Could it do so after bargaining to impasse with the union? Could it do so if the union refused to discuss the matter at all? If Jacobs wanted to adopt a new pension program during the term of the agreement, could it do so without bargaining with the union? Could it do so after bargaining and reaching impasse?

**3. "Zipper" Clauses.** Note that the *Jacobs* Board stated that the parties could avoid midterm discussion of any issue not contained in the agreement by so specifying in the "terms of the contract" itself. The *Jacobs* case thereby stimulated use of provisions called "zipper clauses" because they seek to "zip up" the agreement to preclude any further bargaining during its term. A typical clause follows:

> The parties acknowledge that during the negotiations which resulted in this Agreement, each had the unlimited right and opportunity to make demands and proposals with respect to any subject or matter . . . , and that the understanding and agreements arrived at by the parties . . . are set forth in this Agreement. Therefore, the Company and the Union, for the life of this Agreement, each voluntarily and unqualifiedly waives the right, and each

agrees that the other shall not be obligated, to bargain collectively with respect to any subject or matter referred to, or covered in this Agreement, or with respect to any subject or matter not specifically referred to or covered by this Agreement even though such subject or matter may not have been within the knowledge or contemplation of either or both of the parties at the time they negotiated or signed this Agreement.

It appears settled that "general" zipper clauses constitute a waiver of either side's right to insist on bargaining over its proposals to add new terms, but do not relieve the other side (usually the employer) of its duty to bargain before initiating unilateral changes in existing conditions of employment. See, e.g., International Union, UAW v. NLRB, 765 F.2d 175, 182-183 (D.C. Cir. 1985) ("*Milwaukee Spring II*") (enforcing Board decision excerpted at page 512 below).

Can a zipper clause, by rendering all mandatory subjects of bargaining "contained in" the agreement, at least in certain circumstances, also be read to preclude an employer's midterm modification of a mandatory subject even after bargaining to impasse? Does the zipper clause thus give the union, as well as the employer, the right to refuse to bargain over wages and working conditions during the agreement's term? See CBS Corp. f/k/a Westinghouse Corp., 326 N.L.R.B. 861 (1998), where the Board found that the employer's midterm subcontracting of unit work violated §8(a)(5) because "the [zipper] clauses in this case operate with respect to matters that were 'discussed' during the negotiation of the contracts" and the employer had expressly represented to union negotiators that it "had considered but rejected the possibility of outsourcing unit work. After the Union had been given this assurance, the Union did not pursue further the issue of subcontracting." See also infra note 3, page 517.

**4. Unilateral Changes During Term of Agreement.** The Board holds that employers, regardless of the presence of a zipper clause, must bargain to impasse before taking unilateral action on topics not covered by an agreement absent contract language (perhaps supported by bargaining history) that manifests a "clear and unmistakable" relinquishment of bargaining rights with respect to the particular matter involved. Compare Radioear Corp., 214 N.L.R.B. 362 (1974), with Unit Drop Division, Eaton, Yale & Towne, Inc., 171 N.L.R.B. 600 (1968), enforced in relevant part, 412 F.2d 108 (7th Cir. 1969); and NLRB v. Auto Crane Co., 536 F.2d 310 (10th Cir. 1975). Some courts, however, have held the "clear and unmistakable" standard to be inappropriate where the employer has some basis in the contract to claim authority to effect the change. See infra note 4b, page 518. Consider the following hypotheticals.

a. An employer, who suffered large losses, unilaterally discontinued a long-standing practice (not mentioned in the collective agreement) of giving all personnel a large turkey at Christmas. Does the zipper clause quoted in note 3 protect the employer against a §8(a)(5) charge based on the employer's failure to bargain with the incumbent union over this action? Would it be material if the union in bargaining for the current agreement had made, but dropped, a request for a maintenance-of-benefits clause, without, however, mentioning the turkeys to the employer? Cf. Aeronca, Inc. v. NLRB, 650 F.2d 501 (4th Cir. 1981). But cf. Columbus & Southern Ohio Electric Co., 270 N.L.R.B. 686 (1984); Benchmark Industries, Inc., 270 N.L.R.B. 22 (1984).

b. Suppose the incumbent union makes a midterm request that the employer, for the first time, give each of its employees a Christmas turkey. Would the zipper clause justify the employer's refusal to discuss that request? See generally W.B. Nelson & R.T. Howard, The Duty to Bargain During the Term of an Existing Agreement, 27 Lab. L.J. 573 (1976); Note, Mid-term Modification of Terms and Conditions of Employment, 1972 Duke L.J. 813.

**5. "Bargainability" of "Zipper" Clauses.** Is the zipper clause quoted in note 3 a subject of bargaining upon which a party may insist to the point of impasse? See NLRB v. Tomco Communications, Inc., 567 F.2d 871 (9th Cir. 1978).

**6. Midterm Strikes.** A strike during the term of an agreement may constitute a breach of the agreement's no-strike clause even if the strike is over a subject requiring bargaining under *Jacobs.* In addition, strikes during the notice and cooling-off periods of §8(d) are unprotected. In NLRB v. Lion Oil Co., 352 U.S. 282 (1957), the Court held that where the contract provides for a reopener period on one or more terms, the union may strike (assuming proper notice and exhaustion of the cooling-off period) without running afoul of §8(d). See Speedrack, Inc., 293 N.L.R.B. 1054 (1989); Hydrologics, Inc., 293 N.L.R.B. 1060 (1989). See also Note on Impasse Procedures, supra pages 459-460.

### Milwaukee Spring Division of Illinois Coil Spring Co. ("*Milwaukee Spring II*")

*268 N.L.R.B. 601 (1984), enforced sub nom. International Union, UAW v. NLRB, 765 F.2d 175 (D.C. Cir. 1985)*

[In *Milwaukee Spring I,* 265 N.L.R.B. 206 (1982), the Board (3-0) had held that respondent violated §§8(a)(1), (3) and (5) by deciding—during the term of a collective bargaining agreement and without the union's consent—to transfer its assembly operations from its unionized Milwaukee Spring facility to its unorganized McHenry Spring facility. While review was pending in the Seventh Circuit, a newly reconstituted Board requested and received remand of the case. Upon reconsideration, the Board (3-1), with three Reagan appointees making up the majority, reversed its original decision.]

. . . Illinois Coil Spring Company consists of three divisions—Holly Spring, McHenry Spring, and Respondent (Milwaukee Spring). . . . [A]lthough collectively the four entities are a single employer, each location constitutes a separate bargaining unit. Respondent . . . employed about 99 bargaining unit employees . . . in eight departments, including [assembly operations and molding operations].

The Union has represented Respondent's bargaining unit employees for a number of years. The most recent contract became effective on 1 April 1980, and remained in effect until at least 31 March 1983. The contract contains specific wage and benefits provisions. The contract also provides that the Company "recognizes the Union as the sole and exclusive collective bargaining agent for all production and maintenance employees in the Company's plant at Milwaukee, Wisconsin."

On 26 January 1982 Respondent asked the Union to forgo a scheduled wage increase and to grant other contract concessions. In March, because Respondent lost a major customer, it proposed to the Union relocating its assembly operations to the nonunionized McHenry facility, located in McHenry, Illinois, to obtain relief from the comparatively higher assembly labor costs at Milwaukee Spring. Respondent also advised the Union that it needed wage and benefit concessions to keep its molding operations in Milwaukee viable. On 23 March the Union rejected the proposed reduction in wages and benefits. On 29 March Respondent submitted to the Union a document entitled "Terms Upon Which Milwaukee Assembly Operations Will Be Retained in Milwaukee." On 4 April the Union rejected the Company's proposal for alternatives to relocation and declined to bargain further over the Company's decision to transfer its assembly operations. The Company then announced its decision to relocate the Milwaukee assembly operations to the McHenry facility.

The parties stipulated that the relocation decision was economically motivated and was not the result of union animus . . . [and] that Respondent has satisfied its obligation to bargain with the Union over the decision . . . and has been willing to engage in effects bargaining with the Union.

. . . Generally, an employer may not unilaterally institute changes regarding mandatory subjects before reaching a good-faith impasse in bargaining. Section 8(d) imposes an additional requirement when a collective-bargaining agreement is in effect and an employer seeks to "modif[y] . . . the terms and conditions contained in" the contract: the employer must obtain the union's consent before implementing the change. If the employment conditions the employer seeks to change are not "contained in" the contract, however, the employer's obligation remains the general one of bargaining in good faith to impasse over the subject before instituting the proposed change.

Applying these principles . . . , before the Board may hold that Respondent violated §8(d), the Board first must identify a specific term "contained in" the contract that the Company's decision to relocate modified. . . . [W]e have searched the contract in vain for a provision requiring bargaining unit work to remain in Milwaukee.

*Milwaukee Spring I* suggests, however, that the Board may have concluded that Respondent's relocation decision, because it was motivated by a desire to obtain relief from the Milwaukee contract's labor costs, modified that contract's wage and benefits provisions. We believe this reasoning is flawed. While it is true that the Company proposed modifying the wage and benefits provisions of the contract, the Union rejected the proposals. Following its failure to obtain the Union's consent, Respondent, in accord with §8(d), abandoned the proposals to modify the contract's wage and benefits provisions. Instead, Respondent decided to transfer the assembly operations to a different plant where different workers (who were not subject to the contract) would perform the work. In short, Respondent did not disturb the wages and benefits at its Milwaukee facility, and consequently did not violate §8(d) by modifying, without the Union's consent, the wage and benefits provisions contained in the contract.

Nor do we find that Respondent's relocation decision modified the contract's recognition clause. In two previous cases, the Board construed recognition clauses to encompass the duties performed by bargaining unit employees and held that employers' reassignment of work modified those clauses. In both instances, reviewing courts found no basis for reading jurisdictional rights into standard clauses that merely recognized the contracts' coverage of specified employees. Boeing Co., 230 N.L.R.B. 696 (1977), enf. denied 581 F.2d 793 (9th Cir. 1978); University of Chicago, 210 N.L.R.B. 190 (1974), enf. denied 514 F.2d 942 (7th Cir. 1975). We agree with the courts' reasoning.

Language recognizing the Union as the bargaining agent "for all production and maintenance employees in the Company's plant at Milwaukee, Wisconsin," does not state that the functions that the unit performs must remain in Milwaukee. No doubt parties could draft such a clause; indeed, work-preservation clauses are commonplace. It is not for the Board, however, to create an implied work-preservation clause in every American labor agreement based on wage and benefits or recognition provisions, and we expressly decline to do so. . . .

*In Milwaukee Spring I*, the Board also found that Respondent's laying off employees as a consequence of its relocation decision violated §8(a)(3) notwithstanding that the parties stipulated there was no union animus. Invoking the "inherently destructive" doctrine of [NLRB v. Great Dane Trailers, Inc., 388 U.S. 26 (1967), infra page 543], the Board apparently held that the 8(a)(3) violation flowed from the finding that the relocation decision violated §8(a)(5). Accepting this logic for the purposes of our decision only, we conclude that, having found that Respondent complied with its [§8(a)(5)] statutory obligation before deciding to relocate . . . , there is no factual or legal basis for finding that the consequent layoff of employees violated §8(a)(3).

[Decisions like] *Milwaukee Spring I* discourage truthful midterm bargaining over decisions to transfer unit work. [A]n employer contemplating a plant relocation for several reasons, one of which is labor costs, would be likely to admit only the reasons unrelated to labor costs in order to avoid granting the union veto power over the decision. The union, unaware that labor costs were a factor in the employer's decision, would be unlikely to volunteer wage or other appropriate concessions. Even if the union offered to consider wage concessions, the employer might hesitate to discuss such suggestions for fear that bargaining with the union over the union's proposals would be used as evidence that labor costs had motivated the relocation decision.

We believe our holding today avoids this dilemma and will encourage the realistic and meaningful collective bargaining that the Act contemplates. Under our decision, an employer does not risk giving a union veto power over its decision regarding relocation and should therefore be willing to disclose all factors affecting its decision. Consequently, the union will be in a better position to evaluate whether to make concessions. Because both parties will no longer have an incentive to refrain from frank bargaining, the likelihood that they will be able to resolve their differences is greatly enhanced.

Accordingly, for all of the foregoing reasons, we reverse our original Decision and Order and dismiss the complaint.

Member ZIMMERMAN, dissenting. . . .

My colleagues and I apparently agree that if a collective-bargaining agreement contains an applicable work-preservation clause, §8(d) requires the employer to obtain the union's consent prior to any transfer of work regardless of the reasons underlying the transfer. The difference . . . between [us] is that I find §8(d) applicable to other contractual terms. Here, as Respondent's decision was motivated solely by its desire to avoid the wage provisions of the contract, I would find that Respondent is prohibited from implementing its decision without the Union's consent during the term of the collective-bargaining agreement. . . .

. . . I find that Respondent's midterm relocation decision was proscribed under §8(d). . . . Respondent voluntarily obligated itself to pay a certain amount of wages to employees performing assembly work during the term of the contract, and it cannot avoid this obligation merely by unilaterally relocating the work to another of its facilities, just as it could not by unilaterally reducing the wage rate. It is disingenuous to argue . . . that Respondent's relocation decision did not disturb the contractual wages and benefits at the Milwaukee facility. If Respondent had implemented its decision, there would be no assembly employees at the Milwaukee facility to receive the contractual wages and benefits. Rather, all assembly work would be performed at McHenry where Respondent would pay its employees less for the same work. Under these circumstances, my colleagues' conclusion that Respondent left the wage and benefit provisions "intact" at Milwaukee is illogical and without legal significance. . . .

In my view the determinative factor in deciding whether an employer's midterm relocation decision is proscribed under §8(d) is the employer's motive. Where, as here, the decision is controlled by a desire to avoid a contractual term with regard to a mandatory subject of bargaining, such as wages, then the decision [violates] §§8(d) and 8(a)(5), and the employer may not implement the decision during the term of the contract without the union's consent. But where the decision is motivated by reasons unrelated to contract avoidance, then the employer may unilaterally implement its decision after bargaining to impasse with the union.

## *NOTES AND QUESTIONS*

**1. Role of Motive in Interpreting Collective Bargaining Agreement?** Who offers the more persuasive interpretation of the collective bargaining agreement in *Milwaukee Spring*? The Board majority or dissenting Member Zimmerman? Does Member Zimmerman have a convincing basis for concluding that a relocation motivated solely or predominantly by a desire to avoid the terms of an agreement at least presumptively violates §§8(d) and 8(a)(5)? When a relocation is prompted solely by cost savings, consisting primarily of lower labor costs, would the forbidden motive be present?

**2. Statutory or Contractual Remedy?** Note that the disagreement in *Milwaukee Spring* was not about whether Milwaukee Spring's decision to transfer operations was a mandatory subject of bargaining over which it had to bargain to impasse. The dispute was over whether a commitment to continue operations at Milwaukee was "contained in" the agreement and therefore not subject to modification even after bargaining. Why then was this not a question of contract interpretation for an arbitrator with authority to interpret the agreement rather than a question for the Board under its unfair labor practice jurisdiction?

In alleged contract modification cases, the Board generally will not find an unfair labor practice and thus will leave a union to its contractual remedies before an arbitrator if (1) the employer's interpretation of its contractual rights has a "sound arguable basis in the contract" and (2) the employer was not motivated by union animus, acting in bad faith, or in any way seeking to undermine the union's status. See Bath Marine Draftsmen's Ass'n v. NLRB, 475 F.3d 14 (1st Cir. 2007); NLRB v. Solutia, Inc., 699 F.3d 50 (1st Cir. 2012); Int'l Union of Painter & Allied Trades, Dist. 15, Local 159 v. J&R Flooring, Inc., 656 F.3d 867 (9th Cir. 2011); Daycon Prods. Co, 360 N.L.R.B. No. 54 (2014). Furthermore, after *Milwaukee Spring II* the Board will not find a contract modification violation unless it identifies a "specific term contained in the contract" that has been modified.

**3. Effect of Zipper and Management-Rights Clauses on Midterm Bargaining Duties?** The *Milwaukee Spring* case was complicated by the presence of a zipper clause in the collective bargaining agreement at issue. The D.C. Circuit opinion enforcing the Board's order was authored by Judge Edwards, a former professor of labor law, who read the zipper clause not only to free the employer from bargaining over new topics, but also to prevent it from making any unauthorized change in the status quo even after bargaining. This reading required Judge Edwards to infer a rationale that was not express in the Board's decision. Judge Edwards reasoned:

> It could be argued that the Board treated the relocation decision as a subject that was not "contained in" the contract, and thus decided that, since the parties stipulated that they had bargained in good faith to impasse, the Company did not violate section 8(d) by then deciding to relocate. Given the zipper clause, we do not believe this characterization of the Board's analysis to be viable. If relocation is a mandatory subject and it was found either *not* to be contained in the management rights clause or *not* to be an implied management reserved right, the zipper clause would have prevented the Company from unilaterally deciding to relocate the assembly operation during the term of the contract, even after bargaining to impasse. Although a zipper clause may waive the obligation to bargain over all mandatory subjects during the term of an agreement, it surely does not waive the union's right to object to an employer's taking unilateral action with respect to such subjects. Thus, if an employer is not acting on a claim of right under the contract, or pursuant to a reserved management right inferable from the contract, it may not institute changes with respect to mandatory subjects without the consent of the union. Since the Union did not pursue this analysis, and did not rely on the zipper clause to oppose the relocation decision, it is clear that the UAW assumed that the Company acted pursuant to a right under the agreement.

765 F.2d at 182-183. Do you agree?

**4. What If No Bargaining?** Would the company have committed an unfair labor practice if it had implemented the transfer of operations without bargaining to impasse?

a. *Mandatory Bargaining Topic?* The parties stipulated in *Milwaukee Spring* that the decision to transfer operations was a mandatory subject of bargaining. In light of *First National Maintenance* and *Dubuque*, should the employer have conceded the "bargainability" of the decision?

b. *Basis in Contract for Authority to Transfer Operations?* Even assuming that the transfer of operations was a mandatory topic of bargaining, if the collective bargaining agreement contained a clause providing management with some discretion to assign work, could the company have claimed that the transfer did not require bargaining because it was privileged under the agreement to act unilaterally? The Board generally holds that where an employer asserts a contractual defense to a union's charge of a unilateral change without bargaining, the employer must demonstrate the union's "clear and unmistakable" waiver of the union's bargaining rights. See supra note 3, pages 510-511. The D.C. Circuit has ruled, however, that where the bargaining agreement covers the subject matter of the dispute, the Board should interpret the agreement without any presumption against waiver of statutory rights. See, e.g., Enloe Med. Ctr. v. NLRB, 433 F.3d 834 (D.C. Cir. 2005); NLRB v. U.S. Postal Serv., 8 F.3d 832 (D.C. Cir. 1993). Accord, Chicago Tribune Co. v. NLRB, 974 F.2d 933 (7th Cir. 1992). Another appellate court has held that the Board could apply in this context the "sound arguable basis" standard that it would apply in a contract modification case, as explained in note 2 above. See, e.g., *Bath Marine*, supra. But see SW Ambulance & Int'l Ass'n of Fire Fighters Local I-60, 360 N.L.R.B. No. 109 (2014), and Provena St. Joseph Medical Center, 350 N.L.R.B. 880 (2007) (applying "clear and unmistakable" waiver standard).

Consider, moreover, Judge Edwards's willingness in *Milwaukee Spring* to find a contractual basis for the transfer of operations in an implied management rights clause. His opinion acknowledges in a footnote that under this reasoning "if the Company had the contractual right to make the relocation decision, it had no duty to bargain before making that decision." 765 F.2d at 183 n.30. Given the prevalence of management rights clauses and the ease with which employers can claim at least implied authority under the "reserved management rights" theory, does Judge Edwards's approach authorize the Board effectively to eliminate any continuing midterm duty to bargain over mandatory subjects? Is this consistent with the Board's approach in *Jacobs* and its progeny? On the other hand, given the availability of arbitration under almost all collective agreements, is the effective elimination of any midterm bargaining obligation necessarily undesirable? See Harry T. Edwards, Deferral to Arbitration and Waiver of the Duty to Bargain: A Possible Way Out of Everlasting Confusion at the NLRB, 46 Ohio St. L.J. 23, 28 (1985). In fact, the Board normally avoids having to interpret the scope of management's authority under collective agreements through its policy of deferring contract interpretation questions to arbitration when a party so requests. See the materials on arbitration and NLRA claims in Chapter 8 at pages 722-738.

**5. Notice and Cooling-off Periods of §8(d).** An employer who bargains to an impasse over a mandatory subject not contained in the contract must ordinarily comply with the notice and waiting periods prescribed by §8(d) before instituting changes. See Huttig Sash & Door Co., 154 N.L.R.B. 811 (1965), enforced, 377 F.2d 964 (8th Cir. 1967) (involving reduction of premium wages allegedly in violation of the agreement, which also made wage disputes arbitrable).

# 7 Weapons of Economic Conflict: Strikes, Boycotts, and Picketing

## A. STRIKES AND EMPLOYER COUNTERMEASURES

### 1. Economic Pressures and the Duty to Bargain

**NLRB v. Insurance Agents' International Union**
*361 U.S. 477 (1960)*

[See supra pages 411-416.]

***Note: The Role of Economic Conflict in the Bargaining Process and the Causes of Strikes***

The Supreme Court's decision in *Insurance Agents'* emphasizes the central role of strikes and other forms of economic conflict in the collective bargaining process. An underlying premise of labor laws such as the National Labor Relations Act (NLRA) and the Railway Labor Act (RLA) is that collective bargaining "works" as a method of private determination of the terms and conditions of employment only if the parties are able, at some point in the bargaining process, to communicate the intensity of their preferences and test the other side's resolve and bargaining power by engaging in self-help. For labor, the principal economic weapon is the strike—a collective withdrawal of the services of represented employees. The strike also may be supported by ancillary pressures, such as picketing of the struck premises or possibly the operations of suppliers and customers. For management, the principal weapons include maintaining operations in the face of a strike and, occasionally, the lockout—a preemptive refusal to allow represented employees to work pending the resolution of the dispute.

The success of a strike or threat to strike is a function of the union's bargaining power, which in turn depends on a number of factors: (1) the profitability of the firm and its ability to raise prices without losing market position; (2) the ability of the union to impose production losses on the firm (which will vary with the firm's ability to stockpile inventory in anticipation of a strike and to maintain operations with the help of supervisors and managers or replacement workers); (3) the financial resources of the firm to withstand losses incurred during a strike; and (4) the financial resources of represented employees to withstand losses they incur during a strike.

The *Insurance Agents'* decision also illustrates the Supreme Court's position that the use of economic weapons is generally not inconsistent with good-faith bargaining, and should not be regulated through §§8(a)(5) and 8(b)(3) of the Act. Rather, the principal statutory vehicle for regulating bargaining weapons is the antidiscrimination principle embodied in §§8(a)(3) and 8(b)(2). In *Insurance Agents'*, an unprotected partial strike was held not to violate §8(b)(3). Moreover, the Board, with court approval, has made clear that a conventional peaceful strike does not suspend the employer's duty to bargain. See NLRB v. Rutter-Rex Mfg. Co., 245 F.2d 594 (5th Cir. 1957).

Was the *Insurance Agents* Court right to deny the Board the authority to assess whether use of certain economic weapons is consistent with good-faith bargaining? Note that the very use of bargaining weapons may involve changing terms and conditions of employment that ordinarily require good-faith bargaining with the union. See the *Katz* decision, supra page 449. We deal now with the question of what countermeasures employers can take when confronted with a strike.

## 2. Strikers and Replacements

### a. *The* Mackay Radio *Doctrine*

**NLRB v. Mackay Radio & Telegraph Co.**
*304 U.S. 333 (1938)*

[The Mackay Company, an international wireless communications company, employed in its San Francisco office about 60 supervisors, operators, and clerks, many of whom were members of Local No. 3 of the American Radio Telegraphists Association, a national union. After unsuccessful negotiations in New York between the national union and Mackay's parent company for an agreement covering marine and point-to-point operators, the national union called a "general strike" in which Local 3 participated. Mackay, in order to maintain operations, brought in employees from other offices to fill the strikers' places in San Francisco. The strike was unsuccessful. In response to the strikers' inquiries, Mackay stated that they could return in a body, except for 11 strikers who would have to file applications for reinstatement. Thereafter, only five of the replacements wished to remain in San Francisco, and six of the special group of 11 strikers were allowed to return to work, together with the others. The remaining five, who had been prominent in union activities, were denied reinstatement. The Board held that this denial constituted a violation of §§8(1) and 8(3) and ordered reinstatement, with back pay, of the five strikers. The court of appeals denied enforcement of the Board's order and was, in turn, reversed by the Supreme Court. The Court concluded that the strikers remained "employees" under §2(3) of the Act and that the evidence supported the Board's finding of discrimination in the denial of reinstatement to the five strikers.]

ROBERTS, J. . . .

. . . [It was not] an unfair labor practice to replace the striking employees with others in an effort to carry on the business. Although §13 provides, "Nothing in this Act shall be construed so as to interfere with or impede or diminish in any way the right to strike," it does not follow that an employer, guilty of no act denounced by the statute, has lost the right to protect and continue his business by supplying places left vacant by strikers. And he is not bound to discharge those hired to fill the places of strikers, upon the election of the latter to resume their employment, in order to create places for them. The assurance by respondent to those who accepted employment during the strike that if they so desired their places might be permanent was not an unfair labor practice nor was it such to reinstate only so many of the strikers as there were vacant places to be filled. But the claim put forward is that the unfair labor practice indulged by the respondent was discrimination in reinstating striking employees by keeping out certain of them for the sole reason that they had been active in the union. As we have said, the strikers retained, under the Act, the status of employees. Any such discrimination in putting them back to work is, therefore, prohibited by §8. . . .

As we have said, the respondent was not bound to displace men hired to take the strikers' places in order to provide positions for them. It might have refused reinstatement on the ground of skill or ability, but the Board found that it did not do so. It might have resorted to any one of a number of methods of determining which of its striking employees would have to wait because five men had taken permanent positions during the strike, but it is found that the preparation and use of the list, and the action taken by respondent, were with the purpose to discriminate against those most active in the union. There is evidence to support these findings.

### *Note: Reinstatement Rights of Replaced Economic Strikers*

*Mackay Radio* establishes that the NLRA does not prohibit the employer from attempting to maintain operations during an economic strike by hiring permanent replacements. Replaced strikers, however, remain employees, and later decisions of the Supreme Court make clear that they retain certain preferential rights to reinstatement. In NLRB v. Fleetwood Trailer Co., 389

U.S. 375 (1967), the employer, after a strike by about 50 percent of its workforce, maintained operations at a temporarily reduced rate with the help of replacements. When the strike ended, the employer stated that reinstatement of the strikers was not then possible because of a production cutback. Two months later, the employer increased production to the prestrike level. Although the strikers had made known their continuing desire for reinstatement, new employees were hired for jobs for which the strikers were qualified. The Court upheld the Board's finding of violations of §§8(a)(1) and 8(a)(3), reasoning as follows: A striker remains an "employee" under §2(3) of the Act until he has secured regular and substantially equivalent employment. The failure to reinstate had discouraged employees from engaging in protected activity. Accordingly, a violation of §§8(a)(1) and 8(a)(3) was established unless the employer discharged its burden of showing legitimate and substantial business justification, such as the absence of vacancies or the elimination of jobs due, for example, to a decline in demand for the firm's products. Absent such a showing, the employer, without regard to its intent or antiunion motivation, had violated the Act.

In Laidlaw Corp., 171 N.L.R.B. 1366 (1968), enforced, 414 F.2d 99 (7th Cir. 1969), the Board, relying on *Fleetwood Trailer,* ruled that "economic strikers who unconditionally apply for reinstatement at a time when their positions are filled by permanent replacements: (1) remain employees; and (2) are entitled to full reinstatement upon the departure of replacements unless the strikers have in the meantime acquired regular and substantially equivalent employment, or . . . the failure to offer full reinstatement was for legitimate and substantial business reasons."

## *NOTES AND QUESTIONS*

**1. Does *Mackay Radio* Reflect Congressional Intent?** Inasmuch as the *Mackay Radio* Court had before it a case of discriminatory refusal to reinstate certain strikers because of their union activities, the Court's declaration that an employer may maintain operations with the aid of permanent replacements was unnecessary to the decision. Did this declaration reflect congressional intent? In Collective Bargaining or "Collective Begging"?: Reflections on Antistrikebreaker Legislation, 93 Mich. L. Rev. 577 (1994), Professor Estreicher argues that it did. He notes that even though the issue was not squarely addressed in the NLRB ruling below, the General Counsel's brief before the Court conceded the point. See Reply Br. for the National Labor Relations Board at 15-17, *Mackay Radio* (No. 37-706). The permissibility of hiring permanent replacements for strikers was also reflected in the precedents of the first NLRB established under Public Resolution No. 44: "Where the strike was caused by the employer's violation of 7(a), [the] NLRB returned the workers to their jobs without prejudice.

Where there was no such breach, strikers had no legal claim to restoration." Irving Bernstein, The New Deal Collective Bargaining Policy 85 & n.7 (1950). Moreover, Professor Estreicher adds, the Board's concession in the *Mackay Radio* litigation was supported by the legislative history of the NLRA. For a similar account, see Julius G. Getman & Thomas C. Kohler, The Story of *NLRB v. MacKay Radio & Telegraph Co.*: The High Cost of Solidarity 13-54, in Labor Law Stories (Laura Cooper & Catherine L. Fisk eds., 2005).

In any event, if there were any doubt about the congressional understanding in 1935, Congress, in the Taft-Hartley amendments of 1947, entrenched the principle by excluding permanently replaced strikers from eligibility to vote in NLRB elections. In 1959, a limited re-enfranchisement occurred in §9(c)(3): Replaced strikers eligible for reinstatement could vote for up to one year from the commencement of a lawful economic strike. See Joan Flynn, The Economic Strike Bar: Looking Beyond the "Union Sentiments" of Permanent Replacements, 61 Temp. L. Rev. 691, 696-697 (1988) (discussing history of provision and relation to *Mackay*).

**2. "Discrimination" Against Protected Activity?** In those situations where permanent replacements remain on the job, new turnover does not occur, and the post-strike business does not expand to require additional staff, strikers who have been permanently replaced have lost their jobs, for all practical purposes. Is this result a form of "discrimination" in regard to a term of employment that discourages union-related activity or is the employer's justification for replacement in order to maintain operations a legitimate business purpose that over weighs any discouragement?

**3. Are Employers Required to Show that Operations Cannot Be Maintained with Temporary Help Before They Resort to Permanent Replacements?** Even if the hiring of permanent replacements is often justified by employers' legitimate interests in maintaining operations during strikes, should employers be required to show that they cannot maintain operations by other means? See, e.g., Paul C. Weiler, Governing the Workplace: The Future of Labor and Employment Law 267 (1990). Neither the Board nor the courts have required employers to make such a showing before hiring permanent replacements. See, e.g., Hot Shoppes, Inc., 146 N.L.R.B. 802, 805 (1964). Would such an approach require amending the NLRA? Are there other difficulties? Can the Board provide a reasonably prompt hearing early enough in the strike so that employers and employees alike will know whether permanent replacements are likely, and hence will be able to factor in that prospect in shaping their bargaining demands and counterproposals? Are unemployment statistics a good proxy for determining an employer's ability to maintain operations with temporaries, or do we need a better measure of the availability of workers who meet the struck firm's skill and motivational requirements? Which party should bear the burden of persuasion on the issue of availability? See Estreicher, Collective Bargaining or "Collective Begging"?, supra, at 603-605; William R. Corbett, A Proposal for Procedural Limitations on Hiring Permanent Replacements: "A Far, Far Better Thing" Than the Workplace Fairness Act, 72 N.C. L. Rev. 813 (1994).

**4. One-Sided Duty of Loyalty?** Is *Mackay Radio* reconcilable with the Supreme Court's decision in *Jefferson Standard*, supra page 177, holding that employees engaged in product-disparagement picketing in the course of a strike, at least without making clear the connection between the disparagement and the underlying labor dispute, were unprotected against discharge or discipline because they acted inconsistently with their "duty of loyalty" to the firm? Do employers owe a similar duty to their striking employees not to take actions inconsistent with the continuation of the relationship at strike's end? See James B. Atleson, Values and Assumptions in American Labor Law (1983), supra; see also the "bounded conflict" concept developed in Samuel Estreicher, Strikers and Replacements, 3 Lab. Law. 897 (1987).

**5. "Permanent" Replacements?** In what sense are replacements usually "permanent," given the fact that employees generally are hired "at will" and negotiation of individual employment contracts in the union setting may violate the rule of *J.I. Case*, supra page 398? Are replacements generally "permanent" in one sense only—that they have been given assurances by the employer that they will be able to keep their jobs at strike's end as against returning strikers? See O.E. Butterfield, Inc., 319 N.L.R.B. 1004, 1006 (1995) ("mutual understanding" to this effect required, and employer bears burden of proof regarding offer of "permanency"); cf. Jones Plastic & Engineering, 351 N.L.R.B. 61 (2007), enforced sub nom. United Steel, Paper & Forestry, Rubber, Mfg., Energy, Allied Indus. & Service Workers Int'l Union v. NLRB, 544 F.3d 841 (7th Cir. 2008), (an offer of "at will" employment to replacement employees is not inconsistent with a valid offer of "permanent" status, nor does it "detract[] from an otherwise valid showing of permanent replacement status). But even assurances of "permanence" are qualified by two risks: (a) that the strike will later be deemed an unfair labor practice strike, in which case the strikers will be able to retake their prestrike positions, see Note on Unfair Labor Practice Strikes, infra page 532; and (b) that a strike settlement agreement will be negotiated providing for the replacements' displacement, see Note on Strike Settlement Agreements, infra page 528. On whether the NLRA preempts state law suits by permanent replacements who have been "bumped" by returning strikers, see infra pages 870-874.

**6. Determining When "Permanency" Occurs.** On January 1, an employer hires permanent replacements. However, under applicable regulatory requirements all new hires must undergo two months of training before they can be certified for certain operational positions. On February 1, the strikers make an unconditional application for reinstatement. May the employer refuse to reinstate the former strikers to jobs then occupied by the putative permanent replacements, or does the employer's *Mackay* right to decline to bump permanent replacements ripen only at the end of their training period? See Eastern Air Lines, Inc. v. Air Line Pilots Ass'n, 920 F.2d 722 (11th Cir. 1990); Independent Fed'n of Flight Attendants v. TWA, 819 F.2d 839 (8th Cir. 1987); Air Line Pilots Ass'n v. United Air Lines, 802 F.2d 886 (7th Cir. 1986).

**7. Right of Reinstatement Only to Jobs Previously Held?** Does the duty to recall strikers encompass not only their previous or substantially equivalent positions, but also all available jobs for which the returning strikers are qualified? See Rose Printing Co., 304 N.L.R.B. 1076 (1991) (reinstatement obligation limited to previously held or substantially equivalent jobs; employer may, but is not required to, offer former strikers nonequivalent positions for which they are qualified, but striker's acceptance of such position does not extinguish statutory right to subsequent reinstatement to prestrike position or substantially equivalent one); see also Zimmerman Plumbing and Heating Co., 334 N.L.R.B. 586 (2001) (same). An important factor will be whether the employer maintained a prestrike practice of cross-training employees. See Arlington Hotel Co. v. NLRB, 785 F.2d 249 (8th Cir. 1986) (reinstatement to range of jobs for which strikers qualified required where employer had policy of such cross-training). At what point does a "reinstatement" satisfying *Laidlaw* occur? Are strikers fully reinstated when restored to nonequivalent jobs within the unit and told they will be returned to their former jobs when vacancies occur? See NLRB v. American Olean Tile Co., 826 F.2d 1496 (6th Cir. 1987). See generally Douglas E. Ray, Some Overlooked Aspects of the Strike Replacement Issue, 41 Kan. L. Rev. 363, 384-392 (1992).

**8. Duration of *Laidlaw* Rights?** May an employer, arguing administrative burdens, inform unreinstated strikers who have applied for reinstatement that it will maintain a preferential hiring list and attempt to contact former strikers when openings develop, but only for one year? If the costs to employers are nontrivial, must the General Counsel prove discriminatory motive to establish a violation of §8(a)(3)? A violation of §8(a)(1)? Does the obligation to reinstate strikers continue even after the strikers have lost voting rights under §9(c)(3), discussed infra page 560? See Brooks Research & Mfg., 202 N.L.R.B. 634 (1973) (rejecting argument that time limits should be placed on *Laidlaw* rights, such as one-year limit governing replaced strikers' voting rights, but stating that employer might at reasonable intervals require employees on preferential list to indicate whether they still desire reinstatement); see also Thoreson-McCosh, Inc., 329 N.L.R.B. 630 (1999) (duration of *Laidlaw* rights and voting rights remain separate questions).

**9. Full Disclosure?** May an employer lawfully tell employees during an organizing campaign that they are subject to permanent replacement if they go out on an economic strike without at the same time explaining strikers' *Laidlaw* rights to reinstatement? See Eagle Comtronics, Inc., 263 N.L.R.B. 515 (1982) (employer statements that are consistent with the law cannot be characterized as coercive; hence no violation unless employer threatens that in event of strike employees will be deprived of rights in manner inconsistent with *Laidlaw*); see also G.W. Galloway Co., 281 N.L.R.B. 262 (1985) (violation where employer told strikers it "would have to terminate and replace" employees who failed to "go back to work"), enforcement denied on other grounds, 856 F.2d 275 (D.C. Cir. 1988). Should the failure to include an account of *Laidlaw* rights void elections under the *General Shoe* doctrine, supra page 262? See *Eagle Comtronics*, supra.

***Note: Strike Settlement Agreements***

**Waiver of *Laidlaw* Rights?** Can an employer insist, as a condition of agreeing to a strike settlement, that the union waive *Laidlaw* rights for striking employees? Is this a permissive subject? Are there limits on "voluntary" union waivers? In United Aircraft Corp., 192 N.L.R.B. 382, 388 (1971), enforced in part sub nom. International Ass'n of Machinists v. United Aircraft Corp., 534 F.2d 422 (2d Cir. 1975), the Board sustained an agreement that extinguished all reinstatement rights four-and-a-half months after the strike was settled:

> So long, therefore, as the period fixed by the agreement for the reinstatement of economic strikers is not unreasonably short, is not intended to be discriminatory, or misused by either party with the object of accomplishing a discriminatory objective, was not insisted upon by the employer in order to undermine the status of the bargaining representative, and was the result of good-faith bargaining, the Board ought to accept . . . the policies of the Act which . . . includes as a principal objective the encouragement of the practice and procedure of collective bargaining as a means of settling labor disputes.

Does this go too far in allowing unions to pursue their institutional concern for survival over the individual rights of represented employees? See Matthew W. Finkin, The Truncation of *Laidlaw* Rights by Collective Agreement, 3 Indus. Rel. L.J. 591 (1979). The standard for breach of fair representation suits against unions for their negotiation of strike settlement agreements is developed in Air Line Pilots Ass'n v. O'Neill, 499 U.S. 65 (1991), infra page 944.

**Displacement of Replacement Workers.** Typically, a union will be loath to settle a strike without some provision made for restoring strikers to their jobs, even if this means ousting "permanent" replacements from their positions. Although replacements are statutory employees protected from union-based discrimination under §§8(b)(1)(A) and 8(b)(2) and are members of the bargaining unit to whom the union owes a duty of fair representation, there is little litigation challenging a union's disregard of the welfare of replacement workers. The conventional response is that "a union may lawfully seek to parcel out a limited number of jobs between strikers and permanent replacements on a nondiscriminatory basis, such as seniority and/or job classifications." United Steelworkers of Am., Local 8560, Case No. 8-CB-3963 (Advice Mem., Assoc. General Counsel Harold J. Datz), 103 L.R.R.M. 1238 (Dec. 31, 1979).

What rights do the replacement workers have other than duty of fair representation claims against the union? In Belknap, Inc. v. Hale, 463 U.S. 491 (1983), infra page 870, the Court held that damages actions for breach of contract and misrepresentation filed by ousted "permanent" replacements against their employer are not preempted by the NLRA, although the Court left open the question whether an award of specific performance (i.e., reinstatement) would be preempted. For an example of a post-*Belknap* suit by ousted replacements, see Ballwin v. Pirelli Armstrong Tire Corp., 3 S.W.3d 1, 160 L.R.R.M. 2541 (Tenn. Ct. App. 1999). *Belknap* also stated that an employer may make a promise of continued employment subject to any settlement agreement with the union without sacrificing its *Mackay* right to insist on retention of the permanent replacements at strike's end.

### *Note: Proposals to Repeal or Modify* Mackay Radio

The *Mackay Radio* rule has been the subject of considerable critical commentary. In addition to the articles cited in this section, see citations in Michael H. LeRoy, Institutional Signals and Implicit Bargains in the ULP Strike Doctrine: Empirical Evidence of Law as Equilibrium, 51 Hastings L.J. 171, 172-173 n.7 (1999). For a reference to international challenges to the *Mackay Radio* doctrine at the International Labor Organization, see Chapter 15 infra. Do you agree that the law governing the rights of strikers and replacement workers should be changed? If change is desirable, what form should it take? Evaluate the following options as alternatives to maintaining the status quo:

a. Several Canadian provinces and Canada's federal labor code bar the use of permanent replacements. See Brian Langille & Benjamin Oliphant, The Legal Structure of Freedom of Association 15 (May 28, 2013), available at http://www.upf.edu/gredtiss/_pdf/2013-LLRNConf_LangillexOliphant.pdf;

Jiong Tu, The Impact of Replacement Worker Legislation on Work Stoppages and Wage Settlements, in 20 Advances in Industrial and Labor Relations 108-09 (David Lewin & Paul J. Gollan, eds., 2012); see, e.g., Canada Labour Code RSC 1985, c.12, §94(2.1) (as amended 1999) (federal code); Man., The Labour Relations Act §11 (as amended 2014); see also G. Adams, Canadian Labour Law (2d ed., updated May 2002), at ¶11.690. British Columbia and Quebec both go further, however, and also ban both the use of temporary replacements and the transfer of employees from other locations to the struck facility, and either ban or restrict the employer's ability to have the struck work performed by others (such as managers, nonunit employees, or even unit employees) employed at the struck facility. See B.C., Labour Relations Code, §§6(3)(e), 68 (enacted 1993); Que., Labour Code, §§109.1-109.4 (enacted 1978); Adams, supra, at ¶¶10.520, 10.522; Tu, supra, at 109. From 1993 to 1995, Ontario had a law similar to Quebec's. Tu, supra, at 109. However, with the return of the conservative party to power, Ontario reverted to its pre-1993 position by limiting the job protections of employees engaged in a lawful strike to those who have made an unconditional application to return to work within six months of the commencement of the strike. See Ontario's Labour Relations and Employment Statute Law Amendments Act, 1995, §80; see also Brian A. Langille, Global Competition and Canadian Labor Law Reform: Rhetoric and Reality, in Global Competition and the American Employment Landscape: As We Enter the 21st Century, Proc., 52d Ann. N.Y.U. Conf. on Lab 621, 633-636. (Samuel Estreicher ed., 2000).

b. In June 1992, the Senate failed by three votes to pass the Workplace Fairness Act, S. 55, which would have flatly prohibited resort to permanent replacements while continuing to permit the hiring of temporary workers during strikes. The AFL-CIO renewed its effort to secure passage of such legislation the following congressional term, see the Cesar Chavez Workplace Fairness Act of 1994, but could not overcome a threatened Senate filibuster.

c. In a last-minute unsuccessful attempt to overcome the June 1992 Senate filibuster of S. 55, Senators Packwood (R-Or.) and Metzenbaum (D-Ohio), with AFL-CIO backing, offered a compromise that would have made a proffer of binding interest arbitration a mandatory condition to resorting to economic conflict. Under this proposal, an employer that refused to submit the dispute to arbitration or to accept an award that was rendered could not hire permanent replacements; if the union chose to strike without proffering interest arbitration or accepting an award, the employer would be free to use such replacements. See 138 Cong. Rec. S8056-8089 (June 11, 1992) (amendments to S. 55, nos. 2047-2094, submitted by Sen. Packwood).

d. A number of writers have urged a requirement of a showing of "business necessity" before an employer may resort to the hiring of permanent replacements. See, e.g., William B. Gould IV, Agenda for Reform: The

Future of Employment Relationships and the Law 193 (1993); this option is discussed supra note 3, page 525.

e. Some writers have urged a six-month moratorium on the hiring of permanent replacements following the commencement of a lawful economic strike. See, e.g., Estreicher, Collective Bargaining or "Collective Begging"?, supra, at 606-607 (emphasis omitted):

> Even when the employer is able to obtain a declaratory ruling that temporary workers are not available in sufficient number and quality to meet its requirements — or if the administrative difficulties of providing such a ruling argue against requiring a showing of business necessity — there remains a need for a substantial moratorium period during which the process of collective bargaining has a chance to work free of labor-market pressures. I favor the approach that was Ontario law [prior to 1993] — requiring reinstatement of strikers who announce their intention to return to work at any point within the first six months of a strike.
>
> A clearly defined period of immunity from permanent replacement is desirable. It encourages the parties to continue talking even though a strike has occurred, yet preserves the corrective influence of the prospect of permanent replacements. Moreover, it helps avoid mistakes; workers are not rashly betting their jobs. By striking, workers indicate the intensity of their preferences, and test the employer's resolve and ability to operate without them. After six months, any useful information of this type has already been imparted; workers who persist in their demands do so at the peril of losing their jobs if they misjudge their bargaining position.
>
> Advocates of a flat-out repeal of *Mackay Radio* criticize a six-month moratorium rule for allowing employers bent on ousting the union to prolong disputes beyond the sixth month. Six months is, however, a long time in the life of any company to endure the disruption of a strike — particularly during a period when firms maintain "just-in-time" inventory levels. And under my proposal . . . , the Labor Board would be authorized to avoid representational issues in the course of an active strike. Under these restraints, economic factors rather than purely strategic maneuvers are likely to be dominant. If the strike nevertheless persists, we have a fundamental dispute over terms to be resolved in the marketplace. A rule barring the hiring of permanent replacements in such circumstances may strengthen the union's position in a particular dispute; it does not, however, improve the economic position of the union-represented firm or the relationship between the parties.

f. Finally, it has been suggested that the *Mackay* doctrine should be made part of the negotiations process by making the ability to hire striker replacements a mandatory subject of bargaining. See Leonard Bierman & Rafael Gely, Striker Replacements: A Law, Economics, and Negotiations Approach, 68 S. Cal. L. Rev. 363 (1995). For criticism of this approach and the authors' response, see William R. Corbett, Taking the Employer's Gun and Bargaining About Returning It: A Reply to "A Law, Economics, and Negotiations Approach" to Striker Replacement Law, 56 Ohio St. L.J. 1511 (1995);

Bierman & Gely, "Let's Call It a Draw": Striker Replacements and the *Mackay* Doctrine, 58 Ohio St. L.J. 1003 (1997).

### *Note: Unfair Labor Practice Strikes*

The *Mackay* rule discussed above applies only in economic strikes; the respective rights of the employer, the strikers, and the replacements are quite different in the case of an unfair labor practice or "ULP" strike—a strike called or prolonged because of one or more employer unfair labor practices. Where a strike is caused both by a bargaining impasse and an unfair labor practice, it is deemed an unfair labor practice strike as long as the strike was motivated in part by the ULP. See Teamsters Local Union No. 515 v. NLRB (Reichold Chemicals, Inc.), 906 F.2d 719, 723 (D.C. Cir. 1990) ("*Reichold II*") (ULP need not be sole or even the major cause of the strike; it need only be a contributing factor); RGC (USA) Mineral Sands, Inc., 332 N.L.R.B. 1633 (2001) (same), enforced, 281 F.3d 442 (4th Cir. 2002). Similarly, if an employer commits unfair labor practices during an economic strike, a finding of a causal connection between the employer's conduct and a continuation of the strike converts the stoppage into an unfair labor practice strike, even if the unlawful conduct was not the sole or even predominate factor in prolonging the strike. See Soule Glass & Glazing Co. v. NLRB, 652 F.2d 1055, 1079-1080 (1st Cir. 1981); F.L. Thorpe & Co. v. NLRB, 71 F.3d 282, 286-287 (8th Cir. 1995). Strikers who are replaced following conversion of the strike are treated as unfair labor practice strikers. See Hormigonera Del Toa, Inc., 311 N.L.R.B. 956, 957 (1993); Sunol Valley Golf Club, 310 N.L.R.B. 357, 371 (1993), enforced sub nom. Ivaldi v. NLRB, 48 F.3d 444 (9th Cir. 1995). For further discussion of the conversion doctrine, see Frank H. Stewart, Conversion of Strikes: Economic to Unfair Labor Practice: I & II, 45 Va. L. Rev. 1322 (1959); 49 Va. L. Rev. 1297 (1963).

Determining the "cause" of a strike is crucial for the following reasons. First, an employer is required to displace or "bump" even ostensibly "permanent" replacements to make room for unfair labor practice strikers who have made an unconditional application for reinstatement. See Mastro Plastics Corp. v. NLRB, 350 U.S. 270, 278 (1956); see also, e.g., Pirelli Cable Corp. v. NLRB, 141 F.3d 503, 515 (4th Cir. 1998). If the employer fails to do so (perhaps in the mistaken belief that the strike is an economic rather than a ULP strike), the strikers are entitled to back pay from the date of the unconditional application to return. See General Industrial Employees Union, Local 42 v. NLRB, 951 F.2d 1308, 1311 (D.C. Cir. 1991). In contrast, permanently replaced economic strikers are not entitled to bump their replacements and will receive no back pay absent a violation of their *Laidlaw* rights.

Second, unfair labor practice strikers can vote irrespective of the length of the strike, whereas under §9(c)(3) permanently replaced economic strikers lose their right to vote if a strike has gone on for more than 12 months.

See Thoreson-McCosh, Inc., 329 N.L.R.B. 630 (1999) (reaffirming rule of Wahl Clipper Corp., 195 N.L.R.B. 634 (1972)). Moreover, only permanent—as opposed to temporary—replacements have voting rights. See Tampa Sand & Material Co., 137 N.L.R.B. 1549 (1962). Hence, replacements for ULP strikers cannot vote, whereas replacements for economic strikers may vote if they have been offered "permanent" status.

Third, a strike called to protest an unfair labor practice, unlike an economic strike, does not necessarily violate a conventional no-strike clause in a collective bargaining agreement. In *Mastro Plastics,* the Court held that a standard no-strike clause did not waive the employees' right to strike over the employer's attempt "by coercion, [to] oust[] the employees' lawful bargaining representative and, by threats of discharge, [to] cause[] the employees to sign membership cards in a new union." 350 U.S. at 285. *Mastro* has been extended to less serious ULPs. See, e.g., Arlan's Dep't Store, 133 N.L.R.B. 802 (1961). Some decisions explain that the standard clause embodies a waiver of the right to strike over violations that "depend[] upon competing interpretations of a contract, either one of which would be valid." Dow Chemical Co. v. NLRB, 636 F.2d 1352, 1360 (3d Cir. 1980).

Fourth, a ULP strike does not constitute a strike whose object is the "termination or modification" of an agreement triggering the notice and cooling-off obligations of §8(d). See *Mastro Plastics,* supra. See generally Michael C. Harper, Union Waiver of Employee Rights Under the NLRA: Part I, 4 Indus. Rel. L.J. 335 (1982).

Finally, some older judicial precedent held that the Board has greater authority to reinstate ULP strikers who have engaged in picket-line misconduct than economic strikers who have engaged in similar misconduct. See NLRB v. Thayer Co., 213 F.2d 748 (1st Cir. 1954) (in case of ULP strikers, Board should balance seriousness of employee misconduct against employer misconduct that led to strike). Since the mid-1980s, however, the Board has generally declined to draw such a distinction. See Clear Pine Mouldings, Inc., 268 N.L.R.B. 1044 (1984), enforced, 765 F.2d 148 (9th Cir. 1985); Albin Renauer, Note, Reinstatement of Unfair Labor Practice Strikers Who Engage in Strike-Related Misconduct: Repudiation of the *Thayer* Doctrine by *Clear Pine Mouldings,* 8 Indus. Rel. L.J. 226 (1986); but see M.P.C. Plating, Inc. v. NLRB, 953 F.2d 1018, 1022 (6th Cir. 1992).

## *NOTES AND QUESTIONS*

**1. Determining the Cause of a Strike.** The Board and the courts have frequently clashed over Board determinations that a strike was an unfair labor practice strike rather than an economic strike. See, e.g., California Acrylic Indus. d/b/a Cal Spas v. NLRB, 150 F.3d 1095 (9th Cir. 1998); *Pirelli*

*Cable,* 141 F.3d 503. What factors should the Board and courts look to in determining the cause of a strike? See California Acrylic, 150 F.3d 1095 (1998) (looking to timing of strike, content of union leaflets and picket signs, employee statements at rally on day of strike vote, and employee statements on unemployment insurance claim forms); see also F.L. Thorpe, 71 F.3d at 287 (regarding possible "conversion" of strike, noting that certain ULPs such as unlawful withdrawal of recognition are presumed to prolong a strike).

Some decisions have expressed similar skepticism regarding Board determinations that a strike that began as an economic strike was later converted to a ULP strike, and have often reversed those determinations. See, e.g., *F.L. Thorpe,* supra; NLRB v. Harding Glass Co., 80 F.3d 7 (1st Cir. 1996); *Soule Glass,* 652 F.2d 1055.

**2. "Second-Best" Rule?** Is the special treatment of unfair labor practice strikers defensible? Is it a "second-best" response to the slowness of NLRB procedures or the *Mackay* doctrine? Is it a deterrent to bad-faith bargaining by employers? See Ray, Some Overlooked Aspects of the Strike Replacement Issue, at 365-366, 375; see also Corbett, A Proposal for Procedural Limitations on Hiring Permanent Replacements, at 849 & n.183. Does the degree of uncertainty attending the Board's rules and their application in the bargaining context create a real risk that employees will go on strike on a gamble that their economic strike will be treated as an unfair labor practice strike? Are there ways to improve Board procedures to provide an early determination of the strike's "cause"? See Corbett, supra; Note, The Unfair Labor Practice Strike: A Critique and a Proposal for Change, 46 N.Y.U. L. Rev. 988 (1971).

**3. "Bargainability" of Proposals to Waive Right to Engage in Unfair Labor Practice Strikes?** Does an employer violate §8(a)(5) by bargaining to impasse over a clause seeking a waiver of the right to engage in an unfair labor practice strike during the contract's term? See *Reichold II,* 906 F.2d 719. Is this an area like basic §8(a)(3) protections against discriminatory discipline in which union-negotiated waivers should not be permitted at all or substantially limited? Does the answer depend in part on the scope of the waiver sought by the employer? See Harper, Union Waiver of Employee Rights, supra.

### *Note: Honoring Picket Lines*

The success of a strike often depends on the striking union's ability to encourage other employees—both of the struck employer and other firms—to refuse to cross its picket line. It is fairly well established that even a single employee's decision to refuse to cross a picket line is "concerted" activity for "mutual aid and protection" within §7. As Judge Learned

Hand observed in NLRB v. Peter Cailler Kohler Swiss Chocolates Co., 130 F.2d 503, 505-506 (2d Cir. 1942):

> When all the other workmen in a shop make common cause with a fellow workman over his separate grievance, and go out on strike in his support, they engage in a "concerted activity" for "mutual aid or protection," although the aggrieved workman is the only one of them who has any immediate stake in the outcome. The rest know that by their action each one of them assures himself, in case his turn ever comes, of the support of the one whom they are all then helping, and the solidarity so established is "mutual aid" in the most literal sense, as nobody doubts. So too of those engaged in a "sympathetic strike," or secondary boycott; the immediate quarrel does not itself concern them, but by extending the number of those who will make the enemy of one the enemy of all, the power of each is vastly increased.

See generally Richard M. Fischl, Self, Other and Section 7: Mutualism and Protected Protest Activities Under the National Labor Relations Act, 89 Colum. L. Rev. 789 (1989). There are a number of reasons why the refusal to cross a picket line nonetheless may be *unprotected* concerted activity. First, the picket itself may be illegal — for example, a secondary boycott violative of §8(b)(4) — in which case the employee refusing to cross the line makes common cause with unlawful activity. Contractual provisions purporting to protect employees honoring secondary pickets may also be unlawful. See infra note 9, page 631.

Second, the employee through his or her bargaining representative may have waived any §7 right to honor another union's picket line by agreement. The Board once oscillated from one administration to the next over whether the conventional no-strike clause should be read to contain a waiver of the right to engage in a sympathy strike. See Indianapolis Power & Light Co. (II) v. NLRB, 898 F.2d 524, 526-527 (7th Cir. 1990) (discussing series of Board cases). The Board's current rule is that such a clause is presumed to cover sympathy strikes unless the contract as a whole or extrinsic evidence demonstrates otherwise. See Indianapolis Power & Light Co. (II), 291 N.L.R.B. 145 (1988) (enforced by decision cited above). However, in *Indianapolis Power II* the Board also found the presumption overcome by evidence that the parties had "agree[d] to disagree" regarding the clause's scope. Because there was no mutual intent to include sympathy strikes within the clause, there was no "clear and unmistakable" waiver of the employees' statutory rights. See 291 N.L.R.B. at 1041; see also 898 F.2d at 528 (where extrinsic evidence exists, burden is on employer to prove that sympathy strikes are covered by clause, in essence negating presumption); Children's Hospital of Oakland v. California Nurses Ass'n, 283 F.3d 1188, 1194-1195 (9th Cir. 2002) (deeming the Board's presumption of little if any practical significance). For the view that employee rights to engage in a protected sympathy strike should never be waivable, see Harper, Union Waiver of Employee Rights, supra, at 372-380.

Even if the activity is protected, *Mackay Radio* makes clear that employers may take some measures to ensure continued production or deliveries. The Board has consistently taken the view that employers generally lack justification to permanently replace or discharge employees who refuse to cross a picket line. See, e.g., Western Stress, Inc., 290 N.L.R.B. 678 (1988). However, the courts have given greater weight to the employer's interest in avoiding the delay and loss of business attending its employees honoring of a "stranger" picket line, and are more likely to sustain permanent replacement and in some circumstances discharge. See, e.g., NLRB v. Browning-Ferris Indus., Chem. Servs., Inc., 700 F.2d 385 (7th Cir. 1983) (Posner, J.); Business Servs. by Manpower, Inc. v. NLRB, 784 F.2d 442 (2d Cir. 1986) (Friendly, J.) (rejecting per se rule barring discharge of an employee for refusing to cross a stranger picket line in a case where (1) §7 rights were deemed "thin" because the picket line was informational only, and (2) replacements were impractical because the employer was in the business of providing temporary help).

### *b. The Role of Impact Analysis*

**NLRB v. Erie Resistor Corp.**
*373 U.S. 221 (1963)*

WHITE, J.

The question before us is whether an employer commits an unfair labor practice under §8(a) of the [NLRA] . . . when he extends a 20-year seniority credit to strike replacements and strikers who leave the strike and return to work. . . .

Erie Resistor Corporation and Local 613 of the [IUE] were bound by a collective bargaining agreement which was due to expire on March 31, 1959. In January 1959, both parties met to negotiate new terms but, after extensive bargaining, they were unable to reach agreement. Upon expiration of the contract, the union, in support of its contract demands, called a strike which was joined by all of the 478 employees in the unit.

The company, under intense competition and subject to insistent demands from its customers to maintain deliveries, decided to continue production operations. Transferring clerks, engineers and other nonunit employees to production jobs, the company managed to keep production at about 15% to 30% of normal during the month of April. On May 3, however, the company notified the union members that it intended to begin hiring replacements and that strikers would retain their jobs until replaced. The plant was located in an area classified by the United States Department of Labor as one of severe unemployment and the company had in fact received applications for employment as early as a week or two after the strike began.

Replacements were told that they would not be laid off or discharged at the end of the strike. To implement that assurance, particularly in view of the 450 employees already laid off on March 31, the company notified the union that it intended to accord the replacements some form of super-seniority. At regular bargaining sessions between the company and the union, the union made it clear that, in its view, no matter what form the super-seniority plan might take, it would necessarily work an illegal discrimination against the strikers. As negotiations advanced on other issues, it became evident that super-seniority was fast becoming the focal point of disagreement. On May 28, the company informed the union that it had decided to award 20 years'[3] additional seniority both to replacements and to strikers who returned to work, which would be available only for credit against future layoffs and which could not be used for other employee benefits based on years of service. The strikers, at a union meeting the next day, unanimously resolved to continue striking now in protest against the proposed plan as well.

The company made its first official announcement of the super-seniority plan on June 10, and by June 14, 34 new employees, 47 employees recalled from layoff status and 23 returning strikers had accepted production jobs. The union, now under great pressure, offered to give up some of its contract demands if the company would abandon super-seniority or go to arbitration on the question, but the company refused. In the following week, 64 strikers returned to work and 21 replacements took jobs, bringing the total to 102 replacements and recalled workers and 87 returned strikers. When the number of returning strikers went up to 125 during the following week, the union capitulated. A new labor agreement on the remaining economic issues was executed on July 17, and an accompanying settlement agreement was signed providing that the company's replacement and job assurance policy should be resolved by the [NLRB] and the federal courts but was to remain in effect pending final disposition.

Following the strike's termination, the company reinstated those strikers whose jobs had not been filled (all but 129 were returned to their jobs). At about the same time, the union received some 173 resignations from membership. By September of 1959, the production unit work force had reached a high of 442 employees, but by May of 1960, the work force had gradually slipped back to 240. Many employees laid off during this cutback

---

3. The figure of 20 years was developed from a projection, on the basis of expected orders, of what the company's work force would be following the strike. As of March 31, the beginning of the strike, a male employee needed seven years' seniority to avoid layoff and a female, nine years.

period were reinstated strikers whose seniority was insufficient to retain their jobs as a consequence of the company's super-seniority policy.

The union filed a charge . . . alleging that awarding super-seniority during the course of the strike constituted an unfair labor practice and that the subsequent layoff of the recalled strikers pursuant to such a plan was unlawful. The Trial Examiner found that the policy was promulgated for legitimate economic reasons,[4] not for illegal or discriminatory purposes, and recommended that the union's complaint be dismissed. The Board could not agree with the Trial Examiner's conclusion that specific evidence of subjective intent to discriminate against the union was necessary to finding that super-seniority granted during a strike is an unfair labor practice. Its consistent view, the Board said, had always been that super-seniority, in circumstances such as these, was an unfair labor practice. . . .

The Court of Appeals rejected as unsupportable the rationale of the Board that a preferential seniority policy is illegal however motivated.

> We are of the opinion that inherent in the right of an employer to replace strikers during a strike is the concomitant right to adopt a preferential seniority policy which will assure the replacements some form of tenure, provided the policy is adopted *solely* to protect and continue the business of the employer. . . . It consequently denied the Board's petition for enforcement and remanded the case for further findings. . . .

We think the Court of Appeals erred in holding that, in the absence of a finding of specific illegal intent, a legitimate business purpose is always a defense to an unfair labor practice charge. Cases in this Court dealing with unfair labor practices have recognized the relevance and importance of showing the employer's intent or motive to discriminate or to interfere with union rights. But specific evidence of such subjective intent is "not an indispensable element of proof of violation." Radio Officers v. Labor Board, 347 U.S. 17, 44. "Some conduct may by its very nature contain the implications of the required intent; the natural foreseeable consequences of certain action may warrant the inference." . . . Teamsters Local v. Labor Board, 365 U.S. 667, 675.

Though the intent necessary for an unfair labor practice may be shown in different ways, proving it in one manner may have far different weight and far different consequences than proving it in another. When specific

---

4. The Examiner had relied upon the company's employment records for his conclusion that the replacement program was ineffective until the announcement of the super-seniority awards. The General Counsel, to show that such a plan was not necessary for that purpose, pointed to the facts that the company had 300 unprocessed job applications when the strike ended, that the company declared to the union it could have replaced all the strikers and that the company did not communicate its otherwise well-publicized policy to replacements before they were hired but only after they accepted jobs.

evidence of a subjective intent to discriminate or to encourage or discourage union membership is shown, and found, many otherwise innocent or ambiguous actions may, without more, be converted into unfair labor practices [citing cases involving the discharge of employees, the subcontracting of union work, and the movement of a plant to another town]. Such proof itself is normally sufficient to destroy the employer's claim of a legitimate business purpose, if one is made, and provides strong support to a finding that there is interference with union rights or that union membership will be discouraged. Conduct which on its face appears to serve legitimate business ends in these cases is wholly impeached by the showing of an intent to encroach upon protected rights. The employer's claim of legitimacy is totally dispelled.

The outcome may well be the same when intent is founded upon the inherently discriminatory or destructive nature of the conduct itself. The employer in such cases must be held to intend the very consequences which foreseeably and inescapably flow from his actions and if he fails to explain away, to justify or to characterize his actions as something different than they appear on their face, an unfair labor practice charge is made out. *Radio Officers v. Labor Board,* supra. But, as often happens, the employer may counter by claiming that his actions were taken in the pursuit of legitimate business ends and that his dominant purpose was not to discriminate or to invade union rights but to accomplish business objectives acceptable under the Act. Nevertheless, his conduct *does* speak for itself—it *is* discriminatory and it *does* discourage union membership and whatever the claimed overriding justification may be, it carries with it unavoidable consequences which the employer not only foresaw but which he must have intended. As is not uncommon in human experience, such situations present a complex of motives and preferring one motive to another is in reality the far more delicate task, reflected in part in decisions of this Court, of weighing the interests of employees in concerted activity against the interest of the employer in operating his business in a particular manner and of balancing in the light of the Act and its policy the intended consequences upon employee rights against the business ends to be served by the employer's conduct. This essentially is the teaching of the Court's prior cases dealing with this problem and, in our view, the Board did not depart from it.

The Board made a detailed assessment of super-seniority and, to its experienced eye, such a plan had the following characteristics:

(1) Super-seniority affects the tenure of all strikers whereas permanent replacement, proper under *Mackay,* affects only those who are, in actuality, replaced. It is one thing to say that a striker is subject to loss of his job at the strike's end but quite another to hold that in addition to the threat of replacement, all strikers will at best return to their jobs with seniority inferior to that of the replacements and of those who left the strike.

(2) A super-seniority award necessarily operates to the detriment of those who participated in the strike as compared to nonstrikers.

(3) Super-seniority made available to striking bargaining unit employees as well as to new employees is in effect offering individual benefits to the strikers to induce them to abandon the strike.

(4) Extending the benefits of super-seniority to striking bargaining unit employees as well as to new replacements deals a crippling blow to the strike effort. At one stroke, those with low seniority have the opportunity to obtain the job security which ordinarily only long years of service can bring, while conversely, the accumulated seniority of older employees is seriously diluted. This combination of threat and promise could be expected to undermine the strikers' mutual interest and place the entire strike effort in jeopardy. The history of this strike and its virtual collapse following the announcement of the plan emphasize the grave repercussions of super-seniority.

(5) Super-seniority renders future bargaining difficult, if not impossible, for the collective bargaining representative. Unlike the replacement granted in *Mackay* which ceases to be an issue once the strike is over, the plan here creates a cleavage in the plant continuing long after the strike is ended. Employees are henceforth divided into two camps: those who stayed with the union and those who returned before the end of the strike and thereby gained extra seniority. This breach is reemphasized with each subsequent layoff and stands as an ever-present reminder of the dangers connected with striking and with union activities in general.

In the light of this analysis, super-seniority by its very terms operates to discriminate between strikers and nonstrikers, both during and after a strike, and its destructive impact upon the strike and union activity cannot be doubted. The origin of the plan, as respondent insists, may have been to keep production going and it may have been necessary to offer super-seniority to attract replacements and induce union members to leave the strike. But if this is true, accomplishment of respondent's business purpose inexorably was contingent upon attracting sufficient replacements and strikers by offering preferential inducements to those who worked as opposed to those who struck. We think the Board was entitled to treat this case as involving conduct which carried its own indicia of intent and which is barred by the Act unless saved from illegality by an overriding business purpose justifying the invasion of union rights. The Board concluded that the business purpose asserted was insufficient to insulate the super-seniority plan from the reach of §8(a)(1) and §8(a)(3), and we turn now to a review of that conclusion.

The Court of Appeals and respondent rely upon *Mackay* as precluding the result reached by the Board but we are not persuaded. . . . *Mackay* did not deal with super-seniority, with its effects upon all strikers, whether replaced or not, or with its powerful impact upon a strike itself. Because the employer's interest must be deemed to outweigh the damage to concerted activities caused by permanently replacing strikers does not mean it also outweighs the far greater encroachment resulting from super-seniority in addition to permanent replacement.

We have no intention of questioning the continuing vitality of the *Mackay* rule, but we are not prepared to extend it to the situation we have here. To do so would require us to set aside the Board's considered judgment that the Act and its underlying policy require, in the present context, giving more weight to the harm wrought by super-seniority than to the interest of the employer in operating its plant during the strike by utilizing this particular means of attracting replacements. We find nothing in the Act or its legislative history to indicate that super-seniority is necessarily an acceptable method of resisting the economic impact of a strike, nor do we find anything inconsistent with the result which the Board reached. . . .

. . . [B]ecause the Board's judgment was that the claimed business purpose would not outweigh the necessary harm to employee rights — a judgment which we sustain — it could properly put aside evidence of respondent's motive and decline to find whether the conduct was or was not prompted by the claimed business purpose. . . .

[The opinion of Justice Harlan, concurring, is omitted.]

## *NOTES AND QUESTIONS*

**1. Reconciling *Mackay Radio*?** Is the Board's distinguishing of *Mackay Radio,* recounted by the Court in *Erie Resistor,* convincing? Is the impact of superseniority on strikers materially different than the hiring of permanent replacements? Is the employer's business purpose in *Erie Resistor* less compelling than in *Mackay Radio*?

**2. Does *Erie Resistor* Require Intent for a §8(a)(3) Violation?** Does *Erie Resistor* hold that §8(a)(3) has been violated even if the employer sincerely believes it needs to offer superseniority to permanent replacements in order to maintain operations? If the employer can prove that such an offer was in fact necessary to accomplish that objective? If so, can the approach in *Erie Resistor* be squared with an intent-based interpretation of §8(a)(3)?

**3. Market-Based Checks on Bargaining Demands?** Are the cases reconcilable on a conception of the strike that views the hiring of replacements as a means of providing a market-based check on bargaining demands? Consider Estreicher, Strikers and Replacements, supra, at 902:

> The willingness of workers to cross picket lines and offer their services on the basis of the employer's final offer tells us something about the economic reasonableness of the union's demands. But if exceptional lures are

> required — in *Erie Resistor*, twenty years' super-seniority — the employer is doing more than providing a market check on union demands; he is taking extraordinary measures, not at all reflective of what his practices will be at strike's end, to beat back the strike. Such devices distort the collective bargaining process.

Does this rationale explain the view expressed in Burlington Homes, Inc., 246 N.L.R.B. 1029 (1979), that an employer violates §8(a)(3) by offering higher wages to replacements than it had offered to the union? But note that in Detroit Newspaper Agency, 327 N.L.R.B. 871 (1999), a §8(a)(5) case, the Board stated that an employer need not bargain with the union over the replacements' terms and conditions. In *Detroit Newspaper*, however, the replacements were paid *less* than the wage rate under the expired contract. Would offering a higher wage to replacements than had been offered to the union in its final offer violate the employer's obligation under *Katz*, supra page 449?

**4. Recall Rights for Laid-off Replacements?** In Giddings & Lewis, Inc., 255 N.L.R.B. 742, 744-745 (1981), the employer had established a layoff and recall policy that recalled laid-off replacements ahead of former strikers. The Board found a violation:

> [An employer may not] escape its *Laidlaw* obligation by merely stating that laid-off employees have a reasonable expectancy of recall. . . . [T]he General Counsel has specifically denied that it is seeking recall of unreinstated strikers after layoffs of relatively short duration such as would result from acts of God, brief parts or materials shortages, or relatively short-term loss of business. We agree that an employer should not have to disrupt its existing work force in such circumstances. However, Respondent's stated policy gives recall preference to laid-off employees over unreinstated strikers regardless of the length or the cause of the layoff. . . .
>
> We are not holding that Respondent was required to give preference to strikers or to place nonstrikers and replacements in a subordinate position with respect to recall rights. Certainly, Respondent could have considered many factors unrelated to concerted activity. Instead it [has] chosen to establish certain classifications of employees, classified unreinstated strikers on the basis of their protected activity, and proposed to treat them less favorably solely because they had been engaged in a strike. Respondent, in effect, has set up two unequal classes of employees with respect to recall rights, separated only on the basis of whether or not they participated in a strike. Thus, the seniority rights of the employees involved were established on the basis of invidious considerations, and Respondent's policy is unlawful on its face under well-established precedent.

Viewing the Board's approach as inconsistent with *Mackay Radio,* the Seventh Circuit denied enforcement: "Employers attempting to hire replacement workers could guarantee them employment only until a layoff occurred. Such replacements could hardly be called 'permanent.'" Giddings & Lewis, Inc. v. NLRB, 675 F.2d 926, 930 (7th Cir. 1982).

In Aqua-Chem, Inc., 288 N.L.R.B. 1108, 1109-1110 (1988), enforced, 910 F.2d 1487 (7th Cir. 1990), the Board adopted a position closer to that of the Seventh Circuit in finding that employers could extend recall rights to laid-off replacement workers if they had a "reasonable expectancy of recall," based on factors including "the employer's past business experience, the employer's future plans, the length of the layoff, the circumstances of the layoff, and what the employee was told regarding the likelihood of recall."

Does the court's *Giddings & Lewis* decision and the Board's subsequent retreat in *Aqua-Chem*

> misconstrue the *Mackay Radio* right, which has nothing to do with ensuring that the employer will in fact be able to obtain permanent replacements in a particular case[?] *Mackay Radio* simply permits the employer to insist on the replacements' retention at the strike's end—to resist the union's demand that the replacements be ousted. *Mackay Radio* does not, however, authorize any and all means—whether enhanced compensation or preferential seniority—that may be necessary to attract replacement workers and encourage them to brave union picket lines. Estreicher, Strikers and Replacements, supra, at 902-903. See also Matthew W. Finkin, Labor Policy and the Enervation of the Economic Strike, 1990 U. Ill. L. Rev. 547, 559-562.

## NLRB v. Great Dane Trailers

*388 U.S. 26 (1967)*

WARREN, C.J. . . .

The issue here is whether, in the absence of proof of an antiunion motivation, an employer may be held to have violated §§8(a)(3) and (1) . . . when it refused to pay striking employees vacation benefits accrued under a terminated collective bargaining agreement while it announced an intention to pay such benefits to striker replacements, returning strikers, and nonstrikers who had been at work on a certain date during the strike.

The respondent company and the union entered into a collective bargaining agreement which was effective by its terms until March 31, 1963. The agreement contained a commitment by the company to pay vacation benefits to employees who met certain enumerated qualifications. In essence, the company agreed to pay specified vacation benefits to employees who, during the preceding year, had worked at least 1,525 hours. It was also provided that, in the case of a "lay-off, termination or quitting," employees who had served more than 60 days during the year would be entitled to pro-rata shares of their vacation benefits. Benefits were to be paid on the Friday nearest July 1 of each year.

The agreement was temporarily extended beyond its termination date, but on April 30, 1963, the union gave the required 15 days' notice of intention to strike over issues which remained unsettled at the bargaining table. Accordingly, on May 16, 1963, approximately 350 of the company's 400 employees commenced a strike which lasted until December 26, 1963. The company continued to operate during the strike, using nonstrikers, persons hired as replacements for strikers, and some original strikers who had later abandoned the strike and returned to work. On July 12, 1963, a number of the strikers demanded their accrued vacation pay from the company. The company rejected this demand, basing its response on the assertion that all contractual obligations had been terminated by the strike and, therefore, none of the company's employees had a right to vacation pay. Shortly thereafter, however, the company announced that it would grant vacation pay—in the amounts and subject to the conditions set out in the expired agreement—to all employees who had reported for work on July 1, 1963. The company denied that these payments were founded on the agreement and stated that they merely reflected a new "policy" which had been unilaterally adopted.

. . . [T]he Court of Appeals held that, although discrimination between striking and nonstriking employees had been proved, the Board's conclusion that the company had committed an unfair labor practice was not well-founded inasmuch as there had been no affirmative showing of an unlawful motivation to discourage union membership or to interfere with the exercise of protected rights. . . .

The unfair labor practice charged here is grounded primarily in §8(a)(3) which requires specifically that the Board find a discrimination and a resulting discouragement of union membership. . . . There is little question but that the result of the company's refusal to pay vacation benefits to strikers was discrimination in its simplest form. . . . Some employees who met the conditions specified in the expired collective bargaining agreement were paid accrued vacation benefits in the amounts set forth in that agreement, while other employees who also met the conditions but who had engaged in protected concerted activity were denied such benefits. Similarly, there can be no doubt but that the discrimination was capable of discouraging membership in a labor organization within the meaning of the statute. Discouraging membership in a labor organization "includes discouraging participation in concerted activities . . . such as a legitimate strike." Labor Board v. Erie Resistor Corp., 373 U.S. 221, 233 (1963). The act of paying accrued benefits to one group of employees while announcing the extinction of the same benefits for another group of employees who are distinguishable only by their participation in protected concerted activity surely may have a discouraging effect on either present or future concerted activity.

But inquiry under §8(a)(3) does not usually stop at this point. The statutory language "discrimination . . . to . . . discourage" means that the finding of a violation normally turns on whether the discriminatory conduct was motivated by an antiunion purpose. . . . It was upon the motivation element that the Court of Appeals based its decision not to grant enforcement, and it is to that element which we now turn. . . . We noted in *Erie Resistor*, at 227, that proof of an antiunion motivation may make unlawful certain employer conduct which would in other circumstances be lawful. Some conduct, however, is so "inherently destructive of employee interests" that it may be deemed proscribed without need for proof of an underlying improper motive. Labor Board v. Brown, [380 U.S. 278, 287 (1965)]; American Ship Building Co. v. Labor Board, [380 U.S. 300, 311 (1965)]. That is, some conduct carries with it "unavoidable consequences which the employer not only foresaw but which he must have intended" and thus bears "its own indicia of intent." Labor Board v. Erie Resistor Corp., at 228, 231. If the conduct in question falls within this "inherently destructive" category, the employer has the burden of explaining away, justifying or characterizing "his actions as something different than they appear on their face," and if he fails, "an unfair labor practice charge is made out." Id., at 228. And even if the employer does come forward with counter explanations for his conduct in this situation, the Board may nevertheless draw an inference of improper motive from the conduct itself and exercise its duty to strike the proper balance between the asserted business justifications and the invasion of employee rights in light of the Act and its policy. Id., at 229. On the other hand, when "the resulting harm to employee rights is . . . comparatively slight, and a substantial and legitimate business end is served, the employers' conduct is prima facie lawful," and an affirmative showing of improper motivation must be made. *Labor Board v. Brown*, at 289; *American Ship Building Co. v. Labor Board*, at 311-313.

From this review of our recent decisions, several principles of controlling importance here can be distilled. First, if it can reasonably be concluded that the employer's discriminatory conduct was "inherently destructive" of important employee rights, no proof of an antiunion motivation is needed and the Board can find an unfair labor practice even if the employer introduces evidence that the conduct was motivated by business considerations. Second, if the adverse effect of the discriminatory conduct on employee rights is "comparatively slight," an antiunion motivation must be proved to sustain the charge *if* the employer has come forward with evidence of legitimate and substantial business justifications for the conduct. Thus, in either situation, once it has been proved that the employer engaged in discriminatory conduct which could have adversely affected employee rights to *some* extent, the burden is upon the employer to establish that he was motivated by legitimate objectives since proof of motivation is most accessible to him.

Applying the principles to this case then, it is not necessary for us to decide the degree to which the challenged conduct might have affected employee rights. As the Court of Appeals correctly noted, the company came forward with no evidence of legitimate motives for its discriminatory conduct. 363 F.2d, at 134. The company simply did not meet the burden of proof, and the Court of Appeals misconstrued the function of judicial review when it proceeded nonetheless to speculate upon what *might have* motivated the company. Since discriminatory conduct carrying a potential for adverse effect upon employee rights was proved and no evidence of a proper motivation appeared in the record, the Board's conclusions were supported by substantial evidence, Universal Camera Corp. v. Labor Board, 340 U.S. 474 (1951), and should have been sustained.

The judgment of the Court of Appeals is reversed and the case is remanded with directions to enforce the Board's order.

[The opinion of Justice Harlan, with whom Justice Stewart joined, dissenting, is omitted.]

## *NOTES AND QUESTIONS*

**1. Impact vs. Intent?** *Great Dane Trailers* posits the existence of two categories of conduct differentiated by the severity of injury to employee interests. Does the Court's distinction provide a workable guide for deciding future cases? Are the differential consequences of inclusion in one category or the other warranted by the language of §§8(a)(3) or 8(a)(1)? Consistent with the Court's emphasis in some cases on motive? With the imposition of the burden of persuasion on the General Counsel by §10(c) of the Act? Would it be preferable for the Court to abandon the requirement that motive is a necessary element and to hold that legality may turn on a judgment of whether injury to union or employee interests is warranted by countervailing employer interests? Under this approach, the presence of anti-union motive would provide an independent basis for illegality (regardless of any balancing of interests), but would not be a required element of a violation. Should the Board have the same latitude in balancing interests in the bargaining context as it has been accorded in the organizational context? See generally Estreicher, Strikers and Replacements, supra; Leonard S. Janofsky, New Concepts in Interference and Discrimination Under the NLRA: The Legacy of *American Ship Building* and *Great Dane Trailers,* 70 Colum. L. Rev. 81 (1970); Thomas G.S. Christensen & Andrea Svanoe, Motive and Intent in the Commission of Unfair Labor Practices, 77 Yale L.J. 1269 (1968).

**2. Arguable Contract Justification Defense?** If the company in *Great Dane Trailers* had come forward with evidence demonstrating that (a) the refusal to pay vacation benefits was based solely on a good-faith interpretation of the expired contract and (b) its reading of the contract was reasonable and at least arguably correct, would the company have discharged the burden of proof assigned by the Court? Would such proof have provided a defense to liability? Did the employer in any event violate §8(a)(5) by failing to bargain to impasse over the elimination of the vacation pay provision?

**3. "Penalty" for Striking?** Assume that the employer in *Great Dane* had simply eliminated vacation pay for all employees, whether or not they reported to work on July 1, 1963. Aside from any duty to bargain over such a change, would the employer also have violated §8(a)(3) on the theory that eliminating an accrued benefit of this type penalizes employees for their willingness to engage in concerted activity? Would the "discrimination" element of §8(a)(3) be satisfied in such a case? Consider also the following:

a. *Withholding Service Credits.* In light of *Erie Resistor* and *Great Dane Trailers,* what types of benefits may an employer lawfully withhold from striking employees? The employer does not have to pay strikers for days not worked and presumably it would not have to provide for accrual of service credits affecting the size of retirement benefits for days out on strike. Can the employer also suspend service credits affecting strikers' seniority standing for purposes of determining layoff, priority for picking vacation days, or the length of paid vacations? See General Elec. Co., 80 N.L.R.B. 510 (1948); Illinois Bell Tel. Co., 179 N.L.R.B. 681 (1969), enforced, 446 F.2d 815 (7th Cir. 1971); Texaco, Inc. v. NLRB, 700 F.2d 1039 (5th Cir. 1983). What criteria should determine whether a struck employer's withholding of such credits is a "penalty" for legally protected activity and thus violative of §8(a)(3) or rather a privileged response to business considerations?

b. *Productivity/Work Continuity Requirements.* A company has a practice of giving annual Christmas bonuses to its employees based on a five-factor formula: (1) overall company-wide results, (2) overall company-wide productivity, (3) results at each of its five plants, (4) productivity at the individual plants, and (5) continuity of work at each plant. The production and maintenance workers at one of the plants engaged in a 57-day economic strike during the year, resulting in lower than normal output and productivity. Does the company violate §8(a)(3) in withholding a Christmas bonus from all unit employees at a plant that was on strike during the year? See Pittsburgh-Des Moines Steel Co. v. NLRB, 284 F.2d 74 (9th Cir. 1960).

c. *Probationary Rules.* May employers apply otherwise lawful probationary rules to economic strikers—for example, requiring striking probationary employees to begin the company's standard probationary period anew upon return from a strike? See, e.g., Freezer Queen Foods, Inc., 249 N.L.R.B. 330 (1980); Kansas City Power & Light Co. v. NLRB, 641 F.2d 553 (8th Cir. 1981).

**4. *Great Dane*'s Implication for the *Mackay Radio* Doctrine?** Does *Great Dane Trailers* require reconsideration of at least the presumption in *Mackay Radio* that employers always have a legitimate business purpose in maintaining operations through the use of permanent replacements? Does the "inherently destructive" formulation indeed challenge the entire *Mackay* doctrine? If so, does the continuing validity of *Mackay* call into question the coherence of the *Great Dane* test, which suggests that a "destructive" impact on §7 rights, standing alone, is sufficient to establish an 8(a)(3) violation, regardless of the countervailing weight of the employer's interests?

**5. Permanent Subcontracting of Unit Work Under *Great Dane*?** In International Paper Co. v. NLRB, 115 F.3d 1045 (D.C. Cir. 1997), discussed further infra note 3, page 576, the D.C. Circuit rejected the Board's determination that an employer's permanent subcontracting of unit work during a lawful lockout was "inherently destructive" of employee rights and violated §8(a)(3) without proof of anti-union motive. In rejecting the Board's reliance on *Great Dane,* the court noted that the Supreme Court had found inherently destructive conduct only where "the employer treated employees within a bargaining unit differently depending on the degree of their union activity." Id. at 1050 (citing *Erie Resistor, Great Dane,* and *Metropolitan Edison,* supra page 214). Since the employer's conduct did not fit that mold, the court declined to find a violation absent specific proof of anti-union animus.

## Trans World Airlines, Inc. v. Independent Federation of Flight Attendants

*489 U.S. 426 (1989)*

Justice O'Connor delivered the opinion of the Court.

We decide today whether, at the end of a strike, an employer is required by the Railway Labor Act (RLA or Act), 44 Stat. 577, as amended, 45 U.S.C. §151 et seq., to displace employees who worked during the strike in order to reinstate striking employees with greater seniority.

I

In March 1984, Trans World Airlines, Inc. (TWA), and the Independent Federation of Flight Attendants (IFFA or Union) began negotiations pursuant to §6 of the RLA, 45 U.S.C. §156, on a new collective bargaining agreement to replace their prior agreement due to expire on July 31, 1984. The existing collective bargaining agreement created a complex system of bidding the general effect of which was to insure that those flight attendants with the greatest seniority would have the best opportunity to obtain their preferred job assignments, flight schedules, and bases of operation as vacancies appeared, and to insure that senior flight attendants would be least affected by the periodic furloughs endemic to the airline industry. Thus, for example, should a job vacancy appear at the highly desirable Los Angeles or San Francisco bases of operation or "domiciles," the most senior qualified flight attendant who bid on such a vacancy would be entitled to it. Conversely, should a reduction in force eliminate a position in the Los Angeles domicile, the furloughed flight attendant could opt to displace the most junior attendant of equal rank in the entire system or the most junior attendant of lower rank either at the same domicile or in the entire system.

For two years TWA and the Union unsuccessfully bargained over wages and working conditions not including the seniority bidding system. They pursued all the required dispute resolution mechanisms of the RLA, including direct negotiation, 45 U.S.C. §152 Second, mediation, 45 U.S.C. §155 First, and the final 30-day "cooling off" period. Ibid. By early 1986 a strike seemed imminent, and on March 7, 1986, the Union went out on strike.

TWA informed its flight attendants before and during the strike that it would continue operations by hiring permanent replacements for striking flight attendants, by continuing to employ any flight attendant who chose not to strike, and by rehiring any striker who abandoned the strike and made an unconditional offer to return to any available vacancies. TWA also informed its flight attendants that any vacancies created as a result of the strike would be filled by application of the seniority bidding system to all working flight attendants and that such job and domicile assignments would remain effective after the strike ended. Thus, at the conclusion of the strike, senior full-term strikers would not be permitted to displace permanent replacements or junior nonstriking flight attendants and could be left without an opportunity to return to work. TWA's promise not to displace working flight attendants after the strike created two incentives specifically linked to the seniority bidding system: it gave senior flight attendants an incentive to remain at, or return to, work in order to retain their prior jobs and domicile assignments; it gave junior flight attendants an incentive to remain at, or return to, work in order to obtain job and domicile assignments that were previously occupied by more senior, striking flight attendants.

As promised, TWA continued its operations during the 72-day strike by utilizing approximately 1,280 flight attendants who either did not strike or returned to work before the end of the strike and by hiring and fully training approximately 2,350 new flight attendants, some 1,220 of whom were hired during the first few days of the strike. On May 17, 1986, the Union made an unconditional offer to TWA on behalf of the approximately 5,000 flight attendants who had remained on strike to return to work. TWA accepted the offer but refused the Union's May 27th demand that TWA displace those prestrike employees who were working as of May 17th ("crossover" employees). Accordingly, TWA initially recalled only the 197 most senior full-term strikers to fill available job and domicile vacancies. By the terms of a post-strike arbitral agreement, these strikers and all subsequently reinstated full-term strikers returned to work as vacancies arose and with precisely the seniority they would have had if no strike had occurred. In May 1988, more than 1,100 full-term strikers had been reinstated with full seniority.

. . . At the same time, the Union filed the instant action contending that, even assuming the strike was economic, the full-term strikers were entitled to reinstatement either under the terms of the prestrike collective bargaining agreement or under the RLA itself. On cross motions for partial summary judgment, the District Court held that the full-term strikers were not entitled to displace either the junior crossovers or the 1,220 new hires employed by TWA immediately after the strike commenced. . . .

. . . The Court of Appeals, however, reversed the District Court's ruling that more senior full-term strikers could not displace junior crossovers. . . .

. . . Today, we reverse the Court of Appeals . . . and hold that an employer is not required by the RLA to lay off junior crossovers in order to reinstate more senior full-term strikers at the conclusion of a strike.

The Union relies on [NLRB v. Erie Resistor Corp., 373 U.S. 221 (1963)] to distinguish junior crossovers from new hires under the NLRA. . . .

[However,] it is clear that reinstated full-term strikers lost no seniority either in absolute or relative terms. Thus, unlike the situation in *Erie Resistor*, any future reductions in force at TWA will permit reinstated full-term strikers to displace junior flight attendants exactly as would have been the case in the absence of any strike. Similarly, should any vacancies develop in desirable job assignments or domiciles, reinstated full-term strikers who have bid on those vacancies will maintain their priority over junior flight attendants, whether they are new hires, crossovers, or full-term strikers. In the same vein, periodic bids on job scheduling will find senior reinstated full-term strikers maintaining their priority over all their junior colleagues. In short, once reinstated, the seniority of full-term strikers is in no way affected by their decision to strike.

Nevertheless, [the Union] argues that TWA's refusal to displace junior crossovers will create a "cleavage" between junior crossovers and reinstated full-term strikers at TWA "long after the strike is ended." This is the case because desirable job assignments and domiciles that would have been occupied by the most senior flight attendants had there been no strike will continue to be held by those who did not see the strike through to its conclusion. For example, the senior full-term striker who worked in the Los Angeles domicile before the strike may have been replaced by a junior crossover. As poststrike vacancies develop in TWA's work force, permitting reinstatement of full-term strikers, they are not likely to occur in the most desirable domiciles. Thus, it is unlikely that the senior full-term striker would be reinstated back to her preferred domicile. Resentful rifts among employees will also persist after the strike, the Union argues, because TWA's prestrike assurance of nondisplacement to junior crossovers, unlike the same assurance to new hires, "set up a competition *among* those individuals who participated in the original decision to strike, and thereby undermined the group's ability to take the collective action that it is the very purpose of the [RLA] to protect."

We reject this effort to expand *Erie Resistor.* Both the RLA and the NLRA protect an employee's right to choose not to strike, 45 U.S.C. §152 Fourth; 29 U.S.C. §157, and, thereby, protect employees' rights to "the benefit of their individual decisions not to strike. . . ." Accordingly, in virtually every strike situation there will be some employees who disagree with their union's decision to strike and who cannot be required to abide by that decision. It is the inevitable effect of an employer's use of the economic weapons available during a period of self-help that these differences will be exacerbated and that poststrike resentments may be created. Thus, for example, the employer's right to hire permanent replacements in order to continue operations will inevitably also have the effect of dividing striking employees between those who, fearful of permanently losing their jobs, return to work and those who remain stalwart in the strike. In such a situation, apart from the "pressure on the strikers *as a group* to abandon the strike," to which the dissent refers, a "competition" may arise *among* the striking employees to return to work in order to avoid being displaced by a permanent replacement. Similarly, employee awareness that an employer may decide to transfer working employees to necessary positions previously occupied by more senior striking employees will isolate employees fearful of losing those positions and employees coveting those positions from employees more committed to the strike. Conversely, a policy such as TWA employed here, in creating the incentive for individual strikers to return to work, also "puts pressure on the strikers *as a group* to abandon the strike," in the same manner that the hiring of permanent replacements does.

None of these scenarios, however, present the prospect of a continuing diminution of seniority upon reinstatement at the end of the strike that was central to our decision in *Erie Resistor.* All that has occurred is that the employer has filled vacancies created by striking employees. Some of these vacancies will be filled by newly hired employees, others by doubtless more experienced and therefore more needed employees who either refused to strike or abandoned the strike. . . . The positions occupied by newly hired replacements, employees who refused to strike, and employees who abandoned the strike are simply not "available positions" to be filled. As noted above, those positions that were available at the conclusion of the strike were filled "according to some principle, such as seniority, that is neutral. . . ." That the prospect of a reduction in available positions may divide employees and create incentives among them to remain at work or abandon a strike before its conclusion is a secondary effect fairly within the arsenal of economic weapons available to employers during a period of self-help.

To distinguish crossovers from new hires in the manner IFFA proposes would have the effect of penalizing those who decided not to strike in order to benefit those who did. Because permanent replacements need not be discharged at the conclusion of a strike in which the union has been unsuccessful, a certain number of prestrike employees will find themselves without work. We see no reason why those employees who chose not to gamble on the success of the strike should suffer the consequences when the gamble proves unsuccessful. Requiring junior crossovers, who cannot themselves displace the newly hired permanent replacements, and "who rank lowest in seniority," to be displaced by more senior full-term strikers is precisely to visit the consequences of the lost gamble on those who refused to take the risk. While the employer and union in many circumstances may reach a back-to-work agreement that would displace crossovers and new hires or an employer may unilaterally decide to permit such displacement, nothing in the NLRA or the federal common law we have developed under the statute requires such a result. . . .

Justice BRENNAN, with whom Justice MARSHALL joins, dissenting. . . .

The employer's promise to members of the bargaining unit that they will not be displaced at the end of a strike if they cross the picket lines addresses a far different incentive to the bargaining-unit members than does the employer's promise of permanence to new hires. The employer's threat to hire permanent replacements from outside the existing work force puts pressure on the strikers *as a group* to abandon the strike before their positions are filled by others. But the employer's promise to members of the striking bargaining unit that if they abandon the strike (or refuse to join it at the outset) they will retain their jobs at strike's end in preference to more senior workers who remain on strike produces an additional dynamic: now there is also an incentive for *individual* workers to seek to save (or improve) their own positions at the expense of other members of the striking bargaining unit. We have previously observed that offers of "individual benefits to strikers to induce them to abandon the strike . . . could be expected to undermine the strikers' mutual interest and place the entire strike effort in jeopardy." NLRB v. Erie Resistor Corp., 373 U.S. 221, 230-231 (1963). Such a "divide and conquer" tactic thus "strike[s] a fundamental blow to union . . . activity and the collective bargaining process itself."

Justice BLACKMUN, . . . dissenting. . . .

In his dissent, Justice Brennan does not reach the question whether a carrier who offers permanence to replacements and crossovers is entitled to a presumption of business necessity. Indeed, he would not even *permit* TWA to make a case-specific showing that its crossover policy was necessary for its continued operation during the strike. Here, our positions differ: I would require the carrier to prove the business necessity of offering permanence to replacements and crossovers on the facts of each case. . . .

Because the Court of Appeals found TWA's conduct unlawful without considering whether TWA's crossover policy was "truly necessary" for continued operations during the strike, I would vacate the judgment of the Court of Appeals and direct that court to remand the case for consideration of that issue. Inasmuch as this Court is now reversing outright, I dissent.

## *NOTES AND QUESTIONS*

**1. Refusal to "Expand" *Erie Resistor*?** Is the *TWA* decision consistent with *Erie Resistor*? Does *TWA* create the same kind of enduring cleavage between senior employees who stayed out on strike and junior employees enjoying superior job security because they did not support the strike as concerned the *Erie Resistor* Court? Would a different result in *TWA* necessarily have strengthened the strike weapon? Would employees be more or less willing to vote to strike were they to know that if they returned to work during the strike they would have less job protection than new hires engaged during a strike? On the other hand, didn't the junior employees returning to work cast their lot with the other striking employees by joining the strike in the first instance? Should employees be permitted to abandon in midstream a collective representation mechanism they freely selected? Does the answer depend on whether the employees in question had a right to vote on the employer's final offer and strike authorization? Does it also depend on whether employees are free not to strike without inviting union discipline? See Pattern Makers' League of North Am. v. NLRB, 473 U.S. 95 (1985), infra page 926 (crossovers may escape discipline by resigning from union).

**2. Impact on Market-Based Check on Bargaining Demands?** Employers often face considerable difficulty hiring trained, educated, and motivated workers off the street. These difficulties are particularly formidable where employers use internal labor markets to encourage employees to acquire firm-specific skills. In the *TWA* case, the employer faced also the additional hurdle of meeting training certification requirements of the Federal Aviation Administration. By allowing TWA to treat junior crossover employees more favorably than senior employees remaining on strike, did the Court permit a distortion of the bargaining process that resembles the extraordinary lure used in *Erie Resistor*? See Estreicher, Collective Bargaining or "Collective Begging," supra.

### c. *The Effect of* Radio Mackay *on the Union's Majority Status*

As noted earlier, an economic strike does not suspend an employer's duty to bargain, but permanent replacements, as well as the strikers they replace, are considered members of the bargaining unit and are entitled to vote in Board elections (including decertification elections). What effect, then, is the hiring of replacements likely to have on the incumbent union's majority status and the employer's duty to bargain during (and after) an economic strike?

**NLRB v. Curtin Matheson Scientific, Inc.**
*494 U.S. 775 (1990)*

MARSHALL, J. . . .

I

. . . The Board has long presumed that new employees hired in nonstrike circumstances support the incumbent union in the same proportion as the employees they replace. . . . [I]n Cutten Supermarket, 220 N.L.R.B. 507 (1975), the Board [stated] that striker replacements, like new employees generally, are presumed to *support* the union in the same ratio as the strikers they replaced. Id., at 509. . . . [In] 1980, the Board reiterated that . . . presumption. . . . Pennco, Inc., 250 N.L.R.B. 716, 717-718 (1980), enf'd, 684 F.2d 340 (CA6).

In 1987, after several Courts of Appeals rejected the Board's approach, the Board determined that no universal generalizations could be made about replacements' union sentiments that would justify a presumption either of support for or of opposition to the union. Station KKHI, 284 N.L.R.B. 1339 (1987). On the one hand, the Board found that the prounion presumption lacked empirical foundation because "incumbent unions and strikers sometimes have shown hostility toward the permanent replacements," and "replacements are typically aware of the union's primary concern for the striker's welfare, rather than that of the replacements." Id., at 1344. On the other hand, the Board found that an antiunion presumption was "equally unsupportable" factually. Ibid. The Board observed that a striker replacement "may be forced to work for financial reasons, or may disapprove of the strike in question but still desire union representation and would support other union initiatives." Ibid. Moreover, the Board found as a matter of policy that adoption of an antiunion presumption would "substantially impair the employees' right to strike by adding to the risk of replacement the risk of loss of the bargaining representative as soon as replacements equal in number to the strikers are willing to cross the picket line." Ibid. See also Pennco, Inc., 250 N.L.R.B., at 717. Accordingly, the Board held that it would not apply any presumption regarding striker replacements' union sentiments, but would determine their views on a case-by-case basis. 284 N.L.R.B., at 1344-1345.

## II

We . . . turn to the Board's application of its *Station KKHI* no-presumption approach in this case. . . . In 1970, the Board certified Teamsters Local 968, General Drivers, Warehousemen and Helpers (hereinafter Union) as the collective-bargaining agent for respondent's production and maintenance employees. On May 21, 1979, the most recent bargaining agreement between respondent and the Union expired. Respondent made its final offer for a new agreement on May 25, but the Union rejected that offer. Respondent then locked out the 27 bargaining-unit employees. On June 12, respondent renewed its May 25 offer, but the Union again rejected it. The Union then commenced an economic strike. The record contains no evidence of any strike-related violence or threats of violence.

Five employees immediately crossed the picket line and reported for work. On June 25, while the strike was still in effect, respondent hired 29 permanent replacement employees to replace the 22 strikers. . . . On July 20, . . . respondent withdrew recognition from the Union and refused to bargain further, stating that it doubted that the Union was supported by a majority of the employees in the unit. . . . As of July 20, the bargaining unit consisted of 19 strikers, 25 permanent replacements, and the 5 employees who had crossed the picket line at the strike's inception.

On July 30, the Union filed an unfair labor practice charge with the Board. Following an investigation, the General Counsel issued a complaint, alleging that respondent's withdrawal of recognition . . . violated §§8(a)(1) and 8(a)(5) of the NLRA. In its defense to the charge, respondent claimed that it had a reasonably based, good-faith doubt of the Union's majority status. . . . The Board, however, [held] that respondent lacked sufficient objective basis to doubt the Union's majority support. 287 N.L.R.B. 350 (1987).

First, the Board noted that the crossover of 5 of the original 27 employees did not in itself support an inference that the 5 had repudiated the Union, because their failure to join the strike may have "indicate[d] their economic concerns rather than a lack of support for the union." 287 N.L.R.B., at 352. Second, the Board found that the resignation from their jobs of two of the original bargaining-unit employees, including the chief shop steward, after the commencement of the strike did not indicate opposition to the Union, but merely served to reduce the size of the bargaining unit as of the date of respondent's withdrawal of recognition. Ibid. Third, the Board discounted statements made by six employees to a representative of respondent during the strike. Although some of these statements may have indicated rejection of the Union as the bargaining representative, the Board noted, others "appear[ed] ambiguous at best." Id., at 353. Moreover, the Board stated, "[e]ven attributing to them the meaning most favorable to the Respondent, it would merely signify that 6 employees of a total bargaining unit of approximately 50 did not desire to keep the Union as the collective-bargaining representative." Ibid.

Finally, regarding respondent's hiring of striker replacements, the Board stated that, in accordance with the *Station KKHI* approach, it would "not use any presumptions with respect to [the replacements'] union sentiments," but would instead "take a case-by-case approach [and] require additional evidence of a lack of union support on the replacements' part in evaluating the significance of this factor in the employer's showing of good-faith doubt." 287 N.L.R.B., at 352. The Board noted that respondent's only evidence of the replacements' attitudes toward the Union was its employee relations director's account of a conversation with one of the replacements. The replacement employee reportedly told her that he had worked in union and nonunion workplaces and did not see any need for a union as long as the company treated him well; in addition, he said that he did not think the Union in this case represented the employees. Id., at 351. The Board did not determine whether this statement indicated the replacement employee's repudiation of the Union, but found that the statement was, in any event, an insufficient basis for "inferring the union sentiments of the replacement employees as a group." 287 N.L.R.B., at 353.

The Board therefore concluded that "the evidence [was] insufficient to rebut the presumption of the Union's continuing majority status." Ibid. Accordingly, the Board held that respondent had violated §§8(a)(1) and 8(a)(5) by withdrawing recognition from the Union . . . [and] ordered respondent to bargain with the Union on request. . . .

The Court of Appeals . . . refused to enforce the Board's order, holding that respondent was justified in doubting the Union's majority support. 859 F.2d 362 (CA5 1988). Specifically, the court rejected the Board's decision not to apply any presumption in evaluating striker replacements' union sentiments and endorsed the [presumption] that striker replacements oppose the union.

### III

. . . [U]nder its no-presumption approach, the Board "take[s] into account the particular circumstances surrounding each strike and the hiring of replacements, while retaining the longstanding requirement that the employer must come forth with some objective evidence to substantiate his doubt of continuing majority status." 859 F.2d, at 370 (Williams, J., dissenting).[8]

We find the Board's no-presumption approach rational as an empirical matter. . . . Although replacements often may not favor the incumbent union, the Board reasonably concluded, in light of its long experience in addressing these issues, that replacements may in some circumstances desire union representation despite their willingness to cross the picket line. Economic concerns, for instance, may force a replacement employee to work for a struck employer even though he otherwise supports the union and wants the benefits of union representation. . . . In addition, a replacement, like a nonstriker or a strike crossover, may disagree with the purpose or strategy of the particular strike and refuse to support that strike, while still wanting that union's representation at the bargaining table.

Respondent insists that the interests of strikers and replacements are diametrically opposed and that unions inevitably side with the strikers. For instance, respondent argues, picket-line violence often stems directly from the hiring of replacements. Furthermore, unions often negotiate with employers for strike settlements that would return the strikers to their jobs, thereby displacing some or all of the replacements. . . . Respondent asserts that replacements, aware of the union's loyalty to the strikers, most likely would not support the union. See, e.g., Leveld Wholesale, Inc., 218 N.R.L.B. 1314, 1350 (1975) ("Strike replacements can reasonably foresee that, if the union is successful, the strikers will return to work and the strike replacements will be out of a job"). In a related argument, respondent contends that the Board's no-presumption approach is irreconcilable with the Board's decisions holding that employers have no duty to bargain with a striking union over replacements' employment terms because the "inherent conflict" between strikers and replacements renders the union incapable of

---

8. . . . The American Federation of Labor and Congress of Industrial Organizations, as amicus curiae, urges us to reject the good-faith doubt standard and hold that an employer, before withdrawing recognition of the union, must show actual loss of majority status through a Board-conducted election. See also Flynn, The Economic Strike Bar: Looking Beyond the "Union Sentiments" of Permanent Replacements, 61 Temple L. Rev. 691, 720 (1988). This Court has never expressly considered the validity of the good-faith doubt standard. . . . We decline to address that issue here, as both parties assume the validity of the standard, and resolution of the issue is not necessary to our decision. . . . [In Levitz Furniture Co. of the Pacific, 333 N.L.R.B. 717, 725 (2001), the Board adopted the "actual loss of majority" view for unilateral withdrawal of recognition. — Eds.]

"bargain[ing] simultaneously in the best interests of both strikers and their replacements." Service Electric Co., 281 N.L.R.B. 633, 641 (1986).

These arguments do not persuade us that the Board's position is irrational. Unions do not inevitably demand displacement of all strike replacements. . . .

[E]ven if the interests of strikers and replacements conflict *during* the strike, those interests may converge *after* the strike, once job rights have been resolved. Thus, while the strike continues, a replacement worker whose job appears relatively secure might well want the union to continue to represent the unit regardless of the union's bargaining posture during the strike. Surely replacement workers are capable of looking past the strike in considering whether or not they desire representation by the union. . . . The Board's refusal to adopt an antiunion presumption is also consistent with the Act's "overriding policy" of achieving "'industrial peace.'" . . .

The Board's approach to determining the union views of strike replacements . . . limits employers' ability to oust a union without adducing any evidence of the employees' union sentiments and encourages negotiated solutions to strikes. It was reasonable for the Board to conclude that the antiunion presumption, in contrast, could allow an employer to eliminate the union merely by hiring a sufficient number of replacement employees. That rule thus might encourage the employer to avoid good-faith bargaining over a strike settlement, and instead to use the strike as a means of removing the union altogether. . . . Restricting an employer's ability to use a strike as a means of terminating the bargaining relationship serves the policies of promoting industrial stability and negotiated settlements. . . .

Furthermore, it was reasonable for the Board to decide that the antiunion presumption might chill employees' exercise of their statutory . . . right to strike. . . . If an employer could remove a union merely by hiring a sufficient number of replacements, employees considering a strike would face not only the prospect of being permanently replaced, but also a greater risk that they would lose their bargaining representative, thereby diminishing their chance of obtaining reinstatement through a strike settlement. It was rational for the Board to conclude, then, that adoption of the antiunion presumption could chill employees' exercise of their right to strike.[13]

We therefore find, in light of the considerable deference we accord Board rules, that the Board's approach is consistent with the Act. . . .

Chief Justice REHNQUIST, concurring.

The Board's "no-presumption" rule seems to me to press to the limit the deference to which the Board is entitled in assessing industrial reality,

---

13. . . . We need not determine whether the Board's policy considerations *alone* would justify its refusal to adopt the presumption urged by respondent because we find the Board's decision not irrational as a factual matter.

but for the reasons stated [by] the Court I agree that limit is not exceeded. . . . It appears that another of the Board's rules prevents the employer from polling its employees unless it first establishes a good-faith doubt of majority status. See Texas Petrochemicals Corp., 296 N.L.R.B. 1057, 1064 (1989) (the standard for employer polling is the same as the standard for withdrawal of recognition). I have considerable doubt whether the Board may[, as some of its recent decisions suggest,] insist that good-faith doubt be determined only on the basis of sentiments of individual employees, and at the same time bar the employer from using what might be the only effective means of determining those sentiments. But that issue is not before us today.

[The dissenting opinion of Justice BLACKMUN is omitted.]

Justice SCALIA, with whom Justices O'CONNOR and KENNEDY join, dissenting.

. . . Since the principal employment-related interest of strike replacements (to retain their jobs) is almost invariably opposed to the principal interest of the striking union (to replace them with its striking members) it seems to me impossible to conclude on this record that the employer did not have a reasonable, good-faith doubt regarding the union's majority status. The Board's factual finding being unsupported by substantial evidence, it cannot stand. . . .

[T]he burden upon the employer here was not to demonstrate 100% assurance that a majority of the bargaining unit did not support the union, but merely "reasonable doubt" that they did so. It seems to me absurd to deny that it sustained that burden. . . .

Of course the Board may choose to implement . . . policy . . . by *forbidding* a *rational* inference, just as it may do so by *requiring a nonrational* one (which is what a presumption of law is). And perhaps it could lawfully have reached the outcome it did here [by] saying that *even though* it must reasonably be inferred that an employer has good-faith doubt of majority status when more than half of the bargaining unit are strike replacements whose job rights have not been resolved, we will not permit that inference to be made. . . . But that is not what the agency did here. . . .

## *NOTES AND QUESTIONS*

**1. Ascertaining Preferences of Replacements and Crossovers or Promoting the Continuation of Bargaining Relationships?** How convincing do you find the Board's arguments, accepted by the Court, that it is unable to make generalizations about the replacements' union sentiments? Is the Board's no-presumption approach best understood as reflecting a policy of not allowing an economic strike routinely to become the means of ousting an incumbent union? See Estreicher, Strikers and Replacements, supra.

**2. An "Economic Strike Bar"?** As discussed in Chapter 4, under its "contract bar," the Board declines to hear representational questions for the first three years of a facially valid collective bargaining agreement. Could it also decline to entertain representational questions in the middle of an active strike in order to promote a model of the bargaining process in which strikes are a means of resolving disputes rather than an occasion for terminating relationships? See Estreicher, Strikers and Replacements, supra, at 904-905; Flynn, The Economic Strike Bar, supra. Are there aspects of the majority decision that support such an approach? Why has the Board not taken this more direct approach? If the Board were to bar challenges to the union's majority status during the term of a strike, should or must there be a time limit on the length of such a bar? See Estreicher, supra, at 905:

> Congress, I think, has given us the answer in section 9(c)(3): one year from the commencement of the strike. After the one-year period, the strikers no longer enjoy voting rights, and although they remain statutory employees the Board can no longer forestall a resolution of the representation question.

**3. A Ban on Withdrawals of Recognition During an Active Strike?** Consider an alternative approach to either the no-presumption rule or the "economic strike bar": one that would prevent employers from testing a union's representational authority during a strike by withdrawing recognition rather than petitioning for an election. See footnote 8 of the Court's opinion. On the other hand, would holding an election in the midst of a strike be good policy? Given the Board's blocking charge policy, discussed supra page 233, how likely do you think it is that a decertification election would proceed during a strike? How strong is the union's incentive to file ULP charges in an attempt to block the election in this situation? What types of charges do you think a union might file (whether for strategic or other purposes)? See Joan Flynn, *Allentown Mack* and Economic Strikes: And Now for the Bad News, 49 Lab. L.J. 1205, 1209 (1998).

## 3. Lockouts

**American Ship Building Co. v. NLRB**
*380 U.S. 300 (1965)*

STEWART, J. . . .

The question presented is . . . whether an employer commits an unfair labor practice under §§8(a)(1) and 8(a)(3) of the Act when he temporarily lays off or "locks out" his employees during a labor dispute to bring economic pressure in support of his bargaining position. . . .

The American Ship Building Company operates four shipyards on the Great Lakes—at Chicago, at Buffalo, and at Toledo and Lorain, Ohio. The company is primarily engaged in the repairing of ships, a highly seasonal business concentrated in the winter months when the freezing of the Great Lakes renders shipping impossible. What limited business is obtained during the shipping season is frequently such that speed of execution is of the utmost importance to minimize immobilization of the ships.

Since 1952 the employer has engaged in collective bargaining with a group of eight unions. . . . [T]he employer had contracted with the unions on five occasions, each agreement having been preceded by a strike. The particular chapter of the collective bargaining history with which we are concerned opened shortly before May 1, 1961, when the unions notified the company of their intention to seek modification of the current contract, due to expire on August 1.

. . . [O]n August 9, after extended negotiations, the parties separated without having resolved substantial differences on the central issues dividing them and without having specific plans for further attempts to resolve them — a situation which the trial examiner found was an impasse. Throughout the negotiations, the employer displayed anxiety as to the unions' strike plans, fearing that the unions would call a strike as soon as a ship entered the Chicago yard or delay negotiations into the winter to increase strike leverage. The union negotiator consistently insisted that it was his intention to reach an agreement without calling a strike; however, he did concede incomplete control over the workers — a fact borne out by the occurrence of a wildcat strike in February 1961. Because of the danger of an unauthorized strike and the consistent and deliberate use of strikes in prior negotiations, the employer remained apprehensive of the possibility of a work stoppage.

In light of the failure to reach an agreement and the lack of available work, the employer decided to lay off certain of its workers. On August 11 the employees received a notice which read: "Because of the labor dispute which has been unresolved since August 1, 1961, you are laid off until further notice." The Chicago yard was completely shut down and all but two employees laid off at the Toledo yard. A large force was retained at Lorain to complete a major piece of work there and the employees in the Buffalo yard were gradually laid off as miscellaneous tasks were completed. Negotiations were resumed shortly after these layoffs and continued for the following two months until a two-year contract was agreed upon on October 27. The employees were recalled the following day.

Upon claims filed by the unions, the General Counsel of the Board issued a complaint charging the employer with violations of §§8(a)(1), (3), and (5). The trial examiner found that although there had been no work in the Chicago yard since July 19, its closing was not due to lack of work. Despite similarly slack seasons in the past, the employer had for 17 years retained a nucleus crew to do maintenance work and remain ready to take such work as might come in. The examiner went on to find that the employer was reasonably apprehensive of a strike at some point. Although the unions had given assurances that there would be no strike, past bargaining history was thought to justify continuing apprehension that the unions would fail to make good their assurances. It was further found that the employer's primary purpose in locking out its employees was to avert peculiarly harmful economic consequences which would be imposed on it and its customers if a strike were called either while a ship was in the yard during the shipping season or later when the yard was fully occupied. . . .

A three-to-two majority of the Board rejected the trial examiner's conclusion that the employer could reasonably anticipate a strike. Finding the unions' assurances sufficient to dispel any such apprehension, the Board was able to find only one purpose underlying the layoff: a desire to bring economic pressure to secure prompt settlement of the dispute on favorable terms. The Board did not question the examiner's finding that the layoffs had not occurred until after a bargaining impasse had been reached. Nor did the Board remotely suggest that the company's decision to lay off its employees was based either on union hostility or a desire to avoid its bargaining obligations under the Act. The Board concluded that the employer "by curtailing its operations at the South Chicago yard with the consequent layoff of the employees, coerced employees in the exercise of their bargaining rights in violation of §8(a)(1) of the Act, and discriminated against its employees within the meaning of §8(a)(3) of the Act." 142 N.L.R.B., at 1364-1365.

The difference between the Board and the trial examiner is thus a narrow one turning on their differing assessments of the circumstances which the employer claims gave it reason to anticipate a strike. Both the Board and the examiner assumed, within the established pattern of Board analysis, that if the employer had shut down its yard and laid off its workers solely for the purpose of bringing to bear economic pressure to break an impasse and secure more favorable contract terms, an unfair labor practice would be made out. . . .

The Board has, however, exempted certain classes of lockouts from proscription. "Accordingly, it has held that lockouts are permissible to safeguard against . . . loss where there is reasonable ground for believing that a strike was threatened or imminent." Ibid. Developing this distinction in its rulings, the Board has approved lockouts designed to prevent seizure of a plant by a sitdown strike, Link-Belt Co., 26 N.L.R.B. 227; to forestall repetitive disruptions of an integrated operation by "quickie" strikes, International Shoe Co., 93 N.L.R.B. 907; to avoid spoilage of materials which would result from a sudden work stoppage, Duluth Bottling Assn., 48 N.L.R.B. 1335; and to avert the immobilization of automobiles brought in for repair, Belts Cadillac Olds, Inc., 96 N.L.R.B. 268. In another distinct class of cases the Board has sanctioned the use of the lockout by a multiemployer bargaining unit as a response to a whipsaw strike against one of its members.

Buffalo Linen Supply Co., 109 N.L.R.B. 447, rev'd sub nom. Truck Drivers Union v. Labor Board, 231 F.2d 110, rev'd, 353 U.S. 87.

. . . What we are here concerned with is the use of a temporary layoff of employees solely as a means to bring economic pressure to bear in support of the employer's bargaining position, after an impasse has been reached. This is the only issue before us, and all that we decide.[8]

. . . The Board's position [that the employer violated §8(a)(1)] is premised on the view that the lockout interferes with two of the rights guaranteed by §7: the right to bargain collectively and the right to strike. In the Board's view, the use of the lockout "punishes" employees for the presentation of and adherence to demands made by their bargaining representatives and so coerces them in the exercise of their right to bargain collectively. It is important to note that there is here no allegation that the employer used the lockout in the service of designs inimical to the process of collective bargaining. There was no evidence and no finding that the employer was hostile to its employees' banding together for collective bargaining or that the lockout was designed to discipline them for doing so. It is therefore inaccurate to say that the employer's intention was to destroy or frustrate the process of collective bargaining. What can be said is that it intended to resist the demands made of it in the negotiations and to secure modification of these demands. We cannot see that this intention is in any way inconsistent with the employees' rights to bargain collectively.

Moreover, there is no indication, either as a general matter or in this specific case, that the lockout will necessarily destroy the unions' capacity for effective and responsible representation. The unions here involved have vigorously represented the employees since 1952, and there is nothing to show that their ability to do so has been impaired by the lockout. Nor is the lockout one of those acts which are demonstrably so destructive of collective bargaining that the Board need not inquire into employer motivation, as might be the case, for example, if an employer permanently discharged his unionized staff and replaced them with employees known to be possessed of a violent antiunion animus. Cf. Labor Board v. Erie Resistor Corp., 373 U.S. 221. The lockout may well dissuade employees from adhering to the position which they initially adopted in the bargaining, but the right to bargain collectively does not entail any "right" to insist on one's position free from economic disadvantage. Proper analysis of the problem demands that the simple intention to support the employer's bargaining position as to compensation and the like be distinguished from a hostility to the process of

---

8. Contrary to the views expressed in a concurring opinion filed in this case, we intimate no view whatever as to the consequences which would follow had the employer replaced its employees with permanent replacements or even temporary help. Cf. Labor Board v. Mackay Radio & Telegraph Co., 304 U.S. 333.

collective bargaining which could suffice to render a lockout unlawful. See Labor Board v. Brown, 380 U.S. 278.

The Board has taken the complementary view that the lockout interferes with the right to strike protected under §§7 and 13 of the Act in that it allows the employer to preempt the possibility of a strike and thus leave the union with "nothing to strike against." . . . It is true that recognition of the lockout deprives the union of exclusive control of the timing and duration of work stoppages calculated to influence the result of collective bargaining negotiations, but there is nothing in the statute which would imply that the right to strike "carries with it" the right exclusively to determine the timing and duration of all work stoppages. The right to strike as commonly understood is the right to cease work—nothing more. No doubt a union's bargaining power would be enhanced if it possessed not only the simple right to strike but also the power exclusively to determine when work stoppages should occur, but the Act's provisions are not indefinitely elastic, content-free forms to be shaped in whatever manner the Board might think best conforms to the proper balance of bargaining power.

Thus, we cannot see that the employer's use of a lockout solely in support of a legitimate bargaining position is in any way inconsistent with the right to bargain collectively or with the right to strike. Accordingly, we conclude that on the basis of the findings made by the Board in this case, there has been no violation of §8(a)(1). . . .

. . . [T]his lockout [also] does not fall into that category of cases arising under §8(a)(3) in which the Board may truncate its inquiry into employer motivation. As this case well shows, use of the lockout does not carry with it any necessary implication that the employer acted to discourage union membership or otherwise discriminate against union members as such. The purpose and effect of the lockout were only to bring pressure upon the union to modify its demands. Similarly, it does not appear that the natural tendency of the lockout is severely to discourage union membership while serving no significant employer interest.

There is of course no question that the Board is entitled to the greatest deference in recognition of its special competence in dealing with labor problems. In many areas its evaluation of the competing interests of employer and employee should unquestionably be given conclusive effect in determining the application of §§8(a)(1), (3), and (5). However, we think that the Board construes its functions too expansively when it claims general authority to define national labor policy by balancing the competing interests of labor and management.

. . . Sections 8(a)(1) and (3) do not give the Board a general authority to assess the relative economic power of the adversaries in the bargaining process and to deny weapons to one party or the other because of its assessment of that party's bargaining power. Labor Board v. Brown, 380 U.S. 278. In this case the Board has, in essence, denied the use of the bargaining lockout to the employer because of its conviction that use of this device would give the employer "too much power." In so doing, the Board has stretched §§8(a)(1) and (3) far beyond their functions of protecting the rights of employee organization and collective bargaining. . . .

We are unable to find that any fair construction of the provisions relied on by the Board in this case can support its finding of an unfair labor practice. Indeed, the role assumed by the Board in this area is fundamentally inconsistent with the structure of the Act and the function of the sections relied upon. The deference owed to an expert tribunal cannot be allowed to slip into a judicial inertia which results in the unauthorized assumption by an agency of major policy decisions properly made by Congress. Accordingly, we hold that an employer violates neither §8(a)(1) nor §8(a)(3) when, after a bargaining impasse has been reached, he temporarily shuts down his plant and lays off his employees for the sole purpose of bringing economic pressure to bear in support of his legitimate bargaining position.

[Justice White joined in reversing the Board on the ground that the closing of the shipyard had resulted from the lack of repair work caused by the bargaining deadlock and the fear of a strike rather than from an effort to exert economic pressure against the union. After urging that the Court had unnecessarily reached the issue of the validity of bargaining lockouts, he expressed his dissent from the Court's general position.]

. . . Until today the employer's true motive or sole purpose has not always been determinative of the impact on employee rights. Republic Aviation Corp. v. Labor Board, 324 U.S. 793; Radio Officers' Union v. Labor Board, 347 U.S. 17; Labor Board v. Truck Drivers Union, 353 U.S. 87; Labor Board v. Erie Resistor Corp., 373 U.S. 221; Labor Board v. Burnup & Sims, Inc., 379 U.S. 21. The importance of the employer's right to hire replacements to continue operations, or of his right to fire employees he has good reason to believe are guilty of gross misconduct, was not doubted in *Erie Resistor* and *Burnup & Sims.* Nonetheless the Board was upheld in its determination that the award of superseniority to strike replacements and discharge of the suspected employee were unfair labor practices. Of course, such conduct is taken in the pursuit of legitimate business ends, but nonetheless the "conduct *does* speak for itself . . . it carries with it unavoidable consequences which the employer not only foresaw but which he must have intended." *Erie Resistor,* 373 U.S., at 228. I would have thought it apparent that loss of jobs for an indefinite period, and the threatened loss of jobs, which the Court's decision assuredly sanctions, . . . because of the union's negotiating activity, itself protected conduct under §7, hardly encourage affiliation with a union. . . .

[The opinion of Justice GOLDBERG, with whom Chief Justice WARREN joined, concurring in the result, is omitted.]

### *Note: Lockouts in Multiemployer Bargaining Units*

In NLRB v. Truck Drivers Local Union No. 449 (*Buffalo Linen*), 353 U.S. 87 (1957), a number of laundry companies belonged to a multiemployer association for the purpose of bargaining with a single union toward a comprehensive agreement for all employees of all of the member companies. During negotiations the union called a so-called "whipsaw strike" against one of the companies in the hope of securing a favorable agreement with that company and then using the whipsaw tactic against the other companies in turn. The nonstruck companies, however, locked out their employees in order to maintain a common front among all of the members of the association. The Board held that such a multiemployer lockout in response to a whipsaw strike should be included within an expanded category of "defensive" lockouts, which previously had been limited to lockouts in anticipation of a strike that was timed to cause undue harm to the company. The Supreme Court upheld the Board's approach as within its policymaking discretion (id. at 96):

> Although the Act protects the right of the employees to strike in support of their demands, this protection is not so absolute so as to deny self-help by employers when legitimate interests of employees and employers collide. Conflict may arise, for example, between the right to strike and the interest of small employers in preserving multiemployer bargaining as a means of bargaining on an equal basis with a large union and avoiding the competitive disadvantages resulting from nonuniform contractual terms. The ultimate problem is the balancing of the conflicting legitimate interests. The function of striking that balance to effectuate national labor policy is often a difficult and delicate responsibility, which the Congress committed primarily to the National Labor Relations Board, subject to limited judicial review.

In NLRB v. Brown, 380 U.S. 278 (1965), handed down the same day as the *American Ship* decision, the union, after a deadlock in contract negotiations, struck Food Jet, Inc., a member of the multiemployer bargaining unit, and the nonstruck members of the unit imposed a lockout. Despite the strike, Food Jet continued to operate with supervisors and temporary replacements, as did the nonstruck members. The Board held that the nonstruck members' use of temporary replacements in tandem with the defensive lockout violated §§8(a)(1) and 8(a)(3). The court of appeals denied enforcement and the Supreme Court (per Justice Brennan) affirmed (id. at 284):

> In the circumstances of this case, we do not see how the continued operations of respondents and their use of temporary replacements imply hostile motivation any more than the lockout itself; nor do we see how they are inherently more destructive of employee rights. Rather, the compelling inference is that this was all part and parcel of respondents' defensive measure to preserve the multiemployer group in the face of the whipsaw strike. Since

Food Jet legitimately continued business operations, it is only reasonable to regard respondents' action as evincing concern that the integrity of the employer group was threatened unless they also managed to stay open for business during the lockout. For with Food Jet open for business and respondents' stores closed, the prospect that the whipsaw strike would succeed in breaking up the employer association was not at all fanciful. The retail food industry is very competitive and repetitive patronage is highly important. Faced with the prospect of a loss of patronage to Food Jet, it is logical that respondents should have been concerned that one or more of their number might bolt the group and come to terms with the Local, thus destroying the common front essential to multiemployer bargaining. . . .

## *NOTES AND QUESTIONS*

**1. Pre-Impasse Lockouts.** Would the lockout in *American Ship* have been lawful if it had taken place before a bargaining impasse occurred? Given the Court's general rejection of the distinction between offensive and defense lockouts, is there any basis in the language of the statute, particularly §8(d), for requiring an employer to bargain to impasse before engaging in a bargaining lockout, especially in light of the traditional rule that pre-impasse strikes are lawful? In Darling & Co., 171 N.L.R.B. 801 (1968), enforced sub nom. Lane v. NLRB, 418 F.2d 1208 (D.C. Cir. 1969), the Board (4-1) stated: "the absence of an impasse does not itself make a lockout unlawful any more than the mere existence of an impasse automatically renders a lockout lawful." The Board reaffirmed this position in Harter Equipment, 280 N.L.R.B. 597, 598 n.6 (1986) ("The Board has held that the absence of impasse does not of itself make a lockout in support of bargaining demands unlawful [citing *Darling & Co.*]; neither does the absence of any reasonable fear of strike."), enforced sub nom. Operating Engineers Local 825 v. NLRB, 829 F.2d 458 (3d Cir. 1987).

Should the Board revisit its rules and require a bargaining impasse before resort to a strike or lockout? Note that under the Railway Labor Act, the parties cannot resort to economic self-help until the National Mediation Board has declared an impasse and proffers interest arbitration; even after such a proffer has been made and declined, the parties are subject to additional "cooling-off" periods. Does the Board have authority after *American Ship* to prohibit pre-impasse strikes or lockouts? If it does, what provision, if any, should be made for lockouts in anticipation of imminent strikes?

**2. Lockout Coupled with Hiring of Replacement Workers?**

a. *Temporary Replacements.* Is *Brown* limited to the multiemployer bargaining context, or may a single employer bargaining with a single union lock out its employees and then proceed to maintain operations with temporary replacements? Does this depend on whether the lockout is considered "defensive" rather than "offensive"? Should employers be permitted at the same time to adopt both offensive measures (by locking out in support of their bargaining position) and defensive measures (hiring temporary replacements to maintain operations)? Is there anything in *American Ship* that speaks to this issue?

How should the Court's *Great Dane* test be applied to this question? (Note that *American Ship* was decided after *Erie Resistor* but before *Great Dane.*) Does an employer's use of temporary replacements after locking out unit employees constitute action with an "inherently destructive" or "comparatively slight" impact on §7 rights? In any event, what would be the employer's legitimate business justification? The Board's current position is that the use of temporary replacements during an otherwise lawful lockout does not violate §8(a)(3), absent proof of anti-union motivation. See *Harter Equipment,* 280 N.L.R.B. 597 (1986), enforced sub nom. Local 825, IUOE v. NLRB, 829 F.3d 458 (3d Cir. 1987). Some courts, while affirming the Board's basic position, suggest some conditions on the use of this bargaining tactic:

> The pressure Harter brought to bear in this case also was not destructive of the employees' rights due to the use of temporary employees. In Inter-Collegiate Press [v. NLRB, 486 F.2d 837 (8th Cir. 1973)], the court noted three considerations in evaluating whether the use of temporary replacements had an inherently destructive or comparatively slight effect on employee rights. The court considered the duration of temporary employment and whether a definite date of termination had been communicated to the union and employees, and found that a definite date of duration for the temporary hires had been communicated. Second, the court noted that the option of returning to work was available to the employees upon their acceptance of the employer's terms, and third, the employer had agreed to continue in effect the union-security clause from the old contract.
>
> In this case, the ALJ considered these factors and found that although the advertisements for the replacement workers did not state that the positions were temporary, it was indeed the company's intention to return the regular employees to work at the conclusion of the dispute. In regard to the second factor, the ALJ . . . found that the union could have returned its members to work on terms less profitable than desired. As for the union-security clause, the company had agreed to the latest of a series of union proposed security clauses, only to have it withdrawn by the union. Thus, the company in effect had agreed to such a clause.

Local 825, 829 F.3d at 462. But cf. International Bhd. of Boilermakers, Local 88 v. NLRB, 858 F.2d 756 (D.C. Cir. 1988) (not referring to the *Harter* court's considerations). Did the *Harter* court claim questionable authority in suggesting that the employer's agreement to continue a particular term, the union security clause, might be a condition for using otherwise legal bargaining tactics?

b. *Permanent Replacements.* Is it lawful for an employer to hire permanent replacements after locking out its employees? Is this any different from an outright discharge for organizing or pressing disagreements with the employer? See International Paper Co. v. NLRB, 115 F.3d 1045, 1051 & nn.4-5 (D.C. Cir. 1997) (leaving open the question); but see Harborlite Corp., 357 N.L.R.B. 151 (2011). On the assumption that an employer violates the Act by offensively locking out its union-represented employees and then permanently replacing them, what if the employer acts in anticipation of an imminent strike deadline? Reconsider these questions after reading the note on *International Paper,* infra page 576. Should it matter if some employees have engaged in substantial violence during negotiations? See Johns-Manville Prods. Corp. v. NLRB, 557 F.2d 1126 (5th Cir. 1977) (employer's lockout and hiring of permanent replacements justified by employees' in-plant sabotage).

**3. "Mutual Aid" Pacts.** Employers in various industries have agreed to "mutual aid pacts," which call for nonstruck employers to pay to struck employers a share of the increased revenues accruing to the former because of a strike or which provide for payments to the struck firm out of "insurance funds" contributed by the participating employers. In Operating Engineers Local 12, 187 N.L.R.B. 430 (1970), the NLRB held that employer strike insurance programs are not subjects of mandatory bargaining and that a union's insistence on the elimination of such insurance violated §8(b)(3). Cf. Air Line Pilots Ass'n v. CAB, 502 F.2d 453 (D.C. Cir. 1974), where the court upheld the Civil Aeronautics Board's approval of the airlines' mutual aid pact as consistent with the national policy permitting parties to marshal economic resources to resolve labor disputes. For discussion of antitrust issues, see infra Chapter 10.

**4. Impact vs. Intent.** Does *American Ship* undermine the theoretical basis for continuing to insist that the only limit on the use of bargaining weapons is the antidiscrimination principle? What is left of that principle if, as the Court holds, the employer's desire to inflict the cost of disagreement on the union and its represented employees does not constitute unlawful motivation under §8(a)(3)? Does *Great Dane Trailers* provide a coherent answer? Do *Brown* and *Bonanno Linen,* supra page 497, suggest that good-faith bargaining principles under §§8(a)(5) and 8(b)(3) provide a preferable analytical approach for considering the legality of bargaining weapons? See Estreicher, Strikers and Replacements, supra.

**5. Partial Lockouts?** Assume that an employer is engaged in bargaining with a union that represents operators and maintenance personnel in the same unit. After impasse, the employer locks out only the maintenance workers. Has the employer violated §§8(a)(3) or 8(a)(5)? If the union calls the operators out on strike in response to the partial lockout, can the employer respond by maintaining operations with temporary help? With permanent replacements? Would the answer be the same if, instead of the partial lockout, the employer had temporarily suspended certain holiday and vacation benefits (not otherwise on the table) pending resolution of the contract dispute? Cf. United States Pipe and Foundry Co., 180 N.L.R.B. 325 (1969), enforced sub nom. Local 155, Int'l Molders v. NLRB, 442 F.2d 742 (1971); NLRB v. Great Falls Employers' Council, Inc., 277 F.2d 772 (9th Cir. 1960). If the concern is with the employer being able effectively, through a partial lockout, to compel a strike and hire permanent replacements for strikers, would it not be more direct to simply ban hiring of permanent replacements in the case of any lockout, partial or otherwise?

Are partial lockouts problematic for the additional reason that they create cleavages within the bargaining unit? In Bunting Bearings Corp., 343 N.L.R.B. No. 64 (2004), enforcement denied and remanded sub nom. United Steel, Paper, etc. Workers v. NLRB, 179 Fed. Appx. 61 (D.C. Cir. 2006) (unpublished), the Board held that the employer acted lawfully in selectively locking out only nonprobationary unit employees after a bargaining impasse. The Board majority reasoned that even if the probationary employees were not yet union members and all of the locked-out nonprobationary employees were, the parties' CBA treated probationary employees differently by making them subject to dismissal at will and excluding them from certain benefits, and the union also treated them differently by not including them in its post-lockout strike vote. The D.C. Circuit denied enforcement and remanded, stating as follows:

> In *Great Dane*, the Supreme Court held that if an employer has "engaged in discriminatory conduct which could have adversely affected employee rights to some extent," the employer must "establish that he was motivated by legitimate objectives." We reject the Board majority's contention that the Union failed to establish that Bunting's conduct was discriminatory—as the dissenting Board member explained, "no authority holds that [the Union] must initially do more than what [it] has done here: show a (perfect) correlation between union membership and which employees were locked out." . . . [T]he burden was on Bunting to present evidence showing that the lockout was motivated by legitimate objectives. Bunting did not even attempt to do this. In the absence of such an attempt, it was not appropriate for the ALJ or the Board to "speculate upon what might have motivated" Bunting. Great Dane, 388 U.S. at 34-35.

Id. at 63.

For similar rulings, see Local 15, IBEW v. Midwest Generation, 429 F.3d 651 (7th Cir. 2005) (employer violated §8(a)(3) in locking out employees who sought to return to work after the union had ended the strike without also locking out employees who returned before union halted the strike; employer presented no "operational needs" to justify partial lockout); Wayneview Care Center, 356 N.L.R.B. No. 30 (2010) ("even if the lockouts had been lawful at their inception, beginning September 6, 2005, [the employers] began allowing some employees but not others to return to work. The lockouts thus became partial lockouts. As found by the [ALJ, the employers] failed to show a legitimate and substantial business justification for reinstating some employees, but not others."), enforced, 664 F.3d 341 (D.C. Cir. 2011).

## 4. Subcontracting Struck Work

**Land Air Delivery, Inc. v. NLRB**
*862 F.2d 354 (D.C. Cir. 1988)*

Silberman, Circuit Judge. . . .

Land Air Delivery, Inc. is an air freight motor carrier that engages in the pickup and delivery of small packages for overnight carriers. In 1973, the Board certified Teamsters Local 41 as the exclusive bargaining agent of "[a]ll truck drivers and warehousemen" employed by Land Air. In 1975, the Board clarified the bargaining unit by excluding independent contractors who transported freight for Land Air. At the time of the strike that led to this litigation, Land Air employed 13 bargaining unit truckdrivers and used an additional group of independent contractor drivers.

The unit employees were covered by the Teamsters' National Master Freight Agreement ("NMFA"), which was effective from March 1, 1982 to March 31, 1985. The extent of Land Air's use of independent contractors was a major issue in the 1982 negotiations for a new contract. Petitioner presented at least three subcontracting proposals to the union during their negotiations, and the union rejected each one. The union insisted upon the more restrictive subcontracting language provided in Article 32 of the NMFA, which prohibited the subcontracting of work that employees in the bargaining unit performed. The parties eventually reached a bargaining impasse in late 1982 over the subcontracting language (and over an acceptable grievance machinery), and the union struck to enforce its demands. After three days, Land Air agreed to the subcontracting language in the NMFA.

In November 1984, the union notified the company that the union had authorized a strike, pursuant to the terms of the NMFA, to protest both the company's failure to comply with certain grievance awards and its refusal to take a deadlocked grievance to the next step of the grievance procedure. All 13 unit employees struck, and Land Air immediately hired replacement workers. To continue its business during the strike in Kansas City, Land Air used a mix of employees from other locations, its contractors and contractor drivers, newly-hired employees, and its own staff and supervisors. The company hired eight new employees in November and December 1984; three of these employees were terminated in December 1984, and five were terminated on March 28, 1985. Thus, as of March 28, 1985, Land Air had terminated all of its replacement employees.

The company also signed agreements with 12 independent contractors between February 20 and March 1, 1985. Five of these persons had not been contractors before the strike, and all 12 contractors continued to work for Land Air after the end of the strike. Although the exact timing is not clear from the record, the combination of subcontracting on February 20 and March 1 and termination of replacement employees on March 28 resulted in the elimination of all bargaining unit positions by March 1985.

The strike lasted almost five months, until April 1985, and it resulted in violent action by the strikers against replacement workers and company property. During the course of the strike, Land Air filed an unfair labor practice charge against the union stemming from these acts of violence and coercion. On February 4, 1985, the union entered into an informal settlement agreement, which contained a nonadmission clause, and it also issued a Notice to Employees and Members that it would not engage in coercive acts.

The strike ended on April 9, 1985, when the union members offered orally to return to work unconditionally. At that time, the general manager of Land Air informed the former strikers that there was no work for them. On April 11, the union's business agent communicated the same unconditional offer to Land Air by mail. Land Air took no action to reinstate the striking employees, and the union filed a charge against the company alleging that it had committed an unfair labor practice by refusing to reinstate the strikers. The Board's regional director dismissed the charge, finding that "the subject strike was an economic strike giving the employees the right to reinstatement only at such time when positions became available." Because Land Air had not hired any new employees since the unconditional offer of April 9, the regional director concluded that the company's refusal to reinstate the strikers was not a violation of the Act. . . .

. . . On February 20, 1986, the union filed an amended charge[, which resulted in the issuance of a complaint] alleging violations of sections 8(a)(1), (3), and (5), and specifying:

> On or about February 1, 1985, [Land Air] by its officers, agents and representatives subcontracted out bargaining unit work without notice to or bargaining with the Union.

> On or about April 9, 1985, [Land Air] by its officers, agents and representatives failed and refused to reinstate striking employees who had made an unconditional offer to return to work.

The administrative law judge found that Land Air had violated sections 8(a)(1), (3), and (5) of the Act by permanently subcontracting unit work without prior bargaining. He determined that by March 1985, petitioner had contracted out all bargaining unit positions. He ordered the company to reinstate nine strikers and directed that they receive backpay from Land Air (four of the striking employees were not ordered reinstated because of specific instances of employee misconduct). . . . The Board affirmed the ALJ's findings on these issues, and Land Air petitions this court for review.

## II

Petitioner contends that as a matter of law an employer is entitled to replace economic strikers permanently with subcontractors *at any time* during the strike without bargaining with the union over that decision. The Board, on the other hand, appears to maintain that an employer is *never* (even during an economic strike) permitted to subcontract permanently, without bargaining over the decision.[3] We reject petitioner's contention, and do not find it necessary, in order to resolve this case, to pass on the Board's proposition. Even if pressing "business necessity" would justify permanently contracting out unit work, Land Air has not shown such necessity here.

. . . Land Air claims that [NLRB v. Mackay Radio, 304 U.S. 333 (1938),] in effect "trumps" [Fibreboard Paper Prods. Corp. v. NLRB, 379 U.S. 203 (1964),] because there is no meaningful distinction between replacing strikers with permanent employees and replacing them with permanent subcontractors. We see at least a theoretical distinction, however, and that difference probably has practical consequences.

A permanent subcontract diminishes the bargaining unit by the scope of the subcontract. Contracting out all bargaining unit work, as occurred in this case, completely destroys the bargaining unit. Although as a practical matter it may be true that total replacement of strikers by new permanent

---

3. The Board urged that an employer has two options when faced with an economic strike: (1) it can hire permanent employee replacements or (2) it can contract out the work on a temporary basis. But cf. Elliott River Tours, Inc., 246 N.L.R.B. 935 (1979) (Board countenanced contracting out for two years, which exceeded the duration of the strike, because subcontractor demanded long term as condition for taking on the work). In view of *Elliott River Tours*, we do not take the Board's current position to preclude argument that at least long-term subcontracting is available in special circumstances, i.e., when permanent replacements or temporary subcontractors are not viable options.

employees will often result in a decertification of the union, there is a legal difference between the employer unilaterally dissolving the unit by contracting out its work and the employees in the unit themselves decertifying the union. Until decertification, the employer is obliged to bargain with the striking union over all terms and conditions of employment in the bargaining unit, and his obligation would be lessened if a portion of the work of the unit were permanently subcontracted. Bringing on permanent replacements, moreover, does not necessarily lead to the extinction of the bargaining unit. A striking union might be able to gain the allegiance of at least some of the replacement employees who, combined with strikers, could provide the union with continued majority support. We think, therefore, that the Board is within its authority to treat permanent subcontracting during a strike differently from the use of permanent employee replacements for purposes of section 8(a)(5) of the Act.

Despite our conclusion that permanent subcontracting is not legally equivalent to the use of permanent replacements, we still must confront the question whether permanent subcontracting violated the NLRA under the circumstances of this case. Petitioner relies for support primarily on the decision of the Ninth Circuit in Hawaii Meat Company v. NLRB, 321 F.2d 397 (9th Cir. 1963), where the court held that an employer's unilateral decision to subcontract work permanently during an economic strike did not violate section 8(a)(5). . . . In *Hawaii Meat,* the employer determined before the strike to subcontract permanently its hauling operations in the event of a strike, and it notified the union of its plans just before the strike. It was undisputed that the employer's purpose in subcontracting was totally defensive—to keep its plant operating during the strike. Id. at 399. The court rejected the Board's finding of a violation of section 8(a)(5), because to require an employer to bargain to impasse over a subcontracting decision under those exigent circumstances would be to give the union a practical veto over the decision. As the court observed, the union could easily delay an impasse and thereby prevent the employer from continuing business during the strike. See id. at 400. We read *Hawaii Meat,* then, to stand for no more than the proposition that an employer may not be obliged to bargain with a union about permanent subcontracting during a strike when that subcontracting is necessary to the business purpose of keeping the plant continuously in operation and time of decision is of the essence.

Although the Board has permitted unilateral subcontracting that extends beyond the end of a strike in a case where the subcontractor insisted on such an arrangement, see Elliott River Tours, 246 N.L.R.B. 935 (1979) (two year subcontract), it does not appear to have accepted even our narrow reading of *Hawaii Meat* that permanent subcontracting may be undertaken without first bargaining when needed to continue operations. See supra note 3. It is unnecessary for us to pass on the Board's reluctance to endorse *Hawaii Meat,* however, because it is clear to us that the ALJ was amply supported in his finding that petitioner's decision was not motivated by business necessity.

The subcontracting at issue in this case took place more than three months after the strike started, and Land Air had successfully operated during that entire period with a mixture of employees from other locations, prestrike contractors, new employees, and office staff and supervisors. Although the employer pointed to violence by union members and large security expenses as the business reason for the decision, the subcontracting did not take place until after the union had settled the employer's unfair labor practice charge stemming from the violence. Thus, since the ALJ found no evidence of violence after the entry of the settlement agreement, it was reasonable for him to conclude that the contracting out was not an effort to avoid violence. (If the ALJ's determination were unsupported, we would have quite a different case.) And, despite petitioner's contention that the employees themselves asked to be converted to subcontractors, the ALJ found that the employees had not demanded subcontractor status as a condition for their continued service. . . .

In the context of the past years of dispute between petitioner and the union over the degree of subcontracting, Land Air's decision to subcontract all of its driving work during the union's ineffective strike hardly looks motivated by business necessity. Rather, it appears that petitioner seized the opportunity it thought legally available to fashion a final solution to the dispute over the use of independent contractors. There is no reason to believe that negotiation with the union over that issue was any more inappropriate or anomalous in March 1985 than it had been in previous years. See American Cyanamid Co. v. NLRB, 592 F.2d 356, 361 (7th Cir. 1979). . . .

## *NOTES AND QUESTIONS*

**1. Duty to Bargain over Employer's Countermeasures to a Strike?** Is the Board's position in *Land Air* consistent with its position that an employer does not have to bargain over the terms of employment of replacement workers? See Service Elec. Co., 281 N.L.R.B. 633 (1986), discussed in *Curtin Matheson*, supra page 554; Detroit Newspaper Agency, 327 N.L.R.B. 871 (1999). Is a union ever likely to agree on the use of countermeasures against its strike?

When an employer decides to use permanent subcontractors, especially where it makes this decision prior to the strike as in *Hawaii Meat*, are we in the realm of employer counter measures to a strike (where bargaining is not required) or in the realm of permanent changes in terms and conditions of employment (where bargaining typically is required)? If bargaining is required, then the need to use such subcontractors to maintain operations would presumably be irrelevant.

**2. Strategic Use of "Permanent" Subcontractors?** If the hiring of permanent replacements during an economic strike is permissible, what justification is there for treating permanent subcontracting differently? Is it easier for an employer to maintain operations through such subcontracting rather than by selecting and training its own temporary hires? Is there a greater danger that the employer will act strategically, invoking the "permanency" of the subcontracting not out of necessity to maintain operations but rather to penalize strikers? It is assumed that the offer of permanency enhances the employer's ability to attract qualified replacement workers. Is the same true of an offer of permanency to subcontractors? How should the *Great Dane Trailers* test be applied to this case? See, e.g., Capehorn Industry, Inc., 336 N.L.R.B. 364 (2001).

**3. Permanent Subcontracting During a Lockout?** May an employer permanently subcontract out the work of employees whom it has locked out during collective bargaining? In International Paper Co., 319 N.L.R.B. 1253 (1995), the Board held that such conduct violated §8(a)(3) because it was "inherently destructive" of employees' §7 rights. The D.C. Circuit reversed, however. 115 F.3d 1045 (1997). In the court's view, as long as bargaining obligations are satisfied, an employer may implement a permanent subcontract during a lockout, just as it may do outside of the lockout context. In its view, the impact on §7 rights of implementation during a lockout is not so different as to render the employer's conduct "inherently destructive."

Did the court give adequate consideration to the ability of an employer to act strategically by locking out employees, then implementing a "permanent" subcontract that it can reverse once the union submits to its terms? Indeed, in *International Paper* itself the employer's agreement with the subcontractor provided that the end of the lockout "would constitute cause to terminate the permanent subcontract without penalty." 115 F.3d at 1047.

## B. REGULATION OF COLLECTIVE ACTION BY LABOR ORGANIZATIONS

### 1. Constitutional Limitations on Government Regulation

**Teamsters, Local 695 v. Vogt, Inc.**
*354 U.S. 284 (1957)*

Frankfurter, J. . . .

Respondent owns and operates a gravel pit in Oconomowoc, Wisconsin, where it employs 15 to 20 men. Petitioner unions sought unsuccessfully to induce some of respondent's employees to join the unions and commenced to picket the entrance to respondent's place of business with signs reading, "The men on this job are not 100% affiliated with the AFL." In consequence, drivers of several trucking companies refused to deliver and haul goods to and from respondent's plant, causing substantial damage to respondent. Respondent thereupon sought an injunction to restrain the picketing.

The trial court did not make the finding, requested by respondent:

> That the picketing of plaintiff's premises has been engaged in for the purpose of coercing, intimidating and inducing the employer to force, compel, or induce its employees to become members of defendant labor organizations, and for the purpose of injuring the plaintiff in its business because of its refusal to in any way interfere with the rights of its employees to join or not to join a labor organization.

It nevertheless held that by virtue of Wis. Stat. §103.535, prohibiting picketing in the absence of a "labor dispute," the petitioners must be enjoined from maintaining any pickets near respondent's place of business, from displaying at any place near respondent's place of business signs indicating that there was a labor dispute between respondent and its employees or between respondent and any of the petitioners, and from inducing others to decline to transport goods to and from respondent's business establishment. . . .

. . . Although the trial court had refused to make the finding requested by respondent, the [state] Supreme Court, noting that the facts as to which the request was made were undisputed, drew the inference from the undisputed facts and itself made the finding. It canvassed the whole circumstances surrounding the picketing and held that "One would be credulous, indeed, to believe under the circumstances that the union had no thought of coercing the employer to interfere with its employees in their right to join or refuse to join the defendant union." Such picketing, the court held, was for "an unlawful purpose," since Wis. Stat. §111.06(2)(b) made it an unfair labor practice for an employee individually or in concert with others to "coerce, intimidate or induce any employer to interfere with any of his employees in the enjoyment of their legal rights . . . or to engage in any practice with regard to his employees which would constitute an unfair labor practice if undertaken by him on his own initiative." . . . [T]he Wisconsin Supreme Court therefore affirmed the granting of the injunction. . . .

. . . [I]n passing on a restrictive instead of a permissive state statute, th[is] Court made sweeping pronouncements about the right to picket in holding unconstitutional a statute that had been applied to ban all picketing, with "no exceptions based upon either the number of persons engaged in the proscribed activity, the peaceful character of their demeanor, the nature of their dispute with an employer, or the restrained character and the accurateness of the terminology used in notifying the public of the facts of the dispute." Thornhill v. Alabama, 310 U.S. 88, 99. As the statute dealt at large with all picketing, so the Court broadly assimilated peaceful picketing in general to freedom of speech, and as such protected against abridgment by the Fourteenth Amendment. . . .

Soon, however, the Court came to realize that the broad pronouncements, but not the specific holding, of *Thornhill* had to yield "to the impact of facts unforeseen," or at least not sufficiently appreciated. . . . Cases reached the Court in which a State had designed a remedy to meet a specific situation or to accomplish a particular social policy. These cases made manifest that picketing, even though "peaceful," involved more than just communication of ideas and could not be immune from all state regulation. "Picketing by an organized group is more than free speech, since it involves patrol of a particular locality and since the very presence of a picket line may induce action of one kind or another, quite irrespective of the nature of the ideas which are being disseminated." Bakery Drivers Local v. Wohl, 315 U.S. 769, 776 (concurring opinion); see Carpenters Union v. Ritter's Cafe, 315 U.S. 722, 725-728. . . .

The implied reassessments of the broad language of the *Thornhill* case were finally generalized in a series of cases sustaining injunctions against peaceful picketing, even when arising in the course of a labor controversy, when such picketing was counter to valid state policy in a domain open to state regulation. The decisive reconsideration came in Giboney v. Empire Storage & Ice Co., 336 U.S. 490. A union, seeking to organize peddlers, picketed a wholesale dealer to induce it to refrain from selling to nonunion peddlers. The state courts, finding that such an agreement would constitute a conspiracy in restraint of trade in violation of the state antitrust laws, enjoined the picketing. This Court affirmed unanimously. . . .

The Court . . . concluded that it was "clear that appellants were doing more than exercising a right of free speech or press. . . . They were exercising their economic power together with that of their allies to compel Empire to abide by union rather than by state regulation of trade." Id., at 503. . . .

[Our decisions have] established a broad field in which a State, in enforcing some public policy, whether of its criminal or its civil law, and whether announced by its legislature or its courts, could constitutionally enjoin peaceful picketing aimed at preventing *effectuation of that policy*. . . .

Of course, the mere fact that there is "picketing" does not automatically justify its restraint without an investigation into its conduct and purposes. . . . In this case, the circumstances set forth in the opinion of the Wisconsin Supreme Court afford a rational basis for the inference it drew concerning the purpose of the picketing. No question was raised here concerning the breadth of the injunction, but of course its terms must be read in the light of the opinion of the Wisconsin Supreme Court, which justified it on the ground that the picketing was for the purpose of coercing the employer to coerce his employees. . . .

WHITTAKER, J. took no part in the consideration or decision of this case.

DOUGLAS, J. with whom the Chief Justice and BLACK, J., concur, dissenting.

. . . [W]here, as here, there is no rioting, no mass picketing, no violence, no disorder, no fisticuffs, no coercion — indeed nothing but speech — the principles announced in *Thornhill* and *Swing* should give the advocacy of one side of a dispute First Amendment protection. . . .

Today, the Court [holds that state] courts and state legislatures are free to decide whether to permit or suppress any particular picket line for any reason other than a blanket policy against all picketing. I would adhere to the principle announced in *Thornhill.* I would adhere to the result reached in *Swing.* I would return to the test enunciated in *Giboney* — that this form of expression can be regulated or prohibited only to the extent that it forms an essential part of a course of conduct which the State can regulate or prohibit. I would reverse the judgment below.

## *NOTES AND QUESTIONS*

**1. Status of Labor Picketing Under the First Amendment.** Under *Vogt* and antecedent decisions, labor picketing appears to have been treated as a form of economic pressure subject to reasonable state regulation rather than as a form of communication generally exempt from regulation by virtue of the First Amendment. This treatment of labor picketing was reaffirmed by the Court in NLRB v. Retail Stores, 447 U.S. 607 (1980), infra page 613. By contrast, picketing by political groups is generally treated as expression fully protected by the First Amendment. What is the justification, if any, for the apparently special status of labor picketing? Consider the following rationales:

a. Labor Picketing "calls for an automatic response to a signal, rather than a reasoned response to an idea." Retail Stores, 447 U.S. at 619 (Stevens, J., concurring). But doesn't protected expression often take the form of reference to symbols and intuitive appeals to solidarity? See, e.g., Tinker v. Des Moines Indep. Community Sch. Dist., 393 U.S. 503 (1969) (protecting the wearing of black armbands to symbolize opposition to Vietnam War); Stromberg v. California, 283 U.S. 359 (1931) (protecting the display of a red flag "as a sign, symbol or emblem of opposition to organized government").

b. "Labor picketing is 'speech plus' activity because it involves martial aspects." Does this justify anything more than regulation to ensure that picketers do not interfere with access and egress? See, e.g., NAACP v.

Claiborne Hardware Co., 458 U.S. 886 (1982) (protecting peaceful picketing of businesses by civil rights groups and holding that state could impose liability only on those who threatened or engaged in violence).

c. Labor Picketing is a "form of pressure [that] is applied by closely knit, powerful organizations. . . ." It is supported by a system of power based upon common economic interests, loyalties, social pressures, economic sanctions, and bureaucratic force. A labor picket is thus not so much a rational appeal to persuasion as a "signal for the application of immediate and enormous economic leverage, based upon an already prepared position." Thomas I. Emerson, The System of Freedom of Expression 445 (1970). Does this justify regulation of picketing aimed at the general public rather than labor groups? See Archibald Cox, Freedom of Expression in the Burger Court, 94 Harv. L. Rev. 1, 36-37 (1980). Moreover, even where aimed at labor groups, is the mere appeal to the labor community regulable, or need there be proof of prior agreements among labor organizations to honor each other's picket lines? Is this what Justice Douglas means by expression that "forms an essential part of a course of conduct which the State can regulate or prohibit"? See Michael C. Harper, The Consumer's Emerging Right to Boycott: *NAACP v. Claiborne Hardware* and Its Implications for American Labor Law, 93 Yale L.J. 409 (1984).

d. "Labor picketing can be regulated as part of an integrated scheme which affirmatively protects labor groups in their right to organize and pursue economic objectives by concerted action." Can constitutional rights be traded away in this manner? Even if government can repeal the Wagner Act and other affirmative protections, does that fact give government the authority to condition those protections on a waiver of generally applicable constitutional rights?

**2. Is Worker Center Picketing "Labor Picketing"?** Many worker centers advocate on behalf of low-wage workers, but do so without the intention to become the bargaining representative of the majority of employees. They often address a wide array of issues that affect low-wage workers such as housing, education, immigrant rights and workplace concerns. Cf. Kati L. Griffith, The NLRA Defamation Defense: Doomed Dinosaur or Diamond in the Rough?, 59 Am. U. L. Rev. 1 (2009). If a worker center pickets an employer to protest the employer's underpayment of minimum wages, would it be considered labor picketing and receive truncated protection under the First Amendment? Can it be considered labor picketing without the prospect of other unions refusing to cross the picket line? Does it matter that the worker center is demanding compliance with existing minimum wage law, rather than pushing for terms and conditions above statutory minima? Would it matter that the worker center otherwise spent most of its energies focused on education and advocacy on behalf of legislative changes? Consider these questions in light of the justifications listed in the preceding note. Worker centers and the relationship between labor law and immigration will be taken up in Chapter 14 infra.

**3. The Canadian Approach.** In 2002, the Supreme Court of Canada unanimously held that per se bans on secondary picketing conflict with the Canadian Charter of Rights and Freedoms by inadequately protecting freedom of expression. See Pepsi-Cola Canada Beverages (West) Ltd. v. Retail, Wholesale & Dept. Store Union, Local 558, 2002 SCC 8, 2002 Can. Sup. Ct. LEXIS 9. The Court adopted a "wrongful action" model that allows picketing (whether primary or secondary) to be outlawed where it constitutes either criminal or tortious conduct. Here, it noted that tortious conduct includes not only trespass, nuisance, intimidation, defamation, and misrepresentation, but also the tort of "inducing breach of contract." The Court also indicated that provincial legislatures and courts remained free to "supplement" the wrongful action approach and develop their own policies regarding secondary picketing, although they must "respect the Charter value of free expression and be prepared to justify limiting it."

**4. Producer vs. Consumer Boycotts.** In International Longshoremen's Ass'n v. Allied Int'l, Inc., 456 U.S. 212 (1982), a case arising out of the protest by the International Longshoremen's Association (ILA) against the Soviet invasion of Afghanistan, longshoremen along the East and Gulf coast refused to handle cargo arriving from or destined for the Soviet Union. Allied, an American company, imported Russian wood products on ships operated by Waterman, which in turn employed Clark, a stevedoring company under contract with the ILA. The union boycott disrupted Allied's shipments, and Allied filed secondary boycott charges under §8(b)(4) and brought an action for damages under §303. The Supreme Court held that the ILA boycott was an illegal secondary boycott. The Court also summarily dismissed the union's First Amendment contention (456 U.S. at 226):

> We have consistently rejected the claim that secondary picketing by labor unions in violation of §8(b)(4) is protected activity under the First Amendment. . . . It would seem even clearer that conduct designed not to communicate but to coerce merits still less consideration under the First Amendment. The labor laws reflect a careful balancing of interests. . . . There are many ways in which a union and its individual members may express their opposition to Russian foreign policy without infringing upon the rights of others.

By contrast, in *NAACP v. Claiborne Hardware Co.*, supra, the Court held that an NAACP boycott of white businesses was constitutionally protected activity despite threats by an NAACP official, Charles Evers, that "[i]f we catch any of you going into any of them racist stores, we're gonna break your goddam neck." The Court explained (458 U.S. at 928):

> [T]he emotionally charged rhetoric of Charles Evers' speeches did not transcend the bounds of protected speech. . . . The lengthy addresses generally contained an impassioned plea for black citizens to unify, to support and respect each other, and to realize the political and economic power available to them. In the course of those pleas, strong language was used. If the language had been followed by acts of violence, a substantial question would be presented whether Evers could be held liable for the consequences of that unlawful conduct. In this case, however, . . . [the] acts of violence . . . occurred weeks or months after [the] speech. . . . An advocate must be free to stimulate his audience with spontaneous and emotional appeals for unity and action in a common cause.

Is there a principled distinction between the two cases? Note, that the ILA boycott had a purely political objective whereas the NAACP boycott (despite the Court's willingness to attach the "political" label) was prompted in large part by economic objectives. Does this argue for a greater level of constitutional protection for the ILA boycott than it received? See Laurence H. Tribe, Constitutional Choices 201 (1985): "The contrast between *ILA* and *Claiborne* illustrates the utter manipulability of the political-economic distinction and the Court's hostility [to] the First Amendment rights of unions." Do you agree? Consider the following distinction:

> . . . Our society should be more concerned about the coercive impact of business boycotts, or even employee boycotts, than about the effects of consumer boycotts. Consumer boycotts deserve protection in our democracy in part because every consumer has roughly the same economic voting potential. When a group of consumers of personal goods and services exerts leverage over economic, political, or social decisions, other individuals with equally intense feelings can respond roughly in proportion to their numbers. By contrast, individuals as producers and owners of capital have specialized and very unequal market power. By threatening to withhold their services or capital, some individuals can exert disproportionate leverage over important social decisions. Consumers, who are not in special economic roles, cannot effectively counter these threats even though their feelings may be equally intense.
>
> Thus, while the Supreme Court found illegal the longshoremen's refusal to handle cargo destined to or arriving from the Soviet Union following the Soviet invasion of Afghanistan, that decision is fully consistent with *Claiborne Hardware*. The longshoremen, by virtue of their specialized role in the economy, have a potential influence on American foreign policy drastically disproportionate to their numbers in our society.

Harper, The Consumer's Emerging Right to Boycott, supra, at 426-427.

**5. Political Boycotts and Exposure to the Antitrust Laws.** Does the First Amendment insulate from antitrust regulation union boycotts appealing to union members and supporters to withhold their patronage from particular companies rather than their services? Do such boycotts have to have purely political purposes to be constitutionally protected or can they also be motivated by economic considerations? Cf. Missouri v. National Org. of Women, Inc., 620 F.2d 1301 (8th Cir. 1980) (immunizing from Sherman Act challenge campaign to encourage supporters of a proposed Equal Rights Amendment to the Constitution to withhold convention business from nonratifying states). But cf. generally Ronald E. Kennedy, Political Boycotts: The Sherman Act and the First Amendment, 55 S. Cal. L. Rev. 983 (1982) (urging a "rule of reason" analysis rather than a per se exemption for political boycotts).

**6. Handbilling.** Should labor handbilling receive greater First Amendment protection than labor picketing? See Edward J. DeBartolo Corp. v. Florida Gulf Coast Bldg. & Constr. Trades Council, 485 U.S. 568 (1988), infra page 618; see also Warshawsky & Co. v. NLRB, 182 F.3d 948 (D.C. Cir. 1999).

**7. Stationary Protests.** Should passive techniques of communication that do not require interaction with consumers or bystanders, such as large banners or inflated figures, receive greater First Amendment protection than labor picketing? What about a mock funeral procession? See Overstreet v. United Bhd. of Carpenters, 409 F.3d 1199 (9th Cir. 2005); Kentov v. Sheet Metal Workers, 418 F.3d 1259 (11th Cir. 2005); see also infra page 622, note 4.

**8. Picketing at Residences or Other Sites Remote from the Primary Dispute.** Does the limited constitutional protection of picketing arising from labor disputes extend to picketing at places physically remote from the establishment involved in the dispute, for example, at the residence of the owner or chief executive of the employer or the school attended by his child? See Carey v. Brown, 447 U.S. 455, 470 (1980) (Illinois statute prohibiting residential picketing but exempting "peaceful picketing of a place of employment involved in a labor dispute" declared invalid on equal protection grounds, but with the Court noting that "[w]e are not to be understood to imply, however, that residential picketing is beyond the reach of uniform and non-discriminatory regulation"); Frisby v. Schultz, 487 U.S. 474 (1988) (local ordinance prohibiting focused picketing around the residence of any individual is narrowly tailored and does not violate the First Amendment).

**9. Libel.** Does the First Amendment bar an injunction against picketing with libelous placards during a labor dispute? Against a union's distribution of libelous leaflets to pedestrians adjacent to an employer's premises? See Old Dominion Branch No. 496, Letter Carriers v. Austin, 418 U.S. 264 (1974); Linn v. Plant Guard Workers, 383 U.S. 53 (1966).

## 2. Secondary Pressures

Although "secondary boycotts" were generally illegal at common law, that term was ill defined. See Charles O. Gregory & Harold A. Katz, Labor and the Law 39-51, 120-157 (3d ed. 1979); Robert C. Barnard & Robert W. Graham, Labor and the Secondary Boycott, 15 Wash. L. Rev. 137 (1940). Its core meaning, however, was reflected in a standard definition appearing in Felix Frankfurter & Nathan Greene, The Labor Injunction 43 (1930): "a combination to influence A by exerting some sort of economic or social pressure against persons who deal with A." The proscription of secondary boycotts by unions was designed to bar the deliberate extension of labor's pressures, such as strikes and picketing, beyond the employer with whom a union had a dispute (the primary employer) to other firms doing business with the primary employer but unable directly to settle the primary dispute (the secondary employers).

Section 8(b)(4)(A) of the Taft-Hartley Act did not use the term "secondary boycotts," but its legislative history showed that Congress's purpose had been to reinstate union liabilities for such boycotts under the NLRA rather than under the Sherman Act. Recall that the Supreme Court in 1941 virtually eliminated those liabilities by ruling that the Norris-LaGuardia Act immunized unions against antitrust liability, criminal and civil, for secondary boycotts. See *United States v. Hutcheson*, supra page 42.

The principal statutory provisions on the secondary boycott prohibition are now embodied in §§8(b)(4)(A)-(B), 8(e), and 10(*l*) of the NLRA and §303 of the LMRA. Section 8(b)(4)(B) prohibits a union from pressuring secondary employers to "cease doing business" with the primary employer. Section 8(e) declares unlawful certain contractual provisions thought to further secondary objectives, and §8(b)(4)(A) prohibits a strike for the purpose of securing an agreement violative of §8(e). Section 10(*l*) obligates the Board to give priority to charges alleging violations of §§8(b)(4), 8(e), and 8(b)(7), and requires NLRB Regional Directors to seek interim injunctive relief in the district courts if they have "reasonable cause to believe that such charge is true." Finally, §303, in a departure from the NLRA's exclusive administrative enforcement of unfair labor practice charges, permits employers and others injured by §8(b)(4) violations to sue directly in federal court to recover damages.

To establish a violation of §8(b)(4), a union must be shown to have used improper means in support of an improper objective. Two types of pressures are proscribed: (1) pressures directed at employees of "any person" to induce a work stoppage (§8(b)(4)(i)), and (2) pressures directed at "any person" (presumably representatives of employers) that amount to threats, coercion, or restraint of such person (§8(b)(4)(ii)). In addition, these methods must be used in the service of an improper object. Under clause (A), the principal prohibited object is forcing an employer to enter into a §8(e) agreement or to join a union. Under clause (B) — the hallmark secondary boycott provision — the prohibited object is forcing any person "to cease handling products of any other employer" or "to cease doing business with any other person." Clause (C), a forerunner to §8(b)(7), is concerned with forcing an employer to recognize or bargain with a union if another union has been certified.

There are three provisos to §8(b)(4). The first, applicable in terms only to §8(b)(4)(B), preserves otherwise lawful primary strikes or primary picketing. The second and third provisos apply to §8(b)(4) as a whole. The second proviso states that the section does not make it unlawful to honor a picket line maintained at the premises of another employer; the third protects certain nonpicketing publicity.

### *a. The Primary/Secondary Distinction*

**Howard Lesnick, The Gravamen of the Secondary Boycott***
*62 Colum. L. Rev. 1361, 1412-1414 (1962)*

If a company finds that one of its customers or suppliers has been shut by a strike, normal business relations between the two employers automatically cease; employees of the company seeking to enter the struck plant will find it closed, and the strikers will, of course, not be performing whatever work has been necessary to the doing of business with the secondary. The extent of injury to that company will depend on the particular economic relationships. It may or may not feel compelled to seek to induce the other employer to settle the dispute. In either event, the pressure generated flows entirely from the disruption of the struck employer's business. If, now, the struck employer is continuing to operate, but the employees of the secondary refuse to enter, the effect on the company is no different. In the one case, the gates are physically locked; in the other, though literally open, they are in effect impassable. The legislative policy, for the most part protecting successful strike activity despite the described effect on secondary employers, suggests the inapplicability of a policy designed to protect secondary and not primary employers from identical effects flowing from wholly or partially unsuccessful strike activity.

Suppose, however, that a picket induces one of the company's drivers not only to turn away from the struck plant, but to refuse to make deliveries to any other company, so long as his employer continues to attempt to deal with the struck company. Such pressure, whatever its strength, is "essentially

* [The following essay offers an insightful analysis of the underlying rationale of the secondary boycott provision, even if it does not reflect existing law in every respect. — Eds.]

different" in that it does not grow out of the interference with the primary's business threatened by the strike against it. It seeks to jump that hurdle and conscript the neutral by subjecting it to independent, directly applied loss of service that would not otherwise be suffered even were the struck plant to cease operations entirely. Here, I submit, the protection afforded to secondary employers by §8(b)(4) is called into play, and that afforded the strike by the Act is not at stake.

A similar analysis can be made as to secondary site picketing. An employer who processes materials manufactured by another will feel significantly the loss of trade flowing from the shutting down by a strike of the manufacturer's operations. If the strike fails to close the primary's doors, but "roving situs" pickets induce secondary employees to refuse to unload goods delivered by the primary's nonstriking employees, the effect on the secondary is largely the same as if the delivery, by reason of the success of the strike, could not have been attempted. But if the pickets induce secondary employees to quit all work, whether connected with the primary or not, or induce employees of third persons to refuse to enter the secondary premises, pressure wholly apart from that which could attend the disruption of the primary's business is felt.

In considering the applicability of this analysis to secondary site activities, however, complicating considerations arise. When no primary employees are present at the secondary site, the Act plainly condemns inducement of secondary employees to refuse to work on materials coming there from the primary, even though the inducement be only "partial," that is, limited to those materials. Yet it is clear that the strike, if successful in closing down the primary employer's business, would deprive the secondary of the opportunity to work on such "hot goods." The suggested rationale, then, can not encompass all secondary employee refusals to work that are no broader than those which would "automatically" be occasioned by the disruption of the primary's operation through a wholly successful strike. Only the effect of loss of the primary's employees may be considered. The crucial question, thus modified, is: does the picketing union intend to subject the secondary employer to a loss of the services of his employees broader in impact than would be directly caused by the unavailability, as a result of the complete success of the strike, of the services of the primary employees? If so, the picketing is secondary; otherwise, it is primary.

### *Note: The Relationship Between Theories of the Strike and the Permissible Scope of Secondary Pressures*

Professor Lesnick explains why §8(b)(4) has not been read to reach appeals to employees of a neutral employer to not cross picket lines to pick up goods being produced at a struck employer's plant. See NLRB v.

International Rice Milling, 341 U.S. 665 (1951). He also correctly notes, however, that §8(b)(4) condemns pressures exerted at the premises of the secondary employer when the primary employer's workers are not present at the secondary site. Thus, the law does not always permit the striking union to attempt by secondary pressures to approximate the effects on the secondary employer that would flow from a fully successful shutdown of production at the primary employer. Consider Professor Weiler's proposal:

> In the vast majority of strikes, . . . including those causing the greatest external damage, our society recognizes and accepts the notion that harm to such innocent parties is the price that must be paid to maintain our system of free collective bargaining. Only in the secondary boycott situation — in which the employer has been able to operate during the strike — does the NLRB step in to protect ostensibly "innocent" parties. In this case, not only does the law intervene, but it goes out of its way to insure that the secondary employer does not suffer even the rather insignificant harm caused by its own workers' refusal to handle a single struck product that may constitute only a tiny share of its overall business. Whatever the manifest justification for Section 8(b)(4), its latent function and practical impact are to tilt the balance of power even further toward the employer in those disputes in which *Mackay Radio* makes a significant difference in the employer's arsenal: strikes involving small units of unskilled workers struggling for first contracts in settings of low union density and high unemployment.
>
> I suggest, then, a single change in the current scope of our anti-boycott law. This law should characterize as *primary* activity a request by a striking union to other workers not to provide services to or handle products from the affected operations of a struck employer. Such a hands-off legal posture toward the efforts of striking workers would correspond to the similar stance the law now takes toward the employer's effort to continue operating during the strike.

Paul C. Weiler, Governing the Workplace: The Future of Labor and Employment Law 267, 271-272 (1990).

Would this proposal permit a union to seek to induce employees of retailers to refuse to handle the primary's struck product? Does the proposal draw a distinction between the primary's products and the primary's services? Would it, for example, permit a union to seek to prevent secondary employees from working in a plant cleaned by substitutes for striking employees of an industrial cleaner? Do appeals to secondary employees not to use goods or services from a struck employer often disrupt the secondary's operations to a greater extent than would a completely successful primary strike?

What is the justification for the underlying premise of both the Lesnick and Weiler articles — that a union should be able to attempt by secondary pressures to bring about what it could not accomplish directly by a strike of the primary facility? Is it a notion of parity of weaponry in an economic struggle? Under this logic, if the employer is permitted to attempt to maintain operations during a strike, then the employees should be allowed all means short of violence or physical obstruction "to foil the employer's continuing to operate." See Weiler, supra, at 271. Professor Weiler would not support an extension of the boycott to include the entire line of business of the secondary firm because this would expose the third party to greater harm than would be occasioned by a fully successful primary strike. But why adopt this limitation if the union needs to extend its dispute, perhaps because employees of the secondary firm are willing to work on the struck goods?

If, however, the strike is viewed as a means of testing not only the resolve of the parties but also the reasonableness in the marketplace of the positions of the parties, should any appeals to other employees not substituting for strikers be permitted, whether at secondary or primary sites? Where the union is unable to halt production at the primary employer because substitute sources for the services of represented workers are readily obtainable on the terms offered to and rejected by the union, why permit the union additional leverage by means of alliances with other labor groups? But does this position adequately give effect to a view of the congressional purpose that would permit labor groups, within certain limits, to attempt to alter market outcomes?

### *b. "Ally" Doctrine*

Any attempt to apply the primary/secondary distinction requires an initial definition of who is the "primary" employer. If the picketing takes places at the premises of another firm that is deemed to be an "ally" of the struck employer, the statutory prohibition of secondary-situs picketing does not apply.

### **NLRB v. Business Machine, Local 459 (*Royal Typewriter Co.*)**
*228 F.2d 553 (2d Cir. 1955)*

LUMBARD, J. . . .

The [NLRB] now seeks enforcement of an order directing the Union to cease and desist from certain picketing. . . .

The findings of the Board . . . disclose the following [virtually undisputed] facts. On about March 23, 1954, the Union, being unable to reach agreement with Royal on the terms of a contract, called the Royal service personnel out on strike. The service employees customarily repair typewriters either at Royal's branch offices or at its customers' premises. Royal has several arrangements under which it is obligated to render service to its customers. First, Royal's warranty on each new machine obligates it to provide free inspection and repair for one year. Second, for a fixed periodic fee Royal contracts to service machines not under warranty. Finally, Royal is committed to repairing typewriters rented from it or loaned by it to replace machines undergoing repair. Of course, in addition Royal provides repair services on call by noncontract users.

During the strike Royal differentiated between calls from customers to whom it owed a repair obligation and others. Royal's office personnel were instructed to tell the latter to call some independent repair company listed in the telephone directory. Contract customers, however, were advised to select such an independent from the directory, to have the repair made, and to send a receipted invoice to Royal for reimbursement for reasonable repairs within their agreement with Royal. Consequently many of Royal's contract customers had repair services performed by various independent repair companies. In most instances the customer sent Royal the unpaid repair bill and Royal paid the independent company directly. Among the independent companies paid directly by Royal for repairs made for such customers were Typewriter Maintenance and Sales Company and Tytell Typewriter Company. . . .

. . . [T]he Union picketed some of Royal's larger customers whom it had reason to believe were having independent companies do repair work on Royal contract machines. This picketing continued until restrained on June 15, 1954 by a temporary injunction issued by the District Court for the Southern District of New York. . . .

[T]he Board found that the picketing of these companies took place before entrances "commonly used by members of the public, by employees of the picketed firm, and by employees of any other tenants of the building, and also by deliverymen making light deliveries." There was no evidence that the picketing took place at entrances used exclusively by employees. . . .

From April 13th until April 23rd, . . . the pickets carried signs reading . . . (with the picketed customer's name inserted):

Royal Business Machines In<br>
N.Y. Life Ins. Co.<br>
are being repaired by<br>
Scab Labor<br>
Local 459, IUE-CIO

Sometime after April 23rd the words "Notice to the Public Only" were added to the signs in large letters at the top. . . . The picketing was carried on during ordinary business hours. . . .

One of the picketed customers, Charles Pfizer, did agree to discontinue doing business with Royal and the Union withdrew its pickets. There is no evidence to indicate that this came about through any pressure on or from any of Pfizer's employees.

The Board found, and it is conceded, that an object of the picketing of Royal's customers was to induce the customers to cease doing business with Royal. The Union contended that it sought to do this only by embarrassing the firms picketed and bringing its grievance to the attention of the customers of those firms and the general public. The Trial Examiner found that the picketing constituted inducement and encouragement of employees, that the Union's professed intent not to influence employees was no defense, and that the picketing was therefore unlawful. These findings the Board adopted.

During May 1954 the Union also picketed four independent typewriter repair companies who had been doing work covered by Royal's contracts pursuant to the arrangement described above. The Board found this picketing unlawful with respect to Typewriter Maintenance and Tytell. . . . In each instance the picketing, which was peaceful and orderly, took place before entrances used in common by employees, deliverymen and the general public. The signs read substantially as follows (with the appropriate repair company name inserted):

Notice To The Public Only
Employees Of Royal Typewriter Co.
On Strike
Tytell Typewriter Company Employees Are Being Used
As Strikebreakers

---

Business Machine & Office Appliance Mechanics Union,
Local 459, IUE-CIO

Both before and after this picketing, . . . Tytell and Typewriter Maintenance did work on Royal accounts and received payment directly from Royal. . . . [E]ach independent serviced various of Royal's customers on numerous occasions and received payment directly from Royal.

With one exception there was no evidence that the picketing of either the customers or the repair companies resulted in a strike or refusal to work by any employee. . . . [N]o employee ceased work or refused to operate any Royal typewriter or other machine. . . .

. . . [T]he Trial Examiner and the Board found that both the customer picketing and the repair company picketing violated §8(b)(4)[(A)]. . . . [T]he Board's finding with respect to the repair company picketing cannot be sustained. The independent repair companies were so allied with Royal that the Union's picketing of their premises was not prohibited by §8(b)(4)(A).*

---

* [Reference to §8(b)(4)(A) is to the 1947 text. As a result of the 1959 Landrum-Griffin amendments, this provision is now labeled §8(b)(4)(B).—Eds.]

We approve the "ally" doctrine which had its origin in a well reasoned opinion by Judge Rifkind in the Ebasco case, Douds v. Metropolitan Federation of Architects, Engineers, Chemists & Technicians, Local 231, D.C.S.D.N.Y. 1948, 75 F. Supp. 672, 676. Ebasco, a corporation engaged in the business of providing engineering services, had a close business relationship with Project, a firm providing similar services. Ebasco subcontracted some of its work to Project and when it did so Ebasco supervised the work of Project's employees and paid Project for the time spent by Project's employees on Ebasco's work plus a factor for overhead and profit. When Ebasco's employees went on strike, Ebasco transferred a greater percentage of its work to Project, including some jobs that had already been started by Ebasco's employees. When Project refused to heed the Union's request to stop doing Ebasco's work, the Union picketed Project and induced some of Project's employees to cease work. On these facts Judge Rifkind found that Project was not "doing business" with Ebasco within the meaning of §8(b)(4)(A) and that the Union had therefore not committed an unfair labor practice under that section. He reached this result by looking to the legislative history of the Taft-Hartley Act and to the history of the secondary boycotts which it sought to outlaw. He determined that Project was not a person "'wholly unconcerned in the disagreement between an employer and his employees'" such as §8(b)(4)(A) was designed to protect. . . .

Here there was evidence of only one instance where Royal contacted an independent (Manhattan Typewriter Service, not named in the complaint) to see whether it could handle some of Royal's calls. Apart from that incident there is no evidence that Royal made any arrangement with an independent directly. It is obvious, however, that what the independents did would inevitably tend to break the strike. As Judge Rifkind pointed out in the *Ebasco* case: "The economic effect upon Ebasco's employees was precisely that which would flow from Ebasco's hiring strikebreakers to work on its own premises." And at 95 Cong. Rec. (1949) page 8709 Senator Taft said: "The spirit of the Act is not intended to protect a man who . . . is with a primary employer and taking his work and doing the work which he is unable to do because of the strike." . . .

. . . [T]he picketing of the independent typewriter companies was not the kind of secondary activity which §8(b)(4)(A) of the Taft-Hartley Act was designed to outlaw. Where an employer is attempting to avoid the economic impact of a strike by securing the services of others to do his work, the striking union obviously has a great interest, and we think a proper interest, in preventing those services from being rendered. This interest is more fundamental than the interest in bringing pressure on customers of the primary employer. Nor are those who render such services completely uninvolved in the primary strike. By doing the work of the primary employer they secure benefits themselves at the time that they aid the primary employer. The ally employer may easily extricate himself from the dispute and insulate himself from picketing by refusing to do that work. A case may arise where the ally employer is unable to determine that the work he is doing is "farmed-out." We need not decide whether the picketing of such an employer would be lawful, for that is not the situation here. The existence of the strike, the receipt of checks from Royal, and the picketing itself certainly put the independents on notice that some of the work they were doing might be work farmed-out by Royal. Wherever they worked on new Royal machines they were probably aware that such machines were covered by a Royal warranty. But in any event, before working on a Royal machine they could have inquired of the customer whether it was covered by a Royal contract and refused to work on it if it was. There is no indication that they made any effort to avoid doing Royal's work. The Union was justified in picketing them in order to induce them to make such an effort. We therefore hold that an employer is not within the protection of §8(b)(4)(A) when he knowingly does work which would otherwise be done by the striking employees of the primary employer and where this work is paid for by the primary employer pursuant to an arrangement devised and originated by him to enable him to meet his contractual obligations. The result must be the same whether or not the primary employer makes any direct arrangement with the employers providing the services. . . .

Hand, J. (concurring). . . .

[I]t seems to me that both "independents" had so far associated themselves with Royal in the controversy with its employees as to forfeit their privilege as neutrals. After the picketing began both necessarily knew of the strike against Royal; indeed, the Union's representative spoke to each of them. I altogether agree that they were nevertheless entitled to do work for Royal's customers. One does not make oneself a party to the dispute with a primary employer by taking over the business that the strike has prevented him from doing. On the other hand if a secondary employer, knowing of the strike, not only accepts the customer of the primary employer but takes his pay, not from the customer but from the primary employer, I do not see any relevant difference in doing so from accepting a subcontract from the primary employer, which would certainly forfeit the exemption. As I understand §8(b)(4)(A), it is meant to protect from industrial pressure employers, who have not made common cause with the primary employer. The theory is that they should be free to carry on their businesses without being subject to sanctions that are reasonable between parties to the dispute. When, however, a secondary employer accepts business for which the primary employer pays him, although it is not an inevitable inference that, but for the strike, the primary employer would have done the business himself, I see no reason why he should not be compelled to prove that the primary employer would not have done it, if he could have. Therefore I think that, even though the Union meant to induce a strike of the "independents" employees, it was within its rights.

[The concurring opinion of Justice MEDINA is omitted.]

## *NOTES AND QUESTIONS*

**1. Elements of a §8(b)(4)(B) Violation.** A violation of what is now §8(b)(4)(B) requires two elements: (1) the use of prohibited means, here picketing seeking to induce employees of the target to withhold their services (2) in support of a prohibited object. The principal issue in *Royal* is whether the union picketed the independent repair companies for a prohibited object. The existence of an ally relationship would mean either that those companies were not other "person[s]" or there was no "cease doing business" objective for §8(b)(4)(B) purposes. Although the court states that "there was no evidence that the picketing of either the customers or the repair companies resulted in a strike or refusal to work by any employee" and that "no employee ceased work or refused to operate any Royal typewriter or other machine," it is not clear why this was relevant to the legal issue in the case. As Judge Hand notes, the union plainly "meant to induce a strike of the independents' employees," and that would have been sufficient for a violation had the repair companies not been found to be allies.

The court states that the Board's "finding [of a violation] with respect to the repair company picketing cannot be sustained," but appears to leave undisturbed the agency's finding with respect to the customer picketing. Do you understand why the customer picketing was problematic under §8(b)(4)(B)?

**2. What Made the Independent Repair Companies "Allies" of Royal?**

a. If Royal had told its customers only that it would honor its warranty and would pay them directly the fair costs of repairs covered by the warranty, would the union have been privileged to induce a strike against independent companies doing repair work for Royal's customers? Would it be material whether Royal volunteered that information or disclosed it only to inquiring customers? Whether the repairers were aware of the strike or the continued applicability of Royal's warranty and the company's intention to honor it by direct payments to its own customers?

b. Suppose that Royal's customers had set off against their liabilities to Royal the amounts they paid to independent repairers for work covered by Royal's warranty. Would the union have violated the Act by picketing the employee entrances of the independents making repairs for such customers?

c. Suppose Royal's products had not been warranted but that Royal, like distributors of Ford cars, supplied repair services to its customers. Would independents who, during a strike against Royal, performed repair work for Royal's customers be covered by the "ally" doctrine?

**3. Scope of the Appeal to Employees of the Ally?** If *R-2* is an "ally" performing *R-1*'s struck work, can the union in a primary dispute with *R-1* urge *R-2*'s employees to suspend all work for *R-2* even on jobs for other firms, or is the permissible scope of the appeal limited to the "struck work"? Under §8(b)(4), if *R-2* is an "ally," does this mean that there is no "cease doing business" object with respect to *R-1* or that *R-2* is not another "person" under the statute? Is there any way of reading the statute such that *R-2* is an "ally" for only part of its work and not the remainder? See Shopmen's Local 501, Iron Workers (Oliver Whyte Co.), 120 N.L.R.B. 856 (1958).

**4. "Integrated Enterprise" Ally.** Consider a manufacturer of refrigerators whose production and maintenance employees are on strike. The law is clear that the union can post picket lines around the primary employer's manufacturing facilities urging clerical, marketing, and engineering employees not represented by the union to refuse to cross the lines. See the proviso to §8(b)(4); see also Note on Honoring Picket Lines, supra page 534. Even without the proviso, the union's pressures are plainly not directed to "any person" other than the primary employer.

The result would be the same even if the manufacturer decided to establish separate corporate entities comprised, respectively, of its clerical, marketing, and engineering departments. Because of (a) common ownership, (b) common control, and (c) integrated operations, the union would still be dealing with the same employer for purposes of §8(b)(4). If the result were otherwise, firms would be able by a mere organizational change to confine the effects of labor disputes.

But how far should this "integrated enterprise" doctrine extend? Businesses have not been deemed "allies" for purposes of secondary boycott law simply because they have common owners. Should common ownership and common control together suffice? See Bachman Machine Co. v. NLRB, 266 F.2d 599 (8th Cir. 1959) (rejecting the Board's view that common ownership and control warranted treating two companies not engaged in an integrated enterprise as allies or a single enterprise); Electrical Workers IBEW Local 2208, 285 N.L.R.B. 834, 838 (1987) ("[C]ommon ownership and potential control of the day-to-day activities of corporate divisions are not to be accorded weight"). The Office of the General Counsel released an advice memorandum in 2013 clarifying the circumstances required for a finding of an ally relationship: "[D]aily operations and centralized control of labor relations policies are of paramount importance. Specifically, there must be substantial, actual, and active control, rather than merely the potential to control, the working conditions of the primary employer's employees." Teamsters Local 519, Cases 10-CC-109738, 06-CC-109839, 09-CC-109842, NLRB Office of the General Counsel Advice Memorandum (Sept. 4, 2013). Are joint employers, as discussed on supra pages 250-252, neutral allies even when not providing struck work? If so, are they allies only with respect to disputes involving jointly employed employees?

**5. Corporate Parents and Subsidiaries.** Consider AFTRA v. NLRB, 462 F.2d 887 (D.C. Cir. 1972). There, the American Federation of Television and Radio Artists (AFTRA), having struck WBAL-TV, Baltimore, owned by the Hearst Corporation, picketed *Baltimore News American,* a newspaper also owned by Hearst. The *News American* and WBAL were separate, though unincorporated, divisions of Hearst, a Delaware corporation headquartered in New York. There was no overlap in the management of the divisions, and the management of each division had complete control over day-to-day operations. Each division had its own workforce and controlled its own budget but had to obtain approval from New York for capital expenditures. Hearst did not maintain a corporate-wide labor relations and personnel policy, although the same outside labor law firm represented both divisions. Did AFTRA violate §8(b)(4)(B)?

Does it make sense to treat Hearst and its other divisions as "neutrals" in the WBAL-TV strike? Would evidence of the parent's involvement in the subsidiary's labor relations suffice for "ally" status? See Royal Typewriter Co. v. NLRB, 533 F.2d 1030 (8th Cir. 1976). Is it required? However much day-to-day autonomy the divisions may have enjoyed, is it likely the corporate parent exercised no influence over bargaining positions taken in the WBAL-TV negotiations? See generally Jay S. Siegel, Conglomerates, Subsidiaries, Divisions and the Secondary Boycott, 9 Ga. L. Rev. 329 (1975); Michael H. Levin, "Wholly Unconcerned": The Scope and Meaning of the Ally Doctrine Under Section 8(b)(4) of the NLRA, 119 U. Pa. L. Rev. 283 (1970).

### c. *"Common-Situs" Problems*

A second exception to the ban on secondary-situs picketing occurs when the employees of the primary employer are performing work at the premises of a secondary employer — the so-called "common-situs" situation.

**Sailors' Union of the Pacific and Moore Dry Dock**
*92 N.L.R.B. 547 (1950)*

[Samsoc, a Greek-controlled corporation, entered into a six-year contract to carry gypsum from Mexico to Kaiser plants in California. This agreement contemplated that an American ship, previously operated by a Kaiser subsidiary under a contract with the respondent union, would be replaced by a Samsoc ship, *S.S. Phopho.* Samsoc arranged with Moore Dry Dock to perform the major work required to convert that ship into a gypsum carrier and for the right to place a crew on board for training two weeks before the completion of the work. After Samsoc had hired a predominantly Greek crew at approximately one-half the union scale, the union requested but was denied bargaining rights with respect to the ship's crew. The union's petition for an election, filed on February 24, 1950, was dismissed because a foreign ship was involved. Meanwhile, on February 17, 1950, the union had stationed pickets at the shipyard's entrance after having been denied permission to picket immediately adjacent to the dock where the *Phopho* was located. The union also advised various unions representing Moore's employees that the *Phopho* was "hot" and requested their cooperation. On February 21, Moore's employees stopped work on the *Phopho* but continued all other work throughout the picketing.]

Section 8(b)(4)(A) is aimed at secondary boycotts and secondary strike activities. It was not intended to proscribe primary action by a union having a legitimate labor dispute with an employer. Picketing at the premises of a primary employer is traditionally recognized as primary action even though it is "necessarily designed to induce and encourage third persons to cease doing business with the picketed employer." . . . Hence, if Samsoc, the owner of the *S.S. Phopho,* had had a dock of its own in California to which the *Phopho* had been tied up while undergoing conversion by Moore Dry Dock employees, picketing by the Respondent at the dock site would unquestionably have constituted *primary* action, even though the Respondent might have expected that the picketing would be more effective in persuading Moore employees not to work on the ship than to persuade the seamen aboard the *Phopho* to quit that vessel. The difficulty in the present case arises therefore, not because of any difference in picketing objectives, but from the fact that the *Phopho* was not tied up at its own dock, but at that of Moore, while the picketing was going on in front of the Moore premises.

In the usual case, the situs of a labor dispute is the premises of the primary employer. Picketing of the premises is also picketing of the situs. . . . But in some cases the situs of the dispute may not be limited to a fixed location; it may be ambulatory. Thus . . . the Board [has] held that the truck upon which a truck driver worked was the situs of a labor dispute between him and the owner of the truck. Similarly, we hold . . . that, as the *Phopho* was the place of employment of the seamen, it was the situs of the dispute between Samsoc and the Respondent over working conditions aboard that vessel.

When the situs is ambulatory, it may come to rest temporarily at the premises of another employer. The perplexing question is: Does the right to picket follow the situs while it is stationed at the premises of a secondary employer, when the only way to picket that situs is in front of the secondary employer's premises? Admittedly, no easy answer is possible. Essentially the problem is one of balancing the right of a union to picket at the site of its dispute as against the right of a secondary employer to be free from picketing in a controversy in which it is not directly involved.

When a secondary employer is harboring the situs of a dispute between a union and a primary employer, the right of neither the union to picket nor of the secondary employer to be free from picketing can be absolute. The enmeshing of premises and situs qualifies both rights. . . . [W]e believe that picketing of the premises of a secondary employer is primary if it meets the following conditions: (a) The picketing is strictly limited to times when the situs of dispute is located on the secondary employer's premises; (b) at the time of the picketing the primary employer is engaged in its normal business at the situs; (c) the picketing is limited to places reasonably close to the location of the situs; and (d) the picketing discloses clearly that the dispute is with the primary employer. All these conditions were met in the present case.

(a) During the entire period of the picketing the *Phopho* was tied up at a dock in the Moore shipyard.

(b) Under its contract with Samsoc, Moore agreed to permit the former to put a crew on board the *Phopho* for training purposes during the last 2 weeks before the vessel's delivery to Samsoc. At the time the picketing started on February 17, . . . 90 percent of the conversion job had been completed, practically the entire crew had been hired, the ship's oil bunkers had been filled, and other stores were shortly to be put aboard. . . . The crew were . . . getting the ship ready for sea. They were on board to serve the purposes of Samsoc, the *Phopho*'s owners, and not Moore. . . . The multitudinous steps of preparation, including hiring and training a crew and putting stores aboard, are as much a part of the normal business of a ship as the voyage itself. We find, therefore, that during the entire period of the picketing, the *Phopho* was engaged in its normal business.

(c) Before placing its pickets outside the entrance to the Moore shipyard, the Respondent Union asked, but was refused, permission to place its pickets at the dock where the *Phopho* was tied up. The Respondent therefore posted its pickets at the yard entrance which, as the parties stipulated, was as close to the *Phopho* as they could get under the circumstance.

(d) Finally, by its picketing and other conduct the Respondent was scrupulously careful to indicate that its dispute was solely with the primary employer, the owners of the *Phopho*. Thus the signs carried by the pickets said only that the *Phopho* was unfair to the Respondent. The *Phopho* and not Moore was declared "hot." Similarly, in asking cooperation of other unions, the Respondent clearly revealed that its dispute was with the *Phopho*. Finally, Moore's own witnesses admitted that no attempt was made to interfere with other work in progress in the Moore yard.

. . . We are not holding . . . that a union which has a dispute with a shipowner over working conditions of seamen aboard a ship may lawfully picket the premises of an independent shipyard to which the shipowner has delivered his vessel for overhaul and repair. We are only holding that, if a shipyard permits the owner of a vessel to use its dock for the purpose of readying the ship for its regular voyage by hiring and training a crew and putting stores aboard ship, a union representing seamen may then, within the careful limitations laid down in this decision, lawfully picket in front of the shipyard premises to advertise its dispute with the shipowner. . . .

[The dissenting opinion by Members Reynolds and Murdock is omitted.]

## *NOTES AND QUESTIONS*

**1. Must Primary Employees Be Present and Doing Related Work?** Do the *Moore Dry Dock* criteria require that employees of the primary employer be present at the "ambulatory situs" for picketing to be legal? What if the secondary employees are doing work that could be carried on in the absence of the primary employees? Were Moore Dry Dock's employees doing work that required the presence of the Samsoc employees?

**2. Element of Necessity?** *Moore Dry Dock* involved a situation of "ambulatory situs" picketing in the sense that the *S.S. Phopho*, the situs of the primary dispute, had no fixed location. Because of this factor, secondary-situs picketing was unavoidable. Do the *Moore Dry Dock* criteria thus carry an implicit requirement that the union must show that "effective" picketing could not take place at the primary location? For a time, the Board so held. See Washington Coca-Cola, 197 N.L.R.B. 299 (1953), enforced sub nom. Brewery Drivers, Local 67 v. NLRB, 220 F.2d 380 (D.C. Cir. 1955). However, the D.C. Circuit took issue with this position in Sales Drivers, Local 859 v. NLRB, 229 F.2d 514, 517 (D.C. Cir. 1955). And the Board came to agree that the accessibility of a primary employer's business situs to union picketing was only one of the relevant factors. See Local 861, Electrical Workers (Plauche Elec.), 135 N.L.R.B. 250 (1962). For an argument that the Board should completely disregard this factor, see Lesnick, Gravamen of the Secondary Boycott, supra, at 1425-1426.

**3. Strict Liability?** If the picketing union requests that the secondary employees continue all work except that involving the primary employer, should ambulatory picketing in compliance with *Moore Dry Dock* become illegal if secondary employees refuse to do any work of any kind while the picketing continues? Compare Seafarers Indus. Union v. NLRB, 265 F.2d 585 (D.C. Cir. 1959), with Superior Derrick Corp. v. NLRB, 273 F.2d 891 (5th Cir. 1960). Would it be material that *R-1* could easily be picketed at a fixed situs?

## NLRB v. Denver Building & Construction Trades Council
*341 U.S. 675 (1951)*

BURTON, J.

The principal question here is whether a labor organization committed an unfair labor practice, within the meaning of §8(b)(4)(A), . . . by engaging in a strike, an object of which was to force the general contractor on a construction project to terminate its contract with a certain subcontractor on that project. . . . [W]e hold that such an unfair labor practice was committed.

. . . Doose & Lintner was the general contractor for the construction of a commercial building. . . . It awarded a subcontract for electrical work . . . , in an estimated amount of $2,300, to Gould & Preisner, a firm which for 20 years had employed nonunion workmen on construction work. . . . The latter's employees proved to be the only nonunion workmen on the project. Those of the general contractor and of the other subcontractors were members of unions affiliated with the respondent Denver Building and Construction Trades Council. . . . A representative of one of those unions told Gould that he did not see how the job could progress with Gould's nonunion men on it. Gould insisted that they would complete the electrical work unless bodily put off. The representative replied that the situation would be difficult for both Gould & Preisner and Doose & Lintner.

January 8, 1948, the [Council] instructed [its] representative "to place a picket on the job stating that the job was unfair" to it. In keeping with the Council's practice, each affiliate was notified of that decision. That notice was a signal in the nature of an order to the members of the affiliated unions to leave the job and remain away until otherwise ordered. Representatives of the Council and each of the respondent unions visited the project and reminded the contractor that Gould & Preisner employed nonunion workmen and said that union men could not work on the job with nonunion men. They further advised that if Gould & Preisner's men did work on the job, the Council and its affiliates would put a picket on it to notify their members that nonunion men were working on it and that the job was unfair. All parties stood their ground.

January 9, the Council posted a picket at the project carrying a placard stating "This Job Unfair to Denver Building and Construction Trades Council." He was paid by the Council and his picketing continued from January 9 through January 22. During that time the only persons who reported for work were the nonunion electricians of Gould & Preisner. January 22, before Gould & Preisner had completed its subcontract, the general contractor notified it to get off the job so that Doose & Lintner could continue with the project. January 23, the Council removed its picket and shortly thereafter the union employees resumed work on the project.

Gould & Preisner protested this treatment but its workmen were denied entrance to the job. . . .

[The court of appeals rejected the Board's finding that the respondents' activity was secondary and denied enforcement of the Board's order.]

A.

We must first determine whether the strike in this case had a proscribed object. . . .

. . . [Here] there was a longstanding labor dispute between the Council and Gould & Preisner due to the latter's practice of employing nonunion workmen on construction jobs in Denver. The respondent labor organizations contend that they engaged in a primary dispute with Doose & Lintner alone, and that they sought simply to force Doose & Lintner to make the project an all-union job. If there had been no contract between Doose & Lintner and Gould & Preisner there might be substance in their contention that the dispute involved no boycott. If, for example, Doose & Lintner had been doing all the electrical work on this project through its own nonunion employees, it could have replaced them with union men and thus disposed of the dispute. However, the existence of the Gould & Preisner subcontract presented a materially different situation. The nonunion employees were employees of Gould & Preisner. The only way that respondents could attain their purpose was to force Gould & Preisner itself off the job. This, in turn, could be done only through Doose & Lintner's termination of Gould & Preisner's subcontract. The result is that the Council's strike, in order to attain its ultimate purpose, must have included among its objects that of forcing Doose & Lintner to terminate that subcontract. On that point, the Board adopted the following finding: "That *an* object, if not the only object, of what transpired with respect to . . . Doose & Lintner was to force or require them to cease doing business with Gould & Preisner seems scarcely open to question, in view of all of the facts. And it is clear at least as to Doose & Lintner, that that purpose was achieved." (Emphasis supplied.) 82 N.L.R.B. at 1212.

We accept this crucial finding. . . .

B.

We hold also that a strike with such an object was an unfair labor practice within the meaning of §8(b)(4)(A).

It is not necessary to find that the *sole* object of the strike was that of forcing the contractor to terminate the subcontractor's contract. . . .

We agree with the Board . . . that the fact that the contractor and subcontractor were engaged on the same construction project, and that the contractor had some supervision over the subcontractor's work, did not eliminate the status of each as an independent contractor or make the employees of one the employees of the other. The business relationship between independent contractors is too well established in the law to be overridden without clear language doing so. The Board found that the relationship between Doose & Lintner and Gould & Preisner was one of "doing business" and we find no adequate reason for upsetting that conclusion. . . .

The judgment of the Court of Appeals accordingly is reversed and the case is remanded to it for proceedings not inconsistent with this opinion.

JACKSON, J., would affirm the judgment of the Court of Appeals.

DOUGLAS, J., with whom REED, J., joins, dissenting.

The employment of union and nonunion men on the same job is a basic protest in trade union history. That was the protest here. The union was not out to destroy the contractor because of his antiunion attitude. The union was not pursuing the contractor to other jobs. All the union asked was that union men not be compelled to work alongside nonunion men on the same job. . . .

The picketing would undoubtedly have been legal if there had been no subcontractor involved—if the general contractor had put nonunion men on the job. The presence of a subcontractor does not alter one whit the realities of the situation; the protest of the union is precisely the same. In each the union was trying to protect a job on which union men were employed. If that is forbidden, the Taft-Hartley Act makes the right to strike, guaranteed by §13, dependent on fortuitous business arrangements that have no significance so far as the evils of the secondary boycott are concerned. I would give scope to both §8(b)(4) and §13 by reading the restrictions of §8(b)(4) to reach the case where an industrial dispute spreads from the job to another front.

## *NOTES AND QUESTIONS*

**1. Should Doose & Lintner Have Been Viewed as the "Primary" Employer?** Note that if Doose & Lintner, the general contractor, had been viewed as the primary employer, and if the union had appealed only to its employees, the picketing would have been lawful under *Moore Dry Dock.* Why does the Court hold that the union's dispute was with the subcontractor rather than with the general contractor who selected the subcontractors for the site?

The Court acknowledges that if the general contractor had used its employees for the electrical work initially, the union could have sought to pressure it to use union employees. Does the situation change materially because the general contractor lets out the work to an independent business that uses nonunion labor?

**2. Integrated-Enterprise Ally?** Isn't the construction site a classic case of an integrated enterprise where interdependent groups of workers help produce a common product? If in the refrigerator manufacturer's example (see supra note 4, page 594), a union could picket the entire facility even where the manufacturer decides to convert its clerical, marketing, and engineering departments into commonly owned separate entities, why is a union not permitted to picket an entire construction site in a case like *Denver Trades*?

**3. "Common-Situs" Legislation.** In 1975, legislation passed both Houses of Congress (see H.R. 5900, 94th Cong., 1st Sess.) that would have permitted construction-site work stoppages "directed at any of several employers who are in the construction industry and are jointly engaged as joint venturers or in the relationship of contractor and subcontractor in . . . construction, alteration, painting, or repair" at the site. President Ford vetoed the legislation on the ground that it would lead to continued inflation in the construction industry.

**4. Rights of Nonunion Subcontractors?** Should *Denver Trades* be viewed as a decision that enables nonunion subcontractors to bid on and obtain work on projects controlled by union-represented general contractors? By creating opportunities for competition between union-represented and nonunion subcontractors, does the ruling help reduce construction costs for consumers? Are such concerns properly addressed through application of the secondary boycott provisions of the labor laws?

## Local 761, International Union of Electrical, Radio & Machine Workers v. NLRB (*General Electric*)
*366 U.S. 667 (1961)*

Frankfurter, J. . . .

General Electric Corporation operates a plant outside of Louisville, Kentucky, where it manufactures washers, dryers, and other electrical household appliances. The square-shaped, thousand-acre, unfenced plant is known as Appliance Park. A large drainage ditch makes ingress and egress impossible except over five roadways across culverts, designated as gates.

Since 1954, General Electric sought to confine the employees of independent contractors, described hereafter, who work on the premises of the Park, to the use of Gate 3-A and confine its use to them. The undisputed reason for doing so was to insulate General Electric employees from the frequent labor disputes in which the contractors were involved. Gate 3-A is 550 feet away from the nearest entrance available for General Electric employees, suppliers, and deliverymen. Although anyone can pass the gate without challenge, the roadway leads to a guardhouse where identification must be presented. Vehicle stickers of various shapes and colors enable a guard to check on sight whether a vehicle is authorized to use Gate 3-A. Since January 1958, a prominent sign has been posted at the gate which states: "GATE 3-A FOR EMPLOYEES OF CONTRACTORS ONLY—G.E. EMPLOYEES USE OTHER GATES." On rare occasions, it appears, a General Electric employee was allowed to pass the guardhouse, but such occurrence was in violation of company instructions. There was no proof of any unauthorized attempts to pass the gate during the strike in question.

The independent contractors are utilized for a great variety of tasks on the Appliance Park premises. Some do construction work on new buildings; some install and repair ventilating and heating equipment; some engage in retooling and rearranging operations necessary to the manufacture of new models; others do "general maintenance work." These services are contracted to outside employers either because the company's employees lack the necessary skill or manpower, or because the work can be done more economically by independent contractors. The latter reason determined the contracting of maintenance work for which the Central Maintenance department of the company bid competitively with the contractors. While some of the work done by these contractors had on occasion been previously performed by Central Maintenance, the findings do not disclose the number of employees of independent contractors who were performing these routine maintenance services, as compared with those who were doing specialized work of a capital-improvement nature.

The Union, petitioner here, is the certified bargaining representative for the production and maintenance workers who constitute approximately 7,600 of the 10,500 employees of General Electric at Appliance Park. On July 27, 1958, the Union called a strike because of 24 unsettled grievances with the company. Picketing occurred at all the gates, including Gate 3-A, and continued until August 9 when an injunction was issued by a Federal District Court. The signs carried by the pickets at all gates read: "LOCAL 761 ON STRIKE G.E. UNFAIR." Because of the picketing, almost all of the employees of independent contractors refused to enter the company premises.

Neither the legality of the strike or of the picketing at any of the gates except 3-A nor the peaceful nature of the picketing is in dispute. The sole claim is that the picketing before the gate exclusively used by employees of independent contractors was conduct proscribed by §8(b)(4)(A). . . .

The Board . . . held that, since only the employees of the independent contractors were allowed to use Gate 3-A, the Union's object in picketing there was "to enmesh these employees of the neutral employers in its dispute with the Company," thereby constituting a violation of §8(b)(4)(A) because the independent employees were encouraged to engage in a concerted refusal to work "with an object of forcing the independent contractors to cease doing business with the Company."

The Court of Appeals . . . granted enforcement of the Board's order. . . .

The Board's application of the *Dry Dock* standards to picketing at the premises of the struck employer was made . . . explicit in Retail Fruit & Vegetable Clerks (Crystal Palace Market), 116 N.L.R.B. 856. The owner of a large common market operated some of the shops within, and leased out others to independent sellers. The union, although given permission to picket the owner's individual stands, chose to picket outside the entire market. The Board held that this action was violative of §8(b)(4)(A) in that the union did not attempt to minimize the effect of its picketing, as required in a common-situs case, on the operations of the neutral employers utilizing the market. "We believe . . . that the foregoing principles should apply to all common situs picketing, including cases where, as here, the picketed premises are owned by the primary employer." 116 N.L.R.B., at 859. . . . [T]he Ninth Circuit, in enforcing the Board's order, specifically approved its disavowance of an ownership test. 249 F.2d 591. . . .

In rejecting the ownership test in situations where two employers were performing work upon a common site, the Board was naturally guided by this Court's opinion in [NLRB v. International Rice Milling Co., 341 U.S. 665 (1951)], in which we indicated that the location of the picketing at the primary employer's premises was "not necessarily conclusive" of its legality. 341 U.S., at 671. Where the work done by the secondary employees is unrelated to the normal operations of the primary employer, it is difficult to perceive how the pressure of picketing the entire situs is any less on the neutral employer merely because the picketing takes place at property owned by the struck employer. The application of the *Dry Dock* tests to limit the picketing effects to the employees of the employer against whom the dispute is directed carried out the "dual congressional objectives of preserving the right of labor organizations to bring pressure to bear on offending employers in primary labor disputes and of shielding unoffending employers and others from pressures in controversies not their own." Labor Board v. Denver Building [ & Constr. Council, 341 U.S. 675, 692 (1951)].

. . . [T]he question [here] is whether the Board may apply the *Dry Dock* criteria so as to make unlawful picketing at a gate utilized exclusively by employees of independent contractors who work on the struck employer's premises. The effect of such a holding would not bar the union from picketing at all gates used by the employees, suppliers, and customers of the struck employer. Of course an employer may not, by removing all his employees from the situs of the strike, bar the union from publicizing its cause. . . . The basis of the Board's decision in this case would not remotely have that effect, nor any such tendency for the future.

The Union claims that, if the Board's ruling is upheld, employers will be free to erect separate gates for deliveries, customers, and replacement workers which will be immunized from picketing. This fear is baseless. The key to the problem is found in the type of work that is being performed by those who use the separate gate. It is significant that the Board has since applied its rationale, first stated in the present case, only to situations where the independent workers were performing tasks unconnected to the normal operations of the struck employer — usually construction work on his buildings. In such situations, the indicated limitations on picketing activity respect the balance of competing interests that Congress has required the Board to enforce. On the other hand, if a separate gate were devised for regular plant deliveries, the barring of picketing at that location would make a clear invasion on traditional primary activity of appealing to neutral employees whose tasks aid the employer's everyday operations. The 1959 Amendments . . . , which removed the word "concerted" from the boycott provisions, included a proviso that "nothing contained in this clause (B) shall be construed to make unlawful, where not otherwise unlawful, any primary strike or primary picketing." . . . The proviso was directed against the fear that the removal of "concerted" from the statute might be interpreted so that "the picketing at the factory violates §8(b)(4)(A) because the pickets induce the truck drivers employed by the trucker not to perform their usual services where an object is to compel the trucking firm not to do business with the . . . manufacturer during the strike." . . . 105 Cong. Rec. 16589. . . .

The foregoing course of reasoning would require that the judgment below sustaining the Board's order be affirmed but for one consideration, even though this consideration may turn out not to affect the result. The legal path by which the Board and the Court of Appeals reached their decisions did not take into account that if Gate 3-A was . . . used by employees of independent contractors who performed conventional maintenance work necessary to the normal operations of General Electric, the use of the gate would have been a mingled one outside the bar of §8(b)(4)(A). In short, such mixed use of this portion of the struck employer's premises would not bar picketing rights of the striking employees. While the record shows some such mingled use, it sheds no light on its extent. It may well turn out to be that the instances of these maintenance tasks were so insubstantial as to be treated by the Board as de minimis. We cannot here guess at the quantitative aspect of this problem. It calls for Board determination. For determination of the questions thus raised, the case must be remanded by the Court of Appeals to the Board.

The Chief Justice and Black, J., concur in the result.
[The dissenting opinion of Justice Douglas is omitted.]

## *NOTES AND QUESTIONS*

1. ***General Electric* on Remand.** Upon remand of the *General Electric* case, the Trial Examiner recommended dismissal of the complaint, reasoning that the work of rearranging and enlarging the conveyor system in two appliance departments was "related to GE's normal operation" since the conveyor system was essential for the resumption of production of finished products. The Board rejected this reasoning but not the result; it relied not on the conveyor work but on the installation of showers and miscellaneous repairs and alterations performed by subcontractors, which involved a total cost of approximately $15,000, and which, the Board emphasized, had in the past been done by GE's employees. It concluded that these jobs were "necessarily related to GE's normal operations" and that the picketing had, accordingly, been "primary." See Local 761, International Union of Elec., Radio & Machine Workers (General Electric), 138 N.L.R.B. 342 (1962).

2. **"Reserve Gate" Exception to Lawful Primary-Situs Picketing.** Why does the Court hold that a primary employer who also owns the site can insulate from union pressures some of the on-site work of its subcontractors? *Moore Dry Dock* requires a union to avoid appeals to secondary employees, but that case involved secondary-situs picketing. Why does *Moore Dry Dock* apply at all to picketing at the premises of the primary employer? Do you understand the rationale behind Justice Frankfurter's limits on the use of reserve gates? Why are employees engaged in unrelated work—"tasks unconnected to the normal operations of the employer" and of a kind that would not require curtailment of its regular operations—shielded from union pressures?

3. **Lessor-Lessee Relationships.** Consider the *General Electric* Court's discussion of Retail Fruit & Vegetable Clerks (Crystal Palace Market), 116 N.L.R.B. 856 (1956), enforced, 249 F.2d 591 (9th Cir. 1957). The Board held that the union could not picket the entire site even though its dispute was with the owner of the market. Would the case have come out differently if the owner had not provided direct access to its stands? Does a different analysis apply to a dispute between the owner of an office building and a union representing employees engaged in cleaning the building, where the building provides separate entrances for its commercial tenants? Can the union lawfully picket the entire building?

4. **Relationship of *General Electric* to *Moore Dry Dock*.** If *General Electric* modifies *Moore Dry Dock* (see note 2 supra), is the modification limited to

common-situs picketing on premises owned by the primary employer? For instance, if employees of a General Electric subcontractor doing conventional maintenance work necessary to GE's normal operations were on strike and GE had directed its own workers to use a separate gate, could the striking workers legally picket that gate?

In United Steelworkers of Am. v. NLRB (Carrier Corp.), 376 U.S. 492 (1964), the union's dispute was with Carrier and its pickets extended to a railroad right of way used for deliveries to Carrier and other companies. The railroad spur ran across a public road and through a gate onto Carrier's property. The gate was accessible only to railroad employees. The Supreme Court, agreeing with the Board, held that the union did not violate §8(b)(4) because the gate was "a situs . . . proximate and related to the employer's day-to-day operations." However, the Board has limited *Carrier Corp.* to its facts and has applied *General Electric* in other cases where the primary employer owns the premises subjected to picketing.

**5. Revisiting Common-Situs Picketing in the Construction Industry?** Does *General Electric* require a reexamination of the holding in *Denver Trades*? Consider Markwell & Hartz, Inc. v. NLRB, 387 F.2d 79 (5th Cir. 1967). In that case the general contractor, Markwell & Hartz, entered into a recognition agreement with the United Mine Workers before beginning the work involved. (Prehire contracts are lawful in the construction industry under §8(f).) Markwell & Hartz subcontracted 20 percent of the work, including the pile driving to Binnings and the electrical work to Barnes. Both of these subcontractors' employees were represented by the Building and Construction Trades Council. The Council, in the course of a dispute with Markwell & Hartz, picketed the entire site, even though Markwell & Hartz had clearly marked one gate for the exclusive use of its own employees and three gates for the exclusive use of subcontractors. Binnings's and Barnes's employees honored the picket lines. Did the Council violate §8(b)(4)(B)? In *Markwell & Hartz*, the Fifth Circuit (2-1) sustained a Board order finding a violation.

The Board continues to hold that appeals to secondary employees at construction sites are illegal without regard to whether those employees are doing work that is related to work being done by employees of the primary employer. This has been true even in the unusual case where the labor dispute has been with a general contractor who owns the construction site. See Carpenters Local 470 (Mueller-Anderson, Inc.), 224 N.L.R.B. 315 (1976), enforced, 564 F.2d 1360 (9th Cir. 1977). Do these cases suggest that a different set of rules applies to construction industry picketing (*Denver Trades* and *Moore Dry Dock*) than to picketing on manufacturing sites (*General Electric*)? If so, what is the justification for this special treatment?

### d. *Appeals to Customers of Secondary Employers*

The 1959 amendments to §8(b)(4) sought to close certain loopholes in the Taft-Hartley version of the section (then denominated as §8(b)(4)(A)). First, to prevent unions from inducing a secondary work stoppage of employees not covered by the NLRA such as supervisors, government, and railway workers, Congress expanded the prohibition to reach union-induced work stoppages of "any individual employed by any person engaged in commerce or in an industry affecting commerce." Second, it deleted the word "concerted" in order to reach union-induced work stoppages of even a single individual. In addition, Congress added a second means of violating the secondary-boycott prohibition in addition to union-induced work stoppages (§8(b)(4)(i)): union pressures "to threaten, coerce, or restrain" employers and their representatives even where no work stoppage was threatened (§8(b)(4)(ii)).

#### *Note:* **Servette-DeBartolo** *and the "Publicity" Proviso to §8(b)(4)*

Because of perceived constitutional difficulties with applying the secondary-boycott prohibition to union appeals to the general public that do not involve the threat of work stoppages associated with picket lines, Congress also included a "publicity" proviso to §8(b)(4). The Supreme Court's first opportunity to construe the proviso was presented by NLRB v. Servette, 377 U.S. 46 (1964). Servette was a wholesale distributor of specialty products to retail supermarkets. A union engaged in a dispute with Servette asked supermarket managers to discontinue stocking merchandise supplied by Servette, warning that if the managers did not comply the union would handbill the market asking customers not to purchase items distributed by Servette. Servette argued that the appeal to managers constituted an attempt to induce managers to refuse to perform their work in violation of §8(b)(4)(i), and that the handbilling warning was threatening and coercive in violation of §8(b)(4)(ii). Servette also maintained the appeal did not come within the "publicity" proviso because the products in question were not "produced" by it.

The Supreme Court disagreed. Although the managers were "individuals" encompassed by clause (i), the union was not seeking to induce a managers' work stoppage, but rather they "were asked to make a managerial decision which the Board found was within their authority to make." The handbilling warning did not constitute unlawful means under clause (ii) because of the "publicity" proviso. Reading the proviso in a nonliteral fashion, the Court found that the legislative purpose required construing the word "produced" to reach distribution (377 U.S. at 55):

> The proviso was the outgrowth of a profound Senate concern that the unions' freedom to appeal to the public for support of their case be adequately safeguarded. . . . It would fall far short of achieving this basic purpose if the

proviso applied only to situations in which the union's labor dispute is with the manufacturer or processor.

In Edward J. DeBartolo Corp. v. NLRB, 463 U.S. 147 (1983), H.J. High Construction Co. (High) was a general contractor retained by H.M. Wilson Company to build a department store in a Tampa, Florida, shopping center owned by DeBartolo. Most of the 85 tenants in the mall signed a lease providing for payment of a minimum rent plus a percentage of gross sales, as well as a proportionate share of the upkeep of common areas. The local building trades council, contending that High was paying below-standard wages and benefits, handbilled all four entrances to the shopping center, asking the readers not to patronize any of the stores in the mall until DeBartolo promised that all construction would be done by contractors paying union wages and benefits. The handbills explicitly disclaimed any purpose of inducing a work stoppage. Without deciding whether the handbilling constituted a form of "coercion" or "restraint" violative of §8(b)(4)(ii), the NLRB held that the handbilling was protected by the "publicity" proviso because High was a "producer" of the construction of the Wilson store and DeBartolo and the other tenants were in a "symbiotic" relationship with High because they would benefit from High's "product." 252 N.L.R.B. 702 (1980). The court of appeals agreed. 662 F.2d 264 (4th Cir. 1981).

The Supreme Court unanimously reversed. While agreeing that the High-Wilson relationship fell within the "producer-distributor" relationship contemplated by the proviso, the Court (per Justice Stevens) held that the handbills went beyond the reach of the proviso because they urged a boycott of the products sold by Wilson's cotenants (463 U.S. at 156):

> ... [T]he Board did not find that any product produced by High was being distributed by DeBartolo or any of Wilson's cotenants. Instead, it relied on the theory that there was a symbiotic relationship between them and Wilson, and that DeBartolo and Wilson's cotenants would derive substantial benefit from High's work. That form of analysis would almost strip the distribution requirement of its limiting effect. It diverts the inquiry away from the relationship between the primary and secondary employers and toward the relationship between two secondary employers. It then tests that relationship by a standard so generous that it will be satisfied by virtually any secondary employer that a union might want consumers to boycott.

The Court purported not to decide whether the union's handbilling was covered by §8(b)(ii) — a point that the Board also had left open — and, if so, whether it was protected by the First Amendment. For discussion of a later phase of this litigation, see infra pages 618-620.

### NLRB v. Fruit & Vegetable Packers, Local 760 (*Tree Fruits*)
*377 U.S. 58 (1964)*

BRENNAN, J.

The question . . . is whether the respondent unions violated [§8(b)(4)(ii)(B)] when they limited their secondary picketing of retail stores to an appeal to the customers of the stores not to buy the products of certain firms against which one of the respondents was on strike.

Respondent Local 760 called a strike against fruit packers and warehousemen doing business in Yakima, Washington.[2] The struck firms sold Washington State apples to the Safeway chain of retail stores in and about Seattle. . . . Local 760, aided by respondent Joint Council, instituted a consumer boycott against the apples in support of the strike. They placed pickets who walked back and forth before the customers' entrances of 46 Safeway stores in Seattle. The pickets — two at each of 45 stores and three at the 46th store — wore placards and distributed handbills which appealed to Safeway customers, and to the public generally, to refrain from buying Washington State apples, which were only one of numerous food products sold in the stores.[3] Before the pickets appeared at any store, a letter was delivered to the store manager informing him that the picketing was only an appeal to his customers not to buy Washington State apples, and that the pickets were being expressly instructed "to patrol peacefully in front of the customer entrances of the store, to stay away from the delivery entrances and not to

---

2. The firms, 24 in number, are members of the Tree Fruits Labor Relations Committee, Inc. [the members' collective bargaining agent]. . . . The strike was called in a dispute over the terms of the renewal of a collective bargaining agreement.

3. The placard worn by each picket stated: "To the Consumer: Non-Union Washington State apples are being sold at this store. Please do not purchase such apples. Thank you. Teamsters Local 760, Yakima, Washington."

A typical handbill read:

DON'T BUY WASHINGTON STATE APPLES

*The 1960 Crop of Washington State Apples Is Being Packed by Non-Union Firms*

Included in this non-union operation are twenty-six firms in the Yakima Valley with which there is a labor dispute. These firms are charged with being

UNFAIR

by their employees who, with their union, are on strike and have been *replaced by non-union strike-breaking workers* employed undersubstandard wage scales and working conditions. In justice to these striking union workers who are attempting to protect their living standards and their right to engage in good-faith collective bargaining, we request that you

DON'T BUY WASHINGTON STATE APPLES

Teamsters Union Local 760
*Yakima, Washington*

This is not a strike against any store or market.

(P.S. — PACIFIC FRUIT & PRODUCE CO. is the only firm packing Washington State Apples under a union contract.)

interfere with the work of your employees, or with deliveries to or pickups from your store." A copy of written instructions to the pickets—which included the explicit statement that "you are also forbidden to request that the customers not patronize the store"—was enclosed with the letter. Since it was desired to assure Safeway employees that they were not to cease work, and to avoid any interference with pickups or deliveries, the pickets appeared after the stores opened for business and departed before the stores closed. At all times during the picketing, the store employees continued to work, and no deliveries or pickups were obstructed. Washington State apples were handled in normal courses by both Safeway employees and the employees of other employers involved. Ingress and egress by customers and others was not interfered with in any manner.

. . . The Board held . . . [that] consumer picketing in front of a secondary establishment is prohibited. 132 N.L.R.B. 1172, 1177. . . . [T]he Court of Appeals . . . set aside the Board's order and remanded. The court rejected the Board's construction and held that the statutory requirement of a showing that respondents' conduct would "threaten, coerce, or restrain" Safeway could only be satisfied by affirmative proof that a substantial economic impact on Safeway had occurred, or was likely to occur as a result of the conduct. . . .

The Board's reading of the statute—that the legislative history and the phrase "other than picketing" in the proviso reveal a congressional purpose to outlaw all picketing directed at customers at a secondary site—necessarily rested on the finding that Congress determined that such picketing always threatens, coerces or restrains the secondary employer. We therefore have a special responsibility to examine the legislative history for confirmation that Congress made that determination. Throughout the history of federal regulation of labor relations, Congress has consistently refused to prohibit peaceful picketing except where it is used as a means to achieve specific ends which experience has shown are undesirable. "In the sensitive area of peaceful picketing Congress has dealt explicitly with isolated evils which experience has established flow from such picketing." Labor Board v. Drivers Local Union, 362 U.S. 274, 284. We have recognized this congressional practice and have not ascribed to Congress a purpose to outlaw peaceful picketing unless "there is the clearest indication in the legislative history," ibid., that Congress intended to do so as regards the particular ends of the picketing under review. Both the congressional policy and our adherence to this principle of interpretation reflect concern that a broad ban against peaceful picketing might collide with the guarantees of the First Amendment.

We have examined the legislative history of the amendments to §8(b)(4), and conclude that it does not reflect with the requisite clarity a congressional plan to proscribe all peaceful consumer picketing at secondary sites, and, particularly, any concern with peaceful picketing when it is limited, as here, to persuading Safeway customers not to buy

Washington State apples when they traded in the Safeway stores. All that the legislative history shows in the way of an "isolated evil" believed to require proscription of peaceful consumer picketing at secondary sites, was its use to persuade the customers of the secondary employer to cease trading with him in order to force him to cease dealing with, or to put pressure upon, the primary employer. This narrow focus reflects the difference between such conduct and peaceful picketing at the secondary site directed only at the struck product. In the latter case, the union's appeal to the public is confined to its dispute with the primary employer, since the public is not asked to withhold its patronage from the secondary employer, but only to boycott the primary employer's goods. On the other hand, a union appeal to the public at the secondary site not to trade at all with the secondary employer goes beyond the goods of the primary employer, and seeks the public's assistance in forcing the secondary employer to cooperate with the union in its primary dispute. This is not to say that this distinction was expressly alluded to in the debates. It is to say, however, that the consumer picketing carried on in this case is not attended by the abuses at which the statute was directed. . . .

We come then to the question whether the picketing in this case, confined as it was to persuading customers to cease buying the product of the primary employer, falls within the area of secondary consumer picketing which Congress did clearly indicate its intention to prohibit under §8(b)(4)(ii). We hold that it did not fall within that area, and therefore did not "threaten, coerce, or restrain" Safeway. While any diminution in Safeway's purchases of apples due to a drop in consumer demand might be said to be a result which causes respondents' picketing to fall literally within the statutory prohibition, "it is a familiar rule, that a thing may be within the letter of the statute and yet not within the statute, because not within its spirit, nor within the intention of its makers." Holy Trinity Church v. United States, 143 U.S. 457, 459. When consumer picketing is employed only to persuade customers not to buy the struck product, the union's appeal is closely confined to the primary dispute. The site of the appeal is expanded to include the premises of the secondary employer, but if the appeal succeeds, the secondary employer's purchases from the struck firms are decreased only because the public has diminished its purchases of the struck product. On the other hand, when consumer picketing is employed to persuade customers not to trade at all with the secondary employer, the latter stops buying the struck product, not because of a falling demand, but in response to pressure designed to inflict injury on his business generally. In such case, the union does more than merely follow the struck product; it creates a separate dispute with the secondary employer.

We disagree therefore with the Court of Appeals that the test of "to threaten, coerce, or restrain" for the purposes of this case is whether Safeway suffered or was likely to suffer economic loss. A violation of §8(b)(4)(ii)(B) would not be established, merely because respondents' picketing was effective to reduce Safeway's sales of Washington State apples, even if this led or might lead Safeway to drop the item as a poor seller.

The judgment of the Court of Appeals is vacated and the case is remanded with direction to enter judgment setting aside the Board's order.

DOUGLAS, J., took no part in the consideration or decision of this case.

[Justice Black, concurring, declared that §8(b)(4)(ii)(B) must be read as proscribing the consumer picketing in question but that that section so construed violated the First Amendment.]

HARLAN, J., whom STEWART, J., joins, dissenting. . . .

The difference to which the Court points between a secondary employer merely lowering his purchases of the struck product to the degree of decreased consumer demand and such an employer ceasing to purchase one product because of consumer refusal to buy any products, is surely too refined in the context of reality. . . . Because of the very nature of picketing there may be numbers of persons who will refuse to buy at all from a picketed store, either out of economic or social conviction or because they prefer to shop where they need not brave a picket line. Moreover, the public can hardly be expected always to know or ascertain the precise scope of a particular picketing operation. Thus in cases like this, the effect on the secondary employer may not always be limited to a decrease in his sales of the struck product. And even when that is the effect, the employer may, rather than simply reducing purchases from the primary employer, deem it more expedient to turn to another producer whose product is approved by the union.

The distinction drawn by the majority becomes even more tenuous if a picketed retailer depends largely or entirely on sales of the struck product. . . . To be sure Safeway is a multiple article seller, but it cannot well be gainsaid that the rule laid down by the Court would be unworkable if its applicability turned on a calculation of the relation between total income of the secondary employer and income from the struck product. [Justice Harlan further argued that the statute, construed so as to prohibit all customer picketing, did not violate the First Amendment.]

## NLRB v. Retail Store Employees Union, Local 1001
**(*Safeco Title Insurance Co.*)**
*447 U.S. 607 (1980)*

[Following a bargaining impasse, the union struck Safeco Title Insurance Company, which, however, maintained operations. In addition to Safeco's Seattle office, the union picketed five local title companies whose sale of Safeco policies constituted over 90 percent of their business.

The pickets' signs asked customers to cancel, or not to buy, Safeco policies. The Supreme Court, disagreeing with the court of appeals, upheld the Board's position that the picketing violated the Act.]

POWELL, J. . . .

Although [NLRB v. Fruit & Vegetable Packers, Local 760 (*Tree Fruits*), 377 U.S. 58 (1964),] suggested that secondary picketing against a struck product and secondary picketing against a neutral party were "poles apart," id., at 70, the courts soon discovered that product picketing could have the same effect as an illegal secondary boycott. In Hoffman ex rel. NLRB v. Cement Masons Local 337, 468 F.2d 1187 (CA9 1972), cert. denied, 411 U.S. 986 (1973), for example, a union embroiled with a general contractor picketed the housing subdivision that he had constructed for a real estate developer. Pickets sought to persuade prospective purchasers not to buy the contractor's houses. The picketing was held illegal because purchasers "could reasonably expect that they were being asked not to transact any business whatsoever" with the neutral developer. 468 F.2d, at 1192.[7] . . .

*Cement Masons* highlights the critical difference between the picketing in this case and . . . *Tree Fruits.* The product picketed in *Tree Fruits* was but one item among the many that made up the retailer's trade. 377 U.S., at 60. . . . In this case, . . . the title companies sell only the primary employer's product and perform the services associated with it. Secondary picketing against consumption of the primary product leaves responsive consumers no realistic option other than to boycott the title companies altogether. If the appeal succeeds, each company "stops buying the struck product, not because of a falling demand, but in response to pressure designed to inflict injury on [its] business generally." Thus, "the union does more than merely follow the struck product; it creates a separate dispute with the secondary employer." Id., at 72. . . .

As long as secondary picketing only discourages consumption of a struck product, incidental injury to the neutral is a natural consequence of an effective primary boycott. . . . But the Union's secondary appeal against the central product sold by the title companies in this case is "reasonably calculated to induce customers not to patronize the neutral parties at all." 226 N.L.R.B., at 757. The resulting injury to their businesses is distinctly different from the injury that the Court considered in *Tree Fruits.* Product picketing that reasonably can be expected to threaten neutral parties with

---

7. The so-called merged product cases also involve situations where an attempt to follow the struck product inevitably encourages an illegal boycott of the neutral party. See K & K Construction Co. v. NLRB, 592 F.2d 1228, 1231-1234 (CA3 1979); American Bread Co. v. NLRB, 411 F.2d 147, 154-155 (CA6 1969); Honolulu Typographical Union No. 37 v. NLRB, 131 U.S. App. D.C. 1, 3-4, 401 F.2d 952, 954-955 (1968); Note, Consumer Picketing and the Single-Product Secondary Employer, 47 U. Chi. L. Rev. 112, 132-136 (1979). [Footnote relocated in text. — EDS.]

ruin or substantial loss simply does not square with the language or the purpose of §8(b)(4)(ii)(B). Since successful secondary picketing would put the title companies to a choice between their survival and the severance of their ties with Safeco, the picketing plainly violates the statutory ban on the coercion of neutrals with the object of "forcing or requiring [them] to cease . . . dealing in the [primary] produc[t] . . . or to cease doing business with" the primary employer. §8(b)(4)(ii)(B); see *Tree Fruits*, 377 U.S., at 68.[11]

The Court of Appeals suggested that application of §8(b)(4)(ii)(B) to the picketing . . . might violate the First Amendment. We think not. Although the Court recognized in *Tree Fruits* that the Constitution might not permit "a broad ban against peaceful picketing," the Court left no doubt that Congress may prohibit secondary picketing calculated "to persuade the customers of the secondary employer to cease trading with him in order to force him to cease dealing with, or to put pressure upon, the primary employer." 377 U.S., at 63. Such picketing spreads labor discord by coercing a neutral party to join the fray. In Electrical Workers v. NLRB, 341 U.S. 694, 705 (1951), this Court expressly held that a prohibition on "picketing in furtherance of [such] unlawful objectives" did not offend the First Amendment. See American Radio Assn. v. Mobile S.S. Assn., 419 U.S. 215, 229-231 (1974); Teamsters v. Vogt, Inc., 354 U.S. 284 (1957). We perceive no reason to depart from that well-established understanding. As applied to picketing that predictably encourages consumers to boycott a secondary business, §8(b)(4)(ii)(B) imposes no impermissible restrictions upon constitutionally protected speech.

Accordingly, the judgment of the Court of Appeals is reversed, and the case is remanded with directions to enforce the [NLRB's] order.

[Justices Blackmun and Stevens, in separate concurrences, objected to the Court's perfunctory rejection of the First Amendment claim. Justice Blackmun noted that he concurred in the result "only because I am reluctant to hold unconstitutional Congress' striking of the delicate balance between union freedom of expression and the ability of neutral employers, employees, and consumers to be free from coerced participation in industrial strife." Justice Stevens stated that picketing involves a mixture of conduct and communication; the First Amendment does not invalidate

---

11. The picketing in *Tree Fruits* and the picketing in this case are relatively extreme examples of the spectrum of conduct that the Board and the courts will encounter in complaints charging violations of §8(b)(4)(ii)(B). If secondary picketing were directed against a product representing a major portion of a neutral's business, but significantly less than that represented by a single dominant product, neither *Tree Fruits* nor today's decision necessarily would control. The critical question would be whether, by encouraging customers to reject the struck product, the secondary appeal is reasonably likely to threaten the neutral party with ruin or substantial loss. Resolution of the question in each case will be entrusted to the Board's expertise.

the statute, which bans only the union's conduct, that is, a signal calling for an automatic response rather than a reasoned response to an idea.]

[Justice Brennan, joined by Justices White and Marshall, dissented, stating that "the conceptual underpinnings of [the Court's] new standard are seriously flawed": First, the harmfulness of a primary product boycott is not necessarily correlated with the percentage of the secondary firm's business represented by that product. Second, a single-product retailer always suffers some harm from a successful primary product boycott even though union activity is not focused on him; §8(b)(4)'s prohibition against coercion of neutral parties "is mismatched to the goal of averting that harm." Finally, because of the Court's imprecise standard, unions would no longer be able to shelter their secondary picketing by restricting their appeals to a boycott of the primary product. Unions will be forced to speculate about the ratio "sufficient . . . to trigger the displeasure of the courts or the . . . Board." Moreover, the Court's reference to "ruin or substantial loss . . . leaves one wondering whether unions will . . . have to inspect balance sheets to determine whether the primary product they wish to picket is too profitable for the secondary firm."]

## *NOTES AND QUESTIONS*

**1. Interpreting §8(b)(4)(ii)(B).** Who has the better reading of the statute in *Tree Fruits*: Justice Brennan for the majority or Justice Harlan in dissent?

**2. Costs of Avoiding Constitutional Questions.** Would it have been better to have avoided a strained reading of the statute and tackled head-on the First Amendment issue in *Tree Fruits*? Did the Court's compromise in that case encourage a perfunctory consideration of the constitutional question in *Safeco*? See Samuel Estreicher, Judicial Nullification: Guido Calabresi's Uncommon Common Law for a Statutory Age, 57 N.Y.U. L. Rev. 1126, 1149 n.72 (1982).

**3. Perfunctory Dismissal of the Constitutional Claim?**

a. What reasons does Justice Powell give for rejecting the union's First Amendment claim in *Safeco*? Do any of the cases cited by the Court deal with consumer, as opposed to producer, boycotts? Do any of the arguments for regulating labor picketing, surveyed supra pages 579-580, apply to consumer appeals?

b. Is the basis for regulation a concern that (1) work stoppages may occur irrespective of the message on the placards or (2) consumers will not read the message on the placards and will boycott the target store entirely out of fear of the picketing? Would the courts permit a ban on picketing by nonlabor groups on the basis of similar projections of possible consequences? Is there a difference for constitutional purposes between picketing for an economic objective and picketing for an exclusively social or political purpose? See James Gray Pope, Labor-Community Coalitions and Boycotts: The Old Labor Law, the New Unionism, and the Living Constitution, 69 Tex. L. Rev. 889 (1991); Harper, The Consumer's Emerging Right to Boycott, supra, at 437-448; Theodore J. St. Antoine, Free Speech or Economic Weapon?—The Persisting Problem of Picketing, 16 Suffolk U. L. Rev. 883 (1982). The Court in other contexts has afforded speech and other political acts motivated by self-interest as much protection as those motivated by altruism. See, e.g., First National Bank v. Bellotti, 435 U.S. 765 (1978); Eastern R.R. Presidents Conference v. Noerr Motor Freight, 365 U.S. 127, 138 (1961).

**4. Neutral Sellers or Integrated-Enterprise Allies?** Note that over 90 percent of the business of the five title companies was derived from the sale of Safeco insurance; that Safeco owned substantial stock in the five companies; and that one Safeco officer served on each of the boards of the five companies. The D.C. Circuit below (in a portion of its opinion not reviewed by the Supreme Court) held that the five companies were nevertheless independent entities. 627 F.2d 1133, 1137-1139 (1979). Did the "struck product" picketing in *Safeco* expose the title companies to any greater impact than would have flowed from a shutdown of production at Safeco?

**5. Motive vs. Impact.** Is *Safeco* faithful to the theory of *Tree Fruits*? Does a violation of §8(b)(4) turn on the union's objective or the impact felt by the ostensibly neutral enterprise? Even where the dominant product of the neutral business is provided by the primary employer, does the union's objective change from one directed at the primary to one directed at the secondary employer, as long as the union avoids any inducement of work stoppages at the secondary and confines its appeal to the struck product?

**6. "Merged Product" Cases.** A union involved in a strike with a bakery pickets two restaurants urging a boycott of the bread offered customers for no separate charge with each meal. If the union's placards make clear that they are seeking a boycott only of the bread "sold" by the restaurants, has the union violated §8(b)(4)? Does footnote 7 of the Court's opinion in *Safeco* resolve this issue?

**7. Consumer Picketing in the Absence of a Primary Dispute.** A union, representing employees of New York metropolitan area bottlers and distributors, pickets retail stores in the area with placards stating, "Buy Local." No work stoppages occur. Has the union violated §8(b)(4), even though it has no identifiable primary dispute with any employer? Is it sufficient that one object of the picketing is to cause the retail stores to cease doing business with nonlocal suppliers? See Soft Drink Workers Union Local 812, Teamsters v. NLRB, 657 F.2d 1252 (D.C. Cir. 1980). Does *Safeco,* in combination with the *Allied International* case, supra note 4, page 581, make clear that the picketing is unlawful? If you were the union's attorney, what advice would you give your client to minimize legal difficulties in pursuing its campaign?

## Edward J. DeBartolo Corp. v. Florida Gulf Coast Building & Construction Trades Council

*485 U.S. 568 (1988)*

WHITE, J. . . .

On remand, the Board held that the union's handbilling was proscribed by §8(b)(4)(ii)(B). 273 N.L.R.B. 1431 (1985). It stated that under its prior cases "handbilling and other activity urging a consumer boycott constituted coercion." The Board reasoned that "[a]ppealing to the public not to patronize secondary employers is an attempt to inflict economic harm on the secondary employers by causing them to lose business," and "such appeals constitute 'economic retaliation' and are therefore a form of coercion." It viewed the object of the handbilling as attempting "to force the mall tenants to cease doing business with DeBartolo in order to force DeBartolo and/or Wilson's not to do business with High." The Board observed that it need not inquire whether the prohibition of this handbilling raised serious questions under the First Amendment, for "the statute's literal language and the applicable case law require[d]" a finding of a violation. Finally, it reiterated its longstanding position that "as a congressionally created administrative agency, we will presume the constitutionality of the Act we administer."

The Court of Appeals for the Eleventh Circuit denied enforcement of the Board's order. Because there would be serious doubts about whether §8(b)(4) could constitutionally ban peaceful handbilling not involving nonspeech elements, such as patrolling, the court applied our decision in NLRB v. Catholic Bishop of Chicago, 440 U.S. 490 (1979), to determine if there was a clear congressional intent to proscribe such handbilling. . . .

We agree . . . that this case calls for the invocation of the *Catholic Bishop* rule, for the Board's construction of the statute, as applied in this case, poses serious questions of the validity of §8(b)(4) under the First Amendment. The handbills involved here truthfully revealed the existence of a labor dispute and urged potential customers of the mall to follow a wholly legal course of action, namely, not to patronize the retailers doing business in the mall. The handbilling was peaceful. No picketing or patrolling was involved. On its face, this was expressive activity arguing that substandard wages should be opposed by abstaining from shopping in a mall where such wages were paid. Had the union simply been leafletting the public generally, including those entering every shopping mall in town, pursuant to an annual educational effort against substandard pay, there is little doubt that legislative proscription of such leaflets would pose a substantial issue of validity under the First Amendment. The same may well be true in this case, although here the handbills called attention to a specific situation in the mall allegedly involving the payment of unacceptably low wages by a construction contractor.

That a labor union is the leafletter and that a labor dispute was involved does not foreclose this analysis. We do not suggest that communications by labor unions are never of the commercial speech variety and thereby entitled to a lesser degree of constitutional protection. The handbills involved here, however, do not appear to be typical commercial speech such as advertising the price of a product or arguing its merits, for they pressed the benefits of unionism to the community and the dangers of inadequate wages to the economy and the standard of living of the populace. Of course, commercial speech itself is protected by the First Amendment, Virginia Pharmacy Bd. v. Virginia Citizens Consumer Council, Inc., 425 U.S. 748, 762 (1976), and however these handbills are to be classified, the Court of Appeals was plainly correct in holding that the Board's construction would require deciding serious constitutional issues. . . .

The case turns on whether handbilling such as involved here must be held to "threaten, coerce, or restrain any person" to cease doing business with another, within the meaning of §8(b)(4)(ii)(B). We note first that "induc[ing] or encourag[ing]" employees of the secondary employer to strike is proscribed by §8(b)(4)(i). But more than mere persuasion is necessary to prove a violation of §8(b)(4)(ii): that section requires a showing of threats, coercion, or restraints. Those words, we have said, are "nonspecific, indeed vague," and should be interpreted with "caution" and not given a "broad sweep," [NLRB v. Drivers, 362 U.S. 274, 290 (1960)]; and in applying §8(b)(1)(A) they were not to be construed to reach peaceful recognitional picketing. Neither is there any necessity to construe such language to reach the handbills involved in this case. There is no suggestion that the leaflets had any coercive effect on customers of the mall. There was no violence, picketing, or patrolling and only an attempt to persuade customers not to shop in the mall. . . .

. . . It is urged that [NLRB v. Retail Store Employees (Safeco), 447 U.S. 607 (1980)] rules this case because the union sought a general boycott of all tenants in the mall. But "picketing is qualitatively 'different from other modes of communication.'" Babbitt v. Farm Workers, 442 U.S. 289, 311, n.17 (1979) (quoting Hughes v. Superior Court, 339 U.S. 460, 465 (1950)), and *Safeco* noted that the picketing there actually threatened the neutral with ruin or substantial loss. As Justice Stevens pointed out in his concurrence in *Safeco,* picketing is a "mixture of conduct and communication" and the conduct element "often provides the most persuasive deterrent to third persons about to enter a business establishment." Handbills containing the same message, he observed, are "much less effective than labor picketing" because they "depend entirely on the persuasive force of the idea." . . .

It is nevertheless argued that the second proviso to §8(b)(4) makes clear that that section, as amended in 1959, was intended to proscribe nonpicketing appeals such as handbilling urging a consumer boycott of a neutral employer. . . . By its terms, the proviso protects nonpicketing communications directed at customers of a distributor of goods produced by an employer with whom the union has a labor dispute. Because handbilling and other consumer appeals not involving such a distributor are not within the proviso, the argument goes, those appeals must be considered coercive within the meaning of §8(b)(4)(ii). Otherwise, it is said, the proviso is meaningless, for if handbilling and like communications are never coercive and within the reach of the section, there would have been no need whatsoever for the proviso.

This approach treats the proviso as establishing an exception to a prohibition that would otherwise reach the conduct excepted. But this proviso has a different ring to it. It states that §8(b)(4) "shall not be construed" to forbid certain described nonpicketing publicity. That language need not be read as an exception. It may indicate only that without the proviso, the particular nonpicketing communication the proviso protects might have been considered to be coercive, even if other forms of publicity would not be. Section 8(b)(4), with its proviso, may thus be read as not covering nonpicketing publicity, including appeals to customers of a retailer as they approach the store, urging a complete boycott of the retailer because he handles products produced by nonunion shops.

The Board's reading of §8(b)(4) would make an unfair labor practice out of any kind of publicity or communication to the public urging a consumer boycott of employers other than those the proviso specifically deals with. On the facts of this case, newspaper, radio, and television appeals not to patronize the mall would be prohibited; and it would be an unfair labor practice for unions in their own meetings to urge their members not to shop in the mall. Nor could a union's handbills simply urge not shopping at a department store because it is using a nonunion contractor, although the union could safely ask the store's customers not to buy there because it is selling mattresses not carrying the union label. It is difficult, to say the least, to fathom why Congress would consider appeals urging a boycott of a distributor of a nonunion product to be more deserving of protection than nonpicketing persuasion of customers of other neutral employers such as that involved in this case. . . .

## *NOTES AND QUESTIONS*

**1. Does the First Amendment Bar Regulation of Union Boycotts?** Is it clear, as the Court seems to suggest, that the First Amendment would bar prohibition of labor-induced consumer boycotts? Consider the following argument for a constitutional right to engage in consumer boycotts:

> Joining a consumer boycott should be conceived as a constitutionally protected political act by which individuals can influence their society. . . .
>
> Concerted refusals to patronize can provide a means to affect decisions about society even when they are not intended to influence governmental decisions. Decisions made by targets of boycotts—who is employed, how they are employed, where capital is allocated, and what is produced—can be as important to our society and the lives of its members as decisions made by government officials. Furthermore, the impact of a consumer's vote in the marketplace through a boycott is proportional to dollars withheld and it is unmediated by representatives sensitive to other interests. Nor is the impact lost if a majority of consumers do not join the concert; it is only lessened. Finally, concerted refusals to deal can be utilized by minorities who, because of imperfections in our political process, lack an influence over governmental policy proportionate to their numbers.

Harper, The Consumer's Emerging Right to Boycott, supra, at 422-423. See also Michael C. Harper, First Amendment Protection for Union Appeals to Consumers, 27 Wis. J. L. Gender & Soc'y 176, 178 (2012) (elaborating why *DeBartolo* and Local Union No. 1506, 355 N.L.R.B. 797 (2010), discussed infra, "require and deserve the First Amendment support on which they rely.").

**2. Rendering the Publicity Proviso Superfluous?** Is the publicity proviso simply a clarification of the reach of the ban on secondary appeals to consumers, or does it carve out an area of protection that otherwise would be prohibited by §8(b)(4)? Has the Court essentially construed the publicity proviso to have no independent significance?

**3. Picketing vs. Handbilling.** If no work stoppages occur, is consumer product picketing (targeted only at consumers) really any different from consumer handbilling? Conversely, should handbilling aimed at neutral employees that is intended to or that does induce a strike be treated any differently from picketing seeking or inducing a similar response? See Warshawsky & Co. v. NLRB, 182 F.3d 948 (D.C. Cir. 1999) (distinguishing *DeBartolo* on basis that union handbilling at issue directly induced or encouraged a secondary strike and was therefore unlawful; First Amendment does not protect communications aimed at neutral employees merely because they take form of handbilling rather than picketing).

**4. Bannering.** For several years, the Carpenters Union has had a labor dispute with three contracting companies — Brady, Precision, and E&K — objecting to their use of nonunion employees and their alleged failure to meet local labor standards — especially wage standards — on construction projects in the Phoenix, Los Angeles, and San Diego metropolitan areas. Trying to induce Brady, Precision, and E&K to change their labor practices, by influencing the contracting practices of companies that do business with them ("the Retailers"), the Carpenters sent the Retailers letters promising an "aggressive public information campaign against [Brady, Precision, or E&K]," including "highly visible banner displays" at the Retailers' places of business. The letters urged the Retailers "to not allow [Brady, Precision, or E&K] to perform any work on any of your projects unless and until it generally meets area labor standards." When the Retailers did not respond, the Carpenters decided to protest at the site of 18 Retailers that continued to contract with Brady, Precision, or E&K. Near each Retailer, the Carpenters set up a 4-foot by 15-foot banner that read "SHAME ON [NAME OF RETAILER]" in large red letters, with the words "LABOR DISPUTE" in somewhat smaller black letters on either side of that text. No other words or images appeared on the banners. Standing on the public sidewalk, individual union members held the banners anywhere from 20 to several hundred feet from the Retailers' entrances. The members also distributed handbills to passing pedestrians, explaining the nature of the "labor dispute." The handbills specified that their underlying complaint was with Brady, Precision, and E&K, and that the Carpenters believed that by using the service of those three contractors the Retailers were aiding them in undermining regional labor standards. Have the Carpenters violated §8(b)(4)(B)? Is there any reason to treat the banners differently than handbilling? See Overstreet v. United Bhd. of Carpenters, 409 F.3d 1199 (9th Cir. 2005); Davidoff v. Minneapolis Bldg. & Constr. Trades Council, 550 F.2d 407 (8th Cir. 1977). Is it significant that bannering is typically stationary activity? Does the result differ if the union uses a moving display but without blocking access or egress, any shouting, or any moving back and forth as is typical in a picket line? See Kentov v. Sheet Metal Workers Ass'n, 418 F.3d 1259 (11th Cir. 2005).

In United Bhd. of Carpenters & Joiners of Am., Local Union No. 1506 v. Eliason & Knuth of Ariz., Inc., 355 N.L.R.B. 797, 797 (2010), the Board upheld the legality of large stationary banners announcing a "labor dispute" and urging a consumer boycott:

> The language of the Act and its legislative history do not suggest that Congress intended Section 8(b)(4)(ii)(B) to prohibit the peaceful stationary display of a banner. Furthermore, a review of Board and court precedent demonstrates that the nonconfrontational display of stationary banners at issue here is not comparable to the types of conduct found to "threaten,

coerce, or restrain" a neutral employer under Section 8(b)(4)(ii)(B)—picketing and disruptive or otherwise coercive nonpicketing conduct.

**5. Union Lobbying.** Union lobbying helped defeat state legislation that would have allowed Louisiana's public service commission to regulate rates charged by an electrical generating cooperative. To repay the union for its effort, the cooperative terminated its contract with Brown & Root, a nonunion subcontractor. Did the union violate §8(b)(4)? See Brown & Root, Inc. v. Louisiana State AFL-CIO, 10 F.3d 316 (5th Cir. 1994).

### e. *"Hot Cargo" Clauses*

**National Woodwork Manufacturers Ass'n v. NLRB**
*386 U.S. 612 (1967)*

BRENNAN, J. . . .

Frouge Corporation, a Bridgeport, Connecticut, concern, was the general contractor on a housing project in Philadelphia. Frouge had a collective bargaining agreement with the Carpenters' International Union under which Frouge agreed to be bound by the rules and regulations agreed upon by local unions with contractors in areas in which Frouge had jobs. Frouge was therefore subject to the provisions of a collective bargaining agreement between the Union and an organization of Philadelphia contractors, the General Building Contractors Association, Inc. A sentence in a provision of that agreement entitled Rule 17 provides that ". . . No member of this District Council will handle . . . any doors . . . which have been fitted prior to being furnished on the job. . . ."[2]

Frouge's Philadelphia project called for 3,600 doors. Customarily, before the doors could be hung on such projects, "blank" or "blind" doors would be mortised for the knob, routed for the hinges, and beveled to make them fit between jambs. These are tasks traditionally performed in the Philadelphia area by the carpenters employed on the jobsite. However, precut and prefitted doors ready to hang may be purchased from door manufacturers. Although Frouge's contract and job specifications did not

---

2. "The full text of Rule 17 is as follows:

"No employee shall work on any job on which cabinet work, fixtures, millwork, sash, doors, trim or other detailed millwork is used unless the same is Union-made and bears the Union Label of the United Brotherhood of Carpenters and Joiners of America. No member of this District Council will handle material coming from a mill where cutting out and fitting has been done for butts, locks, letter plates, or hardware of any description, nor any doors or transoms which have been fitted prior to being furnished on job, including base, chair, rail, picture moulding, which has been previously fitted. This section to exempt partition work furnished in sections."

The [NLRB] determined that the first sentence violated §8(e), 149 N.L.R.B. 646, 655-656, and the Union did not seek judicial review of that determination.

call for premachined doors, and "blank" or "blind" doors could have been ordered, Frouge contracted for the purchase of premachined doors from a Pennsylvania door manufacturer which is a member of the National Woodwork Manufacturers Association. . . . The Union ordered its carpenter members not to hang the doors when they arrived at the jobsite. Frouge thereupon withdrew the prefabricated doors and substituted "blank" doors which were fitted and cut by its carpenters on the jobsite.

The National Woodwork Manufacturers Association [charged] . . . that by including the "will not handle" sentence of Rule 17 in the collective bargaining agreement the Union [violated] §8(e) [by] entering into an "agreement . . . whereby [the] employer . . . agrees to cease or refrain from handling . . . any of the products of any other employer . . . ," and [also charged] that in enforcing the sentence against Frouge, the Union [violated] §8(b)(4)(B) [by] "forcing or requiring any person to cease using . . . the products of any other . . . manufacturer. . . ." The [NLRB] dismissed the charges, 149 N.L.R.B. 646. The Board [concluded] that the "will not handle" sentence in Rule 17 was language used by the parties to protect and preserve cutting out and fitting as unit work to be performed by the jobsite carpenters. The Board also [concluded] that both the sentence of Rule 17 itself and its maintenance against Frouge were therefore "primary" activity outside the prohibition of §§8(e) and 8(b)(4)(B). . . .

[The Court, reversing the Seventh Circuit, upheld the Board's position.]

Even on the doubtful premise that the words of §8(e) unambiguously embrace the sentence of Rule 17,[4] this does not end inquiry into Congress' purpose in enacting the section. . . .

Strongly held opposing views have invariably marked the controversy over labor's use of the boycott to further its aims by involving an employer in disputes not his own. But congressional action to deal with such conduct has stopped short of proscribing identical activity having the object of pressuring the employer for agreements regulating relations between him and his own employees. That Congress meant §§8(e) and 8(b)(4)(B) to prohibit only "secondary" objectives clearly appears from an examination of the history of congressional action on the subject. . . .

The Landrum-Griffin Act amendments in 1959 were adopted only to close various loopholes in the application of §8(b)(4)(A). . . .

---

4. The statutory language of §8(e) is far from unambiguous. It prohibits agreements to "cease . . . from handling . . . any of the products of *any other employer*. . . ." (Emphasis supplied.) Since both the product and its source are mentioned, the provision might be read not to prohibit an agreement relating solely to the nature of the product itself, such as a work-preservation agreement, but only to prohibit one arising from an objection to the other employers or a definable group of employers who are the source of the product, for example, their nonunion status.

Section 8(e) simply closed still another loophole. In Local 1976, United Brotherhood of Carpenters v. Labor Board (Sand Door), 357 U.S. 93, the Court held that it was no defense to an unfair labor practice charge under §8(b)(4)(A) that the struck employer had agreed, in a contract with the union, not to handle nonunion material. However, the Court emphasized that the mere execution of such a contract provision (known as a "hot cargo" clause because of its prevalence in Teamsters Union contracts), or its voluntary observance by the employer, was not unlawful under §8(b)(4)(A). Section 8(e) was designed to plug this gap in the legislation by making the "hot cargo" clause itself unlawful. The *Sand Door* decision was believed by Congress not only to create the possibility of damage actions against employers for breaches of "hot cargo" clauses, but also to create a situation in which such clauses might be employed to exert subtle pressures upon employers to engage in "voluntary" boycotts. Hearings in late 1958 before the Senate Select Committee explored seven cases of "hot cargo" clauses in Teamsters Union contracts, the use of which the Committee found conscripted neutral employers in Teamsters organizational campaigns.

This loophole-closing measure likewise did not expand the type of conduct which §8(b)(4)(A) condemned. Although the language of §8(e) is sweeping, it closely tracks that of §8(b)(4)(A), and just as the latter and its successor §8(b)(4)(B) did not reach employees' activity to pressure their employer to preserve for themselves work traditionally done by them, §8(e) does not prohibit agreements made and maintained for that purpose. . . .

Moreover, our decision in [Fibreboard Paper Products Corp. v. NLRB, 379 U.S. 203 (1964)] implicitly recognizes the legitimacy of work preservation clauses like that involved here. Indeed, in the circumstances presented in *Fibreboard,* we held that bargaining on the subject was made mandatory by §8(a)(5) of the Act, concerning as it does "terms and conditions of employment," §8(d). *Fibreboard* involved an alleged refusal to bargain with respect to the contracting-out of plant maintenance work previously performed by employees in the bargaining unit. . . . It would therefore be incongruous to interpret §8(e) to invalidate clauses over which the parties may be mandated to bargain and which have been successfully incorporated through collective bargaining in many of this Nation's major labor agreements. . . .

The determination whether the "will not handle" sentence of Rule 17 and its enforcement violated §8(e) and §8(b)(4)(B) cannot be made without an inquiry into whether, under all the surrounding circumstances,[38] the Union's objective was preservation of work for Frouge's employees, or

38. As a general proposition, such circumstances might include the remoteness of the threat of displacement by the banned product or services, the history of labor relations between the union and the employers who would be boycotted, and the economic personality of the industry. See Comment, 62 Mich. L. Rev. 1176, 1185 et seq. (1964).

whether the agreements and boycott were tactically calculated to satisfy union objectives elsewhere. Were the latter the case, Frouge, the boycotting employer, would be a neutral bystander, and the agreement or boycott would . . . become secondary. There need not be an actual dispute with the boycotted employer, here the door manufacturer, for the activity to fall within this category, so long as the tactical object of the agreement and its maintenance is that employer, or benefits to other than the boycotting employees or other employees of the primary employer[,] thus making the agreement or boycott secondary in its aim. The touchstone is whether the agreement or its maintenance is addressed to the labor relations of the contracting employer vis-à-vis his own employees. This will not always be a simple test to apply. But "[h]owever difficult the drawing of lines more nice than obvious, the statute compels the task." Local 761, Electrical Workers v. Labor Board, 366 U.S. 667, 674.

That the "will not handle" provision was not an unfair labor practice in these cases is clear. The finding of the Trial Examiner, adopted by the Board, was that the objective of the sentence was preservation of work traditionally performed by the jobsite carpenters. This finding is supported by substantial evidence, and therefore the Union's making of the "will not handle" agreement was not a violation of §8(e).

Similarly, the Union's maintenance of the provision was not a violation of §8(b)(4)(B). The Union refused to hang prefabricated doors whether or not they bore a union label, and even refused to install prefabricated doors manufactured off the jobsite by members of the Union. This and other substantial evidence supported the finding that the conduct of the Union on the Frouge jobsite related solely to preservation of the traditional tasks of the jobsite carpenters. . . .

[The Appendix to the Court's opinion, the concurring memorandum of Justice Harlan, and the dissenting opinion of Justice Stewart joined by Justices Black, Douglas, and Clark, are omitted.]

## *NOTES AND QUESTIONS*

**1. Pressure by Co-employees.** In a companion case, Houston Insulation Contractors Ass'n v. NLRB, 386 U.S. 664 (1967), the employer had purchased precut asbestos fittings in violation of its agreement with Local 22, requiring cutting at the employer's Houston shop. Co-employees, members of a sister local, refused to install the precut fittings at another location in Texas. The Court, affirming the NLRB's dismissal of a complaint under §8(b)(4)(B), reasoned that action supporting co-employees is not secondary even though the economic interests of the sympathetic employees are not directly involved; the opinion did not mention control relationships between the employer's operations.

Compare the ownership and control branch of the "ally" doctrine, supra note 4, page 594.

**2. "Union Signatory" vs. "Union Standards" Clauses.** The cases draw a distinction between a "union signatory" clause like that in the first sentence of Rule 17, which is viewed as necessarily having a secondary object because it seeks to influence labor relations of other employers, and a "union standards" clause, which on its face does not necessarily have a secondary object because the clause is aimed at preserving standards that obtain at the signatory employer. The latter is not per se unlawful, absent other evidence of a secondary object. Does *National Woodwork* essentially reinforce this distinction? Consider a clause that states:

> If the employer does not have sufficient equipment to make all deliveries itself, it may contract with any cartage company whose truck drivers enjoy the same or greater wages and other benefits as provided in this agreement for employees making deliveries.

See Meat & Highway Drivers v. NLRB, 335 F.2d 709, 715-717 (D.C. Cir. 1964) (involving a manufacturer employing its own truck drivers but occasionally engaging other trucking companies, including nonunion ones, to deliver its products). In determining the circumstances under which such a clause would be compatible with §8(e), review footnote 38 in *National Woodwork.*

**3. "Work Preservation" vs. "Work Acquisition."** Suppose Frouge's employees had not previously done the work of finishing doors, but the union, in order to counteract a decline in employment or to provide work for more members, strikes for and secures a clause assigning such work to the bargaining unit. Has the union violated §8(b)(4)(A) or §8(e)? Is there anything in those statutory provisions or the policy of protecting "neutrals" that warrants a distinction between work preservation and work acquisition? Does that distinction rest on a fear that work acquisition would cause undue friction or on a desire to limit resistance to technological change, especially in the construction trades? Are these considerations material under controlling provisions?

**4. Redefining "Traditional" Work in Light of Technology.** Under the distinction between work preservation and work acquisition, legality of an agreement under §8(e) may turn on whether the disputed work is defined as that performed in the bargaining unit before the use of new technology, rather than as work performed outside the bargaining unit as a result of technological innovation. The difficulties involved are illustrated by the litigation arising from the increased use of maritime containers—large reusable metal receptacles that can hold tons of cargo and can be loaded or unloaded away from the pier, thus making the movement of cargo much more economical but cutting into the jobs of longshoremen, who formerly handled cargo piece by piece at piers. This development led to the "Rules for Containers" negotiated by marine shipping companies and the International Longshoreman's Association (ILA), providing essentially that if containers owned or leased by shipping companies were to be stuffed (loaded) or stripped (unloaded) within a radius of less than 50 miles of a local port area by anyone other than the employees of the cargo's beneficial owner, the work was deemed to be work that should have been done at the pier by ILA labor. The Rules also provided for "liquidated damages" for containers violative of the rules and for royalty payments on any container passing over a pier intact.

The NLRB invalidated these rules under §8(e), as well as union action to enforce them under §8(b)(4)(B), finding that unlawful work acquisition was involved. See, e.g., International Longshoremen's Ass'n (Dolphin Forwarding, Inc.), 236 N.L.R.B. 525 (1978), enforcement denied, 613 F.2d 890 (D.C. Cir. 1979). The Supreme Court (5-4) rejected the Board's definition of the disputed work, vacated its order, and remanded the case to the Board. See NLRB v. International Longshoremen's Ass'n, 447 U.S. 490 (1980). The Court observed that the Board had ignored whether the disputed work was the functional equivalent of work traditionally done by longshoremen. Similarly, the Court emphasized that the Board must focus on the work of the bargaining unit employees, not on the work of other employees who may be doing the same or similar work, and must decide "whether the historical and functional relationship" between the traditional work and the work reserved for the bargaining unit "can support the conclusion that the objective of the agreement was work-preservation rather than the satisfaction of union goals elsewhere." The Court noted that "the question is not whether the rules represent the most rational or efficient response to innovation but whether they are a legally permissible effort to preserve jobs."

On remand and consolidation of other cases, the NLRB in general upheld the Rules for Containers as having an overall work-preservation objective under the Supreme Court's approach. Nonetheless, the Board found an unlawful objective and invalidated the Rules in the two respects in which they had sought to reserve for longshoremen work made superfluous by the new technology. International Longshoremen's Ass'n (N.Y. Shipping Ass'n), 266 N.L.R.B. 230 (1983).

The Supreme Court, reviewing the Rules for Containers for the second time, held that the Rules were lawful in their entirety. Justice Brennan's opinion states that the Board's ruling of partial invalidity erred in assuming that "eliminated work" could never be the object of a lawful work-preservation agreement. In the Court's view, the evidence indicated only a primary objective of preserving longshore work. NLRB v. International Longshoremen's Ass'n, 473 U.S. 61, 80-82 (1985).

**5. Recapture of Work Formerly Done.** In applying the rationale of *National Woodwork*, should recapture of work formerly done be treated as "work preservation" or "work acquisition"? See American Boiler Mfrs. Ass'n v. NLRB, 404 F.2d 547 (8th Cir. 1968), upholding a clause banning use of prefabricated material that had reduced bargaining unit work by 60 to 85 percent and indicating that "work preservation" includes "recapture," at least where employees had not lost all the work before the disputed clause had been negotiated. See also Retail Clerks Local 1288 v. NLRB, 390 F.2d 858, 861 (D.C. Cir. 1968) ("fairly claimable" work may lawfully be recaptured); Newspaper and Mail Deliverers' Union of New York (New York Post), 337 N.L.R.B. 608 (2002) (distinguishing between "fairly claimable" work that union is attempting to "retain or recapture" and work that the union is attempting to "obtain").

**6. Barring Subcontracting by Particular Employers vs. Barring Subcontracting by Any Employer**. In Teamsters, Local 251, 356 N.L.R.B. No. 135 (2011), the clause between the general contractor and the union provided that the trucking services of two companies, Northeast and Cullion, "will not be utilized." The Board ruled that this clause violated §8(e): "That the May 1999 agreement does not bar all subcontracting or name any other companies — despite the fact that [the union] was aware that J.H. Lynch used other subcontractors — belies [the union's] contention that its primary dispute was with J.H. Lynch and not with Northeast or Cullion. The terms of the . . . agreement make clear that its purpose was not to preserve work for bargaining-unit members at J.H. Lynch but was 'tactically calculated to satisfy union objectives elsewhere.'" The First Circuit, however, denied enforcement with respect to one of the subcontractors. NLRB v. Int'l Bhd. of Teamsters, Local 251, 691 F.3d 49 (1st Cir. 2012). In its view, the May 1999 agreement did not provide substantial evidence of "impermissible intent." Other aspects of the record showed that the union intended the agreement to protect union jobs. The court enforced the Board's order with respect to the other subcontractor because the union did not challenge that ruling.

**7. "Union Signatory" Restrictions on Sale of Business.** A collective agreement provided that the owner and operator of American flagships should not sell a vessel without giving prior notice to the union and without securing from the transferee a commitment to observe all provisions of the agreement. The Board found that the provision violated §8(e) and declined to defer to an arbitration award enforcing it against a transferee. Concluding that maritime buyers and sellers are "doing business" within the meaning of §8(e), the Board noted that sales of United States flag vessels (about 200 annually) are "fairly common." The Board rejected the union's defense of lawful work preservation, and noted that after a sale the clause did not require the retention of the existing crew but only that replacements belong to the signatory union. See NMU (Commerce Tankers Corp.), 196 N.L.R.B. 110 (1972), enforced, 486 F.2d 907 (2d Cir. 1973). The reach of *Commerce Tankers* was substantially narrowed in Operating Eng'rs Local 701 (Tru-Mix Constr. Co.), 221 N.L.R.B. 751, 752-753 (1975) (upholding the provision of a collective agreement extending the agreement to purchasers of the entire business): "[In *Commerce Tankers*] the Board held that the sale of vessels in the maritime industry was a fairly common occurrence and did not 'represent a novel situation but occurs in the normal course of doing business.' That concept would seem inapplicable to a situation, as here, where an entire business entity may be transferred from one person to another." For the antitrust issues involved, see Commerce Tankers v. NMU, 553 F.2d 793 (2d Cir. 1977).

**8. Restrictions on Investments in Other Firms.** The Board has consistently held that a "dual shop" or "integrity" clause barring an employer from forming or participating in the formation of a nonunion subsidiary that would operate in the same industry violates §8(e). See, e.g., Operating Engineers Local 520 (Massman Construction), 327 N.L.R.B. 1257 (1999); Carpenters District Council of Northeast Ohio (Alessio Construction), 310 N.L.R.B. 1023 (1993); Sheet Metal Workers Union Local No. 91 (The Schebler Co.), 294 N.L.R.B. 766 (1989), enforced in part, 905 F.2d 417 (D.C. Cir. 1990). In Heartland Industrial Partners, LLC, 348 N.L.R.B. 1081 (2006), the Board (2-1) upheld the facial validity of an agreement between the Steelworkers Union and Heartland, an investment firm, that governed future acquisitions by Heartland. The agreement consisted of two parts: a Side Letter and a Framework for a Constructive Collective-Bargaining Relationship ("Framework"). Under the Side Letter, no less than six months after Heartland made an investment in a "covered business entit[y]" ("CBE") — defined as an entity in which Heartland had a 50 percent ownership interest or 50 percent voting power, or otherwise had the power to direct its management — the Union could notify Heartland of its intention to organize the CBE, and Heartland would then cause the CBE to execute a Framework agreement with the Union, which would contain card-check and neutrality provisions. The Board majority reasoned that the agreement did not by its terms evidence a "cease doing business" objective: "On their face, they do not require Heartland to choose between inducing a CBE to become unionized or severing its relationship with the CBE. Crucially, the challenged clauses also do not — on their face — require Heartland to sever its relationship with a CBE that does not become bound" by the card-check and neutrality agreement. The Board conceded that the card-check and neutrality provisions provided for binding arbitration but seized on the fact that they did not specify the remedy an arbitrator would have to award for violations; hence there was no basis for assuming that an arbitrator would order Heartland to cease doing business with a CBE. See Road Sprinkler Fitters, 357 N.L.R.B. No. 176, 4-5 (2011) (reiterating support for *Heartland*).

**9. "Picket Line" Clauses.** Clauses purporting to shelter employees from discipline for refusing to cross "secondary" picket lines may run afoul of §8(e). See, e.g., Truck Drivers Local 413 v. NLRB, 334 F.2d 539 (D.C. Cir. 1964). Should the invalidity of the clause automatically divest the employees of statutory protection against discipline for refusing to cross such lines?

**10. "Featherbedding" and Work Preservation.** Does the law encourage unions to adopt suboptimal means of ensuring job security for its members by limiting their ability to use economic pressure to obtain new work opportunities as opposed to rules seeking to secure traditional work more efficiently done elsewhere? See also materials on featherbedding, infra pages 642-647.

**11. The Grievance Arbitration Process and §8(e).** The Board has ruled that a facially valid contract clause may nonetheless violate §8(e) if an arbitrator construes it to have a meaning that is impermissible under §8(e). The arbitrator's construction is viewed as providing the "agreement" necessary for a §8(e) violation. See *New York Post,* supra note 5, 337 N.L.R.B. 608; Sheet Metal Workers Local 27 (Thomas Roofing), 321 N.L.R.B. 540 (1996); see, e.g., Teamsters Local 277 (J & J Farms Creamery Co.), 335 N.L.R.B. 1031 (2001) (subcontracting clause as interpreted by arbitrator is not limited to preservation of unit work, as award limits potential subcontractors to those that have contract with union; union's attempt to enforce arbitral award therefore violates §8(e)). The Board has also held that a union violates §8(b)(4) by filing a grievance based on a reading of a contract clause that would effectively convert the clause into an unlawful one under §8(e). *New York Post,* supra; Elevator Constructors (Long Elevator), 289 N.L.R.B. 1095 (1988), enforced, 902 F.2d 1297 (8th Cir. 1990).

**12. Reform of §8(e)?** Consider the following argument for reform of §8(e):

> [Another] area for expanding the realm of contract is to revisit the legislative judgment in 1959 that employers and unions cannot enter into "hot cargo" agreements. Contracts should not be enforceable where the costs are principally visited on neutral third parties. Congress was particularly concerned that the Teamsters union was using its leverage over carriers virtually to compel the unionization of employees of firms using those carriers and otherwise disrupt those businesses in the service of disputes over which they had no control. But the "hot cargo" ban in §8(e) of the NLRA also prohibits

> agreements when the costs will be either directly borne, or ultimately absorbed, by the contracting parties. For example, unions in the construction industry cannot trade wage concessions for agreements from employers that they will not establish nonunion subsidiaries competing for work in the union's geographical jurisdiction.

Samuel Estreicher, Freedom of Contract and Labor Law Reform: Opening Up the Possibilities for Value-Added Unionism, 71 N.Y.U. L. Rev. 827 (1996).

### *Note: "Right to Control" Doctrine of* NLRB v. Enterprise Association of Steam Pipefitters

In NLRB v. Enterprise Ass'n of Steam Pipefitters, 429 U.S. 507 (1977), Austin, the general contractor for the construction of a home for the aged, awarded a subcontract to Hudik for heating, ventilation, and air conditioning work. That contract specified that Austin should buy and install climate control units manufactured by the Slant/Fin Company, and that the manufacturer should cut and thread the internal piping in these units. Those specifications conflicted with Rule IX of the collective agreement between Hudik and Enterprise Association (the union for the steamfitters employed by Hudik), which required the threading and cutting to be done on the job site. When the prethreaded units arrived there, the union steamfitters refused to install them; the union representative told Austin that the factory installation of the internal piping violated the union's agreement with Hudik. Austin's charge ultimately brought the dispute to the NLRB. The Board conceded that the union's refusal had been based on a valid work-preservation clause covering work traditionally performed by Hudik's employees. It stressed, however, that Hudik did not control the assignment of this work; accordingly, an object of the union's pressure was either forcing Hudik to terminate its subcontract with Austin or forcing Austin to change its manner of doing business. That pressure, according to the Board, was exerted on Hudik for its effect on other employers and was, accordingly, secondary and violative of §8(b)(4)(B). A divided court of appeals set aside the Board's order, reasoning that a strike to compel an employer to honor a lawful work-preservation agreement made for their benefit is not against a "neutral," but is "primary." The Supreme Court reversed (6-3), finding that the Board's emphasis on right to control was not "erroneous as a matter of law." The Court added that under Local 1976, United Bhd. of Carpenters v. Labor Board (Sand Door & Plywood Co.), 357 U.S. 93 (1958), which had been essentially approved in the Landrum-Griffin amendments to the NLRA, even a valid work-preservation agreement does not provide a defense to a §8(b)(4) charge. Here, the fact that Austin controlled the disputed assignment of work meant that any labor pressure against Hudik necessarily included an object of ceasing to do business with Austin in violation of §8(b)(4)(B).

Justice Brennan, joined by Justices Stewart and Marshall, dissented on the following grounds: Under *National Woodwork*, Rule IX (requiring on-the-site threading) had been "primary" because it had been designed to benefit Hudik's own employees and not to affect another employer's personnel policies. Accordingly, the union's pressure to get, or to enforce, such a clause was also "primary." It was inconsistent with *National Woodwork* to hold that because Austin, not Hudik, had the right to control the assignment of the disputed work, Austin was the target of the union's pressure. Hudik was not a neutral even after his contract with Austin, which he knew conflicted with his contract with the union, since Hudik could have negotiated with the union over premium pay or other substitutes for the lost work. Furthermore, *Sand Door* was distinguishable since the provision there barred the use of doors from nonunion suppliers and was secondary. Accordingly, despite the legality of the secondary clause in *Sand Door* (under the law then in effect), pressure to enforce it was illegal. By contrast, the *Enterprise* clause was primary as well as lawful, as was the pressure to enforce it.

## *NOTES AND QUESTIONS*

1. **Union's Alternatives?** Suppose that in *Enterprise Ass'n* the union had given Hudik the option of installing the pre-threaded units, provided that the steamfitters received premium pay for that work, and upon the employer's rejection of that option, the union had refused to allow the steamfitters to install those units. Any difference in result? Cf. Carpenters, Local 742 (J.L. Simmons Co.), 237 N.L.R.B. 564 (1978). If the union had obtained an arbitration award assessing damages against Hudik, would seeking the arbitration or the award itself violate §8(b)(4)(B)? On the effect of the construction industry proviso, see infra pages 635-636.

2. **Picketing the General Contractor?** Could the union have picketed the general contractor, Austin, for the purpose of requiring changed specifications designed to increase work for the signatory subcontractor, Hudik? Even if Austin were already unionized? What if the specifications were dictated by the owner's architect? Could the architect be picketed? Would this mean that a union can picket a customer of its employer to force the customer to send business to the employer, thus expanding job opportunities for its members? On the other hand, if the union cannot picket Austin, who is the "primary" employer in the case?

3. **Why Is "Right to Control" Relevant?** Consider the analysis in Douglas L. Leslie, Right to Control: A Study in Secondary Boycotts and Labor Antitrust, 89 Harv. L. Rev. 904 (1976):

> . . . In the right to control situation, general contractors' forbearance from using prefabricated goods is not merely an inevitable byproduct of the union's success in its dispute with the subcontractor. The very purpose of the work stoppage against the reneging subcontractor is to police a cartel which in turn will coerce general contractors, as a class, to give up prefabricated goods. Moreover, the coercion of the general contractors is essential to the causal chain whereby the union attains its ultimate end of work preservation; the union will succeed only if the generals are compelled, by the threat of a collective refusal to supply essential jobsite services, to exercise their discretion by forgoing prefabricated materials.
>
> Finally, one reason to permit unions to exert pressure on their immediate employers regardless of incidental effects on outsiders is to avoid hampering the collective bargaining process. Underlying such a policy is an implicit assumption that collective bargaining between the union and the subcontractor is an appropriate procedure for resolving the issue underlying work preservation disputes: the proper accommodation between technological progress and job security. But . . . this assumption is unwarranted in the right to control situation. The subcontractor and the union do not have adverse interests on this issue; collective bargaining in the right to control situation does not involve the give and take between parties representing all relevant interests that national labor policy assumes. If this is true, it is difficult to see how labor policy is furthered by allowing the union to strike the subcontractor. . . .

Does Professor Leslie's analysis reflect policies embodied in §8(e), as opposed to the antitrust laws? Does the language of or congressional purpose behind §§8(b)(4)(B) and 8(e) support reading these provisions to restrict union pressure on the employer of the employees that the union is attempting to benefit?

### *Note: Industry-Wide Provisos to §8(e)*

The garment and construction industries differ in their structure and history and in the obstacles they have presented to union organization. These factors help account for differences in the scope of the exemptions from the prohibitions of §8(e) applicable to those two industries.

**Garment Industry Proviso.** The garment industry proviso is the broader one; it embodies an exemption from §8(b)(4)(B), as well as from §8(e), and provides that the NLRA shall not be a bar to enforcement of hot cargo clauses by strikes or other economic pressures. This broader scope is attributable to the structure of the garment industry and the organizing weapons unions used there. Garment manufacturers, seeking to avoid unionization, became "jobbers," farming out manufacturing work to contractors. The intense competition among the latter was linked to the low wages they paid. Faced with practical difficulties in reaching contractors' employees directly, unions pressured jobbers and manufacturers to do business only with unionized contractors. The legislative history indicates that Congress intended the garment industry proviso to continue to permit unions to use those organizational weapons. Thus, in the garment industry it is lawful to enter into an agreement not to contract with nonunion shops, for a union to induce a work stoppage for the purpose of securing such an agreement (which, if the agreement were illegal, would otherwise violate §8(b)(4)(A)), and for a union to induce a work stoppage for the purpose of forcing a manufacturer or jobber to cease doing business with a nonunion contractor (which would otherwise violate §8(b)(4)(B)).

**Construction Industry Proviso.** Largely because of frictions between union construction workers working alongside nonunion workers on the same construction site, the proviso to §8(e) permits agreements "relating to the contracting or subcontracting of work to be done at the site of the construction." There are several limitations to the proviso that should be borne in mind. First, the proviso does not protect agreements barring use at the construction site of materials made elsewhere by a nonunion company. Second, whereas a strike to obtain a hot cargo clause relating to job-site work is lawful, a strike to obtain a hot cargo clause relating to off-site work violates §8(b)(4)(A) and subjects the union to damages under §303. Third, a strike to enforce a lawful hot cargo clause violates §8(b)(4)(B) because it has as one of its objects requiring the signatory employer to cease doing business with the nonunion contractor, even if the latter is performing work at the job site. A demand for arbitration or a lawsuit or other measures not constituting proscribed means under clauses (i) or (ii) of §8(b)(4) would be lawful. See, e.g., Northeastern Indiana Bldg. & Constr. Trades Council, 148 N.L.R.B. 854 (1964), enforcement denied on other grounds, 352 F.2d 696 (D.C. Cir. 1965).

In Connell Constr. Co. v. Plumbers, Local 100, 421 U.S. 616 (1975), excerpted infra page 823, the union sought to organize plumbing and mechanical subcontractors in the Dallas, Texas, area. It picketed a construction site under the supervision of the general contractor, Connell Construction, until the latter agreed to use only subcontractors that were under contract with the union. The hot cargo agreement was limited in terms to mechanical subcontracting work performed only at the job site. Nevertheless, the Court (per Justice Powell) held that the agreement fell outside of the construction industry proviso because the union represented no employees of Connell or of other contractors on the job site, and hence the congressional concern with avoiding job-site frictions was absent. Fearful that such agreements would allow unions to engage in "top-down" organizing of entire construction sites without even consulting the wishes of the affected employees, the Court construed the proviso to "extend[] only to agreements in the context of collective-bargaining relationships and . . . possibly to common-situs relationships on particular jobsites as well." Id. at 633.

In Woelke & Romero Framing, Inc. v. NLRB, 456 U.S. 645 (1982), the Court answered the question it left open in *Connell*—whether hot cargo clauses negotiated in the context of a collective bargaining relationship fell outside of the shelter of the §8(e) proviso if they were not limited to particular job sites where union and nonunion workers would have to work alongside one another. Reviewing the pertinent legislative history, the *Woelke & Romero* Court deemphasized both the job-site friction and top-down organizing concerns identified in *Connell*:

> The proviso helps mitigate the impact of the [NLRB v. Denver Building & Construction Trades Council, 341 U.S. 675 (1951)] decision; although it does not overrule the ban on picketing, it confirms that construction industry unions may enter into agreements that would prohibit the subcontracting of jobsite work to nonunion firms. However, . . . the proviso was not designed solely as a response to the *Denver Building Trades* problem. And even as a response to *Denver Building Trades,* the proviso is only partly concerned with jobsite friction. . . . [W]e believe that Congress endorsed subcontracting agreements obtained in the context of a collective bargaining relationship—and decided to accept whatever top-down pressure such clauses might entail. Congress concluded that the community of interests on the construction jobsite justified the top-down organizational consequences that might attend the protection of legitimate collective-bargaining objectives.

456 U.S. at 662-663.

## *NOTES AND QUESTIONS*

**1. Impact on *Denver Trades*?** In light of *Woelke & Romero,* could the union in *Denver Trades* have obtained a contract with the general contractor barring use of nonunion electrical subcontractors? A work stoppage to enforce such an agreement would clearly violate §8(b)(4)(B), but could the union induce a work stoppage to obtain such a clause? The latter question was expressly reserved in *Woelke & Romero.* See 456 U.S. at 665-666 & n.17. Would it be material that compliance with such a clause could require the contracting employer to sever preexisting relationships with a nonunion contractor? Cf. Los Angeles Bldg. & Constr. Trades Council (Gasket Mfg. Co.), 175 N.L.R.B. 242 (1969).

**2. Construction Industry Proviso and "Right to Control"?** A collective bargaining agreement between a construction union and a construction subcontractor provides for premium pay for installation of prefabricated climate-control units on a construction job, regardless of whether the subcontractor has the "right to control" the decision to use such units. Is the agreement sheltered by the construction industry proviso?

**3. Section 8(e) and "Double-Breasting."** For discussion of the impact of §8(e) on union efforts to regulate "double-breasted" operations, see supra pages 629-630 and infra note 7, page 784.

### *Note: Remedies for Union Unfair Labor Practices*

**Section 10(*l*) Injunctions.** For charges alleging violations of §§8(b)(4)(A)-(C), 8(e), and 8(b)(7), the Regional Director is required upon finding "reasonable cause to believe such charge is true" to seek immediate interim injunctive relief in the federal district courts. The provision differs from the so-called discretionary preliminary injunction authorized by §10(j) for all other unfair labor practices in that (1) the Regional Director can act without authorization by the Board and (2) the seeking of an injunction is mandatory upon a "reasonable cause" finding. "When confronted with a petition for an injunction under section 10(*l*), the function of the District Court is not to determine whether an unfair labor practice has in fact been committed, but simply whether there is reasonable cause to believe a violation of [the NLRA] has occurred. . . . In addition . . . , the Board must show that equitable relief is 'just and proper' under the circumstances." Kentov v. Sheet Metal Workers, supra, 418 F.3d at 1263, quoting Dowd v. International Longshoremen's Ass'n, 975 F.2d 779, 783 (11th Cir. 1992).

**Section 303 Damages Actions.** In the one exception to the exclusive administrative enforcement scheme of the NLRA, §303 of the Labor Management Relations Act of 1947 authorizes "[w]hoever shall be injured in his business or property by reason of any violation" of §8(b)(4) to recover damages in the federal district courts. Such actions may be brought by "primary" and "secondary" employers, see, e.g., United Brick & Clay Workers v. Deena Artware, Inc., 198 F.2d 637 (6th Cir. 1952), as well as third parties suffering direct and foreseeable injuries as a result of the union's unlawful conduct, see, e.g., W.J. Milner & Co. v. IBEW Local 349, 476 F.2d 8 (5th Cir. 1973) (business losses incurred by exclusive sales agent of primary employer, even though agent was not target of union's secondary pressures).

Neither punitive damages, see Local 20, Teamsters v. Morton, 377 U.S. 252 (1964), nor an injunction, see, e.g., Amalgamated Ass'n of Street, Elec., Ry. & Motor Coach Employees v. Dixie Motor Coach Corp., 170 F.2d 902 (8th Cir. 1948), may be obtained in a private §303 action. However, where state law authorizes punitive damages or injunctive relief for state law torts, the federal court may be able to award such relief in the exercise of its supplemental jurisdiction but generally only for violent conduct occurring in the course of the union's secondary pressures. Attorneys' fees are not available for prevailing parties. See Summit Valley Indus., Inc. v. Local 112, United Bhd. of Carpenters & Joiners, 456 U.S. 717 (1982).

Section 303 actions and Board proceedings under §8(b)(4) are independent and can be instituted at the same time. Recovery under §303 need not await resolution of the §8(b)(4) complaint. See International Longshoremen's & Warehousemen's Union v. Juneau Spruce Corp., 342 U.S. 237 (1952). Where the Board rules on a §8(b)(4) complaint before a final judgment is obtained in a §303 action, most courts hold that the Board determination will preclude relitigation of the same issues in the court proceeding. See, e.g., Paramount Transp. System v. Teamsters, Local 150, 436 F.2d 1064 (9th Cir. 1971).

## 3. Work-Assignment Disputes

Work-assignment disputes have for many years created thorny problems. At common law, courts disagreed over the legality of strikes and picketing to secure the assignment of work. See 1 L. Teller, Labor Disputes & Collective Bargaining §131(1940). Later, United States v. Hutcheson, 312 U.S. 219 (1941), supra page 42, precluded the use of the Sherman Act against such stoppages. After World War II ended, such disputes proliferated, and Congress in 1947, by enacting §§8(b)(4)(D), 10(k), 10(*l*), and 303, sought to promote orderly resolution of the underlying disputes and to avert resulting work stoppages. The materials below will explore the effect and the interplay of those sections (as amended in 1959).

### NLRB v. Plasterers' Local Union No. 79
*404 U.S. 116 (1971)*

White, J.

When a charge is filed under §8(b)(4)(D) . . . , the provision banning so-called jurisdictional disputes, the Board must under §10(k) "hear and determine the dispute out of which [the] unfair labor practice shall have arisen, unless . . . the parties to such dispute" adjust or agree upon a method for the voluntary adjustment of the dispute. The issue here is whether an employer, picketed to force reassignment of work, is a "party" to the "dispute" for purposes of §10(k). When the two unions involved, but not the employer, have agreed upon a method of settlement, must the Board dismiss the §10(k) proceedings or must it proceed to determine the dispute with the employer being afforded a chance to participate?

Texas State Tile & Terrazzo Co. (Texas State) and Martini Tile & Terrazzo Co. (Martini) are contractors in Houston, Texas, engaged in the business of installing tile and terrazzo. Both have collective-bargaining agreements with the [Tile Setters' Local Union No. 20] and have characteristically used members of the Tile Setters union for laying tile and also for work described in the collective-bargaining contract as applying "a coat or coats of mortar, prepared to proper tolerance to receive tile on floors, walls and ceiling regardless of whether the mortar coat is wet or dry at the time the tile is applied to it."

This case arose when [Plasterers' Local Union No. 79] picketed the job sites of Texas State and Martini claiming that the work of applying the mortar to receive tile was the work of the Plasterers' union and not of the Tile

Setters. Neither Texas State nor Martini had a collective-bargaining contract with the Plasterers or regularly employed workers represented by that union.

Before the Texas State picketing began, the Plasterers submitted their claim to the disputed work to the National Joint Board for Settlement of Jurisdictional Disputes (Joint Board), a body established by the Building Trades Department, AFL-CIO, and by certain employer groups. Both the Plasterers' and the Tile Setters' locals were bound by Joint Board decisions because their international unions were members of the AFL-CIO's Building Trades Department. Neither Texas State nor Martini had agreed to be bound by Joint Board procedures and decisions, however. The Joint Board found the work in dispute to be covered by an agreement of August 1917, between the two international unions, and awarded the work to the Plasterers. When Texas State and the Tile Setters refused to acquiesce in the Joint Board decision and change the work assignment, the Plasterers began the picketing of Texas State which formed the basis for the §8(b)(4)(D) charges. The Plasterers also picketed a jobsite where Martini employees, members of the Tile Setters, were installing tile, although this dispute had not been submitted to the Joint Board.

Martini and Southwestern Construction Co., the general contractor that had hired Texas State, filed §8(b)(4)(D) . . . charges against the Plasterers, and the NLRB's Regional Director noticed a consolidated §10(k) hearing to determine the dispute. Southwestern, Texas State, Martini, and the two unions participated in the hearing. A panel of the Board noted that the Tile Setters admitted being bound by Joint Board procedures, but deemed the Joint Board decision to lack controlling weight, and "after taking into account and balancing all relevant factors" awarded the work to the Tile Setters.[9] When the Plasterers refused to indicate that they would abide by the Board's award, a §8(b)(4)(D) complaint was issued against them, and they were found to have committed an unfair labor practice by picketing to force Texas State and Martini to assign the disputed work to them. In making both the §10(k) and §8(b)(4)(D) decisions, the Board rejected the Plasterers'

---

9. The NLRB considered the collective-bargaining agreements among the parties, industry and area practice, relative skills and efficiency of operation, past practices of the employers, agreements between the Plasterers and the Tile Setters, the Joint Board award (the NLRB refused to give this controlling weight because of its "ambiguous nature") and concluded:

"Tile setters are at least as skilled in the performance of the work as plasterers, and both Texas Tile and Martini, which assigned them to the work, have been satisfied with both the quality of their work and the cost of employing them. Moreover, the instant assignments of the disputed work to tile setters are consistent with the explicit provisions of the collective-bargaining agreement between the Tile Setters and Texas Tile and Martini, are consistent with the past practice of the Employers, and are not inconsistent with area or industry practice. . . ." The Board's decision in the §10(k) proceeding is reported at 167 N.L.R.B. 185 (1967) and its decision and order in the unfair labor practice proceeding are reported at 172 N.L.R.B. Nos. 70, 72 (1968).

contention that even though the employer had not agreed to be bound by the Joint Board decision, the provisions of §10(k) precluded a subsequent Board decision because the competing unions had agreed upon a voluntary method of adjustment.

On petition to review by the Plasterers and cross petition to enforce by the Board, a divided panel of the Court of Appeals set aside the order of the Board. . . . It concluded that the Board may not make a §10(k) determination of a jurisdictional dispute where the opposing unions have agreed to settle their differences through binding arbitration. Both the Board and the employers petitioned for certiorari, and we granted the petitions.

Section 8(b)(4)(D) makes it an unfair labor practice for a labor organization to strike or threaten or coerce an employer or other person in order to force or require an employer to assign particular work to one group of employees rather than to another, unless the employer is refusing to honor a representation order of the Board. On its face, the section would appear to cover any union challenge to an employer work assignment where the prohibited means are employed. NLRB v. Radio & Television Broadcast Engineers Union, Local 1212, 364 U.S. 573, 576 (1961) (hereinafter *CBS*). As the charging or intervening party, the employer would normally be a party to any proceedings under that section. Section 8(b)(4)(D), however, must be read in light of §10(k) with which it is interlocked. *CBS*, supra, at 576. When a §8(b)(4)(D) charge is filed and there is reasonable cause to believe that an unfair labor practice has been committed, issuance of the complaint is withheld until the provisions of §10(k) have been satisfied. That section directs the Board to "hear and determine" the dispute out of which the alleged unfair labor practice arose; the Board is required to decide which union or group of employees is entitled to the disputed work in accordance with acceptable, Board-developed standards, unless the parties to the underlying dispute settle the case or agree upon a method for settlement. Whether the §8(b)(4)(D) charge will be sustained or dismissed is thus dependent on the outcome of the §10(k) proceeding. The Board allows an employer to fully participate in a §10(k) proceeding as a party. If the employer prefers the employees to whom he has assigned the work, his right to later relief against the other union's picketing is conditioned upon his ability to convince the Board in the §10(k) proceeding that his original assignment is valid under the criteria employed by the Board. . . .

The phrase "parties to the dispute" giving rise to the picketing must be given its commonsense meaning corresponding to the actual interests involved here. . . . Section 10(k) does not expressly or impliedly deny party status to an employer, and since the section's adoption in 1947, the Board has regularly accorded party status to the employer and has refused to dismiss the proceeding when the unions, but not the employer, have agreed to settle.

The Court of Appeals rejected this construction of §10(k). Its reasoning, which we find unpersuasive, was that because the employer is not bound by the §10(k) decision, he should have no right to insist upon participation. But the §10(k) decision standing alone, binds no one. No cease-and-desist order against either union or employer results from such a proceeding; the impact of the §10(k) decision is felt in the §8(b)(4)(D) hearing because for all practical purposes the Board's award determines who will prevail in the unfair labor practice proceeding. If the picketing union persists in its conduct despite a §10(k) decision against it, a §8(b)(4)(D) complaint issues and the union will likely be found guilty of an unfair labor practice and be ordered to cease and desist. On the other hand, if that union wins the §10(k) decision and the employer does not comply, the employer's §8(b)(4)(D) case evaporates and the charges he filed against the picketing union will be dismissed. Neither the employer nor the employees to whom he has assigned the work are legally bound to observe the §10(k) decision, but both will lose their §8(b)(4)(D) protection against the picketing which may, as it did here, shut down the job. The employer will be under intense pressure practically to conform to the Board's decision. This is the design of the Act. Congress provided no other way to implement the Board's §10(k) decision. . . .

## *NOTES AND QUESTIONS*

**1. Board's Multifactor §10(k) Inquiry.** The Board's approach to §10(k) determinations, set forth in Machinists, Lodge 1743 (J.A. Jones Constr.), 135 N.L.R.B. 1402 (1962), was developed after extensive consideration and discussion with union leaders and employers following the *CBS* decision. Subsequently, the Board retained its case-by-case approach, adding to the relevant factors "safety" and, in connection with the introduction of new technology, the issue of whether employees previously performing the given function would be displaced. See Laborers District Council (Anjo Constr.), 265 N.L.R.B. 186 (1982); Philadelphia Typographical Union, Local 2, 142 N.L.R.B. 36 (1963).

Reviewing courts have generally upheld the Board's §10(k) awards, but not without criticism of its lack of standards for weighing the pertinent factors and its failure to follow its own precedents. See NLRB v. Teamsters Local 584, 535 F.2d 205, 207-208 (2d Cir. 1976).

**2. Deference to Employer Assignments?** In approximately 95 percent of the decisions during the three years after the *CBS* decision (1961), the Board upheld the employer's assignment of the disputed work. Given the Board's §10(k) criteria, is this tendency surprising? Is it desirable?

See Supp. Report of the Special "10(k)" Committee, ABA Lab. Rel. Section 437, 438 (1964).

**3. Section 10(k) and Arbitration.** The interplay between §10(k) and the arbitration process is discussed in Carey v. Westinghouse Elec. Corp., 375 U.S. 261 (1964), infra page 723.

**4. Tensions with §§8(a)(3) and 8(b)(2).** The Board has sought to avoid tensions with §§8(a)(3) and 8(b)(2) by awarding disputed work to employees represented by the winning union and not to that union or to its members as such. See, e.g., Operative Plasterers Local 179 (Bertolini Bros. Co.), 194 N.L.R.B. 403, 405 (1971). Nevertheless, compliance with a §10(k) award may result in discharge of, or failure to hire, members of the losing union because of a strike, actual or threatened, by the prevailing union, thereby raising questions under §§8(a)(3) and 8(b). The Board, however, has held that when the actions of all parties, including discharges, are part and parcel of a bona fide work-assignment dispute, §§10(k) and 8(b)(4)(D) are the exclusive remedies. See Brady-Hamilton Stevedore Co., 198 N.L.R.B. 147 (1972), enforced sub nom. Operating Engrs. Local 701 v. NLRB, 504 F.2d 1222 (9th Cir. 1974).

**5. Liability for Damages Under §303?** The *Plasterers* case declared that a union would not violate §8(b)(4)(D) by picketing in order to enforce a §10(k) award. But what of liability under §303(a) for damages caused by a strike or picketing by the prevailing union before it was awarded the work in a §10(k) proceeding or, indeed, thereafter? Cf. Local 714 v. Sullivan Transfer, Inc., 650 F.2d 669 (5th Cir. 1981).

## 4. "Featherbedding" and Make-Work Practices

"Featherbedding" refers to practices such as make-work rules, excessive staffing, production quotas, and resistance to technological improvements. Such practices, like limitations on subcontracting and work-assignment disputes, reflect the desire of employees for job security or increased employment and of unions for institutional survival and growth. Featherbedding is an old phenomenon and has not been confined to the unionized sector. But the power of labor organizations can institutionalize obstructions to efficiency and shield them against the pressure of market forces for considerably longer periods.

It is conceivable that the parties sometimes resort to work rules and restrictive practices as an indirect method of negotiating "efficient"—that is, "off-the-demand curve"—bargains. For further discussion, see I.M. McDonald & Robert M. Solow, Wage Bargaining and Employment,

71 Am. Econ. Rev. 896 (1981). But see Andrew J. Oswald, Efficient Contracts Are on the Labour Demand Curve, 1 Labour Econ. 85 (1993). However, the traditional response of the legal system is that featherbedding is contrary to the public interest because it inhibits productivity and a rising standard of living. That assessment led many courts, at common law, to condemn as unlawful and enjoinable strikes to impose make-work practices. See Haverhill Strand Theater v. Gillen, 229 Mass. 413, 118 N.E. 671 (1918) (union enjoined from enforcing rule requiring the hiring of a minimum of five musicians where employer desired services of single musician); Opera on Tour v. Weber, 285 N.Y. 348, 34 N.E.2d 349 (1941) (despite state counterpart of Norris-LaGuardia Act, injunction upheld against stagehands' strike inspired by musicians in protest against use by traveling opera company of recorded music rather than live orchestra). By the early 1940s, however, the courts were beginning to hold that union work stoppages and other pressures to secure restrictive work rules were immune from Sherman Act liability and injunctions by virtue of the Norris-LaGuardia Act and §20 of the Clayton Act. See United States v. American Federation of Musicians, 47 F. Supp. 304 (N.D. Ill. 1942), affirmed per curiam, 318 U.S. 741 (1943).

Congress in the same period was beginning to legislate against certain union abuses. The Lea Act of 1946, 47 U.S.C. §506, amended the Communications Act of 1934 to provide for fines and imprisonment for inducing radio broadcasters to employ "any . . . persons in excess of the number of employees needed . . . to perform actual services" or to require payments in lieu of employing excess personnel. See United States v. Petrillo, 332 U.S. 1 (1947). The Hobbs Act was enacted to outlaw certain extortionate practices. See infra note 5, page 647. Also, in the Taft-Hartley amendments, Congress added §8(b)(6), which prohibits unions from causing employers to pay, "in the nature of an exaction, for services which are not performed or not to be performed." The House bill would also have barred union-induced "featherbedding practice[s]"—defined as requirements to employ any person "in excess of the number of employees reasonably required by [the] employer to perform actual services." H.R. Rep. No. 245, 80th Cong., 1st Sess. 25, 50, 61 (1947). This provision did not survive because of concerns expressed by the Senate conferees that "it was almost impossible for the courts to determine the exact number of men required in hundreds of industries and all kinds of functions." 93 Cong. Rec. 6601, 6603 (June 5, 1947).

## NLRB v. Gamble Enterprises, Inc.
*345 U.S. 117 (1953)*

BURTON, J.

For generations professional musicians have faced a shortage in the local employment needed to yield them a livelihood. They have been confronted with the competition of military bands, traveling bands, foreign musicians on tour, local amateur organizations and, more recently, technological developments in reproduction and broadcasting. To help them conserve local sources of employment, they developed local protective societies. Since 1896, they also have organized and maintained on a national scale the American Federation of Musicians, affiliated with the American Federation of Labor. By 1943, practically all professional instrumental performers and conductors in the United States had joined the Federation, establishing a membership of over 200,000, with 10,000 more in Canada.

The Federation uses its nationwide control of professional talent to help individual members and local unions. It insists that traveling band contracts be subject to its rules, laws and regulations. Article 18, §4, of its By-Laws provides: "Traveling members cannot, without the consent of a Local, play any presentation performances in its jurisdiction unless a local house orchestra is also employed."

. . . For more than 12 years the Palace Theater in Akron, Ohio, has been one of an interstate chain of theaters managed by respondent, Gamble Enterprises, Inc. . . . Before the decline of vaudeville and until about 1940, respondent employed a local orchestra of nine union musicians to play for stage acts at that theater. When a traveling band occupied the stage, the local orchestra played from the pit for the vaudeville acts and, at times, augmented the performance of the traveling band.

Since 1940, respondent has used the Palace for showing motion pictures with occasional appearances of traveling bands. Between 1940 and 1947, the local musicians, no longer employed on a regular basis, held periodic rehearsals at the theater and were available when required. When a traveling band appeared there, respondent paid the members of the local orchestra a sum equal to the minimum union wages for a similar engagement but they played no music.

The Taft-Hartley Act, containing §8(b)(6), . . . took effect August 22. Between July 2 and November 12, seven performances of traveling bands were presented on the Palace stage. Local musicians were neither used nor paid on those occasions. They raised no objections and made no demands for "stand-by" payments. However, in October, 1947, the American Federation of Musicians, Local No. 24, of Akron, Ohio . . . opened negotiations with respondent for the latter's employment of a pit orchestra of local musicians whenever a traveling band performed on the stage. The pit orchestra was to play overtures, "intermissions" and "chasers" (the latter while patrons were leaving the theater). The union required acceptance of this proposal as a condition of its consent to local appearances of traveling bands. Respondent declined the offer and a traveling band scheduled to appear November 20 canceled its engagement on learning that the union had withheld its consent.

May 8, 1949, the union made a new proposal. It sought a guaranty that a local orchestra would be employed by respondent on some number of occasions having a relation to the number of traveling band appearances. This and similar proposals were declined on the ground that the local orchestra was neither necessary nor desired. Accordingly, in July, 1949, the union again declined to consent to the appearance of a traveling band desired by respondent and the band did not appear.

[The Board, with one dissent, dismissed a complaint of the union's violation of §8(b)(6) but was reversed by the court of appeals.]

We accept the finding of the Board . . . that the union was seeking actual employment for its members and not mere "stand-by" pay. . . . [The union] has . . . consistently negotiated for actual employment in connection with traveling band and vaudeville appearances. It has suggested various ways in which a local orchestra could earn pay for performing competent work and, upon those terms, it has offered to consent to the appearance of traveling bands which are Federation-controlled. . . .

Since we and the Board treat the union's proposals as in good faith contemplating the performance of actual services, we agree that the union has not, on this record, engaged in a practice proscribed by §8(b)(6). It has remained for respondent to accept or reject the union's offers on their merits in the light of all material circumstances. We do not find it necessary to determine also whether such offers were "in the nature of an exaction." We are not dealing here with offers of mere "token" or nominal services. The proposals before us were appropriately treated by the Board as offers in good faith and substantial performances by competent musicians. There is no reason to think that sham can be substituted for substance under §8(b)(6) any more than under any other statute. Payments for "standing-by," or for the substantial equivalent of "standing-by," are not payments for services performed, but when an employer receives a bona fide offer of competent performance of relevant services, it remains for the employer, through free and fair negotiation, to determine whether such offer shall be accepted and what compensation shall be paid for the work done.

[The dissenting opinions of Justice Jackson and Justice Clark (joined by Chief Justice Vinson) are omitted.]

## *NOTES AND QUESTIONS*

**1. Penalties vs. Staffing Rules.** Could the American Federation of Musicians (AFM) have lawfully promoted jobs for local musicians by imposing higher rates for the services of traveling bands when a local band was not also employed? If the Supreme Court had condemned the arrangement challenged in the *Gamble* case, would the alternative just suggested also be illegal? What considerations are likely to impel a union to impose unneeded employees rather than to secure higher rates for a reduced complement? For discussion of AFM policies, see Vern Countryman, The Organized Musicians: Pt. I, 16 U. Chi. L. Rev. 56 (1948); Robert A. Gorman, The Recording Musician and Union Power: A Case Study of the American Federation of Musicians, 37 Sw. L.J. 697 (1983).

**2. Requiring the Setting of "Bogus" Type.** In American Newspaper Publ'g Ass'n v. NLRB, 345 U.S. 100 (1953), a companion case to *Gamble Enterprises*, the Court, agreeing with the Board, held that §8(b)(6) did not prohibit the practice of the International Typographical Union (ITU) of setting "bogus" type. That practice had begun with the introduction of the linotype machine in 1890, which had permitted one newspaper to set type for a given advertisement and to produce a mat that other papers could use to print the same advertisement. In order to avoid the loss of work for compositors, the ITU had secured the agreement of newspaper publishers to permit their compositors, at their regular rates of pay, to set type for a bogus copy of an advertisement despite the use of a mat. After being set, the bogus type was promptly melted. The bogus work, done during slack time, took from 2 to 5 percent of a printer's time. The *American Newspaper* Court held that §8(b)(6) prohibited only payments "in the nature of an exaction" when no services at all are performed, and that the provision "leaves to collective bargaining the determination of what, if any work, including bona fide "made work," shall be included as compensable services." Id. at 111. In 1974, the New York City local of the typographical union agreed with the leading local newspapers to the elimination of "bogus" work and the reduction of "featherbedding" in exchange for what was described as a "lifetime guarantee of employment"; this agreement was ratified by an overwhelming majority of the members.

**3. Bona Fide Offer of "Relevant Services"?** Lathers Local 46 (Expanded Metal Eng'g Co.), 207 N.L.R.B. 631 (1973), is one of the Board's rare holdings of a §8(b)(6) violation. Some manufacturing had been done by a unit employee represented by the Teamsters, which had a collective agreement with the employer. The lathers' local, despite the employer's statement that he had no work for a lather, forced the employer to hire a lather who was paid $400 per week but did no lathering. As suggested by the local's business agent, that employee was assigned odd office jobs, some of which he could not perform and others of which he rejected as "demeaning." The Board concluded that the union's demand had not been, in the language of the *Gamble Enterprises* case, "a *bona fide* offer of competent performance of *relevant* services." See also Teamsters Local 456 (J.R. Stevenson Corp.), 212 N.L.R.B. 968 (1974) (construction contractor's $20,000-a-year employee serving as union's agent in checking union cards of incoming truck drivers had not provided the "relevant services" to employer required under §8(b)(6)).

Are situations where a union insists on unwanted employees (such as musical groups) whose services are allegedly "irrelevant" to the employer's enterprise distinguishable?

**4. Application.** A play that does not call for any music has been running in a Chicago theater for 40 weeks. The theater has agreed with the AFM to guarantee six musicians 46 weeks of work so long as they perform in accordance with the theater's directions. Pursuant to that agreement, the theater has paid the musicians a weekly stipend even though they have not performed or even appeared at the theater while the play has been running. The individual musicians have telephoned the theater each week and offered to perform but have been told that their services are not needed. Has the union violated §8(b)(6)? Would your answer be affected if the Chicago agreement had been executed after the New York cast, which was to perform in Chicago, had, without any music, played to capacity crowds for two years in New York?

**5. Hobbs Act.** The Hobbs Act, 18 U.S.C. §1951, has been construed to make it a criminal offense for individuals by violence, actual or threatened, to compel wage payments for "imposed, unwanted, superfluous and fictitious services." See United States v. Green, 350 U.S. 415 (1956) (threats of union force or violence to induce payment for unwanted services of particular groups of workers on construction site). On the applicability of the Hobbs Act to improper means used by management to secure employees' agreement to reduction of collectively bargained benefits, see United States v. Russo, 708 F.2d 209 (6th Cir. 1983).

## 5. Union Violence

Union violence on picket lines can pose a serious problem. See, e.g., Brown & Sharpe Mfg. Co., 299 N.L.R.B. 586 (1990) (violence directed at replacement workers); see generally Armand J. Thieblot & Thomas R. Haggard, Union Violence: The Record and Response by Courts, Legislatures, and the NLRB (1983). Federal regulation, however, is limited. A union violates §8(b)(1) when its agents use physical violence or the threats of violence to coerce employees in the exercise of their §7 rights. See, e.g., Perry Norvell Co., 80 N.L.R.B. 225 (1948). Picketing in front of the homes of nonstriking unit employees was held to be unlawful coercion in Communications Workers of Am., Local 1118, 305 N.L.R.B. 770 (1991). Ordinary principles of agency law determine whether the union is responsible for the acts of its agents. See NLRA §2(13); see, e.g., Longshoremen's Local

6 (Sunset Line & Twine Co.), 79 N.L.R.B. 1487 (1948). Federal criminal process, however, is generally unavailable because the Hobbs Act has been construed to be inapplicable to deliberate destruction of the employer's property occurring in the course of an otherwise lawful strike for higher wages. See United States v. Enmons, 410 U.S. 396 (1976); see generally Note, Labor Violence and the Hobbs Act: A Judicial Dilemma, 67 Yale L.J. 325 (1957). The Hobbs Act's relevance to union violence was further narrowed in Scheidler v. National Org. for Women, 537 U.S. 393 (2003) ("extortion" within meaning of Hobbs Act requires "obtaining" of property; depriving another of property right of exclusive control over their business assets held insufficient).

The Board has declined in cases of union violence to require the union to reimburse employee victims for lost pay (caused by the union's blocking of access to the plant) or for physical or mental injury. As explained in Union de Tronquistas Local 901 (Lock Joint Pipe & Co.), 202 N.L.R.B. 399 (1973), the Board believes that damages assessments will be difficult in strike situations where tempers run high and violence by individuals will be attributed erroneously to unions. The Board concludes that conventional remedies, such as the cease-and-desist order, court-enforced contempt sanctions, and §10(j) injunctions, will ordinarily suffice.

Notwithstanding some overlap with §8(b)(1) of the NLRA, states may regulate and enjoin violence and other threats to public order occurring in the context of labor disputes. See International Union, United Automobile Workers v. Russell, 356 U.S. 634 (1958); Youngdahl v. Rainfair, Inc., 355 U.S. 131 (1957); United Constr. Workers v. Laburnum Constr. Corp., 347 U.S. 656 (1954). The question of federal preemption of state law is taken up in Chapter 11.

# 8 The Enforcement of Collective Bargaining Agreements

## A. THE GRIEVANCE ARBITRATION MACHINERY

Disputes about rights, duties, and expectations under a collective bargaining agreement are normal. Most such disputes are settled informally, but almost every agreement provides for the channeling of unresolved disputes through a formal grievance system culminating in final, binding arbitration.

Most collective agreements provide for ad hoc selection of a single arbitrator. If the parties cannot agree on the arbitrator, an outside agency, such as the Federal Mediation and Conciliation Service or the American Arbitration Association, may be authorized to appoint the arbitrator or to recommend a panel from which the parties choose by alternately striking names or by some other procedure. Other agreements provide for a tripartite board, which acts by majority vote and which is composed of representatives of each side and a neutral who acts as chairperson. This type of arrangement is sometimes viewed as contributing to mediation or informal settlement.

Some agreements, particularly those applicable to large enterprises and multiemployer bargaining units, provide for a "permanent" umpire or impartial chairman appointed for a fixed term or for so long as neither party requests his removal. Such an arrangement avoids the delays involved in ad hoc selections, educates the umpire about the practices, personalities, and problems involved, and frequently promotes helpful mediation and counseling by the umpire. Arbitration proceedings are designed to be more informal than judicial proceedings and are not in general bound by the rules of evidence or the other procedural rules governing actions at law. Nevertheless, objections based on the rules of evidence, such as hearsay, are frequent. Normally arbitrators overrule such objections but indicate that they will "go to the weight." Arbitrators are drawn from a broad variety of occupations and their competence, values, and styles are quite diverse. They are not bound by prior awards — not even, as a formal matter, by those involving the same agreement; as a practical matter, however, prior awards under the same agreement are very influential. Arbitration awards are seldom published and are substantially immune from correction by reviewing courts.

The grievance arbitration process, as an adjunct to the collective agreement, has customarily been hailed as a major accomplishment of American industrial relations. This process is extremely important to a worker's sense of independence and dignity and to his actual and perceived protection against arbitrary action by supervisors. When coupled with a no-strike clause, as it typically is, it provides both a forum for orderly protest against managerial action and an alternative to strikes and other forms of disruption; it is a substitute not only for litigation but also, and more importantly, for economic conflict.

The literature on arbitration is extensive. Among the books relatively general in their approach are Elkouri & Elkouri, How Arbitration Works (7th ed. 2012); Owen Fairweather, Practice and Procedure in Labor Arbitration (4th ed. 1999).

## 1. Discharge and Discipline

### Inter-Pack Corp.

*87 Lab. Arb. Rep. 1232 (1986)*

Brown, Arbitrator: — [The issue is: — ]

Did the company have just cause to suspend [grievant J] for two weeks because of excessive absenteeism? . . .

#### Statement of Facts

. . . [Grievant J] is a Dye Cutter Operator who was hired on June 3, 1985. On Friday, February 7, 1986 she reported for work at 6:30 A.M. but she left work at 8:00 A.M. because she was sick. On Monday 2-10-86 she was suspended for excessive absenteeism.

The production manager gave the grievant the following letter on February 10, 1986:

> Your attention is directed to Work Rules Group III#1, which deals with absenteeism. Since January 2, 1986, you have compiled the following recorded [sic]:
> 1-6-86 Personal business
> 2-3-86 Did not report

2-7-86 Went home early 8:05 A.M.

Out of a total of 27 work days, you have had a problem on 3 days or 11% of the time.

Failure to correct this situation leaves me with no alternative, but to issue a disciplinary layoff of 2 weeks; commencing February 10, 1986 and ending February 23, 1986 at 12 midnight. You may report for work at 6:30 A.M. on February 24, 1986.

On that same day the grievant filed the following grievance:

Nature of Grievance: Unjustified layoff. The understanding has always been that all employees records have cleared on the 1st of Jan. of each year. Other employees have been written up, then given 3 day layoff, then 14 day layoff and not 14 day layoff first.

Settlement Desired: Returned to work and made whole for all losses.

The employer has relied on the work rules which have been posted and shown to all new employees including the grievant in 1985. These rules state the following:

Violation of the following rules will result in disciplinary action as follows:
First offense — written warning
Second offense — disciplinary lay off not to exceed two weeks
Third offense — discharge

1.) *Excessive absenteeism.* Unless there are unusual or special circumstances excessive absenteeism is an unexcused absence rate of 5% or more or a total absence rate, whether excused or unexcused, of 8% or more. An absence will be excused only if the employee presents evidence (doctor's slip, etc.) that the absence was unavoidable. Notice of unavoidable absences must be given to the company as soon as possible, but not later than the starting time of the shift which will be missed.

2.) *Tardiness.* If an employee must be unavoidably late to work he must notify the company prior to the starting of his shift with the reason for tardiness and the approximate time he can report to work.

3.) *Unauthorized absence.* From work station during working hours. Employees are expected to remain on the job during working hours except for rest periods and lunch period, unless a supervisor authorizes the employee to leave the job. Employees are expected to be on the job at the shift starting time, at the end of rest periods and at the end of the lunch period. Wasting time or loitering outside the employee's work area is prohibited.

The grievant's supervisor testified that the grievant had started to miss time from work in September after she had completed her probationary period. He said he verbally warned her that she should improve her attendance or she would receive a written warning. On October 18, 1985 he did issue the following letter of warning to the grievant:

> Your attention is directed to Work Rules Group III#1, which deals with absenteeism. Since 9-9-85 you have compiled the following record:
> 9-9 Did not report
> 10-7 Went home early 7:00 A.M.
> 10-8 Called in sick
> 10-9 Called in sick
> Out of a total of 30 work days, you have had a problem on 4 days or 13.3% of the time.
> Failure to correct this situation will result in further disciplinary action.

This written reprimand was not the subject of a grievance. Then on November 20, [1985,] the grievant left work early to go to Court. On December 4th the grievant was injured on the job and she left work early and in the next few days she was off on a medical leave. Then she missed three days for her grandmother's funeral. The grievant was [then put] on a two week disciplinary suspension until February 23, 1986. The supervisor stated that the union protested the length of the suspension assessed against the grievant. They stated that she was absent January 6th to go to court. The company replied that there was no subpoena and the grievant's court appearance was a personal matter.

The production manager stated that he had calculated that the grievant had been absent 11% of the time from 1-2-86 to 2-7-86. He said that therefore she had violated rule number one of the company's work rules. He also noted that in February, 1986 the grievant had only eight months seniority. He felt that such a new employee should get the maximum disciplinary time off as a final step to straighten out her attendance on the job. He said that this approach has apparently worked because the grievant has had a good attendance record since this discipline. . . .

## Discussion

. . . The employer's excessive absenteeism rule is a "no fault" attendance policy in that an employee may be disciplined even if his or her absences have been excused. . . .

An employer may use a variety of factors to determine which disciplinary action within the published range of penalties is appropriate. The work rules here state that a second offense will result in a disciplinary lay off not to exceed two weeks. Normally the employee's past record, the employee's length of service, aggravating or mitigating circumstances and the degree of fault involved are elements taken into account in deciding the severity of a penalty. . . .

. . . [T]he fact that two other employees got three days off for their second violation of the rule against excessive absenteeism and the grievant got two weeks off for the same offense means nothing until the circumstances of the three cases are compared. All three employees were disciplined within a six month period so the time frame for comparison is the same. On 9/3/85 [co-worker G] was suspended for three days when he had been absent five separate days without report in 30 work days for a rate of 16.6%. The local president was suspended for three days on 10-18-85 for three days absent without report in 30 work days for a rate of 10.0%. The grievant was given a two week suspension on 2-7-86 for three days absent in 27 work days for an 11% rate. One day absent was a "did not report." One day off was to go to court and one day she left early because she was ill. The grievant had eight months' seniority at the time of her [suspension]. The union president had six years seniority and [co-worker G] had two years seniority when they were disciplined. There is no showing that any of these employees had any problem at work other than their poor attendance in 1985 and 1986.

The three employees all had relatively good work records. While the local president had long service with the company, there is little significant difference between eight months and two years seniority. Thus the [principal] reason cited by the company to treat the grievant differently seems weak.

A basic comparison of the substance of the offenses favors the grievant. Her absences were under more mitigating circumstances. She told her employer in advance of her January court date. She tried to work in February and she had to leave early. A day of early departure should not be given the same weight as a full day's absence. Employees ought to be encouraged to try to come to work even if their ability to last the full day is in doubt. Further, a day for personal business, planned for in advance, ought not to be weighted the same as an unscheduled absence because with prior notice the employer is better able to accommodate for such absence. Finally, a "did not report" day off is the most disturbing unexcused absence because the employee has violated the call-in requirements as well as failing to come to work. Using these standards both [co-worker G] and the local president had aggravated second offenses, while the grievant had "special circumstances," as the term is used in rule number one. The employer's application of the penalty in this rule was arbitrary and discriminatory here. (Sprague Devices, Inc., 79 LA 543 (Mulhall, 1982)).

The company has the management right to suspend employees for just cause. However, the concept of just cause requires that an employer dispense discipline evenhandedly. (McCabe Hamilton & Renny Company, Limited, 78 LA 592 (Tsukiyama, 1982)). The arbitrator does not exceed his authority, nor does he usurp management's function when he interprets and applies the just cause provision in a discipline provision or in the management's rights' clause. (Worthington Corp., 24 LA 1 (McGoldnick, 1955)). The mere fact that a two weeks penalty is published as a possible punishment does not mean that such a suspension can not be too severe under some circumstances. (North West Publications Inc., 43 LA 1197 (Sembower, 1964)). The arbitrator here decides that under the circumstances of this case the two week penalty was too severe.

The grievant's penalty should have been only three days off. Her excessive absenteeism did warrant discipline. Three days off would have been a severe penalty under the circumstances and that would have sufficiently recognized low seniority. Two weeks off under these facts was a disciplinary action well beyond a range of reasonableness. The three day suspension to other employees who had engaged in more aggravated misconduct created no precedent but it did provide a basis for comparison of the employer's consistent action in such cases. The grievant should be made whole. (Washington Hospital Center, 75 LA 32 (Rothchild, 1980)).

## *NOTES AND QUESTIONS*

**1. "Just Cause."** Consider one arbitrator's summary of the factors that support a showing of just cause for suspension or termination: (1) "The employee was forewarned of the consequences of his actions"; (2) "The employer's rules are reasonably related to business efficiency and the performance the employer might expect from an employee"; (3) "An effort was made before discipline to determine whether the employee was guilty as charged"; (4) "The investigation was conducted fairly and objectively"; (5) "Substantial evidence of the employee's guilt was obtained"; (6) "The rule was applied fairly and without discrimination"; and (7) "The degree of discipline was reasonably related to the seriousness of the employee's offense and the employee's past record." Enterprise Wire Co., 46 Lab. Arb. (BNA) 359, 362-365 (1966). On which of these factors did arbitrator Brown rely in *Inter-Pack*? Should all these factors be relevant in every case? Regardless of any limiting language in the collective agreement being applied? Should the list be treated as exclusive?

**2. Consistent Application of Company Rules.** Given arbitrator Brown's stress on the company's relatively lenient treatment of the other two employees guilty of excessive absenteeism, might his decision result in the company being more consistently harsh in the future? Do rulings like *Inter-Pack* require employers to reject claims for leniency? How do employees benefit from a requirement of consistency? Are such rulings important to protect employees from the bias or personal animus of supervisors? Do they help ensure employees fair notice of the grounds for discipline?

**3. Exemplary Punishment.** Ten employees are guilty of a breach of the no-strike clause in a collective agreement; all ten could properly be discharged. The company president needs their production to fill an urgent order but does not wish to overlook completely their breach of contract. She proposes to draw one of the ten names out of a hat and to discharge the employee whose name is drawn. Would such a discharge violate the agreement's just cause provision?

**4. Effect of Tightening Up Enforcement of Company Policy.** Suppose an employer that in the past has enforced leniently absenteeism rules now unilaterally announces that in the future it will enforce the rules more strictly in order to reduce production losses. Do the employees who are subjected to the stricter policy have a claim under a conventional "just cause" provision? Do they have a claim of midterm modification in violation of §8(a)(5) of the NLRA? Would it matter if the reason for the employer's new policy was simply a change in management policy rather than an attempt to avert significant losses?

**5. "No Fault" Absenteeism Policy.** Inter-Pack's "no fault" attendance policy permitted discipline even for excused absences. Are there grounds other than possible inconsistent application on which the union could challenge application of the policy in particular cases? See generally K. Don Scott & G. Stephen Taylor, An Analysis of Absenteeism Cases Taken to Arbitration: 1975-1981, 38 Arb. J. 61 (Sept. 1983) (concluding that arbitrators also take into account such things as employee awareness about the policy and whether managers adhere to the policy themselves).

**6. Individualized Justice?** Should the personal situation of the grievant be relevant in determining whether discharge, as opposed to some lesser penalty, is warranted? Do arbitrators have the authority to demand greater justification for the discharge of an employee with many dependents? Of an employee with an outstanding record of community service or religious commitment? Of an employee whose disability or age would make reemployment more difficult?

**7. "Progressive" Discipline.** What purposes are served by the aspect of Inter-Pack's rule that provides for progressively more serious discipline for each successive offense? Does such a system benefit the employer as well as employees? What are the costs of such a system?

a. Should arbitrators interpret just-cause provisions in collective agreements to require that employees be disciplined only in a progressive fashion, even where the collective agreement and employer policies do not expressly state such a requirement? What if the employer in the past had consistently discharged employees for the first violation of even minor rules, such as those governing tardiness? Should it matter whether the union had objected in the past to discharges that were not preceded by written or oral warnings?

Whether the union had sought unsuccessfully to negotiate a formal progressive discipline system?

b. Do progressive discipline systems place employees in "double jeopardy" for rule infractions? See, e.g., Diamond Gardner Corp. v. United Papermakers, Local 1009, 32 Lab. Arb. Rep. (BNA) 581 (1959) (Smith, Arb.) (since prior reprimand was disciplinary action that could be held against grievant in weighing subsequent infractions, an additional punishment could be imposed later). But cf. Titanium Metals Corp., 121 Lab. Arb. Rep. (BNA) 1441 (2006) (Franckiewicz, Arb.) (imposing discipline for recorded earlier tardiness to justify enhanced discipline for later absenteeism was form of double jeopardy); General Servs. Admin. v. American Fed'n of Gov't Employees, 75 Lab. Arb. Rep. (BNA) 1158, 1160 (1980) (Lubic, Arb.) ("In grievance-arbitration, . . . 'double jeopardy' has been held to mean that once discipline for a given offense has been imposed and accepted it cannot be increased").

c. Do principles of progressive discipline work equally well where performance standards are qualitative and subjective? How should arbitrators treat discharges of professional and managerial employees for poor performance when prior counseling did not make clear that their jobs were in jeopardy unless performance improved? See Samuel Estreicher, Absenteeism and Incompetence: The Role of the Courts, in Proc., 35th Ann. N.Y.U. Conf. on Lab. 335 (Bruno Stein ed., 1983).

**8. Discharges for Off-premises Criminal Activity?** Arbitrators are generally reluctant to uphold discharges or other discipline for off-premises criminal activity. Some require "proof of actual detriment or harm [to the employer], or convincing proof from which detriment or harm can be readily or reasonably discerned." Fairmont Gen. Hosp. v. National Union of Hosp. & Health Care Employees, 91 Lab. Arb. Rep. (BNA) 930 (1988) (Hunter, Arb.) (finding no just cause for hospital's discharge of a practical nurse for pleading guilty to a misdemeanor shoplifting charge).

**9. "Obey Now, Grieve Later."** Should employees be obligated to obey orders and rules until they are found invalid? Most arbitrators follow a qualified "obey now, grieve later" principle, commonly not invoking the rule where work assignments are claimed to be illegal, immoral, or a threat to health or safety. Is the general rule an appropriate reading of the joint expectations of the parties to the labor agreement? Will the ex post remedies awarded by arbitrators sufficiently deter employers' application of unreasonable rules?

**10. Burdens of Proof.**

a. *Who Has the Burden of Persuasion?* Although some arbitrators shift to the union the burden of proving that the employer's punishment is too severe, arbitrators consistently place the burden of proving "just cause" for discipline on the employer. In nondiscipline cases, arbitrators frequently place at least the burden of coming forward (and often the burden of persuasion as well) on the party that has initiated the arbitration. Professor Benjamin Aaron urged avoiding the burden of proof issue in nondiscipline cases: "To insist that the complaining party carries the burden of proof in such cases is manifestly absurd. Neither side has a burden of proof or disproof, but both have an obligation to cooperate in an effort to give the arbitrator as much guidance as possible." See Benjamin Aaron, Some Procedural Problems in Arbitration, 10 Vand. L. Rev. 733, 740-742 (1957). Is Professor Aaron's approach realistic for all cases?

b. *What Is the Standard of Proof?* In the absence of explicit contractual language, arbitrators choose between three standards: preponderance of the evidence, clear and convincing evidence, and proof beyond a reasonable doubt. They are more likely to choose a stricter standard when the alleged employee conduct constitutes criminal behavior or involves moral turpitude, and/or provokes discharge rather than some lesser discipline. See Elkouri & Elkouri, supra, at 949-952. Why are these factors relevant to the standard of proof? Most factual questions in contractual disputes are settled under a preponderance of the evidence standard. Why should discipline disputes be exceptions?

**11. Exclusion of Improperly Obtained Evidence?** The prohibition of unreasonable searches and seizures contained in the Fourth Amendment of the U.S. Constitution does not apply to private employers. Yet some arbitrators have interpreted a just cause provision to incorporate Fourth Amendment principles in considering challenges to company investigatory practices or rules. See, e.g., Omnisource Corp., 113 Lab. Arb. Rep. (BNA) 862 (2000) (Loeb, Arb.); Bakery, Confectionery & Tobacco Workers, Local 111 v. Wheatland Farms, 91-2 Lab. Arb. Awards (CCH) ¶8469 (1991) (Nelson, Arb.) (both finding suspicionless drug and alcohol testing rule an unreasonable exercise of management discretion). Furthermore, while most arbitrators admit evidence garnered from unconsented searches, some arbitrators will use Fourth Amendment standards to exclude evidence that would not be admissible in a criminal proceeding. See, e.g., Imperial Glass Corp. v. American Flint Glass Workers, Local 503, 61 Lab. Arb. Rep. (BNA) 1180 (1973) (Gibson, Arb.).

For discussions of the extent to which not only rules excluding improperly obtained evidence but also other protections from the Constitution's Bill of Rights, such as the privilege against self-incrimination and the right of confrontation, should provide standards for arbitrators, see, e.g., Harry T. Edwards, Due Process Considerations in Labor Arbitration, 25 Arb. J. 141 (1970); John Silard, Rights of the Accused Employee in Company

Disciplinary Investigations, in Proc., 22d Ann. N.Y.U. Conf. on Lab. 217, 219-226 (T. Christensen & A. Christensen eds. 1970).

**12. Rules of Evidence?** To what extent should rules of evidence used in judicial proceedings be applied by arbitrators? Among the traditionally cited advantages of arbitration are its relative informality and simplicity and consequent accessibility to nonlawyers. Can these advantages be maintained if arbitrators apply traditional rules of evidence? Rule 28 of the American Arbitration Association's Voluntary Arbitration Rules provides that the "arbitrator shall be the judge of the relevance and materiality of the evidence offered and conformity to legal rules of evidence shall not be necessary." Furthermore, arbitrators often consider hearsay and other evidence that might otherwise be considered inadmissible in court. See, e.g., Associated Cleaning Consultants & Servs. v. International Bhd. of Painters Local 327, 94 Lab. Arb. Rep. (BNA) 1246 (1990) (Lubow, Arb.). Nevertheless, some commentators have lamented that the increased formalization and duration of many labor arbitrations are due at least in part to the increasing tendency of the parties to rely on lawyers in these proceedings. See, e.g., Reginald Alleyne, Delawyerizing Labor Arbitration, 50 Ohio St. L.J. 93 (1989). Is increased formality necessary to ensure that individual employees are treated fairly? If arbitration becomes more expensive for both employers and unions because of increased formality, will employees benefit in the aggregate?

**13. Reliance on Other Arbitration Awards?** Many arbitrators treat opinions of other arbitrators interpreting other collective bargaining agreements as persuasive authority. Arbitrators, however, are not bound by prior awards on similar issues under other contracts or by the ostensible weight of authority on a particular issue. Stare decisis principles cannot be strictly applied in arbitration because each arbitrator is given independent authority under a particular contract. Moreover, only a very small proportion of arbitration awards are ultimately published.

Arbitrators do give substantial deference to earlier awards involving the same parties, the same contract provision, and the same issue. Should they be required to give such prior awards res judicata or collateral estoppel effect? See United Automobile, Aerospace & Agricultural Implement Workers of America v. Dana Corp., 278 F.3d 548, 555-557 (6th Cir. 2002) (arbitrator is not bound by prior arbitral award unless collective bargaining agreement so stipulates; preclusive effect of prior award is determination to be made by arbitrator); see also W.R. Grace & Co. v. Rubber Workers, 461 U.S. 757 (1983). For commentary on this issue, see Timothy J. Heinsz, Grieve It Again: Of Stare Decisis, Res Judicata and Collateral Estoppel in Labor Arbitration, 38 B.C. L. Rev. 275 (1997). For treatment of judicial review of arbitration awards, see infra pages 690-695.

### 2. SUBCONTRACTING

**Allis-Chalmers Manufacturing Co.**
*39 Lab. Arb. Rep. 1213 (BNA) (1962)*

SMITH, Arbitrator: —

. . . [T]he Union protests the contracting out of certain work. Grievance No. 1802-59-B concerns the use of an outside contractor to perform certain janitorial work. . . . Grievance No. 1183-262-A concerns two "subcontracts" for production work. One was for the manufacture of certain "operating mechanisms," which were components of power transformers. The other was for the manufacture of certain "stationary contacts," which were components of electrical equipment.

With respect to Grievance No. 1802-59-B, the parties stipulated as follows at the hearing: . . . "[O]n October 29 and 30, 1960, the Company called in an outside contractor, Don's Window Cleaning Company, to have janitorial work performed in the plant. . . . This work was normally and customarily performed by employees in the bargaining unit. At [that] time . . . there were employees from the bargaining unit on layoff." . . .

With respect to Grievance No. 1183-262-A . . . :

. . . The "operating mechanisms" operate the tap changing mechanism of a power transformer. In August, 1961, the mechanism was redesigned, and the first nine required thereafter were manufactured in the Company's shops in November or December, 1961. The next required lot consisted of 33 mechanisms. Outside bids were obtained for their manufacture, exclusive of the steel castings which were to be purchased by the Company from an outside source, as in the past, but including some tooling to be supplied by the Company, and a contract for the work was let to Kramer Industries. Kramer's bid was $175 each for the work it was to do. Taking into account the cost of the castings and of the tooling, the Company thus acquired the mechanisms for a cost of $197.90 each, as compared with a cost of $490 each for the nine mechanisms which had been manufactured in the Company's shops. . . .

The initial question . . . is whether, as the Company contends, the . . . grievances fall outside the jurisdictional authority of the Referee. The Company relies upon Paragraph 167 of the Agreement, which provided as follows:

> The jurisdictional authority of the Impartial Referee is defined as and limited to the determination of any grievance which is a controversy between the parties or between the Company and employees covered by this agreement concerning compliance with any provision of this agreement and is submitted to him consistent with the provisions of this agreement.

. . . This contention . . . is without merit and must be rejected. . . . The Paragraph does not state that a grievance must concern and involve a "provision" which explicitly touches the subject matter of the grievance. It simply says, in effect, that the grievance must involve a controversy concerning compliance with "any provision" of the Agreement. This language does not foreclose the consideration of a claim based on the theory that one or more cited provisions of the Agreement give rise to an implied limitation or restriction on managerial action. There can be no doubt that in the area of contractual obligations generally it is frequently necessary, in order to give effect to the intent of the parties, to determine whether the specific provisions of the agreement, fairly and properly construed, import obligations not specifically stated. This is true at least as much in the case of labor agreements as in the case of other kinds of contracts.

The Referee therefore concludes that the instant grievances present claims which are within his jurisdiction to decide. The basic issue is whether, from the provisions defining the bargaining unit, specifying the wage structure, providing seniority rights, and otherwise providing rights and benefits to employees, there arises an implied prohibition upon the contracting out of work of kinds normally and customarily done by employees in the bargaining unit. This is a contention which involves a controversy concerning compliance with a provision of the Agreement alleged to be implicit in the specified provisions.

Insofar as the Union's case is predicated . . . on the broad proposition that the labor agreement, taken as a whole or in the light of the specific provisions cited, gives rise to an implied absolute and unqualified prohibition upon the contracting out of work normally and customarily performed by employees in the bargaining unit, the contention must be dismissed as untenable. . . .

. . . The present Referee, while rejecting the Union's view that there exists an absolute (implied) prohibition on the contracting out of work of kinds regularly and normally performed by bargaining unit employees, likewise rejects the Company's view that it has complete freedom in this respect. "[A] standard of 'good faith' may be applicable, difficult of definition as this may be." Upon further reflection, he is prepared now to say that he thinks this standard is implicit in the union-management relationship represented by the parties' Agreement, in view of the quite legitimate interests and expectations which the employees and the Union have in protecting the fruits of their negotiations with the Company.

"Past practice" in subcontracting for services and for the manufacturing of components may properly be taken into account as a factor negating the existence of any broad, implied limitation on subcontracting, but not as eliminating the restriction altogether. Moreover, an unsuccessful Union attempt to negotiate into the contract specific restrictions on subcontracting, as was the case in the parties' negotiations of their 1959-1961

Agreement, is likewise a fact which may help to support the claim that the parties have recognized that the Company has substantial latitude in the matter of subcontracting. Yet it would be unrealistic to interpret futile bargaining efforts as meaning the parties were in agreement that the Agreement implies no restriction at all. Parties frequently try to solidify through bargaining a position which they could otherwise take, or to broaden rights which otherwise might arguably exist. Thus, the Referee does not find either in the evidence of past practice here adduced or in the history of the negotiations of the 1959-1961 Agreement, a satisfactory basis for concluding that the Company has complete, untrammeled freedom in the matter of subcontracting. . . .

Real difficulty arises, however, in attempting to lay down a set of specific criteria to be used in determining whether, in a subcontracting situation, an employer has acted in bad faith. . . . In general, it seems . . . that "good faith" is present when the managerial decision to contract out work is made on the basis of a rational consideration of factors related to the conduct of an efficient, economical operation, and with some regard for the interests and expectations of the employees affected by the decision, and that "bad faith" is present when the decision is arbitrary (i.e., lacks any rational basis) or fails to take into account at all the interests and expectations of employees affected. Without attempting anything like a complete "catalog," the following would appear, at least prima facie, to be instances of bad faith: (1) To negotiate a collective agreement . . . covering classifications of work while withholding from the Union the fact that the employer contemplates, in the immediate future, a major change in operations which will eliminate such work; (2) entering into a "subcontracting" arrangement which is a subterfuge, in the sense that the "employees" of the ostensible "subcontractor" become in substance the employees of the employer; (3) the commingling of employees of a subcontractor, working under a different set of wages or other working conditions, regularly and continuously with employees of the employer performing the same kinds of work; (4) contracting out work for the specific purpose of undermining or weakening the Union or depriving employees of employment opportunities. On the other hand, the Referee does not consider that it is per se arbitrary, unreasonable, or an act of bad faith to contract out work primarily to reduce production costs. After all, a prime managerial obligation is to conduct an efficient and profitable enterprise, and doing so serves, in the long run, the best interests of employees as well as stockholders. . . .

### Particular Grievances

(1) *The "janitorial" work.* The only part of [this] work . . . protested is floor cleaning. Company testimony is to the effect that this work (in addition

to other work) was "let" to the outside contractor, rather than assigned at least in part to bargaining unit employees, on an overtime basis, because of these considerations: (1) The necessity of insuring that the work would be completed over the weekend; (2) lack of certainty as to when the floor washing would take place; (3) lack of certainty as to how many people would be required to do such work; (4) the difficulty of getting unit personnel to come in "on emergencies" or on overtime; (5) the inability of some of the unit personnel to handle "scrubbing machines"; (6) the necessity of coordinating the floor cleaning with the moving and other operations involved; (7) the limitations, under State law, of the number of hours which women could be required to work consecutively; and (8) safety factors. Economic considerations, such as the overtime premium payments which would have been required, were not, apparently, involved in the determination.

The Union does not claim that these considerations were not the factors motivating the decision. Its claim is that the Company judgment concerning some of them (e.g., the difficulty of coordinating the work of Company employees with the work of employees of the outside contractor) was unsound. It seems to the Referee, however, that the factors which management took into account were within the range of considerations which could rationally be taken into account, and that there is no evidence that the total judgment reached was either arbitrary or unreasonable, or failed to take into account the natural desires of unit personnel to avail themselves of an overtime opportunity. On the whole, the conclusion must be that there is no evidence of bad faith.

(2) *The contracting out of work on components.* . . . Company testimony indicates that the primary reason for the subcontracting to Kramer Company was economic—i.e., the fact that the price for the component as bid by the contractor, taken together with other applicable cost factors, would be substantially lower than the costs previously experienced by the Company in manufacturing the mechanism. Another consideration was apparently the fact that, according to the Company, planned time schedules were not met in connection with its earlier manufacture of this component.

. . . Company testimony is to the effect that the primary consideration motivating the decision to have Fansteel Metallurgical Company process the components, complete, was the shorter procurement cycle which would and did result, namely, 60 days as compared with 120 days under the prior practice. In addition, according to the Company, the unit cost was reduced from $3.37 to $2.02.

The Union does not contend that these considerations did not, in fact, motivate the decisions to contract out the work in question. . . .

As in the case of the janitorial work, the Referee concludes that the considerations which management took into account, although in these instances primarily or partially economic, indicate that its decisions were not arbitrary or unreasonable, and were not taken in bad faith. No ulterior purpose is indicated in terms either of the status of the Union or of employees in the bargaining unit, nor is there any showing, if this has relevance, that the effect of such subcontracting was to curtail bargaining unit jobs in any substantial way.

## *NOTES AND QUESTIONS*

1. **"Bad-Faith" Subcontracting?** Is arbitrator Smith's definition of bad-faith subcontracting guided by some underlying principle? On the one hand, he states that it is not "an act of bad faith to contract out work primarily to reduce production costs." Yet, on the other hand, he suggests that it would be "bad faith" for the employer to have employees of an "ostensible" subcontractor work completely under the control of the employer, or to commingle the subcontractor's employees, working under a different set of wages, with employees of the employer. What distinguishes these cases?

2. **Range of Arbitrator Views.** Although the "bad-faith" standard enjoys some support, see, e.g., Hughes Electron Dynamics, 115 Lab. Arb. Rep. (BNA) 473 (2001) (Richman, Arb.), as acknowledged by arbitrator Smith, not all arbitrators take this approach. Some are more restrictive of employer discretion to subcontract. See, e.g., Mead Corp. v. United Paperworkers Int'l Union, Local 1430, 75 Lab. Arb. Rep. (BNA) 665, 667 (1980) (Gross, Arb.) ("contracting out of unit work merely because someone else will do it cheaper constitutes an improper evasion of contractual obligations and, in that sense, it does not matter whether the company acted in good faith or bad faith since the result is the same"). Others are more permissive. See, e.g., American Sugar Refining Co. v. United Packinghouse Workers, Local 1101, 37 Lab. Arb. Rep. (BNA) 334, 337 (1961) (Beatty, Arb.) ("When an arbitrator finds that the parties have not dealt with the subject of contracting-out in their working agreement, but that the employer is nevertheless prohibited from contracting-out . . . unless he acts in good faith . . . , the arbitrator may be in outer space and reading the stars instead of the contract."). See generally Anthony V. Sinicropi, Revisiting an Old Battleground: The Subcontracting Dispute, Proc., 32d Ann. Meeting, Nat'l Acad. of Arbs. 125 (1979); Saul Wallen, How Issues of Subcontracting and Plant Removal Are Handled by Arbitrators, 19 Indus. & Lab. Rel. Rev. 265 (1966).

Does the range of arbitrator views on the permissibility of subcontracting in the absence of express contractual restrictions make it difficult for the parties to determine how to deal with the subject at the bargaining table? Would it be preferable for the arbitrator community to develop a consensus view on the subject? Would such an approach facilitate collective bargaining or harden issues that the parties would prefer to handle in a more oblique fashion?

**3. NLRA Remedies?** Could the union in *Allis-Chalmers* have secured any relief under the NLRA? What if it were determined that Allis-Chalmers failed arbitrator's Smith criteria for good-faith contracting because "the 'employees' of the ostensible 'subcontractor' [became] in substance the employees of the employer"? Does the presence of a statutory violation depend on whether the employer's decision to contract out work is consistent with past practice? Does the absence of express contractual language restricting subcontracting doom any argument that the employer engaged in a midterm modification of a mandatory subject "contained in" the contract? If the union has a statutory remedy in principle, is it nevertheless required to process its claim, at least initially, in the arbitration proceeding? See prior discussion of *Westinghouse Elec.*, page 481, and midterm bargaining obligations, page 505, and treatment below of the NLRB's concurrent authority over certain contract disputes, page 722.

**4. Did the Arbitrator Have Jurisdiction?** Note that arbitrator Smith first rejects the company's claim that the union's grievance was outside his jurisdiction. Was Smith's rejection of this claim consistent with his ruling for the company on the merits? How can the company challenge the arbitrator's definition of his own jurisdiction? See infra page 690.

**5. Transfer of Work.** An arbitrator is presented with a union's challenge of an employer's transfer of production from a plant in New York to a plant in North Carolina, with resultant layoffs in New York. The evidence suggests that the employer was primarily motivated by the prospect of lower labor costs in North Carolina. The collective agreement covering the New York plant is silent with respect to work transfers but contains a recognition clause, a clause barring discharge without good cause, and a clause barring layoffs "except for lack of work." How should the arbitrator rule? Would proof that the employer was in financial distress be essential? Would your answer change if the New York plant was technologically obsolete, or if the transfer occurred soon after collective negotiations that did not mention transfer? Cf. Kenton Mfg. Co. v. Amalgamated Clothing & Textile Workers Union, 76 Lab. Arb. Rep. (BNA) 817 (1981) (Hannan, Arb.). Consider also *Milwaukee Spring II*, supra page 512.

**6. "Reserved" Management Rights?** The *Allis-Chalmers* decision represents an example of an at least implicit rejection of the "reserved management rights" principle, often asserted by employers in arbitration and accepted by some arbitrators. Under this principle, limitations on the discretion of management to control employees and the workplace must be expressly stated in the collective agreement or be based on some external source of law. Some arbitrators are more qualified in their application of reserved-rights doctrine or reject it altogether. They may use negotiating history to clarify the meaning of ambiguous or general terms in collective agreements. Perhaps most often, they find an intent to bind the employer by consistently applied and mutually accepted past practices. Recall also the discussion of management-rights clauses in *Milwaukee Spring II,* supra page 512.

## B. ARBITRATION AND THE COURTS

### 1. Enforcement of the Agreement to Arbitrate

**Textile Workers Union v. Lincoln Mills of Alabama**
*353 U.S. 448 (1957)*

Douglas, J. . . .

The agreement [in question] provided that there would be no strikes or work stoppages and that grievances would be handled pursuant to a specified procedure. The last step in the grievance procedure — a step that could be taken by either party — was arbitration.

This controversy involves several grievances that concern work loads and work assignments. The grievances were processed through the various steps in the grievance procedure and were finally denied by the employer. The union requested arbitration, and the employer refused. Thereupon the union brought this suit in the District Court to compel arbitration.

The District Court concluded that it had jurisdiction and ordered the employer to comply with the grievance arbitration provisions of the collective bargaining agreement. The Court of Appeals reversed by a divided vote. It held that, although the District Court had jurisdiction to entertain the suit, the court had no authority founded either in federal or state law to grant the relief. . . .

The starting point of our inquiry is §301 of the [Labor Management Relations Act (LMRA)] of 1947. . . .

From the face of the Act it is apparent that §301(a) and §301(b) supplement one another. Section 301(b) makes it possible for a labor organization, representing employees in an industry affecting commerce, to sue and be sued as an entity in the federal courts. Section 301(b) in other words provides the procedural remedy lacking at common law. Section 301(a) certainly does something more than that. Plainly, it supplies the basis upon which the federal district courts may take jurisdiction and apply the procedural rule of §301(b). The question is whether §301(a) is more than jurisdictional.

Congress was . . . interested in promoting collective bargaining that ended with agreements not to strike. . . .

Plainly the agreement to arbitrate grievance disputes is the quid pro quo for an agreement not to strike. Viewed in this light, the legislation does more than confer jurisdiction in the federal courts over labor organizations. It expresses a federal policy that federal courts should enforce these agreements on behalf of or against labor organizations and that industrial peace can be best obtained only in that way. . . .

It seems, therefore, clear to us that Congress adopted a policy which placed sanctions behind agreements to arbitrate grievance disputes, by implication rejecting the common-law rule, discussed in Red Cross Line v. Atlantic Fruit Co., 264 U.S. 109, against enforcement of executory agreements to arbitrate. We would undercut the Act and defeat its policy if we read §301 narrowly as only conferring jurisdiction over labor organizations.

The question then is, what is the substantive law to be applied in suits under §301(a)? We conclude that the substantive law to apply . . . is federal law, which the courts must fashion from the policy of our national labor laws. The [LMRA] expressly furnishes some substantive law. It points out what the parties may or may not do in certain situations. Other problems will lie in the penumbra of express statutory mandates. Some will lack express statutory sanction but will be solved by looking at the policy of the legislation and fashioning a remedy that will effectuate that policy. The range of judicial inventiveness will be determined by the nature of the problem. Federal interpretation of the federal law will govern, not state law. But state law, if compatible with the purpose of §301, may be resorted to in order to find the rule that will best effectuate the federal policy. Any state law applied, however, will be absorbed as federal law and will not be an independent source of private rights. . . .

The question remains whether jurisdiction to compel arbitration of grievance disputes is withdrawn by [Norris-LaGuardia]. . . . Section 7 of that Act prescribes stiff procedural requirements for issuing an injunction in a labor dispute. The kinds of acts which had given rise to abuse of the power to enjoin are listed in §4. The failure to arbitrate was not a part and parcel of the abuses against which the Act was aimed. Section 8 of [Norris-LaGuardia] does, indeed, indicate a congressional policy toward settlement of labor disputes by arbitration, for it denies injunctive relief to any person who has failed to make "every reasonable effort" to settle the dispute by negotiation, mediation, or "voluntary arbitration." Though a literal reading might bring the dispute within the terms of the Act (see Cox, Grievance Arbitration in the Federal Courts, 67 Harv. L. Rev. 591, 602-604), we see no justification in policy for restricting §301(a) to damage suits, leaving specific performance of a contract to arbitrate grievance disputes to the inapposite procedural requirements of that Act. Moreover, we held in Virginian R. Co. v. System Federation, 300 U.S. 515, and in Graham v. Brotherhood of Firemen, 338 U.S. 232, 237, that the Norris-LaGuardia Act does not deprive federal courts of jurisdiction to compel compliance with the mandates of the Railway Labor Act. The mandates there involved concerned racial discrimination. Yet those decisions were not based on any peculiarities of the Railway Labor Act. We followed the same course in Syres v. Oil Workers International Union, 350 U.S. 892, which was governed by the [NLRA]. There an injunction was sought against racial discrimination in application of a collective bargaining agreement; and we allowed the injunction to issue. The congressional policy in favor of the enforcement of agreements to arbitrate grievance disputes being clear, there is no reason to submit them to the requirements of §7 of the Norris-LaGuardia Act.

[The concurring opinion of Justice Burton, joined by Justice Harlan, and the dissenting opinion of Justice Frankfurter, are omitted.]

## *NOTES AND QUESTIONS*

**1. Federal Common Law-Making Authority.** Does §301(a) of the LMRA express more than a grant of jurisdiction to federal courts? If not, on what basis does the Court assert authority to formulate a federal common law to interpret and enforce collective bargaining agreements? If the Court asserted no such authority, would the grant of jurisdiction in the absence of diversity of citizenship of the parties be permissible under Article III of the Constitution? Could the federal common law under §301(a) recognized in *Lincoln Mills* also be invoked as a basis for formulating federal tort principles barring interference with collective bargaining agreements? Cf. Granite Rock Co. v. Teamsters, 561 U.S. 287 (2010) (declining to recognize a federal common law tort claim for interference with contractual relations).

**2. Is Judicial Enforcement of Arbitration Promises Wise Labor Policy?** The Court's decision in *Lincoln Mills* was in part a response to the common law rule in many states that executory promises to arbitrate are not enforceable. Was the Court right that judicial enforcement of such promises was necessary to the promotion of collective bargaining relationships? Consider the views of the late Harry Shulman, former Dean of Yale Law School, in Reason, Contract, and Law in Labor Relations, 68 Harv. L. Rev. 999, 1024 (1955):

> [Arbitration] is a means of making collective bargaining work and thus preserving private enterprise in a free government. When it works fairly well, it

> does not need the sanction of the law or contracts or the law of arbitration. It is only when the system breaks down completely that the courts' aid in these respects is invoked. But the courts cannot, by occasional sporadic decision, restore the parties' continuing relationship; and their intervention in such cases may seriously affect the going systems of self-government. When their autonomous system breaks down, might not the parties better be left to the usual methods for adjustment of labor disputes rather than to court actions on the contract or on the arbitration award?

Parties generally can settle their disputes but some issues cannot be resolved without a third party decisionmaker. If arbitration promises are not enforceable, what "usual methods for adjustment of labor disputes" do the parties have?

**3. Union's Capacity to Sue and Be Sued.** The Taft-Hartley Congress also sought in §301(b) to ensure that unions, though unincorporated associations at common law, could sue and be sued as entities in §301 actions. However, any judgment obtained in a §301 action against the union would be enforceable only against assets of the union; it "shall not be enforceable against any individual member or his assets." (Recall the *Danbury Hatters* case, supra page 23.)

**4. "Quid Pro Quo" for Arbitration?** Does the inclusion of an arbitration clause in a collective bargaining agreement necessarily mean that the union agrees not to strike over any dispute that is subject to arbitration? See *Note: Teamsters v. Lucas Flour,* infra page 703.

**5. The Scope of §301 Jurisdiction.** In decisions after *Lincoln Mills,* the Supreme Court has ruled as follows:

a. *Concurrent Jurisdiction.* State courts have concurrent jurisdiction over actions within the ambit of §301 but are required to apply federal law. Local 174, Teamsters v. Lucas Flour Co., 369 U.S. 95 (1962).

b. *Suits by Individual Employees.* Section 301 grants federal courts jurisdiction over actions brought by an employee to enforce individual rights arising under a collective agreement. See Smith v. Evening News Ass'n, 371 U.S. 195 (1962). Such actions are also governed by federal law. See Humphrey v. Moore, 375 U.S. 335, 344 (1964). An individual employee, however, cannot sue an employer for breach of a collective bargaining agreement without first exhausting contractual grievance arbitration remedies. See Republic Steel Corp. v. Maddox, 379 U.S. 650 (1965).

c. *Suits Arising Under Union Constitutions.* A union constitution is a "contract between labor organizations" within the meaning of §301(a). Therefore, a suit brought by a local union against its parent international, alleging a violation of the international's constitution, is within the §301 jurisdiction of the federal courts. See United Ass'n of Journeymen & Apprentices of Plumbers v. Local 334, 452 U.S. 615 (1981). Also within §301 jurisdiction is a suit by a union member against his union based on alleged violations of the union's constitution. See Wooddell v. International Bhd. of Elec. Workers, Local 71, 502 U.S. 93 (1991). See James Pfander, Federal Jurisdiction Over Union Constitutions After *Wooddell*, 37 Vill. L. Rev. 443 (1992).

**6. NLRA Claims or Defenses in §301 Actions.**

a. An employer defends an action on a collective agreement on the ground that the agreement—which recognized the union as the exclusive representative for all employees in the unit—is illegal because the union lacked majority support when the agreement was negotiated. Is the court to decide the issue of majority support? To ignore it unless the NLRB has invalidated the agreement? To retain jurisdiction but defer disposition until the NLRB has resolved that issue? See, e.g., Glaziers & Glassworkers Local Union 767 v. Custom Auto Glass Distribs., 689 F.2d 1339 (9th Cir. 1982) (employer may not assert defense; representational issues are within Board's jurisdiction to decide).

b. In an action brought by a union, the employer defends on the ground that the union is seeking to enforce a clause proscribed by §8(a)(3) or by §8(e) of the NLRA. Should the court pass on either of those defenses? See Kaiser Steel Corp. v. Mullins, 455 U.S. 72, 86 (1982) ("where a §8(e) defense is raised by a party which §8(e) was designed to protect, and where the defense is not directed to a collateral matter but to the portion of the contract for which enforcement is sought, a court must entertain the defense"). Cf. Burke v. French Equip. Rental, 687 F.2d 307, 311 (9th Cir. 1982) (finding error in trial court's considering §8(e) defense in pension trustees' suit against construction contractor for delinquent payments, which did not involve effort to enforce the allegedly illegal self-help clause, and declaring "we find no indication in *Kaiser* that the Court meant to sweep away the entire jurisprudence of judicial deference to the expertise of the NLRB").

## United Steelworkers of America v. American Manufacturing Co.
*363 U.S. 564 (1960)*

DOUGLAS, J.

This suit was brought by petitioner union in the District Court to compel arbitration of a "grievance" that petitioner, acting for one Sparks, a union member, had filed with the respondent, Sparks' employer. The employer defended on the ground (1) that Sparks is estopped from making his claim because he had a few days previously settled a workmen's compensation claim against the company on the basis that he was permanently partially disabled, (2) that Sparks is not physically able to do the work, and (3) that this type of dispute is not arbitrable under the collective bargaining agreement in question.

The agreement provided that during its term there would be "no strike," unless the employer refused to abide by a decision of the arbitrator. The agreement sets out a detailed grievance procedure with a provision for arbitration (regarded as the standard form) of all disputes between the parties "as to the meaning, interpretation and application of the provisions of this agreement."[1]

The agreement reserves to the management power to suspend or discharge any employee "for cause."[2] It also contains a provision that the employer will employ and promote employees on the principle of seniority "where ability and efficiency are equal." Sparks left his work due to an injury and while off work brought an action for compensation benefits. The case was settled, Sparks' physician expressing the opinion that the injury had made him 25% "permanently partially disabled." That was on September 9. Two weeks later the union filed a grievance which charged that Sparks was entitled to return to his job by virtue of the seniority provision of the collective bargaining agreement. Respondent refused to arbitrate and this action was brought. The District Court held that Sparks, having accepted the settlement on the basis of permanent partial disability, was estopped to claim any seniority or employment rights and granted the motion for summary judgment. The Court of Appeals affirmed, for different reasons. After reviewing the evidence it held that the grievance is "a frivolous, patently baseless one, not subject to arbitration under the collective bargaining agreement." . . .

---

1. The relevant arbitration provisions read as follows:

"Any disputes, misunderstandings, differences or grievances arising between the parties as to the meaning, interpretation and application of the provisions of this agreement, which are not adjusted as herein provided, may be submitted to the Board of Arbitration for decision. . . .

"The arbitrator may interpret this agreement and apply it to the particular case under consideration but shall, however, have no authority to add to, subtract from, or modify the terms of the agreement. . . ."

2. "The Management of the works, the direction of the working force, plant layout and routine of work, including the right to hire, suspend, transfer, discharge or otherwise discipline any employee for cause, such cause being: infraction of company rules, inefficiency, insubordination, contagious disease harmful to others, and any other ground or reason that would tend to reduce or impair the efficiency of plant operation; and to lay off employees because of lack of work, is reserved to the Company, provided it does not conflict with this agreement. . . ."

... [T]he policy [of LMRA, §203(d)] can be effectuated only if the means chosen by the parties for settlement of their differences under a collective bargaining agreement is given full play.

A state decision that held to the contrary announced a principle that could only have a crippling effect on grievance arbitration. The case was International Assn. of Machinists v. Cutler-Hammer, Inc., 271 App. Div. 917, 67 N.Y.S.2d 317, aff'd 297 N.Y 519, 74 N.E.2d 464. It held that "If the meaning of the provision of the contract sought to be arbitrated is beyond dispute, there cannot be anything to arbitrate and the contract cannot be said to provide for arbitration." 271 App. Div., at 918, 67 N.Y.S.2d, at 318. The lower courts in the instant case had a like preoccupation with ordinary contract law. The collective agreement requires arbitration of claims that courts might be unwilling to entertain. In the context of the plant or industry the grievance may assume proportions of which judges are ignorant. Yet, the agreement is to submit all grievances to arbitration, not merely those that a court may deem to be meritorious. There is no exception in the "no strike" clause and none therefore should be read into the grievance clause, since one is the quid pro quo for the other. . . . The function of the court is very limited when the parties have agreed to submit all questions of contract interpretation to the arbitrator. It is confined to ascertaining whether the party seeking arbitration is making a claim which on its face is governed by the contract. Whether the moving party is right or wrong is a question of contract interpretation for the arbitrator. In these circumstances the moving party should not be deprived of the arbitrator's judgment, when it was his judgment and all that it connotes that was bargained for.

The courts, therefore, have no business weighing the merits of the grievance, considering whether there is equity in a particular claim, or determining whether there is particular language in the written instrument which will support the claim. The agreement is to submit all grievances to arbitration, not merely those which the court will deem meritorious. The processing of even frivolous claims may have therapeutic values of which those who are not a part of the plant environment may be quite unaware.

The union claimed in this case that the company had violated a specific provision of the contract. The company took the position that it had not violated that clause. There was, therefore, a dispute between the parties as to "the meaning, interpretation and application" of the collective bargaining agreement. Arbitration should have been ordered. . . .

Reversed.

[Justices Frankfurter and Whittaker concurred in the result.]

Black, J., took no part in the consideration or decision of this case.

[Justice Brennan, with whom Justice Harlan joined, wrote a concurring opinion, which is excerpted at page 677, below.]

**United Steelworkers of America v. Warrior & Gulf Navigation Co.**
*363 U.S. 574 (1960)*

DOUGLAS, J.

Respondent transports steel and steel products by barge and maintains a terminal at Chicksaw, Alabama, where it performs maintenance and repair work on its barges. The employees at that terminal constitute a bargaining unit covered by a collective bargaining agreement negotiated by petitioner union. Respondent between 1956 and 1958 laid off some employees, reducing the bargaining unit from 42 to 23 men. This reduction was due in part to respondent contracting maintenance work, previously done by its employees, to other companies. The latter used respondent's supervisors to lay out the work and hired some of [respondent's] laid-off employees (at reduced wages). Some were in fact assigned to work on respondent's barges. A number of employees signed a grievance which petitioner presented to respondent, the grievance reading:

> We are hereby protesting the Company's actions, of arbitrarily and unreasonably contracting out work to other concerns, that could and previously has been performed by Company employees.
>
> This practice becomes unreasonable, unjust and discriminatory in lieu [sic] of the fact that at present there are a number of employees that have been laid off for about 1 and 1/2 years or more for allegedly [sic] lack of work.
>
> Confronted with these facts we charge that the Company is in violation of the contract by inducing a partial lockout, of a number of the employees who would otherwise be working were it not for this unfair practice.

The collective agreement had both a "no strike" and a "no lockout" provision. It also had a grievance procedure which provided in relevant part as follows:

> Issues which conflict with any Federal statute in its application as established by Court procedure or matters which are strictly a function of management shall not be subject to arbitration under this section.
>
> Should differences arise between the Company and the Union or its members employed by the Company as to the meaning and application of the provisions of this Agreement, or should any local trouble of any kind arise, there shall be no suspension of work on account of such differences but an earnest effort shall be made to settle such differences immediately in the following manner: [Details of grievance procedure are omitted — EDS.]

Settlement of this grievance was not had and respondent refused arbitration. This suit was then commenced by the union to compel it.

The District Court granted respondent's motion to dismiss the complaint. It held after hearing evidence, much of which went to the merits of the grievance, that the agreement did not "confide in an arbitrator the right to review the defendant's business judgment in contracting out work." It further held that "the contracting out of repair and maintenance work, as well as construction work, is strictly a function of management not limited in any respect by the labor agreement involved here." The Court of Appeals affirmed by a divided vote, the majority holding that the collective agreement had withdrawn from the grievance procedure "matters which are strictly a function of management" and that contracting out fell in that exception. . . .

We held in [*Lincoln Mills*], 353 U.S. 448, that a grievance arbitration provision in a collective agreement could be enforced by reason of §301(a) of the [Act] and that the policy to be applied in enforcing this type of arbitration was that reflected in our national labor laws. Id., at 456-457. The present federal policy is to promote industrial stabilization through the collective bargaining agreement. Id., at 453-454. A major factor in achieving industrial peace is the inclusion of a provision for arbitration of grievances in the collective bargaining agreement.

Thus the run of arbitration cases, illustrated by Wilko v. Swan, 346 U.S. 427, becomes irrelevant to our problem. There the choice is between the adjudication of cases or controversies in courts with established procedures or even special statutory safeguards on the one hand and the settlement of them in the more informal arbitration tribunal on the other. In the commercial case, arbitration is the substitute for litigation. Here arbitration is the substitute for industrial strife. Since arbitration of labor disputes has quite different functions from arbitration under an ordinary commercial agreement, the hostility evinced by courts toward arbitration of commercial agreements has no place here. For arbitration of labor disputes under collective bargaining agreements is part and parcel of the collective bargaining process itself.

The collective bargaining agreement states the rights and duties of the parties. It is more than a contract; it is a generalized code to govern a myriad of cases which the draftsmen cannot wholly anticipate. See Shulman, Reason, Contract, and Law in Labor Relations, 68 Harv. L. Rev. 999, 1004-1005. The collective agreement covers the whole employment relationship. It calls into being a new common law—the common law of a particular industry or of a particular plant. As one observer has put it:[6]

> . . . [I]t is not unqualifiedly true that a collective bargaining agreement is simply a document by which the union and employees have imposed upon management limited, express restrictions of its otherwise absolute right to manage the enterprise, so that an employee's claim must fail unless he can point to a specific contract provision upon which the claim is founded. There

6. Cox, Reflections Upon Labor Arbitration, 72 Harv. L. Rev. 1482, 1498-1499 (1959).

> are too many people, too many problems, too many unforeseeable contingencies to make the words of the contract the exclusive source of rights and duties. One cannot reduce all the rules governing a community like an industrial plant to fifteen or even fifty pages. Within the sphere of collective bargaining, the institutional characteristics and the governmental nature of the collective bargaining process demand a common law of the shop which implements and furnishes the context of the agreement. We must assume that intelligent negotiators acknowledged so plain a need unless they stated a contrary rule in plain words.

A collective bargaining agreement is an effort to erect a system of industrial self-government. When most parties enter into contractual relationship they do so voluntarily, in the sense that there is no real compulsion to deal with one another, as opposed to dealing with other parties. This is not true of the labor agreement. The choice is generally not between entering or refusing to enter into a relationship, for that in all probability preexists the negotiations. Rather it is between having that relationship governed by an agreed-upon rule of law or leaving each and every matter subject to a temporary resolution dependent solely upon the relative strength, at any given moment, of the contending forces. The mature labor agreement may attempt to regulate all aspects of the complicated relationship, from the most crucial to the most minute over an extended period of time. Because of the compulsion to reach agreement and the breadth of the matters covered, as well as the need for a fairly concise and readable instrument, the product of negotiations (the written document) is, in the words of the late Dean Shulman, "a compilation of diverse provisions: some provide objective criteria almost automatically applicable; some provide more or less specific standards which require reason and judgment in their application; and some do little more than leave problems to future consideration with an expression of hope and good faith." Shulman, supra, at 1005. Gaps may be left to be filled in by reference to the practices of the particular industry and of the various shops covered by the agreement. Many of the specific practices which underlie the agreement may be unknown, except in hazy form, even to the negotiators. Courts and arbitration in the context of most commercial contracts are resorted to because there has been a breakdown in the working relationship of the parties; such resort is the unwanted exception. But the grievance machinery under a collective bargaining agreement is at the very heart of the system of industrial self-government. Arbitration is the means of solving the unforeseeable by molding a system of private law for all the problems which may arise and to provide for their solution in a way which will generally accord with the variant needs and desires of the parties. The processing of disputes through the grievance machinery is actually a vehicle by which meaning and content are given to the collective bargaining agreement.

Apart from matters that the parties specifically exclude, all of the questions on which the parties disagree must therefore come within the scope of the grievance and arbitration provisions. . . . The grievance procedure is, in other words, a part of the continuous collective bargaining process. It, rather than a strike, is the terminal point of a disagreement.

The labor arbitrator performs functions which are not normal to the courts; the considerations which help him fashion judgments may indeed be foreign to the competence of courts. . . .

The labor arbitrator's source of law is not confined to the express provisions of the contract, as the industrial common law — the practices of the industry and the shop — is equally a part of the collective bargaining agreement although not expressed in it. The labor arbitrator is usually chosen because of the parties' confidence in his knowledge of the common law of the shop and their trust in his personal judgment to bring to bear considerations which are not expressed in the contract as criteria for judgment. The parties expect that his judgment of a particular grievance will reflect not only what the contract says but, insofar as the collective bargaining agreement permits, such factors as the effect upon productivity of a particular result, its consequence to the morale of the shop, his judgment whether tensions will be heightened or diminished. For the parties' objective in using the arbitration process is primarily to further their common goal of uninterrupted production under the agreement, to make the agreement serve their specialized needs. The ablest judge cannot be expected to bring the same experience and competence to bear upon the determination of a grievance, because he cannot be similarly informed.

The Congress, however, has by §301 . . . assigned the courts the duty of determining whether the reluctant party has breached his promise to arbitrate. For arbitration is a matter of contract and a party cannot be required to submit to arbitration any dispute which he has not agreed so to submit. Yet, to be consistent with congressional policy in favor of settlement of disputes by the parties through the machinery of arbitration, the judicial inquiry under §301 must be strictly confined to the question whether the reluctant party did agree to arbitrate the grievance or did agree to give the arbitrator power to make the award he made. An order to arbitrate the particular grievance should not be denied unless it may be said with positive assurance that the arbitration clause is not susceptible of an interpretation that covers the asserted dispute. Doubts should be resolved in favor of coverage.[7]

We do not agree with the lower courts that contracting-out grievances were necessarily excepted from the grievance procedure of this agreement.

---

7. . . . Where the assertion by the claimant is that the parties excluded from court determination not merely the decision of the merits of the grievance but also the question of arbitrability, vesting the power to make both decisions in the arbitrator, the claimant must bear the burden of a clear demonstration of that purpose.

To be sure, the agreement provides that "matters which are strictly a function of management shall not be subject to arbitration." But it goes on to say that if "differences" arise or if "any local trouble of any kind" arises, the grievance procedure shall be applicable. . . .

"Strictly a function of management" might be thought to refer to any practice of management in which, under particular circumstances prescribed by the agreement, it is permitted to indulge. But if courts, in order to determine arbitrability, were allowed to determine what is permitted and what is not, the arbitration clause would be swallowed up by the exception. Every grievance in a sense involves a claim that management has violated some provision of the agreement.

Accordingly, "strictly a function of management" must be interpreted as referring only to that over which the contract gives management complete control and unfettered discretion. Respondent claims that the contracting out of work falls within this category. Contracting out work is the basis of many grievances; and that type of claim is grist in the mills of the arbitrators. A specific collective bargaining agreement may exclude contracting out from the grievance procedure. Or a written collateral agreement may make clear that contracting out was not a matter for arbitration. In such a case a grievance based solely on contracting out would not be arbitrable. Here, however, there is no such provision. Nor is there any showing that the parties designed the phrase "strictly a function of management" to encompass any and all forms of contracting out.* In the absence of any express provision excluding a particular grievance from arbitration, we think only the most forceful evidence of a purpose to exclude the claim from arbitration can prevail, particularly where, as here, the exclusion clause is vague and the arbitration clause quite broad. Since any attempt by a court to infer such a purpose necessarily comprehends the merits, the court should view with suspicion an attempt to persuade it to become entangled in the construction of the substantive provisions of a labor agreement, even through the back door of interpreting the arbitration clause, when the alternative is to utilize the services of an arbitrator.

The grievance alleged that the contracting out was a violation of the collective bargaining agreement. There was, therefore, a dispute "as to the meaning and application of the provisions of this Agreement" which the parties had agreed would be determined by arbitration. . . .

Reversed.

---

* [The management-rights clause in *Warrior & Gulf*, 68 F. Supp. 702, 704 (S.D. Ala. 1958), provided: "The management of the Company and the direction of the working forces, including the right to hire, suspend or discharge for proper cause, or transfer, and the right to relieve employees from duty because of lack of work, or for other legitimate reasons, is vested exclusively in the Company, provided that this will not be used for purposes of discrimination against any member of the Union." — Eds.]

FRANKFURTER, J., concurs in the result.

BLACK, J., took no part in the consideration or decision of this case.

BRENNAN, J., with whom HARLAN, J., joins, concurring. . . .

. . . If a court may delve into the merits to the extent of inquiring whether the parties have expressly agreed whether or not contracting out was a "function of management," why was it error for the lower court here to evaluate the evidence of bargaining history for the same purpose? Neat logical distinctions do not provide the answer. The Court rightly concludes that appropriate regard for the national labor policy and the special factors relevant to the labor arbitral process, admonish that judicial inquiry into the merits of this grievance should be limited to the search for an explicit provision which brings the grievance under the cover of the exclusion clause since "the exclusion clause is vague and arbitration clause quite broad." The hazard of going further into the merits is amply demonstrated by what the courts below did. On the basis of inconclusive evidence, those courts found that Warrior was in no way limited by any implied covenants of good faith and fair dealing from contracting out as it pleased—which would necessarily mean that Warrior was free completely to destroy the collective bargaining agreement by contracting out all the work. . . .

Justice WHITTAKER dissented.

## *NOTES AND QUESTIONS*

**1. "Steelworkers Trilogy."** The preceding two cases, along with the *Enterprise Wheel & Car Corp.* case, infra page 690, are known as the "*Steelworkers Trilogy.*" These decisions quickly generated an extensive literature, including Benjamin Aaron, Arbitration in the Federal Courts: Aftermath of the Trilogy, 9 UCLA L. Rev. 360 (1962); Bernard D. Meltzer, The Supreme Court, Arbitrability and Collective Bargaining, 28 U. Chi. L. Rev. 464 (1961); Paul R. Hays, The Supreme Court and Labor Law, October Term, 1959, 60 Colum. L. Rev. 901 (1960); Symposium, Arbitration and the Courts, 58 Nw. U. L. Rev. 466 (1963). See also Symposium on Labor Arbitration Thirty Years After the *Steelworkers Trilogy*, 66 Chi.-Kent L. Rev. 551 (1990).

**2. Why Oust the Courts?** Why should courts not be involved in screening out grievances for lacking merit? Is the Court simply concerned that courts will make mistakes and refuse to require arbitration of some grievances that in fact do have merit because judges are biased or lack the presumed ability of arbitrators to access the "common law of the shop"? Is the Court suggesting that there are reasons to arbitrate even grievances that are in fact lacking in merit?

**3. Who Decides Arbitrability?** Note the holding in *Warrior & Gulf* that the question of an arbitrator's substantive jurisdiction is for the courts to decide, albeit with a presumption in favor of arbitrability. Note further that in footnote 7 the Court clearly indicates that this holding expresses only a presumption that could be overcome by a "clear demonstration" that the parties intended the arbitrator to decide the jurisdictional issue. These principles, as well as the basic holding of *Warrior & Gulf,* were later reaffirmed in AT&T v. Communication Workers of Am., 475 U.S. 643 (1986). See generally William B. Gould IV, Judicial Review of Labor Arbitration Awards—Thirty Years of the *Steelworkers Trilogy:* The Aftermath of *AT&T* and *Misco,* 64 Notre Dame L. Rev. 464 (1989).

If a court has first ruled in favor of arbitration under the *Warrior & Gulf* presumption, is the arbitrator still free to find that the dispute is not subject to arbitration as "strictly a function of management" or must the arbitrator decide on the merits that the subcontracting did not violate the labor agreement? Does it matter whether an arbitrator is bound by a judicial determination of arbitrability, given the arbitrator's authority over the merits? For the arbitrator's actual ruling in this case, see Warrior & Gulf Navigation Co. v. United Steelworkers of Am., 36 Lab. Arb. Rep. (BNA) 695 (1961) (Holly, Arb.).

**4. Who Decides When an Arbitration Agreement Was Formed?** A union, while on strike, negotiates a collective bargaining agreement with the employer, but continues striking to obtain an agreement to hold strikers, the local union, and the international union harmless for any damages caused by the strike. The new collective agreement includes a no-strike clause that the employer wishes to enforce to obtain damages against the union. The agreement also includes an arbitration clause. The union claims that the new agreement was not adequately ratified for valid formation until after the strike ceased and asks that the arbitrator determine the date when the contract was ratified. Is the question of when the agreement was validly ratified and formed an aspect of the question of arbitrability for the courts to decide, or rather a dispute for the arbitrator to decide? In Granite Rock Co. v. Teamsters, 561 U.S. 287, 303-304 (2010), the Court held that the issue was for the courts: "For purposes of determining arbitrability, *when* a contract is formed can be as critical as *whether* it was formed." Determining the formation date of the agreement was necessary "to determine whether the parties consented to arbitrate matters" that arise under the agreement.

**5. Does the Presumption of Arbitrability Apply with Equal Force in Deciding Whether a Contact was Formed or When it was Formed?** Should a court apply the same presumption of arbitrability to issues involving formation of the collective agreement, including the date of formation, as to other questions about the scope of the agreement to arbitrate? Are formation questions as likely to implicate the merits of the underlying dispute? In *Granite Rock*, the Court acknowledged a "presumption of arbitrability," but stressed the consensual nature of arbitration and stated in a footnote: "[a]lthough *Warrior & Gulf* contains language that might in isolation be misconstrued as establishing a presumption that labor disputes are arbitrable whenever they are not expressly excluded from an arbitration clause," the *Warrior & Gulf* Court found "the dispute arbitrable only after determining that the parties' arbitration clause could be construed under standard principles of contract interpretation to cover it." 561 U.S. at 301-302, 130 S. Ct. at 2858-2859 and n.8.

**6. Default Rules Subject to Contractual Modification?** Do *American Mfg.* and *Warrior & Gulf* establish background or default rules for what the courts should presume is the intended reach of arbitration clauses in labor agreements in the absence of express language to the contrary? If so, do the default rules reflect the likely intention of the parties in most cases? Are there other justifications for reading private agreements in this manner? Is the history of labor dissatisfaction with judicial resolution of disputes relevant to this question? Fears of midterm strikes over disputes that could be resolved in arbitration? See generally Michael C. Harper, Limiting Section 301 Preemption: Three Cheers for the *Trilogy*, Only One for *Lingle* and *Lueck*, 66 Chi.-Kent L. Rev. 685 (1990).

How might the parties contract around the *American Mfg.* and *Warrior & Gulf* rules? For instance, what if the agreement in *American Mfg.* stated that "meritless" grievances should not be arbitrated? What if the provision stated that the parties "are not to be required to arbitrate grievances that a court deems to be without merit"? What if it stated that "in defining arbitral jurisdiction the courts are not to apply any presumption that the parties want any particular dispute to be arbitrated"?

**7. Judicial Enforcement in the Absence of an Arbitration Clause?** In *Warrior & Gulf* Justice Douglas praises arbitration as a "substitute for industrial strife" and bases the presumption in favor of arbitration at least in part on a national labor policy to avoid such strife. If the parties to a collective agreement do not provide for arbitration as a means of resolving disputes during the term of the agreement but reserve the right to resort to economic weapons, should the courts then apply a presumption that the parties intended that the agreement should be directly enforceable in court rather than only through self-help remedies? See Groves v. Ring Screw Works, 498 U.S. 168 (1990) ("the parties may expressly agree to resort to economic warfare rather than to mediation, arbitration, or judicial review, but the statute surely does not favor such an agreement").

*Note: "Procedural Arbitrability"*

As explained above, courts generally decide whether a given dispute is subject to arbitration ("substantive arbitrability"). Does the same hold true for determinations of whether procedural prerequisites to arbitration set forth in the labor agreement have been met ("procedural arbitrability")? In John Wiley & Sons v. Livingston, 376 U.S. 543 (1964), the company argued that the dispute was not arbitrable because the union had failed to meet certain of these prerequisites. The Court held that issues of procedural arbitrability should be addressed to the arbitrator:

> *Once it is determined, as we have, that the parties are obligated to submit the subject matter of a dispute to arbitration,* "procedural" questions which grow out of the dispute and bear on its final disposition should be left to the arbitrator. . . . [T]he opportunities for deliberate delay and the possibility of well-intentioned but no less serious delay created by separation of the "procedural" and "substantive" elements of a dispute are clear. While the courts have the task of determining "substantive arbitrability," there will be cases in which arbitrability of the subject matter is unquestioned but a dispute arises over the procedures to be followed. In all of such cases, acceptance of Wiley's position would produce the delay attendant upon judicial proceedings preliminary to arbitration.

Id. at 557-558 (emphasis supplied).

The *Wiley* Court relied in part on the fact that the procedural arguments of the company in that case were intertwined with the merits of the dispute for which the union sought arbitration. The union's grievance contended that the company should have continued in force the job security, seniority, and certain benefit provisions of the collective agreement after its merger with another company. The union argued that the company's refusal to recognize it after the merger rendered futile adherence to the early steps in the grievance procedure and that time limitations in the procedure were not controlling because the company's total rejection of the agreement made its alleged violations "continuing." The Court asserted that the union's defenses to the company's procedural arguments could not be fully resolved without treatment of the merits of the dispute on whether the collective agreement should apply after the merger.

Does *Wiley* require arbitral resolution of procedural issues, such as the application of filing deadlines that are entirely separable from the merits of the dispute? What if resolution of the procedural issue turns on the application of general legal or equitable principles, like laches, rather than on an interpretation of the terms of the agreement? In Operating Engineers Local 150 v. Flair Builders, 406 U.S. 487 (1972), the Court held that it was for the arbitrator, rather than a court, to resolve the employer's claim that a union demand to arbitrate was barred by laches (regardless of any contractual time limits) because the union had not demanded arbitration for three years after the employer's first alleged breach. What might be the rationale for this holding?

**Litton Financial Printing Division v. NLRB**
*501 U.S. 190 (1991)*

KENNEDY, J. . . .

## I

Petitioner Litton operated a check printing plant in Santa Clara, California. The plant utilized both cold-type and hot-type printing processes. Printing Specialties & Paper Products Union No. 777, Affiliated With District Council No. 1 (Union), represented the production employees at the plant. The Union and Litton entered into a collective-bargaining agreement which, with extensions, remained in effect until October 3, 1979. Section 19 of the Agreement is a broad arbitration provision:

> Differences that may arise between the parties hereto regarding this Agreement and any alleged violations of the Agreement, the construction to be placed on any clause or clauses of the Agreement shall be determined by arbitration in the manner hereinafter set forth.

Section 21 of the Agreement sets forth a two-step grievance procedure, at the conclusion of which, if a grievance cannot be resolved, the matter may be submitted for binding arbitration.

Soon before the Agreement was to expire, an employee sought decertification of the Union. The Board conducted an election on August 17, 1979, in which the Union prevailed by a vote of 28 to 27. On July 2, 1980, after much postelection legal maneuvering, the Board issued a decision to certify the Union. No contract negotiations occurred during this period of uncertainty over the Union's status.

Litton decided to test the Board's certification decision by refusing to bargain with the Union. The Board rejected Litton's position and found its refusal to bargain an unfair labor practice. Litton Financial Printing Division, 256 N.L.R.B. 516 (1981). Meanwhile, Litton had decided to eliminate its cold-type operation at the plant, and in late August and early September of 1980, laid off 10 of the 42 persons working in the plant at that time. The laid off employees worked either primarily or exclusively with the cold-type operation, and included six of the eleven most senior employees in the plant. The layoffs occurred without any notice to the Union.

The Union filed identical grievances on behalf of each laid off employee, claiming a violation of the Agreement, which had provided that "in case of layoffs, lengths of continuous service will be the determining factor if other things such as aptitude and ability are equal." Litton refused to submit to the grievance and arbitration procedure or to negotiate over the decision to lay off the employees, and took a position later interpreted by the Board as a refusal to arbitrate under any and all circumstances. It offered instead to negotiate concerning the effects of the layoffs.

On November 24, 1980, the General Counsel for the Board issued a complaint alleging that Litton's refusal to process the grievances amounted to an unfair labor practice within the meaning of §§8(a)(1) and (5) of the NLRA. On September 4, 1981, an Administrative Law Judge found that Litton had violated the NLRA by failing to process the grievances. . . .

Over six years later, the Board affirmed in part and reversed in part the decision of the Administrative Law Judge. 286 N.L.R.B. 817 (1987). The Board found that Litton had a duty to bargain over the layoffs, and violated §8(a) by failure to do so. Based upon well-recognized Board precedent that the unilateral abandonment of a contractual grievance procedure upon expiration of the contract violates §§8(a)(1) and (5), the Board held that Litton had improperly refused to process the layoff grievances. . . . The Board proceeded to apply its recent decision in Indiana & Michigan Electric Co., 284 N.L.R.B. 53 (1987), which contains the Board's current understanding of the principles of postexpiration arbitrability and of our opinion in Nolde Bros., Inc. v. Bakery Workers, 430 U.S. 243 (1977). The Board held that Litton's "wholesale repudiation" of its obligation to arbitrate any contractual grievance after the expiration of the Agreement also violated §§8(a)(1) and (5), as the Agreement's broad arbitration clause lacked

> language sufficient to overcome the presumption that the obligation to arbitrate imposed by the contract extended to disputes arising under the contract and occurring after the contract had expired. Thus, [Litton] remained "subject to a potentially viable contractual commitment to arbitrate even after the [Agreement] expired." (286 N.L.R.B., at 818 (citation omitted).)

Litton did not seek review of, and we do not address here, the Board's determination that Litton committed an unfair labor practice by its unilateral abandonment of the grievance process and wholesale repudiation of any postexpiration obligation to arbitrate disputes.

In fashioning a remedy, the Board went on to consider the arbitrability of these particular layoff grievances. Following *Indiana & Michigan*, the Board declared its determination to order arbitration "only when the grievances at issue 'arise under' the expired contract." 286 N.L.R.B., at 821. In finding that the dispute about layoff was outside this category, the Board reasoned as follows:

> The conduct that triggered the grievances . . . occurred after the contract had expired. The right to layoff by seniority if other factors such as ability and experience are equal is not "a right worked for or accumulated over time." *Indiana & Michigan,* supra at 61. And, as in *Indiana & Michigan Electric,* there is no indication here that "the parties contemplated that such rights could ripen or remain enforceable even after the contract expired." Id. (citation omitted). Therefore, [Litton] had no contractual obligation to arbitrate the grievances. (286 N.L.R.B., at 821-822.)

Although the Board refused to order arbitration, it did order Litton to process the grievances through the two-step grievance procedure, to bargain with the Union over the layoffs, and to provide a limited backpay remedy.

The Board sought enforcement of its order, and both the Union and Litton petitioned for review. The Court of Appeals enforced the Board's order, with the exception of that portion holding the layoff grievances not arbitrable. On that question, the Court of Appeals was willing to "assume without deciding that the Board's *Indiana & Michigan* decision is a reasonably defensible construction of the section 8(a)(5) duty to bargain." The court decided, nevertheless, that the Board had erred, because the right in question, the right to layoff in order of seniority if other things such as aptitude and ability are equal, did arise under the Agreement. . . .

## II

Sections 8(a)(5) and 8(d) of the NLRA, 29 U.S.C. §§158(a)(5) and (d), require an employer to bargain "in good faith with respect to wages, hours, and other terms and conditions of employment." The Board has taken the position that it is difficult to bargain if, during negotiations, an employer is free to alter the very terms and conditions that are the subject of those negotiations. The Board has determined, with our acceptance, that an employer commits an unfair labor practice if, without bargaining to impasse, it effects a unilateral change of an existing term or condition of employment. See NLRB v. Katz, 369 U.S. 736 (1962). In *Katz* the union was newly certified and the parties had yet to reach an initial agreement. The *Katz* doctrine has been extended as well to cases where, as here, an existing agreement has expired and negotiations on a new one have yet to be completed. See, e.g., Laborers Health and Welfare Trust Fund v. Advanced Lightweight Concrete Co., 484 U.S. 539, 544, n.6 (1988). . . .

The Board has ruled that most mandatory subjects of bargaining are within the *Katz* prohibition on unilateral changes. The Board has identified some terms and conditions of employment, however, which do not survive expiration of an agreement for purposes of this statutory policy. For instance, it is the Board's view that union security and dues check-off provisions are excluded from the unilateral change doctrine because of statutory provisions which permit these obligations only when specified by the express terms of a collective-bargaining agreement. See 29 U.S.C. §158(a)(3) (union security conditioned upon agreement of the parties); 29 U.S.C. §186(c)(4) (dues check-off valid only until termination date of agreement); *Indiana & Michigan*, 284 N.L.R.B., at 55. . . . Also, in recognition of the statutory right to strike, no-strike clauses are excluded from the unilateral change doctrine, except to the extent other dispute resolution methods survive expiration of the agreement. See 29 U.S.C. §§158(d)(4), 163 (union's statutory right to strike); Southwestern Steel & Supply, Inc. v. NLRB, 806 F.2d 1111, 1114 (1986).

In Hilton-Davis Chemical Co., 185 N.L.R.B. 241 (1970), the Board determined that arbitration clauses are excluded from the prohibition on unilateral changes, reasoning that the commitment to arbitrate is a "voluntary surrender of the right of final decision which Congress . . . reserved to [t]he parties. . . . [A]rbitration is, at bottom, a consensual surrender of the economic power which the parties are otherwise free to utilize." Id., at 242. The Board further relied upon our statements acknowledging the basic federal labor policy that "arbitration is a matter of contract and a party cannot be required to submit to arbitration any dispute which he has not agreed so to submit." United Steelworkers of America v. Warrior & Gulf Navigation Co., 363 U.S. 574, 582 (1960). . . .

We think the Board's decision in *Hilton-Davis Chemical Co.* is both rational and consistent with the Act. The rule is grounded in the strong statutory principle, found in both the language of the NLRA and its drafting history, of consensual rather than compulsory arbitration. . . .

In the absence of a binding method for resolution of postexpiration disputes, a party may be relegated to filing unfair labor practice charges with the Board if it believes that its counterpart has implemented a unilateral change in violation of the NLRA. If, as the Union urges, parties who favor labor arbitration during the term of a contract also desire it to resolve postexpiration disputes, the parties can consent to that arrangement by explicit agreement. Further, a collective-bargaining agreement might be drafted so as to eliminate any hiatus between expiration of the old and execution of the new agreement, or to remain in effect until the parties bargain to impasse. Unlike the Union's suggestion that we impose arbitration of postexpiration disputes upon parties once they agree to arbitrate disputes arising under a contract, these alternatives would reinforce the statutory policy that arbitration is not compulsory.

## IV

The duty not to effect unilateral changes in most terms and conditions of employment, derived from the statutory command to bargain in good faith, is not the sole source of possible constraints upon the employer after the expiration date of a collective-bargaining agreement. A similar duty may arise as well from the express or implied terms of the expired agreement itself. This, not the provisions of the NLRA, was the source of the obligation which controlled our decision in Nolde Bros., Inc. v. Bakery Workers, 430 U.S. 243 (1977). . . .

In *Nolde Bros.* a union brought suit under §301 of the Labor Management Relations Act, 29 U.S.C. §185, to compel arbitration. Four days after termination of a collective-bargaining agreement, the employer decided to cease operations. The employer settled employee wage claims, but refused to pay severance wages called for in the agreement, and declined to arbitrate the resulting dispute. The union argued that these wages

> "were in the nature of 'accrued' or 'vested' rights, earned by employees during the term of the contract on essentially the same basis as vacation pay, but payable only upon termination of employment." (*Nolde Bros.*, 430 U.S., at 248).

We agreed that

> "whatever the outcome, the resolution of that claim hinges on the interpretation ultimately given the contract clause providing for severance pay. The dispute therefore, although arising *after* the expiration of the collective-bargaining contract, clearly arises *under* that contract." (Id., at 249 (emphasis in original).)

We acknowledged that "the arbitration duty is a creature of the collective-bargaining agreement" and that the matter of arbitrability must be determined by reference to the agreement, rather than by compulsion of law. Id., at 250-251. With this understanding, we held that the extensive obligation to arbitrate under the contract in question was not consistent with an interpretation that would eliminate all duty to arbitrate as of the date of expiration. That argument, we noted,

> "would preclude the entry of a post-contract arbitration order even when the dispute arose during the life of the contract but arbitration proceedings had not begun before termination. The same would be true if arbitration processes began but were not completed, during the contract's term." (Id., at 251. . . . )

We found a presumption in favor of postexpiration arbitration of matters unless "negated expressly or by clear implication," ibid., but that conclusion was limited by the vital qualification that arbitration was of matters and disputes arising out of the relation governed by contract. . . .

. . . The object of an arbitration clause is to implement a contract, not to transcend it. *Nolde Bros.* does not announce a rule that postexpiration grievances concerning terms and conditions of employment remain arbitrable.

A rule of that sweep in fact would contradict the rationale of *Nolde Bros.* The *Nolde Bros.* presumption is limited to disputes arising under the contract. A postexpiration grievance can be said to arise under the contract only where it involves facts and occurrences that arose before expiration, where an action taken after expiration infringes a right that accrued or vested under the agreement, or where, under normal principles of contract interpretation, the disputed contractual right survives expiration of the remainder of the agreement. . . .

. . . Rights which accrued or vested under the agreement will, as a general rule, survive termination of the agreement. And of course, if a collective-bargaining agreement provides in explicit terms that certain benefits continue after the agreement's expiration, disputes as to such continuing benefits may be found to arise under the agreement, and so become subject to the contract's arbitration provisions. See United Steelworkers of America v. Fort Pitt Steel Casting, Division of Conval-Penn, Inc., 598 F.2d 1273 (CA3 1979) (agreement provided for continuing medical benefits in the event of postexpiration labor dispute).

Finally, as we found in *Nolde Bros.*, structural provisions relating to remedies and dispute resolution — for example, an arbitration provision — may in some cases survive in order to enforce duties arising under the contract. *Nolde Bros.*' statement to that effect under §301 of the LMRA is similar to the rule of contract interpretation which might apply to arbitration provisions of other commercial contracts. We presume as a matter of contract interpretation that the parties did not intend a pivotal dispute resolution provision to terminate for all purposes upon the expiration of the agreement.

The Union . . . argue[s] that we err in reaching the merits of the issue whether the post-termination grievances arise under the expired agreement because, it is said, that is an issue of contract interpretation to be submitted to an arbitrator in the first instance. Whether or not a company is bound to arbitrate, as well as what issues it must arbitrate, is a matter to be determined by the court, and a party cannot be forced to "arbitrate the arbitrability issue." AT&T Technologies, Inc. v. Communication Workers of America, 475 U.S. 643, 651. We acknowledge that where an effective bargaining agreement exists between the parties, and the agreement contains a broad arbitration clause, "there is a presumption of arbitrability in the sense that '[a]n order to arbitrate the particular grievance should not be denied unless it may be said with positive assurance that the arbitration clause is not susceptible of an interpretation that covers the asserted dispute.'" Id., at 650 (quoting Steelworkers v. Warrior & Gulf Navigation, 363 U.S. 564, 582-583 (1960)). But we refuse to apply that presumption wholesale in the context of an expired bargaining agreement, for to do so would make limitless the contractual obligation to arbitrate. Although "[d]oubts should be resolved in favor of coverage," *AT&T Technologies*, supra, 475 U.S., at 650, we must determine whether the parties agreed to arbitrate this dispute, and we cannot avoid that duty because it requires us to interpret a provision of a bargaining agreement.

We apply these principles to the layoff grievances in the present case. The layoffs took place almost one year after the Agreement had expired. It follows that the grievances are arbitrable only if they involve rights which accrued or vested under the Agreement, or rights which carried over after expiration of the Agreement, not as legally imposed terms and conditions of employment but as continuing obligations under the contract.

The contractual right at issue, that "in case of layoffs, lengths of continuous service will be the determining factor if other things such as aptitude and ability are equal," involves a residual element of seniority. Seniority provisions, the Union argues, "create a form of earned advantage, accumulated over time, that can be understood as a special form of deferred compensation for time already worked." Leaving aside the question whether a provision requiring all layoffs to proceed in inverse order of seniority would support an analogy to the severance pay at issue in *Nolde Bros.*, which was viewed as a form of deferred compensation, the layoff provision here cannot be so construed, and cannot be said to create a right that vested or accrued during the term of the Agreement, or a contractual obligation that carries over after expiration.

The order of layoffs under the Agreement was to be determined primarily with reference to "other factors such as aptitude and ability." Only where all such factors were equal was the employer required to look to seniority. Here, any arbitration proceeding would of necessity focus upon whether aptitude and ability—and any unenumerated "other factors"—were equal long after the Agreement had expired, as of the date of the decision to lay employees off and in light of Litton's decision to close down its cold-type printing operation.

The important point is that factors such as aptitude and ability do not remain constant, but change over time. They cannot be said to vest or accrue or be understood as a form of deferred compensation. Specific aptitudes and abilities can either improve or atrophy. And the importance of any particular skill in this equation varies with the requirements of the employer's business at any given time. Aptitude and ability cannot be measured on some universal scale, but only by matching an employee to the requirements of an employer's business at that time. We cannot infer an intent on the part of the contracting parties to freeze any particular order of layoff or vest any contractual right as of the Agreement's expiration.[4]

---

4. Although our decision that the dispute does not rise under the Agreement does, of necessity, determine that as of August 1980 the employees lacked any vested contractual right to a particular order of layoff, the Union would remain able to argue that the failure to lay off in inverse order of seniority if "other things such as aptitude and ability" were equal amounted to an unfair labor practice, as a unilateral change of a term or condition of employment. We do not decide whether, in fact, the layoffs were out of order.

## V

For the reasons stated, we reverse the judgment of the Court of Appeals to the extent that the Court of Appeals refused to enforce the Board's order in its entirety and remanded the cause for further proceedings.

Justice MARSHALL, with whom Justice BLACKMUN and Justice SCALIA join, dissenting. . . .

As the majority appears to concede, and as the Board has held, an unconditional seniority provision can confer a seniority right that is "capable of accruing or vesting to some degree during the life of the contract." United Chrome Products, Inc., 288 N.L.R.B. 1176, 1177 (1988). . . . The fact that, despite the volatility in individual rank, the seniority guarantee might nevertheless vest under the contract means that what vests is not the employee's seniority rank or his right to job security but rather the right to have the *standard* of seniority applied to layoffs.

In my view, a provision granting only "qualified" seniority may vest in the same way. . . . Under this view, a laid off employee would have the opportunity to prove to the arbitrator that he should not have been laid off under the terms of the contract because other factors such as aptitude and ability *were* equal at the time he was laid off.

[The dissenting opinion of Justice Stevens, with whom Justices Blackmun and Scalia join, is omitted.]

## *NOTES AND QUESTIONS*

**1. "Wholesale Repudiation"?** How do you understand the Board's *Indiana & Michigan* "wholesale repudiation" standard? After *Litton*, if an employer is willing to arbitrate postexpiration grievances that it judges to be arbitrable under the *Litton* standards, does its refusal to arbitrate grievances that it erroneously, but in good faith, deems to be nonarbitrable constitute an unfair labor practice as well as a breach of contract? See *Indiana & Mich.*, 284 N.L.R.B. at 60 n.7 ("We will continue to consider the facts of each case and find no violation where the contract may have been breached but the conduct complained of does not amount to a wholesale repudiation of a contractual commitment to arbitrate.").

**2. What Happened to the Presumption of Arbitrability?** What is the *Litton* Court's justification for not applying the *Warrior & Gulf* presumption of arbitrability to postexpiration grievances? Is there less reason to trust arbitrators in such cases? To be concerned about judicial involvement in the resolution of the merits? To presume that the parties expected arbitration to be available?

**3. Did the Seniority Claim Involve a "Vested" or an "Accrued" Right?** Are you persuaded by the *Litton* Court's application of its vested or accrued right standard, or by Justice Marshall's argument that the seniority right invoked by the union might have been vested? See generally Gary Minda, Arbitration in the Post-Cold-War Era—Justice Kennedy's View of Post-expiration Arbitrability in *Litton Financial Printing Division v. NLRB*, 22 Stetson L. Rev. 83 (1992). If the clause at issue in *Litton* had been a "strict-seniority" clause, rather than an "equal ability," qualified-seniority clause, would the Court's decision have been different?

**4. Other "Vested" or "Accrued" Rights?** Aside from pension benefits and severance pay, are there other benefits that might vest or accrue during the prior contract's term? Vacation pay? Holiday pay? Sick pay? Medical benefits? Protection from unjust discharge? Protection from work loss due to subcontracting? Annual promotion to a new pay grade?

**5. Implications of *Litton* for the Merits of Contractual Claims?** Is *Litton* only about the presumption of arbitrability and postexpiration disputes, or does the decision also have implications for decisions on the merits?

a. Assume that a court decides that a postexpiration claim for vacation pay must be arbitrated because the right to such pay had accrued or vested under the agreement before its expiration. Is the arbitrator free to find for the company because in his view the right to vacation pay did not vest? Is the arbitrator confined to what the *Litton* Court calls "normal principles of contract interpretation" in deciding whether "the disputed contractual right survives expiration of the remainder of the agreement"?

b. Do *Litton*'s teachings as to the arbitrability of postexpiration disputes also control how courts are to decide breach of contract issues? For instance, what if the union after *Litton* attempted to argue to a court, rather than to an arbitrator, that the company's refusal to use seniority to determine layoff priority was a breach of contract? Would this claim have to be arbitrated under the *Steelworker Trilogy*?

**6. Implications of *Litton* for the Union's NLRA Claim?** Does footnote 4 in the *Litton* opinion mean that even though the company had no contractual duty to arbitrate the layoff decision after contract termination, the company had a statutory duty to continue using seniority to determine layoffs that could not be unilaterally changed under *Katz* without bargaining to impasse?

**7. Contracting Out of Postexpiration Arbitration?** What sort of contractual language would be sufficient to preclude arbitration of any grievance after contract expiration? Cf. M&G Polymers USA, LLC v. Tackett, 135 S. Ct. 926 (2015) (concluding that retiree healthcare benefits survive expiration of collective bargaining agreement if parties' intent is explicit in the contract).

## 2. Judicial Review of Arbitration Awards

### a. *Effectuation of the Parties' Intent*

**United Steelworkers of America v. Enterprise Wheel & Car Corp.**
*363 U.S. 593 (1960)*

Douglas, J.

Petitioner union and respondent during the period relevant here had a collective bargaining agreement which provided that any differences "as to the meaning and application" of the agreement should be submitted to arbitration and that the arbitrator's decision "shall be final and binding on the parties." . . . The agreement [also] stated:

> Should it be determined by the Company or by an arbitrator in accordance with the grievance procedure that the employee has been suspended unjustly or discharged in violation of the provisions of this Agreement, the Company shall reinstate the employee and pay full compensation at the employee's regular rate of pay for the time lost. . . .

A group of employees left their jobs in protest against the discharge of one employee. A union official advised them at once to return to work. An official of respondent at their request gave them permission and then rescinded it. The next day they were told that they did not have a job any more "until this thing was settled one way or the other."

A grievance was filed; and when respondent finally refused to arbitrate, this suit was brought for specific enforcement of the arbitration provisions of the agreement. The District Court ordered arbitration. The arbitrator found that the discharge of the men was not justified, though their conduct, he said, was improper. In his view the facts warranted at most a suspension of the men for 10 days each. After their discharge and before the arbitration award the collective bargaining agreement had expired. The union, however, continued to represent the workers at the plant. The arbitrator rejected the contention that expiration of the agreement barred reinstatement of the employees. He held that the provision of the agreement above quoted imposed an unconditional obligation on the employer. He awarded reinstatement with back pay minus pay for a 10-day suspension and such sums as these employees received from other employment.

Respondent refused to comply with the award. Petitioner moved the District Court for enforcement. [It] directed respondent to comply. The Court of Appeals, while agreeing that the District Court had jurisdiction to enforce an arbitration award under a collective bargaining agreement, held that the failure of the award to specify the amounts to be deducted from the back pay rendered the award unenforceable. That defect, it agreed, could be remedied by requiring the parties to complete the arbitration. It went on to hold, however, that an award for back pay subsequent to the date of termination of the collective bargaining agreement could not be enforced. It also held that the requirement for reinstatement of the discharged employees was likewise unenforceable because the collective bargaining agreement had expired. . . .

The refusal of courts to review the merits of an arbitration award is the proper approach to arbitration under collective bargaining agreements. The federal policy of settling labor disputes by arbitration would be undermined if courts had the final say on the merits of the awards. . . .

When an arbitrator is commissioned to interpret and apply the collective bargaining agreement, he is to bring his informed judgment to bear in order to reach a fair solution of a problem. This is especially true when it comes to formulating remedies. There the need is for flexibility in meeting a wide variety of situations. The draftsmen may never have thought of what specific remedy should be awarded to meet a particular contingency. Nevertheless, an arbitrator is confined to interpretation and application of the collective bargaining agreement; he does not sit to dispense his own brand of industrial justice. He may of course look for guidance from many sources, yet his award is legitimate only so long as it draws its essence from the collective bargaining agreement. When the arbitrator's words manifest an infidelity to this obligation, courts have no choice but to refuse enforcement of the award.

The opinion of the arbitrator in this case, as it bears upon the award of back pay beyond the date of the agreement's expiration and reinstatement, is ambiguous. It may be read as based solely upon the arbitrator's view of the requirements of enacted legislation, which would mean that he exceeded the scope of the submission. Or it may be read as embodying a construction of the agreement itself, perhaps with the arbitrator looking to "the law" for help in determining the sense of the agreement. A mere ambiguity in the opinion accompanying an award, which permits the inference that the arbitrator may have exceeded his authority, is not a reason for refusing to enforce the award. Arbitrators have no obligation to the court to give their reasons for an award. To require opinions free of ambiguity may lead arbitrators to play it safe by writing no supporting opinions. This would be undesirable for a well-reasoned opinion tends to engender confidence in the integrity of the process and aids in clarifying the underlying agreement. Moreover, we see no reason to assume that this arbitrator has abused the trust the parties confided in him and has not stayed within the areas marked out for his consideration. It is not apparent that he went beyond the submission. The Court of Appeals' opinion refusing to enforce the reinstatement and partial back pay portions of the award was not based upon any finding that the arbitrator did not premise his award on his construction of the contract. It merely disagreed with the arbitrator's construction of it.

The collective bargaining agreement could have provided that if any of the employees were wrongfully discharged, the remedy would be reinstatement and back pay up to the date they were returned to work. Respondent's major argument seems to be that by applying correct principles of law to the interpretation of the collective bargaining agreement it can be determined that the agreement did not so provide, and that therefore the arbitrator's decision was not based upon the contract. The acceptance of this view would require courts, even under the standard arbitration clause, to review the merits of every construction of the contract. This plenary review by a court of the merits would make meaningless the provisions that the arbitrator's decision is final, for in reality it would almost never be final. . . . [T]he question of interpretation of the collective bargaining agreement is a question for the arbitrator. It is the arbitrator's construction which was bargained for; and so far as the arbitrator's decision concerns construction of the contract, the courts have no business overruling him because their interpretation of the contract is different from his. . . .

FRANKFURTER, J., concurs in the result.

BLACK, J., took no part in the consideration or decision of this case.

[The dissenting opinion of Justice Whittaker is omitted.]

## *NOTES AND QUESTIONS*

**1. Effectuating the Background Assumptions of the Parties?** Is the limited judicial review of arbitration awards envisioned in *Enterprise Wheel* a background or default rule for what the courts should presume is the meaning of collective agreements in the absence of express language to the contrary? If so, how might employers or unions contract around this presumption? What reasons, other than the likely intent of the parties, does the Court give for restricting judicial review of arbitration awards?

**2. Promoting Finality of Arbitration Awards?** Consider the following argument for the narrow judicial review of arbitration awards:

> If reviewing courts provide losing parties with the least encouragement to ignore the finality of labor arbitration decisions, the negative consequences for harmonious labor-management relations would be significant. It can easily take a year or more to obtain a district court decision with respect to a challenged arbitral award, and an additional year may be expended if appellate court review is thereafter sought. "[E]ven if the outcome of judicial

> intercession is enforcement of the award, litigation is of itself damaging to the values the award is designed to serve."

Charles B. Craver, Labor Arbitration as a Continuation of the Collective Bargaining Process, 66 Chi.-Kent L. Rev. 571, 588 (1990) (quoting Bernard Dunau, Scope of Judicial Review of Labor Arbitration Awards, in Proc., 24th Ann. N.Y.U. Conf. on Lab. 175, 177 (1972)). See also Douglas E. Ray, Protecting the Parties' Bargain After *Misco*: Court Review of Labor Arbitration Awards, 64 Ind. L.J. 1, 12-13 (1988) (empirical study finding that district court review of arbitration awards in 1985 added 456 days to the process).

**3. The Award Must "Draw Its Essence" from the Contract?** The Court states that an arbitral award is legitimate only so long as it "draws its essence from the collective bargaining agreement," and cautions that an arbitrator "does not sit to dispense his own brand of industrial justice." Some decisions have invoked these phrases to justify the refusal to enforce an award found to be based on what the courts regard to be an implausible interpretation of a collective agreement and hence to reflect the arbitrator's "brand of industrial justice." The Sixth Circuit, for instance, at one point stated that it would refuse to enforce an award when: "(1) it conflicts with express terms of the agreement; (2) it imposes additional requirements not expressly provided for in the agreement; (3) it is not rationally supported by or derived from the agreement; or (4) it is based on general considerations of fairness and equity instead of the exact terms of the agreement." See, e.g., Michigan Family Resources, Inc. v. Service Employees International Union Local 517M, 438 F.3d 653, 656 (6th Cir. 2006); Cement Divisions, National Gypsum Co. v. United Steelworkers of Am., Local 135, 793 F.2d 759, 766 (6th Cir. 1986). Was the Court of Appeals' approach consistent with *Enterprise Wheel*?

In Michigan Family Resources, Inc. v. SEIU, Local 517M, 475 F.3d 747, 753 (6th Cir. 2007) (en banc), the Sixth Circuit overruled *Cement Divisions* and its progeny within the Circuit. The court stated that it instead would refuse to enforce an award only if the arbitrator acted "outside his authority" or dishonestly or was not "arguably construing or applying the contract." It will not reject even "silly" or "serious" errors of interpretation by arbitrators chosen by the parties. Is this approach consistent with *Enterprise Wheel*?

Should *Enterprise Wheel* be understood as setting forth the minimal requirement that the arbitrator understood that his role was to interpret the collective agreement and to ground his award in the agreement and not his own views of industrial justice? Is it sufficient that the arbitrator acted with the requisite subjective intent? For the view that the arbitrator's role as the parties' designated reader or interpreter of the collective agreement precludes substantive review by the courts, see Theodore St. Antoine,

Judicial Review of Labor Arbitration Awards: A Second Look at *Enterprise Wheel* and Its Progeny, 75 Mich. L. Rev. 1137 (1977).

**4. Awards Referring to or Based on External Law.** The language in *Enterprise Wheel* requiring arbitrators to draw the "essence" of their awards from the agreement would seem to preclude them from basing an award for a contractual violation directly on external law. The Supreme Court, however, has held that in certain circumstances parties to a collective bargaining agreement can assign individual employees' non-NLRA statutory claims to arbitration. See 14 Penn Plaza LLC v. Pyett, 556 U.S. 247 (2009), considered infra at 738-747. Furthermore, arbitrators often consider external law under the assumption that the parties would want an ambiguous provision in their private agreement to be interpreted consistently with public law. See Robert G. Howlett, The Arbitrator, the NLRB, and the Courts, Proc., 20th Ann. Meeting, Nat'l Acad. of Arbs. 67, 83, 85 (1967). Should judicial deference to arbitral interpretations of external law depend on whether the agreement expressly incorporates or refers to external law? Should a court not defer to an arbitral award that is based on an interpretation of external law that the court determines is incorrect, even if the award does not require the parties to violate external law?

**5. Applications.**

a. *Arbitral Reduction of Penalty for Misconduct.* A significant number of judicial decisions refusing to enforce arbitral awards express dissatisfaction with an arbitrator's questioning of the severity of an employer's penalty for employee activity acknowledged both to have occurred and to justify some discipline, especially when the agreement explicitly allows for imposition of the penalty meted out. See, e.g., Poland Spring Corp. v. United Food & Commercial Workers Int'l Union, 314 F.3d 29 (1st Cir. 2002); Delta Queen Steamboat Co. v. District 2, 889 F.2d 599 (5th Cir. 1989); Georgia-Pacific Corp. v. Local 27, United Paperworkers, 864 F.2d 940 (1st Cir. 1988). See also infra page 696 (discussing "public policy" challenges to awards reinstating employees who have engaged in, e.g., illegal drug use).

Assume that an employee is discharged for falsely reporting that he was injured and unable to report for work on a day he uses to compete in an amateur golf tournament. Assume further that after concluding that the employee lied to the employer to free himself for the tournament, an arbitrator orders the employee's reinstatement without back pay. The arbitrator acknowledges that the agreement states that "any employee may be discharged for just cause" and that "some of the causes for immediate discharge are . . . dishonesty," but reasons that suspensions have been the usual penalty for similar though not identical dishonest actions and that the employee in this case has an otherwise unblemished and long work record. The arbitrator further maintains that the collective agreement means that dishonesty may be cause for discharge in an appropriate case rather than in all cases. Does a court have authority after *Enterprise Wheel* to vacate the award? If so, on what ground? What if the arbitrator's decision states that there was "just cause" for discipline but concludes that discharge was nonetheless excessive?

b. *Clauses Seeking to Restrict Arbitral Discretion.* Suppose a clause provides that "an arbitrator shall not have authority to consider past practice or bargaining history in construing this agreement." Is there an argument for permitting broader judicial review of arbitral interpretations of such ostensibly unambiguous clauses limiting the arbitrator's own discretion than of similar clauses restricting the employer's authority? See Anheuser-Busch, Inc. v. Teamsters Local Union No. 744, 280 F.3d 1133 (7th Cir. 2002) (overturning award based on past practice but contrary to express terms of agreement stating that "the written agreement constitutes the full and complete agreement between the parties and supersedes all prior agreements . . . , oral or written, including all practices not specifically preserved by the express provisions of this Agreement"); see also Pennsylvania Power Co. v. IBEW, 276 F.3d 174 (3d Cir. 2001) (similar). If a distinction should be made, how should courts treat arbitrators' interpretations of more ambiguous limits on arbitral authority, such as clauses providing that "the arbitrator shall have no power to add to, delete from or modify, in any way, any of the provisions of this agreement"? Or "the arbitrator shall have power to interfere only on the basis of express language in agreement not subject to interpretation"? See Salem Hospital v. Massachusetts Nurses Ass'n, 449 F.3d 234 (1st Cir. 2006) (refusing to enforce because court found language to be subject to interpretation).

**6. Remand or Decide?** If a court determines that an arbitrator has not acted within the scope of her authority or has ignored the contract to "dispense" her own "brand of industrial justice," should the court decide the case itself or remand for another arbitral decision? In a case stressing that courts should consider only whether the arbitrator attempted to construe and apply the contract and should not review arbitral awards on the merits even for "serious" errors or "irrational" factual findings, the Supreme Court in a per curiam summary reversal of a court of appeals for inappropriate review opined that "[e]ven when the arbitrator's award may properly be vacated, the appropriate remedy is to remand the case for further arbitration proceedings." Major League Baseball Players Ass'n v. Garvey, 532 U.S. 504 (2001).

### b. *Public Policy Considerations*

**Eastern Associated Coal Corp. v. United Mine Workers, District 17**
*531 U.S. 57 (2000)*

BREYER, J. . . .

A labor arbitrator ordered an employer to reinstate an employee driver who had twice tested positive for marijuana. The question before us is whether considerations of public policy require courts to refuse to enforce that arbitration award. We conclude that they do not. . . .

#### I

Petitioner, Eastern Associated Coal Corp., and respondent, United Mine Workers of America, are parties to a collective-bargaining agreement with arbitration provisions. The agreement specifies that, in arbitration, in order to discharge an employee, Eastern must prove it has "just cause." Otherwise the arbitrator will order the employee reinstated. The arbitrator's decision is final.

James Smith worked for Eastern as a member of a road crew, a job that required him to drive heavy truck-like vehicles on public highways. As a truck driver, Smith was subject to Department of Transportation (DOT) regulations requiring random drug testing of workers engaged in "safety-sensitive" tasks. 49 CFR §§382.301, 382.305 (1999).

In March 1996, Smith tested positive for marijuana. Eastern sought to discharge Smith. The union went to arbitration, and the arbitrator concluded that Smith's positive drug test did not amount to "just cause" for discharge. Instead the arbitrator ordered Smith's reinstatement, provided that Smith (1) accept a suspension of 30 days without pay, (2) participate in a substance-abuse program, and (3) undergo drug tests at the discretion of Eastern (or an approved substance-abuse professional) for the next five years.

Between April 1996 and January 1997, Smith passed four random drug tests. But in July 1997 he again tested positive for marijuana. Eastern again sought to discharge Smith. The union again went to arbitration, and the arbitrator again concluded that Smith's use of marijuana did not amount to "just cause" for discharge, in light of two mitigating circumstances. First, Smith had been a good employee for 17 years. And, second, Smith had made a credible and "very personal appeal under oath . . . concerning a personal/family problem which caused this one time lapse in drug usage."

The arbitrator ordered Smith's reinstatement provided that Smith (1) accept a new suspension without pay, this time for slightly more than three months; (2) reimburse Eastern and the union for the costs of both arbitration proceedings; (3) continue to participate in a substance-abuse program;

(4) continue to undergo random drug testing; and (5) provide Eastern with a signed, undated letter of resignation, to take effect if Smith again tested positive within the next five years.

Eastern brought suit in federal court seeking to have the arbitrator's award vacated, arguing that the award contravened a public policy against the operation of dangerous machinery by workers who test positive for drugs. The District Court, while recognizing a strong regulation-based public policy against drug use by workers who perform safety-sensitive functions, held that Smith's conditional reinstatement did not violate that policy. And it ordered the award's enforcement.

The Court of Appeals for the Fourth Circuit affirmed on the reasoning of the District Court. 188 F.3d 501 (1999) (unpublished). . . . We now affirm the Fourth Circuit's determination.

## II

Eastern claims that considerations of public policy make the arbitration award unenforceable. In considering this claim, we must assume that the collective-bargaining agreement itself calls for Smith's reinstatement. That is because both employer and union have granted to the arbitrator the authority to interpret the meaning of their contract's language, including such words as "just cause." . . . Eastern does not claim here that the arbitrator acted outside the scope of his contractually delegated authority. Hence we must treat the arbitrator's award as if it represented an agreement between Eastern and the union as to the proper meaning of the contract's words "just cause." . . .

We must then decide whether a contractual reinstatement requirement would fall within the legal exception that makes unenforceable "a collective bargaining agreement that is contrary to public policy." W. R. Grace & Co. v. Rubber Workers, 461 U.S. 757, 766 (1983). The Court has made clear that any such public policy must be "explicit," "well defined," and "dominant." Ibid. It must be "ascertained 'by reference to the laws and legal precedents and not from general considerations of supposed public interests.' " Ibid. . . . ; accord, [United Paperworkers Int'l Union v. Misco, Inc., 484 U.S. 29, 43 (1987)]. And, of course, the question to be answered is not whether Smith's drug use itself violates public policy, but whether the agreement to reinstate him does so. To put the question more specifically does a contractual agreement to reinstate Smith with specified conditions run contrary to an explicit, well-defined, and dominant public policy, as ascertained by reference to positive law and not from general considerations of supposed public interests? See *Misco*, supra, at 43.

### III

Eastern initially argues that the District Court erred by asking, not whether the award is "contrary to" public policy "as ascertained by reference" to positive law, but whether the award "violates" positive law, a standard Eastern says is too narrow. We believe, however, that the District Court correctly articulated the standard set out in *W. R. Grace* and *Misco* and applied that standard to reach the right result.

We agree, in principle, that courts' authority to invoke the public policy exception is not limited solely to instances where the arbitration award itself violates positive law. Nevertheless, the public policy exception is narrow and must satisfy the principles set forth in *W. R. Grace* and *Misco*. Moreover, in a case like the one before us, where two political branches have created a detailed regulatory regime in a specific field, courts should approach with particular caution pleas to divine further public policy in that area.

Eastern asserts that a public policy against reinstatement of workers who use drugs can be discerned from an examination of that regulatory regime, which consists of the Omnibus Transportation Employee Testing Act of 1991 and DOT's implementing regulations. The Testing Act embodies a congressional finding that "the greatest efforts must be expended to eliminate the . . . use of illegal drugs, whether on or off duty, by those individuals who are involved in [certain safety-sensitive positions, including] the operation of . . . trucks." Pub. L. 102-143, §2(3). The Act adds that "increased testing" is the "most effective deterrent" to "use of illegal drugs." §2(5). It requires the Secretary of Transportation to promulgate regulations requiring "testing of operators of commercial motor vehicles for the use of a controlled substance." 49 U.S.C. §31306(b)(1)(A). It mandates suspension of those operators who have driven a commercial motor vehicle while under the influence of drugs. 49 U.S.C. §31310(b)(1)(A) (requiring suspension of at least one year for a first offense); §31310(c)(2) (requiring suspension of at least 10 years for a second offense). And DOT's implementing regulations set forth sanctions applicable to those who test positive for illegal drugs.

In Eastern's view, these provisions embody a strong public policy against drug use by transportation workers in safety-sensitive positions and in favor of random drug testing in order to detect that use. Eastern argues that reinstatement of a driver who has twice failed random drug tests would undermine that policy—to the point where a judge must set aside an employer-union agreement requiring reinstatement.

Eastern's argument, however, loses much of its force when one considers further provisions of the Act that make clear that the Act's remedial aims are complex. The Act says that "rehabilitation is a critical component of any testing program," §2(7), that rehabilitation "should be made available to individuals, as appropriate," ibid., and that DOT must promulgate regulations for "rehabilitation programs," 49 U.S.C. §31306(e). The DOT regulations specifically state that a driver who has tested positive for drugs cannot return to a safety-sensitive position until (1) the driver has been evaluated by a "substance abuse professional" to determine if treatment is needed; (2) the substance-abuse professional has certified that the driver has followed any rehabilitation program prescribed; and (3) the driver has passed a return-to-duty drug test. In addition, (4) the driver must be subject to at least six random drug tests during the first year after returning to the job. Neither the Act nor the regulations forbid an employer to reinstate in a safety-sensitive position an employee who fails a random drug test once or twice. The congressional and regulatory directives require only that the above-stated prerequisites to reinstatement be met.

Moreover, when promulgating these regulations, DOT decided not to require employers either to provide rehabilitation or to "hold a job open for a driver" who has tested positive, on the basis that such decisions "should be left to management/driver negotiation." 59 Fed. Reg. 7502 (1994). That determination reflects basic background labor law principles, which caution against interference with labor-management agreements about appropriate employee discipline. . . .

We believe that these expressions of positive law embody several relevant policies. As Eastern points out, these policies include Testing Act policies against drug use by employees in safety-sensitive transportation positions and in favor of drug testing. They also include a Testing Act policy favoring rehabilitation of employees who use drugs. And the relevant statutory and regulatory provisions must be read in light of background labor law policy that favors determination of disciplinary questions through arbitration when chosen as a result of labor-management negotiation.

The award before us is not contrary to these several policies, taken together. The award does not condone Smith's conduct or ignore the risk to public safety that drug use by truck drivers may pose. Rather, the award punishes Smith by suspending him for three months, thereby depriving him of nearly $9,000 in lost wages; it requires him to pay the arbitration costs of both sides; it insists upon further substance-abuse treatment and testing; and it makes clear (by requiring Smith to provide a signed letter of resignation) that one more failed test means discharge.

The award violates no specific provision of any law or regulation. It is consistent with DOT rules requiring completion of substance-abuse treatment before returning to work, for it does not preclude Eastern from assigning Smith to a non-safety-sensitive position until Smith completes the prescribed treatment program. It is consistent with the Testing Act's 1-year and 10-year driving license suspension requirements, for those requirements apply only to drivers who, unlike Smith, actually operated vehicles under the influence of drugs. See 49 U.S.C. §§31310(b), (c). The award is also consistent with the Act's rehabilitative concerns, for it requires substance-abuse treatment and testing before Smith can return to work.

The fact that Smith is a recidivist—that he has failed drug tests twice—is not sufficient to tip the balance in Eastern's favor. The award punishes Smith more severely for his second lapse. And that more severe punishment, which included a 90-day suspension, would have satisfied even a "recidivist" rule that DOT once proposed but did not adopt—a rule that would have punished two failed drug tests, not with discharge, but with a driving suspension of 60 days. 57 Fed. Reg. 59585 (1992). Eastern argues that DOT's withdrawal of its proposed rule leaves open the possibility that discharge is the appropriate penalty for repeat offenders. That argument fails, however, because DOT based its withdrawal, not upon a determination that a more severe penalty was needed, but upon a determination to leave in place, as the "only driving prohibition period for a controlled substances violation," the "completion of rehabilitation requirements and a return-to-duty test with a negative result." 59 Fed. Reg. 7493 (1994).

Regarding drug use by persons in safety-sensitive positions, then, Congress has enacted a detailed statute. And Congress has delegated to the Secretary of Transportation authority to issue further detailed regulations on that subject. . . . Neither Congress nor the Secretary has seen fit to mandate the discharge of a worker who twice tests positive for drugs. We hesitate to infer a public policy in this area that goes beyond the careful and detailed scheme Congress and the Secretary have created.

We recognize that reasonable people can differ as to whether reinstatement or discharge is the more appropriate remedy here. But both employer and union have agreed to entrust this remedial decision to an arbitrator. We cannot find in the Act, the regulations, or any other law or legal precedent an "explicit," "well defined," "dominant" public policy to which the arbitrator's decision "runs contrary." *Misco*, 484 U.S. at 43; *W.R. Grace*, 461 U.S. at 766. We conclude that the lower courts correctly rejected Eastern's public policy claim.

Justice Scalia, with whom Justice Thomas joins, concurring in the judgment.

I concur in the Court's judgment, because I agree that no public policy prevents the reinstatement of James Smith to his position as a truck driver, so long as he complies with the arbitrator's decision, and with those requirements set out in the Department of Transportation's regulations. I do not endorse, however, the Court's statement that "we agree, in principle, that courts' authority to invoke the public policy exception is not limited solely to instances where the arbitration award itself violates positive law." No case is cited to support that proposition, and none could be. . . . After its dictum opening the door to flaccid public policy arguments of the sort presented by petitioner here, the Court immediately posts a giant "Do Not Enter" sign. "The public policy exception," it says, "is narrow and must satisfy the principles set forth in *W.R. Grace*," which require that the applicable public policy be "explicit," "well defined," "dominant," and "ascertained 'by reference to the laws and legal precedents and not from general considerations of supposed public interests.'" W.R. Grace & Co. v. Rubber Workers, 461 U.S. 757, 766 (1983) (quoting Muschany v. United States, 324 U.S. 49, 66 (1945)). It is hard to imagine how an arbitration award could violate a public policy, identified in this fashion, without actually conflicting with positive law. If such an award could ever exist, it would surely be so rare that the benefit of preserving the courts' ability to deal with it is far outweighed by the confusion and uncertainty, and hence the obstructive litigation, that the Court's Delphic "agreement in principle" will engender. . . .

## *NOTES AND QUESTIONS*

**1. Prior Supreme Court Rulings.** *Eastern Coal* was the Court's third major attempt to define when courts may refuse to enforce arbitration awards as contrary to public policy. In W.R. Grace & Co. v. Rubber Workers, 461 U.S. 757, 766 (1983), the Court stated in declining to overturn an arbitrator's award that the public policy must be "well defined and dominant" and "ascertained 'by reference to . . . laws and legal precedents and not from general considerations of supposed public interests.'" (internal citation omitted). Four years later, in United Paperworkers Int'l Union v. Misco, Inc., 484 U.S. 29 (1987), the Court reviewed an arbitral award requiring reinstatement with back pay of Isiah Cooper, who had been found in the back seat of a car in the company parking lot with a burning marijuana cigarette in the front ashtray. The arbitrator ordered reinstatement because he found insufficient evidence that Cooper violated the contractual rule against use or possession of drugs on company property, but the Fifth Circuit refused to enforce the award. Noting that Cooper's job involved operating hazardous machinery, it ruled that his reinstatement violated the public policy "against the operation of dangerous machinery by persons under the influence of drugs or alcohol." The Supreme Court reversed. Invoking *W.R. Grace,* the Court vacated the order because the lower court had made "no attempt to review existing laws and legal precedents in order to demonstrate that they establish [such] a 'well defined and dominant policy.'" Id. at 42. The *Misco* Court declined, however, to address the union's position that courts may refuse to enforce arbitration awards on public policy grounds only when the award "violates a statute, regulation, or other manifestation of positive law, or compels conduct by the employer that would violate such a law." Id. at 45 n.12. In granting certiorari in *Eastern Coal,* the Court appeared poised to answer the question left unresolved in *Misco.*

**2. Leaving the Door Open to Violations of "Public Policy" Not Based on Positive Law?** Why did the *Eastern Coal* Court not close the door completely to claims that an arbitral award that does not violate positive law (or require the employer to do so) nonetheless violates some broader notion of public policy? What precisely is being left open? Is Justice Scalia correct that the Court did little more than create an opportunity for "obstructive litigation" here?

**3. Applications.**

a. An arbitrator finds that a nuclear power plant machinist, in order to escape the lunch-time rush, intentionally circumvents an interlock system designed to keep the plant's secondary containment area pressurized as an insulation from any leak from the primary containment area around the nuclear core. Nonetheless, the arbitrator stresses the employee's previous unblemished record and rejects the employer's discharge of the employee for breaching a clear company safety rule, which was issued to conform to regulations promulgated by the Nuclear Regulatory Commission (NRC). The NRC reprimanded the company for violation of the rule in this instance, but its regulations focus on the company's responsibility and do not address whether dismissal is required for employees who violate safety rules. See Iowa Elec. Light & Power Co. v. Local Union 204, Int'l Bhd. of Elec. Workers, 834 F.2d 1424 (8th Cir. 1987).

b. An arbitrator finds that an employee was discharged because he continued to refuse to pay court-ordered child support to a sister of the employee's supervisor. The arbitrator finds the discharge to be without a job-related just cause and orders the employee reinstated. The employer argues that the discharge was based on the employee's violation of a clearly enunciated public policy and a court order and should be upheld.

c. Based on principles of progressive discipline, an arbitrator overturns the discharge of an employee who was caught for the first time operating dangerous machinery while under the influence of drugs. The company argues that retention of this employee exposes it to a greater risk of liability under federal occupational safety laws and state tort laws. Should it matter whether retention of the employee would increase the company's risk of liability not only because of the greater chance that he would perform his job negligently, but also because federal law might view his retention as itself a negligent act on the part of the company? See Georgia Power Co. v. Int'l Bhd. of Elec. Workers Local 84, 707 F. Supp. 531 (N.D. Ga. 1989), affirmed, 896 F.2d 507 (11th Cir. 1990).

d. An arbitrator finds that an employee has been guilty of multiple sexual assaults on a coworker (pinching and touching body parts). The arbitrator, however, refuses to accept the employer's discharge of the guilty employee and instead directs that he be given a limited suspension and the opportunity for rehabilitation. See Chrysler Motors v. International Union, Allied Indus. Workers of Am., 959 F.2d 685 (7th Cir. 1992); Communication Workers of Am. v. Southeastern Elec. Coop., 882 F.2d 467 (10th Cir. 1989).

Should it matter whether the employee had been found guilty of prior sexual harassment at the same workplace but saved from dismissal by a previous arbitrator? See Newsday, Inc. v. Long Island Typographical Union, No. 915, 915 F.2d 840 (2d Cir. 1990). Whether the reviewing court would conclude that the employer's failure to discharge the guilty employee would provide grounds to hold the employer vicariously liable to a victim of harassment under federal or state employment discrimination law or state tort law?

## 3. No-Strike Obligations

### *Note:* Teamsters v. Lucas Flour

In Local 174, Teamsters v. Lucas Flour Co., 369 U.S. 95 (1962), the agreement contained an arbitration clause that provided that "during such arbitration, there shall be no suspension of work." The agreement did not otherwise expressly bar midterm strikes. The union struck for eight days to force the employer to rehire an employee who had been discharged for unsatisfactory work. After the strike ended, the dispute was submitted to arbitration, and the arbitral panel sustained the discharge. The Court (per Justice Stewart) held that the strike violated an implied no-strike obligation and upheld a judgment for damages caused by the strike:

> The collective bargaining contract expressly imposed upon both parties the duty of submitting the dispute in question to final and binding arbitration. [The courts of appeals] have held that a strike to settle a dispute which a collective bargaining agreement provides shall be settled exclusively and finally by compulsory arbitration constitutes a violation of the agreement. . . . We approve that doctrine. To hold otherwise would obviously do violence to accepted principles of traditional contract law. Even more in point, a contrary view would be completely at odds with the basic policy of national labor legislation to promote the arbitral process as a substitute for economic warfare. . . .
>
> What has been said is not to suggest that a no-strike agreement is to be implied beyond the area which it has been agreed will be exclusively covered by compulsory terminal arbitration.

Id. at 105, 106. Justice Black dissented:

> I had supposed . . . that the job of courts enforcing contracts was to give legal effect to what the contracting parties actually agree to do, not to what courts think they ought to do. In any case, I have been unable to find any accepted principle of contract law—traditional or otherwise—that permits courts to change completely the nature of a contract by adding new promises that the parties themselves refused to make in order that the new court-made contract

> might better fit into whatever social, economic, or legal policies the courts believe to be so important that they should have been taken out of the realm of voluntary contract by the legislative body and furthered by compulsory legislation. . . .
>
> The history of industrial relations in this country emphasizes the great importance to unions of the right to strike as well as an understandable desire on the part of employers to avoid such work stoppages. Both parties to collective bargaining discussions have much at stake as to whether there will be a no-strike clause in any resulting agreement. It is difficult to believe that the desire of employers to get such a promise and the desire of the union to avoid giving it are matters which are not constantly in the minds of those who negotiate these contracts. In such a setting, to hold — on the basis of no evidence whatever — that a union, without knowing it, impliedly surrendered the right to strike by virtue of "traditional contract law" or anything else is to me just fiction. It took more than 50 years for unions to have written into federal legislation the principle that they have a right to strike. I cannot understand how anyone familiar with that history can allow that legislatively recognized right to be undercut on the basis of the attenuated implications the Court uses here. . . .

Id. at 108-109.

### Boys Markets, Inc. v. Retail Clerks Union, Local 770
*398 U.S. 235 (1970)*

BRENNAN, J. . . .

[W]e reexamine the holding of Sinclair Refining Co. v. Atkinson, 370 U.S. 195 (1962), that the anti-injunction provisions of the Norris-LaGuardia Act preclude a federal district court from enjoining a strike in breach of a no-strike obligation under a collective bargaining agreement, even though that agreement contains provisions, enforceable under §301(a) . . . , for binding arbitration of the grievance dispute concerning which the strike was called. . . . Having concluded that *Sinclair* was erroneously decided and that subsequent events have undermined its continuing validity, we overrule that decision. . . .

#### I

. . . [P]etitioner and respondent were parties to a collective bargaining agreement which provided, inter alia, that all controversies concerning its interpretation or application should be resolved by adjustment and arbitration procedures set forth therein and that, during the life of the contract, there should be "no cessation or stoppage of work, lockout, picketing or boycotts. . . ." The dispute arose when petitioner's frozen foods supervisor and certain members of his crew who were not members of the bargaining unit began to rearrange merchandise in the frozen food cases of one of petitioner's supermarkets. A union representative insisted that the food cases be stripped of all merchandise and be restocked by union personnel. When petitioner did not accede to the union's demand, a strike was called and the union began to picket petitioner's establishment. Thereupon petitioner demanded that the union cease the work stoppage and picketing and sought to invoke the grievance and arbitration procedures specified in the contract.

The following day, since the strike had not been terminated, petitioner filed a complaint in California Superior Court seeking a temporary restraining order, a preliminary and permanent injunction, and specific performance of the contractual arbitration provision. The state court issued a temporary restraining order forbidding continuation of the strike and also an order to show cause why a preliminary injunction should not be granted. Shortly thereafter, the union removed the case to the Federal District Court and there made a motion to quash the state court's temporary restraining order. In opposition, petitioner moved for an order compelling arbitration and enjoining continuation of the strike. Concluding that the dispute was subject to arbitration under the collective bargaining agreement and that the strike was in violation of the contract, the District Court ordered the parties to arbitrate the underlying dispute and simultaneously enjoined the strike [and] all picketing in the vicinity of petitioner's supermarket. . . .

. . . *Lincoln Mills* held generally that "the substantive law to apply in suits under §301(a) is federal law, which the courts must fashion from the policy of our national labor laws," 353 U.S., at 456, and more specifically that a union can obtain specific performance of an employer's promise to arbitrate grievances. We rejected the contention that the anti-injunction proscriptions of [Norris-LaGuardia] prohibited this type of relief, noting that a refusal to arbitrate was not "part and parcel of the abuses against which the Act was aimed," id., at 458, and that the Act itself manifests a policy determination that arbitration should be encouraged. See [Norris-LaGuardia §8]. Subsequently in the *Steelworkers Trilogy* we emphasized the importance of arbitration . . . and cautioned the lower courts against usurping the functions of the arbitrator.

Serious questions remained, however, concerning the role that state courts were to play in suits involving collective bargaining agreements. Confronted with some of these problems in Charles Dowd Box Co. v. Courtney, 368 U.S. 502 (1962), we held that Congress clearly intended *not* to disturb the preexisting jurisdiction of the state courts over suits for violations of collective bargaining agreements. . . .

Shortly after the decision in *Dowd Box*, we sustained, in Teamsters Local 174 v. Lucas Flour Co., 369 U.S. 95 (1962), an award of damages by a state court to an employer for a breach by the union of a no-strike provision in its contract. . . . [W]e did not consider the applicability of the Norris-LaGuardia Act to state court proceedings because the employer's prayer for relief sought only damages and not specific performance of a no-strike obligation.

Subsequent to the decision in *Sinclair*, we held in Avco Corp. v. Aero Lodge 735, [390 U.S. 557 (1968),] that §301(a) suits initially brought in state courts may be removed to the designated federal forum under the federal question removal jurisdiction delineated in 28 U.S.C. §1441. In so holding, however, the Court expressly left open the questions whether state courts are bound by the anti-injunction proscriptions of the Norris-LaGuardia Act and whether federal courts, after removal of a §301(a) action, are required to dissolve any injunctive relief previously granted by the state courts. . . .

The decision in *Avco*, viewed in the context of *Lincoln Mills* and its progeny, has produced an anomalous situation which, in our view, makes urgent the reconsideration of *Sinclair*. The principal practical effect of *Avco* and *Sinclair* taken together is nothing less than to oust state courts of jurisdiction in §301(a) suits where injunctive relief is sought for breach of a no-strike obligation. Union defendants can, as a matter of course, obtain removal to a federal court[11] and there is obviously a compelling incentive for them to do so in order to gain the advantage of the strictures upon injunctive relief which *Sinclair* imposes on federal courts. The sanctioning of this practice, however, is wholly inconsistent with our conclusion in *Dowd Box* that the congressional purpose embodied in §301(a) was to *supplement*, and not to encroach upon, the preexisting jurisdiction of the state courts. It is ironic indeed that the very provision that Congress clearly intended to provide additional remedies for breach of collective bargaining agreements has been employed to displace previously existing state remedies. We are not at liberty thus to depart from the clearly expressed congressional policy to the contrary.

On the other hand, to the extent that widely disparate remedies theoretically remain available in state, as opposed to federal, courts, the federal policy of labor law uniformity elaborated in *Lucas Flour Co.*, is seriously offended. . . .

Furthermore, the existing scheme, with the injunction remedy technically available in the state courts but rendered inefficacious by the removal device, assigns to removal proceedings a total unintended function. . . .

It is undoubtedly true that each of the foregoing objections to *Sinclair-Avco* could be remedied either by overruling *Sinclair* or by extending that decision to the States. [However,] we agree with Chief Justice Traynor of the California Supreme Court that "whether or not Congress could deprive state

11. Section 301(a) suits require neither the existence of diversity of citizenship nor a minimum jurisdictional amount in controversy. All §301(a) suits may be removed pursuant to 28 U.S.C. §1441.

courts of the power to give such [injunctive] remedies when enforcing collective bargaining agreements, it has not attempted to do so either in the Norris-LaGuardia Act or §301." McCarroll v. Los Angeles County Dist. Council of Carpenters, 49 Cal. 2d 45, 63, 315 P.2d 322, 332 (1957).

An additional reason for not resolving the existing dilemma by extending *Sinclair* to the States is the devastating implications for the enforceability of arbitration agreements and their accompanying no-strike obligations if equitable remedies were not available. As we have previously indicated [in *Lincoln Mills,* 353 U.S. at 455,] a no-strike obligation, express or implied, is the quid pro quo for an undertaking by the employer to submit grievance disputes to the process of arbitration. Any incentive for employers to enter into such an arrangement is necessarily dissipated if the principal and most expeditious method by which the no-strike obligation can be enforced is eliminated. While it is of course true . . . that other avenues of redress, such as an action for damages, would remain open to an aggrieved employer, an award of damages after a dispute has been settled is no substitute for an immediate halt to an illegal strike. Furthermore, an action for damages prosecuted during or after a labor dispute would only tend to aggravate industrial strife and delay an early resolution of the difficulties between employer and union. . . .

. . . [B]ecause *Sinclair,* in the aftermath of *Avco,* casts serious doubts upon the effective enforcement of a vital element of stable labor-management relations—arbitration agreements with their attendant no-strike obligations—we conclude that *Sinclair* does not make a viable contribution to federal labor policy.

## IV

[As the *Sinclair* dissent stated, t]he literal terms of §4 of the Norris-LaGuardia Act must be accommodated to the subsequently enacted provisions of §301(a) . . . and the purposes of arbitration. . . .

The Norris-LaGuardia Act was responsive to a situation totally different from that which exists today. In the early part of this century, the federal courts generally were regarded as allies of management in its attempt to prevent the organization and strengthening of labor unions; and in this industrial struggle the injunction became a potent weapon that was wielded against the activities of labor groups. The result was a large number of sweeping decrees, often issued ex parte, drawn on an ad hoc basis without regard to any systematic elaboration of national labor policy. . . .

As labor organizations grew in strength and developed toward maturity, congressional emphasis shifted from protection of the nascent labor movement to the encouragement of collective bargaining and to administrative techniques for the peaceful resolution of industrial disputes. This shift in emphasis was accomplished, however, without extensive revision of many of the older enactments, including the antiinjunction section of the Norris-LaGuardia Act. Thus it became the task of the courts to accommodate, to reconcile the older statutes with the more recent ones. . . .

. . . We conclude, therefore, that the unavailability of equitable relief in the arbitration context presents a serious impediment to the congressional policy favoring the voluntary establishment of a mechanism for the peaceful resolution of labor disputes, that the core purpose of the Norris-LaGuardia Act is not sacrificed by the limited use of equitable remedies to further this important policy, and consequently that the Norris-LaGuardia Act does not bar the granting of injunctive relief in the circumstances of the instant case.

## V

Our holding . . . is a narrow one. We do not undermine the vitality of the Norris-LaGuardia Act. We deal only with the situation in which a collective bargaining contract contains a mandatory grievance adjustment or arbitration procedure. Nor does it follow from what we have said that injunctive relief is appropriate as a matter of course in every case of a strike over an arbitrable grievance. The dissenting opinion in *Sinclair* suggested the following principles for the guidance of the district courts in determining whether to grant injunctive relief—principles that we now adopt:

> A District Court entertaining an action under §301 may not grant injunctive relief against concerted activity unless and until it decides that the case is one in which an injunction would be appropriate despite the Norris-LaGuardia Act. When a strike is sought to be enjoined because it is over a grievance which both parties are contractually bound to arbitrate, the District Court may issue no injunctive order until it first holds that the contract *does* have that effect; and the employer should be ordered to arbitrate, as a condition of his obtaining an injunction against the strike. Beyond this, the District Court must, of course, consider whether issuance of an injunction would be warranted under ordinary principles of equity—whether breaches are occurring and will continue, or have been threatened and will be committed; whether they have caused or will cause irreparable injury to the employer; and whether the employer will suffer more from the denial of an injunction than will the union from its issuance.

370 U.S., at 228. (Emphasis in original.)

In the present case there is no dispute that the grievance in question was subject to adjustment and arbitration under the collective bargaining agreement and that the petitioner was ready to proceed with arbitration at the time an injunction against the strike was sought and obtained. The District Court also concluded that, by reason of respondent's violations of its no-strike obligation, petitioner "has suffered irreparable injury and will continue to suffer irreparable injury." Since we now overrule *Sinclair,* the holding of the Court of Appeals in reliance on *Sinclair* must be reversed. Accordingly, we reverse . . . and remand the case with directions to enter a judgment affirming the order of the District Court.

[The concurring opinion of Justice Stewart is omitted.]

Justice MARSHALL did not participate in the case.

Justice BLACK, dissenting.

. . . Although §301(a) . . . explicitly waives the diversity and amount-in-controversy requirements for federal jurisdiction, it says nothing at all about granting injunctions. Eight years ago this Court considered the relation of these two statutes: after full briefing and argument, relying on the language and history of the Acts, the Court decided that Congress did not wish this later statute to impair in any way Norris-LaGuardia's explicit prohibition against injunctions in labor disputes. Sinclair Refining Co. v. Atkinson, 370 U.S. 195 (1962).

Although Congress has been urged to overrule our holding in *Sinclair,* it has steadfastly refused to do so. Nothing in the language or history of the two Acts has changed. Nothing at all has changed, in fact, except the membership of the Court and the personal views of one Justice [Justice Stewart]. I remain of the opinion that *Sinclair* was correctly decided. . . .

Even if the majority were correct, however, in saying that *Sinclair* misinterpreted the Taft-Hartley and Norris-LaGuardia Acts, I should be compelled to dissent. I believe that both the making and the changing of laws which affect the substantial rights of the people are primarily for Congress, not this Court. Most especially is this so when the laws involved are the focus of strongly held views of powerful but antagonistic political and economic interests. . . .

The only "subsequent event" to which the Court can point is our decision in *Avco*. . . .

*Avco* does make any effort to enforce a no-strike clause in a state court removable to a federal court, but it does not follow [as the Court maintains] that the no-strike clause is unenforceable. Damages may be awarded; the union may be forced to arbitrate. And the employer may engage in self-help. The Court would have it that these techniques are less effective than an injunction. That is doubtless true. But the harshness and effectiveness of injunctive relief—and opposition to "government by injunction"—were the precise reasons for the congressional prohibition in the Norris-LaGuardia Act. The effect of the *Avco* decision is, indeed, to highlight the limited remedial powers of federal courts. But if the Congress is unhappy with these powers as this Court defined them, then the Congress may act; this Court should not. . . .

[The dissenting opinion of Justice White is omitted.]

## *NOTES AND QUESTIONS*

1. **Stare Decisis.** Do you think the Court gave sufficient weight to the principle of stare decisis in *Boys Markets*? Should this principle normally be given greater or lesser weight by the Court in a statutory interpretation case like *Boys Markets* than in a constitutional interpretation case? Did it make a difference in *Boys Markets* that the Court was employing authority, which it had claimed in *Lincoln Mills*, to fashion federal common law under §301 to govern the interpretation of collective bargaining agreements? Does §301 vest the Court with any lawmaking authority to modify other provisions of federal labor law like the Norris-LaGuardia Act? Are you persuaded that the Court's decision in *Avco* "ma[de] urgent the reconsideration of *Sinclair*"? What was the most persuasive policy basis for the Court's overruling of *Sinclair*? Is *Boys Markets* an example of "judicial updating" of a statute perceived by the Court to be outmoded? See generally James J. Brudney, A Famous Victory: Collective Bargaining Protections and the Statutory Aging Process, 74 N.C. L. Rev. 939, 1020-1034 (1996). Is that an appropriate judicial function?

2. **Implied No-Strike Clauses and *Boys Markets* Injunctions.** The no-strike provision upon which an award of damages was sustained in *Lucas Flour* was in part inferred by the Court from an express commitment to submit "any difference as to the true interpretation" of the agreement to binding arbitration. 369 U.S. at 96. Do *Lucas Flour* and *Boys Markets* mean that even in the absence of an express no-strike provision, a federal court may enjoin a strike over a dispute that a collective agreement states shall be exclusively resolved by arbitration? See Gateway Coal Co. v. United Mine Workers, 414 U.S. 368 (1974) (yes). Conversely, are *all* strikes in breach of an express no-strike clause enjoinable under *Boys Markets*? Cf. *Buffalo Forge*, infra page 712. See also note 3 below.

3. **Availability of a *Boys Markets* Injunction in the Absence of a Binding Arbitration Clause?** A collective agreement contains a no-strike clause but does not provide for ultimate resolution of disputes through binding arbitration by a neutral third party. It instead requires a series of meetings on grievances between employer and union representatives before either party can exert economic pressure. Can the employer obtain an injunction against a strike that occurs before the union has exhausted this meeting process or are injunctions available under *Boys Markets* only to support an arbitration process? See American Tel. & Tel. Co. v. Communications Workers of Am., 985 F.2d 855 (6th Cir. 1993) (exception only available when dispute is subject to arbitration). Consider again after reading the Court's *Buffalo Forge* decision, infra page 712.

**4. Safety Disputes.** In *Gateway Coal,* supra note 2, coal miners struck to protest the employer's reinstatement of two foremen who had been suspended for falsifying air flow records important to monitoring the mine's safety. The Court found the underlying dispute clearly arbitrable and upheld an injunction barring the strike, ordering the union to arbitrate, and providing for suspension of the foremen pending the arbitral award. It announced that the usual presumption of arbitrability applies to a safety dispute and that the implied exemption of certain safety disputes from *Boys Markets* injunctions under LMRA §502 requires objective evidence of abnormally dangerous working conditions, as distinguished from an honest, but unjustifiable, belief in their existence. The Court concluded:

> On the facts of this case, we think it clear that §502 did not deprive the District Court of authority to enforce the contractual no-strike obligation. The union inferred from the foremen's failure to record the reduced airflow on the morning of April 15 that their return to the job created an abnormally dangerous working condition. One may doubt whether this assertion alone could suffice to invoke the protection of §502. In any event, the District Court resolved the issue by expressly conditioning injunctive relief on the suspension of the two foremen pending decision by the impartial umpire.

414 U.S. at 387. *Gateway* is criticized in James B. Atleson, Threats to Health and Safety: Employee Self-Help Under the NLRA, 59 Minn. L. Rev. 647 (1975). For treatment of the protection provided by OSHA regulations to employees who refuse to work because of "a reasonable apprehension of death or serious injury," see Whirlpool Corp. v. Marshall, 445 U.S. 1 (1980).

**5. Employer's Duty to Arbitrate in the Face of a Strike in Breach of the No-Strike Clause?** Nearly 220 union workers leave work in protest of the Needham Packing Company's discharge of another worker. The company advises the workers that the discharge would be handled in accordance with the grievance procedure set forth in the collective agreement and that the protesting strikers would be terminated if they do not return to work. The workers do not return. The company terminates them and hires permanent replacements. The union then files grievances over the initial and subsequent discharges. The company thereupon informs the union that it will no longer process these or any grievances, that it is "repudiating and terminating the labor agreement," and that it will no longer recognize or deal with the union. The union sues in federal court to compel arbitration. The company argues that the union's faithful observance of the no-strike clause is a condition precedent to the employer's duty to arbitrate and that the breach of the clause justified the employer's total repudiation of the contract. How should the court rule? How should the court treat §8 of the Norris-LaGuardia Act? See Local 721, United Packinghouse Workers v. Needham Packing Co., 376 U.S. 247 (1964) (company must arbitrate). See generally Clyde W. Summers, Collective Agreements and the Law of Contracts, 78 Yale L.J. 525, 542-547 (1969); David E. Feller, A General Theory of the Collective Bargaining Agreement, 61 Cal. L. Rev. 663, 792-799 (1973).

**6. Conditioning the Grant of the *Boys Markets* Injunction?** A federal district court, enjoining a strike protesting a railroad's elimination of jobs and change in working hours, conditions the injunction on the carrier's rescinding the job changes or paying the adversely affected employees the wages they would have otherwise received, pending a determination by the adjustment board to which the underlying dispute had been submitted. Should the Supreme Court uphold the trial court's discretion to impose the condition? See Brotherhood of Locomotive Eng'rs v. Missouri-Kansas-Texas R.R., 363 U.S. 528 (1962) (upholding trial court's discretion).

### Buffalo Forge Co. v. United Steelworkers of America
*428 U.S. 397 (1976)*

WHITE, J. . . .

The issue . . . is whether a federal court may enjoin a sympathy strike pending the arbitrator's decision as to whether the strike is forbidden by the express no-strike clause contained in the collective bargaining contract to which the striking union is a party.

#### I

The Buffalo Forge Company . . . operates three separate plant and office facilities in the Buffalo, New York area. For some years production and maintenance (P&M) employees at the three locations have been represented by the United Steelworkers . . . and its Local Unions No. 1874 and No. 3732 (the Union). The United Steelworkers is a party to the two separate collective bargaining agreements between the locals and the employer. The contracts contain identical no-strike clauses,[1] as well as grievance and

---

1. Section 14.b. of each agreement provides: "There shall be no strikes, work stoppages or interruption or impeding of work. No Officers or representatives of the Union shall authorize, instigate, aid or condone any such activities. No employee shall participate in any such activity. The Union recognizes its possible liabilities for violation of this provision and will use its influence to see that work stoppages are prevented." . . .

arbitration provisions for settling disputes over the interpretation and application of each contract. The latter provide:

> 26. Should differences arise between the [employer] and any employee covered by this Agreement as to the meaning and application of the provisions of this Agreement, or should any trouble of any kind arise in the plant, there shall be no suspension of work on account of such differences, but an earnest effort shall be made to settle such differences immediately [under the six-step grievance and arbitration procedure provided in sections 27 through 32].[2]

Shortly before this dispute arose, the United Steelworkers and two other locals not parties to this litigation were certified to represent the employer's "office clerical-technical" (O&T) employees at the same three locations. On November 16, 1974, after several months of negotiations looking toward their first collective bargaining agreement, the O&T employees struck and established picket lines at all three locations. On November 18, P&M employees at one plant refused to cross the O&T picket line for the day. Two days later, the employer learned that the P&M employees planned to stop work at all three plants the next morning. In telegrams to the Union, the employer stated its position that a strike by the P&M employees would violate the no-strike clause and offered to arbitrate any dispute which had led to the planned strike. The next day, at the Union's direction, the P&M employees honored the O&T picket line and stopped work at the three plants. They did not return to work until December 16, the first regular working day after the District Court denied the employer's prayer for a preliminary injunction.

The employer's complaint under §301(a) [, filed] . . . on November 26, claimed the work stoppage was in violation of the no-strike clause. Contending in the alternative that the work strike was caused by a specific incident involving P&M truck drivers' refusal to follow a supervisor's instructions to cross the O&T picket line, and that the question whether the P&M employees' work stoppage violated the no-strike clause was itself arbitrable, the employer requested damages, a temporary restraining order and a preliminary injunction against the strike and an order compelling the parties to submit any "underlying dispute" to the contractual grievance and arbitration procedures. The Union's position was that the work stoppage did not violate the no-strike clause. It offered to submit that question to arbitration "on one day's notice," but opposed the prayer for injunctive relief.

After denying the temporary restraining order and finding that the P&M work stoppage was not the result of the specific refusal to cross the

---

2. The final step in the six-part grievance procedure is provided for in §32: "In the event the grievance involved a question as to the meaning and application of the provisions of this Agreement, and has not been previously satisfactorily adjusted, it may be submitted to arbitration upon written notice of the Union or the Company." . . .

O&T picket line, the District Court concluded that the P&M employees were engaged in a sympathy action in support of the striking O&T employees. The District Court then held itself forbidden to issue an injunction by §4 of the Norris-LaGuardia Act because the P&M employees' strike was not over an "arbitrable grievance" and hence was not within the "narrow" exception to the Norris-LaGuardia Act established in [*Boys Markets*], 398 U.S. 235 (1970).

On the employer's appeal from the denial of a preliminary injunction, . . . the parties stipulated that the District Court's findings of fact were correct, that the Union had authorized and directed the P&M employees' work stoppage, that the O&T employees' strike and picket line were bona fide, primary and legal, and that the P&M employees' work stoppage, though ended, might "be resumed at any time in the near future at the direction of the International Union, or otherwise."

. . . The Court of Appeals affirmed. . . . [We] now affirm the judgment of the Court of Appeals.

## II

. . . Whether the sympathy strike the Union called violated the no-strike clause, and the appropriate remedies if it did, are subject to the agreed-upon dispute-settlement procedures of the contract and are ultimately issues for the arbitrator. The employer thus was entitled to invoke the arbitral process to determine the legality of the sympathy strike and to obtain a court order requiring the Union to arbitrate if the Union refused to do so. Furthermore, were the issue arbitrated and the strike found illegal, the relevant federal statutes as construed in our cases would permit an injunction to enforce the arbitral decision.

The issue in this case arises because the employer not only asked for an order directing the Union to arbitrate but prayed that the strike itself be enjoined pending arbitration and the arbitrator's decision whether the strike was permissible under the no-strike clause. . . .

*Boys Markets* plainly does not control this case. The District Court found, and it is not now disputed, that the strike was not *over* any dispute between the Union and the employer that was even remotely subject to the arbitration provisions of the contract. . . . The strike had neither the purpose nor the effect of denying or evading an obligation to arbitrate or of depriving the employer of his bargain. Thus, had the contract not contained a no-strike clause or had the clause expressly excluded sympathy strikes, there would have been no possible basis for implying from the existence of an arbitration clause a promise not to strike that could have been violated by the sympathy strike in this case. Gateway Coal Co. v. Mine Workers, [414 U.S. 368, 382 (1974)].

Nor was the injunction authorized solely because it was alleged that the sympathy strike called by the Union violated the express no-strike provision of the contract. Section 301 . . . assigns a major role to the courts in enforcing collective bargaining agreements, but aside from the enforcement of the arbitration provisions of such contracts, within the limits permitted by *Boys Markets,* the Court has never indicated that the courts may enjoin actual or threatened contract violations despite the Norris-LaGuardia Act. . . .

. . . Here the Union struck, and the parties were in dispute whether the sympathy strike violated the Union's no-strike undertaking. Concededly, that issue was arbitrable. . . . But the Union does not deny its duty to arbitrate; in fact, it denies that the employer ever demanded arbitration. However that may be, it does not follow that the District Court was empowered not only to order arbitration but to enjoin the strike pending the decision of the arbitrator, despite the express prohibition of §4(a) of [Norris-LaGuardia]. . . . If an injunction could issue against the strike in this case, so in proper circumstances could a court enjoin any other alleged breach of contract pending the exhaustion of the applicable grievance and arbitration provisions even though the injunction would otherwise violate one of the express prohibitions of [§4]. The court in such cases would be permitted, if the dispute was arbitrable, to hold hearings, make findings of fact, interpret the applicable provisions of the contract and issue injunctions so as to restore the status quo ante or to otherwise regulate the relationship of the parties pending exhaustion of the arbitration process. This would cut deeply into the policy of the Norris-LaGuardia Act and make the courts potential participants in a wide range of arbitrable disputes under the many existing and future collective bargaining contracts, not just for the purpose of enforcing promises to arbitrate, which was the limit of *Boys Markets,* but for the purpose of preliminarily dealing with the merits of the factual and legal issues that are subjects for the arbitrator and of issuing injunctions that would otherwise be forbidden by the Norris-LaGuardia Act.

This is not what the parties have bargained for. Surely it cannot be concluded here, as it was in *Boys Markets,* that such injunctions pending arbitration are essential to carry out promises to arbitrate and to implement the private arrangements for the administration of the contract. As is typical, the agreement in this case outlines the prearbitration settlement procedures and provides that if the grievance "has not been . . . satisfactorily adjusted," arbitration may be had. Nowhere does it provide for coercive action of any kind, let alone judicial injunctions, short of the terminal decision of the arbitrator. The parties have agreed to grieve and arbitrate, not to litigate. They have not contracted for a judicial preview of the facts and the law. Had they anticipated additional regulation of their relationships pending arbitration, it seems very doubtful that they would have resorted to litigation rather than to private arrangements. . . .

The dissent suggests that injunctions should be authorized in cases such as this at least where the violation, in the court's view, is clear and the court is sufficiently sure that the parties seeking the injunction will win before the arbitrator. But this would still involve hearings, findings and judicial interpretations of collective bargaining contracts. It is incredible to believe that the courts would always view the facts and the contract as the arbitrator would; and it is difficult to believe that the arbitrator would not be heavily influenced or wholly preempted by judicial views of the facts and the meaning of contracts if this procedure is to be permitted. Injunctions against strikes, even temporary injunctions, very often permanently settle the issue; and in other contexts time and expense would be discouraging factors to the losing party in court in considering whether to relitigate the issue before the arbitrator.

. . . We agree with the Court of Appeals that there is no necessity here, such as was found to be the case in *Boys Markets*, to accommodate the policies of the Norris-LaGuardia Act to the requirements of §301 by empowering the District Court to issue the injunction sought by the employer . . .

STEVENS, J., with whom BRENNAN, MARSHALL, and POWELL, JJ., join, dissenting.

. . . In this case, the question whether the sympathy strike violates the no-strike clause is an arbitrable issue. If the court had the benefit of an arbitrator's resolution of the issue in favor of the employer, it could enforce that decision just as it could require the parties to submit the issue to arbitration. And if the agreement were so plainly unambiguous that there could be no bona fide issue to submit to the arbitrator, there must be the same authority to enforce the parties' bargain pending the arbitrator's final decision. . . .

. . . In the present case, an interim determination of the no-strike question by the court neither usurps nor precludes a decision by the arbitrator. By definition, issuance of an injunction pending the arbitrator's decision does not supplant a decision that he otherwise would have made. Indeed, it is the ineffectiveness of the damage remedy for strikes pending arbitration that lends force to the employer's argument for an injunction. The court does not oust the arbitrator of his proper function but fulfills a role that he never served.

## *NOTES AND QUESTIONS*

**1. What If the Injunction Would Not Interfere with Arbitration?** The *Buffalo Forge* Court reasoned that the lower court should not have enjoined the strike pending arbitration in that case because the strike was not over any underlying dispute subject to arbitration and because issuance of an injunction required the court to deal preliminarily "with the merits of the factual and legal issues that are subjects for the arbitrator." Would the Court's reasoning apply equally to a decree enjoining a union's continuation of a sympathy strike after an arbitrator had ruled that the sympathy strike was indeed covered by a no-strike provision? To an injunction pending arbitration if the union had explicitly pledged to arbitrate the issue of a sympathy strike's legality before instituting a strike? See Norman L. Cantor, Strikes over Non-Arbitrable Labor Disputes, 23 B.C. L. Rev. 633, 636-639 (1982).

**2. What If the Picketing Union's Dispute Were Arbitrable?** Would the case have come out differently if the picketing union's underlying dispute had itself been arbitrable? Indeed, what if the agreements for both the union honoring the picket line and the picketing union contained identical terms and covered employees in the same job categories? See Cedar Coal v. UMW, 560 F.2d 1153 (4th Cir. 1977) (interpreting *Buffalo Forge* to allow injunctions when underlying dispute is arbitrable).

**3. "Reverse" *Boys Markets* Injunctions.** Under *Boys Markets* and *Buffalo Forge,* how should the courts treat a union's request for an injunction of a company's change in working conditions pending an arbitration process that will consider whether the changes are consistent with the collective agreement? The circuit courts generally agree that when normal equitable standards are met, injunctions are appropriate where "necessary to prevent conduct by the party enjoined from rendering the arbitral process a hollow formality" because without the injunction in such circumstances an "arbitral award when rendered could not return the parties substantially to the status quo ante." Lever Bros. Co. v. Chemical Workers Local 217, 554 F.2d 115 (4th Cir. 1976). See also Oil, Chemical and Atomic Workers Int'l Union v. Amoco Oil Co., 885 F.2d 697, 702 (10th Cir. 1989); Independent Oil & Chemical Workers of Quincy, Inc. v. Procter & Gamble Mfg., 864 F.2d 927, 930 (1988). Under this standard, some courts have granted injunctions against major business transformations such as the sale or relocation of operations that allegedly violate contractual commitments expressly dealing with such decisions. See, e.g., Local Lodge No. 1266, Int'l Ass'n of Machinists v. Panoramic Corp., 668 F.2d 276 (7th Cir. 1981) (sale of division, if not enjoined, would present arbitrator with fait accompli). However, they have not issued injunctions merely to ensure that employees will not suffer some injury pending arbitration that might not be compensated fully by the contract remedies invoked by arbitrators. See, e.g., Aluminum Workers, Local Union No. 215 v. Consolidated Aluminum Corp., 696 F.2d 437 (6th Cir. 1982) (injunction not justified by "repossessions, foreclosures, and injury to credit status" that could result from discharges).

**4. Norris-LaGuardia Requirements.** For the general applicability of the requirements and limitations of §§7, 8, and 9 of Norris-LaGuardia to prayers for injunctions against unions and employers, see United Parcel Serv. (New York) v. Local 804, Teamsters, 698 F.2d 100 (2d Cir. 1983); UAW v. Lester Eng'g Co., 718 F.2d 818 (6th Cir. 1983); Armco, Inc. v. United Steelworkers of America, Local 169, 280 F.3d 669 (6th Cir. 2002).

**5. Unfair Labor Practice Strikes and the Scope of No-Strike Clauses.** In Arlan's Dep't Store, 133 N.L.R.B. 802 (1961), the Board held that strikes against "serious unfair labor practices"—defined as practices "destructive of the foundation on which collective bargaining must rest"—are "immune from general no strike clauses." Under what circumstances can an employer obtain a *Boys Markets* injunction against what purports to be an unfair labor practice strike? See, e.g., Dow Chem. Co., 244 N.L.R.B. 1060, enforcement denied, 636 F.2d 1352 (3d Cir. 1980).

**6. Availability of *Boys Markets* Injunctions for Certain Postexpiration Strikes?** The collective agreement between the company and the union included broad clauses prohibiting strikes "during the life of the agreement" and providing for binding arbitration of "any grievance." The agreement also provided that employees were not to be discharged or otherwise disciplined except for just cause. Three weeks before the expiration of the agreement the company discharged three bargaining unit employees, citing excessive absenteeism. The union immediately filed a grievance, claiming that the discharged employees' records were no worse than a number of other employees who had not been discharged. After exhausting the final step in the grievance system a week after the expiration of the agreement, but without requesting arbitration, the union commences a strike in protest of the discharges. The employer petitions a federal court for an injunction of the strike and damages. How should the court respond? See Goya Foods, Inc., 238 N.L.R.B. 1465 (1978) (holding that a no-strike clause can be violated after expiration of the agreement by a strike over a matter that could still be arbitrated under that agreement). Is *Goya Foods* required by *Lucas Flour*, supra page 703? Can the decision be reconciled with the Board's usual requirement that a waiver of statutory rights must be "clear and unmistakable"? With the Board's general rule that no-strike promises do not persist after the expiration date of a contract?

### *Note: Political Boycotts and the Norris-LaGuardia Act*

President Carter, on January 4, 1980, imposed an embargo on grain shipments to the Soviet Union, following the Soviet intervention in Afghanistan. On January 9, the International Longshoremen's Association (ILA) announced that its members would not handle any cargo going to or coming from the Soviet Union or carried on Russian ships. Thereupon, an ILA local refused to load superphosphoric acid, used in agricultural fertilizers, onto three ships that had arrived at the terminal operated by Jacksonville Bulk Terminals, Inc. (JBT). The collective agreement between the union and JBT contained a broad no-strike clause banning "any strike of any kind" and channeled all disputes through a grievance procedure culminating in arbitration. JBT sued under LMRA §301, alleging a violation of the no-strike pledge and requesting an order against the union compelling arbitration, injunctive relief against the stoppage pending arbitration, and damages. The Fifth Circuit affirmed the district court's arbitration order but reversed its grant of injunctive relief. It rejected the district court's conclusion that the Norris-LaGuardia Act is inapplicable to politically motivated strikers, and held that an injunction pending arbitration was not warranted because the underlying dispute was not arbitrable.

In Jacksonville Bulk Terminals, Inc. v. International Longshoremen's Ass'n, 457 U.S. 702 (1982), the Supreme Court, in an opinion by Justice Marshall, first addressed the employer's argument that the political motivation of the union placed the work stoppage controversy in that case outside the reach of §4 of the Norris-LaGuardia Act. The Court noted that §4 covers any "case involving or growing out of any labor dispute" and that §13(c) of the Act "broadly defines the term 'labor dispute' to include 'any controversy concerning terms or conditions of employment.'" The Court stressed that this language "does not except labor disputes having their genesis in political protests. Nor is there any basis in the statutory language for the argument that the Act requires that *each* dispute relevant to the case be a labor dispute. The Act merely requires that the case involve 'any' labor dispute." The Court therefore concluded that the "critical element in determining whether the provisions of [the Act] apply is whether 'the employer-employee relationship [is] the matrix of the controversy.' . . . In this case, the employer and the union representing its employees are the disputants, and their dispute concerns the interpretation of the labor contract that defines their relationship. Thus, the employer-employee relationship is the matrix of this controversy."

The Court then addressed the employer's argument that the work stoppage in that case was not within the *Buffalo Forge* exception to *Boys Markets* injunctions. The employer contended that "in addition to the political dispute, disputes concerning both the management-rights clause and the work-conditions clause underlie the work stoppage, and that at least one of these disputes is arguably arbitrable." The Court disagreed. It instead reaffirmed *Buffalo Forge*'s rule that the dispute that must be arbitrable is the dispute that "triggered" the work stoppage. In this case the "underlying dispute, whether viewed as an expression of the Union's 'moral outrage' at Soviet military policy or as an expression of sympathy for the people of Afghanistan, is plainly not arbitrable under the collective bargaining agreement."

## *NOTES AND QUESTIONS*

**1. Any Limits to Norris-LaGuardia's Reach?** Given the Court's conclusion that a strike in protest of Soviet military action comes within the reach of Norris-LaGuardia as long as the "employer-employee relationship" is "the matrix of the controversy," does every strike trigger the Norris-LaGuardia Act?

**2. An Explanation of *Buffalo Forge*?** Does the reasoning of *Jacksonville Bulk Terminals* help answer the questions posed concerning *Buffalo Forge* in note 1 at page 716.

**3. Secondary Boycott?** In International Longshoremen's Ass'n v. Allied Int'l, Inc., 456 U.S. 212 (1982), the Court held that the same boycott at issue in *Jacksonville Bulk Terminals* fell "squarely" within the scope of the NLRA's prohibition of secondary boycotts. The Court concluded that it "was [not] a defense that the reason for the boycott was not a labor dispute with a primary employer but was rather a political dispute with a foreign nation."

**4. "Wildcat" Strikes.** An employer announces that it intends to change certain work schedules, claiming unilateral authority to do so by a broad management-rights clause in its collective agreement. The union accepts the employer's interpretation of the collective agreement while at the same time obtaining employer concessions on some work rules that had been in contention. However, a large part of the bargaining unit goes out on strike against the direction of union leadership. The strikers claim to be protesting the union's acceptance of the work schedule changes. There are broad arbitration and no-strike clauses in the collective agreement. The employer seeks an injunction of the work stoppage in federal district court. Should the court grant the injunction? See Complete Auto Transit, Inc. v. Reis, 614 F.2d 1110, 1114 (6th Cir. 1980), affirmed on other grounds, 451 U.S. 401 (1981) (dicta stating that strike over dissatisfaction with union representation is not arbitrable and thus not enjoinable). Can the employer take any other action to discourage the strike?

### *Note: Union and Individual Employee Liability for Breach of No-Strike Obligations*

In *Complete Auto Transit,* the Supreme Court held that the third sentence of §301(b) of the LMRA "clearly reveals Congress' intent to shield individual employees from liability for damages arising from their breach of the no-strike clause of a collective bargaining agreement, whether or not the union participated in or authorized the illegality." The *Complete Auto Transit* decision was an elaboration of the Court's earlier decision in Atkinson v. Sinclair Refining Co., 370 U.S. 238 (1962), which read §301(b) as an attempt to insulate individual employees from the harsh effects of being liable for the often major damages incurred by employers during strikes. *Atkinson* decided only that officers and members of a union should be protected when the union may be liable for violation of a no-strike clause, but *Complete Auto Transit* applied the same reasoning to wildcat strikes for which a union could not be held liable.

In Carbon Fuel Co. v. United Mine Wkrs., 444 U.S. 212 (1979), the Court also read §§301(b) and (e) to limit the "responsibility of unions for strikes in breach of contract to cases when the union may be found responsible according to the common-law rule of agency." The Court stressed that Congress "provided in §301(b) that a union 'shall be bound by the acts of its agents,' and in §301(e) provided that the common law of agency shall govern 'in determining whether any person is acting as an "agent" of another person.'" The Court found that the United Mine Workers International Union was not liable for wildcat strikes in violation of a no-strike agreement and engaged in by three of its locals, absent evidence that the International had "instigated, supported, ratified, or encouraged any of the work stoppages." The Court rejected the employer's "suggestion that Congress' policy in favor of arbitration extends to imposing an obligation on the [International], which agreed to arbitrate grievances, to use reasonable means to try to control the locals' actions in contravention of that agreement."

The three local unions in *Carbon Fuel* did not seek review of the judgments against the them aggregating $722,347.43, The Fourth Circuit sustained those judgments on a 'mass action' theory, holding the locals responsible for most of the wildcat strikes. 582 F.2d 1346 (1978). The theory was based on the assumption "that large groups of men do not act collectively without leadership and that a functioning union must be held responsible for the mass action of its members." After the Supreme Court's decision in *Carbon Fuel*, should a local union be held liable for damages resulting from a "mass action" unauthorized strike that its officers did not instigate, support, ratify, or encourage? What if the union demonstrated in court that its officers used all reasonable means to prevent and end the wildcat activity? See Consolidation Coal Co. v. Local 2216, UMW, 779 F.2d 1274 (7th Cir. 1985) ("mass action" theory could not be a basis of union liability independent of agency principles because it would be against the "American system of jurisprudence" to conclude "that a local union should be considered guilty of orchestrating a strike until it proves itself innocent"; mass action, however, could provide some evidence of union authorization or ratification); Consolidation Coal Co. v. UMW, Local 1261, 725 F.2d 1258 (10th Cir. 1984) (collecting conflicting decisions).

## C. ARBITRATION AND THE NLRB

### 1. Arbitration and Unfair Labor Practice Charges Under the NLRA

#### *Note: The NLRB's Authority over Disputes Raising Contractual Issues*

**Background.** The Board does not have authority to adjudicate violations of collective agreements, and arbitrators are not given jurisdiction to enforce the NLRA. Nevertheless, the coexistence of public and private labor-management dispute resolution mechanisms presents special problems of coordination.

As we have seen, the application of the NLRA often turns on the meaning of particular collective agreements. For instance, whether an employer has committed a §8(a)(5) violation by unilaterally changing a working condition subject to mandatory bargaining may depend on whether a collective agreement is read to preserve management's authority to make such a change. And whether the employer may make the change even after bargaining to impasse with the union may turn on whether the collective bargaining agreement is read to contain a commitment not to make the change during the agreement's term. The question arises, therefore, whether the Labor Board should delegate resolution of the issues of contractual interpretation to the private contractual interpretation system (generally arbitration) chosen by the parties, or whether federal law requires the Board to render an independent interpretation of collective agreements when statutory obligations turn on the meaning of such arguments.

Moreover, the Board's resolution of an unfair labor practice charge may require a factual determination similar to one that would be made by an arbitrator in resolving a parallel grievance under the relevant collective agreement. For instance, many §8(a)(3) charges that an employer has discriminated against employees for union-related activity turn on questions of intent and employer justification that are also likely to be considered during the arbitration of grievances challenging the employer's action under a collective agreement. In such cases, should grievants be able to seek a remedy from both the Board and an arbitrator, or should they be forced to choose only one forum? If they should be forced to choose, should the law direct them to one forum or the other? What degree of deference, if any, does the Board owe the arbitrator's determination or vice versa?

**Concurrent Jurisdiction.** The Supreme Court has not definitively answered most of these questions. In a series of cases in the mid-1960s, however, it did indicate that the Board and the contractual grievance and arbitration system have concurrent legal jurisdiction over a broad range of disputes.

*Carey v. Westinghouse.* In Carey v. Westinghouse Elec. Corp., 375 U.S. 261 (1964), the Court held that an employer should be compelled to arbitrate a grievance filed by a union representing the employer's production and maintenance workers charging that the employer had assigned production and maintenance work to a group of employees represented by a second union. The employer had argued that arbitration should not be compelled because the controversy "presented a representation matter" within the jurisdiction of the NLRB under §10(k). The Court agreed that the matter could be within the Board's purview, regardless of whether it was really a work assignment dispute concerning which bargaining unit should perform the work or a representational dispute concerning which union should represent particular employees. If a work assignment dispute, the Board would have authority to resolve the dispute under §10(k) if one of the unions conducted a strike to compel the employer to assign work to members of its bargaining unit. If a representational dispute, either union could invoke the Board's authority to have its certification clarified, or the production and maintenance union could charge the employer with a midterm modification in violation of §8(d). However, the existence of a possible remedy under the NLRA does not modify the §301 policy favoring arbitration.

Three years later, in NLRB v. C & C Plywood, 385 U.S. 421 (1967), the Court held that the Board had jurisdiction over a §8(a)(5) charge that an employer had unilaterally changed wages during the term of a collective agreement, even though adjudication of the charge required the Board to consider the employer's argument that a term of the agreement gave it authority to make the change. The lower court had ruled that the "Board did not have jurisdiction to find the respondent had violated §8(a) . . . because the existence . . . of an unfair labor practice [did] not turn entirely upon the provisions of the Act, but arguably upon a good-faith dispute as to the correct meaning of the provisions of the collective agreement." The Supreme Court reversed, stressing (at 428) that:

> [I]in this case the Board has not construed a labor agreement to determine the extent of the contractual rights which were given the union by the employer. It has not imposed its own view of what the terms and conditions of the labor agreement should be. It has done no more than merely enforce a statutory right which Congress considered necessary to allow labor and management to get on with the process of reaching fair terms and conditions of employment. . . . The Board's interpretation went only so far as was necessary to determine that the union did not agree to give up these statutory safeguards. Thus, the Board, in necessarily construing a labor agreement to decide this unfair labor practice case, has not exceeded the jurisdiction laid out for it by Congress.

*Acme Industrial.* In NLRB v. Acme Industrial Co., 385 U.S. 432 (1967), the Court upheld the Board's extension of *Truitt* (see supra page 440) to requests for information that the Board found relevant to the union's enforcement of a collective agreement. The company argued that the Board should have awaited an arbitrator's determination of the relevance of the requested information before enforcing the union's statutory rights under §8(a)(5).

*Acme Industrial* and *C & C Plywood* thus suggest that the Board has authority to interpret collective agreements in the course of resolving unfair labor practice complaints, without requiring complainants to first obtain interpretations of the agreements from arbitrators or courts.

**Permissibility of NLRB Delegation of Authority?** The question, however, remains whether the Board has discretion to delegate decision-making authority to the private dispute resolution process chosen by the parties to collective agreements. This issue was for some time debated extensively both within the Board and between the Board and the federal courts of appeals. The position settled upon by the Board in the mid-1980s and adhered to since is set out in the following cases.

### a. *Pre-Arbitral or* Collyer *Deferral*

**United Technologies Corp.**
*268 N.L.R.B. 557 (1984)*

On 6 November 1981 the Union filed a third-step grievance alleging that the Respondent, through its general foreman, Peterson, intimidated, coerced, and harassed shop steward Wilson and employee Sherfield at a first-step grievance meeting by threatening [to discipline] Sherfield if she appealed her grievance to the second step.[2] The remedy the Union sought was that "the Company immediately stop these contract violations and . . . Peterson be properly disciplined and reinstructed for his misuse, abuse, and violation of the contract." The Respondent denied the Union's grievance at the third step, and the Union withdrew it on 27 January 1982

2. The grievance that was the subject of the first-step meeting alleged that Sherfield had been "repeatedly harassed, intimidated, and discriminated against" by her foreman, Cote, and that Cote had engaged in an "act of aggression" against her . . . [i.e.,] Cote had responded to Sherfield's request for certain parts by allegedly tossing a bag of parts weighing approximately one-third of an ounce at her workbench. . . . [D]uring the first-step meeting, Cote apologized to Sherfield, whereupon General Foreman Peterson denied the grievance and urged everyone to return to work. Shop steward Wilson and Sherfield indicated that they would appeal the grievance to the second step. Peterson then told Sherfield that the Company had been nice to her and that they had not disciplined her in the past because of her [rejected parts]. Wilson stated that Peterson's statement could be construed as a threat. Peterson denied that he was threatening Sherfield; rather, he said he was merely telling Sherfield what could and would happen.

"without prejudice." The next day, the Respondent filed its own grievance alleging that "[n]otwithstanding the union's mistake in its allegations concerning General Foreman Peterson, it has refused to withdraw, with prejudice, its grievance." The Union denied the Respondent's grievance. . . . Following [Respondent's appeal and] a fourth-step meeting, the Union again denied the Respondent's grievance and refused the Respondent's request [for] arbitration. Thereafter, the Union filed the charge in [this case]. . . .

. . . [T]he concept of judicial and administrative deference to the arbitral process and the notion that courts should support, rather than interfere with, this method of dispute resolution have become entrenched in American jurisprudence. . . . [T]he Board has played a key role in fostering a climate in which arbitration could flourish. Thus, as early as 1943[7] the Board [expressed sympathy for] the concept of prospective deference to contractual grievance machinery. . . .

The Board [embraced the concept of deference] with renewed vigor in the seminal case of Collyer Insulated Wire,[8] [and] dismissed a complaint alleging unilateral changes in wages and working conditions in violation of §8(a)(5) in deference to the parties' grievance-arbitration machinery. The *Collyer* majority articulated several factors favoring deferral: The dispute arose . . . [during] a long and productive collective-bargaining relationship; there was no claim of employer animosity to the employees' exercise of protected rights; the parties' contract provided [broadly] for arbitration . . . ; the arbitration clause clearly encompassed the dispute . . . ; the employer had asserted its willingness to [arbitrate] the dispute; and [it] was eminently well suited to resolution by arbitration. . . . [T]he *Collyer* majority was holding the parties to their bargain by directing them to avoid substituting the Board's processes for their own mutually agreed-upon method for dispute resolution. . . .

. . . In *National Radio*[11] the Board extended the deferral policy to cases involving 8(a)(3) allegations [in that case, the disciplinary suspension and discharge of an active union adherent]. . . .

. . . [H]owever, the Board in *General American Transportation*[, 228 N.L.R.B. 808 (1977),] abruptly changed course. . . . Indeed, by deciding to decline to defer cases alleging violations of §§8(a)(1) and (3) and 8(b)(1)(A) and (2), the *General American Transportation* majority essentially emasculated the Board's deferral policy. . . . [Its] reasons . . . are largely unsupportable. *Collyer* worked well because it was premised on sound legal and

7. Consolidated Aircraft Corp., 47 N.L.R.B. 694, 706 (1943), enfd. in pertinent part, 141 F.2d 785 (9th Cir. 1944).

8. 192 N.L.R.B. 837 (1971).

11. National Radio Co., 198 N.L.R.B. 527 (1972).

pragmatic considerations. . . . [W]e believe it deserves to be . . . infused with renewed life.

. . . Where an employer and a union have voluntarily [created] dispute resolution machinery culminating in final and binding arbitration, it is contrary to the basic principles of the Act for the Board to jump into the fray prior to an honest attempt by the parties to resolve their disputes through that machinery. . . . [T]he statutory purpose of encouraging the practice and procedure of collective bargaining is ill-served by permitting the parties to ignore their agreement and to petition this Board in the first instance for remedial relief. . . .

. . . [D]eferral is not akin to abdication. It is merely the prudent exercise of restraint, a postponement of the use of the Board's processes to give the parties' own dispute resolution machinery a chance to succeed. The Board's processes may always be invoked if the arbitral result is inconsistent with the standards of *Spielberg*. . . .[18]

The facts of the instant case make it eminently well suited for deferral. The dispute centers on a statement a single foreman made to a single employee and a shop steward during . . . a routine first-step grievance meeting allegedly concerning possible adverse consequences . . . [from] the employee's [decision] to process her grievance to the next step. The statement is alleged to be a threat violative of §8(a)(1) [but it] is also . . . clearly cognizable under the broad grievance-arbitration provision of [the] . . . bargaining agreement.[20] Moreover, Respondent has expressed its willingness, indeed its eagerness, to arbitrate the dispute.

. . . [W]e believe it would best effectuate the purposes and policies of the Act to defer this case to the arbitral forum . . . , under the principles of *Collyer* and *National Radio*.[22]

The complaint is dismissed, provided that: Jurisdiction . . . is hereby retained for the limited purpose of entertaining an appropriate and timely motion for further consideration upon a proper showing that either (a) the dispute has not, with reasonable promptness after the issuance of this . . . Order, either been resolved . . . in the grievance procedure or submitted . . . to arbitration, or (b) the grievance or arbitration procedures have not been fair and regular or have reached a result . . . repugnant to the Act.

---

18. Spielberg Mfg. Co., 112 N.L.R.B. 1080 (1955).

20. . . . [Article] IV of the contract states that "the company and the union recognize that employees covered by this agreement may not be discriminated against in violation of the [NLRA]. . . ." [Plainly] the parties contemplated that disputes such as the one here be resolved under the grievance-arbitration machinery.

22. The Respondent must, of course, waive any timeliness provisions of the grievance-arbitration clauses of the collective-bargaining agreement so that the Union's grievance may be processed in accordance with the following Order.

Member ZIMMERMAN, dissenting. . . .

. . . Former Chairman Murphy explained in her determinative concurring opinion [in *General American Transportation*] the fundamental reasons for a pre-arbitral deferral policy which distinguishes between unfair labor practices involving disputes between contracting parties about their collective-bargaining agreement and unfair labor practices involving disputes about individual employees' statutory rights:

> [T]he Board should stay its processes in favor of the parties' grievance arbitration machinery only in those situations where the dispute is essentially between the contracting parties and where there is no alleged interference with individual employees' basic rights under §7 of the Act. Complaints alleging violations of §§8(a)(5) and 8(b)(3) fall squarely into this category, while complaints alleging violations of §§8(a)(3), (a)(1), (b)(1)(A), and (b)(2) clearly do not. . . .

Now, after 6 years [under] . . . *General American Transportation*, without any intervening judicial criticism, the majority has overruled that case and has returned to *National Radio*. The majority cites no specific evidence that General American Transportation actually has had any adverse effect upon private grievance and arbitration systems. . . .

Employees' §7 rights are public rights charged to the Board's protection. . . .

. . . Implicit in [my colleagues'] reasoning is that an exclusive collective-bargaining representative may waive an individual employee's right to seek initial redress of interference with §7 rights before the Board.[8] A union may, of course, agree to waive some individual statutory rights.[9] But in my view a union cannot waive an individual employee's right to choose a statutory forum in which to initiate and litigate an unfair labor practice issue. Even if it could, such a waiver would have to be a "clear and unmistakable" one. Here, however, the majority forces individual employees to litigate statutory rights in a contractual forum . . . without [determining] that there has been a "clear and unmistakable" waiver of the right to resort first and exclusively to the Board. My colleagues simply assume that the mere existence of a contractual grievance and arbitration procedure proves a waiver.

. . . The arbitration process is not designed to and is not particularly adept at protecting employee statutory or public rights. First, a union,

---

8. The majority erroneously states that its expansive application of *Collyer* neither waives nor even diminishes individual statutory rights. At the very least, however, an individual employee's right to elect the statutory forum first will be waived. Moreover, because *Collyer*-ized cases are subject to only a limited review under *Spielberg*, an individual's right to full de novo consideration of the statutory issue before the Board will also be waived.

9. Metropolitan Edison Co. v. NLRB, 103 S. Ct. 1467 (1983) [supra page 214].

without breaching its duty of fair representation, might not vigorously support an employee's claim in arbitration inasmuch as the union, in balancing individual and collective interests, might trade off an employee's statutory right in favor of some other benefits for employees in the bargaining unit as a whole. Second, because arbitrators' competency is primarily in "the law of the shop, not the law of the land," they may lack the competency to resolve the statutory issue(s) involved in the dispute. Third, even if the arbitrator is conversant with the Act, he is limited to determining the dispute in accordance with the parties' intent under the collective-bargaining agreement. Finally, because the arbitrator's function is to effectuate the parties' intent rather than to enforce the Act, he may issue a ruling that is inimical to the public policies underlying the Act, thereby depriving an employee of his protected statutory rights.

## *NOTES AND QUESTIONS*

**1. Effect of "No Discrimination" Clause?** The Board in *United Technologies* states that the complained-of supervisor harassment is subject to the grievance arbitration process under the contract clause quoted in footnote 20, which specifically prohibits discrimination in violation of the NLRA. Would an arbitration decision under this clause necessarily decide the same issue that would have been before the Board had it not deferred the case? Would the arbitrator necessarily use the same standards in deciding the case? Would the Board have deferred to arbitration if there had been no such "no discrimination" clause in the contract?

**2. Deferral and Waiver of the Right to Pursue a Statutory Claim Before the NLRB.** Does deferral under *Collyer* necessarily mean that the Board treats a bargaining representative's agreement to an arbitration clause as a waiver of individual employees' rights to have certain unfair labor practice charges decided initially through Board processes? See Michael C. Harper, Union Waiver of Employee Rights Under the NLRA: Part II, A Fresh Approach to Board Deferral to Arbitration, 4 Indus. Rel. L.J. 680 (1981); Harry T. Edwards, Deferral to Arbitration and Waiver of the Duty to Bargain: A Possible Way Out of Everlasting Confusion at the NLRB, 46 Ohio St. L.J. 23 (1985). If waiver is a necessary basis for Board deferral, is it reasonable for the Board to consider a union's negotiation of an arbitration clause to constitute a "clear and unmistakable" waiver of any statutory right to invoke Board processes? See Michael C. Harper, A New Board Policy on Deferral to Arbitration: Acknowledging and Delimiting Union Waiver of Employee Statutory Rights, 5 Fla. Int'l L. Rev. 685, 689-690 (2010).

**3. Distinctions Among Types of Unfair Labor Practice Charges?** Does the distinction offered by NLRB Chair Murphy in *General American Transportation* between types of unfair labor practice charges suggest an appropriate standard for deferral? Should all rights protected by §§8(a)(5) and 8(b)(3) be waivable by bargaining representatives? Should all rights protected by §§8(a)(3), 8(a)(1), 8(b)(1)(A), and 8(b)(2) be nonwaivable? Are there reasons for the Board to be more willing to defer cases like *Collyer*, where an employer invokes a collective bargaining agreement as a defense to a §8(a)(5) charge of unilateral action, than to defer §§8(a)(1) or 8(a)(3) cases? Compare Hammontree v. NLRB, 894 F.2d 438 (D.C. Cir. 1990) (panel decision holding Board may defer only in cases turning on interpretation of collective agreement), with Hammontree v. NLRB, 925 F.2d 1486 (D.C. Cir. 1991) (en banc reversal upholding Board's *United Technologies* deferral policy).

**4. Substantive Conceptions of the Duty to Bargain and the Scope of NLRB Deferral.** Evaluate the following argument: "An employer who is willing to submit to arbitration a dispute over some unilateral change in working conditions during the term of a collective agreement should not be held to have violated §8(a)(5) unless the change may threaten the entire collective bargaining relationship. Relatively minor contract violations should not be considered a violation of §8(a)(5). Therefore, Board deferral to arbitration in the typical §8(a)(5) case reflects a sensible substantive interpretation of the Act." Does this argument apply to cases like *Milwaukee Spring*, supra page 585, where the §8(a)(5) charge is that the company was constrained by the collective agreement from making some unilateral change even after bargaining with the union to impasse? Should the *Milwaukee Spring* case itself have been deferred to arbitration? See Edwards, Deferral to Arbitration, supra, at 34-35.

**5. *Dubo* Deferral.** Where the grievance arbitration process has already been initiated, the Board will hold in abeyance unfair labor practice charges that might, for all practical purposes, be resolved in that process. See Dubo Mfg., 142 N.L.R.B. 431 (1963). How broadly should *Dubo* be applied? For instance, assume that in a case like *Carey*, supra page 723, while arbitration is being pursued between one of the contesting unions and the employer, the employer asks the Board to clarify the certifications of the unions. Should the Board defer action on the employer's petition until learning the outcome of the arbitration? Consider also an unfair labor practice case that presents several closely related matters, only some of which are resolvable through an already initiated arbitration process.

**6. Effect of Board's Refusal to Defer?** Should a §301 court compel arbitration after the Board has refused to defer an unfair labor practice charge based on the same occurrence? For instance, what if the Board notes a conflict of interest between the employee filing the charge and the union that would represent him in arbitration? See Teamsters Local 807 v. Regional Import & Export Trucking Co., 944 F.2d 1037 (7th Cir. 1991) (enforcing agreement to arbitrate, noting that the arbitration procedure could avoid the conflict perceived by the Board). What if the Board, after refusing to defer, decides the unfair labor practice charge on its merits? See United Food & Commercial Workers Local 400 v. Shoppers Food Warehouse Corp., 35 F.3d 958 (4th Cir. 1994) (holding that arbitration clause should be enforced because any "direct and immediate" conflict with a ruling of the Board is only speculative until arbitrator has ruled).

### b. *Post-Arbitral or* Spielberg *Deference*

**Olin Corp.**
*268 N.L.R.B. 573 (1984)*

. . . [T]he Union is the exclusive collective-bargaining representative of Respondent's approximately 260 production and maintenance employees. [Article XIV ("Strikes and Lockouts")] of the 1980-1983 collective-bargaining agreement [provided]:

> During the life of the Agreement, the Company will not conduct a lock-out at the Plant and neither the Local Union nor the International Union, nor any officer or representative of either, will cause or permit its members to cause any strike, slowdown or stoppage (total or partial) of work or any interference, directly or indirectly, with the full operation of the plant.

Employee Spatorico was president of the Union from 1976 until his termination in December 1980. On the morning of 17 December, Respondent suspended two pipefitters for refusing to perform a job that they felt was more appropriately millwright work. A "sick out" ensued during which approximately 43 employees left work that day with medical excuses. Respondent gave formal written reprimands to 39 of the [participants]. In a letter dated 29 December, Respondent notified Spatorico that he was discharged based on his entire record and in particular for threatening the sick out, participating in [it], and failing to prevent it.

Spatorico's discharge was grieved and arbitrated. . . . [T]he arbitrator found that a sick out had occurred . . . , that Spatorico "at least partially caused or participated" in it, and that he failed to try to stop it until after it had occurred. The arbitrator concluded that Spatorico's conduct contravened his obligation under article XIV . . . [and] stated, "Union officers implicitly have an affirmative duty not to cause strikes which are in violation of the clause, not to participate in such strikes and to try to stop them when they occur." Accordingly, the arbitrator found that Spatorico had been appropriately discharged.

Noting that the unfair labor practice charges had been referred to arbitration under Dubo Mfg. Corp., 142 N.L.R.B. 431 (1963), the arbitrator . . . found "no evidence that the company discharged the grievant for his legitimate Union activities." The arbitrator [reiterated] that Spatorico had been discharged for participating in and failing to stop the sick out because Spatorico "is a Union officer but the contract's no strike clause *specifically* prohibits such activity by Union officers." (Emphasis added.)

[The ALJ rejected deference on these grounds: the arbitrator's failure to consider the unfair labor practice "in a serious way"; his lack of competence to decide that issue because he was limited to contract interpretation; and his failure to refer explicitly to the statutory right and waiver questions raised by the unfair labor practice charge.]

. . . On the merits, however, the judge agreed with the arbitrator's conclusion in that he found Spatorico's "participation in the strike was inconsistent with his manifest contractual obligation to attempt to stem the tide of unprotected activity." The judge concluded that article XIV . . . was sufficiently clear and unmistakable to waive, at the least, the sort of conduct in which Spatorico engaged, that, therefore, "Spatorico exposed himself to the greater liability permitted by the Supreme Court" in Metropolitan Edison Co. v. NLRB, 103 S. Ct. 1467 (1983), and that Respondent did not violate §§8(a)(3) and (1) . . . by discharging him while merely reprimanding other employees.

We agree with the judge that the complaint should be dismissed. We do so, however, without reaching the merits because we would defer to the arbitrator's award consistent with the standards set forth in Spielberg Mfg. Co. [112 N.L.R.B. 1080 (1955)]. . . . [I]n *Spielberg*, the Board held that it would defer to an arbitration award where the proceedings appear to have been fair and regular, all parties have agreed to be bound, and the decision of the arbitrator is not clearly repugnant to the purposes and policies of the Act. The Board in *Raytheon Co.*[3] further conditioned deferral on the arbitrator's having considered the unfair labor practice issue. Consistent application of the *Raytheon* requirement has proven elusive, and as illustrated by . . . *Propoco*,[4] its scope has expanded considerably.

. . . [T]he *Propoco* majority . . . [formulated] a standard of review that arbitration awards are appropriate for deferral only when the Board determines on de novo consideration that the award disposes of the issues just as

3. 140 N.L.R.B. 883 (1963).

4. Propoco, Inc., 263 N.L.R.B. 136 (1982), enforced with unpublished, nonprecedential opinion, Case No. 83-4058 (2d Cir. 1983). See also American Freight System, 264 N.L.R.B. 126 (1982).

the Board would have. This approach of determining the merits *before* considering the appropriateness of deferral was applied here by the judge, and he predictably reached a decision not to defer. The judge's decision here, like so many other past decisions of this sort, [frustrates] the declared purpose of *Spielberg* to recognize the arbitration process as an important aspect of the national labor policy. . . .

Accordingly, we adopt the following standard for deferral to arbitration awards. We would find that an arbitrator has adequately considered the unfair labor practice if (1) the contractual issue is factually parallel to the unfair labor practice issue, and (2) the arbitrator was presented generally with the facts relevant to resolving the unfair labor practice. In this respect, differences, if any, between the contractual and statutory standards of review should be weighed by the Board as part of its determination under the *Spielberg* standards of whether an award is "clearly repugnant" to the Act. And, with regard to the inquiry into the "clearly repugnant" standard, we would not require an arbitrator's award to be totally consistent with Board precedent. Unless the award is "palpably wrong,"[7] i.e., unless the arbitrator's decision is not susceptible to an interpretation consistent with the Act, we will defer.

Finally, . . . the party seeking to have the Board reject deferral and consider the merits of a given case [must] show that the above standards for deferral have not been met. Thus, the party seeking to have the Board ignore the determination of an arbitrator has the burden of affirmatively demonstrating the defects in the arbitral process or award.

. . . [I]f a respondent establishes that an arbitration concerning the matter before the Board has taken place, the burden of persuasion rests with the General Counsel to demonstrate . . . deficiencies in the arbitral process requiring the Board to ignore the determination of the arbitrator and subject the case to de novo review.

. . . [W]e find [here] that the arbitral proceeding has met the *Spielberg* standards for deferral, and that the arbitrator adequately considered the unfair labor practice issue. First, . . . the contractual and statutory issues were factually parallel. Indeed, the arbitrator noted that the factual questions [before him] were "1) whether . . . there was a sick out and 2) whether the grievant caused, participated in or failed to attempt to stop [it], i.e., whether the grievant failed to meet the obligation imposed upon him by Article XIV." These factual questions are coextensive with those that would be considered by the Board in a decision on the statutory question—i.e.,

7. International Harvester Co., 138 N.L.R.B. 923, 929 (1962), aff'd sub nom. Ramsey v. NLRB, 327 F.2d 784 (7th Cir. 1964), cert. denied, 377 U.S. 1003 (1964), quoted in former Member Penello's dissenting opinion in Douglas Aircraft Co., 234 N.L.R.B. 578, 581 (1978), enf. denied, 609 F.2d 352 (9th Cir. 1979).

whether the collective-bargaining agreement clearly and unmistakably proscribed the behavior engaged in by . . . Spatorico on 17 December 1980.

Second, . . . the arbitrator was presented generally with the facts relevant to resolving the unfair labor practice. . . . [T]he General Counsel has not shown that the arbitrator was lacking any evidence relevant to the determination . . . of the obligations imposed by the no-strike clause . . . and to the determination of the nexus between that clause and Spatorico's conduct. Thus the evidence before the arbitrator was essentially the same evidence necessary for determination of the merits of the unfair labor practice charge.

Finally, we turn to whether the arbitrator's award is clearly repugnant to the purposes and policies of the Act. . . . [T]he Supreme Court in *Metropolitan Edison Co.*, supra, recently addressed the merits of the substantive issue involved here. . . . [T]he Court found that the Union had not clearly and explicitly waived the §7 rights of its employee officials, and accordingly that the employer violated §§8(a)(3) and (1) . . . by disciplining the officials more severely than rank-and-file employees. The Court noted, however, that a "union and an employer reasonably could choose to secure the integrity of a no-strike clause by requiring union officials to take affirmative steps to end unlawful work stoppages," and that a union lawfully may bargain away the statutory protection accorded union officials in order to secure gains it considers more valuable to its members. A union's "decision to undertake such contractual obligations," the Court added, "promotes labor peace and clearly falls within the range of reasonableness accorded bargaining representatives."

Article XIV of the parties' contract here, in addition to a general no-strike/no-lockout obligation similar to the clause . . . in *Metropolitan Edison,* includes a proscription that "neither the Local Union nor the International Union, nor any officer or representative of either, will cause or permit its members to cause any strike, slowdown or stoppage (total or partial) of work or any interference, directly or indirectly, with the full operation of the plant." Certainly, were we reviewing the merits, Board members might differ as to the standards of specificity required for contractual language waiving statutory rights and as to whether the above language meets those standards at least as applied to employee Spatorico. The question of waiver, however, is also a question of contract interpretation. An arbitrator's interpretation of the contract is what the parties here have bargained for. . . . Particularly in view of the additional proscriptions in the no-strike clause quoted above, the arbitrator here had a reasonable basis for finding . . . that the clause "specifically prohibits" union officers from engaging in activity of the sort engaged in by Spatorico. We find that the arbitrator's contractual interpretation is not clearly repugnant to either the letter or the spirit of . . . *Metropolitan Edison.* . . .

Member ZIMMERMAN, dissenting in part. . . .

. . . Under the [majority's] new standard . . . an arbitrator need no longer actually consider and pass upon the unfair labor practice issue before the Board defers to his award. Instead, the Board will now presume that the unfair labor practice issue has been "adequately considered" by the arbitrator, and it will defer to an arbitration award if (1) the contractual issue is factually parallel to the unfair labor practice issue and (2) the arbitrator was presented generally with the facts relevant to resolving [that issue]. . . .

. . . First, and most importantly, the new standard expands the Board's deferral policy beyond permissible statutory bounds. For all the reasons stated by the Board in the long line of cases upon which I rely, . . . the use of a presumption here to justify deferral amounts to an abdication by this Board of its obligation under §10(a) . . . to protect employees' rights and the public interest by preventing and remedying unfair labor practices. Nowhere in the Act itself, its legislative history, or in its judicial interpretation is there authority for the proposition that the Federal labor policy favoring arbitration requires or permits the Board to abstain from effectuating the equally important Federal labor policy entrusted to the Board under §10(a).

Second, . . . the overwhelming weight of judicial precedent stands for the proposition that the Board *has no authority to defer* if it does not have some affirmative proof that an unfair labor practice issue was presented to and considered by an arbitrator. . . .

[Third,] the majority's new rule [involves] the inequity of requiring that "the party seeking to have the Board reject deferral . . . show that the above standards for deferral have not been met." . . . To invoke a presumption and shift the burden of disproving a naked defense claim to the General Counsel amounts to an abuse of the Board's discretion. In effect, once the existence of an arbitration award has been proved by a respondent, the majority will transform an affirmative defense into part of the General Counsel's prima facie case. . . .

A fourth major criticism . . . involves the relationship of this [new] standard to the expansion of prearbitral deferral policy announced . . . today in *United Technologies*, [supra page 724]. In that decision, my colleagues seek to temper the broadened "postponement of the use of the Board's processes" by noting that those processes "may always be invoked if the arbitral result is inconsistent with the standards of *Spielberg*." The majority's reversal of policy in this case, however, suggests that such postarbitral review will be of scant significance. . . .

## *NOTES AND QUESTIONS*

**1. "Palpably Wrong."** What does the *Olin* Board mean when it states that an arbitration award that otherwise meets the *Spielberg* standards should be given deference by the Board unless it is "clearly repugnant" to the Act by being "palpably wrong"? Should the Board assume, in the absence of clear evidence to the contrary, that the arbitrator reasonably applied to the case the same legal principles that the Board would have applied had it considered the matter de novo? For instance, does the Board in fact conclude that the arbitrator in *Olin* applied the same standard of "clear and unmistakable" waiver of the statutory right to strike that it would have applied under *Metropolitan Edison* and other cases? Or is the Board satisfied as long as the arbitrator did not stray too far from the Board's standard?

**2. Deference to Arbitrator Selection of Remedies?** Does *Olin* mean that the Board should defer to an arbitrator's selection of remedies as well as his or her factual findings and contract interpretations? For instance, assume that an arbitrator determines that an employee was discharged primarily because of her involvement in protected activities, but that the employee should be denied back pay because her related "insubordination" justified some punishment. Should the Board defer to the arbitrator's balance of remedies, even if it would have ordered back pay as well as reinstatement on the basis of the facts as found by the arbitrator? Cf. Darr v. NLRB, 801 F.2d 1404 (D.C. Cir. 1986) (questioning deference to arbitrator's compromise remedy), on remand sub nom. Cone Mills Corp., 298 N.L.R.B. 661 (1990).

**3. "Factually Parallel."** Consider the application of *Olin* to a typical §8(a)(3) charge that does not turn on the interpretation of any contract provision, but that does present issues that may be factually parallel to those that were presented in arbitration under the contract. How would the General Counsel go about proving that the issues before the arbitrator were not factually parallel to those that would be before the Board, or that the arbitrator was not presented generally with the facts relevant to resolving the unfair labor practice charge? Would it be enough to demonstrate that the arbitrator did not address the possibility of the employee being fired because of union activity? To show that the union did not argue any case of union-related discrimination to the arbitrator? Or would the General Counsel have to show that the facts relevant to proving union-related discrimination were not before the arbitrator? Should the burden of proof on these issues of parallelism be on the General Counsel, as *Olin* held, or on the party seeking deference?

**4. Implications of *Olin*?** Given *United Technologies* and *Olin*, (a) What steps should be taken in arbitration by the employer and arbitrator, with a view to avoiding relitigation before the NLRB concerning a discharge that might be attacked as prompted, in whole or in part, by the employee's protected activities? (b) What steps should be taken by the union either to secure arbitral consideration of the claim of a pretextual discharge or to preserve the opportunity to secure the NLRB's resolution of the claim? Do *United Technologies* and *Olin* cause most §8(a)(3) and §8(a)(1) cases during the term of collective agreements to be decided by arbitrators? If so, is this desirable?

**5. Independent §8(a)(5) Violation Despite No Contractual Restriction?** Consider post-arbitration consideration of a §8(a)(5) refusal-to-bargain case like *Collyer.* If an arbitrator rules that a collective agreement does not restrict an employer's unilateral change in work rules or its decision to subcontract some of the bargaining unit work, should the Board defer because the issue before it is factually parallel, or does the §8(a)(5) charge present a discrete legal issue? See, e.g., Kohler Mix Specialties, Inc., 332 N.L.R.B. 630, 631 (2000). What if the arbitrator, however, based on an express or an implied management-rights clause, interpreted the agreement to permit any management decisions not expressly prohibited by the agreement? See supra note 3, page 517.

**6. *Spielberg* Deference in §8(a)(4) Cases?** Should the Board defer to arbitration awards to resolve charges under §8(a)(4)? See Filmation Assocs., 227 N.L.R.B. 1721 (1977) (Board will not defer on §8(a)(4) charges or on other charges "closely intertwined" therewith); Equitable Gas Co. v. NLRB, 966 F.2d 861 (4th Cir. 1992) (approving *Filmation* rule).

**7. Deference to Joint Labor-Management Committees?** Should the Board be more hesitant to defer to awards rendered by joint labor-management grievance committees than by third-party arbitrators? Should it matter whether a bipartite committee issues a written opinion with its award? See Taylor v. NLRB, 786 F.2d 1516 (11th Cir. 1986) (generally rejecting *Olin,* and noting the "practical reality" that individual rights are often bargained away in bipartite proceedings). But cf. General Drivers, Warehousemen & Helpers Local Union No. 89 v. Riss & Co., Inc., 372 U.S. 517 (1962) (final and binding award of bipartite committee held enforceable by §301 court). See also Douglas Ray, Individual Rights and NLRB Deferral to the Arbitration Process: A Proposal, 28 B.C. L. Rev. 1, 15-16 (1986).

**8. Deference to Union-Management Settlements?** When, if ever, should the Board defer to pre-arbitration settlements between unions and employers? Can it do so based on standards analogous to those pronounced in *Olin,* that is, where the grievance proceedings were fair and regular, where all parties had agreed to be bound, where the outcome reached is not palpably wrong, and where the unfair labor practice issue was considered in the settlement process? See Alpha Beta Co., 273 N.L.R.B. 1546 (1985), enforced sub nom. Mahon v. NLRB, 808 F.2d 1342 (9th Cir. 1987) (adopting these standards); United States Postal Serv., 300 N.L.R.B. 196 (1990) (similar holding even though individual employee grievant did not consent to the settlement); Plumbers and Pipefitters Local 520 v. NLRB, 955 F.2d 744 (D.C. Cir. 1992) (approving application of these standards). But see Roadway Express, Inc. v. NLRB, 647 F.2d 415, 425 (4th Cir. 1981) ("the failure of [an employee] to agree to [a] settlement is a good basis for refusal to defer").

How can the "palpably wrong" standard be applied to settlements that do not reach legal conclusions? In *Alpha Beta*, supra, the Board stated that a settlement will not be judged "palpably wrong" if it is arrived at through a process in which both sides make concessions. Does evidence of compromise establish the suitability of deference? Furthermore, how can the Board determine whether statutory issues were considered, or even could have been considered, in reaching a settlement without the benefit of the record of an arbitration hearing? In its *Postal Serv.* decision, supra, the Board explained that it will be satisfied "when the contractual issue and the unfair labor practice issue are factually parallel, and the parties were generally aware of the facts relevant to resolving the unfair labor practice [claim]." Is there reason to believe that the Board can at least count on the parties in most cases to present the relevant statutory concerns? If the Board did not defer to settlements, would it discourage the settlement of grievances and thus impede the arbitration process?

**9. Court-Mandated Deference?** Does a court have any basis for *requiring* the Board to defer to an arbitral decision where the Board has declined to do so, or do *C & C Plywood* and *Acme* suggest that deference is a matter for the discretion of the Board? See NLRB v. Aces Mechanical Corp., 837 F.2d 570 (2d Cir. 1988) (denying enforcement of a §8(a)(3) order because the Board's refusal to defer to arbitration award upholding discipline was arbitrary in light of the Board's precedents).

**10. A New Standard.** On December 15, 2015, as this edition went to press, the Board (3-2) overruled the *Olin* standard in *Babcock & Wilcox Constr. Co.*, 361 N.L.R.B. No. 132 (2014). Although finding that deferral was appropriate in the case before it, the majority announced a new standard: The agency will defer to an arbitral award if the party who urges such deferral establishes that (1) the arbitrator was "explicitly authorized to decide the statutory issue, either in the collective-bargaining agreement or by agreement of the parties in the particular case"; (2) the arbitrator was presented with and considered the statutory issue, or was prevented from doing so by the party opposing deferral; and (3) Board law "reasonably permits the award." It did not, however, address the deferral standard in NLRA §8(a)(5) cases. How, if at all, might this new standard alter your responses to the questions posed above? Will the parties often expressly authorize arbitrators to decide unfair labor practice issues? If not, will the Board be engaging in post-award review in nearly every case brought by the party who lost in arbitration?

## 2. Arbitration and Claims Under Statutes Other than the NLRA

### 14 Penn Plaza LLC v. Pyett
*556 U.S. 247 (2009)*

Thomas, J. . . .

The question presented by this case is whether a provision in a collective-bargaining agreement that clearly and unmistakably requires union members to arbitrate claims arising under the Age Discrimination in Employment Act of 1967 (ADEA), is enforceable. The United States Court of Appeals for the Second Circuit held that this Court's decision in Alexander v. Gardner-Denver Co., 415 U.S. 36 (1974), forbids enforcement of such arbitration provisions. We disagree and reverse the judgment of the Court of Appeals.

#### I

Respondents are members of the Service Employees International Union, Local 32BJ (Union). Under the National Labor Relations Act (NLRA), the Union is the exclusive bargaining representative of employees within the building-services industry in New York City, which includes building cleaners, porters, and doorpersons. . . . Since the 1930's, the Union has engaged in industry-wide collective bargaining with the Realty Advisory Board on Labor Relations, Inc. (RAB), a multiemployer bargaining association for the New York City real-estate industry. The agreement between the Union and the RAB is embodied in their Collective Bargaining Agreement for Contractors and Building Owners (CBA). The CBA requires union members to submit all claims of employment discrimination to binding arbitration under the CBA's grievance and dispute resolution procedures:

> "§30 NO DISCRIMINATION. There shall be no discrimination against any present or future employee by reason of race, creed, color, age, disability, national origin, sex, union membership, or any other characteristic protected

> by law, including, but not limited to, claims made pursuant to Title VII of the Civil Rights Act, the Americans with Disabilities Act, the Age Discrimination in Employment Act, the New York State Human Rights Law, the New York City Human Rights Code, . . . or any other similar laws, rules, or regulations. All such claims shall be subject to the grievance and arbitration procedures (Articles V and VI) as the sole and exclusive remedy for violations. Arbitrators shall apply appropriate law in rendering decisions based upon claims of discrimination."

Petitioner 14 Penn Plaza LLC is a member of the RAB. It owns and operates the New York City office building where, prior to August 2003, respondents worked as night lobby watchmen and in other similar capacities. Respondents were directly employed by petitioner Temco Service Industries, Inc. (Temco), a maintenance service and cleaning contractor. In August 2003, with the Union's consent, 14 Penn Plaza engaged Spartan Security, a unionized security services contractor and affiliate of Temco, to provide licensed security guards to staff the lobby and entrances of its building. Because this rendered respondents' lobby services unnecessary, Temco reassigned them to jobs as night porters and light duty cleaners in other locations in the building. Respondents contend that these reassignments led to a loss in income, caused them emotional distress, and were otherwise less desirable than their former positions.

At respondents' request, the Union filed grievances challenging the reassignments. The grievances alleged that petitioners: (1) violated the CBA's ban on workplace discrimination by reassigning respondents on account of their age; (2) violated seniority rules by failing to promote one of the respondents to a handyman position; and (3) failed to equitably rotate overtime. After failing to obtain relief on any of these claims through the grievance process, the Union requested arbitration under the CBA.

After the initial arbitration hearing, the Union withdrew the first set of respondents' grievances—the age-discrimination claims—from arbitration. Because it had consented to the contract for new security personnel at 14 Penn Plaza, the Union believed that it could not legitimately object to respondents' reassignments as discriminatory. But the Union continued to arbitrate the seniority and overtime claims, and, after several hearings, the claims were denied.

In May 2004, while the arbitration was ongoing but after the Union withdrew the age-discrimination claims, respondents filed a complaint with the Equal Employment Opportunity Commission (EEOC) alleging that petitioners had violated their rights under the ADEA. Approximately one month later, the EEOC issued a Dismissal and Notice of Rights, which explained that the agency's "'review of the evidence . . . fail[ed] to indicate that a violation ha[d] occurred,'" and notified each respondent of his right to sue.

Respondents thereafter filed suit against petitioners in the United States District Court for the Southern District of New York, alleging that their reassignment violated the ADEA and state and local laws prohibiting age discrimination. Petitioners filed a motion to compel arbitration of respondents' claims pursuant to §3 and §4 of the Federal Arbitration Act (FAA), 9 U.S.C. §§3, 4. The District Court denied the motion because under Second Circuit precedent, "even a clear and unmistakable union-negotiated waiver of a right to litigate certain federal and state statutory claims in a judicial forum is unenforceable." Respondents immediately appealed the ruling under §16 of the FAA, which authorizes an interlocutory appeal of "an order . . . refusing a stay of any action under section 3 of this title" or "denying a petition under section 4 of this title to order arbitration to proceed." 9 U.S.C. §§16(a)(1)(A)-(B).

The Court of Appeals affirmed. According to the Court of Appeals, it could not compel arbitration of the dispute because *Gardner-Denver,* which "remains good law," held "that a collective bargaining agreement could not waive covered workers' rights to a judicial forum for causes of action created by Congress." The Court of Appeals observed that the *Gardner-Denver* decision was in tension with this Court's more recent decision in Gilmer v. Interstate/Johnson Lane Corp., 500 U.S. 20 (1991), which "held that an individual employee who had agreed individually to waive his right to a federal forum *could* be compelled to arbitrate a federal age discrimination claim." . . .

## II

. . . [T]he Union and the RAB, negotiating on behalf of 14 Penn Plaza, collectively bargained in good faith and agreed that employment-related discrimination claims, including claims brought under the ADEA, would be resolved in arbitration. This freely negotiated term between the Union and the RAB easily qualifies as a "conditio[n] of employment" that is subject to mandatory bargaining under §159(a). . . . The decision to fashion a CBA to require arbitration of employment-discrimination claims is no different from the many other decisions made by parties in designing grievance machinery.

* * *

The *Gilmer* Court's interpretation of the ADEA fully applies in the collective-bargaining context. Nothing in the law suggests a distinction between the status of arbitration agreements signed by an individual employee and those agreed to by a union representative. This Court has required only that an agreement to arbitrate statutory antidiscrimination claims be "explicitly stated" in the collective-bargaining agreement. *Wright* [v. Universal Maritime Serv. Corp,], 525 U.S., [70,] 80 [(1998)]. The

CBA under review here meets that obligation. Respondents incorrectly counter that an individual employee must personally "waive" a "[substantive] right" to proceed in court for a waiver to be "knowing and voluntary" under the ADEA. As explained below, however, the agreement to arbitrate ADEA claims is not the waiver of a "substantive right" as that term is employed in the ADEA. Indeed, if the "right" referred to in §626(f)(1) included the prospective waiver of the right to bring an ADEA claim in court, even a waiver signed by an individual employee would be invalid as the statute also prevents individuals from "waiv[ing] rights or claims that may arise after the date the waiver is executed." §626(f)(1)(C).

Examination of the two federal statutes at issue in this case, therefore, yields a straightforward answer to the question presented: The NLRA provided the Union and the RAB with statutory authority to collectively bargain for arbitration of workplace discrimination claims, and Congress did not terminate that authority with respect to federal age-discrimination claims in the ADEA. . . . The CBA's arbitration provision is also fully enforceable under the *Gardner-Denver* line of cases. . . .

The [*Gardner-Denver*] Court . . . explained that the employee had not waived his right to pursue his Title VII [race discrimination] claim in federal court by participating in an arbitration that was premised on the same underlying facts as the Title VII claim. Thus, whether the legal theory of preclusion advanced by the employer rested on "the doctrines of election of remedies" or was recast "as resting instead on the doctrine of equitable estoppel and on themes of res judicata and collateral estoppel," it could not prevail in light of the collective-bargaining agreement's failure to address arbitration of Title VII claims. See [415 U.S. at] at 46, n. 6 ("[W]e hold that the federal policy favoring arbitration does not establish that an arbitrator's resolution of a *contractual* claim is dispositive of a statutory claim under Title VII" (emphasis added)).

. . . In Barrentine v. Arkansas-Best Freight System, Inc., 450 U.S. 728 (1981), the Court considered "whether an employee may bring an action in federal district court, alleging a violation of the minimum wage provisions of the Fair Labor Standards Act, . . . after having unsuccessfully submitted a wage claim based on the same underlying facts to a joint grievance committee pursuant to the provisions of his union's collective-bargaining agreement." The Court held that the unsuccessful arbitration did not preclude the federal lawsuit. Like the collective-bargaining agreement in *Gardner-Denver*, the arbitration provision under review in *Barrentine* did not expressly reference the statutory claim at issue. . . .

McDonald v. West Branch, 466 U.S. 284 (1984), was decided along similar lines. The question presented in that case was "whether a federal court may accord preclusive effect to an unappealed arbitration award in a case brought under 42 U.S.C. §1983." The Court declined to fashion such a rule, again explaining that "because an arbitrator's authority derives solely from the contract, an arbitrator may not have authority to enforce §1983" when that provision is left unaddressed by the arbitration agreement. . . .

The facts underlying *Gardner-Denver*, *Barrentine*, and *McDonald* reveal the narrow scope of the legal rule arising from that trilogy of decisions. Summarizing those opinions in *Gilmer*, this Court made clear that the *Gardner-Denver* line of cases "did not involve the issue of the enforceability of an agreement to arbitrate statutory claims." Those decisions instead "involved the quite different issue whether arbitration of contract-based claims precluded subsequent judicial resolution of statutory claims. Since the employees there had not agreed to arbitrate their statutory claims, and the labor arbitrators were not authorized to resolve such claims, the arbitration in those cases understandably was held not to preclude subsequent statutory actions." *Gardner-Denver* and its progeny thus do not control the outcome where, as is the case here, the collective-bargaining agreement's arbitration provision expressly covers both statutory and contractual discrimination claims.

We recognize that apart from their narrow holdings, the *Gardner-Denver* line of cases included broad dicta that was highly critical of the use of arbitration for the vindication of statutory antidiscrimination rights. That skepticism, however, rested on a misconceived view of arbitration that this Court has since abandoned.

First, the Court in *Gardner-Denver* erroneously assumed that an agreement to submit statutory discrimination claims to arbitration was tantamount to a waiver of those rights. . . .

The Court was correct in concluding that federal antidiscrimination rights may not be prospectively waived, but it confused an agreement to arbitrate those statutory claims with a prospective waiver of the substantive right. The decision to resolve ADEA claims by way of arbitration instead of litigation does not waive the statutory right to be free from workplace age discrimination; it waives only the right to seek relief from a court in the first instance. . . .

Second, *Gardner-Denver* mistakenly suggested that certain features of arbitration made it a forum "well suited to the resolution of contractual disputes," but "a comparatively inappropriate forum for the final resolution of rights created by Title VII." According to the Court, the "factfinding process in arbitration" is "not equivalent to judicial factfinding" and the "informality of arbitral procedure . . . makes arbitration a less appropriate forum for final resolution of Title VII issues than the federal courts." The Court also questioned the competence of arbitrators to decide federal statutory claims. . . .

These misconceptions have been corrected. For example, the Court has "recognized that arbitral tribunals are readily capable of handling the factual and legal complexities of antitrust claims, notwithstanding the absence of judicial instruction and supervision" and that "there is no reason to assume at the outset that arbitrators will not follow the law." . . . An arbitrator's capacity to resolve complex questions of fact and law extends with equal force to discrimination claims brought under the ADEA. Moreover, the recognition that arbitration procedures are more streamlined than federal litigation is not a basis for finding the forum somehow inadequate; the relative informality of arbitration is one of the chief reasons that parties select arbitration. . . .

Third, the Court in *Gardner-Denver* raised in a footnote a "further concern" regarding "the union's exclusive control over the manner and extent to which an individual grievance is presented." 415 U.S., at 58, n. 19. The Court suggested that in arbitration, as in the collective-bargaining process, a union may subordinate the interests of an individual employee to the collective interests of all employees in the bargaining unit. . . .

We cannot rely on this judicial policy concern as a source of authority for introducing a qualification into the ADEA that is not found in its text. . . .

The conflict-of-interest argument also proves too much. Labor unions certainly balance the economic interests of some employees against the needs of the larger work force as they negotiate collective-bargain agreements and implement them on a daily basis. But this attribute of organized labor does not justify singling out an arbitration provision for disfavored treatment. This "principle of majority rule" to which respondents object is in fact the central premise of the NLRA. [citations omitted] It was Congress' verdict that the benefits of organized labor outweigh the sacrifice of individual liberty that this system necessarily demands. Respondents' argument that they were deprived of the right to pursue their ADEA claims in federal court by a labor union with a conflict of interest is therefore unsustainable; it amounts to a collateral attack on the NLRA.

In any event, Congress has accounted for this conflict of interest in several ways. As indicated above, the NLRA has been interpreted to impose a "duty of fair representation" on labor unions, which a union breaches "when its conduct toward a member of the bargaining unit is arbitrary, discriminatory, or in bad faith." Marquez v. Screen Actors, 525 U.S. 33, 44 (1998). . . . Respondents in fact brought a fair representation suit against the Union based on its withdrawal of support for their age-discrimination claims. Given this avenue that Congress has made available to redress a union's violation of its duty to its members, it is particularly inappropriate to ask this Court to impose an artificial limitation on the collective-bargaining process.

In addition, a union is subject to liability under the ADEA if the union itself discriminates against its members on the basis of age. See 29 U.S.C. §623(d). . . . Union members may also file age-discrimination claims with the EEOC and the National Labor Relations Board, which may then seek judicial intervention under this Court's precedent. See EEOC v. Waffle House, Inc., 534 U.S. 279, 295-296, 122 S. Ct. 754, 151 L. Ed. 2d 755

(2002). In sum, Congress has provided remedies for the situation where a labor union is less than vigorous in defense of its members' claims of discrimination under the ADEA.

### III

. . . Respondents also argue that the CBA operates as a substantive waiver of their ADEA rights because it not only precludes a federal lawsuit, but also allows the Union to block arbitration of these claims. Petitioners contest this characterization of the CBA, and offer record evidence suggesting that the Union has allowed respondents to continue with the arbitration even though the Union has declined to participate. But not only does this question require resolution of contested factual allegations, it was not fully briefed to this or any court and is not fairly encompassed within the question presented, see this Court's Rule 14.1(a). Thus, although a substantive waiver of federally protected civil rights will not be upheld, we are not positioned to resolve in the first instance whether the CBA allows the Union to prevent respondents from "effectively vindicating" their "federal statutory rights in the arbitral forum," Green Tree Financial Corp.-Ala. v. Randolph, 531 U.S. 79, 90 (2000). Resolution of this question at this juncture would be particularly inappropriate in light of our hesitation to invalidate arbitration agreements on the basis of speculation. See id., at 91.

### IV

We hold that a collective-bargaining agreement that clearly and unmistakably requires union members to arbitrate ADEA claims is enforceable as a matter of federal law. The judgment of the Court of Appeals is reversed, and the case is remanded for further proceedings consistent with this opinion.

[The dissenting opinion of Justice Stevens is omitted.]

[The dissenting opinion of Justice Souter, joined by Justices Stevens, Ginsburg, and Breyer, is omitted.]

## *NOTES AND QUESTIONS*

**1. Union Response to *Penn Plaza*.** Should unions negotiate clauses assigning statutory claims to arbitration under collective agreements? Might doing so expose unions to duty of fair representation (DFR) claims by any employee who is not satisfied with the handling of a statutory-based grievance? See infra pages 960-975. How might unions protect themselves from such claims? Is the union subject to a DFR claim even if it allows the employee to pursue his grievance, including statutory grounds, to arbitration? What if the union also declines to provide representation or pay its share of the costs of the arbitration? What if, on the other hand, the union does not agree to allow the case to go to arbitration? Does the *Penn Plaza* decision suggest that an employee who could not present a statutory claim to an impartial arbitrator would not sacrifice the opportunity to litigate in court, or is the employee bound by the labor agreement and remitted only to his remedies against the union?

In New York City, Local 32 B-J of the SEIU and the Realty Advisory Board have negotiated a "*Pyett* Protocol" making available an arbitration forum (at the parties' cost) for cases where the union's represented members are under an FAA-based obligation to arbitrate their statutory claim but the union declines to proceed to arbitration. See Terry Meginniss & Paul Salvatore, Response to an Unresolved Issue from Pyett: The NYC Real Estate Industry Protocol, ch. 11 in The Challenge for Collective Bargaining: Proc. of the N.Y.U. 65th Ann. Conf. on Labor (Michael Z. Green ed. 2013).

**2. Might Unions and Represented Employees Benefit from *Penn Plaza*?** Does *Penn Plaza* offer unions a bargaining chip in negotiations with employers who benefit from having employment disputes resolved more efficiently through arbitration rather than in court? Would a ruling that prevented unions from assigning statutory claims to arbitration have instead increased the costs of collective bargaining and the incentives to avoid unions, since the Court in *Gilmer* had allowed nonunion employers to require individual employees to agree to send statutory claims to binding arbitration? See Estreicher, Win-Win Labor Law Reform, 10 Lab. Law. 667, 675-676 (1994). Indeed, would a ruling that prevented unions from assigning statutory claims to arbitration have meant that unionized employers could have bound individual applicants for employment to compulsory arbitration agreements without bargaining with the union that represents the unit employees? In Air Line Pilots Ass'n, Int'l v. Northwest Airlines, Inc., 199 F.3d 477 (D.C. Cir. 1999), adopted by the court en banc, 211 F.3d 1312 (D.C. Cir. 2000), a Railway Labor Act case decided before *Penn Plaza*, the court ruled that a unionized employer was free of bargaining obligations on the arbitration of statutory claims.

**3. Relevance for Board Deference and Deferral to Arbitration?** Does *Penn Plaza* support or suggest modifications in the Board's deference and deferral doctrines? Is it relevant that the Board's doctrines in some cases seem to accept union waiver of employee substantive rights under the NLRA, see note 2 supra page 728, while the *Penn Plaza* Court only accepts union waiver of the procedural right to press a substantive claim in court? Is it also relevant that Board processes, unlike the private judicial rights of action deemed waivable in *Penn Plaza*, are public administrative processes akin to the EEOC's public rights of action, which the Court has held not to be subject to waiver. See EEOC v. Waffle House, Inc., 534 U.S. 279 (2002). For a fuller exploration of these questions, see Harper, A New Board Policy on Deferral to Arbitration, supra and Estreicher, Labor Law Reform, supra.

**4. Scope of Judicial Review of Arbitration Awards on Statutory Claims.** Presumably, the Court's holding in Hines v. Anchor Motor Freight, Inc., 424 U.S. 554 (1976), see infra page 970, offers an employee the opportunity to relitigate a statutory, as well as a contractual, claim where the employee can establish the union's breach of its duty of fair representation in conducting the arbitration of the claim. On what grounds might a party to the arbitration of a statutory, rather than a contractual, claim obtain judicial *review* of the arbitrator's award? The Federal Arbitration Act (FAA), which was applied in *Gilmer* and which Penn Plaza invoked to impel Pyett to arbitrate under the collective agreement, provides for judicial vacation of an award only on the limited grounds of (1) being "procured by corruption, fraud, or undue means"; (2) "evident partiality or corruption in the arbitrators[s]"; (3) the arbitrator(s) being "guilty of misconduct in refusing to postpone the hearing, upon sufficient cause shown, or in refusing to hear evidence pertinent and material to the controversy; or of any other misbehavior by which the rights of any party have been prejudiced"; or (4) the arbitrator(s) having "exceeded their powers, or so imperfectly executed them that a mutual, final, and definite award upon the subject matter submitted was not made." See 9 U.S.C. §10. The Supreme Court also has stated, without elaboration, that arbitration awards issued under the authority of the FAA can be vacated for being in "manifest disregard" of the law. First Options of Chicago Inc. v. Kaplan, 514 U.S. 938, 942 (1995) (citing Wilko v. Swan, 346 U.S. 427, 436-437 (1953)). But cf. Stolt-Nielson S.A. v. AnimalFeeds Int'l Corp., 559 U.S. 662, 672 n.3 (2010) (declining to decide whether "manifest disregard" standard "survives" either "as an independent ground for review or as a judicial gloss on the enumerated grounds for vacatur" set forth in the FAA). Does the rationale of *Penn Plaza* require that courts be allowed to review awards to ensure that substantive legal rights have not been sacrificed in the arbitral forum? If so, does this also require at least some limited review of factual findings? See generally Estreicher, Judicial Review of Arbitration Awards Resolving Statutory Claims, Chapter 28 in Alternative Dispute Resolution in the Employment Arena, in Proc. N.Y.U. 53d Ann. Conf. on Labor 789-814 (S. Estreicher & D. Sherwyn, eds., 2004).

Might the parties to a collective bargaining agreement expand the grounds for judicial review of arbitration awards on statutory claims? In Hall Street Assocs. v. Mattel, Inc., 552 U.S. 576 (2008), the Court held that the grounds for the expedited judicial review available under the FAA cannot be expanded by agreement of the parties. The Court left open whether an agreement providing for enhanced review could be enforced under other law, such as state statutory or common law. Might the Court fashion federal common law pursuant to §301 of the LMRA to allow parties to expand the grounds for judicial review of awards based on arbitration founded in collective bargaining agreements?

**5. Conditioning Employment on Waiver of Class Actions on Statutory Claims?** Does an employer violate NLRA 8(a)(1) by requiring employees to sign an arbitration agreement that precludes the filing of class actions or collective claims in in any forum? In 2012, a divided Board concluded that such an agreement was an unlawful interference with employees' Section 7 rights. D.R. Horton, Inc., 357 N.L.R.B. No. 184 (2012), enforcement denied 737 F.3d 344 (5th Cir. 2014). In the majority's view, the collective action waiver wrested from employees an unlawful waiver of their right under §7 to pursue litigation or arbitration on a group basis concerning legal claims that affect terms and conditions of employment. The *D.R. Horton* Board reasoned that its decision fell within an FAA exception because the collective action waiver required employees to forgo their substantive NLRA rights to protected concerted activity. The Fifth Circuit disagreed, ruling that the class action provision waived a procedural right, not a substantive right. D.R. Horton, Inc. v. NLRB, 737 F.3d 344 (5th Cir. 2013). Murphy Oil USA, 361 N.L.R.B. No. 72 (2014) (reaffirming its 2012 *D.R. Horton, Inc.* decision).

Although the Board has consistently held that employees cannot be discharged or disciplined for filing lawsuits or participating in arbitrations on a group basis, *D.R. Horton* is the first instance where the agency has asserted authority under Section 7 to regulate rules established by the employer with its non-union employees governing the forum and procedures for litigation and arbitration. Would there still be a *D.R. Horton* concern if the collective action waiver provided employees a period of time to opt out of a non-collective dispute resolution program? The Board is likely to confront this issue soon. Compare 24 Hour Fitness USA, Inc., No. 20-CA-35419 (Nov. 6, 2012) (ALJ decision that an employer's collective action waiver interfered with employee rights, despite the company's inclusion of a provision giving employees a 30-day period to opt out of the dispute resolution program), with Bloomingdale's Inc., No. 31-CA-71281 (June 25, 2013) (ALJ ruling that a retailer's class action waiver did not interfere with employee rights because agreement's opt-out process made the collective action waiver voluntary).

# 9 Problems of Business Transformation

## A. SUCCESSORSHIP

### 1. Obligations Under the NLRA

**NLRB v. Burns International Security Services, Inc.**
*406 U.S. 272 (1972)*

White, J. . . .

The issues . . . are whether Burns refused to bargain with a union representing a majority of employees in an appropriate unit and whether the [NLRB] could order Burns to observe the terms of a collective bargaining contract signed by the union and Wackenhut that Burns had not voluntarily assumed. Resolution turns to a great extent on the precise facts involved here.

I

The Wackenhut Corp. provided protection services at the Lockheed plant for five years before Burns took over this task. On February 28, 1967, a few months before the changeover of guard employers, a majority of the Wackenhut guards selected the union as their exclusive bargaining representative in a Board election after Wackenhut and the union had agreed that the Lockheed plant was the appropriate bargaining unit. On March 8, the Regional Director certified the union as the exclusive bargaining representative for these employees and, on April 29, Wackenhut and the union entered into a three-year collective bargaining contract.

Meanwhile, since Wackenhut's one-year service agreement to provide security protection was due to expire on June 30, Lockheed had called for bids from various companies supplying these services, and both Burns and Wackenhut submitted estimates. At a prebid conference attended by Burns on May 15, a representative of Lockheed informed the bidders that Wackenhut's guards were represented by the union, that the union had recently won a Board election and been certified, and that there was in existence a collective bargaining contract between Wackenhut and the [United Plant Guard Workers (UPG)]. . . . Lockheed then accepted Burns' bid, and on May 31 Wackenhut was notified that Burns would assume responsibility for protection services on July 1. Burns chose to retain 27 of the Wackenhut guards, and it brought in 15 of its own guards from other Burns locations.

During June, when Burns hired the 27 Wackenhut guards, it supplied them with membership cards of the American Federation of Guards (AFG), another union with which Burns had collective bargaining contracts at other locations, and informed them that they had to become AFG members to work for Burns, that they would not receive uniforms otherwise, and that Burns "could not live with" the existing contract between Wackenhut and the union. On June 29, Burns recognized the AFG on the theory that it had obtained a card majority. On July 12, however, the UPG demanded that Burns recognize it as the bargaining representative of Burns' employees at Lockheed and that Burns honor the collective bargaining agreement between it and Wackenhut. When Burns refused, the UPG filed unfair labor practice charges, and Burns responded by challenging the appropriateness of the unit and by denying its obligation to bargain.

The Board . . . found the Lockheed plant an appropriate unit and held that Burns had violated §§8(a)(2) and 8(a)(1) . . . by unlawfully recognizing and assisting the AFG . . . ; and that it had violated §§8(a)(5) and 8(a)(1) by failing to recognize and bargain with the UPG and by refusing to honor the collective bargaining agreement that had been negotiated between Wackenhut and UPG.

Burns did not challenge the §8(a)(2) unlawful assistance finding . . . but sought review of the unit determination and the order to bargain and observe the preexisting collective bargaining contract. The Court of Appeals accepted the Board's unit determination and enforced the Board's order insofar as it related to the finding of unlawful assistance of a rival union and the refusal to bargain, but it held that the Board had exceeded its powers in ordering Burns to honor the contract executed by Wackenhut.

## II

We address first Burns' alleged duty to bargain with the union. . . .

The trial examiner first found that the unit designated by the regional director was an appropriate unit for bargaining. . . .

The trial examiner then found, inter alia, that Burns "had in its employ a majority of Wackenhut's former employees," and that these employees had already expressed their choice of a bargaining representative in an election held a short time before. Burns was therefore held to have a duty to bargain. . . .

The Board, without revision, accepted the trial examiner's findings and conclusions with respect to the duty to bargain, and we see no basis for setting them aside. In an election held but a few months before, the union had been designated bargaining agent for the employees in the unit and a majority of these employees had been hired by Burns for work in the identical unit. It is undisputed that Burns knew all the relevant facts in this regard and was aware of the certification and of the existence of a collective bargaining contract. In these circumstances, it was not unreasonable for the Board to conclude that the union certified to represent all employees in the unit still represented a majority of the employees and that Burns could not reasonably have entertained a good-faith doubt about that fact. Burns' obligation to bargain with the union over terms and conditions of employment stemmed from its hiring of Wackenhut's employees and from the recent election and Board certification. It has been consistently held that a mere change of employers or of ownership in the employing industry is not such an "unusual circumstance" as to affect the force of the Board's certification within the normal operative period if a majority of employees after the change of ownership or management were employed by the preceding employer. . . .

. . . It would be a wholly different case if the Board had determined that because Burns' operational structure and practices differed from those of Wackenhut, the Lockheed bargaining unit was no longer an appropriate one. Likewise, it would be different if Burns had not hired employees already represented by a union certified as a bargaining agent,[3] and the Board recognized as much at oral argument. But where the bargaining unit remains unchanged and a majority of the employees hired by the new employer are represented by a recently certified bargaining agent there is little basis for faulting the Board's implementation of the express mandates of §8(a)(5) and §9(a) by ordering the employer to bargain with the incumbent union. . . .

### III

It does not follow, however, from Burns' duty to bargain that it was bound to observe the substantive terms of the collective bargaining contract

---

3. The Board has never held that the [NLRA] itself requires that an employer who submits the winning bid for a service contract or who purchases the assets of a business be obligated to hire all of the employees of the predecessor though it is possible that such an obligation might be assumed by the employer. But cf. Chemrock Corp., 151 N.L.R.B. 1074 (1965). However, an employer who declines to hire employees solely because they are members of a union commits a §8(a)(3) unfair labor practice. . . .

the union had negotiated with Wackenhut and to which Burns had in no way agreed. . . .

Section 8(d) . . . was enacted in 1947 because Congress feared that "the present Board has gone very far, in the guise of determining whether or not employers had bargained in good faith, in setting itself up as the judge of what concessions an employer must make and of the proposals and counter-proposals that he may or may not make. . . . [U]nless Congress writes into the law guides for the Board to follow, the Board may attempt to . . . control more and more the terms of collective bargaining agreements." H.R. Rep. No. 245, 80th Cong., 1st Sess., 19-20 (1947).

This history was reviewed in detail and given controlling effect in H.K. Porter Co. v. NLRB, 397 U.S. 99 (1970). There this Court, while agreeing that the employer violated §8(a)(5) by adamantly refusing to agree to a dues checkoff, intending thereby to frustrate the consummation of any bargaining agreement, held that the Board had erred in ordering the employer to agree to such a provision. . . .

These considerations . . . underlay the Board's prior decisions, which until now have consistently held that, although successor employers may be bound to recognize and bargain with the union, they are not bound by the substantive provisions of a . . . contract negotiated by their predecessors but not agreed to or assumed by them. . . .

The Board, however, has now departed from this view and argues that the same policies that mandate a continuity of bargaining obligation also require that successor employers be bound to the terms of a predecessor's collective bargaining contract. It asserts that the stability of labor relations will be jeopardized and that employees will face uncertainty and a gap in the bargained-for terms and conditions of employment, as well as the possible loss of advantages gained by prior negotiations, unless the new employer is held to have assumed, as a matter of federal labor law, the obligations under the contract entered into by the former employer. . . . [T]he Board notes that in John Wiley & Sons, Inc. v. Livingston, 376 U.S. 543, 550 (1964), the Court declared that "a collective bargaining agreement is not an ordinary contract" but is, rather, an outline of the common law of a particular plant or industry. . . . The Board contends that the same factors that the Court emphasized in *Wiley*, the peaceful settlement of industrial conflicts and "protection [of] the employees [against] a sudden change in the employment relationship," id., at 549, require that Burns be treated under the collective bargaining contract exactly as Wackenhut would have been if it had continued protecting the Lockheed plant.

We do not find *Wiley* controlling . . . here. *Wiley* arose in the context of a §301 suit to compel arbitration, not in the context of an unfair labor practice proceeding where the Board is expressly limited by the provisions of §8(d). That decision emphasized "[t]he preference of national labor policy for arbitration as a substitute for tests of strength before contending forces" and held only that the agreement to arbitrate, "construed in the context of a national labor policy," survived the merger and left to the arbitrator, subject to judicial review, the ultimate question of the extent to which, if any, the surviving company was bound by other provisions of the contract. Id., at 549, 551.

*Wiley*'s limited accommodation between the legislative endorsement of freedom of contract and the judicial preference for peaceful arbitral settlement of labor disputes does not warrant the Board's holding that the employer commits an unfair labor practice unless he honors the substantive terms of the preexisting contract. The present case does not involve a §301 suit, nor does it involve the duty to arbitrate. Rather, the claim is that Burns must be held bound by the contract executed by Wackenhut, whether Burns has agreed to it or not and even though Burns made it perfectly clear that it had no intention of assuming that contract. *Wiley* suggests no such open-ended obligation. Its narrower holding dealt with a merger occurring against a background of state law that embodied the general rule that in merger situations the surviving corporation is liable for the obligations of the disappearing corporation. See N.Y. Stock Corp. Law §90 (1951); 15 W. Fletcher, Private Corporations §7121 (1961 rev. ed.). Here there was no merger or sale of assets, and there were no dealings whatsoever between Wackenhut and Burns. On the contrary, they were competitors for the same work, each bidding for the service contract at Lockheed. Burns purchased nothing from Wackenhut and became liable for none of its financial obligations. Burns merely hired enough of Wackenhut's employees to require it to bargain with the union as commanded by §8(a)(5) and §9(a). But this consideration is a wholly insufficient basis for implying either in fact or in law that Burns had agreed or must be held to have agreed to honor Wackenhut's collective bargaining contract.

. . . [T]he Board failed to heed the admonitions of the *H.K. Porter* case. Preventing industrial strife is an important aim of federal labor legislation, but Congress has not chosen to make the bargaining freedom of employers and unions totally subordinate to this goal. . . . This bargaining freedom means both that parties need not make any concessions as a result of Government compulsion and that they are free from having contract provisions imposed upon them against their will. . . .

. . . [H]olding either the union or the new employer bound to the substantive terms of an old collective bargaining contract may result in serious inequities. A potential employer may be willing to take over a moribund business only if he can make changes in corporate structure, composition of the labor force, work location, task assignment, and nature of supervision. Saddling such an employer with the terms and conditions of employment contained in the old collective bargaining contract may make these changes impossible and may discourage and inhibit the transfer of capital. On the other hand, a union may have made concessions to a small or failing employer that it would be unwilling to make to a large or economically successful firm. The congressional policy manifest in the Act is to enable the parties to negotiate for any protection either deems appropriate, but to allow the balance of bargaining advantage to be set by economic power realities. Strife is bound to occur if the concessions that must be honored do not correspond to the relative economic strength of the parties.

The Board's position would also raise new problems, for the successor employer would be circumscribed in exactly the same way as the predecessor under the collective bargaining contract. It would seemingly follow that employees of the predecessor would be deemed employees of the successor, dischargeable only in accordance with provisions of the contract and subject to the grievance and arbitration provisions thereof. Burns would not have been free to replace Wackenhut's guards with its own except as the contract permitted. Given the continuity of employment relationship, the preexisting contract's provisions with respect to wages, seniority rights, vacation privileges, pension and retirement fund benefits, job security provisions, work assignments and the like would devolve on the successor. Nor would the union commit a §8(b)(3) unfair labor practice if it refused to bargain for a modification of the agreement effective prior to the expiration date of the agreement. A successor employer might also be deemed to have inherited its predecessor's preexisting contractual obligations to the union that had accrued under past contracts and that had not been discharged when the business was transferred. . . . Finally, a successor will be bound to observe the contract despite good-faith doubts about the union's majority during the time that the contract is a bar to another representation election, Ranch-Way, Inc., 183 N.L.R.B. No. 116 (1970). . . .

In many cases, of course, successor employers will find it advantageous not only to recognize and bargain with the union but also to observe the preexisting contract rather than to face uncertainty and turmoil. Also, in a variety of circumstances involving a merger, stock acquisition, reorganization, or assets purchase, the Board might properly find as a matter of fact that the successor had assumed the obligations under the old contract. Cf. Oilfield Maintenance Co., 142 N.L.R.B. 1384 (1963). Such a duty does not, however, ensue as a matter of law from the mere fact that an employer is doing the same work in the same place with the same employees as his predecessor. . . . We accordingly set aside the Board's finding of a §8(a)(5) unfair labor practice insofar as it rested on a conclusion that Burns was required to but did not honor the collective bargaining contract executed by Wackenhut.

## IV

It therefore follows that the Board's order requiring Burns to "give retroactive effect to all the clauses of said [Wackenhut] contract and, with interest of 6 percent, make whole its employees for any losses suffered by reason of Respondent's [Burns's] refusal to honor, adopt and enforce said contract" must be set aside.

Although Burns had an obligation to bargain with the union concerning wages and other conditions of employment when the union requested it to do so, this case is not like a §8(a)(5) violation where an employer unilaterally changes a condition of employment without consulting a bargaining representative. It is difficult to understand how Burns could be said to have *changed* unilaterally any preexisting term or condition of employment without bargaining when it had no previous relationship whatsoever to the bargaining unit and, prior to July 1, no outstanding terms and conditions of employment from which a change could be inferred. . . .

Although a successor employer is ordinarily free to set initial terms on which it will hire the employees of a predecessor, there will be instances in which it is perfectly clear that the new employer plans to retain all of the employees in the unit and in which it will be appropriate to have him initially consult with the employees' bargaining representative before he fixes terms. In other situations, however, it may not be clear until the successor employer has hired his full complement of employees that he has a duty to bargain with a union, since it will not be evident until then that the bargaining representative represents a majority of the employees in the unit. . . . Here, for example, Burns' obligation to bargain with the union did not mature until it had selected its force of guards late in June. The Board quite properly found that Burns refused to bargain on July 12 when it rejected the overtures of the union. It is true that the wages it paid when it began protecting the Lockheed plant on July 1 differed from those specified in the Wackenhut . . . agreement, but there is no evidence that Burns ever unilaterally changed the terms and conditions of employment it had offered to potential employees in June after its obligation to bargain . . . became apparent. If the union had made a request to bargain after Burns had completed its hiring and if Burns had negotiated in good faith and had made offers to the union which the union rejected, Burns could have unilaterally initiated such proposals as the opening terms and conditions of employment on July 1 without committing an unfair labor practice. Cf. NLRB v. Katz, 369 U.S. 736, 745 n.12 (1962). . . . The Board's order requiring Burns to make whole its employees for any losses suffered by reason of Burns' refusal to honor and enforce the contract, cannot therefore be sustained on the ground that Burns unilaterally changed existing terms and conditions of employment, thereby committing an unfair labor practice which required monetary restitution in these circumstances.

[The dissenting opinion of Justice Rehnquist, with whom Chief Justice Burger and Justices Brennan and Powell join, . . . dissenting in part, is omitted.]

## NOTES AND QUESTIONS

**1. Different Aspects of the "Successorship" Question.** *Burns* involves several aspects of the "successorship" question: (1) Is there a duty to hire the predecessor's employees? (2) Is there a duty to bargain with the union that had been the bargaining agent for the predecessor's employees? (3) Is there a duty to maintain the terms and conditions of the predecessor's unexpired collective bargaining agreement? See generally Samuel Estreicher, Successorship Obligations, in Labor Law and Business Change: Theoretical and Transactional Perspectives, ch. 4 (Samuel Estreicher & Daniel G. Collins eds., 1988).

**2. Relevance of Absence of Privity Between Wackenhut and Burns?** In his separate opinion in *Burns*, Justice Rehnquist argues that Burns presented a weak case for the imposition of any duties on the new employer because Burns did not purchase the assets of Wackenhut or have any other relationship with Wackenhut other than hiring some of its old employees and performing some work that Wackenhut had previously performed. Does the majority opinion in *Burns* rest in any way on the absence of a relationship between Burns and Wackenhut or on the fact that Burns and Wackenhut had presented rival bids for the same work?

**3. Sale of Assets vs. Sale of Controlling Interest in Stock or Merger.** *Burns* sets the general framework for sales of a company's assets; in such circumstances, the seller and purchaser remain distinct entities; the seller's obligations as a general matter are not assumed by the buyer unless expressly assumed. When the transaction involves a sale of a controlling interest of the stock of a corporation, the seller's obligations are carried by the continuing corporation or other business entity. *Burns* does not apply in the latter setting; the continuing corporation is bound not only by the duty to bargain with an incumbent union, but also by the terms of any existing collective agreement.

**4. Why No Purchaser Obligation to Maintain Terms?** Could the Court have held in *Burns* that the principle of *Katz*, supra page 449—that terms and conditions of employment may not be altered absent bargaining to impasse—applies to new employers that take over an appropriate bargaining unit in the same manner that it applies to employers whose employees in an appropriate unit have selected a new bargaining representative? Presumably, application of this principle would also require the continuation of employment for the predecessor's workforce. Can the justification for the Court's implicit rejection of this approach lie in freedom of contract principles, as suggested by the Court's reference to

*H.K. Porter*, supra page 429, even though the parties would be as free to negotiate new terms as would any other parties in a new collective bargaining relationship? Should it matter whether the new employer is a competitive bidder as in *Burns*? See generally Michael C. Harper, Defining the Economic Relationship Appropriate for Collective Bargaining, 39 B.C. L. Rev. 329, 356-363 (1998).

**5. Impact of *Burns* on Hiring Decisions.**

a. *Why No Duty to Hire Predecessor Employees?* Justice White for the Court holds that a new owner should be free to hire an entirely new workforce, although it may not in doing so discriminate in violation of §8(a)(3). Does the decision adequately protect the predecessor's employees from loss of their jobs due to their prior decision to seek union representation? Would the Court have struck a better balance between the competing interests had it established a presumption that a nondiscriminating new employer would retain predecessor employees, absent a strong business justification for nonretention? Would such a presumption be equally appropriate in competitive-bidding and consensual-transaction settings? President Obama's Executive Order 13495 of January 30, 2009, 76 Fed. Reg. 6103, requires successor federal government contractors to offer the employees of predecessor contractors "a right of first refusal of employment in positions for which [the] employees are qualified." Consider also N.Y.C. Displaced Building Service Protection Workers Protection Act, N.Y.C. Admin. Code §22-505 (requiring successor building owners, managers and contractors to offer employment to predecessor's employees for a 90-day period).

b. *Proof of Unlawful Motivation.* Once the General Counsel proves the presence of a discriminatory motive, the new employer has the burden of proving that it would have declined to hire the predecessor employees without regard to their representation by union or other concerted activity. See Planned Building Services, Inc., 347 N.L.R.B. 670 (2006). An employer is free to hire, for any business reason, fewer than half of its employees from the previous employer's workforce; but the Board holds, with judicial support, that an employer commits a §8(a)(3) violation by doing so solely in order to avoid a bargaining obligation, even if the new employer does not otherwise take into account union membership or activity. See, e.g., U.S. Marine Corp. v. NLRB, 944 F.2d 1305, 1316-1319 (7th Cir. 1991) (finding discrimination where employer refused to hire more employees from predecessor's workforce after coming close to one-half of its hiring goal); Dasal Caring Ctrs., 280 N.L.R.B. 60, 69 (1986), enforced, 815 F.2d 711 (8th Cir. 1987) (test of discrimination is in part whether new employer "conducted its staffing in a manner precluding the predecessor's employees from being hired as a majority of [its] overall workforce to avoid the

Board's successorship doctrine"). Is the Board's approach consistent with the *Burns* decision? If required by local law to retain the predecessor employees for a period of time, as is true in the New York City building service industry (see note 5a. supra), does the new employer violate §8(a)(3) by hiring an entirely new workforce? See Paulsen v. GVS Properties, LLC. 904 F. Supp. 2d 282 (E.D.N.Y. 2012).

**6. Should Continued Employee Support Have Been Presumed?** Given the Court's assumption that Burns had no obligation to offer continuing employment to the Wackenhut employees, did it make sense for the Court to hold that Burns assumed an obligation to bargain when it hired a majority of its employees from the Wackenhut workforce? Does the fact that a majority of employees in a new bargaining unit comes from a bargaining unit that had been represented by a union agent clearly indicate the sympathies concerning representation of a majority of the new unit? Even ignoring the possibility of substantial employee turnover in the old unit, is it not possible that the employees hired from the old unit disproportionately voted against or had come to disapprove of union representation? Is it a sufficient response that employee turnover does not ordinarily affect the presumption of continued majority support for a union when there is no new employer? That employees are free to petition for decertification?

**7. Under What Circumstances Must the New Employer Initially Consult with the Union?**

a. The *Burns* Court also states that "there will be instances in which it is perfectly clear that the new employer plans to retain all of the employees in the unit and in which it will be appropriate to have him initially consult with the employees' bargaining representative before he fixes terms." Does this caveat apply in every case where the employer desires to hire all the prior employer's employees, even where it has made clear that it is not offering the employees the same terms under which they had been working? The Board holds that a new employer can avoid any duty to consult initially with the union by clearly announcing an intent to establish new terms before attempting to hire former employees. See Nazareth Regional High Sch. v. NLRB, 549 F.2d 873 (2d Cir. 1977); Spruce Up Corp., 209 N.L.R.B. 194 (1974), enforced without opinion, 529 F.2d 516 (4th Cir. 1975).

b. Consider also the following case: Prior to assuming control of operations on July 1, 1992, the new employer contacted the predecessor's employees individually to say it wanted them to apply for positions. The new employer also had several discussions with the union representing the predecessor's employees, including communicating to the union on June 22, 1992, that it wanted the predecessor's employees to serve a probationary period. The new employer did not discuss the possibility of other changes in initial terms of employment until June 23, when it told several of the predecessor's employees that it wanted them to work at reduced wages. Did the new employer violate §8(a)(5) by not first bargaining with the union over any change in wages? By June 22, did the new employer by announcing its intent to rehire the predecessor's employees lose its flexibility to set new wage rates unilaterally? In Canteen Co., 317 N.L.R.B. 1052 (1995), enforced, 103 F.3d 1355 (7th Cir. 1997), a divided Board (3-2) answered these questions in the affirmative. The majority stressed that the new employer had misled the predecessor's employees by failing to announce its intent to set new terms until after the hiring process began. How would you advise new employers desiring exploratory talks with unions to protect themselves from a full bargaining obligation on new terms?

c. Shortly before negotiating to purchase the Monterey newspaper from another publisher, Day Press established a new pay system for any employee newly hired at any of its newspapers. Under the system, Day would pay a new employee within the "pay band" set for the particular job classification for which the employee was hired. The company would decide on the specific wage rate within the band based on the employee's qualifications and on local market conditions. After completing its purchase of Monterey, Day hired a majority of its workers for the Monterey paper from Monterey's prior workforce and promptly recognized the union that represented the Monterey workers in bargaining with the prior publisher. Day, however, implemented its new system so that while it paid retained incumbent Monterey employees in accord with their pay under their collective agreement with the old publisher, it set the pay for the new employees it hired through its discretionary "pay band" system. The union demanded that the employer consult with it before choosing wages within the discretionary bands for new employees. The company claimed a right to set such wages as "initial terms" under *Burns.* Is Day committing an unfair labor practice? See Monterey Newspapers, Inc., 334 N.L.R.B. 1019 (2001) (no).

**8. Remedy for Discriminatory Hiring.** A new employer that would have satisfied the conditions of successorship had it not illegally discriminated in hiring its workforce not only must instate those employees who were discriminatorily denied jobs, but also is required to consult with the union that represented the predecessor's employees before setting its initial terms and conditions of employment. See, e.g., Love's Barbeque Restaurant No. 62, 245 N.L.R.B. 78 (1979), enforced in relevant part sub nom. Kallman v. NLRB, 640 F.2d 1094 (9th Cir. 1981). Furthermore, the Board has held that where unlawful hiring has made it impossible to determine whether the new employer would have hired enough of the predecessor's employees to be deemed a "successor" had it acted lawfully, the new employer has an obligation to bargain with the union before changing the predecessor's terms of employment. See Galloway School Lines, Inc., 321 N.L.R.B. 1422 (1996).

**9. Comparative Perspective.** The labor laws of other major industrial countries tend to require continuity of jobs and negotiated terms of incumbent employees when there is a transfer of ownership of the business or part of a business where they work. Members of the European Community, including Germany and Great Britain, have passed protective legislation to comply with Directives of the Council of Ministers of the European Economic Community. The "Transfer of Undertakings" Directive provides that following "any transfer of an undertaking, business, or part of an undertaking or business to another employer as a result of a legal transfer or merger . . . the transferee shall continue to observe the terms and conditions agreed in any collective agreement on the same terms applicable to the transferor under that agreement, until the date of termination or expiry of the collective agreement or the entry into force or application of another collective agreement." Directive 2001/23/EC, art. 1(1), art. 3(3), 2001 O.J. (L82) 16. The Directive further provides that the "transfer of the undertaking, business or part of the undertaking or business shall not in itself constitute grounds for dismissal by the transferor or the transferee." Id., art. 4(1). In addition, the Directive states that if the "undertaking or business preserves its autonomy, the status and function of the representatives or of the representation of the employees affected by the transfer shall be preserved." Id., art. 6(1). The Directive has been interpreted to apply to asset transfers, including long-term leases, as long as there is a transfer of the business as a going concern engaged in the same or similar activities. See Samuel Estreicher, Global Issues in Labor Law 227 (2007); Roger Blanpain, European Labor Law, 695-720 (12th ed. 2010).

Some Canadian provinces also have implemented legislation that preserves not only the collective bargaining relationship but also any existing collective bargaining agreement, upon the sale or transfer of a business. For instance, §69 of the Ontario Labour Relations Act provides that, absent a substantial change in operations, an employer that acquires a business or a part of a business through any means is bound by its predecessor's bargaining obligations and bargaining agreements. This provision has been applied to cases where the successor failed to hire any of the predecessor's employees. See, e.g., Retail Wholesale Canada, Local 422 v. Nestle Canada, 1999 Carswell Ont. 4753; H.G.R.E., Local 75 v. Accomodex Franchise Management Inc., [1993] O.L.R.B. Rep. 281; Canadian Retail Employees Union, Local 1000A v. More Groceteria Ltd., [1980] C.L.L.C. 14, at 1430 (O.L.R.B.).

## Fall River Dyeing & Finishing Corp. v. NLRB
*482 U.S. 27 (1987)*

BLACKMUN, J. . . .

### I . . .

For almost as long as Sterlingwale had been in existence, its production and maintenance employees had been represented by the United Textile Workers of America, AFL-CIO, Local 292 (Union). The most recent collective-bargaining agreement before Sterlingwale's demise had been negotiated in 1978 and was due to expire in 1981. By an agreement dated October 1980, however, in response to the financial difficulties suffered by Sterlingwale, the Union agreed to amend the 1978 agreement to extend its expiration date by one year, until April 1, 1982, without any wage increase and with an agreement to improve labor productivity. . . .

In late summer 1982, however, Sterlingwale finally went out of business. It made an assignment for the benefit of its creditors, primarily Ansin's mother, who was an officer of the corporation and holder of a first mortgage on most of Sterlingwale's real property, and the Massachusetts Capital Resource Corporation (MCRC), which held a security interest on Sterlingwale's machinery and equipment. Ansin also hired a professional liquidator to dispose of the company's remaining assets, mostly its inventory, at auction.

During this same period, a former Sterlingwale employee and officer, Herbert Chace, and Arthur Friedman, president of one of Sterlingwale's major customers, Marcamy Sales Corporation (Marcamy), formed petitioner Fall River Dyeing & Finishing Corp. . . . Chace and Friedman formed petitioner with the intention of engaging strictly in the commission-dyeing business and of taking advantage of the availability of Sterlingwales's assets and workforce. Accordingly, Friedman had Marcamy acquire from MCRC and Ansin's mother Sterlingwale's plant, real property, and equipment, and convey them to petitioner. Petitioner also obtained some of Sterlingwale's remaining inventory at the liquidator's auction. Chace became petitioner's vice president in charge of operations and Friedman became its president.

In September 1982, petitioner began operating out of Sterlingwale's former facilities and began hiring employees. It advertised for workers and supervisors in a local newspaper, and Chace personally got in touch with several prospective supervisors. Petitioner hired 12 supervisors, of whom eight had been supervisors with Sterlingwale and three had been production employees there. In its hiring decisions for production employees, petitioner took into consideration recommendations from these supervisors and a prospective employee's former employment with Sterlingwale. Petitioner's initial hiring goal was to attain one full shift of workers, which meant from 55 to 60 employees. Petitioner planned to "see how business would be" after this initial goal had been met and, if business permitted, to expand to two shifts. The employees who were hired first spent approximately four to six weeks in start-up operations and an additional month in experimental production.

By letter dated October 19, 1982, the Union requested petitioner to recognize it as the bargaining agent for petitioner's employees and to begin collective bargaining. Petitioner refused the request, stating that, in its view, the request had "no legal basis." At that time, 18 of petitioner's 21 employees were former employees of Sterlingwale. By November of that year, petitioner had employees in a complete range of jobs, had its production process in operation, and was handling customer orders; by mid-January 1983, it had attained its initial goal of one shift of workers. Of the 55 workers in this initial shift, a number that represented over half the workers petitioner would eventually hire, 36 were former Sterlingwale employees. Petitioner continued to expand its workforce, and by mid-April 1983 it had reached two full shifts. For the first time, ex-Sterlingwale employees were in the minority but just barely so (52 or 53 out of 107 employees).

Although petitioner engaged exclusively in commission dyeing, the employees experienced the same conditions they had when they were working for Sterlingwale. The production process was unchanged and the employees worked on the same machines, in the same building, with the same job classifications, under virtually the same supervisors. Over half the volume of petitioner's business came from former Sterlingwale customers, and, in particular, Marcamy.

On November 1, 1982, the Union filed an unfair labor practice charge with the Board, alleging that in its refusal to bargain petitioner had violated §8(a)(1) and (5). . . . [The ALJ] decided that, on the facts of the case, petitioner was a successor to Sterlingwale. [The judge found that] petitioner's duty to bargain arose in mid-January [1983] because former Sterlingwale employees then were in the majority and because the Union's October demand was still in effect. Petitioner thus committed an unfair labor practice in refusing to bargain. In a brief decision and order, the Board, with one member dissenting, affirmed this decision.

The Court of Appeals for the First Circuit, also by a divided vote, enforced the order. . . .

## II

Although our reasoning in *Burns* was tied to the facts presented there, we suggested that our analysis would be equally applicable even if a union with which a successor had to bargain had not been certified just before the transition in employers. . . .

Moreover, in defining "the force of the Board's certification within the normal operative period," 406 U.S., at 279, we referred in *Burns* to two presumptions regarding a union's majority status following certification. See id., at 279, n.3. First, after a union has been certified by the Board as a bargaining-unit representative, it usually is entitled to a conclusive presumption of majority status for one year following the certification. . . . Second, after this period, the union is entitled to a rebuttable presumption of majority support. . . .

The rationale behind the presumptions is particularly pertinent in the successorship situation and so it is understandable that the Court in *Burns* referred to them. During a transition between employers, a union is in a peculiarly vulnerable position. It has no formal and established bargaining relationship with the new employer, is uncertain about the new employer's plans, and cannot be sure if or when the new employer must bargain with it. While being concerned with the future of its members with the new employer, the union also must protect whatever rights still exist for its members under the collective-bargaining agreement with the predecessor employer. Accordingly, during this unsettling transition period, the union needs the presumptions of majority status to which it is entitled to safeguard its members' rights and to develop a relationship with the successor.

The position of the employees also supports the application of the presumptions in the successorship situation. If the employees find themselves in a new enterprise that substantially resembles the old, but without their chosen bargaining representative, they may well feel that their choice of a union is subject to the vagaries of an enterprise's transformation. This feeling is not conducive to industrial peace. In addition, after being hired by a new company following a layoff from the old, employees initially will be concerned primarily with maintaining their new jobs. In fact, they might be inclined to shun support for their former union, especially if they believe that such support will jeopardize their jobs with the successor or if they are inclined to blame the union for their layoff and problems associated with it. Without the presumptions of majority support and with the wide variety of corporate transformations possible, an employer could use a successor enterprise as a way of getting rid of a labor contract and of exploiting the employees' hesitant attitude towards the union to eliminate its continuing presence. . . .

We now hold that a successor's obligation to bargain is not limited to a situation where the union in question has been recently certified. Where, as here, the union has a rebuttable presumption of majority status, this status continues despite the change in employers. And the new employer has an obligation to bargain with that union so long as the new employer is in fact a successor of the old employer and the majority of its employees were employed by its predecessor. . . .

## III

In *Burns* we approved the approach taken by the Board and accepted by courts with respect to determining whether a new company was indeed the successor to the old. 406 U.S., at 280-281, and n.4. This approach, which is primarily factual in nature and is based upon the totality of the circumstances of a given situation, requires that the Board focus on whether the new company has "acquired substantial assets of its predecessor and continued, without interruption or substantial change, the predecessor's business operations." Golden State Bottling Co. v. NLRB, 414 U.S. [163,] 184 [(1973)]. Hence, the focus is on whether there is "substantial continuity" between the enterprises. Under this approach, the Board examines a number of factors: whether the business of both employers is essentially the same; whether the employees of the new company are doing the same jobs in the same working conditions under the same supervisors; and whether the new entity has the same production process, produces the same products, and basically has the same body of customers. See *Burns,* 406 U.S., at 280, n.4. . . .

. . . [W]e find that the Board's determination that there was "substantial continuity" between Sterlingwale and petitioner and that petitioner was Sterlingwale's successor is supported by substantial evidence in the record. Petitioner acquired most of Sterlingwale's real property, its machinery and equipment, and much of its inventory and materials. It introduced no new product line. Of particular significance is the fact that, from the perspective of the employees, their jobs did not change. Although petitioner abandoned converting dyeing in exclusive favor of commission dyeing, this change did not alter the essential nature of the employees' jobs, because both types of dyeing involved the same production process. The job classifications of petitioner were the same as those of Sterlingwale; petitioners' employees worked on the same machines under the direction of supervisors most of whom were former supervisors of Sterlingwale. The record, in fact, is clear that petitioner acquired Sterlingwale's assets with the express purpose of taking advantage of its predecessor's workforce.

We do not find determinative of the successorship question the fact that there was a 7-month hiatus between Sterlingwale's demise and petitioner's start-up. Petitioner argues that this hiatus, coupled with the fact that its employees were hired through newspaper advertisements — not through

Sterlingwale employment records, which were not transferred to it—resolves in its favor the "substantial continuity" question. Yet such a hiatus is only one factor in the "substantial continuity" calculus and thus is relevant only when there are other indicia of discontinuity. Conversely, if other factors indicate a continuity between the enterprises, and the hiatus is a normal start-up period, the "totality of the circumstances" will suggest that these circumstances present a successorship situation. . . .

For the reasons given above, this is a case where the other factors suggest "substantial continuity" between the companies despite the seven-month hiatus. Here, moreover, the extent of the hiatus between the demise of Sterlingwale and the start-up of petitioner is somewhat less than certain. After the February layoff, Sterlingwale retained a skeleton crew of supervisors and employees that continued to ship goods to customers and to maintain the plant. In addition, until the assignment for the benefit of the creditors late in the summer, Ansin was seeking to resurrect the business or to find a buyer for Sterlingwale. The Union was aware of these efforts. Viewed from the employees' perspective, therefore, the hiatus may have been much less than seven months. Although petitioner hired the employees through advertisements, it often relied on recommendations from supervisors, themselves formerly employed by Sterlingwale, and intended the advertisements to reach the former Sterlingwale workforce.

Accordingly, we hold that, under settled law, petitioner was a successor to Sterlingwale. We thus must consider if and when petitioner's duty to bargain arose. . . .

Petitioner contends that the Board's representative complement rule is unreasonable, given that it injures the representation rights of many of the successor's employees and that it places significant burdens upon the successor, which is unsure whether and when the bargaining obligation will arise. . . . According to petitioner, if majority status is determined at the "full complement" stage, all the employees will have a voice in the selection of their bargaining representative, and this will reveal if the union truly has the support of most of the successor's employees.[12] This approach, however, focuses only on the interest in having a bargaining representative selected by the majority of the employees. It fails to take into account the significant interest of employees in being represented as soon as possible. The latter interest is especially heightened in a situation where many of the successor's employees, who were formerly represented by a union, find themselves after the employer transition in essentially the same enterprise, but without their bargaining representative. Having the new employer refuse to bargain with

12. After *Burns*, there was some initial confusion concerning this Court's holding. It was unclear if workforce continuity would turn on whether a majority of the successor's employees were those of the predecessor or on whether the successor had hired a majority of the predecessor's employees. . . . [Footnote relocated in text.—Eds.]

the chosen representative of these employees "disrupts the employees' morale, deters their organizational activities, and discourages their membership in unions." Franks Bros. Co. v. NLRB, 321 U.S. 702, 704 (1944). Accordingly, petitioner's "full complement" proposal must fail.

Nor do we believe that this "substantial and representative complement" rule places an unreasonable burden on the employer. . . .

. . . [I]n this situation the successor is in the best position to follow a rule the criteria of which are straightforward. The employer generally will know with tolerable certainty when all its job classifications have been filled or substantially filled, when it has hired a majority of the employees it intends to hire, and when it has begun normal production. . . .

We therefore hold that the Board's "substantial and representative complement" rule is reasonable in the successorship context. Moreover, its application to the facts of this case is supported by substantial record evidence. The Court of Appeals observed that by mid-January [1983] petitioner "had hired employees in virtually all job classifications, had hired at least fifty percent of those it would ultimately employ in the majority of those classifications, and it employed a majority of the employees it would eventually employ when it reached full complement." At that time petitioner had begun normal production. Although petitioner intended to expand to two shifts, and, in fact, reached this goal by mid-April, that expansion was contingent expressly upon the growth of the business. Accordingly, as found by the Board and approved by the Court of Appeals, mid-January was the period when petitioner reached its "substantial and representative complement." Because at that time the majority of petitioner's employees were former Sterlingwale employees, petitioner had an obligation to bargain with the Union then.

We also hold that the Board's "continuing demand" rule is reasonable in the successorship situation. The successor's duty to bargain at the "substantial and representative complement" date is triggered only when the union has made a bargaining demand. Under the "continuing demand" rule, when a union has made a premature demand that has been rejected by the employer, this demand remains in force until the moment when the employer attains the "substantial and representative complement." . . .

[Justice White joined only Parts I and III of the Court's opinion.]

POWELL, J., with whom THE CHIEF JUSTICE and O'CONNOR, J., join, dissenting. . . .

In my view, the Board's decision to measure the composition of the petitioner work force in mid-January is unsupportable. The substantial and representative complement test can serve a useful role when the hiring process is sporadic, or the future expansion of the work force is speculative. But . . . where it is feasible to wait and examine the full complement — as it was here — it clearly is fairer to both employer and employees to do so. . . .

## *NOTES AND QUESTIONS*

1. **"Substantial Continuity"?** Does the *Fall River* Court's "substantial continuity" test differ from the requirement in *Burns* that the bargaining unit involved in the predecessor situation remains essentially unchanged? If jobs, working conditions, and production processes remain the same, should a change in product line or customers affect the continued appropriateness of union representation? Should a relatively long hiatus before the start-up of a new business? Should the method of recruitment of the new workforce be relevant, if the new employer ends up hiring the prior employer's workers?

2. **Majority of Successor's or of Predecessor's Employees?** Note the issue highlighted in footnote 12 of the *Fall River* majority opinion. Consider the following hypotheticals: First, retailer Big moves into a new town by purchasing one of the stores of retailer Small and immediately tripling the scope of operations. Retailer Big hires for its expanded store all of the employees of retailer Small but also hires twice as many new employees. Does retailer Big have to bargain with the union that represented retailer Small's employees if retailer Big did not in any way change the jobs of these employees or the nature of its operations, other than store size?

Second, retailer Big decides to sell one of its seven stores in Middletown to retailer Little. The seven stores had comprised one bargaining unit represented by one bargaining agent. Retailer Little retains all the employees who had worked for retailer Big and does not otherwise change the nature of operations at the store. Does retailer Little have to bargain with the union that continues to represent the employees at retailer Big's other six stores in Middletown?

Before and after *Fall River*, both the Board and the courts have required that a majority of the successor's employees must have worked for the predecessor. See, e.g., NLRB v. Simon Debartelo Group, 241 F.3d 207 (2d Cir. 2001); Canteen Corp. v. NLRB, 103 F.3d 1355 (7th Cir. 1997); Saks & Co. v. NLRB, 634 F.2d 681 (2d Cir. 1980); Zim's Foodliner, Inc. v. NLRB, 495 F.2d 1131 (7th Cir. 1974). Why is this test preferable to the alternative standard offered in footnote 12 — that a majority of the predecessor's employees have been hired by the successor?

3. **"Substantial and Representative Complement" Rule.** Does the *Fall River* Court's "substantial and representative complement" rule adequately balance relevant labor law goals? Does it give adequate notice to employers of when new bargaining obligations arise? Was the rule appropriately applied in *Fall River*? If the new employer continues the old employer's operations without any break, when should the representative-complement

determination be made? See, e.g., Shares, Inc. v. NLRB, 433 F.3d 939 (7th Cir. 2006) (approving Board's use of date of transfer of control).

**4. Does the Recognition Bar Apply to New Collective Bargaining Relationship with Successor?** Elizabeth's Nursing Homes acquires a facility from Mary's Homes. After hiring most of Mary's employees at the facility, Elizabeth's agrees to recognize the union that had represented the employees in bargaining with Mary's. After three bargaining sessions over the course of three months, Elizabeth's files a petition to decertify the union based on strong evidence that a majority of employees no longer support the union. Should the successor employer, like an employer who newly recognizes a union that has not had prior bargaining status in the same unit, be barred from filing a decertification petition until the expiration of a reasonable period of time for bargaining? The Board has changed position on this issue a number of times, both before and after *Fall River.* See UGL-Unicco Service Co., 357 N.L.R.B. No. 76 (2011) (recounting shifts). The Board in *UGL-UNICCO* held that a successor employer is obligated to provide an incumbent union with a "reasonable period of bargaining" during which no question concerning representation may be raised. The Board also announced that it will apply a bright-line six months definition of "reasonable period" for situations in which the successor employer has adopted existing terms and conditions of employment as the starting point for bargaining. However, where the successor employer unilaterally announces new initial terms and conditions, it will apply a flexible definition of six months to a year, in accord with its *Lee Lumber* rule, see page 352 supra, for a voluntarily recognized union.

**5. Single-Employer Relocations.** How should *Burns* and *Fall River* be applied to plant relocations by an employer in the face of an unexpired collective bargaining agreement? Under what circumstances does an employer have an obligation to continue bargaining or to continue to honor the terms of a collective agreement after relocation of operations to a new facility?

Consider the following situation: Westwood has relocated its business from San Francisco to Hayward, a distance of 30 miles, offering to transfer all employees willing to move to Hayward. The Hayward operations begin with seven long-term San Francisco employees and six new employees who had been hired in San Francisco with the understanding that they would be going to Hayward. Does Westwood have a duty to apply the terms of the unexpired labor agreement to the Hayward facility? To recognize and bargain with the union that represented employees in San Francisco? What if the six new employees had been hired after operations began in Hayward? Does the result change if the workforce expands in Hayward to 20 employees? See Westwood Import Co., Inc. v. NLRB, 681 F.2d 664 (9th Cir.

1982). See also Rock Bottom Stores, Inc., 312 N.L.R.B. 400 (1993), enforced, 51 F.3d 366 (2d Cir. 1995) (employer must honor terms of agreement if operations are substantially the same and if transferring employees make up a substantial percentage — at least 40 percent — of employee complement at new facility).

**6. Successor Liability for Predecessor Unfair Labor Practices.** In Golden State Bottling Co., Inc. v. NLRB, 414 U.S. 168 (1973), cited by the *Fall River* Court, the Court upheld the Board's authority to issue a back pay and reinstatement order against a purchaser of the assets of a business who buys with knowledge of the seller's unremedied unfair labor practices. The *Golden State* Court explained that when a new employer

> has acquired substantial assets of its predecessor and continued without interruption or substantial change the predecessor's business operations, those employees who have been retained will understandably view their job situations as essentially unaltered. . . . To the extent that the employees' legitimate expectation is that the unfair labor practices will be remedied, a successor's failure to do so may result in labor unrest as the employees engage in collective action to force remedial action. Similarly, if the employees identify the new employer's labor policies with those of the predecessor but do not take collective action, the successor may benefit from the unfair labor practices due to a continuing deterrent effect on union activities.

Is a competitor obligated to remedy a prior employer's ULPs if, as in *Burns*, it had no contractual relationship with the predecessor? See Glebe Elec., Inc., 307 N.L.R.B. 883 (1992) (some contractual relationship or common pecuniary or security interest is necessary). *Golden State* may apply even where the new employer cannot be ordered to bargain because a majority of its employees were not employed by the predecessor. See St. Mary's Foundry, 284 N.L.R.B. 221 (1987), enforced, 860 F.2d 679 (6th Cir. 1988).

Does *Golden State* apply if no NLRB order had issued against the predecessor at the time of the business transfer? What if no charge had even been filed against the predecessor before transfer of the business? See NLRB v. General Wood Preserving Co., 905 F.2d 803 (4th Cir. 1990) (charge not required; actual knowledge of conduct of predecessor employer may suffice). In *General Wood Preserving* the successor had knowledge of the underlying conduct because he had been present as an employee and consultant at the time. See also NLRB v. St. Marys Foundry Co., 860 F.2d 679 (6th Cir. 1988) (when successor knows of allegations against predecessor "he undertakes the business with notice of the risk that those allegations may ripen into findings of unfair labor practices which will have to be remedied, and that he may be held liable for the remedy, just as surely as if he purchased with knowledge that formal charges had been filed."); S. Bent & Bros., 336 N.L.R.B. 788, 790 (2001) (stating that it is well-settled that "the Board does not consider whether the successor has seen the particular charges or complaints, but rather, whether the successor was aware of conduct that the Board ultimately found unlawful.").

## 2. Obligations Under the Collective Bargaining Agreement

### Howard Johnson Co. v. Hotel and Restaurant Employees
*417 U.S. 249 (1974)*

Marshall, J.

. . . Prior to the sale at issue here, the Grissoms . . . had operated a Howard Johnson's Motor Lodge and an adjacent Howard Johnson's Restaurant in Belleville, Michigan, under franchise agreements with the petitioner. Employees at both the restaurant and motor lodge were represented by the respondent Hotel & Restaurant Employees & Bartenders International Union. The Grissoms had entered into separate collective-bargaining agreements with the Union covering employees at the two establishments. Both agreements contained dispute settlement procedures leading ultimately to arbitration. Both agreements also provided that they would be binding upon the employer's "successors, assigns, purchasers, lessees or transferees."

On June 16, 1972, the Grissoms entered into an agreement with Howard Johnson to sell it all of the personal property used in connection with operation of the restaurant and motor lodge. The Grissoms retained ownership of the real property, leasing both premises to Howard Johnson. Howard Johnson did not agree to assume any of the Grissoms' obligations, except for four specific contracts relating to operation of the restaurant and motor lodge. On June 28, Howard Johnson mailed the Grissoms a letter, which they later acknowledged and confirmed, clarifying that "[i]t was understood and agreed that the Purchaser . . . would not recognize and assume any labor agreements between the Sellers . . . and any labor organizations," and that it was further agreed that "the Purchaser does not assume any obligations or liabilities of the Sellers resulting from any labor agreements. . . ."

. . . After reaching agreement with the Grissoms, Howard Johnson began hiring its own work force. It placed advertisements in local newspapers, and posted notices in various places, including the restaurant and motor lodge. It began interviewing prospective employees on July 10, hired its first employees on July 18, and began training them at a Howard Johnson facility in Ann Arbor on July 20. Prior to the sale, the Grissoms had 53 employees. Howard Johnson commenced operations with 45 employees,

33 engaged in the restaurant and 12 in the motor lodge. Of these, only nine of the restaurant employees and none of the motor lodge employees had previously been employed by the Grissoms. None of the supervisory personnel employed by the Grissoms were hired by Howard Johnson.

The Union filed this action in the state courts on July 21. Characterizing Howard Johnson's failure to hire all of the employees of the Grissoms as a "lockout" in violation of the collective-bargaining agreements, the Union sought a temporary restraining order enjoining this "lockout" and an order compelling Howard Johnson and the Grissoms to arbitrate the extent of their obligations to the Grissom employees under the bargaining agreements. . . .

The defendants subsequently removed this action to the federal courts on the ground that it was brought under §301 of the Labor Management Relations Act, 29 U.S.C. §185. At a hearing before the District Court on August 7, the Grissoms admitted that they were required to arbitrate in accordance with the terms of the collective-bargaining agreements they had signed and that an order compelling arbitration should issue. On August 22, the District Court . . . held that Howard Johnson was also required to arbitrate the extent of its obligations to the former Grissom employees. The court denied, however, the Union's motion for a preliminary injunction requiring the Company to hire all the former Grissom employees, and granted a stay of its arbitration order pending appeal. Howard Johnson appealed the order compelling arbitration, but the Court of Appeals affirmed. . . .

Both courts below relied heavily on this Court's decision in John Wiley & Sons v. Livingston, 376 U.S. 543 (1964). In *Wiley*, the union representing the employees of a corporation which had disappeared through a merger sought to compel the surviving corporation, which had hired all of the merged corporation's employees and continued to operate the enterprise in a substantially identical form after the merger, to arbitrate under the merged corporation's collective-bargaining agreement. As *Wiley* was this Court's first experience with the difficult "successorship" question, its holding was properly cautious and narrow:

> We hold that the disappearance by merger of a corporate employer which has entered into a collective bargaining agreement with a union does not automatically terminate all rights of the employees covered by the agreement, and that, in appropriate circumstances, present here, the successor employer may be required to arbitrate with the union under the agreement. (Id., at 548.)

Mr. Justice Harlan, writing for the Court, emphasized "the central role of arbitration in effectuating national labor policy" and preventing industrial strife, and the need to afford some protection to the interests of the employees during a change of corporate ownership. Id., at 549. . . .

The courts below held that *Wiley* rather than *Burns* was controlling here on the ground that *Burns* involved an NLRB order holding the employer bound by the substantive terms of the collective-bargaining agreement, whereas this case, like *Wiley*, involved a §301 suit to compel arbitration. Although this distinction was in fact suggested by the Court's opinion in *Burns*, we do not believe that the fundamental policies outlined in *Burns* can be so lightly disregarded. . . . We find it unnecessary, however, to decide in the circumstances of this case whether there is any irreconcilable conflict between *Wiley* and *Burns*. We believe that even on its own terms, *Wiley* does not support the decision of the courts below. . . .

. . . *Wiley* involved a merger, as a result of which the initial employing entity completely disappeared. In contrast, this case involves only a sale of some assets, and the initial employers remain in existence as viable corporate entities, with substantial revenues from the lease of the motor lodge and restaurant to Howard Johnson. Although we have recognized that ordinarily there is no basis for distinguishing among mergers, consolidations, or purchases of assets in the analysis of successorship problems, see Golden State Bottling Co. v. NLRB, 414 U.S. 168, 182-183, n.5 (1973), we think these distinctions are relevant here for two reasons. First, the merger in *Wiley* was conducted "against a background of state law that embodied the general rule that in merger situations the surviving corporation is liable for the obligations of the disappearing corporation," *Burns*, 406 U.S., at 286, which suggests that holding Wiley bound to arbitrate under its predecessor's collective-bargaining agreement may have been fairly within the reasonable expectations of the parties. Second, the disappearance of the original employing entity in the *Wiley* merger meant that unless the union were afforded some remedy against Wiley, it would have no means to enforce the obligations voluntarily undertaken by the merged corporation, to the extent that those obligations vested prior to the merger or to the extent that its promises were intended to survive a change of ownership. Here, in contrast, because the Grissom corporations continue as viable entities with substantial retained assets, the Union does have a realistic remedy to enforce their contractual obligations. Indeed, the Grissoms have agreed to arbitrate the extent of their liability to the Union and their former employees; presumably this arbitration will explore the question whether the Grissoms breached the successorship provisions of their collective-bargaining agreements, and what the remedy for this breach might be.

Even more important, in *Wiley* the surviving corporation hired all of the employees of the disappearing corporation. Although, under *Burns*, the surviving corporation may have been entitled to make substantial changes in its operation of the enterprise, the plain fact is that it did not. As the arbitrator in *Wiley* subsequently stated:

> Although the Wiley merger was effective on October 2, 1961, the former Interscience employees continued to perform the same work on the same products under the same management at the same work place as before the change in the corporate employer. (Interscience Encyclopedia, Inc., 55 Lab. Arb. 210, 218 (1970).)[4] . . .

Here, however, Howard Johnson decided to select and hire its own independent work force to commence its operation of the restaurant and motor lodge.[5] It therefore hired only nine of the 53 former Grissom employees and none of the Grissom supervisors. The primary purpose of the Union in seeking arbitration here with Howard Johnson is not to protect the rights of Howard Johnson's employees; rather, the Union primarily seeks arbitration on behalf of the former Grissom employees who were not hired by Howard Johnson. It is the Union's position that Howard Johnson was bound by the pre-existing collective-bargaining agreement to employ all of these former Grissom employees, except those who could be dismissed in accordance with the "just cause" provision or laid off in accordance with the seniority provision. . . .

What the Union seeks here is completely at odds with the basic principles this Court elaborated in *Burns*. . . . Clearly, *Burns* establishes that Howard Johnson had the right not to hire any of the former Grissom employees, if it so desired.[8] The Union's effort to circumvent this holding by

---

4. Subsequently, the Interscience plant was closed and the former Interscience employees were integrated into Wiley's work force. The arbitrator, relying in part on the NLRB's decision in *Burns*, held that the provisions of the Interscience collective-bargaining agreement remained in effect for as long as Wiley continued to operate the former Interscience enterprise as a unit in substantially the same manner as prior to the merger, but that the integration of the former Interscience employees into Wiley's operations destroyed this continuity of identity and terminated the effectiveness of the bargaining agreement. 55 Lab. Arb., at 218-220.

5. It is important to emphasize that this is not a case where the successor corporation is the "alter ego" of the predecessor, where it is "merely a disguised continuance of the old employer." Southport Petroleum Co. v. NLRB, 315 U.S. 100, 106 (1942). Such cases involve a mere technical change in the structure or identity of the employing entity, frequently to avoid the effect of the labor laws, without any substantial change in its ownership or management. In these circumstances, the courts have had little difficulty holding that the successor is in reality the same employer and is subject to all the legal and contractual obligations of the predecessor.

8. . . . Of course, it is an unfair labor practice for an employer to discriminate in hiring or retention of employees on the basis of union membership or activity under §8(a)(3) of the National Labor Relations Act, 29 U.S.C. §158(a)(3). Thus, a new owner could not refuse to hire the employees of his predecessor solely because they were union members or to avoid having to recognize the union. . . . There is no suggestion in this case that Howard Johnson in any way discriminated in its hiring against the former Grissom employees because of their union membership, activity, or representation.

asserting its claims in a §301 suit to compel arbitration rather than in an unfair labor practice context cannot be permitted.

We do not believe that *Wiley* requires a successor employer to arbitrate in the circumstances of this case. The Court there held that arbitration could not be compelled unless there was "substantial continuity of identity in the business enterprise" before and after a change of ownership, for otherwise the duty to arbitrate would be "something imposed from without, not reasonably to be found in the particular bargaining agreement and the acts of the parties involved." 376 U.S., at 551. This continuity of identity in the business enterprise necessarily includes, we think, a substantial continuity in the identity of the work force across the change in ownership. . . .

Since there was plainly no substantial continuity of identity in the work force hired by Howard Johnson with that of the Grissoms, and no express or implied assumption of the agreement to arbitrate, the courts below erred in compelling the Company to arbitrate the extent of its obligations to the former Grissom employees. Accordingly, the judgment of the Court of Appeals must be reversed.

[The dissenting opinion of Justice Douglas is omitted.]

## *NOTES AND QUESTIONS*

**1. Rationale for Distinguishing *Wiley*.**

a. *Sale of Assets vs. Merger.* If Howard Johnson had acquired the Grissoms' property through a merger rather than through a purchase of assets, would the Court have upheld the order to arbitrate? Even if Howard Johnson had retained only a few ex-Grissom employees? The merger statute applicable in *Wiley* was not atypical. While a purchaser of assets does not assume a seller's liabilities absent an explicit agreement, state corporate law generally provides that all premerger assets and liabilities (including unexpired executory contracts) become assets and liabilities of the surviving corporation after a merger. See, e.g., Revised Model Bus. Corp. Act §11.07(a)(3)-(4) (2000); Cal. Corp. Code §1107(a) (2014); Del. Code Ann. tit. 8, §259(a) (2014); N.Y. Bus. Corp. Law §906(b) (Consol. 2014).

b. *Continuing Workforce and Operations.* If Howard Johnson had hired all of the Grissom employees and had otherwise maintained the continuity of operations of the restaurant and motor lodge, would the Court have ordered arbitration? Or is the obligation to arbitrate under *Wiley* generally not applicable to a purchaser of assets who does not otherwise assume obligations under the collective agreement, regardless of the continuity of the work force and the enterprise? See, e.g., AmeriSteel Corp. v. Int'l Bhd. of Teamsters, 267 F.3d 264 (3d Cir. 2001); Local 7-517 v. Uno-Ven Co., 170

F.3d 779 (7th Cir. 1999) (both finding no duty to arbitrate despite continuity in work force and operations).

**2. Stock Purchasers.** What if Howard Johnson had acquired the Grissoms' business by purchasing from the Grissoms all of the stock in a corporation that owned their business? Those who obtain control of a business through purchase of its stock are generally viewed as successor employers suable under §301 for any violations of the unexpired labor agreement. See, e.g., Amalgamated Clothing & Textile Workers v. Ratner Corp., 602 F.2d 1363 (9th Cir. 1979) (stock transfer combined with reorganization as holding company). Should it matter whether the new owner makes a major alteration in the business, or should the question of the continued applicability of the collective agreement always be sent to the arbitrator? See supra note 3, page 756.

**3. Enforcing Contractual Obligations Against the Buyer?** Does *Howard Johnson* permit unions and employers, by sufficiently explicit language in a collective agreement, to require future purchasers of the employer's operations to continue to employ an incumbent workforce in accord with the terms of the agreement? Would there be any basis in general contract law for enforcing such an obligation directly against the assets purchaser who does not otherwise assume the obligations of the labor agreement? When would it be of any practical significance that the obligations of the seller's labor agreement are enforceable only against the seller, absent an assuming purchaser? See infra note 6, page 776.

**4. State Law Requirements.** Note that the *Howard Johnson* Court distinguished the merger in *Wiley* as being conducted "against a background of state law that embodied the general rule that in merger situations the surviving corporation is liable for the obligations of the disappearing corporation. . . ." Does this language mean that state law may regulate the labor law obligations of purchasers of assets? Illinois law, for instance, provides that "[w]here a collective bargaining agreement between an employer and a labor organization contains a successor clause, such clause shall be binding upon and enforceable against any successor employer who succeeds to the contracting employer's business, until the expiration date of the agreement therein stated." The statutory definition of successor includes "any purchaser . . . [that] conducts or will conduct substantially the same business operation, or offer the same service, and use the same physical facilities, as the contracting employer." Ill. Stat. ch. 820, §10/1(a) & (b) (2014). See also Minn. Stat. §338.02. Could state law take the further step of imposing collective agreements on successor employers even in the absence of any "successor" language in the seller's labor agreement? Delaware law, for instance, provides that collective bargaining agreements survive "any merger, consolidation, joint venture, lease, sale, dividend exchange, mortgage, pledge, transfer or other disposition (in one transaction or a series of transactions) whether with a subsidiary or otherwise." Del. Code Ann. tit. 19, §706 (2014).

Would these laws necessarily result in the imposition of obligations on new employers where, as in *Howard Johnson,* the purchasers hire a substantially new workforce? Does *Howard Johnson* reflect a policy balance under federal labor law that preempts or displaces any state law like that cited above? See Commonwealth Edison Co. v. Int'l Bhd. of Electrical Workers, Local 15, 961 F. Supp. 1169 (N.D. Ill. 1997) (holding Illinois law preempted); Steelworkers v. St. Gabriel's Hosp., 871 F. Supp. 335 (D. Minn. 1994) (holding Minnesota law preempted); Eileen Silverstein, Against Preemption in Labor Law, 24 Conn. L. Rev. 1 (1991); Note, Labor Policy and Private Determination of Successor Liability: Illinois' Successor Clause Statute, 67 Wash. U. L.Q. 575 (1989); see generally the discussion of preemption of state law in Chapter 11.

**5. Successor's Tacit Assumption of the Collective Bargaining Agreement?** Howard Johnson, of course, could have agreed to be bound by the Grissoms' collective agreements after the transfer of ownership. Should a new owner also be bound by the old owner's agreement when it acts in accord with the agreement for a period of time by initially hiring the old owner's employees and by compensating and governing them in compliance with the agreement? See, e.g., New England Mechanical, Inc. v. Laborers Local Union 294, 909 F.2d 1339, 1343 (9th Cir. 1990) (employer may indicate its intent to be bound by acting in accord with old agreement). Cf. Note 7 at page 758 supra for employer's obligation to consult with union when it makes a clear plan to retain employees.

**6. Remedy Against the Seller.** Consider next the possibility (as suggested by the *Howard Johnson* Court at footnote 3 and accompanying text) of unions and employees having a remedy against the seller for failing to fulfill a contractual promise to obtain the agreement of the purchaser to assume the predecessor's collective bargaining agreements.

a. *Types of Clauses.* Allegations that such promises have been made may rest on a variety of clauses in collective agreements:

1. One type involves boilerplate recitals, whether in the preamble to the labor agreement or its penultimate paragraph, that the contract is binding on the parties and their "successors or assigns."
2. A second type of provision might be termed the "evasion" clause, in which the employer promises not to transfer any operation "for the purpose of defeating or evading the agreement."

3. A third is the explicit successorship clause, in which the employer expressly agrees to transfer the operation only to a purchaser who will assume the labor contract.

Estreicher, Successorship Obligations, in Labor Law and Business Change, supra, at 63, 68-69.

b. "*Reverse* Boys Market" *Injunctions.* Should courts issue "reverse *Boys Markets*" injunctions pending arbitration, see supra page 717, to restrain sales that may violate successorship promises in collective agreements? See, e.g., Local Lodge No. 1266, Int'l Ass'n of Machinists v. Panoramic Corp., 668 F.2d 276 (7th Cir. 1981); United Steelworkers of America v. Cooper-Standard Automotive of Bowling Green, Ohio, 175 L.R.R.M. 3249 (N.D. Ind. 2004) (both issuing injunctions). In which situations, if any, will allowing the sale to proceed and remitting the union to pursue its arbitral remedies against the seller inadequately protect the contractual rights of the seller's employees?

**7. Mandatory Subject of Bargaining?** Should union proposals for successorship clauses be mandatory topics of bargaining? Is the reasoning of the Court in *Burns* instructive on this question? See Lone Star Steel Co. v. NLRB, 639 F.2d 545 (10th Cir. 1980) (finding a successorship clause a mandatory topic).

**8. "Cease Doing Business" Clauses.** Do clauses that compel the signatory employer to cease doing business with prospective purchasers who are unwilling to sign agreements with the union run afoul of §8(e)? Note that in footnote 3 the *Howard Johnson* Court cited Commerce Tankers Corp., 196 N.L.R.B. 1100 (1972), enforced, 486 F.2d 907 (2d Cir. 1973), which held that successorship clauses do not violate §8(e) where sales of plants or parts of plants do not occur in the normal course of the signatory employer's business.

**9. "Alter Ego" Relationships.** Consider footnote 5 in the *Howard Johnson* decision. The Board applies a multifactor test for alter ego status, considering whether the two enterprises have substantially identical management, business purpose, operation, equipment, customers, and supervision, as well as ownership. Does a "substantial" change in actual ownership matter when the individuals in effective control of the first firm remain in control of the second? See, e.g., NLRB v. Omnitest Inspection Servs., Inc., 937 F.2d 112 (3d Cir. 1991); J.M. Tanaka Constr., Inc. v. NLRB, 675 F.2d 1029 (9th Cir. 1982) (both holding that common formal ownership is not a necessary prerequisite to alter ego relationship). What if ownership, as well as control and operations, is identical, but the new enterprise has not been established to avoid labor-related obligations? Compare Stardyne Inc. v. NLRB, 41 F.3d 141 (3d Cir. 1994) (finding of intent to evade bargaining obligations is not prerequisite to imputing alter ego status), with Alkire v. NLRB, 716 F.2d 1014 (4th Cir. 1983) (to be alter ego employer must have been able to reasonably foresee that transfer of work could avoid duty imposed by NLRA).

**10. WARN Act Requirements.** The Worker Adjustment and Retraining Notification Act (WARN), see supra note 5, page 491, expressly imposes on the seller "of a part or all of an employer's business" the obligation to provide workers 60-days "notice for any plant closing or mass layoff . . . up to and including the effective date of the sale." However, "[a]fter the effective date of the sale . . . , the purchaser shall be responsible for providing notice. . . ." 29 U.S.C. 2101(b)(1). See Wilson v. Airtherm Products, Inc., 436 F.3d 906 (8th Cir. 2006) (seller not liable for failure to give notice of plant closing when it sold business as a going concern, terminated its employees on date of sale, and had no reason to anticipate that buyer would close plant). In *Wilson* the buyer had assured the seller that it would hire enough of the seller's employees to avoid a "mass layoff," as defined in the WARN Act. What if the seller had good reason before the sale to believe that the buyer would effect a "mass layoff" by not hiring the seller's employees?

## B. SIMULTANEOUS OPERATION OF UNION AND NONUNION ENTERPRISES

The NLRA does not prohibit an employer from operating both a union and a nonunion plant in the same geographical area. If a union successfully organizes the employees at only one of two plants of the same employer, and the Board has determined that the single plant is an appropriate bargaining unit, the union will have to organize the second plant to become the representative of its employees. As we have seen, the NLRA would prohibit the employer from shifting work from the union to the nonunion plant simply because of the union's presence at the first plant; however, after meeting any bargaining obligations, the employer would be able to shift work to the nonunion plant in order to operate more efficiently with lower labor costs. In order to prevent such a shift, the union would have to negotiate a work-preservation clause. Moreover, if the employer commenced operations at the nonunion plant after the unionization of its first plant, the union generally would not be able to claim representation of the new employees at the second plant without demonstrating majority support at that location. Absent such a showing, the Board would have to determine whether the second plant's workforce "accreted" to that of the first under a variant of the "community of interests" criteria that requires an "overwhelming" community of interest. See page 249 supra.

In industries such as construction where companies contract to do work on a project-by-project basis at various and noncontinuous sites, collective bargaining agreements with unions typically cover all work done by the company within a particular geographical area. All workers within the area are part of the bargaining unit and are usually referred to the company from a union hiring hall. Under such agreements, a unionized company must anticipate using union labor at any site at which it bids for work.

Since at least the early 1970s, however, owners of unionized contractors have formed separate nonunion companies to bid for work in the same geographical area. Unions have attempted to challenge this practice, termed "double-breasting," by arguing that in such instances the nonunion company should be subject to the contractual obligations of the labor agreement with the unionized employer. The general rule is that a new construction company is required to assume the labor agreement of a commonly owned competing company only when the two companies are found to be a "single employer" or the second company is determined to be the "alter ego" of the first.

**South Prairie Construction Co. v. Local No. 627, International Union of Operating Engineers**
*425 U.S. 800 (1976)*

PER CURIAM.

Respondent Union filed a complaint in 1972 with the National Labor Relations Board alleging that South Prairie Construction Co. (South Prairie) and Peter Kiewit Sons' Co. (Kiewit) had violated §8(a)(5) and (1) of the National Labor Relations Act, . . . by their continuing refusal to apply to South Prairie's employees the collective-bargaining agreement in effect between the Union and Kiewit. The Union first asserted that since South Prairie and Kiewit are wholly owned subsidiaries of Peter Kiewit Sons, Inc. (PKS), and engage in highway construction in Oklahoma, they constituted a single "employer" within the Act for purposes of applying the Union-Kiewit agreement. That being the case, the Union contended, South Prairie was obligated to recognize the Union as the representative of a bargaining unit drawn to include South Prairie's employees. Disagreeing with the Administrative Law Judge on the first part of the Union's claim, the Board concluded that South Prairie and Kiewit were in fact separate employers, and dismissed the complaint.

On the facts of this case, the Union first had to establish that Kiewit and South Prairie were a single "employer." If it succeeded, the existence of a violation under §8(a)(5) would then turn on whether under §9 the "employer unit" was the "appropriate" one for collective-bargaining purposes.

On the Union's petition for review, the Court of Appeals for the District of Columbia Circuit canvassed the facts of record. It discussed, inter alia, the manner in which Kiewit, South Prairie, and PKS functioned as entities; PKS' decision to activate South Prairie, its nonunion subsidiary, in a State where historically Kiewit had been the only union highway contractor among the latter's Oklahoma competitors; and the two firms' competitive bidding patterns on Oklahoma highway jobs after South Prairie was activated in 1972 to do business there.

Stating that it was applying the criteria recognized by this Court in Radio Union v. Broadcast Service, 380 U.S. 255 (1965), the Court of Appeals disagreed with the Board and decided that on the facts presented Kiewit and South Prairie were a single "employer."[3] It reasoned that in addition to the "presence of a very substantial qualitative degree of centralized control of labor relations," the facts "evidence a substantial qualitative degree of interrelation of operations and common management — one that we are satisfied would not be found in the arm's length relationship existing among unintegrated companies." 518 F.2d 1040, 1046, 1047 (1975). The Board's finding to the contrary was, therefore, in the view of the Court of Appeals "not warranted by the record." 518 F.2d at 1047.

Having set aside this portion of the Board's determination, however, the Court of Appeals went on to reach and decide the second question presented by the Union's complaint which had not been passed upon by the Board. The court decided that the employees of Kiewit and South Prairie constituted the appropriate unit under §9 of the Act for purposes of collective bargaining. On the basis of this conclusion, it decided that these firms had committed an unfair labor practice by refusing "to recognize Local 627 as the bargaining representative of South Prairie's employees or to extend the terms of the Union's agreement with Kiewit to South Prairie's employees." 518 F.2d, at 1050. The case was remanded to the Board for "issuance and enforcement of an appropriate order against . . . Kiewit and South Prairie." Ibid. . . .

The Court of Appeals was evidently of the view that since the Board dismissed the complaint it had necessarily decided that the employees of Kiewit and South Prairie would not constitute an appropriate bargaining unit under §9. . . . The Board's cases hold that especially in the construction industry a determination that two affiliated firms constitute a single

3. "[I]n determining the relevant employer, the Board considers several nominally separate business entities to be a single employer where they comprise an integrated enterprise, N.L.R.B. Twenty-first Ann. Rep. 14-15 (1956). The controlling criteria, set out and elaborated in Board decisions, are interrelation of operations, common management, centralized control of labor relations and common ownership." 380 U.S., at 256.

employer "does not necessarily establish that an employer wide unit is appropriate, as the factors which are relevant in identifying the breadth of an employer's operation are not conclusively determinative of the scope of an appropriate unit." Central New Mexico Chapter, National Electrical Contractors Assn., Inc., 152 N.L.R.B. 1604, 1608 (1965). See also B & B Industries, Inc., 162 N.L.R.B. 832 (1967).

The Court of Appeals reasoned that the Board's principal case on the "unit" question, Central New Mexico Chapter, supra, was distinguishable because there the two affiliated construction firms were engaged in different types of contracting. It thought that this fact was critical to the Board's conclusion in that case that the employees did not have the same "community of interest" for purposes of identifying an appropriate bargaining unit. Whether or not the Court of Appeals was correct in this reasoning, we think that for it to take upon itself the initial determination of this issue was "incompatible with the orderly function of the process of judicial review." NLRB v. Metropolitan Ins. Co., 380 U.S. 438, 444 (1965). Since the selection of an appropriate bargaining unit lies largely within the discretion of the Board, whose decision, "if not final, is rarely to be disturbed," Packard Motor Co. v. NLRB, 330 U.S. 485, 491 (1947), we think the function of the Court of Appeals ended when the Board's error on the "employer" issue was "laid bare." FPC v. Idaho Power Co., 344 U.S. 17, 20 (1952). . . .

## *NOTES AND QUESTIONS*

**1. Finding "Single Employer" Status.** As stated in *South Prairie* in footnote 3, the factors considered by the Board when determining whether two firms are to be considered a "single employer" are: the interrelation of operations of the two businesses, the extent of common ownership and control, the degree to which there is centralized control of labor relations, and whether there is common management.

The Board generally has found dual operations by the same ownership to constitute a single employer only in cases where day-to-day control of labor relations is centralized or where the commonly owned nonunion firm directly assumes work formerly done by the union firm, such as through subcontracting. See Stephen F. Befort, Labor Law and the Double-Breasted Employer: A Critique of the Single Employer and Alter Ego Doctrines and a Proposed Reformulation, 1987 Wis. L. Rev. 67. If management of the firms is separated at some level, the fact of common ownership and thus potential common control is not sufficient. See, e.g., Mercy Hospital of Buffalo, 336 N.L.R.B. 1282, 1283-84 (2001) (common ownership not determinative in absence of centralized control of labor relations); Crest Floors & Plastics, Inc., 274 N.L.R.B. 1230, 1248 (1985), enforced, 785 F.2d 314 (9th Cir. 1986). Nor is the mere potential for the union firm to perform work being performed by the nonunion firm sufficient. See, e.g., Western Union Corp., 224 N.L.R.B. 274 (1976), affirmed, 571 F.2d 665 (D.C. Cir. 1978).

**2. Appropriate Bargaining Unit Requirement.** As stressed in *South Prairie,* a finding of "single employer" status does not necessarily lead to the extension of the labor agreement to both companies. The NLRB also must find under its normal standards that the two firms constitute an appropriate bargaining unit. In what kinds of cases should the Board find that employees of two construction firms that it deems to be a "single employer" are not appropriately combined in one bargaining unit? Should the Board apply a rebuttable presumption in favor of single employer-wide bargaining units, for instance, where two firms of a "single employer" do the same kind of construction with the same kind of equipment in the same geographical area?

**3. Use of the "Alter Ego" Doctrine in Double-Breasting Cases.** The Board also may impose a unionized employer's collective bargaining agreement on a commonly owned and managed nonunion employer when it finds sufficient identity between the two employers to conclude that the second is the alter ego of the first. See Crawford Door Sales Co., 226 N.L.R.B. 1144 (1976); supra note 9, page 777. Although a finding of alter ego status is sufficient to extend the agreement without any further inquiry into the appropriateness of an extended unit, see Carpenters' Local Union No. 1478 v. Stevens, 743 F.2d 1271, 1277 (9th Cir. 1984), the Board does not find alter ego status in cases where it would not find a single unit to be appropriate. Single employer and alter ego analysis indeed are not sharply distinguished in more recent Board decisions. See, e.g., Cannelton Industries, Inc., 339 N.L.R.B. 996 (2003).

**4. Distinguishing Joint Employers.** "Single employer" status should not be confused with "joint employer" status, see pages 250-252 supra. The status of employers as joint derives from their sharing control over employment terms and conditions of the same group of employees. Fully independent companies with separate management as well as ownership may be joint employers where they share such control. Such companies, however, would not be a single employer of all the employees of each company, as South Prairie and Kiewit were found to be by the court. Conversely, if South Prairie and Kiewit, though commonly owned, were not a single employer because each independently managed and set terms for two separate groups of employees, they also would not be joint employers of either group of employees.

**5. Proposed Legislation Against Double-Breasting.** From time to time, union representatives have urged legislation to expand the "single employer" doctrine. For instance, H.R. 931, 101st Cong., 1st Sess. at 2-3 (1989), would have added the following language to the NLRA's definition of employer: "Any two or more business entities engaged primarily in the building and construction industry, performing work within the geographical area covered by a collective bargaining agreement to which any of the entities is a party, performing the type of work described in such agreement, and having, directly or indirectly, substantial common ownership, substantial common management, or substantial common control, shall be deemed a single employer." This bill also would have amended §8(d) to include within the duty to bargain "the duty to apply the terms of a collective bargaining agreement between [a business entity comprising part of a single employer in the building and construction industry] and a labor organization to all other business entities comprising the single employer and performing the work described in the collective bargaining agreement within the geographical area covered by the agreement."

Is there a good reason why an entrepreneur who operates a unionized construction firm should not be able to operate a potentially competitive new firm with new employees free of any collective bargaining obligations, when an entrepreneur new to the market would have such freedom? Consider the competitive position in the Oklahoma construction market of Peter Kiewit Sons in the *South Prairie* case. Is your answer affected by whether the second business is established only to avoid having to pay the union scale on jobs where competitive nonunion bids are expected? By whether the entrepreneur uses equipment or other capital from the first business to operate the second?

**6. Section 301 Actions.** In addition to bringing unfair labor practice charges before the Board, a union might bring a §301 action to try to compel a newly established nonunion firm to observe the terms of an agreement that the union has with another competitive firm with common ownership. In light of *South Prairie,* which issues are properly decided by the §301 court, and which are within the Board's "primary jurisdiction" to decide? Compare Brown v. Sandino Materials, 250 F.3d 120 (2d Cir. 2001), and Carpenters Local Union No. 1846 v. Pratt-Farnsworth, Inc., 690 F.2d 489, 513-514 (5th Cir. 1982) (court may determine appropriateness of bargaining unit), with UA Local 343 v. Nor-Cal Plumbing, Inc., 48 F.3d 1465 (9th Cir. 1994), and Teamsters Local No. 70 v. California Consolidators, 693 F.2d 81, 82-83 (9th Cir. 1982) (unit determination must be made by Board). Should a court enforce an arbitration award requiring both employers to observe the terms of an agreement only if the award properly applied the Board's single employer or alter ego doctrines? See Gateway Structures, Inc. v. Carpenters Conference Bd., 779 F.2d 485 (9th Cir. 1985).

**7. Contractual Responses to Double-Breasting.** Section 8(e) may impede unions from contracting to restrict the ability of employers to invest in competitive nonunion firms. Consider, for instance, a clause in a collective agreement that provides for liquidated damages and a right to rescind the labor agreement if the employer has an ownership interest in any business entity "that engages in work within the scope of the agreement and that uses employees whose wage package, hours, and working conditions are inferior to those prescribed in the agreement." See, e.g., Sheet Metal Workers Local Union No. 91, 305 N.L.R.B. 1055 (1991) (finding such a clause violative of §8(e) because of its secondary objectives). But see Becker Elec. Co. v. Electrical Workers (IBEW) Local 212, 927 F.2d 895 (6th Cir. 1991) (clause that extends terms of agreement to work "heretofore" performed by the unit when performed by any entity owned by the employer or over which the employer exercises management or control does not violate §8(e) because of work preservation, rather than work acquisition purpose); Painters District Council 51, 321 N.L.R.B. 158 (1996) (following *Becker*); Virginia Sprinkler Co. v. Sprinkler Fitters Local Union 669, 868 F.2d 116 (4th Cir. 1989) (clause limited to imposing terms on any "single or joint employer" does not violate §7 right to refrain from bargaining or abridge Board's authority to define appropriate bargaining unit). Should Congress amend §8(e) to make it easier for unions to contract to restrict double-breasting? For discussion of §8(e), see supra pages 623-628.

**8. Employer's Disclosure Obligations.** Is a union legally entitled during bargaining to obtain information concerning the employer's relationship with another employer that the union reasonably believes is its alter ego? See, e.g., Brisco Sheet Metal, Inc., 307 N.L.R.B. 361 (1992); Maben Energy Corp., 295 N.L.R.B. 149 (1989) (yes). See supra pages 440-449.

**9. Double-Breasting Outside of the Construction Industry.** Should "double-breasted" operations in industries outside construction where firms do not directly bid on jobs receive different legal treatment? Consider the following hypothetical: Central Trucking, a unionized carrier, has been losing business on some of its major routes to a competitor, Mid-American Freight. In response, Central's holding company establishes a separate subsidiary, Democratic Express, which employs a new workforce at lower wages and benefits than those provided in Central's collective bargaining agreements. Democratic Express offers lower rates and has taken business from both Mid-American and Central. Democratic also has purchased some trucks and other equipment from Central but has totally separate management. Officers of the holding company of Central and Democratic state that Democratic was formed to compete more effectively in the market shared by Central and Mid-American. The unions representing

Central's employees have filed unfair labor practice charges against Democratic and the holding company, arguing that Democratic should be treated as a single employer with Central and should abide by the terms of Central's collective agreements. How should the Board rule? Does the analysis differ from a case in the construction industry?

## C. BANKRUPTCY, CHAPTER 11 REORGANIZATIONS, AND COLLECTIVE BARGAINING AGREEMENTS

An employer may attempt to escape the terms of a collective agreement by filing for bankruptcy and reorganization under Chapter 11 of the Bankruptcy Code. 11 U.S.C. §§1101-1174. Chapter 11 allows economically troubled businesses to avoid liquidation by filing for bankruptcy and presenting a plan for reorganization that specifies what each class of creditors is to be paid. Under §365 of the Bankruptcy Code, a party that has filed under Chapter 11 "may assume or reject any executory contract" subject to the approval of the bankruptcy court. Since the courts have viewed unexpired collective bargaining agreements, on which performance remains due on both sides, as executory contracts for purposes of §365, Chapter 11 may provide an escape from collective agreements.

Chapter 11 petitions are generally not attractive options for companies that are economically healthy. See James J. White, The *Bildisco* Case and the Congressional Response, 30 Wayne L. Rev. 1169, 1186-1189 (1984). However, with the upheaval in the American economy that began during the 1970s, including the deregulation of some heavily unionized industries and increased product market competition in others, companies in economic difficulty increasingly resorted to Chapter 11. As a result, in the late 1970s and early 1980s, a series of courts of appeals decisions addressed the standards by which bankruptcy courts were to treat debtors' attempts to reject collective agreements through Chapter 11. These decisions culminated in a 1984 Supreme Court decision, NLRB v. Bildisco, 465 U.S. 513.

### *Note:* **NLRB v. Bildisco** *and the Congressional Response*

The *Bildisco* Court unanimously agreed that Congress intended §365 to apply to collective bargaining agreements, despite the prohibition of unilateral terminations embodied in §8(d) of the NLRA. The Court also agreed with the courts of appeals that "because of the special nature of a collective-bargaining contract, and the consequent 'law of the shop' which it creates, a somewhat stricter standard should govern the decision of the Bankruptcy Court to allow rejection of a collective-bargaining agreement" than the deferential business-judgment standard used for commercial executory contracts. However, the Court rejected a proposed standard barring rejection of agreements absent proof that "reorganization will fail unless rejection is permitted." Rather, the bankruptcy court should permit rejection "if the debtor can show that the collective-bargaining agreement burdens the estate, and that after careful scrutiny, the equities balance in favor of rejecting the labor contract." Although this standard seems quite elastic, the Court further explained that "[s]ince the policy of Chapter 11 is to permit successful rehabilitation of debtors," the "Code does not authorize freewheeling consideration of every conceivable equity, but rather only how the equities relate to the success of the reorganization." The Court cautioned, however, that "[b]efore acting on a petition to modify or reject a collective-bargaining agreement, . . . the Bankruptcy Court should be persuaded that reasonable efforts to negotiate a voluntary modification have been made and are not likely to produce a prompt and satisfactory solution." The Court indicated that such reasonable efforts need not include full bargaining to impasse.

The *Bildisco* decision also addressed an additional issue: "whether the NLRB can find a debtor-in-possession guilty of an unfair labor practice for unilaterally rejecting or modifying a collective bargaining agreement before formal rejection by the Bankruptcy Court." By a 5-4 vote, the Court answered this question in the negative, finding that the rehabilitative purpose of Chapter 11 would be disserved if collective bargaining agreements remained enforceable contracts within the meaning of §8(d) after the filing of a petition in bankruptcy.

Unions condemned the *Bildisco* decision, especially its allowance of unilateral changes before a bankruptcy court has approved rejection of the collective agreement. In part because Congress was simultaneously under independent pressure to amend the Code to secure the constitutionality of the jurisdiction of bankruptcy courts, the unions succeeded in convincing Congress to also amend the Code's treatment of collective bargaining agreements. Section 1113 of the Code, enacted in 1984, embodies this amendment.

Section 1113 modifies the unanimous approach taken by the Court in the first part of *Bildisco.* It confirms that the bankruptcy court can reject a collective bargaining agreement and adopts *Bildisco*'s "balance of the equities" standard for doing so. However, §1113 provides that this balance must "clearly" favor rejection and specifies further prerequisites. Subsequent to filing a Chapter 11 petition and before filing an application for rejection of a collective agreement, a company must "make a proposal to the authorized representative . . . based on the most complete and reliable information available at the time of such proposal, which provides for those necessary modifications in the employees benefits, and protections that are necessary to permit the reorganization of the debtor." The proposal also must assure "that all creditors, the debtor and all of the affected parties are treated fairly and equitably," and the company must provide "the representative of the employees with such information as is necessary to evaluate the proposal."

Furthermore, until commencement of the court's hearing on the rejection petition, the company must "meet, at reasonable times, with the authorized representative to confer in good faith in attempting to reach mutually satisfactory modifications" of the agreement. Rejection is further conditioned on the union refusing to accept the company's modification proposal "without good cause."

In addition, §1113 displaces *Bildisco*'s second holding, which had permitted unilateral terminations or modifications of collective agreements upon the filing of a bankruptcy petition and before court approval of a request to reject the agreement. After §1113, absent bankruptcy court authorization, the NLRB may find an employer's unilateral modification or termination of a collective agreement after filing a bankruptcy petition to constitute a §8(a)(5) violation. See, e.g., Crest Litho, 308 N.L.R.B. 108 (1992). Section 1113, however, establishes explicit time limits for the bankruptcy court to hear and rule on a rejection application. A hearing on rejection ordinarily must be held within 14 days of the application, and if the court does not rule within a short period after commencement of the hearing (normally 30 days), the company or trustee may alter or terminate the contract pending the ruling. Furthermore, the court may, after notice and hearing, authorize the company to make interim changes in the collective agreement before its final ruling on rejection, "if essential to the continuation of the debtor's business, or in order to avoid irreparable damage to the estate."

## *NOTES AND QUESTIONS*

**1. Remaining Issues.** Section 1113 poses a number of difficult interpretive issues. They include the following:

a. *"Necessary" Modifications?* Concerning the proposal that a company seeking reorganization must make to a union prior to filing a petition for rejection, when are modifications in employee benefits and protections "necessary" to permit a reorganization? Compare Wheeling-Pittsburgh Steel Corp. v. United Steelworkers, 791 F.2d 1074, 1088-1089 (3d Cir. 1986) ("necessary" means "essential" to preventing the debtor's liquidation), with Truck Drivers Local 807 v. Carey Transp., Inc., 816 F.2d 82, 89-90 (2d Cir. 1987) ("necessary" does not mean "absolutely minimal," and long-term viability must be considered). *Truck Drivers* has been more influential. See, e.g., In re Mile High Systems, Inc., 899 F.2d 887, 892-893 (10th Cir. 1990). In order to meet the "necessary" standard, should any proposal have to contain a "snap-back" provision to restore sacrificed benefits in the event that the company's financial condition improves more rapidly than anticipated? Is the length of the proposed contract relevant to this question? If one proposed modification among many cannot be shown to be "necessary" to a successful reorganization, must the entire petition for rejection be denied? See In re Royal Composing Room, Inc., 848 F.2d 345 (2d Cir. 1988) ("focus should be on the proposal as a whole").

b. *"Fairly and Equitably" Treated?* What is added by the requirement that the proposal to the union must assure that all "affected parties are treated fairly and equitably"? Does this require the company to reduce the benefits of all unionized employees by a similar percentage? Must all creditors be disadvantaged in some comparable way? See, e.g., In re Garofalo's Finer Foods, Inc., 117 B.R. 363 (Bankr. N.D. Ill. 1990).

c. *Disclosure Obligations?* Does §1113's information disclosure provision embody NLRA good-faith bargaining standards developed under the *Truitt* decision, supra page 440, and thus require the release of data by employers who claim a financial inability to pay what the union seeks? Note that §1113(d)(3) provides that the bankruptcy court may enter a protective order to "prevent disclosure of information [that] . . . could compromise the position of the debtor with respect to its competitors in the industry in which it is engaged."

d. *"Confer in Good Faith"?* Does §1113's requirement that the company "meet at reasonable times" and "confer in good faith" with a union representative mean that the rejection of an agreement should not be permitted unless the company seeking reorganization meets NLRA standards of good-faith bargaining under §8(d) of the NLRA? Must there be bargaining to impasse? Or might standards of good-faith bargaining, or the definition of impasse, be adjusted in this context?

e. *Union's Refusal to Accept Proposed Modification "Without Good Cause"?* When does a union's refusal to accept a company's modification proposal constitute a refusal "without good cause"? Presumably "good cause" would be present if the company's proposal were not "necessary" or "fair and equitable," or if the company did not provide necessary information or otherwise confer in good faith. But if all of these requirements are met, should the court still evaluate the merits of the union's bargaining position to determine whether its refusal to accept the proposal was in good faith or at least reasonable? Would such an inquiry have any precedent in federal labor law? See, e.g., In re Maxwell Newspapers, Inc., 981 F.2d 85 (2d Cir. 1992) (requiring union to agree to necessary and fair proposal or to present adequate alternative); In re Allied Delivery Sys. Co., 49 B.R. 700, 704 (Bankr. N.D. Ohio 1985) (no good cause if proposal is necessary, fair, and equitable).

f. *"Balance of the Equities."* How is the bankruptcy court to determine whether the "balance of the equities clearly favors rejection" of the collective bargaining agreement? Does the addition of the word "clearly" mean anything more than that the agreement should not be rejected when the equities are in balance? Should the bankruptcy court weigh most heavily how important rejection is to successful rehabilitation of the debtor company? How much weight, if any, should the court give to factors such as the likelihood of a strike after abrogation of any no-strike clause in the rejected agreement, the absolute and relative (to other creditors) impact on the unionized employees, or the possibility that the debtor is trying to get rid of the union? See *Truck Drivers*, supra (listing as factors, inter alia, likelihood and consequence of strike, and good or bad faith of parties). Should the court also consider whether the collective bargaining agreement has already been breached by the debtor-in-possession? See United Steelworkers of America v. Unimet Corp., 842 F.2d 879 (6th Cir. 1988); Bill D. Bensinger, Modification of Collective Bargaining Agreements: Does a Breach Bar Rejection?, 13 Am. Bankr. Inst. L. Rev. 809 (2005).

g. *"Essential to the Continuation of the Employer's Business."* When should the bankruptcy court find it "essential to the continuation of the employer's business" to authorize the implementation of interim changes in the collective agreement pending a ruling on an application for rejection of the agreement? Should the standard for such interim releases be more stringent than that for rejection? Should the interim changes permitted ever be greater than those requested in a proposal to the union?

**2. Remedies for §1113 Violations.** Does the limited remedial response available to the bankruptcy court—refusal to approve rejection of the labor agreement—suggest that the procedural requirements of §1113 are not meaningful in practice? Will bankruptcy court judges be likely to refuse a petition to reject a collective agreement when rejection seems necessary to a successful reorganization, simply because the debtor company, for example, failed to provide full information to the union or failed to exhaust its bargaining obligations?

**3. Effect of Rejection of the Collective Agreement.** Section 1113 does not directly address the obligations of the debtor company after its application for rejection has been approved. Approval of rejection terminates the collective bargaining agreement, but *Bildisco* made clear that it does not abrogate the obligation of the debtor to deal with the union as the employees' bargaining agent. Approval of rejection also does not automatically change the terms and conditions of employment contained in the agreement.

If the bankruptcy court has approved interim changes in employment conditions pending its ruling on the rejection petition, these interim changes presumably constitute a new status quo that the employer can maintain until a new contract is negotiated or further changes are justified after bargaining to impasse. See In re D.O. & W. Coal Co., 93 B.R. 454 (Bankr. W.D. Va. 1988) (interim relief order continues in effect after expiration of labor agreement and becomes part of status quo that employer must observe). See generally Donald B. Smith & Richard A. Bales, Reconciling Labor and Bankruptcy Law, 2001 MSU L. Rev. 1146; Martha S. West, Life After *Bildisco*: Section 1113 and the Duty to Bargain in Good Faith, 47 Ohio St. L.J. 65, 151-159 (1986); Harvey R. Miller & Debra A. Dandenau, Bankruptcy Reorganization and Rejection of Collective Bargaining Agreements— An Alternative to Oppressive Labor Contracts, in Labor Law and Business Change: Theoretical and Transactional Perspectives, ch. 16 (Samuel Estreicher & Daniel G. Collins eds., 1988), and Michael E. Abram & Babette Ceccotti, Protecting Union Interests in Employer Bankruptcy, in id., ch. 17.

**4. Relevance of Norris-LaGuardia Act.** Does the Norris-LaGuardia Act bar a bankruptcy court from enjoining a strike whose object is to compel a debtor company to abide by its pre-reorganization petition obligations pending a ruling on the employer's application for rejection? What if the strike that the bankruptcy court is asked to enjoin seeks to influence the negotiation of a new agreement *after* rejection has been approved? Cf. In re Northwest Airlines, 349 B.R. 338 (S.D.N.Y. 2006) (after bankruptcy court's approval of rejection, enjoining strike as a violation of Railway Labor Act's prohibition of self-help until Act's settlement procedures are exhausted).

# 10 | Labor and the Antitrust Laws

## A. ORIGINS OF LABOR'S ANTITRUST EXEMPTION

**Apex Hosiery v. Leader**
*310 U.S. 469 (1940)*

[See pages 38-42 supra.]

**United States v. Hutcheson**
*312 U.S. 219 (1941)*

[See pages 42-46 supra.]

*NOTES AND QUESTIONS*

**1. Reach of *Apex Hosiery*?** What is the scope of the antitrust exemption recognized in the *Apex Hosiery* case? In what sense is it broader than the exemption recognized in *Hutcheson*? Narrower?

**2. Reach of *Hutcheson*?** Why did Justice Frankfurter not simply rely on the *Apex Hosiery* decision in *Hutcheson*? Why does the Court require that the union "act[] in its self-interest"? That it "does not combine with non-labor groups"? Do these two conditions indicate that there is no basis for concern that labor is aiding a business conspiracy? Are there agreements between unions and nonlabor groups, including many collective bargaining agreements, through which the unions clearly are not offering such help? See discussion of the "nonstatutory" exemption infra page 799.

**3. Basis for the *Hutcheson* Exemption.** On which statute is the exemption articulated in *Hutcheson* based? Are you convinced by Justice Frankfurter's argument that the Norris-LaGuardia Act, though ostensibly only about limitations on injunctions, also affects government criminal prosecutions? Does *Hutcheson* in effect overrule the interpretation of the Clayton Act given in *Duplex Printing*?

## B. UNILATERAL UNION ACTION AND AGREEMENTS WITH "LABOR GROUPS": THE "STATUTORY" EXEMPTION

When a union representing employees (as defined in the National Labor Relations Act (NLRA) and the Railway Labor Act (RLA)) or engaged in "labor disputes" within the reach of §13 of the Norris-LaGuardia Act acts unilaterally, *Hutcheson* makes clear that it enjoys an immunity from the antitrust laws. The Supreme Court in Connell Constr. Co. v. Plumbers, Local 100, 421 U.S. 616, 621-622 (1975), infra page 823, uses the term "statutory" exemption to refer to the antitrust immunity grounded in §§6 and 20 of the Clayton Act and the Norris-LaGuardia Act for unions acting on their own and without combination with "nonlabor groups." What does "labor group" mean in the *Hutcheson* formulation? Does labor's "statutory" exemption also cover union efforts to regulate independent businesses that are thought either to be in job and wage competition with union members or to function as intermediaries in the labor market? The Court grappled with this question in the case that follows.

### H.A. Artists & Associates, Inc. v. Actors' Equity Association
*451 U.S. 704 (1981)*

Justice STEWART delivered the opinion of the Court.

The respondent Actors' Equity Association (Equity) is a union representing the vast majority of stage actors and actresses in the United States. It enters into collective-bargaining agreements with theatrical producers that specify minimum wages and other terms and conditions of employment for those whom it represents. The petitioners are independent theatrical agents who place actors and actresses in jobs with producers. The Court of Appeals for the Second Circuit held that the respondents' system of regulation of theatrical agents is immune from antitrust liability by reason of the statutory labor exemption from the antitrust laws. . . .

#### I

Equity is a national union that has represented stage actors and actresses since early in this century. Currently representing approximately 23,000 actors and actresses, it has collective-bargaining agreements with virtually all major theatrical producers in New York City, on and off Broadway, and with most other theatrical producers throughout the United States. The terms negotiated with producers are the minimum conditions of employment (called "scale"); an actor or actress is free to negotiate wages or terms more favorable than the collectively bargained minima.

Theatrical agents are independent contractors who negotiate contracts and solicit employment for their clients. The agents do not participate in the negotiation of collective-bargaining agreements between Equity and the theatrical producers. If an agent succeeds in obtaining employment for a client, he receives a commission based on a percentage of the client's earnings. Agents who operate in New York City must be licensed as employment agencies and are regulated by the New York City Department of Consumer Affairs pursuant to New York law, which provides that the maximum commission a theatrical agent may charge his client is 10% of the client's compensation. . . .

The essential elements of Equity's regulation of theatrical agents have remained unchanged since 1928. A member of Equity is prohibited, on pain of union discipline, from using an agent who has not, through the mechanism of obtaining an Equity license (called a "franchise"), agreed to comply with the regulations. The most important of the regulations requires that a licensed agent must renounce any right to take a commission on an employment contract under which an actor or actress receives scale wages. To the extent a contract includes provisions under which an actor or actress will sometimes receive scale pay—for rehearsals or "chorus" employment, for example—and sometimes more, the regulations deny the agent any commission on the scale portions of the contract. Licensed agents are also precluded from taking commissions on out-of-town expense money paid to their clients. Moreover, commissions are limited on wages within 10% of scale pay, and an agent must allow his client to terminate a representation contract if the agent is not successful in procuring employment within a specified period. Finally, agents are required to pay franchise fees to Equity. . . .

The District Court found, after a bench trial, that Equity's creation and maintenance of the agency franchise system were fully protected by the statutory labor exemption from the antitrust laws, and accordingly dismissed the petitioners' complaint. Among its factual conclusions, the trial court found that in the theatrical industry, agents play a critical role in securing employment for actors and actresses:

> As a matter of general industry practice, producers seek actors and actresses for their productions through agents. Testimony in this case convincingly established that an actor without an agent does not have the same access to producers or the same opportunity to be seriously considered for a part as does an actor who has an agent. Even principal interviews, in which producers

> are required to interview all actors who want to be considered for principal roles, do not eliminate the need for an agent, who may have a greater chance of gaining an audition for his client.
>
> Testimony confirmed that agents play an integral role in the industry; without an agent, an actor would have significantly lesser chances of gaining employment.

The court also found "no evidence to suggest the existence of any conspiracy or illegal combination between Actors' Equity and [the agents' organization] or between Actors' Equity and producers," and concluded that "[t]he Actors' Equity franchising system was employed by Actors' Equity for the purpose of protecting the wages and working conditions of its members."

The Court of Appeals unanimously affirmed the judgment of the District Court. . . .

The Court of Appeals properly recognized that the threshold issue was to determine whether or not Equity's franchising of agents involved any combination between Equity and any "non-labor groups," or persons who are not "parties to a labor dispute." And the court's conclusion that the trial court had not been clearly erroneous in its finding that there was no combination between Equity and the theatrical producers to create or maintain the franchise system is amply supported by the record.

The more difficult problem is whether the combination between Equity and the agents who agreed to become franchised was a combination with a "nonlabor group." The answer to this question is best understood in light of Musicians v. Carroll, 391 U.S. 99. There, four orchestra leaders, members of the American Federation of Musicians, brought an action based on the Sherman Act challenging the union's unilateral system of regulating "club dates," or one-time musical engagements. These regulations, inter alia, enforced a closed shop; required orchestra leaders to engage a minimum number of "sidemen," or instrumentalists; prescribed minimum prices for local engagements;[22] prescribed higher minimum prices for traveling orchestras; and permitted leaders to deal only with booking agents licensed by the union.

Without disturbing the finding of the Court of Appeals that the orchestra leaders were employers and independent contractors, the Court concluded that they were nonetheless a "labor group" and parties to a "labor dispute" within the meaning of the Norris-LaGuardia Act, and thus that their involvement in the union regulatory scheme was not an unlawful

22. These consisted of a minimum scale for sidemen, a "leader's fee," which was twice the sidemen's scale in orchestras of at least four, and an additional 8% for social security, unemployment insurance, and other expenses. In addition, if a leader did not appear but designated a subleader, and four or more musicians performed, the leader was required to pay from his leader's fee 1.5 times the sidemen's scale to the subleader.

combination between "labor" and "nonlabor" groups. The Court agreed with the trial court that the applicable test was whether there was "job or wage competition or some other economic interrelationship affecting legitimate union interests between the union members and the independent contractors." Id., at 106.

The Court also upheld the restrictions on booking agents, who were *not* involved in job or wage competition with union members. Accordingly, these restrictions had to meet the "other economic interrelationship" branch of the disjunctive test quoted above. And the test was met because those restrictions were "'at least as intimately bound up with the subject of wages' . . . as the price floors." Id., at 113 (quoting Teamsters v. Oliver, 362 U.S. 605, 606). The Court noted that the booking agent restrictions had been adopted, in part, because agents had "charged exorbitant fees, and booked engagements for musicians at wages . . . below union scale."

The restrictions challenged by the petitioners in this case are very similar to the agent restrictions upheld in the *Carroll* case. The essential features of the regulatory scheme are identical: members are permitted to deal only with agents who have agreed (1) to honor their fiduciary obligations by avoiding conflicts of interest, (2) not to charge excessive commissions, and (3) not to book members for jobs paying less than the union minimum.[25] And as in *Carroll*, Equity's regulation of agents developed in response to abuses by employment agents who occupy a critical role in the relevant labor market. The agent stands directly between union members and jobs, and is in a powerful position to evade the union's negotiated wage structure.

The peculiar structure of the legitimate theater industry, where work is intermittent, where it is customary if not essential for union members to secure employment through agents, and where agents' fees are calculated as a percentage of a member's wage, makes it impossible for the union to defend even the integrity of the minimum wages it has negotiated without regulation of agency fees. The regulations are "brought within the labor exemption [because they are] necessary to assure that scale wages will be paid. . . ." *Carroll*, 391 U.S., at 112. They "embody . . . a direct frontal attack upon a problem thought to threaten the maintenance of the basic wage structure." Teamsters v. Oliver, 358 U.S. 283, 294. Agents must, therefore, be considered a "labor group," and their controversy with Equity is plainly a "labor dispute" as defined in the Norris-LaGuardia Act: "representation of

---

25. . . . The petitioners argue that theatrical agents are indistinguishable from "numerous [other] groups of persons who merely supply products and services to union members" such as landlords, grocers, accountants, and lawyers. But it is clear that agents differ from these groups in two critical respects: the agents control access to jobs and negotiation of the terms of employment. For the actor or actress, therefore, agent commissions are not merely a discretionary expenditure of disposable income, but a virtually inevitable concomitant of obtaining employment.

persons in negotiating, fixing, maintaining, changing, or seeking to arrange terms or conditions of employment, regardless of whether or not the disputants stand in the proximate relation of employer and employee." 29 U.S.C. §113(c).

Agents perform a function — the representation of union members in the sale of their labor — that in most nonentertainment industries is performed exclusively by unions. In effect, Equity's franchise system operates as a substitute for maintaining a hiring hall as the representative of its members seeking employment.

Finally, Equity's regulations are clearly designed to promote the union's legitimate self-interest. In a case such as this, where there is no direct wage or job competition between the union and the group it regulates, the *Carroll* formulation to determine the presence of a nonlabor group — whether there is "some . . . economic interrelationship affecting legitimate union interests . . . ," 391 U.S., at 106 . . . — necessarily resolves this issue.

The question remains whether the fees that Equity levies upon the agents who apply for franchises are a permissible component of the exempt regulatory system. We have concluded that Equity's justification for these fees is inadequate. Conceding that *Carroll* did not sanction union extraction of franchise fees from agents, Equity suggests, only in the most general terms, that the fees are somehow related to the basic purposes of its regulations: elimination of wage competition, upholding of the union wage scale, and promotion of fair access to jobs. But even assuming that the fees no more than cover the costs of administering the regulatory system, this is simply another way of saying that without the fees, the union's regulatory efforts would not be subsidized — and that the dues of Equity's members would perhaps have to be increased to offset the loss of a general revenue source. If Equity did not impose these franchise fees upon the agents, there is no reason to believe that any of its legitimate interests would be affected. . . .

[The opinion of Justice Brennan, with whom The Chief Justice and Justice Marshall join, concurring in part and dissenting in part, is omitted.]

## *NOTES AND QUESTIONS*

**1. What If the Agents Were Not a "Labor Group"?** Why was it necessary to find that the agents are a "labor group"? Is there any reason to suspect that the union regulated the agents in order to help cartelize the agents' commercial market rather than to secure control of the actors' labor market? Consider whether the nonstatutory exemption, treated infra, would have applied.

**2. Can the Agents Bargain Collectively?** In what sense are agents a "labor group"? Could agents organize themselves and insist on collective bargaining with actors and/or producers, free of antitrust exposure? Cf. Los

Angeles Meat & Provisions Drivers v. United States, 371 U.S. 94 (1962); Columbia Rivers Packers Ass'n v. Hinton, 315 U.S. 143 (1942).

**3. Can a "Labor Group" Combine with Those Having "Independent Contractor" Status Under the NLRA?** In Home Box Office, Inc. v. Directors Guild of Am., Inc., 531 F. Supp. 578 (S.D.N.Y 1982), a transmitter of pay-television programs brought an action to enjoin a television directors' union from enforcing certain agreements with, inter alia, freelance directors and producer-directors by which the latter would refuse to sell their services except on terms stipulated in the union's agreements with production companies. Negotiations between plaintiff Home Box Office (HBO) and the union failed to result in an agreement, and the union directed its members not to work for HBO or other nonsignatories or face union-imposed fines. The district court noted that in some respects the freelance directors were independent contractors: (a) they could accept or reject offers to direct particular shows; (b) they contracted to work on an individual program rather than for a fixed period; (c) they could accept more than one assignment simultaneously from different employers; and (d) they had discretion over who their assistants would be and over how they would perform their directing role in the show. In other respects, however, the freelance directors resembled traditional employees of the production companies for whom they worked: (a) they risked no capital and did not share in profits; (b) they did not control the time or the place of their work; (c) they had no "right to control" the creative elements of the shows they directed; and (d) they functioned in a manner similar to staff directors. District Judge Sofaer concluded (at 597) that the freelance directors were a "labor group":

> [F]reelance directors are employees, not independent contractors or entrepreneurs. Yet even without regard to that conclusion, the similarity of function and overlap of capacities among staff and freelance directors creates a mutuality of interest that readily justifies their bargaining collectively. If minimum wages or other conditions of employment differed materially for these two groups, the terms of employment enjoyed by the more advantaged group could well be affected by the availability of directorial services in the other group at lower prices. Staff and freelance directors are to a considerable extent interchangeable; indeed, employer decisions more than anything else determine throughout the industry whether a set of directors is on staff or freelance. Thus, staff and freelance directors are in much stronger job competition than were the musicians and bandleaders in . . . *Carroll*, which permitted a bargaining combination of the two groups.

**4. "Contingent" Workforce.** Does the result in *Home Box Office* change if standard industry practice is to use only freelance directors with no competing group of staff directors? What if the freelance directors are not considered employees under the NLRA? Does the definition of "labor dispute" in §13 of the Norris-LaGuardia demarcate the outer bounds of labor's "statutory" exemption from the antitrust laws? Consider this question in light of the increasing use by American firms of so-called "contingent" workers, performing services previously done by in-house employees. See supra pages 250-252.

**5. Regulation of Agents by Sports Unions.** Unions that represent players in collective bargaining with the major professional sports leagues also regulate the agents who negotiate individual contracts for the players. Unlike Actors' Equity, however, the sports unions do not regulate through control of their membership, but rather directly by asserting their authority as exclusive bargaining representatives to determine who may negotiate for bargaining unit members with the clubs. Is this form of regulation entitled to the statutory exemption provided in *H.A. Artists*? See, e.g., Collins v. National Basketball Players Ass'n, 850 F. Supp. 1468 (D. Colo. 1991).

**6. Union Price Setting for Labor Groups?** Note that in *Carroll* the union was permitted to set prices for band engagements. The Court justified this practice on the ground that labor costs were the principal determinant of prices:

> [T]he price of the product—here the price for an orchestra for a club date—represents almost entirely the scale wages of the sidemen and the leader. Unlike most industries, except for [an] 8% charge [to cover employment taxes and other expenses], there are no other costs contributing to the price. Therefore, if leaders cut prices, inevitably wages must be cut.

391 U.S. at 112. Justice White dissented on this point (at 116-117):

> The union has of course a full right to impose on this leader, who is in effect an employer, its minimum scale for work by sidemen and subleaders. The musicians union, however, goes further. It requires that, for an engagement of four or more musicians, the leader charge his customer not less than the sideman's scale times the number of musicians (including the subleader), plus double the sideman's scale to compensate the leader, of which one-fourth—plus the sideman's scale—goes to the subleader. The union is clearly requiring that the leader charge his customer more than the total of the leader's wage bill, even though the leader himself does no "labor group" work.

Does the Court's reluctance in *H.A. Artists* to sustain the union's franchise fees for agents suggest that even in the context of a union's regulation of a "labor group," restrictions that are not necessary to protect wage and job standards of union members are subject to antitrust scrutiny? Reconsider after reading the *Jewel Tea* decision below.

## C. AGREEMENTS WITH "NONLABOR GROUPS": THE "NONSTATUTORY" EXEMPTION

The "statutory" exemption has limited application because unions generally need to obtain agreements with nonlabor groups in order to promote the interest of their members. The need to provide some measure of protection for collective bargaining agreements led to judicial development of a "nonstatutory exemption" in recognition of the fact that "a proper accommodation between the congressional policy favoring collective bargaining under the NLRA and the congressional policy favoring free competition requires that some union-employer agreements be accorded a limited nonstatutory exemption from antitrust sanctions." Connell Constr. v. Plumbers, Local 100, 421 U.S. 616, 622 (1975), infra page 823.

**Allen Bradley Co. v. Local 3, IBEW**
*325 U.S. 797 (1945)*

BLACK, J. . . .

[Petitioners, manufacturers of electrical equipment outside of New York City and, for the most part, outside of New York State as well, brought this action because they had been excluded from the New York City market through activities of respondents and others.]

Respondents are a labor union, its officials and its members. The union, Local No. 3 of the International Brotherhood of Electrical Workers [IBEW], has jurisdiction only over the metropolitan area of New York City. It is therefore impossible for the union to enter into a collective bargaining agreement with petitioners. Some of petitioners do have collective bargaining agreements with other unions, and in some cases even with other locals of the IBEW.

Some of the members of respondent union work for manufacturers who produce electrical equipment similar to that made by petitioners; other members of respondent union are employed by contractors and work on the installation of electrical equipment, rather than in its production.

The union's consistent aim for many years has been to expand its membership, to obtain shorter hours and increased wages, and to enlarge employment opportunities for its members. To achieve this latter goal — that is, to make more work for its own members — the union realized that local manufacturers, employers of the local members, must have the widest possible outlets for their product. The union therefore waged aggressive campaigns to obtain closed-shop agreements with all local electrical equipment manufacturers and contractors. Using conventional labor union methods, such as strikes and boycotts, it gradually obtained more and more closed-shop agreements in the New York City area. Under these agreements, contractors were obligated to purchase equipment from none but local manufacturers who also had closed-shop agreements with Local No. 3; manufacturers obligated themselves to confine their New York City sales to contractors employing the Local's members. In the course of time, this type of individual employer-employee agreement expanded into industry-wide understandings, looking not merely to terms and conditions of employment but also to price and market control. Agencies were set up composed of representatives of all three groups to boycott recalcitrant local contractors and manufacturers and to bar from the area equipment manufactured outside its boundaries. The combination among the three groups, union, contractors, and manufacturers, became highly successful from the standpoint of all of them. . . . Quite obviously, this combination of business men has violated both §§1 and 2 of the Sherman Act, unless its conduct is immunized by the participation of the union. For it intended to and did restrain trade in and monopolize the supply of electrical equipment in the New York City area to the exclusion of equipment manufactured in and shipped from other states, and did also control its price and discriminate between its would-be customers. Apex Hosiery Co. v. Leader, 310 U.S. 469, 512-513 [(1940)]. Our problem in this case is therefore a very narrow one—do labor unions violate the Sherman Act when, in order to further their own interests as wage earners, they aid and abet business men to do the precise things which that Act prohibits? . . .

. . . It has been argued that [the immunity claimed by the defendants] can be inferred from a union's right to make bargaining agreements with its employer. Since union members can without violating the Sherman Act strike to enforce a union boycott of goods, it is said they may settle the strike by getting their employers to agree to refuse to buy the goods. Employers and the union did here make bargaining agreements in which the employers agreed not to buy goods manufactured by companies which did not employ the members of Local No. 3. We may assume that such an agreement standing alone would not have violated the Sherman Act. But it did not stand alone. It was but one element in a far larger program in which contractors and manufacturers united with one another to monopolize all the business in New York City, to bar all other business men from that area, and to charge the public prices above a competitive level. It is true that victory of the union in its disputes, even had the union acted alone, might have added to the cost of goods, or might have resulted in individual refusals of all of their employers to buy electrical equipment not made by Local No. 3. So far as the union might have achieved this result acting alone, it would have been the natural consequence of labor union activities exempted by the Clayton Act from the coverage of the Sherman Act. *Apex Hosiery Co. v. Leader*, supra, 503. But when the unions participated with a combination of business men who had complete power to eliminate all competition among themselves and to prevent all competition from others, a situation was created not included within the exemptions of the Clayton and Norris-LaGuardia Acts. . . .

Respondents objected to the form of the injunction and specifically requested that it be amended so as to enjoin only those prohibited activities in which the union engaged in combination "with any person, firm or corporation which is a nonlabor group. . . ." Without such a limitation, the injunction as issued runs directly counter to the Clayton and the Norris-LaGuardia Acts. The district court's refusal so to limit it was error.

The judgment of the Court of Appeals ordering the action dismissed is accordingly reversed and the cause is remanded to the district court for modification and clarification of the judgment and injunction, consistent with this opinion.

[Urging that the union had been the dynamic force behind the formation of the challenged agreements—a finding made by the trial court (41 F. Supp. 727, 750 (S.D.N.Y. 1941)) and not disturbed on appeal—Justice Murphy dissented; Justice Roberts concurred only in the Court's result.]

## *NOTES AND QUESTIONS*

**1. The Court's Holding?** Which of the following statements best describes the Court's holding in *Allen Bradley?*

a. The arrangement was a sham: Employers used the union as a pretext for cartelizing the product market. See Herbert N. Bernhardt, The *Allen Bradley* Doctrine: An Accommodation of Conflicting Policies, 110 U. Pa. L. Rev. 1094, 1099 (1962).

b. The characteristics of the market restriction determine the scope of labor's exemption: Labor loses its exemption when it is party to market restrictions that businesses on their own might devise without union pressure. See Bernard D. Meltzer, Labor Unions, Collective Bargaining and the Antitrust Laws, 32 U. Chi. L. Rev. 659, 676 (1965).

c. The characteristics of management's behavior control: Management's failure to resist the union's activity indicates a combination violative of the antitrust laws rather than a product of arm's-length collective bargaining. See Ralph K. Winter, Collective Bargaining and Competition: The Application of Antitrust Standards to Union Activities, 73 Yale L.J. 14, 49-50 (1963).

**2. Section 8(e) Liability?** *Allen Bradley* was decided before the Taft-Hartley amendments proscribing secondary pressures by unions. In a portion of its opinion in National Woodwork Manufacturers Ass'n v. NLRB, 386 U.S. 612, 629-631 (1967), supra page 623, the Court distinguished *Allen Bradley* in the following manner:

> . . . [T]he fact is that the boycott in *Allen Bradley* was carried on, not as a shield to preserve the jobs of Local 3 members, traditionally a primary labor activity, but as a sword, to reach out and monopolize all the manufacturing job tasks for Local 3 members. . . . But the boycott in the present case was not used as a sword; it was a shield carried solely to preserve the members' jobs. We therefore have no occasion today to decide the questions which might arise where the workers carry on a boycott to reach out to monopolize jobs or acquire new job tasks when their own jobs are not threatened by the boycotted product.

**3. Alternative Arrangements?** Suppose that the union and the contractors' association in a multiemployer agreement stipulated that the contractors would use only components bearing the Local 3 label, no price-fixing or other forms of market control had occurred, and the union had no agreement with the manufacturers restricting the contractors with whom they could deal. Would the agreement with the contractors, standing alone, be subject to Sherman Act challenge? Would it violate §8(e) of the NLRA? Is it likely the restrictions would benefit any of the signatory employers? Should this be relevant to the issue of antitrust immunity?

### United Mine Workers v. Pennington
*381 U.S. 657 (1965)*

WHITE, J. . . .

This action began as a suit by the trustees of the United Mine Workers of America [UMW] Welfare and Retirement Fund against . . . Phillips Brothers Coal Company . . . seeking to recover some $55,000 in royalty payments [allegedly] due under the trust provisions of the National Bituminous Coal Wage Agreement of 1950, as amended. . . . Phillips filed an answer and a cross claim against UMW, alleging in both that the trustees, the UMW and certain large coal operators had conspired to restrain and to monopolize interstate commerce in violation of §§1 and 2 of the Sherman Antitrust Act, as amended. Actual damages . . . of $100,000 were claimed for the period [from] February 14, 1954 [to] December 31, 1958.

[Phillips's] allegations were essentially as follows: Prior to the 1950 Wage Agreement between the operators and the union, severe controversy had existed in the industry, particularly over wages, the welfare fund and the union's efforts to control the working time of its members. Since 1950, however, relative peace has existed in the industry, all as the result of the 1950 Wage Agreement and its amendments and the additional understandings entered into between UMW and the large operators. Allegedly the parties considered overproduction to be the critical problem of the coal industry. The agreed solution was to be the elimination of the smaller companies, the larger companies thereby controlling the market. More specifically, the union abandoned its efforts to control the working time of the miners, agreed not to oppose the rapid mechanization of the mines which would substantially reduce mine employment, agreed to help finance such mechanization and agreed to impose the terms of the 1950 agreement on all operators without regard to their ability to pay. The benefit to the union was to be increased wages as productivity increased with mechanization, these increases to be demanded of the smaller companies whether mechanized or not. Royalty payments into the welfare fund were to be increased also, and the union was to have effective control over the fund's use. The union and large companies agreed upon other steps to exclude the marketing, production, and sale of nonunion coal. Thus the companies agreed not to lease coal lands to nonunion operators, and in 1958 agreed not to sell or buy coal from such companies. . . .

The complaint survived motions to dismiss and after a five-week trial before a jury, a verdict was returned in favor of Phillips and against the trustees and the union, the damages against the union being fixed in the amount of $90,000, to be trebled under 15 U.S.C. §15 (1958 ed.). The trial court set aside the verdict against the trustees but overruled the union's motion for judgment notwithstanding the verdict or in the alternative for a new trial. The Court of Appeals affirmed. . . .

We first consider UMW's contention that the trial court erred in denying its motion for a directed verdict and for judgment notwithstanding the verdict, since a determination in UMW's favor on this issue would finally resolve the controversy. The question presented by this phase of the case is whether in the circumstances of this case the union is exempt from liability under the antitrust laws. We think the answer is clearly in the negative and that the union's motions were correctly denied. . . .

If the UMW in this case, in order to protect its wage scale by maintaining employer income, had presented a set of prices at which the mine operators would be required to sell their coal, the union and the employers who happened to agree could not successfully defend this contract provision if it were challenged under the antitrust laws by the United States or by some party injured by the arrangement. Cf. Allen Bradley Co. v. Union, 325 U.S. 797. . . . In such a case, the restraint on the product market is direct and immediate, is of the type characteristically deemed unreasonable under the Sherman Act and the union gets from the promise nothing more concrete than a hope for better wages to come.

A major part of Phillips' case, however, was that the union entered into a conspiracy with the large operators to impose the agreed-upon wage and royalty scales upon the smaller, nonunion operators, regardless of their ability to pay and regardless of whether or not the union represented the employees of these companies, all for the purpose of eliminating them from the industry, limiting production and preempting the market for the large, unionized operators. The UMW urges that since such an agreement concerned wage standards, it is exempt from the antitrust laws.

It is true that wages lie at the very heart of those subjects about which employers and unions must bargain and the law contemplates agreements on wages not only between individual employers and a union but agreements between the union and employers in a multiemployer bargaining unit. Labor Board v. Truck Drivers Union, 353 U.S. 87, 94-96. The union benefit from the wage scale agreed upon is direct and concrete and the effect on the product market, though clearly present, results from the elimination of competition based on wages among the employers in the bargaining unit, which is not the kind of restraint Congress intended the Sherman Act to proscribe. Apex Hosiery Co. v. Leader, 310 U.S. 469, 503-504. . . . We think it beyond question that a union may conclude a wage agreement with the multiemployer bargaining unit without violating the antitrust laws and that it may as a matter of its own policy, and not by agreement with all or part of the employers of that unit, seek the same wages from other employers.

This is not to say that an agreement resulting from union-employer negotiations is automatically exempt from Sherman Act scrutiny simply because the negotiations involve a compulsory subject of bargaining, regardless of the subject or the form and content of the agreement. . . . [T]here are limits to what a union or an employer may offer or extract in the name of wages, and because they must bargain does not mean that the agreement reached may disregard other laws. Teamsters Union v. Oliver, 358 U.S. 283, 296. . . .

We have said that a union may make wage agreements with a multi-employer bargaining unit and may in pursuance of its own union interests seek to obtain the same terms from other employers. No case under the antitrust laws could be made out on evidence limited to such union behavior.[2] But we think a union forfeits its exemption from the antitrust laws when it is clearly shown that it has agreed with one set of employers to impose a certain wage scale on other bargaining units. One group of employers may not conspire to eliminate competitors from the industry and the union is liable with the employers if it becomes a party to the conspiracy. This is true even though the union's part in the scheme is an undertaking to secure the

2. Unilaterally, and without agreement with any employer group to do so, a union may adopt a uniform wage policy and seek vigorously to implement it even though it may suspect that some employers cannot effectively compete if they are required to pay the wage scale demanded by the union. The union need not gear its wage demands to wages which the weakest units in the industry can afford to pay. Such union conduct is not alone sufficient evidence to maintain a union-employer conspiracy charge under the Sherman Act. There must be additional direct or indirect evidence of the conspiracy. There was, of course, other evidence in this case, but we indicate no opinion as to its sufficiency.

same wages, hours or other conditions of employment from the remaining employers in the industry.

. . . [T]here is nothing in the labor policy indicating that the union and the employers in one bargaining unit are free to bargain about the wages, hours and working conditions of other bargaining units or to attempt to settle these matters for the entire industry. On the contrary, the duty to bargain unit by unit leads to a quite different conclusion. The union's obligation to its members would seem best served if the union retained the ability to respond to each bargaining situation as the individual circumstances might warrant, without being strait-jacketed by some prior agreement with the favored employers. . . .

. . . [T]he policy of the antitrust laws is clearly set against employer-union agreements seeking to prescribe labor standards outside the bargaining unit. One could hardly contend, for example, that one group of employers could lawfully demand that the union impose on other employers wages that were significantly higher than those paid by the requesting employers, or a system of computing wages that, because of differences in methods of production, would be more costly to one set of employers than to another. The anticompetitive potential of such a combination is obvious, but is little more severe than what is alleged to have been the purpose and effect of the conspiracy in this case to establish wages at a level that marginal producers could not pay so that they would be driven from the industry. And if the conspiracy presently under attack were declared exempt it would hardly be possible to deny exemption to such avowedly discriminatory schemes.

From the viewpoint of antitrust policy, moreover, all such agreements between a group of employers and a union that the union will seek specified labor standards outside the bargaining unit suffer from a more basic defect, without regard to predatory intention or effect in the particular case. For the salient characteristic of such agreements is that the union surrenders its freedom of action with respect to its bargaining policy. Prior to the agreement the union might seek uniform standards in its own self-interest but would be required to assess in each case the probable costs and gains of a strike or other collective action to that end and thus might conclude that the objective of uniform standards should temporarily give way. After the agreement the union's interest would be bound in each case to that of the favored employer group. It is just such restraints upon the freedom of economic units to act according to their own choice and discretion that run counter to antitrust policy. . . .

DOUGLAS, J., with whom BLACK and CLARK, JJ., agree, concurring. As we read the opinion of the Court, it reaffirms the principles of [Allen Bradley Co. v. Local 3, IBEW, 325 U.S. 797 (1945)].

*First.* On the new trial the jury should be instructed that if there were an industry-wide collective bargaining agreement whereby employees and the union agreed on a wage scale that exceeded the financial ability of some operators to pay and that if it was made for the purpose of forcing some employers out of business, the union as well as the employers who participated in the arrangement with the union should be found to have violated the antitrust laws.

*Second.* An industry-wide agreement containing those features is prima facie evidence of a violation. . . .

[Justice Goldberg, in an opinion joined by Justices Harlan and Stewart, concurred in the reversal but dissented from the grounds relied on in the opinion by Justice White. Excerpts from this concurring opinion appear infra page 811.]

## *NOTES AND QUESTIONS*

**1. Subsequent Proceedings.** On remand in *Pennington,* the trial judge, after a bench trial, dismissed the complaint, noting that the Supreme Court's opinion requires "predatory intent to drive small coal operators out of business in order to hold the employer and the union for a violation of the Sherman Act." Lewis v. Pennington, 257 F. Supp. 815, 829 (E.D. Tenn. 1966), affirmed, 400 F.2d 806, 814 (6th Cir. 1968). However, other similarly situated coal companies were successful in their actions against the UMW under the Sherman Act. See, e.g., Tennessee Consol. Coal Co. v. UMW, 416 F.2d 1192 (6th Cir. 1969) (jury trial; damages after reduction with plaintiff's consent and trebling amounted to $1.4 million for one plaintiff plus $150,000 attorney fees and $67,500 for another plaintiff).

**2. Intent vs. Impact?** Did the trial court on remand correctly read *Pennington* to require a finding of "predatory intent"? Should a union be insulated from antitrust liability if it enters into a wage-setting agreement that foreseeably drives some employers from a product market, where its intent is simply to maintain labor standards throughout the industry? Assume, for instance, that a union and a multiemployer group agree to wages that are likely to and do eliminate marginal producers who have not mechanized and whose wages constitute a larger percentage of total costs than do the wages of larger producers who dominate the multiemployer group. Should that agreement be vulnerable to antitrust challenge?

**3. Union "Surrender of Freedom of Action"?** Why does Justice White stress that by the agreements in *Pennington* "the union surrenders its freedom of action with respect to its bargaining policy"? Was the union's willingness to sacrifice its "freedom of action" evidence of an intent to aid larger "favored employers" so as to foreclose competition from smaller employers? Or did the union simply decide that it could better enhance the welfare of represented employees by agreeing to a uniform wage policy, regardless of the economic fate of smaller operators? Reconsider these issues after reading the next principal case.

**4. "Me-Too" vs. "They-Too" Agreements.** A union and an employer (or an employers' association), accounting for 60 percent of the output of a given industry, enter into a collective bargaining agreement with the following "most favored nation" or "me-too" clause: "The union agrees that if it grants an employer competing with the signatory employer (or employers) lower wages or better terms or conditions than those prescribed herein, the union will immediately advise the signatory employer(s) and give them the benefit of such lower wages or more favorable terms and conditions." Would such an agreement be exempt from the Sherman Act? In Dolly Madison Indus., 182 N.L.R.B. 1037 (1970), the NLRB distinguished such a "me-too" clause from the "they-too" clause in *Pennington* and concluded that the former clause, in the absence of a "predatory purpose," would not violate the Sherman Act and was, accordingly, a mandatory subject of bargaining on which the employer could lawfully insist to the point of impasse. Cf. Associated Milk Dealers, Inc. v. Milk Drivers, Local 753, 422 F.2d 546 (7th Cir. 1970) ("most favored nation" clause not illegal per se; predatory purpose must be shown).

Are the objectives of the signatory parties or the probable impact of any agreement on third parties different in the case of "me-too" clauses than in the case of "they-too" clauses? Are "me-too" clauses less likely to be used as part of a predatory campaign to drive out competitors? Does the availability of the less restrictive "me-too" clause, which appears to further at least as well the legitimate interest of the signatory parties in maintaining uniform labor standards, support a finding that the negotiation of any "they-too" clause must have been for a predatory purpose or will have an unnecessary anticompetitive effect?

### Local 189, Meat Cutters v. Jewel Tea Co.
*381 U.S. 676 (1965)*

WHITE, J., announced the judgment of the Court and delivered an opinion in which WARREN, C.J., and BRENNAN, J., join. . . .

[This case] concerns the lawfulness of the following restriction on the operating hours of food store meat departments contained in a collective bargaining agreement executed after joint multiemployer multiunion negotiations: "Market operating hours shall be 9:00 A.M. to 6:00 P.M. Monday through Saturday, inclusive. No customer shall be served who comes into the market before or after the hours set forth above."

This litigation arose out of the 1957 contract negotiations between the representatives of 9,000 Chicago retailers of fresh meat and the seven union petitioners, who are local affiliates of the Amalgamated Meat Cutters and

Butcher Workmen of North America, AFL-CIO, representing virtually all butchers in the Chicago area. During the 1957 bargaining sessions the employer group presented several requests for union consent to a relaxation of the existing contract restriction on marketing hours for fresh meat, which forbade the sale of meat before 9 A.M. and after 6 P.M. in both service and self-service markets. The unions rejected all such suggestions, and their own proposal retaining the marketing-hours restriction was ultimately accepted at the final bargaining session by all but two of the employers, National Tea Co. and Jewel Tea Co. (hereinafter "Jewel"). Associated Food Retailers of Greater Chicago, a trade association having about 1,000 individual and independent merchants as members and representing some 300 meat dealers in the negotiations, was among those who accepted. Jewel, however, asked the union negotiators to present to their membership, on behalf of it and National Tea, a counter-offer that included provision for Friday night operations. At the same time Jewel voiced its belief, as it had midway through the negotiations, that any marketing-hours restriction was illegal. On the recommendation of the union negotiators, the Jewel offer was rejected by the union membership, and a strike was authorized. Under the duress of the strike vote, Jewel decided to sign the contract previously approved by the rest of the industry.

In July 1958 Jewel brought suit against the unions, . . . Associated, and Charles H. Bromann, Secretary-Treasurer of Associated, seeking invalidation under §§1 and 2 of the Sherman Act of the contract provision that prohibited night meat market operations. The gist of the complaint was that the defendants and others had conspired together to prevent the retail sale of fresh meat before 9 A.M. and after 6 P.M. As evidence of the conspiracy Jewel relied in part on the events during the 1957 contract negotiations—the acceptance by Associated of the market-hours restriction and the unions' imposition of the restriction on Jewel through a strike threat. . . .

The complaint [alleged]: In recent years the prepackaged, self-service system of marketing meat had come into vogue, that 174 of Jewel's 196 stores were equipped to vend meat in this manner, and a butcher need not be on duty in a self-service market at the time meat purchases were actually made. The prohibition of night meat marketing unlawfully impeded Jewel in the use of its property and adversely affected the general public in that many persons find it inconvenient to shop during the day. An injunction, treble damages and attorneys' fees were demanded.

. . . After trial, the District judge ruled the "record was devoid of any evidence to support a finding of conspiracy" between Associated and the unions to force the restrictive provision on Jewel. Testing the unions' action standing alone, the trial court found that even in self-service markets removal of the limitation on marketing hours either would inaugurate longer hours and night work for the butchers or would result in butchers' work being done by others unskilled in the trade. Thus, the court concluded, the unions had imposed the marketing-hours limitation to serve their own interests respecting conditions of employment and such action was clearly within the labor exemption of the Sherman Act. . . .

The Court of Appeals reversed the dismissal of the complaint as to both the unions and Associated. . . .

We . . . now reverse the Court of Appeals.

[Part I (reflecting the Court's unanimous position) rejected the union's contention that the case was within the NLRB's "primary and exclusive jurisdiction." The Court suggested, first, that a characterization of the disputed clause as an item of mandatory bargaining would not have controlled the Sherman Act claim. Second, the Board's machinery would not be available when, for example, an agreement challenged under the Sherman Act had been reached without insistent bargaining.]

**II . . .**

It is well at the outset to emphasize that this case comes to us stripped of any claim of a union-employer conspiracy against Jewel. The trial court found no evidence to sustain Jewel's conspiracy claim and this finding was not disturbed by the Court of Appeals. We therefore have a situation where the unions, having obtained a marketing-hours agreement from one group of employers, have successfully sought the same terms from a single employer, Jewel, not as a result of a bargain between the unions and some employers directed against other employers, but pursuant to what the unions deemed to be in their own labor union interests.

Jewel does not allege that it has been injured by the elimination of competition among the other employers within the unit with respect to marketing hours: Jewel complains only of the unions' action in forcing it to accept the same restriction, the unions acting not at the behest of any employer group but in pursuit of their own policies. . . .

We pointed out in *Pennington* that exemption for union-employer agreements is very much a matter of accommodating the coverage of the Sherman Act to the policy of the labor laws. Employers and unions are required to bargain about wages, hours and working conditions, and this fact weighs heavily in favor of antitrust exemption for agreements on these subjects. But neither party need bargain about other matters and either party commits an unfair labor practice if it conditions its bargaining upon discussions of a nonmandatory subject. Labor Board v. Borg-Warner Corp., 356 U.S. 342. Jewel, for example, need not have bargained about or agreed to a schedule of prices at which its meat would be sold and the unions could not legally have insisted that it do so. But if the unions had made such a demand, Jewel had agreed and the United States or an injured party had challenged the agreement under the antitrust laws, we seriously doubt that either the unions or Jewel could claim immunity by reason of the labor exemption, whatever substantive questions of violation there might be.

Thus the issue in this case is whether the marketing-hours restriction, like wages, and unlike prices, is so intimately related to wages, hours and working conditions that the unions' successful attempt to obtain that provision through bona fide, arm's-length bargaining in pursuit of their own labor union policies, and not at the behest of or in combination with nonlabor groups, falls within the protection of the national labor policy and is therefore exempt from the Sherman Act.[5] We think that it is.

The Court of Appeals would classify the marketing-hours restriction with the product-pricing provision and place both within the reach of the Sherman Act. In its view, labor has a legitimate interest in the number of hours it must work but no interest in whether the hours fall in the daytime, in the nighttime or on Sundays. . . .

Contrary to the Court of Appeals, we think that the particular hours of the day and the particular days of the week during which employees shall be required to work are subjects well within the realm of "wages, hours, and other terms and conditions of employment" about which employers and unions must bargain. . . . And, although the effect on competition is apparent and real, perhaps more so than in the case of the wage agreement, the concern of union members is immediate and direct. Weighing the respective interests involved, we think the national labor policy expressed in the National Labor Relations Act places beyond the reach of the Sherman Act union-employer agreements on when, as well as how long, employees must work. An agreement on these subjects between the union and the employers in a bargaining unit is not illegal under the Sherman Act, nor is the union's unilateral demand for the same contract of other employers in the industry. . . .

If it were true that self-service markets could actually operate without butchers, at least for a few hours after 6 P.M., that no encroachment on

5. The crucial determinant is not the form of the agreement—e.g., prices or wages—but its relative impact on the product market and the interests of union members. Thus in Teamsters Union v. Oliver [362 U.S. 605 (1959)], we held that federal labor policy precluded application of state antitrust laws to an employer-union agreement that when leased trucks were driven by their owners, such owner-drivers should receive, in addition to the union wage, not less than a prescribed minimum rental. Though in form a scheme fixing prices for the supply of leased vehicles, the agreement was designed "to protect the negotiated wage scale against the possible undermining through diminution of the owner's wages for driving which might result from a rental which did not cover his operating cost." Id., at 293-294. As the agreement did not embody a "'remote and indirect approach to the subject of wages' . . . but a direct frontal attack upon a problem thought to threaten the maintenance of the basic wage structure established by the collective bargaining contract," id., at 294, the paramount federal policy of encouraging collective bargaining proscribed application of the state law. See also Meat Drivers v. United States, 371 U.S. 94, 98; Milk Wagon Drivers' Union, Local No. 753 v. Lake Valley Farm Products, Inc., 311 U.S. 91.

butchers' work would result and that the workload of butchers during normal working hours would not be substantially increased, Jewel's position would have considerable merit. For then the obvious restraint on the product market — the exclusion of self-service stores from the evening market for meat — would stand alone, unmitigated and unjustified by the vital interests of the union butchers which are relied upon in this case. In such event the limitation imposed by the unions might well be reduced to nothing but an effort by the unions to protect one group of employers from competition by another, which is conduct that is not exempt from the Sherman Act. Whether there would be a violation of §§1 and 2 would then depend on whether the elements of a conspiracy in restraint of trade or an attempt to monopolize had been proved.

Thus the dispute between Jewel and the unions essentially concerns a narrow factual question: Are night operations without butchers, and without infringement of butchers' interests, feasible? The District Court resolved this factual dispute in favor of the unions. It found that "in stores where meat is sold at night it is impractical to operate without either butchers or other employees. Someone must arrange, replenish and clean the counters and supply customer services." Operating without butchers would mean that "their work would be done by others unskilled in the trade," and "would involve an increase in workload in preparing for the night work and cleaning the next morning." Those findings were not disturbed by the Court of Appeals. . . . Our function is limited to reviewing the record to satisfy ourselves that the trial judge's findings are not clearly erroneous. Fed. R. Civ. P. 52(a). [The court concluded that the findings were not clearly erroneous.] . . .

Goldberg, J., with whom Harlan and Stewart, JJ., join, dissenting from the opinion but concurring in the reversal in *Pennington* and concurring in the judgment of the Court in *Jewel Tea*. . . .

. . . [T]he Court should hold that, in order to effectuate congressional intent, collective bargaining activity concerning mandatory subjects of bargaining under the Labor Act is not subject to the antitrust laws. This rule flows directly from the *Hutcheson* holding that a union acting as a union, in the interests of its members, and not acting to fix prices or allocate markets in aid of an employer conspiracy to accomplish these objects, with only indirect union benefits, is not subject to challenge under the antitrust laws. To hold that mandatory collective bargaining is completely protected would effectuate the congressional policies of encouraging free collective bargaining subject only to specific restrictions contained in the labor laws, and of limiting judicial intervention in labor matters via the antitrust route — an intervention which necessarily under the Sherman Act places on judges and juries the determination of "what public policy in regard to the industrial struggle demands." Duplex Co. v. Deering, [254 U.S. 443, 485 (1921)] (dissenting opinion of Brandeis, J.). . . .

DOUGLAS, J., with whom BLACK and CLARK, JJ., concur, dissenting. . . .

. . . [I]n the circumstances of this case the collective bargaining agreement itself, of which the District Court said there was clear proof, was evidence of a conspiracy among the employers with the unions to impose the marketing-hours restriction on Jewel via a strike threat by the unions. This tended to take from the merchants who agreed among themselves their freedom to work their own hours and to subject all who, like Jewel, wanted to sell meat after 6 P.M. to the coercion of threatened strikes, all of which if done in concert only by businessmen would violate the antitrust laws. See Fashion Guild v. Federal Trade Comm'n, 312 U.S. 457, 465. . . .

## *NOTES AND QUESTIONS*

**1. Permissible Product Market Restraints?** Are you convinced by the trial court's findings, relied on by Justice White's opinion for a plurality of the Court, that a direct product market restraint—the limitation on the operating hours of meat departments—was the only way the union could achieve its legitimate labor market objectives of (a) preventing nonbutchers from doing butchers' work, and (b) preventing an increase in the workload of butchers in preparing for and cleaning up after night operations? Could the union just as readily through negotiated work rules have required additional compensation for night work and any additional preparation and cleaning tasks? Does *Jewel Tea*, in effect, permit certain negotiated restraints on product market competition among members of a multiemployer association where (a) the restraints are insisted on by the unions, and (b) the unions can assert plausible employee concerns served by the restraints?

**2. Protecting Other Employers?** What if the trial court had found that the union wanted restraints on the operating hours of meat departments at general food markets not to protect its members directly, but rather to protect the operations of other employers, traditional butcher shops? Should it matter, for purposes of antitrust immunity, whether the union's objective was to serve its membership by protecting businesses whose methods of operation offered more skilled work? As in *Pennington*, supra page 802, the question arises whether antitrust exposure should turn on the objective nature of the restraint, rather than findings of underlying intent subject to the vagaries of the adjudication process.

**3. Does the Mandatory/Permissive Subject Distinction Define Which Subjects Should Be Immune from Antitrust Scrutiny?** Justice Goldberg apparently would shield from all antitrust scrutiny bargaining over mandatory subjects of bargaining. How does Justice White's position differ on this point?

a. Does Justice Goldberg's position adequately explain the result in *Jewel Tea*? Are the operating hours of a retail business a mandatory subject of bargaining?

b. Consider Rule 17 in the *National Woodwork* case, quoted in full supra page 623. What if there were evidence that the provision was included by the union at the insistence of manufacturers of cabinets, fixtures, and doors, with whom the union had other collective bargaining relationships and who sought to exclude lower-cost, easy-to-install products made by competitors? Would the fact that the negotiated provision involved a mandatory subject—the nature of the work performed by unit employees—foreclose all scrutiny under the antitrust laws? Is this consistent with *Pennington*? With *Allen Bradley*?

### *Note: Availability of Statutory Exemption for Employers' Labor Market Restraints and Bargaining Tactics*

The finding of antitrust immunity in *Jewel Tea* seems to be based on a recognition that the labor laws are framed to allow unions to attempt to regulate labor-market competition for the purpose of enhancing represented employees' wages and working conditions. To expose a union's successfully organized labor market to antitrust challenge would undermine this purpose. Does the same reasoning extend to coordinated efforts by unionized employers, including those engaged in multiemployer bargaining, to control a labor market in order to depress wages or other terms or conditions of employment?

This question is not often posed in most industries because unions generally negotiate comprehensive terms, leaving little to no leeway for individualized bargaining. In the sports industry, however, collective bargaining sets minimum terms and it is contemplated that individual talent will seek to negotiate above-scale wages and other terms and conditions. Employers in this industry prefer to restrict the ability of talented players to negotiate freely better terms by playing or threatening to play for other teams. The professional sports leagues, for instance, have established rules restricting players' ability to commence employment with any team of their choice ("draft" rules) and to move between teams ("reserve" or "restricted free agency" rules). Unions in professional sports have resisted these restraints and have attempted to bargain not only for minimum pay scales and collective benefits like pensions, but also for greater freedom for individual players to negotiate competitive contracts. One path of such resistance has been antitrust litigation.

The courts recognized the applicability of the "nonstatutory" antitrust exemption first for employer-proposed labor market restraints that were accepted by a union in a collective agreement, at least if such acceptance was "the product of bona fide arm's-length bargaining." See, e.g., Mackey v. NFL, 543 F.2d 606, 614 (8th Cir. 1976). The rationale for this recognition was grounded in the exclusive bargaining authority of unions as elaborated by the Court in *J.I. Case*, supra page 398; unions cannot bargain effectively for represented employees if they do not have the authority to trade the individual bargaining leverage of some employees for collective benefits. In the following case, however, the Court provided an additional and broader rationale for exempting not only employer-proposed labor market restraints to which unions have agreed after some degree of bargaining, but also restraints imposed unilaterally, after bargaining to impasse, in the course of multiemployer bargaining.

**Brown v. Pro Football, Inc.**
*518 U.S. 231 (1996)*

BREYER, J. . . .

A group of professional football players brought this antitrust suit against football club owners. The club owners had bargained with the players' union over a wage issue until they reached impasse. The owners then had agreed among themselves (but not with the union) to implement the terms of their own last best bargaining offer. The question before us is whether federal labor laws shield such an agreement from antitrust attack. We believe that they do. . . .

## I

. . . In 1987, a collective-bargaining agreement between the National Football League (NFL or League), a group of football clubs, and the NFL Players Association, a labor union, expired. The NFL and the Players Association began to negotiate a new contract. In March 1989, during the negotiations, the NFL adopted Resolution G-2, a plan that would permit each club to establish a "developmental squad" of up to six rookie or "first-year" players who, as free agents, had failed to secure a position on a regular player roster. Squad members would play in practice games and sometimes in regular games as substitutes for injured players. Resolution G-2 provided that the club owners would pay all squad members the same weekly salary.

The next month, April, the NFL presented the developmental squad plan to the Players Association. The NFL proposed a squad player salary of $1,000 per week. The Players Association disagreed. It insisted that the club owners give developmental squad players benefits and protections similar to those provided regular players, and that they leave individual squad members free to negotiate their own salaries.

Two months later, in June, negotiations on the issue of developmental squad salaries reached an impasse. The NFL then unilaterally implemented the developmental squad program by distributing to the clubs a uniform contract that embodied the terms of Resolution G-2 and the $1,000 proposed weekly salary. The League advised club owners that paying developmental squad players more or less than $1,000 per week would result in disciplinary action, including the loss of draft choices.

In May 1990, 235 developmental squad players brought this antitrust suit against the League and its member clubs. The players claimed that their employers' agreement to pay them a $1,000 weekly salary violated the Sherman Act. See 15 U.S.C. §1 (forbidding agreements in restraint of trade). The Federal District Court denied the employers' claim of exemption from the antitrust laws; it permitted the case to reach the jury; and it subsequently entered judgment on a jury treble-damages award that exceeded $30 million. The NFL and its member clubs appealed.

The Court of Appeals (by a split 2-to-1 vote) reversed. The majority interpreted the labor laws as "waiving anti-trust liability for restraints on competition imposed through the collective-bargaining process, so long as such restraints operate primarily in a labor market characterized by collective bargaining." . . . Although we do not interpret the exemption as broadly as did the Appeals Court, we nonetheless find the exemption applicable, and we affirm that court's immunity conclusion.

## II

. . . As a matter of logic, it would be difficult, if not impossible, to require groups of employers and employees to bargain together, but at the same time to forbid them to make among themselves or with each other any of the competition-restricting agreements potentially necessary to make the process work or its results mutually acceptable. . . .

. . . [T]he question before us is one of determining the exemption's scope: Does it apply to an agreement among several employers bargaining together to implement after impasse the terms of their last best good-faith wage offer? We assume that such conduct, as practiced in this case, is unobjectionable as a matter of labor law and policy. On that assumption, we conclude that the exemption applies.

Labor law itself regulates directly, and considerably, the kind of behavior here at issue — the postimpasse imposition of a proposed employment term concerning a mandatory subject of bargaining. Both the Board and the courts have held that, after impasse, labor law permits employers unilaterally to implement changes in pre-existing conditions, but only insofar as the new terms meet carefully circumscribed conditions. For example, the new terms must be "reasonably comprehended" within the employer's preimpasse proposals (typically the last rejected proposals), lest by imposing more or less favorable terms, the employer unfairly undermined the union's status. . . . The collective-bargaining proceeding itself must be free of any unfair labor practice, such as an employer's failure to have bargained in good faith. (citations omitted) These regulations reflect the fact that impasse and an accompanying implementation of proposals constitute an integral part of the bargaining process. See Bonanno Linen Serv., Inc., 243 N.L.R.B. 1093, 1094 (1979) (describing use of impasse as a bargaining tactic), enf'd, 630 F.2d 25 (CA1 1980), aff'd, 454 U.S. 404 (1982); Colorado-Ute Elec. Assn., 295 N.L.R.B. 607, 609 (1989), enf. denied on other grounds, 939 F.2d 1392 (CA10 1991), cert. denied, 504 U.S. 955 (1992).

[N]o one here has argued that labor law does, or should, treat multiemployer bargaining differently in this respect. Indeed, Board and court decisions suggest that the joint implementation of proposed terms after impasse is a familiar practice in the context of multiemployer bargaining. . . . We proceed on that assumption.

Multiemployer bargaining itself is a well-established, important, pervasive method of collective bargaining, offering advantages to both management and labor. See Appendix, infra (multiemployer bargaining accounts for more than 40% of major collective-bargaining agreements, and is used in such industries as construction, transportation, retail trade, clothing manufacture, and real estate, as well as professional sports); NLRB v. Truck Drivers, 353 U.S. 87, 95 (1957) (*Buffalo Linen*) (Congress saw multiemployer bargaining as "a vital factor in the effectuation of the national policy of promoting labor peace through strengthened collective bargaining"); Charles D. Bonanno Linen Service, Inc. v. NLRB, 454 U.S. 404, 409, n.3 (1982) (*Bonanno Linen*) (multiemployer bargaining benefits both management and labor, by saving bargaining resources, by encouraging development of industry-wide worker benefits programs that smaller employers could not otherwise afford, and by inhibiting employer competition at the workers' expense). . . . The upshot is that the practice at issue here plays a significant role in a collective-bargaining process that itself constitutes an important part of the Nation's industrial relations system.

In these circumstances, to subject the practice to antitrust law is to require antitrust courts to answer a host of important practical questions about how collective bargaining over wages, hours, and working conditions is to proceed—the very result that the implicit labor exemption seeks to avoid. And it is to place in jeopardy some of the potentially beneficial labor-related effects that multiemployer bargaining can achieve. . . .

If the antitrust laws apply, what are employers to do once impasse is reached? If all impose terms similar to their last joint offer, they invite an antitrust action premised upon identical behavior (along with prior or accompanying conversations) as tending to show a common understanding or agreement. If any, or all, of them individually impose terms that differ significantly from that offer, they invite an unfair labor practice charge. Indeed, how can employers safely discuss their offers together even before a bargaining impasse occurs? A preimpasse discussion about, say, the practical advantages or disadvantages of a particular proposal invites a later antitrust claim that they agreed to limit the kinds of action each would later take should an impasse occur. The same is true of postimpasse discussions aimed at renewed negotiations with the union. Nor would adherence to the terms of an expired collective-bargaining agreement eliminate a potentially plausible antitrust claim charging that they had "conspired" or tacitly "agreed" to do so, particularly if maintaining the status quo were not in the immediate economic self-interest of some. All this is to say that to permit antitrust liability here threatens to introduce instability and uncertainty into the collective-bargaining process, for antitrust law often forbids or discourages the kinds of joint discussions and behavior that the collective-bargaining process invites or requires.

. . . The labor laws give the Board, not antitrust courts, primary responsibility for policing the collective-bargaining process. And one of their objectives was to take from antitrust courts the authority to determine, through application of the antitrust laws, what is socially or economically desirable collective-bargaining policy. . . .

### III

Nor do we see how an exemption limited by petitioners' principle of labor-management consent could work. One cannot mean the principle literally — that the exemption applies only to understandings embodied in a collective-bargaining agreement — for the collective-bargaining process may take place before the making of any agreement or after an agreement has expired. Yet a multiemployer bargaining process itself necessarily involves many procedural and substantive understandings among participating employers as well as with the union. Petitioners cannot rescue their principle by claiming that the exemption applies only insofar as both labor and management consent to those understandings. Often labor will not (and should not) consent to certain common bargaining positions that employers intend to maintain. Similarly, labor need not consent to certain tactics that this Court has approved as part of the multiemployer bargaining process, such as unit-wide lockouts and the use of temporary replacements. See NLRB v. Brown, 380 U.S. 278, 284 (1965); *Buffalo Linen,* 353 U.S. at 97.

The Solicitor General argues that the exemption should terminate at the point of impasse. After impasse, he says, "employers no longer have a duty under the labor laws to maintain the status quo," and "are free as a matter of labor law to negotiate individual arrangements on an interim basis with the union."

Employers, however, are not completely free at impasse to act independently. The multiemployer bargaining unit ordinarily remains intact; individual employers cannot withdraw. *Bonanno Linen*, 454 U.S. at 410-413. The duty to bargain survives; employers must stand ready to resume collective bargaining. . . .

More importantly, the simple "impasse" line would not solve the basic problem we have described above. Labor law permits employers, after impasse, to engage in considerable joint behavior, including joint lockouts and replacement hiring. . . . Indeed, as a general matter, labor law often limits employers to four options at impasse: (1) maintain the status quo, (2) implement their last offer, (3) lock out their workers (and either shut down or hire temporary replacements), or (4) negotiate separate interim agreements with the union. What is to happen if the parties cannot reach an interim agreement? The other alternatives are limited. Uniform employer conduct is likely. Uniformity — at least when accompanied by discussion of the matter — invites antitrust attack. And such attack would ask antitrust courts to decide the lawfulness of activities intimately related to the bargaining process.

The problem is aggravated by the fact that "impasse" is often temporary. . . . How are employers to discuss future bargaining positions during a temporary impasse? Consider, too, the adverse consequences that flow from failing to guess how an antitrust court would later draw the impasse line. Employers who erroneously concluded that impasse had not been reached would risk antitrust liability were they collectively to maintain the status quo, while employers who erroneously concluded that impasse had occurred would risk unfair labor practice charges for prematurely suspending multiemployer negotiations. . . .

Petitioners also say that irrespective of how the labor exemption applies elsewhere to multiemployer collective bargaining, professional sports is "special." We can understand how professional sports may be special in terms of, say, interest, excitement, or concern. But we do not understand how they are special in respect to labor law's antitrust exemption. . . .

For these reasons, we hold that the implicit ("nonstatutory") antitrust exemption applies to the employer conduct at issue here. That conduct took place during and immediately after a collective-bargaining negotiation. It grew out of, and was directly related to, the lawful operation of the bargaining process. It involved a matter that the parties were required to negotiate collectively. And it concerned only the parties to the collective-bargaining relationship.

Our holding is not intended to insulate from antitrust review every joint imposition of terms by employers, for an agreement among employers could be sufficiently distant in time and in circumstances from the collective-bargaining process that a rule permitting antitrust intervention would not significantly interfere with that process. See, e.g., [Brown v. Pro Football], 50 F.3d [1056,] 1057 (D.C. Cir. 1995) (suggesting that exemption lasts until collapse of the collective-bargaining relationship, as evidenced by decertification of the union); El Cerrito Mill & Lumber Co., 316 N.L.R.B. [1005,] 1006-1007 [1995] (suggesting that "extremely long" impasse, accompanied by "instability" or "defunctness" of multiemployer unit, might justify union withdrawal from group bargaining). We need not decide in this case whether, or where, within these extreme outer boundaries to draw that line. Nor would it be appropriate for us to do so without the detailed views of the Board, to whose "specialized judgment" Congress "intended to leave" many of the "inevitable questions concerning multi-employer bargaining bound to arise in the future." *Buffalo Linen*, 353 U.S. at 96 (internal quotation marks omitted). . . .

Justice STEVENS, dissenting.

In my view . . . neither the policies underlying the [antitrust and labor] statutory schemes, nor the . . . purpose of the nonstatutory exemption, provides a justification for exempting from antitrust scrutiny collective action initiated by employers to depress wages below the level that would be produced in a free market. Nor do those policies support a rule that would allow employers to suppress wages by implementing noncompetitive agreements among themselves on matters that have not previously been the subject of either an agreement with labor or even a demand by labor for inclusion in the bargaining process. That, however, is what is at stake in this litigation.

In light of the accommodation that has been struck between antitrust and labor law policy, it would be most ironic to extend an exemption crafted to protect collective action by employees to protect employers acting jointly to deny employees the opportunity to negotiate their salaries individually in a competitive market. Perhaps aware of the irony, the Court chooses to analyze this case as though it represented a typical impasse in an unexceptional multiemployer bargaining process. In so doing, it glosses over three unique features of the case that are critical to the inquiry into whether the policies of the labor laws require extension of the nonstatutory labor exemption to this atypical case.

First, in this market, unlike any other area of labor law implicated in the cases cited by the Court, player salaries are individually negotiated. The practice of individually negotiating player salaries prevailed even prior to collective bargaining. The players did not challenge the prevailing practice because, unlike employees in most industries, they want their compensation to be determined by the forces of the free market rather than by the process of collective bargaining. Thus, although the majority professes an inability to understand anything special about professional sports that should affect the framework of labor negotiations, in this business it is the employers, not the employees, who seek to impose a noncompetitive uniform wage on a segment of the market and to put an end to competitive wage negotiations.

Second, respondents concede that the employers imposed the wage restraint to force owners to comply with leaguewide rules that limit the number of players that may serve on a team, not to facilitate a stalled bargaining process, or to revisit any issue previously subjected to bargaining. . . .

Third, although the majority asserts that the "club owners had bargained with the players' union over a wage issue until they reached impasse," that hardly constitutes a complete description of what transpired. When the employers' representative advised the union that they proposed to pay the players a uniform wage determined by the owners, the union promptly and unequivocally responded that their proposal was inconsistent with the "principle" of individual salary negotiation that had been accepted in the past and that predated collective bargaining. The so-called "bargaining" that followed amounted to nothing more than the employers' notice to the union that they had decided to implement a decision to replace individual salary negotiations with a uniform wage level for a specific group of players.

## *NOTES AND QUESTIONS*

**1. Do the Antitrust Laws Reach Pure Labor-Market Restraints?** The NFL had argued, in view of *Apex Hosiery*, supra page 38, that the antitrust laws do not reach any limitations on competition in a labor market that do not also directly affect competition in a product market. Is this an appropriate reading of *Apex Hosiery*? Is there a justification for allowing employers to combine with each other, outside of collective bargaining, to regulate wages and other working conditions? For examples of employer-imposed labor-market restraints found to be subject to antitrust challenge, see Radovich v. National Football League, 352 U.S. 445 (1957); Anderson v. Shipowners Ass'n, 272 U.S. 359 (1926); In re High-Tech Employee Antitrust Litigation, No. 11-CV-02509-LHR (N.D. Cal.) (August 8, 2014).

**2. Is the Post-Impasse Unilateral Imposition of Terms by Employers a Necessary Feature of Multiemployer Bargaining?** Consider the Court's explanation of why a multiemployer association would need to be able to impose similar terms at impasse. Note that multiemployer bargaining requires the consent of each member of the multiemployer association as well as of the union. Are employers likely to consent to such bargaining if they are forced to sacrifice their ability to unilaterally impose similar terms after impasse?

Did Justice Stevens in dissent offer a way to distinguish bargaining by sports leagues, where employers seek to impose a noncompetitive wage, from multiemployer bargaining in most industries, where employers resist union efforts to impose a noncompetitive wage? Would recognition of this distinction have enabled the Court to protect necessary employer bargaining tactics in multiemployer bargaining outside of sports without granting the NFL an exemption in *Brown* and allowing the sports industry to impose noncompetitive wages unilaterally? For a further discussion, see Michael C. Harper, Multiemployer Bargaining, Antitrust Law, and Team Sports: The Contingent Choice of a Broad Exemption, 38 Wm. & Mary L. Rev. 1663 (1997).

**3. When Does the Nonstatutory Exemption Apply?**

a. *Relevance of Labor Law Legality?* Does *Brown* require labor law legality as a necessary condition for exemption? Would a bargaining tactic, such as the unilateral imposition of a labor market restraint prior to impasse, that is unlawful under the NLRA not be part of the "lawful operation of the bargaining process," and thus not exempt? Does the converse hold true—that labor law legality is a sufficient condition, so that a practice lawful under the NLRA would be exempt?

b. *Relevance of Voluntary Decertification or Withdrawal of Union as Collective Bargaining Agency?* Is it clear that voluntary decertification of the union would set at least one outer boundary for the exemption, so that especially skilled employees, like the football players in *Brown*, could choose, by rejecting collective bargaining, to seek higher wages through an unrestrained labor market secured by antitrust law? Or could a decertification in anticipation of antitrust litigation and ultimate recertification upon settlement be treated as part of an ongoing collective bargaining process that should be regulated only by labor law? The NFL argued for such treatment in its defense to the players' antitrust suit against the League's post-decertification 2011 lockout. See Brady v. National Football League, 779 F. Supp. 2d 1043 (D. Minn.) (preliminary injunction granted), granting stay pending appeal, 640 F.3d 785 (8th Cir. 2011).

**4. What If There Has Been No Collective Bargaining on the Subject of the Agreement?** Does the nonstatutory exemption protect an employer-promulgated rule over which the union could have bargained but chose not to? This question was posed by a college underclassman's antitrust challenge to an NFL rule excluding from eligibility for its annual draft, and thus from employment as a player, anyone who is not at least three full NFL seasons removed from his high school graduation. In Clarett v. National Football League, 369 F.3d 124 (2d Cir. 2004), the court found that the nonstatutory exemption protected the rule, even though it was not expressly incorporated into the collective bargaining agreement between the NFL and the players' union. The court stressed that the rule was well known to the union, and given that it was a mandatory bargaining subject, the union or the NFL could have forced the other to the bargaining table if either felt that a change was warranted. The eligibility rule was a mandatory subject because it could have tangible effects on the wages and working conditions of current NFL players, including a potential effect on the job security of veteran players. The court noted that the rule was not dissimilar to hiring hall arrangements that have long been recognized as mandatory subjects of bargaining.

**5. Are All Otherwise Legal Multiemployer Bargaining Tactics Antitrust-Exempt?** Does the reasoning of *Brown* extend to all other agreements between members of a multiemployer bargaining association that both are designed to strengthen the association's leverage in collective bargaining and also are legal under the labor laws? Consider, for instance, grocery store chains engaged in multiemployer bargaining with a union that they fear may target a particular company chain with a consumer boycott during a strike. Are these competitors subject to an antitrust challenge if they agree to share revenues during any strike that occurs during the multiemployer bargaining? Should it matter whether the sharing of revenues is to continue for a few weeks after completion of the bargaining process? Whether the agreement includes a competitor that is not part of the multiemployer bargaining unit? See State of California v. Safeway, Inc., 371 F. Supp. 2d 1179 (C.D. Cal. 2005), aff'd, 651 F.3d 1118 (9th Cir. 2011) (en banc) (revenue sharing concerns product market and is not sufficiently connected to bargaining process, especially in light of involvement of competitor not part of the bargaining unit).

Should the availability of the exemption turn on whether the agreement between employers engaged in multiemployer bargaining may result in pressure being exerted on parties outside the collective bargaining process as long as the pressure is intended to affect the process? Consider, for instance, an agreement between members of a multiemployer association of building operators to boycott any cleaning contractor servicing an independent building operator that settles in an agreement with the union. See Sage Realty Corp. v. ISS Cleaning Services Group, Inc., 936 F. Supp. 130 (S.D.N.Y. 1996) (labor exemption applies).

**6. Implications for Agreements Outside Multiemployer Bargaining?** Can the *Brown* decision be extended to render antitrust-immune coordinated bargaining between two or more employers that are not part of a formal multiemployer unit? Does immunity turn on the legality of the coordination under the labor laws? After *Pennington* and *Brown*, do two or more unions lose their antitrust exemption when they agree to coordinate bargaining policy with respect to different bargaining units of the same employer or in the same industry?

### Connell Construction Co. v. Plumbers, Local 100
*421 U.S. 616 (1975)*

POWELL, J. . . .

Local 100 is the bargaining representative for workers in the plumbing and mechanical trades in Dallas. When this litigation began, it was party to a multiemployer bargaining agreement with the Mechanical Contractors Association of Dallas, a group of about 75 mechanical contractors. That contract contained a "most favored nation" clause, by which the union agreed that if it granted a more favorable contract to any other employer it would extend the same terms to all members of the Association.

Connell Construction Co. is a general building contractor in Dallas. It obtains jobs by competitive bidding and subcontracts all plumbing and mechanical work. Connell has followed a policy of awarding these subcontracts on the basis of competitive bids, and it has done business with both union and nonunion subcontractors. Connell's employees are represented by various building trade unions. Local 100 has never sought to represent them or to bargain with Connell on their behalf.

In November 1970, Local 100 asked Connell to agree that it would subcontract mechanical work only to firms that had a current contract with the union. . . .

When Connell refused to sign this agreement, Local 100 stationed a single picket at one of Connell's major construction sites. About 150 workers walked off the job, and construction halted. Connell filed suit in state court to enjoin the picketing as a violation of Texas antitrust laws. Local 100 removed the case to federal court. Connell then signed the subcontracting agreement under protest. It amended its complaint to claim that the agreement violated §§1 and 2 of the Sherman Act and was therefore invalid. Connell sought a declaration to this effect and an injunction against any further efforts to force it to sign such an agreement.

By the time the case went to trial, Local 100 had submitted identical agreements to a number of other general contractors in Dallas. Five others had signed, and the union was waging a selective picketing campaign against those who resisted.

The District Court held that the subcontracting agreement was exempt from federal antitrust laws because it was authorized by the construction industry proviso to §8(e). . . . The court also held that federal labor legislation preempted the State's antitrust laws. . . . [T]he Fifth Circuit affirmed. . . . It held that Local 100's goal of organizing nonunion subcontractors was a legitimate union interest and that its efforts toward that goal were therefore exempt from federal antitrust laws. . . . We reverse on the question of federal antitrust immunity and affirm the ruling on state law preemption. . . .

In this case Local 100 used direct restraints on the business market to support its organizing campaign. The agreements with Connell and other general contractors indiscriminately excluded nonunion subcontractors from a portion of the market, even if their competitive advantages were not derived from substandard wages and working conditions but rather from more efficient operating methods. Curtailment of competition based on efficiency is neither a goal of federal labor policy nor a necessary effect of the elimination of competition among workers. Moreover, competition based on efficiency is a positive value that the antitrust laws strive to protect.

The multiemployer bargaining agreement between Local 100 and the Association, though not challenged in this suit, is relevant in determining the effect that the agreement between Local 100 and Connell would have on the business market. The "most favored nation" clause in the multiemployer agreement promised to eliminate competition between members of the Association and any other subcontractors that Local 100 might organize. By giving members of the Association a contractual right to insist on terms as favorable as those given any competitor, it guaranteed that the union would make no agreement that would give an unaffiliated contractor a competitive advantage over members of the Association. Subcontractors in the Association thus stood to benefit from any extension of Local 100's organization, but the method Local 100 chose also had the effect of sheltering them from outside competition in that portion of the market covered by subcontracting agreements between general contractors and Local 100. In that portion of the market, the restriction on subcontracting would eliminate competition on all subjects covered by the multiemployer agreement, even on subjects unrelated to wages, hours, and working conditions.

Success in exacting agreements from general contractors would also give Local 100 power to control access to the market for mechanical subcontracting work. The agreements with general contractors did not simply prohibit subcontracting to any nonunion firm; they prohibited subcontracting to any firm that did not have a contract with Local 100. The union thus had complete control over subcontract work offered by general contractors that had signed these agreements. Such control could result in significant adverse effects on the market and on consumers — effects unrelated to the union's legitimate goals of organizing workers and standardizing working conditions. For example, if the union thought the interests of its members would be served by having fewer subcontractors competing for the available work, it could refuse to sign collective bargaining agreements with marginal firms. Cf. *Mine Workers v. Pennington* [supra page 802]. Or, since Local 100 has a well-defined geographical jurisdiction, it could exclude "traveling" subcontractors by refusing to deal with them. Local 100 thus might be able to create a geographical enclave for local contractors, similar to the closed market in *Allen Bradley* [supra page 799].

This record contains no evidence that the union's goal was anything other than organizing as many subcontractors as possible. This goal was legal, even though a successful organizing campaign ultimately would reduce the competition that unionized employers face from nonunion firms. But the methods the union chose are not immune from antitrust sanctions simply because the goal is legal. Here Local 100, by agreement with several contractors, made nonunion subcontractors ineligible to compete for a portion of the available work. This kind of direct restraint on the business market has substantial anticompetitive effects, both actual and potential, that would not follow naturally from the elimination of competition over wages and working conditions. It contravenes antitrust policies to a degree not justified by congressional labor policy, and therefore cannot claim a nonstatutory exemption from the antitrust laws.

There can be no argument in this case, whatever its force in other contexts, that a restraint of this magnitude might be entitled to an antitrust exemption if it were included in a lawful collective bargaining agreement. In this case, Local 100 had no interest in representing Connell's employees. The federal policy favoring collective bargaining therefore can offer no shelter for the union's coercive action against Connell or its campaign to exclude nonunion firms from the subcontracting market.

Local 100 nonetheless contends that the kind of agreement it obtained from Connell is explicitly allowed by the construction-industry proviso to §8(e) and that antitrust policy therefore must defer to the NLRA. The majority in the Court of Appeals declined to decide this issue, holding that it was subject to the "exclusive jurisdiction" of the NLRB. 483 F.2d, at 1174. This Court has held, however, that the federal courts may decide labor law questions that emerge as collateral issues in suits brought under independent federal remedies, including the antitrust laws. We conclude that §8(e) does not allow this type of agreement. . . .

If we agreed with Local 100 that the construction-industry proviso authorizes subcontracting agreements with "stranger" contractors, not limited to any particular jobsite, our ruling would give construction unions an almost unlimited organizational weapon. The unions would be free to enlist any general contractor to bring economic pressure on nonunion subcontractors, as long as the agreement recited that it only covered work to be performed on some jobsite somewhere. The proviso's jobsite restriction then would serve only to prohibit agreements relating to subcontractors that deliver their work complete to the jobsite.

Absent a clear indication that Congress intended to leave such a glaring loophole in its restrictions on "top-down" organizing, we are unwilling to read the construction industry proviso as broadly as Local 100 suggests. Instead, we think its authorization extends only to agreements in the context of collective bargaining relationships and, in light of congressional references to the problem in [NLRB v. Denver Building & Construction Trades

Council, 341 U.S. 675 (1951)], possibly to common-situs relationships on particular jobsites as well.

Finally, Local 100 contends that even if the subcontracting agreement is not sanctioned by the construction-industry proviso and therefore is illegal under §8(e), it cannot be the basis for antitrust liability because the remedies in the NLRA are exclusive. This argument is grounded in the legislative history of the 1947 Taft-Hartley amendments. Congress rejected attempts to regulate secondary activities by repealing the antitrust exemptions in the Clayton and Norris-LaGuardia Acts, and created special remedies under the labor law instead. It made secondary activities unfair labor practices under §8(b)(4), and drafted special provisions for preliminary injunctions at the suit of the NLRB and for recovery of actual damages in the district courts. Sections 10(*l*), 303. . . . But whatever significance this legislative choice has for antitrust suits based on those secondary activities prohibited by §8(b)(4), it has no relevance to the question whether Congress meant to preclude antitrust suits based on the "hot-cargo" agreements that it outlawed in 1959. There is no legislative history in the 1959 Congress suggesting that labor-law remedies for §8(e) violations were intended to be exclusive, or that Congress thought allowing antitrust remedies in cases like the present one would be inconsistent with the remedial scheme of the NLRA.

We therefore hold that this agreement, which is outside the context of a collective bargaining relationship and not restricted to a particular jobsite, but which nonetheless obligates Connell to subcontract work only to firms that have a contract with Local 100, may be the basis of a federal antitrust suit because it has a potential for restraining competition in the business market in ways that would not follow naturally from elimination of competition over wages and working conditions. . . .

Neither the District Court nor the Court of Appeals decided whether the agreement between Local 100 and Connell, if subject to the antitrust laws, would constitute an agreement that restrains trade within the meaning of the Sherman Act. The issue was not briefed and argued fully in this Court. Accordingly, we remand for consideration whether the agreement violated the Sherman Act.

DOUGLAS, J., dissenting. . . .

Throughout this litigation, Connell has maintained only that Local 100 coerced it into signing the subcontracting agreement. With the complaint so drawn, I have no difficulty in concluding that the union's conduct is regulated solely by the labor laws. The question of antitrust immunity would be far different, however, if it were alleged that Local 100 had conspired with mechanical subcontractors to force nonunion subcontractors from the market by entering into exclusionary agreements with general contractors like Connell. . . .

[Justice Stewart, joined by Justices Brennan and Marshall, dissented on the following grounds: The LMRA was the only source of remedies for the petitioner. In 1947, Congress had rejected a provision that would have subjected secondary boycotts to customary antitrust remedies. In 1959, Congress had rejected similar proposals, in enacting §8(e) and in extending §303 to provide a damage remedy for secondary pressures designed to force an employer to sign an "illegal 'hot cargo' clause." On the other hand, if the disputed subcontracting agreement were valid, picketing to secure it should also be valid under decisions by the NLRB and the reviewing courts. Finally, activity "authorized" under the NLRA should not, by itself, be a basis for antitrust liability.]

## *NOTES AND QUESTIONS*

### 1. Consistent with *Jewel Tea*?

> [In *Connell*] the union was protecting its wages, hours and working conditions by promoting the use of union subcontractors, as surely as the union in *Jewel Tea* did so by banning the sale of union products after union employees had gone home. Hence, the *Jewel Tea* rule would have upheld the conduct in *Connell.*

Thomas J. Campbell, Labor Law and Economics, 38 Stan. L. Rev. 1003, 1060 (1986). Do you agree, or is *Jewel Tea* distinguishable?

**2. Explaining the Court's Holding.** Does Justice Powell for the Court convincingly explain why Local 100's agreements with Connell and other general contractors are not entitled to the nonstatutory exemption? Consider the following rationales:

a. *Product Market Restraints That "Would Not Follow Naturally from the Elimination of Competition over Wages and Working Conditions"*? Does this language from the majority opinion in *Connell* suggest that union-signatory clauses are more anticompetitive because they seek to advance organizational objectives rather than immediate economic benefits for union-represented employees? Does this make sense from the standpoint of antitrust policy? Does the Court identify any additional product market restraints beyond those involved in satisfying the union's organizational objectives? Is it significant that any additional restraints are merely potential rather than proven to be actually anticompetitive in effect? Consider also the parallel to *Plant v. Woods,* supra pages 16-17.

b. *Absence of a Collective Bargaining Relationship*? Does the absence of a collective bargaining relationship in *Connell,* or its presence in Woelke & Romero Framing, Inc. v. NLRB, 456 U.S. 645 (1982), supra pages 635-636, necessarily affect the anticompetitive impact of union signatory clauses? Could an agreement like that in *Woelke & Romero,* insulated by the §8(e) proviso, still be subject to antitrust challenge?

c. *Is Labor Law Illegality Sufficient for Antitrust Exposure?* The fact that the NLRA prohibits certain union activity does not necessarily foreclose additional sanctions under the antitrust laws. But does the presence of an NLRA violation in a union-employer agreement mean that the agreement and the bargaining process that produced it implicate no federal labor policy that the antitrust laws should accommodate? In considering this question, note that the antitrust laws expose parties to extraordinary remedies, including treble damages, and Congress may have intended a limited regulation of certain organizing tactics by unions. See Douglas L. Leslie, Principles of Labor Antitrust, 66 Va. L. Rev. 1183, 1227-1229 (1980); Theodore St. Antoine, Antitrust Law at the Expense of Labor Law, 62 Va. L. Rev. 603 (1976).

**3. Injunction of Union Picketing?** Could Connell have obtained an injunction under the antitrust laws against union picketing to secure the agreement that Connell challenged in the actual case? See Burlington Northern Santa Fe Railway Co. v. Int'l Bhd. of Teamsters Local 174, 203 F.3d 703 (9th Cir. 2000) (en banc) (Norris-LaGuardia Act precludes private party from bringing antitrust action for injunction even of secondary picketing in labor dispute). The *Burlington Northern* court, however, acknowledged that §10(*l*) of the NLRA directs the Labor Board to seek injunctions of illegal secondary picketing.

**4. Per Se Rule or "Rule of Reason"?** The absence of the labor exemption does not necessarily result in substantive antitrust liability. For a consideration of a "rule of reason" rather than a per se standard, see Larry V. Muko, Inc. v. Southwestern Pa. Bldg. & Constr. Trades Council, 670 F.2d 421 (3d Cir. 1982). See also Adams Constr. Co. v. Georgia Power Co., 733 F.2d 853 (11th Cir. 1984). See generally Milton Handler & William C. Zifchak, Collective Bargaining and the Antitrust Laws: The Emasculation of the Labor Exemption, 81 Colum. L. Rev. 459, 511 (1981); Leslie, Principles of Labor Antitrust, supra, at 1222-1224.

# 11 | Preemption of State Authority

As explained in Chapter 1, until passage of the National Labor Relations Act (NLRA) in 1935, regulation of labor-management relations and of union activity in this country was primarily the province of state law. The enactment of the NLRA represented, of course, a congressional judgment that uniform federal standards were needed in this area. However, apart from special provisions such as §10(b)'s allowance of state laws banning union shop clauses, Congress did not specify in the original NLRA, or its subsequent amendments, the extent to which it intended to displace state law.

In Garner v. Teamsters Union, 346 U.S. 485 (1953), the Court articulated what became, at least for many years, the two most important bases for federal labor preemption. In *Garner*, the Teamsters had peacefully picketed the loading platform of an interstate trucking company to induce the company's employees to join the union. A Pennsylvania court enjoined the picketing, finding a violation of state law because the union intended to coerce the company into compelling its employees to join the union. The Supreme Court set aside the injunction on the ground that Pennsylvania law was preempted by the NLRA. Seizing upon the parties' stipulation that the picketing violated §8(b)(2) of the NLRA, Justice Jackson's opinion for a unanimous Court maintained that the state court decree interfered with the NLRB's "primary jurisdiction" to adjudicate the dispute.

*Garner* also offered a second ground for preemption, beyond congressional reliance on an expert and sensitive agency to develop uniform law. The Court explained that the state's application of its own law potentially could upset the substantive balance of the rights of employees, unions, employers, and the general public that Congress had struck in the NLRA:

> The detailed prescription of a procedure for restraint of specified types of picketing would seem to imply that other picketing is to be free of other methods and sources of restraint. For the policy of the National Labor Management Relations Act is not to condemn all picketing but only that ascertained by its prescribed processes to fall within its prohibitions. Otherwise, it is

> implicit in the Act that the public interest is served by freedom of labor to use the weapon of picketing. For a state to impinge on the area of labor combat designed to be free is quite as much an obstruction of federal policy as if the state were to declare picketing free for purposes or by methods which the federal Act prohibits.

Id. at 499-500.

The materials that follow develop the issues raised by the bases of preemption identified in *Garner* and a third developed in Machinists v. Wisconsin Employment Relations Commission, 427 U.S. 132 (1976), infra page 850. They also present a fourth basis for preemption that has become more salient in recent decades with the growing number of state laws establishing protective labor standards. The Supreme Court in Textile Workers Union v. Lincoln Mills of Alabama, 353 U.S. 448 (1957), supra page 665, and Local 174, Teamsters v. Lucas Flour Co., 369 U.S. 95 (1962), supra page 703, held that §301 of the Labor Management Relations Act (LMRA) authorized the courts to develop a uniform federal common law governing the enforcement of collective bargaining agreements. This §301 jurisprudence raises the question of the extent to which state law can establish causes of action that either require the interpretation of those agreements or in some sense are dependent on the existence of such agreements.

## A. *GARMON* PREEMPTION

### 1. The Basic Framework

**San Diego Building Trades Council v. Garmon**
*359 U.S. 236 (1959)*

Frankfurter, J. . . .

Respondents began an action in the Superior Court for the County of San Diego, asking for an injunction and damages. . . . In March of 1953 the unions sought from respondents an agreement to retain in their employ only those workers who were already members of the unions, or who applied for membership within thirty days. Respondents refused, claiming that none of their employees had shown a desire to join a union, and that, in any event, they could not accept such an arrangement until one of the unions had been designated by the employees as a collective bargaining agent. The unions began at once peacefully to picket the respondent's place of business, and to exert pressure on customers and suppliers in order to persuade them to stop dealing with respondents. . . . On the basis of its findings, the court enjoined the unions from picketing and from the use of other pressures to force an agreement, until one of them had been properly designated as a collective bargaining agent. The court also awarded $1,000 damages for losses found to have been sustained.

At the time the suit in the state court was started, respondents had begun a representation proceeding before the [NLRB]. The Regional Director declined jurisdiction, presumably because the amount of interstate commerce involved did not meet the Board's monetary standards. . . .

[The California Supreme Court upheld the trial court's decree. The U.S. Supreme Court vacated the state court injunction on the authority of Guss v. Utah Labor Relations Bd., 353 U.S. 1 (1957), but left open the viability of the damages award. On remand, the state high court] . . . set aside the injunction, but sustained the award of damages. . . .

We . . . granted certiorari to determine whether the California court had jurisdiction to award damages arising out of peaceful union activity which it could not enjoin. . . .

When it is clear or may fairly be assumed that the activities which a State purports to regulate are protected by §7 of the [NLRA], or constitute an unfair labor practice under §8, due regard for the federal enactment requires that state jurisdiction must yield. To leave the States free to regulate conduct so plainly within the central aim of federal regulation involves too great a danger of conflict between power asserted by Congress and requirements imposed by state law. Nor has it mattered whether the States have acted through laws of broad general application rather than laws specifically directed towards the governance of industrial relations. Regardless of the mode adopted, to allow the States to control conduct which is the subject of national regulation would create potential frustration of national purposes.

At times it has not been clear whether the particular activity regulated by the States was governed by §7 or §8 or was, perhaps, outside both these sections. But courts are not primary tribunals to adjudicate such issues. It is essential to the administration of the Act that these determinations be left in the first instance to the [NLRB]. What is outside the scope of this Court's authority cannot remain within a State's power and state jurisdiction too must yield to the exclusive primary competence of the Board. See, e.g., Garner v. Teamsters Union, 346 U.S. 485, especially at 489-491. . . .

The case before us is such a case. The adjudication in California has throughout been based on the assumption that the behavior of the petitioning unions constituted an unfair labor practice. This conclusion was derived by the California courts from the facts as well as from their view of the Act. It is not for us to decide whether the [NLRB] would have, or should have, decided these questions in the same manner. When an activity is arguably subject to §7 or §8 of the Act, the States as well as the federal courts must defer to the exclusive competence of the [NLRB] if the danger of state interference with national policy is to be averted.

To require the States to yield to the primary jurisdiction of the National Board does not ensure Board adjudication of the status of a disputed activity.

If the Board decides, subject to appropriate federal judicial review, that conduct is protected by §7, or prohibited by §8, then the matter is at an end, and the States are ousted of all jurisdiction. Or, the Board may decide that an activity is neither protected nor prohibited, and thereby raise the question whether such activity may be regulated by the States. However, the Board may also fail to determine the status of the disputed conduct by declining to assert jurisdiction, or by refusal of the General Counsel to file a charge, or by adopting some other disposition which does not define the nature of the activity with unclouded legal significance. . . . [T]he failure of the Board to define the legal significance under the Act of a particular activity does not give the States the power to act. In the absence of the Board's clear determination that an activity is neither protected nor prohibited or of compelling precedent applied to essentially undisputed facts, it is not for this Court to decide whether such activities are subject to state jurisdiction. . . . The governing consideration is that to allow the States to control activities that are potentially subject to federal regulation involves too great a danger of conflict with national labor policy. . . .

. . . It may be that an award of damages in a particular situation will not, in fact, conflict with the active assertion of federal authority. The same may be true of the incidence of a particular state injunction. To sanction either involves a conflict with federal policy in that it involves allowing two law-making sources to govern. In fact, since remedies form an ingredient of any integrated scheme of regulation, to allow the State to grant a remedy here which has been withheld from the [NLRB] only accentuates the danger of conflict.

[Justice Harlan, joined by Justices Clark, Whittaker, and Stewart, concurred on "the narrow ground" that the union's activities could fairly be deemed protected. The concurrence disagreed with the Court's foreclosure of state damage awards for conduct arguably or actually prohibited by the national scheme, and maintained that neither principle nor precedent supported the Court's intimation that the states lacked jurisdiction over conduct neither protected nor prohibited.]

## *NOTES AND QUESTIONS*

**1. The *Garmon* Framework.** The Supreme Court and the lower courts continue to cite *Garmon* as the leading precedent for one of the three basic labor law preemption doctrines: State law and state tribunals cannot regulate conduct that is protected by §7 or prohibited by §8 of the NLRA. Nor (with certain exceptions to be explored later) can the states regulate conduct that is arguably protected or prohibited by the NLRA unless and until the NLRB has determined that the conduct is in fact not protected or prohibited.

**2. Actually-Protected Activity.** The removal of state authority to regulate activity that is in fact protected by §7 seems the least problematic aspect of the *Garmon* doctrine. Once Congress or the NLRB, exercising delegated authority, has made an affirmative decision to protect certain conduct, the states cannot preclude or curb such activity. Which line of reasoning from *Garner* is the basis for this aspect of the *Garmon* holding?

**3. Actually-Prohibited Activity.** Consider the removal of state authority to regulate activity that is prohibited by §8. If the Board has determined that some activity is prohibited by §8, is the preemption of state authority to further punish or remedy such activity necessary to protect the primary jurisdiction of the NLRB? If not, is the preemption of such state authority necessary to protect substantive policy judgments embodied in federal labor law?

Consider, for instance, the Court's decision in Wisconsin Dep't of Industry v. Gould, Inc., 475 U.S. 282 (1986), to preempt under *Garmon* a Wisconsin law barring the state from doing business with companies found by judicially enforced orders of the NLRB to have violated the NLRA in three separate cases within a five-year period. The Court stated:

> [T]here can be little doubt that the NLRA would prevent Wisconsin from forbidding *private parties* within the State to do business with repeat labor law violators. Like civil damages for picketing, which the Court refused to allow in *Garmon*, a prohibition against in-state private contracts would interfere with Congress' "integrated scheme of regulation" by adding a remedy to those prescribed by the NLRA. . . .
>
> Wisconsin . . . contends, however, that the statutory scheme invoked against Gould escapes pre-emption because it is an exercise of the State's spending power rather than its regulatory power. But that seems to us a distinction without a difference, at least in this case, because on its face the debarment statute serves plainly as a means of enforcing the NLRA. The State concedes, as we think it must, that the point of the statute is to deter labor law violations and to reward "fidelity to the law."

475 U.S. at 287 (emphasis in original).

Is it clear how punishing those who have been found to violate the NLRA and rewarding those who have been faithful to its commands upsets the policy judgments embodied in the NLRA? Does Congress's decision to afford only certain remedies for NLRA violations reflect a policy balance that could be upset by a state's provision of additional remedies? For an argument that Congress provided limited remedies not to shield NLRA violators from enhanced state law penalties, but only to ensure that adjudication by the NLRB would be free of any constitutional requirement of jury trials, see Michael H. Gottesman, Rethinking Labor Law Preemption: State Laws

Facilitating Unionization, 7 Yale J. on Reg. 335, 407-409 (1990) (arguing generally that *Garmon* preemption should be applied to state regulation of conduct prohibited by the NLRA only where the regulated activity falls along a "continuum" that Congress intended to totally occupy by protecting conduct up to one point and forbidding it beyond that point).

**4. "Arguably-Protected" and "Arguably-Prohibited" Activity.** Does the Court's "primary jurisdiction" rationale for the preemption of state regulation of conduct that is "arguably protected" or "arguably prohibited" by the Act depend on the presence of a ready mechanism to invoke the Board's potential jurisdiction over the conduct? Consider the following:

> The NLRB is given no power to make [a]declaratory ruling. Indeed, the employer cannot always secure a determination by the Board itself as to whether the employees' conduct is prohibited by §8(b). He can file a charge but there is no further remedy if the General Counsel refuses to issue a complaint upon the ground that the evidence is weak or the case is unimportant, or for any other reason.

Archibald Cox, Labor Decisions of the Supreme Court at the October Term, 1957, 44 Va. L. Rev. 1057, 1065 (1958). For further discussion, see Sears, Roebuck & Co. v. San Diego Cty. Dist. Council, 436 U.S. 180 (1978), infra page 840.

## 2. Exceptions to *Garmon*

### Farmer, Special Administrator v. United Brotherhood of Carpenters
*430 U.S. 290 (1977)*

POWELL, J. . . .

In April 1969 [Hill] filed in Superior Court for the County of Los Angeles an action for damages against the Union, the District Council and the International with which the Union was affiliated, and certain officials of the Union, including Business Agent Daley. In count two of his amended complaint, Hill alleged that the defendants had intentionally engaged in outrageous conduct, threats, and intimidation, and had thereby caused him to suffer grievous emotional distress resulting in bodily injury. In three other counts, he alleged that the Union had discriminated against him in referrals for employment because of his dissident intra-Union political activities, that the Union had breached the hiring hall provisions of the collective-bargaining agreement between it and a contractors association by failing to refer him on a nondiscriminatory basis, and that the failure to comply with the collective-bargaining agreement also constituted a breach of his membership contract with the Union. He sought $500,000 in actual, and $500,000 in punitive, damages.

The Superior Court sustained a demurrer to the allegations of discrimination and breach of contract on the ground that federal law pre-empted state jurisdiction over them, but allowed the case to go to trial on the allegations in count two. Hill attempted to prove that the Union's campaign against him included "frequent public ridicule," "incessant verbal abuse," and refusals to refer him to jobs in accordance with the rules of the hiring hall. The defendants countered with evidence that the hiring hall was operated in a nondiscriminatory manner. The trial court instructed the jury that in order to recover damages Hill had to prove by a preponderance of the evidence that the defendants intentionally and by outrageous conduct had caused him to suffer severe emotional distress. . . .

The jury returned a verdict of $7,500 actual damages and $175,000 punitive damages against the Union, the District Council, and Business Agent Daley, and the trial court entered a judgment on the verdict.

The California Court of Appeal reversed. . . . [It] held that the state courts had no jurisdiction over the complaint since the "crux" of the action concerned employment relations and involved conduct arguably subject to the jurisdiction of the National Labor Relations Board. . . .

[T]he same considerations that underlie the *Garmon* rule[5] have led the Court to recognize exceptions in appropriate classes of cases. We have refused to apply the pre-emption doctrine to activity that would otherwise fall within the scope of *Garmon* if that activity "was a merely peripheral concern of the Labor Management Relations Act . . . [or] touched interests so deeply rooted in local feeling and responsibility that, in the absence of compelling congressional direction, we could not infer that Congress had deprived the States of the power to act." [*Garmon*, 359 U.S. at] 243-244. See, e.g., Linn v. Plant Guard Workers, 383 U.S. 53 (1966) (malicious libel); Automobile Workers v. Russell, 356 U.S. 634 (1958) (mass picketing and threats of violence); Machinists v. Gonzales, 356 U.S. 617 (1958) (wrongful expulsion from union membership). . . .

The nature of the inquiry is perhaps best illustrated by *Linn v. Plant Guard Workers*, supra. Linn, an assistant manager of Pinkerton's National Detective Agency, filed a diversity action in federal court against a union, two of its officers, and a Pinkerton employee, alleging that the defendants had circulated a defamatory statement about him in violation of state law. If unfair labor practice charges had been filed, the Board might have found that the union violated §8 by intentionally circulating false statements during an organizational campaign, or that the issuance of the malicious

5. . . . The branch of the pre-emption doctrine most applicable to the instant case concerns the primary jurisdiction of the National Labor Relations Board. [Footnote relocated in text. — Eds.]

statements during the campaign had such a significant effect as to require that the election be set aside. Under a formalistic application of *Garmon,* the libel suit could have been pre-empted.

But a number of factors influenced the Court to depart from the *Garmon* rule. First, the Court noted that the underlying conduct—the intentional circulation of defamatory material known to be false—was not protected under the Act, 383 U.S., at 61, and there was thus no risk that permitting the state cause of action to proceed would result in state regulation of conduct that Congress intended to protect. Second, the Court recognized that there was "an overriding state interest" in protecting residents from malicious libels, and that this state interest was "deeply rooted in local feeling and responsibility." Id., at 61, 62. Third, the Court reasoned that there was little risk that the state cause of action would interfere with the effective administration of national labor policy. The Board's §8 unfair labor practice proceeding would focus only on whether the statements were misleading or coercive; whether the statements also were defamatory would be of no relevance to the Board's performance of its functions. Id., at 63. Moreover, the Board would lack authority to provide the defamed individual with damages or other relief. Ibid. Conversely, the state-law action would be unconcerned with whether the statements were coercive or misleading in the labor context, and in any event the court would have power to award Linn relief only if the statements were defamatory. Taken together, these factors justified an exception to the pre-emption rule.

The Court was careful, however, to limit the scope of that exception. To minimize the possibility that state libel suits would either dampen the free discussion characteristic of labor disputes or become a weapon of economic coercion, the Court adopted by analogy the standards enunciated in New York Times Co. v. Sullivan, 376 U.S. 254 (1964), and held that state damages actions in this context would escape pre-emption only if limited to defamatory statements published with knowledge or reckless disregard of their falsity. The Court also held that a complainant could recover damages only upon proof that the statements had caused him injury, including general injury to reputation, consequent mental suffering, alienation of associates, specific items of pecuniary loss, or any other form of harm recognized by state tort law. The Court stressed the responsibility of the trial judge to assure that damages were not excessive.

Similar reasoning underlies the exception to the pre-emption rule in cases involving violent tortious activity. Nothing in the federal labor statutes protects or immunizes from state action violence or the threat of violence in a labor dispute, Automobile Workers v. Russell, 356 U.S., at 640 (Warren, C.J., dissenting); Construction Workers v. Laburnum Constr. Corp., 347 U.S. 656, 666 (1954), and thus there is no risk that state damages actions will fetter the exercise of rights protected by the NLRA. On the other hand, our cases consistently have recognized the historic state interest in "such traditionally local matters as public safety and order and the use of streets and highways." Allen-Bradley Local v. Wisconsin Emp. Rel. Bd., 315 U.S. 740, 749 (1942). And, as with the defamation actions preserved by *Linn*, state-court actions to redress injuries caused by violence or threats of violence are consistent with effective administration of the federal scheme: Such actions can be adjudicated without regard to the merits of the underlying labor controversy. . . .

Although cases like *Linn* and *Russell* involve state-law principles with only incidental application to conduct occurring in the course of a labor dispute, it is well settled that the general applicability of a state cause of action is not sufficient to exempt it from pre-emption. "[I]t [has not] mattered whether the States have acted through laws of broad general application rather than laws specifically directed towards the governance of industrial relations." *Garmon*, 359 U.S., at 244. Instead, the cases reflect a balanced inquiry into such factors as the nature of the federal and state interests in regulation and the potential for interference with federal regulation. . . .

No provision of the National Labor Relations Act protects the "outrageous conduct" complained of by petitioner Hill in the second count of the complaint. Regardless of whether the operation of the hiring hall was lawful or unlawful under federal statutes, there is no federal protection for conduct on the part of union officers which is so outrageous that "no reasonable man in a civilized society should be expected to endure it." Thus, as in Linn v. Plant Guard Workers, 383 U.S. 53 (1966), and *Automobile Workers v. Russell*, supra, permitting the exercise of state jurisdiction over such complaints does not result in state regulation of federally protected conduct.

The State, on the other hand, has a substantial interest in protecting its citizens from the kind of abuse of which Hill complained. That interest is no less worthy of recognition because it concerns protection from emotional distress caused by outrageous conduct, rather than protection from physical injury, as in *Russell*, or damage to reputation, as in *Linn*. . . . Although recognition of the tort of intentional infliction of emotional distress is a comparatively recent development in state law, see W. Prosser, Law of Torts, §12, pp. 49-50, 56 (4th ed. 1971), our decisions permitting the exercise of state jurisdiction in tort actions based on violence or defamation have not rested on the history of the tort at issue, but rather on the nature of the State's interest in protecting the health and well-being of its citizens.

There is, to be sure, some risk that the state cause of action for infliction of emotional distress will touch on an area of primary federal concern. Hill's complaint itself highlights this risk. In those counts of the complaint that the trial court dismissed, Hill alleged discrimination against him in hiring hall referrals, which were also alleged to be violations of both the collective-bargaining agreement and the membership contract. These allegations, if sufficiently supported before the National Labor Relations Board, would make out an unfair labor practice[11] and the Superior Court considered them pre-empted by the federal Act. Even in count two of the complaint Hill made allegations of discrimination in "job-dispatching procedures" and "work assignments" which, standing alone, might well be pre-empted as the exclusive concern of the Board. The occurrence of the abusive conduct, with which the state tort action is concerned, in such a context of federally prohibited discrimination suggests a potential for interference with the federal scheme of regulation.

Viewed, however, in light of the discrete concerns of the federal scheme and the state tort law, that potential for interference is insufficient to counterbalance the legitimate and substantial interest of the State in protecting its citizens. If the charges in Hill's complaint were filed with the Board, the focus of any unfair labor practice proceeding would be on whether the statements or conduct on the part of Union officials discriminated or threatened discrimination against him in employment referrals for reasons other than failure to pay Union dues. Whether the statements or conduct of the respondents also caused Hill severe emotional distress and physical injury would play no role in the Board's disposition of the case, and the Board could not award Hill damages for pain, suffering, or medical expenses. Conversely, the state-court tort action can be adjudicated without resolution of the "merits" of the underlying labor dispute. Recovery for the tort of emotional distress under California law requires proof that the defendant intentionally engaged in outrageous conduct causing the plaintiff to sustain mental distress. The state court need not consider, much less resolve, whether a union discriminated or threatened to discriminate against an employee in terms of employment opportunities. To the contrary, the tort action can be resolved without reference to any accommodation of the special interests of unions and members in the hiring hall context.

. . . At the same time, we reiterate that concurrent state-court jurisdiction cannot be permitted where there is a realistic threat of interference with the federal regulatory scheme. Union discrimination in employment opportunities cannot itself form the underlying "outrageous" conduct on which the state-court tort action is based; to hold otherwise would undermine the pre-emption principle. Nor can threats of such discrimination suffice to sustain state-court jurisdiction. It may well be that the threat, or actuality, of employment discrimination will cause a union member considerable emotional distress and anxiety. But something more is required before concurrent state-court jurisdiction can be permitted. Simply stated, it is essential that the state tort be either unrelated to employment discrimination or a function of the particularly abusive manner in which the

11. Discrimination in hiring hall referrals constitutes an unfair labor practice under §§8(b)(1)(A) and 8(b)(2) of the NLRA. See, e.g., Radio Officers v. NLRB, 347 U.S. 17 (1954); Operating Engineers Local 18, 205 N.L.R.B. 901 (1973), enf'd, 500 F.2d 48 (CA6 1974). . . .

discrimination is accomplished or threatened rather than a function of the actual or threatened discrimination itself.

Two further limitations deserve emphasis. Our decision rests in part on our understanding that California law permits recovery only for emotional distress sustained as a result of "outrageous" conduct. The potential for undue interference with federal regulation would be intolerable if state tort recoveries could be based on the type of robust language and clash of strong personalities that may be commonplace in various labor contexts. We also repeat that state trial courts have the responsibility in cases of this kind to assure that the damages awarded are not excessive. See Linn v. Plant Guard Workers, 383 U.S., at 65-66. . . .

Although the second count of petitioner's complaint alleged the intentional infliction of emotional distress, it is clear from the record that the trial of that claim was not in accord with the standards discussed above. The evidence supporting the verdict in Hill's favor focuses less on the alleged campaign of harassment, public ridicule, and verbal abuse, than on the discriminatory refusal to dispatch him to any but the briefest and least desirable jobs; and no appropriate instruction distinguishing the two categories of evidence was given to the jury. The consequent risk that the jury verdict represented damages for employment discrimination rather than for instances of intentional infliction of emotional distress precludes reinstatement of the judgment of the Superior Court. . . .

## *NOTES AND QUESTIONS*

**1. Protecting the Board's "Primary Jurisdiction"?** Given footnote 5, is *Farmer* best understood as a rule protecting the NLRB's primary jurisdiction? If so, why does the Court stress that the state tort action not only be unrelated to employment discrimination per se but also require "outrageous" conduct, beyond that "commonplace in various labor contexts," and in addition not be the basis for "excessive" damage awards? Does the primary-jurisdiction rationale explain the Court's adoption in the *Linn* case of both the *New York Times Co. v. Sullivan* scienter standard and also damages limitations for state law defamation suits concerning statements made during labor disputes? If the primary-jurisdiction rationale does not explain these limitations, what does?

**2. "Peripheral Federal Concern" vs. "Deeply Rooted in Local Feeling."** Is *Farmer* simply an application of a principle, expressed in *Garmon*, that there should be no preemption of state laws that regulate activity that is a "merely peripheral concern" of federal labor law "or" touches interests "deeply rooted in local feeling and responsibility"? How are lower courts to apply this exception? When are state interests sufficiently "deeply rooted"? When are federal interests "merely peripheral"?

**3. General vs. Specific State Law?** Note that the *Farmer* Court states that "the general applicability of a state course of action is not sufficient to exempt it from pre-emption." Is general applicability at least necessary for exemption from preemption? Would a state law that is framed specifically for labor disputes always be preempted? For instance, what if the tort law relied on in *Farmer* had applied only to outrageous conduct by unions? For further treatment of this consideration in preemption analysis, see infra note 4, page 848, and infra note 3, page 855.

**4. An Appropriate Balance?** Given the "outrageous" conduct required by *Farmer* and the pliable standards governing damage awards, will a trial court through instructions and the control of evidence be able to prevent a jury from considering the "actuality of employment discrimination"? Does *Farmer* expose unions to unfounded lawsuits by disgruntled workers seeking to bypass the eligibility rules of union hiring halls? Similarly, does *Linn* create a risk of unfounded suits by unions or employers to gain tactical advantage during organizing campaigns? Indeed, was *Linn* a considerably more difficult case than *Farmer* because it permits lawsuits between employers and unions that could both protract and aggravate labor disputes and also upset the balance of weapons afforded labor and management by federal labor law? See the dissenting opinions in *Linn* of Justices Black and Fortas. 383 U.S. at 67, 69.

**5. Punitive Damages?** Given the limitations on defamation damages imposed by *Linn*, as well as the holding in IBEW v. Foust, 442 U.S. 42 (1979), barring punitive damages against a union for breaching the duty of fair representation, should a court permit the recovery of punitive damages in a case like *Farmer* if the trial is otherwise properly conducted?

## Sears, Roebuck & Co. v. San Diego County District Council of Carpenters
*436 U.S. 180 (1978)*

STEVENS, J. . . .

The question . . . is whether the [NLRA] deprives a state court of the power to entertain an action by an employer to enforce state trespass laws against picketing which is arguably — but not definitely — prohibited or protected by federal law.

## I

On October 24, 1973, two business representatives of respondent Union visited the department store operated by petitioner (Sears) in Chula Vista, Cal., and determined that certain carpentry work was being performed by men who had not been dispatched from the Union hiring hall. Later that day, the Union agents met with the store manager and requested that Sears either arrange to have the work performed by a contractor who employed dispatched carpenters or agree in writing to abide by the terms of the Union's master labor agreement with respect to the dispatch and use of carpenters. The Sears manager stated that he would consider the request, but he never accepted or rejected it.

Two days later the Union established picket lines on Sears' property. The store is located in the center of a large rectangular lot. The building is surrounded by walkways and a large parking area. A concrete wall at one end separates the lot from residential property; the other three sides adjoin public sidewalks which are adjacent to the public streets. The pickets patrolled either on the privately owned walkways next to the building or in the parking area a few feet away. They carried signs indicating that they were sanctioned by the "Carpenters Trade Union." The picketing was peaceful and orderly.

Sears' security manager demanded that the Union remove the pickets from Sears' property. The Union refused, stating that the pickets would not leave unless forced to do so by legal action. On October 29, Sears filed a verified complaint in the Superior Court of California seeking an injunction against the continuing trespass; the court entered a temporary restraining order enjoining the Union from picketing on Sears' property. The Union promptly removed the pickets to the public sidewalks. On November 21, 1973, after hearing argument on the question whether the Union's picketing on Sears' property was protected by state or federal law, the court entered a preliminary injunction. The California Court of Appeal affirmed. . . .

The Supreme Court of California reversed. . . . Because the picketing was both arguably protected by §7 and arguably prohibited by §8, the court held state jurisdiction was pre-empted under [*Garmon*]. . . .

## II

We start from the premise that the Union's picketing on Sears' property after the request to leave was a continuing trespass in violation of state law.

We note, however, that the scope of the controversy in the state court was limited. Sears asserted no claim that the picketing itself violated any state or federal law. It sought simply to remove the pickets from its property to the public walkways, and the injunction issued by the state court was strictly confined to the relief sought. Thus, as a matter of state law, the location of the picketing was illegal but the picketing itself was unobjectionable.

As a matter of federal law, the legality of the picketing was unclear. Two separate theories would support an argument by Sears that the picketing was prohibited by §8 of the NLRA and a third theory would support an argument by the Union that the picketing was protected by §7. Under each of these theories the Union's purpose would be of critical importance.

If an object of the picketing was to force Sears into assigning the carpentry work away from its employees to Union members dispatched from the hiring hall, the picketing may have been prohibited by §8(b)(4)(D). Alternatively, if an object of the picketing was to coerce Sears into signing a prehire or members-only type agreement with the Union, the picketing was at least arguably subject to the prohibition on recognitional picketing contained in §8(b)(7)(C). Hence, if Sears had filed an unfair labor practice charge against the Union, the Board's concern would have been limited to the question whether the Union's picketing had an objective proscribed by the Act; the location of the picketing would have been irrelevant.

On the other hand, the Union contends that the sole objective of its action was to secure compliance by Sears with area standards, and therefore the picketing was protected by §7. Longshoremen v. Ariadne Shipping Co., 397 U.S. 195. Thus, if the Union had filed an unfair labor practice charge under §8(a)(1) when Sears made a demand that the pickets leave its property, it is at least arguable that the Board would have found Sears guilty of an unfair labor practice.

Our second premise, therefore, is that the picketing was both arguably prohibited and arguably protected by federal law. The case is not, however, one in which "it is clear or may fairly be assumed" that the subject matter which the state court sought to regulate—that is, the location of the picketing—is either prohibited or protected by the Federal Act. . . .

## IV

The leading case holding that when an employer grievance against a union may be presented to the [NLRB] it is not subject to litigation in a state tribunal is Garner v. Teamsters, 346 U.S. 485. *Garner* involved peaceful organizational picketing which arguably violated §8(b)(2). . . . A Pennsylvania equity court held that the picketing violated the Pennsylvania Labor Relations Act and therefore should be enjoined. The State Supreme Court reversed because the union conduct fell within the jurisdiction of the [NLRB] to prevent unfair labor practices.

This Court affirmed because Congress had "taken in hand this particular type of controversy . . . [i]n language almost identical to parts of the Pennsylvania statute," 346 U.S. at 488. Accordingly, the State, through its courts, was without power to "adjudge the same controversy and extend its own form of relief." Id., at 489. This conclusion did not depend on any surmise as to "how the [NLRB] might have decided this controversy had petitioners presented it to that body." Ibid. The precise conduct in controversy was arguably prohibited by federal law and therefore state jurisdiction was pre-empted. The reason for pre-emption was clearly articulated:

> A multiplicity of tribunals and a diversity of procedures are quite as apt to produce incompatible or conflicting adjudications as are different rules of substantive law. The same reasoning which prohibits federal courts from intervening in such cases, except by ways of review or on application of the federal Board, precludes state courts from doing so. . . . The conflict lies in remedies. . . . [W]hen two separate remedies are brought to bear on the same activity, a conflict is imminent. Id., at 498-499.

This reasoning has its greatest force when applied to state laws regulating the relations between employees, their union, and their employer. It may also apply to certain laws of general applicability which are occasionally invoked in connection with a labor dispute. Thus, a State's antitrust law may not be invoked to enjoin collective activity which is also arguably prohibited by the federal Act. Capital Service, Inc. v. NLRB, 347 U.S. 501; Weber v. Anheuser Busch, Inc., 348 U.S. 468. In each case, the pertinent inquiry is whether the two potentially conflicting statutes were "brought to bear on precisely the same conduct." Id., at 479.

On the other hand, the Court has allowed a State to enforce certain laws of general applicability even though aspects of the challenged conduct were arguably prohibited by §8 of the NLRA. Thus, for example, the Court has upheld state-court jurisdiction over conduct that touches "interests so deeply rooted in local feeling and responsibility that, in the absence of compelling congressional direction, we could not infer that Congress had deprived the States of the power to act." San Diego Building Trades Council v. Garmon, 359 U.S., at 244. . . .

The critical inquiry, therefore, is not whether the State is enforcing a law relating specifically to labor relations or one of general application but whether the controversy presented to the state court is identical to (as in *Garner*) or different from (as in *Farmer*) that which could have been, but was not, presented to the Labor Board. For it is only in the former situation that a state court's exercise of jurisdiction necessarily involves a risk of interference with the unfair labor practice jurisdiction of the Board which the arguably prohibited branch of the *Garmon* doctrine was designed to avoid.

In the present case, the controversy which Sears might have presented to the Labor Board is not the same as the controversy presented to the state court. If Sears had filed a charge, the federal issue would have been whether the picketing had a recognitional or work-reassignment objective; decision of that issue would have entailed relatively complex factual and legal determinations completely unrelated to the simple question whether a trespass had occurred. Conversely, in the state action, Sears only challenged the location of the picketing; whether the picketing had an objective proscribed by federal law was irrelevant to the state claim. Accordingly, permitting the state court to adjudicate Sears' trespass claim could create no realistic risk of interference with the Labor Board's primary jurisdiction to enforce the statutory prohibition against unfair labor practices.

The reasons why pre-emption of state jurisdiction is normally appropriate when union activity is arguably prohibited by federal law plainly do not apply to this situation; they therefore are insufficient to preclude a State from exercising jurisdiction limited to the trespassory aspects of that activity.

## V

The question whether the arguably protected character of the Union's trespassory picketing provides a sufficient justification for pre-emption of the state court's jurisdiction over Sears' trespass claim involves somewhat different considerations.

Apart from notions of "primary jurisdiction," there would be no objection to state courts' and the NLRB's exercising concurrent jurisdiction over conduct prohibited by the federal Act. But there is a constitutional objection to state-court interference with conduct actually protected by the Act. Considerations of federal supremacy, therefore, are implicated to a greater extent when labor-related activity is protected than when it is prohibited. Nevertheless, several considerations persuade us that the mere fact that the Union's trespass was *arguably* protected is insufficient to deprive the state court of jurisdiction in this case.

. . . [A]t first blush, the primary-jurisdiction rationale provides stronger support for pre-emption in this case when the analysis is focused upon the arguably protected, rather than the arguably prohibited, character of the Union's conduct. For to the extent that the Union's picketing was arguably protected, there existed a potential overlap between the controversy presented to the state court and that which the Union might have brought before the NLRB. Prior to granting any relief from the Union's continuing trespass, the state court was obligated to decide that the trespass was not actually protected by federal law, a determination which might entail an accommodation of Sears' property rights and the Union's §7 rights. In an unfair labor practice proceeding initiated by the Union, the Board might have been required to make the same accommodation.

Although it was theoretically possible for the accommodation issue to be decided either by the state court or by the [NLRB], there was in fact no risk of overlapping jurisdiction in this case. The primary-jurisdiction rationale justifies pre-emption only in situations in which an aggrieved party has a reasonable opportunity either to invoke the Board's jurisdiction himself or else to induce his adversary to do so. In this case, Sears could not directly obtain a Board ruling on the question whether the Union's trespass was federally protected. Such a Board determination could have been obtained only if the Union had filed an unfair labor practice charge alleging that Sears had interfered with the Union's §7 right to engage in peaceful picketing on Sears' property. By demanding that the Union remove its pickets from the store's property, Sears in fact pursued a course of action which gave the Union the opportunity to file such a charge. But the Union's response to Sears' demand foreclosed the possibility of having the accommodation of §7 and property rights made by the [NLRB]; instead of filing a charge with the Board, the Union advised Sears that the pickets would only depart under compulsion of legal process.

In the face of the Union's intransigence, Sears had only three options: permit the pickets to remain on its property; forcefully evict the pickets; or seek the protection of the State's trespass laws. Since the Union's conduct violated state law, Sears legitimately rejected the first option. Since the second option involved a risk of violence, Sears surely had the right—perhaps even the duty—to reject it. Only by proceeding in state court, therefore, could Sears obtain an orderly resolution of the question whether the Union had a federal right to remain on its property.

The primary-jurisdiction rationale unquestionably requires that when the same controversy may be presented to the state court or the NLRB, it must be presented to the Board. But that rationale does not extend to cases in which an employer has no acceptable method of invoking, or inducing the Union to invoke, the jurisdiction of the Board. We are therefore persuaded that the primary-jurisdiction rationale does not provide a *sufficient* justification for pre-empting state jurisdiction over arguably protected conduct when the party who could have presented the protection issue to the Board has not done so and the other party to the dispute has no acceptable means of doing so.

This conclusion does not, however, necessarily foreclose the possibility that pre-emption may be appropriate. The danger of state interference with federally protected conduct is the principal concern of the *Garmon* doctrine. To allow the exercise of state jurisdiction in certain contexts might create a significant risk of misinterpretation of federal law and the consequent prohibition of protected conduct. In those circumstances, it might be reasonable to infer that Congress preferred the costs inherent in a jurisdictional hiatus to the frustration of national labor policy which might accompany the exercise of state jurisdiction. Thus, the acceptability of "arguable protection" as a justification for pre-emption in a given class of cases is, at least in part, a function of the strength of the argument that §7 does in fact protect the disputed conduct.

The Court has held that state jurisdiction to enforce its laws prohibiting violence, defamation, the intentional infliction of emotional distress, or obstruction of access to property is not preempted by the NLRA. But none of those violations of state law involves protected conduct. In contrast, some violations of state trespass laws may be actually protected by §7 of the federal Act.

[The Court observed that in light of cases like NLRB v. Babcock & Wilcox Co., 351 U.S. 105 (1956),] while there are unquestionably examples of trespassory union activity in which the question whether it is protected is fairly debatable, experience under the Act teaches that such situations are rare and that a trespass is far more likely to be unprotected than protected. . . .

If there is a strong argument that the trespass is protected in a particular case, a union can be expected to respond to an employer demand to depart by filing an unfair labor practice charge; the protection question would then be decided by the agency experienced in accommodating the §7 rights of unions and the property rights of employers in the context of a labor dispute. But if the argument for protection is so weak that it has virtually no chance of prevailing, a trespassing union would be well advised to avoid the jurisdiction of the Board and to argue that the protected character of its conduct deprives the state court of jurisdiction.

As long as the union has a fair opportunity to present the protection issue to the [NLRB], it retains meaningful protection against the risk of error in a state tribunal. In this case the Union failed to invoke the jurisdiction of the Labor Board, and Sears had no right to invoke that jurisdiction and could not even precipitate its exercise without resort to self-help. Because the assertion of state jurisdiction in a case of this kind does not create a significant risk of prohibition of protected conduct, we are unwilling to presume that Congress intended the arguably protected character of the Union's conduct to deprive the California courts of jurisdiction to entertain Sears' trespass action.[44]

---

44. The fact that Sears demanded that the Union discontinue the trespass before it initiated the trespass action is critical to our holding. While it appears that such a demand was a precondition to commencing a trespass action under California law, see 122 Cal. Rptr. 449 (1975), in order to avoid a valid claim of pre-emption it would have been required as a matter of federal law in any event. . . .

The judgment of the Supreme Court of California is therefore reversed, and the case is remanded to that court for further proceedings not inconsistent with this opinion.

[Justice Blackmun's concurrence included two points. First, the corollary of the Court's reasoning is this: If, after the employer asks the union to leave his property, the union files and expeditiously pursues an NLRB charge, state jurisdiction is preempted (and states should not act) until the General Counsel declines to issue a complaint or the Board dismisses the complaint and holds the picketing unprotected. Second, the likelihood of frequent state court interference with protected activities will diminish if state courts provide an adversary hearing before restraining union picketing.

Justice Powell, concurring separately, rejected Blackmun's corollary, stressing the slowness of the Board's processes, coupled with the risk of violence in situations where trespass has occurred. The dissenting opinion of Justice Brennan, joined by Justices Stewart and Marshall, is omitted.

On remand, the California Supreme Court reversed the order granting a preliminary injunction, holding that the union's picketing on private property was both lawful under California law and could not be enjoined under the state's anti-injunction statute. Sears, Roebuck & Co. v. San Diego Cty. Dist. Council of Carpenters, 25 Cal. 3d 317, 599 P.2d 676, 158 Cal. 3d 170 (1979).]

## *NOTES AND QUESTIONS*

**1. "Arguably-Protected" Conduct and Employer Remedies.** Does *Sears* hold that state law regulating arguably protected conduct is preempted only when an employer is able to invoke NLRA processes to test the protected status of the activity? Or should the Court's ruling be viewed as limited to those situations, like trespassory "area standards" picketing, where the claim of NLRA protection is relatively weak? After *Lechmere*, supra page 144, can a union's trespassory picketing be classified as "arguably protected"?

**2. When Is Conduct "Arguably" Protected?** Consider the Court's discussion in International Longshoremen's Ass'n v. Davis, 476 U.S. 380 (1986), of how state courts are to determine whether activity is arguably within the jurisdiction of the NLRB:

> If the word "arguably" is to mean anything, it must mean that the party claiming pre-emption is required to demonstrate that his case is one that the Board could legally decide in his favor. That is, a party asserting pre-emption must advance an interpretation of the Act that is not plainly contrary to its

> language and that has not been "authoritatively rejected" by the courts or the Board. . . . The party must put forth enough evidence to enable the court to find that the Board reasonably could uphold a claim based on such an interpretation.

Id. at 395. In *Davis*, the union's claim of preemption turned on whether it was arguable that a particular employee whom the employer claimed was a supervisor was in fact an "employee" protected by §7. The Court concluded that the union had to present evidence supporting its claim that this employee's job was different from that of another employee that the Regional Director had found to be a supervisor, or alternatively had to make a convincing argument that the Director was wrong in his prior determination. It was not enough for the union to assert that the employee was arguably not a supervisor.

**3. *Sears* and the Prohibited-Activity Prong of *Garmon*.** Assume that the NLRB had decided that the picketing was prohibited by the NLRA. Could Sears now bring an action based on trespass for monetary damages against the union? Does the Court's analysis of the arguably-prohibited prong of *Garmon* have relevance for the regulation of conduct that is in fact prohibited by federal law?

**4. General vs. Specific State Law?** Given the *Sears* Court's consideration of the relevance of the "general applicability" of California's trespass law, is a state law specifically directed toward conduct arguably prohibited by federal labor law always preempted? What if California's trespass law had provided for treble damages only against trespassory labor picketing?

**5. Enjoining Preempted State Proceedings.** The Anti-Injunction Act, 28 U.S.C. §2283, which limits federal injunctions against enforcement of state court proceedings, has blocked private litigants from enjoining the enforcement of state court decrees that contravene preemption doctrine. See Amalgamated Clothing Workers v. Richman Bros. Co., 348 U.S. 511 (1955). The Court has held, however, that the Board has authority, notwithstanding the Anti-Injunction Act, to obtain a federal court stay of such proceedings. See NLRB v. Nash-Finch Co., 404 U.S. 138 (1971) (enjoining state court action that would have limited peaceful labor picketing).

## 3. The Problem of Retaliatory Lawsuits

The Board takes the position that retaliatory lawsuits — lawsuits brought for the purpose of retaliating against activity protected by the NLRA—

constitute unfair labor practices that may be enjoined. The Supreme Court in two decisions, however, has read the NLRA, in light of First Amendment concerns, to limit the types of cases in which the Board may seek to enjoin and provide remedies for retaliatory lawsuits as unfair labor practices. BE & K Construction Co. v. NLRB, 536 U.S. 516 (2002); Bill Johnson's Restaurants, Inc. v. NLRB, 461 U.S. 731 (1983).

In *Bill Johnson's*, stressing that the right to petition the government through the courts is strongly protected by the First Amendment, the Court announced that "[t]he filing and prosecution of a well-founded lawsuit may not be enjoined as an unfair labor practice, even if it would not have been commenced but for the plaintiff's desire to retaliate against the defendant for exercising rights protected by the Act." 461 U.S. at 743. Furthermore, although "it is an enjoinable unfair labor practice to prosecute a baseless lawsuit with the intent of retaliating against an employee for the exercise of rights protected by §7," id. at 744, where there are "genuinely disputed material factual issues" or "genuine State-law legal questions," the Board must stay its hand from seeking an injunction until state tribunals have had an opportunity to determine the merit of the suit, id. at 746. The Court also concluded that a suit that proves meritorious cannot be adjudged to be an unfair labor practice, even if filed for a retaliatory purpose.

In *BE & K Construction*, the Court further held that the Board had exceeded its authority in ruling that "all reasonably based but unsuccessful lawsuits filed with a retaliatory purpose" constitute unfair labor practices. 536 U.S. at 531. The Court relied in part on Professional Real Estate Investors, Inc. v. Columbia Pictures Industries, Inc., 508 U.S. 49, 60-61 (1993), in which it had held that to be challenged under the antitrust laws, lawsuits must be "both objectively baseless *and* subjectively motivated by an unlawful purpose." The *BE & K Construction* Court, however, left open whether this same standard applies to the NLRA:

> We do not decide whether the Board may declare unlawful any unsuccessful but reasonably based suits that would not have been filed *but for a motive to impose the costs of the litigation process*, regardless of the outcome, in retaliation for NLRA protected activity, since the Board's standard does not confine itself to such suits. . . .

Id. at 536-537 (emphasis supplied).

On remand, a divided Board (3-2) in BE & K Construction Co., 351 N.L.R.B. 451 (2007) held that an employer's filing of an unsuccessful retaliatory lawsuit against a union does not constitute an unfair labor practice, unless the "lawsuit lacks a reasonable basis, or is objectively baseless, [such that] no reasonable litigant could realistically expect success on the merits." The Board does not apply this standard to retaliatory threats not incidental to the actual filing of a suit. See, e.g., United States Postal Service, 350 N.L.R.B. 125 (2007).

In both *BE & K Construction* and *Bill Johnson's*, the employer's court action had been brought under federal or state laws that were themselves not preempted by the NLRA. What if the employer's suit had been brought under preempted state law? Before finding such a suit an unfair labor practice, is the Board required after *BE & K Construction* to find that the lawsuit was objectively baseless? In *Bill Johnson's*, the Court explained in a footnote, 461 U.S. at 737 n.5, that it was not "dealing with a suit that is claimed to be beyond the jurisdiction of the state courts because of federal-law preemption." If the state court proceeding did seek to regulate arguably protected conduct, the Court indicated that the Board could obtain an injunction of the proceeding under the authority of NLRB v. Nash-Finch, 404 U.S. 138 (1971). Based on this language in *Bill Johnson's*, in Loehmann's Plaza (I), 305 N.L.R.B. 663 (1991), the Board ruled that after the General Counsel issues a complaint charging that a lawsuit has been brought seeking regulation of protected activity, the lawsuit is preempted under *Sears* and *Davis* as potential state regulation of arguably protected conduct. In the Board's view, in such a case it may find that the lawsuit's continuation is itself an unfair labor practice regardless of whether the suit has any merit under state law. In Loehmann's Plaza (II), 316 N.L.R.B. 109 (1995), the Board found the union activity challenged in the state lawsuit to be in fact not protected, and held that the continuation of the lawsuit therefore was not an unfair labor practice. Thus, continuation of a lawsuit after the issuance of the General Counsel's complaint will be found to be unlawful if, but only if, the activity the suit attempts to regulate is ultimately found to be actually protected. Is there any reason that the Board should not apply this doctrine after *BE & K Construction*?

## B. *MACHINISTS* PREEMPTION

### 1. Regulation of Economic Conflict

**Lodge 76, IAM (Machinists) v. Wisconsin Employment Relations Commission**
*427 U.S. 132 (1976)*

Brennan, J. . . .

A collective bargaining agreement between petitioner Local 76 (the Union) and respondent, Kearney and Trecker Corporation (the employer) was terminated by the employer pursuant to the terms of the agreement on June 19, 1971. Good-faith bargaining over the terms of a renewal agreement continued for over a year thereafter, finally resulting in the signing of a new agreement effective July 23, 1972. A particularly controverted issue during negotiations was the employer's demand that the provision of the expired agreement under which, as for the prior 17 years, the basic workday was seven and one-half hours, Monday through Friday, and the basic workweek was 37½ hours, be replaced with a new provision providing a basic workday of eight hours and a basic workweek of 40 hours, and that the terms on which overtime rates of pay were payable be changed accordingly.

A few days after the old agreement was terminated the employer unilaterally began to make changes in some conditions of employment provided in the expired contract, e.g., eliminating the checkoff of Union dues, eliminating the Union's office in the plant and eliminating Union lost time. . . . [I]n March 1972, the employer announced that it would [also] unilaterally implement, as of March 13, 1972, its proposal for a 40-hour week and eight-hour day. [At] a membership meeting on March 7 . . . , strike action was authorized and a resolution was adopted binding union members to refuse to work any overtime, defined as work in excess of seven and one-half hours in any day or 37½ hours in any week. Following the strike vote, the employer offered to "defer the implementation" of its workweek proposal if the Union would agree to call off the concerted refusal to work overtime. The Union, however, refused the offer and indicated its intent to continue the concerted ban on overtime. Thereafter, the employer did not make effective the proposed changes in the workday and workweek before the new agreement became effective on July 23, 1972. Although all but a very few employees complied with the Union's resolution against acceptance of overtime work during the negotiations, the employer did not discipline, or attempt to discipline, any employee for refusing to work overtime.

Instead, while negotiations continued, the employer filed a charge . . . that the Union's resolution violated §8(b)(3) of the [NLRA]. The Regional Director dismissed the charge on the ground that the "policy prohibiting overtime work by its member employees does not appear to be in violation of the Act" and therefore was not conduct cognizable by the Board under NLRB v. Insurance Agents, 361 U.S. 477 (1960) [, supra page 411]. However, the employer also filed a complaint before the Wisconsin Employment Relations Commission charging that the refusal to work overtime constituted an unfair labor practice under state law. . . . [T]he Commission . . . [held] that "the concerted refusal to work overtime is not an activity which is arguably protected under §7 or arguably prohibited under §8 of the [NLRA] and . . . therefore the . . . Commission is not preempted from asserting its jurisdiction to regulate said conduct." . . . The Commission thereupon entered an order that the Union, inter alia, "[i]mmediately cease and desist from authorizing, encouraging or condoning any concerted refusal to accept overtime assignments. . . ." The Wisconsin Circuit Court entered judgment enforcing the Commission's order. The Wisconsin Supreme Court affirmed the Circuit Court. . . . We reverse.

I

We consider first preemption based predominantly on the primary jurisdiction of the Board. This line of preemption analysis was developed in [*Garmon*], 359 U.S. 236. . . . However, a second line of preemption analysis has been developed in cases focusing upon the crucial inquiry whether Congress intended that the conduct involved be unregulated because left "to be controlled by the free play of economic forces." NLRB v. Nash-Finch Co., 404 U.S. 138, 144 (1971). Concededly this inquiry was not made in 1949 in the so-called *Briggs-Stratton* case, Automobile Workers v. Wisconsin Board, 336 U.S. 245 (1949), the decision of this Court heavily relied upon by the court below in reaching its decision that state regulation of the conduct at issue is not preempted by national labor law. . . .

However, the *Briggs-Stratton* holding that state power is not pre-empted as to peaceful conduct neither protected by §7 nor prohibited by §8 of the federal Act, a holding premised on the statement that "[t]his conduct is either governable by the State or it is entirely ungoverned," id., at 254, was undercut by subsequent decisions of this Court. For the Court soon recognized that a particular activity might be "protected" by federal law not only where it fell within §7, but also when it was an activity that Congress intended to be "unrestricted by *any* governmental power to regulate" because it was among the permissible "economic weapons in reserve . . . [the] actual exercise [of which] on occasion by the parties is part and parcel of the system that the Wagner and Taft-Hartley Acts have recognized." NLRB v. Insurance Agents, 361 U.S. [477,] at 488, 489 (1960) (emphasis added). "[T]he legislative purpose may . . . dictate that certain activity 'neither protected nor prohibited' be privileged against state regulation." Hanna Mining Co. v. Marine Engineers, 382 U.S. [181,] 187 [(1965)].

II

. . . [I]n Local 20, Teamsters v. Morton, 377 U.S. 252 (1964), [we] held preempted the application of state law to award damages for peaceful union secondary picketing. Although *Morton* involved conduct neither "protected nor prohibited" by §7 or §8 . . . , we recognized the necessity of an inquiry whether "'Congress occupied the field and closed it to state regulation.'" Id., at 258. Central to *Morton*'s analysis was the observation that "[i]n selecting which forms of economic pressure should be prohibited . . . , Congress struck the 'balance . . . between the uncontrolled power of management and labor to further their respective interests,'" id., at 258-259. . . .

There is simply no question that the Act's processes would be frustrated in the instant case were the State's ruling permitted to stand. The employer in this case invoked the Wisconsin law because it was unable to overcome the union tactic with its own economic self-help means. . . .

Our decisions hold that Congress meant that these activities, whether of employer or employees, were not to be regulable by States any more than by the NLRB, for neither States nor the Board are "afforded flexibility in picking and choosing which economic devices of labor and management would be branded as unlawful." [*Insurance Agents*, 361 U.S. at 498.] . . . To sanction state regulation of such economic pressure deemed by the federal Act "desirabl[y] . . . left for the free play of contending economic forces, . . . is not merely [to fill] a gap [by] outlaw[ing] what federal law fails to outlaw; it is denying to one party to an economic contest a weapon that Congress meant him to have available." Lesnick, Preemption Reconsidered: The Apparent Reaffirmation of *Garmon*, 72 Colum. L. Rev. 469, 478 (1972). Accordingly, such regulation by the State is impermissible because it "'stands as an obstacle to the accomplishment and execution of the full purposes and objectives of Congress.'" Hill v. Florida, 325 U.S. 538, 542 (1945). . . .

*Briggs-Stratton* is today overruled, and . . . we hold further that the Union's refusal to work overtime is peaceful conduct constituting activity which must be free of regulation by the States if the congressional intent in enacting the comprehensive federal law of labor relations is not to be frustrated. . . . [T]he judgment of the Wisconsin Supreme Court is reversed.

POWELL, J., with whom THE CHIEF JUSTICE joins, concurring. . . .

I write to make clear my understanding that the Court's opinion does not, however, preclude the States from enforcing, in the context of a labor dispute, "neutral" state statutes or rules of decision: state laws that are not directed toward altering the bargaining positions of employers or unions but which may have an incidental effect on relative bargaining strength. Except where Congress has specifically provided otherwise, the States generally should remain free to enforce, for example, their law of torts or of contracts, and other laws reflecting neutral public policy.* See Cox, Labor Law Preemption Revisited, 85 Harv. L. Rev. 1337, 1355-1356 (1972).

STEVENS, J., with whom STEWART and REHNQUIST, JJ., join, dissenting. . . .

If adherence to the rule of *Briggs-Stratton* would permit the States substantially to disrupt the balance Congress has struck between union and employer, I would readily join in overruling it. But I am not persuaded that partial strike activity is so essential to the bargaining process that the States should not be free to make it illegal. . . .

---

* State laws should not be regarded as neutral if they reflect an accommodation of the special interests of employers, unions, or the public in areas such as employee self-organization, labor disputes, or collective bargaining in pursuit of collective bargaining goals.

## NOTES AND QUESTIONS

**1. Basis for *Machinists* Preemption?** *Garner* offered two rationales for labor law preemption: (1) the primary jurisdiction of the NLRB, and (2) protection of the substantive balance of rights and responsibilities struck by federal law. Is *Machinists* preemption based on either or both of these rationales?

**2. Determining When Congress Intends to Leave a Field Unregulated?** *Machinists* may have been a more difficult case to find a congressional intent to occupy the "field" of regulation than the *Morton* decision on which it relied. In the 1959 amendments to the NLRA, Congress dealt with recognitional picketing and secondary pressures but did not focus on "partial strikes" or slowdowns. How are the parties, the Board, and the courts to determine whether Congress intends to leave a field unregulated when, as *Machinists* appears to hold, preemption may be found in the absence of evidence of a specific focus by Congress on the activity in question?

a. Is *Machinists* best understood as limited to the arena of bargaining weapons on the premise that Congress intended, as *Insurance Agents,* supra page 411, makes clear, to leave largely unregulated conduct designed to exert pressure in collective bargaining? If so, does this mean that states may regulate employee or union protests of grievances and employer countermeasures during the term of an agreement—say, a walkout over a grievance resulting in damage to unattended equipment? Or would such regulation also be inconsistent with Congress' intent to leave economic pressure unregulated?

b. Does *Machinists* preemption apply to contexts other than the exertion of economic pressure? Consider a state law framed to expand the access of union organizers to private property beyond what federal law requires under *Babcock* and *Lechmere.* The *Garmon* doctrine would not apply because an employer's denial of the required extra access would not be arguably prohibited or protected by the NLRA. Is such a law preempted under *Machinists*? Does non-preemption depend on the courts reading the Supreme Court's decisions on union-organizer access to private property to balance §7 rights with state-defined private property rights rather than with some other implied statutorily recognized employer interest? See note 2, page 150 supra. Is it relevant whether the state law is aimed specifically at union organizing or more broadly grants all solicitors access to certain forms of private property, such as shopping malls? Cf. PruneYard Shopping Ctr. v. Robbins, 447 U.S. 74 (1980) (upholding such a general state law from challenge as an unconstitutional deprivation of property); Northern California Newspaper Organizing Comm. v. Solano Assocs., 239 Cal. Rptr. 227, 193 Cal. App. 3d 1644 (Cal. App. 1 Dist. 1987) (upholding the same state law from an

NLRA preemption challenge). See generally Jeffrey M. Hirsch, Taking State Property Rights Out of Federal Labor Law, 47 B.C. L. Rev. 891 (2006).

c. Does *Machinists* apply to an Oregon law that creates a private right of action for any employee discharged or disciplined for declining to attend a meeting for the communication of an employer's religious or political views? See ORS §659.785. The Oregon law defines political matters to include the decision to support or join a constituent group, and defines constituent groups to include labor organizations. See ORS §659.780. See Paul M. Secunda, Toward the Viability of State-Based Legislation to Address Workplace Captive Audience Meetings in the United States, 29 Comp. Lab. L. & Pol'y J. 209 (2008).

**3. "Neutral" State Laws?** Does Justice Powell's concurring opinion provide an appropriate and workable way to limit the reach of *Machinists* preemption? How does Justice Powell's text apply to the Oregon law described in the last note? For further consideration of Powell's suggestion, see supra note 3, page 840, and note 4, page 848.

**4. Requiring State Regulation?** If only "neutral" state laws are in general not preempted under *Machinists,* are states effectively barred from carving out "labor dispute" exceptions from general criminal trespass laws? See Rum Creek Coal Sales, Inc. v. Caperton, 926 F.2d 353 (4th Cir. 1991) (finding preemption). Does this make sense? Can the NLRA's preemptive reach be read to *require* state regulation of labor activity? Cf. Lividas v. Bradshaw, 512 U.S. 107 (1994), discussed infra note 6, page 881.

**5. Applications.** How far does the reach of *Machinists* preemption extend?

a. *State "Anti-Scab" Laws.* Is a state law that prohibits the hiring of permanent replacements for strikers preempted? What if it prohibits only the hiring of permanent replacements for unfair labor practice strikers? Prohibits only the use of replacements when involving the use of "force or threats" to interfere with peaceful picketing during a labor dispute? See Employers Ass'n, Inc. v. United Steelworkers of Am., 803 F. Supp. 1558 (D. Minn. 1992), affirmed, 32 F.3d 1297 (8th Cir. 1994). See generally Michael H. LeRoy, The *Mackay Radio* Doctrine of Permanent Striker Replacements and the Minnesota Picket Line Peace Act: Questions of Preemption, 77 Minn. L. Rev. 843 (1993). Does the reach of *Machinists* preemption here depend on whether employers have an unlimited right under the NLRA to use replacements during an economic strike, rather than a more limited right to maintain operations through replacements who have been promised they will not be bumped at strike's end? If the latter, can states act to ensure that the availability of striker replacements is not artificially enhanced by use of out-of-state specialty suppliers or by use of those who "customarily and repeatedly" offer themselves as replacements for striking workers? Or are these judgments reserved solely to the NLRB? See Washington v. Labor Ready, Inc., 103 Wash. App. 775, 14 P.3d 828 (2001); Kapiolani Medical Center for Women and Children v. Hawaii, 82 F. Supp. 2d 1151 (D. Haw. 2000).

b. *Requiring Secret-Ballot Certification Elections.* Can states require secret ballot elections as a condition of collective bargaining representation of employees covered by the NLRA? At least four states, Arizona, South Carolina, South Dakota, and Utah, have placed such a requirement in their state constitutions. See NLRB v. Arizona, 2012 WL 3848400 (Sept. 5, 2012) (state constitutional provision not preempted on its face).

c. *State "Successor" Laws.* Can state law require contractors who take over service contracts to hire their predecessor's employees for at least some probationary period? See Washington Serv. Contractors Coalition v. District of Columbia, 54 F.3d 811 (D.C. Cir. 1995) (no preemption). Can state law impose obligations on firms to honor the collective bargaining agreements of employers from whom they have purchased assets and with whose operations they have substantial continuity? See Steelworkers v. St. Gabriel's Hosp., 871 F. Supp. 335 (D. Minn. 1994) (preemption). See also infra note 10, page 882.

d. *State Unemployment Compensation Laws.* The New York Telephone Company brings a suit in a federal district court against the administrators of the New York unemployment compensation fund, seeking an injunction against the enforcement of an increase of the company's taxes toward the fund because of extensive benefits paid to strikers during a seven-month strike against the company. The company contends that the New York law under which the benefits were paid to the strikers should be preempted as inconsistent with "the federal policy favoring the free play of economic forces in the collective bargaining process." The challenged New York law normally authorizes payment of unemployment compensation after approximately one week of the claimant's unemployment. If unemployment is caused by a "strike, lockout, or other industrial controversy," however, there is an additional seven-week waiting period for benefits. Is the New York law preempted under *Machinists*? Is the New York law not "neutral" because it allows payments to strikers? Would it be "neutral" if it prohibited such payments? The Supreme Court ultimately held the law not preempted in part because of a congressional judgment to permit the states "broad freedom in setting up the types of unemployment compensation [systems] they wish," as found in the Social Security Act of 1935, which plays a role in the funding and administration of state unemployment compensation. See New York Telephone Co. v. New York Dep't of Labor, 440 U.S. 519, 537 (1979).

**Building & Construction Trades Council v. Associated Builders & Contractors (Boston Harbor)**
*507 U.S. 218 (1993)*

BLACKMUN, J. . . .

The issue in this litigation is whether the National Labor Relations Act (NLRA), 49 Stat. 449, as amended, 29 U.S.C. §151 et seq., pre-empts enforcement by a state authority, acting as the owner of a construction project, of an otherwise lawful prehire collective-bargaining agreement negotiated by private parties.

I

The Massachusetts Water Resources Authority (MWRA) is an independent government agency charged by the Massachusetts Legislature with providing water-supply services, sewage collection, and treatment and disposal services for . . . eastern . . . Massachusetts. Following a lawsuit arising out of its failure to prevent the pollution of Boston Harbor, in alleged violation of the Federal Water Pollution Control Act, MWRA was ordered to clean up the harbor. The cleanup project was expected to cost $6.1 billion over 10 years. . . . MWRA has primary responsibility for the project. Under its enabling statute and the Commonwealth's public-bidding laws, MWRA provides the funds for construction (assisted by state and federal grants), owns the sewage-treatment facilities to be built, establishes all bid conditions, decides all contract awards, pays the contractors, and generally supervises the project.

In the spring of 1988, MWRA selected Kaiser Engineers, Inc., as its project manager. Kaiser was to be primarily in charge of managing and supervising construction activity. Kaiser also was to advise MWRA on the development of a labor-relations policy that would maintain worksite harmony, labor-management peace, and overall stability throughout the duration of the project. To that end, Kaiser suggested to MWRA that Kaiser be permitted to negotiate an agreement with the Building and Construction Trades Council and affiliated organizations (BCTC) that would assure labor stability over the life of the project. MWRA accepted Kaiser's suggestion, and Kaiser accordingly proceeded to negotiate the Boston Harbor Wastewater Treatment Facilities Project Labor Agreement (Agreement). The Agreement included: recognition of BCTC as the exclusive bargaining agent for all craft employees; use of specified methods for resolving all labor-related disputes; a requirement that all employees be subject to union-security provisions compelling them to become union members within seven days of their employment; the primary use of BCTC's hiring halls to supply the project's craft labor force; a 10-year no-strike commitment; and a requirement that all contractors and subcontractors agree to be bound by the Agreement. MWRA's board of directors approved and adopted the Agreement in May 1989 and directed that Bid Specification 13.1 [requiring bidding contractors to abide by terms of the Agreement] be incorporated into its solicitation of bids for work on the project. . . .

In March 1990, a contractors' association not a party to this litigation filed a charge with the National Labor Relations Board (NLRB) contending that the Agreement violated the NLRA. The NLRB General Counsel refused to issue a complaint, finding: (1) that the Agreement is a valid prehire agreement under §8(f) of the NLRA, 29 U.S.C. §158(f), which authorizes such agreements in the construction industry; and (2) that the Agreement's provisions limiting work on the project to contractors who agree to abide by the Agreement are lawful under the construction-industry proviso to §8(e), 29 U.S.C. §158(e). . . .

Also in March 1990, respondent Associated Builders and Contractors of Massachusetts/Rhode Island, Inc. (ABC), an organization representing non-union construction-industry employers, brought this suit against MWRA, Kaiser, and BCTC, seeking, among other things, to enjoin enforcement of Bid Specification 13.1. . . . Only NLRA pre-emption is at issue here. . . .

## III . . .

Our decisions in this area support the distinction between government as regulator and government as proprietor. We have held consistently that the NLRA was intended to supplant state labor regulation, not all legitimate state activity that affects labor. In *Machinists,* for example, we referred to Congress' pre-emptive intent to "leave some activities unregulated," 427 U.S. at 144 (emphasis added), and held that the activities at issue—workers deciding together to refuse overtime work—were not "regulable by States," id., at 149 (emphasis added). In Golden State [Transit Corp. v. Los Angeles, 475 U.S. 608 (1986) ("*Golden State I*")], we held that the reason Los Angeles could not condition renewal of a taxicab franchise upon settlement of a labor dispute was that "*Machinists* pre-emption . . . precludes state and municipal regulation 'concerning conduct that Congress intended to be unregulated.'" 475 U.S. at 614. . . . We refused to permit the city's exercise of its regulatory power of license nonrenewal to restrict Golden State's right to use lawful economic weapons in its dispute with its union. See 475 U.S. at 615-619. As petitioners point out, a very different case would have been presented had the city of Los Angeles purchased taxi services from Golden State in order to transport city employees. In that situation, if the strike had produced serious interruptions in the services the city had purchased, the city would not necessarily have been pre-empted from advising Golden State that it would hire another company if the labor dispute were not resolved and services resumed by a specific deadline.

In [Wisconsin Dep't of Industry v.] Gould [Inc., 475 U.S. 282 (1986)], we rejected the argument that the State was acting as proprietor rather than regulator for purposes of *Garmon* pre-emption when the State refused to do business with persons who had violated the NLRA three times within five years. We noted in doing so that in that case, "debarment . . . serves plainly as a means of enforcing the NLRA." 475 U.S. at 287. We said there that "the State concedes, as we think it must, that the point of the statute is to deter labor law violations"; we concluded that "no other purpose could credibly be ascribed." Ibid.

. . . The conduct at issue in *Gould* was a state agency's attempt to compel conformity with the NLRA. Because the statute at issue in *Gould* addressed employer conduct unrelated to the employer's performance of contractual obligations to the State, and because the State's reason for such conduct was to deter NLRA violations, we concluded: "Wisconsin 'simply is not functioning as a private purchaser of services,' . . . [and therefore,] for all practical purposes, Wisconsin's debarment scheme is tantamount to regulation." Id., at 289. We emphasized that we were "not saying that state purchasing decisions may never be influenced by labor considerations." Id., at 291.

The conceptual distinction between regulator and purchaser exists to a limited extent in the private sphere as well. A private actor, for example, can participate in a boycott of a supplier on the basis of a labor policy concern rather than a profit motive. See id., at 290. The private actor under such circumstances would be attempting to "regulate" the suppliers and would not be acting as a typical proprietor. The fact that a private actor may "regulate" does not mean, of course, that the private actor may be "pre-empted" by the NLRA; the Supremacy Clause does not require pre-emption of private conduct. Private actors therefore may "regulate" as they please, as long as their conduct does not violate the law. . . . When the State acts as regulator, it performs a role that is characteristically a governmental rather than a private role, boycotts notwithstanding. Moreover, as regulator of private conduct, the State is more powerful than private parties. These distinctions are far less significant when the State acts as a market participant with no interest in setting policy. . . .

## IV

Permitting the States to participate freely in the market-place is not only consistent with NLRA pre-emption principles generally but also, in these cases, promotes the legislative goals that animated the passage of the §§8(e) and (f) exceptions for the construction industry. . . .

It is undisputed that the Agreement between Kaiser and BCTC is a valid labor contract under §§8(e) and (f). As noted above, those sections explicitly authorize this type of contract between a union and an employer like Kaiser, which is engaged primarily in the construction industry, covering employees engaged in that industry.

Of course, the exceptions provided for the construction industry in §§8(e) and (f), like the prohibitions from which they provide relief, are not made specifically applicable to the State. This is because the State is excluded from the definition of the term "employer" under the NLRA, see 29 U.S.C. §152(2), and because the State, in any event, is acting not as an employer but as a purchaser in this case. Nevertheless, the general goals behind passage of §§8(e) and (f) are still relevant to determining what Congress intended with respect to the State and its relationship to the agreements authorized by these sections.

It is evident from the face of the statute that in enacting exemptions authorizing certain kinds of project labor agreements in the construction industry, Congress intended to accommodate conditions specific to that industry. Such conditions include, among others, the short-term nature of employment which makes posthire collective bargaining difficult, the contractor's need for predictable costs and a steady supply of skilled labor, and a longstanding custom of prehire bargaining in the industry. See S. Rep. No. 187, 86th Cong., 1st Sess., 28, 55-56 (1959); H.R. Rep. No. 741, 86th Cong., 1st Sess., 19-20 (1959).

There is no reason to expect these defining features of the construction industry to depend upon the public or private nature of the entity purchasing contracting services. To the extent that a private purchaser may choose a contractor based upon that contractor's willingness to enter into a prehire agreement, a public entity as purchaser should be permitted to do the same. Confronted with such a purchaser, those contractors who do not normally enter such agreements are faced with a choice. They may alter their usual mode of operation to secure the business opportunity at hand, or seek business from purchasers whose perceived needs do not include a project labor agreement. In the absence of any express or implied indication by Congress that a State may not manage its own property when it pursues its purely proprietary interests, and where analogous private conduct would be permitted, this Court will not infer such a restriction. Indeed, there is some force to petitioners' argument that denying an option to public owner-developers that is available to private owner-developers itself places a restriction on Congress' intended free play of economic forces identified in *Machinists.*

## V

In the instant case, MWRA acted on the advice of a manager hired to organize performance of a cleanup job over which, under Massachusetts law, MWRA is the proprietor. There is no question but that MWRA was attempting to ensure an efficient project that would be completed as quickly and effectively as possible at the lowest cost. As petitioners note, moreover, the challenged action in this litigation was specifically tailored to one particular job, the Boston Harbor cleanup project. There is therefore no basis on which to distinguish the incentives at work here from those that operate elsewhere in the construction industry, incentives that this Court has recognized as legitimate. See Woelke & Romero Framing Co. v. NLRB, 456 U.S. [645,] 662, and n.14 [(1982)].

We hold today that Bid Specification 13.1 is not government regulation and that it is therefore subject to neither *Garmon* nor *Machinists* preemption. . . .

## *NOTES AND QUESTIONS*

**1. Is the Intent to Avoid Disruption in a Government Operation Sufficient to Avoid *Machinists* Preemption?** Does the Court's analysis suggest that as long as a state or municipal government authority plausibly claims it is merely seeking to avoid disruption of a government-funded operation by a labor dispute, it may refuse to do business with any private employer involved in such a dispute? Could Wisconsin officials have made such a claim in *Gould*? Could the licensing authority in *Golden State*?

**2. Is *Boston Harbor* Limited to the Construction Industry?** Does *Boston Harbor* allow a state or local government to take any action as a "market participant" that it could have taken had it been a privately-owned market participant? How important to the Court's analysis were the exceptions for the construction industry expressed in §§8(e) and (f) of the NLRA?

**3. Underlying Political Motive of Government Officials?**

a. Even if the Harbor Authority had a proprietary interest in deciding which contractors would do the construction work and the terms under which that work was done, is it likely that the City's political leaders might have influenced the agency to act in a manner favorable to the interests of their labor union supporters? If evidence of such a motive were presented, would it have changed the analysis in *Boston Harbor*?

b. Presumably the *Golden State* decision means that a city cannot condition an approval of a zoning change to allow expansion of a business on the business's resolution of a labor dispute with a union. Should the result be different if the city's politically powerful mayor through mediation induces the employer to agree to the union's terms, conditional on the city's approval of the zoning change? What if the mayor and the city council simply change their position on the zoning change after the employer and union reach agreement and the union then changes its political stance?

See Benjamin I. Sachs, Despite Preemption: Making Labor Law in Cities and States, 124 Harv. L. Rev. 1153 (2011).

**4. Applications.**

a. A Michigan statute bars governmental units in the state from entering into a Project Labor Agreement (PLA) like the one at issue in *Boston Harbor.* Under the statute, bidding on public construction projects must be open to contractors whether or not they are parties to such an agreement. Is the statute preempted under *Machinists*? What if the statute barred any private contractor with a PLA from bidding on a public project and prohibited private projects receiving state grant funds from using project labor agreements? See Michigan Building and Construction Trades Council v. Snyder, 729 F.3d 572 (6th Cir. 2013).

b. After purchasing the *Oakland Tribune,* ANI newspapers terminated the paper's contracts with nine unions, dismissed a majority of its employees, and moved its printing operation out of Oakland. In response, the unions organized a boycott of the paper. The Oakland City Council voted to join the boycott by canceling the city's subscription to receive 13 papers daily and by withdrawing its advertising. The council also passed a resolution urging the citizens of Oakland to join the boycott. ANI seeks an injunction against the City Council's actions, claiming preemption by federal labor law. What result? Does the suggestion in *Boston Harbor* that a private party's participation in a boycott is akin to regulation settle the case? Or is it relevant that the city's subscriptions and advertising have only a minimal economic impact on the newspaper? See Alameda Newspapers, Inc. v. City of Oakland, 95 F.3d 1406 (9th Cir. 1996).

c. The Corporation Counsel of New York City asks your advice on whether the city can refuse to renew its sole-source contract with the private Legal Aid Society if the staff lawyers of the society carry out their threat to decline to provide legal services to criminal defendants in city courts pending the resolution of a contract dispute with the society. What advice do you give?

**5. Presidential Executive Orders.** The NLRA does not restrict the power of Congress to pass other legislation that might shift any balance struck in the NLRA between employee rights and union or employer prerogatives. It may, however, have a kind of preemptive force with respect to presidential executive orders. The President has general authority under procurement law to issue executive orders placing conditions on the hiring and use of federal contractors, but must respect the limits set in other federal legislation. Two issues seem paramount: (1) With respect to the particular executive order, is the President acting in a regulatory or propriety capacity? (2) If the President is acting in a regulatory capacity, is the executive order regulating conduct arguably protected or prohibited by the NLRA or conduct the NLRA intended to leave unregulated? Compare Chamber of Commerce v. Reich, 74 F.3d 1322 (D.C. Cir. 1996) (President Clinton's executive order barring the federal government from contracting with employers who hire permanent replacements during a lawful strike contravened federal labor law policy embodied in the NLRA in favor of allowing economic conflict to be free of any regulation of use of tactics like striking and hiring replacements for strikers), with UAW-Labor Employment & Training Corp. v. Chao, 325 F.3d 360 (D.C. Cir. 2003) (President Bush's executive order mandating that employers that contract with the federal government post notices that "employees cannot be required to join a union or maintain membership in a union in order to retain their jobs" did not contravene federal labor policy embodied in the NLRA).

a. Does federal labor policy bar President Obama's Executive Order 13496 mandating that federal contractors inform workers of their rights under the NLRA?

b. Does federal labor policy bar President Obama's Executive Order 13204 requiring federal contractors who have been awarded contracts in competitive bidding to provide employees of a predecessor contractor a right of first refusal in jobs for which they are qualified?

c. Did federal labor policy preclude President Bush from issuing an executive order prohibiting any federal agency from requiring bidders or contractors on federally funded projects to enter, or prohibiting them from entering, prehire, project labor agreements, like the one at issue in the *Boston Harbor* case? See Building & Construction Trades Dep't v. Allbaugh, 295 F.3d 28 (D.C. Cir. 2002) (upholding President Bush's order).

d. Does federal labor policy bar President Obama from issuing Executive Order 13502 "to encourage executive agencies to consider requiring the use of project labor agreements in connection with large scale construction projects in order to promote economy and efficiency"?

### Chamber of Commerce v. Brown
*554 U.S. 60 (2008)*

STEVENS, J. . . .

A California statute known as "Assembly Bill 1889" (AB 1889) prohibits several classes of employers that receive state funds from using the funds "to assist, promote, or deter union organizing." See Cal. Govt. Code Ann. §§16645-16649 (West Supp. 2008). The question presented to us is whether two of its provisions—§16645.2, applicable to grant recipients, and §16645.7, applicable to private employers receiving more than $10,000 in program funds in any year—are pre-empted by federal law mandating that certain zones of labor activity be unregulated.

## I

As set forth in the preamble, the State of California enacted AB 1889 for the following purpose:

> "It is the policy of the state not to interfere with an employee's choice about whether to join or to be represented by a labor union. For this reason, the state should not subsidize efforts by an employer to assist, promote, or deter union organizing. It is the intent of the Legislature in enacting this act to prohibit an employer from using state funds and facilities for the purpose of influencing employees to support or oppose unionization and to prohibit an employer from seeking to influence employees to support or oppose unionization while those employees are performing work on a state contract." 2000 Cal. Stats. ch. 872, §1.

AB 1889 prohibits certain employers that receive state funds—whether by reimbursement, grant, contract, use of state property, or pursuant to a state program—from using such funds to "assist, promote, or deter union organizing." See Cal. Govt. Code Ann. §§16645.1 to 16645.7. This prohibition encompasses "any attempt by an employer to influence the decision of its employees" regarding "[w]hether to support or oppose a labor organization" and "[w]hether to become a member of any labor organization." §16645(a). The statute specifies that the spending restriction applies to "any expense, including legal and consulting fees and salaries of supervisors and employees, incurred for . . . an activity to assist, promote, or deter union organizing." §16646(a).

Despite the neutral statement of policy quoted above, AB 1889 expressly exempts "activit[ies] performed" or "expense[s] incurred" in connection with certain undertakings that promote unionization, including "[a]llowing a labor organization or its representatives access to the employer's facilities or property," and "[n]egotiating, entering into, or carrying out a voluntary recognition agreement with a labor organization." §§16647(b), (d).

To ensure compliance with the grant and program restrictions at issue in this case, AB 1889 establishes a formidable enforcement scheme. Covered employers must certify that no state funds will be used for prohibited expenditures; the employer must also maintain and provide upon request "records sufficient to show that no state funds were used for those expenditures." §§16645.2(c), 16645.7(b)-(c). If an employer commingles state and other funds, the statute presumes that any expenditures to assist, promote, or deter union organizing derive in part from state funds on a pro rata basis. §16646(b). Violators are liable to the State for the amount of funds used for prohibited purposes plus a civil penalty equal to twice the amount of those funds. §§16645.2(d), 16645.7(d). Suspected violators may be sued by the state attorney general or any private taxpayer, and prevailing plaintiffs are "entitled to recover reasonable attorney's fees and costs." §16645.8(d).

## II

In April 2002, several organizations whose members do business with the State of California (collectively, Chamber of Commerce) brought this action against the California Department of Health Services and appropriate state officials (collectively, the State) to enjoin enforcement of AB 1889. . . .

The District Court granted partial summary judgment in favor of the Chamber of Commerce, holding that the National Labor Relations Act (NLRA or Wagner Act), pre-empts Cal. Govt. Code Ann. §16645.2 (concerning grants) and §16645.7 (concerning program funds) because those provisions "regulat[e] employer speech about union organizing under specified circumstances, even though Congress intended free debate." The Court of Appeals for the Ninth Circuit, after twice affirming the District Court's judgment, granted rehearing en banc and reversed. While the en banc majority agreed that California enacted §§16645.2 and 16645.7 in its capacity as a regulator, and not as a mere proprietor or market participant, it concluded that Congress did not intend to preclude States from imposing such restrictions on the use of their own funds. We . . . now reverse.

. . . [W]e hold that §§16645.2 and 16645.7 are pre-empted under *Machinists* because they regulate within "a zone protected and reserved for market freedom." Building & Constr. Trades Council v. Associated Builders & Contractors of Mass./R. I., Inc., 507 U.S. 218, 227 (1993) *(Boston Harbor)*. We do not reach the question whether the provisions would also be pre-empted under *Garmon*.

## III . . .

From one vantage, §8(c) "merely implements the First Amendment," NLRB v. Gissel Packing Co., 395 U.S. 575, 617(1969), in that it responded to particular constitutional rulings of the NLRB. See S. Rep. No. 80-105, pt. 2, pp 23-24 (1947). But its enactment also manifested a "congressional intent to encourage free debate on issues dividing labor and management." Linn v. Plant Guard Workers, 383 U.S. 53, 62 (1966). . . .

Congress' express protection of free debate forcefully buttresses the pre-emption analysis in this case. Under *Machinists*, congressional intent to shield a zone of activity from regulation is usually found only "implicit[ly] in the structure of the Act," Livadas v. Bradshaw, 512 U.S. 107, 117, n.11 (1994), drawing on the notion that "'[w]hat Congress left unregulated is as important as the regulations that it imposed,'" Golden State Transit Corp. v. Los Angeles, 493 U.S. 103 (1989) *(Golden State II)* (quoting N.Y. Tel. Co. v. N.Y. State DOL, 440 U.S. 519 (1979) (Powell, J., dissenting)). In the case of noncoercive speech, however, the protection is both implicit and explicit. Sections 8(a) and 8(b) demonstrate that when Congress has sought to put limits on advocacy for or against union organization, it has expressly set forth the mechanisms for doing so. Moreover, the amendment to §7 calls attention to the right of employees to refuse to join unions, which implies an underlying right to receive information opposing unionization. Finally, the addition of §8(c) expressly precludes regulation of speech about unionization "so long as the communications do not contain a 'threat of reprisal or force or promise of benefit.'" *Gissel Packing,* 395 U.S., at 618.

. . . California's policy judgment that partisan employer speech necessarily "interfere[s] with an employee's choice about whether to join or to be represented by a labor union," 2000 Cal. Stats. ch. 872, §1, is the same policy judgment that the NLRB advanced under the Wagner Act, and that Congress renounced in the Taft-Hartley Act. To the extent §§16645.2 and 16645.7 actually further the express goal of AB 1889, the provisions are unequivocally pre-empted.

## IV

The Court of Appeals concluded that *Machinists* did not pre-empt §§16645.2 and 16645.7 for three reasons: (1) The spending restrictions apply only to the *use* of state funds, (2) Congress did not leave the zone of activity free from *all* regulation, and (3) California modeled AB 1889 on federal statutes. We find none of these arguments persuasive.

[1.] . . . It is beyond dispute that California enacted AB 1889 in its capacity as a regulator rather than a market participant. AB 1889 is neither "specifically tailored to one particular job" nor a "legitimate response to state procurement constraints or to local economic needs." As the statute's preamble candidly acknowledges, the legislative purpose is not the efficient procurement of goods and services, but the furtherance of a labor policy. See 2000 Cal. Stats. ch. 872, §1. Although a State has a legitimate proprietary interest in ensuring that state funds are spent in accordance with the purposes for which they are appropriated, this is not the objective of AB 1889. In contrast to a neutral affirmative requirement that funds be spent solely for the purposes of the relevant grant or program, AB 1889 imposes a targeted negative restriction on employer speech about unionization. Furthermore, the statute does not even apply this constraint uniformly. Instead of forbidding the use of state funds for *all* employer advocacy regarding unionization, AB 1889 permits use of state funds for *select* employer advocacy activities that promote unions. Specifically, the statute exempts expenses incurred in connection with, *inter alia,* giving unions access to the workplace, and voluntarily recognizing unions without a secret ballot election. §§16647(b), (d). . . .

California's reliance on a "use" restriction rather than a "receipt" restriction is, at least in this case, no more consequential than Wisconsin's reliance on its spending power rather than its police power in [Wis. Dep't of

Indus., Labor & Human Rels. v. Gould, Inc., 475 U.S. 282 [(1986)]. As explained below, AB 1889 couples its "use" restriction with compliance costs and litigation risks that are calculated to make union-related advocacy prohibitively expensive for employers that receive state funds. By making it exceedingly difficult for employers to demonstrate that they have not used state funds and by imposing punitive sanctions for noncompliance, AB 1889 effectively reaches beyond "the use of funds over which California maintains a sovereign interest."

Turning first to the compliance burdens, AB 1889 requires recipients to "maintain records sufficient to show that no state funds were used" for prohibited expenditures, §§16645.2(c), 16645.7(c), and conclusively presumes that any expenditure to assist, promote, or deter union organizing made from "commingled" funds constitutes a violation of the statute, §16646(b). Maintaining "sufficient" records and ensuring segregation of funds is no small feat, given that AB 1889 expansively defines its prohibition to encompass "any expense" incurred in "any attempt" by an employer to "influence the decision of its employees." §§16645(a), 16646(a). Prohibited expenditures include not only discrete expenses such as legal and consulting fees, but also an allocation of overhead, including "salaries of supervisors and employees," for any time and resources spent on union-related advocacy. See §16646(a). The statute affords no clearly defined safe harbor, save for expenses incurred in connection with activities that either favor unions or are required by federal or state law. See §16647.

The statute also imposes deterrent litigation risks. Significantly, AB 1889 authorizes not only the California Attorney General but also any private taxpayer—including, of course, a union in a dispute with an employer—to bring a civil action against suspected violators for "injunctive relief, damages, civil penalties, and other appropriate equitable relief." §16645.8. Violators are liable to the State for three times the amount of state funds deemed spent on union organizing. §§6645.2(d), 16645.7(d), 16645.8(a). Prevailing plaintiffs, and certain prevailing taxpayer intervenors, are entitled to recover attorney's fees and costs, §16645.8(d), which may well dwarf the treble damages award. Consequently, a trivial violation of the statute could give rise to substantial liability. Finally, even if an employer were confident that it had satisfied the recordkeeping and segregation requirements, it would still bear the costs of defending itself against unions in court, as well as the risk of a mistaken adverse finding by the factfinder.

In light of these burdens, California's reliance on a "use" restriction rather than a "receipt" restriction "does not significantly lessen the inherent potential for conflict" between AB 1889 and the NLRA. . . .

[2.] . . . Stressing that the NLRB has regulated employer speech that takes place on the eve of union elections, the Court of Appeals deemed *Machinists* inapplicable because "employer speech in the context of organizing" is not a zone of activity that Congress left free from "*all* regulation." . . .

. . . The NLRB has policed a narrow zone of speech to ensure free and fair elections under the aegis of §9 of the NLRA, 29 U.S.C. §159. Whatever the NLRB's regulatory authority within special settings such as imminent elections, however, Congress has clearly denied it the authority to regulate the broader category of noncoercive speech encompassed by AB 1889. It is equally obvious that the NLRA deprives California of this authority, since "'[t]he States have no more authority than the Board to upset the balance that Congress has struck between labor and management.'" Metropolitan Life Ins. Co. v. Massachusetts, 471 U.S. 724, 751 (1985).

[3.] Finally, the Court of Appeals reasoned that Congress could not have intended to pre-empt AB 1889 because Congress itself has imposed similar restrictions. Specifically, three federal statutes include provisions that forbid the use of particular grant and program funds "to assist, promote, or deter union organizing." We are not persuaded that these few isolated restrictions, plucked from the multitude of federal spending programs, were either intended to alter or did in fact alter the "'wider contours of federal labor policy.'" *Metropolitan Life*, 471 U.S., at 753, 105 S. Ct. 2380, 85 L. Ed. 2d 728.

A federal statute will contract the pre-emptive scope of the NLRA if it demonstrates that "Congress has decided to tolerate a substantial measure of diversity" in the particular regulatory sphere. *N.Y. Tel.*, 440 U.S., at 546 (plurality opinion). . . .

Had Congress enacted a federal version of AB 1889 that applied analogous spending restrictions to *all* federal grants or expenditures, the pre-emption question would be closer. Cf. *Metropolitan Life*, 471 U.S., at 755 (citing federal minimum labor standards as evidence that Congress did not intend to pre-empt state minimum labor standards). But none of the cited statutes is Government wide in scope, none contains comparable remedial provisions, and none contains express pro-union exemptions.

BREYER, J. with whom Justice GINSBURG joins, dissenting.

California's statute differs from the Wisconsin statute [in *Gould*] because it does not seek to compel labor-related activity. Nor does it seek to forbid labor-related activity. It permits all employers who receive state funds to "assist, promote, or deter union organizing." It simply says to those employers, do not do so on our dime. I concede that a federal law that forces States to pay for labor-related speech from public funds would encourage *more* of that speech. But no one can claim that the NLRA is such a law. And without such a law, a State's refusal to pay for labor-related speech does not *impermissibly* discourage that activity. To refuse to pay for an activity (as here) is not the same as to compel others to engage in that activity (as in *Gould*).

. . . California's operative language does not weaken or undercut Congress' policy of "encourag[ing] free debate on issues dividing labor and management." For one thing, employers remain free to spend *their own* money to "assist, promote, or deter" unionization. More importantly,

I cannot conclude that California's statute would weaken or undercut any such congressional policy because Congress itself has enacted three statutes that, *using identical language,* do precisely the same thing. . . .

. . . [T]he law normally gives legislatures broad authority to decide how to spend the people's money. A legislature, after all, generally has the right *not* to fund activities that it would prefer not to fund—even where the activities are otherwise protected. . . .

As far as I can tell, States that *do* wish to pay for employer speech are generally free to do so. They might make clear, for example, through grant-related rules and regulations that a grant recipient can use the funds to pay salaries and overhead, which salaries and overhead might include expenditures related to management's role in labor organizing contests. If so, why should States that do *not* wish to pay be deprived of a similar freedom? Why should they be conscripted into paying?

. . . [T]he regulator/market-participant distinction suggests a false dichotomy. The converse of "market participant" is not necessarily "regulator." A State may appropriate funds without either participating in or regulating the labor market. . . .

The majority further objects to the fact that the statute does not "apply" the constraint "uniformly," because it permits use of state funds for "*select* employer advocacy activities that promote unions." That last phrase presumably refers to an exception in the California statute that permits employers to spend state funds to negotiate a voluntary recognition of a union. But this exception underscores California's basic purpose—maintaining a position of spending neutrality on *contested* labor matters. Where labor and management agree on unionization, there is no conflict.

. . . I agree with the majority that, should the compliance provisions, as a practical matter, unreasonably discourage expenditure of *nonstate* funds, the NLRA may well pre-empt California's statute. But I cannot say on the basis of the record before us that the statute will have that effect.

## *NOTES AND QUESTIONS*

**1. How Broad a Holding?** After *Chamber of Commerce,* would a state law that prohibited only the use of state funds on any expenditure for lawyers or consultant fees involving union organizing be preempted? What if it also prohibited the use of state funds for lawyers and consultants, and other outside expenses, generally? Should it matter whether the statute attempted to control the use of state money by state contractors or just by state grantees? See Healthcare Ass'n of New York State v. Pataki, 471 F.3d 87, 105-106 (2d Cir. 2006) (if labor costs cannot affect a contractor's expense to the state, the state imposes limitations on the use of the contractor's monies rather than the state's).

**2. Application to Federal Executive Orders?** What is the impact of *Chamber of Commerce* on President Obama's Executive Order 13494 directing federal contracting agencies to treat as "unallowable" the costs of any activity undertaken to persuade employees "to exercise or not to exercise . . . the right to organize and bargain collectively through representatives of the employees' own choosing"? The Order states that its purpose is to promote economy and efficiency and "is consistent with the policy of the United States to remain impartial concerning any labor-management dispute involving Government contractors."

**3. "Labor Peace" Agreements.**

a. Does *Chamber of Commerce* preclude the Los Angeles City Council from passing the following "labor peace" ordinance, covering all service contractors and their subcontractors at the city's airports? The ordinance would require each contractor to enter into a "labor peace agreement" with any labor organization expressing interest in representing the contractor's employees at the airports. This agreement would have to include (1) a procedure for determining employee choice of union representation through a card check conducted by a neutral third party; (2) an expedited procedure for resolving through binding arbitration all disputes over application of this procedure; (3) an agreement by the labor organization to forbear from economic action, including strikes, picketing, and boycotts, and a corresponding agreement by the contractor not to engage in any lockouts; and (4) a procedure for resolving through binding arbitration any disputes over the negotiation of any collective bargaining agreement to apply when, and if, the labor organization becomes the exclusive bargaining representative.

b. Can Duluth, Minnesota require hotels and restaurants to accept card-check union recognition as a condition of receiving $50,000 or more in city subsidies?

c. Is it relevant in these cases whether the city ordinances would affect labor relations on work other than that done for the municipalities? See Metropolitan Milwaukee Ass'n of Commerce v. Milwaukee County, 431 F.3d 277 (7th Cir. 2005) (finding preempted ordinance requiring all county contractors that transport elderly and disabled county residents to enter into "labor peace" agreements with organizing unions).

### Belknap, Inc. v. Hale
*463 U.S. 491 (1983)*

[After unsuccessful negotiations for a renewal agreement, employees in the warehouse and maintenance unit struck Belknap, Inc., on February 1. The company immediately granted a wage increase, effective on that date, to employees who stayed on the job; it also advertised in local newspapers for permanent replacements for the strikers. A large number of candidates appeared, and the company hired many new employees. Each new employee signed a statement that he was a permanent replacement for a designated Belknap employee in a designated job classification. The union's March 7 charge that the employer's February unilateral wage increase violated the NLRA led to the issuance of a complaint in April. Following that charge and complaint, Belknap's letters reiterated to the employees: "You will continue to be permanent replacement employees so long as you conduct yourselves in accordance with the policies . . . in effect here at Belknap." Also, "we continue to meet and negotiate in good faith with the Union. . . . However, we have made it clear to the Union that we have no intention of getting rid of the permanent replacements just in order to provide jobs for the replaced strikers if and when the Union calls off the strike." Shortly before the unfair labor practice hearing in July, the Regional Director convened a conference and said that a settlement would lead him to agree to dismiss the charges and complaints against both parties. (The union had also been charged with an unfair labor practice.) The parties ultimately settled the one major unresolved issue — the recall of the strikers — by agreeing that the company would reinstate at least 35 strikers a week.

Replacements laid off to make room for returning strikers sued Belknap in a state court. They alleged that the company had represented that it was hiring permanent employees, knowing that the statement was false and that the plaintiffs would detrimentally rely on it. Alternatively, they claimed that Belknap's firing of them was a breach of contract. Each plaintiff sought $250,000 in compensatory damages and an equal amount in punitive damages. The Kentucky Court of Appeals reversed a summary judgment for Belknap, reasoning that Belknap had not committed any unfair labor practices and, additionally, that preemption was not warranted because the plaintiffs' claims were of only peripheral concern to the NLRA and were deeply rooted in local law. The U.S. Supreme Court affirmed.]

WHITE, J. . . .

We are unpersuaded [by the contention that Congress intended the union's and Belknap's conduct "to be controlled by the free play of economic forces" (quoting from *Machinists*)]. We find unacceptable the notion that the federal law on the one hand insists on promises of permanent employment if the employer anticipates keeping the replacements in preference to returning strikers, but on the other hand forecloses damage suits for the employer's breach of these very promises. Even more mystifying is the suggestion that the federal law shields the employer from damages suits for misrepresentations that are made [while] securing permanent replacements and [that] are actionable under state law.

Arguments that entertaining suits by innocent third parties for breach of contract or for misrepresentation will "burden" the employer's right to hire permanent replacements are no more than arguments that "this is war," that "anything goes," and that promises of permanent employment that under federal law the employer is free to keep, if it so chooses, are essentially meaningless. It is one thing to hold that the federal law intended to leave the employer and the union free to use their economic weapons against one another, but is quite another to hold that either the employer or the union is also free to injure innocent third parties without regard to the normal rules of law governing those relationships. We cannot agree with the dissent that Congress intended such a lawless regime. . . .

An employment contract with a replacement promising permanent employment, subject only to settlement with its employees' union and to a Board unfair labor practice order directing reinstatement of strikers, would not in itself render the replacement a temporary employee subject to displacement by a striker over the employer's objection during or at the end of what is proved to be a purely economic strike. . . .

. . . [T]he employer, although he has prevailed in the strike, may refuse reinstatement only if he has hired replacements on a permanent basis. If he has promised to keep the replacements on in such a situation, discharging them to make way for selected strikers whom he deems more experienced or more efficient would breach his contracts with the replacements. Those contracts, it seems to us, create a sufficiently permanent arrangement to permit the prevailing employer to abide by its promises.[8]

We perceive no substantial impact on the availability of settlement of economic or unfair labor practice strikes if the employer is careful to protect itself against suits like this in the course of contracting with strike replacements. Its risk of liability if it discharges replacements pursuant to a settlement or to a Board order would then be minimal. We fail to understand why in such circumstances the employer would be any less willing to settle the strike than it would be under the regime proposed by Belknap and the Board, which as a matter of law, would permit it to settle without liability for misrepresentation or for breach of contract.

. . . *Machinists* did not deal with solemn promises of permanent employment, made to innocent replacements, that the employer was free to make and keep under federal law. J.I. Case Co. v. NLRB, 321 U.S. 332 (1944), suggests that individual contracts of employment must give way to otherwise valid provisions of the collective bargaining contract, id., at 336-339, but it was careful to say that the Board "has no power to adjudicate the validity or

---

8. The refusal to fire permanent replacements because of commitments made to them in the course of an economic strike satisfies the requirement of NLRB v. Fleetwood Trailer Co., 389 U.S. 375, 380 (1967), that the employer have a "legitimate and substantial justification" for his refusal to reinstate strikers. That the offer and promise of permanent employment are conditional does not render the hiring any less permanent if the conditions do not come to pass. All hirings are to some extent conditional. . . .

effect of such contracts except as to their effect on matters within its jurisdiction." . . . There, the cease-and-desist order, as modified, stated that the discontinuance of the individual contracts was "without prejudice to the assertion of any legal rights the employee may have acquired under such contract or to any defenses thereto by the employer." Id., at 342. . . .

It is said that respondent replacements are employees within the bargaining unit, that the Union is the bargaining representative of petitioner's employees, and the replacements are thus bound by the terms of the settlement negotiated between the employer and "their" representative.[10] The argument is not only that as a matter of federal law the employer cannot be foreclosed from discharging the replacements pursuant to a contract with a bargaining agent, but also that by virtue of the agreement with the Union it is relieved from responding in damages for its knowing breach of contract—that is, that the contracts are not only not specifically enforceable but also may be breached free from liability for damages. We need not address . . . the issue of specific performance since the respondents ask only damages. As to the damages issue . . . such an argument was rejected in *J.I. Case.*

If federal law forecloses this suit, more specific and persuasive reasons than those based on *Machinists* must be identified to support any such result. Belknap insists that the rationale of the *Garmon* decision, properly construed and applied, furnishes these reasons. . . .

. . . It is true that whether the strike was an unfair labor practice strike and whether the offer to replacements was the kind of offer forbidden during such a dispute were matters for the Board. The focus of these determinations, however, would be on whether the rights of strikers were being infringed. Neither controversy would have anything in common with the question whether Belknap made misrepresentations to replacements that were actionable under state law. . . . The strikers cannot secure reinstatement, or indeed any relief, by suing for misrepresentation in state court. The state courts in no way offer them an alternative forum for obtaining relief that the Board can provide. The same was true in *Sears* and *Farmer.* Hence, it appears to us that maintaining the misrepresentation action would not interfere with the Board's determination of matters within its jurisdiction and that such an action is of no more than peripheral concern to the Board and the federal law. At the same time, Kentucky surely has a substantial interest in protecting its citizens from misrepresentations that have caused them grievous harm. . . . The state interests involved in this case

10. The AFL-CIO disavows this argument. It suggests that replacements are bound only by those agreements that a union makes, as the exclusive bargaining agent for the struck employer's workers, regarding the terms and conditions of employment for the employer's workforce after the termination of the strike. . . .

clearly outweigh any possible interference with the Board's function that may result from permitting the action for misrepresentation to proceed. . . .

[The opinions of Justice Blackmun, concurring separately, and of Justice Brennan, joined by Justices Marshall and Powell, dissenting, are omitted.]

## *NOTES AND QUESTIONS*

**1. Effect on Balance of Power?** Does the ruling in *Belknap* affect the employer's ability to attract permanent replacements? The Court assumes not, observing that employers can make conditional offers to replacements without making them vulnerable to automatic displacement by returning economic strikers, whereas a finding of preemption ultimately would have been understood by "many" replacements as preventing them from enforcing any promise of unconditioned permanency. Is this a judgment the Board or the courts should be making?

**2. Effect on Settlement of Strikes?** Might *Belknap* complicate the settlement of some intense strikes because employers who have recruited workers with unconditional offers of continuing employment will have to take into account the prospect of liability from suits by "bumped" replacements? On the other hand, are the costs of prolonged strikes outweighed by the *Belknap* rule's discouragement of employers making purely strategic offers they would never have to keep solely for the purpose of obtaining leverage in an economic dispute with a striking union? Do you think unions and the employees they represent are better off under the *Belknap* rule or a rule preempting state contract and misrepresentation suits? See Samuel Estreicher, Collective Bargaining or "Collective Begging"?: Reflections on Antistrikebreaker Legislation, 93 Mich. L. Rev. 577, 603 n.108 (1994); Note on Strike Settlement Agreements, supra page 528.

**3. Further State Regulation?**

a. *Tort Action Against Unions?* If the replacements had sued the union for intentionally inducing a breach of the replacements' contracts with the employer, would their suits have been preempted? Under *Garmon* or *Machinists*, can state law make actionable a union's attempt to maintain solidarity during a lawful strike?

b. *Reinstatement Remedy?* The Court notes that it need not decide whether the displaced replacements could have asked a state court to order the employer to reinstate them. Would such a suit be preempted?

**4. Suits Based on Individual Contracts in Violation of §8(a)(5).** Does *Belknap* suggest that employees may be able to sue their employers for breaches of other promises in individual employment contracts even when the promises were made without the involvement of the collective bargaining representative and thus at least arguably in violation of §8(a)(5)? Or should *Belknap* be viewed as limited to the context of employer promises made to individuals before they are within a bargaining unit and the exclusive bargaining regime of the NLRA? Note the Court's discussion of the pre-exclusive bargaining individual contracts in *J.I. Case* and consider the following:

> Making promises to represented employees without the consent of their exclusive bargaining representative does and should constitute an unfair labor practice. Unions therefore should be able to seek whatever remedies from the Labor Board necessary and appropriate to prevent such undermining of their status, including the prospective voiding of commitments already made.
>
> However, allowing states to enforce such commitments before the Board has held them invalid neither deprives the Board of jurisdiction to consider later unfair labor practice charges, or encourages further circumvention of bargaining agents. . . . Employees who have been given special promises by their employer will not necessarily look more favorably on their exclusive representative if that representative's status has the legal effect of denying them benefits on which they relied. Only unions protected by section 8(a)(5) of the Labor Act should be able to use its force to secure their status; employers who may be guilty of the section's violation should not be able to use it as a shield against individual employees asserting contractual commitments.

Michael C. Harper, Limiting Section 301 Preemption: Three Cheers for the Trilogy, Only One for *Lingle* and *Lueck*, 66 Chi.-Kent L. Rev. 685, 742-743 (1990). But see Barbieri v. United Technologies Corp., 771 A.2d 915 (Conn. 2001) (individual contracts not superseded by collective agreement, but enforceability was within primary jurisdiction of Board); Beaman v. Yakima Valley Disposal, Inc., 807 P.2d 849 (Wash. 1991) (individual contract action preempted under *Garmon*). See also the discussion of §301 preemption, infra pages 883-894.

### *Note: Preemption of State Regulation of Unionization of Supervisors*

Supervisor unionism is lawful under the NLRA, but supervisors have no federal right to organize or compel bargaining by their employer. The Supreme Court has decided a number of cases defining the extent to which the states may regulate union efforts to organize employees whose supervisory responsibilities may have placed them outside the protection of the NLRA. In Marine Engineers Beneficial Ass'n v. Interlake S.S. Co., 370 U.S. 173 (1962), the union picketed Interlake, causing employees of another company to refuse to unload a vessel. A state court enjoined the picketing. despite the union's argument that its efforts to organize the employer's supervisory marine engineers could not be regulated by the state because its organizing activity was secondary and thus arguably violated §8(b)(4). The state court held that §8(b)(4) did not apply because the union represented only supervisors and thus was not a "labor organization" as defined in §2(5) as an organization in which statutory "employees participate." The Supreme Court reversed, stressing that the definitions of employee, supervisor, and labor organization in the NLRA present difficult issues that under *Garmon*'s primary jurisdiction rationale must first be decided by the NLRB rather than by state courts.

State regulation of supervisor unionism also may raise questions of *Machinists* preemption. In Beasley v. Food Fair of North Carolina, Inc., 416 U.S. 653 (1974), the Court held that North Carolina could not use its "right to work" law to prevent an employer from discharging supervisory employees because of their membership in a union. The Court rested its decision on §14(a) of the NLRA, enacted as part of the Taft-Hartley amendments, which it viewed as an expression of congressional intent to free employers from any compulsion, whether derived from state or federal law, to treat supervisors as employees and thus undermine the employers' ability to insist on the undivided loyalty of their supervisory employees.

In an earlier case, Hanna Mining Co. v. District 2, Marine Engineers Beneficial Ass'n, 382 U.S. 181 (1965), the Court held that a state could enjoin picketing to compel supervisory employees to join a union. The Court rejected the union's argument that §14(a) expressed an intent to have peaceful efforts to organize supervisors free of any form of regulation, federal or state.

Could a state law provide that supervisors have a legal right to form unions and insist on collective bargaining? Would this contravene an implied judgment in the NLRA that employers have a right to preclude unionization of their supervisors? What about a state law providing that graduate students, like those involved in the *NYU* and *Brown* cases, supra pages 109-111, have a right to form unions and engage in collective bargaining?

## 2. "Minimum Terms" Legislation

**Metropolitan Life Insurance Co. v. Massachusetts**
*471 U.S. 724 (1985)*

Blackmun, J. . . .

Massachusetts Gen. Laws Ann., ch. 175, §47B (West Supp. 1985), is typical of mandated-benefit laws currently in place in the majority of States. With respect to a Massachusetts resident, it requires any general health-insurance policy that provides hospital and surgical coverage, or any benefit plan that has such coverage, to provide as well a certain minimum of mental-health protection. In particular, §47B requires that a health-insurance policy provide 60 days of coverage for confinement in a mental hospital, coverage for confinement in a general hospital equal to that provided by the policy for nonmental illness, and certain minimum outpatient benefits. . . .

## II

. . . In 1979, the Attorney General of Massachusetts brought suit in Massachusetts Superior Court for declaratory and injunctive relief to enforce §47B. . . .

## IV

. . . Appellants contend . . . that because mandated-benefit laws require benefit plans whose terms are arrived at through collective bargaining to purchase certain benefits the parties may not have wished to purchase, such laws in effect mandate terms of collective-bargaining agreements. The Supreme Judicial Court of Massachusetts correctly found that "[b]ecause a plan that purchases insurance has no choice but to provide mental health care benefits, the insurance provisions of §47B effectively control the content of insured welfare benefit plans." More precisely, faced with §47B, parties to a collective-bargaining agreement providing for health insurance are forced to make a choice: either they must purchase the mandated benefit, decide not to provide health coverage at all, or decide to become self-insured, assuming they are in a financial position to make that choice. . . .

. . . [A]ppellants do not suggest that §47B alters the balance of power between the parties to the labor contract. Instead, appellants argue that, not only did Congress establish a balance of bargaining power between labor and management in the Act, but it also intended to prevent the States from establishing minimum employment standards that labor and management would otherwise have been required to negotiate from their federally protected bargaining positions, and would otherwise have been permitted to set at a lower level than that mandated by state law. Appellants assert that such state regulation is permissible only when Congress has authorized its enactment. Because welfare benefits are a mandatory subject of bargaining under the labor law, see Chemical & Alkali Workers v. Pittsburgh Plate Glass Co., 404 U.S. 157, 159, and n.1 (1971), and because Congress has never given States the authority to enact health regulations that affect the terms of bargaining agreements, appellants urge that the NLRA pre-empts any state attempt to impose minimum-benefit terms on the parties.

Appellants assume that Congress' ultimate concern in the NLRA was in leaving the parties free to reach agreement about contract terms. The framework established in the NLRA was merely a means to allow the parties to reach such agreement fairly. A law that interferes with the end result of bargaining is, therefore, even worse than a law that interferes with the bargaining process. . . .

The NLRA is concerned primarily with establishing an equitable process for determining terms and conditions of employment, and not with particular substantive terms of the bargain that is struck when the parties are negotiating from relatively equal positions. . . .

One of the ultimate goals of the Act was the resolution of the problem of "depress[ed] wage rates and the purchasing power of wage earners in industry," 29 U.S.C. §151, and "the widening gap between wages and profits," 79 Cong. Rec. 2371 (1935) (remarks of Sen. Wagner), thought to be the cause of economic decline and depression. Congress hoped to accomplish this by establishing procedures for more equitable private bargaining.

The evil Congress was addressing thus was entirely unrelated to local or federal regulation establishing minimum terms of employment. Neither inequality of bargaining power nor the resultant depressed wage rates were thought to result from the choice between having terms of employment set by public law or having them set by private agreement. No incompatibility exists, therefore, between federal rules designed to restore the equality of bargaining power, and state or federal legislation that imposes minimal substantive requirements on contract terms negotiated between parties to labor agreements, at least so long as the purpose of the state legislation is not incompatible with these general goals of the NLRA.

Accordingly, it never has been argued successfully that minimal labor standards imposed by other federal laws were not to apply to unionized employers and employees. See, e.g., Barrentine v. Arkansas-Best Freight System, Inc., 450 U.S. 728, 737, 739 (1981). Cf. Alexander v. Gardner-Denver Co., 415 U.S. 36, 51 (1974). Nor has Congress ever seen fit to exclude unionized workers and employers from laws establishing federal minimal employment standards. We see no reason to believe that for this purpose Congress intended state minimum labor standards to be treated differently from minimum federal standards.

Minimum state labor standards affect union and nonunion employees equally, and neither encourage nor discourage the collective-bargaining processes that are the subject of the NLRA. Nor do they have any but the most indirect effect on the right of self-organization established in the Act. . . .

It would further few of the purposes of the Act to allow unions and employers to bargain for terms of employment that state law forbids employers to establish unilaterally. "Such a rule of law would delegate to unions and unionized employers the power to exempt themselves from whatever state labor standards they disfavored." [Allis-Chalmers Corp. v. Lueck, 471 U.S. 202, 212 (1985).] It would turn the policy that animated the Wagner Act on its head to understand it to have penalized workers who have chosen to join a union by preventing them from benefiting from state labor regulations imposing minimal standards on nonunion employers. . . .

Federal labor law . . . is interstitial, supplementing state law where compatible, and supplanting it only when it prevents the accomplishment of the purposes of the federal Act. . . . "A holding that the States were precluded from acting would remove the backdrop of state law that provided the basis of congressional action . . . and would thereby artificially create a no-law area." Taggart v. Weinacker's, Inc., 397 U.S. 223, 228 (1970) (concurring opinion). . . .

Massachusetts' mandated-benefit law is an insurance regulation designed to implement the Commonwealth's policy on mental-health care, and as such is a valid and unexceptional exercise of the Commonwealth's police power. It was designed in part to ensure that the less wealthy residents of the Commonwealth would be provided adequate mental-health treatment should they require it. Though §47B, like many laws affecting terms of employment, potentially limits an employee's right to choose one thing by requiring that he be provided with something else, it does not limit the rights of self-organization or collective bargaining protected by the NLRA, and is not pre-empted by that Act. . . .

Justice Powell took no part in the decision of these cases.

## *NOTES AND QUESTIONS*

1. **Breadth of *Machinists* Preemption?** Does the ruling in *Metropolitan Life* require a rejection of a broad reading of *Machinists* preemption that would insulate the *processes* of collective bargaining from all state regulation? Or does the Court only hold that a state law may establish general substantive entitlements for all employees, including those represented by unions, as long as it does not directly regulate the processes of collective bargaining?

2. **Minimum-Terms Laws and NLRA Goals.** Is *Metropolitan Life* based on an assumption that state minimum-terms laws advance the NLRA's goal of enhancing the purchasing power of workers? Would the result have been different if it had been shown that employers simply adjust for a mandated increase in one benefit by decreasing some other benefit so that the total package of benefits granted to employees remains the same? Is the Court's assumption rather that workers in general benefit from minimum-benefit laws and that excluding union-represented workers from their coverage could seriously discourage §7 activity, despite any restriction of employee choice?

**3. Is *Teamsters v. Oliver* Still Viable?** In a portion of its opinion not reprinted above, the *Metropolitan Life* Court makes only an oblique reference to Local 24, International Bhd. of Teamsters v. Oliver, 358 U.S. 283 (1959), an earlier decision that seemed to hold that state law could not "be applied to prevent the contracting parties [to collective bargaining agreements] from carrying out their agreement upon a subject matter as to which federal law directs them to bargain." Id. at 295. Inasmuch as health care benefits are clearly within the scope of topics over which federal law makes bargaining mandatory, *Oliver* seemed to provide strong support for the insurance companies' case for preemption in *Metropolitan Life.*

*Oliver* reviewed an Ohio court's decision holding that state antitrust law was violated by a collective agreement that prescribed the "terms and conditions which regulate the minimum rental and certain other terms of lease when a motor vehicle is leased to a carrier by an owner who drives his vehicle in the carrier's service." 358 U.S. at 284-285. The Court found this application of Ohio's law to inhibit collective bargaining over wages because the "union justified the [prescription] as necessary to prevent undermining of the negotiated drivers' wage scale." The union argued that minimum rental fees were necessary to prevent carriers from leasing a vehicle from an owner-driver at a rental below the actual costs of operation, such that the driver's wage, "although nominally the negotiated wage, was actually a wage reduced by the excess of his operating expenses over the rental he received." Id. at 289.

Is *Oliver* still good law? Can the decision be invoked to preempt state laws that either prohibit using collective bargaining to establish particular terms of employment that the employer could have established on its own, or more generally place some limit on the benefits that employees can obtain from their employer through collective bargaining? Does this mean that *Metropolitan Life* and *Oliver* together establish a one-way ratchet: States may set a floor but not a ceiling on collective bargaining outcomes? See Harper, Limiting Section 301 Preemption, supra, at 720-731.

**4. Regulatory Review of Labor Cost-Induced Applications for Rate Increases?** Southwestern Bell negotiates with the Communications Workers a new three-year collective agreement that includes substantial wage increases. Southwestern Bell then applies to the Arkansas Public Service Commission for telephone rate increases to cover increased costs, including those deriving from the new labor agreement. The Commission adjusts Southwestern's requested rate increases downward because it deems the recently negotiated wage increases "unreasonable." Under *Oliver* and *Machinists,* should the Commission's decision be overturned insofar as it relied on an assessment of appropriate wage levels? See Southwestern Bell Tel. Co. v. Arkansas Pub. Serv. Comm'n, 824 F.2d 672 (8th Cir. 1987) (no preemption).

**5. "Conditional" Minimum-Benefit Laws.** The Massachusetts law in *Metropolitan Life* required employers to provide specified mental-health benefits only if they provided general health-care benefits to their employees. Does such a conditional regulation create difficulties for union negotiators that would not be present if state law simply required all employers unconditionally to provide mental-health benefits? See Harper, supra. See also note 3, infra page 888.

**6. Denial of Guarantee of Minimum Benefits to Unionized Employees?** *Metropolitan Life* secured from preemption a state's extension to employees covered by collective agreements of the same minimum benefit extended to employees not covered by such agreements. Can a state, consistent with federal labor law, deny to employees covered by collective agreements any minimum benefit that it extends to employees not working under a collective agreement?

In Lividas v. Bradshaw, 512 U.S. 107 (1994), the Supreme Court, considering a California law imposing penalties on any employer who fails to pay promised wages promptly, unanimously held preempted the California Commissioner of Labor's refusal to enforce the law at the behest of employees whose terms of employment are set in a collective agreement. The Court found the *Lividas* case to be "no different" than Nash v. Florida Industrial Comm'n, 389 U.S. 235 (1967), in which it had held preempted "a state policy of withholding unemployment benefits solely because an employee had filed an unfair labor practice charge with the National Labor Relations Board. . . . Just as the respondent State Commission in [*Nash*] offered an employee the choice of pursuing her unfair labor practice claim or receiving unemployment compensation, the Commissioner has presented Lividas and others like her with the choice of having state-law rights . . . enforced or exercising the right to enter into a collective-bargaining agreement with an arbitration clause." Although the *Lividas* Court cautioned that it did not mean to suggest "that the NLRA automatically defeats all state action taking any account of the collective-bargaining process or every state law distinguishing union-represented employees from others," it offered no limiting principles that might provide guidance in other cases.

In Fort Halifax Packing Co. v. Coyne, 482 U.S. 1 (1987), the Court held that the NLRA did not preempt a Maine statute that required employers, in the event of a plant closing, to make severance payments (at the rate of one week's pay for each year of employment) to employees not covered by an express contract providing for severance pay. Is *Lividas* consistent with *Fort Halifax*? Is it critical to the preemption inquiry that the Maine minimum severance benefit did not apply to any employee "covered by an express contract providing for severance pay," including any individual contract?

**7. Wrongful-Discharge Law and Union-Represented Employees.** Does *Lividas* mean that any state law protecting employees from termination must be applied to union-represented employees without regard to the just cause and arbitration provisions of particular collective agreements? The Montana Wrongful Discharge from Employment Act, for instance, provides employees a remedy for being discharged without "good cause," but exempts from protection employees "covered by a written collective bargaining agreement." Does this statute inhibit employee choice to pursue collective bargaining in the same manner as the California delinquent wage law in *Lividas*? See Anthony Herman, Wrongful Discharge Actions After *Lueck* and *Metropolitan Life Insurance:* The Erosion of Individual Rights and Collective Strength?, 9 Indus. Rel. L.J. 596, 647-650 & n.263 (1987). Might the Montana statute be distinguished as involving a critical workplace condition, the details of which should be determined by collective bargaining when employees have opted for union representation? Is this sort of limiting principle available after *Lividas*? Cf. Barnes v. Stone Container Corp., 942 F.2d 689 (9th Cir. 1991) (preempting under *Machinists* the application of Montana's wrongful discharge statute to a union-represented employee after expiration of a collective agreement while negotiations were ongoing for a new agreement).

**8. Union Standards as Minimum Terms?** Could a local government require all contractors seeking building permits to provide on *private* construction projects for the payment of the "prevailing wage" (as set by reference to the prevailing union wage on public construction projects)? Presumably such an ordinance is a regulatory rather than proprietary action and thus not exempt from preemption under the *Boston Harbor* doctrine. Is it exempt as minimum-terms regulation under *Metropolitan Life*, however? Is it different from "prevailing wage" requirements for public construction in many jurisdictions? See Chamber of Commerce v. Bragdon, 64 F.3d 497 (9th Cir. 1995) (finding preemption).

**9. Minimum Terms for a Particular Labor Group?** In Congress Plaza Hotel v. Shannon, 549 F.3d 1119 (7th Cir. 2008), the court found preempted a state statute that mandated two 15-minute breaks and a 30-minute lunch period for hotel room attendants who cleaned guest rooms in Cook County, Illinois. The court stressed that the statute applied only to one labor group in one industry in one county, and thus concluded that it did not provide a minimum "backdrop" for negotiations, but rather impermissibly set benefits by legislation rather than bargaining. Did the court convincingly distinguish *Metropolitan Life*?

**10. "Successor" Protections as Minimum Terms?** In November 2002, New York City enacted a law, note 5a. at page 757, providing building service employees with protection from loss of employment for 90 days if the building in which they are employed is sold or control is transferred to another entity or if they are employed by a contractor that has been replaced with a different contractor by the owner or manager of the business. Despite the 90-day guarantee, employment is subject to termination for cause or a decision by the new employer to operate with fewer employees. Local 32BJ of the Service Employees International Union lobbied heavily for the law, presumably hoping to preserve the union's representation of employees of large commercial office and residential buildings in the city. Is the law preempted under *Machinists,* or is it a minimum-terms law shielded from preemption under *Metropolitan Life*?

## C. SECTION 301 PREEMPTION

**Allis-Chalmers Corp. v. Lueck**
*471 U.S. 202 (1985)*

BLACKMUN, J. . . .

### I

Respondent Roderick S. Lueck began working for petitioner Allis-Chalmers Corporation in February 1975. He is a member of Local 248 of the [UAW]. Allis-Chalmers and Local 248 are parties to a collective-bargaining agreement. The agreement incorporates by reference a separately negotiated group health and disability plan fully funded by Allis-Chalmers but administered by Aetna Life & Casualty Company. The plan provides that disability benefits are available for non-occupational illness and injury to all employees, such as petitioner, who are represented by the union.

The collective-bargaining agreement also establishes a four-step grievance procedure for an employee's contract grievance. This procedure culminates in final and binding arbitration if the union chooses to pursue the grievance that far. A separate letter of understanding that binds the parties creates a special three-part grievance procedure for disability grievances. The letter establishes a Joint Plant Insurance Committee composed of two representatives designated by the union and two designated by the employer. The Committee has the authority to resolve all disputes involving "any insurance-related issues that may arise from provisions of the [Collective-Bargaining] Agreement." . . .

In July 1981, respondent Lueck suffered a non-occupational back injury while carrying a pig to a friend's house for a pig roast. He notified

Allis-Chalmers of his injury, as required by the claims-processing procedure, and subsequently filed a disability claim with Aetna, also in accordance with the established procedure. After evaluating physicians' reports submitted by Lueck, Aetna approved the claim. Lueck began to receive disability benefits effective from July 20, 1981, the day he filed his claim with Aetna.

According to Lueck, however, Allis-Chalmers periodically would order Aetna to cut off his payments, either without reason, or because he failed to appear for a doctor's appointment, or because he required hospitalization for unrelated reasons. After each termination, Lueck would question the action or supply additional information, and the benefits would be restored. In addition, according to Lueck, Allis-Chalmers repeatedly requested that he be reexamined by different doctors, so that Lueck believed that he was being harassed. All of Lueck's claims were eventually paid, although, allegedly, not until he began this litigation.

Lueck never attempted to grieve his dispute concerning the manner in which his disability claim was handled by Allis-Chalmers and Aetna. Instead, in January 18, 1982, he filed suit against both of them in the [state] Circuit Court, . . . alleging that they "intentionally, contemptuously, and repeatedly failed" to make disability payments under the negotiated disability plan, without a reasonable basis for withholding the payments. This breached their duty "to act in good faith and deal fairly with [Lueck's] disability claims." Lueck alleged that as a result of these bad faith actions he incurred debts, emotional distress, physical impairment, and pain and suffering. He sought both compensatory and punitive damages.

Ruling on cross-motions for summary judgment, the trial court ruled in favor of Allis-Chalmers and Aetna.

The Supreme Court of Wisconsin . . . reversed. The court held . . . that the suit did not arise under §301 of the LMRA, and therefore was not subject to dismissal for failure to exhaust the arbitration procedures established in the collective-bargaining agreement. The court reasoned that a §301 suit arose out of a violation of a labor contract, and that the claim here was a tort claim of bad faith. . . .

## II

. . . Congress did not state explicitly whether and to what extent it intended §301 of the LMRA to pre-empt state law. In such instances courts sustain a local regulation "unless it conflicts with federal law or would frustrate the federal scheme, or unless the courts discern from the totality of the circumstances that Congress sought to occupy the field to the exclusion of the States." Malone v. White Motor Corp., 435 U.S. [497,] 504 [(1978)]. The question posed here is whether this particular Wisconsin tort, as applied, would frustrate the federal labor-contract scheme established in §301.

### III

. . . [Textile Workers v. Lincoln Mills, 353 U.S. 448 (1957), and Teamsters v. Lucas Flour Co., 369 U.S. 95 (1962), establish] that a suit in state court alleging a violation of a provision of a labor contract must be brought under §301 and be resolved by reference to federal law. A state rule that purports to define the meaning or scope of a term in a contract suit therefore is pre-empted by federal labor law.

If the policies that animate §301 are to be given their proper range, however, the pre-emptive effect of §301 must extend beyond suits alleging contract violations. These policies require that "the relationships created by [a collective bargaining] agreement" be defined by application of "an evolving federal common law grounded in national labor policy." Bowen v. United States Postal Service, 459 U.S. 212, 224-225 (1983). The interests in interpretive uniformity and predictability that require that labor-contract disputes be resolved by reference to federal law also require that the meaning given a contract phrase or term be subject to uniform federal interpretation. Thus, questions relating to what the parties to a labor agreement agreed, and what legal consequences were intended to flow from breaches of that agreement, must be resolved by reference to uniform federal law, whether such questions arise in the context of a suit for breach of contract or in a suit alleging liability in tort. Any other result would elevate form over substance and allow parties to evade the requirements of §301 by re-labeling their contract claims as claims for tortious breach of contract.

Were state law allowed to determine the meaning intended by the parties in adopting a particular contract phrase or term, all the evils addressed in *Lucas Flour* would recur. The parties would be uncertain as to what they were binding themselves to when they agreed to create a right to collect benefits under certain circumstances. As a result, it would be more difficult to reach agreement, and disputes as to the nature of the agreement would proliferate. Exclusion of such claims "from the ambit of §301 would stultify the congressional policy of having the administration of collective bargaining contracts accomplished under a uniform body of federal substantive law." Smith v. Evening News Assn., 371 U.S. 195, 200 (1962).

Of course, not every dispute concerning employment, or tangentially involving a provision of a collective-bargaining agreement, is pre-empted by §301 or other provisions of the federal labor law. Section 301 on its face says nothing about the substance of what private parties may agree to in a labor contract. . . . Clearly, §301 does not grant the parties to a collective-bargaining agreement the ability to contract for what is illegal under state law. In extending the pre-emptive effect of §301 beyond suits for breach of contract, it would be inconsistent with congressional intent under that section to pre-empt state rules that proscribe conduct, or establish rights and obligations, independent of a labor contract.

Therefore, state-law rights and obligations that do not exist independently of private agreements, and that as a result can be waived or altered by agreement of private parties, are pre-empted by those agreements. Cf. Malone v. White Motor Corp., 435 U.S., at 504-505 (NLRA pre-emption). Our analysis must focus, then, on whether the Wisconsin tort action for breach of the duty of good faith as applied here confers non-negotiable state law rights on employers or employees independent of any right established by contract, or, instead, whether evaluation of the tort claim is inextricably intertwined with consideration of the terms of the labor contract. If the state tort law purports to define the meaning of the contract relationship, that law is pre-empted. . . .

The Wisconsin court attempted to demonstrate, by a proffered example, the way in which a bad-faith tort claim could be unrelated to any contract claim. It noted that an insurer ultimately could pay a claim as required under a contract, but still cause injury through "unreasonably delaying payment" of the claim. In such a situation, the court reasoned, the state tort claim would be adjudicated without reaching questions of contract interpretation. The court evidently assumed that the only obligations the parties assumed by contract are those expressly recited in the agreement, in this case the right to receive benefit payments for non-occupational injuries. Thus, the court reasoned, the good-faith behavior mandated in the labor agreement was independent of the good-faith behavior required by state insurance law because "[g]ood faith in the labor agreement context means [only] that parties must abide by the specific terms of the labor agreement."

If this is all there is to the independence of the state tort action, that independence does not suffice to avoid the pre-emptive effect of §301. The assumption that the labor contract creates no implied rights is not one that state law may make. Rather, it is a question of federal contract interpretation whether there was an obligation under this labor contract to provide the payments in a timely manner, and, if so, whether Allis-Chalmers' conduct breached that implied contract provision.

The Wisconsin court's assumption that the parties contracted only for the payment of insurance benefits, and that questions about the manner in which the payments were made are outside the contract is, moreover, highly suspect. There is no reason to assume that the labor contract as interpreted by the arbitrator would not provide such relief. . . . [U]nder Wisconsin law it appears that the parties to an insurance contract are free to bargain about what "reasonable" performance of their contract obligation entails. That being so, this tort claim is firmly rooted in the expectations of the parties that must be evaluated by federal contract law.

Because the right asserted not only derives from the contract, but is defined by the contractual obligation of good faith, any attempt to assess liability here inevitably will involve contract interpretation. The parties' agreement as to the manner in which a benefit claim would be handled will necessarily be relevant to any allegation that the claim was handled in a dilatory manner. Similarly, the question whether Allis-Chalmers required Lueck to be examined by an inordinate number of physicians evidently depends in part upon the parties' understanding concerning the medical evidence required to support a benefit claim. These questions of contract interpretation, therefore, underlie any finding of tort liability, regardless of the fact that the state court may choose to define the tort as "independent" of any contract question. Congress has mandated that federal law govern the meaning given contract terms. Since the state tort purports to give life to these terms in a different environment, it is pre-empted.

A final reason for holding that Congress intended §301 to pre-empt this kind of derivative tort claim is that only that result preserves the central role of arbitration in our "system of industrial self-government." Steelworkers v. Warrior & Gulf Navigation Co., 363 U.S. 574, 581 (1960). . . . Perhaps the most harmful aspect of the Wisconsin decision is that it would allow a suit [raising essentially a contract claim] be brought directly in state court without first exhausting the grievance procedures established in the bargaining agreement. . . . Since nearly any alleged willful breach of contract can be restated as a tort claim for breach of a good-faith obligation under a contract, the arbitrator's role in every case could be bypassed easily if §301 is not understood to pre-empt such claims. . . .

We . . . hold that when resolution of a state-law claim is substantially dependent upon analysis of the terms of an agreement made between the parties in a labor contract, that claim must either be treated as a §301 claim, see Avco Corp. v. Aero Lodge 735, 390 U.S. 557 (1968), or dismissed as pre-empted by federal labor-contract law. This complaint should have been dismissed for failure to make use of the grievance procedure established in the collective-bargaining agreement, Republic Steel Corp. v. Maddox, 379 U.S. [650 (1965)], or dismissed as pre-empted by §301. The judgment of the Wisconsin Supreme Court therefore is reversed.

## *NOTES AND QUESTIONS*

**1. Is §301 Preemption Subject to Contractual Modification and Waiver?** Section 301 jurisprudence establishes only presumptions about the intent of the parties to collective agreements, i.e., default rules to be applied in the absence of express agreements to the contrary. Could the parties to a particular collective agreement contract around a *Lueck* preemption by expressly providing that either their entire agreement or a particular clause should be interpreted under state law?

Is the §301 preemption defense also waivable by the failure of a party to raise it in a timely fashion before trial? See Sweeney v. Westvaco Co., 926 F.2d 29 (1st Cir. 1991) (defense may be waived). The Supreme Court held in International Longshoremen's Ass'n v. Davis, 476 U.S. 380 (1986), that the *Garmon* preemption defense is jurisdictional and cannot be waived. Is this true also of a §301 preemption claim?

**2. Preserving the Expectations of the Parties to a Collective Agreement?** Is §301 preemption, as developed in *Lueck*, primarily framed to protect the substantive expectations of the parties to collective bargaining agreements and thus to reduce bargaining costs? Would allowance of state tort actions for bad-faith breach of contract create uncertainty for employers about the potential liabilities to which they are exposed by particular contractual commitments? Would this complicate negotiations and raise the costs to unions of securing certain benefits for their members? Compare Harper, Limiting Section 301 Preemption, at 715-718, with Laura W. Stein, Preserving Unionized Employees' Individual Employment Rights, 17 Berkeley J. Emp. & Lab. L. 1, 36-41 (1996).

**3. Effect of Nonmodifiability of State Laws?** What if Wisconsin tort law had provided that the assumption of an insurance obligation imposes certain additional duties of good faith that cannot be waived or altered? Would the application of this law to an insurance obligation undertaken in a collective bargaining agreement be preempted by federal law? Would this be an example of an "independent" state law obligation referenced in *Lueck* as beyond the reach of §301 preemption? Is the state law obligation "independent," even if nonmodifiable, if it still depends on the existence of an insurance commitment in the labor agreement?

However, if the holding in *Lueck* does not depend on the fact that Wisconsin tort remedies were subject to contractual modification, is it consistent with the Court's decision in *Metropolitan Life*, also authored by Justice Blackmun in the same term as *Lueck*? See Harper, Limiting Section 301 Preemption, at 728-731.

**4. *Lingle* and Rejection of the "Same Factual Considerations" Test.** In Lingle v. Norge Div. of Magic Chef, Inc., 486 U.S. 399 (1988), the Court held that an employee covered by a collective agreement that provides her with a contractual remedy for discharge without just cause may challenge under state law a discharge allegedly in retaliation for filing a worker's compensation claim. The Seventh Circuit had held that Lingle's state law retaliatory discharge claim should be preempted under *Lueck* because it could present "the same factual considerations as the contractual determination of whether Lingle was fired for just cause." 486 U.S. at 408. The Supreme Court read its *Lueck* precedent differently:

> [T]he state-law remedy in this case is "independent" of the collective-bargaining agreement in the sense of "independent" that matters for §301 pre-emption purposes: resolution of the state-law claim does not require construing the collective-bargaining agreement. . . . For while there may be instances in which the National Labor Relations Act pre-empts state law on the basis of the subject matter of the law in question, §301 pre-emption merely ensures that federal law will be the basis for interpreting collective-bargaining agreements, and says nothing about the substantive rights a State may provide to workers when adjudication of those rights does not depend upon the interpretation of such agreements. In other words, even if dispute resolution pursuant to a collective-bargaining agreement, on the one hand, and state law, on the other, would require addressing precisely the same set of facts, as long as the state-law claim can be resolved without interpreting the agreement itself, the claim is "independent" of the agreement for §301 pre-emption purposes.

Id. at 407-410.

**5. Independence vs. Need to Interpret Agreement: The Question of Defenses Based on the Agreement.** The *Lingle* Court's stress on whether resolution of the state law claim requires an interpretation of the collective agreement raises the question of whether the assertion of a defense based on a collective agreement should be a sufficient basis for preemption, even where the plaintiff's affirmative case does not depend on the existence of the agreement. For instance, should an employee be able to proceed with a state law invasion-of-privacy action against his employer's drug testing after the employer asserts that the testing is authorized by a collective bargaining agreement covering the employee? Compare Clark v. Newport News Shipbuilding & Dry Dock Co., 937 F.2d 934 (4th Cir. 1991); Jackson v. Liquid Carbonic Corp., 863 F.2d 111 (1st Cir. 1988) (both finding preemption because "reasonableness" of privacy expectations depend on collectively bargained rules), with Williams v. National Football League, 582 F.3d 863, 879 (8th Cir. 2009) (employer's defenses to liability not relevant to §301 analysis); Cramer v. Consolidated Freightways Corp., 255 F.3d 683 (9th Cir. 2001) (en banc) (no preemption where privacy right is not negotiable, or where no clear waiver in collective agreement). See Harper, supra, at 709-710 (arguing against denying employees causes of action that would be available to them if they were not represented by a union, only because their union *could* have waived their right to bring the actions regardless of whether union actually did so).

**6. Is a Need to Interpret the Collective Agreement Sufficient for §301 Preemption?** Two additional Supreme Court decisions also may suggest that the independence of a state law cause of action from the existence of a collective agreement may save the action from §301 preemption regardless of the need to interpret the agreement in adjudicating the state law claim. In Hawaiian Airlines, Inc. v. Norris, 512 U.S. 246 (1994), the Court held that an employee's claims under Hawaii's wrongful discharge common law and its Whistleblower Protection Act were not preempted by the Railway Labor Act (RLA) requirement that "minor" disputes, which grow "out of grievances or out of the interpretation and application" of collective bargaining agreements, be subject to the Act's mandatory arbitration mechanism. The Court held that RLA preemption is inappropriate where the state cause of action "involves rights and obligations that exist independent of the collective bargaining agreement." The Court described its approach to RLA preemption as "virtually identical" to the §301 preemption standard delineated in *Lueck.*

In Lividas v. Bradshaw, 512 U.S. 107 (1994), discussed supra page 881, the Court held that an employee's right under California law to receive a penalty payment from an employer who failed to pay promised wages promptly was not preempted even though the penalty was based on the level of wages set in a collective bargaining agreement:

> [T]he primary text for deciding whether Livadas was entitled to a penalty was not the Food Store Contract, but a calendar. The only issue raised by Livadas's claim, whether Safeway "willfully failed to pay" her wages promptly upon severance, Cal. Lab. Code Ann. §203 (West 1989), was a question of state law, entirely independent of any understanding embodied in the collective-bargaining agreement between the union and the employer. There is no indication that there was a "dispute" in this case over the amount of the penalty to which Livadas would be entitled, and *Lingle* makes plain in so many words that when liability is governed by independent state law, the mere need to "look to" the collective-bargaining agreement for damages computation is no reason to hold the state-law claim defeated by §301.

Id. at 125-126.

**7. Removal to Federal Court.** The assertion of a *Garmon* or *Machinists* preemption defense to an action in state court has generally not been the basis for removal of the action to federal court. Employment law actions, like other actions brought in state court, are removable only if they present a federal question that is central to the plaintiffs' properly pleaded complaint. The general rule is that an anticipated federal defense does not provide a basis for federal court jurisdiction or removal. However, under what the Supreme Court terms the "complete pre-emption corollary to the well-pleaded complaint rule," the Court has approved a §301 preemption defense as a basis for removal by reading Local 174, Teamsters v. Lucas Flour Co., 369 U.S. 95 (1962), to mean that a federal question is central to any complaint that seeks to enforce obligations created by a collective bargaining agreement. See Avco v. Machinists, 390 U.S. 557, 558 (1968); cf. Franchise Tax Bd. v. Laborers Constr. Vacation Trust for Southern Cal., 463 U.S. 1, 23 (1983). This "complete preemption" basis for removal was limited in Caterpillar Inc. v. Williams, 482 U.S. 386 (1987), where plaintiffs were supervisors outside of the bargaining unit who asserted individual contract claims that they were promised they would be returned to the bargaining unit rather than being laid off. The Court noted that they relied "on contractual agreements made while they were in managerial or weekly salaried positions—agreements in which the collective-bargaining agreement played no part." Id. at 395 n.9. Because plaintiffs' claim did not depend on the collective bargaining agreement, it fell outside of the "complete preemption" doctrine, and the employer's assertion of a §301 preemption defense, consistent with the general rule stated above, did not establish removal jurisdiction.

**8. §301 Preemption of Wrongful-Discharge and Related Actions.** What kinds of wrongful discharge claims are sufficiently independent of the collective bargaining agreement to avoid §301 preemption? Consider the following:

a. *Claims of Discharge in Violation of State Public Policy?* Cf. Martin v. Shaw's Supermarkets, Inc., 105 F.3d 40 (1st Cir. 1997) (finding preemption of workers' compensation retaliation claim where state statute required consistency with collective agreement).

b. *Claims of Discharge in Breach of an Implied Covenant of Good Faith?* See, e.g., Newberry v. Pacific Racing Ass'n, 854 F.2d 1142 (9th Cir. 1988) (finding preemption).

c. *Claims by Employees That Their Employer Committed Intentional Torts Against Them During the Termination of Their Employment?* Compare Shiflett v. I.T.O. Corp., 202 F.3d 260 (4th Cir. 2000) (table decision); McCormick v. AT&T Technologies, Inc., 934 F.2d 531 (4th Cir. 1991) (both finding preemption because collective agreement must be interpreted to determine whether acts were wrongful), with Galvez v. Kuhn, 933 F.2d 773 (9th Cir. 1991) (finding no preemption because cause of action would exist without interpretation of collective agreement).

d. *Claims Against an Employer for Misrepresenting the Terms of a Collective Bargaining Agreement Covering the Employees?* Compare Adkins v. General Motors Corp., 946 F.2d 1201 (6th Cir. 1991) (preempting claim that employer and union fraudulently induced employees to accept collective agreement not in their interest), with Voilas v. Local 731, United Auto Workers, 170 F.3d 367 (3d Cir. 1999); Wells v. General Motors Corp., 881 F.2d 166 (5th Cir. 1989) (both finding claim that employer fraudulently induced acceptance of collectively bargained voluntary termination plan not preempted because based on contractual promises independent of collective agreement).

e. *Claims Based on Written or Oral or Implied Contracts or Promises Made by the Employer with Individual Employees Either Before or During the Term of a Collective Agreement Covering the Employees?* Compare Smith v. Colgate-Palmolive Co., 943 F.2d 764 (7th Cir. 1991) (finding preemption of fraud claim based on promises of job security after relocation to new state because reasonableness of reliance turned on meaning of collective agreement), with Foy v. Pratt & Whitney Group, 127 F.3d 229 (2d Cir. 1997) (finding no preemption of action for misrepresentation in employer's promises of opportunities to transfer to other plants); White v. National Steel Corp., 938 F.2d 474 (4th Cir. 1991) (finding no preemption of action for breach of individual contracts promising right to return to bargaining unit positions from new management positions).

**9. No Preemption of Actions Based on Individual Contracts?** The *Williams* decision, supra note 7, also may have relevance to at least the last question in the preceding note. Consider the following language:

> Caterpillar next relies on this Court's decision in J.I. Case Co. v. NLRB, 321 U.S. 332 (1944), arguing that when respondents returned to the collective-bargaining unit, their individual employment agreements were subsumed into, or eliminated by, the collective-bargaining agreement. Thus, Caterpillar contends, respondents' claims under their individual contracts actually are claims under the collective agreement and pre-empted by §301.
>
> Caterpillar is mistaken. First, *J.I. Case* does not stand for the proposition that all individual employment contracts are subsumed into, or eliminated by, the collective-bargaining agreement. In fact, the Court there held:
>
> > Individual contracts cannot subtract from collective ones, and whether under some circumstances they may add to them in matters covered by the collective bargain, we leave to be determined by appropriate forums under the law of contracts applicable, and to the Labor Board if they constitute unfair labor practices. (321 U.S., at 339.)
>
> Thus, individual employment contracts are not inevitably superseded by any subsequent collective agreement covering an individual employee, and claims based upon them may arise under state law. Caterpillar's basic error is its failure to recognize that a plaintiff covered by a collective-bargaining agreement is permitted to assert legal rights *independent* of that agreement, including state-law contract rights, so long as the contract relied upon is not a collective-bargaining agreement.

482 U.S. at 395-396 (emphasis in original).

### *Note: §301 Suits Against Unions*

The Supreme Court has twice held that claims against unions based on duties allegedly taken on by the unions in collective bargaining agreements must proceed, if at all, as §301 suits or as suits for breach of the duty of fair representation. First, in International Bhd. of Electrical Workers v. Hechler, 481 U.S. 851 (1987), the Court applied *Lueck* to preempt a claim based on Florida's tortious breach-of-contract law against a union for allegedly failing to fulfill a duty assumed under a collective agreement to ensure represented employees a safe workplace. The claim was found to be dependent on the agreement, and thus one that could not proceed independently of federal law, because Florida state law imposed no duty of care on unions to ensure a safe working environment in the absence of a contractual commitment. The *Hechler* Court remanded for the lower courts to decide whether Hechler's suit would have to proceed as a duty of fair representation claim, then time-barred by the short six-month statute of limitations, or whether she might be able to bring a §301 suit against her union, possibly under a third-party beneficiary theory.

Similarly, in United Steelworkers v. Rawson, 495 U.S. 362 (1990), the Court held preempted a state law claim by survivors of several deceased Idaho miners against a union for allegedly negligently inspecting a mine before an accident that caused the miners' deaths. The Court concluded that since the union's participation in mine inspections was made possible by provisions in their collective agreement with the management of the mine, any duty in connection with the inspection had to arise out of the collective agreement and be dependent on an analysis of its terms. The *Rawson* Court also confirmed what it had suggested in *Hechler* about the possibility of a collective agreement being interpreted to impose a greater duty of representation on unions than the statutory obligation defined by duty of fair representation standards. However, if "an employee claims that a union owes him a more far-reaching duty, he must be able to point to language in the collective-bargaining agreement specifically indicating an intent to create obligations enforceable against the union by the individual employees." 495 U.S. at 374. The Court found no such language in the agreement in that case; the provisions relied on by the claimants were "concessions made by the employer to the Union, a limited surrender of the employer's exclusive authority over mine safety" rather than promises from the union to the employer. Id. at 375.

*Hechler* and *Rawson* left some questions in their wake. For instance, if Idaho's law had imposed an affirmative duty on unions to actively secure a safe workplace for represented employees, should a claim that a union had failed to do so be preempted for upsetting the representational balance struck under federal duty of fair representation law? See Nellis v. Air Line Pilots Ass'n, 805 F. Supp. 355 (E.D. Va. 1992) (holding that state law cannot add to federal duty of fair representation regarding union's responsibility to negotiate particular benefits it had promised); Welch v. General Motors Corp., Buick Motor Div., 922 F.2d 287 (6th Cir. 1990) (preempting application of Michigan disability discrimination law to challenge the fairness of union decisions). Should employees be able to enforce any provision in a collective agreement that commits a union to do something, such as maintain plant safety, that could benefit the employees? Cf. Helton v. Hake, 386 F. Supp. 1027 (W.D. Mo. 1974) ("The job steward shall see . . . that no work shall be done in the immediate area of high tension lines until the power has been shut off, or the lines insulated, or the safety of the members of the bargaining unit otherwise provided for."). What could be the theory for such a §301 action? Does a union, when it contracts with an employer as an agent for employees, also thereby make contractual commitments to its principals?

# 12 Limited Sovereignty: The Relationship Between Employee and Bargaining Agent

If the labor laws simply authorized individual employees to designate representatives of their choosing to negotiate individual terms of employment with their employers, there would be no need for a federal overlay on the rules embodied in the common law of agency. However, the labor laws have provided for a more complicated relationship between bargaining representative and represented employee. First, the representative is selected not by the individual but by the majority of employees in an appropriate unit. Second, the law not only prevents the individual employee from revoking the agency, but also places certain durational and other limits on the majority's ability to effect revocation. These features of the statutory agency contemplated by the federal labor laws have been thought to warrant some measure of regulation of the relationship between the bargaining agent and represented employee and the internal governance of the union itself.

There are several sources of law in this area. First, the provisos to NLRA §§8(a)(3) and 8(b)(2), subject to state law constraints authorized by §14(b) of the Act, authorize agreements requiring all bargaining unit employees to pay for the costs of collective representation, while limiting unions' ability to insist that nonmembers undertake other obligations that attach to actual union membership. Second, §§8(b)(1) and 8(b)(2) prohibit union practices that restrain or coerce employees in the exercise of their §7 rights (including the right "to refrain" from concerted activity) or that otherwise discriminate against employees with the object of encouraging (or discouraging) union membership. Third, the courts have read into the NLRA (with later acquiescence by the NLRB) and the Railway Labor Act (RLA) an implied duty of fair representation that the exclusive bargaining representative owes to represented employees as a corollary of the statutory grant of exclusive bargaining status. Fourth, union constitutions have been read to create enforceable rights that may be invoked by members against their unions in litigation pursuant to §301 of the Labor Management

Relations Act of 1947 (LMRA). Fifth, Congress in the Labor-Management Reporting and Disclosure Act of 1959 (LMRDA or Landrum-Griffin Act), 29 U.S.C. §§401-531, established a federal "bill of rights" for union members and set forth ground rules for union elections, union disciplinary boards, and other aspects of internal union governance. Finally, the recurring problem of union corruption has led courts to apply certain other federal laws, notably the Racketeer Influenced and Corrupt Organizations Act of 1970 (RICO), 18 U.S.C. §§1961-1968, to purge unions of the influence of organized crime.

## A. THE UNION'S DUAL CONSTITUENCY

In this section we consider the problems raised by the fact that unions have a dual constituency. On the one hand, unions are private organizations governed by and hopefully responsive to their members. On the other hand, unions as exclusive bargaining agents have a responsibility to all employees in the bargaining unit, whether or not such employees have chosen to become union members. In systems based on "members only" representation, the dual constituency problem is not present because unions are considered to be agents only of their members with no obligations to other workers in the plant. In the United States, however, unions typically negotiate comprehensive agreements at the level of the firm that purport to bind all members in the bargaining unit, whether or not they are members of the union. The tensions created by this combined status of private organization and statutory bargaining agent are the subject of the materials that follow.

### *Note: "Free Riders" and Union Security*

"Union security" arrangements, which require an agreement between the union and the employer, mandate union membership or some form of financial support of the union by employees as a condition of initial or continued employment by the employer. The principal forms of such agreements (without regard to their current legality under the NLRA or state law) have been the following:

(1) The closed shop—requiring membership in the union as a condition of both initial and continued employment.
(2) The union shop—permitting employment of nonmembers but requiring employees to join the union within a specified period and to maintain their membership as a condition of continued employment.
(3) The agency shop—under which members of the bargaining unit need not join the union as a condition of either initial or

continued employment, but must pay initiation fees and dues in order to maintain their employment.

(4) Maintenance of membership—under which employees are not required to join the union, but if they do or, having been a member, fail to resign during a window period, must remain a member for the duration of the agreement as a condition of continued employment.

(5) Preferential hiring—union members are given preference in hiring, but the employer is permitted to hire nonunion personnel if the union fails to supply needed workers. Such arrangements are particularly common in the construction industry, and have sometimes been coupled with union shop provisions.

The Wagner Act allowed "closed shop" agreements, and the labor movement's demands for "union security" received a substantial boost during World War II because the War Labor Board required "maintenance of membership" agreements in all workplaces whose disputes affected the defense effort. See Harry A. Millis & Emily Clark Brown, From the Wagner Act to Taft-Hartley 296-298 (1950). However, closed shop agreements were outlawed by the Taft-Hartley Amendments of 1947. The proviso to §8(a)(3) of the NLRA (and the corresponding proviso to §8(b)(2)) instead allow only union security clauses that require employees to obtain "membership" in the union within 30 days of employment—a requirement interpreted in the *General Motors* case, infra page 902—as limited to meeting the financial obligations of collective representation.

The obligations that a union may impose under §8(a)(3) are also subject to certain qualifications. First, under the §8(a)(3) proviso, the union cannot deny "membership" on grounds other than "the failure of the employee to tender the periodic dues and the initiation fees uniformly required as a condition of acquiring or retaining membership." Second, although the original Taft-Hartley requirement that a majority of the affected employees vote to authorize a union security agreement was repealed in 1951, the provision (currently §9(e)(1)) allowing employees to vote in a secret-ballot election to revoke the union security arrangement was retained. Third, states are permitted under §14(b) of the NLRA to enact "right to work" laws banning union security arrangements. As of late 2014, 24 states, most of them in the South and West and parts of the Midwest, had "right to work" laws on the books. See Right to Work States, http://www.nrtw.org/rtws.htm (last visited Aug. 28, 2014).

Initially, because of fears of "company unions," the RLA prohibited all forms of union security. In 1951, the RLA was amended (§2, Eleventh) to permit agreements that require payment of assessments as well as periodic dues and initiation fees to unions enjoying majority support. Unlike the Taft-Hartley Act, the RLA does not provide a mechanism for employee deauthorization of union security agreements, nor does it give power to the states to outlaw such agreements.

Despite continuing controversy over "compulsory unionism," union security arrangements are commonplace in collective bargaining agreements. It appears that the overwhelming majority of private sector collective bargaining agreements in states that permit union security agreements contain such an agreement. See Bureau of National Affairs (BNA), BNA, Basic Patterns in Union Contracts (1995).

## 1. "Right to Work" Laws: §14(b) states

### a. *Effect of "Right to Work" Laws*

1. *Picketing for Invalid Clauses.* Retail Clerks Local 1625 v. Schermerhorn, 375 U.S. 96 (1963), holds that §14(b) of the NLRA authorizes states to ban both "union shop" and "agency fee" agreements. States enacting such "right to work" laws may enjoin the execution and application of such agreements. However, the states may not enjoin a strike or picketing to obtain such an agreement: "[P]icketing in order to get an employer to execute an agreement to hire all-union labor in violation of a state union-security statute lies exclusively in the federal domain . . . because state power, recognized by §14(b), begins only with actual negotiation and execution of the type of agreement described by §14(b). Absent such an agreement, conduct arguably an unfair labor practice would be a matter for the [NLRB] under *Garmon* [excerpted supra page 830]." 375 U.S. at 105.

2. *User Fees.* Section 14(b) authorizes states to prohibit agreements "requiring membership in a labor organization as a condition of employment." To what extent does this provision authorize states to bar agreements providing for payment of user fees by nonmembers? The Board has held that right to work states may prohibit unions from charging a flat (or graduated) fee for handling grievances. See Hughes Tool Co., 104 N.L.R.B. 318 (1953); Machinists Local 697, 223 N.L.R.B. 832 (1976). Notwithstanding a state right to work law, can a union insist that employees, as a condition of retaining their jobs, pay a "representation fee" consisting of "a pro rata share of the costs directly related to enforcing and servicing the collective bargaining agreement" as determined by an independent audit? The prevailing view is that right to work states may bar such fees. But see Sweeney v. Pence, 2014 U.S. App. LEXIS 16896 (7th Cir. 2014) (Wood. J., arguing in dissent that "nonmembers must pay for the services that the unions are required by law to render them" and that a state law to the contrary goes beyond §14(b) and raises a constitutional problem

because "the state is not entitled to force private organizations or persons to render uncompensated services to others."); Pipefitters Local 141 v. NLRB, 675 F.2d 1257, 1262 (D.C. Cir. 1982) (Mikva, J., arguing in dissent that §14(b) does not authorize states to prohibit representation fees and that union proposals for such clauses are mandatory subjects of bargaining).

3. *Commentary.* For further discussion of "right to work" laws, see generally Thomas Haggard, Compulsory Unionism, The NLRB and the Courts: A Legal Analysis of Union Security Agreements (1977); Frederic Meyers, Right to Work in Practice (1951); Norman Cantor, Uses and Abuses of the Agency Shop, 59 Notre Dame L. Rev. 61 (1983); Joseph R. Grodin & Duane B. Beeson, State Right-to-Work Laws and Federal Labor Policy, 52 Calif. L. Rev. 95 (1964).

### *b. The Justification for "Right to Work" Laws?*

What is the justification for "right to work" laws? Consider the following criticism from a well-known conservative/libertarian economist.

**Mancur Olson, The Logic of Collective Action: Public Goods and the Theory of Groups**
*88-97 (1971 ed.)*

If the conclusion that compulsory membership is usually essential for an enduring, stable labor movement is correct, then it follows that some of the usual arguments against the union shop are fallacious. One of the most common arguments against compulsory unionism, one used even by some professional economists, depends on an analogy with ordinary private business. In essence the argument is that, since a firm must please its customers if it is to retain their patronage, a union should also be forced to stand the test of an open shop, in which case it would still succeed if its performance pleased the potential members. This "right-to-work" argument often comes from those who are most ardent in support of a free-enterprise system based on the "profit motive." But if the same profit motive that is assumed to activate consumers and businessmen also stimulates workers, the enforcement of "right-to-work" laws would bring about the death of trade unions. A rational worker will not voluntarily contribute to a (large) union providing a collective benefit since he alone would not perceptibly strengthen the union, and since he would get the benefits of any union achievements whether or not he supported the union.

Arguments about compulsory union membership in terms of "rights" are therefore misleading and unhelpful. There are of course many intelligent arguments against unions and the union shop. But none of them can rest alone on the premise that the union shop and other forms of compulsory unionism restrict individual freedom, unless the argument is extended to cover all coercion used to support the provision of collective services. There is no less infringement of "rights" through taxation for the support of a police force or a judicial system than there is in a union shop. Of course, law and order are requisites of all organized economic activity; the police force and the judicial system are therefore presumably more vital to a country than labor unions. But this only puts the argument on the proper grounds: do the results of the unions' activities justify the power that society has given them? The debate on the "right-to-work" laws should center, not around the "rights" involved, but on whether or not a country would be better off if its unions were stronger or weaker. . . .

It may seem strange to draw an analogy between the union and the state. Some have supposed . . . that the state must be different in all of the more important respects from every other type of organization. But normally both the union and the state provide mostly common or collective benefits to large groups. Accordingly, the individual union member, like the individual taxpayer, will not be able to see by himself that the collective good is provided, but will, whether he has tried to have this good provided or not, nonetheless get it if it is provided by others. The union member, like the individual taxpayer, has no incentive to sacrifice any more than he is forced to sacrifice. . . .

## *NOTES AND QUESTIONS*

1. **"Right to Refrain"?** As elaborated later in this chapter, the exclusive bargaining representative is under a duty of fair representation that requires nondiscriminatory, fair representation in collective bargaining and grievance adjustment of the interests of unit employees who have eschewed union membership or (in right to work states) have refused to pay for the costs of collective representation. Moreover, employees have a right to obtain a rebate of dues revenues not used for collective bargaining and grievance adjustment functions. See Communication Workers of America v. Beck, infra page 909. Also, under §19 of the NLRA, employees with religious objections to compulsory unionism can be required to make contributions to charities of their choice in lieu of paying union dues. Do these protections suggest that the employees' negative freedom of association—captured by §7's "right to refrain"—is fully vindicated without also giving those employees a right to be "free riders"? See generally Sheldon Leader, Freedom of Association: A Study in Labor

Law and Political Theory, ch. 9 (1992); Samuel Estreicher, Freedom of Contract and Labor Law Reform: Opening Up the Possibilities for Value-Added Unionism, 71 N.Y.U. L. Rev. 827 (1996).

**2. "Winning Hearts and Minds."** The late George Brooks, of Cornell University's School of Industrial and Labor Relations, a former research director for the International Brotherhood of Pulp, Sulfite, and Papermill Workers, argued that compulsory unionism is not in the best interests of either unions or employees. See George W. Brooks, The Strengths and Weaknesses of Compulsory Unionism, 11 N.Y.U. Rev. Law & Soc. Change 29, 32-35 (1982-1983):

> Once the union shop is granted by the employer and embodied in the collective bargaining agreement, the union's revenue is assured without any further effort on the part of union staff and officers. When the checkoff is added, as it is almost universally, the transfer of funds is accomplished with no effort on the part of the union. The irksome and time-consuming task of collecting dues is eliminated. At the same time, that useful conversation between union staff and employee/member is greatly diminished. . . . [T]he relationship between union members and leaders, the very life of the union in the earlier period, was seriously eroded. Officers and stewards no longer bothered to educate new employees on reasons for joining the union. This was not the employer's responsibility. Inevitably, the role of the steward declined, and his status in the union diminished. It became increasingly difficult to get competent persons to serve as stewards. The lines of communication up and down the union structure became less important and sometimes dried up, except when the parties were engaged in negotiations, and there was the possibility of a strike. But contacts before a strike were not substitutes for daily expressions of satisfaction and dissatisfaction to the steward from employees who have the right to leave the union if they feel sufficiently frustrated . . . . We have thus come full circle. Compulsory unionism begins as a device for protecting the union and its members against an anti-union employer. It ends as a device by which the employer protects the union against reluctant or critical members. The erosion of vitality of the union at the workplace is an inevitable consequence. . . .

See also George W. Brooks, Stability Versus Employee Free Choice, 61 Cornell L. Rev. 344 (1976); and The Sources of Vitality in the American Labor Movement (ILR Bull. 41, New York State School of Industrial and Labor Relations, Cornell Univ., 1960). Is it clear that the problems Professor Brooks identifies are caused by union security clauses?

**3. Union Security in Other Countries.**

a. *United Kingdom.* Until 1988, the United Kingdom allowed the closed shop. Bowing to European Union pressure, however, Parliament enacted the Employment Act of 1988, which bars employers from discharging an employee who refuses to join a union, and the Employment Act of 1990, which renders unlawful agreements to refuse employment to a person because he or she is not a union member, declines union membership, or declines to make payments to a union as an alternative to membership. See Leader, Freedom of Association, supra, at 131-132; John T. Addison & W. Stanley Siebert, Union Security in Britain, with an Addendum on New Labour's Reforms, in The Internal Governance and Organizational Effectiveness of Labor Unions, supra, ch. 13 (Samuel Estreicher, Harry C. Katz & Bruce E. Kaufman eds., 2001).

b. *Denmark.* Denmark law permitting the closed shop has been ruled inconsistent with the "negative freedom of association" guaranteed by Article 11 of the European Convention for the Protection of Human Rights and Fundamental Freedoms. See Sorensen v. Denmark and Rasmussen v. Denmark, European Court of Human Rights — Strasbourg (Jan. 11, 2006).

c. *Germany.* Article 9, §3 of the Federal Constitution is interpreted as conferring a "negative freedom of association" that bars both closed shop and agency shop agreements. See Manfred Weiss, Labor Law, in Introduction to German Law, at 304-305 (Mathias Reimann & Joachim Zekoll eds., 2005).

d. *Canada.* By legislation, Canada mandates that all bargaining agreements contain at least an agency shop agreement. Moreover, both closed shop and union shop agreements are lawful. See Daphne Gottlieb Taras & Allen Ponak, Union Security in Canada, in The Internal Governance and Organizational Effectiveness of Labor Unions (2001).

e. *Japan.* Apparently, Japan permits union shop agreements negotiated by majority unions, while allowing employees to resign membership to affiliate with a different organization. Discharges of employees improperly expelled from union membership may be treated as unlawful dismissals. See Tadashi Hanami and Fumito Komiya, Labour Law in Japan 159 (2011).

## 2. The Limits of Compulsory Participation in Non-§14(b) States

### *a. The Obligation to Maintain "Membership"*

**NLRB v. General Motors Corp.**
*373 U.S. 734 (1963)*

White, J.

The issue here is whether an employer commits an unfair labor practice [under §8(a)(5)] when it refuses to bargain with a certified union over the union's proposal for the adoption of the "agency shop." More narrowly, since the employer is not obliged to bargain over a proposal that he commit an unfair labor practice, the question is whether the agency shop is an unfair labor practice under §8(a)(3) . . . or else is exempted from the prohibitions of that section by the proviso thereto. We have concluded that this type of arrangement does not constitute an unfair labor practice and that it is not prohibited by §8.

Respondent's employees are represented by the [UAW] in a single, multiplant, companywide unit. The 1958 agreement . . . provides for maintenance of membership and the union shop. These provisions were not operative, however, in such States as Indiana where state law prohibited making union membership a condition of employment.

In June 1959, the Indiana intermediate appellate court held that an agency shop arrangement would not violate the state right-to-work law. As defined in that opinion, . . . "agency shop" applies to an arrangement under which all employees are required as a condition of employment to pay dues to the union and pay the union's initiation fee, but they need not actually become union members. The union thereafter [proposed] the negotiation of a contractual provision covering Indiana plants "generally similar to that set forth" in the [Indiana court] case. . . . The respondent . . . replied . . . that the proposed agreement would violate the [NLRA] and that respondent must therefore "respectfully decline" . . . to bargain over the proposal.

[Reviewing a claimed violation of §8(a)(5),] the Board . . . assessed the union's proposal as comporting fully with the congressional declaration of policy in favor of union-security contracts and therefore a mandatory subject [of bargaining]. . . . [I]t also stated that it had "no doubt that an agency-shop agreement is a permissible form of union-security within the meaning of §§7 and 8(a)(3). . . ." Accordingly, the Board . . . ordered respondent to bargain. . . .

. . . The Court of Appeals set the order aside on the grounds that the Act tolerates only "an agreement requiring membership in a labor organization as a condition of employment" when such agreements do not violate state right-to-work laws, [but] does not authorize agreements requiring payment of membership dues to a union, in lieu of membership, as a condition of employment. It held that . . . the employer was therefore not obliged to bargain over [the proposed agreement]. We . . . now reverse. . . .

We find nothing in the legislative history . . . indicating that Congress intended the . . . proviso to §8(a)(3) to validate only the union shop and simultaneously to abolish . . . all other union-security arrangements permissible under state law. There is much to be said for the Board's view that, if Congress desired in the Wagner Act to permit a closed or union shop and in the Taft-Hartley Act the union shop, then it also intended to preserve the status of less vigorous, less compulsory contracts which demanded less adherence to the union.

Respondent, however, relies upon the express words of the proviso which allow employment to be conditioned upon "membership": since the union's proposal here does not require actual membership but demands only initiation fees and monthly dues, it is not saved by the proviso.

... [However,] the 1947 amendments not only abolished the closed shop but also made significant alterations in the meaning of "membership" for the purposes of union-security contracts. Under the second proviso to §8(a)(3), the burdens of membership upon which employment may be conditioned are expressly limited to the payment of initiation fees and monthly dues. It is permissible to condition employment upon membership, but membership, insofar as it has significance to employment rights, may in turn be conditioned only upon payment of fees and dues. "Membership" as a condition of employment is whittled down to its financial core. . . .

We are therefore confident that the proposal made by the union here conditioned employment upon the practical equivalent of union "membership," as Congress used that term in the proviso to §8(a)(3). The proposal for requiring the payment of dues and fees imposes no burdens not imposed by a permissible union shop contract and compels the performance of only those duties of membership which are enforceable by discharge under a union shop arrangement. If an employee in a union shop unit refuses to respect any union-imposed obligations other than the duty to pay dues and fees, and membership in the union is therefore denied or terminated, the condition of "membership" for §8(a)(3) purposes is nevertheless satisfied and the employee may not be discharged for nonmembership even though he is not a formal member. Of course, if the union chooses to extend membership even though the employee will meet only the minimum financial burden, and refuses to support or "join" the union in any other affirmative way, the employee may have to become a "member" under a union shop contract, in the sense that the union may be able to place him on its rolls. The agency shop arrangement proposed here removes that choice from the union and places the option of membership in the employee while still requiring the same monetary support as does the union shop. Such a difference between the union and agency shop may be of great importance in some contexts, but for present purposes it is more formal than real. To the extent that it has any significance at all it serves, rather than violates, the desire of Congress to reduce the evils of compulsory unionism while allowing financial support for the bargaining agent.

## *NOTES AND QUESTIONS*

1. **Advantages and Disadvantages of Full Membership?** Although full union members, like their "financial core" counterparts, may be discharged only for a failure to pay union dues and initiation fees, unlike the latter, they may be fined or otherwise sanctioned by the union for other delinquencies, such as failing to perform picket-line duty or to attend

union meetings. In contrast, employees who have declined full membership are not subject to internal union rules or sanctions.

At the same time, employees who are not members of the union have limited rights to participate in decisions that vitally affect their interests. Matters of considerable importance, such as strike votes and contract ratification votes, are governed by union constitutions and by-laws that extend these opportunities for participation, if at all, only to union members. The Board's general position is that such votes are matters of internal union governance and that even unratified contracts can serve as a contract bar to a §9 petition. See, e.g., Appalachian Shale Prods. Co., 121 N.L.R.B. 1160 (1958). Moreover, the Supreme Court's decision in *Borg-Warner,* supra page 460, makes clear that employers may not insist on employee votes as a condition of agreement. See generally Samuel Estreicher, Deregulating Union Democracy, 20 J. Lab. Res. 247 (2000); Alan Hyde, Democracy in Collective Bargaining, 93 Yale L.J. 793 (1984); Matthew W. Finkin, The Limits of Majority Rule in Collective Bargaining, 64 Minn. L. Rev. 183 (1980); Julia Penny Clark, The Duty of Fair Representation: A Theoretical Structure, 51 Tex. L. Rev. 1119 (1973).

Although federal law does not require submission of proposed contracts to employees or even union members (unless required by the union constitution or other rules), the *government* may submit proposed contracts to the affected employees in two circumstances. See LMRA §203(c) (Federal Mediation and Conciliation Service (FMCS) may submit employer's last offer to unit employees as means of inducing settlement, although parties' failure to agree to any procedure suggested by FMCS is not unlawful); see also supra page 460 (vote on employer's last offer required in case of "national emergency strikes").

Union control of rights of participation in economic decision making creates incentives for employees in the bargaining unit to become full-fledged union members in order to have a say in their economic fate. It may also increase the risk that unions may not function as faithful agents of all employees in the bargaining unit. For the view that the NLRA should be amended to give all unit employees irrespective of union membership a statutory right to strike authorization and contract ratification votes, see Estreicher, "Easy In, Easy Out," supra; Estreicher, Deregulating Union Democracy, supra; Labor Law Reform in a World of Competitive Product Markets, 69 Chi.-Kent L. Rev. 3, 42 (1993).

Two possible mitigating doctrines, however, should be kept in mind. First, the union's good-faith bargaining obligation may limit its ability to condition agreement in one bargaining unit on the result of votes taken in other units. See United Paperworkers Int'l Union Local 620, 309 N.L.R.B. 44 (1992) (union's "pool voting" rule violates §8(b)(3)) (criticized in Julius G. Getman & F. Ray Marshall, Industrial Relations in Transition: The Paper Industry Example, 102 Yale L.J. 1803, 1886-1892 (1993)). Second, the union's duty of fair representation, discussed infra pages 938-959, may include an obligation to ascertain employee interests in some circumstances.

See, e.g., Branch 6000, Nat'l Ass'n of Letter Carriers v. NLRB, 595 F.2d 808, 812-813 (D.C. Cir. 1979) (prenegotiation referendum on bargaining policy, as distinguished from contact ratification vote, must be extended to non-members); but see International Longshoreman's Ass'n, Local 1575 (Navieras, NPR, Inc.), 332 N.L.R.B. 1336 (2000) (contract ratification is "purely an internal union affair").

**2. Dues "Uniformly Required"?** Can a union offer its members a partial rebate of the dues ordinarily payable for regular attendance at union meetings? Can it assess a fine against members who fail to attend regularly? Can it lawfully seek or force the discharge of a member who has failed to attend meetings but insists on paying only the reduced dues or refuses to pay the fine? Compare Local 171, Ass'n of Western Pulp Workers (Boise Cascade Corp.), 165 N.L.R.B. 971 (1967) (partial "refund" of dues to members who attend monthly meetings lawful) with, Norris Indus., Thermador Div., 190 N.L.R.B. 479 (1971) (refusal to recall employee suspended from union membership for refusal to pay "assessment" charged to non-attendees unlawful; *Boise Cascade* distinguished on ground that dues there were "uniform" and refund merely lawful use of union funds to stimulate attendance, whereas assessment at issue here was not part of "uniform periodic dues"). Is this distinction a sensible one? What about nonmembers? Should a union be able to charge them an agency fee equivalent to the higher, "no rebate" level of dues, and to force the discharge of a nonmember who insists on paying the lower level available to union members who regularly attend meetings?

### *b. Use of Union Dues*

Do union security clauses that require the payment of union dues without imposing other obligations of union membership abridge the rights of employees who are not members of the union and who object to the use of exacted union dues for purposes that are offensive to their beliefs? Does the First Amendment protect the claims of these objectors? Can the NLRA and RLA be read to protect such claims without reaching the constitutional question? On the assumption that either the Constitution or the labor laws protect such objections, to what purposes may union dues be committed, and what procedures must the union follow? These questions are the subject of the materials that follow.

#### *Note: Nonmembers' Objections to Use of Union Dues Under the Railway Labor Act*

***Railway Employees' Dep't v. Hanson.*** In Railway Employees' Dep't v. Hanson, 351 U.S. 225 (1956), the Supreme Court ruled that because the

RLA preempts all state laws banning union security agreements, the negotiation and enforcement of such provisions in railroad industry contracts involve "governmental action" and are therefore subject to constitutional limitations. *Hanson* upheld the facial constitutionality of §2, Eleventh of the RLA in its bare authorization of union-shop contracts requiring workers to give "financial support" to unions. The Court did not pass on other aspects of forced association or on the issue of the use of exacted money for political causes that are opposed by particular employees.

***Machinists v. Street.*** Those questions were reached in International Ass'n of Machinists v. Street, 367 U.S. 740 (1961), where the Court (per Justice Brennan) held that to avoid constitutional infirmities, §2, Eleventh of the RLA should be read to prohibit a union, over the objections of nonmembers, from spending compelled agency shop fees on political causes. In discussing potential remedies on remand, the *Street* Court rejected the possibility of a blanket injunction against either the collection of all dues from objectors or against all expenditures of funds for the disputed purposes. Justice Brennan made clear that any remedy would accrue only to nonmembers who had made their objections known to the union, and offered the following two suggestions (id. at 774-775):

> One [possible] remedy would be an injunction against expenditure for political causes opposed by each complaining employee of a sum, from those moneys to be spent by the union for political purposes, which is so much of the moneys exacted from him as is the proportion of the union's total expenditures made for such political activities to the union's total budget. . . . A second remedy would be restitution to each individual employee of that portion of his money which the union expended, despite his notification, for the political causes to which he had advised the union he was opposed.

Justice Black, writing separately in *Street,* would have reached the constitutional question, and in his view the First Amendment "deprives the Government of all power to make any person pay out a single penny against his will to be used in any way to advocate doctrines or views he is against, whether economic, scientific, political, religious or any other." Id. at 791. The proper remedy, he argued, would be to forbid enforcement of the union shop clause to bar employment as long as the union continued to spend its funds to support causes objected to by the dissidents.

Justice Frankfurter filed a dissent, joined by Justice Harlan. The dissenters argued that the union security obligations under the RLA were dependent on private agreements rather than government compulsion, and hence did not involve government action implicating constitutional requirements.

***Ellis v. Brotherhood of Railway Clerks.*** The Supreme Court revisited these issues in Ellis v. Brotherhood of Railway, Airline & S.S. Clerks, 466 U.S. 435 (1984). Departing from the implications of *Street,* the Court invalidated the union's remedy for impermissible funding, namely a rebate to an objector paid a year after all his dues had been collected. The Court reasoned that this remedy forced an objector to make an interest-free loan in the amount of the rebate. Less restrictive alternatives, such as advance reduction of dues or interest-bearing escrow accounts, would place only minimal burdens on the union.

The Court also stated that in determining the activities that the RLA authorized to be financed by compulsory dues, "the test must be whether the challenged expenditures are necessarily or reasonably incurred for the purpose of performing the duties of an exclusive representative of the employees in dealing with the employer on labor-management issues." The Court found that the following activities passed this test. (We use the numbers used by the Court to designate the activities described below.)

1. The union's quadrennial national conventions, where officers are elected, bargaining goals established, and overall policy formulated—activities characterized by the Court as essential to the effective discharge of a bargaining agent's duties.

2. Social activities. The 0.7 percent of expenditures designated for refreshments for union business meetings and social activities, which were formally open to nonmembers. The Court deemed these expenditures "de minimis," and found that they promoted closer ties between employees and improved the atmosphere of union meetings.

3. Limited union publications. Under the union's own policy, involuntary payments were not to be used for that part of a publication concerned with "political causes," as distinguished from negotiations, social activities, and recently proposed as well as enacted legislation. Thus, the union rebated to dissenters the proportion of total publication expenses represented by the ratio of "political" linage to total linage. More generally, the Court declared: "If a union cannot spend dissenters' funds for a particular activity . . . spending their funds for writing about that activity [is unjustifiable]."

The Court, however, concluded that the RLA did not authorize use of dissenters' dues to finance the following activities:

4. Organizing employees outside the bargaining unit.

5. Litigation not involving bargaining, grievances, or the duty of fair representation within the bargaining unit. For example, "unless the . . . bargaining unit is directly concerned, objecting employees need not share the costs of the union's challenge to the legality of the airline industry mutual aid pact; [or] of litigation seeking to protect the rights of airline employees generally during bankruptcy proceedings. . . ."

In *Ellis,* the Court rejected a challenge based on the First Amendment, finding that the government's interest in industrial peace that had led to authorization of the union shop also justified the expenditures that the Court had upheld under the statute.

Justice Powell dissented from the Court's disposition concerning the union's quadrennial convention on these grounds: Five prominent politicians plus four Congressmen had made major addresses at the 25th convention, which cost the union $1.8 million in toto. The union had not identified the expenses for these "political activities," in sharp contrast to its handling of publication expenses. Not all the expenses of the convention had the nexus with collective bargaining required under the Court's test.

**Communication Workers of America v. Beck**
*487 U.S. 735 (1988)*

BRENNAN, J. . . .

Section 8(a)(3) of the National Labor Relations Act . . . permits an employer and an exclusive bargaining representative to enter into an agreement requiring all employees in the bargaining unit to pay periodic union dues and initiation fees as a condition of continued employment, whether or not the employees otherwise wish to become union members. Today we must decide whether this provision also permits a union, over the objections of dues-paying nonmember employees, to expend funds so collected on activities unrelated to collective bargaining, contract administration, or grievance adjustment, and, if so, whether such expenditures violate the union's duty of fair representation or the objecting employees' First Amendment rights.

## I

In accordance with §9 of the NLRA, a majority of the employees of American Telephone and Telegraph Company and several of its subsidiaries selected petitioner Communications Workers of America (CWA) as their exclusive bargaining representative. As such, the union is empowered to bargain collectively with the employer on behalf of all employees in the bargaining unit over wages, hours, and other terms and conditions of employment. . . . This broad authority, however, is tempered by the union's "statutory obligation to serve the interests of all members without hostility or discrimination toward any," Vaca v. Sipes, 386 U.S. 171, 177 (1967), a duty that extends not only to the negotiation of the collective-bargaining agreement itself but also to the subsequent enforcement of that agreement, including the administration of any grievance procedure the agreement may establish. [CWA negotiated such a collective agreement with the company. To defray the costs of representation, CWA obtained a union-security clause in the agreement] under which all represented employees, including those who do not wish to become union members, must pay the union "agency fees" in "amounts equal to the periodic dues" paid by union members. Under the clause, failure to tender the required fee may be grounds for discharge.

In June 1976, respondents, 20 employees who chose not to become union members, initiated this suit challenging CWA's use of their agency fees for purposes other than collective bargaining, contract administration, or grievance adjustment (hereinafter "collective-bargaining" or "representational" activities). Specifically, respondents alleged that the union's expenditure of their fees on activities such as organizing the employees of other employers, lobbying for labor legislation, and participating in social, charitable, and political events violated petitioner's duty of fair representation, §8(a)(3) of the NLRA, the First Amendment, and various common-law fiduciary duties. In addition to declaratory relief, respondents sought an injunction barring petitioners from exacting fees above those necessary to finance collective-bargaining activities, as well as damages for the past collection of such excess fees.

The District Court concluded that the union's collection and disbursement of agency fees for purposes other than bargaining unit representation violated the associational and free speech rights of objecting nonmembers, and therefore enjoined their future collection. . . .

A divided panel of the United States Court of Appeals for the Fourth Circuit agreed that respondents stated a valid claim for relief under the First Amendment, but, preferring to rest its judgment on a ground other than the Constitution, concluded that the collection of nonmembers' fees for purposes unrelated to collective bargaining violated §8(a)(3). . . .

On rehearing, the en banc court vacated the panel opinion and by a 6-to-4 vote again affirmed in part, reversed in part, and remanded for further proceedings. . . .

## II . . .

Respondents sought relief on three separate federal claims: that the exaction of fees beyond those necessary to finance collective-bargaining activities violates §8(a)(3); that such exactions violate the judicially created duty of fair representation; and that such exactions violate respondents' First Amendment rights. We think it clear that the courts below properly exercised jurisdiction over the latter two claims, but that the National Labor Relations Board (NLRB or Board) had primary jurisdiction over respondents' §8(a)(3) claim.

The court was not precluded, however, from deciding the merits of this claim insofar as such a decision was necessary to the disposition of respondents' duty-of-fair-representation challenge. . . . The necessity of deciding the scope of §8(a)(3) arises because *petitioners* seek to defend themselves on the ground that the statute authorizes precisely this type of agreement. Under these circumstances, the Court of Appeals had jurisdiction to decide the §8(a)(3) question raised by respondents' duty-of-fair-representation claim.

## III

. . . Taken as a whole, §8(a)(3) permits an employer and a union to enter into an agreement requiring all employees to become union members as a condition of continued employment, but the "membership" that may be so required has been "whittled down to its financial core." NLRB v. General Motors Corp., 373 U.S. 734, 742 (1963). The statutory question presented in this case, then, is whether this "financial core" includes the obligation to support union activities beyond those germane to collective bargaining, contract administration, and grievance adjustment. We think it does not. . . .

. . . [W]e ruled in Railway Employees v. Hanson, 351 U.S. 225 (1956), that because the RLA preempts all state laws banning union-security agreements, the negotiation and enforcement of such provisions in railroad industry contracts involves "governmental action" and is therefore subject to constitutional limitations. Accordingly, in [Machinists v. Street, 367 U.S. 740 (1961),] we interpreted §2, Eleventh to avoid the serious constitutional question that would otherwise be raised by a construction permitting unions to expend governmentally compelled fees on political causes that nonmembers find objectionable. See 367 U.S., at 749. No such constitutional questions lurk here, petitioners contend, for §14(b) of the NLRA expressly preserves the authority of States to outlaw union-security agreements. Thus, petitioners' argument runs, the federal preemption essential to *Hanson*'s finding of governmental action is missing in the NLRA context, and we therefore need not strain to avoid the plain meaning of §8(a)(3) as we did with §2, Eleventh.

We need not decide whether the exercise of rights permitted, though not compelled, by §8(a)(3) involves state action. . . . Even assuming that it does not, and that the NLRA and RLA therefore differ in this respect, we do not believe that the absence of any constitutional concerns in this case would warrant reading the nearly identical language of §8(a)(3) and §2, Eleventh differently. It is, of course, true that federal statutes are to be construed so as to avoid serious doubts as to their constitutionality, and that when faced with such doubts the Court will first determine whether it is fairly possible to interpret the statute in a manner that renders it constitutionally valid. . . . We . . . decline to construe the language of §8(a)(3) differently from that of §2, Eleventh on the theory that our construction of the latter provision was merely constitutionally expedient. Congress enacted the two provisions for the same purpose, eliminating "free riders," and that purpose dictates our construction of §8(a)(3) no less than it did that of §2, Eleventh, regardless of whether the negotiation of union-security agreements under the NLRA partakes of governmental action.

IV

We conclude that §8(a)(3), like its statutory equivalent, §2, Eleventh of the RLA, authorizes the exaction of only those fees and dues necessary to "performing the duties of an exclusive representative of the employees in dealing with the employer on labor-management issues." *Ellis* [v. Railway Clerks.] 466 U.S., [435,] 448 [(1984)].

[Justice Kennedy took no part in the decision in this case.]

[The opinion of Justice Blackmun, with whom Justices O'Connor and Scalia join, concurring in part and dissenting in part is omitted.]

## *NOTES AND QUESTIONS*

**1. First Amendment Interests of Nonmembers?** As noted in *Beck*, the Court had previously held in the *Hanson* case, supra page 906, that the First Amendment applies to union security agreements under RLA §2(11). Are constitutional considerations relevant in the NLRA context? Assuming arguendo that the necessary "state action" is present, consider Justice Frankfurter's dissent in *Street*, as well as Mancur Olson's discussion of the coercive nature of government expenditures on collective goods. Governments supply collective goods, like police and fire protection, and require citizens to pay the cost of those services, whether they desire them or not. This is not thought to raise first amendment issues of "compelled association." Professor Olson suggests unions also supply collective goods to the members of the bargaining unit. If government can expend dissenting taxpayers' monies on wars and a myriad of controversial social causes not endorsed by dissenters, can it require all employees to expend their funds on union activities that some employees do not favor? Is the "free rider" concern or justification sufficient to meet freedom of expression concerns?

The U.S. Supreme Court in 2014 ruled in Harris v. Quinn, 134 S. Ct. 2618, that "free rider" concerns were not sufficient to overcome a First Amendment challenge to Illinois's requirement that homecare providers whose wages are set and funded by the state, must pay agency-shop fees to a union representative. The closely divided *Harris* Court did not overrule Abood v. Detroit Board of Ed., 431 U.S. 209 (1977), which had allowed over First Amendment challenge the compelled payment of agency-shop fees for school employees who in every sense were public employees. Nonetheless, the Court sharply criticized *Abood* and refused to extend its holding to individuals who were not "full-fledged public employees" and who were "almost entirely answerable to the customers and not to the State . . . ."134 S. Ct. at 2622. The *Harris* Court also distinguished private sector employees from those in the public sector whose speech is more likely to involve matters of public concern. The Court stated that free-rider concerns are "generally insufficient to overcome First Amendment objections." Id. at 2627.

**2. Accommodation of Religious Objectors.** Under §19 of the NLRA, enacted in 1974 and amended in 1980 by Pub. L. 96-953, employees with religiously based conscientious objections to joining or providing financial support to unions are given the option of contributing to a charity of their choice a sum equal to union dues and initiation fees. If such an employee requests the union to use the grievance arbitration procedure on the employee's behalf, the union is authorized "to charge the employee for the reasonable cost of using such procedure."

Is the approach of §19 preferable to the rules set forth in *Ellis* as a means of accommodating politically based conscientious objections? Since the Court in *Beck* is construing the NLRA rather than the Constitution directly, should the Court be constrained to follow the approach of §19 rather than craft its own rules of accommodation?

**3. Use of Union Funds for Federal Election Campaigns.** Before the Supreme Court's Citizens United v. FEC, 558 U.S. 310 (2010) ruling, unions could not use their general treasury funds to contribute to federal election campaigns. See §321 of the Federal Election Campaign Act of 1976, 90 Stat. 490, 2 U. S. C. §441b, (traceable to §304 of the Taft-Hartley Act, 61 Stat. 159-160). Unions could communicate with their members with respect to such campaigns and conduct nonpartisan get-out-the-vote campaigns directed to their members. They also could establish "a separate segregated fund to be used for political purposes." In Pipefitters Local 562 v. United States, 407 U.S. 385 (1972), the Court held that union officials could control and administer the separate fund as long as the political monies were segregated from union monies. In *Citizens United* the Supreme Court held violative of the First Amendment the congressional ban on corporate and labor union expenditures from their general treasuries for electioneering communications under 2 U.S.C. §441b. See generally Benjamin I. Sachs, Unions, Corporations, and Political Opt-Out Rights After Citizens United, 112 Colum. L. Rev. 800 (2012).

**4. Executive Orders for Government Contractors.** On April 13, 1992, President George H.W. Bush issued Executive Order 12800, requiring most government contractors and subcontractors to post a notice to employees informing them of their rights under *Beck.* The Department of Labor subsequently issued regulations implementing Executive Order 12800. See 29 C.F.R. Part 470. On February 1, 1993, however, President Clinton issued Executive Order 12,836, withdrawing the previous order. 58 Fed. Reg. 7045 (1993). In 2001, President George Bush reissued his father's directive as Executive Order 13,201. The district court held that the order was "preempted" by the NLRA and enjoined its implementation, but the court of appeals reversed. See UAW-Labor Employment and Training Corp. v. Chao, 325 F.3d 360 (D.C. Cir. 2003) (applying *Garmon* preemption analysis and concluding that the order was not arguably protected or prohibited by the NLRA).

On January 30, 2009, President Obama revoked the Bush administration's executive order and issued Executive Order 13496 requiring federal contractors to post notices of employees' NLRA rights. The Department of Labor regulation implementing Executive Order 13496 does not include notice of *Beck* rights.

**5. Permissible Union-Security Clauses Following *Beck*?** Following *Beck* and *General Motors (GM),* may a union lawfully negotiate a union security clause stating that unit employees must become and remain "members in good standing" of the union within 30 days of beginning employment in order to retain their jobs—without including language explaining that "membership" is limited to "financial core" obligations under *GM,* and that objecting nonmembers need only pay the portion of dues germane to representational activities under *Beck*? Former Board Chair William Gould argued that such clauses should be held facially invalid because they allow employers and unions to sow confusion and "allow[] unions to reap the benefits of that confusion," and proposed that the Board adopt a model union security clause incorporating *GM*'s and *Beck*'s refinements of the statutory language. See Group Health, Inc., 325 N.L.R.B. 342, 345 (1998) (Chairman Gould, concurring). In Marquez v. Screen Actors Guild, Inc., 525 U.S. 33 (1998), however, a unanimous Supreme Court held that the mere negotiation of a clause that tracks the language of §8(a)(3) does not violate the union's duty of fair representation. The Court emphasized that it was not ruling on the enforcement of such a clause or on whether the union had otherwise failed to adequately notify Marquez of her *GM* and *Beck* rights. Following *Marquez,* which did not involve review of an NLRB order, could the Board, as a matter of policy, choose to require greater disclosure in collective bargaining agreements? See Kroger, Inc., 327 N.L.R.B. 1237, 1239 n.3 (1999); Bloom v. NLRB, 209 F.3d 1060 (8th Cir. 2000).

### *Note:* Beck *vs. RLA and Public Sector Precedents*

As the Notes and Questions above suggest, *Beck* raises a host of issues, including: (1) whether the union must notify nonmembers of their right to object to the payment of full dues, and if so in what manner; (2) which expenses are chargeable to objecting nonmembers; and (3) by what means and in what forum (or fora) objecting nonmembers may challenge a union's calculations regarding "chargeable" versus "nonchargeable" expenses. In resolving these issues, the Board and courts have often looked to precedent not only under the RLA, but also to case law construing the requirements of the First Amendment in the public sector, which is discussed at a number of points below.

**Standard for Determining Permissible Expenditures**

a. *"Relevant" or "Germane" vs. "Necessarily or Reasonably Incurred".* Both in *Ellis* and in Lehnert v. Ferris Faculty Ass'n, 500 U.S. 507 (1991), a public-sector case, the Court used two somewhat different verbal formulations interchangeably: (1) expenses "relevant" or "germane" to the union's collective bargaining functions, and (2) expenditures that are "necessarily or reasonably incurred" for purposes of performing the union's bargaining functions. Is there a difference? If so, which test is preferable? In *Lehnert*, the plurality opinion further held that objectors could be charged for activities of the union's state and national affiliates that may be relevant to collective bargaining and that "may ultimately inure to the benefit of the [unit employees]," even if they did not directly benefit those employees in a particular year. See 500 U.S. at 524.

b. *The* California Saw *Test. Beck* speaks in terms of both "activities related to collective bargaining, contract administration and grievance adjustment" and (quoting *Ellis*) activities "necessary to "performing the duties of an exclusive [bargaining] representative. . . ." Again, is there a difference? In California Saw & Knife Works, 320 N.L.R.B. 224 (1995), enforced sub nom. Machinists v. NLRB, 133 F.3d 1012 (7th Cir. 1998), the Board, without discussion, adopted the former formulation as the test under the NLRA.

c. *Aborted* Beck *Rulemaking.* In 1992, the Board initiated a rulemaking proceeding aimed at implementing the *Beck* decision and issued a proposed rule. See Union Dues Regulation, 57 Fed. Reg. 43635 (1992).

Three years later it abandoned this proceeding and determined to proceed by adjudication. See *California Saw*, supra.

**Basic Procedures Under *Beck* and *California Saw***

a. *Notice to Employees.* In *California Saw*, the Board established the following basic rules. Before obligating employees to pay dues under a union security clause, the union must notify them that they have the right to be and remain nonmembers, and that nonmembers have the right to: (1) object to paying for union activities that are not germane to the union's duties as bargaining agent and to obtain a reduction in fees for such activities; (2) be given sufficient information to enable them to intelligently decide whether to object; and (3) be apprised of any internal union procedures for filing objections. See 320 N.L.R.B. at 233.

b. *Objectors' Rights.* Once an employee objects to paying fees for nonrepresentational purposes, the union must: (1) refrain from charging her for the portion of dues expended on such activities; (2) inform her of the percentage of dues that goes to nonrepresentational activities; (3) provide a summary of the major categories of "chargeable" and "nonchargeable" expenses; and (4) supply verified figures demonstrating that the expenditures listed in these categories were indeed made. *California Saw*, supra, at 239-241; see also Ferriso v. NLRB, 125 F.3d 865 (D.C. Cir. 1997); Television & Radio Artists (KGW Radio), 327 N.L.R.B. 474, 477 (1999) (elaborating on verification requirement).

c. *Challenge Procedure.* Finally, the union must also afford objectors a reasonable procedure for challenging the union's allocation of chargeable and nonchargeable expenses. *California Saw*, 320 N.L.R.B. at 242. If the union provides an arbitration procedure for resolution of such challenges, may it require objectors to exhaust that process before they may pursue a judicial remedy? The Supreme Court has held "no" in the RLA context, at least where the employees had never consented to the arbitration procedure. See Air Line Pilots Ass'n v. Miller, 523 U.S. 866 (1998).

d. *Rebate Procedure.* In Chicago Teachers Union, Local No. 1 v. Hudson, 475 U.S. 292 (1986), a unanimous Court held unconstitutional a procedure that did not permit nonmembers to make pre-deduction objections to expenses charged by the union, but rather required the filing of written post-deduction objections, which triggered a three-stage process culminating in arbitration paid for by the union. If an objection was sustained at any stage of this process, the remedy would be an immediate reduction in the amount of future deductions for all nonmembers and a rebate for the objector.

The Court in both *Ellis* and *Hudson* required the union to provide a pre-expenditure procedure to avoid temporary use of the dissidents' funds for purposes to which they object. Is the practical effect of the Court's approach to give dissidents the ability to require the union to escrow the lion's share of their dues pending the vagaries of subsequent litigation? Should the duty of fair representation be read to require that amounts reasonably in dispute be held in escrow until an employee's objections are resolved? See Office & Professional Employees Int'l Union, Local 29 (Dameron Hosp. Ass'n), 331 N.L.R.B. 48 (2000) (declining to pass on issue where union's refusal to place challenged amount in escrow violated its own internal policy).

**Extra-Unit Expenditures**

a. *Litigation and Organizing Expenses.* The Court in *Ellis* held that expenditures for union organizing outside the bargaining unit and extra-unit litigation challenging the airlines' mutual aid pact or protecting employee claims in bankruptcy were not related to or germane to core union functions. 466 U.S. at 453. Are these expenditures clearly unrelated to the welfare of all bargaining unit employees? See *California Saw,* supra, 320 N.L.R.B. at 237 (ruling that unions may charge for extra-unit litigation expenses because such expenses "may ultimately inure to the benefit" of the unit employees).

As to organizing expenses, in United Food & Commercial Workers Locals 951, 7, and 1036 (Meijer, Inc.), 329 N.L.R.B. 730 (1999), enforced in relevant part, 307 F.3d 760 (9th Cir. 2002) (en banc), the Board held (4-1) that, "at least with respect to organizing within the same competitive market as the bargaining unit employer," non-unit organizing expenses are chargeable to objecting nonmembers. In *Meijer,* the Board relied on expert testimony that unions are able to obtain substantially higher wages for the employees they represent when the employees of other employers in the same competitive market (that is, the same industry and relevant geographic area) are also unionized.

As it had in *California Saw,* the Board in *Meijer* again declared itself unbound by *Ellis.* It noted that in finding organizing expenses nonchargeable under the RLA, the *Ellis* Court had placed great weight on the legislative history of §2, Eleventh, and in particular, on the congressional testimony of the president of a major railroad union that the union security agreements permitted by the proposed amendment would not affect unions' bargaining power "one way or the other." The Board noted that the railroad industry was already substantially organized (75-80 percent of railroad employees were already union members) when §2, Eleventh was enacted, thus amply supporting, in its view, the *Ellis* Court's conclusion that extra-unit organizing would afford "only the most attenuated benefits" to those already organized under the RLA. Because industries covered by the NLRA were much more thinly organized, the Board stated, *Ellis*'s rationale for finding organizing expenses nonchargeable under the RLA was inapplicable in the NLRA context.

In upholding the Board in *Meijer*, the Ninth Circuit en banc found the Board's distinguishing of *Ellis* persuasive. Moreover, it stressed that the *Ellis* Court had applied the RLA unaided by the expertise of any administrative agency, while the Labor Board has been delegated authority by Congress to interpret and apply the NLRA. In its view, *Meijer* represented a permissible interpretation of an ambiguous statutory provision under *Chevron*, supra page 75. Given the "extensive economic research and data" relied upon by the Board, the court found the Board's conclusion in *Meijer* not only "reasonable," but "completely in accord with the economic realities of collective bargaining." 307 F.3d at 769.

In 2007, a Board panel (2-1) held that a Teamsters local had violated the Act by charging objecting nonmembers for expenses incurred in organizing employees within the same competitive market, the dairy and cheese processing industry. See Teamsters Local 75 (Schreiber Foods), 349 N.L.R.B. 77 (2007). The majority distinguished *Meijer* on the basis that the union's expert in *Schreiber* had testified only in "general terms" regarding the relationship between the extent of unionization in an industry and the wage rates of represented employees, whereas in *Meijer* the union had presented specific evidence (both through experts and union officials) regarding the effect of the extent of organization of employees in the precise industry at issue, in the same metropolitan area, on negotiated wage rates. In dissent, then-Member Liebman objected to the majority's "apparent[] read[ing of] *Meijer* as requiring, *in each case*, that the union demonstrate empirically that organizing within the industry [in question] leads to increased union wage rates *in that industry*." In Pirlott v. NLRB, 522 F.3d 423 (D.C. Cir. 2008), the court upheld the decision in *Schreiber*, finding that substantial evidence supported the Board's conclusion that the union had failed to present sufficient evidence of a positive correlation between wages and union density in the industry at issue.

b. *Strike Funds.* A unitary national pilots' union has created a strike contingency fund to provide strike support benefits for pilots in bargaining units at other airlines. Does the RLA require the union to rebate to objecting nonmembers the pro rata portion of agency fees attributable to the strike contingency fund? See Crawford v. Air Line Pilots Ass'n, 992 F.2d 1295 (4th Cir. 1993) (en banc). In *Crawford*, the court noted that when one airline obtains a cost-cutting concession from the pilots' union, other airlines attempt to obtain the same or equivalent concessions from their pilots. Hence, a successful strike to forestall concessions at one airline increases the union's chances of fighting off such concessions at other airlines. Would it have made a difference in *Crawford* if the pilots were organized in local or regional unions rather than a single national labor organization—either under the RLA or (again, assuming a different industry) under the NLRA?

### 3. Exposure to Union Discipline

This section addresses NLRA- and RLA-based restrictions on what unions can do to compel represented employees to adhere to union policies. Union members may also have rights against their organizations under the union constitution or the LMRDA; those issues are considered in the next chapter.

**NLRB v. Allis-Chalmers Manufacturing Co.**
*388 U.S. 175 (1967)*

Brennan, J. . . .

Employees at the [Wisconsin] plants of respondent Allis-Chalmers Manufacturing Company were represented by [UAW] locals. . . . Lawful economic strikes were conducted at both plants in support of new contract demands. In compliance with the UAW constitution, the strikes were called with the approval of the International Union after at least two-thirds of the members of each local voted by secret ballot to strike. Some members of each local crossed the picket lines and worked during the strikes. After the strikes were over, the locals [charged] these members . . . with violation of the International constitution and bylaws. The charges were heard by local trial committees in proceedings at which the charged members were represented by counsel. No claim of unfairness in the proceedings is made. The trials resulted in each charged member being found guilty of "conduct unbecoming a Union member" and being fined in a sum from $20 to $100. Some of the fined members did not pay the fines and one of the locals obtained a judgment in the amount of the fine against one of its members, Benjamin Natzke, in a test suit brought in the Milwaukee County Court. An appeal from the judgment is pending in the Wisconsin Supreme Court.

[Allis-Chalmers filed an unfair labor practice charge alleging that the locals had violated §8(b)(1)(A). The Board found no violation, and a Seventh Circuit panel agreed. However, after rehearing en banc, the court, with three judges dissenting, vacated the panel opinion and held that the locals' conduct violated §8(b)(1)(A). The Supreme Court reversed.]

It is highly unrealistic to regard §8(b)(1), and particularly its words "restrain or coerce," as precisely and unambiguously covering the union conduct involved in this case. On its face court enforcement of fines imposed on members for violation of membership obligations is no more conduct to "restrain or coerce" satisfaction of such obligations than court enforcement of penalties imposed on citizens for violation of their obligations as citizens to pay income taxes, or court awards of damages against a contracting party for nonperformance of a contractual obligation voluntarily undertaken. But even if the inherent imprecision of the words "restrain or coerce" may be overlooked, recourse to legislative history to determine the sense in which Congress used the words is not foreclosed. . . .

National labor policy has been built on the premise that by pooling their economic strength and acting through a labor organization freely chosen by the majority, the employees of an appropriate unit have the most effective means of bargaining for improvements in wages, hours, and working conditions. The policy therefore extinguishes the individual employee's power to order his own relations with his employer and creates a power vested in the chosen representative to act in the interests of all employees. . . .

Integral to this federal labor policy has been the power in the chosen union to protect against erosion [of] its status under that policy through reasonable discipline of members who violate rules and regulations governing membership. That power is particularly vital when the members engage in strikes. . . . Provisions in union constitutions and bylaws for fines and expulsion of recalcitrants, including strikebreakers, are therefore commonplace and were commonplace at the time of the Taft-Hartley amendments.

To say that Congress meant in 1947 by the §7 amendments and §8(b)(1)(A) to strip unions of the power to fine members for strikebreaking, however lawful the strike vote, and however fair the disciplinary procedures and penalty, is to say that Congress preceded the Landrum-Griffin amendments with an even more pervasive regulation of the internal affairs of unions. . . . More importantly, it is to say that Congress limited unions in the powers necessary to the discharge of their role as exclusive statutory bargaining agents by impairing the usefulness of labor's cherished strike weapon. It is no answer that the proviso to §8(b)(1)(A) preserves to the union the power to expel the offending member. Where the union is strong and membership therefore valuable, to require expulsion of the member visits a far more severe penalty upon the member than a reasonable fine. Where the union is weak, and membership therefore of little value, the union faced with further depletion of its ranks may have no real choice except to condone the member's disobedience. Yet it is just such weak unions for which the power to execute union decisions taken for the benefit of all employees is most critical to effective discharge of its statutory function. . . .

Cogent support for an interpretation of . . . §8(b)(1) as not reaching the imposition of fines and attempts at court enforcement is the proviso to §8(b)(1). It states that nothing in the section shall "impair the right of a labor organization to prescribe its own rules with respect to the acquisition or retention of membership therein. . . ." Senator Holland offered the proviso during debate and Senator Ball immediately accepted it, stating that it was not the intent of the sponsors in any way to regulate the internal affairs of unions. At the very least it can be said that the proviso preserves the rights of unions to impose fines, as a lesser penalty than expulsion, and to impose fines which carry the explicit or implicit threat of expulsion for nonpayment. Therefore, under the proviso the rule in the UAW constitution governing fines is valid and the fines themselves and expulsion for nonpayment would not be an unfair labor practice. Assuming that the proviso cannot also be read to authorize court enforcement of fines, a question we need not reach, . . . to interpret the body of §8(b)(1) to apply to the imposition and collection of fines would be to impute to Congress a concern with the permissible *means* of enforcement of union fines and to attribute to Congress a narrow and discrete interest in banning court enforcement of such fines. Yet there is not one word in the legislative history evidencing any such congressional concern. . . .

The collective bargaining agreements with the locals incorporate union security clauses. Full union membership is not compelled by the clause: an employee is required only to become and remain "a member of the Union . . . to the extent of paying his dues. . . ." The [Court of Appeals] nevertheless regarded full membership to be "the result not of individual voluntary choice but of the insertion of [this] union security provision in the contract under which a substantial minority of the employees may have been forced into membership." But the relevant inquiry here is not what motivated a member's full membership but whether the Taft-Hartley amendments prohibited disciplinary measures against a full member who crossed his union's picket line. . . . Whether those prohibitions would apply if the locals had imposed fines on members whose membership was in fact limited to the obligation of paying monthly dues is a question not before us and upon which we intimate no view. . . . [Reversed.]

[The concurring opinion of Justice White is omitted.]

BLACK, J., with whom DOUGLAS, HARLAN, and STEWART, JJ., join, dissenting.

. . . Contrary to the Court, I am not at all certain that a union's right under the proviso to prescribe rules for the retention of membership includes the right to restrain a member from working by trying him on the vague charge of "conduct unbecoming a union member" and fining him for exercising his §7 right of refusing to participate in a strike, even though the fine is only enforceable by expulsion from membership. It is one thing to say that Congress did not wish to interfere with the union's power, similar to that of any other kind of voluntary association, to prescribe specific conditions of membership. It is quite another thing to say that Congress intended to leave unions free to exercise a court-like power to try and punish members with a direct economic sanction for exercising their right to work. . . .

. . . [The union security clause] . . . made it necessary for all employees, including the ones involved here, to pay dues and fees to the union. But §8(a)(3) and §8(b)(2) make it clear that "Congress intended to prevent utilization of union security agreements for any purpose other than to compel payment of union dues and fees." [*Radio Officers' Union*], 347 U.S. 17, 41. If the union uses the union security clause to compel employees to pay dues, characterizes such employees as members, and then uses such membership as a basis for imposing court-enforced fines upon those employees unwilling to participate in a union strike, then the union security clause is being used for a purpose other than "to compel payment of union dues and fees." It is being used to coerce employees to join in union activity in violation of §8(b)(2). . . .

**Scofield v. NLRB**
*394 U.S. 423 (1969)*

[In *Scofield*, a union rule barred union members on incentive pay from accepting payment during the regular pay period for production exceeding a union-imposed ceiling. The union required that such excess production be banked and drawn on only when employees had not reached the daily ceiling. The union fined members who made requests to have over-the-ceiling payments during the regular pay period; nonpayment of fines could lead to expulsion from membership for "conduct unbecoming a member." The employer had, without success, bargained for the union's abandonment of the ceiling. Under the parties' union security clause, the employees could pay a "service fee" in lieu of joining the union. The Supreme Court (per Justice White) upheld the Board's dismissal of the complaint:]

The principal contention of the petitioners[, members fined by the union,] is that the rule impedes collective bargaining, a process nurtured in many ways by the Act. But surely this is not the case here. The union has never denied that the ceiling is a bargainable issue. It has never refused to bargain about it as far as this record shows. Indeed, the union has at various times agreed to raise its ceiling in return for an increase in the piece rate, and the ceiling has been regularly used to compute the new piece rate. . . . The company has repeatedly sought an agreement eliminating the piecework ceiling, an agreement which, had it been obtained, unquestionably would have been violated by the union rule. . . . [I]t has signed contracts recognizing the ceiling, has tolerated it, and has cooperated in its administration by honoring requests by employees to bank their pay for over-ceiling work. We discern no basis in the statutory policy encouraging collective bargaining for giving the employer a better bargain than he has been able to strike at the bargaining table. . . .

This leaves the possible argument that because the union has not successfully bargained for a contractual ceiling, it may not impose one on its own members, for doing so will discriminate between members and those others who are free to earn as much as the contract permits. All members of the bargaining unit, however, have the same contractual rights. In dealing with the employer as bargaining agent, the union has accorded all employees uniform treatment. If members are prevented from taking advantage of their contractual rights bargained for all employees it is because they have chosen to become and remain union members. . . . [T]he price of obeying the [instant] rule is not as high as in [NLRB v. Allis-Chalmers Mfg. Co., 388 U.S. 175 (1967)]. There the member could be replaced for his refusal to report to work during a strike; here he need simply limit his production and suffer whatever consequences that conduct may entail. If a member chooses not to engage in this concerted activity and is unable to prevail on the other members to change the rule, then he may leave the union and obtain whatever benefits in job advancement and extra pay may result from extra work, at the same time enjoying the protection from competition, the high piece rate, and the job security which compliance with the union rule by union members tends to promote.

That the choice to remain a member results in differences between union members and other employees raises no serious issue under §8(b)(2) and §8(a)(3) . . . , because the union has not induced the employer to discriminate against the member but has merely forbidden the member to take advantage of benefits which the employer stands willing to confer. . . .

## NLRB v. Boeing Co.
*412 U.S. 67 (1973)*

[The parties' collective agreement, which included a maintenance of membership clause, expired on September 15, 1965. During an 18-day strike over a renewal agreement, 143 employees out of the 1,900 bargaining unit employees crossed the picket lines and worked. Following the execution of a new agreement, the union duly charged the strikebreakers with violating the prohibition of the union constitution against "accepting employment . . . in an establishment in which a strike exists." Under appropriate union procedures, each strikebreaker was found guilty, fined $450, and barred from holding union office for five years. The employees' base pay for a 40-hour week ranged from $95 to $145. The union sued in a state court to collect these fines. The Trial Examiner, finding the fines excessive, upheld the company's §8(b)(1)(A) charge. The Board, however, dismissed the complaint, concluding that Congress had not authorized the NLRB to regulate the size of union fines.]

REHNQUIST, J. . . .

Given the rationale of *Allis-Chalmers* and *Scofield*, the Board's conclusion that §8(b)(1)(A) . . . has nothing to say about union fines of this nature, whatever their size, is correct. Issues as to the reasonableness or unreasonableness of such fines must be decided upon the basis of the law of contracts, voluntary associations, or such other principles of law as may be applied in a forum competent to adjudicate the issue. Under our holding, state courts will be wholly free to apply state law to such issues at the suit of either the union or the member fined. . . .

. . . [T]he Board was warranted in determining that when the union discipline does not interfere with the employee-employer relationship or otherwise violate a policy of the [NLRA], the Congress did not authorize it "to evaluate the fairness of union discipline meted out to protect a legitimate union interest." . . .

[Chief Justice Burger, dissenting, referred to the oddity of a union's supporting state court jurisdiction and stressed the need for uniformity and the Board's expertise. Justice Douglas, joined by Justice Blackmun, also dissented. He urged that the union's fining of employees more than they had earned during the strike was in effect similar to the employer's suspending them without pay after the strike—an action that would plainly be unlawful if undertaken at the union's instigation. He noted that Board jurisdiction over the reasonableness of fines would carry with it publicly provided counsel for indigent and unsophisticated employees.]

## *NOTES AND QUESTIONS*

**1. "Coercion"?** Why does a union's pursuit of court enforcement of fines against members for returning to work during a strike not "coerce" employees in the exercise of their §7 rights? Does *Allis-Chalmers* in effect allow unions a measure of institutional autonomy notwithstanding the literal terms of §8(b)(1)(A)? Do you agree with Justice Black's view that when unions resort to the courts, union discipline is no longer a private, intraorganizational matter, but rather implicates statutory protections? Are the concerns raised by Justice Black overstated in view of the right of union members to resign from the organization at any time—a factor stressed by the Court in *Scofield*? Reconsider this question after reading *Pattern Makers' League of North America v. NLRB*, infra page 926.

Would it have been preferable for the *Allis-Chalmers* Court to employ a balancing test similar to the approach used in *Republic Aviation*, supra page 131, and *Great Dane*, supra page 543? If so, how should the balance be struck between the union's need for solidarity and the individual's interest in working without threat of fines or loss of union membership? See Edward P. Archer, *Allis-Chalmers* Recycled: A Current View of a Union's Right to Fine Employees for Crossing a Picket Line, 7 Ind. L. Rev. 498 (1974).

**2. Union Discipline and Bargaining Duties.**

a. A union unilaterally adopted a rule limiting its members, who had been painting an average of 11.5 rooms per week, to 10 rooms per week. The stated purpose of this rule was to reduce speed-up pressures and to protect the painters' health and the quality of their work. The governing bargaining agreement was silent about production quotas but specified a seven-hour day and five-day work week. While the union and the employer argued over whether the union had violated the agreement, it expired. In subsequent bargaining that led to a strike, the parties were unable to agree on a provision on production quotas, and the renewal agreement again specified only a seven-hour day and five-day work week. After the execution of this agreement, the union threatened members who violated its 10-room rule with expulsion. Some members stopped work after reaching that quota even though they had not worked a full 35-hour week, and production fell below the prior 11.5 average. Has the union committed an unfair labor practice? Cf. Painters Dist. Council (Westgate Painting & Decorating Corp.), 186 N.L.R.B. 964 (1970), enforced, 453 F.2d 783 (2d Cir. 1971).

b. A union fined its members $400 for working during an authorized and lawful strike and brought an action to recover the fines. During negotiations for a renewal agreement, the company insisted that a condition of any agreement was the cancellation of these fines and the acceptance of a clause barring both the union and the company from interfering with the employees' exercise of their §7 rights — including the right to refrain — by means of discipline, fine, or discharge. Has the company violated §8(a)(5)? Cf. Universal Oil Prods. Corp. v. NLRB, 445 F.2d 155 (7th Cir. 1971).

**3. Union Discipline for Refusal to Engage in Unprotected Activity.** Does a union commit an unfair labor practice by fining members for violating a union rule that requires them to engage in activity that is unprotected under the NLRA, such as strikes in breach of a no-strike clause or repeated and concerted refusals to accept overtime work that is mandatory under the contract? Cf. NLRB v. GAIU Local 13-B, 682 F.2d 304 (2d Cir. 1982). What if the union expels rather than fines members in such cases?

**4. Union Discipline for Invoking NLRB Processes.** In NLRB v. Industrial Union of Marine & Shipbuilding Workers, 391 U.S. 418 (1968), the Court sustained the Board's determination that a union rule requiring members to exhaust internal union remedies before filing a charge with the NLRB hindered unimpeded access to the Board's processes, and that the union's attempt to enforce the rule either by fines or expulsion therefore violated §8(b)(1). The Board has upheld the expulsion of a member for filing a decertification petition while finding unlawful the imposition of a fine because of such a filing. See Molders

Local 125 (Blackhawk Tanning Co.), 178 N.L.R.B. 208 (1969), enforced, 442 F.2d 92 (7th Cir. 1971); Marble Finishers Local 89 (Bybee Stone Co.), 265 N.L.R.B. 496 (1982). Is *Blackhawk Tanning* consistent with *Marine & Shipbuilding Workers*?

**5. Union Discipline in Internal Union Political Disputes.** Note Justice Rehnquist's statement for the Court in *Boeing* that "the Board was warranted in determining that when the union discipline does not interfere with the employee-employer relationship or otherwise violate a policy of the [NLRA], the Congress did not authorize it 'to evaluate the fairness of union discipline meted out to protect a legitimate union interest.'" Does this mean that the Board is free to decide that §8(b)(1)(A) does not restrict union discipline for acts implicating internal union democracy or the fairness of internal union procedures? In Office & Professional Employees Int'l Union, Local 251 (Sandia Nat'l Laboratories), 331 N.L.R.B. 1417 (2000), the union had expelled and suspended from office several members who had sought the impeachment of the local's president for his handling of certain union funds. This discipline did not affect in any way the disciplined employees' relationship with their employers. The Board held that "Section 8(b)(1)(A) does not proscribe the wholly intraunion conduct and discipline in this case. . . . [Rather,] Section 8(b)(1)(A)'s proper scope, in union discipline cases, is to proscribe union conduct against union members that impacts on the employment relationship, impairs access to the Board's processes, pertains to unacceptable methods of union coercion, such as physical violence in organizational or strike contexts, or otherwise impairs policies imbedded in the [NLRA]." Is this an appropriate resolution of the competing interests?

**Pattern Makers' League of North America v. NLRB**
*473 U.S. 95 (1985)*

POWELL, J.

The Pattern Makers' League of North America, AFL-CIO (the League), a labor union, provides in its constitution that resignations are not permitted during a strike or when a strike is imminent. The League fined ten of its members who, in violation of this provision, resigned during a strike and returned to work. The [NLRB] held that these fines were imposed in violation of §8(b)(1)(A). . . . We granted a petition for a writ of certiorari in order to decide whether §8(b)(1)(A) reasonably may be construed by the Board as prohibiting a union from fining members who have tendered resignations invalid under the union constitution.

I

The League is a national union composed of local associations (locals). In May 1976, its constitution was amended to provide that:

> No resignation or withdrawal from an Association, or from the League, shall be accepted during a strike or lockout, or at a time when a strike or lockout appears imminent.

This amendment, known as League Law 13, became effective in October 1976, after being ratified by the League's locals. On May 5, 1977, when a collective-bargaining agreement expired, two locals began an economic strike against several manufacturing companies in Rockford, Illinois and Beloit, Wisconsin. Forty-three of the two locals' members participated. In early September 1977, after the locals formally rejected a contract offer, a striking union member submitted a letter of resignation to the Beloit association. He returned to work the following day. During the next three months, ten more union members resigned from the Rockford and Beloit locals and returned to work. On December 19, 1977, the strike ended when the parties signed a new collective-bargaining agreement. The locals notified ten employees who had resigned that their resignations had been rejected as violative of League Law 13. The locals further informed the employees that, as union members, they were subject to sanctions for returning to work. Each was fined approximately the equivalent of his earnings during the strike.

The Rockford-Beloit Pattern Jobbers' Association (the Association) had represented the employers throughout the collective-bargaining process. It filed charges with the Board against the League and its two locals, the petitioners. . . . The Board agreed [with the ALJ] that §8(b)(1)(A) prohibited the union from imposing sanctions on the ten employees. Pattern Makers' League of North America, [265 N.L.R.B. 1332 (1982)].

The [Seventh Circuit] enforced the Board's order. The Court of Appeals stated that by restricting the union members' freedom to resign, League Law 13 "frustrate[d] the overriding policy of labor law that employees be free to choose whether to engage in concerted activities." . . .

II

A

. . . When employee members of a union refuse to support a strike (whether or not a rule prohibits returning to work during a strike), they are refraining from "concerted activity." Therefore, imposing fines on these employees for returning to work "restrain[s]" the exercise of their §7 rights.

Indeed, if the terms "refrain" and "restrain or coerce" are interpreted literally, fining employees to enforce compliance with any union rule or policy would violate the Act. . . .

### B

The Court's reasoning in *Allis-Chalmers* supports the Board's conclusion that petitioners in this case violated §8(b)(1)(A). . . . The Court has emphasized that the crux of *Allis-Chalmers'* holding was the distinction between "internal and external enforcement of union rules. . . ." Scofield v. NLRB, 394 U.S., at 428. See also NLRB v. Boeing Co., 412 U.S. 67, 73 (1973).

The Congressional purpose to preserve unions' control over their own "internal affairs" does not suggest an intent to authorize restrictions on the right to resign. Traditionally, union members were free to resign and escape union discipline. In 1947, union constitutional provisions restricting the right to resign were uncommon, if not unknown. Therefore, allowing unions to "extend an employee's membership obligation through restrictions on resignation" would "expan[d] the definition of internal action" beyond the contours envisioned by the Taft-Hartley Congress. International Assn. of Machinists, Local 1414 (Neufeld Porsche-Audi, Inc.), 270 N.L.R.B. No. 209, p. 11 (1984). . . .

### III

Section 8(b)(1)(A) allows unions to enforce only those rules that "impai[r] no policy Congress has imbedded in the labor laws. . . ." [Scofield v. NLRB, 394 U.S. 423, 430 (1969).] The Board has found union restrictions on the right to resign to be inconsistent with the policy of voluntary unionism implicit in §8(a)(3). See Neufeld Porsche-Audi, 270 N.L.R.B. No. 209 (1984); Machinists Local 1327 (Dalmo Victor II), 263 N.L.R.B [984, 992 (1982)] (Chairman Van de Water and Member Hunter, concurring), enf. denied, 725 F.2d 1212 (9th Cir. 1984). We believe that the inconsistency between union restrictions on the right to resign and the policy of voluntary unionism supports the Board's conclusion that League Law 13 is invalid.

. . . The union security agreements permitted by §8(a)(3) require employees to pay dues, but an employee cannot be discharged for failing to abide by union rules or policies with which he disagrees.

Full union membership thus no longer can be a requirement of employment. If a new employee refuses formally to join a union and subject himself to its discipline, he cannot be fired. Moreover, no employee can be discharged if he initially joins a union, and subsequently resigns. We think it noteworthy that §8(a)(3) protects the employment rights of the dissatisfied member, as well as those of the worker who never assumed full union membership. By allowing employees to resign from a union at any time, §8(a)(3) protects the employee whose views come to diverge from those of his union.

League Law 13 curtails this freedom to resign from full union membership. Nevertheless, the petitioners contend that League Law 13 does not contravene the policy of voluntary unionism imbedded in the Act. They assert that this provision does not interfere with workers' employment rights because offending members are not discharged, but only fined. We find this argument unpersuasive, for a union has not left a "worker's employment rights inviolate when it exacts [his entire] paycheck in satisfaction of a fine imposed for working." Wellington, Union Fines and Workers' Rights, 85 Yale L.J. 1022, 1023 (1976). Congress in 1947 sought to eliminate completely any requirement that the employee maintain full union membership. Therefore, the Board was justified in concluding that by restricting the right of employees to resign, League Law 13 impairs the policy of voluntary unionism.

## IV

. . . Petitioners . . . argue that the proviso to §8(b)(1)(A) expressly allows unions to place restrictions on the right to resign. The proviso states that nothing in §8(b)(1)(A) shall "impair the right of a labor organization to prescribe its own rules with respect to the acquisition or retention of membership therein." Petitioners contend that because League Law 13 places restrictions on the right to withdraw from the union, it is a "rul[e] with respect to the . . . retention of membership," within the meaning of the proviso.

Neither the Board nor this Court has ever interpreted the proviso as allowing unions to make rules restricting the right to resign. Rather, the Court has assumed that "rules with respect to the . . . retention of membership" are those that provide for the expulsion of employees from the union. The legislative history of the Taft-Hartley Act is consistent with this interpretation. . . .

The Board reasonably has concluded that League Law 13 "restrains or coerces" employees, see §8(b)(1)(A), and is inconsistent with the congressional policy of voluntary unionism. . . . [T]he Board's interpretation of the Act merits our deference.

[The concurring opinion of Justice White is omitted.]

BLACKMUN, J., with whom BRENNAN and MARSHALL, JJ., join, dissenting. . . .

To be effective, the decision to strike, like the decision to bargain collectively, must be respected by the minority until democratically revoked.

The employees' collective decision to strike is not taken lightly, and entails considerable costs. See NLRB v. Mackay Radio & Tel. Co., 304 U.S. 333, 345 (1938) (employer has right permanently to replace workers on economic strike). Before workers undertake such a course, it is reasonable that they have some assurance that collectively they will have the means to withstand the pressures the employer is able lawfully to impose on them. A voluntarily and democratically adopted rule prohibiting resignations during a strike is one such means. By ensuring solidarity during a strike, it enforces the union's "legitimate interest in presenting a united front . . . and in not seeing its strength dissipated and its stature denigrated by subgroups within the unit separately pursuing what they see as separate interests." Emporium Capwell Co. v. Western Addition Community Org., 420 U.S. 50, 70 (1975). . . .

[There is no] suggestion in the record before us that the union members here were unaware of the promises they had made to their fellow members. If the dissenting members disagreed either with the decision to enact League Law 13, or with the decision to strike, they were free to try to influence their colleagues to their view. If they did not agree with the enactment of League Law 13, they were free as well to resign from the union when the rule was promulgated over their objection. Once the strike had begun, if they believed that the union officers were no longer acting in their best interest, they were free to try to convince their colleagues to end the strike, to replace their leaders, or even to decertify their union. See *Allis-Chalmers*, 388 U.S., at 191. Having failed to persuade the majority to their view, they should not be free to break their promise to their fellow workers. . . .

[The opinion of Justice Stevens, dissenting, is omitted.]

## *NOTES AND QUESTIONS*

**1. NLRB Discretion?** Is the Board free after *Pattern Makers'* to change its mind and permit reasonable union restrictions on resignation during strikes? In a concurring opinion not reprinted above, Justice White stated that the Board "adopted a sensible construction of the imprecise language of [§§]7 and 8 that is not negated by the legislative history of the Act," but further stated that "were the Board arguing for [the union's] interpretation of the Act, I would accord its view appropriate deference." 473 U.S. at 117.

**2. Waiver?** In view of the often uninformed nature of the decision to become a union member and the ambiguity of union security clauses sanctioned by the *Marquez* decision, supra page 914, the Court is understandably reluctant to equate union membership with a knowing and voluntary waiver of a right to resign held to be implicit in §8(b)(1)(A). But why isn't an employee's participation in a strike vote, particularly when coupled with participation in the early phase of the strike, sufficient to constitute a waiver of the right to resign during the course of a strike? Consider potential alternatives. What "deadline" might unions be allowed to give members for resigning without risk of discipline? Before contract talks have begun? Before an impasse has been declared by either party? Before the union has sought or obtained a strike ratification vote?

**3. Individual Rights vs. Collective Solidarity?** Does *Pattern Makers'* improperly import notions of individual rights to undermine the union's ability to function as an instrument of collective solidarity engaged in an economic struggle with the employer? Should the Board or the Court have recognized limits on the right to exit in the midst of a strike struggle? See David Abraham, Individual Autonomy and Collective Empowerment in Labor Law: Union Membership Resignations and Strikebreaking in the New Economy, 63 N.Y.U. L. Rev. 1268, 1336 (1988).

**4. Resignation and Dues Obligations.** Does a valid resignation from the union automatically free the employee from any obligation to pay dues under the union security clause of a collective bargaining agreement? Consider IBEW, Local No. 2088 (Lockheed Space Operations Co.), 302 N.L.R.B. 322 (1991):

> Explicit language within the checkoff clause authorization clearly setting forth an obligation to pay dues even in the absence of union membership will be required to establish that the employee has bound himself or herself to pay dues even after resignation of membership. If an authorization contains such language, dues may properly continue to be deducted from the employee's earnings and turned over to the union during the entire agreed-upon period of irrevocability, even if the employee states he or she had a change of heart and wants to revoke the authorization.

Id. at 329; see also, e.g., Allied Production Workers Union Local 12 (Northern Engraving Corp.), 337 N.L.R.B. 16, 18 (2001) (*Lockheed* allows employee to be bound to dues obligation post-resignation if there is "clear and unmistakable language"). Why is the obligation to pay dues treated differently than the obligation to remain subject to union rules in the midst of a strike? Is there a basis for such different treatment in the statutory language or purpose? See generally Heidi Marie Werntz, Comment, Waiver of *Beck* Rights and Resignation Rights: Infusing the Union-Member Relationship with Individualized Commitment, 43 Cath. U. L. Rev. 159 (1993).

**5. Resignation and Truly "Internal" Union Discipline.** In Machinists Lodge 1233 (General Dynamics Corp.), 284 N.L.R.B. 1101 (1987), the Board held (2-1) that the union violated §8(b)(1)(A) by fining crossovers who had resigned before returning to work, but had acted lawfully in suspending their voting rights and their eligibility for union office for five years.

## 4. Freedom from Discrimination in Employment Rights

The core policy judgment underlying Taft-Hartley's outlawing of the closed shop is that a worker's employment status should be determined independently of the decision whether or not to join a union or otherwise to engage in concerted activities. Union or agency shop agreements permit the employer to control hiring decisions, and both §§8(a)(3) and 8(b)(2) prohibit discrimination in hiring, promotion, and discipline decisions on the basis of union membership. Difficulties may arise, however, where the union plays a role in hiring decisions through its administration of hiring and referral halls—important institutions in industries such as construction, maritime, and longshoring, where the composition of the employer's labor force shifts with the requirements of particular projects or where employment is characteristically short-term.

### Local 357, Teamsters v. NLRB
*365 U.S. 667 (1961)*

Douglas, J.

Petitioner union (along with the International Brotherhood of Teamsters and a number of other affiliated local unions) executed a three-year . . . agreement with California Trucking Associations, which represented a group of motor truck operators in California. The provisions of the contract relating to hiring of casual or temporary employees were as follows:

> . . . Casual employees shall, wherever the Union maintains a dispatching service, be employed only on a seniority basis in the Industry whenever such senior employees are available. An available list with seniority status will be kept by the Unions, and employees requested will be dispatched upon call to any employer who is a party to this Agreement. Seniority rating of such employees shall begin with a minimum of three months service in the Industry *irrespective of whether such employee is or is not a member of the Union.*
>
> Discharge of any employee by any employer shall be grounds for removal of any employee from seniority status. No casual employee shall be employed by an employer who is a party to this Agreement in violation of seniority status if such employees are available and if the dispatching service for such employees is available. The employer shall first call the Union or the dispatching hall designated by the Union for such help. In the event the employer is notified

> that such help is not available, or in the event the employees called for do not appear for work at the time designated by the employer, the employer may hire from any other available source. (Emphasis added.)

. . . One Slater was a member of the union and had customarily used the hiring hall. But in August 1955 he obtained casual employment with an employer who was party to the hiring-hall agreement without being dispatched by the union. He worked until sometime in November of that year, when he was discharged by the employer on complaint of the union that he had not been referred through the hiring hall arrangement.

Slater made charges against the union and the employer. . . . [T]he Board found that the hiring-hall provision was unlawful per se and that the discharge of Slater on the union's request constituted a violation by the employer of §8(a)(1) and §8(a)(3) and a violation by the union of §8(b)(2) and §8(b)(1)(A). . . . The Board ordered, inter alia, that the company and the union cease giving any effect to the hiring-hall agreement; that they jointly and severally reimburse Slater for any loss sustained by him as a result of his discharge; and that they jointly and severally reimburse all casual employees for fees and dues paid by them to the union beginning six months prior to the date of the filing of the charge. 121 N.L.R.B. 1629.

. . . [T]he Court of Appeals . . . set aside the portion of the order requiring a general reimbursement of dues and fees. By a divided vote it upheld the Board in ruling that the hiring-hall agreement was illegal per se. . . .

Our decision in Carpenters Local 60 v. Labor Board, 365 U.S. 651,* . . . is dispositive of the petition of the Board that asks us to direct enforcement of the order of reimbursement. . . .

The other aspect of the case goes back to the Board's ruling in Mountain Pacific Chapter, 119 N.L.R.B. 883. That decision, rendered in 1958, departed from earlier rulings and held . . . that the hiring-hall agreement, despite the inclusion of a nondiscrimination clause, was illegal per se:

> Here the very grant of work at all depends solely upon union sponsorship, and it is reasonable to infer that the arrangement displays and enhances the Union's power and control over the employment status. . . . The Employers here have surrendered all hiring authority to the Union and have given advance notice via the established hiring hall to the world at large that the Union is arbitrary master and is contractually guaranteed to remain so. From the final authority over hiring vested in the Respondent Union . . . , the inference of encouragement of union membership is inescapable.

---

* [In *Local 60,* decided the same day, the Court ruled that §10(c) did not warrant the Board's reimbursement order, which the Court described as "punitive." The Court noted that no basis existed for concluding that all the casual employees, many of whom had been long-time union members, would have refused to pay dues to the union absent its violations of §8(b)(2).—EDS.]

Id., 896.

The Board went on to say that a hiring-hall arrangement to be lawful must contain protective provisions. Its views were stated as follows:

> We believe, however, that the inherent and unlawful encouragement of union membership that stems from unfettered union control over the hiring process would be negated, and we would find an agreement to be nondiscriminatory on its face, only if the agreement explicitly provided that:
>
> 1. Selection of applicants for referral to jobs shall be on a nondiscriminatory basis and shall not be based on, or in any way affected by, union membership, bylaws, rules, regulations, constitutional provisions, or any other aspect or obligation of union membership, policies, or requirements.
> 2. The employer retains the right to reject any job applicant referred by the union.
> 3. The parties to the agreement post in places where notices to employees and applicants for employment are customarily posted, all provisions relating to the functioning of the hiring arrangement, including the safeguards that we deem essential to the legality of an exclusive hiring agreement.

Id., 897.

The Board recognizes that the hiring hall came into being "to eliminate wasteful, time-consuming, and repetitive scouting for jobs by individual workmen and haphazard uneconomical searches by employers." Id., 896, n.8. The hiring hall at times has been a useful adjunct to the closed shop. But Congress may have thought that it need not serve that cause, that in fact it has served well both labor and management—particularly in the maritime field and in the building and construction industry. In the latter the contractor who frequently is a stranger to the area where the work is done requires a "central source" for his employment needs; and a man looking for a job finds in the hiring hall "at least a minimum guarantee of continued employment."

Congress has not outlawed the hiring hall, though it has outlawed the closed shop except within the limits prescribed in the provisos to §8(a)(3). . . .

There being no express ban of hiring halls in any provisions of the Act, those who add one, whether it be the Board or the courts, engage in a legislative act. The Act deals with discrimination either by the employers or unions that encourages or discourages union membership. As respects §8(a)(3) we said in Radio Officers v. Labor Board, 347 U.S. 17, 42-43:

> . . . [T]his section does not outlaw all encouragement or discouragement of membership in labor organizations; only such as is accomplished

> by discrimination is prohibited. Nor does this section outlaw discrimination in employment as such; only such discrimination as encourages or discourages membership in a labor organization is proscribed.

It is the "true purpose" or "real motive" in hiring or firing that constitutes the test. Id., 43. Some conduct may by its very nature contain the implications of the required intent; the natural foreseeable consequences of certain action may warrant the inference. Id., 45. The existence of discrimination may at times be inferred by the Board, for "it is permissible to draw on experience in factual inquiries." Radio Officers v. Labor Board, supra, at 49.

But surely discrimination cannot be inferred from the face of the instrument when the instrument specifically provides that there will be no discrimination against "casual employees" because of the presence or absence of union membership. The only complaint in the case was by Slater, a union member, who sought to circumvent the hiring-hall agreement. When an employer and the union enforce the agreement against union members, we cannot say without more that either indulges in the kind of discrimination to which the Act is addressed.

It may be that the very existence of the hiring hall encourages union membership. We may assume that it does. The very existence of the union has the same influence. When a union engages in collective bargaining and obtains increased wages and improved working conditions, its prestige doubtless rises and, one may assume, more workers are drawn to it. . . . The truth is that the union is a service agency that probably encourages membership whenever it does its job well. But, as we said in *Radio Officers v. Labor Board,* supra, the only encouragement or discouragement of union membership banned by the Act is that which is "accomplished by discrimination."

Nothing is inferable from the present hiring-hall provision except that employer and union alike sought to route "casual employees" through the union hiring hall and required a union member who circumvented it to adhere to it. . . .

The present agreement for a union hiring hall has a protective clause in it, as we have said; and there is no evidence that it was in fact used unlawfully. We cannot assume that a union conducts its operations in violation of law or that the parties to this contract did not intend to adhere to its express language. Yet we would have to make those assumptions to agree with the Board that it is reasonable to infer the union will act discriminatorily. . . .

Frankfurter, J., took no part in the consideration or decision of this case.

[The concurring opinion of Justice Harlan, with whom Justice Stewart joined, and the opinion of Justice Clark, dissenting in part, are omitted.]

## *NOTES AND QUESTIONS*

1. **Impact vs. Motive.** Is it clear why the Court holds that the Board's regulatory authority over union-administered hiring halls is limited to systems that discriminate, either facially or in their application? Just as employer action is sometimes subject to review for unjustified detrimental impact on §7 rights, as in *Republic Aviation*, supra page 131, could there not be a similar approach under §8(b)(1)(A) to review whether hiring halls unnecessarily encourage union membership or otherwise entrench the union? Would this be consistent with the text of §8(b)(1)(A) which, unlike the employer analogue in §8(a)(1), does not expressly deal with "interference" falling short of restraint or coercion? Or do strong countervailing, legitimate justifications provide the basis for the legality of nondiscriminatory hiring halls?

2. **"Nondiscrimination" and Internal Union Rules.** The NLRB has held that a union by-law that bars union members from working with nonunion employees and that is known to unionized employers does not violate §8(b) in the absence of some direct inducement to the employer to discriminate in employment. American Fed'n of Musicians, 165 N.L.R.B. 798 (1967), enforced sub nom. Glasser v. NLRB, 395 F.2d 401 (2d Cir. 1968). Is such a result realistic? Does the by-law violate the union's duty of fair representation, discussed infra pages 938-959?

3. **"Nondiscrimination" and Referral Fees.** Can a union lawfully decline to refer a qualified nonunion worker who refuses to pay a referral fee levied on those who do not pay union dues? See Operating Eng'rs, 137 N.L.R.B. 1043 (1962).

### ***Note: Superseniority for Union Officers***

"Shop stewards" are employees designated by the union to handle grievances and other union business on the job site. In order to promote continuity, employers and unions sometimes agree to provisions that give such stewards "superseniority" for various purposes. In Dairylea Coop., Inc., 219 N.L.R.B. 656, 658 (1975), enforced sub nom. NLRB v. Milk Drivers & Dairy Employees, Local 338, 531 F.2d 1162 (2d Cir. 1976), the Board held that although clauses providing layoff and recall superseniority for stewards are lawful because stewards benefit all employees, broad grants of superseniority (for purposes such as wages or increased vacation time) violate §8(a)(3):

> [I]n view of the inherent tendency of superseniority clauses to discriminate against employees for union-related reasons . . . we do find that superseniority clauses which are not on their face limited to layoff and recall are presumptively

unlawful, and the burden of rebutting that presumption (i.e., establishing justification) rests on the shoulders of the party asserting their legality.

*Dairylea* applied only to shop stewards who, typically, remain employed by the employer and are not considered officers of the union as such. The Board divided on the extension of *Dairylea* to union officials in United Electrical, Radio & Mach. Workers of Am., Local 623 (Limpco Mfg., Inc.), 230 N.L.R.B. 406 (1977), enforced sub nom. Anna M. D'Amico v. NLRB, 582 F.2d 820 (3d Cir. 1978). *Limpco* involved the local's recording secretary, who assisted stewards in writing grievances but had no direct grievance adjustment or on-the-job contract administration obligations. Two members concluded that superseniority regarding layoff and recall for "functional union officers" is presumptively lawful, while Member Murphy limited the presumption to "stewards and officers whose functions relate in general to furthering the bargaining relationship," 230 N.L.R.B. at 408 n.12. The two dissenters argued that superseniority must be limited to "union officials responsible for the processing of grievances on the job, and whose presence is therefore required for the proper performance of this function[]." Id. at 409. The Third Circuit enforced the Board's order because of credible proof that the individual in question was "officially assigned duties which helped implement the collective bargaining agreement in a meaningful way." 582 F.2d at 825.

In 1983, a reconstituted Board held in Gulton Electro-Voice, Inc., 266 N.L.R.B. 406, enforced sub nom. Local 900, Int'l Union of Electrical, Radio & Mach. Workers v. NLRB, 727 F.2d 1184 (D.C. Cir. 1984), that superseniority must be "limited to employees who, as agents of the union, must be on the job to accomplish their duties directly related to administering the collective-bargaining agreement." The labor agreement in *Gulton* conferred superseniority on the local's recording secretary and financial secretary, officials who play no role in grievance resolution. The agency rejected the argument that superseniority was justified because it helped maintain an effective and efficient bargaining relationship or helped attract better union representatives. These goals, while legitimate, had to be furthered by the union using its own devices rather than through protective job status. The D.C. Circuit enforced the Board's position as a reasonable resolution of the problem and dismissed the union's argument that the employees had waived §7 objections by ratifying the contract that included the superseniority clause. Accord, NLRB v. Local 1131, Local 1161, Int'l Union, United Automobile, Aerospace & Agricultural Implement Workers of Am., 777 F.2d 1131 (6th Cir. 1985).

## *NOTES AND QUESTIONS*

**1. Paying Salaries of Local Union Officers.** Can an employer and union lawfully agree that all officials of the local union will be "on duty in each shift and shall have the right to function at all times on union business on all days their particular shift is in operation"? Is direct compensation of union officials different from granting superseniority to them? Consider also §302 of the LMRA. Is an agreement like that described above lawful under §302? See Caterpillar, Inc. v. UAW, 107 F.3d 1052 (3d Cir. 1997), cert. dismissed, 523 U.S. 1015 (1998); see also infra page 1046.

**2. Differential Extended Leaves of Absences.** Can an employer and union lawfully provide for extended leaves of absences (with reinstatement rights) for up to two years for union business while limiting other leaves to only six months? See WPIX, Inc. v. NLRB, 870 F.2d 858 (2d Cir. 1989) (finding no violation).

**3. Retention of Seniority During Transfers Out of the Bargaining Unit.** The collective bargaining agreement between Clipper City Lodge Local No. 516 and the Manitowoc Engineering Company provides that employees transferred or promoted out of the bargaining unit retain their accrued seniority and can transfer back to the bargaining unit, provided they "maintain membership in the Union or obtain a withdrawal card in accord with the provision of the Union's Constitution." "Membership" is defined as satisfaction of "financial core" obligations in accordance with the *General Motors* decision, supra page 902, and the union constitution states that a withdrawal card "may" issue upon submission of an application and payment of overdue financial obligations. Is the agreement unlawful on its face? Or is its legality dependent on whether the union retains discretion whether to issue withdrawal cards? See NLRB v. Manitowoc Engineering Co., 909 F.2d 963 (7th Cir. 1990).

## B. THE DUTY OF FAIR REPRESENTATION

### 1. Early Judicial Development

**Steele v. Louisville & Nashville R.R.**
*323 U.S. 192 (1944)*

Stone, C.J. . . .

Petitioner, a Negro, is a locomotive fireman . . . , suing on his own behalf and that of his fellow employees who, like petitioner, are Negro firemen employed by the Railroad. Respondent Brotherhood, a labor organization, is, as provided under §2, Fourth of the Railway Labor Act [RLA], the exclusive bargaining representative of the craft of firemen employed by the Railroad. . . . The majority of the firemen . . . are white and are members of the Brotherhood, but a substantial minority are Negroes who, by the constitution and ritual of the Brotherhood, are excluded from its membership. As the membership of the Brotherhood constitutes a majority of all firemen employed on respondent Railroad, and as under §2, Fourth, the members because they are the majority have the right to choose and have chosen the Brotherhood to represent the craft, petitioner and other Negro firemen . . . have been required to accept the Brotherhood as their representative. . . .

On March 28, 1940, the Brotherhood, purporting to act as representative of the entire craft of firemen, without informing the Negro firemen or giving them opportunity to be heard, served a notice on respondent Railroad and on twenty other railroads operating principally in the southeastern part of the United States. The notice announced the Brotherhood's desire to amend the existing collective bargaining agreement [so] as ultimately to exclude all Negro firemen from the service. By established practice on the several railroads so notified only white firemen can be promoted to serve as engineers, and the notice proposed that only "promotable," i.e., white, men should be employed as firemen or assigned to new runs or jobs or permanent vacancies in established runs or jobs.

On February 18, 1941, the railroads and the Brotherhood, as representative of the craft, entered into a new agreement which provided that not more than 50% of the firemen in each class of service in each seniority district of a carrier should be Negroes; that until such percentage should be reached all new runs and all vacancies should be filled by white men; and that the agreement did not sanction the employment of Negroes in any seniority district in which they were not working. The agreement reserved the right of the Brotherhood to negotiate for further restrictions on the employment of Negro firemen. . . . On May 12, 1941, the Brotherhood entered into a supplemental agreement with respondent Railroad further controlling the seniority rights of Negro firemen and restricting their employment. The Negro firemen were not given notice or opportunity to be heard with respect to either of these agreements, which were put into effect before their existence was disclosed. . . .

Until April 8, 1941, petitioner was in a "passenger pool," to which one white and five Negro firemen were assigned. These jobs were highly desirable. . . . Petitioner had performed and was performing his work satisfactorily. Following a reduction in the mileage covered by the pool, all jobs in the pool were, about April 1, 1941, declared vacant. The Brotherhood and the Railroad, acting under the agreement, disqualified all the Negro firemen and replaced them with four white men, members of the Brotherhood, all junior in seniority to petitioner and no more competent or worthy. . . . [P]etitioner was deprived of employment for sixteen days and then was assigned to more arduous, longer, and less remunerative work in local freight service. . . . [He] was later replaced by a Brotherhood member junior to him, and assigned work on a switch engine, which was still harder and less remunerative, until January 3, 1942. On that date, after the bill of complaint in the present suit had been filed, he was reassigned to passenger service. . . .

The Supreme Court of Alabama . . . held . . . that petitioner's complaint stated no cause of action. . . . It thought that the Brotherhood was empowered by the statute to enter into the agreement of February 18, 1941, and that by virtue of the statute the Brotherhood has power by agreement with the Railroad both to create the seniority rights of petitioner and his fellow Negro employees and to destroy them. . . .

If . . . the Act confers this power on the bargaining representative of a craft or class of employees without any commensurate statutory duty toward its members, constitutional questions arise. For the representative is clothed with power not unlike that of a legislature which is subject to constitutional limitations on its power to deny, restrict, destroy or discriminate against the rights of those for whom it legislates and which is also under an affirmative constitutional duty equally to protect those rights. If the Railway Labor Act purports to impose on petitioner and the other Negro members of the craft the legal duty to comply with the terms of a contract whereby the representative has discriminatorily restricted their employment for the benefit and advantage of the Brotherhood's own members, we must decide the constitutional questions which petitioner raises in his pleading.

But we think that Congress, in enacting the Railway Labor Act and authorizing a labor union, chosen by a majority of a craft, to represent the craft, did not intend to confer plenary power upon the union to sacrifice, for the benefit of its members, rights of the minority of the craft, without imposing on it any duty to protect the minority. Since petitioner and the other Negro members of the craft are not members of the Brotherhood or eligible for membership, the authority to act for them is derived not from their action or consent but wholly from the command of the Act. . . .

Unless the labor union representing a craft owes some duty to represent nonunion members of the craft, at least to the extent of not discriminating against them as such in the contracts which it makes as their representative, the minority would be left with no means of protecting their interests. . . . While the majority of the craft chooses the bargaining representative, when chosen it represents . . . the craft or class, and not the majority. The fair interpretation of the statutory language is that the organization chosen to represent a craft is to represent all its members, the majority as well as the minority, and it is to act for and not against those whom it represents. It is a principle of general application that the exercise of a granted power to act in behalf of others involves the assumption toward them of a duty to exercise the power in their interest and behalf, and that such a grant of power will not be deemed to dispense with all duty toward those for whom it is exercised unless so expressed.

We think that the Railway Labor Act imposes upon the statutory representative of a craft at least as exacting a duty to protect equally the interests of the members of the craft as the Constitution imposes upon a legislature to give equal protection to the interests of those for whom it legislates. Congress has seen fit to clothe the bargaining representative with powers comparable to those possessed by a legislative body both to create and restrict the rights of those whom it represents, cf. J.I. Case Co. v. Labor Board, [321 U.S. 332,] 335, but it has also imposed on the representative a corresponding duty. We hold that the language of the Act . . . , read in the light of the purposes of the Act, expresses the aim of Congress to impose on the bargaining representative of a craft or class of employees the duty to exercise fairly the power conferred upon it in behalf of all those for whom it acts, without hostile discrimination against them.

This does not mean that the statutory representative of a craft is barred from making contracts which may have unfavorable effects on some of the members of the craft represented. Variations in the terms of the contract based on differences relevant to the authorized purposes of the contract in conditions to which they are to be applied, such as differences in seniority, the type of work performed, the competence and skill with which it is performed, are within the scope of the bargaining representation of a craft, all of whose members are not identical in their interest or merit. . . . Without attempting to mark the allowable limits . . . , it is enough for present purposes to say that the statutory power to represent a craft and to make contracts as to wages, hours and working conditions does not include the authority to make among members of the craft discriminations not based on such relevant differences. Here the discriminations based on race alone are obviously irrelevant and invidious. Congress plainly did not undertake to authorize the bargaining representative to make such discriminations. . . .

The representative which thus discriminates may be enjoined from so doing, and its members may be enjoined from taking the benefit of such discriminatory action. No more is the Railroad bound by or entitled to take the benefit of a contract which the bargaining representative is prohibited by the statute from making. In both cases the right asserted, which is derived from the duty imposed by the statute on the bargaining representative, is a federal right implied from the statute and the policy which it has adopted. It is the federal statute which condemns as unlawful the Brotherhood's conduct. . . .

[Justice Black concurred in the result. The concurring opinion of Justice Murphy is omitted.]

## *NOTES AND QUESTIONS*

**1. Intervention Out of Necessity?** Although a landmark decision in the history of the struggle against racial discrimination in this country, *Steele* is, in retrospect, a relatively easy case for judicial intervention. Note that the RLA does not contain a set of union unfair practices (other than those arising from bargaining duties) and does not provide for administrative enforcement of the statutory obligation. Moreover, the union was plainly acting in a manner that wholly disregarded the interests of the black firemen, who were not allowed by the union even to become members of the organization. For Congress to provide that such an organization would serve as the ostensible exclusive bargaining agent for the black firemen clearly raised a substantial question of equal protection under the laws. The Supreme Court in later decisions has made clear that the duty of fair representation operates even in less extreme situations as a general obligation of any exclusive bargaining agent.

**2. Adequacy of the *Steele* Solution?** Is the Court's solution to the problem of unfair representation adequate to the task given the fact that (1) the black firemen were excluded from union membership, and (2) the Brotherhood had plainly shown that it represented a constituency that thought it would benefit from subordination of the black firemen? Would a better approach have been to disqualify the Brotherhood from serving as an exclusive bargaining agent under the RLA until it purged itself of racial discrimination? See Karl E. Klare, The Quest for Industrial Democracy and the Struggle Against Racism: Perspectives from Labor Law and Civil Rights Law, 61 Or. L. Rev. 157, 189-190 (1982); Hyde, Democracy in Collective Bargaining, supra, at 819.

**3. Commentary.** For a discussion of the background of *Steele* and the course of the litigation, see Deborah C. Malamud, The Story of *Steele v. Louisville & Nashville Railroad*: White Unions, Black Unions, and the Struggle for Racial Justice on the Rails, in Labor Law Stories 55-105 (Laura J. Cooper & Catherine L. Fisk eds., 2005).

## 2. Unfair Representation and the NLRB

### *Note: The NLRB's* Miranda Fuel *Doctrine*

In Miranda Fuel Co., 140 N.L.R.B. 181 (1962), a member of the union began an extended leave of absence three days early. After receiving complaints from other employees, the union pressed the employer to drop that employee to the bottom of the seniority list—an action not required by the collective agreement. A majority of the Board concluded that the union had violated §§8(b)(1)(A) and 8(b)(2), reasoning as follows: The duty of fair representation is a corollary of the representative's exclusivity under §9(a) and is incorporated into §7. A bargaining agent's breach of that duty, regardless of whether it was influenced by an employee's union activities, therefore infringes on the employee's §7 rights and violates §8(b)(1)(A). Furthermore, a bargaining representative's attempt to secure employer participation or acquiescence in such a violation constitutes a violation of §8(b)(2), and resultant arbitrary employer action is derivatively a violation of §§8(a)(1) and §8(a)(3). The reviewing court denied enforcement of the Board's order in NLRB v. Miranda Fuel Co., 326 F.2d 172 (2d Cir. 1963). One member of the court, Judge Medina, agreed with the Board's dissenting members that "discrimination for reasons wholly unrelated to 'union membership, loyalty . . . , or the performance of union obligations,' is not sufficient to support findings of violations of §§8(a)(3), 8(a)(1), 8(b)(2) and §8(b)(1)(A) of the Act." Id. at 175. Judge Lumbard concurred in the result without reaching the question of whether a union's violation of the duty of fair representation constitutes a per se violation of §8(b)(1). Judge Friendly, dissenting, also passed over that question and the question of a derivative employer violation under §8(a)(1). However, he would have sustained the Board's order on the basis of §§8(b)(2) and 8(a)(3). He read §8(a)(3)'s prohibition of "discrimination" broadly—as encompassing any differential treatment based on invidious or arbitrary considerations, and concluded that the demonstration of union power to bring about such treatment would constitute "encouragement," resulting in a §8(a)(3) violation.

## *NOTES AND QUESTIONS*

1. **Subsequent History.** Although enforcement was denied in *Miranda Fuel*, the Board continues to hold that breach of the duty of fair representation constitutes an unfair labor practice, usually under §8(b)(1)(A). There is substantial judicial acceptance of that approach, dating from Rubber Workers Local 12 v. NLRB, 368 F.2d 12 (5th Cir. 1966). See, e.g., NLRB v. Int'l Bhd. of Elec. Workers, Local Union 16, 425 F.3d 1035, 1040 (7th Cir. 2005). The Supreme Court has assumed in a number of decisions that the NLRA applies to breaches of the duty, but has yet to rule on the precise question.

2. **Employer Discrimination Under the NLRA?** Assume that Judge Friendly's definition of "discrimination" is operative and that an employer, organized or unorganized, discriminates in employment on racial, or on nonracial but invidious, grounds. Would the employer violate the NLRA? Cf. Judge J. Skelly Wright's formulation in United Packinghouse Food & Allied Workers v. NLRB, 416 F.2d 1126 (D.C. Cir. 1969).

### 3. Contract Negotiation

**Air Line Pilots Ass'n v. O'Neill**
*499 U.S. 65 (1991)*

Stevens, J. . . .

I

This case arose out of a bitter confrontation between Continental Airlines, Inc. (Continental) and the union representing its pilots, the Air Line Pilots Association, International (ALPA). On September 24, 1983, Continental filed a petition for reorganization under Chapter 11 of the Bankruptcy Code. Immediately thereafter, with the approval of the Bankruptcy Court, Continental repudiated its collective-bargaining agreement with ALPA and unilaterally reduced its pilots' salaries and benefits by more than half. ALPA responded by calling a strike that lasted for over two years.

Of the approximately 2,000 pilots employed by Continental, all but about 200 supported the strike. By the time the strike ended, about 400 strikers had "crossed over" and been accepted for reemployment in order of reapplication. By trimming its operations and hiring about 1,000 replacements, Continental was able to continue in business. By August 1985, there were 1,600 working pilots and only 1,000 strikers.

The strike was acrimonious, punctuated by incidents of violence, and the filing of a variety of law suits, charges, and countercharges. In August 1985, Continental notified ALPA that it was withdrawing recognition of ALPA as the collective-bargaining agent for its pilots. ALPA responded with a federal lawsuit alleging that Continental was unlawfully refusing to continue negotiations for a new collective-bargaining agreement. In this adversary context, on September 9, 1985, Continental posted its "Supplementary Base Vacancy Bid 1985-5" (85-5 bid) — an act that precipitated, not only an end to the strike, but also the litigation that is now before us.

For many years Continental had used a "system bid" procedure for assigning pilots to new positions. Bids were typically posted well in advance in order to allow time for necessary training without interfering with current service. When a group of vacancies was posted, any pilot could submit a bid specifying his or her preferred position (Captain, First Officer, or Second Officer), base of operations, and aircraft type. In the past, vacant positions had been awarded on the basis of seniority, determined by the date the pilot first flew for Continental. The 85-5 bid covered an unusually large number of anticipated vacancies — 441 future Captain and First Officer positions and an undetermined number of Second Officer vacancies. Pilots were given nine days — until September 18, 1985 — to submit their bids.

Fearing that this bid might effectively lock the striking pilots out of jobs for the indefinite future, ALPA authorized the strikers to submit bids. Several hundred did so, as did several hundred working pilots. Although Continental initially accepted bids from both groups, it soon became concerned about the bona fides of the striking pilots' offer to return to work at a future date. It therefore challenged the strikers' bids in court and announced that all of the 85-5 bid positions had been awarded to working pilots.

At this juncture, ALPA intensified its negotiations for a complete settlement. ALPA's negotiating committee and Continental reached an agreement, which was entered as an order by the Bankruptcy Court on October 31, 1985. The agreement provided for an end to the strike, the disposition of all pending litigation, and reallocation of the positions covered by the 85-5 bid.

The agreement offered the striking pilots three options. Under the first, pilots who settled all outstanding claims with Continental were eligible to participate in the allocation of the 85-5 bid positions. Under the second option, pilots who elected not to return to work received severance pay of $4,000 per year of service (or $2,000 if they had been furloughed before the strike began). Under the third option, striking pilots retained their individual claims against Continental and were eligible to return to work only after all the first option pilots had been reinstated.

Pilots who chose the first option were thus entitled to some of the 85-5 bid positions that, according to Continental, had previously been awarded to working pilots. The first 100 Captain positions were allocated to working pilots and the next 70 Captain positions were awarded, in order of seniority, to returning strikers who chose option one. Thereafter, striking and non-striking pilots were eligible for Captain positions on a one-to-one ratio. The initial base and aircraft type for a returning striker was assigned by Continental, but the assignments for working pilots were determined by their bids. After the initial assignment, future changes in bases and equipment were determined by seniority, and striking pilots who were in active service when the strike began received seniority credit for the period of the strike.

## II

Several months after the settlement, respondents, as representatives of a class of former striking pilots, brought this action against ALPA. In addition to raising other charges not before us, respondents alleged that the union had breached its duty of fair representation in negotiating and accepting the settlement. After extensive discovery, ALPA filed a motion for summary judgment. Opposing that motion, respondents identified four alleged breaches of duty, including the claim that "ALPA negotiated an agreement that arbitrarily discriminated against striking pilots."

The District Court granted the motion. . . .

The Court of Appeals reversed. It first rejected ALPA's argument that a union cannot breach its duty of fair representation without intentional misconduct. The court held that the duty includes "three distinct" components[:] A union breaches the duty if its conduct is either "arbitrary, discriminatory, or in bad faith." [quoting *Vaca v. Sipes*, infra page 960] . . .

Applying [the] arbitrariness test to the facts of this case, the Court of Appeals concluded that a jury could find that ALPA acted arbitrarily because the jury could find that the settlement "left the striking pilots worse off in a number of respects than complete surrender to [Continental]." That conclusion rested on the court's opinion that the evidence suggested that, if ALPA had simply surrendered and made an unconditional offer to return to work, the strikers would have been entitled to complete priority on all the positions covered by the 85-5 bid. . . . In addition, the Court of Appeals ruled that the evidence raised a genuine issue of material fact whether the favored treatment of working pilots in the allocation of 85-5 bid positions constituted discrimination against those pilots who had chosen to strike.

The court held that respondents had raised a jury question whether ALPA had violated its duty to refrain from "arbitrary" conduct, and the court therefore remanded the case for trial. Because it reversed the District Court's grant of summary judgment on the arbitrariness component, the Court of Appeals did not decide whether summary judgment on the fair representation claim might be precluded by the existence of other issues of fact. . . .

## III

ALPA's central argument is that the duty of fair representation requires only that a union act in good faith and treat its members equally and in a nondiscriminatory fashion. The duty, the union argues, does not impose any obligation to provide *adequate* representation. The District Court found that there was no evidence that ALPA acted other than in good faith and without discrimination. Because of its view of the limited scope of the duty, ALPA contends that the District Court's finding, which the Court of Appeals did not question, is sufficient to support summary judgment. . . .

ALPA suggests that a union need owe no enforceable duty of adequate representation because employees are protected from inadequate representation by the union political process. ALPA argues, as has the Seventh Circuit, that employees "do not need . . . protection against representation that is inept but not invidious" because if a "union does an incompetent job . . . its members can vote in new officers who will do a better job or they can vote in another union." Dober v. Roadway Express, Inc., 707 F.2d 292, 295 (CA7 1983). . . .

ALPA relies heavily on language in Ford Motor Co. v. Huffman, 345 U.S. 330 (1953), which, according to the union, suggests that no review of the substantive terms of a settlement between labor and management is permissible. In particular, ALPA stresses our comment in the case that "[a] wide range of reasonableness must be allowed a statutory bargaining representative in serving the unit it represents, subject always to complete good faith and honesty of purpose in the exercise of its discretion." Id., at 338. Unlike ALPA, we do not read this passage to limit review of a union's actions to "good faith and honesty of purpose," but rather to recognize that a union's conduct must also be within "[a] wide range of reasonableness."

Although there is admittedly some variation in the way in which our opinions have described the union's duty of fair representation, we have repeatedly identified three components of the duty, including a prohibition against "arbitrary" conduct. . . .

The union correctly points out, however, that virtually all of [the Court's duty of fair representation] cases can be distinguished because they involved contract administration or enforcement rather than contract negotiation. ALPA argues that the policy against substantive review of contract terms applies directly . . . in the negotiation area. Although this is a possible basis for distinction, none of our opinions has suggested that the duty is governed by a double standard. Indeed, we have repeatedly noted that the *Vaca v. Sipes* standard applies to "challenges leveled not only at a union's contract administration and enforcement efforts but at its negotiation activities as well." Communications Workers v. Beck, 487 U.S. 735, 743 (1988) (internal citation omitted); see also Electrical Workers v. Foust, 442 U.S. 42, 47 (1979); Vaca v. Sipes, 386 U.S., at 177. . . .

We doubt, moreover, that a bright line could be drawn between contract administration and contract negotiation. Industrial grievances may precipitate settlement negotiations leading to contract amendments, and some strikes and strike settlement agreements may focus entirely on questions of contract interpretation. See Conley v. Gibson, 355 U.S. 41, 46 (1957). . . .

We are, therefore, satisfied that the Court of Appeals correctly concluded that the tripartite standard announced in *Vaca v. Sipes* applies to a union in its negotiating capacity. We are persuaded, however, that the Court of Appeals' further refinement of the arbitrariness component of the standard authorizes more judicial review of the substance of negotiated agreements than is consistent with national labor policy.

. . . Congress did not intend judicial review of a union's performance to permit the court to substitute its own view of the proper bargain for that reached by the union. Rather, Congress envisioned the relationship between the courts and labor unions as similar to that between the courts and the legislature. Any substantive examination of a union's performance, therefore, must be highly deferential, recognizing the wide latitude that negotiators need for the effective performance of their bargaining responsibilities . . . . For that reason, the final product of the bargaining process may constitute evidence of a breach of duty only if it can be fairly characterized as so far outside a "wide range of reasonableness," Ford Motor Co. v. Huffman, 345 U.S., at 338, that it is wholly "irrational" or "arbitrary." . . .

For purposes of decision, we may assume that the Court of Appeals was correct in its conclusion that, if ALPA had simply surrendered and voluntarily terminated the strike, the striking pilots would have been entitled to reemployment in the order of seniority. Moreover, we may assume that Continental would have responded to such action by rescinding its assignment of all of the 85-5 bid positions to working pilots. After all, it did rescind about half of those assignments pursuant to the terms of the settlement. Thus, we assume that the union made a bad settlement—one that was even worse than a unilateral termination of the strike.

Nevertheless, the settlement was by no means irrational. A settlement is not irrational simply because it turns out *in retrospect* to have been a bad settlement. Viewed in light of the legal landscape at the time of the settlement, ALPA's decision to settle rather than give up was certainly not illogical. At the time of the settlement, Continental had notified the union that all of the 85-5 bid positions had been awarded to working pilots and was maintaining that none of the strikers had any claim on any of those jobs. . . .

Given the background of determined resistance by Continental at all stages of this strike, it would certainly have been rational for ALPA to recognize the possibility that an attempted voluntary return to work would merely precipitate litigation over the right to the 85-5 bid positions. Because such a return would not have disposed of any of the individual claims of the pilots who ultimately elected option one or option two of the settlement, there was certainly a realistic possibility that Continental would not abandon its bargaining position without a complete settlement.

At the very least, the settlement produced certain and prompt access to a share of the new jobs and avoided the costs and risks associated with major litigation. Moreover, since almost a third of the striking pilots chose the lump-sum severance payment rather than reinstatement, the settlement was presumably more advantageous than a surrender to a significant number of striking pilots. In labor disputes, as in other kinds of litigation, even a bad settlement may be more advantageous in the long run than a good lawsuit. In all events, the resolution of the dispute over the 85-5 bid vacancies was well within the "wide range of reasonableness," 345 U.S., at 338, that a union is allowed in its bargaining.

The suggestion that the "discrimination" between striking and working pilots represented a breach of the duty of fair representation also fails. If we are correct in our conclusion that it was rational for ALPA to accept a compromise between the claims of the two groups of pilots to the 85-5 bid positions, some form of allocation was inevitable. A rational compromise on the initial allocation of the positions was not invidious "discrimination" of the kind prohibited by the duty of fair representation. Unlike the grant of "super seniority" to the cross-over and replacement workers in NLRB v. Erie Resistor Corp., 373 U.S. 221 (1963), this agreement preserved the seniority of the striking pilots after their initial reinstatement. . . . The agreement here only provided the order and mechanism for the reintegration of the returning strikers but did not permanently alter the seniority system. . . .

## *NOTES AND QUESTIONS*

1. **A Meaningful Standard?** Does the "wide range of reasonableness" standard give lower courts any guidance in identifying those union decisions that fail to take account of the interests of some subgroup of represented employees? Is the Court suggesting that a union's decisions in the contract- or settlement-making arena are to be judged only by the highly deferential "rational basis" standard applied to legislative judgments — a standard under which legislation has seldom been found wanting in the modern era? Is the legislative analogy appropriate in light of the union's dual constituency? Should the strength of the analogy turn on the state of union democracy after passage of the LMRDA (as developed in the next chapter)?

2. **Should Judges Assess Union Competence?** Consider the complicated facts of *O'Neill.* Are judges capable of assessing the reasonableness of a union's bargaining strategy on the cold facts of a record long after a dispute has been resolved? Does the *O'Neill* decision provide adequate protection from activist judges, some of whom may be skeptical of the merits of collective representation?

3. **Does a Union Breach Its Duty of Fair Representation When It Subordinates the Interests of Some Members in Order to Retain Its Status as Bargaining Representative?** Assume that a judge is convinced that ALPA's leadership persisted in maintaining a losing strike, resulting in the settlement challenged in the *O'Neill* litigation, because the leadership feared that surrendering would make it vulnerable to decertification. Should the judge find a breach of the duty of fair representation? Can a union justify sacrificing the interests of some employees in order to retain its bargaining status so as to advance the interests of other employees in the long run? Should it matter whether the union sacrifices the interests of a discrete and identifiable group of employees in order to bolster its appeal to a majority?

**4. Does a Union Breach Its Duty When It Subordinates the Interests of Employees in One Bargaining Unit to Serve the Interests of Employees in Other Units?** Should a union's discretion to balance the interests of some employees against the interests of others in order to serve the collective good be limited to employees within defined bargaining units? Or should collective representatives have discretion to balance the interests of employees across units?

a. Consider Aguinaga v. UFCW, 993 F.2d 1463 (10th Cir. 1993). There, John Morrell & Co. had a multiplant master agreement with the United Food and Commercial Workers Union (UFCW) that prohibited the company from decreasing the workforce for the purpose of avoiding any of the provisions of the master agreement and from contracting with other plants within 100 miles of a closed plant to provide services formerly provided by a plant scheduled for closure. As expiration of the master agreement approached in 1982, Morrell sought new language that permitted individual plants to negotiate separate wage rates and benefits independent of the master agreement. UFCW refused and ordered its local at the Rodeo plant to avoid any direct discussions with Morrell. In June 1982, the Rodeo plant was closed, and the employees were paid their severance benefits. In September 1982, settling a strike that had occurred at Morrell's Sioux Falls plant over retention of the master agreement, the UFCW entered into two secret side-letter agreements that had the effect of allowing Morrell to reopen the Rodeo plant as a non-union facility without having to pay the wage rates set in the master agreement or to rehire the old Rodeo employees. The UFCW did not inform the former Rodeo plant employees of the terms of the side-letter agreements. In March 1983, Morrell reopened the Rodeo facility and agreed to let the union represent its workers in exchange for the union's dropping an NLRB charge alleging a unilateral change in conditions of employment at Rodeo. If the UFCW can demonstrate that its conduct was an attempt to gain an advantage with Morrell in bargaining over other Morrell plants, should it be held to have breached its duty of fair representation to the former Rodeo employees? Should the UFCW at least have pressed any meritorious statutory or contractual claims for the former Rodeo employees? Would the result be the same if the union's agreement to allow reopening of the Rodeo facility did not provide for the union's retention of its status as bargaining agent? What if the side-letter agreements had been openly disclosed?

b. Consider the dispute between the United Automobile Workers (UAW) and Caterpillar, a manufacturer of earth-moving machinery. In 1991, the union struck Caterpillar over its refusal to adhere to the "pattern" agreement reached with John Deere, Caterpillar's competitor. Caterpillar maintained that because of its export business, it could not afford to follow the pact agreed to by Deere, which had a principally domestic business. After Caterpillar began hiring permanent replacements, the

UAW urged its members to return to work in April 1992. Do UAW-represented employees who lost their jobs because of the strike have an action against their union if it is shown that UAW's motivation in insisting on the "pattern" agreement with Deere was to preserve the inviolability of pattern bargaining with the Big Three automobile manufacturers, which employ the lion's share of the UAW's membership? What if all that can be shown is that the UAW is willing to sacrifice some jobs at Caterpillar in order to maintain the integrity of its "pattern" agreement with Deere and Caterpillar's other domestic competitors?

**5. The Median Voter Model and the Duty of Fair Representation.** Consider Bruce E. Kaufman & Jorge Martinez-Vasquez, Monopoly, Efficient Contract, and Median Voter Models of Union Wage Determination: A Critical Comparison, 11 J. Lab. Res. 401, 404-405, 414 (1990):

> . . . [U]nder certain conditions it can be shown that the union's preferred wage will be that of the median voter in the union. . . . These conditions are that the union's electoral process is perfectly democratic with elections determined by majority vote and the individual preferences are a function of only a single variable, well-ordered and single-peaked. Given these assumptions, the political pressure on the union leadership to win re-election to office and ratification of new contracts will lead them to select . . . the preferred wage of the median voter, as the union's optimal wage. . . .
>
> . . . [The median voter model] shows, for example, that rigid union wages are to be expected in cyclical downturns, for, in most cases, the layoffs that result do not threaten the job security of the majority of senior union members. When layoffs do threaten a majority of the membership, however, the model shows that the union will actively consider a wage cut.

Does this analysis suggest that normal, well-functioning democratic processes predictably will lead to the sacrifice of the interest of identifiable junior employees? If so, does this necessarily argue for an aggressive use of the duty of fair representation to protect these employees?

**6. Union Referenda and the Legislative Analogy?** When a union delegates decision making to a referendum of its members, should the duty of fair representation require the union to broaden the electorate to include employees of the bargaining unit who have not joined the union? Consider Branch 6000, National Ass'n of Letter Carriers v. NLRB, 595 F.2d 808 (D.C. Cir. 1979). In that case the collective agreement permitted the union to determine annually the employees' wishes as to whether days off should be on a fixed or a rotating basis. The union's referendum meeting on that question excluded nonunion unit employees and denied them the right to vote or be heard. Has the union breached its duty of fair representation? Is the situation distinguishable from contract ratification, which generally may be lawfully restricted to union members?

**Barton Brands, Ltd. v. NLRB**
*529 F.2d 793 (7th Cir. 1976)*

[On August 31, 1969, Glencoe sold all its assets to Barton. Glencoe then had only six active employees and more than 20 employees on layoff. Each company's employees comprised a separate bargaining unit, represented by the union.]

BAUER, J. . . .

Shortly after the sale, Barton and the Union began negotiations regarding integration of the bargaining units at the two plants. At separate meetings for the Barton and Glencoe employees, Paul Kraus, Barton's Chief Operations Officer . . . , explained that Barton's business was expanding and that the firm, among other developments, planned to build a new bottling facility at the site of the Glencoe plant. He told the employees that he felt their best interests would be served if the two units were integrated and the employees' seniority dovetailed; i.e., former Glencoe employees would be given full credit for seniority accumulated at Glencoe and both groups of employees would be placed on one combined seniority list.[5] Both the Barton and Glencoe employees voted in favor of dovetailing and the collective bargaining agreement between Barton and the Union was amended to reflect the plan.

Barton did not build the new facility. Within a year of the purchase, engineering studies showed the site to be unfeasible for bottling. A plan to build on a different site was abandoned when Barton sold its Canadian Mist brand, which accounted for about one-third of its business. Following these events, Barton laid off some employees and other employees began to worry about their job security. One manifestation of this apprehension was a dissatisfaction among some Barton employees with the dovetailing of the former Glencoe employees, which they saw as causing employees to be laid off despite having worked at Barton longer than employees who had received credit for their time worked at Glencoe.

. . . [B]efore June, 1972, the expiration date of the Barton collective bargaining agreement, the Union leadership canvassed the unit employees requesting suggestions for contract changes. One of the suggestions

5. The dovetailing plan benefited the former Glencoe employees by greatly increasing their job security, including the return to work of the laid off employees, and benefited the Barton employees by providing them the opportunity to transfer to the proposed new plant, a right which they were told they would not have if the units remained separate.

received was a proposal that the former Glencoe employees be endtailed; i.e., that they be placed on the seniority list below all Barton employees who were hired before Barton's purchase of Glencoe. The Union presented the proposal to Barton during negotiations. Although Barton first rejected it, expressing some doubts about its legality, the parties ultimately agreed that for the purposes of layoff and recall, the seniority of the former Glencoe employees would be calculated from September 1, 1969, the day Barton acquired the Glencoe site. For all other purposes, including choice of jobs while working, vacations, and other benefits, the dovetail provision remained in effect. The parties reached agreement on September 22, 1972, and the Union membership ratified the contract on October 12.

During the [negotiation and ratification] period . . . , an average of 223 active employees [were] on the Barton payroll, twelve of whom were former Glencoe employees. As a result of the endtailing provision . . . , twelve former Glencoe employees suffered layoffs that would not have occurred if they had been permitted to retain their seniority from Glencoe.

At the request of a laid off former Glencoe employee, the Board's General Counsel filed complaints against the Union and Barton charging them respectively with violations of §§8(b)(2) and 8(b)(1)(A) and §§8(a)(3) and 8(a)(1). . . . The Board, [reversing the ALJ,] found that the Union breached its duty of fair representation by effecting the reduction in seniority and the layoff of the former Glencoe employees "largely, if not solely, for the reason to advance the political cause of Union official Ken Cecil." 213 N.L.R.B. No. 71 at 5. [The agency also] found Barton liable for acquiescing in the Union breach.

The Board reached its finding regarding the Union's motivation on evidence which indicated that Cecil, Vice-President of Local 23 and the highest Union officer at Barton during the period involved, . . . presented the endtailing proposal to the Union contract negotiating committee, and claimed responsibility for the proposal during the contract negotiations and during his successful campaign for reelection to his Union office in November and December, 1972, which immediately followed the signing of the new contract.

. . . [T]he Union alleges that (1) there is not substantial evidence on the record to support the [Board's] finding that the Union changed the Glencoe employees' seniority in order to further Cecil's political ambitions, (2) the change in seniority could not have violated §8(b)(2) . . . since the Glencoe employees were not discriminated against on the basis of union membership or activity, and (3) even if the seniority change was illegal discrimination under §8(b)(2), the Union's good faith is a defense to the charge against it. . . .

. . . The Board's determination that Cecil championed the endtailing of the former Glencoe employees to curry favor with the majority of the Barton employees in order to enhance his candidacy in the upcoming election is sustained by the evidence, but the Board's reasoning that Cecil's efforts are chargeable to the Union as a whole and that the enhancement of the Cecil candidacy was the motivating factor behind the endtailing decision is not borne out by the evidence. . . . Cecil's actions, which the Board attributes to the Union, were not undertaken in his capacity as a union officer but were undertaken in his own behalf as a candidate for union office. The only activity which the Board cites that Cecil undertook in his capacity as an officer was the presenting of the endtailing proposal to the union negotiating committee, an innocent act in which he served as the conduit for a rank and file proposal previously formulated. . . .

. . . The record clearly indicates that the endtailing proposal arose out of rank and file apprehension about job security, not out of a Union desire to reelect Cecil. . . .

This does not necessarily end the case. If we think the Board's order may be sustained on other grounds, we must remand. . . . S.E.C. v. Chenery Corp., 318 U.S. 80 (1943). In this case we think sufficient grounds do exist to support a Board order and we will outline them to justify our remand and to aid the Board in its reconsideration of the case.

The record suggests that the union acted solely on grounds of political expediency in reducing the former Glencoe employees' seniority.[14] While a union may make seniority decisions within "a wide range of reasonableness . . . in serving the [interests of the] unit it represents," Ford Motor Co. v. Huffman, 345 U.S. 330, 338 (1950), such decisions may not be made *solely* for the benefit of a stronger, more politically favored group over a minority group. To allow such arbitrary decisionmaking is contrary to the union's duty of fair representation. . . .

. . . [P]roof of good faith on the part of a union is not a defense to a charge based on the duty of fair representation since arbitrary conduct without evidence of bad faith has been held by this Circuit to constitute a breach of the duty. . . .

Furthermore, the cases cited . . . for the proposition that the endtailing of employees from an acquired firm into a unit of employees from the

---

14. There is no merit to the argument raised by both the Union and Barton that the Glencoe employees received a "windfall" as a result of the initial dovetailing which could properly be revoked. Not only is the windfall characterization an exaggeration since the dovetailing caused Glencoe employees to by-pass other employment when they came to work for Barton, but the original Barton employees voted for the dovetailing to further their own self-interest. See n.5, supra.

The argument that the endtailing is proper since Barton's decision not to build a new bottling plant was a failure to fulfill a condition precedent to the initial dovetailing agreement also is without merit. There is no express condition precedent in the agreement itself and there is nothing in the record which suggests that the building of a new plant was an implied condition precedent.

acquiring firm is permissible are distinguishable from the case at bar. . . . [Those cases] all involved endtailing decisions made at the time of the initial acquisition rather than after the employees had been dovetailed into the acquiring firm's unit. In these cases the affected employees, unlike the employees in the case at bar, did not lose benefits they believed they were entitled to, nor were they prejudiced by relinquishing other employment opportunities in reliance on the dovetailing arrangement. . . .

In summary, since the established seniority rights of a minority of the Barton employees have been abridged . . . for no apparent reason other than political expediency, there seem to be sufficient grounds . . . to support the Board order. We thus are remanding . . . for a determination whether the Union violated its duty of fair representation . . . by successfully negotiating for the endtailing proposal. In making its determination, the Board should consider that in order to be absolved of liability the Union must show some objective justification for its conduct beyond that of placating the desires of the majority of the unit employees at the expense of the minority. . . .

## *NOTES AND QUESTIONS*

**1. Special Status of Seniority-Based Expectations?** Is *Barton Brands* best understood as a case protecting the seniority benefits of the Glencoe employees because of their status as quasi-vested benefits? See Harry H. Wellington, Union Democracy and Fair Representation: Federal Responsibility in a Federal System, 67 Yale L.J. 1327, 1361 (1958) ("some sort of dovetailing would . . . be required to approximate community expectation"). Does this make sense? Are seniority-based expectations immune from modification in collective bargaining? Consider the following hypotheticals:

a. A union representing a multiplant unit negotiates a collective agreement provision specifying the use of endtailing in the event of a merger or consolidation. Yet during the contract term one of the plants is shut down and its employees are transferred to the other plants. The union decides that dovetailing would be fairer, and the employer agrees.

b. Responding to a demand by the employer that staffing levels be cut, the union agrees that, in lieu of layoffs by reverse order of seniority, the employees will share the remaining work so that no one is laid off.

c. The union and the employer agree that veterans returning from the Korean War should receive seniority credit for their years of military service, whether or not they previously worked for the employer. In the ensuing layoffs, employees who worked in the plant during the war are laid off in favor of Korean War veterans who had hardly any past service with the employer. See Ford Motor Co. v. Huffman, 345 U.S. 330 (1964).

**2. Majoritarian Preferences as a Justification for Union Action?** Can *Barton Brands* be better understood as a case rejecting the adequacy of bare majoritarian political power as a rationale for union negotiating positions? Suppose that the union, after considering all factors, including the expansion of Barton's business and the contraction of Glencoe's, the expectations of Barton's long-time employees, and the prospects for industrial peace, had originally rejected dovetailing and the employer had agreed. Would the union have defaulted on its duty of fair representation? See generally Ekas v. Carling Nat'l Breweries, 602 F.2d 664 (4th Cir. 1979); King v. Space Carriers, Inc., 608 F.2d 283 (8th Cir. 1979).

**3. Illusive Quest for Substantive or Procedural Fairness?** Alternatively, do *Barton Brands* and the questions in the preceding notes suggest that the preferences of a majority of employees provide adequate justification for any union strategy? Consider the critique in Mayer G. Freed, Daniel D. Polsby & Matthew L. Spitzer, Unions, Fairness and the Conundrums of Collective Choice, 56 S. Cal. L. Rev. 461, 487-490 (1983):

> [A]ll attempts to define the [duty of fair representation (DFR)] by reference to "vested" or "accrued" rights ultimately fail because they include a concept of "justification" that cannot withstand analysis. . . . Professor Finkin [in the Limits of Majority Rule in Collective Bargaining, 64 Minn. L. Rev. 183] believes, and we agree, that when faced with endtailing/dovetailing issues, the union must be free in the first instance to choose either alternative. Consequently, he recognizes that the *Barton Brands* formulation of the DFR cannot stand without modification. But *Barton Brands* does not deal with the union's decision in the first instance, and in Professor Finkin's view the union was properly subjected to a DFR claim because it "expropriated" the seniority that had already been conferred on the former Glencoe employees. The union had initially made the decision to dovetail; apparently, it was bound thenceforward, unless it could offer a "legitimate" reason for changing the status quo.
>
> If *Barton Brands* illustrates an unjustified "expropriation," what would a justified decision look like? Professor Finkin illustrates with a hypothetical contrasting case, in which a union's decision ought to be allowed because it is not based "solely" on the majority's desire to benefit itself. Suppose that as a result of a "change in technology," a group of employees receives a windfall under the currently operative provisions for compensation. Professor Finkin says that under these circumstances, the wage structure could be changed not only for the future, but retroactively as well. "Such an action would not be an expropriation—a taking by the majority solely to benefit itself—but an accommodation to a relevant change in circumstance."
>
> It is far from clear, however, that the changed-circumstance hypothetical is significantly different from the situation in *Barton Brands.* In the hypothetical, the majority acted because a minority of employees received a greater share of the pie than was initially anticipated, while the majority received a smaller share. The same is true of *Barton Brands.* In either case there is a

> windfall, and subsequent union action to redistribute the consequences. The only distinction — and it should not be crucial — is that in the hypothetical a minority of employees is deprived of a positive windfall, while in *Barton Brands* the minority is being stuck with a negative windfall. Professor Finkin adds that in *Barton Brands*, in contrast to the situation presented in the hypothetical, the affected interest had acquired a special importance because it was seniority, and at the time of the union's novation, layoffs were in the offing. . . . If seniority is especially important in times of economic recession, the majority's justification for its decision to protect itself from layoffs has a strength on the merits that would appear in principle to be identical to the minority's claim to the protection of the same interest.

Is Freed, Polsby, and Spitzer's complete embrace of majority rule consistent with the rationale of the *Steele* decision recognizing the duty of fair representation?

**4. Equal Protection and Principled Democracy as a Model for the Duty of Fair Representation?** Consider the following analysis of how the equal protection model invoked in the seminal *Steele* decision could be used as an alternative to unqualified majoritarianism:

> . . . Under the standard we propose, when a union decision is attacked as a breach of its DFR, the union must assert a principled justification for the decision. This objective element of the DFR inquiry requires that the union's asserted purposes be tested against the requirements of principled democracy and equal respect . . . . The reviewing court or the Board must proceed further to determine whether the asserted principled justification, rather than unequal respect for some employees, was in fact the cause of the union's decision.
>
> . . . The doctrinal structure we have derived from equal protection can be illuminated by analyzing a few examples of union-proposed seniority rules. The general union preference for rules that favor employees with greater tenure ("seniority") is arguably disrespectful of the interests of junior employees. Upon closer inspection, however, it is apparent that seniority is derived from conceptions of the good of the bargaining unit that do not disparage the intrinsic value of junior workers. Preference for senior employees over junior employees in job security and promotional opportunities can be justified by the senior employees' greater aggregate contribution to their firm, by the larger proportion of their lives that they have invested in the workplace, and by a concern for their decreasing job mobility. Moreover, a preference for more senior workers will tend, over time, to benefit most workers.
>
> In addition to meeting a test of facial validity, the union's justification must be credible. A union's assertion of traditional seniority goals might be suspect, for instance, given certain historical circumstances. Consider the case of a union that does not seek preferential treatment for senior workers until immediately after an affirmative action hiring policy is instituted. In such a case, the decisionmaker must be persuaded that the union's sudden desire for

a seniority system is not simply a covert expression of an illegitimate preference for the predominant racial group.

Some seniority-related decisions are not so easily analyzed by reference to traditional and plausible union goals. [Red Ball Motor Freight, 157 N.L.R.B. 1237, enforced, 379 F.2d 137 (D.C. Cir. 1967),] for instance, provides an excellent example of the utility of the insider-outsider perspective. The union that won the merged bargaining-unit election had pledged to grant to all workers from the larger unit seniority over all workers from the smaller unit, regardless of their actual tenure. The union leadership seemed to be motivated solely by a calculation of the political benefits of supporting the interests of a majority bloc of bargaining unit voters. Although the union was probably not hostile toward the employees from the smaller unit, judicial suspicion that the union had devalued their interests was clearly appropriate. The insider-outsider perspective helps to explain why. The fifty employees from the larger unit had never shared a working community with the thirty employees from the smaller unit. For the fifty, the thirty must have been easily regarded as "others," intruders whose interests should not be given equal consideration. The employees of the smaller unit would not have been a suspect group for purposes of equal protection review because their status as "aliens" would expeditiously terminate. Nevertheless, in the DFR context, the foreign origin of the thirty provides evidence that the social empathy on which principled decisionmaking depends was never established.

Michael C. Harper & Ira C. Lupu, Fair Representation as Equal Protection, 98 Harv. L. Rev. 1212, 1237-1239 (1985). Would this approach have enabled the *Barton Brands* court to guide the jury in determining whether the union had breached its duty to the Glencoe "outsiders"? For other discussions, see Alan Hyde, Can Judges Identify Fair Bargaining Procedures?: A Comment on Freed, Polsby & Spitzer, 57 S. Cal. L. Rev. 415 (1984); Mayer G. Freed, Daniel D. Polsby & Matthew L. Spitzer, A Reply to Hyde, Can Judges Identify Fair Bargaining Procedures?, 57 S. Cal. L. Rev. 425 (1984).

**5. "Two-Tier" Agreements.** Beginning in the 1980s, economic pressures on union-organized firms often resulted in concessionary agreements, including two-tier wage structures under which future employees were promised substantially lower wages than those of current employees doing the same work. Some, though not all, of these agreements provided for an upward adjustment of the new-hire rate to equalize the current-employee rate over time. See generally James E. Martin (with Thomas D. Heetderks), Two-Tier Compensation Structures: Their Impact on Unions, Employers and Employees (1990). Do such wage structures violate the union's duty of fair representation to new hires? Does the union's obligation commence only after individuals have been hired into their jobs?

Consider Renneisen v. American Airlines, Inc., 990 F.2d 918 (7th Cir. 1993). There, the Air Line Pilots Association (ALPA) agreed in 1983 negotiations to a wage structure that divided the union into A-scale pilots consisting of American Airline pilots hired before November 4, 1983, who would receive certain wage and benefit guarantees and B-scale pilots hired afterwards who would work without such guarantees. The agreement further provided that the A-scale pilots' guarantees would not be rebargained unless a majority of the A-scale pilots voted to do so. In the actual case, the B-scale pilots brought a suit against their employer. But what if they had sued ALPA for breach of its duty of fair representation? Would *O'Neill* require dismissal of the action? Does the union's self-interest in maintaining a cohesive membership and the fact that B-scale pilots will over time become a majority of the bargaining unit—and hence be in a position to renegotiate the wage structure—save the agreement? For criticism of such agreements, see Note, Two-Tier Wage Discrimination and the Duty of Fair Representation, 98 Harv. L. Rev. 631, 645 (1985).

### *Note: Bargaining for Retirees*

Reconsider the *Pittsburgh Plate Glass* ruling, supra page 470. Although unions are permitted to bargain on the behalf of retirees, the benefits of current retirees are not mandatory subjects of bargaining. The Supreme Court has also suggested (short of holding) that unions may owe no duty of fair representation to retirees. See Schneider Moving & Storage Co. v. Robbins, 466 U.S. 364, 376 n.22 (1984):

> A union's statutory duty of fair representation traditionally runs only to the members of its collective-bargaining unit, and is coextensive with its statutory authority to act as the exclusive representative for all employees within the unit. . . . Even if there were a duty of fair representation here, it would accord the Union wide discretion and would provide only limited protection to trust beneficiaries. A primary union objective is "to maximize overall compensation of its members." . . . Thus, it may sacrifice particular elements of the compensation package "if an alternative expenditure of resources would result in increased benefits for workers in the bargaining unit as a whole."

But cf. Brotherhood of Railroad Trainmen v. Howard, 343 U.S. 768 (1952). Does the union nevertheless assume a duty of fair representation when it elects to bargain on behalf of retirees? See, e.g., Nedd v. UMW, 556 F.2d 190 (3d Cir. 1977).

Is there a significant danger that a union will sacrifice the welfare of retirees in order to enhance the welfare of current employees? Is the danger mitigated by the Court's dictum in *Pittsburgh Plate Glass* that "[u]nder established contract principles, vested retirement rights may not be altered without the pensioner's consent" (404 U.S. at 181 n.20)? By the fact that retirees often retain voting rights in the union and in any contract ratification votes? Should such procedures be required as a precondition to allowing unions to negotiate terms that reduce retirees' prior level of benefits? See generally Robert S. Bates, Jr., Benefits of Retirees: Negotiations and the Duty of Fair Representation, 21 J. Marshall L. Rev. 513 (1988).

In United Auto Workers v. General Motors Corp. the district court certified a settlement class comprised of GM retirees and approved a settlement calling for significant reductions in retiree health care benefits. See UAW v. GMC, 497 F.3d 615, 622 (6th Cir. 2007) (affirming district court ruling). In a separate decision issued the same day, the court dismissed objections by a group of GM retirees appealing a previous denial of their motion to intervene on the ground that the rights of GM retirees were not protected under the agreement. See Federal Court OKs GM-UAW Agreement to Require Retiree Health Care Payments, 2006 Daily Lab. Rep. (BNA) No. 65, at A-7 (Apr. 5, 2006). To reduce the impact of the plan changes on individuals, GM had agreed to create a new independent defined contribution voluntary employee benefit association (VEBA) to which it would contribute $1 billion in each of three years — 2006, 2007, and 2011. See UAW, GM Agreement Would Defer Wage Increases, Add Retiree Health Contributions, 2005 Daily Lab. Rep. (BNA) No. 203, at A-11 (Oct. 21, 2005). Does the use of the settlement class action device obviate concerns about unions negotiating reductions in the benefits of retirees?

Consider also the approach taken in §1114 of the Bankruptcy Code, enacted in 1988, which requires separate representation of the interests of retirees in Chapter 11 proceedings to terminate or modify collective bargaining agreements affecting retiree claims.

## 4. Grievance Adjustment

### Vaca v. Sipes
*386 U.S. 171 (1967)*

White, J.

On February 13, 1962, Benjamin Owens* filed this class action [in a Missouri court] against petitioners, as officers and representatives of the National Brotherhood of Packinghouse Workers and of its Kansas City Local No. 12 (the Union).... Owens, a Union member, alleged that he had been discharged from his employment at Swift & Company's (Swift) Kansas City [plant] in violation of the collective bargaining agreement . . . between Swift and the Union, and that the Union had "arbitrarily,

* [After Owens's death, Sipes, his administrator, was substituted for him as appellant in an appeal from the trial court's setting aside of the jury verdict on the ground that state jurisdiction had been preempted. — Eds.]

capriciously and without just or reasonable reason or cause" refused to take his grievance with Swift to arbitration under the fifth step of the bargaining agreement's grievance procedures. . . .

In mid-1959, Owens, a long-time high blood pressure patient, . . . entered a hospital on sick leave from his employment with Swift. After a long rest . . . , Owens was certified by his family physician as fit to resume his heavy work. . . . However, Swift's company doctor examined Owens upon his return and concluded that his blood pressure was too high to permit reinstatement. After securing a second authorization from another outside doctor, Owens returned to the plant . . . on January 6, 1960. However, on January 8, when the [company] doctor discovered Owens' return, he was permanently discharged on the ground of poor health.

. . . Owens then sought the union's help in securing reinstatement, and a grievance was filed. . . . By mid-November 1960, the grievance had been processed through the third and into the fourth step of the grievance procedure. . . . Swift adhered to its position that Owens' poor health justified his discharge, rejecting numerous medical reports of [his] reduced blood pressure [as not being] based upon sufficiently thorough medical tests.

On February 6, 1961, the Union sent Owens to a new doctor at Union expense "to see if we could get some better medical evidence so that we could go to arbitration. . . ." This examination did not support Owens' position. When the Union received the report, its executive board voted not to take the Owens grievance to arbitration. . . . Union officers suggested to Owens that he accept Swift's offer of referral to a rehabilitation center, and the grievance was suspended for that purpose. Owens rejected this alternative and demanded that the Union take his grievance to arbitration, but the Union refused. With his contractual remedies thus stalled at the fourth step, Owens brought this suit. The grievance was finally dismissed by the Union and Swift shortly before trial began in June 1964.

. . . [T]he trial judge instructed [the jury] that petitioners would be liable if Swift had wrongfully discharged Owens and if the Union had "arbitrarily . . . and without just cause or excuse . . . refused" to press Owens' grievance to arbitration. . . . The jury then returned the general verdict for Owens which eventually was reinstated by the Missouri Supreme Court. . . .

[After finding that Owens's complaint stated a breach of the union's statutory duty of fair representation, the Court traced the history of the Board's *Miranda Fuel* doctrine (supra page 942); noted that Local 12, United Rubber Workers v. NLRB, 368 F.2d 12 (5th Cir. 1966), had upheld the doctrine and had indicated that it would "preempt judicial cognizance of some fair representation suits"; and referred to exceptions to preemption, questioning whether the Board is more expert than the judiciary with respect to fair representation issues.]

In addition to the above considerations, the unique interests served by the duty of fair representation doctrine have a profound effect . . . on the applicability of the preemption rule to this class of cases. . . . The collective bargaining system as encouraged by Congress and administered by the NLRB of necessity subordinates the interests of an individual employee to the collective interests of all employees in a bargaining unit. See, e.g., J.I. Case Co. v. Labor Board, 321 U.S. 332. . . . Were we to hold, as petitioners and the Government urge, that the courts are foreclosed by the NLRB's *Miranda Fuel* decision from this traditional supervisory jurisdiction, the individual employee injured by arbitrary or discriminatory union conduct could no longer be assured of impartial review of his complaint, since the Board's General Counsel has unreviewable discretion to refuse to institute an unfair labor practice complaint. The existence of even a small group of cases in which the Board would be unwilling or unable to remedy a union's breach of duty would frustrate the basic purposes underlying the duty of fair representation doctrine. For these reasons, we cannot assume from the NLRB's tardy assumption of jurisdiction in these cases that Congress, when it enacted NLRA §8(b) in 1947, intended to oust the courts of their traditional jurisdiction to curb arbitrary conduct by the individual employee's statutory representative.

There are also some intensely practical considerations which foreclose preemption of . . . fair representation duty suits, considerations which emerge from the intricate relationship between the duty of fair representation and the enforcement of collective bargaining contracts. For the fact is that the question of whether a union has breached its duty of fair representation will in many cases be a critical issue in a suit under §301 charging an employer with a breach of contract. To illustrate, let us assume a collective bargaining agreement that limits discharges to those for good cause and that contains no grievance, arbitration or other provisions purporting to restrict access to the courts. If an employee is discharged without cause, either the union or the employee may sue the employer under §301. Under this section, courts have jurisdiction . . . even though the conduct of the employer which is challenged as a breach of contract is also arguably an unfair labor practice within the jurisdiction of the NLRB. . . .

The rule is the same with regard to preemption where the bargaining agreement contains grievance and arbitration provisions which are intended to provide the exclusive remedy for breach of contract claims. If an employee is discharged without cause in violation of such an agreement, that the employer's conduct may be an unfair labor practice does not preclude a suit by the union against the employer to compel arbitration of the employee's grievance, the adjudication of the claim by the arbitrator, or a suit to enforce the resulting arbitration award.

However, if the wrongfully discharged employee himself resorts to the courts before the grievance procedures have been fully exhausted, the employer may well defend on the ground that the exclusive remedies provided by such a contract have not been exhausted. Since the employee's claim is based upon breach of the collective bargaining agreement, he is bound by terms of that agreement which govern the manner in which contractual rights may be enforced. For this reason, it is settled that the employee must at least attempt to exhaust exclusive grievance and arbitration procedures established by the bargaining agreement. Republic Steel Corp. v. Maddox, 379 U.S. 650. However, because these contractual remedies have been devised and are often controlled by the union and the employer, they may well prove unsatisfactory or unworkable for the individual grievant. The problem then is to determine under what circumstances the individual employee may obtain judicial review of his breach-of-contract claim despite his failure to secure relief through the contractual remedial procedures.

An obvious situation in which the employee should not be limited to the . . . procedures established by the contract occurs when the conduct of the employer amounts to a repudiation of those contractual procedures. Cf. Drake Bakeries v. Bakery Workers, 370 U.S. 254, 260-263. . . .

. . . [A]nother situation when the employee may seek judicial enforcement of his contractual rights arises if, as is true here, the union has sole power under the contract to invoke the higher stages of the grievance procedure, *and* if, as is alleged here, the employee-plaintiff has been prevented from exhausting his contractual remedies by the union's *wrongful* refusal to process the grievance. It is true that the employer in such a situation may have done nothing to prevent exhaustion of the exclusive contractual remedies. . . . But the employer has committed a wrongful discharge in breach of that agreement, a breach which could be remedied through the grievance process to the employee-plaintiff's benefit were it not for the union's breach of its statutory duty of fair representation to the employee. To leave the employee remediless in such circumstances would . . . be a great injustice. We cannot believe that Congress . . . intended to confer upon unions such unlimited discretion to deprive injured employees of all remedies for breach of contract. Nor do we think that Congress intended to shield employers from the natural consequences of their breaches of bargaining agreements by wrongful union conduct in the enforcement of such agreements.

For these reasons, we think the wrongfully discharged employee may bring an action against his employer in the face of a defense based upon the failure to exhaust contractual remedies, provided the employee can prove that the union as bargaining agent breached its duty of fair representation in its handling of the employee's grievance. We may assume for present purposes that such a breach of duty by the union is an unfair labor practice, as the NLRB and the Fifth Circuit have held. The employee's suit against the employer, however, remains a §301 suit, and the jurisdiction of the courts is no more destroyed by the fact that the employee, as part and parcel of his §301 action, finds it necessary to prove an unfair labor practice by the union, than it is by the fact that the suit may involve an unfair labor practice by the employer himself. The court is free to determine whether the employee is barred by the actions of his union representative, and, if not, to proceed with the case. And if, to facilitate his case, the employee joins the union as a defendant, the situation is not substantially changed. The action is still a §301 suit. . . . And, insofar as adjudication of the union's breach of duty is concerned, the result should be no different if the employee, as Owens did here, sues the employer and the union in separate actions. There would be very little to commend a rule which would permit the Missouri courts to adjudicate the Union's conduct in an action against Swift but not in an action against the Union itself.

. . . [I]t is obvious that the courts will be compelled to pass upon whether there has been a breach of the duty of fair representation in the context of many §301 breach-of-contract actions. If a breach of duty by the union and a breach of contract by the employer are proven, the court must fashion an appropriate remedy. Presumably, in at least some cases, the union's breach of duty will have enhanced or contributed to the employee's injury. What possible sense could there be in a rule which would permit a court that has litigated the fault of employer and union to fashion a remedy only with respect to the employer? Under such a rule, either the employer would be compelled by the court to pay for the union's wrong—slight deterrence, indeed, to future union misconduct—or the injured employee would be forced to go to two tribunals to repair a single injury. Moreover, the Board would be compelled in many cases either to remedy injuries arising out of a breach of contract, a task which Congress has not assigned to it, or to leave the individual employee without remedy for the union's wrong. . . .

Petitioners contend . . . that Owens failed to prove that the Union breached its duty of fair representation in its handling of Owens' grievance. Petitioners also argue that the Supreme Court of Missouri, in rejecting this contention, applied a standard that is inconsistent with governing principles of federal law with respect to the Union's duty to an individual employee in its processing of grievances. . . . We agree with both contentions. . . .

A breach of the statutory duty of fair representation occurs only when a union's conduct toward a member of the collective bargaining unit is arbitrary, discriminatory, or in bad faith. . . .

Though we accept the proposition that a union may not arbitrarily ignore a meritorious grievance or process it in perfunctory fashion, we do not agree that the individual employee has an absolute right to have his grievance taken to arbitration regardless of the provisions of the applicable collective bargaining agreement. . . . [In giving] the union discretion to supervise the grievance machinery and to invoke arbitration, the employer and the union contemplate that each will endeavor in good faith to settle grievances short of arbitration. Through this settlement process, frivolous grievances are ended prior to the most costly and time-consuming step in the grievance procedures. Moreover, both sides are assured that similar complaints will be treated consistently, and major problem areas in the interpretation of the collective bargaining contract can be isolated and perhaps resolved. . . .

If the individual employee could compel arbitration of his grievance regardless of its merit, the settlement machinery provided by the contract would be substantially undermined, thus destroying the employer's confidence in the union's authority. . . . Moreover, under such a rule, a significantly greater number of grievances would proceed to arbitration. This would greatly increase the cost of the grievance machinery and could so overburden the arbitration process as to prevent it from functioning successfully. . . . Nor do we see substantial danger to the interests of the individual employee if his statutory agent is given the contractual power honestly and in good faith to settle grievances short of arbitration. . . .

For these same reasons, the standard applied here by the Missouri Supreme Court cannot be sustained. For if a union's decision that a particular grievance lacks sufficient merit to justify arbitration would constitute a breach of the duty of fair representation because a judge or jury later found the grievance meritorious, the union's incentive to settle such grievances short of arbitration would be seriously reduced. The dampening effect on the entire grievance procedure . . . would surely be substantial. Since the union's statutory duty of fair representation protects the individual employee from arbitrary abuses of the settlement device by providing him with recourse against both employer (in a §301 suit) and union, this severe limitation on the power to settle grievances is neither necessary nor desirable. . . .

. . . [We] cannot uphold the jury's award, for we conclude that as a matter of federal law the evidence does not support a verdict that the Union breached its duty of fair representation. . . .

In administering the grievance and arbitration machinery as statutory agent of the employees, a union must, in good faith and in a nonarbitrary manner, make decisions as to the merits of particular grievances. See Humphrey v. Moore, 375 U.S. 335, 349-350; Ford Motor Co. v. Huffman, 345 U.S. 330, 337-339. In a case such as this, when Owens supplied the Union with medical evidence supporting his position, the Union might well have breached its duty had it ignored Owens' complaint or had it processed the grievance in a perfunctory manner. . . . But here the Union processed the grievance into the fourth step, attempted to gather sufficient evidence to prove Owens' case, attempted to secure for Owens less vigorous work at the plant, and joined in the employer's efforts to have Owens rehabilitated. Only when these efforts all proved unsuccessful did the Union conclude both that arbitration would be fruitless and that the grievance should be dismissed. There was no evidence that any Union officer was personally hostile to Owens or that the Union acted at any time other than in good faith. Having concluded that the individual employee has no absolute right to have his grievance arbitrated under the collective bargaining agreement at issue, and that a breach of the duty of fair representation is not established merely by proof that the underlying grievance was meritorious, we must conclude that that duty was not breached here. . . .

The appropriate remedy for a breach of a union's duty of fair representation must vary with the circumstances of the particular breach. In this case, the employee's complaint was that the Union wrongfully failed to afford him the arbitration remedy against his employer established by the collective bargaining agreement. But the damages sought by Owens were primarily those suffered because of the employer's alleged breach of contract. Assuming for the moment that Owens had been wrongfully discharged, Swift's only defense to a direct action for breach of contract would have been the Union's failure to resort to arbitration, compare Republic Steel Corp. v. Maddox, 379 U.S. 650, with Smith v. Evening News Assn., 371 U.S. 195, and if that failure was itself a violation of the Union's statutory duty to the employee, there is no reason to exempt the employer from contractual damages which he would otherwise have had to pay. The difficulty lies in fashioning an appropriate scheme of remedies.

Petitioners urge that an employee be restricted in such circumstances to a decree compelling the employer and the union to arbitrate the underlying grievance. It is true that the employee's action is based on the employer's alleged breach of contract plus the union's alleged wrongful failure to afford him his contractual remedy of arbitration. For this reason, an order compelling arbitration should be viewed as one of the available remedies when a breach of the union's duty is proved. But we see no reason inflexibly to require arbitration in all cases. In some cases, for example, at least part of the employee's damages may be attributable to the union's breach of duty, and an arbitrator may have no power under the bargaining agreement to award such damages against the union. In other cases, the arbitrable issues may be substantially resolved in the course of trying the fair representation controversy. In such situations, the court should be free to decide the contractual claim and to award the employee appropriate damages or equitable relief. . . .

The governing principle, then, is to apportion liability between the employer and the union according to the damage caused by the fault of each.[18] Thus, damages attributable solely to the employer's breach of contract should not be charged to the union, but increases if any in those damages caused by the union's refusal to process the grievance should

---

18. We are not dealing here with situations where a union has affirmatively caused the employer to commit the alleged breach of contract. In cases of that sort where the union's conduct is found to be an unfair labor practice, the NLRB has found an unfair labor practice by the employer, too, and has held the union and the employer jointly and severally liable for any back pay found owing to the particular employee who was the subject of their joint discrimination. . . . Even if this approach would be appropriate for analogous §301 and breach-of-duty suits, it is not applicable here. Since the Union played no part in Swift's alleged breach of contract and since Swift took no part in the Union's alleged breach of duty, joint liability for either wrong would be unwarranted. [Footnote relocated in text. — EDS.]

not be charged to the employer. In this case, even if the Union had breached its duty, all or almost all of Owens' damages would still be attributable to his allegedly wrongful discharge by Swift. For these reasons, even if the Union here had properly been found liable for a breach of duty, it is clear that the damage award was improper.

[The opinion of Justice Fortas, with whom the Chief Justice and Justice Harlan joined, concurring in the result, is omitted.

Justice Black dissented on these grounds: Owens, despite a judicial determination that he was wrongfully discharged, is left remediless by the Court. The union's good faith decision to forego arbitration, in Justice Black's view, although it might properly shield the union, should not also shield the employer from contract liability. The merits of an employee's grievance should be determined by a jury or an arbitrator, he argued, but under the Court's decision "it will never be determined by either." The dissent discounted the Court's concern that unions need broad discretion over individual grievances: "I simply fail to see how the union's legitimate role as statutory agent is undermined by requiring it to prosecute all serious grievances to a conclusion or allowing the injured employee to sue his employer after he has given the union a chance to act on his behalf." 386 U.S. at 209.]

## *NOTES AND QUESTIONS*

1. **Do Collective Bargaining Agreements Create Individual Rights?** Justice Black's dissent in *Vaca* reflected his view that an employee has vested rights under a labor agreement that are not subject to modification by either signatory without the employee's consent. See also Simmons v. Union News Co., 382 U.S. 884 (1965) (Black, J., dissenting from denial of certiorari). His view seems difficult to reconcile with the *Steelworkers v. American Mfg. Co.* perspective, supra page 669, on grievance arbitration as a continuation of the bargaining process. Was it also rejected by the majority in *Vaca*? In the 1950s, Professor Cox argued that collective bargaining agreements containing a grievance procedure should be presumed to be intended to create obligations for an employer that run only to the union as long as the union fulfills its fiduciary duties to represented employees. Archibald Cox, Rights Under a Labor Agreement, 69 Harv. L. Rev. 601 (1956). Was Professor Cox's view embraced by the *Vaca* majority? Professor Feller, who represented the union in the *Steelworkers* litigation, later asserted the view that collective bargaining agreements create no employee rights, only rules restricting employer discretion in governing the workplace. David Feller, A General Theory of the Collective Bargaining Agreement, 61 Cal. L. Rev. 663, 774, 792, 811 (1973). Does *Vaca* support Professor Feller's theory? See also

Bernard Dunau, Employee Participation in the Grievance Aspect of Collective Bargaining, 50 Colum. L. Rev. 731 (1950).

**2. Contractual Rights of Individual Employees Under the RLA.** The RLA gives a railway worker the right to pursue his own grievance to an adjustment board. Consequently, the Supreme Court ruled that a union's authority to settle a grievance required actual authority, granted by the individual or derived from the union constitution or custom or usage. See Elgin, Joliet & Eastern Ry. Co. v. Burley, 325 U.S. 711 (1945), opinion adhered to, 327 U.S. 661 (1946). In view of the union's duty of fair representation and the 1951 amendment to the RLA authorizing union security agreements, should there be greater judicial willingness to find that a union was authorized to settle an individual's grievance? See Pyzynski v. New York Cent. R.R. Co., 421 F.2d 854 (2d Cir. 1970), indicating that a greater settlement leeway for the union was justified. But cf. Graf v. Elgin, Joliet & Eastern Ry. Co., 697 F.2d 771, 778-781 (7th Cir. 1983), suggesting that an individual employee's RLA right to prosecute his own grievance is an added reason for limiting a railway union's duty of fair representation.

**3. Contract Administration vs. Contract-Making.** Even if individuals do not have wholly vested rights to enforce claims under labor agreements as written, should the union's latitude to compromise contract-based expectations be narrower than the "wide range of reasonableness" applicable to the union's adjustment of conflicting interests in the contract-making phase under *O'Neill*? See Clyde W. Summers, The Individual Employee's Rights Under the Collective Agreement: What Constitutes Fair Representation?, 126 U. Pa. L. Rev. 251 (1977). Would imposing on unions a heavier burden of justification for compromises of contractual claims in contract administration than for compromises of employee interests in contract negotiation undermine the union's role as collective agent? Consider this excerpt from Harper & Lupu, supra, at 1260, 1261-1263:

> Proponents of contractual rights norms tend to overlook the important allocational implications of contract administration within the bargaining unit. Administration may well require a union to make distributional judgments as important as those made in the negotiating stage. Like all contracts, the distributional agreements between employers and unions that emerge from collective labor negotiations require interpretation and elaboration. The need to resolve ambiguities in wording, to fill the interstices of the agreement, and to adjust contract provisions to unforeseen developments is especially great for collective labor agreements because they purport to establish comprehensive governing codes for multifaceted employment relationships.

The existence of the employer as an opposing will reinforces the conclusion that contract administration is part of the continuing political struggle of collective bargaining. Either party to the contract, management or union, can legally modify agreements either by obtaining the other's consent or by persuading the contract arbitrator to adopt a particular interpretation. Management's authority to pursue contract changes that will serve its general interests is undoubted. Dynamic and symmetrical collective bargaining therefore requires that a union have similar authority to continue to serve its conception of its unit's well-being. If the union is bound to advance an individual employee's contractually secured interests at the expense of possible gains to the general community of employees, collective bargaining becomes tilted and asymmetrical—rigid for employees' interests while flexible for those of management. Therefore, even if a collective agreement does create rights that employees may assert against management, these rights should remain within the continuing control of an exclusive representative and thus remain subordinate to that representative's ongoing attempts to advance its conception of the bargaining unit's good. . . .

**4. Placing the Unfairly Represented Employee in a Better Position?** Assume that the union's failure to pursue arbitration is a breach of its duty of fair representation. Does the Court in *Vaca* persuade you that the individual should not be restricted to an order compelling arbitration? Why should the union's breach create for employees something the NLRA does not expressly provide—a private damage remedy against unions? Why should unfairly represented employees have a remedy that fairly represented employees do not enjoy? Moreover, why should the union's breach deprive the employer of the arbitral remedy prescribed by the agreement?

Consider the following proposal from Estreicher, Win-Win Labor Law Reform, at 674-675:

> Under current law, an employee who is fairly represented is limited to the grievance procedure and arbitration remedy set forth in the collective agreement. However, an employee complaining of unfair representation can disregard the finality provisions of the agreement and proceed directly to court. The union will be required to defend its grievance handling and arbitration decisions before a jury, and possibly pay damages if the jury disagrees with its decisions.
>
> The law should be changed to place the unfairly represented employee in the same position as the fairly represented employee: Adjudicated violations of the fair-representation duty should trigger only a rearbitration remedy, provided the union agrees to empower the arbitrator to apportion back-pay responsibility between the employer and the union. For those situations where the breach of the fair-representation duty involves a conflict of interest between the union and the employee—rather than simply a mishandling of the employee's grievance—the employee should be permitted counsel of his or her choice . . . compensated out of union funds.

See also Mitchell H. Rubinstein, Duty of Fair Representation Jurisprudential Reform: The Need to Adjudicate Disputes in Internal Union Review Tribunals and the Forgotten Remedy of Re-Arbitration, 42 U. Mich. J.L. Reform 517 (2009).

**5. Contractual Modification of *Vaca* Rights?** A collective agreement establishes a four-step grievance procedure terminating in arbitration. It provides as follows: (a) All employees shall be bound by agreements or settlements made by the union and the employer with respect to grievances; (b) Failure by the union to process a grievance to the next step of the grievance procedure or to arbitration, within the time limits for such action prescribed herein, shall constitute agreement by the union to the employer's prior disposition of the grievance; (c) No employee shall have the right to maintain a legal action on this agreement, except actions for accrued pay, vacation benefits, or vested pension rights; (d) Any employee complaining of unfair processing of his grievance would have a right of appeal to a union-created Public Review Board comprised of labor relations professionals with no other ties to the union or the employer, see infra note 3, page 1005, and the Board, upon finding a breach of the union's duty of fair representation, would have the authority to reactivate the grievance and compel arbitration. The decisions of the Public Review Board would be final and binding. In light of *Vaca*, would such an agreement be valid insofar as it purports to foreclose individual actions on the agreement? Cf. Clayton v. Int'l Union, United Automobile Workers, 451 U.S. 679 (1987), discussed infra page 980.

### *Note:* Hines v. Anchor Motor Freight, Inc.

In Hines v. Anchor Motor Freight, Inc., 424 U.S. 554 (1976), the company fired eight truck drivers for padding overnight motel expenses. The union did not act on the drivers' suggestion that the motel be investigated; instead, the union reassured the drivers, stating that they should not hire their own lawyer for the joint area committee's hearing of their grievances. The company's strong documentary evidence presented at the hearing was contradicted only by the drivers' denials. After the area committee upheld the discharges, the drivers retained counsel and requested a rehearing based on the motel owner's concession that the motel clerk could have overcharged petitioners, doctored the records, and pocketed the overcharges. The committee denied a rehearing for lack of new evidence. The drivers then sued the company and the union, alleging breach of the contract's "just cause" provision and of the union's duty of fair representation. In a deposition the motel clerk confessed to falsifying the records. Nevertheless, the district court granted summary judgment to the defendants, reasoning that the decision of the "arbitration" committee bound the employees, and finding a failure to show the union's "bad faith, arbitrariness or perfunctoriness." The Sixth Circuit reversed the summary judgment as to the local union but not as to the employer. The Supreme Court, assuming the correctness of the reversal of the summary judgment for the union, reversed the summary judgment for the employer. Justice White, for the Court, extending *Vaca,* declared that a breach of the duty of fair representation, "if it seriously undermines the integrity of the arbitral process[,] also removes the bar of the [contract's] finality provisions." He continued (424 U.S. at 570-572):

> . . . Under the [Court of Appeal's] rule . . . , unless the employer is implicated in the Union's malfeasance or has otherwise caused the arbitral process to err, petitioners would have no remedy against Anchor even though they [prove] the Union's bad faith, the falsity of the charges against them and the breach of contract by Anchor by discharging without cause. This rule would apparently govern even . . . where it is shown that a union has manufactured the evidence and knows . . . that it is false; or even if, unbeknownst to the employer, the union has corrupted the arbitrator to the detriment of disfavored union members. As is the case where there has been a failure to exhaust, . . . we cannot believe that Congress intended to foreclose the employee from his §301 remedy otherwise available against the employer if the contractual processes have been seriously flawed by the union's breach of its duty to represent employees honestly and in good faith and without invidious discrimination or arbitrary conduct. . . .
>
> Petitioners are not entitled to relitigate their discharge merely because they offer newly discovered evidence that . . . they were fired without cause. The grievance processes cannot be expected to be error-free. The finality provision has sufficient force to surmount occasional instances of mistake. But it is quite another matter to suggest that erroneous arbitration decisions must stand even though the employee's representation by the union has been dishonest, in bad faith or discriminatory; for in that event error and injustice of the grossest sort would multiply. The contractual system would then cease to qualify as an adequate mechanism to secure individual redress for damaging failure of the employer to abide by the contract. . . . In our view, enforcement of the finality provision where the arbitrator has erred is conditioned upon the Union's having satisfied its statutory duty fairly to represent the employee in connection with the arbitration proceedings. . . .
>
> Petitioners, if they prove an erroneous discharge and the Union's breach of duty tainting the decision of the joint committee, are entitled to an appropriate remedy against the employer as well as the Union.

Justice Stewart concurred separately. Justice Stevens did not participate in the case.

Justice Rehnquist, joined by Chief Justice Burger, dissented, urging that a remedy against the employer, who had acted in good faith, would be based on the union's ineffectiveness as counsel; would undermine the finality of arbitration awards; and, given the remedy against the union, was unnecessary.

## NOTES AND QUESTIONS

**1. Was *Hines* Required by *Vaca*?** After *Vaca*, could the Court in *Hines* have ruled that the finality provision of the labor agreement shielded the employer from suit by unfairly represented employees?

**2. Does "Perfunctory" Grievance-Handling Encompass "Mere Negligence"?** Some courts have held that references in *Vaca* and *Hines* to "perfunctory" grievance-handling suggest that liability should be imposed on unions for negligence in the discharge of their contract administration function. Consider, for example, the facts in Ruzicka v. General Motors, 523 F.2d 306 (6th Cir. 1975). Ruzicka was fired for being drunk on the job and for verbally abusing his supervisor. Without contesting the underlying facts, Ruzicka filed a grievance asserting that the penalty was too harsh. The union timely filed a demand for arbitration but inexplicably omitted a detailed statement of the grievance as required by the collective agreement. Because of this omission, the grievance could not be processed further, and Ruzicka sued the union. The Sixth Circuit held that "negligent and perfunctory handling" of Ruzicka's grievance constituted unfair representation.

Compare Camacho v. Ritz-Carlton Water Towers, 786 F.2d 242 (7th Cir. 1986). There, the Seventh Circuit took the view that duty of fair representation liability for negligence would embroil the courts in disputes best handled by the grievance process and, moreover, impose costs that employees, acting as a collective body, may not wish to assume:

> The use of a standard based on causation or negligence also would interfere with employees' right to choose the level of care for which they are willing to pay. Business agents . . . usually have many duties in addition to handling grievances. They are not lawyers or private investigators. They may know the ins and outs of the collective bargaining agreement without having a trial lawyer's skills. A union could secure the skills and perseverance of a good litigation team only by paying the steep fees these skills command in the market. A union may choose to rely on part-time, untrained, overworked grievers—with the inevitable difference in the outcome of some cases—rather than purchase a higher quality of representation.

Id. at 244-245.

Although the issue was not squarely before it, the Supreme Court appears to have embraced the no-"mere negligence" liability position in United States v. Rawson, 495 U.S. 362, 372, 373 (1990), where it stated:

"The courts have in general assumed that mere negligence, even in the enforcement of a collective-bargaining agreement, would not state a claim for breach of the duty of fair representation, and we endorse that view today." See also Beavers v. United Paperworkers Int'l Union, Local 1741, 72 F.3d 97, 100 (8th Cir. 1995); Webb v. ABF Freight System, Inc., 155 F.3d 1230, 1240 (10th Cir. 1998) (both citing *Rawson* for proposition that term "perfunctory" does not encompass mere negligence). If negligence is not enough, what would constitute "perfunctory" grievance arbitration processing? See id. ("perfunctory" means the union "acted without concern or solicitude, or gave a claim only cursory attention") (internal citations omitted); see also Peters v. Burlington Northern Railroad Co., 931 F.2d 534, 539-540 (9th Cir. 1990) (reviewing cases, concludes that "mere negligence" and "perfunctory" labels represent opposite ends of a continuum that attempts to separate errors in judgment, e.g., in evaluating merits of grievance, from "inexplicable conduct" such as failure to conduct even minimal investigation of grievance).

Professors Harper and Lupu suggest that an equal protection norm, rather than a minimum competent representation norm, could support rejecting unexplained negligence as a defense for a union's departure from its usual grievance processing standards. Harper & Lupu, supra, at 1276. See also James D. Holzhauer, The Contractual Duty of Competent Representation, 63 Chi.-Kent L. Rev. 255 (1987).

**3. Intraunion Division of Interest.** In Smith v. Hussman Refrigerator Co., 619 F.2d 1229 (8th Cir.) (en banc), rehearing denied and opinion clarified, 633 F.2d 18 (1980), a collective agreement provided: "The Company recognizes the principle of seniority based upon total length of continuous service with the Company. Seniority, skill and ability to perform the work shall be considered by the Company in making promotions, transfers, layoffs and recalls. Where skill and ability to perform are substantially equal, seniority shall govern." The company posted four job openings and, after interviewing candidates, assigned the jobs to four employees with less seniority than several union members who convinced the union to file grievances on their behalf. The union gave no notice of the arbitration to the successful job bidders, and none appeared in the proceeding. The arbitrator ruled in favor of two of the grievants, resulting in a withdrawal of the job assignments from two of the successful bidders. Has the union breached its duty of fair representation if it decided to pursue the grievance solely because the grievants had superior seniority? By failing to inform the successful job bidders of the arbitration? Is there a breach even if the union considered the merits of all the employees involved and decided that, even without regard to seniority, the grievants were as qualified as those who received the positions? Is it relevant to these questions that the seniority provision was negotiated as a compromise, with the union seeking to obtain maximum protection for seniority and the employer maximum discretion to appoint by merit? Should the union be forced into a quasi-judicial role—balancing the interests of the more senior workers against those of the successful job bidders—when the employer will fully represent the opposing interest? See Feller, Theory of the Collective Bargaining Agreement, supra.

**4. Duty to Provide "Fair Process"?** Should the courts and the Board use the duty of fair representation doctrine to require unions to adopt "fair processes" in the handling of grievances? Would a "fair process" rather than a "fair substantive outcome" approach provide a better and more manageable balance between individual and collective interests? See, e.g., Lea A. VanderVelde, A Fair Process Model for the Union's Fair Representation Duty, 67 Minn. L. Rev. 1079 (1983); Ross E. Cheit, Competing Models of Fair Representation: The Perfunctory Processing Cases, 24 B.C. L. Rev. 1 (1982). Or would imposing extra-contractual procedural requirements impede union efforts to achieve collective gains? Instead of judicially imposed procedural requirements, could proceduralist review—whether the union was adhering to its customary procedures, whether the union's procedures were typically used by other labor organizations—be used as a means of identifying improperly motivated union decisions?

**5. Applications.** Should the union be held to have breached its duty of fair representation in the following cases?

a. Acting in good faith, union business agents, without consulting the union's lawyer, fail to take a discharge grievance to arbitration on the ground that "the grievance was a clear loser" and that the employer and the members were getting tired of spending money on "frivolous grievances." After the grievance is time-barred, a lawyer concludes that the odds of winning were no worse than 40-60 and is prepared to sue the union and the employer under the authority of *Vaca v. Sipes*. Would your answer be different if a ten-day suspension were involved? Cf. Curth v. Farady, 401 F. Supp. 678 (E.D. Mich. 1975).

b. Jones, a long-time employee, was fired for drunkenness, and Maverick for fighting. Maverick was unpopular with both his fellow employees and his supervisors because of his radical politics and difficult personality. The union believed that these discharges were close cases, and that it would probably lose both of them in arbitration. The union and the employer agreed that Jones would be reinstated but that Maverick's discharge would stand. Cf. Local 13, Longshoremen's & Warehousemen's Union v. Pacific Maritime Ass'n, 441 F.2d 1061, 1068 (9th Cir. 1971); Harrison v. United Transp. Union, 530 F.2d 558 (4th Cir. 1975).

c. A company suspected that employee dishonesty caused excessive costs at one of its lunch counters. The union initially rejected the company's demand that the crew be wholly or partially replaced. Later, the union, having inspected the company's books and finding evidence of pervasive theft by the employees, agreed to an experimental suspension of five counter employees. Lunch counter costs declined thereafter and, pursuant to its prior agreement with the union, the company terminated all five. They complained that their termination violated the "just cause" provision of the collective agreement, but the union declined to process any of their grievances. Cf. Union News Co. v. Hildreth, 295 F.2d 658 (6th Cir. 1961); Simmons v. Union News Co., 382 U.S. 884 (1965).

## Breininger v. Sheet Metal Workers' Local Union No. 6
*493 U.S. 67 (1989)*

BRENNAN, J. . . .

This case presents two questions under the federal labor laws: first, whether the National Labor Relations Board (NLRB or Board) has exclusive jurisdiction over a union member's claims that his union both breached its duty of fair representation and violated the Labor-Management Reporting and Disclosure Act of 1959 (LMRDA) by discriminating against him in job referrals made by the union hiring hall; and second, whether the union's alleged refusal to refer him to employment through the hiring hall as a result of his political opposition to the union's leadership gives rise to a claim under §§101(a)(5) and 609 of the LMRDA. . . .

### I

Petitioner Lynn L. Breininger was at all relevant times a member of respondent, Local Union No. 6 of the Sheet Metal Workers International Association. Pursuant to a multiemployer collective-bargaining agreement, respondent operates a hiring hall through which it refers both members and nonmembers of the union for construction work. Respondent maintains an out-of-work list of individuals who wish to be referred to jobs. When an employer contacts respondent for workers, he may request certain persons by name. If he does not, the union begins at the top of the list and attempts to telephone in order each worker listed until it has satisfied the employer's request. The hiring hall is not the exclusive source of employment for sheet metal workers; they are free to seek employment through other mechanisms, and employers are not restricted to hiring only those persons recommended by the union. Respondent also maintains a job referral list under the Specialty Agreement, a separate collective-bargaining agreement negotiated to cover work on siding, decking, and metal buildings.

Petitioner alleges that respondent refused to honor specific employer requests for his services and passed him over in making job referrals. He also contends that respondent refused to process his internal union grievances regarding these matters. . . .

The District Court held that it lacked jurisdiction to entertain petitioner's suit because "discrimination in hiring hall referrals constitutes an unfair labor practice" [over which the NLRB has exclusive jurisdiction]. . . .

The Court of Appeals affirmed in a brief per curiam opinion. With respect to the fair representation claim, the court noted that "circuit courts have consistently held that . . . fair representation claims must be brought before the Board" and that "if the employee fails affirmatively to allege that his employer breached the collective bargaining agreement, which [petitioner] failed to do in this case, he cannot prevail." . . . In regard to the LMRDA count, the Court of Appeals found that "discrimination in the referral system, because it does not breach the employee's membership rights, does not constitute 'discipline' within the meaning of the LMRDA" and that "hiring hall referrals are not a function of union membership since referrals are available to nonmembers as well as members." . . .

## II

. . . [W]e reject the notion that the NLRB ought to possess exclusive jurisdiction over fair representation complaints in the hiring hall context because it has had experience with hiring halls in the past. As an initial matter, we have never suggested that the [Vaca v. Sipes, 386 U.S. 171 (1967)] rule contains exceptions based on the subject matter of the fair representation claim presented, the relative expertise of the NLRB in the particular area of labor law involved, or any other factor. . . .

Our reasoning in *Vaca* in no way implies . . . that a fair representation action *requires* a concomitant claim against an employer for breach of contract. Indeed, the earliest fair representation suits involved claims against unions for breach of the duty in *negotiating* a collective-bargaining agreement, a context in which no breach-of-contract action against an employer is possible. See Ford Motor Co. v. Huffman, 345 U.S. 330 (1953); Steele v. Louisville & Nashville R. Co., 323 U.S. 192 (1944).

Respondent argues that the concern in *Vaca* that suits against the employer and union be heard together in the same forum is applicable to the hiring hall situation, because any action by petitioner against an employer would be premised not on §301 but rather on the contention that the employer had knowledge of the union conduct violating §8(b)(1)(A) and acted on that knowledge in making an employment decision. The employer would thereby violate NLRA §8(a)(3), see Wallace

Corp. v. NLRB, 323 U.S. 248, 255-256 (1944), and be held jointly and severally liable with the union, *but only in a suit before the Board.* In the hiring hall environment, permitting courts to hear fair representation claims against the union would create the danger of bifurcated proceedings before a court and the NLRB. The absence of a §301 claim, according to respondent, requires that we hold that the NLRB possesses exclusive jurisdiction over petitioner's fair representation suit. . . .

The situation in the instant case is entirely different [from that in *Vaca*]. In the hiring hall context, the Board may bring a claim alleging a violation of §8(b)(1)(A) against the union, and a parallel suit against the employer under §8(a)(3), without implicating the duty of fair representation at all. Or, as in the instant case, an employee may bring a claim solely against the union based on its wrongful refusal to refer him for work. While in *Vaca* an allegation that the union had breached its duty of fair representation was a necessary component of the §301 claim against the employer, the converse is not true here: a suit against the union need not be accompanied by an allegation that an employer breached the contract, since whatever the employer's liability, the employee would still retain a legal claim against the union. The fact that an employee *may* bring his fair representation claim in federal court in order to join it with a §301 claim does not mean that he *must* bring the fair representation claim before the Board in order to "join" it with a hypothetical unfair labor practice case against the employer that was never actually filed.

. . . Because federal-court jurisdiction exists over a fair representation claim regardless of whether it is accompanied by a breach-of-contract claim against an employer under §301, and because a fair representation claim is a separate cause of action from any possible suit against the employer, we decline to adopt a rule that exclusive jurisdiction lies in the NLRB over any fair representation suit whose hypothetical accompanying claim against the employer might be raised before the Board. . . .

Respondent contends that even if jurisdiction in federal court is proper, petitioner has failed to allege a fair representation claim for two reasons.

First, respondent notes that we have interpreted NLRA §8(a)(3) to forbid employer discrimination in hiring only when it is intended to discriminate on a union-related basis. See, e.g., NLRB v. Brown, 380 U.S. 278, 286 (1965). Respondent maintains that symmetry requires us to interpret §8(b)(2) as forbidding only discrimination based on union-related criteria and not any other form of maladministration of a union job referral system. Respondent contends that under this standard it committed no unfair labor practice in this case. The LMRA, according to respondent, reflects a purposeful congressional decision to limit the scope of §8(b)(2) to instances where a union discriminates solely on the basis of union membership or lack thereof. This decision would be negated if the duty of fair representation were construed as extending further than the unfair labor practice provisions of the NLRA.

We need not decide the appropriate scope of §8(b)(1)(A) and 8(b)(2) because we reject the proposition that the duty of fair representation should be defined in terms of what is an unfair labor practice. Respondent's argument rests on a false syllogism: (a) because Miranda Fuel Co., 140 N.L.R.B. 181 (1962), enf. denied, 326 F.2d 172 (CA2 1963), establishes that a breach of the duty of fair representation is also an unfair labor practice, and (b) the conduct in this case was not an unfair labor practice, therefore (c) it must not have been a breach of the duty of fair representation either. The flaw in the syllogism is that there is no reason to equate breaches of the duty of fair representation with unfair labor practices, especially in an effort to *narrow* the former category.

The duty of fair representation is not intended to mirror the contours of §8(b); rather, it arises independently from the grant under §9(a) of the NLRA of the union's exclusive power to represent all employees in a particular bargaining unit. . . .

Respondent's argument assumes that enactment of the LMRA in 1947 somehow limited a union's duty of fair representation according to the unfair labor practices specified in §8(b). We have never adopted such a view, and we decline to do so today.

Second, respondent insists that petitioner has failed to state a claim because in the hiring hall setting a union is acting essentially as an employer in matching up job requests with available personnel. Because a union does not "represent" the employees as a bargaining agent in such a situation, respondent argues that it should be relieved entirely of its duty of fair representation.

We cannot accept this proposed analogy. Only because of its status as a Board-certified bargaining representative and by virtue of the power granted to it by the collective-bargaining agreement does a union gain the ability to refer workers for employment through a hiring hall. Together with this authority comes the responsibility to exercise it in a nonarbitrary and nondiscriminatory fashion, because the members of the bargaining unit have entrusted the union with the task of representing them. That the particular function of job referral resembles a task that an employer might perform is of no consequence. The key is that the union is administering a provision of the contract, something that we have always held is subject to the duty of fair representation. "The undoubted broad authority of the union as exclusive bargaining agent in the negotiation *and administration* of a collective bargaining contract is accompanied by a responsibility of equal scope, the responsibility and duty of fair representation." . . .

The union's assumption in the hiring hall of what respondent believes is an "employer's" role in no way renders the duty of fair representation inapplicable. When management administers job rights outside the hiring hall setting, arbitrary or discriminatory acts are apt to provoke a strong reaction through the grievance mechanism. In the union hiring hall, however, there is no balance of power. If respondent is correct that in a hiring hall the union has assumed the mantle of employer, then the individual employee stands alone against a single entity: the joint union/employer. . . . In sum, if a union does wield additional power in a hiring hall by assuming the employer's role, its responsibility to exercise that power fairly *increases* rather than *decreases.* That has been the logic of our duty of fair representation cases since Steele v. Louisville & Nashville R. Co., 323 U.S., at 200.

We reject respondent's contention that petitioner's complaint fails to state a fair representation claim.

[Part III of this opinion is reproduced in the next chapter, on internal union governance (Chapter 13), infra page 999.]

## *NOTES AND QUESTIONS*

1. **Asymmetrical Duty.** Federal labor law does not prohibit employers from refusing to hire workers because of the personal animus of managers. Why then should federal law prohibit such discrimination on the part of unions?

2. **Reach of *Breininger's* Holding?** Does *Breininger* mean that unions have enforceable obligations under the duty of fair representation whenever they exercise any power normally retained by employers? Consider, for instance, a union that has been vested with authority to monitor the safety of the workplace. Would imposition of duty of fair representation liability discourage unions from seeking such authority to benefit employees in the health and safety area? Are the concerns different here than with respect to the imposition of liability on unions for the operation of hiring halls? For grievance processing?

3. **Would NLRB Regulation Be Preferable?** The Court's decision in *Breininger* is arguably attributable to the limitation on the Board's authority to regulate union hiring halls recognized in Local 357, Teamsters v. NLRB, supra page 932. Would it have been preferable to enlarge the Board's authority to regulate union maladministration of hiring halls under §§8(b)(1) and 8(b)(2) so that employee claims would have the benefit of the Board's expertise, and unions and employers alike could benefit from the General Counsel's authority to screen weak claims?

4. **"Heightened" Union Responsibility in Hiring-Hall Context?** In *O'Neill,* supra page 944, the Court stated that the three-part *Vaca v. Sipes* standard "applies to *all union activity.*" 499 U.S. at 67 (emphasis

added). Recall also that in *United States v. Rawson*, supra note 2, page 972, the Court endorsed the view that mere negligence does not breach the duty of fair representation. Do these decisions indicate that merely negligent conduct in the operation of a hiring hall does not violate the duty of fair representation? Ruling in a case involving a union's negligent failure in operating an exclusive hiring hall to refer an employee to a job in the proper order, the Board thought so. See Steamfitters Local Union No. 342 (Contra Costa Electric, Inc.), 329 N.L.R.B. 688 (1999) (overruling Iron Workers Local 118 (California Erectors), 309 N.L.R.B. 808 (1992)). The D.C. Circuit reversed and remanded, however, noting that *O'Neill* and *Rawson* were not hiring-hall cases, and pointing to the Court's statement in *Breininger* that "'if a union does wield additional power in a hiring hall by assuming the employer's role, its responsibility to exercise that power fairly *increases* rather than *decreases*.'" Jacoby v. NLRB, 233 F.3d 611, 616 (D.C. Cir. 2000). On remand, accepting the court's decision as the law of the case, the Board reaffirmed its earlier holding that inadvertent errors in the operation of an exclusive hall stemming from mere negligence do not violate the duty of fair representation. See 336 N.L.R.B. 549 (2001), petition for review denied, 325 F.3d 301, 308-309 (D.C. Cir. 2003) ("a union must operate a hiring hall with 'objective, consistent standards,' without discrimination, and without 'causing or attempting to cause an employer to discriminate against an employee,'" but one unintentional act of maladministration does not contravene "heightened duty standard").

## 5. Procedural Aspects of Duty of Fair Representation Suits

### a. *Exhaustion of Internal Union Remedies*

As explained in *Vaca v. Sipes*, an employee asserting a claim based on a violation of the collective agreement must exhaust his contractual remedies before bringing a §301 action. Under Clayton v. International Union, United Automobile Workers, 451 U.S. 679, 685 (1981), he is not required to exhaust his internal union remedies "where an internal union appeals procedure cannot result in reactivation of the employee's grievance or an award of the complete relief sought in his §301 suit. . . ." The Court did not foreclose an exhaustion requirement in other cases:

> . . . Concededly, a requirement that aggrieved employees exhaust internal remedies might lead to nonjudicial resolution of some contractual grievances. . . . However, we decline to impose a universal exhaustion requirement lest employees with meritorious §301 claims be forced to exhaust themselves and their resources by submitting their claims to potentially lengthy

> internal union procedures that may not be adequate to redress their underlying grievances.
>
> [C]ourts have discretion to decide whether to require exhaustion of internal union procedures. In exercising this discretion, at least three factors should be relevant: first, whether union officials are so hostile to the employee that he could not hope to obtain a fair hearing on his claim; second, whether the internal union appeals procedures would be inadequate either to reactivate the employee's grievance or to award him the full relief he seeks under §301; and third, whether exhaustion of internal procedures would unreasonably delay the employee's opportunity to obtain a judicial hearing on the merits of his claim. If any of these factors are found to exist, the court may properly excuse the employee's failure to exhaust.

Id. at 689. In this case, however, while the union's Public Review Board could award back pay, it lacked the power to reinstate the employee or reactivate his grievance (which had lapsed for failure to satisfy the 15-day filing requirement of the labor agreement). Justice Powell's dissent argued that the claim against either defendant did not mature until after completion of the internal appeals.

### b. *Statute of Limitations*

In DelCostello v. Teamsters, 462 U.S. 151 (1983), the Court (per Justice Brennan) held that the six-month statute of limitations in §10(b) of the NLRA governs "hybrid §301" suits like those in *Vaca* and *Hines.*

### c. *Damages*

Plaintiffs in fair representation litigation can recover compensatory damages and demand a jury trial. See Teamsters Local No. 391 v. Terry, 494 U.S. 558 (1990). However, they may not recover punitive damages. In International Brotherhood of Electrical Workers v. Foust, 442 U.S. 42, 50-52 (1979), the Court held that the interest in deterring future breaches by the union was outweighed by the debilitating impact that "unpredictable and potentially substantial" awards of punitive damages would have on union treasuries and union discretion in deciding which claims to pursue.

### d. *Allocation of Damages*

Despite the implications of *Foust,* in Bowen v. United States Postal Serv., 459 U.S. 212 (1983), the Supreme Court (per Justice Powell) held that in "hybrid" §301 suits, where the employee successfully sues the employer for a breach of the collective agreement and the union for a breach of its duty of fair representation, an allocation of damages between employer and union is required:

> . . . The interests . . . identified in *Vaca* [supra page 960] provide a measure of [the] principle for apportioning damages. Of paramount importance is the right of the employee . . . to be made whole. In determining the degree to which the employer or the union should bear the employee's damages, the Court held that the employer should not be shielded from the "natural consequences" of its breach by wrongful union conduct. . . . The Court noted, however, that the employer may have done nothing to prevent exhaustion. Were it not for the union's failure to represent the employee fairly, the employer's breach "could [have been] remedied through the grievance process to the employee-plaintiff's benefit." The fault that justifies dropping the bar to the employee's suit for damages also requires the union to bear some responsibility for increases in the employee's damages resulting from its breach. To hold otherwise would make the employer alone liable for the consequences of the union's breach of duty.

Id. at 222. Justice White (joined by Justices Marshall, Blackmun, and Rehnquist) issued a partial dissent, arguing that the employer should be primarily responsible for a wrongful discharge it caused and had full power to correct at any point in the proceeding. The Board has also adopted the *Bowen-Vaca* standard for the assessment of relief against unions in §8(b) cases based on a breach of the duty of fair representation. See Iron Workers Local Union 377 (Alamillo Steel Corp.), 326 N.L.R.B. 375 (1998).

*Bowen* should be contrasted with Northwest Airlines, Inc. v. Transport Workers, 451 U.S. 77 (1981), where an employer held liable to female employees because collectively bargained wage differentials violated the Equal Pay Act and Title VII was denied a right to contribution from the union despite the latter's significant joint responsibility for the unlawful differentials. Unions, however, can be sued directly under Title VII for discriminatory employment decisions they help bring about. See Goodman v. Lukens Steel Co., 482 U.S. 656, 669 (1987).

# 13 Regulation of Union Government and Administration

This chapter considers issues of internal union governance — the relationship of the union member to his or her labor organization. We begin with a discussion of the union's control over who may join the organization.

### *Note: Union Control over Admission to Membership*

Courts historically refused to require unions to admit individuals to membership on the view that as private organizations they should be afforded the same freedom as social clubs and churches. This freedom has been qualified in the case of unions by the statutory duty of fair representation, see supra page 938, and by a number of laws like §703(c) of Title VII of the Civil Rights Act of 1964, 42 U.S.C. §2000e, which prohibits discriminatory membership decisions on account of race, color, religion, national origin, and sex. See, e.g., Local 28, Sheet Metal Workers v. EEOC, 478 U.S. 421 (1986).

The considerable latitude unions enjoy over membership decisions raises difficulties in at least two areas. First, where unions effectively control who can be employed through their administration of hiring halls, arbitrary refusal to admit qualified applicants into membership may result in discriminatory allocation of employment opportunities, notwithstanding the formal guarantees of §§8(b)(2) and 8(a)(3) of the NLRA. See Directors Guild of Am. v. Superior Court of Los Angeles Cty., 64 Cal. 2d 42, 409 P.2d 934 (1966). Second, even where unions do not control access to jobs, often the only effective means represented employees have of influencing the decisions of their union is through the exercise of their rights as members to vote on whether to accept a contract, whether to strike, and who shall represent the union at the bargaining table. These rights of economic participation are often limited to those who are members of the labor organization. See infra pages 1029-1036.

In the Labor-Management Reporting and Disclosure Act of 1959 (LMRDA or Landrum-Griffin Act), Congress decided to regulate some of the internal decisions of unions but declined to create a federal right to union membership. Senator McClellan's original bill (S. 1137, 86th Cong., 1st Sess. (1959)) contained the following provision, §101(2), which was dropped from the LMRDA as enacted: "... Every person who meets the reasonable qualifications uniformly prescribed by a labor organization shall be eligible for membership and admitted to membership in such organization."

## A. FREE SPEECH AND ASSEMBLY

The impetus for the LMRDA of 1959 originated with disclosures by Senator McClellan's special committee of significant misuse of union funds, influence of racketeers, and union collusion with employers. The hearings did not focus on internal union democracy. Although Senator McClellan's initial bill included, as Title I, a "Bill of Rights" for union members, the bill as it emerged from the Senate Labor Committee did not include this Title. It was reincorporated in modified form on the Senate and House floors.

### 1. Union Controls on Speech by Rank-and-File Members

**Salzhandler v. Caputo**
*316 F.2d 445 (2d Cir. 1963)*

Lumbard, C.J. . . .

Salzhandler, a member of Local 442, Brotherhood of Painters, Decorators & Paperhangers of America, brought suit in the district court following the decision of a Trial Board of the union's New York District Council No. 9 that he had untruthfully accused . . . Webman, the president of the local, of the crime of larceny. The Trial Board found that Salzhandler's "unsupported accusations" violated the union's constitution which prohibited "conduct unbecoming a member . . . ," "acts detrimental to . . . interests of the Brotherhood," "libeling, slandering . . . fellow members [or] officers of local unions" and "acts and conduct . . . inconsistent with the duties, obligations and fealty of a member."

. . . [A]t the times in question [Salzhandler] was serving a three-year term [as financial secretary] which was to end June 30, 1962. His weekly compensation as an officer was $35, of which $25 was salary and $10 was for expenses. . . .

. . . In going over the union's checks in July 1960 Salzhandler noticed that two checks, one for $800 and one for $375, had been drawn to cover the expenses of Webman and one Max Schneider at two union conventions to which they were elected delegates. The $800 check, drawn on August 21, 1959 to Webman's order, was endorsed by Webman and his wife. The $375 check, drawn on March 4, 1960 to "Cash," was likewise endorsed by Webman and his wife. Schneider's endorsement did not appear on either check. Schneider had died on May 31, 1960. . . .

In November 1960 Salzhandler distributed to members of the local a leaflet which accused Webman of improper conduct with regard to union funds and of referring to members of the union by such names as "thieves, scabs, robbers, scabby bosses, bums, pimps, f-bums, [and] jail birds." Attached to the leaflet were photostats of the four checks. . . . The leaflet also branded Webman as a "petty robber" of the two $6 checks. . . .

On December 13, 1960, Webman filed charges against Salzhandler with the New York District Council No. 9 . . . , alleging that Salzhandler had violated the union constitution, §267, by libeling and slandering him in implying that he, Webman, had not reimbursed Max Schneider for convention expenses, and that he had been a "petty robber" in causing the two $6 checks to be deposited in the Michael Schneider fund, rather than being paid over to the two widows. The charge went on to state that Salzhandler was guilty of "acts and conduct inconsistent with the duties, obligations and fealty of a member or officer of the Brotherhood" and that the net effect of the leaflet was untruthfully to accuse an officer of the union of the crime of larceny. For over six hours on the evening of February 23, 1961, Salzhandler was tried by a five-member Trial Board of the District Council. . . . Salzhandler was represented by a union member who was not a lawyer. At the trial, Webman introduced the leaflet. Salzhandler produced the photostats and was questioned by the Trial Board. Webman's witnesses testified that the convention expenditures were approved by the membership. Salzhandler produced three witnesses who testified that Webman had called members names as alleged in the leaflet.

Not until April 2, 1961 did Salzhandler receive notice of the Trial Board's decision and his removal from office and this was from a printed postal card mailed to all members: "By a decision of the Trial Committee . . . , Sol Saltzhandler [sic] is no longer Financial Secretary of Local Union 442."

Thereafter, on April 4, the District Council mailed to Salzhandler only the final paragraph of its five page "Decision" which read as follows:

> It is our decision that Brother Solomon Salzhandler be prohibited from participating in the affairs of L.U. 442, or of any other Local Union of the Brotherhood, or of District Council 9, for . . . five (5) years. He shall not be permitted during that period to attend meetings of L.U. 442, to vote on any matter, to have the floor at any meeting of any other Local Union affiliated with the District Council, or to be a candidate for any position in any local

> Union or in the District Council. In all other respects, Brother Salzhandler's rights and obligations as a member of the Brotherhood shall be continued.

Salzhandler did not receive a copy of the full opinion of the Trial Board until after this action was commenced on June 14, 1961. . . .

Judge Wham dismissed the complaint [based on LMRDA §102], holding that the Trial Board's conclusion that the leaflet was libelous was sufficiently supported by the evidence. He went further, however, and made an independent finding that the statements were, in fact, libelous. The court held, as a matter of law, that "The rights accorded members of labor unions under [LMRDA] Title I . . . do not include the right . . . to libel or slander officers of the union." We do not agree.

The LMRDA . . . was designed to protect the rights of union members to discuss freely and criticize the management of their unions and the conduct of their officers. The legislative history and the extensive [prior] hearings abundantly evidence the intention of the Congress to prevent union officials from using their disciplinary powers to silence criticism and punish those who dare to question and complain. The statute is clear and explicit. . . . [The court here quoted §§101(a)(1) and (2), 102, and 609.]

. . . In a proviso to §101(a)(2), there are two express exceptions to the broad rule of free expression. One relates to "the responsibility of every member toward the organization as an institution." The other deals with interference with the union's legal and contractual obligations. . . .

The expression of views by Salzhandler did not come within either exception in the proviso to §101(a)(2). The leaflet did not interfere in any way with the union's legal or contractual obligations and the union has never claimed that it did. Nor could Salzhandler's charges against Webman be construed as a violation of the "responsibility of every member toward the organization as an institution." Quite the contrary; it would seem clearly in the interest of proper and honest management of union affairs to permit members to question the manner in which the union's officials handle the union's funds and how they treat the union's members. . . .

The union argues that there is a public interest in promoting the monolithic character of unions in their dealings with employers. But the Congress weighed this factor and decided that the desirability of protecting the democratic process within the unions outweighs any possible weakening of unions in their dealings with employers which may result from the freer expression of opinions within the unions. . . .

. . . Here Salzhandler's charges against Webman related to the handling of union funds; they concerned the way the union was managed. The Congress has decided that it is in the public interest that unions be democratically governed and toward that end that discussion should be free and untrammeled and that reprisals within the union for the expression of views should be prohibited. It follows that although libelous statements may be made the basis of civil suit . . . , the union may not subject a member to any disciplinary action on a finding . . . that such statements are libelous. . . .

## *NOTES AND QUESTIONS*

**1. Justification for Regulating Internal Union Decisions?** What is the justification for regulating the membership decisions of a private labor organization that are in conformity with its own internal rules? Is the economic power of unions over membership decisions a sufficient reason? Is regulation appropriate because union power may derive in significant part from government regulation, via the exclusivity principle and the protection of concerted activity? Is it critical that employees in a union shop do not escape the reach of the union's power by being expelled or by resigning from the union's membership? Do these considerations adequately distinguish other private associations with delegated regulatory power, like state bar associations?

**2. Nature of Sanction: Fines vs. Expulsion?** Should unions have greater latitude to expel than to impose judicially enforceable fines on members for conduct inimical to the union's goals? Consider the NLRB decisions drawing this distinction under §8(b)(1)(A), cited infra note 2, page 925.

**3. Applications.** In light of *Salzhandler*, can a union, after proper notice and hearing, fine or expel a union member for the following conduct?

a. She circulates libelous statements about fiscal irregularities on the part of union officials among the general public while the union is on strike or while it is engaged in an organizational campaign.

b. She becomes president of a rival union, which has filed an election petition regarding her unit with the NLRB. Compare Ferguson v. International Ass'n of Bridge, Structural & Ornamental Ironworkers, 854 F.2d 1169 (9th Cir 1998) ("dual unionism" activity not protected), with Lodge 702, IAM v. Loudermilk, 444 F.2d 719 (5th Cir. 1971) (union cannot fine member for such conduct where membership is compulsory).

c. She urges during a union meeting, and elsewhere, that an ongoing strike is in breach of contract and tries to start a back-to-work movement. Would it be material whether her construction of the agreement was right or wrong?

d. She advocates "communist ideas," thereby violating a provision of the union constitution barring members from "advocating . . . communism, fascism, nazism, or any other totalitarian philosophy . . . or giving support to these 'isms' or to movements . . . inimical to the union or its established policies and laws." Does it make a difference if the disputed advocacy occurred during a campaign for union office, during a union meeting, or at the workplace? Cf. Turner v. Air Transport Lodge 1894, IAM, 590 F.2d 409 (2d Cir. 1978).

e. In her individual capacity, a union official publicly supports the Republican candidate for President after the union's executive board voted that the union should support the Democratic candidate. Should it be contrary to public policy, under state law, to remove the official from her union office? To expel her from membership? Cf. Morgan v. Local 1150, IUE, 16 L.R.R.M. 720 (Super. Ct. Ill. 1945), reversed on other grounds, 331 Ill. App. 21, 72 N.E.2d 59 (1946). Same answer under the LMRDA?

4. **Must the Union Maintain an Open Forum for Dissident Views?** Is a union newsletter that frequently publishes favorable accounts of the activities of incumbent officers an "open forum" required by §101(a)(2) to publish the views of dissidents? See Shimman v. Miller, 995 F.2d 651 (6th Cir. 1993) (so holding). See also infra note 5, page 1022.

5. **Is Democracy Good for Union Effectiveness?** Consider Benjamin C. Sigal, Freedom of Speech and Union Discipline: The "Right" of Defamation and Disloyalty, in Proc., 17th N.Y.U. Conf. on Lab. 367, 370, 371 (T.G.S. Christensen ed., 1964):

> In considering the problem of democracy in a labor union, it is an oversimplification to give major emphasis to its aspect as a political institution. It is still primarily an economic institution, whose effectiveness depends on its potential fighting qualities. . . . The enterprises with which they deal are directed by very small groups of men, who can act quickly without the inhibitions of democratic controls. Unions must be able, therefore, to exercise discipline over their members, and to respond quickly and decisively to counter employer tactics if they are to cope successfully with emergency and crisis situations. Internal division in crucial situations may render them impotent. . . .
>
> . . . The union is not the workers' economic legislature, policeman, or judge. Under optimum conditions, it is a recognized participant in establishing those laws, a lookout rather than a policeman, and an advocate rather than a judge. Furthermore, the extent to which it introduces an element of democracy into the government of industry is the consequence of its economic power, not its moral posture.

6. **Commentary.** For general assessments of LMRDA regulation of internal union democracy, see Symposium, Union Governance and Democracy, 21 J. Lab. Res. (Parts I & II, 2000); The Internal Governance and Organizational Effectiveness of Labor Unions: Essays in Honor of George Brooks (Samuel Estreicher, Harry C. Katz & Bruce E. Kaufman eds., 2001).

### *Note: Procedural Aspects of Title I Actions*

**Exhaustion of Internal Union Remedies.** Although Title I authorizes a private right of action without any prior investigation or other involvement by the Secretary of Labor, §101(a)(4) requires exhaustion of "reasonable hearing procedures (but not to exceed a four-month lapse of time)." Even though the exhaustion proviso does not appear in §102, which establishes the right to sue for §101 violations—and the bill that was reported out of the House Labor Committee (H.R. 8342) provided for exhaustion of internal remedies in §102—the courts have held that "the broad language in §101(a)(4) includes suits instituted against labor unions in any court on any claim." Detroy v. American Guild of Variety Artists, 286 F.2d 75, 77 (2d Cir. 1961). However, the duty to exhaust is not absolute. In *Detroy*, which involved the placing of a union member's name on a "National Unfair List" without notice or hearing, the court held that exhaustion was not required because (1) a speedy judicial remedy was needed to undo the blacklisting; (2) the internal remedy had not been brought to the member's attention; and (3) the union's constitution did not provide a clear means of obtaining review of unfair listing decisions.

Union discipline for failure to exhaust internal remedies has been held barred by §101(a)(4). See Ryan v. International Bhd. of Electrical Workers, 361 F.2d 942 (7th Cir. 1966). Cf. NLRB v. Industrial Union of Marine & Shipbuilding Workers, 391 U.S. 418, 427-428 (1968), note 4, supra page 925.

**Statute of Limitations.** In Reed v. United Transp. Union, 488 U.S. 319 (1989), the Court (per Justice Brennan) held that "free speech" claims under Title I are governed by state general or residual personal-injury statutes of limitations. The borrowing of the NLRA statute of limitations for §301 duty of fair representation suits in *DelCostello v. Teamsters,* supra page 981, was treated as "a closely circumscribed exception to the general rule that statutes of limitations are to be borrowed from state law."

**Damages and Right to a Jury Trial.** Title I authorizes the recovery of damages. Where legal relief is sought, a jury trial may be demanded. In Wooddell v. International Bhd. of Elec. Workers, Local 71, 502 U.S. 93 (1991), Wooddell claimed that because of his dissident activities, he was discriminated against in job referrals from the union hiring hall in violation of rights under Title I and the union constitution. The Court held that his claim for lost wages should not be treated as one for equitable relief—restitution incidental to a claim for reinstatement to a position from which he had been terminated. Because he was claiming a discriminatory refusal to refer him to jobs he never obtained, his claim rather was analogous to one for damages for personal injury, and hence was legal in nature, entitling him to a jury trial.

**Attorneys' Fees.** In Hall v. Cole, 412 U.S. 1 (1973), the Court held that an award of attorneys' fees is permissible in a §102 suit addressing a violation of §101(a)(2). The respondent, at a regular membership meeting, introduced resolutions critical of the officers' undemocratic and short-sighted actions. These resolutions were defeated, and the union expelled the respondent from membership for violating a rule against "malicious vilification" of any officer. A federal district court ordered respondent's reinstatement; the court found no damages but ordered the union to pay him $5,500 in counsel fees. The Supreme Court, per Justice Brennan, upheld that award, reasoning that §102 permits an award of fees and that the instant award was not an abuse of discretion. The Court observed that the respondent, by vindicating his own right to free speech guaranteed by §101(a)(2), had rendered a substantial service to the union as an institution and to its members. Accordingly, under the "common benefit theory," an award of counsel fees fell within the traditional equitable authority of federal courts. The Court rejected the contention that the express authorization of counsel fees in §§201(c) and 501(b) of the LMRDA, coupled with the absence of authorization in §102, indicated an intent to preclude fee-shifting under §102.

## 2. Union Controls on Speech by Officials and Staff

**Finnegan v. Leu**
*456 U.S. 431 (1982)*

Burger, C.J.

The question presented . . . is whether the discharge of a union's appointed business agents by the union president, following his election over the candidate supported by the business agents, violated the [LMRDA]. The Court of Appeals held that the Act did not protect the business agents from discharge. . . .

In December 1977, respondent Harold Leu defeated Omar Brown in an election for the presidency of Local 20 of the International Brotherhood of Teamsters, Chauffeurs, Warehousemen and Helpers of America, a labor organization representing workers in a 14-county area of northwestern Ohio. During the vigorously contested campaign, petitioners, then business agents of Local 20, openly supported the incumbent president, Brown. Upon assuming office in January 1978, Leu discharged petitioners and the Local's other business agents, all of whom had been appointed by Brown following his election in 1975. Leu explained that he felt the agents were loyal to Brown, not to him, and therefore would be unable to follow and implement his policies and programs.

Local 20's bylaws—which were adopted by, and may be amended by, a vote of the union membership—provide that the president shall have authority to appoint, direct, and discharge the Union's business agents. . . . The duties of the business agents include participation in the negotiating of collective-bargaining agreements, organizing of union members, and processing of grievances. In addition, the business agents, along with the president, other elected officers, and shop stewards, sit as members of the Stewards Council, the legislative assembly of the Union. Petitioners had come up through the union ranks, and as business agents they were also members of Local 20. Discharge from their positions as business agents did not render petitioners ineligible to continue their union membership.

Petitioners filed suit in the United States District Court, alleging that they had been terminated from their appointed positions in violation of the [LMRDA §§101(a)(1), 101(a)(2), 102, and 609]. The District Court granted summary judgment for respondents Leu and Local 20, holding that the Act does not protect a union employee from discharge by the president of the union if the employee's rights as a union member are not affected. . . . [T]he Sixth Circuit affirmed. . . .

The [LMRDA] was the product of congressional concern with widespread abuses of power by union leadership. . . .

Sections 101(a)(1) and (2) . . . , on which petitioners rely, guarantee equal voting rights, and rights of speech and assembly, to "[e]very *member* of a labor organization" (emphasis added). In addition, §609 of the Act renders it unlawful for a union or its representatives "to fine, suspend, expel, or otherwise discipline any of its *members* for exercising any right to which he is entitled under the provisions of this Act." (Emphasis added.) It is readily apparent, both from the language of these provisions and from the legislative history of Title I, that it was rank-and-file union members—not union officers or employees, as such—whom Congress sought to protect.

Petitioners held a dual status as both employees and members of the Union. As *members* of Local 20, petitioners undoubtedly had a protected right to campaign for Brown and support his candidacy. At issue here is whether they were thereby immunized from discharge at the pleasure of the president from their positions as appointed union *employees.*

Petitioners contend that discharge from a position as a union employee constitutes "discipline" [under] §609; and that termination of union employment is therefore unlawful when predicated upon an employee's exercise of rights guaranteed to members under the Act. However, we conclude that the term "discipline," as used in §609, refers only to retaliatory actions that affect a union member's rights of status *as a member* of the union. Section 609 speaks in terms of disciplining "members"; and the three disciplinary sanctions specifically enumerated—fine, suspension, and expulsion—are all punitive actions taken against union members as members. In contrast, discharge from union employment does not impinge upon the incidents of union membership, and affects union members only to the extent that they happen also to be union employees. We discern nothing in §609, or its legislative history, to support petitioners' claim that Congress intended to establish a system of job security or tenure for appointed union employees. . . .

We hold, therefore, that removal from appointive union employment is not within the scope of those union sanctions explicitly prohibited by §609.

Our analysis is complicated, however, by the fact that §102 provides independent authority for a suit against a union based on an alleged violation of Title I of the Act. Section 102 states that

> [a]ny person whose rights secured by the provisions of this title have been infringed by any violation of this title may bring a civil action in a district court of the United States for such relief (including injunctions) as may be appropriate.

Although the intended relationship between §§102 and 609 is not entirely clear, it seems evident that a litigant may maintain an action under §102—to redress an "infringement" of "rights secured" under Title I—without necessarily stating a violation of §609.

The question still remains, however, whether petitioners' "rights secured" under Title I were "infringed" by the termination of their union employment. Petitioners, as union members, had a right under §§101(a)(1) and (2) to campaign for Brown and to vote in the union election, but they were not prevented from exercising those rights. Rather, petitioners allege only an *indirect* interference with their membership rights, maintaining that they were forced to "choos[e] between their rights of free expression . . . and their jobs." See Retail Clerks Union Local 648 v. Retail Clerks International Ass'n, 299 F. Supp. 1012, 1021 ([D.D.C.] 1969).

We need not decide whether the retaliatory discharge of a union member from union office—even though not "discipline" prohibited under §609—might ever give rise to a cause of action under §102. For whatever limits Title I places on a union's authority to utilize dismissal from union office as "part of a purposeful and deliberate attempt . . . to suppress dissent within the union," cf. Schonfeld v. Penza, 477 F.2d 899, 904 (CA2 1973), it does not restrict the freedom of an elected union leader to choose a staff whose views are compatible with his own.[11] Indeed, neither the language nor the legislative history of the Act suggests that it was intended even to address the issue of union patronage. To the contrary, the Act's overriding objective

11. We leave open the question whether a different result might obtain in a case invoking nonpolicymaking and nonconfidential employees.

was to ensure that unions would be democratically governed, and responsive to the will of the union membership as expressed in open, periodic elections. See Wirtz v. Hotel Employees, 391 U.S. 492, 497 (1968). Far from being inconsistent with this purpose, the ability of an elected union president to select his own administrators is an integral part of ensuring a union administration's responsiveness to the mandate of the union election. . . .

[The opinion of Justice Blackmun, with whom Justice Brennan joins, concurring, is omitted.]

### Sheet Metal Workers' International Ass'n v. Lynn
*488 U.S. 347 (1989)*

MARSHALL, J.

. . . The question presented in this case is whether the removal of an elected business agent, in retaliation for statements he made at a union meeting in opposition to a dues increase sought by the union trustee, violated the LMRDA. . . .

#### I

In June 1981, respondent Edward Lynn was elected to a 3-year term as a business representative of petitioner Local 75 of the Sheet Metal Workers' International Association (Local), an affiliate of petitioner Sheet Metal Workers' International Association (International). Lynn was instrumental in organizing fellow members of the Local who were concerned about a financial crisis plaguing the Local. These members, who called themselves the Sheet Metal Club Local 75 (Club), published leaflets that demonstrated, on the basis of Department of Labor statistics, that the Local's officials were spending far more than the officials of two other sheet metal locals in the area. The Club urged the Local's officials to reduce expenditures rather than increase dues in order to alleviate the Local's financial problems. A majority of the Local's members apparently agreed, for they defeated three successive proposals to increase dues.

Following the third vote, in June 1982, the Local's 17 officials, including Lynn, sent a letter to the International's general president, requesting that he "immediately take whatever action [is] . . . necessary including, but not limited to, trusteeship to put this local on a sound financial basis." Invoking his authority under the International's constitution, the general president responded by placing the Local under a trusteeship and by delegating to the trustee, Richard Hawkins, the authority "to supervise and direct" the affairs of the Local, "including, but not limited to, the authority to suspend local union . . . officers, business managers, or business representatives." Art. 3, §2(c), Constitution and Ritual of the Sheet Metal Workers' International

Association, Revised and Amended by Authority of the Thirty-Fifth General Convention, St. Louis, Missouri (1978).

Within a month of his appointment, Hawkins decided that a dues increase was needed to rectify the Local's financial situation. Recognizing that he lacked authority to impose a dues increase unilaterally, Hawkins prepared a proposal to that effect which he submitted to and which was approved by the Local's executive board. A special meeting was then convened to put the dues proposal to a membership vote. Prior to the meeting, Hawkins advised Lynn that he expected Lynn's support. Lynn responded that he first wanted a commitment to reduce expenditures, which Hawkins declined to provide. Lynn thus spoke in opposition to the dues proposal at the special meeting. The proposal was defeated by the members in a secret ballot vote. Five days later, Hawkins notified Lynn that he was being removed "indefinitely" from his position as business representative specifically because of his outspoken opposition to the dues increase.

After exhausting his intraunion remedies, Lynn brought suit in District Court under §102 of the LMRDA, 29 U.S.C. §412, claiming, inter alia, that his removal from office violated §101(a)(2), the free speech provision of Title I of the LMRDA, 29 U.S.C. §411(a)(2). The District Court granted summary judgment for petitioners, reasoning that, under *Finnegan v. Leu*, supra, "[a] union member's statutory right to oppose union policies affords him no protection against dismissal from employment as an agent of the union because of such opposition."

The Court of Appeals for the Ninth Circuit reversed. The court held that *Finnegan* did not control where the dismissed union employee was an elected, rather than an appointed, official because removal of the former "can only impede the democratic governance of the union."

## II . . .

### A

Petitioners argue that Lynn's Title I rights were not "infringed" for purposes of §102 because Lynn, like other members of the Local, was not prevented from attending the special meeting, expressing his views on Hawkins' dues proposal, or casting his vote, and because he remains a member of the Local. Under this view, Lynn's status as an elected, rather than an appointed, official is essentially immaterial and the loss of union employment cannot amount to a Title I violation.

This argument is unpersuasive. In the first place, we acknowledged in *Finnegan* that the business agents' Title I rights had been interfered with, albeit indirectly, because the agents had been forced to choose between their rights and their jobs. See id., at 440, 442. This was so even though the business agents were not actually prevented from exercising their Title I rights. The same is true here. Lynn was able to attend the special meeting, to express views in opposition to Hawkins' dues proposal, and to cast his vote. In taking these actions, Lynn "was exercising . . . membership right[s] protected by section 101(a)." Given that Lynn was removed from his post as a direct result of his decision to express disagreement with Hawkins' dues proposal at the special meeting, and that his removal presumably discouraged him from speaking out in the future, Lynn paid a price for the exercise of his membership rights.

This is not, of course, the end of the analysis. Whether such interference with Title I rights gives rise to a cause of action under §102 must be judged by reference to the LMRDA's basic objective: "to ensure that unions [are] democratically governed, and responsive to the will of the union membership as expressed in open, periodic elections." *Finnegan,* 456 U.S., at 441. In *Finnegan,* this goal was furthered when the newly elected union president discharged the appointed staff of the ousted incumbent. Indeed, the basis for the *Finnegan* holding was the recognition that the newly elected president's victory might be rendered meaningless if a disloyal staff were able to thwart the implementation of his programs. While such patronage-related discharges had some chilling effect on the free speech rights of the business agents, we found this concern outweighed by the need to vindicate the democratic choice made by the union electorate.

The consequences of the removal of an elected official are much different. To begin with, when an elected official like Lynn is removed from his post, the union members are denied the representative of their choice. Indeed, Lynn's removal deprived the membership of his leadership, knowledge, and advice at a critical time for the Local. His removal, therefore, hardly was "an integral part of ensuring a union administration's responsiveness to the mandate of the union election." Ibid.; see also Wirtz v. Hotel Employees, 391 U.S. 492, 497 (1968).

Furthermore, the potential chilling effect on Title I free speech rights is more pronounced when elected officials are discharged. Not only is the fired official likely to be chilled in the exercise of his own free speech rights, but so are the members who voted for him. See Hall v. Cole, 412 U.S. 1, 8 (1973). Seeing Lynn removed from his post just five days after he led the fight to defeat yet another dues increase proposal,[6] other members of the Local may well have concluded that one challenged the union's hierarchy, if at all, at one's peril. This is precisely what Congress sought to prevent when it passed

---

6. There is no suggestion that Lynn's speech in opposition to the dues increase contravened any obligation properly imposed upon him as an elected business agent of the Local.

the LMRDA. . . . We thus hold that Lynn's retaliatory removal stated a cause of action under §102.[7] . . .

Petitioners next contend that, even if the removal of an elected official for the exercise of his Title I rights ordinarily states a cause of action under §102, a different result obtains here because Lynn was removed during a trusteeship lawfully imposed under Title III of the LMRDA. . . .

We disagree. In the first place, we find nothing in the language of the LMRDA or its legislative history to suggest that Congress intended Title I rights to fall by the wayside whenever a trusteeship is imposed. Had Congress contemplated such a result, we would expect to find some discussion of it in the text of the LMRDA or its legislative history. Given Congress' silence on this point, a trustee's authority under Title III ordinarily should be construed in a manner consistent with the protections provided in Title I. . . .

Whether there are any circumstances under which a trustee acting pursuant to Title III can override Title I free speech rights is a question we need not confront. Section 101(a)(3) of Title I, 29 U.S.C. §411(a)(3), guarantees to the members of a local union the right to vote on any dues increase, and, as petitioners conceded at oral argument, this critical Title I right does not vanish with the imposition of a trusteeship. A trustee seeking to restore the financial stability of a local union through a dues increase thus is required to seek the approval of the union's members. In order to ensure that the union members' democratic right to decide on a dues proposal is meaningful, the right to exchange views on the advantages and disadvantages of such a measure must be protected. A trustee should not be able to control the debate over an issue which, by statute, is beyond his control.

In the instant case, Lynn's statements concerning the proposed dues increase were entitled to protection. Petitioners point to nothing in the International's constitution to suggest that the nature of Lynn's office changed once the trusteeship was imposed, so that Lynn was obligated to support Hawkins' positions. Thus, at the special meeting, Lynn was free to express the view apparently shared by a majority of the Local's members that the best solution to the Local's financial problems was not an increase in dues, but a reduction in expenditures. Under these circumstances, Hawkins violated Lynn's Title I rights when he removed Lynn from his post.

---

7. In reaching this conclusion, we reject petitioners' contention that a union official must establish that his firing was part of a systematic effort to stifle dissent within the union in order to state a claim under §102. Although in *Finnegan* we noted that a §102 claim might arise if a union official were dismissed "as 'part of a purposeful and deliberate attempt . . . to suppress dissent within the union,'" 456 U.S., at 441, quoting Schonfeld v. Penza, 477 F.2d 899, 904 (CA2 1973), we did not find that this constituted the *only* situation giving rise to a §102 claim. We merely stated that we did not have such a case before us, and that we expressed no view as to its proper resolution. 456 U.S., at 441. Likewise, we explicitly reserved the question "whether a different result might obtain in a case involving nonpolicymaking and nonconfidential employees." Id., at 441, n.11.

Justice KENNEDY took no part in the consideration or decision of this case.

Justice WHITE, concurring in the judgment.

. . . In the case before us, the speech for which respondent was removed was also speech in the capacity of a member. The duties of a union business agent are defined in the union constitution. Those duties relate primarily to collective bargaining and administering the collective-bargaining contract. They do not seem to include supporting the union president's proposal to increase union dues; and if they did, I am not so sure that respondent would have spoken out against the dues increase at all. . . .

In this case, unlike *Finnegan,* respondent was not discharged by an incoming elected president with power to appoint his own staff, but by a trustee whose power to dismiss and appoint officers, for all that is shown here, went no further than the Local's president to discharge for cause, i.e., for incompetence or other behavior disqualifying them for the tasks they were expected to perform as officers. Respondent's speech opposing the dues increase was the speech of a member about a matter the members were to resolve, and there is no countervailing interest rooted in union democracy that suffices to override that protection.

Thus, I doubt that resolution of cases like this turns on whether an officer is elected or appointed. Rather its inquiry is whether an officer speaks as a member or as an officer in discharge of his assigned duties. If the former, he is protected by Title I. If the latter, the issue becomes whether other considerations deprive the officer/member of the protections of that Title.

## *NOTES AND QUESTIONS*

**1. Union Officials Exercising Rights as Members?** Should the nature of the union official's position or the reason for his or her removal from office control? Is Justice White's position, concurring in *Lynn,* preferable to the majority's distinction between appointed officials and elected officials? Would the result in *Finnegan* have been different if the appointed business agents had been removed for speaking at a membership meeting against a dues increase proposed by Leu, the new local president?

Are courts likely to be able to devise workable standards for distinguishing between "insubordination" by a union official and that official's exercise of "freedom of speech" in his capacity as a union member? Pertinent variables are explored in James G. Pope, Free Speech Rights of Union Officials Under the LMRDA, 18 Harv. C.R.-C.L. L. Rev. 525 (1983).

**2. Nonpolicymaking Union Employees.** The *Finnegan* Court in footnote 11 leaves open whether a union might dismiss appointed "nonpolicymaking and nonconfidential employees" because of their speech. Should there be such an exception to the *Finnegan* holding? In Franza v. International Bhd. of Teamsters, 869 F.2d 41 (2d Cir. 1988), the court held that a nonsupervisory auditor of a benefit plan who claimed retaliatory discharge for backing an incumbent union president had no claim under Title I:

> Here, where Franza's status as a member is unrelated to his employment by the Plan, his loss of that employment is not the infringement of a right to which Title I's protections attach. Hence, the test is not whether the employee is or is not in a policymaking position; rather the question is whether membership rights in the union were directly infringed by action taken with respect to a union member's employment status.

Id. at 48. Contrast Elrod v. Burns, 427 U.S. 347 (1976) (First Amendment bars patronage dismissal of nonpolicymaking employees).

If the exception does obtain, which union officials should be treated as serving in a nonpolicymaking and nonconfidential capacity? For instance, shop stewards are typically working employees who are selected as union representatives responsible for the initial fielding of grievances. Are such stewards "policymaking" union officials subject to removal under *Finnegan*? Are *elected* stewards offered greater protection by the rationale in *Lynn*? See Brett v. Hotel, Motel, Restaurant, Construction Camp Employees, Local 879, 828 F.2d 1409, 1414-1415 (9th Cir. 1987) (distinguishing *Finnegan* in this manner). Would union members receive a different message from the removal of a dissident who had been appointed a steward as opposed to the removal of a dissident who had been elected? Cf. Adams-Lundy v. Flight Attendants, 731 F.2d 1154 (5th Cir. 1984). If not, what is the justification for offering less protection to appointed stewards?

Can union officials with access to confidential information be dismissed for their speech even if they are not in policy making roles? See, e.g., Hodge v. Drivers, Salesmen, Warehousemen, Milk Processors, Cannery, Dairy Employees & Helpers' Local Union 695, 707 F.2d 961 (7th Cir. 1983) (union secretary); Brewer v. General Drivers, Warehousemen & Helpers Local Union 89, 190 F. Supp. 2d 966 (W.D. Ken. 2002) (bookkeeper/office manager).

**3. "Purposeful and Deliberate Attempt . . . to Suppress Dissent"?** Note that the Court in *Finnegan* reserves deciding what limits Title I places on a "union's authority to utilize dismissal from union office as 'part of a purposeful and deliberate attempt . . . to suppress dissent within the union.'" Does this suggest that the dismissal of even policymaking appointed officials might be a violation of Title I if part of a broader scheme to eliminate dissent in the union? If so, what needs to be shown to establish such a scheme? See Carlton v. Local No. 7 United Food &

Commercial Workers Int'l Union, 43 Fed. Appx. 289 (10th Cir. 2002) (more than dismissal of political opponents and public criticisms required); Harvey v. Hollenback, 113 F.3d 639, 644 (6th Cir. 1997) ("plaintiffs face an uphill battle in proving such a scheme").

**4. Applicability of NLRA?** A union removes a steward for filing, at the request of other employees, what higher union officials consider to be unjustifiable grievances against the company; the union removes another steward for filing, again at another employee's request, charges against the union for breach of its duty of fair representation. Has the union violated the NLRA? Cf. NLRB v. Local 212, UAW, 690 F.2d 82 (6th Cir. 1982) (enforcing Board's finding of ULP; *Finnegan* is not relevant to NLRA). If a union removes a shop steward because he filed a charge against the union with the NLRB, the union may be liable as an employer for retaliation violative of §§8(a)(1), (3), and (4). See NLRB v. Aeronautical Industrial Dist. Lodge No. 91, 934 F.2d 1288 (2d Cir. 1991).

## B. "DUE PROCESS" IN UNION TRIBUNALS

### 1. "Otherwise Disciplined"

**Breininger v. Sheet Metal Workers' Local Union No. 6***
*493 U.S. 67 (1989)*

Brennan, J. . . .

#### III

The Court of Appeals rejected petitioner's LMRDA claim on the ground that petitioner had failed to show that he was "otherwise disciplined" within the meaning of LMRDA §§101(a)(5) and 609. . . . These provisions make it unlawful for a union to "fin[e], suspen[d], expe[l], or otherwise disciplin[e]" any of its members for exercising rights secured under the LMRDA. The Court of Appeals reasoned that because "[h]iring hall referrals . . . are available to nonmembers as well as to members," and the hiring hall was not an exclusive source of employment for sheet metal workers, petitioner did not suffer discrimination on the basis of rights he held by virtue of his *membership* in the union. We affirm the Court of Appeals' conclusion, although we do not adopt its reasoning. . . .

---

* [See also supra pages 975-980. — Eds.]

[W]e find that by using the phrase "otherwise discipline," Congress did not intend to include all acts that deterred the exercise of rights protected under the LMRDA, but rather meant instead to denote only punishment authorized by the union as a collective entity to enforce its rules. . . .

Our construction of the statute is buttressed by its structure. First, the specifically enumerated types of discipline — fine, expulsion, and suspension — imply some sort of established disciplinary process rather than ad hoc retaliation by individual union officers. Second, §101(a)(5) includes procedural protections — "written specific charges" served before discipline is imposed, "a reasonable time" in which to prepare a defense, and a "full and fair hearing" — that would not apply to instances of unofficial, sub rosa discrimination. These protections contemplate imposition of discipline through the type of procedure we encountered in Boilermakers v. Hardeman, 401 U.S. 233, 236-237 (1971) (expulsion after trial before union committee, with subsequent internal union review). The fact that §101(a)(5) does not prohibit union discipline altogether, but rather seeks to provide "safeguards against improper disciplinary action," indicates that "discipline" refers to punishment that a union can impose by virtue of its own authority over its members. A hiring hall could hardly be expected to provide a hearing before every decision *not* to refer an individual to a job. . . .

In the instant case, petitioner alleged only that the union business manager and business agent failed to refer him for employment because he supported one of their political rivals. He did not allege acts by the union amounting to "discipline" within the meaning of the statute. According to his complaint, he was the victim of the personal vendettas of two union officers. The opprobrium of the union *as an entity*, however, was not visited upon petitioner. He was not punished by any tribunal, nor was he the subject of any proceedings convened by respondent. In sum, petitioner has not alleged a violation of §§101(a)(5) and 609, and the Court of Appeals correctly dismissed his claim under the LMRDA.

Justice Stevens, with whom Justice Scalia joins, concurring in part and dissenting in part. . . .

The Court states that the discriminatory use of the hiring hall to punish petitioner does not constitute discipline because it is not an "established disciplinary process" or imposed by "any tribunal" or as the result of "any proceeding." But, as Congress was well aware, discipline can be imposed informally as well as formally and pursuant to unwritten practices similar to those petitioner has alleged as well as to a formal established policy. The language and structure of the Act do not evince any intention to restrict its coverage to sanctions that are imposed by tribunals or as the result of proceedings. That Congress specified detailed procedures to be followed in disciplinary proceedings does not mean that no procedures need be followed when discipline is imposed without any proceeding whatsoever. . . . By holding that the informally imposed sanctions alleged here are not covered by the LMRDA, the Court ironically deprives union members of the protection of the Act's procedural safeguards at a time when they are most needed — when the union or its officers act so secretly and so informally that the member receives no advance notice, no opportunity to be heard, and no explanation for the union's action.

## *NOTES AND QUESTIONS*

**1. Why No "Discipline"?** Why does the Court find that the union officials' failure to refer Breininger for employment was not "discipline" within the meaning of the statute? Because the officials did not initiate some disciplinary process? Because the union did not make a formal decision to not refer him?

On which side of the line drawn in *Breininger* do the following actions by union officials fall? (a) An employee is denied readmission to union membership because of an unwritten union rule preventing the reinstatement of membership for 12 months after a resignation; (b) An employee is denied a pension account because of union officials' failure to credit him for all his years of service; (c) An employee is maliciously accused by union officials of violent behavior toward fellow employees. See Wall v. Construction & General Laborers' Union, Local 230, 175 L.R.R.M. 2900 (Conn. 2004).

**2. "Infringement" vs. "Discipline."** Does *Breininger* limit only the reach of the procedural protections imposed by §101(a)(5), or does it also limit the substantive rights established in §101(a)? Section 102 of the LMRDA authorizes suits alleging that a member's Title I rights have been "infringed." Does *Breininger* limit the meaning of "infringement" as well as that of "discipline" so that §102 must be read coextensively with §101(a)(5)? Doing so would permit union officials to punish members for the exercise of their Title I rights as long as the sanction does not involve formal union discipline. For the general view that *Breininger* does not have this effect, see Guidry v. International Union of Operating Engineers, Local 406, 907 F.2d 1491, 1493 (5th Cir. 1990): "A litigant may successfully seek redress under section 102 for an infringement of [equal rights under §101(a)(1) and the right to free speech under §101(a)(2)] even if no unlawful 'discipline' is shown."

**3. Preemption of State Law Remedies?** Could Breininger have brought an action against the union or its officers pursuant to state law? Section 103 of the LMRDA preserves state law remedies from preemption by the LMRDA. Does the availability of a federal claim for breach of the duty of fair representation, however, preclude any type of action based on state law? See supra, pages 883-894. What is the practical significance of the Court's sustaining the fair representation claim while rejecting the LMRDA claim?

## 2. "A Full and Fair Hearing"

### International Brotherhood of Boilermakers v. Hardeman
*401 U.S. 233 (1971)*

Brennan, J. . . .

. . . Respondent, George Hardeman, is a boilermaker. He was [in October 1960] a member of petitioner's Local Lodge 112. On October 3, he went to the union hiring hall to see Herman Wise, business manager of the Local Lodge and the official responsible for referring workmen for jobs. Hardeman had talked to a friend of his, an employer who had promised to ask for him by name for a job in the vicinity. He sought assurance from Wise that he would be referred for the job. When Wise refused to make a definite commitment, Hardeman threatened violence if no work was forthcoming in the next few days.

On October 4, Hardeman returned to the hiring hall and waited for a referral. None was forthcoming. The next day, in his words, he "went to the hall . . . and waited from the time the hall opened until we had the trouble. . . ." When Wise came out of his office to go to a local jobsite, . . . Hardeman handed him a copy of a telegram asking for Hardeman by name. As Wise was reading the telegram, Hardeman began punching him in the face.

Hardeman was tried for this conduct on charges of creating dissension and working against the interest and harmony of the Local Lodge, and threatening and using force to restrain an officer of the Local Lodge from properly discharging the duties of his office. The trial committee found him "guilty as charged," and the Local Lodge sustained the finding and voted his expulsion for an indefinite period. International union review of this action, instituted by Hardeman, modified neither the verdict nor the penalty. Five years later, Hardeman brought this suit alleging that petitioner violated §101(a)(5) by denying him a full and fair hearing in the union disciplinary proceedings. . . .

II

. . . [Hardeman] was charged with violation of Art. XIII, §1, of the Subordinate Lodge Constitution, which forbids attempting to create dissension or working against the interest and harmony of the union, and carries a penalty of expulsion. He was also charged with violation of Art. XII, §1, of the Subordinate Lodge By-Laws, which forbids the threat or use of force against any officer of the union in order to prevent him from properly discharging the duties of his office; violation may be punished "as warranted by the offense." Hardeman's conviction on both charges was upheld in internal union procedures for review.

The trial judge instructed the jury that "whether or not [respondent] was rightfully or wrongfully discharged or expelled is a pure question of law for me to determine." He assumed, but did not decide, that the transcript of the union disciplinary hearing contained evidence adequate to support conviction of violating Art. XII. He held, however, that there was no evidence at all in the transcript of the union disciplinary proceedings to support the charge of violating Art. XIII . . . . Since the union tribunal had returned only a general verdict, and since one of the charges was thought to be supported by no evidence whatsoever, the trial judge held that Hardeman had been deprived of the full and fair hearing guaranteed by §101(a)(5). The Court of Appeals affirmed. . . .

We find nothing in either the language or the legislative history of §101(a)(5) that could justify . . . a substitution of judicial for union authority to interpret the union's regulations in order to determine the scope of offenses warranting discipline of union members. . . .

We think that this is sufficient to indicate that §101(a)(5) was not intended to authorize courts to determine the scope of offenses for which a union may discipline its members.[11] And if a union may discipline its members for offenses not proscribed by written rules at all, it is surely a futile exercise for a court to construe the written rules in order to determine whether particular conduct falls within or without their scope.

Of course, §101(a)(5)(A) requires that a member subject to discipline be "served with written specific charges." These charges must be, in Senator McClellan's words, "specific enough to inform the accused member of the offense that he had allegedly committed." Where, as here, the union's charges make reference to specific written provisions, §101(a)(5)(A) obviously empowers the federal courts to examine those provisions and determine whether the union member had been misled or otherwise prejudiced in the presentation of his defense. But it gives courts no warrant to scrutinize the union regulations in order to determine whether particular conduct may be punished at all.

---

11. State law, in many circumstances, may go further. See Summers, The Law of Union Discipline: What the Courts Do in Fact, 70 Yale L.J. 175 (1960). But Congress, which preserved state law remedies by §103 of the LMRDA, 29 U.S.C. §413, was well aware that even the broad language of Senator McClellan's original proposal was more limited in scope than much state law. See 105 Cong. Rec. 6481-6489.

Respondent does not suggest, and cannot discern, any possibility of prejudice in the present case. Although the notice of charges with which he was served does not appear as such in the record, the transcript of the union hearing indicates that the notice did not confine itself to a mere statement of citation of the written regulations that Hardeman was said to have violated: the notice appears to have contained a detailed statement of the facts relating to the fight that formed the basis for the disciplinary action. Section 101(a)(5) requires no more.

### III

There remains only the question whether the evidence in the union disciplinary proceedings was sufficient to support the finding of guilt. Section 101(a)(5)(C) of the LMRDA guarantees union members a "full and fair" disciplinary hearing, and the parties and the lower federal courts are in full agreement that this guarantee requires the charging party to provide some evidence at the disciplinary hearing to support the charges made. This is the proper standard of judicial review. We have repeatedly held that conviction on charges unsupported by any evidence is a denial of due process, Thompson v. Louisville, 362 U.S. 199, 206 (1960); . . . ; and . . . §101(a)(5)(C) may fairly be said to import a similar requirement into union disciplinary proceedings. Senator Kuchel, who first introduced the provision, characterized it on the Senate floor as requiring the "usual reasonable constitutional basis" for disciplinary action, 105 Cong. Rec. 6720, and any lesser standard would make useless §101(a)(5)(A)'s requirement of written specific charges. A stricter standard, on the other hand, would be inconsistent with the apparent congressional intent to allow unions to govern their own affairs, and would require courts to judge the credibility of witnesses on the basis of what would be at best a cold record.

Applying this standard to the present case, we think there is no question that the charges were adequately supported. Respondent was charged with having attacked Wise without warning, and with continuing to beat him for some time. Wise so testified at the disciplinary hearing, and his testimony was fully corroborated by one other witness to the altercation. Even Hardeman, although he claimed he was thereafter held and beaten, admitted having struck the first blow. . . . [T]here is no question but that the charges were supported by "some evidence."

## *NOTES AND QUESTIONS*

**1. Principled Nonintervention?** Does the limited judicial review prescribed in *Hardeman* give adequate weight to the limitations of union adjudicatory processes? The impact of *Hardeman* on the willingness of lower courts to engage in procedural review of union discipline, absent evidence of "built-in bias," is surveyed in Risa L. Lieberwitz, Due Process and the LMRDA: An Analysis of Democratic Rights in the Union and the Workplace, 29 B.C. L. Rev. 21, 45 (1987).

**2. Elements of a Full and Fair Hearing?** Section 101(a)(5) specifies that members subject to discipline must be served in writing with specific charges and be given a reasonable time to prepare a defense. What other elements are necessary for a hearing to be "full and fair"? Presumably the member must have an opportunity to present evidence and to confront his or her accusers. Does the member have a right to outside counsel if the union constitution bars outside representation? See, e.g., Cornelio v. Metropolitan Dist. Council of Philadelphia, United Bhd. of Carpenters & Joiners of Am., 243 F. Supp. 126 (E.D. Pa. 1965), aff'd per curiam, 358 F.2d 728 (3d Cir. 1966).

**3. Public Review Boards.** Some unions, notably the United Auto Workers, have established "public review boards," composed of outsiders, such as university personnel, arbitrators, and clergy members, to serve as a final appellate body with respect to union disciplinary decisions. See Walter E. Oberer (the first director of the UAW Board), Voluntary Impartial Review of Labor: Some Reflections, 58 Mich. L. Rev. 55 (1959); George W. Brooks, Impartial Public Review of Internal Union Disputes: Experiment in Democratic Self-Discipline, 22 Ohio St. L.J. 64 (1961). Present members of the Public Review Board are Interim Provost Harry C. Katz (Cornell University) and Professors Janice R. Bellace (Univ. of Pennsylvania Wharton School), James J. Brudney (Fordham Univ. Law) and Maria L. Ontiveros (Univ. of San Francisco Law).

## C. ELECTIONS, REFERENDA, AND PARTICIPATORY INTERESTS

### *Note: The Enforcement Scheme of Title IV of the LMRDA*

Unlike the private-action remedies provided in Titles I and V of the LMRDA, enforcement of Title IV is vested exclusively with the Secretary of Labor. Section 401(c) creates only a narrow exception to the administrative enforcement scheme, allowing direct suits by candidates to compel union compliance with reasonable requests for distribution of campaign literature. The public justification given by the LMRDA's sponsors for the absence of a private right of action in Title IV was to minimize unwarranted judicial interference with internal union affairs.

Under §402 a union member challenging the results of an election must first invoke his internal union remedies and then file a complaint with the Secretary. The Secretary "shall investigate the complaint and, if he finds probable cause to believe that a violation of this title has occurred, he shall, within sixty days after the filing of such a complaint," bring a civil action to set aside the election. Section 402(c) instructs the district court to set aside the election if it finds on a preponderance of the evidence that a Title IV violation "may have affected the outcome of an election."

**Exhaustion and the Scope of Title IV Actions.** In Hodgson v. Local 6799, United Steelworkers, 403 U.S. 333 (1971), an unsuccessful candidate for local union president challenged through the union's internal procedures the incumbent's use of union facilities to prepare campaign material, but his subsequent complaint to the Secretary also alleged that the union's rule conditioning eligibility for office on attendance at one-half of the local's meetings constituted an additional violation of §401(g). The Secretary brought suit on both grounds, but the Supreme Court held that the Secretary could sue only for violations raised during internal union appeals: "To accept [the Secretary's contention] that a union member need not protest this violation to his union before complaining to the Secretary would be needlessly to weaken union self-government." Id. at 340. The dissenting opinions of Justices Brennan and White urged that the exhaustion requirement should apply only to grounds for setting aside an election and not to the terms governing a new election, which must conform to Title IV as well as to the union's constitution and by-laws. Their position was embraced later by the Court in Trbovich v. United Mine Workers, 404 U.S. 528, 537 n.8 (1972).

In Wirtz v. Local 125, Laborers Int'l Union, 389 U.S. 477 (1968), a union member protested that a local union had violated §401(e) by paying the per capita dues of selected delinquent members and then permitting them to vote in a run-off election. The Secretary was permitted to challenge the general election as well as the run-off, even though the internal union complaint made reference only to the run-off. The controlling consideration for the Court was that the member's protest had given the union fair notice that the earlier election had the same unlawful taint as the run-off.

**Limits on the Secretary's Discretionary Authority.** Although the Secretary of Labor has considerable enforcement discretion under Title IV, the Supreme Court in a pair of rulings recognized a few qualifying principles. In *Trbovich v. United Mine Workers*, supra, the Court held that a union member whose complaint to the Secretary initiated the Secretary's Title IV challenge to an election had a right to intervene in that action. The Court noted that Congress lodged Title IV challenges within the Secretary's discretion in order (1) to screen out frivolous claims and (2) to consolidate in one action all meritorious claims challenging a single election. However, once the Secretary decides to bring a Title IV action, those screening and consolidation objectives have been served, and there is no reason to believe that Congress intended to foreclose participation by union members in the litigation. Nevertheless, such intervention is to be limited to the presentation of evidence and argument in support of the grounds for setting aside the election identified in the Secretary's complaint.

In Dunlop v. Bachowski, 421 U.S. 560 (1975), the Court conceded that the Secretary has substantial leeway in determining both the probability that a Title IV violation affected an election's outcome and the probability of success of any litigation, but held that the Secretary's exercise of discretion not to sue is subject to limited judicial review. The Court ruled (1) that the Secretary must furnish the complainant and the court with a statement of the grounds for the Secretary's refusal to sue under §402(b) and the essential facts and inferences upon which the decision was based; and (2) that a refusal to sue is subject to the narrow "arbitrary and capricious" standard of §706(2)(A) of the Administrative Procedure Act. The Court emphasized that judicial review should normally be confined to examining the statement of reasons and should not extend to the factual basis of the Secretary's findings as to the existence of violations or their impact on the election. Moreover, it left open the authority of the district court to order the Secretary to sue if his refusal was deemed "arbitrary." For a decision finding the Secretary's statement of reasons insufficient under *Bachowski,* see Harrington v. Chao, 280 F.3d 50 (1st Cir. 2002). See generally Note, *Dunlop v. Bachowski* and the Limits of Judicial Review Under Title IV of the LMRDA: A Proposal for Administrative Reform, 86 Yale L.J. 885 (1977).

## 1. Eligibility Requirements

### Local 3489, United Steelworkers of America v. Usery
*429 U.S. 305 (1977)*

Brennan, J.

The Secretary of Labor brought this action in the District Court for the Southern District of Indiana under §402(b) of the LMRDA, to invalidate the 1970 election of officers of Local 3489, United Steelworkers of America. The Secretary alleged that a provision of the Steelworkers' International constitution, binding on the Local, that limits eligibility for local union office to members who have attended at least one-half of the regular meetings of the Local for three years previous to the election (unless prevented by union activities or working hours), violated §401(e). . . . The District Court dismissed the complaint, finding no violation of the Act. The [Seventh Circuit] reversed. . . .

## I

At the time of the challenged election, there were approximately 660 members in good standing of Local 3489. The Court of Appeals found that 96.5% of these members were ineligible to hold office, because of failure to satisfy the meeting-attendance rule. Of the 23 eligible members, nine were incumbent union officers. The Secretary argues, and the Court of Appeals held, that the failure of 96.5% of the local members to satisfy the meeting-attendance requirement, and the rule's effect of requiring potential insurgent candidates to plan their candidacies as early as 18 months in advance of the election when the reasons for their opposition might not have yet emerged,[5] established that the requirement has a substantial anti-democratic effect on local union elections. Petitioners argue that the rule is reasonable because it serves valid union purposes, imposes no very burdensome obligation on the members, and has not proved to be a device that entrenches a particular clique of incumbent officers in the local.

## II

The opinions in three cases decided in 1968 have identified the considerations pertinent to the determination whether the attendance rule violates §401(e). Wirtz v. Hotel Employees, 391 U.S. 492; Wirtz v. Bottle Blowers Assn., 389 U.S. 463; Wirtz v. Laborers' Union, 389 U.S. 477.

. . . The injunction in §401(e) that "every member in good standing shall be eligible to be a candidate and to hold office" is made expressly "subject to . . . reasonable qualifications uniformly imposed." But "Congress plainly did not intend that the authorization . . . of 'reasonable qualifications' . . . should be given a broad reach. . . ." The basic objective of Title IV of the LMRDA is to guarantee "free and democratic" union elections modeled on "political elections in this country" where "the assumption is that voters will exercise common sense and judgment in casting their ballots." 391 U.S., at 504. Thus, Title IV is not designed merely to protect the right of a union member to run for a particular office in a particular election. "Congress emphatically asserted a vital public interest in assuring free and democratic union elections that transcends the

5. Regular meetings were held on a monthly basis. Thus, in order to attend half of the meetings in a three-year period, a previously inactive member desiring to run for office would have to begin attending 18 months before the election.

narrower interest of the complaining union member." *Wirtz v. Bottle Blowers Assn.*, supra, at 475; *Wirtz v. Laborers' Union*, supra, at 483. The goal was to "protect the rights of rank-and-file members to participate fully in the operation of their union through processes of democratic self-government, and, through the election process, to keep the union leadership responsive to the membership." *Wirtz v. Hotel Employees*, supra, at 497.

Whether a particular qualification is "reasonable" [under] §401(e) must therefore "be measured in terms of its consistency with the Act's command to unions to conduct 'free and democratic' union elections." 391 U.S., at 499. Congress was not concerned only with corrupt union leadership. Congress chose the goal of "free and democratic" union elections as a preventive measure "to curb the possibility of abuse by benevolent as well as malevolent entrenched leadership." Id., at 503. *Hotel Employees* expressly held that that check was seriously impaired by candidacy qualifications which substantially deplete the ranks of those who might run in opposition to incumbents, and therefore held invalid the candidacy limitation there involved that restricted candidacies for certain positions to members who had previously held union office. "Plainly, given the objective of Title IV, a candidacy limitation which renders 93% of union members ineligible for office can hardly be a 'reasonable qualification.'" Id., at 502.

## III

. . . [W]e conclude that here, too, the antidemocratic effects of the meeting-attendance rule outweigh the interests urged in its support. Like the bylaw in *Hotel Employees*, an attendance requirement that results in the exclusion of 96.5% of the members from candidacy for union office hardly seems to be a "reasonable qualification" consistent with the goal of free and democratic elections. . . .

Petitioners argue, however, that the bylaw held violative of §401(e) in *Hotel Employees* differs significantly from the attendance rule here. Under the *Hotel Employees* bylaw no member could assure by his own efforts that he would be eligible for union office, since others controlled the criterion for eligibility. Here, on the other hand, a member can assure himself of eligibility for candidacy by attending some 18 brief meetings over a three-year period. In other words, the union would have its rule treated not as excluding a category of member from eligibility, but simply as mandating a procedure to be followed by any member who wishes to be a candidate.

Even examined from this perspective, however, the rule has a restrictive effect on union democracy. In the absence of a permanent "opposition party" within the union, opposition to the incumbent leadership is likely to emerge in response to particular issues at different times, and member interest in changing union leadership is therefore likely to be at its highest only shortly before elections. Thus it is probable that to require that a member decide upon a potential candidacy at least 18 months in advance of an election when no issues exist to prompt that decision may not foster but discourage candidacies and to that extent impair the general membership's freedom to oust incumbents in favor of new leadership.

Nor are we persuaded by petitioners' argument that the Secretary has failed to show an antidemocratic effect because he has not shown that the incumbent leaders of the union became "entrenched" in their offices as a consequence of the operation of the attendance rule. The reasons for leaderships becoming entrenched are difficult to isolate. The election of the same officers year after year may be a signal that antidemocratic election rules have prevented an effective challenge to the regime, or might well signal only that the members are satisfied with their stewardship; if elections are uncontested, opposition factions may have been denied access to the ballot, or competing interests may have compromised differences before the election to maintain a front of unity. Conversely, turnover in offices may result from an open political process, or from a competition limited to candidates who offer no real opposition to an entrenched establishment. But Congress did not saddle the courts with the duty to search out and remove improperly entrenched union leaderships. Rather, Congress chose to guarantee union democracy by regulating not the results of a union's electoral procedure but the procedure itself. . . .

Petitioners next argue that the rule is reasonable within §401(e) because it encourages attendance at union meetings, and assures more qualified officers by limiting election to those who have demonstrated an interest in union affairs, and are familiar with union problems. But the rule has plainly not served these goals. It has obviously done little to encourage attendance at meetings, which continue to attract only a handful of members.[8] . . .

As for assuring the election of knowledgeable and dedicated leaders, the election provisions of the LMRDA express a congressional determination that the best means to this end is to leave the choice of leaders to the membership in open democratic elections, unfettered by arbitrary exclusions. Pursuing this goal by excluding the bulk of the membership from eligibility for office, and thus limiting the possibility of dissident candidacies, runs directly counter to the basic premise of the statute. We therefore conclude that Congress, in guaranteeing every union member the opportunity to hold office, subject only to "reasonable qualifications," disabled unions from establishing eligibility qualifications as sharply restrictive of the openness of the union political process as is petitioners' attendance rule.

---

8. Attendance at Local 3489's meetings averages 47 out of approximately 660 members. There is no indication in the record that this total represents a significant increase over attendance before the institution of the challenged rule.

[The dissent of Justice Powell, joined by Justices Stewart and Rehnquist, is omitted.]

## *NOTES AND QUESTIONS*

**1. Facial Validity vs. Effect.** Is the following approach to eligibility requirements consistent with *Local 3489*? "It is not the facial reasonableness or unreasonableness of a requirement which determines its validity, but its antidemocratic effect." Brock v. International Org. of Masters, Mates & Pilots, 842 F.2d 70, 73 (4th Cir. 1988) (rejecting Secretary of Labor's challenge to requirement that candidates must be members in good standing for 24 months, without providing "grace" period). Is this approach required by *Local 3489*?

**2. Meeting-Attendance Requirement.** In Doyle v. Brock, 821 F.2d 778 (D.C. Cir. 1987), a divided panel of the D.C. Circuit overturned the Secretary of Labor's refusal to sue to enjoin a meeting-attendance requirement that candidates attend at least one-half of the monthly meetings in the prior year, a requirement that resulted in the disqualification of a high percentage of candidates. Judge Silberman, dissenting, argued that *Local 3489* did not create a per se rule. See id. at 787-789. The Labor Department's regulation adopted after *Doyle* states that an attendance requirement must be reasonable and that "reasonableness must be gauged in the light of all the circumstances of the particular case," including burden, excuse provisions, and impact. See 29 C.F.R. §452.38(a). In a footnote, the regulation also states that the exclusion of a "large portion of members" alone may render an attendance requirement unreasonable. Id. at n.25. Citing the Secretary's reluctance to embrace a flat-percentage test for identifying unreasonable attendance rules, the First Circuit in Herman v. Springfield, Mass. Area, Local 497, 201 F.3d 1 (1st Cir. 2000) (per Judge Boudin), rejected the agency's challenge to a rule that disqualified 96 percent of the membership by requiring attendance at three meetings in the prior 12-month period. Compare Judge Posner's opinion in Herman v. Local 1011, United Steelworkers of America, 207 F.3d 924, 927-928 (7th Cir. 2000) ("Requiring attendance at eight meetings in two years imposes a burden because it compels the prospective candidate not only to sacrifice what may be scarce free time . . . but also, if he is disinclined to attend meetings for any reason other than to be able to run for union office, to make up his mind whether to run many months before the election.").

If substantial disqualification of members alone condemns an attendance requirement, can any such requirement stand given the generally sparse attendance at union meetings? Should a union's ability to ensure the minimal sophistication of its leadership thus be frustrated? On the other hand, if attendance is a good proxy for familiarity with union affairs, can't incumbents argue to the membership that they should not vote for candidates with poor attendance records? If the members nevertheless vote against the incumbents, aren't they saying something about the quality of the union's leadership and the futility of attending meetings?

**3. Competency Requirement.** The Laborers union has a rule that a candidate for local office "shall be literate and otherwise competent to perform the duties for which he is a candidate." At the behest of a candidate disqualified under this rule, the Secretary of Labor brought an action claiming a violation of §401(e) because of the vague, subjective quality of the competency requirement; competency, in the Secretary's view, should be judged by the membership. Does the rule violate §401(e)? Does the answer depend on whether the rule results in the disqualification of a substantial portion of the membership? See Donovan v. Local Union No. 120, Laborers Int'l Union, 683 F.2d 1095 (7th Cir. 1982).

**4. Continuous Employment in the Craft Requirement.** Can a union limit eligibility for union office to members who have been continuously employed in the craft for 24 months? If valid, does the rule become problematic if the union executive board retains discretion to grant leaves of absence? See Brock v. Local 630 of the International Bhd. of Teamsters, 662 F. Supp. 118 (C.D. Cal. 1987). Can a union apply such a rule in the case of a member laid off for lack of work who wishes to continue dues payments so that she remains a member in good standing? See Reich v. Teamsters Local 30, 6 F.3d 978 (3d Cir. 1993) (rejecting Secretary of Labor's challenge).

**5. Potential Conflicts of Interest.** Is §401(e) violated by a union constitutional provision rendering any member ineligible for union office for two years after applying for a management position, whether or not successfully? Compare Martin v. Branch 419, National Ass'n of Letter Carriers, 965 F.2d 61 (6th Cir. 1992) (no), with McLaughlin v. American Postal Workers Union, Miami Area Local, 680 F. Supp. 1519 (S.D. Fla. 1988) (yes). Would the rule pass muster if limited to union members who previously obtained management positions and later returned to the status of nonsupervisory worker?

**6. "May Have Affected the Outcome"?** Section 402(c)(2) of the LMRDA requires finding that any violation of §401 "may have affected the outcome of an election" before a court may void the results and order a new election. In Wirtz v. Hotel, Motel & Club Employees Union, Local 6, 391 U.S. 492 (1968), the Court considered the effect of §401(c)(2) on elections involving by-laws that restrict eligibility to a small percentage of members. The district court, in finding the outcome of the election "not affected" by the violation of §401, had relied on these factors: (a) the insurgents' poor electoral showing; (b) the absence of evidence that any ineligible nominee had been a proven vote-getter; (c) the lack of a substantial issue or grievance against the incumbents; and (d) the overwhelming advantage enjoyed by the "Administration Party" because of their full slate. Rejecting the lower court's reasoning, the Court suggested that in vote-tampering cases §401(c)(2) ordinarily should not result in invalidation of the election when the margin of victory substantially exceeds the number of disputed ballots. However, union rules or practices that work a wholesale exclusion from the ballot could support a finding that the election outcome "may have [been] affected" absent "tangible evidence against [that] reasonable possibility." Id. at 507.

**7. Reasonable Accommodation?** In Donovan v. Air Transport Dist. Lodge 146, IAM, 754 F.2d 621 (5th Cir. 1985), the court held that (1) unions must either accommodate members whose work schedules prevent their attending and participating fully in nomination meetings or assert some valid reason for nonaccommodation, and (2) the Secretary had authority to invalidate not only the challenged election but also other elections tainted by the challenged procedure, regardless of the complainant's entitlement to vote in other elections.

**8. Additional Procedural Requirements.** On the union's duty to keep a reasonably up-to-date list of members receiving election notices, see Reich v. Machinists Dist. Lodge 720, 11 F.3d 1496 (9th Cir. 1993), and to give timely notice of voting balloting instructions, see Dole v. Local Union 317, 711 F. Supp. 577 (N.D. Ala. 1989).

**9. Affirmative Action.** A predominantly white union with approximately 50,000 members, consisting primarily of public school teachers (but covered by the LMRDA), amended its constitution by majority vote so as to guarantee 8 percent of the seats in its "Representative Assembly" (numbering approximately 600) to members of four minority groups— blacks, Asians, Hispanics, and American Indians. If the regular election procedures do not place those minorities in 8 percent of the assembly seats, the amendment directs the board of directors to appoint additional minority members to reach that goal. The amendment also increases the board of directors from 50 to 54, reserving the four new places for members of the same minority groups and providing that those places are to be in addition to those won by minorities through the regular procedures.

The Secretary of Labor sues for an injunction against the application of this amendment in an upcoming election, urging that it does not embody "reasonable qualifications uniformly imposed" under §401(e), and that it denies members the right to vote for candidates of their choice. How should the court rule? Would it be material if there were evidence that the union had in the past discriminated against members of the minority groups involved or that the proportion of those groups who were union members or public school teachers in the region involved was greater than 8 percent? Compare Donovan v. Illinois Education Ass'n, 667 F.2d 638 (7th Cir. 1982) (reversing the court below and invalidating similar by-laws), with United Steelworkers v. Weber, 443 U.S. 193 (1979).

## 2. Overlap Between Titles I and IV of the LMRDA

**Calhoon v. Harvey**
*379 U.S. 134 (1964)*

Black, J. . . .

The respondents, three members of District No. 1, National Marine Engineers' Beneficial Association, filed a complaint in Federal District Court against the union, its president and its secretary-treasurer, alleging that certain provisions of the union's bylaws and national constitution violated the Act in that they infringed "the right of members of defendant District No. 1, NMEBA, to nominate candidates in elections of defendant, . . . guaranteed to each member of defendant, and to each plaintiff, by §101(a)(1). . . ." It was alleged that §102 . . . gave the District Court jurisdiction [over] the controversy. The union bylaws complained of deprived a member of the right to nominate anyone for office but himself. The national constitution in turn provided that no member could be eligible for nomination or election to a full-time elective office unless he had been a member of the national union for five years and had served 180 days or more of seatime in each of two of the preceding three years on vessels covered by collective bargaining agreements with the national or its subsidiary bodies. . . . [R]espondents asked that the union be enjoined from preparing for or conducting any election until it revised its system of elections so as to afford each of its members a fair opportunity to nominate any persons "meeting fair and reasonable eligibility requirements for any or all offices to be filled by such election."

The union moved to dismiss the complaint on the grounds that (1) the court lacked jurisdiction over the subject matter, and (2) the complaint failed to state a claim upon which relief could be granted. The District Court dismissed for want of "jurisdiction," holding that the alleged conduct of the union, even if true, failed to show a denial of the equal rights of all members of the union to vote for or nominate candidates guaranteed by §101(a)(1) . . . so as to give the District Court jurisdiction of the controversy under §102. . . . The Court of Appeals reversed, holding that "the complaint alleged a violation of §101(a)(1) and that federal jurisdiction existed under §102." . . .

## I

Jurisdiction of the District Court under §102 . . . depends entirely upon whether this complaint showed a violation of rights guaranteed by §101(a)(1), for we disagree with the Court of Appeals' holding that jurisdiction under §102 can be upheld by reliance in whole or in part on allegations which in substance charge a breach of Title IV rights. An analysis and understanding of the meaning of §101(a)(1) and of the charges of the complaint are therefore essential to a determination of this issue. Respondents charge that the bylaws and constitutional provisions referred to above infringed their right guaranteed by §101(a)(1) to nominate candidates. The result of their allegations here, however, is an attempt to sweep into the ambit of their right to sue in federal court if they are denied an equal opportunity to nominate candidates under §101(a)(1), a right to sue if they are not allowed to nominate anyone they choose regardless of his eligibility and qualifications under union restrictions. But Title IV, not Title I, sets standards for eligibility and qualifications of candidates and officials and provides its own separate and different administrative and judicial procedure for challenging those standards. And the equal-rights language of §101(a)(1) would have to be stretched far beyond its normal meaning to hold that it guarantees members not just a right to "nominate candidates," but a right to nominate anyone, without regard to valid union rules. . . .

[Section 101(a)(1)] is no more than a command that members and classes of members shall not be discriminated against in their right to nominate and vote. And Congress carefully prescribed that even this right against discrimination is "subject to reasonable rules and regulations" by the union. The complaining union members here have not been discriminated against in any way and have been denied no privilege or right to vote or nominate which the union has granted to others. They have indeed taken full advantage of the uniform rule limiting nominations by nominating themselves for office. It is true that they were denied their request to be candidates, but that denial was not a discrimination against their right to nominate, since the same qualifications were required equally of all members. Whether the eligibility requirements set by the union's constitution and bylaws were reasonable and valid is a question separate and distinct from whether the right to nominate on an equal basis given by §101(a)(1) was violated. The District Court therefore was without jurisdiction to grant the relief requested here unless, as the Court of Appeals held, the "*combined* effect of the eligibility requirements and the restriction to self-nomination" is to be considered in determining whether §101(a)(1) has been violated.

## II

We hold that possible violations of Title IV of the Act regarding eligibility are not relevant in determining whether . . . a district court has jurisdiction under §102 of Title I. . . . Title IV sets up a statutory scheme governing the election of union officers, fixing the terms during which they hold office, requiring that elections be by secret ballot, regulating the handling of campaign literature, requiring a reasonable opportunity for the nomination of candidates, authorizing unions to fix "reasonable qualifications uniformly imposed" for candidates, and attempting to guarantee fair union elections in which all the members are allowed to participate. Section 402 . . . , as has been pointed out, sets up an exclusive method for protecting Title IV rights, by permitting an individual member to file a complaint with the Secretary of Labor challenging the validity of any election because of violations of Title IV. . . . It is apparent that Congress decided to utilize the special knowledge and discretion of the Secretary of Labor in order best to serve the public interest. Cf. San Diego Building Trades Council v. Garmon, 359 U.S. 236, 242. In so doing Congress, with one exception not here relevant, decided not to permit individuals to block or delay union elections by filing federal-court suits for violations of Title IV. Reliance on the discretion of the Secretary is in harmony with the general congressional policy to allow unions great latitude in resolving their own internal controversies, and, where that fails, to utilize the agencies of Government most familiar with union problems to aid in bringing about a settlement through discussion before resort to the courts. Without setting out the lengthy legislative history . . . , we are satisfied that the Act itself shows clearly by its structure and language that the disputes here, basically relating . . . to eligibility of candidates for office, fall squarely within Title IV . . . and are to be resolved by the administrative and judicial procedures set out in that Title.

Accordingly, the judgment of the Court of Appeals is reversed and that of the District Court is affirmed. . . .

Douglas, J. would affirm the judgment of the Court of Appeals for the reasons stated in its opinion as reported in 324 F.2d 486.

Stewart, J., whom Harlan, J. joins, concurring. . . .

After today, simply by framing its discriminatory rules in terms of eligibility, a union can immunize itself from preelection attack in a federal court even though it makes deep incursions on the equal right of its members to nominate, to vote, and to participate in the union's internal affairs. . . .

Nonetheless, the Court finds a "general congressional policy" to avoid judicial resolution of internal union disputes. That policy, the Court says, was designed to limit the power of individuals to block and delay elections by seeking injunctive relief. Such an appraisal might have been accurate before the addition of Title I, but it does not explain the emphasis on prompt judicial remedies there provided. In addition to the injunctive relief authorized by §102 and the saving provisions of §103, §101(a)(4) modifies the traditional requirement of exhausting internal remedies before resort to litigation. Even §403 is not conclusive on the elimination of preelection remedies. At the least, state-court actions may be brought in advance of an election to "enforce the constitution and bylaws." And as to federal courts, it is certainly arguable that recourse through the Secretary of Labor is the exclusive remedy only after the election has been held. By reading Title I rights so narrowly, and by construing Title IV to foreclose absolutely preelection litigation in the federal courts, the Court sharply reduces meaningful protection for many of the rights which Congress was so assiduous to create.[7] By so simplifying the tangled provisions of the Act, the Court renders it virtually impossible for the aggrieved union member to gain a hearing when it is most necessary—when there is still an opportunity to make the union's rules comport with the requirements of the Act.

My difference with the Court does not reach to the disposition of this particular case. Whether stated in terms of restrictions on the right to nominate, or in terms of limitations on eligibility for union office, I think the rules of a labor organization would operate illegally to curtail the members' equal right to nominate within the meaning of Title I only if those rules effectively distorted the basic democratic process. The line might be a shadowy one in some cases. But I think that in this case the respondents did not allege in their complaint nor demonstrate in their affidavits that this line was crossed. . . .

### Local No. 82, Furniture & Piano Moving Drivers v. Crowley
*467 U.S. 526 (1984)*

[While insurgents were seeking office, several members, including Crowley, were excluded from a meeting of the local (to nominate candidates for its executive board) because they could not produce a computerized receipt showing their dues payment. Another dispute concerned the office for which insurgent Lynch had been nominated. The insurgents claimed

7. The Court's reading of federal-court remedies available under Title I and Title IV is particularly restrictive because of the limited powers of the district judge once the balloting has occurred. Under §402(c), the court is confined to setting the election aside only if "the violation of §401 may have affected the outcome." For the aggrieved union member, this protection may be totally inadequate. The function of nominating a candidate is not always to gain the office. A faction may be vitally interested in appearing on the ballot merely to show that it is part of the political structure of the union. Under the Court's view, until such a faction approaches majority status, judicial relief in the federal courts will be absent. . . .

that he was a nominee for secretary-treasurer; but the incumbent secretary-treasurer, who was also presiding, declared himself the only nominee for that office and named Lynch as a nominee for president (as did the ballot). The local denied the protests of several members and distributed mail ballots (the traditional voting method), which were to be counted by December 13, 1980. On December 1, after the ballots had been distributed, the plaintiffs sued in a federal district court, alleging that the local and its officers, by the computerized receipts requirement, had violated (i) the plaintiffs' "equal rights . . . to nominate candidates [and] to attend membership meetings" under §101(a)(1), and (ii) their right to freedom of expression at union meetings under §101(a)(2). They also alleged that the defendants had violated §101(a)(1) by excluding Lynch as a nominee for secretary-treasurer. Under the district court's temporary restraining order of December 12, the ballots were to be sealed and delivered to the court. By that time, many if not most ballots had been returned and were to have been counted by the union the next day. Following hearings and negotiations, the court, invoking its jurisdiction under Title I, invalidated the ballots and selected outside arbitrators to conduct another election. The Secretary of Labor intervened on defendants' behalf in their appeal. Rejecting the argument that Title IV barred the relief granted below, the court of appeals affirmed. The Supreme Court reversed.]

BRENNAN, J. . . .

. . . This case requires . . . that we decide whether Title I remedies are available to aggrieved union members while a union election is being conducted.

It is useful to begin by noting what the plain language of the Act clearly establishes about the relationship between the remedies provided under Title I and Title IV. First, the exclusivity provision included in §403 of Title IV plainly bars Title I relief when an individual union member challenges the validity of an election that has already been completed.[16] Second, the full panoply of Title I rights are available to individual union members "prior to the conduct" of a union election. . . .

Even if the plain meaning of the "already conducted" language of §403 could be read not to preclude other remedies until the actual tabulation and certification of ballots has been completed, we would hesitate to find such an interpretation determinative. [S]uch an approach would ignore the

16. . . . The exclusivity provision of Title IV may not bar post-election relief for Title I claims or other actions that do not directly challenge the validity of an election already conducted. See, e.g., Ross v. Electrical Workers, 513 F.2d 840 (CA9 1975) (common law tort claim); Amalgamated Clothing Workers Rank and File Committee v. Amalgamated Clothing Workers, 473 F.2d 1303 (CA3 1973) (Title I claim).

limitation on judicial remedies . . . included in Title I, which allows a district court to award only "appropriate" relief. . . .

. . . [T]hroughout the Congressional discussions preceding enactment of both Title I and Title IV, Congress clearly indicated its intent to consolidate challenges to union elections with the Secretary of Labor, and to have the Secretary supervise any new elections necessitated by violations of the Act. This strongly suggests that, even when Title I violations are properly alleged and proven, Congress would not have considered a court order requiring and judicially supervising a new election to be "appropriate" relief under Title I. At the same time, there is nothing in the legislative history suggesting that Congress intended to foreclose all access to federal courts under Title I during an election, especially when a statutory violation could be corrected without any major delay or disruption to an ongoing election. We therefore conclude that whether a Title I suit may properly be maintained by individual union members during the course of a union election depends upon the nature of the relief sought by the Title I claimants.

. . . Although the enactment of Title I offered additional protection to union members, including . . . various statutory safeguards . . . during . . . a union election, there is no direct evidence . . . that Congress believed that enforcement of Title I would either require or allow courts to pre-empt the expertise of the Secretary and supervise their own elections. In the absence of such legislative history, and given the clear congressional preference expressed in Title IV for supervision of new elections by the Secretary of Labor, we are compelled to conclude that Congress did not consider court supervision of union elections to be an "appropriate" remedy for a Title I suit filed during . . . a union election.

That is not to say that a court has no jurisdiction over otherwise proper Title I claims that are filed during . . . a lengthy union election. The important congressional policies underlying enactment of Title I . . . likewise compel us to conclude that appropriate relief under Title I may be awarded by a court while an election is being conducted. Individual union members may properly allege violations of Title I that are easily remediable under that title without substantially delaying or invalidating an ongoing election. For example, union members might claim that they did not receive election ballots distributed by the union because of their opposition to the incumbent officers running for reelection. Assuming that such union members prove a statutory violation under Title I, a court might appropriately order the union to forward ballots to the claimants before completion of the election. To foreclose a court from ordering such Title I remedies during an election would not only be inefficient, but also would frustrate the purposes that Congress sought to serve by including Title I in the LMRDA. Indeed, eliminating all Title I relief in this context might preclude aggrieved union members from ever obtaining relief for statutory violations, since the more drastic remedies under Title IV are ultimately dependent upon a showing that a violation "may have affected the outcome" of the election. . . .

In sum, whether suits alleging violations of Title I . . . may properly be maintained during the course of a union election depends upon the appropriateness of the remedy required to eliminate the claimed statutory violation. If the remedy sought is invalidation of the election already being conducted with court supervision of a new election, then union members must utilize the remedies provided by Title IV. For less intrusive remedies sought during an election, however, a district court retains authority to order appropriate relief under Title I. . . .

. . . [T]h[e]proceedings [in this case] demonstrate why they are inconsistent with the policies underlying the LMRDA. For example, the temporary restraining order and preliminary injunction issued by the court delayed the union election that was originally scheduled for December 1980 for one full year. Among other consequences, this left the incumbent union officers in power beyond the scheduled expiration of their terms. Cf. §401(b) (officers shall be elected not less than once every three years). If the procedures under Title IV had been properly followed, the December 1980 election would have been presumed valid, see §402(a), and new officers would have replaced the incumbents. Moreover, the expertise of the Secretary in supervising elections was completely ignored. Not only did the court acting alone decide that a new election was required, but its order established procedures for that election and appointed an outside arbitrator to supervise their implementation. This action by the District Court directly interfered with the Secretary's exclusive responsibilities for supervising new elections, and was inconsistent with the basic objectives of the LMRDA enforcement scheme. . . .

[The dissenting opinion of Justice Stevens is omitted.]

## *NOTES AND QUESTIONS*

**1. Race to the Courthouse?** Under *Crowley*, does a dissident candidate's ability to vindicate his Title I rights depend on whether he or she can get to the courthouse in time to prevent an election from commencing? Or does *Crowley* actually obviate such a race by precluding any injunction that would delay or disrupt an election? Compare, e.g., Sickman v. Communications Workers of America, Local 13000, 162 L.R.R.M. 2935 (E.D. Pa. 1999) (granting injunction to place additional name on ballot because it would not disrupt election), with Conway v. Int'l Ass'n of Heat & Frost Insulators, 169 L.R.R.M. 3160, 2001 WL 1867408 (N.D. Ohio 2001) (denying injunction to place name on ballot because no longer practical). On the issues raised by *Calhoon*, and partially answered in *Crowley*, see Samuel Estreicher, Note, Pre-Election Remedies Under the Landrum-Griffin Act, 74 Colum. L. Rev. 1105 (1974).

**2. Candidacy Requirements Infringing Title I Free Speech Rights?** Driscoll, a union member, after exhausting his internal union remedies, filed a complaint with the Secretary of Labor pursuant to §402, charging that §401 was violated by the union's requirement that all candidates for union office execute a non-Communist affidavit, and asking for invalidation of that requirement in future elections. The Secretary declined to sue, whereupon Driscoll filed an action alleging, inter alia, violations of §101(a)(1), (2), and (5) of the LMRDA. The district court, relying on *Calhoon v. Harvey,* dismissed for want of jurisdiction under Title I over restrictions on eligibility for union office. Driscoll urged that *Calhoon* was not applicable because the affidavit requirement directly infringed his right to free speech protected by Title I.

In Driscoll v. International Union of Operating Engineers, Local 139, 484 F.2d 682 (7th Cir. 1973), the court of appeals rejected that contention. It held that plaintiff did not fall within the one exception to the "broad mandate of *Calhoon*" that the court was prepared to recognize: Title I jurisdiction would exist to protect what also appeared to be Title IV rights, when removal of a union official and a declaration of his future ineligibility were part of a deliberate attempt to suppress dissent in the context of long-standing factionalism, as in Schonfeld v. Penza, 477 F.2d 899 (2d Cir. 1973) (sustaining an injunction against disciplinary action and staying the election of a successor for the removed officer). For the Supreme Court's treatment of the approach in *Schonfeld,* see footnote 7 of *Sheet Metal Workers' International Ass'n v. Lynn,* supra page 996. See also note 3, supra page 998. Without citing *Schonfeld,* a divided panel of the Second Circuit appears to have rejected even this limited exception to the "mandate of *Calhoon.*" See Members for a Better Union v. Gus Bevona, 152 F.3d 58 (2d Cir. 1998) (despite finding that previous vote on constitutional amendments violated Title I rights and that there was a genuine threat of future violations, the district court lacked jurisdiction to prescribe the time, location, and procedure for a second vote). Did *Crowley,* in any event, foreclose the *Schonfeld* exception?

**3. Ballot Tampering.** Before ballots in a union election have been counted, one of the ballot boxes disappears for a few hours. After the box reappears and the ballots are about to be counted, dissidents allege an effective deprivation of their right to vote under §101(a)(1) and bring an action to restrain the counting of the ballots. Does the court have jurisdiction to hear the case after *Crowley*?

**4. Distribution of Campaign Literature.** Section 401(c) allows bona-fide candidates to sue directly in court to compel the union's compliance with "all reasonable requests" to distribute, at the candidates' expense, campaign literature on their behalf. In International Org. of Masters,

Mates & Pilots v. Brown, 498 U.S. 466 (1991), a dissident candidate sought early access (before the deadline for making nominations) to the union's membership mailing list. The union denied the request because it had not yet held its nominating convention and designated an agency for handling mailing requests. The Court (per Justice Stevens) affirmed an injunction ordering the union to turn over the mailing list. The unanimous opinion held that (1) the plaintiff was a "bona fide candidate for office" because he met the union's eligibility requirements even though his candidacy had not been certified by the union's postconvention meeting of a ballot committee, as required by the union's constitution, and (2) his request was "reasonable" within the meaning of §401(c) and thus prevailed even over an equally reasonable union rule curtailing the period during which campaign literature may be mailed. *Brown* did not expressly deal with whether the dissident candidate had a right under §401(c) to direct access to the membership list, although the Court did affirm a preliminary injunction that differed from the plaintiff's request by directing the union "to deliver the names and addresses of the Union members to a mailing service acceptable to the parties." Id. at 469. For a decision requiring only such indirect access, see McCafferty v. Local 254, Service Employees Int'l Union, 186 F.3d 52 (1st Cir. 1999). On whether attorneys' fees are available to candidates bringing §401(c) suits under the "common benefit" rationale of *Hall v. Cole*, supra page 990, see, e.g., Mims v. Teamsters Local No. 728, 821 F.2d 1568 (11th Cir. 1987).

**5. Incumbent's Use of Union Newspaper.** In Yablonski v. United Mine Workers, 305 F. Supp. 868 (D.D.C. 1969), after Jock Yablonski, a member of the UMW's executive board, announced his candidacy for the UMW's presidency, then occupied by Tony Boyle, the UMW's newspaper (the *Journal*), which the union regularly sent to its members, gave Boyle an unusual amount of favorable coverage, while not even mentioning Yablonski's activities. Yablonski sued the UMW in a federal district court, alleging a violation of LMRDA §§401(c) and 501, and requesting a temporary injunction directing the defendants to give Yablonski equal treatment in the future and to compensate for past inequality by devoting one-half of each of the next two issues to material that he supplied. The court found that the defendants had used the *Journal* as a campaign instrument for Boyle in violation of §401(c), and that the usual standards for injunctive relief had been satisfied. Nevertheless, the court denied the requested relief because such relief was not authorized by §401(c) and conflicted with the First Amendment. Furthermore, §401(g) is enforceable only by the Secretary of Labor in a §402 action and, indeed, §401(g) might be violated by granting the specific relief requested by the plaintiffs. The court, however, did enjoin the defendants from discriminatory use of the membership lists and, specifically, from using the *Journal* so as to advance Boyle's candidacy.

The course of the *Yablonski* litigation suggests the limitations of pre-election relief against incumbents' abuse of their position for electioneering purposes. The original complaint was filed August 26, 1969. The district court's opinion was handed down September 15, 1969; an appeal resulted in a remand for clarification, which the district court issued on November 4, just slightly more than one month before the December 9 election. See Yablonski v. United Mine Workers, 305 F. Supp. 876 (1969). That election, a much closer one than usual for the UMW, resulted in Yablonski's defeat by almost a two-to-one margin. The Secretary of Labor successfully sought the invalidation of the election, stressing the incumbents' exploitation of the *Journal.* See Hodgson v. Mine Workers, 344 F. Supp. 17 (D.D.C. 1972).

Yablonski, his wife, and his daughter were murdered after he had challenged the election through the union's internal procedures. In 1973, Boyle was linked to the conspiracy to kill the Yablonskis; he was subsequently convicted on three counts of first-degree murder. See Commonwealth v. Boyle, 498 Pa. 486, 447 A.2d 250 (1982). In part because of the events surrounding the Yablonski candidacy, the membership voted in a reform slate headed by Arnold Miller. See Paul F. Clark, The Miners' Fight for Democracy: Arnold Miller and the Reform of the United Mine Workers (1981).

The relief granted in Hodgson v. Mine Workers, 344 F. Supp. at 36, included the following:

> Commencing with the July 1, 1972 issue of the UMWA Journal up to and including the last issue prior to the supervised election, equal space for the presentation of news concerning, and the political views of, bona fide candidates will be made available in each issue under a format subject to the approval of the Secretary of Labor. Slates of candidates may combine their allotted space and present their views as a slate.

Is this relief compatible with the First Amendment? Cf. Miami Herald Publishing Co. v. Tornillo, 418 U.S. 241 (1974).

**6. Secretary of Labor's Preballoting Authority.** The investigatory authority conferred on the Secretary by LMRDA §601 extends to violations of Title IV, and his accompanying subpoena authority has been held not to depend on the filing of a complaint by a union member or a showing of probable cause. See Local 57, IUOE v. Wirtz, 346 F.2d 552 (1st Cir. 1965); Laurence H. Silberman & George B. Dreisen, The Secretary and the Law: Preballoting Investigations Under the Landrum-Griffin Act, 7 Ga. L. Rev. 1 (1972); Joseph L. Rauh, Jr., LMRDA—Enforce It or Repeal It, 5 Ga. L. Rev. 643 (1971).

**7. Title V.** On the overlap between Titles IV and V, see Peter J. Laughran, Contesting Misuse of Union Funds in Union Election

Challenges: Expanded Remedies Under Title V of the Labor-Management Reporting and Disclosure Act, 22 Colum. J.L. & Soc. Probs. 181 (1989). See also materials on Title V, infra pages 1041-1044.

**United Steelworkers of America v. Sadlowski**
*457 U.S. 102 (1982)*

MARSHALL, J. . . .

In this case, we confront the question whether §101(a)(2) of the Labor-Management Reporting and Disclosure Act of 1959 (LMRDA), 29 U.S.C. §411(a)(2), precludes the membership of a union from adopting a rule that prohibits candidates for union office from accepting campaign contributions from nonmembers. . . .

## I

### A

Petitioner United Steelworkers of America (USWA), a labor organization with 1,300,000 members, conducts elections for union president and other top union officers every four years. The elections for these officers are decided by referendum vote of the membership. In the 1977 election, which was hotly contested, two candidates ran for president: respondent Edward Sadlowski, Jr., the Director of USWA's largest District, and Lloyd McBride, another District Director. Both Sadlowski and McBride headed a slate of candidates for the other top union positions.

McBride was endorsed by the incumbent union leadership, and received substantial financial support from union officers and staff. Sadlowski, on the other hand, received much of his financial support from sources outside the union. During the campaign, the question whether candidates should accept contributions from persons who were not members of the union was vigorously debated. The McBride slate contended that outsider participation in USWA elections was dangerous for the union. McBride ultimately defeated Sadlowski by a fairly wide margin—57% to 43%. The other candidates on the McBride slate won by similar margins.

After the elections, union members continued to debate the question whether outsider participation in union campaigns was desirable. This debate was finally resolved in 1978, when USWA held its biennial Convention. The Convention, which consists of approximately 5,000 delegates elected by members of USWA's local unions, is USWA's highest governing body. At the 1978 Convention, several local unions submitted resolutions recommending amendment of the USWA Constitution to include an "outsider rule" prohibiting campaign contributions by nonmembers. The union's International Executive Board also recommended a ban on nonmember contributions. Acting on the basis of these recommendations, the Convention's Constitution Committee proposed to the Convention that it adopt an outsider rule. After a debate on the floor of the Convention, the delegates by a margin of roughly 10 to 1 voted to include such a rule in the Constitution.

The outsider rule, Article V, §27 of the USWA Constitution, provides in pertinent part:

> Sec. 27. No candidate (including a prospective candidate) for any position set forth in Article IV, Section 1, and supporter of a candidate may solicit or accept financial support, or any other direct or indirect support of any kind (except an individual's own volunteered personal time) from any non-member. (USWA Const. Art. V, §27.)

Section 27 confers authority upon the International Executive Board to adopt regulations necessary to implement the provision. It also creates a Campaign Contribution Administrative Committee, consisting of three "distinguished, impartial" nonmembers to administer and enforce the provision. Id. The Committee may order a candidate to cease and desist from conduct that breaches §27, and may declare a candidate disqualified. Its decisions are final and binding. . . .

In October 1979, Sadlowski and several other individuals filed suit against USWA in the United States District Court for the District of Columbia. [The district court granted the plaintiffs' motion for summary judgment and the court of appeals affirmed, relying on both §101(a)(2) of the LMRDA (the "freedom of speech and assembly" provision) and §101(a)(4) (the "right to sue" provision).]

### II . . .

#### A

At the outset, we address respondents' contention that this case can be resolved simply by reference to First Amendment law. Respondents claim that §101(a)(2) confers upon union members rights equivalent to the rights established by the First Amendment. They further argue that in the context of a political election, a rule that placed substantial restrictions on a candidate's freedom to receive campaign contributions would violate the First Amendment. Thus, a rule that substantially restricts contributions in union campaigns must violate §101(a)(2). We are not persuaded by this argument. In light of the legislative history, we do not believe that

§101(a)(2) should be read as incorporating the entire body of First Amendment law, so that the scope of protections afforded by the statute coincides with the protections afforded by the Constitution. . . . Rather, Congress' decision to include a proviso covering "reasonable" rules refutes that proposition. . . . Union rules, by contrast, are valid under §101(a)(2) so long as they are reasonable; they need not pass the stringent tests applied in the First Amendment context. . . .

To determine whether a union rule is valid under the statute, we first consider whether the rule interferes with an interest protected by the first section of §101(a)(2). If it does, we then determine whether the rule is "reasonable" and thus sheltered by the proviso to §101(a)(2). . . .

Applying this form of analysis here, we conclude that the outsider rule is valid. Although it may limit somewhat the ability of insurgent union members to wage an effective campaign, an interest deserving some protection under the statute, it is rationally related to the union's legitimate interest in reducing outsider interference with union affairs. . . .

An examination of the policies underlying the LMRDA indicates that the outsider rule may have some impact on interests that Congress intended to protect under §101(a)(2). . . .

The interest in fostering vigorous debate during election campaigns may be affected by the outsider rule. If candidates are not permitted to accept contributions from persons outside the union, their ability to criticize union policies and to mount effective challenges to union leadership may be weakened. Restrictions that limit access to funds may reduce the number of issues discussed, the attention that is devoted to each issue, and the size of the audience reached. . . .

Although the outsider rule does affect rights protected by the statute, as a practical matter the impact may not be substantial. Respondents, as well as the Court of Appeals, suggest that incumbents have a large advantage because they can rely on their union staff during election campaigns. Challengers cannot counter this power simply by seeking funds from union members; the rank-and-file cannot provide sufficient support. Thus, they must be permitted to seek funds from outsiders. In fact, however, the rank-and-file probably can provide support. The USWA is a very large union whose members earn sufficient income to make campaign contributions. Requiring candidates to rely solely on contributions from members will not unduly limit their ability to raise campaign funds. Uncontradicted record evidence discloses that challengers have been able to defeat incumbents or administration-backed candidates, despite the absence of financial support from nonmembers.

In addition, although there are undoubtedly advantages to incumbency, see Hall v. Cole, 412 U.S., at 13, 93 S. Ct., at 631, respondents and the Court of Appeals may overstate those advantages. Staff employees are forbidden by §401(g) of the LMRDA, 29 U.S.C. §481(g), and by internal USWA rules from campaigning on union time or from using union funds, facilities, or equipment for campaign purposes. Staff officers have [their own] contractual right to choose whether or not to participate in any USWA campaign without being subjected to discipline or reprisal for their decision. Indeed, USWA elections have frequently involved challenges to incumbents by members of the staff. Many of these challenges have been successful. . . .

Although the outsider rule may implicate rights protected by §101(a)(2), it serves a legitimate purpose that is clearly protected under the statute. The union adopted the rule because it wanted to ensure that nonmembers do not unduly influence union affairs. USWA feared that officers who received campaign contributions from nonmembers might be beholden to those individuals and might allow their decisions to be influenced by considerations other than the best interests of the union. The union wanted to ensure that the union leadership remained responsive to the membership. An examination of the policies underlying the LMRDA reveals that this is a legitimate purpose that Congress meant to protect.

Evidence that Congress regarded the desire to minimize outsider influence as a legitimate purpose is provided by the history to Title I. On the Senate floor, Senator McClellan argued that a bill of rights for union members was necessary because some unions had been "invaded" or "infiltrated" by outsiders who had no interest in the members but rather had seized control for their own purposes. 2 Leg. Hist. 1097-1100. . . . It is true that Senator McClellan was particularly concerned about infiltration of unions by racketeers. . . . However, his statements also indicate a more general desire to ensure that union members, and not outsiders, control the affairs of their union.

Indeed, specific provisions contained in Title IV provide support for our conclusion that the outsider rule serves a legitimate and protected purpose. Section 401(g), 29 U.S.C. §481(g), prohibits the use of employer as well as union funds in election campaigns. This ban reflects a desire to minimize the danger that employers will influence the outcome of union elections.

Finally, respondents contend that USWA could simply have required that candidates for union office reveal the sources of their funds. But a disclosure rule, by itself, would not have solved the problem. Candidates who received such funds might still be beholden to outsiders. A disclosure requirement ensures only that union members know about this possibility when they cast their votes. It does not eradicate the threat of outside influence. . . .

Justice WHITE, with whom THE CHIEF JUSTICE, Justice BRENNAN, and Justice BLACKMUN join, dissenting.

It goes without saying that running for office in a union with 1.3 million members spread throughout the United States and Canada requires a substantial war chest if the campaign is to be effective and to have any reasonable chance of succeeding. Attempting to unseat the incumbents of union office is a substantial undertaking. . . . [T]here is no permanent opposition party within the union. There is only a one-party system consisting of the union's incumbent officers and hired staff all controlled from the top down . . . . The union involved in this case has some 30 elected positions, its president appoints more than 1,500 office and field staff, and salaries and expenses for union personnel in 1978 totalled over $37 million.

Thus, in the best of circumstances, the role of the challenger is very difficult. And if one keeps in mind that Congress intended to give the challenger a fair chance even in a union controlled by unscrupulous leaders with an iron grip on the staff and a willingness to employ means both within and without the law, it is wholly unrealistic to confine the challenger to financial support garnered within the union.

## *NOTES AND QUESTIONS*

1. **Relevance of First Amendment and Government Analogy?** Should the Court have imposed First Amendment standards on the Steelworkers given the benefits conferred on the union by government regulation?

2. **The Advantages of Incumbency vs. "Outsider" Support?** Can an argument be made that unions must be open to outside influence because of the special advantages of incumbency in union office? Would the position of the *Sadlowski* majority or that of the dissenters better promote the ability of all members of the Steelworkers' constituency to influence union decision making?

3. **Employer-Funded Advocacy Groups.** The National Right to Work Legal Defense and Education Foundation is a tax-exempt, nonprofit organization that opposes "compulsory unionism." The Foundation has financed test cases brought by workers against labor unions in order to challenge the obligation to pay dues or the use of compelled dues for political activities. Many of the Foundation's contributors are either employers under contract with unions or competitors of such employers. A group of national labor unions sues in a federal district court for a declaratory judgment and an injunction, claiming that the Foundation is violating LMRDA §101(a)(4) by financing suits (other than as a party) brought by employees and union members against unions. Does the complaint state a claim? See United Auto Workers v. National Right to Work Legal Defense & Educ. Found., 781 F.2d 928 (D.C. Cir. 1986) (holding that §101(a)(4) does not extend to the Foundation's support of an individual employee's litigation against unions because the Foundation's litigation program is independent and not under the control of interested employers).

*Note: Referenda*

**Special Meetings of the Membership.** An arbitration board denied the grievances of plaintiffs, who had been discharged because they had breached a no-strike clause. Plaintiffs attacked the award, asserting newly discovered evidence of an arbitrator's bias, but the union's president refused to support their challenge. Although plaintiffs met the union constitution's requirements for a special meeting, the local's president refused to call one. Moreover, at the next regular meeting he denied plaintiffs permission to ask the membership for support of their claim. Plaintiffs sue in a federal district court, claiming that the president's refusals violated their rights under §101(a)(2). The union moves to dismiss, urging that the allegations do not state a federal claim. What result? Cf. Yanity v. Benware, 376 F.2d 197 (2d Cir. 1967).

Suppose a special meeting had been called but had been adjourned as soon as the plaintiffs had sought to raise the arbitration question. Would §§101(a)(1) or (a)(2) have been violated? Must the right to call meetings be enforced to give effect to those sections of the LMRDA? Can the provisions of the union constitution be a source of rights federally protected under §101 rather than only a potential limitation on such rights? If so, what result if the union constitution had not provided for special meetings? Does §101(a) at least require that the union call meetings in accordance with the union's own rules?

**Voting in Person.** In McGinnis v. Teamsters Local 710, 774 F.2d 196 (7th Cir. 1985), the court held that §101(a)(1) was violated by a local's by-law requiring its members to vote in person, in Chicago, on amendments to the local's "Constitution and By-Laws." The court, noting that from 25 to 40 percent of the members lived and worked more than 100 miles from Chicago, held that the union's grant of a right to vote must "be extended on an equal basis and in a meaningful manner." The local's "facially neutral" voting policy had a disparate impact on members living far from Chicago because of the significant expenses of their voting in Chicago. See Gurton v. Arons, 329 F.2d 371 (2d Cir. 1964).

### 3. Ratification Votes

**American Postal Workers Union, Headquarters Local 6885 v. American Postal Workers Union**
*665 F.2d 1096 (D.C. Cir. 1981)*

[The Postal Reorganization Act of 1970 (PRA), 39 U.S.C. §§101-5605, provides that the NLRA is applicable to postal labor relations, but only to the extent that it is consistent with the PRA. See id. at §1209(a). The American Postal Workers Union (APWU) was created in July 1971 by the merger of four national unions, each representing one craft in the Postal Service. Negotiations between the APWU and the U.S. Postal Service produced a "National Agreement" in 1971; the Agreement was not submitted to union members for approval. In 1972, the APWU constitution was amended to include Article XIX, which required "[a]pproval [of future contracts] by a majority of the union members voting who are covered by the proposed agreement." At that time, the APWU represented only employees covered by the National Agreement. Beginning in 1973, the APWU was selected as the bargaining representative for some smaller "non-mail processing units" in the Postal Service. The APWU interpreted Article XIX as applying only to national units; consequently, collective bargaining agreements negotiated for the "non-mail processing units" were not subject to ratification votes.

The APWU was certified in 1977 as the representative of the Postal Service's research and development employees in Rockville, Md. In 1978, as both sides prepared for fact-finding after negotiations had been suspended, the APWU and the Postal Service reached a tentative agreement. A local union (Local 6885) and its members sued in a federal district court, alleging that by not submitting the proposed agreement to the local's members for ratification (and by related actions), the APWU (a) breached its promise to the local and violated Article XIX of its constitution, (b) violated LMRDA §101(a)(1), and (c) breached both its duty of fair representation and its fiduciary obligation. The trial court's summary judgment dismissed all claims against the union defendants. Plaintiffs appealed, and nonunion members of the bargaining unit intervened, adopting those of plaintiffs' arguments that applied to them.]

Mikva, J. . . .

. . . We find no need to interpret article XIX of the APWU constitution or to rule on the reasonableness of appellees' construction. Even if appellants have no ratification right under the literal terms of the constitution, they do have such a right under section 101(a)(1) of the LMRDA. . . .

This provision itself accords no voting rights to a union membership, but it does mandate that rights given to some members be available to all. The Ninth Circuit has described section 101(a)(1) as protecting union members from "denial of a voting right given to any other member or class of members." [Stelling v. IBEW, Local 1547, 587 F.2d 1379, 1385 (9th Cir. 1978).] . . .

. . . The APWU has in effect created two classes of members, only one of which is entitled to ratify its collective bargaining agreements. Such classifications, unless within the scope of the statute's proviso regarding "reasonable rules and regulations," are impermissible under section 101(a)(1):

"while a union may set up procedural and even substantive conditions or restrictions on the members' right to vote, it may not do so indefinitely or arbitrarily so as to establish a permanent special class of membership not entitled to an equal vote." Acevedo v. Bookbinders Local 25, 196 F. Supp. 308, 311 (S.D.N.Y. 1961). . . .

The APWU's refusal to permit Local 6885 to approve its contract, while requiring ratification votes on the national agreement, is therefore contrary to section 101(a)(1) if it cannot be justified as a "reasonable" distinction. In ruling for appellees on this issue, the court below held:

> Rather than discrimination, such a provision merely enables the unions to deal flexibly in their selection of bargaining methods . . . [citing Byrom v. American Postal Workers Union, Civ. No. 78-4268, slip op. at 7 (S.D.N.Y. Oct. 2, 1979)].

This rationale was more fully explained in *Byrom,* in which the court noted that contract ratification is a method of collective bargaining. The other general method of negotiating contracts—giving the bargaining representative final authority to bind the membership—may be more or less advantageous relative to the ratification method, depending on the circumstances of the particular situation. The court in *Byrom,* followed by the court below, inferred that Congress did not intend by section 101(a)(1) to limit a union's flexibility in selecting bargaining methods.

We are not persuaded that this notion of flexibility rises to the level of a "reasonable" justification for discriminating against non-mail processing units in the exercise of ratification rights. No evidence in the record explains why ratification was inappropriate for the Local 6885 bargaining agreement, or even for nonnational contracts generally. No differences between such contracts and the ratified national agreements were articulated by appellees, by the court below, or by the court in *Byrom.* In fact, there is no indication that the desire to preserve flexibility even motivated the discrimination challenged by appellants. . . .

[Appellants] have a very substantial interest . . . in the bargaining agreement governing their own employment. Once the union acted to permit some of its members to approve or reject their contracts, section 101(a)(1) directed that similar rights be given appellants—in the absence of a reasonable rationale for discriminating. Neither the vague, broad notion of flexibility nor the formalistic adherence to outmoded interpretations of article XIX's language provides sufficient justification for denying appellants an opportunity to ratify their contract. The court below therefore erred in granting summary judgment on this question. We remand for fuller consideration of the local's allegations and the union's defenses.

[On remand, in Local 6885 v. Postal Workers, 113 L.R.R.M. 2433, 1982 WL 2198 (D.D.C. 1982), the court granted the intervenors' (nonunion members') motion for summary judgment, reasoning as follows: Ratification was not an internal union affair but had important external ramifications for "perhaps the most important topic in any bargaining session—wages (merit pay increases and save grade provisions)." The court added:]

It certainly would not follow from this reasoning that the APWU would owe the interveners a duty of fair representation with respect to *any* union matter which had an effect, no matter how attenuated, on their wages or salaries. Here, however, the ratification phase had such direct consequences on the wages of the interveners that it must be considered to be inextricably connected with the bargaining phase. Thus, the duty of fair representation . . . would also extend, in this instance, to the ratification phase. If the Court were to rule otherwise, the duty of fair representation owed to the interveners in the bargaining phase would be seriously diluted, in the same way that the force of [§101(a)(1)] would be "substantially vitiate[d]" if the plaintiff local were not guaranteed the right of ratification that other locals were. Since the union admittedly breached its duty to the local with respect to the ratification phase, it was certainly foreseeable that the damages flowing from that breach would affect the non-member employees as well. If the union's failure to submit the contract for ratification showed a disregard of the interests of the local, it certainly also showed a similar disregard for the interests of the interveners.

## *NOTES AND QUESTIONS*

**1. "Reasonable" Basis for Discrimination Between Members?** The *American Postal Workers Union* court, relying on the nondiscrimination mandate in §101(a)(1) of the LMRDA, rejects bargaining "flexibility" as a "reasonable" justification for discrimination "against non-mail processing units in the exercise of ratification rights." What might be a "reasonable" justification for discriminatory ratification provisions in a union's constitution or by-laws? Would it be reasonable to exclude members who are temporary or casual workers and thus who would not be significantly affected by the agreement to be ratified? Should it matter if most of the membership is excluded as casual workers? See Sergeant v. Inlandboatmen's Union of the Pacific, 346 F.3d 1196 (9th Cir. 2003) (finding "reasonable" exclusion of voluntary casual workers from ratification vote in part because of, rather than in spite of, the fact that nearly half of the workers are excluded).

**2. Rights of Nonunion Members?** On remand, the district court in *American Postal Workers Union* appears to have rested its judgment for the intervenors, who were not union members, on the international's violation of rights conferred on union members by the LMRDA and by the union constitution. (a) Is that approach justifiable? (b) Suppose that the union had submitted the tentative agreement for ratification at a meeting open only to union members. Would the union have violated its duty of fair representation? What if the proposed agreement had a different impact on union members and nonmembers? Or if the union had solicited the views of nonmembers and had advised the voting members accordingly?

Does the district court's opinion on remand support a general right of nonunion members to participate in a contract ratification vote if union members enjoy such right? If not, what is the holding of the trial court?

**3. Do Union Members Have a Right to a Contract Ratification Vote?** Even in the absence of a union constitutional provision conferring a ratification vote, can such a right be derived from §101(a)(1) or from the duty of fair representation? Compare Sim v. New York Mailers' Union Number 6, 166 F.3d 465 (2d Cir. 1999), with Branch 6000, National Ass'n of Letter Carriers v. NLRB, 595 F.2d 808 (D.C. Cir. 1979).

Although acknowledging the absence of supporting case law, Professor Hyde would derive from the values of the LMRDA rights of members to "democratic collective bargaining." These include (1) "an opportunity to express their views on prospective bargaining demands"; (2) a membership vote at open meetings on the union's prioritized list of bargaining demands; (3) membership participation in the selection of negotiators; and (4) a membership ratification vote of the proposed settlement, "following full and honest disclosure of its provisions, strengths, and weaknesses." Alan Hyde, Democracy in Collective Bargaining, 93 Yale L.J. 793, 845-848 (1984). Is there a plausible argument for reading the LMRDA or the duty of fair representation to impose any of these requirements? If not, would statutory change along these lines be desirable? If there is to be statutory change, should such participational opportunities be limited to union members rather than be available to all employees represented by the particular union? See also infra note 8.

**4. One-Time Practices of the Teamsters Union.** Although the Teamsters Union has been substantially reformed in recent years, infra page 1049, it may be useful to consider some of its former practices, criticized by Paul Alan Levy (a lawyer for Teamsters for a Democratic Union) in Membership Rights in Union Referenda to Ratify Collective Bargaining Agreements, 4 Hofstra Lab. L.J. 225, 238-257 (1987).

a. A national Teamsters contract typically consists of a national master agreement that is negotiated between the union's national negotiating committee and the national employers' association and a set of supplementary agreements for various regional areas and various job classifications. The Teamsters constitution requires a membership ratification vote, but the union construes this requirement to authorize it to submit both the national agreement and all of its supplements to all members affected by all agreements as a single package for an up-or-down vote on the entire package. The effect of this interpretation is that the members vote not only on the supplements that govern their working conditions but also on the supplements that govern working conditions in other regions and other job classifications. By contrast, the United Auto Workers allows local memberships to vote separately on the local supplements affecting only their working conditions. Is there any basis for legal intervention? See Davey v. Fitzsimmons, 413 F. Supp. 670 (D.D.C. 1976).

b. In 1984, negotiations for midterm modification of the national agreement with United Parcel Service, the union sent mail ballots calling for a quick vote on the proposed contract (extending the term of the agreement for three additional years in exchange for a $1,000 one-time bonus payment) before most locals had a chance to hold meetings and hear opposing views. Do the courts have authority under Title I of the LMRDA to require that any vote on contract terms be "meaningful" or "fair"? See Bauman v. Presser, 117 L.R.R.M. 2393 (D.D.C. 1984), appeal dismissed, 119 L.R.R.M. 2247 (D.C. Cir. 1985). For other procedural failures in connection with ratification votes, see Sako v. Teamsters Local 705, 125 L.R.R.M. 2372 (N.D. Ill. 1987); Maoilo v. Klipa, 655 F. Supp. 1139 (W.D. Pa. 1987); Livingston v. Iron Workers, 647 F. Supp. 723 (W.D.N.C. 1986).

c. In the 1985 referendum for ratification of the proposed national master freight contract, which contained wage increases for senior employees but cut wages and fringes for employees without seniority status called "casuals," the union decided not to send ballots to the casual employees. On the assumption that the union constitution permits exclusion of casuals from a right to vote, do they nevertheless have a claim under the LMRDA or the duty of fair representation to the extent they spend a significant number of days each year working as casuals? Cf. Alvey v. General Elec. Co., 622 F.2d 1279 (7th Cir. 1980); Turner v. Dempster, 569 F. Supp. 683 (N.D. Cal. 1983), affirmed, 743 F.2d 1301 (9th Cir. 1984); Acevedo v. Bookbinders Local 25, 196 F. Supp. 308 (S.D.N.Y 1961); Williams v. Int'l Typographers Union, 423 F.2d 1295 (10th Cir. 1970).

**5. Access to Mailing Lists.** In Carothers v. Presser, 818 F.2d 926 (D.C. Cir. 1987), the court held that §101(a) does not grant members an independent right of access to their union's mailing list for disseminating members' views on a contract proposal submitted for ratification. Dissidents, however, may be entitled to such access when the union is guilty of an independent violation, for example, denying an "equal right to vote" by using such lists to urge a favorable vote while denying similar use to dissidents.

**6. Dues Increases.** Section 101(a)(3)(A) requires secret-ballot membership votes for increases in local union dues. Can the international president, invoking his authority under the international constitution, veto a dues reduction voted on by members of a local? See Moore v. Local Union 569 of the International Bhd. of Elec. Workers, 989 F.2d 1534 (9th Cir. 1993).

**7. Recall of Union Officers.** Section 401(h) authorizes the removal "for cause shown and after hearing" of elected local union officers by the members in a secret-ballot vote, if the Secretary of Labor finds that the local's constitution and by-laws do not provide "an adequate procedure for the removal of elected officers guilty of serious misconduct." (For the Secretary's regulations for determining the adequacy of removal procedures, see 29 C.F.R. §§417.1-417.25.) Title IV does not require an election or other procedure for removing international or national union officers, and it has been held that even where the international constitution provides for such a procedure, Title IV standards need not be met. See BLE Int'l Reform Comm. v. Sytsma, 802 F.2d 180 (6th Cir. 1986).

**8. Economic Participation Rights as Rights of All Unit Employees?** Should federal law be amended to give all unit employees, regardless of union membership, participational rights in unions' economic decisions, such as contract ratification votes? Consider Samuel Estreicher, Deregulating Union Democracy, 21 J. Lab. Res. 247, 255-256 (2000):

> One mistake of the current regime is worrying about the form that permissible labor organizations can take. As long as workers are provided low-cost opportunities to cast secret ballot votes on the economic issues most directly of concern to them, the law should be indifferent as to the form [and] the internal structure of labor organizations. . . .
>
> Under this [proposal,] individuals, for-profit companies (whether they issue stock or not), nonprofit associations with limited membership rights under state law, nonprofit associations with ancillary employment referral and other for-profit labor market functions, and traditional nonprofit membership organizations voluntarily conforming to the LMRDA—all could compete for authority to act as exclusive bargaining agents. . . .
>
> Participational rights in critical economic decisions directly affecting the welfare of bargaining unit employees [would] be divorced from membership in the labor organization. . . .
>
> The NLRA and Railway Labor Act would also be amended to provide that all bargaining unit employees subject to an exclusive bargaining agency would have statutory rights, whether they are union members or not, to vote [by] secret ballot on the following critical economic decisions: (1) whether to have a collective representative, who it should be, and whether to approve the dues proposed to be assessed by that representative; (2) whether to reauthorize the bargaining agency within a definite period of time, say, two or three years; (3) whether to approve or disapprove of the employer's final offer; (4) whether to authorize a strike; and (5) whether to ratify the proposed contract.

> With the possible exception of the initial vote on collective representation, all of the votes on the other critical economic decisions, including reauthorization of the bargaining agency, would require no showing of interest, no effort on the part of the affected employees to organize their colleagues or attend meetings as a precondition to exercise of the franchise.

This proposal is criticized in Michael J. Goldberg, Derailing Union Democracy: Why Deregulation Would Be a Mistake, 23 Berk. J. Emp. & Lab. L. 137 (2002).

## D. LOCAL-INTERNATIONAL DISPUTES: TRUSTEESHIPS AND RELATED MATTERS

International unions control their subordinate local and regional unions through a variety of means. On economic issues where the employer is national in scope, as we have seen in the case of the Teamsters and Automobile Workers unions, the international is likely to negotiate a national agreement with supplementary agreements negotiated at the local level. Where local unions do their own bargaining, the international's representatives may play the leading role at the bargaining table; in other situations the international requires submission of all locally negotiated pacts for approval. Other points of control include disposition of the union's strike treasury and rules governing geographical work jurisdiction of local unions.

An international union also can exercise disciplinary control over a local union by expelling it from membership in the international, by forcing it to merge with another local, or by imposing a trusteeship. The latter involves sending a representative of the international to direct the affairs and treasury of the local union. The international union's constitution may authorize suspension of democratic procedures and empower the trustee to negotiate directly with employers. The trusteeship device, though necessary in many situations, has been subject to abuse, whether to loot local treasuries, to entrench officials friendly to the international, or to control local delegates to an international convention.

Title III of the LMRDA attempts to curb those abuses. Under §302, trusteeships may be set up only in accordance with the union's constitution and by-laws and only for designated purposes. Section 303 prohibits the counting of any votes from trusteed locals in a convention or election of a national officer unless the delegates from the local were elected by the local's members in a secret ballot. This section also proscribes the transfer from the trusteed local to the international of funds in excess of assessments applicable to non-trusteed locals. The statute imposes reporting requirements, and allows any member or subordinate body to sue in federal court or to request investigation and suit by the Secretary of Labor to enforce §§302 and 303.

**United Brotherhood of Carpenters v. Brown**
*343 F.2d 872 (10th Cir. 1965)*

[In 1960, Local 201 applied for the formation of a district council, to be composed of local unions located around Wichita, Kansas. Such a council was designed primarily to permit employees to work in the council area without paying a "service permit fee" that otherwise would be required, and to help provide personnel for area missile sites. Such a council would have substantially benefited the members of Local 201, because it was the biggest local in the area, but its territory included only three of the missile sites. After Local 201's members voted overwhelmingly for forming the council, it was established, with by-laws providing for a per capita tax of $4 as well as monthly dues of $8 per member, an increase of $2.20. The dues increase encountered opposition within the local. In two separate secret-ballot votes in July and October 1961, the local rejected the dues increase. At the October meeting, Local 201's members also voted in favor of disaffiliating from the district council. The General President of the United Brotherhood, pursuant to his authority under the union constitution, ordered affiliation of Local 201 with the council and the increase in the local's dues. Upon the local's noncompliance, the international's executive board, after a hearing, recommended that (1) Local 201 "be placed under the complete supervision" of the General Office; (2) the supervisor should replace all the local's officers; and (3) the president's directive be obeyed. Mack, appointed as trustee, took the foregoing actions and also negotiated a new collective agreement. Following related state court litigation, a federal district court held that the trusteeship was invalid and should be revoked and that the dues increase, not having been decided by secret ballot, was unlawful.]

Hill, J. . . .

The basic issue . . . is, of course, the validity of the trusteeship imposed upon Local 201 by United Brotherhood. . . . [Section 302] provides that a trusteeship may be established and administered by a labor organization over its subordinate body ". . . only in accordance with the constitution and bylaws of the organization which has assumed trusteeship. . . ." The statute is mandatory . . . and has . . . removed whatever inherent power an international union had prior to its enactment to impose such a trusteeship. Unless the constitution and bylaws of the parent organization make provision therefor, such organization has no power to establish a trusteeship over a subordinate body. . . . [No specific provision of the constitution and bylaws of United Brotherhood authorizes] it to impose a trusteeship on any of its subordinate local unions.

It is suggested, however, that United Brotherhood's power to impose the trusteeship in question may be derived from the general authority granted to it in sections 6B[10] and 6D[11] of its Constitution and Laws, as implemented by the provision in section 10K, which empowers the General Executive Board "... to take such action as is necessary and proper for the welfare ..." of the national union. Appellant's argument is that while its constitution and laws do not specifically grant it the authority to impose trusteeships, such authority may be implied from sections 6B, 6D and 10K and that implied authority is sufficient. We do not agree .... Obviously, a trusteeship cannot conform to the constitution and bylaws of a labor organization where, as here, the constitution and bylaws make no provision for trusteeships. We think the statute not only contemplates, but requires, more than some vague general reference to the effect that the parent organization shall have power to take such action as is necessary and proper for its welfare. It requires at the very least that the organization's constitution and bylaws set forth the circumstances under which a trusteeship may be established over its local unions and the matter or procedure in which it is to be imposed....

A second limitation upon the imposition of trusteeships is that under §302 it must be for one of the following purposes: (1) To correct corruption or financial malpractice; (2) to assure the performance of collective bargaining agreements or other duties of a bargaining representative; or (3) to restore democratic procedures, or otherwise carry out the legitimate objects of the labor organization. Congress recognized that the use of trusteeships by an international union is a particularly effective device for the maintenance of order within the organization.... But, Congress also recognized that "... in some instances trusteeships have been used as a means of consolidating the power of corrupt union officers, plundering and dissipating the resources of local unions, and preventing the growth of competing political elements within the organization." 2 U.S. Code Cong. & Adm. News, 86th Cong., 1st Sess., 1959, p. 2333. To preserve the legitimate use of trusteeships, Congress in enacting §302 enumerated the purposes for which a trusteeship could be imposed in a language of a broad and general nature. However, in order to prevent their misuse, Congress obviously intended those purposes to have limitations as well and therefore in determining whether a particular case meets the test, the statute must be construed in the light of the various other provisions of the Act.

The purpose of the Act as a whole is not only to stop and prevent outrageous conduct by thugs and gangsters but also to stop lesser forms

10. "The right is reserved to the United Brotherhood through the International Body to regulate and determine all matters pertaining to the various branches and subdivisions of the trade."

11. "The right is reserved to establish jurisdiction over any Local or Auxiliary Unions, District, State or Provincial Councils whose affairs are conducted in such a manner as to be detrimental to the welfare of the members and to the best interests of the International Body."

of objectionable conduct by those in positions of trust and to protect democratic processes within union organizations. . . .

. . . The trial court found, and the evidence confirms, that United Brotherhood established the trusteeship over Local 201 because it would not affiliate with the District Council and would not raise its dues. The court also found, and the evidence shows, that it was not imposed because of "dissension" within the local union. The result is that the trusteeship was established for the purposes of affiliating Local 201 with the District Council and raising the dues of its membership. In determining whether these are proper purposes under §302, we must remember that a majority of the local membership consistently voted against having anything to do with the District Council and on at least two occasions, by secret ballot, voted against the proposal to raise the monthly dues. We must also remember that [LMRDA §101 was] designed to afford them protection in that respect. Under these circumstances, we have no hesitancy in holding that the purposes for which this trusteeship was imposed do not fall within any of the categories set forth in §302. . . .

## *NOTES AND QUESTIONS*

**1. Preserving Existing Bargaining Structure or Stifling Dissent?** Contrast the principal case with Carpenters Local 1302 v. United Bhd. of Carpenters, 477 F.2d 612 (2d Cir. 1973), where the international union imposed a trusteeship on a local that insisted, contrary to the international's instructions, in filing an NLRB petition that sought separate certification of shipyard carpenters as a means of disaffiliating itself from a Metal Trades Council. The Council, comprised of 11 local unions, had exclusive recognition on an employer-wide basis for 8,000 shipyard employees for over 25 years. The court of appeals agreed that the trusteeship had been established for a valid purpose. Judge Hays wrote for the majority:

> Not only would separate bargaining negotiations delay the execution of a collective agreement, but disaffiliation by the Local might well lead to attempts at disaffiliation by other locals . . . and the undermining of the Council's position as a bargaining representative. Such a development would almost inevitably result in instability of the whole bargaining relationship with the eleven locals vying to outdo one another and resorting to strikes to accomplish their aim. It was to avoid just such results that the Metal Trades [Council] was organized.
>
> Thus the trusteeship was imposed to prevent the destruction of the existing bargaining unit and to preserve the status of the certified bargaining

> representative. The International action was designed . . . to carry out "the legitimate object" of the organization within the meaning of Section 302.

Id. at 614, 615. Was the international's purpose in *Brown* distinguishable under §302 from the parent union's purpose in *Local 1302*?

**2. Valid Purposes Under §302.** Assume that the international union in *Brown* in establishing the trusteeship had followed its own constitution and by-laws and had otherwise met the procedural stipulations of §304(c). Should the trusteeship still have been treated as invalid because of its purposes? Does the *Brown* court hold that an international can never force a local union to adopt collective bargaining strategies rejected by the local's membership? Should §302 be so interpreted?

**3. What Constitutes a "Trusteeship"?** An international union may take various steps that may restrict a local's autonomy or destroy it completely. The applicability of Title III to such steps turns on whether these acts amount to a "trusteeship," as defined in LMRDA §3(h). In light of that definition, consider under what circumstances the following acts would constitute the imposition of a "trusteeship":

a. The international revokes the charter of a local for engaging in an economic strike forbidden by the international and charters a new local with jurisdiction embracing that of the "revoked" local. See the long and interesting saga reported in Parks v. IBEW, 314 F.2d 886 (4th Cir. 1963), and compare Local 2 v. International Bhd. of Telephone Workers, 261 F. Supp. 433 (D. Mass. 1966).

b. An international directs the merger of one local with a considerably larger one. Cf. Brewery Bottlers Local 1345 v. International Bhd. of Teamsters, 202 F. Supp. 464 (E.D.N.Y 1962). See also Musicians Local 10 v. American Fed'n of Musicians, 57 L.R.R.M. 2227 (N.D. Ill. 1964), upholding a trusteeship imposed in order to merge two racially segregated locals pursuant to a merger plan providing that during a transitional period specified officers should be elected by members formerly belonging to the smaller black local. Cf. Daye v. Tobacco Workers Union, 234 F. Supp. 815 (D.D.C. 1964).

**4. Relationship Between Titles I and III.** Sometimes trusteeships are improperly imposed to curb dissident campaigns in local unions. The courts generally have declined to find a private right of action under Title III, remitting the dissident candidate to his or her rights under Titles I and IV. See, e.g., Ross v. Hotel Employees & Restaurant Employees Int'l Union, 266 F.3d 236, 257 (3d Cir. 2001) ("Relief under §304 must be sought on behalf of the local union organization and the entire membership must reap its benefits.").

## E. FISCAL AND FIDUCIARY RESPONSIBILITY

In addition to highlighting corruption in some unions, the McClellan Committee reported the subversion of employee self-determination and independent collective bargaining through organization of, and secret payments to, "spontaneous" anti-union committees composed of employees; the replacement of militant unions by friendly ones; sweetheart contracts; and other abuses by unions, employers, and labor relations consultants. See Select Comm. on Improper Activities in the Labor or Management Field, Interim Report, S. Rep. No. 1417, 85th Cong., 2d Sess. (1958).

The protection of dissent and of union elections provided by the LMRDA might indirectly curb such abuses on the part of union officials by encouraging exposure of misconduct and discipline or electoral defeat of offenders. The statute also mounted a more direct attack by means of the following interrelated measures: (1) provisions in Title V making certain financial malpractices federal criminal offenses (see §§501(c) and 503) and barring certain ex-convicts from holding office (see §504); (2) reporting and disclosure requirements applicable to unions, their officers, and employers (see Title II); (3) the imposition of a general fiduciary obligation on union officials, enforceable under certain circumstances by a union member in the federal courts (see §501); (4) amendments to §302 of the LMRA; and (5) compulsory bonding of union personnel handling union finances and property (see §502).

### 1. Reporting Requirements

Sections 201(a) and (b) of the Act mandate that "every labor organization" file with the Secretary of Labor a range of information to make transparent the union's operations and financial condition and to deter the misuse of union funds. Section 201(a), for instance, requires the filing of the address where records are kept, the name and title of each officer, the fees and dues required of members, and procedures for determining memberships, levying assessments, participation in benefit plans, disbursements of funds, financial audits, calling of meetings, selection and removal of officers, disciplining of members, authorizations of bargaining demands and strikes, and ratification of contracts. Section 201(b) requires the annual filing of financial reports "as may be necessary accurately to disclose its financial condition and operations."

The level of detail in annual financial reporting required of unions with more than $250,000 of annual receipts was significantly increased by new regulations of the Secretary of Labor promulgated on October 9, 2003. The new regulations require the identification and specification of the purpose of individual receipts and disbursements of $5,000 or more. They also require each union officer and employee to provide an accounting that estimates the portion of work time spent on corresponding activities. Union leaders have claimed that the new reporting obligations are unnecessarily burdensome, but the regulations have been upheld as within the Secretary's discretion. AFL-CIO v. Chao, 409 F.3d 377 (D.C. Cir. 2005).

Supplementing the disclosure requirements is the investigative power conferred on the Secretary of Labor by §601 of the LMRDA. Section 201(c) of the statute also entitles union members "for just cause to examine any books, records, and accounts necessary to verify" reports required of labor organizations by Title II of the Act. Similar rights existed at common law. See, e.g., Mooney v. Local 284, Bartenders Union, 48 Cal. 2d 841, 313 P.2d 857 (1957) (by analogy to shareholder's right to inspect corporate books for "proper purpose," union member requesting accounting of expenses and income—after union had unexplained operating deficit for several months—held entitled to inspect books without exhausting internal remedies). Regarding survival of common law rights, see LMRDA §§603(a), 205, and 201(c). For an exploration of problems arising under §201(c), see Fruit & Vegetable Packers & Warehousemen Local 760 v. Morley, 378 F.2d 738 (9th Cir. 1967); Landry v. Sabine Independent Seamen's Ass'n, 623 F.2d 347 (5th Cir. 1980). Insurgents, through §201(c), may secure information useful in criticizing and challenging incumbents. Furthermore, rival unions, reform groups, and employers may, through §205(a), secure similarly useful information through the reports that Title II requires unions to file annually with the Department of Labor.

Sections 203(a)(4) and (b) of the LMRDA require the filing of reports by employers and consultants of any arrangements for activities that have as "an object" the direct or indirect persuasion of employees with respect to the exercise or non-exercise of their organizational and bargaining rights ("persuader" activity). The Act, however, in §203(c), exempts the "giving or agreeing to give advice" from the reporting requirement of §203. In Auto Workers v. Dole, 869 F.2d 616 (D.C. Cir. 1989), the court agreed that the Secretary of Labor could treat as within the "advice" exemption activities of consultants providing materials to be used by employers to discourage unionization (even fully scripted speeches for supervisors to deliver), as long as the materials are submitted to the employer "for his use, and the employer is free to accept or reject the oral or written materials submitted to him." Material disseminated by the consultant directly to employees, however, is reportable activity. In fall 2010, the Department of Labor published a notice of intent to conduct notice-and-comment rulemaking on a narrowed interpretation of §203(c). See U.S. Dep't of Labor, Office of Labor-Management Standards (RIN: 1245-AA03).

## 2. Fiduciary Obligations

Section 501 states that "officers, agents, shop stewards, and other representatives of a labor organization occupy positions of trust in relation to such organization and its members as a group." It also commands these representatives "to hold its money and property solely for the benefit of the organization and its members" and "to refrain from dealing with such organization as an adverse party or in behalf of an adverse party in any matter connected with his duties." Courts applying this provision must fashion federal law drawing from the common law experience of state courts with fiduciary duties.

### *NOTES AND QUESTIONS*

1. **Applications.** Consider whether §501 should apply to alleged misconduct of the following kind:

a. Union officials generate liability for the union by a strike that flagrantly violates a no-strike pledge or the statutory proscription against secondary boycotts.

b. Union officials enter into sweetheart contracts and are paid off by employers. See Schonfeld v. Rarback, 61 L.R.R.M. 2043 (S.D.N.Y 1965); see also Echols v. Cook, 56 L.R.R.M. 3030 (N.D. Ga. 1962).

c. Union officials, by massive mismanagement, bring about the actuarial insolvency of a union-established pension fund. Cf. Hood v. Journeymen Barbers, 454 F.2d 1347 (7th Cir. 1972).

d. Union officials impose a trusteeship on a local union in order to countermand a vote to withdraw the designation of the international's national plan as the pension plan to which employers would have to make contributions under collective agreements. There is no evidence that the international president or other union officials would derive any personal gain from the designation of the national plan. See Pignotti v. Local 3, Sheet Metal Workers, 477 F.2d 825 (8th Cir. 1973) (president breached his fiduciary duties by allowing his "personal feelings" to interfere with his duties). Do you agree that the president's irrational loyalty to the national plan constituted a breach of his fiduciary duty?

2. **Use of Union Funds to Pay for Legal Fees Incurred Defending Union Officers.** Do union officers breach their duties under §501 by using union funds to pay for legal fees in the defense of criminal or civil actions brought against them for alleged fraudulent use of union money? See Highway Truck Drivers & Helpers, Local 107 v. Cohen, 182 F. Supp. 608, affirmed, 284 F.2d 182 (3d Cir. 1960) (finding violation of §501). Was

*Cohen* rightly decided? Should it have mattered in *Cohen* that the membership had authorized the use of union funds through a resolution adopted in accordance with the union constitution and bylaws? Should a union not be able to use its assets to purchase insurance to defend and indemnify officials when charged with personal misconduct under color of their union authority? Is it relevant to these questions that §501 states that "a general exculpatory resolution of a governing body purporting to relieve any [union representative] of liability for breach of the duties declared by this section shall be void as against public policy"? Should it be relevant that state law generally provides for indemnification of expenses (including attorneys' fees) as of right when the director or officer of a corporation has been successful in fiduciary litigation? See, e.g., 8 Del. Code 145 (2002); Waltuch v. Conticommodity Services, Inc., 88 F.3d 87 (2d Cir. 1996).

**3. Exculpation vs. Ratification?** A union amends its pension plan for elected union officers to extend coverage to certain appointed union officials, such as the assistant to the president, organizer, executive secretary, publicity director, and editor of union newspapers. After the district court finds that the pension plan amendment was not authorized by the union constitution, the constitution is amended to permit such pension coverage and to validate retroactively all benefits paid under the plan. Is the amendment ineffective as an attempt to exculpate a prior fiduciary violation? Should it matter whether the union's initial view of its constitutional authority was reasonably arguable, even if erroneous? See Morrissey v. Curran, 423 F.2d 393 (2d Cir. 1970).

**4. Union Counsel Representing Officers?** Tucker v. Shaw, 378 F.2d 304 (2d Cir. 1967), raised the question of whether a union's regularly retained counsel could represent the union's officers in a suit brought against them under LMRDA §§501(a) and (b). The plaintiffs sought, among other relief, to recover, on behalf of the union, union funds allegedly diverted for the defendants' personal purposes. In barring the union's counsel from representing the officers, the court noted that the union's interest in the outcome of the litigation might well be adverse to that of the officers; that the attorney's familiarity with the facts involved in the litigation "might unfairly tip the scales against plaintiffs at the outset"; and that because of this familiarity with the facts, the attorney was a likely witness in the case. See also Yablonski v. UMW, 448 F.2d 1175 (D.C. Cir. 1971); Weaver v. UMW, 492 F.2d 580 (D.C. Cir. 1973). Was this case rightly decided? When independent counsel must be retained to represent the union's interest, who chooses such counsel?

## 3. Regulation of Employee Welfare and Pension Funds

Section 302 of the LMRA was designed to shield collective bargaining against bribery and extortion and to protect jointly administered health and welfare funds against dissipation. Successive amendments to that section tightened proscriptions of bribery and extortion and expanded the purposes permissible for funds to which employers may make payments and in whose administration unions participate.

Union-negotiated pension and welfare funds, in which unions retain some administrative role, are regulated by §302(c)(5) of the LMRDA, which requires, inter alia, that "employees and employers are equally represented in the administration of such fund[s]," id. §302(c)(5)(B). The Taft-Hartley provision was supplemented by the Welfare and Disclosure Act of 1958, the 1962 amendments to which included, inter alia, criminal penalties for gross abuses, such as embezzlement and kickbacks.

Several other federal statutes also have had a limited impact on health and welfare funds. LMRDA §501 has served as the basis for federal enforcement of fiduciary obligations of union trustees of health and welfare funds. See Hood v. Journeymen Barbers, 454 F.2d 1347 (7th Cir. 1972).

Responding to the loss of pensions by some employees as a result of under-funded plans, Congress enacted comprehensive regulation of all private employee pension and welfare benefit plans, whether negotiated through collective bargaining or otherwise. This statute, the Employee Retirement Income Security Act of 1974 (ERISA), 29 U.S.C. §§1161 et seq., imposes far-reaching and complex standards regarding investments, funding, employee eligibility, disclosure, and reporting. The problem of employer withdrawal from underfunded multiemployer pension plans led to the Multiemployer Pension Plan Amendments Act of 1980, 29 U.S.C. §§1381 et seq.; see generally Alicia H. Munnell & Jean-Pierre Aubry, Private Sector Multiemployer Pension Plans—A Primer (No. 14-13, Aug. 2014, Center for Retirement Research at Boston College). A significant interrelationship* between the regulation of such plans and the NLRA is reflected in NLRB v. Amax Coal Co., 453 U.S. 322 (1981), which dealt with the status of trustees selected by an employer under §302(c)(5) of the LMRA. Although that section refers to such trustees as "the representatives of the employer," the Court emphasized that the fiduciary duty of such trustees was directly antithetical to that of an agent of the appointing party. Hence, the Court, agreeing with the NLRB, ruled broadly that they were not employer "representatives for the purposes of collective bargaining" under NLRA §8(b)(1)(B); consequently, union insistence that management appoint or retain particular trustees for a §302(c)(5) trust does not violate §8(b)(1)(B).

---

* See also Walsh v. Schlecht, 429 U.S. 401 (1977), involving the interrelationship between §8(e) of the NLRA and §302(c)(5).

Justice Stevens, dissenting in *Amax Coal*, objected that the Court's opinion would be read as permitting a union "to exercise an economic veto over an employer's selection of the management trustees" under §302(c)(5). Although those appointees are fiduciaries, they frequently exercise broad discretion over questions such as level of employer contributions, eligibility requirements, and benefit standards, on which management and union representatives could legitimately differ. Consequently, in the dissent's view, the Court's approach undercuts the purposes behind the requirement in §302(c)(5)(B) for equal employer representation in fund administration.

The Court in *Amax* considered the applicability of §8(b)(1)(B) but not of §8(b)(3). Is §8(b)(3) violated by a union's strike to veto an employer's appointee or to press its own candidate?

## 4. Corruption

### *Note: §302 of the LMRA*

In an attempt to deal with the problem of union corruption, §302(a) broadly restricts payments by an employer (or its representative) to representatives of its employees or any labor organization that represents or seeks to represent its employees. Under §302(c) Congress delineated certain exceptions from the §302(a) ban:

(1) payments made to employee representatives as compensation for their services as an employee of the employer;
(2) payments in satisfaction of an arbitration award in settlement of a dispute "in the absence of fraud or duress";
(3) payments for commodities at market price "in the regular course of business";
(4) payments for union dues pursuant to a "written assignment" from the employee that shall not be irrevocable for a period of more than a year or the duration of the collective agreement, whichever occurs sooner;
(5) payments to a trust fund "established by such representative for the sole and exclusive benefit of the employees, their families and dependents" for medical insurance, pensions, etc., subject to certain provisos;
(6) payments to a trust fund "established by such representative" for pooled vacation, holiday, severance, or similar benefits, or to defray the cost of apprenticeship programs, subject to a proviso;
(7) payments to a "pooled or individual" trust fund "established by such representative" for employee scholarships, child care centers, and housing assistance, subject to a proviso;

(8) payments to a trust fund "established by such representative" for defraying the cost of legal services for employees and their families, subject to certain provisos, including a ban on payment for legal services to initiate any proceeding against the employer (other than workers' compensation claims) or labor organization; or

(9) payments to a plant, area, or industry-wide labor-management committee for purposes set forth in §5(b) of the Labor Management Cooperation Act of 1978.

A particularly interesting issue involves the legality under §302(c)(1) of employer grants of paid leaves of absence to employees to function as full-time union grievance chairs. Early Third Circuit authority striking down such arrangements in Trailways, Inc. v. Joint Council, Amalgamated Transit Union, 785 F.2d 1011 (3d Cir. 1986), was overturned in Caterpillar, Inc. v. UAW, 107 F.3d 1052 (3d Cir. 1997), cert. denied, 523 U.S. 1015 (1998). Section 302(c)(1) exempts from the general prohibition of employer payments to unions in §302(a) payments by the employer "to any representative of his employees . . . who is also an employee or former employee of such employer, as compensation for, or by reason of, his service as an employee of such employer. . . ." The *Caterpillar* court (per Judge Nygaard) held:

> We believe that the payments at issue here, while they were not compensation for hours worked in the past, certainly were "by reason" of that service. We reach this conclusion because the payments arose, not out of some "back-door deal" with the union, but out of the collective bargaining agreement itself. Caterpillar was willing to put that costly benefit on the table, which strongly implies that the employees had to give up something in the bargaining process that they otherwise could have received. Thus, every employee implicitly gave up a small amount in current wages and benefits in exchange for a promise that, if he or she should someday be elected grievance chairperson, Caterpillar would continue to pay his or her salary.

107 F.3d at 1056.

Courts have recently addressed whether, or to what extent, §302 applies to neutrality agreements between employers and unions. See Chapter 5 for further discussion of neutrality agreements. In Mulhall v. Unite Here Local 355, 667 F.3d 1211 (11th Cir. 2012), cert. denied, 134 S. Ct. 822 (2013), the court concluded that the terms of neutrality agreements can include "a thing of value" and thus violate §302. The employer entered into an agreement giving the union access rights to the workforce and providing for neutrality by both sides during the authorization card solicitation process and the union agreed to give financial support of a ballot initiative that the employer favored. Other Courts of Appeals have held that neutrality agreements lacking immediate financial benefits to the union fall outside the scope of §302.

See, e.g., Adcock v. Freightliner LLC, 550 F. 3d 369 (4th Cir. 2008). See also Unite Here Local 355 v. Mulhall, 134 S. Ct. 594 (2013) (dismissing writ of certiorari as improvidently granted). Justices Breyer, Sotomayor, and Kagan dissented from the dismissal and would have requested briefing on, among other things, whether §302 authorizes a private right of action. Id. at 594-595.

Criminal penalties for violations are provided in §302(d). See, e.g., United States v. Phillips, 19 F.3d 1565 (11th Cir. 1994) (steel producer's payment of unearned pension credits retroactive to time negotiators left the company to become union officials, and failure to notify pension plan participants that plan had been amended to provide for such payments; term "willfully" in §302(d)(2) does not require proof of evil purpose, only that defendant "knowingly and intentionally committed acts which constitute the offense charged and that such acts were not committed accidentally or by some mistake").

### *Note: The Racketeer Influenced and Corrupt Organizations Act of 1970*

In 1970, Congress passed the Racketeer Influenced and Corrupt Organizations Act (RICO), Pub. L. No. 91-452, 84 Stat. 922 (codified in scattered sections of 7, 15, 18 & 49 U.S.C.; the principal provisions are at 18 U.S.C. §§1961-1968). RICO §1962 created four new crimes consisting of improper relationships between "persons" and "enterprises." Both terms are defined broadly. Subsection (a) makes unlawful a person's investment of income derived from a "pattern of racketeering activity" or through "collection of an unlawful debt" or the profits from such income for the purpose of acquiring an interest in, establishing, or operating an enterprise affecting interstate or foreign commerce. Subsection (b) declares it unlawful for a person through a pattern of racketeering or the collection of an unlawful debt to acquire or maintain an interest in such an enterprise. Under subsection (c) it is unlawful for any person "associated with any enterprise" to conduct the enterprise or to participate in its conduct through a pattern of racketeering activity or collection of an unlawful debt. Conspiracies to violate any of the substantive subsections are unlawful under subsection (d).

Predicate acts of "racketeering activity" are defined in two ways. 18 U.S.C. §1961(1)(A)-(B). First, RICO defines a predicate act as

> [a]ny act or threat involving murder, kidnapping, gambling, arson, robbery, bribery, extortion, dealing in obscene matter, or dealing in narcotic or other dangerous drugs, which is chargeable under State law and punishable by imprisonment of more than one year.

Second, RICO incorporates violations of specified federal statutes prohibiting bribery, extortion, fraud, obstruction of justice, and various crimes of vice. The most important of these in the labor relations context are mail fraud (18 U.S.C. §1341), wire fraud (§1343), unlawful welfare fund payments (§1954), Hobbs Act violations (§1951), prohibited payments and loans to labor organizations (indictable offenses under §302(d) of the LMRA, 29 U.S.C. §186(d)), and embezzlement from union funds (29 U.S.C. §501(c)).

Sections 1963 and 1964 set forth penalties and remedies, including both criminal prosecution and civil actions (the latter providing for treble damages and reasonable attorneys' fees).

In recent years the federal government has used RICO's civil provisions to "reorganize" various labor unions. The Government's first victory occurred in United States v. Local 560, Int'l Bhd. of Teamsters, 581 F. Supp. 279 (D.N.J. 1984), affirmed, 780 F.2d 267 (3d Cir. 1985). In that case a district court removed the leadership of a Union City, New Jersey, Teamsters local and imposed a judicial trusteeship, finding that members of the local executive board facilitated a takeover of the local by organized-crime interests and by use or threat of force or fear of economic harm undermined union democracy in the local. The court ruled that the "extortion of membership rights" protected by LMRDA §§101(a)(1) and (2) constitutes a Hobbs Act violation and thereby satisfies the predicate-act requirement of RICO §1962(b). Similar relief was obtained against other unions in United States v. Local 30, United Slate, Tile & Composition Roofers Ass'n, 686 F. Supp. 1139, 1171 (E.D. Pa. 1988), affirmed, 871 F.2d 401 (3d Cir. 1989); United States v. Bonanno Organized Crime Family, 683 F. Supp. 1411, 1453-1454 (E.D.N.Y. 1988) (consent judgment against Teamsters Local 814).

Perhaps the most celebrated success of the "civil RICO" effort was the consent decree negotiated between the Teamsters international union and the government in 1989. (The provisions of the decree are described in United States v. International Bhd. of Teamsters, 905 F.2d 610, 613 (2d Cir. 1990).) Acting pursuant to the decree, the government in December 1991 conducted and supervised a direct, secret-ballot election of the membership for the union's International General President and International General Executive Board — the first election of its kind in the union's history. The winner of the election for international president was Ron Carey, the leader of a Long Island local of United Parcel Services employees, who was supported by the dissidents of Teamsters for a Democratic Union. See James B. Jacobs & Kerry T. Cooperman, Breaking the Devil's Pact: The Battle to Free the Teamsters from the Mob (2011); George Kannar, Making the Teamsters Safe for Democracy, 102 Yale L.J. 1645 (1993). Carey was later replaced by James Hoffa, Jr.

For generally positive accounts of the government's use of RICO provisions to cleanse labor unions of the influence of organized labor, see, e.g., James B. Jacobs & Ellen Peters, Labor Racketeering: The Mafia and Unions, 30 Crime & Just. 229 (2003); and Professor Jacobs's Gotham Unbound: How New York City Was Liberated from the Grip of Organized Crime (1999) (with

Colleen Friel & Robert Radick); Busting the Mob: United States v. Cosa Nostra (1994) (with Christopher Panarella & Jay Worthington); and Corruption and Racketeering in the New York City Construction Industry: The Final Report of the New York State Organized Crime Task Force (1990) (with Ronald Goldstock, Martin Marcus & Thomas D. Thacher II). A broad role for civil RICO is advocated in Randy M. Mastro et al., Private Plaintiffs' Use of Equitable Remedies Under the RICO Statute: A Means to Reform Corrupted Labor Unions, 24. U. Mich J.L. Reform 571 (1991).

For critical views of the government's RICO litigation, see Howard S. Siminoff & Theodore M. Lieverman, The RICO-ization of Federal Labor Law: An Argument for Broad Preemption, 8 Lab. Law. 335 (1992); Victoria T.G. Bassetti, Weeding RICO Out of Garden Variety Labor Disputes, 92 Colum. L. Rev. 103 (1992); Scott D. Miller, RICO's Application to Labor's Illegal Strike Conduct: Reconciling RICO with the NLRA, 11 Hamline J. Pub. L. & Pol'y 233 (1990).

For new uses of RICO to pursue immigration law claims against employers, see Samuel Estreicher & Joseph J. Bernasky, RICO Usage Against Employers for Immigration Misdeeds, N.Y.L.J., Jan. 16, 2007 and supra note 3, pages 1069-1070; and for labor-management claims generally, see James J. Brudney, Collateral Conflict: Employer Claims of RICO Extortion Against Union Comprehensive Campaigns, 83 S. Cal. L. Rev. 731 (2010).

### *Note: State Regulation of Union Corruption*

Section 504(a) of the LMRDA bars individuals convicted of certain crimes from serving as an officer of, or in any position of responsibility with, a union for a period of five years. In Brown v. Hotel and Restaurant Employees, Local 54, 468 U.S. 491 (1984), the Court (per Justice O'Connor) held that, in light of the express disclaimer of preemption in §603(a), states enjoy some latitude in regulating the responsibilities and qualifications of union officials. *Brown* upheld New Jersey's annual registration requirement for labor organizations representing or seeking to represent casino industry employees, which disqualified union officers, agents, or "principal employee[s]" who were convicted for a list of enumerated offenses or "any other offense which indicates that licensure of the applicant would be inimical to the policy of this act and to casino operations." N.J. Stat. Ann 5:12-86(c)(4). The *Brown* Court emphasized that the disqualification provision "does not implicate the employees' express Sec. 7 right to select a particular labor union as their collective-bargaining representative, but only their subsidiary right to select the officials of that union organization." 468 U.S. at 509. A separate provision that denied non-complying labor organizations the right to receive dues from represented casino employees was remanded by the Court, for a determination of whether this provision "will effectively prevent the union from performing its statutory functions as bargaining representative for its members." Id. at 513.

# 14 | Labor Law and Immigration

This chapter focuses on the relationship between immigration and labor law in the United States. Millions of immigrants labor in U.S. workplaces each year. From 2010-2012, the U.S. admitted approximately two million foreign temporary workers and trainees per year. See Off. of Immigr. Stat., U.S. Dep't. of Homeland Sec., Nonimmigrant Admissions by Class of Admission: Fiscal Years 2010 to 2012. By conservative estimates, an additional eight million workers labor in the United States, even though as a matter of immigration law they do not have proper authorization to be present in the U.S. These workers are often referred to as "unauthorized" or "undocumented." See Jeffrey S. Passel & D'Vera Cohn, Unauthorized Immigrant Population: National and State Trends, 2010, Pew Hispanic Center, 2011, at 17, Table 6.

These individuals' dual identity as immigrants on the one hand, and workers on the other, raises a number of labor law questions. To what extent do federal immigration policies aimed to deter unauthorized immigration conflict with NLRA protections of the unauthorized? Is immigration law a labor law issue, such that the NLRA could protect some forms of collective advocacy about immigration policy from employer interference? To what extent does the NLRA protect organizing efforts by immigrant workers in support of their demands for better wages and working conditions, sometimes with the assistance of worker centers or other alternative labor groups? This chapter addresses these and other questions. It also serves as a review of many of the traditional labor law themes that are covered in previous chapters and as an opportunity to explore the outer limits of labor law in the contemporary period.

## A. THE NLRA AND UNAUTHORIZED IMMIGRANTS

**Sure-Tan, Inc. v. NLRB**
*467 U.S. 883 (1984)*

O'CONNOR, J.

Petitioners are two small leather processing firms. . . . In July 1976, a union organization drive was begun. Eight employees signed cards authorizing the Chicago Leather Workers Union, Local 431, Amalgamated Meatcutters and Butcher Workmen of North America (Union), to act as their collective-bargaining representative. Of the 11 employees then employed by petitioners, most were Mexican nationals present illegally in the United States without visas or immigration papers authorizing them to work. The Union ultimately prevailed in [an NLRB] election. . . .

Two hours after the election, petitioners' president, John Surak, addressed a group of employees, including some of the undocumented aliens involved in this case. He asked the employees why they had voted for the Union and cursed them for doing so. He then inquired as to whether they had valid immigration papers. Many of the employees indicated that they did not.

Petitioners filed with the Board objections to the election, arguing that six of the seven eligible voters were illegal aliens. Surak executed an accompanying affidavit which stated that he had known about the employees' illegal presence in this country for several months prior to the election. . . .

[T]he Board's Acting Regional Director notified petitioners that their objections were overruled and that the Union would be certified as the employees' collective-bargaining representative. The next day, Surak sent a letter to the [Immigration and Naturalization Services (INS)] asking that the agency check into the status of a number of petitioners' employees as soon as possible. In response to the letter, INS agents visited petitioners' premises on February 18, 1977, to investigate the immigration status of all Spanish-speaking employees. The INS agents discovered that five employees were living and working illegally in the United States and arrested them. Later that day, each employee executed an INS form, acknowledging illegal presence in the country and accepting INS's grant of voluntary departure as a substitute for deportation. By the end of the day, all five employees were on a bus ultimately bound for Mexico. . . .

[T]he Board affirmed the ALJ's conclusion that petitioners had violated §§8(a)(1) and (3) by requesting the INS to investigate the status of their Mexican employees "solely because the employees supported the Union" and "with full knowledge that the employees in question had no papers or work permits." . . . The Board, therefore, agreed with the ALJ's finding that "the discriminatees' subsequent deportation was the proximate result of the discriminatorily motivated action by [petitioners] and constitutes a constructive discharge." . . .

On appeal, the Court of Appeals enforced the Board's order. . . . The court fully agreed that petitioners had violated the NLRA by constructively discharging their undocumented alien employees. . . .

We first consider the predicate question whether the NLRA should apply to unfair labor practices committed against undocumented aliens. The Board has consistently held that undocumented aliens are "employees" within the meaning of §2(3) of the Act. That provision broadly provides that "[t]he term 'employee' shall include any employee," 29 U.S.C. §152(3), subject only to certain specifically enumerated exceptions. . . . Since the task of defining the term "employee" is one that "has been assigned primarily to the agency created by Congress to administer the Act," NLRB v. Hearst Publications, Inc., 322 U.S. 111, 130 (1944), the Board's construction of that term is entitled to considerable deference, and we will uphold any interpretation that is reasonably defensible. . . .

The terms and policies of the Act fully support the Board's interpretation in this case. The breadth of §2(3)'s definition is striking: the Act squarely applies to "any employee." The only limitations are specific exemptions for agricultural laborers, domestic workers, individuals employed by their spouses or parents, individuals employed as independent contractors or supervisors, and individuals employed by a person who is not an employer under the NLRA. See 29 U.S.C. §152(3). Since undocumented aliens are not among the few groups of workers expressly exempted by Congress, they plainly come within the broad statutory definition of "employee."

Similarly, extending the coverage of the Act to such workers is consistent with the Act's avowed purpose of encouraging and protecting the collective-bargaining process. . . . As this Court has previously recognized: "[A]cceptance by illegal aliens of jobs on substandard terms as to wages and working conditions can seriously depress wage scales and working conditions of citizens and legally admitted aliens; and employment of illegal aliens under such conditions can diminish the effectiveness of labor unions." De Canas v. Bica, 424 U.S. 351, 356-357 (1976). If undocumented alien employees were excluded from participation in union activities and from protections against employer intimidation, there would be created a subclass of workers without a comparable stake in the collective goals of their legally resident co-workers, thereby eroding the unity of all the employees and impeding effective collective bargaining. See NLRB v. Jones & Laughlin Steel Corp., 301 U.S. 1, 33 (1937). Thus, the Board's categorization of undocumented aliens as protected employees furthers the purposes of the NLRA.

Counterintuitive though it may be, we do not find any conflict between application of the NLRA to undocumented aliens and the mandate of the Immigration and Nationality Act (INA), 66 Stat. 163, as amended, 8 U.S.C. §1101 et seq. This Court has observed that "[t]he central concern of the INA is with the terms and conditions of admission to the country and the subsequent treatment of aliens lawfully in the country." De Canas v. Bica, 424

U.S., at 359. The INA evinces "at best evidence of a peripheral concern with employment of illegal entrants." Id., at 360. For whatever reason, Congress has not adopted provisions in the INA making it unlawful for an employer to hire an alien who is present or working in the United States without appropriate authorization. While it is unlawful to "concea[l], harbo[r], or shiel[d] from detection" any alien not lawfully entitled to enter or reside in the United States, see 8 U.S.C. §1324(a)(3), an explicit proviso to the statute explains that "employment (including the usual and normal practices incident to employment) shall not be deemed to constitute harboring." Ibid. See De Canas v. Bica, supra, at 360, and n. 9. Moreover, Congress has not made it a separate criminal offense for an alien to accept employment after entering this country illegally. See 119 Cong. Rec. 14184 (1973) (remarks of Rep. Dennis). Since the employment relationship between an employer and an undocumented alien is hence not illegal under the INA, there is no reason to conclude that application of the NLRA to employment practices affecting such aliens would necessarily conflict with the terms of the INA.

We find persuasive the Board's argument that enforcement of the NLRA with respect to undocumented alien employees is compatible with the policies of the INA. A primary purpose in restricting immigration is to preserve jobs for American workers; immigrant aliens are therefore admitted to work in this country only if they "will not adversely affect the wages and working conditions of the workers in the United States similarly employed." 8 U.S.C. §1182(a)(14). See S. Rep. No. 748, 89th Cong., 1st Sess., 15 (1965). Application of the NLRA helps to assure that the wages and employment conditions of lawful residents are not adversely affected by the competition of illegal alien employees who are not subject to the standard terms of employment. If an employer realizes that there will be no advantage under the NLRA in preferring illegal aliens to legal resident workers, any incentive to hire such illegal aliens is correspondingly lessened. In turn, if the demand for undocumented aliens declines, there may then be fewer incentives for aliens themselves to enter in violation of the federal immigration laws. The Board's enforcement of the NLRA as to undocumented aliens is therefore clearly reconcilable with and serves the purposes of the immigration laws as presently written.

Accepting the premise that the provisions of the NLRA are applicable to undocumented alien employees, we must now address the more difficult issue whether, under the circumstances of this case, petitioners committed an unfair labor practice by reporting their undocumented alien employees to the INS in retaliation for participating in union activities. Section 8(a)(3) makes it an unfair labor practice for an employer "by discrimination in regard to hire or tenure of employment or any term or condition of employment to encourage or discourage membership in any labor organization." 29 U.S.C. §158(a)(3). The Board, with the approval of lower courts, has long held that an employer violates this provision not only when, for the purpose of discouraging union activity, it directly dismisses an employee, but also when it purposefully creates working conditions so intolerable that the employee has no option but to resign—a so-called "constructive discharge." . . .

Petitioners do not dispute that the anti-union animus element of this test was, as expressed by the lower court, "flagrantly met." . . . "The record is replete with examples of Sure-Tan's blatantly illegal course of conduct to discourage its employees from supporting the Union." . . . Petitioners contend, however, that their conduct in reporting the undocumented alien workers did not force the workers' departure from the country; instead, they argue, it was the employees' status as illegal aliens that was the actual "proximate cause" of their departure. . . .

This argument is unavailing. According to testimony by an INS agent before the ALJ, petitioners' letter was the sole cause of the investigation during which the employees were taken into custody. This evidence was undisputed by petitioners and amply supports the ALJ's conclusion that "but for [petitioners'] letter to Immigration, the discriminatees would have continued to work indefinitely." . . . And there can be little doubt that Surak foresaw precisely this result when, having known about the employees' illegal status for some months, he notified the INS only after the Union's electoral victory was assured. . . .

We observe that the Board quite properly does not contend that an employer may never report the presence of an illegal alien employee to the INS. See, e. g., Bloom/Art Textiles, Inc., 225 N.L.R.B. 766 (1976) (no violation of Act for employer to discharge illegal alien who was a union activist where the evidence showed that the reason for the discharge was not the employee's protected collective activities, but the employer's concern that employment of the undocumented worker violated state law). The reporting of any violation of the criminal laws is conduct which ordinarily should be encouraged, not penalized. . . . It is only when the evidence establishes that the reporting of the presence of an illegal alien employee is in retaliation for the employee's protected union activity that the Board finds a violation of §8(a)(3). Absent this specific finding of anti-union animus, it would not be an unfair labor practice to report or discharge an undocumented alien employee. . . . Such a holding is consistent with the policies of both the INA and the NLRA. . . .

## *NOTES AND QUESTIONS*

**1. Unauthorized Workers as Statutory "Employees"?** What are the reasons that the *Sure-Tan* Court advances for including unauthorized workers in the NLRA's definition of "employee"? In 1986, with the Immigration Reform and Control Act (IRCA), Congress amended immigration law to include, among other things, (1) a requirement that employers verify the immigration status of their employees and (2) sanctions against employers who knowingly employ unauthorized immigrants. IRCA also included sanctions for unauthorized immigrants who knowingly use fraudulent documents to gain employment. See Pub. L. No. 99-603, 100 Stat. 3359 (1986), codified at 8 U.S.C. §1324(a) et seq. Does IRCA undermine *Sure-Tan*'s reasoning as to the NLRA's coverage of unauthorized workers?

**2. Immigration-related Retaliation.** Recall that unlawful NLRA retaliation occurs when an employer discriminates "in regard to hire or tenure of employment or any term or condition of employment to encourage or discourage membership in any labor organization." 29 U.S.C. §158(a)(3). According to the *Sure-Tan* Court, why did the employer's communication with U.S. immigration authorities fall within this definition? Would an employer's verbal threat to call immigration authorities in response to a union organizing effort also fall within this definition? See NLRB Assoc. Gen. Couns. Mem. OM 11-62 (June 7, 2011) (noting that U and T visas are sometimes available for immigrant workers when employers engage in "egregious conduct" such as "interfering with protected activity through illegal threats of retaliation such as threats to call immigration authorities"); Laura Francis, Immigrant Workers Claim Retaliation, Seek Executive Action to Prevent More, 2014 Daily Lab. Rep. (BNA) No. 149, at A6 (August 4, 2014) (NLRB regional director is alleging that a D.C.-area construction contractor threatened immigration-related retaliation if immigrant workers voted in favor of a union).

**3. NLRB Remedial Authority and Immigration Law: Backpay Relief for Individuals Not Authorized to Work in the U.S.?** Should unauthorized individuals not legally entitled to work in the United States be able to obtain make-whole relief under the NLRA if their employer discharges them for attempting to organize a union, or for engaging in other conduct protected by §7? In a portion of the opinion omitted here, the *Sure-Tan* Court concluded that the Board lacked authority to award backpay and reinstatement remedies to unauthorized immigrant employees, at least if they were outside the country and could not legally reenter. In the case excerpted below, the Court considered the remedies issue again in a post-IRCA context involving an employee who was inside the U.S.

## Hoffman Plastic Compounds, Inc. v. NLRB
*535 U.S. 137 (2002)*

REHNQUIST, C.J.

The National Labor Relations Board (Board) awarded backpay to an undocumented alien who has never been legally authorized to work in the

United States. We hold that such relief is foreclosed by federal immigration policy, as expressed by Congress in the Immigration Reform and Control Act of 1986 (IRCA).

Petitioner Hoffman Plastic Compounds, Inc. (petitioner or Hoffman), custom-formulates chemical compounds for businesses. . . . In May 1988, petitioner hired Jose Castro. . . . Before being hired for this position, Castro presented documents that appeared to verify his authorization to work in the United States. In December 1988, the United Rubber, Cork, Linoleum, and Plastic Workers of America, AFL-CIO, began a union-organizing campaign at petitioner's production plant. Castro and several other employees supported the organizing campaign and distributed authorization cards to co-workers. In January 1989, Hoffman laid off Castro and other employees engaged in these organizing activities.

Three years later, in January 1992, respondent Board found that Hoffman unlawfully selected four employees, including Castro, for layoff "in order to rid itself of known union supporters" in violation of §8(a)(3) of the National Labor Relations Act (NLRA). . . . To remedy this violation, the Board ordered that Hoffman (1) cease and desist from further violations of the NLRA, (2) post a detailed notice to its employees regarding the remedial order, and (3) offer reinstatement and backpay to the four affected employees. . . . Hoffman entered into a stipulation with the Board's General Counsel and agreed to abide by the Board's order.

In June 1993, the parties proceeded to a compliance hearing before an Administrative Law Judge (ALJ) to determine the amount of backpay owed to each discriminatee. . . . Castro testified that he was born in Mexico and that he had never been legally admitted to, or authorized to work in, the United States. . . . He admitted gaining employment with Hoffman only after tendering a birth certificate belonging to a friend who was born in Texas. . . . He also admitted that he used this birth certificate to fraudulently obtain a California driver's license and a Social Security card, and to fraudulently obtain employment following his layoff by Hoffman. . . . Neither Castro nor the Board's General Counsel offered any evidence that Castro had applied or intended to apply for legal authorization to work in the United States. . . . Based on this testimony, the ALJ found the Board precluded from awarding Castro backpay or reinstatement as such relief would be . . . in conflict with IRCA, which makes it unlawful for employers knowingly to hire undocumented workers or for employees to use fraudulent documents to establish employment eligibility. . . .

In September 1998, four years after the ALJ's decision, and nine years after Castro was fired, the Board reversed with respect to backpay. . . . Citing its earlier decision in A.P.R.A. Fuel Oil Buyers Group, Inc., 320 N.L.R.B. 408 (1995), the Board determined that "the most effective way to accommodate and further the immigration policies embodied in [IRCA] is to provide the protections and remedies of the [NLRA] to undocumented workers in the same manner as to other employees." . . . The Board thus found that Castro was entitled to $66,951 of backpay, plus interest. . . . It calculated this backpay award from the date of Castro's termination to the date Hoffman first learned of Castro's undocumented status, a period of 4½ years. . . .

Hoffman filed a petition for review of the Board's order in the Court of Appeals. A panel of the Court of Appeals denied the petition for review. . . . We granted certiorari . . . and now reverse. . . .

This case exemplifies the principle that the Board's discretion to select and fashion remedies for violations of the NLRA, though generally broad . . . is not unlimited, see, e.g., NLRB v. Fansteel Metallurgical Corp., 306 U.S. 240, 257-258 (1939); Southern S.S. Co. v. NLRB, 316 U.S. 31, 46-47 (1942) . . . Since the Board's inception, we have consistently set aside awards of reinstatement or backpay to employees found guilty of serious illegal conduct in connection with their employment. . . .

Though we found that the employer had committed serious violations of the NLRA, the Board had no discretion to remedy those violations by awarding reinstatement with backpay to employees who themselves had committed serious criminal acts. Two years later, in Southern S.S. Co., supra, the Board awarded reinstatement with backpay to five employees whose strike on shipboard had amounted to a mutiny in violation of federal law. We set aside the award, saying: "It is sufficient for this case to observe that the Board has not been commissioned to effectuate the policies of the Labor Relations Act so single-mindedly that it may wholly ignore other and equally important [c]ongressional objectives." 316 U.S., at 47.

Although the Board had argued that the employees' conduct did not in fact violate the federal mutiny statute, we rejected this view, finding the Board's interpretation of a statute so far removed from its expertise merited no deference from this Court. Id., at 40-46. Since Southern S.S. Co., we have accordingly never deferred to the Board's remedial preferences where such preferences potentially trench upon federal statutes and policies unrelated to the NLRA. Thus, we have precluded the Board from enforcing orders found in conflict with the Bankruptcy Code . . . rejected claims that federal antitrust policy should defer to the NLRA . . . and precluded the Board from selecting remedies pursuant to its own interpretation of the Interstate Commerce Act. . . .

The Board cites our decision in ABF Freight System, Inc. v. NLRB, 510 U.S. 317 . . . (1994), as authority for awarding backpay to employees who violate federal laws. In ABF Freight, we held that an employee's false testimony at a compliance proceeding did not require the Board to deny reinstatement with backpay. The question presented was "a narrow one," id. at 322, limited to whether the Board was obliged to "adopt a rigid rule" that employees who testify falsely under oath automatically forfeit NLRA remedies, id., at 325. There are significant differences between that case and this. First, we expressly did not address whether the Board could award backpay to an employee who engaged in "serious misconduct" unrelated to internal Board proceedings, id., at 322, n. 7, such as threatening to kill a supervisor . . . or stealing from an employer. . . . Second, the challenged order did not implicate federal statutes or policies administered by other federal agencies, a "most delicate area" in which the Board must be "particularly careful in its choice of remedy." . . . Third, the employee misconduct at issue, though serious, was not at all analogous to misconduct that renders an underlying employment relationship illegal under explicit provisions of federal law. . . . For these reasons, we believe the present case is controlled by the *Southern S.S. Co.* line of cases, rather than by *ABF Freight.*

We need not resolve [whether *Sure-Tan's* holding on NLRA backpay applies here]. For whether isolated sentences from *Sure-Tan* definitively control, or count merely as persuasive dicta in support of petitioner, we think the question presented here better analyzed through a wider lens, focused as it must be on a legal landscape now significantly changed.

The *Southern S.S. Co.* line of cases established that where the Board's chosen remedy trenches upon a federal statute or policy outside the Board's competence to administer, the Board's remedy may be required to yield. Whether or not this was the situation at the time of *Sure-Tan,* it is precisely the situation today. In 1986, two years after *Sure-Tan,* Congress enacted IRCA, a comprehensive scheme prohibiting the employment of illegal aliens in the United States. . . . As we have previously noted, IRCA "forcefully" made combating the employment of illegal aliens central to "[t]he policy of immigration law." . . . It did so by establishing an extensive "employment verification system," . . . designed to deny employment to aliens who (a) are not lawfully present in the United States, or (b) are not lawfully authorized to work in the United States. . . . This verification system is critical to the IRCA regime. To enforce it, IRCA mandates that employers verify the identity and eligibility of all new hires by examining specified documents before they begin work. . . . If an alien applicant is unable to present the required documentation, the unauthorized alien cannot be hired. . . .

Similarly, if an employer unknowingly hires an unauthorized alien, or if the alien becomes unauthorized while employed, the employer is compelled to discharge the worker upon discovery of the worker's undocumented status. . . . Employers who violate IRCA are punished by civil fines . . . and may be subject to criminal prosecution . . . IRCA also makes it a crime for an unauthorized alien to subvert the employer verification system by tendering fraudulent documents. . . . It thus prohibits aliens from using or attempting to use "any forged, counterfeit, altered, or falsely made document" or "any document lawfully issued to or with respect to a person other than the possessor" for purposes of obtaining employment in the United States. . . . Aliens who use or attempt to use such documents are subject to fines and criminal prosecution. . . . There is no dispute that Castro's use of false documents to obtain employment with Hoffman violated these provisions.

Under the IRCA regime, it is impossible for an undocumented alien to obtain employment in the United States without some party directly contravening explicit congressional policies. Either the undocumented alien tenders fraudulent identification, which subverts the cornerstone of IRCA's enforcement mechanism, or the employer knowingly hires the undocumented alien in direct contradiction of its IRCA obligations. The Board asks that we overlook this fact and allow it to award backpay to an illegal alien for years of work not performed, for wages that could not lawfully have been earned, and for a job obtained in the first instance by a criminal fraud. We find, however, that awarding backpay to illegal aliens runs counter to policies underlying IRCA, policies the Board has no authority to enforce or administer. Therefore, as we have consistently held in like circumstances, the award lies beyond the bounds of the Board's remedial discretion.

The Board contends that awarding limited backpay to Castro "reasonably accommodates" IRCA, because, in the Board's view, such an award is not "inconsistent" with IRCA. . . . The Board argues that because the backpay period was closed as of the date Hoffman learned of Castro's illegal status, Hoffman could have employed Castro during the backpay period without violating IRCA. . . . The Board further argues that while IRCA criminalized the misuse of documents, "it did not make violators ineligible for back pay awards or other compensation flowing from employment secured by the misuse of such documents." . . . This latter statement, of course, proves little: The mutiny statute in *Southern S.S. Co.*, and the INA in *Sure-Tan*, were likewise understandably silent with respect to such things as backpay awards under the NLRA. What matters here, and what sinks both of the Board's claims, is that Congress has expressly made it criminally punishable for an alien to obtain employment with false documents. There is no reason to think that Congress nonetheless intended to permit backpay where but for an employer's unfair labor practices, an alien-employee would have remained in the United States illegally, and continued to work illegally, all the while successfully evading apprehension by immigration authorities. Far from "accommodating" IRCA, the Board's position, recognizing employer misconduct but discounting the misconduct of illegal alien employees, subverts it.

Indeed, awarding backpay in a case like this not only trivializes the immigration laws, it also condones and encourages future violations. The Board admits that had the INS detained Castro, or had Castro obeyed the law and departed to Mexico, Castro would have lost his right to backpay. . . . Castro thus qualifies for the Board's award only by remaining inside the United States illegally. . . . Similarly, Castro cannot mitigate damages, a duty our cases require . . . without triggering new IRCA violations, either by tendering false documents to employers or by finding employers willing to ignore IRCA and hire illegal workers. The Board here has failed to even consider this tension. . . .

We therefore conclude that allowing the Board to award backpay to illegal aliens would unduly trench upon explicit statutory prohibitions critical to federal immigration policy, as expressed in IRCA. It would encourage the successful evasion of apprehension by immigration authorities, condone prior violations of the immigration laws, and encourage future violations. However broad the Board's discretion to fashion remedies when dealing only with the NLRA, it is not so unbounded as to authorize this sort of an award.

Lack of authority to award backpay does not mean that the employer gets off scot-free. The Board here has already imposed other significant sanctions against Hoffman — sanctions Hoffman does not challenge. . . . These include orders that Hoffman cease and desist its violations of the NLRA, and that it conspicuously post a notice to employees setting forth their rights under the NLRA and detailing its prior unfair practices. . . . Hoffman will be subject to contempt proceedings should it fail to comply with these orders. . . . We have deemed such "traditional remedies" sufficient to effectuate national labor policy regardless of whether the "spur and catalyst" of backpay accompanies them. . . . As we concluded in *Sure-Tan,* "in light of the practical workings of the immigration laws," any "perceived deficienc[y] in the NLRA's existing remedial arsenal" must be "addressed by congressional action," not the courts. . . .

BREYER, J., with whom STEVENS, J., SOUTER, J., and GINSBURG, J., join, dissenting.

Without the possibility of the deterrence that backpay provides, the Board can impose only future-oriented obligations upon law-violating employers — for it has no other weapons in its remedial arsenal. And in the absence of the backpay weapon, employers could conclude that they can violate the labor laws at least once with impunity. . . . Hence the backpay remedy is necessary; it helps make labor law enforcement credible; it makes clear that violating the labor laws will not pay.

Where in the immigration laws can the Court find a "policy" that might warrant taking from the Board this critically important remedial power? Certainly not in any statutory language. The immigration statutes say that an employer may not knowingly employ an illegal alien, that an alien may not submit false documents, and that the employer must verify documentation. . . . They provide specific penalties, including criminal penalties, for violations. . . . But the statutes' language itself does not explicitly state how a violation is to [a]ffect the enforcement of other laws, such as the labor laws. What is to happen, for example, when an employer hires, or an alien works, in violation of these provisions? Must the alien forfeit all pay earned? May the employer ignore the labor laws? More to the point, may the employer violate those laws with impunity, at least once — secure in the knowledge that the Board cannot assess a monetary penalty? The immigration statutes' language simply does not say.

Nor can the Court comfortably rest its conclusion upon the immigration laws' purposes. For one thing, the general purpose of the immigration statute's employment prohibition is to diminish the attractive force of employment, which like a "magnet" pulls illegal immigrants towards the United States. . . . To permit the Board to award backpay could not significantly increase the strength of this magnetic force, for so speculative a future possibility could not realistically influence an individual's decision to migrate illegally. . . .

To *deny* the Board the power to award backpay, however, might very well increase the strength of this magnetic force. That denial lowers the cost to the employer of an initial labor law violation (provided, of course, that the only victims are illegal aliens). It thereby increases the employer's incentive to find and to hire illegal-alien employees. Were the Board forbidden to assess backpay against a *knowing* employer—a circumstance not before us today . . . —this perverse economic incentive, which runs directly contrary to the immigration statute's basic objective, would be obvious and serious. But even if limited to cases where the employer did not know of the employee's status, the incentive may prove significant—for, as the Board has told us, the Court's rule offers employers immunity in borderline cases, thereby encouraging them to take risks, i.e., to hire with a wink and a nod those potentially unlawful aliens whose unlawful employment (given the Court's views) ultimately will lower the costs of labor law violations. . . . The Court has recognized these considerations in stating that the labor laws must apply to illegal aliens in order to ensure that "there will be no advantage under the NLRA in preferring illegal aliens" and therefore there will be "fewer incentives for aliens themselves to enter." Sure-Tan, supra, at 893-894. The Court today accomplishes the precise opposite.

## *NOTES AND QUESTIONS*

**1. Continued Coverage of Unauthorized Workers as Statutory "Employees"?** Since *Hoffman,* the courts of appeals have continued to hold that unauthorized individuals are "employees" under the NLRA, despite the Board's inability to award reinstatement or backpay to them. See, e.g., Agri Processor Co. v. NLRB, 514 F.3d 1, 5 (D.C. Cir. 2008) ("[T]he NLRA's plain language, as applied by the Supreme Court in *Sure-Tan,* continues to control after IRCA . . .".).

**2. Likely Impact of Denial of NLRB Backpay Awards?** Does the majority or the dissent have the better of the argument about *Hoffman*'s effect on immigration law and labor law? With respect to immigration law, is the denial of NLRA backpay likely to encourage or discourage the employment of unauthorized employees? How, if at all, will it affect the incentives of employers and unauthorized job seekers? With respect to labor law, what is the majority's response to the dissent's critique that withholding backpay undermines the deterrent effect of NLRB orders in cases involving unlawfully discharged unauthorized employees? For a systematic review of IRCA's legislative history regarding the relationship between IRCA and labor and employment law protections, see Kati L. Griffith, When Federal Immigration Exclusion Meets Subfederal Workplace Inclusion: A Forensic Approach to Legislative History, 18 N.Y.U. J. Leg. & Pub. Pol'y (forthcoming 2015). Is *Hoffman* likely to have a significant impact on the exercise of §7 rights by employees in the American workplace?

**3. Other NLRB Remedies for the Unauthorized?** Besides cease and desist orders and notice posting, what remedies could the NLRB fashion in these cases that would not conflict with *Hoffman*? Consider Mezonos Maven Bakery, 357 N.L.R.B. No. 47, at 9 (2011) (Members Liebman and Pearce, concurring):

> It is arguable, for example, that a remedy that requires payment by the employer of backpay equivalent to what it would have owed to an undocumented discriminatee would not only be consistent with *Hoffman*, but would advance Federal labor and immigration policy objectives. Such backpay could be paid, for example, into a fund to make whole discriminatees whose backpay the Board had been unable to collect. . . . [W]e would be willing to consider in a future case any remedy within our statutory powers that would prevent an employer that discriminates against undocumented workers because of their protected activity from being unjustly enriched by its unlawful conduct.

The Court's decision in Phelps Dodge v. NLRB, 313 U.S. 177 (1941), discussed supra pages 124-125, stands for the proposition that the NLRB can sometimes direct remedies that would not directly benefit the charging parties because they had received employment elsewhere. The *Phelps Dodge* Court found permissible a hiring order that did not help the immediate claimants, stating that the Board "does not exist for the adjudication of private rights; it acts in a public capacity to give effect to the declared public policy of the Act." Id. at 193 (internal citation marks omitted). But is the proposed remedy "punitive," and thus inconsistent with Republic Steel Corp. v. NLRB, 311 U.S. 7 (1940)? In that case, the "Board, in providing for back pay, directed the company to deduct from the payments to the reinstated employees the amounts they had received for work performed upon 'work relief projects' and to pay over such amounts to the appropriate governmental agencies." The Supreme Court held that the order exceeded the Board's remedial authority as a punitive measure "for the purpose of redressing, not an injury to the employees, but an injury to the public. . . ." Id. at 8, 9-10.

**4. Does *Hoffman* Apply Where the Employer, not the Employee, Violates IRCA?** In *Hoffman*, the employee violated IRCA by submitting fraudulent documents to gain employment. Does *Hoffman*'s disallowance of the backpay remedy apply where the employee did not violate IRCA but the employer did? The Board answered this question in the affirmative in Mezonos Maven Bakery, 357 N.L.R.B. No. 47 (2011), enforced sub nom. Palma v. NLRB, 723 F.3d 176 (2d Cir. 2013). Does *Hoffman* compel this result?

**5. Evidentiary and Compliance Implications of *Hoffman*?** Post-*Hoffman*, an employee's lack of authorization to work in the U.S. during the backpay period is a potential affirmative defense to backpay. In Flaum Appetizing Corp., 357 N.L.R.B. No. 162, at 5 (2011) the Board concluded that the employer has the burden to plead specific facts about immigration status and cannot engage in an immigration status "fishing expedition." Once an immigration status affirmative defense is properly raised, how should the Board determine an employee's immigration status? In NLRB v. Domsey Trading Corp., 636 F.3d 33, 39 (2011) the Second Circuit held that "employers may cross-examine backpay applicants with regard to their immigration status" during compliance proceedings and left "it to the Board to fashion evidentiary rules consistent with *Hoffman*." Can immigration law experts play a role? See id. ("[T]he ALJ should have permitted Domsey to introduce the testimony of its immigration expert"). Would a Social Security Administration (SSA) "No Match" letter, which identifies a mismatch between SSA records and an employer's SSA submission, be sufficient evidence of immigration status? So far, the answer is no. See Tuv Taam Corp., 340 N.L.R.B. 756, at 760 (2003) (concluding that a SSA letter is not "legally cognizable evidence regarding the immigration status of . . . discriminatees," in part because the letter explicitly states that it "does not imply" that anyone "intentionally provided incorrect information."); Aramark Facility Serv. v. SEIU Local 1877, 530 F.3d 817, 826 (9th Cir. 2008) (affirming an arbitrator's ruling that an employer's terminations in response to an SSA No Match letter violated the collective bargaining agreement's "just cause" provision and stating that "SSN mismatches could generate a no-match letter for many reasons, including typographical errors, name changes, compound last names prevalent in immigrant communities, and inaccurate or incomplete employer records."). Can an employer's unsupported assertions of an immigration status-based affirmative defense to backpay constitute an unfair labor practice? NLRB Assoc. Gen. Couns. Mem. OM 12-55 (May 4, 2012) ("Regions may consider whether a charged party commits an independent violation of Section 8(a)(1) where, without evidence . . . it issues Board subpoenas for the employee's work authorization documents for purposes of harassing the employee"). Can an employer condition reinstatement of an illegally terminated employee on re-verification of the employee's work authorization? See id. (a reinstatement offer can no longer be conditioned on re-verification).

**6. Bargaining Unit Determination Issues?** Do unauthorized immigrants share a community of interest with their authorized counterparts? Do they have the same expectation of continued employment in the future? Does this matter? See Agri Processor Co. v. NLRB, 514 F.3d 1 (D.C. Cir. 2008) (finding unlawful an employer's refusal to bargain with a newly certified union because of the unauthorized status of some bargaining unit members and concluding that authorized and unauthorized employees share a community of interest related to wages, benefits, working conditions and supervision).

**7. Impact of Hoffman/IRCA on Employment Law?** Are monetary remedies available to unauthorized immigrants for violations of other employment laws? So far, courts have limited IRCA and *Hoffman*'s impact where the underlying claim is for pay for work performed as opposed to a remedy for lost income as a result of an otherwise unlawful discharge. See Lucas v. Jerusalem Cafe, LLC, 721 F.3d 927, 937 (8th Cir. 2013) ("[W]e hold that unauthorized aliens may sue under the [Fair Labor Standards Act] . . . to recover statutory damages for work actually performed"). Similar distinctions are made for labor-related claims brought under state law. See Salas v. Sierra Chemical Co., 59 Cal. 4th 407, 414 (Cal. 2014) ("state law employee protections and remedies" extend to all workers "regardless of immigration status" except for reinstatement remedies and remedies that provide "lost pay damages for any period after the employer's discovery of an employee's ineligibility to work in the United States"); Madeira v. Affordable Hous. Found., 469 F.3d 219, 248, 254 (2d Cir. 2006) (damages for lost future earnings at U.S. pay rates may be available under New York's scaffolding law in some cases but, to avoid conflict with IRCA, juries are instructed "to consider the workers' removeability in calculating what, if any, compensation to award"). See generally Kati L. Griffith, U.S. Migrant Worker Law: The Interstices of Immigration Law and Labor and Employment Law, 31 Comp. Lab. L. & Pol'y J. 125, 145-52 (2009) and her Comment, A Supreme Stretch: The Supremacy Clause in the Wake of IRCA and Hoffman Plastic Compounds, 41 Cornell Int'l L.J. 127 (2008) (arguing for a narrow reading of IRCA's preemptive effects on state and local workplace protections). For an argument that IRCA and unsettled post-*Hoffman* case law creates a formidable disincentive for unauthorized immigrants to come forward with federal and state employment law claims, see Kati L. Griffith, Discovering "Immployment" Law: The Constitutionality of Subfederal Immigration Regulation at Work, 29 Yale L. & Pol'y Rev. 389, 431-441 (2011).

**8. President Obama's November 2014 Executive Actions on Immigration.** In November 2014, President Obama announced a series of executive actions on immigration covering a variety of issues, the most important of which for present purposes include an expansion of the deferred action plan both for a potentially large number of unauthorized immigrants who arrived in the U.S. as children and also for parents of U.S. citizens and lawful permanent residents. See series of executive actions listed on U.S. Department of Homeland Security (DHS) web site, http://www.dhs.gov/immigrationaction?utm_source=hp_feature&utm_medium=web&utm_campaign=dhs_hp. According to DHS, "[d]eferred action does not confer any form of legal status in this country . . . it simply means that, for a specified period of time, an individual is permitted to be lawfully present in the United States." See DHS Memorandum, Executive Action: Expand Deferred Action for Childhood Arrivals (DACA) Program, 2, (Nov. 20, 2014). Those who apply for deferred action are eligible, however, to apply for work authorization. See id.; 8 C.F.R. §1274a.12(c)(14) ("An alien who has been granted deferred action" can gain work authorization "if the alien establishes an economic necessity for employment"). How would *Hoffman*'s holding that unauthorized employees cannot receive NLRA backpay or reinstatement for NLRA §8(a)(3) violations apply to an unauthorized immigrant who receives deferred action and temporarily gains work authorization as a result of President Obama's executive action?

**9. Violation of International Norm of "Freedom of Association"?** Responding to the application of the Confederation of Mexican Workers and the AFL-CIO, the International Labour Organization (ILO)'s Committee on Freedom of Association issued a report in 2003 that criticized *Hoffman.* See ILO, Comm. On Freedom of Association, Case No. 2227, Report No. 332 (Nov. 2003) (stating unauthorized employees' access to cease and desist orders and notice posting is "likely to afford little protection to undocumented workers who can be indiscriminately dismissed for exercising freedom of association rights without any direct penalty aimed a dissuading such action"). For another criticism of *Hoffman* by an international body, see Inter-American Court of Human Rights, Legal Condition and Rights of Undocumented Migrant Workers, Consultative Opinion OC-18/03 (September 17, 2003). The next chapter will more fully discuss cross-border labor law instruments and their authority.

## B. THE NLRA AND IMMIGRATION ADVOCACY

In the last decade, U.S. labor unions have been involved in immigration reform advocacy efforts at the national and local levels. See, e.g., Laura Francis, AFL-CIO Launches Immigration Ad Campaign Targeting Republicans for Stalling Legislation, 2013 Daily Lab. Rep. (BNA) No. 216, at A10 (Nov. 6, 2014). As part of these initiatives, union members, and other worker advocates, have often encouraged their co-workers to take action on this policy issue. These efforts raise the question of whether, or under what circumstances, the NLRA can protect workplace-related political advocacy about immigration policy. We previously discussed political advocacy outside of the immigration context, supra pages 183-192.

**Memorandum GC 08-10 from NLRB Gen. Counsel Ronald Meisburg to All Regional Directors re: Unfair Labor Practice Charges Involving Political Advocacy**
*July 22, 2008,*[1]

In late 2006, we considered a series of charges involving discipline of employees who had participated in nationwide and local demonstrations organized to protest pending legislative proposals that would impose greater restrictions and penalties on immigrant employees and their employers. Consideration of those cases prompted a review of agency law and policy in political advocacy cases. . . .

In Eastex, Inc. v. NLRB [437 U.S. 556 (1978), supra page 183] the Supreme Court endorsed the Board's view that employees are protected under the "mutual aid or protection" clause of Section 7 when they seek to "improve their lot as employees through channels outside the immediate employee-employer relationship." At the same time, the Court cautioned against extending this principle so far that nearly all forms of political activity — no matter how attenuated from employees' workplace interests — might be deemed protected. The important question of where, and on what basis, to draw the line between protected concerted activity and unprotected political activity can be a difficult one. . . .

The Board has long extended this Section 7 protection beyond the confines of the employment relationship to concerted political advocacy when the subject of that advocacy has a direct nexus to employee working conditions.

Thus, over thirty years ago, the Board held that a Kaiser Engineers employee who wrote to members of Congress on behalf of his fellow employees, opposing a competitor company's efforts to obtain resident visas for foreign engineers, was engaged in protected activity under Section 7 [Kaiser Engineers, 213 N.L.R.B. 752, 755 (1974), enfd. 538 F.2d 1379 (9th Cir. 1976)]. The letter was motivated by a concern that an influx of foreign engineers would threaten U.S. engineers' job security and therefore was for the "mutual aid or protection" of the Kaiser engineers and their "fellow engineers in the profession."

The Supreme Court upheld this approach in *Eastex*. . . .

In numerous subsequent cases, the Board has found that employee appeals to legislators or governmental agencies were protected, so long as the substance of those appeals was directly related to employee working conditions. . . .

---

1. *Available at* http://www.nlrb.gov/reports-guidance/general-counsel-memos.

### Application to Current Political Advocacy Concerns

. . . [I]t is clear from the analytical framework set forth above that participation in such demonstrations did in fact fall within the scope of the "mutual aid or protection" clause. These demonstrations were in protest, *inter alia,* of proposed legislation that would require prospective employees to obtain a variety of clearances before they could work in this country and would mandate that prospective employers verify each employee's paperwork or risk steep penalties.

Over a period of several months, thousands of employees across the country, many of them immigrants, took time off from work to attend rallies and, in many instances, to also demonstrate through their absence from work the role of immigrants in the workforce. These demonstrations focused upon pending legislation that both supporters and detractors agreed were designed to eliminate the employment of illegal immigrants. Moreover, many observers predicted that the potential penalties would cause employers to forgo hiring even lawful immigrants in order to avoid inadvertent violations. Protesting employees therefore were concerned by predictions that employers would decline to hire immigrant employees altogether rather than risk violating the proposed law. In this manner, the proposed legislation could directly affect their job opportunities and job security. This is the same type of concern that was the focus of the protected employee political advocacy in Kaiser Engineers.

In sum, immigrant employees and even non-immigrant employees could reasonably believe that the bill could impact their interests as employees. For these reasons, employee attendance at and support of these demonstrations in our view was within the scope of the "mutual aid or protection" clause. . . .

Once we have determined that a particular political advocacy falls within the "mutual aid or protection" clause, we must then ascertain whether the means employed to carry out that advocacy is protected . . . The immigration demonstrations . . . involved . . . leaving or absenting oneself from work to attend a political demonstration. . . . [T]hough their subject is related to employee working conditions, the immediate employer may lack the ability to address the underlying grievance. . . . [W]hen employees leave work in support of a political cause, either to mobilize public sentiment or to urge governmental action (in either case a matter outside their employer's control), they are not withholding their services as an economic weapon in the employment relationship . . . It is hardly unprecedented to find that conduct with a protected object may nonetheless be unprotected because of the means employed. . . .

We can distill the following principles from these lines of Board authority:

[N]on-disruptive political advocacy for or against a specific issue related to a specifically identified employment concern, that takes place during the employees' own time and in nonwork areas, is protected;

> [O]n-duty political advocacy for or against a specific issue related to a specifically identified employment concern is subject to restrictions imposed by lawful and neutrally applied work rules; and
>
> [L]eaving or stopping work to engage in political advocacy for or against a specific issue related to a specifically identified employment concern may also be subject to restrictions imposed by lawful and neutrally-applied work rules. . . .

## *NOTES AND QUESTIONS*

**1. Connection to Worker Interests "As Employees"?** The Supreme Court's *Eastex* decision, supra page 183, reminds us that some workplace-related political advocacy is protected concerted activity "for mutual aid or protection" as long as it sufficiently relates to "employees' interests as employees." What was the connection between the immigration proposals described in the Meisburg Memo and employees' interests as employees? What was the connection in *Kaiser*, which is cited in the memo?

**2. Advocacy for Immigration Reform as Protected Activity?** Recent proposals for "comprehensive immigration reform" typically include changes to work visa programs, a legalization program for the unauthorized population and increased enforcement efforts through employer verification of immigration status and border patrol measures. For instance, the proposed W visa program would create a new visa category for low-skilled non-agricultural workers. See Border Security, Economic Opportunity, and Immigration Modernization Act of 2013, S. 744, 113th Cong. (2013) §§4701-4703. Unlike former visa programs for low-skilled laborers, W visa holders could change employers during the term of the visa. §4703(i). The proposed bill would create the Bureau of Immigration and Labor Market as "an independent statistical agency within U.S. Citizenship and Immigration Services." §4701(b). Among other things the Bureau would "devise a methodology" to identify which occupations are experiencing labor shortages and to help determine the cap on visas each year. §§4701-4703. Does the W visa proposal relate to employees' interests "as employees"? What about heightened immigration enforcement initiatives and the proposal to legalize millions of unauthorized immigrants? See generally Kati L. Griffith & Tamara L. Lee, Immigration Advocacy as Labor Advocacy, 33 Berkeley J. Emp. & Lab. L. 73 (2012).

**3. Advocacy Related to Other Non-NLRA Laws?** Advocacy related to other non-NLRA federal statutes may implicate labor issues as well. The Victims of Trafficking and Violence Protection Act of 2000 includes protections against "severe forms" of labor trafficking, which is defined as "the recruitment, harboring, transportation, provision or obtaining of a person for labor or services, through the use of force, fraud, or coercion for the purpose of subjection to involuntary servitude, peonage, debt bondage, or slavery." 22 U.S.C. §7102 (2006). When, if at all, would collective advocacy relating to labor trafficking protections sufficiently relate to employees' interests "as employees"? What about the Racketeer Influenced and Corrupt Organizations Act (RICO)? See 18 U.S.C. §1961(1)(B), (F) (2006) ("racketeering activity" includes immigration law violations "relating to fraud and misuse of visa, permits, and other documents," "relating to bringing in and harboring certain aliens," "relating to aiding or assisting certain aliens to enter the United States," and "relating to importation of alien for immoral purpose"). Employee litigants have invoked RICO in cases alleging that their employers' immigration violations depressed their wages. See Trollinger v. Tyson Foods, Inc., 370 F.3d 602 (6th Cir. 2004) (concluding that authorized worker plaintiffs had standing); Simpson v. Sanderson Farms, Inc., 744 F. 3d 702 (11th Cir. 2014) (concluding that authorized worker plaintiffs did not have standing). Are employees engaged in protected activity when they strike, or attend a rally, in support of litigation under these laws? What if they are simply circulating a leaflet describing developments in such litigation during non-working time in non-work areas?

**4. Immigration and Labor Standards.** The relationship between immigration and labor standards is often at the heart of policy debates about immigration. Does immigration actually harm U.S. labor standards, such as wages and unemployment levels? Labor economists have opposing views on the issue. Compare George J. Borjas, The Labor Demand Curve Is Downward Sloping: Reexamining the Impact of Immigration on the Labor Market, 118 Q.J. Econ. 1335, 1336 (2003) ("[T]he evidence consistently suggests that immigration has indeed harmed the employment opportunities of competing native workers"); with David Card, Is the New Immigration Really So Bad?, 115 Econ. J. 300, 320-323 (2005) (concluding that the effect on low-skill native workers is very slight and there is "no strong evidence that immigration has overall effects on aggregate employment, participation, unemployment and wages").

## C. THE NLRA AND IMMIGRANT WORKER CENTERS

Low-wage immigrant workers are increasingly engaging in organizing activities with the assistance of "worker centers." Difficult to define, these centers are often described as "community-based and community-led organizations that engage in a combination of service, advocacy, and organizing to provide support to low-wage workers." Janice Fine, Worker Centers: Organizing Communities at the Edge of the Dream (2006); see also U.S. Chamber of Commerce, The New Model of Representation: An Overview of Leading Worker Centers (2014) (distinguishing between worker centers that are "community-based organizations" and worker centers that are the "new face of traditional labor unions"). These centers raise a number of questions about the applicability of the NLRA.

**Restaurant Opportunities Center of NY**
*2006 NLRB GCM LEXIS 52 (2006)*

. . . The Region submitted these cases for advice on whether: (1) Restaurant Opportunities Center of New York (ROCNY) is a labor organization under Section 2(5) of the Act; (2) ROCNY's conduct to force the Employers to enter into lawsuit settlement agreements that set numerous terms and conditions of employment is recognitional picketing in violation of Section 8(b)(7)(C); (3) ROCNY's conduct constitutes attempts to force representation on employees absent majority support in violation of Section 8(b)(1)(A); and (4) ROCNY's conduct seeks to force the Employers to discriminate against employees on the basis of ROCNY membership in violation of Section 8(b)(2). . . .

Section 8(b) applies only to a "labor organization" or its agents. Section 2(5) defines a labor organization as an organization in which employees participate and that exists for the purpose, at least in part, of "dealing with employers" over grievances, labor disputes, or terms and conditions of employment. It is undisputed that ROCNY is an organization in which employees participate. Thus, it easily meets the first requirement of labor organization status. However, as most of ROCNY's activities consist of social advocacy, legal services, and job-support services for restaurant workers that do not fall within the purview of Section 2(5), the question is whether, in its role as legal advocate, ROCNY's attempt to settle employment discrimination claims has constituted "dealing with" the Employers over terms and conditions of employment under Section 2(5).

. . . The "dealing with" requirement has been defined broadly—an organization may satisfy the "dealing with" requirement without formally bargaining for a collective-bargaining agreement. What is required is a "bilateral mechanism" of proposals from the group or organization, "coupled with real or apparent consideration of those proposals by management." However, the required element of dealing only exists when the bilateral mechanism of offer and consideration of proposals entails a "pattern or practice" that extends "over time." An isolated instance of exchanging proposals, or a single attempt to deal with an employer over a discrete issue does not establish a pattern or practice of dealing. . . .

ROCNY's attempts to negotiate settlement agreements with the Employers here were discrete, non-recurring transactions with each Employer. The parties' discussions were limited to settling legal claims raised by employees. Granted, the parties' discussions stretched over a period of time. But the settlement of lawsuits is not generally something that can be accomplished in a single meeting. Although stretching over a period of time, the parties' dealings were limited to a single context or a single issue — resolving ROCNY's attempts to enforce employment laws. Nothing in the tentative agreement discussed by the parties implies an ongoing or recurring pattern of dealing over employment terms and conditions, beyond the resolution of the current dispute. Indeed, even the subjects that were explicitly left open-ended in the proposed agreement with Daniel, such as Daniel's new promotion policy and language policy, were intended to be developed by Daniel in conjunction with the EEOC, without further input from ROCNY.

This is the case even with regard to the arbitration provisions in the proposed settlement agreement with Daniel. These provisions, which allow the parties to raise alleged contract violations for adjudication by a third party for the effective period of the settlement agreement, are merely contract enforcement mechanisms that do not imply a continuing practice of "dealing." They do not entail further "back and forth" between the parties, nor do they contemplate any bilateral offer or consideration of new proposals. Rather, the arbitration provisions are strictly adjudicatory enforcement mechanisms that do not involve any further "dealing" under Section 2(5). . . .

Therefore, absent evidence that ROCNY has engaged in a pattern of dealing with employers over time, rather than discrete instances of lawsuit-settlement negotiations arising out of charges with a federal law enforcement agency, we conclude that ROCNY is not a Section 2(5) labor organization. . . .

Even if it were to be established that ROCNY is a Section 2(5) labor organization, we conclude that ROCNY's picketing in support of lawsuit settlement is not recognitional; thus, the charges in the instant cases should be dismissed on that basis as well, absent withdrawal.

Section 8(b)(7)(C) makes it unlawful for a labor organization to picket an unorganized employer with the goal of either organizing the employer's employees or obtaining voluntary recognition from the employer, without an election petition being filed within a reasonable period of time not to exceed 30 days.

Here, ROCNY has engaged in mass demonstrations near the entrances to the Employers' restaurants that have included chanting, noisemaking, handbilling, and, at Daniel, picket signs. Although the demonstrators have been mostly confined to defined spaces behind police barricades, instead of patrolling back and forth, at least some of the conduct falls within the Board's definition of picketing. . . . Because of the presence of crowds near the restaurant entrance, the use of picket signs, and the confrontational chanting and noisemaking, the activity at Daniel has clearly constituted picketing.

Moreover, this picketing has taken place on a weekly basis for a period longer than 30 days. Thus, the critical issue is whether ROCNY's picketing has a recognitional object. Recognitional picketing has been defined as "any picketing that seeks to establish a union in a continuing relationship with an employer with regard to matters which could substantially affect terms and conditions of employment." In determining whether picketing is recognitional, the Board considers the totality of the circumstances, including the language on the picket signs and the union's prior and contemporaneous conduct or statements.

In the instant cases, there is no evidence that ROCNY has demanded recognition as collective-bargaining representative of any of the Employers' employees; ROCNY's demands have been limited to negotiating the settlement of the employees' [employment-discrimination] claims as their legal advocate. At Daniel, for example, the handbills distributed during ROCNY's picketing refer to the claims of racial and national origin discrimination and [employment-discrimination] litigation. The picket signs protest alleged discriminatory practices, except for a single picket sign that appeared in a few instances that read "Organizing is a Right." Thus, the object of the picketing and other conduct, as discerned from the overall circumstances, is to publicize the discrimination claims and pressure the Employers to engage in or resume settlement negotiations.

[W]e conclude here that, merely by seeking settlement of employment lawsuits, even with an ongoing oversight role, ROCNY is not seeking recognition and bargaining under Section 8(b)(7).

Further, there is no evidence that ROCNY's settlement attempts conceal a recognitional purpose broader than just the settlement of the outstanding legal claims. ROCNY's proposals seem reasonably related to the claims of mass discrimination and disparate treatment raised by employees. They are aimed at fostering job actions based on objective, non-discriminatory bases, giving all employees equal opportunities in job promotions and scheduling, and redressing the alleged underpayment of the "back of the house" positions in which most employees of color (and claimants) are employed. In addition, the proposed arbitration clause is merely an enforcement mechanism like those routinely included in settlement agreements.

Therefore, even if ROCNY were a labor organization, we would dismiss the Section 8(b)(7)(C) allegation because its picketing to encourage settlement of outstanding discrimination claims is not picketing for a recognitional purpose.

## *NOTES AND QUESTIONS*

**1. Worker Centers as NLRA "Labor Organizations"?** Section 2(5) of the NLRA broadly defines a "labor organization" as an "organization of any kind, or any agency or employee representation committee or plan, in which employees participate and which exists for the purpose, in whole or in part, of dealing with employers concerning grievances, labor disputes, wages, rates of pay, hours of employment, or conditions of work." Was ROCNY "dealing with" employers? The Board's *Electromation* decision, 309 N.L.R.B. 990, 997 (1992), states that "dealing with" involves "the creation of a bilateral process . . . on the basis of employee-initiated proposals." Is arbitration of the terms of a settlement agreement a "bilateral process"? See also NLRB v. Cabot Carbon, 360 U.S. 203, 212-213 (1959) (determining that "dealing with" is broader than the phrase "collective bargaining."); Center for United Labor Action, 219 N.L.R.B. 873, 873 (1975) ("Support for a cause, no matter how active it may become, does not rise to the level of representation unless it can be demonstrated that the organization in question is expressly or implicitly seeking to deal with the employer over matters affecting the employees."). What if ROCNY started a new campaign against the restaurant that made specific demands about working conditions that went beyond the settlement agreement? What if there was a new campaign seeking a revision of the agreement? What if ROCNY provided ongoing advocacy services for employees claiming violations of the settlement agreement? What if ROCNY charged a user fee for these services? What if ROCNY was pressuring the restaurant to adopt a "code of conduct," similar to the New York Green Grocer Code of Conduct, set forth in the Statutory Supplement? In what ways do traditional unions operate differently than ROCNY? If unions had no need to obtain a union security agreement, could they simply rechristen themselves as "worker centers"?

**2. Worker Center Exposure to Sections 8(a)(2) and 8(b)?** If ROCNY is an NLRA "labor organization," it would be subject to the NLRA's 8(a)(2) and 8(b) unfair labor practice provisions. With respect to 8(a)(2), what if the employer held regular meetings with ROCNY to discuss terms and conditions of employment at the workplace? Would that constitute unlawful employer interference? See pages 219-230 supra. With respect to 8(b), were ROCNY's protest activities to encourage public pressure for a legal settlement and its ongoing role in settlement arbitrations instances of unlawful "organizational or recognitional picketing"? See pages 384-395 supra. What if the picketing was not related to a legal settlement and instead included general pleas for the employer to improve wages? What criteria should the Board use to determine whether a worker center is picketing for organizational or recognitional purposes?

**3. LMRDA Implications?** The applicability of the NLRA's 8(b) and 8(a)(2) provisions is not the only issue at stake. Worker centers that fall within the Landrum-Griffin definition of a "labor organization" may be subject to Landrum-Griffin's extensive requirements. See generally Chapter 13 supra. The LMRDA definition largely tracks the language of NLRA section 2(5) referenced above but adds that "[a] labor organization shall be deemed to be engaged in an industry affecting commerce if," it falls within any of the five listed categories, including "a national or international labor organization or a local labor organization recognized or acting as the representative of employees" or an entity that "has chartered a local labor organization or subsidiary body which is representing or actively seeking to represent employees . . .". See 29 U.S.C. §402(i)(j). Under what circumstances, would a worker center fit within this definition? Does it matter that Congress, when passing the LMRDA amendments in 1959, found "from recent investigations" that labor organizations had been involved in "a number of instances of breach of trust, corruption . . . and other failures to observe high standards of responsibility and ethical conduct . . ."? See 29 U.S.C. §401(b). Consider the LMRDA's statement that "[e]very member of a labor organization shall have equal rights and privileges within such organization to nominate candidates, to vote in elections . . . to attend membership meetings and to participate in the deliberations and voting upon the business of such meetings. . . ." 29 U.S.C. §411(a)(1). What would this provision mean for worker centers that do not have members and/or do not hold elections?

**4. The NLRA's Relevance Regardless of the "Labor Organization" Issue.** As you will recall, the NLRA protects employees who engage in protected concerted activity, regardless of whether there is a union, worker center or other labor group present. Thus, section 8(a)'s protections do not turn on whether worker centers are NLRA "labor organizations" or whether the employees want to eventually gain bargaining authority. Indeed, a handful of worker centers have made meritorious section 8(a) charges on behalf of employees. See, e.g., Greater Omaha Packing Co., Inc. 360 N.L.R.B. No. 62 (2014); Babi I, 358 N.L.R.B. No. 148 (2012); Kati L. Griffith, Worker Center Organizing: Is Federal Labor Law a Friend or Foe?, Paper Presented at NYU Center for Labor & Employment Law (Nov. 6, 2014)(collecting publically available cases involving worker center organizing and NLRA 8(a)(1) claims). Moreover, as Professor Griffith has argued, the NLRA's "defamation defense" also has relevance regardless of whether worker centers are NLRA labor organizations. Based on the Supreme Court's *Linn* decision, discussed supra pages 835-840, a heightened standard of proof is required in defamation cases that arise out of an NLRA "labor dispute." Thus, when worker centers engage in aggressive speech and "tough talk" to pressure an employer, the *Linn* defamation defense may apply as long as the dispute involves collective activity about terms and conditions of employment. See Kati L. Griffith, The NLRA Defamation Defense: Doomed Dinosaur or Diamond in the Rough?, 59 Am. U. L. Rev. 1 (2009).

# 15 | Cross-Border Labor Law

So far, our study of the National Labor Relations Act has focused primarily on private-sector labor relations within the borders of the United States. In recent decades, economic globalization — characterized by the increased flow of goods, capital, services, and information across national borders — has raised new challenges and questions for domestic labor law. When, if ever, can the NLRA reach conduct that occurs outside of the United States? Can foreign complainants bring legal claims in U.S. courts against U.S-based companies for labor abuses that occur abroad? What connections have been made between trade law and labor standards? What role can international institutions play in promoting labor standards that transcend national boundaries? Even when international labor standards are not legally enforceable, can they still have an effect on labor relations? Are there private initiatives that promote cross-border labor rights? It is impossible to comprehensively cover the topic of cross-border labor law in one chapter. Instead, the goal here is to provide a general framework for understanding the legal instruments and central debates in this evolving and dynamic area, especially as they relate to freedom of association.

## A. LITIGATION IN U.S. LABOR FORUMS

### 1. Extraterritorial Application of the NLRA

Generally speaking, the NLRA does not apply outside of the borders of the United States. Nonetheless, as the next three cases illustrate, it is not always easy to demarcate the line between domestic and extraterritorial application.

**Asplundh Tree Expert Co. v. NLRB**
*365 F.3d 168 (3d Cir. 2004)*

McKee, J. . . .

. . . Asplundh provides tree trimming services throughout the eastern United States and maintains it principal place of business in Willow Grove, Pennsylvania. Much of Asplundh's work is performed for utility companies [in the United States] that need to keep their power lines cleared of tree limbs. One of Asplundh's operations is based in Cincinnati, Ohio, where it primarily performs line clearance work for the Cincinnati Gas & Electric Company. . . .

Asplundh also offers its services to utilities and other entities in other states. In that capacity, it assigns its employees to perform work related to storms, natural disasters and natural emergencies. Several provincial governments in Canada retained Asplundh to assist in clearing electrical lines, trimming tree limbs and cleaning streets after a major ice storm struck eastern Canada in January 1998. Ottawa, Ontario was among the entities that contracted for Asplundh's services following that storm, and on January 12, Asplundh's Cincinnati operation prepared to send 10 crews of 2 employees each to that Canadian City.

Asplundh does not require its employees to travel outside of their locality for emergency storm cleanup work like the Ottawa assignment. Instead, employees volunteer for such work, and are compensated in part by a per diem covering their food and lodging while working away from home. On January 13, a group of 20 employees met in a parking lot before leaving for Ottawa. At the meeting, Supervisor Darrell Lewis told the employees that they would receive per diem payments in the amount of $25 for food and that Asplundh would pay up to $75 per day for hotel rooms. The group left for Ottawa later that day in a caravan of Asplundh trucks. Lewis did not travel to Ottawa, and Foreman Ronald Lacey was therefore left in charge of the assignment. . . .

Once in Ottawa, Lacey reserved hotel rooms for all of the employees which he paid for at a negotiated price of $61 per room per night. That rate was obviously less than the $75 per night Lewis had told the employees was available for their lodging. Concomitantly, some of the employees began to feel that the $25 per diem for food was insufficient to cover the high cost of food in Ottawa.

At least four employees — Brinson, Crabtree, Shane Duff and Ron Noble — met on the first night in Ottawa and discussed their dissatisfaction with the problems they had encountered en route as well as the amount of their per diem. . . .

On the morning of January 17, Brinson phoned Lacey and told him that the employees wanted a $14 increase in their per diem payments — the difference between the $75 authorized for hotel rooms and the actual

$61 room cost. Brinson also indicated that the employees might not work if their per diem payments were not increased. Lacey then called Cincinnati and spoke with Lewis, the supervisor. Lacey told Lewis of the employees' request and of the possibility that they might not work if their concerns were not addressed. Lewis instructed Lacey not to raise the per diem payments and told Lacey that "if they're not going to take the trucks out, that means they quit."

Lacey went to the hotel lobby to meet with the employees, placed another call to Lewis, then handed Brinson the phone. Lewis told Brinson that the employees were "whiny cry babies" and were "making the Company look bad." Lewis then told Brinson that a number of crews would be laid off when they returned to Cincinnati and that the Ottawa employees were making it easier for Lewis to decide whom to lay off. . . .

Lacey . . . approached Brinson, who was standing with Crabtree, Duff and Noble, and asked them what they were going to do. Brinson said that they still wanted to discuss their situation before going to work. Lacey responded by demanding Brinson's truck keys. After Brinson handed over his keys, Lacey asked Crabtree what he wanted to do. Crabtree replied" "I'm with Denis [Brinson]. I still think we need to have something done about this." Lacey then asked Crabtree for his keys, and after Crabtree gave them to Lacey, Lacey said "this means you quit." Lacey also admonished Brinson and Crabtree for sticking up for their fellow employees and then told them to "get home the best what you f . . . g can." . . .

Soon thereafter, Brinson and Crabtree returned to Cincinnati by bus. Once back in Cincinnati, Brinson repeatedly offered to return to work, but neither he nor Crabtree were ever allowed to return to their jobs with Asplundh. . . .

On May 29, 1998, Brinson filed a charge with the Board alleging that Asplundh "discharged its employees [Brinson and Crabtree] because of their protected, concerted activities." . . . On November 30, 2001, the Board [found that the Asplundh violated the NLRA and] . . . ordered Asplundh to cease and desist from engaging in unfair labor practices and from interfering with employees in the exercise of the rights guaranteed by §7 of the NLRA, 29 U.S.C. §157. The Board also ordered Asplundh to reinstate Brinson and Crabtree, make them whole, remove any reference to improper conduct from their personnel files, and post a remedial notice at its Cincinnati location. . . .

. . . [W]e must first resolve Asplundh's challenge to the Board's exercise of jurisdiction over an unfair labor practices charge arising from "offending" conduct that occurred in Canada.

Although Congress undoubtedly has the authority "to enforce its laws beyond territorial boundaries of the United States[,] . . . whether Congress has in fact exercised that authority . . . is a matter of statutory construction." EEOC v. Arabian American Oil Co., ("ARAMCO"), 499 U.S. 244, 248 (1991).

Moreover, "it is a longstanding principle of American law 'that legislation of Congress, unless a contrary intent appears, is meant to apply only within the territorial jurisdiction of the United States.'" Id. (quoting Foley Bros., Inc. v. Filardo, 336 U.S. 281, 285 (1949)).

As *ARAMCO* teaches, we begin our analysis with the language of the NLRA. Section 10 of that Act provides that "the Board is empowered, as hereinafter provided, to prevent any person from engaging in any unfair labor practice (listed in section 158) affecting commerce." 29 U.S.C. §160(a). Admittedly, the NLRA defines the jurisdictional terms "affecting commerce" and "commerce" very broadly. "'Affecting commerce' means in commerce, or burdening or obstructing commerce or the free flow of commerce, or having led or tending to lead to a labor dispute burdening or obstructive commerce or in the free flow of commerce." 29 U.S.C. §152(7). . . .

Thus, a literal reading of the jurisdiction and definitional provision of the NLRA seems to not only favor the NLRB's extraterritorial exercise of jurisdiction, it seems to dictate that result and end our jurisdictional inquiry. However, in interpreting this seemingly broad language, we are not free to ignore the Supreme Court's interpretation of the similarly broad jurisdictional reach of Title VII in *ARAMCO*. . . .

The Court held that the wording of Title VII was not sufficient to rebut the presumption against extraterritoriality and support a conclusion that Congress intended to empower the Equal Employment Opportunity Commission to exercise jurisdiction beyond the United States, despite the broad definitions suggesting the contrary. The Court buttressed reliance on [the] presumption against extraterritorial jurisdiction by noting that Congress had not included any mechanism for extraterritorial enforcement of the Act's protections. . . .

Similarly, in enacting the NLRA, Congress included no mechanism for extraterritorial enforcement, and did not provide a method for resolving any conflicts with labor laws of other nations.

Given the obvious potential for conflict where United States companies employ workers oversees, this omission strikes us as more than a mere oversight. It is consistent with the Supreme Court's conclusion that broad definitional language is little more than "boilerplate" in the absence of an express manifestation of extraterritorial intent. . . .

. . . We believe the Board's "policy" argument is nothing more than a "balancing of contacts" test that the Supreme Court has already rejected in a case it decided before *ARAMCO*.

In McCulloch v. Sociedad Nacional de Marineros de Honduras, 372 U.S. 10 (1963), an American corporation, United Fruit, was the beneficial owner of a number of cargo vessels which made regular sailings between the United States, Latin America and other ports transporting the American corporation's products. Each vessel was legally owned by a foreign subsidiary of the American corporation, flew the flag of a foreign nation, carried a foreign crew and had other contacts with the nation of its flag. A portion of United Fruit's fleet of beneficially owned vessels consisted of vessels legally owned by Empresa Hondurena de Vapores, a Honduran corporation. However, all of the stock of that Honduran corporation was owned by United Fruit. The crews on the vessels were recruited by Empresa Hondurena in Honduras and all of the crewmen were Honduran citizens who claimed Honduras as their residence and home port with the exception of one Jamaican. The crew's wages, terms and conditions of employment, etc., were controlled by a bargaining agreement between Empresa Hondurena and a Honduran union, Sociedad Nacional de Marineros de Honduras. The agreement was governed by Honduran labor law.

However, United Fruit, the parent corporation of Empresa Hondurena, determined the ports of call of the vessels, their cargoes and sailings, and integrated the Honduran vessels into its broader fleet organization. The Honduran vessels made regular and periodic stops at various ports between Central and South America as well as ports in the United States.

An American maritime union, the National Maritime Union of America, AFL-CIO, filed a petition seeking certification as the representative of the crewmen employed on certain of the Honduran vessels. The NLRB granted the union's petition for certification, asserting jurisdiction based on its finding that the vessels' "maritime operations involved substantial United States contacts, outweighing the numerous foreign contacts present." Sociedad, the Honduran union, responded by seeking an injunction to prevent the regional director of the NLRB from holding an election, and the district court granted the Honduran union's request for relief.

There, as here, the inquiry turned on "the coverage of the [NLRA]." . . .

The Court . . . noted that using the Board's "balancing of contacts" test to determine jurisdiction

> might require that the Board inquire into the internal discipline and order of all foreign vessels calling at American ports. Such activity would raise considerable disturbance not only in the field of maritime law but in our international relations as well. In addition, enforcement of Board orders would project the courts into application of the sanctions of the Act to foreign-flag ships on a purely ad hoc weighing of contacts basis. This would inevitably lead to embarrassment in foreign affairs and be entirely infeasible in actual practice.

Consequently, the Supreme Court rejected the Board's "balancing of contacts" test and concluded that the question before it was "more basic; namely, whether the Act as written was intended to have any application to foreign registered vessels employing alien seamen." In other words, the inquiry turned on statutory construction rather than an analysis of the comparative impact the Board's exercise of jurisdiction would have on the jurisdictions potentially affected by the underlying dispute or the Board's action. After examining the language in the NLRA, the Court concluded "that the jurisdictional provisions of the Act do not extend to maritime operations of foreign-flag ships employing alien seamen."

Thus, after *McCulloch*, the Board's "balancing of contacts" cannot be used to manufacture jurisdiction in the absence of clearly expressed congressional intent to extend the NLRA to United States citizens temporarily working abroad for a United States employer. . . .

Finally, we are mindful of the fact that Congress knows how to provide for extraterritorial application of its enactments when it intends them to operate outside of the United States. . . . However, Congress has never amended the NLRA to provide for extraterritorial application under any circumstances despite the Court's decision in *McCulloch* over 40 years ago expressly limiting the territorial reach of the NLRA. . . .

Despite the broad "boilerplate" definitions in the NLRA, we can discover no clear[l]y expressed congressional intention that that Act was intended to apply to employees working temporarily outside of the United States for United States employers. Therefore, we hold the Board did not have jurisdiction over the unfair labor practices charge here. . . .

## *NOTES AND QUESTIONS*

**1. Did *Asplundh* Require an "Extraterritorial Application" of the NLRA?** Except for the temporary assignment in Canada, the employees worked primarily in the United States. The employees' concerted activity, which occurred in Canada, involved a dispute about a promise that the employer made before the employees left the United States. Asplundh presumably made the decisions to lay off the two employees within the United States. Moreover, the NLRA's remedies would not have required the employer to take actions outside of the territorial boundaries of the United States. According to the *Asplundh* court, which aspect of the relevant conduct required extraterritorial application of United States labor law? Is the court concluding that the NLRA never applies to employees working temporarily outside of the United States?

**2. Was Reliance on *McCulloch* Warranted?** In a footnote at the end of the *Asplundh* decision, the court stated:

> Extraterritorial application of the NLRA here certainly does not appear to create the potential for international discord that was so evident from the circumstances in *McCulloch.* There, recognition of the union by the NLRB would have created a direct conflict with the Honduran Labor Code that

> recognized Sociedad as the sole Honduran bargaining agent. The facts thus presented "the presence of highly charged international circumstances". . . . The presumption against extraterritorial application of congressional enactments is, in large measure, based upon the notion that legislation is nearly always enacted in response to domestic concerns. . . . The difficulties . . . with an ad hoc approach to these difficult issues certainly mitigates against creating exceptions to the extraterritorial reach of the NLRA to accommodate the kind of dispute before us here . . .

*Asplundh*, 365 F.3d at 180 n. 16. As alluded to in the footnote, resistance to applying the NLRA extraterritorially is often rooted in the notion that Congress intended the NLRA to apply only to relationships between U.S.-based employers and employees, thus avoiding foreign relations problems. Didn't *Asplundh* involve such a relationship? Would the assertion of NLRA jurisdiction in *Asplundh* have strained relations with Canada?

**3. Was Reliance on *ARAMCO*'s Presumption Against Extraterritorial Application Warranted?** The *Asplundh* court relied heavily on the presumption against extraterritorial application as expressed in the *ARAMCO* decision, a Title VII of the Civil Rights Act of 1964 case which involved a U.S. citizen working abroad for a U.S. company for four years before his termination. Does the presumption apply any time an employment relationship has any contact with a foreign jurisdiction, or does it apply only when the employment relationship involves regular, ongoing contact?

## Dowd v. International Longshoremen's Ass'n
*975 F.2d 779 (11th Cir. 1992)*

BIRCH, J. . . .

. . . For the past several years, Florida grapefruit has been shipped to Japan from Fort Pierce and Port Canaveral pursuant to agreements between American exporters and Japanese importers. The International Longshoremen's Association ("ILA") is engaged in a labor dispute with Coastal Stevedoring Company ("Coastal") and Port Canaveral Stevedoring Limited ("Canaveral"), which operate from Fort Pierce and Port Canaveral respectively. Both Coastal and Canaveral use non-union labor to load shipments of grapefruit bound for Japan, where the fruit is unloaded by employees of Japanese stevedoring companies.

Prior to the 1990-1991 shipping season, ILA delegates visited Japan and met with representatives of the National Council of Dockworkers' Unions of Japan, the Japan Labor Union Association, and the Japan Seamen's Union (collectively, the "Japanese Unions"). The ILA expressed its concern over the use of non-union labor at several Florida ports and requested the assistance of the Japanese Unions in pressuring participants in the citrus trade to use stevedoring companies which employ union labor. In various communications, widely disseminated among participants in the grapefruit export industry, Japanese Union officials requested that importers ensure that the fruit they purchased was loaded in Florida by stevedoring companies that hire union employees. Further, these communications warned that dockworkers belonging to the Japanese Unions would refuse to unload fruit loaded in American ports by non-union labor. In a letter dated October 4, 1990, ILA president John M. Bowers informed Toshio Kamezaki, president of the National Council of Dockworkers' Unions of Japan, of ILA's plans to picket Coastal and Canaveral. He stated that "your further support in denying the unloading and landing of these picketed products in your country will also be most helpful to the members of the International Longshoremen's Association." . . .

Several Japanese importers expressed their concern to Florida exporters and stevedoring companies that Japanese dockworkers would not handle fruit loaded in Florida by non-union labor. Subsequent communications reveal that, as a result, at least one ship was diverted from Fort Pierce, where it would have been handled by non-union labor, to Tampa, where it was loaded by longshoremen represented by ILA. In a letter to the National Council of Dockworkers' Unions of Japan dated November 6, 1990, ILA special consultant Ernest Lee noted that the diversion of this ship to Tampa was "a direct result of your very timely and effective notices to relevant parties in Japan of your support for our efforts." Further, Lee noted that "your continued efforts on our behalf will be most appreciated." These efforts continued with demonstrated success. After news of the boycott threatened by the Japanese Unions on behalf of ILA filtered through the industry, neither Canaveral nor Coastal handled another shipment of citrus bound for Japan for the remainder of the 1990-1991 export season.

On June 14, 1991, the Board filed a petition for injunction pursuant to section 10(l) of the NLRA alleging that there was reasonable cause to believe that ILA had threatened, coerced, or restrained neutral persons to cease doing business with Coastal and Canaveral in violation of NLRA section 8(b)(4)(ii) and that injunctive relief was just and proper.

. . . [T]he district court . . . ordered ILA, pending a final adjudication by the Board, to refrain from threatening persons neutral to the dispute with Coastal and Canaveral and to repudiate its written request soliciting the aid of the Japanese Unions. . . .

Section 8(b)(4)(ii)(B) of the NLRA prohibits coercion or refusals to deal aimed at employers or others not principally involved in an underlying labor dispute, i.e., "secondary" or "neutral" employers, while preserving the right of labor organizations to bring such pressure against employers primarily involved in the dispute. Section 10(l) of the NLRA is thus an exception to the general prohibition in the Norris-LaGuardia Act, 29 U.S.C. §101 et seq. (1988) against federal injunctions in labor disputes. Section 10(l) authorizes the district court to grant interim injunctive relief pending the Board's resolution of charges involving certain labor practices, such as the secondary boycott at issue here, which are likely to have a particularly disruptive effect upon the flow of commerce. 29 U.S.C. §160(l). . . .

ILA argues that it did not "threaten, coerce, or restrain" any person in commerce, as required to find a violation of section 8(b)(4)(ii), but merely requested the aid of the Japanese Unions, who in turn threatened various Japanese importers. The Board urges us to attribute the conduct of the Japanese Unions to ILA . . . ILA maintains that the record is devoid of any evidence that the dealings between ILA and the Japanese Unions satisfy the formal requisites of an agency. . . .

We uphold the injunction upon the agency theory proposed by the Board in its petition. . . . When adjudicating an unfair labor practice under the NLRA, common law concepts of agency are to be applied broadly to effectuate the statutory purpose. In condemning certain unfair labor practices by an employer, the Supreme Court stated:

> The employer, however, may be held to have assisted the formation of a union even though the acts of the so-called agents were not expressly authorized or might not be attributable to him on strict application of the rules of respondeat superior. We are dealing here not with private rights nor with technical concepts pertinent to an employer's legal responsibility to third persons for acts of his servants, but with a clear legislative policy to free the collective bargaining process from all taint of an employer's compulsion, domination, or influence.

International Ass'n of Machinists, 311 U.S. 72, 80 (1940). . . .

Initially, we find reasonable grounds to support the Board's theory of agency. ILA does not attempt to dispute that the Japanese Unions acted at ILA's request as communicated by its representatives sent to Japan and in two subsequent letters. Further, the pressure by the Japanese Unions clearly was exerted on behalf of ILA. Mustering the finer distinctions of the law of agency, ILA first contends that there was no formal agency relationship because ILA had no right to control the actions of the Japanese Unions. Second, emphasizing that an agent performs a task in the principal's stead, ILA argues that, since it had no power to direct Japanese dockworkers to refuse to unload goods, it could not be a principal for purposes of delegating that power to the Japanese Unions. In the context of the NLRA, we find these arguments unpersuasive.

. . . ILA admittedly had no legal power to compel the Japanese Unions to assist in the dispute with Coastal and Canaveral. This lack of legal obligation, while perhaps dispositive in some theoretical suit between ILA and the Japanese Unions for breach of an agency agreement, does not allow ILA to avoid responsibility for violations of the NLRA conducted on its behalf and at its request. Several precedents involving employer and union responsibility for the unfair labor practices of another actor are instructive. The former Fifth Circuit held that where an employer encouraged the local Chamber of Commerce director to campaign against the formation of a union and failed to effectively disavow such interference, the employer was responsible for the director's conduct, despite the fact that the director was not the employer's formal agent. Cagle's, Inc. v. NLRB, 588 F.2d 943, 947-48 (5th Cir.1979). The court found that the employer had engaged in unfair labor practices despite the fact that the employer obviously had no more legal power to compel the director of the Chamber of Commerce to join the anti-union effort than ILA enjoyed over the Japanese Unions. Similarly, the NLRB found an employer responsible for the anti-union activities of a community organization where the employer encouraged the efforts of the organization and failed to rebut the statement in the propaganda distributed by the organization warning that the employer would close its manufacturing plant if a union was organized. Star Kist Samoa, Inc., 237 N.L.R.B. 238 (1978). In that case the employer had no right to demand or control the actions of the community organization. Under the liberal application of agency concepts appropriate in the labor context, a contractual right to control and direct the performance of another is not required to impose responsibility under section 8(b) where an employer or union has encouraged or requested another to engage in unfair labor practices on its behalf.

. . . ILA contends that, even if the actions of the Japanese Unions could be attributed to ILA, these acts occurred outside the geographic territory of the United States and therefore beyond the intended application of the NLRA. ILA directs our attention to the recent decision of the Supreme Court in EEOC v. Arabian American Oil Co., 111 S. Ct. 1227 (1991) [("*ARAMCO*")] and to a line of cases founded on Benz v. Compania Naviera Hidalgo, S.A., 353 U.S. 138 (1957) limiting the application of the NLRA. . . .

The Supreme Court has held that the NLRA does not regulate the practices of owners of foreign vessels which are temporarily present in an American port with regard to foreign employees working on these vessels. McCulloch v. Sociedad Nacional de Marineros de Honduras, 372 U.S. 10 (1963). Further, the NLRA does not encompass picketing by an American labor union at an American port where such picketing is aimed at altering the employment relationship between owners of foreign vessels and foreign seamen. American Radio Ass'n v. Mobile S.S. Ass'n, Inc., 419 U.S. 215 (1974); Windward Shipping (London), Ltd. v. American Radio Ass'n, 415 U.S. 104 (1974); Benz v. Compania Naviera Hidalgo, S.A., 353 U.S. at 142-46.

ILA argues that the presumption against the extraterritorial application of statutes affirmed in *ARAMCO*, coupled with the cases in the *Benz* and *McCulloch* line, dictate that the conduct described in the Board's petition for injunction is not regulated by the NLRA. . . .

... The *Benz* cases do not represent generally applicable boundaries of commerce, but instead a judgment that Congress did not intend to interfere with the internal operation of foreign vessels. As the Court explained in *Windward Shipping*:

> ... Those cases which deny jurisdiction to the NLRB recognize that Congress, when it used the words "in commerce" in the LMRA, simply did not intend that Act to erase longstanding principles of comity and accommodation in international maritime trade.

415 U.S. at 112-13. International Longshoremen's Ass'n v. Allied Int'l, Inc., 456 U.S. 212 (1982) provided the Court with another opportunity to amplify *Benz* and *McCulloch.* The Court held that ILA's refusal to unload cargo shipped from the Soviet Union in protest of the Afghanistan invasion violated the secondary boycott provisions of the NLRA.

Unlike the situation in every case from *Benz* through *Mobile,* the ILA's refusal to unload Allied's shipments in no way affected the maritime operations of foreign ships. The boycott here did not aim at altering the terms of employment of foreign crews on foreign-flag vessels. It did not seek to extend the bill of rights developed for American workers and American employers to foreign seamen and foreign shipowners. The longstanding tradition of restraint in applying the laws of this country to ships of a foreign country—a tradition that lies at the heart of *Benz* and every subsequent decision—therefore is irrelevant to this case.

Most recently, in *ARAMCO,* the Court confirmed that the presumption against extraterritorial application is in fact a presumption that Congress intended to avoid "clashes between our laws and those of other nations which could result in international discord." ...

Guided by these precedents, we hold that the alleged violation of section 8(b)(4)(ii) by ILA falls within the scope of the NLRA. Specifically, the Board's exercise of jurisdiction is supported by several factors: (1) the NLRA is here applied, as Congress intended, to protect persons in commerce from a secondary boycott, (2) the conduct was intended and had the effect of creating an unlawful secondary boycott in the United States, (3) certain significant conduct in furtherance of the secondary boycott occurred within the geographic territory of the United States, and (4) the fact that the Board is acting against a domestic labor organization subject to regulation under the NLRA.

Although the NLRA was not intended to regulate the relationship between foreign seamen and the owners of foreign vessels, section 8(b)(4) was designed to limit the scope of primary labor disputes and to shield "unoffending employers and others from pressure in controversies not their own." NLRB v. Denver Bldg. & Constr. Trades Council, 341 U.S. 675, 692 (1951). The protection of neutral entities such as the Canaveral Port Authority, which received a tariff on vessels loaded by Canaveral, as well as the exporters who did business with Canaveral and Coastal falls squarely within the purposes of the NLRA. Further, foreign corporations, such as the shippers and importers involved in the Florida citrus trade, who do business in the United States are "within commerce" for the purposes of enjoying the protection against secondary boycotts in section 8(b)(4). This case thus contrasts sharply with *McCulloch*, in which the Court considered the jurisdiction of the Board to order an election among foreign seamen employed aboard a Honduran ship. There the Court, emphasizing that the NLRA was enacted as "a bill of rights both for American workingmen and for their employers," held that the NLRA did not contemplate the internal management and affairs of foreign vessels. Here we are confronted with the Board's application of section 8(b)(4) on behalf of the very parties which Congress intended to protect. Further, the present action does not involve the prospect of interfering with the internal operation of foreign vessels or offending in any fashion the principles of international comity which guided the Court in *Benz* and its progeny.

Since the object and effect of the conduct in question was to implement a secondary boycott within the United States, we do not believe the location of that conduct is determinative. Where the object of the unlawful threats and coercion is to gain an advantage in a domestic labor dispute by pressuring neutrals which are protected under the NLRA, the fact that the principal threats by the Japanese Unions were uttered overseas is of little significance. . . .

Moreover, significant actions taken in this country by ILA support the Board's jurisdiction. Although the initial meeting between ILA representatives and those of the Japanese Unions occurred in Japan, ILA repeated and affirmed its request in the October letter mailed from New York. Further, ILA ratified the actions of the Japanese Unions in the November letter mailed from Washington, D.C. Therefore, some of the actions upon which ILA's liability is based occurred within the United States, and the NLRA is properly invoked to reach such conduct.

Finally, we consider it appropriate that the NLRA is here applied to regulate the conduct of a domestic labor organization operating in the United States. ILA may not immunize its unfair labor practices by the simple device of selecting a foreign intermediary or by confining its coercion and threats to those participants in the flow of commerce between the United States and Japan who happen to reside in the latter country.

### *Note:* International Longshoremen's Ass'n v. NLRB, *56 F.3d 205 (D.C. Cir. 1995)*

[After the NLRB issued a final order in the case excerpted above, the ILA challenged it in the U.S. Court of Appeals for the D.C. Circuit. Portions of the opinion are presented below. — EDS.]

. . . Because we hold that the Board erred in attributing the actions of the Japanese unions to the ILA, we grant the petition for review and remand the case to the Board.

. . . [NLRA Section 8(b)(4)(i)] specifically targets union actions to engage in, or induce or encourage others employed in commerce to engage in, a strike or refusal to work on goods . . . and section 8(b)(4)(ii) prohibits union actions to threaten or coerce persons engaged in commerce . . . where in either case the object of such action is to force a person to cease using or otherwise dealing in the products of another . . . In this case, the ILA did neither.

The undisputed facts reveal that the ILA merely requested assistance from Japanese labor unions in its dispute with two nonunion stevedoring companies engaged in Florida's citrus fruit export trade. In response, the Japanese unions gave notice that their members would refuse to unload any fruit in Japan that had been loaded in Florida by nonunion workers. As a consequence of this threat, all Florida-Japan citrus shipments were redirected to new ports of embarkment during the 1990-1991 export season. The parties adversely affected by these actions — the two stevedoring companies and one neutral party — filed unfair labor practice charges against the ILA.

Upon reviewing the unfair labor practice charges, the Board held that the ILA had violated the prohibition against secondary boycotts. In reaching this conclusion, however, the Board could not rely on section 8(b)(4)(i), for, although the ILA arguably induced or encouraged other employees to refuse to handle goods, the employees to whom the ILA's entreaties were addressed were Japanese longshoremen, who are not employed by a person "engaged in commerce" as the Act requires. 29 U.S.C. §158(b)(4)(i). Nor could the Board find that the ILA's actions, standing alone, fell within the scope of section 8(b)(4)(ii), because the Japanese unions, not the ILA, issued the alleged threats that created the boycott. Nevertheless, the Board held that the ILA's actions fell within the scope of section 8(b)(4)(ii) pursuant to a theory of agency law. Under this theory, the Board held that the Japanese unions acted as the agents of the ILA merely because the ILA requested the Japanese unions' actions and benefited from the results of those actions.

In its petition for review, the ILA claims that the Board's agency theory is untenable. We agree. Not only is the Board's theory completely without support in nearly 50 years of NLRB and judicial precedent interpreting the secondary boycott provision of the NLRA, but it flies in the face of the common law agency principles that Congress sought to incorporate into the Act. Put simply, the ILA and the Japanese unions were completely independent entities; neither exercised any control over the other. If they were bound together at all, it was by a spirit of labor solidarity, but such a spiritual link is too frail to render one union the agent of another. Thus, we reject the Board's theory and remand the case for further consideration. . . .

In its petition for review, the ILA presents a two-pronged attack on the Board's decision. First, the ILA argues that the Board's action constituted an impermissible extraterritorial application of the NLRA, because the threats giving rise to the unfair labor practice charge in this case occurred in Japan. Second, it contends that the Board erred in holding that the Japanese unions were acting as the agents of the ILA when they threatened to boycott products loaded by nonunion labor. [With respect to the first prong] we need not resolve that issue to dispose of this case. We are required to address the question whether the NLRA reaches acts taken in Japan by Japanese unions only if we first agree with the Board that the Japanese unions served as the agents of the ILA in undertaking the conduct at issue, for only then are actions occurring on foreign soil potentially brought within the purview of the Act. We will indulge an assumption that the Board has applied the NLRA only domestically in this case, for our conclusion with respect to the Board's agency theory fully resolves the dispute between the parties. . . .

. . . [A]s the Board has acknowledged, this case gives rise to an unfair labor practice under NLRA section 8(b)(4)(ii)(B) only if the threats issued by the Japanese unions somehow may be attributed to the ILA. Accordingly, we turn to the parties' agency law arguments.

In considering questions of agency under the NLRA, we must construe section 2(13), which provides that, "in determining whether any person is acting as an 'agent' of another person so as to make such other person responsible for his acts, the question of whether the specific acts performed were actually authorized or subsequently ratified shall not be controlling." 29 U.S.C. §152(13). Congress added this provision to the Act as part of the LMRA, and the legislative history of that statute makes clear that it was designed to render "both employers and labor organizations . . . responsible for the acts of their agents in accordance with the ordinary common law rules of agency." H.R. Conf. Rep. No. 510, 80th Cong., 1st Sess. 36 (1947). . . .

. . . [I]n our view, the Japanese unions were in no sense the agents of the ILA. It is a fundamental principle of hornbook agency law that an agency relationship arises only where the principal "has the right to control the conduct of the agent with respect to matters entrusted to him." Restatement (Second) of Agency §14 (1958) . . . Here, the ILA exercised no control over the conduct of the Japanese unions. To the contrary, the ILA and the Japanese unions are completely independent entities, bound together only by the fact that both seek to further the goals of organized labor worldwide. We discern nothing in the law of agency to support a theory transforming one union into the agent of another based upon the spirit of labor solidarity alone. . . .

Equally inapposite are cases in which courts have held employers responsible for the actions of employees and others conducting anti-union campaigns. Chief among such cases are the Supreme Court's decisions in International Ass'n of Machinists v. NLRB, 311 U.S. 72 (1940), and H.J. Heinz Co. v. NLRB, 311 U.S. 514 (1941). . . .

[T]he holdings of *International Association of Machinists* and its progeny turn upon the reasonable perceptions of those involved in the collective bargaining process. Thus, the courts in those cases held employers liable for the unlawful conduct of third parties when, under all the circumstances, employees reasonably could have believed that such third parties were acting for and on behalf of the employer. . . . Here, by contrast, nothing in the record suggests that any party perceived the Japanese unions to be the agents of the ILA, nor that such a perception would have been reasonably justified had it arisen. Thus, nothing in this line of precedent supports the theory that one union may become the agent of a second, completely independent union merely by responding to a request for assistance in a labor dispute. . . .

. . . Instead, the NLRA's secondary boycott provision targets specific union conduct by means of carefully circumscribed legislative language, and we would subvert rather than effectuate the statute by allowing the Board to nullify its express limitations through the application of an infinitely malleable agency theory. We are not shaken in this conclusion by the Board's claim that legal principles in the labor arena must expand to address newly emerging problems on an international scale. If the nation's increasingly global economy requires an expansion of federal labor law, it is for Congress — not the Board or the federal courts — to make the necessary changes.

## *NOTES AND QUESTIONS*

**1. Relevance of the Foreign-Flag Shipping Cases?** *McCulloch* and its progeny are cases where an extraterritoriality problem is found even though the underlying facts transpire within the United States. In ILA v. Allied Int'l, Inc., 456 U.S. 212 (1982), which is relied upon in *Dowd,* the Supreme Court held that the NLRA did have jurisdiction to enjoin the longshoremen union's refusal to handle goods going to or coming from the Soviet Union. The *Dowd* court found *McCulloch* inapposite because "the ILA's refusal to unload Allied's shipments in no way affected the maritime operations of foreign ships. The boycott here did not intend to change terms of employment for foreign crews on foreign-flag vessels. It did not seek to extend the bill of rights developed for workers in America to foreign seamen and foreign shipowners . . . [T]his drama was 'played out by an all-American cast.'" Wasn't the drama in *Asplundh* also played out by an all-American cast?

**2. Role of Agency Principles in Identifying an Extraterritorial Application of the NLRA?** Which is more convincing, the *Dowd* court's view that the Japanese unionists were agents of the ILA for NLRA purposes or the D.C. Circuit's approach that "[i]f they were bound together at all, it was by a spirit of labor solidarity [and that] such a spiritual link is too frail to render one union the agent of another."? Is the *Dowd* court correct in its premise that if the Japanese unionists were acting as agents of the ILA, the *ARAMCO* presumption against extraterritorial application of the NLRA would not have been triggered? Didn't the underlying events still occur in Japan? Was the intended effect of the ILA boycott in reducing trade in Florida citrus sufficient to bring the case presumptively within §8(b)(4)?

## 2. Alien Tort Statute (ATS)

Typically, U.S. courts do not entertain claims based entirely in international law. The Alien Tort Statute is a notable exception. Originally part of the Judiciary Act of 1789, the ATS states that "[t]he district courts shall have original jurisdiction of any civil action by an alien for a tort only, committed in violation of the law of nations or a treaty of the United States." 28 U.S.C. §1350. In the last two decades, foreign litigants have brought ATS claims against U.S. companies and their suppliers in an attempt to hold them liable for labor abuses that occurred abroad. The excerpt below is from such a case.

### Aldana v. Del Monte Fresh Produce, N.A., Inc.
*416 F.3d 1242 (11th Cir. 2005)*

Per Curiam

. . . Because the district court granted Del Monte's motion to dismiss, the facts are taken from the well pleaded allegations of the complaint. . . . Plaintiffs are seven Guatemalan citizens currently residing in the United States. Del Monte is a Delaware company; its principal place of business is in Coral Gables, Florida. In Guatemala, Plaintiffs were officers in SITRABI, a national trade union of plantation workers. At the time in question, they represented workers on a Bandegua banana plantation in the municipality of Morales, Izabal. Bandeuga is a wholly-owned subsidiary of Del Monte.

SITRABI and Bandegua were negotiating a new collective bargaining agreement for workers at the plantation. While those negotiations were ongoing, Bandegua terminated 918 workers. SITRABI responded by filing a complaint in the Labor Court of Guatemala. Negotiations continued.

Plaintiffs allege that on or before 13 October 1999, Bandegua hired or established an agency relationship with a private, armed security force. Private security forces are permitted and regulated in Guatemala. According to Plaintiffs, on 13 October 1999, Del Monte agents met with the security force "to plan violent action against the Plaintiffs and other SITRABI leaders." Plaintiffs do not allege that government officials attended the meeting.

According to Plaintiffs, at 5:45 p.m. the security force, which is described as "a gang of over 200 heavily armed men," arrived at SITRABI's headquarters in Morales, Izabal. There, the security force held two Plaintiffs hostage, threatened to kill them, and shoved them with guns. Throughout the evening, other SITRABI leaders were lured, abducted or otherwise forced to the headquarters and similarly detained. Once the seven SITRABI leaders were in the headquarters, "a leader of the security force . . . who claimed to be the President of the [municipal] Chamber of Commerce," blamed Plaintiffs for the area's economic decline. The official also explained that Plaintiffs' union activity could cause Del Monte to abandon the plantation. Later, a mayoral candidate appeared. While the candidate was at SITRABI headquarters, the security force "reached a consensus that the two main leaders of SITRABI [both of whom are Plaintiffs in this case] would be taken to a radio station . . . where they would be forced to denounce the union." Plaintiffs also allege that the actual Mayor of Morales participated. He, along with "several other armed aggressors," allegedly accompanied Plaintiffs to a radio station. There, Plaintiffs, at gunpoint, announced the labor dispute was over and that they were resigning.

Members of the security force then forced the two Plaintiffs back to the headquarters. At headquarters, they received a facsimile of a "model resignation form," purportedly sent from Del Monte or Bandegua. The Plaintiffs then signed the letters at gunpoint and were released — after being detained for more than eight hours — at 2:00 a.m. on 14 October 1999. The leader of the security force allegedly threatened to kill Plaintiffs if they failed to leave Guatemala or relocated to Mexico. Plaintiffs now live in the United States.

Based on these allegations, Plaintiffs brought twelve claims against Del Monte and Bandegua in the district court. That court granted Del Monte's motion to dismiss for failure to state a claim. Plaintiffs have appealed the dismissal of their claims brought under the Alien Tort Act, 28 U.S.C. §1350 ("ATA"). . . .

The Alien Tort Act provides that "the district courts shall have original jurisdiction of any civil action by an alien for a tort only, committed in violation of the law of nations or a treaty of the United States." 28 U.S.C. §1350 (2005). To obtain relief under the ATA, plaintiffs must be (1) an alien, (2) suing for a tort, which was (3) committed in violation of international law. Abebe-Jira v. Negewo, 72 F.3d 844, 848 (11th Cir. 1996). The first two elements are not disputed. Del Monte does challenge Plaintiffs' contention that the underlying acts show a violation of the laws of nations: prohibitions against (1) cruel, inhuman, degrading treatment or punishment; (2) arbitrary detention; and (3) crimes against humanity.

The Supreme Court recently interpreted the Alien Tort Act in Sosa v. Alvarez-Machain, 542 U.S. 692 (2004). There, the Court explained that the ATA is jurisdictional in nature but that it also provides a cause of action "for the modest number of international law violations with a potential for personal liability at the time [of its enactment]." 124 S. Ct. at 2761. According to the Court, causes of action under the ATA are not static; new ones may be recognized, if the claim is "based on the present-day law of nations to rest on a norm of international character accepted by the civilized world and defined with a specificity comparable to the features of the 18th century paradigms we have recognized." 124 S. Ct. at 2761-62. But the Court said that federal courts should exercise "great caution" when considering new causes of action, and maintain "vigilant doorkeeping . . . thus [opening the door] to a narrow class of international norms [recognized] today." 124 S. Ct. at 2763, 2764.

Based largely on our reading of *Sosa,* we agree with the district court's dismissal of Plaintiffs' non-torture claims under the Alien Tort Act. We see no basis in law to recognize Plaintiffs' claim for cruel, inhuman, degrading treatment or punishment. In reaching this conclusion, we acknowledge that two district courts of this Circuit recognized such a cause of action. But [these decisions] relied on the International Covenant on Civil and Political Rights, Mehinovic, 198 F. Supp. 2d at 1347, Cabello, 157 F. Supp. 2d at 1361. *Sosa* explains that the International Covenant did not "create obligations enforceable in the federal courts." 124 S. Ct. at 2767. Accordingly, we affirm the district court's decision on the cruel, inhuman, degrading treatment or punishment claims.

We do the same for Plaintiffs' claim for arbitrary detention. In *Sosa,* the Court determined that "a single illegal detention of less than a day . . . violates no norm of customary international law so well defined as to support the creation of a federal remedy." The detention alleged here was more frightening than the one in *Sosa;* still, the short time of the detention here causes the legal principle announced by the Court in *Sosa* to guide us. We, therefore, affirm the district court's conclusion.

We also agree with the district court's dismissal of the crimes against humanity claim. . . . [T]o the extent that crimes against humanity are recognized as violations of international law, they occur as a result of "widespread or systematic attack" against civilian populations. See Cabello v. Fernandez-Larios, 402 F.3d 1148, 1161 (11th Cir. 2005). . . . Plaintiffs' reliance—found exclusively in the appellate brief—on alleged systematic and widespread efforts against organized labor in Guatemala is too tenuous to establish a prima facie case. . . .

## *NOTES AND QUESTIONS*

**1. What is the "Law of Nations"?** The "law of nations" is a term used by early international law writers and in the Founding era for what we would today call international law. In its *Sosa v. Alvarez-Machain* decision (cited above), the Supreme Court limited the reach of the ATS.

It concluded that federal courts should not recognize ATS claims "for violations of any international law norm with less definite content and acceptance among civilized nations than the historical paradigms familiar when [ATS] was enacted." Sosa, 542 U.S. at 732. The Court referred to piracy, offenses against ambassadors, and violations of safe-conduct as exemplars of these paradigms and held that an arbitrary detention that lasted less than a day did not constitute one of these paradigm offenses.

**2. Can Violations of Freedom of Association Rise to the Level of Violations of the Law of Nations?** The *Aldana* court concluded that the actions against trade unionists in Guatemala did not involve violations of *Sosa*-compliant norms and hence did not come within the ATS. As we discuss International Labor Organization (ILO) conventions and principles below, ask whether norms like the freedom to join organizations of mutual interest free of government control or restraint could satisfy *Sosa.*

**3. Extraterritorial Application of the ATS?** In Kiobel v. Royal Dutch Petroleum Co., 133 S. Ct. 1659 (2013), the U.S. Supreme Court further circumscribed the ATS's potential reach:

> [P]etitioners' case seeking relief for violations of the law of nations occurring outside the United States is barred. . . . [E]ven where the claims touch and concern the territory of the United States, they must do so with sufficient force to displace the presumption against extraterritorial application. . . . Corporations are often present in many countries, and it would reach too far to say that mere corporate presence suffices. If Congress were to determine otherwise, a statute more specific than the ATS would be required.

Id. at 1669. If corporate presence in a country does not suffice, what kind of corporate involvement is necessary to reach the level of "touch[ing] and concern[ing] the territory of the United States"? What degree of control by a U.S. parent employer of the actions of foreign subsidiaries, or other companies operating abroad, is sufficient to trigger the "touch and concern" criterion?

## B. LABOR STANDARDS IN U.S. TRADE LAW

The connection between labor standards and trade is a major area of the emerging field of cross-border labor law. The World Trade Organization (WTO), discussed infra note 6, page 1108, has refused to incorporate a "social clause" that addresses labor standards through trade law. At its 1996 Singapore Conference, for instance, the WTO stated, "[w]e believe that economic growth and development fostered by increased trade . . . contribute to the promotion of [labor] standards. We reject the use of labor standards for protectionist purposes, and agree that the comparative advantage of countries, particularly low-wage developing countries, must in no way be put into question." WTO Singapore Ministerial Declaration, 36 I.L.M. 220, 221 (1997) (adopted Dec. 13, 1996). Nonetheless, as illustrated in this part, the U.S. government increasingly includes consideration of labor standards as part of U.S. trade policy at the regional and bilateral levels.

## 1. Unilateral Trade Preference Programs

### *Note: The Generalized System of Preferences (GSP)*, 19 U.S.C. §§2461 et seq., Stat. Supp.

Congress created the Generalized System of Preferences (GSP), a unilateral trade preference program, as part of the Trade Act of 1974. Under the GSP, the United States can give preferential tariff treatment to some developing nations as an exception to the World Trade Organization (WTO)'s principles of equal treatment in trade. The WTO allows preferential tariff treatment in these circumstances to help stimulate the economic development of under-developed nations by providing additional access to markets. The GSP Renewal Act of 1984, Pub. L. 98-573, 98 Stat. 3019, signed by President Ronald Reagan, added a "labor rights clause" to the GSP. As a result, the U.S cannot grant preferential status to a country that "has not taken or is not taking steps to afford internationally recognized worker rights to workers in the country . . .". 19 U.S.C. §2462(b)(2)(G). Internationally recognized worker rights include "the right of association" and "the right to organize and bargain collectively," but the statute does not otherwise elaborate the definition. 19 U.S.C. §2467(4)(A)(B); see Stat. Supp.

**GSP-Compliance Mechanisms.** The United States Trade Representative (USTR) administers the GSP. USTR chairs the Trade Policy Staff Committee (TPSC), an interagency committee which responds to petitions for review of a country's status under the GSP. The GSP's regulations state that during annual and general reviews "any person may file a request to have the GSP status of any eligible beneficiary developing country reviewed with respect to any of the designation criteria listed [including internationally recognized worker rights]." 15 C.F.R. §2007.0. The TPSC "shall hold public hearings in order to provide the opportunity for public testimony on petitions and requests filed . . . Unless subject to additional review, the TPSC shall prepare recommendations for the President on any modifications to the GSP." 15 C.F.R. §2007.2.

For the period spanning from 1985 through 2011, the AFL-CIO, the International Labor Rights Fund (ILRF) and other groups filed 178 "internationally recognized worker rights" GSP petitions relating to 56 GSP beneficiary countries. During this period, ninety-one of these petitions were accepted for review and the U.S. government ultimately suspended GSP benefits in sixteen cases. See Layna Mosley & Lindsay Tello, The Politics of Petitions: Interest Groups and Labor Rights in the General System of Preferences (Jan. 12, 2014) (unpublished manuscript) (on file with the Leitner program, Yale University).

**The Bangladesh GSP Case.** In 2013, the U.S. suspended Bangladesh's GSP status based on concerns about internationally recognized worker rights. See Generalized System of Preferences (GSP), 78 Fed. Reg. 40822 (U.S.T.R. July 8, 2013) (2012 annual GSP review) (also noting that worker rights-related GSP reviews were underway for Fiji, Georgia, Iraq, Niger, the Philippines, and Uzbekistan). Bangladesh's GSP status had been under "continuing review" since the USTR accepted the AFL-CIO's 2007 GSP petition against Bangladesh. The 2007 petition highlighted government harassment of trade unions and labor violations in Bangladesh's export processing zones, ready-made garment industry and shrimp and fish processing industry. See AFL-CIO, Petition to Remove Bangladesh from the List of Eligible Beneficiary Developing Countries Pursuant to 19 U.S.C. 2462(d) of the GSP (June 22, 2007). In 2011 the AFL-CIO updated its petition, arguing that labor problems were intensifying:

> [Ready-made garment industry] [S]everal factory fires have taken the lives of dozens of workers; unpaid wages have led desperately poor workers with no other alternatives to take to the streets; and the Bangladesh Center for Worker Solidarity (BCWS), one of the few independent entities advocating for workers' rights in the garment sector was de-registered and its leaders arrested on numerous, baseless charges. We are deeply concerned that they may not be afforded the due process protections required under international law. . . .
>
> [Shrimp and fish processing industry] [W]e have recently seen the nascent unions formed in this sector busted. In several factories, the employers fired the leaders of the incipient trade unions. In some cases, these workers were told that they could only return if they renounced their union activity.

AFL-CIO, 2011 Update of the AFL-CIO's 2007 Petition to Remove Bangladesh from the List of Eligible Beneficiary Developing Countries Under the Generalized System of Preferences (April 2011). To improve the situation, the AFL-CIO requested that Bangladesh agree to register independent unions, halt the arrests and intimidation of union leaders, and increase workplace safety inspections.

Ongoing reviews prompted by these GSP petitions, as well as the April 2013 devastating Rana Plaza factory collapse which claimed over 1,100 garment workers' lives, led to the removal of Bangladesh from the GSP. Since April 2013, the U.S. has engaged in various consultations and negotiations with Bangladesh to increase transparency and improve labor rights according to a set of benchmarks. In July 2014, U.S. Trade Representative Michael Froman noted that there had been "a significant increase in the registration of unions" recently, but that there are ongoing concerns "about the large number of factories that have yet to be inspected, the lack of progress on needed labor law reforms, and continuing reports of harassment of and violence against labor activists who are attempting to exercise their rights." See U.S.T.R. Press Release, GSP Action Plan Review Finds More Needs to be Done to Improve Worker Rights and Worker Safety in Bangladesh (July 2014).

**Status of the GSP**. As of the writing of this edition, the U.S. has not renewed the GSP since it terminated on July 31, 2013. 19 U.S.C. §2465. The GSP has experienced lapses in the past, however, and Congress has typically applied GSP's benefits retroactively. See Office of the U.S. Trade Representative, GSP Expiration: Frequently Asked Questions, available at http://www.ustr.gov/sites/default/files/03112014-FAQs-on-GSP-Expiration.pdf.

**Other Unilateral Trade Preference Programs?** The U.S. also links trade preferences to labor rights through other initiatives, such as the African Growth and Opportunity Act, 19 U.S.C. §3703(a)(1)(F); the Andean Trade Preference Act, 19 U.S.C. §3202(c)(7); and the Caribbean Basin Initiative, 19 U.S.C. §2702(b)(7).

## 2. Regional Trade Agreements

### AFL-CIO et al., Public Submission to the Office of Trade & Labor Affairs Under Chapters 16 (Labor) and 20 (Dispute Settlement) DR-CAFTA Concerning the Failure of the Government of Guatemala to Effectively Enforce Its Labor Laws and Comply With Its Commitments Under the ILO Declaration on Fundamental Principles and Rights at Work

*Apr. 23, 2008*

On March 10, 2005, the government of Guatemala ratified the Dominican Republic-Central America Free Trade Agreement (DR-CAFTA), which entered into force between the United States and Guatemala on July 1, 2006. The AFL-CIO, STEPQ, SITRABI, SITRAINPROCSA [and other unions] together file this petition with the Department of Labor's Office of Trade and Labor Affairs (OTLA).

This petition sets forth several serious and repeated failures by the Government of Guatemala to effectively enforce its own labor laws and outlines ways in which the government is falling short of its commitment to "respect, promote and realize" core workers' rights, as outlined in the ILO Declaration on Fundamental Principles and Rights at Work. . . .

. . . The level of physical violence against trade unionists increased markedly in 2006-08. Violations of freedom of association and collective bargaining continue apace, and access to fair and efficient administrative or judicial tribunals remains elusive. This petition includes [the following] individual cases:

STEPQ (UNION OF PORT QUETZAL COMPANY WORKERS): The employer: a) failed to bargain in good faith as required by law, b) unlawfully dismissed union members and subsequently failed to reinstate workers pursuant to a judicial order, and c) attempted to form a management-dominated union in order to displace STEPQ as the legally recognized bargaining agent. The government failed to effectively enforce the law as to each of these violations. Some evidence suggests that the government may also have had some involvement in the assassination of the union's General Secretary, Pedro Zamora. The assassination of Mr. Zamora is a serious criminal offense. Further, his murder also violated his right to free association, as well as the associational rights of the members of the union. The government has failed to adequately investigate the death threats toward, and the assassination of, Mr. Zamora. The government has also failed to adequately investigate death threats against other members of the union.

SITRABI (UNION OF IZABAL BANANA WORKERS): In this case: a) the employer failed to adhere to the terms of the collective bargaining agreement, particularly on various wage-related provisions, b) several union officers were threatened and assaulted, and c) a union officer was murdered on company property, which was guarded at all times by the employer. The murder of the union officer violated his individual right to free association, as well as the associational rights of the members of the union. The government also failed to launch an adequate investigation into the death threats and murder.

SITRAINPROCSA: The employer: a) refused to bargain with the legally recognized union, b) illegally suspended and then dismissed two elected officers of the union, c) undertook a campaign to illegally dismiss certain union members, and d) sold the factory to another owner, which then refused to recognize the existing union. The government failed to enforce the law as to any of these violations by the employer. . . . These . . . cases represent only a handful of the many labor law violations in Guatemala. . . .

. . . [The] cases herein demonstrate that the government of Guatemala has failed to honor its commitments under DR-CAFTA. Each case, together and individually, sets forth facts more than sufficient to establish a recurring course of action or inaction on the part of the government. The failure to effectively enforce labor laws also affects trade between the United States and Guatemala. The U.S. government should immediately invoke the Cooperative Labor Consultations mechanism under Article 16.6 of DR-CAFTA and require that the government of Guatemala take all measures necessary and consistent with domestic and international labor law to remedy the claims herein. If the consultations fail to bring about a resolution, the U.S. government should invoke the dispute settlement mechanism and proceed forward until such time that the government of Guatemala complies with its laws. . . .

## *NOTES AND QUESTIONS*

**1. Trade and Labor Connection?** Note the complaint's statement that Guatemala's failure to enforce domestic labor laws affects trade between the two countries. What are the ways that the cases cited in the complaint could affect trade? Or is "trade" affected any time a party to the agreement fails to comply with the agreement's labor provisions? See CAFTA-DR, Stat. Supp. The North American Free Trade Agreement (NAFTA), 32 I.L.M. 605 (1993), which went into effect in 1994, was the United States' first regional trade agreement to tie labor standards to trade. NAFTA allows the U.S., Canada and Mexico to trade with each other tariff free. U.S. labor organizations, concerned that U.S. companies would move to Mexico to take advantage of lower labor standards and then trade their products back to the U.S. tariff free, resisted the passage of NAFTA and pressed for the inclusion of labor standards if the Agreement went forward. NAFTA ultimately included labor standards provisions, referred to as the North American Agreement on Labor Cooperation (NAALC). See 32 I.L.M. 1499 (1993); Stat. Supp.

**2. CAFTA-DR: An Improvement From a Labor-Standards Perspective?** NAFTA states that each party to the agreement "shall promote compliance with and effectively enforce its labor law." See Stat. Supp. Over a decade after NAFTA, the U.S. ratified CAFTA-DR, the agreement at issue in the Guatemala case excerpted above. Unlike NAFTA, this treaty explicitly references the International Labor Organization's (ILO's) labor standards, discussed below. Signatories "reaffirm their obligations as members of [the ILO] and their commitments under the ILO Declaration of Fundamental Principles and Rights at Work and its Follow-Up" and "strive to ensure that such labor principles and the internationally recognized labor rights [such as freedom of association and collective bargaining] . . . are recognized and protected by its laws." CAFTA-DR Art. 16.1.1. As you review the

ILO materials below and in your Statutory Supplement, consider to what extent CAFTA-DR's directive that governments "strive to ensure" that ILO standards are protected is substantively different from NAFTA's requirement that each party effectively enforce its own labor laws.

**3. Consultations.** The CAFTA-DR complaint against Guatemala excerpted above requests consultations, a common mechanism under CAFTA-DR, NAFTA and other cross-border labor law instruments. Are consultations between government officials an enforcement mechanism? Consider the recommended consultations that resulted from a 2007 NAALC submission against Mexico. In this case, the U.S. Department of Labor's Office of Trade and Labor Affairs (OTLA), which handles complaints under regional trade agreements, noted freedom of association concerns raised by the Mexican officials' response to an organizing effort among textile workers in Hidalgo Mexico. OTLA recommended:

> [c]onsultations between the [OTLA and its Mexican equivalent] on . . . [c]ompliance with procedural requirements in Mexico's labor law, and measures taken to prevent unwarranted delays and to improve coordination between federal and state authorities in the administration of labor justice procedures; [t]ransparency in the union representation process, including the establishment of a publicly available registry of unions and collective bargaining agreements . . . [a]ccess to Mexican authorities responsible for relevant law enforcement.

Office of Trade and Labor Affairs, Public Report of Review of Office of Trade and Labor Affairs Submission 2005-03 (Hidalgo), 1 (Aug. 31, 2007) at ii. What effect, if any, could this recommendation have on workers and employers? Could the imposition of a NAALC review, which subjects the government and parties to information requests and interviews with OTLA, lead to changes? Could publicity about the NAALC review and recommendations have an effect?

**4. Arbitration.** The CAFTA-DR complaint requests arbitration if the consultations do not "bring about a resolution." Unlike NAALC, which was a "side agreement" to NAFTA, CAFTA-DR Article 16 permits use of the trade agreement's mandatory dispute-settlement procedures and fines for some labor controversies. Notably, CAFTA-DR limits arbitration to cases where a party "fail[s] to effectively enforce its labor laws, through a sustained or recurring course of action or inaction, in a manner affecting trade between the Parties . . ." and does not apply to cases where a party does not comply with ILO standards. Other than the potential for arbitration, NAFTA-like mechanisms, such as government-to-government consultations and recommendations, are CAFTA-DR's main implementation measures.

**5. Outcome of CAFTA-DR Complaint Against Guatemala?** In response to the complaint against Guatemala the U.S. Department of Labor issued a report in 2009 finding inadequacies in Guatemala's protection of union members from violence and other forms of retaliation. The U.S. requested an arbitral panel to resolve the matter in 2011, after it determined that Guatemala had not responded to the report adequately and consultations with the Guatemalan government failed to resolve the matter. The parties subsequently suspended the work of the arbitral panel to negotiate an Enforcement Plan. In 2013, the parties agreed to a plan, which included specific timelines and benchmarks related to labor law enforcement and transparency in Guatemala. The benchmarks include additional resources to the Ministry of Labor, increased labor inspections, additional monitoring of court orders and criminal prosecutions of employers who fail to comply with court orders. See USTR, Exec. Office of the President, Mutually Agreed Enforcement Action Plan between the Government of the United States and the Government of Guatemala ("Enforcement Plan") (2013). In September 2014, the U.S. determined that Guatemala had not complied with the Enforcement Plan within the relevant timeline and requested that the arbitral panel move forward with its dispute-settlement process. See U.S.T.R. Press Release, United States Proceeds With Labor Enforcement Case Against Guatemala (September 2014).

**6. NAFTA as Paradigm-Shifting?** Since NAFTA, labor standards have played a role in negotiations over trade agreements that involve the United States. Labor standards are part of ongoing negotiations regarding the Trans-Pacific Partnership (TPP), a proposed regional trade agreement between the U.S. and ten other countries. Similarly, the United States increasingly seeks to include freedom of association and other labor standards protections in the main body of bilateral free trade agreements. In fact, the U.S. Model Bilateral Investment Treaty refers to commitments to ILO labor standards to enforce existing labor laws and allows parties to "make a written request for consultations with the other Party regarding any matter arising under this Article." See U.S.T.R., Model Bilateral Investment Treaty (2012).

**7. Labor Standards and U.S. Trade with China?** China has become a major trading partner of the United States and manufacturing site for companies exporting goods to the United States. China allows one union, the All-China Federation of Trade Unions, and actively (and sometimes violently) suppresses any effort at independent unionism. Concerns about China's labor rights record have often surfaced in the trade policy arena. In 2004, the AFL-CIO unsuccessfully invoked Section 301 of the Trade Act of 1974, 19 U.S.C. §2411 (2006), to petition the U.S. government to impose trade sanctions against China. The Trade Act of 1974 gives the U.S. Trade

Representative the authority to impose sanctions against a country for an "unreasonable" practice burdening U.S. commerce, 19 U.S.C. §2411(b), including "a persistent pattern of conduct . . . that denies workers the right of association," (d)(3)(B)(iii)(I). When denying the AFL-CIO's petition for an investigation, a spokesman for the U.S. Trade Representative stated, "[c]learly China has much more to do in the area of labor rights, and we will keep up the pressure on China to do so. . . . A Section 301 investigation will neither shed more light on this problem nor lead to a more effective approach for addressing Chinese workers' rights and labor conditions." See U.S.T.R., Press Release, Statement from USTR Spokesman Regarding China Labor Petition (July 2006).

## C. LABOR STANDARDS OF INTERNATIONAL INSTITUTIONS

So far, the cross-border legal instruments discussed in this chapter have been linked explicitly to U.S. legal fora and/or U.S. laws. International institutions, to which the U.S. is a party, also promote labor standards that cross borders.

### 1. Standards for Nation States

The International Labor Organization (ILO) is widely acknowledged as the central international institution focusing on international labor standards. It promulgates internationally-recognized labor standards ("conventions"), supervises their application and provides technical assistance to member countries. Consider the following ILO case, which addressed whether the U.S. Supreme Court's *Lechmere* decision, supra pages 144-149, complies with ILO freedom of association and collective bargaining standards.

**ILO, Comm. On Freedom of Association**
*Case No. 1523, Report No. 284 (1992)*[1]

. . . The United States has not ratified the Freedom of Association and Protection of the Right to Organise Convention, 1948 ([ILO Convention] No. 87) or the Right to Organise and Collective Bargaining Convention, 1949 ([ILO Convention] No. 98).

1. http://www.ilo.org/dyn/normlex/en/f?p=1000:50001:0::NO:50001:P50001_COMPLAINT_FILE_ID:2896543.

. . . [T]he [United Food and Commercial Workers International Union (UFCW)] alleges that . . . freedom of communication is absolutely essential to the free exercise of organisational rights [under Conventions No. 87 and No. 98]. If employees are to fully exercise these rights, they must have a full and fair opportunity to be informed of the benefits and liabilities of joining a union. As stated by the US Supreme Court (Central Hardware Company v. NLRB, 407 U.S. 539, 543 (1972)), "organizational rights are not viable in a vacuum; their effectiveness depends in some measure on the ability of employees to learn the advantages and disadvantages of organization from others". Because non-employee union organisers are specially trained and experienced in apprising employees of the benefits accruing from unionisation, their role is absolutely critical in ensuring that employees have full access to information. The Supreme Court has also stated that the NLRA "guarantees both the right of union officials to discuss organisation with employees and the right of employees to discuss organisation among themselves". . . . [T]he UFCW stated that [*Lechmere*] will have a devastating impact on freedom of association rights for workers in the United States. According to the UFCW, the Lechmere case struck down all recent NLRB precedents which maintained a balance between organisational rights provided for in section 7 of the NLRA and property interests; in effect, the Supreme Court has now declared that private property will assume absolute priority over rights of freedom of association, whenever union organisers are involved.

. . . [T]he Government replies that its laws are generally in compliance with ILO Conventions Nos. 87 and 98. . . . In assessing the rights of non-employee union representatives to have access to employees on an employer's property, the NLRB accommodates the employees' rights, the employers' private property rights, and considers whether there is a reasonable alternative means of communication with the employees. . . . [T]he decision in *Lechmere* is nothing more than a reaffirmation of a unanimous decision issued in 1956 by the Supreme Court (NLRB v. Babcock and Wilcox) from which the NLRB deviated recently. In any event, if the *Lechmere* precedent has any significance under United States labour law, it will take years before its true impact is known. . . . [T]he United States labour law system has been shown to be extremely effective in resolving unfair labour practice charges through investigation, conciliation, and decision and order on the merits. . . .

### [The Committee's Recommendations]

. . . In the light of its foregoing conclusions, the Committee invites the Governing Body to approve the following recommendations: (a) The Committee requests the Government to guarantee access of trade union representatives to workplaces, with due respect for the rights of property and management, so that trade unions can communicate with workers, in order to apprise them of the potential advantages of unionisation. . . .

## NOTES AND QUESTIONS

1. **Origins, Purposes, and Structure of the ILO.** Part XIII of the Treaty of Versailles created the ILO in 1919, in the wake of World War I and the Bolshevik Revolution in Russia. After World War II, the ILO reaffirmed its Constitution at its 1944 General Conference, held in Philadelphia, and became a specialized agency of the United Nations. Review the Preamble to the ILO's Constitution, in the Statutory Supplement, and compare the ILO's purposes to the NLRA's purposes.

As of 2014, 185 governments are members of the ILO. The tripartite General Conference serves as the organization's policymaking body. Each member state can send two government representatives, one employer representative and one worker representative as delegates to the Conference. ILO Constitution, Art. 3 ¶¶1, 5. Each of these delegates can vote on matters that come before the Conference. For the ILO to adopt a convention, a two-thirds vote of Conference delegates present is required. Id. at Art. 19 ¶2. The ILO also has a 56-member executive Governing Body, consisting of government representatives from 28 ILO member states. Ten of these representatives "shall be appointed by the Members of chief industrial importance." Id. at Art. 7 ¶2. The Governing Body includes 14 employer representatives and 14 employee representatives, which are elected by the employer and employee delegates to the ILO General Conference. Id. at Article 7 ¶2. The Governing Body appoints a Director-General, which runs the International Labor Office in Geneva. Id. at Art. 8.

2. **An ILO Case Based on Conventions the U.S. Has Not Ratified.** The U.S. is currently active in the ILO and a member of its Governing Body. As of 2014, it has ratified 14 of 189 ILO conventions. As the ILO *Lechmere* case illustrates, however, the United States has declined to ratify ILO Conventions No. 87 (on freedom of association) and No. 98 (on the right to organize and engage in collective bargaining). If the U.S. has not ratified these conventions, what is the basis for the case above? To answer this question, a basic understanding of the ILO's convention-ratification procedures and the ILO's Committee on Freedom of Association (CFA) is necessary.

The ILO's Constitution states that when the ILO's General Conference adopts a convention, each of the members "undertakes that it will . . . bring the Convention before the authority or authorities within whose competence the matter lies, for the enactment of legislation or other action."

Art. 19 ¶¶5(b) & 6(b). If the member "does not obtain the consent of the authority or authorities within whose competence the matter lies, no further obligation shall rest upon the Member," except to report the extent of its efforts "at appropriate intervals as requested by the Governing Body." Art. 19 ¶5(e). Governments that ratify a convention have essentially entered into a binding treaty obligation. See Art. 20. They are required to submit annual reports about their application of the convention. Art. 22. When a member state brings a complaint against another member for failure to observe a Convention both members have ratified, a Commission of Inquiry (Art. 26) can be appointed and may make a report with recommendation (Art. 28). If the member state does not accept the recommendation, it can propose to turn the case over to the International Court of Justice (ICJ). Art. 29.

In 1951, the ILO's Governing Body created the Committee on Freedom of Association (CFA) to process most complaints about freedom of association, regardless of whether a member state has ratified the Convention at issue. The CFA receives complaints against member states from member states as well as employer and employee organizations. The CFA is comprised of an independent chairperson and three representatives each from governments, employers and workers that are also members of the Governing Body. If the CFA finds a violation of its freedom of association and collective bargaining conventions, it issues a report and makes findings and recommendations to governments about how to respond. See ILO, Special Procedures for the Examination in the ILO of Complaints Alleging Violations of Freedom of Association, http://www.ilo.org/dyn/normlex/en/f?p=1000:62:0::NO:62:P62_LIST_ENTRIE_ID:2565060:NO.

**3. The United States' Resistance to Adopting Conventions 87 and 98?** The United States' position, as stated in the ILO *Lechmere* decision, is that its laws "are generally in compliance with ILO Conventions" and thus they do not need ratification. Commentators have argued that there may be other reasons for the United States' resistance. See Steve Charnovitz, The ILO Convention on Freedom of Association and its Future in the United States, 102 Am. J. Int'l L. 90 (2008) ("The reluctance . . . can also be attributed to the existence of detailed, contentious federal labor law regulating the same issues covered by the ILO conventions."); Lance Compa, Unfair Advantage: Workers' Freedom of Association in the United States Under International Human Rights Standards (2000) (U.S. laws are not in compliance with ILO's freedom of association principles); Edward E. Potter, Freedom of Association, The Right to Organize and Collective Bargaining: The Impact on U.S. Law and Practice of Ratification of ILO Conventions No. 87 and No. 98 (Labor Policy Association, 1984) (arguing against signing on to these conventions because, among other things, doing so would subvert employers' property and speech rights).

**4. Import of CFA Cases.** What does the ILO's *Lechmere* decision tell us about the meaning of the ILO's freedom of association and collective bargaining protections and the ways it balances them with employer interests? What authority, if any, does its decision rely on? Review the text of Conventions 87 and 98, in the Statutory Supplement, and consider whether the ILO's definitions of these protections differ from the NLRA's definitions. For instance, are NLRA exclusions for independent contractors, domestic workers and agricultural workers in conflict with the text of Convention No. 87? Besides the ILO's *Lechmere* case, American unions have brought several cases against the United States, alleging that various aspects of American labor law are not in compliance with ILO's freedom of association and collective bargaining protections. See, e.g, ILO, Comm. On Freedom of Association, Case No. 2547, Report No. 371 (March 2014) (referring to the Board's *Brown* decision, supra page 110, on graduate student teaching assistants as NLRA employees); ILO, Comm. On Freedom of Association, Case No. 1543, Report No. 278 (June 1991) (regarding *Mackay Radio,* supra pages 522-524).

**5. Freedom of Association as a Human Right.** The ILO has contributed to a growing jurisprudence of labor rights as human rights. Along with the creation of the CFA in 1951, the ILO's 1998 Declaration on Fundamental Principles and Rights at Work gave freedom of association and the right to collective bargaining a "special status." The 1998 Declaration, which the United States agreed to, obligates all ILO member states "to respect, to promote and to realize, in good faith and in accordance with the Constitution [of the ILO]" freedom of association and the right to organize and engage in collective bargaining. The 1998 Declaration, however, also explicitly states that it is not binding. See Stat. Supp.

Other United Nations documents include freedom of association within a human rights framework. See Universal Declaration of Human Rights (1948), Art. 23 ¶4 ("Everyone has the right to form and to join trade unions for the protection of his interests"); the International Covenant on Economic, Social, and Cultural Rights (1966), Art. 8 ("The right of everyone to form trade unions and join the trade union of his choice, subject only to the rules of the organization concerned, for the promotion and protection of his economic and social interests. . . . The right to strike, provided that it is exercised in conformity with the laws of the particular country"). While the United States has not ratified the United Nations instruments cited above, it ratified the International Covenant on Civil and Political Rights (ICCPR, 1966) in 1992. See 31 I.L.M. 648. Article 22 of ICCPR states that every person "shall have the right to freedom of association with others, including the right to form and join trade unions for the protection of his interests" and that "[n]o restrictions may be placed on the exercise of this right other than those which are prescribed by law and which are necessary in a democratic society in the interests of national security or public safety . . . or the protection of the rights and freedoms of others . . .". When ratifying ICCPR in 1992, the United States Senate declared that Articles 1 through 27 are not self-executing and require implementing legislation, which has not occurred. See 31 I.L.M. 648. See also Sosa v. Alvarez-Machain, 542 U.S. 692, 735 (2004) (ICCPR creates no specific obligation enforceable in U.S. courts). See generally James A. Gross & Lance Compa, Human Rights in Labor and Employment Relations: International and Domestic Perspectives (2009); Samuel Estreicher, Global Issues in Labor Law (2007).

**6. The ILO and the World Trade Organization (WTO).** Two years before the issuance of the ILO's 1998 Declaration, the World Trade Organization's (WTO), under pressure to address labor standards, declared that the ILO is the more appropriate forum to discuss international labor standards. At its 1996 Singapore Conference, the WTO resisted proposed linkages between trade and labor standards and stated that the ILO "is the competent body to set and deal with these standards. . . ." WTO Singapore Ministerial Declaration, 36 I.L.M. 220, 221 (1997) (adopted Dec. 13, 1996). For a discussion of the relationship between trade and labor standards, the WTO's separation of these areas notwithstanding, see supra pages 1095-1103.

## 2. Standards for Employers

While the focus thus far has been standard setting for nation states, international institutions also promulgate freedom of association labor standards directed at employers.

### *Note: OECD Guidelines for Multinational Enterprises*

The Organization for Economic Cooperation and Development (OECD), which promotes economic cooperation among advanced industrial countries (including the United States), originally issued Guidelines for Multinational Enterprises in 1976. Its latest update is set forth in the Statutory Supplement.

**The U.S.'s Position with Respect to the OECD's Guidelines.** The U.S., a member of the OECD since its founding in the early 1960s, has pledged to promote the OECD's Guidelines. The U.S. Department of State describes the Guidelines as "voluntary recommendations to multinational enterprises (MNE) on responsible business conduct in . . . areas, including human rights, employment . . . [and] supply chain management . . . [which] have received broad support internationally, and are the only multilateral, comprehensive code of conduct that 44 national governments [including the U.S.] have pledged to promote." See U.S. Department of State, OECD Guidelines, http://www.state.gov/e/eb/oecd/usncp/index.htm.

**OECD Compliance Mechanisms.** The Guidelines allow submissions directly against multinational companies. Each signatory country identifies a "National Contact Point" (NCP), who receives allegations regarding the Guidelines. NCPs do not have enforcement powers. They are authorized to facilitate the voluntary mediation of allegations and can ultimately refer the complaint to the OECD's Committee on Investment and Multinational Enterprises (CIME). In the United States, the NCP is located in the U.S. Department of State and often relies on the Federal Mediation and Conciliation Service (FMCS) to mediate conflicts.

**Supply-Chain Accountability?** While the OECD refers to, but does not define, "supply chain" in the Guidelines, a multinational enterprise's (MNE's) "supply chain" is often described broadly as "the network of organizations that cooperate to transform raw materials into finished goods and services for customers." See OECD, Roundtable on Corporate Responsibility: Supply Chains and the OECD Guidelines for Multinational Enterprises, BSR Discussion Paper on Responsible Supply Chain Management, (July 2010). Thus, a MNE's business relationships in the supply chain can "take a variety of forms including, for example, franchising, licensing or subcontracting." Commentary on General Policies, OECD Guidelines, at 22.

Based on your reading of the OECD's Guidelines, set forth in the Statutory Supplement, can the Guidelines hold enterprises accountable for the actions of their business partners in the supply chain? The commentary attached to the Guidelines' General Policies states that the Guidelines apply to "adverse impacts that are either caused or contributed to by the enterprise, or are directly linked to their operations, products or services by a business relationship [which includes entities in the supply chain]." Commentary on General Policies ¶14. According to the commentary, contributing to "an adverse impact should be interpreted as a substantial contribution, meaning an activity that causes, facilitates or incentivizes another entity to cause an adverse impact and does not include minor or trivial contributions." Id. The commentary acknowledges "that there are practical limitations on the ability of enterprises to effect change in the behavior of their suppliers. . . . However, enterprises can also influence suppliers through contractual arrangements such as management contracts, pre-qualification requirements for potential suppliers, voting trusts, and license or franchise agreements." Id. at ¶21. Does the commentary change your original answer in any way?

**Other Labor Standards for Employers Promulgated by International Institutions?** In 1977, the ILO's Governing Body adopted a non-binding Tripartite Declaration of Principles Concerning Multinational Enterprises and Social Policy (MNE Declaration). It was most recently amended in March 2006. Similar to the OECD's Guidelines, it is a voluntary instrument focusing mainly on the activities of multinational enterprises.

**U.S. Unions Turning to the OECD's Guidelines and the ILO's MNE Declaration.** In the last two decades, U.S. labor unions and their allies have increasingly turned to cross-border labor law strategies to supplement their domestic efforts. In a recent OECD case, the UAW and a global union federation representing Nissan/Renault workers worldwide requested mediation from the U.S.'s NCP regarding a labor dispute in Canton, Mississippi. See Press Release, April 28, 2014, Mississippi workers and UAW turn to OECD process in Nissan rights dispute, http://dobetternissan.org/2014/04/mississippi-workers-and-uaw-turn-to-oecd-process-in-nissan-rights-dispute. The unions' stated reasons for making the request included encouraging mediation of the dispute and involving "other countries that have a stake because of Nissan/Renault's cross-national ownership structure (Japan, France, Netherlands)." Id. For a discussion about how OECD Guidelines affect businesses that operate internationally, see Michael Sherrard & Gerlind Wisskirchen, Next Up For North American Employers and Unions? International and Corporate Social Responsibility, 29 A.B.A. J. Lab. & Emp. L. 245 (2014).

## D. PRIVATE SECTOR INITIATIVES

### *Note: International Framework Agreements*

International Framework Agreements (IFAs), sometimes referred to as Global Framework Agreements, are private agreements that emerge from negotiations between multinational enterprises and global union federations. Unlike corporate codes of conduct, which are unilateral company initiatives that seek to impose social standards (such as freedom of association) on their supply chain partners, these agreements are bilateral. They are framework agreements about fundamental rights, not about specific conditions of work at a particular facility, and often involve an ongoing negotiating and oversight relationship between the parties.

To date, most IFAs involve European companies. See César F. Rosado Marzán, Soft Means and Hard Challenges: Fundamental Discrepancies and the Promise of Non-Binding Arbitration for International Framework Agreements, 98 Minn. L. Rev. 1749, 1762 (2014). The agreement presented in the Statutory Supplement is one of the few existing IFAs that involves a

U.S.-based company. It is an IFA between Chiquita Brands and two unions—the International Union of Food, Agricultural, Hotel, Restaurant, Catering, Tobacco & Allied Workers Association (IUF) and the Coordinadora Latinamericana de Sindicatos Bananeros (COLSIBA). After reading the Chiquita IFA, consider the questions below.

**Supply-Chain Responsibility?** According to the Chiquita IFA, what responsibility does Chiquita have for companies it partners with along the supply chain? In contrast, an IFA between Royal Bam and the Building and Woodworker's International union states that Royal Bam "considers the respect for workers' rights to be a crucial element in sustainable development and will therefore refrain from using the services of those trading partners, subcontractors and suppliers which do not respect the criteria listed above." See Royal Bam IFA (2006), available at http://www.bwint.org/default.asp?Index=128&Language=FR. What obligation does this give Royal Bam? While IFAs are widely viewed as lacking enforcement teeth, some suppliers have lost contracts as a result, at least in part, becasue of IFA commitments. See International Metalworkers' Federation, Background to International Framework Agreements in the IMF (Germany 2006).

**Compliance Mechanisms?** According to the text of the Chiquita IFA, how is the agreement enforced? What power does the Review Committee have? What might the unions do if they do not feel the Review Committee is properly "enforcing" the terms of the IFA?

While arguments that corporate codes of conduct give rise to legal obligations enforceable in U.S. courts have not gained much traction, see Doe v. Wal-Mart, 572 F.3d 677 (9th Cir. 2009), arguments that IFAs are enforceable in U.S. courts have not been tested. See, e.g., Alvin L. Goldman, Enforcement of International Framework Agreements Under U.S. Law, 33 Comp. Lab. L. & Pol'y J. 605, 632-34 (2012) (noting that some IFAs possibly could be enforced in U.S. courts under contract law, labor law or other legal theories but "that the legal hurdles are very significant").

**Other Multiple-Party Private Agreements?** Private multi-stakeholder agreements initiated by nonprofit organizations, rather than 64 global unions, have also emerged in recent years and include freedom of association protections. The Worker Rights Consortium (WRC), for instance, was a central player in an agreement involving a Fruit of the Loom subsidiary (Russell Athletic). The WRC, which has over 174 university and college affiliates, describes itself as "an independent labor rights monitoring organization . . . [whose] primary focus is the labor practices of factories that make university-related apparel." See WRC Mission, available at http://www.workersrights.org/about/. The WRC's campaign targeted

Russell/Fruit of the Loom because of reports that it had closed its Honduras-based *Jerzees Nuevo Dia* factory in response to a union organizing effort. Under the agreement, "not only will Russell Athletic reopen the factory near its former site, offer positions with back pay to all the former workers, and collectively bargain with the union . . . , the company will ensure workers' freedom of association at all of its facilities in Honduras." Susan Hobbs, Russell Factory in Honduras to Reopen in Response to U.S. Student Pressure (BNA Daily Labor Report November 23, 2009). The *Jerzees* workers and Russell Athletic subsequently signed a collective bargaining agreement. See Business Wire, Fruit of the Loom, Inc. Named Recipient of the Secretary of State's Award for Corporate Excellence; Company Honored for Ground-Breaking Efforts at Garment Manufacturing Facilities in Honduras (Jan. 29, 2014).

**Can Voluntary Labor Standards Ever Lead to Enforceable Labor Standards?** Consider Professor Estlund's view:

> [A] recurring dilemma . . . flows from the voluntariness that is a defining feature of *private* transnational social regulation. Regulated entities must be induced to submit to private regulation. Stakeholders' efforts to ratchet up the strength and efficacy of regulatory regimes are thus in tension with their efforts to induce voluntary submission to those regimes. That tension is bound to constrain efforts to secure enforceable commitments. . . .

Cynthia L. Estlund, Enforcement of Private Transnational Labor Regulation: A New Frontier in the Anti-Sweatshop Movement?, in Fabrizio Cafaggi, The Enforcement of Transnational Private Regulation 238 (2012).

# Table of Cases

*Principal cases are indicated by italics.*

# Table of Authorities

*Principal authorities are in italics.*

Atleson, Threats to Health and Safety: Employee Self-Help Under the NLRA, 59 Minn. L. Rev. 647 (1975), 711

____________, Values and Assumptions in American Labor Law (1983), 526

____________, Work Group Behavior and Wildcat Strikes: The Causes and Functions of Industrial Civil Disobedience, 34 Ohio St. L.J. 751 (1973), 410

Barenberg, Democracy and Domination in the Law of Workplace Cooperation: From Bureaucratic to Flexible Production, 94 Colum. L. Rev. 753 (1994), 220

____________, The Political Economy of the Wagner Act: Power, Symbol and Workplace Cooperation, 106 Harv. L. Rev. 1379 (1993), 220

Barnard & Graham, Labor and the Secondary Boycott, 15 Wash. L. Rev. 137 (1940), 584

Barron, A Theory of Protected Employer Rights: A Revisionist Analysis of the Supreme Court's Interpretation of the National Labor Relations Act, 59 Tex. L. Rev. 421 (1981), 131

Bassetti, Weeding RICO Out of Garden Variety Labor Disputes, 92 Colum. L. Rev. 103 (1992), 1050

Bates, Jr., Benefits of Retirees: Negotiations and the Duty of Fair Representation, 21 J. Marshall L. Rev. 513 (1988), 960

Becker, "Better Than a Strike": Protecting New Forms of Collective Work Stoppages Under the National Labor Relations Act, 61 U. Chi. L. Rev. 351 (1994), 177

____________, Democracy in the Workplace: Union Representation Elections and Federal Labor Law, 77 Minn. L. Rev. 495 (1993), 270–271

Befort, Labor Law and the Double-Breasted Employer: A Critique of the Single Employer and Alter Ego Doctrines and a Proposed Reformulation, 1987 Wis. L. Rev., 781

Bensinger, Modification of Collective Bargaining Agreements: Does A Breach Bar Rejection?, 13 Am. Bankr. Inst. L. Rev. 809 (2005), 789

Bensman, D., The Practice of Solidarity: American Hat Finishers in the Nineteenth Century (1985), 24

Berman, E., Labor and the Sherman Act (1930), 25

Bernhardt, The *Allen Bradley* Doctrine: An Accommodation of Conflicting Policies, 110 U. Pa. L. Rev. 1094 (1962), 801

Bernstein, D., *Lochner's* Legacy, 82 Tex. L. Rev. 1 (2003), 21

Bernstein, I., The Lean Years: A History of the American Worker, 1920-1933 (1960), 36

____________, The New Deal Collective Bargaining Policy (1950), 34, 48, 49, 50, 397, 525

____________, Turbulent Years: A History of the American Worker, 1933-1941 (1970), 50, 51, 219, 402

Bernstein, M., The NLRB's Adjudication-Rule Making Dilemma Under the Administrative Procedure Act, 79 Yale L.J. 571 (1970), 71

Berul, To Bargain or Not to Bargain Should Not Be the Question: Deterring Section 8(a)(5) Violations in First-Time Bargaining Situations Through a Liberalized Standard for the Award of Litigation and Negotiation Costs, 18 Lab. Law. 27 (2002), 436, 437

Bierman, Justice Thomas and *Lechmere, Inc. v. NLRB:* A Reply to Professor Robert A. Gorman, 10 Hofstra Lab. L.J. 299 (1992), 152

Bierman & Gely, "Let's Call It a Draw": Striker Replacements and the *Mackay* Doctrine, 58 Ohio St. L.J. 1003 (1997), 532

____________, Striker Replacements: A Law, Economics, and Negotiations Approach, 68 S. Cal. L. Rev. 363 (1995), 531

Black & Hosea, First Contract Legislation in Manitoba: A Model for the United States?, 45 Lab. L.J. 33 (1994), 439

Blanpain, R., European Labor Law (12th ed. 2010), 760

Cheit, Competing Models of Fair Representation: The Perfunctory Processing Cases, 24 B.C. L. Rev. 1 (1982), 974

Christensen & Svanoe, Motive and Intent in the Commission of Unfair Labor Practices: The Supreme Court and the Fictive Formality, 77 Yale L.J. 1269 (1968), 131, 546

Clark, The Duty of Fair Representation: A Theoretical Structure, 51 Tex. L. Rev. 1119 (1973), 905

____________, The Miners' Fight for Democracy: Arnold Miller and the Reform of the United Mine Workers (1981), 1023

Cleared for Takeoff: Airline Labor Relations Since Deregulation (Jean T. McKelvey ed., 1988), 49

Cohen, C., Neutrality Agreements: Will the NLRB Sanction Its Own Obsolescence?, 16 Lab. Law. 201 (2000), 474

Cohen, Santucci, Jr. & Fritts, Resisting Its Own Obsolescence—How the National Labor Relations Board is Questioning the Existing Law of Neutrality Agreements, 20 Notre Dame J.L., Ethics & Pub. Pol'y 521 (2006), 380

____________, A Proposal for Procedural Limitations on Hiring Permanent Replacements: "A Far, Far Better Thing" Than the Workplace Fairness Act, 72 N.C. L. Rev. 813 (1994), 526, 534

____________, Taking the Employer's Gun and Bargaining About Returning It: A Reply to "A Law, Economics, and Negotiations Approach" to Striker Replacement Law, 56 Ohio St. L.J. 1511 (1995), 531

Compa, L., Unfair Advantage: Workers' Freedom of Association in the United States Under International Human Rights Standards (2000), 1106

Countryman, The Organized Musicians: Pt. I, 16 U. Chi. L. Rev. 56 (1948), 646

Cox, Freedom of Expression in the Burger Court, 94 Harv. L. Rev. 1 (1980), 580

____________, Labor Decisions of the Supreme Court at the October Term, 1957, 44 Va. L. Rev. 1057 (1958), 466, 834

____________, Rights Under A Labor Agreement, 69 Harv. L. Rev. 601 (1956), 967

Cox & Dunlop, Regulation of Collective Bargaining by the National Labor Relations Board, 63 Harv. L. Rev. 389 (1950), 425

Crain, Building Solidarity Through Expansion of NLRA Coverage: A Blueprint for Worker Empowerment, 74 Minn. L. Rev. 953 (1990), 93

Craver, Labor Arbitration as a Continuation of the Collective Bargaining Process, 66 Chi. Kent L. Rev. 571 (1990), 693

Cullen, D., National Emergency Strikes (1968), 460

Davies, Strike Season: Protecting Labor-Management Conflict in the Age of Terror, 93 Geo. L.J. 1783 (2005), 459, 460

Despax, M. & Rojot, J., France, in International Encyclopedia of Labour Law (Blanpain ed., 1987), 503

DHS Memorandum, Executive Action: Expand Deferred Action for Childhood Arrivals (DACA) Program, 2, (Nov. 2014), 1066

Dickens, W., Union Representation Elections: Campaign and Vote (Oct. 1980) (unpublished Ph.D. dissertation, Department of Economics, Massachusetts Institute of Technology), 296

Dunau, Employee Participation in the Grievance Aspect of Collective Bargaining, 50 Colum. L. Rev. 731 (1950), 968

____________, Scope of Judicial Review of Labor Arbitration Awards, in Proc., 24th Ann. N.Y.U. Conf. on Lab. 175 (1972), 693

____________, Some Aspects of the Current Interpretation of Section 8(b)(7), 52 Geo. L.J. 220 (1964), 393, 394

____________, Models of Workplace Representation for an Era of Global Labor and Product Market Competition, in Labour Law: Human Rights and Social Justice 51 (Blanpain ed., 2001), 64, 65

____________, Note, Pre-Election Remedies Under the Landrum-Griffin Act, 74 Colum. L. Rev. 1105 (1974), 1020

____________, Platonic Guardians of Democracy: John Hart Ely's Role for the Supreme Court in the Constitution's Open Texture, 56 N.Y.U. L. Rev. 547 (1981), 22

____________, Policy Oscillation at the Labor Board: A Plea for Rulemaking, 37 Admin. L. Rev. 163 (1985), 71, 209, 293

____________, The Second Circuit and the NLRB 1980-81: A Case Study in Judicial Review of Agency Action, 48 Brook. L. Rev. 1063 (1982), 74

____________, Strikers and Replacements, 3 Lab. Law. 897 (1987), 131, 177, 181, 526, 541, 546, 559, 560, 569

____________, Successorship Obligations, in Labor Law and Business Change: Theoretical and Transactional Perspectives (Estreicher & Collins eds., 1988), 756, 777

____________, "Think Global, Act Local": Employee Representation in a World of Global Labor and Product Market Competition, 4 Va. L. & Bus. Rev. 91 (Spring 2009), 65

____________, Trade Unionization Under Globalization: The Demise of Voluntarism?, 54 St. Louis U. L.J. 415 (Winter 2010), 65

____________, Win-Win Labor Law Reform, 10 Lab. Law. 667 (1994), 745, 969

Estreicher & Bernasky, RICO Usage Against Employers for Immigration Misdeeds, N.Y. L.J., Jan. 16, 2007, 1050

Estreicher & Bodie, Review Essay—Administrative Delay at the NLRB: Some Modest Proposals, 23 J. Lab. Res. 87 (2002), 70, 73

Estreicher & Revesz, Nonacquiescence by Federal Administrative Agencies, 98 Yale L.J. 679 (1989), 69, 437

Estreicher, S. & Schwab, S., Foundations of Labor and Employment Law (2000), 64, 503

Estreicher & Telsey, A Recast *Midwest Piping* Doctrine: The Case for Judicial Acceptance, 36 Lab. L.J. 14 (1985), 378

Fairweather, O., Practice and Procedure in Labor Arbitration (4th ed. 1999), 650

Farber & Krueger, Union Membership in the United States: The Decline Continues, in Employee Representation: Alternatives and Future Directions (Kaufman & Kleiner eds., 1993), 64

Farber & Western, Accounting for the Decline of Unions in the Private Sector, 1973-1998, 22 J. Lab. Res. 459 (2001), 64

Federal Court OKs GM-UAW Agreement to Require Retiree Health Care Payments, 2006 Daily Lab. Rep. (BNA) No. 65, at A-7 (Apr. 5, 2006), 960

Feller, A General Theory of the Collective Bargaining Agreement, 61 Cal. L. Rev. 663 (1973), 712, 967, 974

Ferguson, The Eyes of the Needles: A Sequential Model of Union Organizing Drives, 1999-2004, 62 Indus. & Lab. Rel. Rev. 3 (2008), 433

Fine, J., Worker Centers: Organizing Communities at the Edge of the Dream (2006), 1070

Finkin, The Limits of Majority Rule in Collective Bargaining, 64 Minn. L. Rev. 183 (1980), 905

____________, The Road Not Taken: Some Thoughts on Nonmajority Employee Representation, 69 Chi.-Kent L. Rev. 195 (1993), 403, 404

____________, The Truncation of *Laidlaw* Rights by Collective Agreement, 3 Indus. Rel. L.J. 591 (1979), 528

Fischl, Self, Other and Section 7: Mutualism and Protected Protest Activities Under the National Labor Relations Act, 89 Colum. L. Rev. 789 (1989), 535

Northrup, The Railway Labor Act—Time for Repeal?, 13 Harv. J.L. & Soc. Pol'y 441 (1990), 49, 454

Note, *Dunlop v. Bachowski* and the Limits of Judicial Review Under Title IV of the LMRDA: A Proposal for Administrative Reform, 86 Yale L.J. 885 (1977), 1007

Note, Labor Policy and Private Determination of Successor Liability: Illinois' Successor Clause Statute, 67 Wash. U. L.Q. 575 (1989), 776

Note, Labor Violence and the Hobbs Act: A Judicial Dilemma, 67 Yale L.J. 325 (1957), 648

Note, Mid-term Modification of Terms and Conditions of Employment, 1972 Duke L.J., 512

Note, Private Abridgement of Speech and the State Constitution, 90 Yale L.J. 165 (1980), 154

Note, Two-Tier Wage Discrimination and the Duty of Fair Representation, 98 Harv. L. Rev. 631 (1985), 959

Note, The Unfair Labor Practice Strike: A Critique and a Proposal for Change, 46 N.Y.U. L. Rev. 988 (1971), 534

Oberer, Voluntary Impartial Review of Labor: Some Reflections, 58 Mich. L. Rev. 55 (1959), 1005

OECD, Roundtable on Corporate Responsibility: Supply Chains and the OECD Guidelines for Multinational Enterprises, BSR Discussion Paper on Responsible Supply Chain Management (July 2010), 1109

Office of Immigration Statistics, U.S. Dep't of Homeland Sec., Nonimmigrant Admissions by Class of Admission: Fiscal Years 2010 to 2012, 1051

Office of Trade & Labor Affairs, Public Report of Review of Office of Trade and Labor Affairs Submission 2005-03 (Hidalgo), 1 (Aug. 31, 2007), 1101

Olson, M., *The Logic of Collective Action: Public Goods and the Theory of Groups (1971), 899*

Osterman, How Common Is Workplace Transformation and Who Adopts It?, 47 Indus. & Lab. Rel. Rev. 173 (1994), 227

Oswald, Efficient Contracts Are on the Labour Demand Curve, 1 Labour Econ. 85 (1993), 643

Passel & Cohn, Unauthorized Immigrant Population: National and State Trends, 2010, at 17, tbl. 6 (Pew Hispanic Ctr. 2011), 1051

Pawlenko, Reevaluating Inter-Union Competition: A Proposal to Resurrect Rival Unionism, 8 U. Pa. J. Lab. & Emp. L. 65 (2006), 60, 337

Peck, The Atrophied Rule Making Powers of the National Labor Relations Board, 70 Yale L.J. 729 (1961), 72

Pelling, H., American Labor (1960), 4

Pen, VW Issues Policy Offering Groups Varying Levels of Management-Worker Engagement, 2014 Daily Lab. Rep. (BNA) No. 218, at A9 (2014), 229

Perlman, S., A Theory of the Labor Movement (1928), 4

Pfander, Federal Jurisdiction Over Union Constitutions After *Wooddell*, 37 Vill. L. Rev. 443 (1992), 669

Pope, Free Speech Rights of Union Officials Under the LMRDA, 18 Harv. C.R.-C.L. L. Rev. 525 (1983), 997

____________, Labor-Community Coalitions and Boycotts: The Old Labor Law, the New Unionism, and the Living Constitution, 69 Tex. L. Rev. 889 (1991), 617

Potter, E., Freedom of Association, The Right to Organize and Collective Bargaining: The Impact on U.S. Law and Practice of Ratification of ILO Conventions No. 87 and No. 98 (Labor Pol'y Ass'n 1984), 1106

Press Release, Mississippi Workers and UAW Turn to OECD Process in Nissan Rights Dispute (Apr. 28, 2014), http://dobetternissan.org/2014/04/mississippi-workers-and-uaw-turn-to-oecd-process-in-nissan-rights-dispute, 1110

Rabban, Distinguishing Excluded Managers from Covered Professionals Under the NLRA, 89 Colum. L. Rev. 1775 (1989), 92

Rabin-Margalioth, The Significance of Worker Attitudes: Individualism as a Cause for Labor's Decline, 16 Hofstra Lab. & Emp. L.J. 133 (1998), 64

Rauh, Jr., LMRDA—Enforce It or Repeal It, 5 Ga. L. Rev. 643 (1971), 1023

Ray, Individual Rights and NLRB Deferral to the Arbitration Process: A Proposal, 28 B.C. L. Rev. 1 (1986), 737

____________, Industrial Stability and Decertification Elections: Need for Reform, 1984 Ariz. State L.J., 340

____________, Protecting the Parties' Bargain After *Misco:* Court Review of Labor Arbitration Awards, 64 Ind. L.J. 1 (1988), 693

____________, Some Overlooked Aspects of the Strike Replacement Issue, 41 Kan. L. Rev. 363 (1992), 527, 534

Renauer, Note, Reinstatement of Unfair Labor Practice Strikers Who Engage in Strike-Related Misconduct: Repudiation of the *Thayer* Doctrine by *Clear Pine Mouldings*, 8 Indus. Rel. L.J. 226 (1986), 533

Rogers, Reforming U.S. Labor Relations, 69 Chi.-Kent L. Rev. 97 (1993), 503

Rosado Marzán, Soft Means and Hard Challenges: Fundamental Discrepancies and the Promise of Non-Binding Arbitration for International Framework Agreements, 98 Minn. L. Rev. 1749 (2014), 1110

Rose & Chaison, Canadian Labor Policy as a Model for Legislative Reform in the United States, 46 Lab. L.J. 259 (1995), 439

Rubinstein, Duty of Fair Representation Jurisprudential Reform: The Need to Adjudicate Disputes in Internal Union Review Tribunals and the Forgotten Remedy of Re-Arbitration, 42 U. Mich. J.L. Reform 517 (2009), 970

Sachs, B., Card Check 2.0, in Labor and Employment Law Initiatives and Proposals Under the Obama Administration: Proc. of the N.Y.U. 62d Ann. Conf. on Labor (Eigen & Estreicher eds., 2011), 62

____________, Despite Preemption: Making Labor Law in Cities and States, 124 Harv. L. Rev. 1153 (2011), 862

____________, Enabling Employee Choice: A Structural Approach to the Rules of Union Organizing, 123 Harv. L. Rev. 655 (2010), 62

____________, Unions, Corporations, and Political Opt-Out Rights After Citizens United, 112 Colum. L. Rev. 800 (2012), 914

St. Antoine, Antitrust Law at the Expense of Labor Law, 62 Va. L. Rev. 603 (1976), 828

____________, Free Speech or Economic Weapon?—The Persisting Problem of Picketing, 16 Suffolk U. L. Rev. 883 (1982), 617

____________, Judicial Review of Labor Arbitration Awards: A Second Look at *Enterprise Wheel* and Its Progeny, 75 Mich. L. Rev. 1137 (1977), 693–694

Schwab, Collective Bargaining and the Coase Theorem, 72 Cornell L. Rev. 245 (1987), 495, 510

Scott & Taylor, An Analysis of Absenteeism Cases Taken to Arbitration: 1975-1981, 38 Arb. J. 61 (Sept. 1983), 655

Secunda, The Contemporary "Fist Inside the Velvet Glove"—Employer Captive Audience Meetings Under the NLRA, 5 Fla. Int'l U. L. Rev. 385 (2010), 269

____________, Toward the Viability of State-Based Legislation to Address Workplace Captive Audience Meetings in the United States, 29 Comp. Lab. L. & Pol'y J. 209 (2008), 855

Sexton, First Contract Arbitration in Canada, 38 Lab. L.J. 508 (1987), 439

# Index